W9-DAQ-833

George A.
Rawlyk Library
Crandall University

Speech and Language Processing

"This book is an absolute necessity for instructors at all levels, as well as an indispensible reference for researchers. Introducing NLP, computational linguistics, and speech recognition comprehensively in a single book is an ambitious enterprise. The authors have managed it admirably, paying careful attention to traditional foundations, relating recent developments and trends to those foundations, and tying it all together with insight and humor. Remarkable."
  – Philip Resnik, University of Maryland

"...ideal for ... linguists who want to learn more about computational modeling and techniques in language processing; computer scientists building language applications who want to learn more about the linguistic underpinnings of the field; speech technologists who want to learn more about language understanding, semantics and discourse; and all those wanting to learn more about speech processing. For instructors ... this book is a dream. It covers virtually every aspect of NLP... What's truly astounding is that the book covers such a broad range of topics, while giving the reader the depth to understand and make use of the concepts, algorithms and techniques that are presented... ideal as a course textbook for advanced undergraduates, as well as graduate students and researchers in the field."
  – Johanna Moore, University of Edinburgh

"*Speech and Language Processing* is a comprehensive, reader-friendly, and up-to-date guide to computational linguistics, covering both statistical and symbolic methods and their application. It will appeal both to senior undergraduate students, who will find it neither too technical nor too simplistic, and to researchers, who will find it to be a helpful guide to the newly established techniques of a rapidly growing research field."
  – Graeme Hirst, University of Toronto

"The field of human language processing encompasses a diverse array of disciplines, and as such is an incredibly challenging field to master. This book does a wonderful job of bringing together this vast body of knowledge in a form that is both accessible and comprehensive. Its encyclopedic coverage makes it a must-have for people already in the field, while the clear presentation style and many examples make it an ideal textbook."
  – Eric Brill, Microsoft Research

This is quite simply the most complete introduction to natural language and speech technology ever written. Virtually every topic in the field is covered, in a prose style that is both clear and engaging. The discussion is linguistically informed, and strikes a nice balance between theoretical computational models, and practical applications. It is an extremely impressive achievement.
  – Richard Sproat, AT&T Labs – Research

**PRENTICE HALL SERIES
IN ARTIFICIAL INTELLIGENCE**
Stuart Russell and Peter Norvig, Editors

GRAHAM	ANSI *Common Lisp*
RUSSELL & NORVIG	*Artificial Intelligence: A Modern Approach*
JURAFSKY & MARTIN	*Speech and Language Processing*

Speech and Language Processing

An Introduction to Natural Language Processing, Computational Linguistics, and Speech Recognition

Daniel Jurafsky and James H. Martin

University of Colorado, Boulder

Contributing writers:
Andrew Kehler, Keith Vander Linden, and Nigel Ward

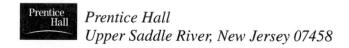

Prentice Hall
Upper Saddle River, New Jersey 07458

Library of Congress Cataloging-in-Publication Data

Jurafsky, Daniel S. (Daniel Saul)
    Speech and Langauge Processing / Daniel Jurafsky, James H. Martin.
        p. cm.
    Includes bibliographical references and index.
    ISBN 0-13-095069-6

Editor-in-Chief: *Marcia Horton*
Publisher: *Alan Apt*
Editorial/production supervision: *Scott Disanno*
Editorial assistant: *Toni Holm*
Executive managing editor: *Vince O'Brien*
Cover design director: *Heather Scott*
Cover design execution: *John Christiana*
Manufacturing manager: *Trudy Pisciotti*
Manufacturing buyer: *Pat Brown*
Assistant vice-president of production and manufacturing: *David W. Riccardi*

Cover design: *Daniel Jurafsky, James H. Martin, and Linda Martin.* The front cover drawing
is the action for the Jacquard Loom (Usher, 1954). The back cover drawing is Alexander
Graham Bell's Gallows telephone (Rhodes, 1929).

This book was set in Times-Roman, TIPA (IPA), and PMC (Chinese) by the authors using
LATEX2e.

© 2000 by Prentice-Hall, Inc.
Pearson Higher Education
Upper Saddle River, New Jersey 07458

The author and publisher of this book have used their best efforts in preparing this book.
These efforts include the development, research, and testing of the theories and programs to
determine their effectiveness. The author and publisher shall not be liable in any event for
incidental or consequential damages in connection with, or arising out of, the furnishing,
performance, or use of these programs.

All rights reserved. No part of this book may be reproduced, in any form or by any means,
without permission in writing from the publisher.

Printed in the United States of America

10 9 8 7 6 5 4 3 2 1
ISBN 0-13-095069-6

Prentice-Hall International (UK) Limited, *London*
Prentice-Hall of Australia Pty. Limited, *Sydney*
Prentice-Hall Canada, Inc., *Toronto*
Prentice-Hall Hispanoamericana, S.A., *Mexico*
Prentice-Hall of India Private Limited, *New Delhi*
Prentice-Hall of Japan, Inc., *Tokyo*
Prentice-Hall Asia Pte. Ltd., *Singapore*
Editora Prentice-Hall do Brasil, Ltda., *Rio de Janeiro*

For my parents, Ruth and Al Jurafsky — D.J.

For Linda — J.M.

Summary of Contents

Contents

Foreword

Linguistics has a hundred-year history as a scientific discipline, and computational linguistics has a forty-year history as a part of computer science. But it is only in the last five years that language understanding has emerged as an industry reaching millions of people, with information retrieval and machine translation available on the internet, and speech recognition becoming popular on desktop computers. This industry has been enabled by theoretical advances in the representation and processing of language information.

Speech and Language Processing is the first book to thoroughly cover language technology, at all levels and with all modern technologies. It combines deep linguistic analysis with robust statistical methods. From the point of view of levels, the book starts with the word and its components, moving up to the way words fit together (or syntax), to the meaning (or semantics) of words, phrases and sentences, and concluding with issues of coherent texts, dialog, and translation. From the point of view of technologies, the book covers regular expressions, information retrieval, context free grammars, unification, first-order predicate calculus, hidden Markov and other probabilistic models, rhetorical structure theory, and others. Previously you would need two or three books to get this kind of coverage. *Speech and Language Processing* covers the full range in one book, but more importantly, it relates the technologies to each other, giving the reader a sense of how each one is best used, and how they can be used together. It does all this with an engaging style that keeps the reader's interest and motivates the technical details in a way that is thorough but not dry. Whether you're interested in the field from the scientific or the industrial point of view, this book serves as an ideal introduction, reference, and guide to future study of this fascinating field.

Peter Norvig & Stuart Russell, Editors
Prentice Hall Series in Artificial Intelligence

Preface

This is an exciting time to be working in speech and language processing. Historically distinct fields (natural language processing, speech recognition, computational linguistics, computational psycholinguistics) have begun to merge. The commercial availability of speech recognition and the need for Web-based language techniques have provided an important impetus for development of real systems. The availability of very large on-line corpora has enabled statistical models of language at every level, from phonetics to discourse. We have tried to draw on this emerging state of the art in the design of this pedagogical and reference work:

1. *Coverage*

   In attempting to describe a unified vision of speech and language processing, we cover areas that traditionally are taught in different courses in different departments: speech recognition in electrical engineering; parsing, semantic interpretation, and pragmatics in natural language processing courses in computer science departments; and computational morphology and phonology in computational linguistics courses in linguistics departments. The book introduces the fundamental algorithms of each of these fields, whether originally proposed for spoken or written language, whether logical or statistical in origin, and attempts to tie together the descriptions of algorithms from different domains. We have also included coverage of applications like spelling-checking and information retrieval and extraction as well as areas like cognitive modeling. A potential problem with this broad-coverage approach is that it required us to include introductory material for each field; thus linguists may want to skip our description of articulatory phonetics, computer scientists may want to skip such sections as regular expressions, and electrical engineers skip the sections on signal processing. Of course, even in a book this long, we didn't have room for everything. Thus this book should not be considered a substitute for important relevant courses in linguistics, automata and formal language theory, or, especially, statistics and information theory.

2. *Emphasis on practical applications*

   It is important to show how language-related algorithms and techniques (from HMMs to unification, from the lambda calculus to transformation-based learning) can be applied to important real-world problems: spelling checking, text document search, speech recogni-

tion, Web-page processing, part-of-speech tagging, machine translation, and spoken-language dialogue agents. We have attempted to do
this by integrating the description of language processing applications
into each chapter. The advantage of this approach is that as the relevant
linguistic knowledge is introduced, the student has the background to
understand and model a particular domain.

3. *Emphasis on scientific evaluation*
The recent prevalence of statistical algorithms in language processing and the growth of organized evaluations of speech and language
processing systems has led to a new emphasis on evaluation. We
have, therefore, tried to accompany most of our problem domains with
a **Methodology Box** describing how systems are evaluated (e.g., including such concepts as training and test sets, cross-validation, and
information-theoretic evaluation metrics like perplexity).

4. *Description of widely available language processing resources*
Modern speech and language processing is heavily based on common resources: raw speech and text corpora, annotated corpora and
treebanks, standard tagsets for labeling pronunciation, part-of-speech,
parses, word-sense, and dialogue-level phenomena. We have tried to
introduce many of these important resources throughout the book (e.g.,
the Brown, Switchboard, callhome, ATIS, TREC, MUC, and BNC corpora) and provide complete listings of many useful tagsets and coding
schemes (such as the Penn Treebank, CLAWS C5 and C7, and the
ARPAbet) but some inevitably got left out. Furthermore, rather than
include references to URLs for many resources directly in the textbook, we have placed them on the book's Web site, where they can
more readily updated.

The book is primarily intended for use in a graduate or advanced undergraduate course or sequence. Because of its comprehensive coverage and
the large number of algorithms, the book is also useful as a reference for
students and professionals in any of the areas of speech and language processing.

Overview of the Book

The book is divided into four parts in addition to an introduction and end
matter. Part I, "Words", introduces concepts related to the processing of
words: phonetics, phonology, morphology, and algorithms used to process
them: finite automata, finite transducers, weighted transducers, *N*-grams,

and Hidden Markov Models. Part II, "Syntax", introduces parts-of-speech and phrase structure grammars for English and gives essential algorithms for processing word classes and structured relationships among words: part-of-speech taggers based on HMMs and transformation-based learning, the CYK and Earley algorithms for parsing, unification and typed feature structures, lexicalized and probabilistic parsing, and analytical tools like the Chomsky hierarchy and the pumping lemma. Part III, "Semantics", introduces first order predicate calculus and other ways of representing meaning, several approaches to compositional semantic analysis, along with applications to information retrieval, information extraction, speech understanding, and machine translation. Part IV, "Pragmatics", covers reference resolution and discourse structure and coherence, spoken dialogue phenomena like dialogue and speech act modeling, dialogue structure and coherence, and dialogue managers, as well as a comprehensive treatment of natural language generation and of machine translation.

Using this Book

The book provides enough material to be used for a full-year sequence in speech and language processing. It is also designed so that it can be used for a number of different useful one-term courses:

NLP	NLP	Speech + NLP	Comp. Linguistics
1 quarter	1 semester	1 semester	1 quarter
1. Intro	1. Intro	1. Intro	1. Intro
2. Regex, FSA	2. Regex, FSA	2. Regex, FSA	2. Regex, FSA
8. POS tagging	3. Morph., FST	3. Morph., FST	3. Morph., FST
9. CFGs	6. N-grams	4. Comp. Phonol.	4. Comp. Phonol.
10. Parsing	8. POS tagging	5. Prob. Pronun.	10. Parsing
11. Unification	9. CFGs	6. N-grams	11. Unification
14. Semantics	10. Parsing	7. HMMs & ASR	13. Complexity
15. Sem. Analysis	11. Unification	8. POS tagging	16. Lex. Semantics
18. Discourse	12. Prob. Parsing	9. CFGs	18. Discourse
20. Generation	14. Semantics	10. Parsing	19. Dialogue
	15. Sem. Analysis	12. Prob. Parsing	
	16. Lex. Semantics	14. Semantics	
	17. WSD and IR	15. Sem. Analysis	
	18. Discourse	19. Dialogue	
	20. Generation	21. Mach. Transl.	
	21. Mach. Transl.		

Selected chapters from the book could also be used to augment courses in Artificial Intelligence, Cognitive Science, or Information Retrieval.

Acknowledgments

The three contributing writers for the book are Andy Kehler, who wrote Chapter 18 (Discourse), Keith Vander Linden, who wrote Chapter 20 (Generation), and Nigel Ward, who wrote most of Chapter 21 (Machine Translation). Andy Kehler also wrote Section 19.4 of Chapter 19. Paul Taylor wrote most of Section 4.7 and Section 7.8.

Dan would like to thank his parents for encouraging him to do a really good job of everything he does, finish it in a timely fashion, and make time for going to the gym. He would also like to thank Nelson Morgan, for introducing him to speech recognition and teaching him to ask "but does it work?"; Jerry Feldman, for sharing his intense commitment to finding the right answers and teaching him to ask "but is it really important?"; Chuck Fillmore, his first advisor, for sharing his love for language and especially argument structure, and teaching him to always go look at the data, (and all of them for teaching by example that it's only worthwhile if it's fun); and Robert Wilensky, his dissertation advisor, for teaching him the importance of collaboration and group spirit in research. He is also grateful to the CU Lyric Theater program and the casts of *South Pacific*, *Gianni Schicchi*, *Guys and Dolls*, *Gondoliers*, *Iolanthe*, and *Oklahoma*, and to Doris and Cary, Elaine and Eric, Irene and Sam, Susan and Richard, Lisa and Mike, Mike and Fia, Erin and Chris, Eric and Beth, Pearl and Tristan, Bruce and Peggy, Ramon and Rebecca, Adele and Ali, Terry, Kevin, Becky, Temmy, Lil, Lin and Ron and David, Mike, and Jessica and Bill, and all their families for providing lots of emotional support and often a place to stay during the writing.

Jim would like to thank his parents for encouraging him and allowing him to follow what must have seemed like an odd path at the time. He would also like to thank his thesis advisor, Robert Wilensky, for giving him his start in NLP at Berkeley; Peter Norvig, for providing many positive examples along the way; Rick Alterman, for encouragement and inspiration at a critical time; and Chuck Fillmore, George Lakoff, Paul Kay, and Susanna Cumming for teaching him what little he knows about linguistics. He'd also like to thank Michael Main for covering for him while he shirked his departmental duties. Finally, he'd like to thank his wife Linda for all her support and patience through all the years it took to complete this book.

Boulder is a very rewarding place to work on speech and language processing. We'd like to thank our colleagues here for their collaborations, which have greatly influenced our research and teaching: Alan Bell, Barbara Fox, Laura Michaelis and Lise Menn in linguistics; Clayton Lewis, Gerhard

Fischer, Mike Eisenberg, Mike Mozer, Liz Jessup, and Andrzej Ehrenfeucht in computer science; Walter Kintsch, Tom Landauer, and Alice Healy in psychology; Ron Cole, John Hansen, and Wayne Ward in the Center for Spoken Language Understanding, and our current and former students in the computer science and linguistics departments: Marion Bond, Noah Coccaro, Michelle Gregory, Keith Herold, Michael Jones, Patrick Juola, Keith Vander Linden, Laura Mather, Taimi Metzler, Douglas Roland, and Patrick Schone.

This book has benefited from careful reading and enormously helpful comments from a number of readers and from course-testing. We are deeply indebted to colleagues who each took the time to read and give extensive comments and advice, which vastly improved large parts of the book, including Alan Bell, Bob Carpenter, Jan Daciuk, Graeme Hirst, Andy Kehler, Kemal Oflazer, Andreas Stolcke, and Nigel Ward. Our editor Alan Apt, our series editors Peter Norvig and Stuart Russell, and our production editor Scott DiSanno made many helpful suggestions on design and content. We are also indebted to many friends and colleagues who read individual sections of the book or answered our many questions for their comments and advice, including the students in our classes at the University of Colorado, Boulder, and in Dan's classes at the University of California, Berkeley, and the LSA Summer Institute at the University of Illinois at Urbana-Champaign, as well as

Yoshi Asano, Todd M. Bailey, John Bateman, Giulia Bencini, Lois Boggess, Michael Braverman, Nancy Chang, Jennifer Chu-Carroll, Noah Coccaro, Gary Cottrell, Gary Dell, Jeff Elman, Robert Dale, Dan Fass, Bill Fisher, Eric Fosler-Lussier, James Garnett, Susan Garnsey, Dale Gerdemann, Dan Gildea, Michelle Gregory, Nizar Habash, Jeffrey Haemer, Jorge Hankamer, Keith Herold, Beth Heywood, Derrick Higgins, Erhard Hinrichs, Julia Hirschberg, Jerry Hobbs, Fred Jelinek, Liz Jessup, Aravind Joshi, Terry Kleeman, Jean-Pierre Koenig, Kevin Knight, Shalom Lappin, Julie Larson, Stephen Levinson, Jim Magnuson, Jim Mayfield, Lise Menn, Laura Michaelis, Corey Miller, Nelson Morgan, Christine Nakatani, Mike Neufeld, Peter Norvig, Mike O'Connell, Mick O'Donnell, Rob Oberbreckling, Martha Palmer, Dragomir Radev, Terry Regier, Ehud Reiter, Phil Resnik, Klaus Ries, Ellen Riloff, Mike Rosner, Dan Roth, Patrick Schone, Liz Shriberg, Richard Sproat, Subhashini Srinivasin, Paul Taylor, Wayne Ward, Pauline Welby, Dekai Wu, and Victor Zue.

We'd also like to thank the Institute of Cognitive Science and the Departments of Computer Science and Linguistics for their support over the years. We are also very grateful to the National Science Foundation: Dan Jurafsky's time on the book was supported in part by NSF CAREER Award IIS-9733067 and Andy Kehler was supported in part by NSF Award IIS-9619126.

Daniel Jurafsky
James H. Martin
Boulder, Colorado

1 INTRODUCTION

Dave Bowman: Open the pod bay doors, HAL.
HAL: I'm sorry Dave, I'm afraid I can't do that.
Stanley Kubrick and Arthur C. Clarke,
screenplay of *2001: A Space Odyssey*

The HAL 9000 computer in Stanley Kubrick's film *2001: A Space Odyssey* is one of the most recognizable characters in twentieth-century cinema. HAL is an artificial agent capable of such advanced language-processing behavior as speaking and understanding English, and at a crucial moment in the plot, even reading lips. It is now clear that HAL's creator Arthur C. Clarke was a little optimistic in predicting when an artificial agent such as HAL would be available. But just how far off was he? What would it take to create at least the language-related parts of HAL? Minimally, such an agent would have to be capable of interacting with humans via language, which includes understanding humans via **speech recognition** and **natural language understanding** (and, of course, **lip-reading**), and of communicating with humans via **natural language generation** and **speech synthesis**. HAL would also need to be able to do **information retrieval** (finding out where needed textual resources reside), **information extraction** (extracting pertinent facts from those textual resources), and **inference** (drawing conclusions based on known facts).

Although these problems are far from completely solved, much of the language-related technology that HAL needs is currently being developed, with some of it already available commercially. Solving these problems, and others like them, is the main concern of the fields known as Natural Language Processing, Computational Linguistics, and Speech Recognition and Synthesis, which together we call **Speech and Language Processing**. The goal of this book is to describe the state of the art of this technology

at the start of the twenty-first century. The applications we will consider
are all of those needed for agents like HAL as well as other valuable areas
of language processing such as **spelling correction**, **grammar checking**,
information retrieval, and **machine translation**.

1.1   KNOWLEDGE IN SPEECH AND LANGUAGE PROCESSING

By speech and language processing, we have in mind those computational
techniques that process spoken and written human language, *as language*.
As we will see, this is an inclusive definition that encompasses everything
from mundane applications such as word counting and automatic hyphenation, to cutting edge applications such as automated question answering on
the Web, and real-time spoken language translation.

What distinguishes these language processing applications from other
data processing systems is their use of *knowledge of language*. Consider the
Unix wc program, which is used to count the total number of bytes, words,
and lines in a text file. When used to count bytes and lines, wc is an ordinary
data processing application. However, when it is used to count the words
in a file it requires *knowledge about what it means to be a word*, and thus
becomes a language processing system.

Of course, wc is an extremely simple system with an extremely limited and impoverished knowledge of language. More-sophisticated language
agents such as HAL require much broader and deeper knowledge of language. To get a feeling for the scope and kind of knowledge required in
more-sophisticated applications, consider some of what HAL would need to
know to engage in the dialogue that begins this chapter.

To determine what Dave is saying, HAL must be capable of analyzing
an incoming audio signal and recovering the exact sequence of words Dave
used to produce that signal. Similarly, in generating its response, HAL must
be able to take a sequence of words and generate an audio signal that Dave
can recognize. Both of these tasks require knowledge about **phonetics and
phonology**, which can help model how words are pronounced in colloquial
speech (Chapters 4 and 5).

Note also that unlike Star Trek's Commander Data, HAL is capable
of producing contractions like *I'm* and *can't*. Producing and recognizing
these and other variations of individual words (e.g., recognizing that *doors* is
plural) requires knowledge about **morphology**, which captures information
about the shape and behavior of words in context (Chapters 2 and 3).

Moving beyond individual words, HAL must know how to analyze the structure underlying Dave's request. Such an analysis is necessary among other reasons for HAL to determine that Dave's utterance is a request for action, as opposed to a simple statement about the world or a question about the door, as in the following variations of his original statement.

HAL, the pod bay door is open.

HAL, is the pod bay door open?

In addition, HAL must use similar structural knowledge to properly string together the words that constitute its response. For example, HAL must know that the following sequence of words will not make sense to Dave, despite the fact that it contains precisely the same set of words as the original.

I'm I do, sorry that afraid Dave I'm can't.

The knowledge needed to order and group words together comes under the heading of **syntax**.

Of course, simply knowing the words and the syntactic structure of what Dave said does not tell HAL much about the nature of his request. To know that Dave's command is actually about opening the pod bay door, rather than an inquiry about the day's lunch menu, requires knowledge of the meanings of the component words, the domain of **lexical semantics**, and knowledge of how these components combine to form larger meanings, **compositional semantics**.

Next, despite its bad behavior, HAL knows enough to be polite to Dave. It could, for example, have simply replied *No* or *No, I won't open the door*. Instead, it first embellishes its response with the phrases *I'm sorry* and *I'm afraid*, and then only indirectly signals its refusal by saying *I can't*, rather than the more direct (and truthful) *I won't*.[1] The appropriate use of this kind of polite and indirect language comes under the heading of **pragmatics**.

Finally, rather than simply ignoring Dave's command and leaving the door closed, HAL chooses to engage in a structured conversation relevant to Dave's initial request. HAL's correct use of the word *that* in its answer to Dave's request is a simple illustration of the kind of between-utterance device common in such conversations. Correctly structuring these such conversations requires knowledge of **discourse conventions**.

To summarize, the knowledge of language needed to engage in complex language behavior can be separated into six distinct categories.

---

[1] For those unfamiliar with HAL, it is neither sorry nor afraid, nor is it incapable of opening the door. It has simply decided in a fit of paranoia to kill its crew.

- Phonetics and Phonology — The study of linguistic sounds
- Morphology — The study of the meaningful components of words
- Syntax — The study of the structural relationships between words
- Semantics — The study of meaning
- Pragmatics — The study of how language is used to accomplish goals
- Discourse — The study of linguistic units larger than a single utterance

1.2   AMBIGUITY

AMBIGUITY

A perhaps surprising fact about the six categories of linguistic knowledge is that most or all tasks in speech and language processing can be viewed as resolving **ambiguity** at one of these levels. We say some input is ambiguous if there are multiple alternative linguistic structures than can be built for it. Consider the spoken sentence *I made her duck*. Here's five different meanings this sentence could have (there are more), each of which exemplifies an ambiguity at some level:

(1.1) I cooked waterfowl for her.

(1.2) I cooked waterfowl belonging to her.

(1.3) I created the (plaster?) duck she owns.

(1.4) I caused her to quickly lower her head or body.

(1.5) I waved my magic wand and turned her into undifferentiated waterfowl.

These different meanings are caused by a number of ambiguities. First, the words *duck* and *her* are morphologically or syntactically ambiguous in their part-of-speech. *Duck* can be a verb or a noun, while *her* can be a dative pronoun or a possessive pronoun. Second, the word *make* is semantically ambiguous; it can mean *create* or *cook*. Finally, the verb *make* is syntactically ambiguous in a different way. *Make* can be transitive, that is, taking a single direct object (1.2), or it can be ditransitive, that is, taking two objects (1.5), meaning that the first object (*her*) got made into the second object (*duck*). Finally, *make* can take a direct object and a verb (1.4), meaning that the object (*her*) got caused to perform the verbal action (*duck*). Furthermore, in a spoken sentence, there is an even deeper kind of ambiguity; the first word could have been *eye* or the second word *maid*.

We will often introduce the models and algorithms we present throughout the book as ways to **resolve** or **disambiguate** these ambiguities. For example deciding whether *duck* is a verb or a noun can be solved by **part-of-speech tagging**. Deciding whether *make* means "create" or "cook" can be solved by **word sense disambiguation**. Resolution of part-of-speech and word sense ambiguities are two important kinds of **lexical disambiguation**. A wide variety of tasks can be framed as lexical disambiguation problems. For example, a text-to-speech synthesis system reading the word *lead* needs to decide whether it should be pronounced as in *lead pipe* or as in *lead me on*. By contrast, deciding whether *her* and *duck* are part of the same entity (as in (1.1) or (1.4)) or are different entity (as in (1.2)) is an example of **syntactic disambiguation** and can be addressed by **probabilistic parsing**. Ambiguities that don't arise in this particular example (like whether a given sentence is a statement or a question) will also be resolved, for example by **speech act interpretation**.

1.3   MODELS AND ALGORITHMS

One of the key insights of the last 50 years of research in language processing is that the various kinds of knowledge described in the last sections can be captured through the use of a small number of formal models, or theories. Fortunately, these models and theories are all drawn from the standard toolkits of Computer Science, Mathematics, and Linguistics and should be generally familiar to those trained in those fields. Among the most important elements in this toolkit are **state machines**, **formal rule systems**, **logic**, as well as **probability theory** and other machine learning tools. These models, in turn, lend themselves to a small number of algorithms from well-known computational paradigms. Among the most important of these are **state space search** algorithms and **dynamic programming** algorithms.

In their simplest formulation, state machines are formal models that consist of states, transitions among states, and an input representation. Some of the variations of this basic model that we will consider are **deterministic** and **non-deterministic finite-state automata**, **finite-state transducers**, which can write to an output device, **weighted automata**, **Markov models**, and **hidden Markov models**, which have a probabilistic component.

Closely related to these somewhat procedural models are their declarative counterparts: formal rule systems. Among the more important ones we will consider are **regular grammars** and **regular relations**, **context-free grammars**, **feature-augmented grammars**, as well as probabilistic variants of them all. State machines and formal rule systems are the main tools used when dealing with knowledge of phonology, morphology, and syntax.

The algorithms associated with both state-machines and formal rule systems typically involve a search through a space of states representing hypotheses about an input. Representative tasks include searching through a space of phonological sequences for a likely input word in speech recognition, or searching through a space of trees for the correct syntactic parse of an input sentence. Among the algorithms that are often used for these tasks are well-known graph algorithms such as **depth-first search**, as well as heuristic variants such as **best-first**, and **A* search**. The dynamic programming paradigm is critical to the computational tractability of many of these approaches by ensuring that redundant computations are avoided.

The third model that plays a critical role in capturing knowledge of language is logic. We will discuss **first order logic**, also known as the **predicate calculus**, as well as such related formalisms as feature-structures, semantic networks, and conceptual dependency. These logical representations have traditionally been the tool of choice when dealing with knowledge of semantics, pragmatics, and discourse (although, as we will see, applications in these areas are increasingly relying on the simpler mechanisms used in phonology, morphology, and syntax).

Probability theory is the final element in our set of techniques for capturing linguistic knowledge. Each of the other models (state machines, formal rule systems, and logic) can be augmented with probabilities. One major use of probability theory is to solve the many kinds of ambiguity problems that we discussed earlier; almost any speech and language processing problem can be recast as: "given *N* choices for some ambiguous input, choose the most probable one".

Another major advantage of probabilistic models is that they are one of a class of **machine learning** models. Machine learning research has focused on ways to automatically learn the various representations described above; automata, rule systems, search heuristics, classifiers. These systems can be trained on large corpora and can be used as a powerful modeling technique, especially in places where we don't yet have good causal models. Machine learning algorithms will be described throughout the book.

1.4   LANGUAGE, THOUGHT, AND UNDERSTANDING

To many, the ability of computers to process language as skillfully as we do will signal the arrival of truly intelligent machines. The basis of this belief is

the fact that the effective use of language is intertwined with our general cognitive abilities. Among the first to consider the computational implications of this intimate connection was Alan Turing (1950). In this famous paper, Turing introduced what has come to be known as the **Turing Test**. Turing   TURING TEST
began with the thesis that the question of what it would mean for a machine to think was essentially unanswerable due to the inherent imprecision in the terms *machine* and *think*. Instead, he suggested an empirical test, a game, in which a computer's use of language would form the basis for determining if it could think. If the machine could win the game it would be judged intelligent.

In Turing's game, there are three participants: two people and a computer. One of the people is a contestant and plays the role of an interrogator. To win, the interrogator must determine which of the other two participants is the machine by asking a series of questions via a teletype. The task of the machine is to fool the interrogator into believing it is a person by responding as a person would to the interrogator's questions. The task of the second human participant is to convince the interrogator that the other participant is the machine, and that they are human.

The following interaction from Turing's paper illustrates the kind of interactions he had in mind. Clearly a convincing simulation of humanity doesn't require being an expert in all domains:

Q: Please write me a sonnet on the topic of the Forth Bridge.
A: Count me out on this one. I never could write poetry.
Q: Add 34957 to 70764.
A: (Pause about 30 seconds and then give answer as) 105621.

Turing predicted that roughly by the end of the twentieth century a machine with 10 gigabytes of memory would have around a 30% chance of fooling a human interrogator after 5 minutes of questioning. Given the fact that you can fool some of the people all the time, it is not clear how rigorous this particular standard is. Nevertheless, the critical issue for Turing was that using language as humans do is sufficient, by itself, as an operational test for intelligence.

Surprisingly, many of the issues raised by Turing became relevant as early as 1966 in the context of the ELIZA program (Weizenbaum, 1966). ELIZA was an early natural language processing system capable of carrying on a limited form of conversation with a user. Consider the following session with a version of ELIZA that imitated the responses of a Rogerian psychotherapist.

User[1]:	You are like my father in some ways.
ELIZA[1]:	WHAT RESEMBLANCE DO YOU SEE
User[2]:	You are not very aggressive but I think you don't want me to notice that.
ELIZA[2]:	WHAT MAKES YOU THINK I AM NOT AGGRESSIVE
User[3]:	You don't argue with me.
ELIZA[3]:	WHY DO YOU THINK I DON'T ARGUE WITH YOU
User[4]:	You are afraid of me.
ELIZA[4]:	DOES IT PLEASE YOU TO BELIEVE I AM AFRAID OF YOU

As we will discuss in more detail in Chapter 2, ELIZA is a remarkably simple program that makes use of pattern-matching to process the input and translate it into suitable outputs. The success of this simple technique in this domain is due to the fact that ELIZA doesn't actually need to *know* anything to mimic a Rogerian psychotherapist. As Weizenbaum notes, this is one of the few dialogue genres where the listener can act as if they know nothing of the world.

ELIZA's deep relevance to Turing's ideas is that many people who interacted with ELIZA came to believe that it really *understood* them and their problems. Indeed, Weizenbaum (1976) notes that many of these people continued to believe in ELIZA's abilities even after the program's operation was explained to them. In more recent years, Weizenbaum's informal reports have been repeated in a somewhat more controlled setting. Since 1991, an event known as the Loebner Prize competition has attempted to put various computer programs to the Turing test. Although these contests have proven to have little scientific interest, a consistent result over the years has been that even the crudest programs can fool some of the judges some of the time (Shieber, 1994). Not surprisingly, these results have done nothing to quell the ongoing debate over the suitability of the Turing test as a test for intelligence among philosophers and AI researchers (Searle, 1980).

Fortunately, for the purposes of this book, the relevance of these results does not hinge on whether or not computers will ever be intelligent, or understand natural language. Far more important is recent related research in the social sciences that has confirmed another of Turing's predictions from the same paper.

> Nevertheless I believe that at the end of the century the use of words and educated opinion will have altered so much that we will be able to speak of machines thinking without expecting to be contradicted.

It is now clear that regardless of what people believe or know about the inner workings of computers, they talk about them and interact with them as social entities. People act toward computers as if they were people; they are polite to them, treat them as team members, and expect among other things that computers should be able to understand their needs, and be capable of interacting with them naturally. For example, Reeves and Nass (1996) found that when a computer asked a human to evaluate how well the computer had been doing, the human gives more positive responses than when a different computer asks the same questions. People seemed to be afraid of being impolite. In a different experiment, Reeves and Nass found that people also give computers higher performance ratings if the computer has recently said something flattering to the human. Given these predispositions, speech and language-based systems may provide many users with the most natural interface for many applications. This fact has led to a long-term focus in the field on the design of **conversational agents**, artificial entities that communicate conversationally.

1.5   THE STATE OF THE ART AND THE NEAR-TERM FUTURE

> We can only see a short distance ahead, but we can see plenty there that needs to be done.
>
> Alan Turing.

This is an exciting time for the field of speech and language processing. The recent commercialization of robust speech recognition systems, and the rise of the Web, have placed speech and language processing applications in the spotlight, and have pointed out a plethora of exciting possible applications. The following scenarios serve to illustrate some current applications and near-term possibilities.

A Canadian computer program accepts daily weather data and generates weather reports that are passed along unedited to the public in English and French (Chandioux, 1976).

The *Babel Fish* translation system from Systran handles over 1,000,000 translation requests a day from the AltaVista search engine site.

A visitor to Cambridge, Massachusetts, asks a computer about places to eat using only spoken language. The system returns relevant information from a database of facts about the local restaurant scene (Zue et al., 1991).

These scenarios represent just a few of applications possible given current technology. The following, somewhat more speculative scenarios, give some feeling for applications currently being explored at research and development labs around the world.

A computer reads hundreds of typed student essays and grades them in a manner that is indistinguishable from human graders (Landauer et al., 1997).

An automated reading tutor helps improve literacy by having children read stories and using a speech recognizer to intervene when the reader asks for reading help or makes mistakes (Mostow and Aist, 1999).

A computer equipped with a vision system watches a short video clip of a soccer match and provides an automated natural language report on the game (Wahlster, 1989).

A computer predicts upcoming words or expands telegraphic speech to assist people with a speech or communication disability (Newell et al., 1998; McCoy et al., 1998).

1.6   SOME BRIEF HISTORY

Historically, speech and language processing has been treated very differently in computer science, electrical engineering, linguistics, and psychology/cognitive science. Because of this diversity, speech and language processing encompasses a number of different but overlapping fields in these different departments: **computational linguistics** in linguistics, **natural language processing** in computer science, **speech recognition** in electrical engineering, **computational psycholinguistics** in psychology. This section summarizes the different historical threads which have given rise to the field of speech and language processing. This section will provide only a sketch; see the individual chapters for more detail on each area and its terminology.

Foundational Insights: 1940s and 1950s

The earliest roots of the field date to the intellectually fertile period just after World War II that gave rise to the computer itself. This period from the 1940s through the end of the 1950s saw intense work on two foundational paradigms: the **automaton** and **probabilistic** or **information-theoretic models**.

The automaton arose in the 1950s out of Turing's (1936) model of algorithmic computation, considered by many to be the foundation of modern computer science. Turing's work led first to the **McCulloch-Pitts neuron** (McCulloch and Pitts, 1943), a simplified model of the neuron as a kind of computing element that could be described in terms of propositional logic, and then to the work of Kleene (1951) and (1956) on finite automata and regular expressions. Shannon (1948) applied probabilistic models of discrete Markov processes to automata for language. Drawing the idea of a finite-state Markov process from Shannon's work, Chomsky (1956) first considered finite-state machines as a way to characterize a grammar, and defined a finite-state language as a language generated by a finite-state grammar. These early models led to the field of **formal language theory**, which used algebra and set theory to define formal languages as sequences of symbols. This includes the context-free grammar, first defined by Chomsky (1956) for natural languages but independently discovered by Backus (1959) and Naur et al. (1960) in their descriptions of the ALGOL programming language.

The second foundational insight of this period was the development of probabilistic algorithms for speech and language processing, which dates to Shannon's other contribution: the metaphor of the **noisy channel** and **decoding** for the transmission of language through media like communication channels and speech acoustics. Shannon also borrowed the concept of **entropy** from thermodynamics as a way of measuring the information capacity of a channel, or the information content of a language, and performed the first measure of the entropy of English using probabilistic techniques.

It was also during this early period that the sound spectrograph was developed (Koenig et al., 1946), and foundational research was done in instrumental phonetics that laid the groundwork for later work in speech recognition. This led to the first machine speech recognizers in the early 1950s. In 1952, researchers at Bell Labs built a statistical system that could recognize any of the 10 digits from a single speaker (Davis et al., 1952). The system had 10 speaker-dependent stored patterns roughly representing the first two vowel formants in the digits. They achieved 97–99% accuracy by choosing the pattern which had the highest relative correlation coefficient with the input.

The Two Camps: 1957–1970

By the end of the 1950s and the early 1960s, speech and language processing had split very cleanly into two paradigms: symbolic and stochastic.

The symbolic paradigm took off from two lines of research. The first was the work of Chomsky and others on formal language theory and generative syntax throughout the late 1950s and early to mid 1960s, and the work of many linguistics and computer scientists on parsing algorithms, initially top-down and bottom-up and then via dynamic programming. One of the earliest complete parsing systems was Zelig Harris's Transformations and Discourse Analysis Project (TDAP), which was implemented between June 1958 and July 1959 at the University of Pennsylvania (Harris, 1962).[2] The second line of research was the new field of artificial intelligence. In the summer of 1956 John McCarthy, Marvin Minsky, Claude Shannon, and Nathaniel Rochester brought together a group of researchers for a two-month workshop on what they decided to call artificial intelligence (AI). Although AI always included a minority of researchers focusing on stochastic and statistical algorithms (include probabilistic models and neural nets), the major focus of the new field was the work on reasoning and logic typified by Newell and Simon's work on the Logic Theorist and the General Problem Solver. At this point early natural language understanding systems were built, These were simple systems that worked in single domains mainly by a combination of pattern matching and keyword search with simple heuristics for reasoning and question-answering. By the late 1960s more formal logical systems were developed.

The stochastic paradigm took hold mainly in departments of statistics and of electrical engineering. By the late 1950s the Bayesian method was beginning to be applied to the problem of optical character recognition. Bledsoe and Browning (1959) built a Bayesian system for text-recognition that used a large dictionary and computed the likelihood of each observed letter sequence given each word in the dictionary by multiplying the likelihoods for each letter. Mosteller and Wallace (1964) applied Bayesian methods to the problem of authorship attribution on *The Federalist* papers.

The 1960s also saw the rise of the first serious testable psychological models of human language processing based on transformational grammar, as well as the first on-line corpora: the Brown corpus of American English, a 1 million word collection of samples from 500 written texts from different genres (newspaper, novels, non-fiction, academic, etc.), which was assembled at Brown University in 1963–64 (Kučera and Francis, 1967; Francis, 1979; Francis and Kučera, 1982), and William S. Y. Wang's 1967 DOC (Dictionary on Computer), an on-line Chinese dialect dictionary.

Four Paradigms: 1970–1983

The next period saw an explosion in research in speech and language processing and the development of a number of research paradigms that still dominate the field.

---

[2] This system was reimplemented recently and is described by Joshi and Hopely (1999) and Karttunen (1999), who note that the parser was essentially implemented as a cascade of finite-state transducers.

The **stochastic** paradigm played a huge role in the development of speech recognition algorithms in this period, particularly the use of the Hidden Markov Model and the metaphors of the noisy channel and decoding, developed independently by Jelinek, Bahl, Mercer, and colleagues at IBM's Thomas J. Watson Research Center, and by Baker at Carnegie Mellon University, who was influenced by the work of Baum and colleagues at the Institute for Defense Analyses in Princeton. AT&T's Bell Laboratories was also a center for work on speech recognition and synthesis; see Rabiner and Juang (1993) for descriptions of the wide range of this work.

The **logic-based** paradigm was begun by the work of Colmerauer and his colleagues on Q-systems and metamorphosis grammars (Colmerauer, 1970, 1975), the forerunners of Prolog, and Definite Clause Grammars (Pereira and Warren, 1980). Independently, Kay's (1979) work on functional grammar, and shortly later, Bresnan and Kaplan's (1982) work on LFG, established the importance of feature structure unification.

The **natural language understanding** field took off during this period, beginning with Terry Winograd's SHRDLU system, which simulated a robot embedded in a world of toy blocks (Winograd, 1972a). The program was able to accept natural language text commands *(Move the red block on top of the smaller green one)* of a hitherto unseen complexity and sophistication. His system was also the first to attempt to build an extensive (for the time) grammar of English, based on Halliday's systemic grammar. Winograd's model made it clear that the problem of parsing was well-enough understood to begin to focus on semantics and discourse models. Roger Schank and his colleagues and students (in what was often referred to as the *Yale School*) built a series of language understanding programs that focused on human conceptual knowledge such as scripts, plans and goals, and human memory organization (Schank and Albelson, 1977; Schank and Riesbeck, 1981; Cullingford, 1981; Wilensky, 1983; Lehnert, 1977). This work often used network-based semantics (Quillian, 1968; Norman and Rumelhart, 1975; Schank, 1972; Wilks, 1975c, 1975b; Kintsch, 1974) and began to incorporate Fillmore's notion of case roles (Fillmore, 1968) into their representations (Simmons, 1973).

The logic-based and natural-language understanding paradigms were unified on systems that used predicate logic as a semantic representation, such as the LUNAR question-answering system (Woods, 1967, 1973).

The **discourse modeling** paradigm focused on four key areas in discourse. Grosz and her colleagues introduced the study of substructure in discourse, and of discourse focus (Grosz, 1977a; Sidner, 1983), a number of researchers began to work on automatic reference resolution (Hobbs, 1978), and the **BDI** (Belief-Desire-Intention) framework for logic-based work on speech acts was developed (Perrault and Allen, 1980; Cohen and Perrault, 1979).

Empiricism and Finite State Models Redux: 1983–1993

This next decade saw the return of two classes of models which had lost popularity in the late 1950s and early 1960s, partially due to theoretical arguments against them such as Chomsky's influential review of Skinner's *Verbal Behavior* (Chomsky, 1959b). The first class was finite-state models, which began to receive attention again after work on finite-state phonology and morphology by Kaplan and Kay (1981) and finite-state models of syntax by Church (1980). A large body of work on finite-state models will be described throughout the book.

The second trend in this period was what has been called the "return of empiricism"; most notably here was the rise of probabilistic models throughout speech and language processing, influenced strongly by the work at the IBM Thomas J. Watson Research Center on probabilistic models of speech recognition. These probabilistic methods and other such data-driven approaches spread into part-of-speech tagging, parsing and attachment ambiguities, and connectionist approaches from speech recognition to semantics.

This period also saw considerable work on natural language generation.

The Field Comes Together: 1994–1999

By the last five years of the millennium it was clear that the field was vastly changing. First, probabilistic and data-driven models had become quite standard throughout natural language processing. Algorithms for parsing, part-of-speech tagging, reference resolution, and discourse processing all began to incorporate probabilities, and employ evaluation methodologies borrowed from speech recognition and information retrieval. Second, the increases in the speed and memory of computers had allowed commercial exploitation of a number of subareas of speech and language processing, in particular speech recognition and spelling and grammar checking. Speech and language processing algorithms began to be applied to Augmentative and Alternative Communication (AAC). Finally, the rise of the Web emphasized the need for language-based information retrieval and information extraction.

On Multiple Discoveries

Even in this brief historical overview, we have mentioned a number of cases of multiple independent discoveries of the same idea. Just a few of the "multiples" to be discussed in this book include the application of dynamic programming to sequence comparison by Viterbi, Vintsyuk, Needleman and Wunsch, Sakoe and Chiba, Sankoff, Reichert *et al.*, and Wagner and Fischer (Chapters 5 and 7); the HMM/noisy channel model of speech recognition by Baker and by Jelinek, Bahl, and Mercer (Chapter 7); the development of context-free grammars by Chomsky and by Backus and Naur (Chapter 9); the proof that Swiss-German has a non-context-free syntax by Huybregts and by Shieber (Chapter 13); the application of unification to language processing by Colmerauer *et al.* and by Kay in (Chapter 11).

Are these multiples to be considered astonishing coincidences? A well-known hypothesis by sociologist of science Robert K. Merton (1961) argues, quite the contrary, that

> all scientific discoveries are in principle multiples, including those that on the surface appear to be singletons.

Of course there are many well-known cases of multiple discovery or invention; just a few examples from an extensive list in Ogburn and Thomas (1922) include the multiple invention of the calculus by Leibnitz and by Newton, the multiple development of the theory of natural selection by Wallace and by Darwin, and the multiple invention of the telephone by Gray and Bell.[3] But Merton gives an further array of evidence for the hypothesis that multiple discovery is the rule rather than the exception, including many cases of putative singletons that turn out be a rediscovery of previously unpublished or perhaps inaccessible work. An even stronger piece of evidence is his ethnomethodological point that scientists themselves act under the assumption that multiple invention is the norm. Thus many aspects of scientific life are designed to help scientists avoid being "scooped"; submission dates on journal articles; careful dates in research records; circulation of preliminary or technical reports.

---

[3] Ogburn and Thomas are generally credited with noticing that the prevalence of multiple inventions suggests that the cultural milieu and not individual genius is the deciding causal factor in scientific discovery. In an amusing bit of recursion, however, Merton notes that even this idea has been multiply discovered, citing sources from the 19th century and earlier!

A Final Brief Note on Psychology

Many of the chapters in this book include short summaries of psychological research on human processing. Of course, understanding human language processing is an important scientific goal in its own right and is part of the general field of cognitive science. However, an understanding of human language processing can often be helpful in building better machine models of language. This seems contrary to the popular wisdom, which holds that direct mimicry of nature's algorithms is rarely useful in engineering applications. For example, the argument is often made that if we copied nature exactly, airplanes would flap their wings; yet airplanes with fixed wings are a more successful engineering solution. But language is not aeronautics. Cribbing from nature is sometimes useful for aeronautics (after all, airplanes do have wings), but it is particularly useful when we are trying to solve human-centered tasks. Airplane flight has different goals than bird flight; but the goal of speech recognition systems, for example, is to perform exactly the task that human court reporters perform every day: transcribe spoken dialog. Since people already do this well, we can learn from nature's previous solution. Since an important application of speech and language processing systems is for human-computer interaction, it makes sense to copy a solution that behaves the way people are accustomed to.

1.7   SUMMARY

This chapter introduces the field of speech and language processing. The following are some of the highlights of this chapter.

- A good way to understand the concerns of speech and language processing research is to consider what it would take to create an intelligent agent like HAL from 2001: A Space Odyssey.

- Speech and language technology relies on formal models, or representations, of knowledge of language at the levels of phonology and phonetics, morphology, syntax, semantics, pragmatics and discourse. A small number of formal models including state machines, formal rule systems, logic, and probability theory are used to capture this knowledge.

- The foundations of speech and language technology lie in computer science, linguistics, mathematics, electrical engineering and psychology. A small number of algorithms from standard frameworks are used throughout speech and language processing,

- The critical connection between language and thought has placed speech and language processing technology at the center of debate over intelligent machines. Furthermore, research on how people interact with complex media indicates that speech and language processing technology will be critical in the development of future technologies.

- Revolutionary applications of speech and language processing are currently in use around the world. Recent advances in speech recognition and the creation of the World-Wide Web will lead to many more applications.

BIBLIOGRAPHICAL AND HISTORICAL NOTES

Research in the various subareas of speech and language processing is spread across a wide number of conference proceedings and journals. The conferences and journals most centrally concerned with computational linguistics and natural language processing are associated with the Association for Computational Linguistics (ACL), its European counterpart (EACL), and the International Conference on Computational Linguistics (COLING). The annual proceedings of ACL and EACL, and the biennial COLING conference are the primary forums for work in this area. Related conferences include the biennial conference on Applied Natural Language Processing (ANLP) and the conference on Empirical Methods in Natural Language Processing (EMNLaP). The journal *Computational Linguistics* is the premier publication in the field, although it has a decidedly theoretical and linguistic orientation. The journal *Natural Language Engineering* covers more practical applications of speech and language research.

Research on speech recognition, understanding, and synthesis is presented at the biennial International Conference on Spoken Language Processing (ICSLP) which alternates with the European Conference on Speech Communication and Technology (EUROSPEECH). The IEEE International Conference on Acoustics, Speech, and Signal Processing (IEEE ICASSP) is held annually, as is the meeting of the Acoustical Society of America. Speech journals include *Speech Communication*, *Computer Speech and Language*, and the *IEEE Transactions on Pattern Analysis and Machine Intelligence*.

Work on language processing from an Artificial Intelligence perspective can be found in the annual meetings of the American Association for Artificial Intelligence (AAAI), as well as the biennial International Joint Conference on Artificial Intelligence (IJCAI) meetings. The following artificial intelligence publications periodically feature work on speech and language processing: *Artificial Intelligence*, *Computational Intelligence*, *IEEE Transactions on Intelligent Systems*, and the *Journal of Artificial Intelligence Research*. Work on cognitive modeling of language can be found at the annual meeting of the Cognitive Science Society, as well as its journal *Cognitive Science*. An influential series of invitation-only workshops was held by ARPA, called variously the *DARPA Speech and Natural Language Processing Workshop* or the *ARPA Workshop on Human Language Technology*.

There are a fair number of textbooks available covering various aspects of speech and language processing. Manning and Schütze (1999) (*Foundations of Statistical Language Processing*) focuses on statistical models of tagging, parsing, disambiguation, collocations, and other areas. Charniak (1993) (*Statistical Language Learning*) is an accessible, though older and less-extensive, introduction to similar material. Allen (1995) (*Natural Language Understanding*) provides extensive coverage of language processing from the AI perspective. Gazdar and Mellish (1989) (*Natural Language Processing in Lisp/Prolog*) covers especially automata, parsing, features, and unification. Pereira and Shieber (1987) gives a Prolog-based introduction to parsing and interpretation. Russell and Norvig (1995) is an introduction to artificial intelligence that includes chapters on natural language processing. Partee et al. (1990) has a very broad coverage of mathematical linguistics. Cole (1997) is a volume of survey papers covering the entire field of speech and language processing. A somewhat dated but still tremendously useful collection of foundational papers can be found in Grosz et al. (1986) (*Readings in Natural Language Processing*).

Of course, a wide-variety of speech and language processing resources are now available on the World-Wide Web. Pointers to these resources are maintained on the home-page for this book at:

```
http://www.cs.colorado.edu/~martin/slp.html
```

Part I

WORDS

Words are the fundamental building block of language. Every human language, spoken, signed, or written, is composed of words. Every area of speech and language processing, from speech recognition to machine translation to information retrieval on the Web, requires extensive knowledge about words. Psycholinguistic models of human language processing and models from generative linguistics are also heavily based on lexical knowledge.

The six chapters in this part introduce computational models of the spelling, pronunciation, and morphology of words and cover three important real-world tasks that rely on lexical knowledge: automatic speech recognition (ASR), text-to-speech synthesis (TTS), and the correction of spelling errors. Finally, these chapters define perhaps the most important computational model for speech and language processing: the automaton. Four kinds of automata are covered: finite-state automata (FSAs) and regular expressions, finite-state transducers (FSTs), weighted transducers, and the Hidden Markov Model (HMM), as well as the N-gram model of word sequences.

2 REGULAR EXPRESSIONS AND AUTOMATA

In the old days, if you wanted to impeach a witness you had to go back and fumble through endless transcripts. Now it's on a screen somewhere or on a disk and I can search for a particular word — say every time the witness used the word glove *— and then quickly ask a question about what he said years ago. Right away you see the witness get flustered.*

Johnnie L. Cochran Jr., attorney, *New York Times*, 9/28/97

Imagine that you have become a passionate fan of woodchucks. Desiring more information on this celebrated woodland creature, you turn to your favorite Web browser and type in *woodchuck*. Your browser returns a few sites. You have a flash of inspiration and type in *woodchucks*. This time you discover "interesting links to woodchucks and lemurs" and "all about Vermont's unique, endangered species". Instead of having to do this search twice, you would have rather typed one search command specifying something like *woodchuck with an optional final s*. Furthermore, you might want to find a site whether or not it spelled *woodchucks* with a capital *W* (*Woodchuck*). Or perhaps you might want to search for all the prices in some document; you might want to see all strings that look like *$199* or *$25* or *$24.99*. In this chapter we introduce the **regular expression**, the standard notation for characterizing text sequences. The regular expression is used for specifying text strings in situations like this Web-search example, and in other information retrieval applications, but also plays an important role in word-processing (in PC, Mac, or UNIX applications), computation of frequencies from corpora, and other such tasks.

After we have defined regular expressions, we show how they can be implemented via the **finite-state automaton**. The finite-state automaton is not only the mathematical device used to implement regular expressions, but also one of the most significant tools of computational linguistics. Variations of automata such as finite-state transducers, Hidden Markov Models, and N-gram grammars are important components of the speech recognition and synthesis, spell-checking, and information-extraction applications that we will introduce in later chapters.

2.1   REGULAR EXPRESSIONS

> SIR ANDREW: Her C's, her U's and her T's: why that?
> Shakespeare, *Twelfth Night*

REGULAR
EXPRESSION

One of the unsung successes in standardization in computer science has been the **regular expression** (**RE**), a language for specifying text search strings. The regular expression languages used for searching texts in UNIX (vi, Perl, Emacs, grep), Microsoft Word (version 6 and beyond), and Word-Perfect are almost identical, and many RE features exist in the various Web search engines. Besides this practical use, the regular expression is an important theoretical tool throughout computer science and linguistics.

STRINGS

A regular expression (first developed by Kleene (1956) but see the History section for more details) is a formula in a special language that is used for specifying simple classes of **strings**. A string is a sequence of symbols; for the purpose of most text-based search techniques, a string is any sequence of alphanumeric characters (letters, numbers, spaces, tabs, and punctuation). For these purposes a space is just a character like any other, and we represent it with the symbol ␣.

Formally, a regular expression is an algebraic notation for characterizing a set of strings. Thus they can be used to specify search strings as well as to define a language in a formal way. We will begin by talking about regular expressions as a way of specifying searches in texts, and proceed to other uses. Section 2.3 shows that the use of just three regular expression operators is sufficient to characterize strings, but we use the more convenient and commonly-used regular expression syntax of the Perl language throughout this section. Since common text-processing programs agree on most of the syntax of regular expressions, most of what we say extends to all UNIX, Microsoft Word, and WordPerfect regular expressions. Appendix A shows the few areas where these programs differ from the Perl syntax.

CORPUS

Regular expression search requires a **pattern** that we want to search for, and a **corpus** of texts to search through. A regular expression search function will search through the corpus returning all texts that contain the pattern. In an information retrieval (IR) system such as a Web search engine, the texts might be entire documents or Web pages. In a word-processor, the texts might be individual words, or lines of a document. In the rest of this chapter, we will use this last paradigm. Thus when we give a search pattern, we will assume that the search engine returns the *line of the document* returned. This is what the UNIX `grep` command does. We will underline the exact part of the pattern that matches the regular expression. A search can be designed to return all matches to a regular expression or only the first match. We will show only the first match.

Basic Regular Expression Patterns

The simplest kind of regular expression is a sequence of simple characters. For example, to search for *woodchuck*, we type `/woodchuck/`. So the regular expression `/Buttercup/` matches any string containing the substring *Buttercup,* for example the line *I'm called little Buttercup*) (recall that we are assuming a search application that returns entire lines). From here on we will put slashes around each regular expression to make it clear what is a regular expression and what is a pattern. We use the slash since this is the notation used by Perl, but the slashes are *not* part of the regular expressions.

The search string can consist of a single letter (like `/!/`) or a sequence of letters (like `/urgl/`); The *first* instance of each match to the regular expression is underlined below (although a given application might choose to return more than just the first instance):

RE	Example Patterns Matched
`/woodchucks/`	"interesting links to woodchucks and lemurs"
`/a/`	"Mary Ann stopped by Mona's"
`/Claire_says,/`	"Dagmar, my gift please," Claire says,"
`/song/`	"all our pretty songs"
`/!/`	"You've left the burglar behind again!" said Nori

Regular expressions are **case sensitive**; lowercase `/s/` is distinct from uppercase `/S/`; (`/s/` matches a lower case *s* but not an uppercase *S*). This means that the pattern `/woodchucks/` will not match the string *Woodchucks*. We can solve this problem with the use of the square braces `[` and `]`. The string of characters inside the braces specify a **disjunction** of characters to match. For example Figure 2.1 shows that the pattern `/[wW]/` matches patterns containing either *w* or *W*.

RE	Match	Example Patterns
/[wW]oodchuck/	Woodchuck or woodchuck	"Woodchuck"
/[abc]/	'a', 'b', *or* 'c'	"In uomini, in soldati"
/[1234567890]/	any digit	"plenty of 7 to 5"

Figure 2.1   The use of the brackets [] to specify a disjunction of characters.

The regular expression /[1234567890]/ specified any single digit. While classes of characters like digits or letters are important building blocks in expressions, they can get awkward (e.g., it's inconvenient to specify

/[ABCDEFGHIJKLMNOPQRSTUVWXYZ]/

RANGE

to mean "any capital letter"). In these cases the brackets can be used with the dash (-) to specify any one character in a **range**. The pattern /[2-5]/ specifies any one of the characters *2*, *3*, *4*, or *5*. The pattern /[b-g]/ specifies one of the characters *b*, *c*, *d*, *e*, *f*, or *g*. Some other examples:

RE	Match	Example Patterns Matched
/[A-Z]/	an uppercase letter	"we should call it 'Drenched Blossoms'"
/[a-z]/	a lowercase letter	"my beans were impatient to be hoed!"
/[0-9]/	a single digit	"Chapter 1: Down the Rabbit Hole"

Figure 2.2   The use of the brackets [] plus the dash - to specify a range.

The square braces can also be used to specify what a single character *cannot* be, by use of the caret ^. If the caret ^ is the first symbol after the open square brace [, the resulting pattern is negated. For example, the pattern /[^a]/ matches any single character (including special characters) except *a*. This is only true when the caret is the first symbol after the open square brace. If it occurs anywhere else, it usually stands for a caret; Figure 2.3 shows some examples.

RE	Match (single characters)	Example Patterns Matched
[^A-Z]	not an uppercase letter	"Oyfn pripetchik"
[^Ss]	neither 'S' nor 's'	"I have no exquisite reason for't"
[^\.]	not a period	"our resident Djinn"
[e^]	either 'e' or '^'	"look up ^ now"
a^b	the pattern 'a^b'	"look up a^ b now"

Figure 2.3   Uses of the caret ^   for negation or just to mean ^ .

The use of square braces solves our capitalization problem for *wood-chucks*. But we still haven't answered our original question; how do we specify both *woodchuck* and *woodchucks*? We can't use the square brackets, because while they allow us to say "s or S", they don't allow us to say "s or nothing". For this we use the question-mark /?/, which means "the preceding character or nothing", as shown in Figure 2.4.

RE	Match	Example Patterns Matched
woodchucks?	woodchuck or woodchucks	"woodchuck"
colou?r	color or colour	"colour"

Figure 2.4   The question-mark ? marks optionality of the previous expression.

We can think of the question-mark as meaning "zero or one instances of the previous character". That is, it's a way of specifying how many of something that we want. So far we haven't needn't to specify that we want more than one of something. But sometimes we need regular expressions that allow repetitions of things. For example, consider the language of (certain) sheep, which consists of strings that look like the following:

baa!
baaa!
baaaa!
baaaaa!
baaaaaa!
. . .

This language consists of strings with a *b*, followed by at least two *a*s, followed by an exclamation point. The set of operators that allow us to say things like "some number of *a*s" are based on the asterisk or *, commonly called the **Kleene** * (pronounced "cleany star"). The Kleene star means "zero or more occurrences of the immediately previous character or regular expression". So /a*/ means "any string of zero or more *a*s". This will match *a* or *aaaaaa* but it will also match *Off Minor*, since the string *Off Minor* has zero *a*s. So the regular expression for matching one or more *a* is /aa*/, meaning one *a* followed by zero or more *a*s. More complex patterns can also be repeated. So /[ab]*/ means "zero or more *a*s or *b*s" (not "zero or more right square braces"). This will match strings like *aaaa* or *ababab* or *bbbb*.

KLEENE *

We now know enough to specify part of our regular expression for prices: multiple digits. Recall that the regular expression for an individual digit was /[0-9]/. So the regular expression for an integer (a string of digits) is /[0-9][0-9]*/. (Why isn't it just /[0-9]*/)?

Sometimes it's annoying to have to write the regular expression for digits twice, so there is a shorter way to specify "at least one" of some character. This is the **Kleene +**, which means "one or more of the previous character". Thus the expression /[0-9]+/ is the normal way to specify "a sequence of digits". There are thus two ways to specify the sheep language: /baaa*!/ or /baa+!/.

KLEENE +

One very important special character is the period (/./, a **wildcard** expression that matches any single character (*except* a carriage return):

RE	Match	Example Patterns
/beg.n/	any character between *beg* and *n*	begin, beg'n, begun

Figure 2.5   The use of the period . to specify any character.

The wildcard is often used together with the Kleene star to mean "any string of characters". For example suppose we want to find any line in which a particular word, for example *aardvark*, appears twice. We can specify this with the regular expression /aardvark.*aardvark/.

ANCHORS

Anchors are special characters that anchor regular expressions to particular places in a string. The most common anchors are the caret ^ and the dollar-sign $. The caret ^ matches the start of a line. The pattern /^The/ matches the word *The* only at the start of a line. Thus there are three uses of the caret ^: to match the start of a line, as a negation inside of square brackets, and just to mean a caret. (What are the contexts that allow Perl to know which function a given caret is supposed to have?). The dollar sign $ matches the end of a line. So the pattern ␣$ is a useful pattern for matching a space at the end of a line, and /^The dog\.$/ matches a line that contains only the phrase *The dog*. (We have to use the backslash here since we want the . to mean "period" and not the wildcard).

There are also two other anchors: \b matches a word boundary, while \B matches a non-boundary. Thus /\bthe\b/ matches the word *the* but not the word *other*. More technically, Perl defines a word as any sequence of digits, underscores or letters; this is based on the definition of "words" in programming languages like Perl or C. For example, /\b99/ will match the string *99* in *There are 99 bottles of beer on the wall* (because 99 follows a space) but not *99* in *There are 299 bottles of beer on the wall* (since 99 follows a number). But it will match *99* in *$99* (since *99* follows a dollar sign ($), which is not a digit, underscore, or letter).

Disjunction, Grouping, and Precedence

Suppose we need to search for texts about pets; perhaps we are particularly interested in cats and dogs. In such a case we might want to search for either the string *cat* or the string *dog*. Since we can't use the square-brackets to search for "cat or dog" (why not?) we need a new operator, the **disjunction** operator, also called the **pipe** symbol |. The pattern /cat|dog/ matches either the string cat or the string dog.

DISJUNCTION

Sometimes we need to use this disjunction operator in the midst of a larger sequence. For example, suppose I want to search for information about pet fish for my cousin David. How can I specify both *guppy* and *guppies*? We cannot simply say /guppy|ies/, because that would match only the strings *guppy* and *ies*. This is because sequences like guppy take **precedence** over the disjunction operator |. In order to make the disjunction operator apply only to a specific pattern, we need to use the parenthesis operators (and). Enclosing a pattern in parentheses makes it act like a single character for the purposes of neighboring operators like the pipe | and the Kleene *. So the pattern /gupp(y|ies)/ would specify that we meant the disjunction only to apply to the suffixes y and ies.

PRECEDENCE

The parenthesis operator (is also useful when we are using counters like the Kleene*. Unlike the | operator, the Kleene* operator applies by default only to a single character, not a whole sequence. Suppose we want to match repeated instances of a string. Perhaps we have a line that has column labels of the form *Column 1 Column 2 Column 3*. The expression /Column␣[0-9]+␣*/ will not match any column; instead, it will match a column followed by any number of spaces! The star here applies only to the space ␣ that precedes it, not the whole sequence. With the parentheses, we could write the expression /(Column␣[0-9]+␣*)*/ to match the word *Column*, followed by a number and optional spaces, the whole pattern repeated any number of times.

This idea that one operator may take precedence over another, requiring us to sometimes use parentheses to specify what we mean, is formalized by the **operator precedence hierarchy** for regular expressions. The following table gives the order of RE operator precedence, from highest precedence to lowest precedence:

OPERATOR
PRECEDENCE

Parenthesis	( )
Counters	* + ? { }
Sequences and anchors	the ^my end$
Disjunction		

Thus, because counters have a higher precedence than sequences, /the*/ matches *theeeee* but not *thethe*. Because sequences have a higher precedence than disjunction, /the|any/ matches *the* or *any* but not *theny*.

Patterns can be ambiguous in another way. Consider the expression /[a-z]*/ when matching against the text *once upon a time*. Since /[a-z]*/ matches zero or more letters, this expression could match nothing, or just the first letter *o*, or *on*, or *onc*, or *once*. In these cases regular expressions always match the *largest* string they can; we say that patterns are **greedy**, expanding to cover as much of a string as they can.

GREEDY

A Simple Example

Suppose we wanted to write a RE to find cases of the English article *the*. A simple (but incorrect) pattern might be:

/the/

One problem is that this pattern will miss the word when it begins a sentence and hence is capitalized (i.e., *The*). This might lead us to the following pattern:

/[tT]he/

But we will still incorrectly return texts with the embedded in other words (e.g., *other* or *theology*). So we need to specify that we want instances with a word boundary on both sides:

/\b[tT]he\b/

Suppose we wanted to do this without the use of /\b/? We might want this since /\b/ won't treat underscores and numbers as word boundaries; but we might want to find *the* in some context where it might also have underlines or numbers nearby (*the_* or *the25*). We need to specify that we want instances in which there are no alphabetic letters on either side of the *the*:

/[^a-zA-Z][tT]he[^a-zA-Z]/

But there is still one more problem with this pattern: it won't find the word *the* when it begins a line. This is because the regular expression [^a-zA-Z], which we used to avoid embedded *the*s, implies that there must be some single (although non-alphabetic) character before the the. We can avoid this by specifying that before the *the* we require *either* the beginning-of-line or a non-alphabetic character:

```
/(^|[^a-zA-Z])[tT]he[^a-zA-Z]/
```

A More Complex Example

Let's try out a more significant example of the power of REs. Suppose we want to build an application to help a user buy a computer on the Web. The user might want "any PC with more than 500 MHz and 32 Gb of disk space for less than $1000". In order to do this kind of retrieval we will first need to be able to look for expressions like *500 MHz* or *32 Gb* or *Compaq* or *Mac* or *$999.99*. In the rest of this section we'll work out some simple regular expressions for this task.

First, let's complete our regular expression for prices. Here's a regular expression for a dollar sign followed by a string of digits. Note that Perl is smart enough to realize that $ here doesn't mean end-of-line; how might it know that?

```
/$[0-9]+/
```

Now we just need to deal with fractions of dollars. We'll add a decimal point and two digits afterwards:

```
/$[0-9]+\.[0-9][0-9]/
```

This pattern only allows *$199.99* but not *$199*. We need to make the cents optional, and make sure we're at a word boundary:

```
/\b$[0-9]+(\.[0-9][0-9])?\b/
```

How about specifications for processor speed (in megahertz = MHz or gigahertz = GHz)? Here's a pattern for that:

```
/\b[0-9]+ *(MHz|[Mm]egahertz|GHz|[Gg]igahertz)\b/
```

Note that we use / */ to mean "zero or more spaces", since there might always be extra spaces lying around. Dealing with disk space (in Gb = gigabytes), or memory size (in Mb = megabytes or Gb = gigabytes), we need to allow for optional gigabyte fractions again (*5.5 Gb*). Note the use of ? for making the final s optional:

```
/\b[0-9]+␣*(Mb|[Mm]egabytes?)\b/
/\b[0-9](\.[0-9]+)?␣*(Gb|[Gg]igabytes?)\b/
```

Finally, we might want some simple patterns to specify operating systems and vendors:

```
/\b(Win95|Win98|WinNT|Windows␣*(NT|95|98|2000)?)\b/
/\b(Mac|Macintosh|Apple)\b/
```

Advanced Operators

RE	Expansion	Match	Example Patterns
\d	[0-9]	any digit	Party␣of␣5
\D	[^0-9]	any non-digit	Blue␣moon
\w	[a-zA-Z0-9␣]	any alphanumeric or space	Daiyu
\W	[^\w]	a non-alphanumeric	!!!!
\s	[␣\r\t\n\f]	whitespace (space, tab)	
\S	[^\s]	Non-whitespace	in␣Concord

Figure 2.6　　Aliases for common sets of characters.

There are also some useful advanced regular expression operators. Figure 2.6 shows some useful aliases for common ranges, which can be used mainly to save typing. Besides the Kleene * and Kleene +, we can also use explicit numbers as counters, by enclosing them in curly brackets. The regular expression /{3}/ means "exactly 3 occurrences of the previous character or expression". So /a\.{24}z/ will match *a* followed by 24 dots followed by *z* (but not *a* followed by 23 or 25 dots followed by a *z*).

A range of numbers can also be specified; so /{n,m}/ specifies from n to m occurrences of the previous char or expression, while /{n,}/ means at least n occurrences of the previous expression. REs for counting are summarized in Figure 2.7.

Finally, certain special characters are referred to by special notation based on the backslash (\). The most common of these are the **newline** character \n and the **tab** character \t. To refer to characters that are special themselves, (like ., *, [, and \), precede them with a backslash, (i.e., /\./, /*/, /\[/, and /\\/).

NEWLINE

RE	Match
*	zero or more occurrences of the previous char or expression
+	one or more occurrences of the previous char or expression
?	exactly zero or one occurrence of the previous char or expression
{n}	*n* occurrences of the previous char or expression
{n,m}	from *n* to *m* occurrences of the previous char or expression
{n,}	at least *n* occurrences of the previous char or expression

Figure 2.7   Regular expression operators for counting.

RE	Match	Example Patterns Matched
*	an asterisk "*"	"K*A*P*L*A*N"
\.	a period "."	"Dr. Livingston, I presume"
\?	a question mark	"Would you light my candle?"
\n	a newline	
\t	a tab	

Figure 2.8   Some characters that need to be backslashed.

The reader should consult Appendix A for further details of regular expressions, and especially for the differences between regular expressions in Perl, UNIX, and Microsoft Word.

Regular Expression Substitution, Memory, and ELIZA

An important use of regular expressions is in **substitutions**. For example, the Perl substitution operator s/regexp1/regexp2/ allows a string characterized by one regular expression to be replaced by a string characterized by a different regular expression:

SUBSTITUTION

```
s/colour/color/
```

It is often useful to be able to refer to a particular subpart of the string matching the first pattern. For example, suppose we wanted to put angle brackets around all integers in a text, changing e.g., *the 35 boxes* to *the <35> boxes*. We'd like a way to refer back to the integer we've found so that we can easily add the brackets. To do this, we put parentheses (and) around the first pattern, and use the **number** operator \1 in the second pattern to refer back. Here's how it looks:

```
s/([0-9]+)/<\1>/
```

The parenthesis and number operators can also be used to specify that a certain string or expression must occur twice in the text. For example, suppose we are looking for the pattern "the Xer they were, the Xer they will be", where we want to constrain the two X's to be the same string. We do this by surrounding the first X with the parenthesis operator, and replacing the second X with the number operator \1, as follows:

```
/the (.*)er they were, the \1er they will be/
```

Here the \1 will be replaced by whatever string matched the first item in parentheses. So this will match *The bigger they were, the bigger they will be* but not *The bigger they were, the faster they will be.*

The number operator can be used with other numbers: if you match two different sets of parenthesis, \2 means whatever matched the *second* set. For example

```
/the (.*)er they (.*), the \1er they \2/
```

REGISTERS will match *The bigger they were, the bigger they were* but not *The bigger they were, the bigger they will be.* These numbered memories are called **registers** (e.g. register 1, register 2, register 3, etc). This memory feature is not part of every regular expression language and is often considered an "extended" feature of regular expressions.

Substitutions using memory are very useful in implementing a simple natural-language understanding program like ELIZA (Weizenbaum, 1966). Recall that ELIZA simulated a Rogerian psychologist and could carry on conversations with the user like the following:

User$_1$:   Men are all alike.
ELIZA$_1$:   IN WHAT WAY
User$_2$:   They're always bugging us about something or other.
ELIZA$_2$:   CAN YOU THINK OF A SPECIFIC EXAMPLE
User$_3$:   Well, my boyfriend made me come here.
ELIZA$_3$:   YOUR BOYFRIEND MADE YOU COME HERE
User$_4$:   He says I'm depressed much of the time.
ELIZA$_4$:   I AM SORRY TO HEAR YOU ARE DEPRESSED.

Eliza worked by having a cascade of regular expression substitutions that each matched some part of the input lines and changed them. The first substitutions changed all instances of *my* to *YOUR*, and *I'm* to *YOU ARE*, and so on. The next set of substitutions looked for relevant patterns in the input and created an appropriate output; here are some examples:

```
s/.* YOU ARE (depressed|sad) .*/I AM SORRY TO HEAR YOU ARE \1/
```

```
s/.* YOU ARE (depressed|sad) .*/WHY DO YOU THINK YOU ARE \1/
s/.* all .*/IN WHAT WAY/
s/.* always .*/CAN YOU THINK  OF A SPECIFIC EXAMPLE/
```

Since multiple substitutions could apply to a given input, substitutions were assigned a rank and were applied in order. Creation of such patterns is addressed in Exercise 2.2.

2.2   FINITE-STATE AUTOMATA

The regular expression is more than just a convenient metalanguage for text searching. First, a regular expression is one way of describing a **finite-state automaton** (**FSA**). Finite-state automata are the theoretical foundation of a good deal of the computational work we will describe in this book. Any regular expression can be implemented as a finite-state automaton (except regular expressions that use the memory feature; more on this later). Symmetrically, any finite-state automaton can be described with a regular expression. Second, a regular expression is one way of characterizing a particular kind of formal language called a **regular language**. Both regular expressions and finite-state automata can be used to described regular languages. The relation among these three theoretical constructions is sketched out in Figure 2.9.

FINITE-STATE
AUTOMATON
FSA

REGULAR
LANGUAGE

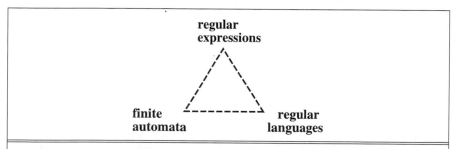

Figure 2.9   The relationship between finite automata, regular expressions, and regular languages; figure suggested by Martin Kay.

This section will begin by introducing finite-state automata for some of the regular expressions from the last section, and then suggest how the mapping from regular expressions to automata proceeds in general. Although we begin with their use for implementing regular expressions, FSAs have a wide variety of other uses that we will explore in this chapter and the next.

Using an FSA to Recognize Sheeptalk

After a while, with the parrot's help, the Doctor got to learn the language of the animals so well that he could talk to them himself and understand everything they said.

Hugh Lofting, *The Story of Doctor Dolittle*

Let's begin with the "sheep language" we discussed previously. Recall that we defined the sheep language as any string from the following (infinite) set:

baa!
baaa!
baaaa!
baaaaa!
baaaaaa!

...

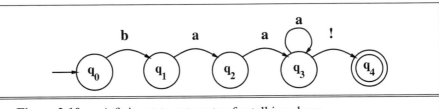

Figure 2.10   A finite-state automaton for talking sheep.

The regular expression for this kind of "sheeptalk" is /baa+!/. Figure 2.10 shows an **automaton** for modeling this regular expression. The automaton (i.e., machine, also called **finite automaton, finite-state automaton**, or **FSA**) recognizes a set of strings, in this case the strings characterizing sheep talk, in the same way that a regular expression does. We represent the automaton as a directed graph: a finite set of vertices (also called nodes), together with a set of directed links between pairs of vertices called arcs. We'll represent vertices with circles and arcs with arrows. The automaton has five **state**s, which are represented by nodes in the graph. State 0 is the **start state** which we represent by the incoming arrow. State 4 is the **final state** or **accepting state**, which we represent by the double circle. It also has four **transitions**, which we represent by arcs in the graph.

The FSA can be used for recognizing (we also say **accepting**) strings in the following way. First, think of the input as being written on a long tape

AUTOMATON

STATE
START STATE

broken up into cells, with one symbol written in each cell of the tape, as in Figure 2.11.

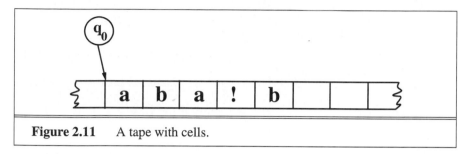

Figure 2.11   A tape with cells.

The machine starts in the start state (q_0), and iterates the following process: Check the next letter of the input. If it matches the symbol on an arc leaving the current state, then cross that arc, move to the next state, and also advance one symbol in the input. If we are in the accepting state (q_4) when we run out of input, the machine has successfully recognized an instance of sheeptalk. If the machine never gets to the final state, either because it runs out of input, or it gets some input that doesn't match an arc (as in Figure 2.11), or if it just happens to get stuck in some non-final state, we say the machine **rejects** or fails to accept an input.

We can also represent an automaton with a **state-transition table**. As in the graph notation, the state-transition table represents the start state, the accepting states, and what transitions leave each state with which symbols. Here's the state-transition table for the FSA of Figure 2.10.

State	Input		
	b	a	!
0	1	0	0
1	0	2	0
2	0	3	0
3	0	3	4
4:	0	0	0

Figure 2.12   The state-transition table for the FSA of Figure 2.10.

We've marked state 4 with a colon to indicate that it's a final state (you can have as many final states as you want), and the 0 indicates an illegal or missing transition. We can read the first row as "if we're in state 0 and we see the input **b** we must go to state 1. If we're in state 0 and we see the input **a** or **!**, we fail".

More formally, a finite automaton is defined by the following five parameters:

- Q: a finite set of N states $q_0, q_1, \ldots, q_N$
- Σ: a finite input alphabet of symbols
- q_0: the start state
- F: the set of final states, $F \subseteq Q$
- $\delta(q, i)$: the transition function or transition matrix between states. Given a state $q \in Q$ and an input symbol $i \in \Sigma$, $\delta(q, i)$ returns a new state $q' \in Q$. δ is thus a relation from $Q \times \Sigma$ to Q;

For the sheeptalk automaton in Figure 2.10, $Q = \{q_0, q_1, q_2, q_3, q_4\}$, $\Sigma = \{a, b, !\}$, $F = \{q_4\}$, and $\delta(q, i)$ is defined by the transition table in Figure 2.12.

Figure 2.13 presents an algorithm for recognizing a string using a state-transition table. The algorithm is called D-RECOGNIZE for "deterministic recognizer". A **deterministic** algorithm is one that has no choice points; the algorithm always knows what to do for any input. The next section will introduce non-deterministic automata that must make decisions about which states to move to.

DETERMINIS-
TIC

D-RECOGNIZE takes as input a tape and an automaton. It returns *accept* if the string it is pointing to on the tape is accepted by the automaton, and *reject* otherwise. Note that since D-RECOGNIZE assumes it is already pointing at the string to be checked, its task is only a subpart of the general problem that we often use regular expressions for, finding a string in a corpus. (The general problem is left as an exercise to the reader in Exercise 2.9.)

D-RECOGNIZE begins by initializing the variable *index* the beginning of the tape, and *current-state* to the machine's initial state. D-RECOGNIZE then enters a loop that drives the rest of the algorithm. It first checks whether it has reached the end of its input. If so, it either accepts the input (if the current state is an accept state) or rejects the input (if not).

If there is input left on the tape, D-RECOGNIZE looks at the transition table to decide which state to move to. The variable *current-state* indicates which row of the table to consult, while the current symbol on the tape indicates which column of the table to consult. The resulting transition-table cell is used to update the variable *current-state* and *index* is incremented to move forward on the tape. If the transition-table cell is empty then the machine has nowhere to go and must reject the input.

Figure 2.14 traces the execution of this algorithm on the sheep language FSA given the sample input string *baaa!*.

function D-RECOGNIZE(*tape, machine*) **returns** accept or reject

> *index* ← Beginning of tape
> *current-state* ← Initial state of machine
> **loop**
>   **if** End of input has been reached **then**
>   **if** current-state is an accept state **then**
>   **return** accept
>   **else**
>   **return** reject
>   **elsif** *transition-table[current-state,tape[index]]* is empty **then**
>   **return** reject
>   **else**
>   *current-state* ← *transition-table[current-state,tape[index]]*
>   *index* ← *index* + 1
> **end**

Figure 2.13   An algorithm for deterministic recognition of FSAs. This algorithm returns *accept* if the entire string it is pointing at is in the language defined by the FSA, and *reject* if the string is not in the language.

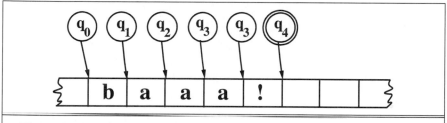

Figure 2.14   Tracing the execution of FSA #1 on some sheeptalk.

Before examining the beginning of the tape, the machine is in state q_0. Finding a *b* on input tape, it changes to state q_1 as indicated by the contents of *transition-table*$[q_0,b]$ in Figure 2.12 on page 35. It then finds an *a* and switches to state q_2, another *a* puts it in state q_3, a third *a* leaves it in state q_3, where it reads the "!", and switches to state q_4. Since there is no more input, the `End of input` condition at the beginning of the loop is satisfied for the first time and the machine halts in q_4. State q_4 is an accepting state, and so the machine has accepted the string *baaa!* as a sentence in the sheep language.

The algorithm will fail whenever there is no legal transition for a given combination of state and input. The input *abc* will fail to be recognized since there is no legal transition out of state q_0 on the input a, (i.e., this entry of the transition table in Figure 2.12 on page 35 has a $\emptyset$). Even if the automaton had allowed an initial *a* it would have certainly failed on *c*, since *c* isn't even in the sheeptalk alphabet!. We can think of these "empty" elements in the table as if they all pointed at one "empty" state, which we might call the **fail state** or **sink state**. In a sense then, we could view any machine with empty transitions *as if* we had augmented it with a fail state, and drawn in all the extra arcs, so we always had somewhere to go from any state on any possible input. Just for completeness, Figure 2.15 shows the FSA from Figure 2.10 with the fail state q_F filled in.

FAIL STATE

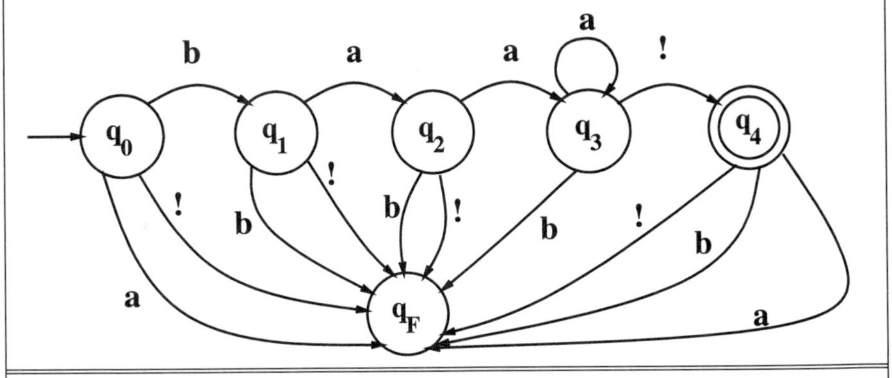

Figure 2.15   Adding a fail state to Figure 2.10.

Formal Languages

We can use the same graph in Figure 2.10 as an automaton for GENERATING sheeptalk. If we do, we would say that the automaton starts at state q_0, and crosses arcs to new states, printing out the symbols that label each arc it follows. When the automaton gets to the final state it stops. Notice that at state 3, the automaton has to chose between printing out a **!** and going to state 4, or printing out an **a** and returning to state 3. Let's say for now that we don't care how the machine makes this decision; maybe it flips a coin. For now, we don't care which exact string of sheeptalk we generate, as long as it's a string captured by the regular expression for sheeptalk above.

> **Key Concept #1. Formal Language:** A model which can both gener-
> ate and recognize all and only the strings of a formal language acts as
> a *definition* of the formal language.

A **formal language** is a set of strings, each string composed of symbols FORMAL LANGUAGE
from a finite symbol-set called an **alphabet** (the same alphabet used above ALPHABET
for defining an automaton!). The alphabet for the sheep language is the set
$\Sigma = \{a, b, !\}$. Given a model m (such as a particular FSA), we can use $L(m)$
to mean "the formal language characterized by m". So the formal language
defined by our sheeptalk automaton m in Figure 2.10 (and Figure 2.12) is the
infinite set:

$$L(m) = \{baa!, baaa!, baaaa!, baaaaa!, baaaaaa!, \dots\} \qquad (2.1)$$

The usefulness of an automaton for defining a language is that it can
express an infinite set (such as this one above) in a closed form. Formal
languages are not the same as **natural languages**, which are the kind of NATURAL LANGUAGES
languages that real people speak. In fact, a formal language may bear no
resemblance at all to a real language (e.g., a formal language can be used
to model the different states of a soda machine). But we often use a formal
language to model part of a natural language, such as parts of the phonology,
morphology, or syntax. The term **generative grammar** is sometimes used
in linguistics to mean a grammar of a formal language; the origin of the term
is this use of an automaton to define a language by generating all possible
strings.

Another Example

In the previous examples our formal alphabet consisted of letters; but we
can also have a higher level alphabet consisting of words. In this way we
can write finite-state automata that model facts about word combinations.
For example, suppose we wanted to build an FSA that modeled the subpart
of English dealing with amounts of money. Such a formal language would
model the subset of English consisting of phrases like *ten cents*, *three dollars*, *one dollar thirty-five cents* and so on.

We might break this down by first building just the automaton to account for the numbers from 1 to 99, since we'll need them to deal with cents.
Figure 2.16 shows this.

We could now add *cents* and *dollars* to our automaton. Figure 2.17
shows a simple version of this, where we just made two copies of the automaton in Figure 2.16 and appended the words *cents* and *dollars*.

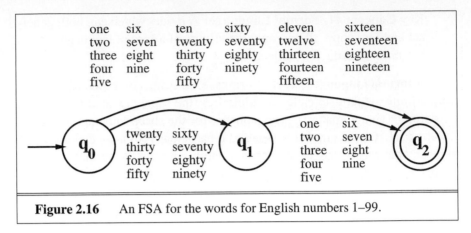

Figure 2.16   An FSA for the words for English numbers 1–99.

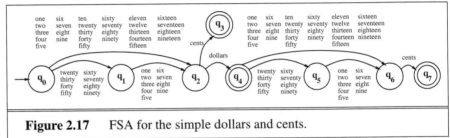

Figure 2.17   FSA for the simple dollars and cents.

We would now need to add in the grammar for different amounts of dollars; including higher numbers like *hundred*, *thousand*. We'd also need to make sure that the nouns like *cents* and *dollars* are singular when appropriate (*one cent*, *one dollar*), and plural when appropriate (*ten cents*, *two dollars*). This is left as an exercise for the reader (Exercise 2.3). We can think of the FSAs in Figure 2.16 and Figure 2.17 as simple grammars of parts of English. We will return to grammar-building in Part II of this book, particularly in Chapter 9.

Non-Deterministic FSAs

Let's extend our discussion now to another class of FSAs: **non-deterministic FSAs** (or **NFSAs**). Consider the sheeptalk automaton in Figure 2.18, which is much like our first automaton in Figure 2.10:

The only difference between this automaton and the previous one is that here in Figure 2.18 the self-loop is on state 2 instead of state 3. Consider using this network as an automaton for recognizing sheeptalk. When we get to state 2, if we see an **a** we don't know whether to remain in state

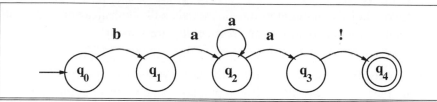

Figure 2.18   A non-deterministic finite-state automaton for talking sheep (NFSA #1). Compare with the deterministic automaton in Figure 2.10.

2 or go on to state 3. Automata with decision points like this are called **non-deterministic FSAs** (or **NFSAs**). Recall by contrast that Figure 2.10 specified a **deterministic** automaton, i.e., one whose behavior during recognition is fully *determined* by the state it is in and the symbol it is looking at. A deterministic automaton can be referred to as a **DFSA**. That is not true for the machine in Figure 2.18 (NFSA #1).

NON-DETERMINISTIC
NFSA

DFSA

There is another common type of non-determinism, caused by arcs that have no symbols on them (called **ε-transitions**). The automaton in Figure 2.19 defines the exact same language as the last one, or our first one, but it does it with an ε-transition.

ε-TRANSITION

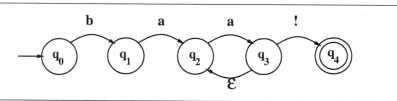

Figure 2.19   Another NFSA for the sheep language (NFSA #2). It differs from NFSA #1 in Figure 2.18 in having an ε-transition.

We interpret this new arc as follows: If we are in state 3, we are allowed to move to state 2 *without* looking at the input, or advancing our input pointer. So this introduces another kind of non-determinism — we might not know whether to follow the ε-transition or the ! arc.

Using an NFSA to Accept Strings

If we want to know whether a string is an instance of sheeptalk or not, and if we use a non-deterministic machine to recognize it, we might follow the wrong arc and reject it when we should have accepted it. That is, since there is more than one choice at some point, we might take the wrong choice. This problem of choice in non-deterministic models will come up again and again as we build computational models, particularly for parsing.

There are three standard solutions to this problem:

- **Backup:** Whenever we come to a choice point, we could put a *marker* to mark where we were in the input, and what state the automaton was in. Then if it turns out that we took the wrong choice, we could back up and try another path.

- **Look-ahead:** We could look ahead in the input to help us decide which path to take.

- **Parallelism:** Whenever we come to a choice point, we could look at every alternative path in parallel.

We will focus here on the backup approach and defer discussion of the look-ahead and parallelism approaches to later chapters.

The backup approach suggests that we should blithely make choices that might lead to deadends, knowing that we can always return to unexplored alternative choices. There are two keys to this approach: we need to remember all the alternatives for each choice point, and we need to store sufficient information about each alternative so that we can return to it when necessary. When a backup algorithm reaches a point in its processing where no progress can be made (because it runs out of input, or has no legal transitions), it returns to a previous choice point, selects one of the unexplored alternatives, and continues from there. Applying this notion to our non-deterministic recognizer, we need only remember two things for each choice point: the state, or node, of the machine that we can go to and the corresponding position on the tape. We will call the combination of the node and position the **search-state** of the recognition algorithm. To avoid confusion, we will refer to the state of the automaton (as opposed to the state of the search) as a **node** or a **machine-state**. Figure 2.21 presents a recognition algorithm based on this approach.

SEARCH-
STATE

Before going on to describe the main part of this algorithm, we should note two changes to the transition table that drives it. First, in order to represent nodes that have outgoing ε-transitions, we add a new ε-**column** to the transition table. If a node has an ε-transition, we list the destination node in the ε-column for that node's row. The second addition is needed to account for multiple transitions to different nodes from the same input symbol. We let each cell entry consist of a list of destination nodes rather than a single node. Figure 2.20 shows the transition table for the machine in Figure 2.18 (NFSA #1). While it has no ε-transitions, it does show that in machine-state

	Input
State	b a ! ε
0	1 0 0 0
1	0 2 0 0
2	0 2,3 0 0
3	0 0 4 0
4:	0 0 0 0

Figure 2.20   The transition table from NFSA #1 in Figure 2.18.

q_2 the input a can lead back to q_2 or on to q_3.

Figure 2.21 shows the algorithm for using a non-deterministic FSA to recognize an input string. The function ND-RECOGNIZE uses the variable *agenda* to keep track of all the currently unexplored choices generated during the course of processing. Each choice (search state) is a tuple consisting of a node (state) of the machine and a position on the tape. The variable *current-search-state* represents the branch choice being currently explored.

ND-RECOGNIZE begins by creating an initial search-state and placing it on the agenda. For now we don't specify what order the search-states are placed on the agenda. This search-state consists of the initial machine-state of the machine and a pointer to the beginning of the tape. The function NEXT is then called to retrieve an item from the agenda and assign it to the variable *current-search-state*.

As with D-RECOGNIZE, the first task of the main loop is to determine if the entire contents of the tape have been successfully recognized. This is done via a call to ACCEPT-STATE?, which returns *accept* if the current search-state contains both an accepting machine-state and a pointer to the end of the tape. If we're not done, the machine generates a set of possible next steps by calling GENERATE-NEW-STATES, which creates search-states for any ε-transitions and any normal input-symbol transitions from the transition table. All of these search-state tuples are then added to the current agenda.

Finally, we attempt to get a new search-state to process from the agenda. If the agenda is empty we've run out of options and have to reject the input. Otherwise, an unexplored option is selected and the loop continues.

It is important to understand why ND-RECOGNIZE returns a value of reject only when the agenda is found to be empty. Unlike D-RECOGNIZE, it does not return reject when it reaches the end of the tape in an non-accept machine-state or when it finds itself unable to advance the tape from some

machine-state. This is because, in the non-deterministic case, such road-
blocks only indicate failure down a given path, not overall failure. We can
only be sure we can reject a string when all possible choices have been examined and found lacking.

---

function ND-RECOGNIZE(*tape, machine*) **returns** accept or reject

  agenda ← {(Initial state of machine, beginning of tape)}
  current-search-state ← NEXT(*agenda*)
  loop
    if ACCEPT-STATE?(*current-search-state*) returns true **then**
      return accept
    else
      agenda ← *agenda* ∪ GENERATE-NEW-STATES(*current-search-state*)
    if *agenda* is empty **then**
      return reject
    else
      current-search-state ← NEXT(*agenda*)
  end

function GENERATE-NEW-STATES(*current-state*) **returns** a set of search-
states

  current-node ← the node the current search-state is in
  index ← the point on the tape the current search-state is looking at
  return a list of search states from transition table as follows:
    (*transition-table[current-node,ε], index*)
    ∪
    (*transition-table[current-node, tape[index]], index + 1*)

function ACCEPT-STATE?(*search-state*) **returns** true or false

  current-node ← the node search-state is in
  index ← the point on the tape search-state is looking at
  if *index* is at the end of the tape **and** *current-node* is an accept state of machine
  then
    return true
  else
    return false

Figure 2.21   An algorithm for NFSA recognition. The word *node* means
a state of the FSA, while *state* or *search-state* means "the state of the search
process", i.e., a combination of *node* and *tape-position*.

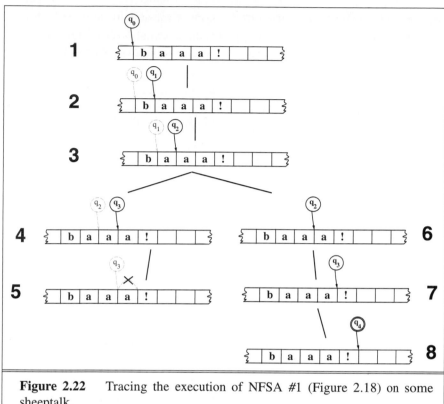

Figure 2.22   Tracing the execution of NFSA #1 (Figure 2.18) on some sheeptalk.

Figure 2.22 illustrates the progress of ND-RECOGNIZE as it attempts to handle the input baaa!. Each strip illustrates the state of the algorithm at a given point in its processing. The *current-search-state* variable is captured by the solid bubbles representing the machine-state along with the arrow representing progress on the tape. Each strip lower down in the figure represents progress from one *current-search-state* to the next.

Little of interest happens until the algorithm finds itself in state q_2 while looking at the second a on the tape. An examination of the entry for transition-table$[q_2,a]$ returns both q_2 and q_3. Search states are created for each of these choices and placed on the agenda. Unfortunately, our algorithm chooses to move to state q_3, a move that results in neither an accept state nor any new states since the entry for transition-table$[q_3, a]$ is empty. At this point, the algorithm simply asks the agenda for a new state to pursue. Since the choice of returning to q_2 from q_2 is the only unexamined choice on the agenda it is returned with the tape pointer advanced to the next a. Somewhat diabolically, ND-RECOGNIZE finds itself faced with the same choice. The entry for transition-table[q_2,a] still indicates that looping back to q_2 or advancing to q_3 are valid choices. As before, states representing both are placed on the agenda. These search states are not the same as the previous ones since their tape index values have advanced. This time the agenda provides the move to q_3 as the next move. The move to q_4, and success, is then uniquely determined by the tape and the transition-table.

Recognition as Search

ND-RECOGNIZE accomplishes the task of recognizing strings in a regular language by providing a way to systematically explore all the possible paths through a machine. If this exploration yields a path ending in an accept state, it accepts the string, otherwise it rejects it. This systematic exploration is made possible by the agenda mechanism, which on each iteration selects a partial path to explore and keeps track of any remaining, as yet unexplored, partial paths.

STATE-SPACE SEARCH

Algorithms such as ND-RECOGNIZE, which operate by systematically searching for solutions, are known as **state-space search** algorithms. In such algorithms, the problem definition creates a space of possible solutions; the goal is to explore this space, returning an answer when one is found or rejecting the input when the space has been exhaustively explored. In ND-RECOGNIZE, search states consist of pairings of machine-states with positions on the input tape. The state-space consists of all the pairings of machine-state and tape positions that are possible given the machine in question. The goal of the search is to navigate through this space from one state to another looking for a pairing of an accept state with an end of tape position.

The key to the effectiveness of such programs is often the *order* in which the states in the space are considered. A poor ordering of states may lead to the examination of a large number of unfruitful states before a successful solution is discovered. Unfortunately, it is typically not possible to tell a good choice from a bad one, and often the best we can do is to insure that each possible solution is eventually considered.

Careful readers may have noticed that the ordering of states in ND-RECOGNIZE has been left unspecified. We know only that unexplored states are added to the agenda as they are created and that the (undefined) function NEXT returns an unexplored state from the agenda when asked. How should the function NEXT be defined? Consider an ordering strategy where the states that are considered next are the most recently created ones. Such a policy can be implemented by placing newly created states at the front of the agenda and having NEXT return the state at the front of the agenda when called. Thus the agenda is implemented by a **stack**. This is commonly referred to as a **depth-first search** or **Last In First Out (LIFO)** strategy.   DEPTH-FIRST

Such a strategy dives into the search space following newly developed leads as they are generated. It will only return to consider earlier options when progress along a current lead has been blocked. The trace of the execution of ND-RECOGNIZE on the string `baaa!` as shown in Figure 2.22 illustrates a depth-first search. The algorithm hits the first choice point after seeing `ba` when it has to decide whether to stay in q_2 or advance to state q_3. At this point, it chooses one alternative and follows it until it is sure it's wrong. The algorithm then backs up and tries another older alternative.

Depth first strategies have one major pitfall: under certain circumstances they can enter an infinite loop. This is possible either if the search space happens to be set up in such a way that a search-state can be accidentally re-visited, or if there are an infinite number of search states. We will revisit this question when we turn to more complicated search problems in parsing in Chapter 10.

The second way to order the states in the search space is to consider states in the order in which they are created. Such a policy can be implemented by placing newly created states at the back of the agenda and still have NEXT return the state at the front of the agenda. Thus the agenda is implemented via a **queue**. This is commonly referred to as a **breadth-first**   BREADTH-FIRST
search or **First In First Out (FIFO)** strategy. Consider a different trace of the execution of ND-RECOGNIZE on the string `baaa!` as shown in Figure 2.23. Again, the algorithm hits its first choice point after seeing `ba` when it had to decide whether to stay in q_2 or advance to state q_3. But now rather than picking one choice and following it up, we imagine examining all possible choices, expanding one ply of the search tree at a time.

Like depth-first search, breadth-first search has its pitfalls. As with depth-first if the state-space is infinite, the search may never terminate. More importantly, due to growth in the size of the agenda if the state-space is even moderately large, the search may require an impractically large amount of memory. For small problems, either depth-first or breadth-first search strategies may be adequate, although depth-first is normally preferred for its more efficient use of memory. For larger problems, more complex search techniques such as **dynamic programming** or **A*** must be used, as we will see in Chapters 7 and 10.

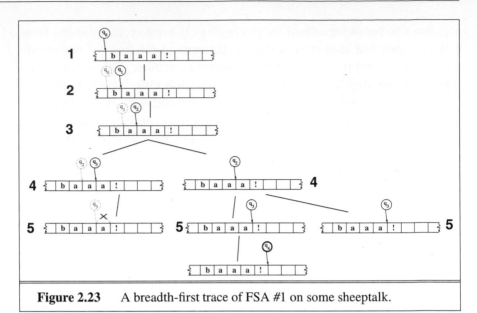

Figure 2.23   A breadth-first trace of FSA #1 on some sheeptalk.

Relating Deterministic and Non-Deterministic Automata

It may seem that allowing NFSAs to have non-deterministic features like ε-transitions would make them more powerful than DFSAs. In fact this is not the case; for any NFSA, there is an exactly equivalent DFSA. In fact there is a simple algorithm for converting an NFSA to an equivalent DFSA, although the number of states in this equivalent deterministic automaton may be much larger. See Lewis and Papadimitriou (1981) or Hopcroft and Ullman (1979) for the proof of the correspondence. The basic intuition of the proof is worth mentioning, however, and builds on the way NFSAs parse their input. Recall that the difference between NFSAs and DFSAs is that in an NFSA a state q_i may have more than one possible next state given an input i (for example q_a and q_b). The algorithm in Figure 2.21 dealt with this problem by choosing either q_a or q_b and then *backtracking* if the choice turned out to be wrong. We mentioned that a parallel version of the algorithm would follow both paths (toward q_a and q_b) simultaneously.

The algorithm for converting a NFSA to a DFSA is like this parallel algorithm; we build an automaton that has a deterministic path for every path our parallel recognizer might have followed in the search space. We imagine following both paths simultaneously, and group together into an equivalence class all the states we reach on the same input symbol (i.e., q_a and q_b). We now give a new state label to this new equivalence class state (for example

q_{ab}). We continue doing this for every possible input for every possible group of states. The resulting DFSA can have as many states as there are distinct sets of states in the original NFSA. The number of different subsets of a set with N elements is 2^N, hence the new DFSA can have as many as 2^N states.

2.3   REGULAR LANGUAGES AND FSAS

As we suggested above, the class of languages that are definable by regular expressions is exactly the same as the class of languages that are characterizable by finite-state automata (whether deterministic or non-deterministic). Because of this, we call these languages the **regular languages**. In order to give a formal definition of the class of regular languages, we need to refer back to two earlier concepts: the alphabet Σ, which is the set of all symbols in the language, and the *empty string* ε, which is conventionally not included in Σ. In addition, we make reference to the *empty set* $\emptyset$ (which is distinct from ε). The class of regular languages (or **regular sets**) over Σ is then formally defined as follows: [1]

REGULAR
LANGUAGES

1. $\emptyset$ is a regular language
2. $\forall a \in \Sigma \cup \varepsilon$, $\{a\}$ is a regular language
3. If L_1 and L_2 are regular languages, then so are:
    (a) $L_1 \cdot L_2 = \{xy \mid x \in L_1, y \in L_2\}$, the **concatenation** of L_1 and L_2
    (b) $L_1 \cup L_2$, the **union** or **disjunction** of L_1 and L_2
    (c) L_1^*, the **Kleene closure** of L_1

All and only the sets of languages which meet the above properties are regular languages. Since the regular languages are the set of languages characterizable by regular expressions, it must be the case that all the regular expression operators introduced in this chapter (except memory) can be implemented by the three operations which define regular languages: concatenation, disjunction/union (also called "|"), and Kleene closure. For example all the counters (*,+, {n,m}) are just a special case of repetition plus Kleene *. All the anchors can be thought of as individual special symbols. The square braces [] are a kind of disjunction (i.e., [ab] means "*a* or *b*", or the disjunction of *a* and *b*). Thus it is true that any regular expression can be turned into a (perhaps larger) expression which only makes use of the three primitive operations.

---

[1] Following van Santen and Sproat (1998), Kaplan and Kay (1994), and Lewis and Papadimitriou (1981).

Regular languages are also closed under the following operations (Σ^* means the infinite set of all possible strings formed from the alphabet Σ):

- **intersection**: if L_1 and L_2 are regular languages, then so is $L_1 \cap L_2$, the language consisting of the set of strings that are in both L_1 and L_2.
- **difference**: if L_1 and L_2 are regular languages, then so is $L_1 - L_2$, the language consisting of the set of strings that are in L_1 but not L_2.
- **complementation**: If L_1 is a regular language, then so is $\Sigma^* - L_1$, the set of all possible strings that aren't in L_1.
- **reversal**: If L_1 is a regular language, then so is L_1^R, the language consisting of the set of reversals of all the strings in L_1.

The proof that regular expressions are equivalent to finite-state automata can be found in Hopcroft and Ullman (1979), and has two parts: showing that an automaton can be built for each regular language, and conversely that a regular language can be built for each automaton. We won't give the proof, but we give the intuition by showing how to do the first part: take any regular expression and build an automaton from it. The intuition is inductive: for the base case we build an automaton to correspond to regular expressions of a single symbol (e.g., the expression a) by creating an initial state and an accepting final state, with an arc between them labeled a. For the inductive step, we show that each of the primitive operations of a regular expression (concatenation, union, closure) can be imitated by an automaton:

- **concatenation**: We just string two FSAs next to each other by connecting all the final states of FSA$_1$ to the initial state of FSA$_2$ by an ε-transition.

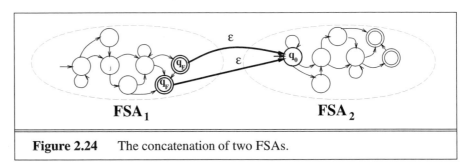

Figure 2.24   The concatenation of two FSAs.

- **closure**: We connect all the final states of the FSA back to the initial states by ε-transitions (this implements the repetition part of the Kleene *), and then put direct links between the initial and final states by ε-

transitions (this implements the possibly of having *zero* occurrences). We'd leave out this last part to implement Kleene-plus instead.

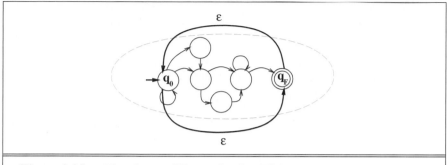

Figure 2.25   The closure (Kleene *) of an FSA.

- **union**: We add a single new initial state q'_0, and add new transitions from it to all the former initial states of the two machines to be joined.

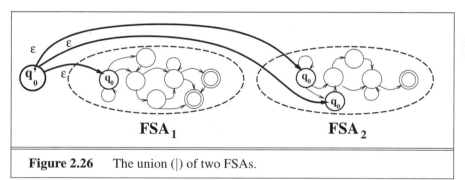

Figure 2.26   The union (|) of two FSAs.

2.4 SUMMARY

This chapter introduced the most important fundamental concept in language processing, the **finite automaton**, and the practical tool based on automaton, the **regular expression**. Here's a summary of the main points we covered about these ideas:

- The **regular expression** language is a powerful tool for pattern-matching.
- Basic operations in regular expressions include **concatenation** of symbols, **disjunction** of symbols ([], |, and .), **counters** (*, +, and

{n,m}), **anchors** (^, $) and precedence operators ((,)).

- Any regular expression can be realized as a **finite state automaton (FSA)**.

- Memory (\1 together with ()) is an advanced operation that is often considered part of regular expressions, but which cannot be realized as a finite automaton.

- An automaton implicitly defines a **formal language** as the set of strings the automaton **accepts**.

- An automaton can use any set of symbols for its vocabulary, including letters, words, or even graphic images.

- The behavior of a **deterministic** automaton (**DFSA**) is fully determined by the state it is in.

- A **non-deterministic** automaton (**NFSA**) sometimes has to make a choice between multiple paths to take given the same current state and next input.

- Any **NFSA** can be converted to a **DFSA**.

- The order in which a **NFSA** chooses the next state to explore on the agenda defines its **search strategy**. The **depth-first search** or **LIFO** strategy corresponds to the agenda-as-stack; the **breadth-first search** or **FIFO** strategy corresponds to the agenda-as-queue.

- Any regular expression can be automatically compiled into a **NFSA** and hence into a **FSA**.

BIBLIOGRAPHICAL AND HISTORICAL NOTES

Finite automata arose in the 1950s out of Turing's (1936) model of algorithmic computation, considered by many to be the foundation of modern computer science. The Turing machine was an abstract machine with a finite control and an input/output tape. In one move, the Turing machine could read a symbol on the tape, write a different symbol on the tape, change state, and move left or right. (Thus the Turing machine differs from a finite-state automaton mainly in its ability to change the symbols on its tape).

Inspired by Turing's work, McCulloch and Pitts built an automata-like model of the neuron (see von Neumann, 1963, p. 319). Their model, which is now usually called the **McCulloch-Pitts neuron** (McCulloch and Pitts, 1943), was a simplified model of the neuron as a kind of "computing element" that could be described in terms of propositional logic. The model was a binary device, at any point either active or not, which took excitatory and inhibitory input from other neurons and fired if its activation passed some fixed threshold. Based on the McCulloch-Pitts neuron, Kleene (1951) and (1956) defined the finite automaton and regular expressions, and proved their equivalence. Non-deterministic automata were introduced by Rabin and Scott (1959), who also proved them equivalent to deterministic ones.

Ken Thompson was one of the first to build regular expressions compilers into editors for text searching (Thompson, 1968). His editor *ed* included a command "g/regular expression/p", or Global Regular Expression Print, which later became the UNIX `grep` utility.

There are many general-purpose introductions to the mathematics underlying automata theory; such as Hopcroft and Ullman (1979) and Lewis and Papadimitriou (1981). These cover the mathematical foundations the simple automata of this chapter, as well as the finite-state transducers of Chapter 3, the context-free grammars of Chapter 9, and the Chomsky hierarchy of Chapter 13. Friedl (1997) is a very useful comprehensive guide to the advanced use of regular expressions.

The metaphor of problem-solving as search is basic to Artificial Intelligence (AI); more details on search can be found in any AI textbook such as Russell and Norvig (1995).

EXERCISES

2.1 Write regular expressions for the following languages: You may use either Perl notation or the minimal "algebraic" notation of Section 2.3, but make sure to say which one you are using. By "word", we mean an alphabetic string separated from other words by white space, any relevant punctuation, line breaks, and so forth.

    a. the set of all alphabetic strings.

    b. the set of all lowercase alphabetic strings ending in a *b*.

    c. the set of all strings with two consecutive repeated words (e.g., "Humbert Humbert" and "the the" but not "the bug" or "the big bug").

d. the set of all strings from the alphabet a, b such that each a is immediately preceded and immediately followed by a b.

e. all strings which start at the beginning of the line with an integer (i.e., 1,2,3,...,10,...,10000,...) and which end at the end of the line with a word.

f. all strings which have both the word *grotto* and the word *raven* in them. (but not, for example, words like *grottos* that merely *contain* the word *grotto*).

g. write a pattern which places the first word of an English sentence in a register. Deal with punctuation.

2.2 Implement an ELIZA-like program, using substitutions such as those described on page 32. You may choose a different domain than a Rogerian psychologist, if you wish, although keep in mind that you would need a domain in which your program can legitimately do a lot of simple repeating-back.

2.3 Complete the FSA for English money expressions in Figure 2.16 as suggested in the text following the figure. You should handle amounts up to $100,000, and make sure that "cent" and "dollar" have the proper plural endings when appropriate.

2.4 Design an FSA that recognizes simple date expressions like *March 15, the 22nd of November, Christmas*. You should try to include all such "absolute" dates, (e.g. not "deictic" ones relative to the current day like *the day before yesterday*). Each edge of the graph should have a word or a set of words on it. You should use some sort of shorthand for classes of words to avoid drawing too many arcs (e.g., furniture → desk, chair, table).

2.5 Now extend your date FSA to handle deictic expressions like *yesterday, tomorrow, a week from tomorrow, the day before yesterday, Sunday, next Monday, three weeks from Saturday*.

2.6 Write an FSA for time-of-day expressions like *eleven o'clock, twelve-thirty, midnight*, or *a quarter to ten* and others.

2.7 (Due to Pauline Welby; this problem probably requires the ability to knit.) Write a regular expression (or draw an FSA) which matches all knitting patterns for scarves with the following specification: *32 stitches wide, K1P1 ribbing on both ends, stockinette stitch body, exactly two raised stripes*. All knitting patterns must include a cast-on row (to put the correct number of stitches on the needle) and a bind-off row (to end the pattern and prevent un-raveling). Here's a sample pattern for one possible scarf matching the above description:[2]

1. Cast on 32 stitches.   *cast on; puts stitches on needle*
2. K1 P1 across row (i.e. do (K1 P1) 16 times). *K1P1 ribbing*
3. Repeat instruction 2 seven more times.   *adds length*
4. K32, P32.   *stockinette stitch*
5. Repeat instruction 4 an additional 13 times. *adds length*
6. P32, P32.   *raised stripe stitch*
7. K32, P32.   *stockinette stitch*
8. Repeat instruction 7 an additional 251 times. *adds length*
9. P32, P32.   *raised stripe stitch*
10. K32, P32.   *stockinette stitch*
11. Repeat instruction 10 an additional 13 times. *adds length*
12. K1 P1 across row.   *K1P1 ribbing*
13. Repeat instruction 12 an additional 7 times. *adds length*
14. Bind off 32 stitches.   *binds off row: ends pattern*

2.8 Write a regular expression for the language accepted by the NFSA in Figure 2.27.

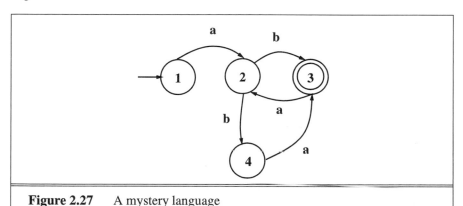

Figure 2.27   A mystery language

2.9 Currently the function D-RECOGNIZE in Figure 2.13 only solves a sub-part of the important problem of finding a string in some text. Extend the algorithm to solve the following two deficiencies: (1) D-RECOGNIZE cur-rently assumes that it is already pointing at the string to be checked, and (2)

---

[2] *Knit* and *purl* are two different types of stitches. The notation K*n* means do *n* knit stitches. Similarly for purl stitches. Ribbing has a striped texture—most sweaters have ribbing at the sleeves, bottom, and neck. Stockinette stitch is a series of knit and purl rows that produces a plain pattern— socks or stockings are knit with this basic pattern, hence the name.

D-RECOGNIZE fails if the string it is pointing includes as a proper substring a legal string for the FSA. That is, D-RECOGNIZE fails if there is an extra character at the end of the string.

2.10   Give an algorithm for negating a deterministic FSA. The negation of an FSA accepts exactly the set of strings that the original FSA rejects (over the same alphabet), and rejects all the strings that the original FSA accepts.

2.11   Why doesn't your previous algorithm work with NFSAs? Now extend your algorithm to negate an NFSA.

3 MORPHOLOGY AND FINITE-STATE TRANSDUCERS

A writer is someone who writes, and a stinger is something that stings. But fingers don't fing, grocers don't groce, haberdashers don't haberdash, hammers don't ham, and humdingers don't humding.

Richard Lederer, *Crazy English*

Chapter 2 introduced the regular expression, showing for example how a single search string could help a web search engine find both *woodchuck* and *woodchucks*. Hunting for singular or plural woodchucks was easy; the plural just tacks an *s* on to the end. But suppose we were looking for another fascinating woodland creatures; let's say a *fox*, and a *fish*, that surly *peccary* and perhaps a Canadian *wild goose*. Hunting for the plurals of these animals takes more than just tacking on an *s*. The plural of *fox* is *foxes*; of *peccary*, *peccaries*; and of *goose*, *geese*. To confuse matters further, fish don't usually change their form when they are plural (as Dr. Seuss points out: *one fish two fish, red fish, blue fish*).

It takes two kinds of knowledge to correctly search for singulars and plurals of these forms. **Spelling rules** tell us that English words ending in -*y* are pluralized by changing the -*y* to -*i*- and adding an -*es*. **Morphological rules** tell us that *fish* has a null plural, and that the plural of *goose* is formed by changing the vowel.

The problem of recognizing that *foxes* breaks down into the two morphemes *fox* and -*es* is called **morphological parsing**.

> **Key Concept #2.** **Parsing** means taking an input and producing some sort of structure for it.

PARSING

We will use the term parsing very broadly throughout this book, including many kinds of structures that might be produced; morphological, syntactic,

STEMMING

SURFACE

PRODUCTIVE

semantic, pragmatic; in the form of a string, or a tree, or a network. In the information retrieval domain, the similar (but not identical) problem of mapping from *foxes* to *fox* is called **stemming**. Morphological parsing or stemming applies to many affixes other than plurals; for example we might need to take any English verb form ending in *-ing* (*going*, *talking*, *congratulating*) and parse it into its verbal stem plus the *-ing* morpheme. So given the **surface** or **input form** *going*, we might want to produce the parsed form VERB-go + GERUND-ing. This chapter will survey the kinds of morphological knowledge that needs to be represented in different languages and introduce the main component of an important algorithm for morphological parsing: the **finite-state transducer**.

Why don't we just list all the plural forms of English nouns, and all the *-ing* forms of English verbs in the dictionary? The major reason is that *-ing* is a **productive** suffix; by this we mean that it applies to every verb. Similarly *-s* applies to almost every noun. So the idea of listing every noun and verb can be quite inefficient. Furthermore, productive suffixes even apply to new words (so the new word *fax* automatically can be used in the *-ing* form: *faxing*). Since new words (particularly acronyms and proper nouns) are created every day, the class of nouns in English increases constantly, and we need to be able to add the plural morpheme *-s* to each of these. Additionally, the plural form of these new nouns depends on the spelling/pronunciation of the singular form; for example if the noun ends in *-z* then the plural form is *-es* rather than *-s*. We'll need to encode these rules somewhere. Finally, we certainly cannot list all the morphological variants of every word in morphologically complex languages like Turkish, which has words like the following:

(3.1) uygarlaştıramadıklarımızdanmışsınızcasına

uygar	*+laş*	*+tır*	*+ama*	*+dık*	*+lar*	*+ımız*
civilized	+BEC	+CAUS	+NEGABLE	+PPART	+PL	+P1PL

+dan	*+mış*	*+sınız*	*+casına*
+ABL	+PAST	+2PL	+AsIf

"(behaving) as if you are among those whom we could not civilize/cause to become civilized"

The various pieces of this word (the **morphemes**) have these meanings:

+BEC	is "become" in English
+CAUS	is the causative voice marker on a verb
+NEGABLE	is "not able" in English

+PPart	marks a past participle form
+P1PL	is 1st person pl possessive agreement
+2PL	is 2nd person pl
+ABL	is the ablative (from/among) case marker
+AsIf	is a derivational marker that forms an adverb from a finite verb form

In such languages we clearly need to parse the input since it is impossible to store every possible word. Kemal Oflazer (personal communication), who came up with this example, notes that verbs in Turkish have 40,000 forms not counting derivational suffixes; adding derivational suffixes allows a theoretically infinite number of words. This is true because, for example, any verb can be "causativized" like the example above, and multiple instances of causativization can be embedded in a single word (*You cause X to cause Y to . . . do W*). Not all Turkish words look like this; Oflazer finds that the average Turkish word has about three morphemes (a root plus two suffixes). Even so, the fact that such words are possible means that it will be difficult to store all possible Turkish words in advance.

Morphological parsing is necessary for more than just information retrieval. We will need it in machine translation to realize that the French words *va* and *aller* should both translate to forms of the English verb *go*. We will also need it in spell checking; as we will see, it is morphological knowledge that will tell us that *misclam* and *antiundoggingly* are not words.

The next sections will summarize morphological facts about English and then introduce the **finite-state transducer**.

3.1   SURVEY OF (MOSTLY) ENGLISH MORPHOLOGY

Morphology is the study of the way words are built up from smaller meaning-bearing units, **morphemes**. A morpheme is often defined as the minimal meaning-bearing unit in a language. So for example the word *fox* consists of a single morpheme (the morpheme *fox*) while the word *cats* consists of two: the morpheme *cat* and the morpheme *-s*.

MORPHEMES

As this example suggests, it is often useful to distinguish two broad classes of morphemes: **stems** and **affixes**. The exact details of the distinction vary from language to language, but intuitively, the stem is the "main" morpheme of the word, supplying the main meaning, while the affixes add "additional" meanings of various kinds.

STEMS

AFFIXES

Affixes are further divided into **prefixes**, **suffixes**, **infixes**, and **circumfixes**. Prefixes precede the stem, suffixes follow the stem, circumfixes do both, and infixes are inserted inside the stem. For example, the word *eats* is composed of a stem *eat* and the suffix *-s*. The word *unbuckle* is composed of a stem *buckle* and the prefix *un-*. English doesn't have any good examples of circumfixes, but many other languages do. In German, for example, the past participle of some verbs formed by adding *ge-* to the beginning of the stem and *-t* to the end; so the past participle of the verb *sagen* (to say) is *gesagt* (said). Infixes, in which a morpheme is inserted in the middle of a word, occur very commonly for example in the Philipine language Tagalog. For example the affix *um*, which marks the agent of an action, is infixed to the Tagalog stem *hingi* "borrow" to produce *humingi*. There is one infix that occurs in some dialects of English in which taboo morpheme like "f**king" or "bl**dy" or others like it are inserted in the middle of other words ("Man-f**king-hattan", "abso-bl**dy-lutely"[1]) (McCawley, 1978).

Prefixes and suffixes are often called **concatenative morphology** since a word is composed of a number of morphemes concatenated together. A number of languages have extensive **non-concatenative morphology**, in which morphemes are combined in more complex ways. The Tagalog infixation example above is one example of non-concatenative morphology, since two morphemes (*hingi* and *um*) are intermingled. Another kind of non-concatenative morphology is called **templatic morphology** or **root-and-pattern** morphology. This is very common in Arabic, Hebrew, and other Semitic languages. In Hebrew, for example, a verb is constructed using two components: a root, consisting usually of three consonants (CCC) and carrying the basic meaning, and a template, which gives the ordering of consonants and vowels and specifies more semantic information about the resulting verb, such as the semantic voice (e.g., active, passive, middle). For example the Hebrew tri-consonantal root *lmd*, meaning 'learn' or 'study', can be combined with the active voice CaCaC template to produce the word *lamad*, 'he studied', or the intensive CiCeC template to produce the word *limed*, 'he taught', or the intensive passive template CuCaC to produce the word *lumad*, 'he was taught'.

A word can have more than one affix. For example, the word *rewrites* has the prefix *re-*, the stem *write*, and the suffix *-s*. The word *unbelievably* has a stem (*believe*) plus three affixes (*un-*, *-able*, and *-ly*). While English doesn't tend to stack more than four or five affixes, languages like Turkish can have words with nine or ten affixes, as we saw above. Languages

---

[1] Alan Jay Lerner, the lyricist of My Fair Lady, bowdlerized the latter to *abso-bloomin'lutely* in the lyric to "Wouldn't It Be Loverly?" (Lerner, 1978, p. 60).

that tend to string affixes together like Turkish does are called **agglutinative** languages.

There are two broad (and partially overlapping) classes of ways to form words from morphemes: **inflection** and **derivation**. Inflection is the combination of a word stem with a grammatical morpheme, usually resulting in a word of the same class as the original stem, and usually filling some syntactic function like agreement. For example, English has the inflectional morpheme -*s* for marking the **plural** on nouns, and the inflectional morpheme -*ed* for marking the past tense on verbs. Derivation is the combination of a word stem with a grammatical morpheme, usually resulting in a word of a *different* class, often with a meaning hard to predict exactly. For example the verb *computerize* can take the derivational suffix -*ation* to produce the noun *computerization*.

INFLECTION

DERIVATION

Inflectional Morphology

English has a relatively simple inflectional system; only nouns, verbs, and sometimes adjectives can be inflected, and the number of possible inflectional affixes is quite small.

English nouns have only two kinds of inflection: an affix that marks **plural** and an affix that marks **possessive**. For example, many (but not all) English nouns can either appear in the bare stem or **singular** form, or take a plural suffix. Here are examples of the regular plural suffix -*s*, the alternative spelling -*es*, and irregular plurals:

PLURAL

SINGULAR

		Regular Nouns	Irregular Nouns	
Singular	cat	thrush	mouse	ox
Plural	cats	thrushes	mice	oxen

While the regular plural is spelled -*s* after most nouns, it is spelled -*es* after words ending in -*s* (*ibis/ibises*) , -*z*, (*waltz/waltzes*) -*sh*, (*thrush/thrushes*) -*ch*, (*finch/finches*) and sometimes -*x* (*box/boxes*). Nouns ending in -*y* preceded by a consonant change the -*y* to -*i* (*butterfly/butterflies*).

The possessive suffix is realized by apostrophe + -*s* for regular singular nouns (*llama's*) and plural nouns not ending in -*s* (*children's*) and often by a lone apostrophe after regular plural nouns (*llamas'*) and some names ending in -*s* or -*z* (*Euripides' comedies*).

English verbal inflection is more complicated than nominal inflection. First, English has three kinds of verbs; **main verbs**, (*eat, sleep, impeach*), **modal verbs** (*can, will, should*), and **primary verbs** (*be, have, do*) (using

REGULAR

the terms of Quirk et al., 1985). In this chapter we will mostly be concerned with the main and primary verbs, because it is these that have inflectional endings. Of these verbs a large class are **regular**, that is to say all verbs of this class have the same endings marking the same functions. These regular verbs (e.g. *walk*, or *inspect*), have four morphological forms, as follow:

Morphological Form Classes	Regularly Inflected Verbs			
stem	walk	merge	try	map
-s form	walks	merges	tries	maps
-ing participle	walking	merging	trying	mapping
Past form or *-ed* participle	walked	merged	tried	mapped

These verbs are called regular because just by knowing the stem we can predict the other forms, by adding one of three predictable endings, and making some regular spelling changes (and as we will see in Chapter 4, regular pronunciation changes). These regular verbs and forms are significant in the morphology of English first because they cover a majority of the verbs, and second because the regular class is **productive**. As discussed earlier, a productive class is one that automatically includes any new words that enter the language. For example the recently-created verb *fax* (*My mom faxed me the note from cousin Everett*), takes the regular endings *-ed*, *-ing*, *-es*. (Note that the *-s* form is spelled *faxes* rather than *faxs*; we will discuss spelling rules below).

IRREGULAR
VERBS

The **irregular verbs** are those that have some more or less idiosyncratic forms of inflection. Irregular verbs in English often have five different forms, but can have as many as eight (e.g., the verb *be*) or as few as three (e.g. *cut* or *hit*). While constituting a much smaller class of verbs (Quirk et al. (1985) estimate there are only about 250 irregular verbs, not counting auxiliaries), this class includes most of the very frequent verbs of the language.[2] The table below shows some sample irregular forms. Note that an irregular

PRETERITE

verb can inflect in the past form (also called the **preterite**) by changing its vowel (*eat/ate*), or its vowel and some consonants (*catch/caught*), or with no ending at all (*cut/cut*).

---

[2] In general, the more frequent a word form, the more likely it is to have idiosyncratic properties; this is due to a fact about language change; very frequent words preserve their form even if other words around them are changing so as to become more regular.

Morphological Form Classes	Irregularly Inflected Verbs		
stem	eat	catch	cut
-s form	eats	catches	cuts
-ing participle	eating	catching	cutting
Past form	ate	caught	cut
-ed participle	eaten	caught	cut

The way these forms are used in a sentence will be discussed in Chapters 8–12 but is worth a brief mention here. The -s form is used in the "habitual present" form to distinguish the third-person singular ending (*She jogs every Tuesday*) from the other choices of person and number (*I/you/we/they jog every Tuesday*). The stem form is used in the infinitive form, and also after certain other verbs (*I'd rather walk home, I want to walk home*). The -ing participle is used when the verb is treated as a noun; this particular kind of nominal use of a verb is called a **gerund** use: *Fishing is fine if you live near water.* The -ed participle is used in the **perfect** construction (*He's eaten lunch already*) or the passive construction (*The verdict was overturned yesterday.*).

GERUND

PERFECT

In addition to noting which suffixes can be attached to which stems, we need to capture the fact that a number of regular spelling changes occur at these morpheme boundaries. For example, a single consonant letter is doubled before adding the -ing and -ed suffixes (*beg/begging/begged*). If the final letter is "c", the doubling is spelled "ck" (*picnic/picnicking/picnicked*). If the base ends in a silent -e, it is deleted before adding -ing and -ed (*merge/-merging/merged*). Just as for nouns, the -s ending is spelled -es after verb stems ending in -s (*toss/tosses*) , -z, (*waltz/waltzes*) -sh, (*wash/washes*) -ch, (*catch/catches*) and sometimes -x (*tax/taxes*). Also like nouns, verbs ending in -y preceded by a consonant change the -y to -i (*try/tries*).

The English verbal system is much simpler than for example the European Spanish system, which has as many as fifty distinct verb forms for each regular verb. Figure 3.1 shows just a few of the examples for the verb *amar*, 'to love'. Other languages can have even more forms than this Spanish example.

Derivational Morphology

While English inflection is relatively simple compared to other languages, derivation in English is quite complex. Recall that derivation is the combi-

Present Indicative	Imper.	Imperfect Indicative	Future	Preterite	Present Subjnct.	Conditional	Imperfect Subjnct.	Future Subjnct.
amo		amaba	amaré	amé	ame	amaría	amara	amare
amas	ama	amabas	amarás	amaste	ames	amarías	amaras	amares
	ames							
ama		amaba	amará	amó	ame	amaría	amara	amáreme
amamos		amábamos	amaremos	amamos	amemos	amaríamos	amáramos	amáremos
amáis	amad	amabais	amaréis	amasteis	améis	amaríais	amarais	amareis
	amáis							
aman		amaban	amarán	amaron	amen	amarían	amaran	amaren

Figure 3.1   To love in Spanish.

nation of a word stem with a grammatical morpheme, usually resulting in a word of a *different* class, often with a meaning hard to predict exactly.

NOMINALIZATION

A very common kind of derivation in English is the formation of new nouns, often from verbs or adjectives. This process is called **nominalization**. For example, the suffix *-ation* produces nouns from verbs ending often in the suffix *-ize* (*computerize* → *computerization*). Here are examples of some particularly productive English nominalizing suffixes.

Suffix	Base Verb/Adjective	Derived Noun
-ation	computerize (V)	computerization
-ee	appoint (V)	appointee
-er	kill (V)	killer
-ness	fuzzy (A)	fuzziness

Adjectives can also be derived from nouns and verbs. Here are examples of a few suffixes deriving adjectives from nouns or verbs.

Suffix	Base Noun/Verb	Derived Adjective
-al	computation (N)	computational
-able	embrace (V)	embraceable
-less	clue (N)	clueless

Derivation in English is more complex than inflection for a number of reasons. One is that it is generally less productive; even a nominalizing suffix like *-ation*, which can be added to almost any verb ending in *-ize*, cannot be added to absolutely every verb. Thus we can't say *eatation* or *spellation* (we use an asterisk (*) to mark "non-examples" of English). Another is that there are subtle and complex meaning differences among nominalizing suffixes. For example *sincerity* has a subtle difference in meaning from *sincereness*.

3.2 FINITE-STATE MORPHOLOGICAL PARSING

Let's now proceed to the problem of parsing English morphology. Consider a simple example: parsing just the productive nominal plural (*-s*) and the verbal progressive (*-ing*). Our goal will be to take input forms like those in the first column below and produce output forms like those in the second column.

Input	Morphological Parsed Output
cats	`cat +N +PL`
cat	`cat +N +SG`
cities	`city +N +PL`
geese	`goose +N +PL`
goose	(`goose +N +SG`) or (`goose +V`)
gooses	`goose +V +3SG`
merging	`merge +V +PRES-PART`
caught	(`catch +V +PAST-PART`) or (`catch +V +PAST`)

The second column contains the stem of each word as well as assorted morphological **features**. These features specify additional information about the stem. For example the feature `+N` means that the word is a noun; `+SG` means it is singular, `+PL` that it is plural. We will discuss features in Chapter 11; for now, consider `+SG` to be a primitive unit that means "singular". Note that some of the input forms (like *caught* or *goose*) will be ambiguous between different morphological parses.

FEATURES

In order to build a morphological parser, we'll need at least the following:

1. **lexicon:** the list of stems and affixes, together with basic information about them (whether a stem is a Noun stem or a Verb stem, etc.).

   LEXICON

2. **morphotactics:** the model of morpheme ordering that explains which classes of morphemes can follow other classes of morphemes inside a word. For example, the rule that the English plural morpheme follows the noun rather than preceding it.

   MORPHOTACTICS

3. **orthographic rules:** these **spelling rules** are used to model the changes that occur in a word, usually when two morphemes combine (e.g., the

$y \rightarrow ie$ spelling rule discussed above that changes *city* + *-s* to *cities* rather than *citys*).

The next part of this section will discuss how to represent a simple version of the lexicon just for the sub-problem of morphological recognition, including how to use FSAs to model morphotactic knowledge. We will then introduce the finite-state transducer (FST) as a way of modeling morphological features in the lexicon, and addressing morphological parsing. Finally, we show how to use FSTs to model orthographic rules.

The Lexicon and Morphotactics

A lexicon is a repository for words. The simplest possible lexicon would consist of an explicit list of every word of the language (*every* word, i.e., including abbreviations ("AAA") and proper names ("Jane" or "Beijing") as follows:

    a
    AAA
    AA
    Aachen
    aardvark
    aardwolf
    aba
    abaca
    aback
    ...

Since it will often be inconvenient or impossible, for the various reasons we discussed above, to list every word in the language, computational lexicons are usually structured with a list of each of the stems and affixes of the language together with a representation of the morphotactics that tells us how they can fit together. There are many ways to model morphotactics; one of the most common is the finite-state automaton. A very simple finite-state model for English nominal inflection might look like Figure 3.2.

The FSA in Figure 3.2 assumes that the lexicon includes regular nouns (**reg-noun**) that take the regular *-s* plural (e.g., *cat, dog, fox, aardvark*). These are the vast majority of English nouns since for now we will ignore the fact that the plural of words like *fox* have an inserted *e*: *foxes*. The lexicon also includes irregular noun forms that don't take *-s*, both singular **irreg-sg-noun** (*goose, mouse*) and plural **irreg-pl-noun** (*geese, mice*).

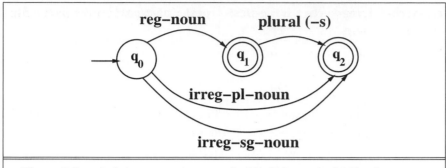

Figure 3.2   A finite-state automaton for English nominal inflection.

reg-noun	irreg-pl-noun	irreg-sg-noun	plural
fox	geese	goose	-s
cat	sheep	sheep	
dog	mice	mouse	
aardvark			

A similar model for English verbal inflection might look like Figure 3.3.

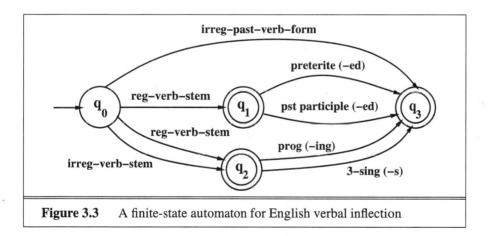

Figure 3.3   A finite-state automaton for English verbal inflection

This lexicon has three stem classes (reg-verb-stem, irreg-verb-stem, and irreg-past-verb-form), plus four more affix classes (*-ed* past, *-ed* participle, *-ing* participle, and third singular *-s*):

reg-verb-stem	irreg-verb-stem	irreg-past-verb	past	past-part	pres-part	3sg
walk fry talk impeach	cut speak sing sang spoken	caught ate eaten	-ed	-ed	-ing	-s

English derivational morphology is significantly more complex than English inflectional morphology, and so automata for modeling English derivation tend to be quite complex. Some models of English derivation, in fact, are based on the more complex context-free grammars of Chapter 9 (Sproat, 1993; Orgun, 1995).

As a preliminary example, though, of the kind of analysis it would require, we present a small part of the morphotactics of English adjectives, taken from Antworth (1990). Antworth offers the following data on English adjectives:

> big, bigger, biggest
> cool, cooler, coolest, coolly
> red, redder, reddest
> clear, clearer, clearest, clearly, unclear, unclearly
> happy, happier, happiest, happily
> unhappy, unhappier, unhappiest, unhappily
> real, unreal, really

An initial hypothesis might be that adjectives can have an optional prefix (*un-*), an obligatory root (*big, cool*, etc) and an optional suffix (*-er, -est*, or *-ly*). This might suggest the the FSA in Figure 3.4.

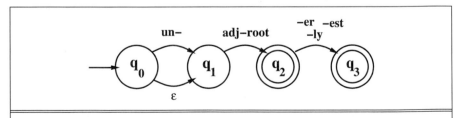

Figure 3.4   An FSA for a fragment of English adjective morphology: Antworth's Proposal #1.

Alas, while this FSA will recognize all the adjectives in the table above, it will also recognize ungrammatical forms like *unbig*, *redly*, and *realest*. We need to set up classes of roots and specify which can occur with which suffixes. So **adj-root**$_1$ would include adjectives that can occur with *un-* and *-ly* (*clear*, *happy*, and *real*) while **adj-root**$_2$ will include adjectives that can't (*big*, *cool*, and *red*). Antworth (1990) presents Figure 3.5 as a partial solution to these problems.

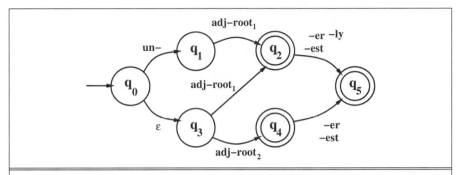

Figure 3.5   An FSA for a fragment of English adjective morphology: Antworth's Proposal #2.

This gives an idea of the complexity to be expected from English derivation. For a further example, we give in Figure 3.6 another fragment of an FSA for English nominal and verbal derivational morphology, based on Sproat (1993), Bauer (1983), and Porter (1980). This FSA models a number of derivational facts, such as the well known generalization that any verb ending in *-ize* can be followed by the nominalizing suffix *-ation* (Bauer, 1983; Sproat, 1993)). Thus since there is a word *fossilize*, we can predict the word *fossilization* by following states q_0, q_1, and q_2. Similarly, adjectives ending in *-al* or *-able* at q_5 (*equal, formal, realizable*) can take the suffix *-ity*, or sometimes the suffix *-ness* to state q_6 (*naturalness, casualness*). We leave it as an exercise for the reader (Exercise 3.2) to discover some of the individual exceptions to many of these constraints, and also to give examples of some of the various noun and verb classes.

We can now use these FSAs to solve the problem of **morphological recognition**; that is, of determining whether an input string of letters makes up a legitimate English word or not. We do this by taking the morphotactic FSAs, and plugging in each "sub-lexicon" into the FSA. That is, we expand each arc (e.g., the **reg-noun-stem** arc) with all the morphemes that make up the set of **reg-noun-stem**. The resulting FSA can then be defined at the level of the individual letter.

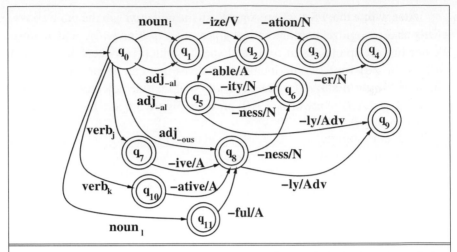

Figure 3.6   An FSA for another fragment of English derivational morphology.

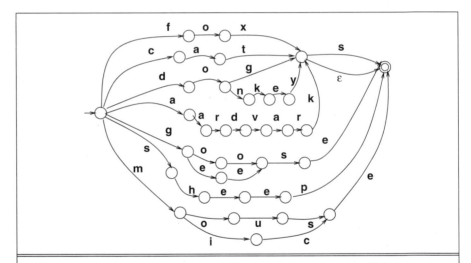

Figure 3.7   Compiled FSA for a few English nouns with their inflection. Note that this automaton will incorrectly accept the input *foxs*. We will see beginning on page 76 how to correctly deal with the inserted *e* in *foxes*.

Figure 3.7 shows the noun-recognition FSA produced by expanding the Nominal Inflection FSA of Figure 3.2 with sample regular and irregular nouns for each class. We can use Figure 3.7 to recognize strings like *aardvarks* by simply starting at the initial state, and comparing the input letter by letter with each word on each outgoing arc, and so on, just as we saw in Chapter 2.

Morphological Parsing with Finite-State Transducers

Now that we've seen how to use FSAs to represent the lexicon and incidentally do morphological recognition, let's move on to morphological parsing. For example, given the input *cats*, we'd like to output cat +N +PL, telling us that cat is a plural noun. We will do this via a version of **two-level morphology**, first proposed by Koskenniemi (1983). Two-level morphology represents a word as a correspondence between a **lexical level**, which represents a simple concatenation of morphemes making up a word, and the **surface** level, which represents the actual spelling of the final word. Morphological parsing is implemented by building mapping rules that map letter sequences like *cats* on the surface level into morpheme and features sequences like cat +N +PL on the lexical level. Figure 3.8 shows these two levels for the word *cats*. Note that the lexical level has the stem for a word, followed by the morphological information +N +PL which tells us that *cats* is a plural noun.

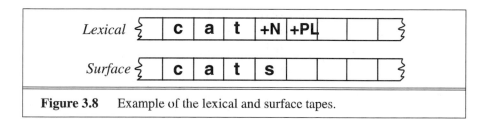

Figure 3.8   Example of the lexical and surface tapes.

     The automaton that we use for performing the mapping between these two levels is the **finite-state transducer** or **FST**. A transducer maps between one set of symbols and another; a finite-state transducer does this via a finite automaton. Thus we usually visualize an FST as a two-tape automaton which recognizes or generates *pairs* of strings. The FST thus has a more general function than an FSA; where an FSA defines a formal language by defining a set of strings, an FST defines a *relation* between sets of strings. This relates to another view of an FST; as a machine that reads one string and generates another. Here's a summary of this four-fold way of thinking about transducers:

- **FST as recognizer:** a transducer that takes a pair of strings as input and outputs *accept* if the string-pair is in the string-pair language, and a *reject* if it is not.
- **FST as generator:** a machine that outputs pairs of strings of the language. Thus the output is a yes or no, and a pair of output strings.
- **FST as translator:** a machine that reads a string and outputs another string
- **FST as set relater:** a machine that computes relations between sets.

An FST can be formally defined in a number of ways; we will rely on the following definition, based on what is called the **Mealy machine** extension to a simple FSA:

MEALY
MACHINE

- Q: a finite set of N states $q_0, q_1, \ldots, q_N$
- Σ: a finite alphabet of complex symbols. Each complex symbol is composed of an input-output pair $i : o$; one symbol i from an input alphabet I, and one symbol o from an output alphabet O, thus $\Sigma \subseteq I \times O$. I and O may each also include the epsilon symbol ε.
- q_0: the start state
- F: the set of final states, $F \subseteq Q$
- $\delta(q, i : o)$: the transition function or transition matrix between states. Given a state $q \in Q$ and complex symbol $i : o \in \Sigma$, $\delta(q, i : o)$ returns a new state $q' \in Q$. δ is thus a relation from $Q \times \Sigma$ to Q.

Where an FSA accepts a language stated over a finite alphabet of single symbols, such as the alphabet of our sheep language:

$$\Sigma = \{b, a, !\} \tag{3.2}$$

an FST accepts a language stated over *pairs* of symbols, as in:

$$\Sigma = \{a : a, \ b : b, \ ! : !, \ a : !, \ a : \varepsilon, \ \varepsilon : !\} \tag{3.3}$$

In two-level morphology, the pairs of symbols in Σ are also called **feasible pairs**.

FEASIBLE
PAIRS

Where FSAs are isomorphic to regular languages, FSTs are isomorphic to **regular relations**. Regular relations are sets of pairs of strings, a natural extension of the regular languages, which are sets of strings. Like FSAs and regular languages, FSTs and regular relations are closed under union, although in general they are not closed under difference, complementation and intersection (although some useful subclasses of FSTs *are* closed under these operations; in general FSTs that are not augmented with the ε

REGULAR
RELATIONS

are more likely to have such closure properties). Besides union, FSTs have two additional closure properties that turn out to be extremely useful:

- **inversion**: The inversion of a transducer T (T^{-1}) simply switches the input and output labels. Thus if T maps from the input alphabet I to the output alphabet O, T^{-1} maps from O to I.   INVERSION

- **composition**: If T_1 is a transducer from I_1 to O_1 and T_2 a transducer from I_2 to O_2, then $T_1 \circ T_2$ maps from I_1 to O_2.   COMPOSITION

Inversion is useful because it makes it easy to convert a FST-as-parser into an FST-as-generator. Composition is useful because it allows us to take two transducers that run in series and replace them with one more complex transducer. Composition works as in algebra; applying $T_1 \circ T_2$ to an input sequence S is identical to applying T_1 to S and then T_2 to the result; thus $T_1 \circ T_2(S) = T_2(T_1(S))$. We will see examples of composition below.

We mentioned that for two-level morphology it's convenient to view an FST as having two tapes. The **upper** or **lexical tape**, is composed from   LEXICAL TAPE
characters from the left side of the $a : b$ pairs; the **lower** or **surface** tape, is composed of characters from the right side of the $a : b$ pairs. Thus each symbol $a : b$ in the transducer alphabet Σ expresses how the symbol a from one tape is mapped to the symbol b on the another tape. For example $a : \varepsilon$ means that an a on the upper tape will correspond to *nothing* on the lower tape. Just as for an FSA, we can write regular expressions in the complex alphabet Σ. Since it's most common for symbols to map to themselves, in two-level morphology we call pairs like $a : a$ **default pairs**, and just refer to   DEFAULT PAIRS
them by the single letter a.

We are now ready to build an FST morphological parser out of our earlier morphotactic FSAs and lexica by adding an extra "lexical" tape and the appropriate morphological features. Figure 3.9 shows an augmentation of Figure 3.2 with the nominal morphological features (+SG and +PL) that correspond to each morpheme. Note that these features map to the empty string ε or the word/morpheme boundary symbol # since there is no segment corresponding to them on the output tape.

In order to use Figure 3.9 as a morphological noun parser, it needs to be augmented with all the individual regular and irregular noun stems, replacing the labels **regular-noun-stem** etc. In order to do this we need to update the lexicon for this transducer, so that irregular plurals like *geese* will parse into the correct stem goose +N +PL. We do this by allowing the lexicon to also have two levels. Since surface *geese* maps to underlying goose, the new lexical entry will be "g:g o:e o:e s:s e:e". Regular forms are

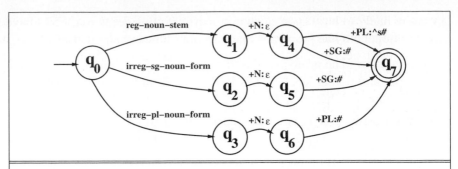

Figure 3.9   A transducer for English nominal number inflection T_{num}. Since both q_1 and q_2 are accepting states, regular nouns can have the plural suffix or not. The morpheme-boundary symbol ˆ and word-boundary marker # will be discussed below.

simpler; the two-level entry for *fox* will now be "f:f o:o x:x", but by relying on the orthographic convention that f stands for f:f and so on, we can simply refer to it as fox and the form for *geese* as "g o:e o:e s e". Thus the lexicon will look only slightly more complex:

reg-noun	irreg-pl-noun	irreg-sg-noun
fox	g o:e o:e s e	goose
cat	sheep	sheep
dog	m o:i u:ε s:c e	mouse
aardvark		

Our proposed morphological parser needs to map from surface forms like *geese* to lexical forms like goose +N +SG. We could do this by **cascading** the lexicon above with the singular/plural automaton of Figure 3.9. Cascading two automata means running them in series with the output of the first feeding the input to the second. We would first represent the lexicon of stems in the above table as the FST T_{stems} of Figure 3.10. This FST maps e.g. *dog* to **reg-noun-stem**. In order to allow possible suffixes, T_{stems} in Figure 3.10 allows the forms to be followed by the wildcard @ **symbol**; @:@ stands for "any feasible pair". A pair of the form @:x, for example will mean "any feasible pair which has x on the surface level", and correspondingly for the form x:@. The output of this FST would then feed the number automaton T_{num}.

Instead of cascading the two transducers, we can **compose** them using the composition operator defined above. Composing is a way of taking a

@ SYMBOL

cascade of transducers with many different levels of inputs and outputs and
converting them into a single "two-level" transducer with one input tape and
one output tape. The algorithm for composition bears some resemblance to
the algorithm for determinization of FSAs from page 48; given two automata
T_1 and T_2 with state sets Q_1 and Q_2 and transition functions δ_1 and δ_2, we
create a new possible state (x,y) for every pair of states $x \in Q_1$ and $y \in Q_2$.
Then the new automaton has the transition function:

$$\delta_3((x_a,y_a),i:o) = (x_b,y_b) \text{ if }$$
$$\exists c \text{ s.t. } \delta_1(x_a,i:c) = x_b$$
$$\text{and } \delta_2(y_a,c:o) = y_b \tag{3.4}$$

The resulting composed automaton, $T_{lex} = T_{num} \circ T_{stems}$, is shown in
Figure 3.11 (compare this with the FSA lexicon in Figure 3.7 on page 70).[3]
Note that the final automaton still has two levels separated by the :. Because
the colon was reserved for these levels, we had to use the | symbol in T_{stems}
in Figure 3.10 to separate the upper and lower tapes.

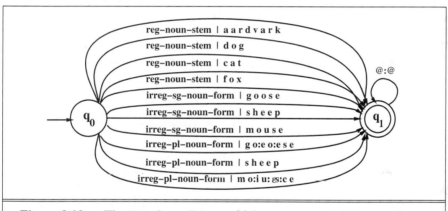

Figure 3.10   The transducer T_{stems}, which maps roots to their root-class.

This transducer will map plural nouns into the stem plus the morphological marker +PL, and singular nouns into the stem plus the morpheme
+SG. Thus a surface *cats* will map to cat +N +PL as follows:

    c:c a:a t:t +N:ε +PL:^s#

That is, c maps to itself, as do a and t, while the morphological feature
+N (recall that this means "noun") maps to nothing (ε), and the feature +PL

---

[3] Note that for the purposes of clear exposition, Figure 3.11 has not been minimized in the
way that Figure 3.7 has.

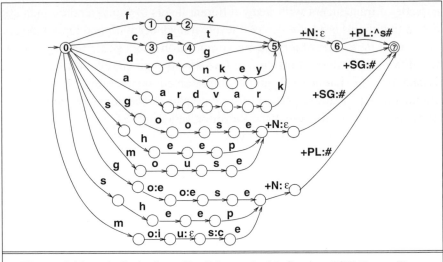

Figure 3.11   A fleshed-out English nominal inflection FST $T_{lex} = T_{num} \circ T_{stems}$.

MORPHEME
BOUNDARY
#
WORD
BOUNDARY

(meaning "plural") maps to ^s. The symbol ^ indicates a **morpheme boundary**, while the symbol **#** indicates a **word boundary**, Figure 3.12 refers to tapes with these morpheme boundary markers as **intermediate** tapes; the next section will show how the boundary marker is removed.

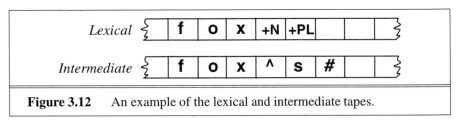

Figure 3.12   An example of the lexical and intermediate tapes.

Orthographic Rules and Finite-State Transducers

The method described in the previous section will successfully recognize words like *aardvarks* and *mice*. But just concatenating the morphemes won't work for cases where there is a spelling change; it would incorrectly reject an input like *foxes* and accept an input like *foxs*. We need to deal with the fact that English often requires spelling changes at morpheme boundaries by introducing **spelling rules** (or **orthographic rules**). This section introduces a number of notations for writing such rules and shows how to implement the rules as transducers. Some of these spelling rules:

SPELLING
RULES

Name	Description of Rule	Example
Consonant doubling	1-letter consonant doubled before *-ing/-ed*	beg/begging
E deletion	Silent e dropped before *-ing* and *-ed*	make/making
E insertion	e added after *-s,-z,-x,-ch*, *-sh* before *-s*	watch/watches
Y replacement	*-y* changes to *-ie* before *-s*, *-i* before *-ed*	try/tries
K insertion	verbs ending with *vowel* + *-c* add *-k*	panic/panicked

We can think of these spelling changes as taking as input a simple concatenation of morphemes (the "intermediate output" of the lexical transducer in Figure 3.11) and producing as output a slightly-modified, (correctly-spelled) concatenation of morphemes. Figure 3.13 shows the three levels we are talking about: lexical, intermediate, and surface. So for example we could write an E-insertion rule that performs the mapping from the intermediate to surface levels shown in Figure 3.13. Such a rule might say some-

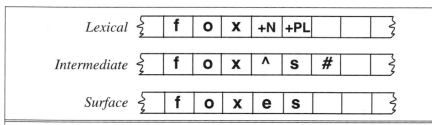

Figure 3.13   An example of the lexical, intermediate, and surface tapes. Between each pair of tapes is a two-level transducer; the lexical transducer of Figure 3.11 between the lexical and intermediate levels, and the E-insertion spelling rule between the intermediate and surface levels. The E-insertion spelling rule inserts an *e* on the surface tape when the intermediate tape has a morpheme boundary ^ followed by the morpheme *-s*.

thing like "insert an *e* on the surface tape just when the lexical tape has a morpheme ending in *x* (or *z*, etc) and the next morpheme is *-s*". Here's a formalization of the rule:

$$\varepsilon \rightarrow e\, / \left\{ \begin{array}{c} x \\ s \\ z \end{array} \right\} \, {}^{\wedge}\underline{} s\# \qquad\qquad (3.5)$$

This is the rule notation of Chomsky and Halle (1968); a rule of the form $a \rightarrow b/c\underline{}d$ means "rewrite a as b when it occurs between c and *d*". Since the symbol ε means an empty transition, replacing it means inserting something. The symbol ^ indicates a morpheme boundary. These boundaries are deleted by including the symbol ^:ε in the default pairs for the transducer; thus morpheme boundary markers are deleted on the surface level by default. (Recall that the colon is used to separate symbols on the intermediate and surface forms). The # symbol is a special symbol that marks a word boundary. Thus (3.5) means "insert an *e* after a morpheme-final *x*, *s*, or *z*, and before the morpheme *s*". Figure 3.14 shows an automaton that corresponds to this rule.

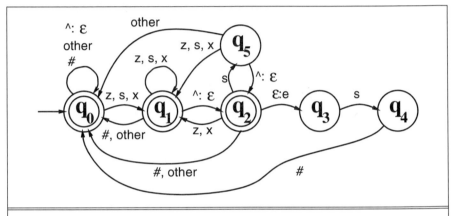

Figure 3.14   The transducer for the E-insertion rule of (3.5), extended from a similar transducer in Antworth (1990).

The idea in building a transducer for a particular rule is to express only the constraints necessary for that rule, allowing any other string of symbols to pass through unchanged. This rule is used to insure that we can only see the ε:*e* pair if we are in the proper context. So state q_0, which models having seen only default pairs unrelated to the rule, is an accepting state, as is q_1, which models having seen a *z*, *s*, or *x*. q_2 models having seen the morpheme boundary after the *z*, *s*, or *x*, and again is an accepting state. State q_3 models having just seen the E-insertion; it is not an accepting state, since the insertion is only allowed if it is followed by the *s* morpheme and then the end-of-word symbol #.

The *other* symbol is used in Figure 3.14 to safely pass through any parts of words that don't play a role in the E-insertion rule. *other* means "any feasible pair that is not in this transducer"; it is thus a version of @:@ which is context-dependent in a transducer-by-transducer way. So for example when leaving state q_0, we go to q_1 on the *z*, *s*, or *x* symbols, rather than following the *other* arc and staying in q_0. The semantics of *other* depends on what symbols are on other arcs; since *#* is mentioned on some arcs, it is (by definition) not included in *other*, and thus, for example, is explicitly mentioned on the arc from q_2 to q_0.

A transducer needs to correctly reject a string that applies the rule when it shouldn't. One possible bad string would have the correct environment for the E-insertion, but have no insertion. State q_5 is used to insure that the *e* is always inserted whenever the environment is appropriate; the transducer reaches q_5 only when it has seen an *s* after an appropriate morpheme boundary. If the machine is in state q_5 and the next symbol is *#*, the machine rejects the string (because there is no legal transition on *#* from q_5). Figure 3.15 shows the transition table for the rule which makes the illegal transitions explicit with the "–" symbol.

State \ Input	s : s	x : x	z : z	^:ε	ε : e	#	other
q_0:	1	1	1	0	-	0	0
q_1:	1	1	1	2	-	0	0
q_2:	5	1	1	0	3	0	0
q_3	4	-	-	-	-	-	-
q_4	-	-	-	-	-	0	-
q_5	1	1	1	2	-	-	0

Figure 3.15   The state-transition table for E-insertion rule of Figure 3.14, extended from a similar transducer in Antworth (1990).

The next section will show a trace of this E-insertion transducer running on a sample input string.

3.3   COMBINING FST LEXICON AND RULES

We are now ready to combine our lexicon and rule transducers for parsing and generating. Figure 3.16 shows the architecture of a two-level morphology system, whether used for parsing or generating. The lexicon transducer maps between the lexical level, with its stems and morphological features, and an intermediate level that represents a simple concatenation of morphemes. Then a host of transducers, each representing a single spelling rule constraint, all run in parallel so as to map between this intermediate level and the surface level. Putting all the spelling rules in parallel is a design choice;

we could also have chosen to run all the spelling rules in series (as a long cascade), if we slightly changed each rule.

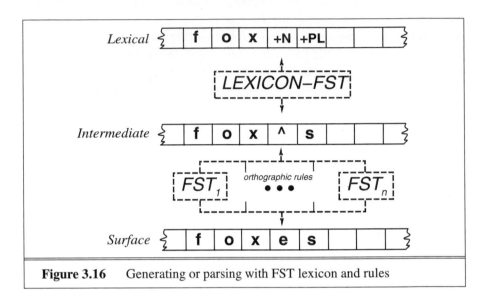

Figure 3.16   Generating or parsing with FST lexicon and rules

The architecture in Figure 3.16 is a two-level cascade of transducers. Recall that a cascade is a set of transducers in series, in which the output from one transducer acts as the input to another transducer; cascades can be of arbitrary depth, and each level might be built out of many individual transducers. The cascade in Figure 3.16 has two transducers in series: the transducer mapping from the lexical to the intermediate levels, and the collection of parallel transducers mapping from the intermediate to the surface level. The cascade can be run top-down to generate a string, or bottom-up to parse it; Figure 3.17 shows a trace of the system *accepting* the mapping from *fox^s* to *foxes*.

The power of finite-state transducers is that the exact same cascade with the same state sequences is used when the machine is generating the surface tape from the lexical tape, or when it is parsing the lexical tape from the surface tape. For example, for generation, imagine leaving the Intermediate and Surface tapes blank. Now if we run the lexicon transducer, given fox +N +PL, it will produce *fox^s#* on the Intermediate tape via the same states that it accepted the Lexical and Intermediate tapes in our earlier example. If we then allow all possible orthographic transducers to run in parallel, we will produce the same surface tape.

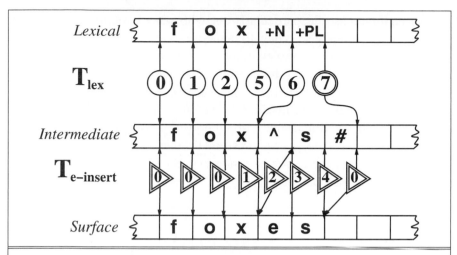

Figure 3.17   Accepting *foxes*: The lexicon transducer T_{lex} from Figure 3.11 cascaded with the E-insertion transducer in Figure 3.14.

Parsing can be slightly more complicated than generation, because of the problem of **ambiguity**. For example, *foxes* can also be a verb (albeit a rare one, meaning "to baffle or confuse"), and hence the lexical parse for *foxes* could be fox +V +3SG as well as fox +N +PL. How are we to know which one is the proper parse? In fact, for ambiguous cases of this sort, the transducer is not capable of deciding. **Disambiguating** will require some external evidence such as the surrounding words. Thus *foxes* is likely to be a noun in the sequence *I saw two foxes yesterday*, but a verb in the sequence *That trickster foxes me every time!*. We will discuss such disambiguation algorithms in Chapters 8 and 17. Barring such external evidence, the best our transducer can do is just enumerate the possible choices; so we can transduce *foxˆs#* into both fox +V +3SG and fox +N +PL.

There is a kind of ambiguity that we need to handle: local ambiguity that occurs during the process of parsing. For example, imagine parsing the input verb *assess*. After seeing *ass*, our E-insertion transducer may propose that the *e* that follows is inserted by the spelling rule (for example, as far as the transducer is concerned, we might have been parsing the word *asses*). It is not until we don't see the # after *asses*, but rather run into another *s*, that we realize we have gone down an incorrect path.

Because of this non-determinism, FST-parsing algorithms need to incorporate some sort of search algorithm. Exercise 3.8 asks the reader to modify the algorithm for non-deterministic FSA recognition in Figure 2.21 in Chapter 2 to do FST parsing.

AMBIGUITY

DISAMBIGUAT-ING

Running a cascade, particularly one with many levels, can be unwieldy. Luckily, we've already seen how to compose a cascade of transducers in series into a single more complex transducer. Transducers in parallel can be combined by **automaton intersection**. The automaton intersection algorithm just takes the Cartesian product of the states, i.e., for each state q_i in machine 1 and state q_j in machine 2, we create a new state q_{ij}. Then for any input symbol a, if machine 1 would transition to state q_n and machine 2 would transition to state q_m, we transition to state q_{nm}.

Figure 3.18 sketches how this intersection ($\wedge$) and composition ($\circ$) process might be carried out.

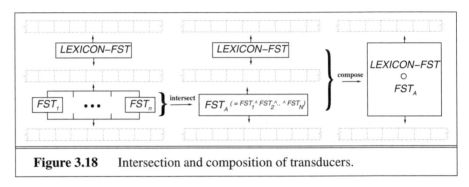

Figure 3.18   Intersection and composition of transducers.

Since there are a number of rule$\rightarrow$FST compilers, it is almost never necessary in practice to write an FST by hand. Kaplan and Kay (1994) give the mathematics that define the mapping from rules to two-level relations, and Antworth (1990) gives details of the algorithms for rule compilation. Mohri (1997) gives algorithms for transducer minimization and determinization.

3.4   LEXICON-FREE FSTS: THE PORTER STEMMER

While building a transducer from a lexicon plus rules is the standard algorithm for morphological parsing, there are simpler algorithms that don't require the large on-line lexicon demanded by this algorithm. These are used especially in Information Retrieval (IR) tasks (Chapter 17) in which a user needs some information, and is looking for relevant documents (perhaps on the web, perhaps in a digital library database). She gives the system a query with some important characteristics of documents she desires, and the IR system retrieves what it thinks are the relevant documents. One common

type of query is Boolean combinations of relevant **keywords** or phrases, e.g.   KEYWORDS
(*marsupial OR kangaroo OR koala*). The system then returns documents that
have these words in them. Since a document with the word *marsupials* might
not match the keyword *marsupial*, some IR systems first run a stemmer on
the keywords and on the words in the document. Since morphological parsing in IR is only used to help form equivalence classes, the details of the
suffixes are irrelevant; what matters is determining that two words have the
same stem.

One of the most widely used such **stemming** algorithms is the simple   STEMMING
and efficient Porter (1980) algorithm, which is based on a series of simple
cascaded rewrite rules. Since cascaded rewrite rules are just the sort of thing
that could be easily implemented as an FST, we think of the Porter algorithm
as a lexicon-free FST stemmer (this idea will be developed further in the
exercises (Exercise 3.7). The algorithm contains rules like:

(3.6) ATIONAL $\rightarrow$ ATE (e.g., relational $\rightarrow$ relate)

(3.7) ING $\rightarrow$ ε if stem contains vowel (e.g., motoring $\rightarrow$ motor)

The algorithm is presented in detail in Appendix B.

Do stemmers really improve the performance of information retrieval
engines? One problem is that stemmers are not perfect. For example Krovetz
(1993) summarizes the following kinds of errors of omission and of commis-
sion in the Porter algorithm:

Errors of Commission		Errors of Omission	
organization	organ	European	Europe
doing	doe	analysis	analyzes
generalization	generic	matrices	matrix
numerical	numerous	noise	noisy
policy	police	sparse	sparsity
university	universe	explain	explanation
negligible	negligent	urgency	urgent

Krovetz also gives the results of a number of experiments testing whether
the Porter stemmer actually improved IR performance. Overall he found
some improvement, especially with smaller documents (the larger the document, the higher the chance the keyword will occur in the exact form used
in the query). Since any improvement is quite small, IR engines often don't
use stemming.

3.5 HUMAN MORPHOLOGICAL PROCESSING

In this section we look at psychological studies to learn how multi-morphemic words are represented in the minds of speakers of English. For example, consider the word *walk* and its inflected forms *walks*, and *walked*. Are all three in the human lexicon? Or merely *walk* plus as well as *-ed* and *-s*? How about the word *happy* and its derived forms *happily* and *happiness*? We can imagine two ends of a theoretical spectrum of representations. The **full list-**

FULL LISTING **ing** hypothesis proposes that all words of a language are listed in the mental lexicon without any internal morphological structure. On this view, morphological structure is simply an epiphenomenon, and *walk*, *walks*, *walked*, *happy*, and *happily* are all separately listed in the lexicon. This hypothesis is certainly untenable for morphologically complex languages like Turkish (Hankamer (1989) estimates Turkish as 200 billion possible words). The

MINIMUM
REDUNDANCY **minimum redundancy** hypothesis suggests that only the constituent morphemes are represented in the lexicon, and when processing *walks*, (whether for reading, listening, or talking) we must access both morphemes (*walk* and *-s*) and combine them.

Most modern experimental evidence suggests that neither of these is completely true. Rather, some kinds of morphological relationships are mentally represented (particularly inflection and certain kinds of derivation), but others are not, with those words being fully listed. Stanners et al. (1979), for example, found that derived forms (*happiness*, *happily*) are stored separately from their stem (*happy*), but that regularly inflected forms (*pouring*) are not distinct in the lexicon from their stems (*pour*). They did this by using a repetition priming experiment. In short, repetition priming takes advantage of the fact that a word is recognized faster if it has been seen before (if it is

PRIMED **primed**). They found that *lifting* primed *lift*, and *burned* primed *burn*, but for example *selective* didn't prime *select*. Figure 3.19 sketches one possible representation of their finding:

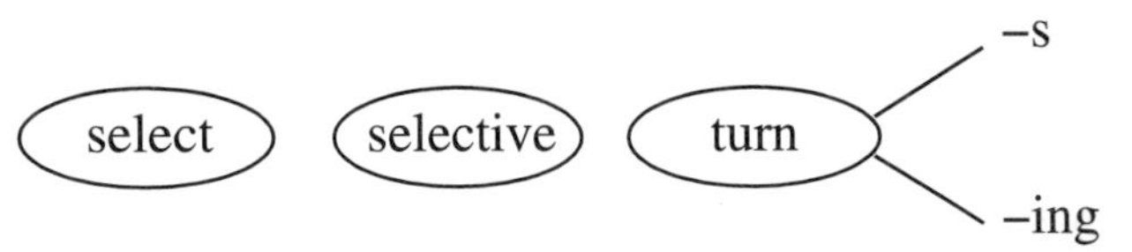

Figure 3.19   Stanners et al. (1979) result: Different representations of inflection and derivation.

In a more recent study, Marslen-Wilson et al. (1994) found that *spoken* derived words can prime their stems, but only if the meaning of the derived form is closely related to the stem. For example *government* primes *govern*, but *department* does not prime *depart*. Grainger et al. (1991) found similar results with prefixed words (but not with suffixed words). Marslen-Wilson et al. (1994) represent a model compatible with their own findings as follows:

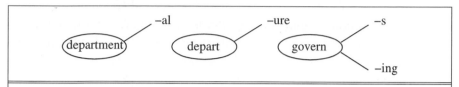

Figure 3.20   Marslen-Wilson et al. (1994) result: Derived words are linked to their stems only if semantically related

Other evidence that the human lexicon represents some morphological structure comes from **speech errors**, also called **slips of the tongue**. In normal conversation, speakers often mix up the order of the words or initial sounds:

if you <u>break</u> it it'll <u>drop</u>
I don't have time to <u>work</u> to watch television because I have to <u>work</u>

But inflectional and derivational affixes can also appear separately from their stems, as these examples from Fromkin and Ratner (1998) and Garrett (1975) show:

it's <u>not</u> only us who have screw <u>looses</u> (for "screws loose")
word<u>s</u> of rule formation (for "rules of word formation")
easy enough<u>ly</u> (for "easily enough")
which by its<u>elf</u> is the most <u>un</u>implausible sentence you can imagine

The ability of these affixes to be produced separately from their stem suggests that the mental lexicon must contain some representation of the morphological structure of these words.

In summary, these results suggest that morphology does play a role in the human lexicon, especially productive morphology like inflection. They also emphasize the important of semantic generalizations across words, and suggest that the human auditory lexicon (representing words in terms of their sounds) and the orthographic lexicon (representing words in terms of letters) may have similar structures. Finally, it seems that many properties of language processing, like morphology, may apply equally (or at least similarly) to language **comprehension** and language **production**.

3.6 SUMMARY

This chapter introduced **morphology**, the arena of language processing dealing with the subparts of words, and the **finite-state transducer**, the computational device that is commonly used to model morphology. Here's a summary of the main points we covered about these ideas:

- **Morphological parsing** is the process of finding the constituent **morphemes** in a word (e.g., `cat +N +PL` for *cats*).

- English mainly uses **prefixes** and **suffixes** to express **inflectional** and **derivational** morphology.

- English **inflectional** morphology is relatively simple and includes person and number agreement (*-s*) and tense markings (*-ed* and *-ing*).

- English **derivational** morphology is more complex and includes suffixes like *-ation, -ness, -able* as well as prefixes like *co-* and *re-*.

- Many constraints on the English **morphotactics** (allowable morpheme sequences) can be represented by finite automata.

- **Finite-state transducers** are an extension of finite-state automata that can generate output symbols.

- **Two-level morphology** is the application of finite-state transducers to morphological representation and parsing.

- **Spelling rules** can be implemented as transducers.

- There are automatic transducer-compilers that can produce a transducer for any simple rewrite rule.

- The lexicon and spelling rules can be combined by **composing** and **intersecting** various transducers.

- The **Porter algorithm** is a simple and efficient way to do **stemming**, stripping off affixes. It is not as accurate as a transducer model that includes a lexicon, but may be preferable for applications like **information retrieval** in which exact morphological structure is not needed.

BIBLIOGRAPHICAL AND HISTORICAL NOTES

Despite the close mathematical similarity of finite-state transducers to finite-state automata, the two models grew out of somewhat different traditions. Chapter 2 described how the finite automaton grew out of Turing's (1936) model of algorithmic computation, and McCulloch and Pitts finite-state-like models of the neuron. The influence of the Turing machine on the transducer was somewhat more indirect. Huffman (1954) proposed what was essentially a state-transition table to model the behavior of sequential circuits, based on the work of Shannon (1938) on an algebraic model of relay circuits. Based on Turing and Shannon's work, and unaware of Huffman's work, Moore (1956) introduced the term **finite automaton** for a machine with a finite number of states with an alphabet of input symbols and an alphabet of output symbols. Mealy (1955) extended and synthesized the work of Moore and Huffman.

The finite automata in Moore's original paper, and the extension by Mealy differed in an important way. In a Mealy machine, the input/output symbols are associated with the transitions between states. The finite-state transducers in this chapter are Mealy machines. In a Moore machine, the input/output symbols are associated with the state; we will see examples of Moore machines in Chapter 5 and Chapter 7. The two types of transducers are equivalent; any Moore machine can be converted into an equivalent Mealy machine and vice versa.

Many early programs for morphological parsing used an **affix-stripping** approach to parsing. For example Packard's (1973) parser for ancient Greek iteratively stripped prefixes and suffixes off the input word, making note of them, and then looked up the remainder in a lexicon. It returned any root that was compatible with the stripped-off affixes. This approach is equivalent to the **bottom-up** method of parsing that we will discuss in Chapter 10.

AMPLE (A Morphological Parser for Linguistic Exploration) (Weber and Mann, 1981; Weber et al., 1988; Hankamer and Black, 1991) is another early bottom-up morphological parser. It contains a lexicon with all possible surface variants of each morpheme (these are called **allomorphs**), together with constraints on their occurrence (for example in English the *-es* allomorph of the plural morpheme can only occur after s, x, z, sh, or ch). The system finds every possible sequence of morphemes which match the input and then filters out all the sequences which have failing constraints.

An alternative approach to morphological parsing is called *generate-and-test* or *analysis-by-synthesis* approach. Hankamer's (1986) keCi is a morphological parser for Turkish which is guided by a finite-state representation of Turkish morphemes. The program begins with a morpheme that might match the left edge of the word, and applies every possible phonological rule to it, checking each result against the input. If one of the outputs succeeds, the program then follows the finite-state morphotactics to the next morpheme and tries to continue matching the input.

The idea of modeling spelling rules as finite-state transducers is really based on Johnson's (1972) early idea that phonological rules (to be discussed in Chapter 4) have finite-state properties. Johnson's insight unfortunately did not attract the attention of the community, and was independently discovered by Roland Kaplan and Martin Kay, first in an unpublished talk (Kaplan and Kay, 1981) and then finally in print (Kaplan and Kay, 1994) (see page 15 for a discussion of multiple independent discoveries). Kaplan and Kay's work was followed up and most fully worked out by Koskenniemi (1983), who described finite-state morphological rules for Finnish. Karttunen (1983) built a program called KIMMO based on Koskenniemi's models. Antworth (1990) gives many details of two-level morphology and its application to English. Besides Koskenniemi's work on Finnish and that of Antworth (1990) on English, two-level or other finite-state models of morphology have been worked out for many languages, such as Turkish (Oflazer, 1993) and Arabic (Beesley, 1996). Antworth (1990) summarizes a number of issues in finite-state analysis of languages with morphologically complex processes like infixation and reduplication (e.g., Tagalog) and gemination (e.g., Hebrew). Karttunen (1993) is a good summary of the application of two-level morphology specifically to phonological rules of the sort we will discuss in Chapter 4. Barton et al. (1987) bring up some computational complexity problems with two-level models, which are responded to by Koskenniemi and Church (1988).

Students interested in further details of the fundamental mathematics of automata theory should see Hopcroft and Ullman (1979) or Lewis and Papadimitriou (1981). Mohri (1997) and Roche and Schabes (1997b) give additional algorithms and mathematical foundations for language applications, including, for example, the details of the algorithm for transducer minimization. Sproat (1993) gives a broad general introduction to computational morphology.

EXERCISES

3.1 Add some adjectives to the adjective FSA in Figure 3.5.

3.2 Give examples of each of the noun and verb classes in Figure 3.6, and find some exceptions to the rules.

3.3 Extend the transducer in Figure 3.14 to deal with `sh` and `ch`.

3.4 Write a transducer(s) for the K insertion spelling rule in English.

3.5 Write a transducer(s) for the consonant doubling spelling rule in English.

3.6 The Soundex algorithm (Odell and Russell, 1922; Knuth, 1973) is a method commonly used in libraries and older Census records for representing people's names. It has the advantage that versions of the names that are slightly misspelled or otherwise modified (common, for example, in handwritten census records) will still have the same representation as correctly-spelled names. (e.g., Jurafsky, Jarofsky, Jarovsky, and Jarovski all map to J612).

    a. Keep the first letter of the name, and drop all occurrences of non-initial a, e, h, i, o, u, w, y

    b. Replace the remaining letters with the following numbers:

        b, f, p, v → 1
        c, g, j, k, q, s, x, z → 2
        d, t → 3
        l → 4
        m, n → 5
        r → 6

    c. Replace any sequences of identical numbers with a single number (i.e., 666 → 6)

    d. Convert to the form `Letter Digit Digit Digit` by dropping digits past the third (if necessary) or padding with trailing zeros (if necessary).

The exercise: write a FST to implement the Soundex algorithm.

3.7 Implement one of the steps of the Porter Stemmer as a transducer.

3.8   Write the algorithm for parsing a finite-state transducer, using the pseu-do-code introduced in Chapter 2. You should do this by modifying the algo-rithm ND-RECOGNIZE in Figure 2.21 in Chapter 2.

3.9   Write a program that takes a word and, using an on-line dictionary, computes possible anagrams of the word, each of which is a legal word.

3.10   In Figure 3.14, why is there a z, s, x arc from q_5 to q_1?

4 COMPUTATIONAL PHONOLOGY AND TEXT-TO-SPEECH

You like po-tay-to and I like po-tah-to.
You like to-may-to and I like to-mah-to.
Po-tay-to, po-tah-to,
To-may-to, to-mah-to,
Let's call the whole thing off!

> George and Ira Gershwin, *Let's Call the*
> *Whole Thing Off* from *Shall We Dance*,
> 1937

The debate between the "whole language" and "phonics" methods of teaching reading to children seems at very glance like a purely modern educational debate. Like many modern debates, however, this one recapitulates an important historical dialectic, in this case in writing systems. The earliest independently-invented writing systems (Sumerian, Chinese, Mayan) were mainly logographic: one symbol represented a whole word. But from the earliest stages we can find, most such systems contain elements of syllabic or phonemic writing systems, in which symbols are used to represent the sounds that make up the words. Thus the Sumerian symbol pronounced *ba* and meaning "ration" could also function purely as the sound /ba/. Even modern Chinese, which remains primarily logographic, uses sound-based characters to spell out foreign words and especially geographical names. Purely sound-based writing systems, whether syllabic (like Japanese *hiragana* or *katakana*), alphabetic (like the Roman alphabet used in this book), or consonantal (like Semitic writing systems), can generally be traced back to these early logo-syllabic systems, often as two cultures came together. Thus the Arabic, Aramaic, Hebrew, Greek, and Roman systems all derive from a West Semitic script that is presumed to have been modified by Western Semitic mercenaries from a cursive form of Egyptian hieroglyphs. The

Japanese syllabaries were modified from a cursive form of a set of Chinese characters which were used to represent sounds. These Chinese characters themselves were used in Chinese to phonetically represent the Sanskrit in the Buddhist scriptures that were brought to China in the Tang dynasty.

Whatever its origins, the idea implicit in a sound-based writing system, that the spoken word is composed of smaller units of speech, is the Ur-theory that underlies all our modern theories of phonology. In the next four chapters we begin our exploration of these ideas, as we introduce the fundamental insights and algorithms necessary to understand modern speech recognition and speech synthesis technology, and the related branch of linguistics called **computational phonology**.

Let's begin by defining these areas. The core task of automatic speech recognition is take an acoustic waveform as input and produce as output a string of words. Conversely, the core task of text-to-speech synthesis is to take a sequence of text words and produce as output an acoustic waveform. The uses of speech recognition and synthesis are manifold, including automatic dictation/transcription, speech-based interfaces to computers and telephones, voice-based input and output for the disabled, and many others that will be discussed in greater detail in Chapter 7.

This chapter will focus on an important part of both speech recognition and text-to-speech systems: how words are pronounced in terms of individual speech units called **phones**. A speech recognition system needs to have a pronunciation for every word it can recognize, and a text-to-speech system needs to have a pronunciation for every word it can say. The first section of this chapter will introduce **phonetic alphabets** for describing pronunciation, part of the field of **phonetics**. We then introduce **articulatory phonetics**, the study of how speech sounds are produced by articulators in the mouth.

PHONETICS
ARTICULATORY
PHONETICS

Modeling pronunciation would be much simpler if a given phone was always pronounced the same in every context. Unfortunately this is not the case. As we will see, the phone [t] is pronounced very differently in different phonetic environments. **Phonology** is the area of linguistics that describes the systematic way that sounds are differently realized in different environments, and how this system of sounds is related to the rest of the grammar. The next section of the chapter will describe the way we write **phonological rules** to describe these different realizations.

COMPUTATIONAL
PHONOLOGY

We next introduce an area known as **computational phonology**. One important part of computational phonology is the study of computational mechanisms for modeling phonological rules. We will show how the spelling-rule transducers of Chapter 3 can be used to model phonology. We then discuss computational models of **phonological learning**: how phonological rules can be automatically induced by machine learning algorithms.

Finally, we apply the transducer-based model of phonology to an important problem in text-to-speech systems: mapping from strings of letters to strings of phones. We first survey the issues involved in building a large pronunciation dictionary, and then show how the transducer-based lexicons and spelling rules of Chapter 3 can be augmented with pronunciations to map from orthography to pronunciation.

This chapter focuses on the non-probabilistic areas of computational linguistics and pronunciations modeling. Chapter 5 will turn to the role of probabilistic models, including such areas as probabilistic models of pronunciation variation and probabilistic methods for learning phonological rules.

4.1   SPEECH SOUNDS AND PHONETIC TRANSCRIPTION

The study of the pronunciation of words is part of the field of **phonetics**, the study of the speech sounds used in the languages of the world. We will be modeling the pronunciation of a word as a string of symbols which represent **phones** or **segments**. A phone is a speech sound; we will represent phones with phonetic symbols that bears some resemblance to a letter in an alphabetic language like English. So for example there is a phone represented by *l* that usually corresponds to the letter *l* and a phone represented by *p* that usually corresponds to the letter *p*. Actually, as we will see later, phones have much more variation than letters do. This chapter will only briefly touch on other aspects of phonetics such as **prosody**, which includes things like changes in pitch and duration.

This section surveys the different phones of English, particularly American English, showing how they are produced and how they are represented symbolically. We will be using two different alphabets for describing phones. The first is the **International Phonetic Alphabet (IPA)**. The IPA is an evolving standard originally developed by the International Phonetic Association in 1888 with the goal of transcribing the sounds of all human languages. The IPA is not just an alphabet but also a set of principles for transcription, which differ according to the needs of the transcription, so the same utterance can be transcribed in different ways all according to the principles of the IPA. In the interests of brevity in this book we will focus on the symbols that are most relevant for English; thus Figure 4.1 shows a subset of the IPA symbols for transcribing consonants, while Figure 4.2 shows a subset of the IPA

PHONETICS

PHONES

IPA

IPA Symbol	ARPAbet Symbol	Word	IPA Transcription	ARPAbet Transcription
[p]	[p]	parsley	[ˈparsli]	[p aa r s l iy]
[t]	[t]	tarragon	[ˈtærəgɑn]	[t ae r ax g aa n]
[k]	[k]	catnip	[ˈkætnɨp]	[k ae t n ix p]
[b]	[b]	bay	[beɪ]	[b ey]
[d]	[d]	dill	[dɪl]	[d ih l]
[g]	[g]	garlic	[ˈgɑrlɨk]	[g aa r l ix k]
[m]	[m]	mint	[mɪnt]	[m ih n t]
[n]	[n]	nutmeg	[ˈnʌtmɛg]	[n ah t m eh g]
[ŋ]	[ng]	ginseng	[ˈdʒɪnsɨŋ]	[jh ih n s ix ng]
[f]	[f]	fennel	[ˈfɛnl̩]	[f eh n el]
[v]	[v]	clove	[kloʊv]	[k l ow v]
[θ]	[th]	thistle	[ˈθɪsl̩]	[th ih s el]
[ð]	[dh]	heather	[ˈhɛðɚ]	[h eh dh axr]
[s]	[s]	sage	[seɪdʒ]	[s ey jh]
[z]	[z]	hazelnut	[ˈheɪzl̩nʌt]	[h ey z el n ah t]
[ʃ]	[sh]	squash	[skwɑʃ]	[s k w a sh]
[ʒ]	[zh]	ambrosia	[æmˈbroʊʒə]	[ae m b r ow zh ax]
[tʃ]	[ch]	chicory	[ˈtʃɪkɚi]	[ch ih k axr iy]
[dʒ]	[jh]	sage	[seɪdʒ]	[s ey jh]
[l]	[l]	licorice	[ˈlɪkɚɨʃ]	[l ih k axr ix sh]
[w]	[w]	kiwi	[ˈkiwi]	[k iy w iy]
[r]	[r]	parsley	[ˈpɑrsli]	[p aa r s l iy]
[j]	[y]	yew	[yu]	[y uw]
[h]	[h]	horseradish	[ˈhɔrsrædɪʃ]	[h ao r s r ae d ih sh]
[ʔ]	[q]	uh-oh	[ʔʌʔoʊ]	[q ah q ow]
[ɾ]	[dx]	butter	[ˈbʌɾɚ]	[b ah dx axr]
[ɾ̃]	[nx]	wintergreen	[wɪ̃ɾ̃ɚgrin]	[w ih nx axr g r i n]
[l̩]	[el]	thistle	[ˈθɪsl̩]	[th ih s el]

Figure 4.1   IPA   and   ARPAbet   symbols   for   transcription   of   English consonants.

symbols for transcribing vowels.[1] These tables also give the ARPAbet symbols; ARPAbet (Shoup, 1980) is another phonetic alphabet, but one that is specifically designed for American English and which uses ASCII symbols;

---

[1]   For simplicity we use the symbol [r] for the American English "r" sound, rather than the more-standard IPA symbol [ɹ].

it can be thought of as a convenient ASCII representation of an American-English subset of the IPA. ARPAbet symbols are often used in applications where non-ASCII fonts are inconvenient, such as in on-line pronunciation dictionaries.

IPA Symbol	ARPAbet Symbol	Word	IPA Transcription	ARPAbet Transcription
[i]	[iy]	lily	[ˈlɪli]	[l ih l iy]
[ɪ]	[ih]	lily	[ˈlɪli]	[l ih l iy]
[eɪ]	[ey]	daisy	[ˈdeɪzi]	[d ey z i]
[ɛ]	[eh]	poinsettia	[pɔmˈsɛriə]	[p oy n s eh dx iy ax]
[æ]	[ae]	aster	[ˈæstɚ]	[ae s t axr]
[ɑ]	[aa]	poppy	[ˈpɑpi]	[p aa p i]
[ɔ]	[ao]	orchid	[ˈɔrkɨd]	[ao r k ix d]
[ʊ]	[uh]	woodruff	[ˈwʊdrʌf]	[w uh d r ah f]
[oʊ]	[ow]	lotus	[ˈloʊrəs]	[l ow dx ax s]
[u]	[uw]	tulip	[ˈtulɨp]	[t uw l ix p]
[ʌ]	[uh]	buttercup	[ˈbʌrɚˌkʌp]	[b uh dx axr k uh p]
[ɝ]	[er]	bird	[ˈbɝd]	[b er d]
[aɪ]	[ay]	iris	[ˈaɪrɨs]	[ay r ix s]
[aʊ]	[aw]	sunflower	[ˈsʌnflaʊɚ]	[s ah n f l aw axr]
[ɔɪ]	[oy]	poinsettia	[pɔmˈsɛriə]	[p oy n s eh dx iy ax]
[ju]	[y uw]	feverfew	[fivɚfju]	[f iy v axr f y u]
[ə]	[ax]	woodruff	[ˈwʊdrəf]	[w uh d r ax f]
[ɨ]	[ix]	tulip	[ˈtulɨp]	[t uw l ix p]
[ɚ]	[axr]	heather	[ˈhɛðɚ]	[h eh dh axr]
[ʉ]	[ux]	dude[2]	[dʉd]	[d ux d]

Figure 4.2   IPA and ARPAbet symbols for transcription of English vowels.

Many of the IPA and ARPAbet symbols are equivalent to the Roman letters used in the orthography of English and many other languages. So for example the IPA and ARPAbet symbol [p] represents the consonant sound at

---

[2] The last phone, [ʉ]/[ux], is quite rare in general American English and indeed is an "extension" not present in the original ARPAbet. Labov (1994) notes that the realization of a fronted [uw] as [ux] has made it more common in (at least) Western and Northern Cities dialects of American English starting in the late 1970s. This fronting was first called to public by imitations and recordings of 'Valley Girls' speech by Moon Zappa (Zappa and Zappa, 1982). Nevertheless, for most speakers [uw] is still much more common than [ux] in words like *dude*.

the beginning of *platypus*, *puma*, and *pachyderm*, the middle of *leopard*, or the end of *antelope* (note that the final orthographic *e* of *antelope* does not correspond to any final vowel; the *p* is the last sound).

The mapping between the letters of English orthography and IPA symbols is rarely as simple as this, however. This is because the mapping between English orthography and pronunciation is quite opaque; a single letter can represent very different sounds in different contexts. Figure 4.3 shows that the English letter *c* is represented as IPA [k] in the word *cougar*, but IPA [s] in the word *civet*. Besides appearing as *c* and *k*, the sound marked as [k] in the IPA can appear as part of *x* (*fox*), as *ck* (*jackal*), and as *cc* (*raccoon*). Many other languages, for example Spanish, are much more transparent in their sound-orthography mapping than English.

Word	jackal	raccoon	cougar	civet
IPA	[ˈdʒæ.kl̩]	[ræˈkun]	[ˈku.gɚ]	[ˈsɪ.vɨt]
ARPAbet	[jh ae k el]	[r ae k uw n]	[k uw g axr]	[s ih v ix t]

Figure 4.3   The mapping between IPA symbols and letters in English orthography is complicated; both IPA [k] and English orthographic [c] have many alternative realizations.

The Vocal Organs

ARTICULATORY PHONETICS   We turn now to **articulatory phonetics**, the study of how phones are produced, as the various organs in the mouth, throat, and nose modify the airflow from the lungs.

Sound is produced by the rapid movement of air. Most sounds in human spoken languages are produced by expelling air from the lungs through the windpipe (technically the **trachea**) and then out the mouth or nose. As it passes through the trachea, the air passes through the **larynx**, commonly known as the Adam's apple or voicebox. The larynx contains two small folds of muscle, the **vocal folds** (often referred to non-technically as the **vocal cords**) which can be moved together or apart. The space between these

GLOTTIS   two folds is called the **glottis**. If the folds are close together (but not tightly closed), they will vibrate as air passes through them; if they are far apart, they won't vibrate. Sounds made with the vocal folds together and vibrating

VOICED   are called **voiced**; sounds made without this vocal cord vibration are called

UNVOICED   **unvoiced** or **voiceless**. Voiced sounds include [b], [d], [g], [v], [z], and all

VOICELESS   the English vowels, among others. Unvoiced sounds include [p], [t], [k], [f], [z], and others.

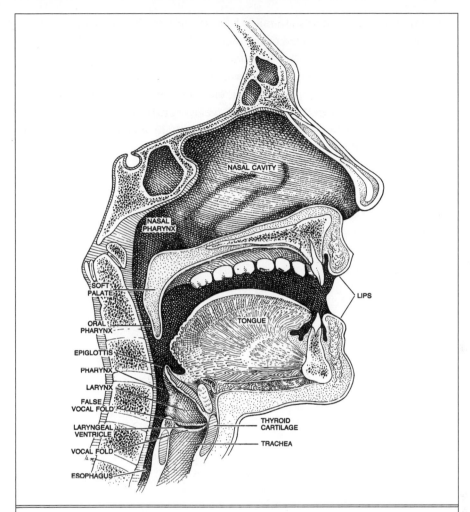

Figure 4.4   The vocal organs, shown in side view. Drawing by Laszlo Kubinyi from Sundberg (1977), ©Scientific American.

The area above the trachea is called the **vocal tract**, and consists of the **oral tract** and the **nasal tract**. After the air leaves the trachea, it can exit the body through the mouth or the nose. Most sounds are made by air passing through the mouth. Sounds made by air passing through the nose are called **nasal sounds**; nasal sounds use both the oral and nasal tracts as resonating cavities; English nasal sounds include *m*, and *n*, and *ng*.

NASAL
SOUNDS

Phones are divided into two main classes: **consonants** and **vowels**. Both kinds of sounds are formed by the motion of air through the mouth,

CONSONANTS

VOWELS

throat or nose. Consonants are made by restricting or blocking the airflow in some way, and may be voiced or unvoiced. Vowels have less obstruction, are usually voiced, and are generally louder and longer-lasting than consonants. The technical use of these terms is much like the common usage; [p], [b], [t], [d], [k], [g], [f], [v], [s], [z], [r], [l], etc., are consonants; [aa], [ae], [aw], [ao], [ih], [aw], [ow], [uw], etc., are vowels. **Semivowels** (such as [y] and [w]) have some of the properties of both; they are voiced like vowels, but they are short and less syllabic like consonants.

Consonants: Place of Articulation

PLACE

Because consonants are made by restricting the airflow in some way, consonants can be distinguished by where this restriction is made: the point of maximum restriction is called the **place of articulation** of a consonant. Places of articulation, shown in Figure 4.5, are often used in automatic speech recognition as a useful way of grouping phones together into equivalence classes:

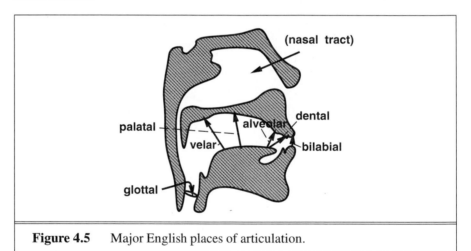

Figure 4.5   Major English places of articulation.

LABIAL

- **labial:** Consonants whose main restriction is formed by the two lips coming together have a **bilabial** place of articulation. In English these include [p] as in *possum*, [b] as in *bear*, and [m] as in *marmot*. The English **labiodental** consonants [v] and [f] are made by pressing the bottom lip against the upper row of teeth and letting the air flow through the space in the upper teeth.

DENTAL

- **dental:** Sounds that are made by placing the tongue against the teeth are dentals. The main dentals in English are the [θ] of _thing_ or the [ð] of _though_, which are made by placing the tongue behind the teeth with the tip slightly between the teeth.

- **alveolar:** The alveolar ridge is the portion of the roof of the mouth just behind the upper teeth. Most speakers of American English make the phones [s], [z], [t], and [d] by placing the tip of the tongue against the alveolar ridge. ALVEOLAR

- **palatal:** The roof of the mouth (the **palate**) rises sharply from the back of the alveolar ridge. The **palato-alveolar** sounds [ʃ] (_shrimp_), [tʃ] (_chinchilla_), [ʒ] (_Asian_), and [dʒ] (_jaguar_) are made with the blade of the tongue against this rising back of the alveolar ridge. The palatal sound [y] of _yak_ is made by placing the front of the tongue up close to the palate. PALATAL
PALATE

- **velar:** The **velum** or soft palate is a movable muscular flap at the very back of the roof of the mouth. The sounds [k] (_cuckoo_), [g] (_goose_), and [ŋ] (_kingfisher_) are made by pressing the back of the tongue up against the velum. VELAR
VELUM

- **glottal:** The glottal stop [ʔ] is made by closing the glottis (by bringing the vocal folds together). GLOTTAL

Consonants: Manner of Articulation

Consonants are also distinguished by _how_ the restriction in airflow is made, for example whether there is a complete stoppage of air, or only a partial blockage, etc. This feature is called the **manner of articulation** of a conso- MANNER nant. The combination of place and manner of articulation is usually suffi- cient to uniquely identify a consonant. Here are the major manners of artic- ulation for English consonants:

- **stop:** A stop is a consonant in which airflow is completely blocked STOP for a short time. This blockage is followed by an explosive sound as the air is released. The period of blockage is called the **closure** and the explosion is called the **release**. English has voiced stops like [b], [d], and [g] as well as unvoiced stops like [p], [t], and [k]. Stops are also called **plosives**. It is possible to use a more narrow (detailed) tran- scription style to distinctly represent the closure and release parts of a stop, both in ARPAbet and IPA-style transcriptions. For example the closure of a [p], [t], or [k] would be represented as [pcl], [tcl], or [kcl] (respectively) in the ARPAbet, and [p̚], [t̚], or [k̚] (respectively) in IPA style. When this form of narrow transcription is used, the un-marked ARPABET symbols [p], [t], and [k] indicate purely the release of the consonant. We will not be using this narrow transcription style in this chapter.

NASALS

- **nasals:** The nasal sounds [n], [m], and [ŋ] are made by lowering the velum and allowing air to pass into the nasal cavity.

FRICATIVE

- **fricative:** In fricatives, airflow is constricted but not cut off completely. The turbulent airflow that results from the constriction produces a characteristic "hissing" sound. The English labiodental fricatives [f] and [v] are produced by pressing the lower lip against the upper teeth, allowing a restricted airflow between the upper teeth. The dental fricatives [θ] and [ð] allow air to flow around the tongue between the teeth. The alveolar fricatives [s] and [z] are produced with the tongue against the alveolar ridge, forcing air over the edge of the teeth. In the palato-alveolar fricatives [ʃ] and [ʒ] the tongue is at the back of the alveolar ridge forcing air through a groove formed in the tongue. The higher-pitched fricatives (in English [s], [z], [ʃ] and [ʒ]) are called **sibilants**. Stops that are followed immediately by fricatives are called **affricates**; these include English [tʃ] (*chicken*) and [dʒ] (*giraffe*).

SIBILANTS

APPROXIMANT

- **approximant:** In approximants, the two articulators are close together but not close enough to cause turbulent airflow. In English [y] (*yellow*), the tongue moves close to the roof of the mouth but not close enough to cause the turbulence that would characterize a fricative. In English [w] (*wormwood*), the back of the tongue comes close to the velum. American [r] can be formed in at least two ways; with just the tip of the tongue extended and close to the palate or with the whole tongue bunched up near the palate. [l] is formed with the tip of the tongue up against the alveolar ridge or the teeth, with one or both sides of the tongue lowered to allow air to flow over it. [l] is called a **lateral** sound because of the drop in the sides of the tongue.

TAP

FLAP

- **tap:** A tap or **flap** [ɾ] is a quick motion of the tongue against the alveolar ridge. The consonant in the middle of the word *lotus* ([loʊɾəs]) is a tap in most dialects of American English; speakers of many British dialects would use a [t] instead of a tap in this word.

Vowels

Like consonants, vowels can be characterized by the position of the articulators as they are made. The two most relevant parameters for vowels are what is called vowel **height**, which correlates roughly with the location of the highest part of the tongue, and the shape of the lips (rounded or not). Figure 4.6 shows the position of the tongue for different vowels.

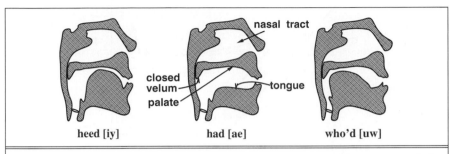

Figure 4.6   Positions of the tongue for three English vowels, high front [iy], low front [ae] and high back [uw]; tongue positions modeled after Ladefoged (1996).

In the vowel [i], for example, the highest point of the tongue is toward the front of the mouth. In the vowel [u], by contrast, the high-point of the tongue is located toward the back of the mouth. Vowels in which the tongue is raised toward the front are called **front vowels**; those in which the tongue is raised toward the back are called **back vowels**. Note that while both [ɪ] and [ɛ] are front vowels, the tongue is higher for [ɪ] than for [ɛ]. Vowels in which the highest point of the tongue is comparatively high are called **high vowels**; vowels with mid or low values of maximum tongue height are called **mid vowels** or **low vowels**, respectively.

Figure 4.7 shows a schematic characterization of the vowel height of different vowels. It is schematic because the abstract property **height** only correlates roughly with actual tongue positions; it is in fact a more accurate reflection of acoustic facts. Note that the chart has two kinds of vowels: those in which tongue height is represented as a point and those in which it is represented as a vector. A vowels in which the tongue position changes markedly during the production of the vowel is **diphthong**. English is particularly rich in diphthongs; many are written with two symbols in the IPA (for example the [eɪ] of *hake* or the [oʊ] of *cobra*).

The second important articulatory dimension for vowels is the shape of the lips. Certain vowels are pronounced with the lips rounded (the same lip shape used for whistling). These **rounded** vowels include [u], [ɔ], and the diphthong [oʊ].

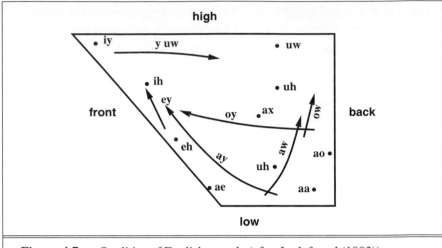

Figure 4.7   Qualities of English vowels (after Ladefoged (1993)).

Syllables

SYLLABLE

Consonants and vowels combine to make a **syllable**. There is no completely agreed-upon definition of a syllable; roughly speaking a syllable is a vowel-like sound together with some of the surrounding consonants that are most closely associated with it. The IPA period symbol [.] is used to separate syllables, so *parsley* and *catnip* have two syllables (['par.sli] and ['kæt.nɪp] respectively), *tarragon* has three ['tæ.rə.gan], and *dill* has one ([dɪl]). A syl-

ONSET

CODA

SYLLABIFICATION

lable is usually described as having an optional initial consonant or set of consonants called the **onset**, followed by a vowel or vowels, followed by a final consonant or sequence of consonants called the **coda**. Thus d is the onset of [dɪl], while l is the coda. The task of breaking up a word into sylla-bles is called **syllabification**. Although automatic syllabification algorithms exist, the problem is hard, partly because there is no agreed-upon definition of syllable boundaries. Furthermore, although it is usually clear how many syllables are in a word, Ladefoged (1993) points out there are some words (meal, teal, seal, hire, fire, hour) that can be viewed either as having one syllable or two.

ACCENTED

In a natural sentence of American English, certain syllables are more **prominent** than others. These are called **accented** syllables. Accented sylla-bles may be prominent because they are louder, they are longer, they are as-sociated with a pitch movement, or any combination of the above. Since ac-cent plays important roles in meaning, understanding exactly why a speaker chooses to accent a particular syllable is very complex. But one important factor in accent is often represented in pronunciation dictionaries. This factor is called **lexical stress**. The syllable that has lexical stress is the one that will be louder or longer if the word is accented. For example the word *parsley* is stressed in its first syllable, not its second. Thus if the word *parsley* is accented in a sentence, it is the first syllable that will be stronger. We write the symbol ['] before a syllable to indicate that it has lexical stress (e.g. ['par.sli]). This difference in lexical stress can affect the meaning of a word. For example the word *content* can be a noun or an adjective. When pronounced in isolation the two senses are pronounced differently since they have different stressed syllables (the noun is pronounced ['kɑn.tɛnt]) and the adjective [kən.'tɛnt]. Other pairs like this include *object* (noun ['ɑb.dʒɛkt] and verb [əb.'dʒɛkt]); see Cutler (1986) for more examples. Automatic disambiguation of such **homographs** is discussed in Chapter 17. The role of prosody is taken up again in Section 4.7.

LEXICAL
STRESS

HOMOGRAPHS

4.2   THE PHONEME AND PHONOLOGICAL RULES

> *'Scuse me, while I kiss the sky*
> Jimi Hendrix, *Purple Haze*
> *'Scuse me, while I kiss this guy*
> Common mis-hearing of same lyrics

All [t]s are not created equally. That is, phones are often produced differently in different contexts. For example, consider the different pronunciations of [t] in the words *tunafish* and *starfish*. The [t] of *tunafish* is **aspirated**. Aspiration is a period of voicelessness after a stop closure and before the onset of voicing of the following vowel. Since the vocal cords are not vibrating, aspiration sounds like a puff of air after the [t] and before the vowel. By contrast, a [t] following an initial [s] is **unaspirated**; thus the [t] in *starfish* ([stɑrfɪʃ]) has no period of voicelessness after the [t] closure. This variation in the realization of [t] is predictable: whenever a [t] begins a word or unreduced syllable in English, it is aspirated. The same variation occurs for [k]; the [k] of *sky* is often mis-heard as [g] in Jimi Hendrix's lyrics because [k] and [g] are both unaspirated. In a very detailed transcription system we could use the symbol for aspiration [ʰ] after any [t] (or [k] or [p]) which begins a word or unreduced syllable. The word *tunafish* would be transcribed [tʰunəfɪʃ] (the ARPAbet does not have a way of marking aspiration).

UNASPIRATED

There are other contextual variants of [t]. For example, when [t] occurs between two vowels, particularly when the first is stressed, it is pronounced as a tap. Recall that a tap is a voiced sound in which the top of the tongue is curled up and back and struck quickly against the alveolar ridge. Thus the word *buttercup* is usually pronounced [bʌɾɚkʌp]/[b uh dx axr k uh p] rather than [bʌtɚkʌp]/[b uh t axr k uh p].

Another variant of [t] occurs before the dental consonant [θ]. Here the [t] becomes dentalized ([t̪]). That is, instead of the tongue forming a closure against the alveolar ridge, the tongue touches the back of the teeth.

PHONEME

ALLOPHONES

How do we represent this relation between a [t] and its different realizations in different contexts? We generally capture this kind of pronunciation variation by positing an abstract class called the **phoneme**, which is realized as different **allophones** in different contexts. We traditionally write phonemes inside slashes. So in the above examples, /t/ is a phoneme whose allophones include [tʰ], [ɾ], and [t̪]. A phoneme is thus a kind of generalization or abstraction over different phonetic realizations. Often we equate the phonemic and the lexical levels, thinking of the lexicon as containing transcriptions expressed in terms of phonemes. When we are transcribing the pronunciations of words we can choose to represent them at this broad phonemic level; such a **broad transcription** leaves out a lot of predictable phonetic detail. We can also choose to use a **narrow transcription** that includes more detail, including allophonic variation, and uses the various diacritics. Figure 4.8 summarizes a number of allophones of /t/; Figure 4.9 shows a few of the most commonly used IPA diacritics.

NARROW
TRANSCRIPTION

Phone	Environment	Example	IPA
[tʰ]	in initial position	*toucan*	[tʰukʰæn]
[t]	after [s] or in reduced syllables	*starfish*	[stɑrfiʃ]
[ʔ]	word-finally or after vowel before [n]	*kitten*	[kʰɪʔn]
[ʔt]	sometimes word-finally	*cat*	[kʰæʔt]
[ɾ]	between vowels	*buttercup*	[bʌɾɚkʰʌp]
[t˺]	before consonants or word-finally	*fruitcake*	[frut˺kʰeɪk]
[t̪]	before dental consonants ([θ])	*eighth*	[eɪt̪θ]
[]	sometimes word-finally	*past*	[pæs]

Figure 4.8   Some allophones of /t/ in General American English.

The relationship between a phoneme and its allophones is often captured by writing a **phonological rule**. Here is the phonological rule for dentalization in the traditional notation of Chomsky and Halle (1968):

$$/t/ \rightarrow [\underset{\sqcap}{t}] \; / \; \underline{\quad} \; \theta \tag{4.1}$$

In this notation, the surface allophone appears to the right of the arrow, and the phonetic environment is indicated by the symbols surrounding the underbar (___). These rules resemble the rules of two-level morphology of Chapter 3 but since they don't use multiple types of rewrite arrows, this rule is ambiguous between an obligatory or optional rule. Here is a version of the flapping rule:

$$/\left\{ \begin{array}{c} t \\ d \end{array} \right\}/ \; \rightarrow \; [\mathrm{r}] \; / \; \acute{V} \; \underline{\quad} \; V \tag{4.2}$$

Diacritics			Suprasegmentals		
˚	Voiceless	[ḁ]	ˈ	Primary stress	[ˈpu.mə]
ʰ	Aspirated	[pʰ]	ˌ	Secondary stress	[ˈfoʊrəˌgræf]
ˌ	Syllabic	[l̩]	ː	Long	[aː]
~	Nasalized	[æ̃]	ˑ	Half long	[aˑ]
̚	Unreleased	[t̚]	.	Syllable break	[ˈpu.mə]
̪	Dental	[t̪]			

Figure 4.9   Some of the IPA diacritics and symbols for suprasegmentals.

4.3   PHONOLOGICAL RULES AND TRANSDUCERS

Chapter 3 showed that spelling rules can be implemented by transducers. Phonological rules can be implemented as transducers in the same way; indeed the original work by Johnson (1972) and Kaplan and Kay (1981) on finite-state models was based on phonological rules rather than spelling rules. There are a number of different models of **computational phonology** that use finite automata in various ways to realize phonological rules. We will describe the **two-level morphology** of Koskenniemi (1983) used in Chapter 3, but the interested reader should be aware of other recent models.[3] While Chapter 3 gave examples of two-level rules, it did not talk about the

---

[3] One example is Bird and Ellison's (1994) model of the multi-tier representations of autosegmental phonology in which each phonological tier is represented by a finite-state automaton, and autosegmental association by the synchronization of two automata.

motivation for these rules, and the differences between traditional ordered rules and two-level rules. We will begin with this comparison.

As a first example, Figure 4.10 shows a transducer which models the application of the simplified flapping rule in (4.3):

$$/t/ \rightarrow [\text{ɾ}] / \acute{V} \underline{\quad} V \qquad\qquad (4.3)$$

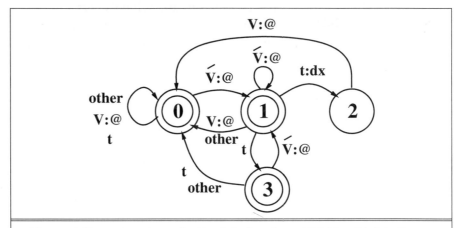

Figure 4.10   Transducer for English Flapping: ARPAbet "dx" indicates a flap, and the "other" symbol means "any feasible pair not used elsewhere in the transducer". "@" means "any symbol not used elsewhere on any arc".

The transducer in Figure 4.10 accepts any string in which flaps occur in the correct places (after a stressed vowel, before an unstressed vowel), and rejects strings in which flapping doesn't occur, or in which flapping occurs in the wrong environment. Of course the factors that flapping are actually a good deal more complicated, as we will see in Section 5.7.

In a traditional phonological system, many different phonological rules apply between the lexical form and the surface form. Sometimes these rules interact; the output from one rule affects the input to another rule. One way to implement rule-interaction in a transducer system is to run transducers in a *cascade*. Consider, for example, the rules that are needed to deal with the phonological behavior of the English noun plural suffix *-s*. This suffix is pronounced [ɨz] after the phones [s], [ʃ], [z], or [ʒ] (so *peaches* is pronounced [pitʃɨz], and *faxes* is pronounced [fæksɨz]), [z] after voiced sounds (*pigs* is pronounced [pɪgz]), and [s] after unvoiced sounds (*cats* is pronounced [kæts]). We model this variation by writing phonological rules for the realization of the morpheme in different contexts. We first need to choose one of these three forms (s, z, and ɨz) as the "lexical" pronunciation of the suffix; we chose z only because it turns out to simplify rule writing. Next we write two phonological rules. One, similar to the E-insertion spelling rule of page 77, inserts a [ɨ] after a morpheme-final sibilant and before the plural morpheme [z]. The other makes sure that the -s suffix is properly realized as [s] after unvoiced consonants.

$$\varepsilon \; \rightarrow \; ɨ \; / \; [\text{+sibilant}] \; \char"02C6 \; \underline{\quad} \; z \; \# \qquad\qquad (4.4)$$

$$z \; \rightarrow \; s \; / \; [\text{-voice}] \; \char"02C6 \; \underline{\quad} \; \# \qquad\qquad\qquad (4.5)$$

These two rules must be *ordered*; rule (4.4) must apply before (4.5). This is because the environment of (4.4) includes z, and the rule (4.5) changes z. Consider running both rules on the lexical form *fox* concatenated with the plural -*s*:

Lexical form:	fɑksˆz
(4.4) applies:	fɑksˆɨz
(4.5) doesn't apply:	fɑksˆɨz

If the devoicing rule (4.5) was ordered first, we would get the wrong result (what would this incorrect result be?). This situation, in which one rule destroys the environment for another, is called **bleeding**:[4]

Lexical form:	fɑksˆz
(4.5) applies:	fɑksˆs
(4.4) doesn't apply:	fɑksˆs

As was suggested in Chapter 3, each of these rules can be represented by a transducer. Since the rules are ordered, the transducers would also need to be ordered. For example if they are placed in a **cascade**, the output of the first transducer would feed the input of the second transducer.

Many rules can be cascaded together this way. As Chapter 3 discussed, running a cascade, particularly one with many levels, can be unwieldy, and so transducer cascades are usually replaced with a single more complex transducer by **composing** the individual transducers.

Koskenniemi's method of **two-level morphology** that was sketchily introduced in Chapter 3 is another way to solve the problem of rule ordering. Koskenniemi (1983) observed that most phonological rules in a grammar are independent of one another; that feeding and bleeding relations between

---

[4] If we had chosen to represent the lexical pronunciation of -*s* as [s] rather than [z], we would have written the rule inversely to voice the -*s* after voiced sounds, but the rules would still need to be ordered; the ordering would simply flip.

rules are not the norm.[5] Since this is the case, Koskenniemi proposed that phonological rules be run in parallel rather than in series. The cases where there is rule interaction (feeding or bleeding) we deal with by slightly modifying some rules. Koskenniemi's two-level rules can be thought of as a way of expressing **declarative constraints** on the well-formedness of the lexical-surface mapping.

Two-level rules also differ from traditional phonological rules by explicitly coding when they are obligatory or optional, by using four differing **rule operators**; the ⇔ rule corresponds to traditional **obligatory** phonological rules, while the ⇒ rule implements **optional rules**:

Rule type	Interpretation
$a:b \Leftarrow c \_\_ d$	a is **always** realized as b in the context $c \_\_ d$
$a:b \Rightarrow c \_\_ d$	a may be realized as b **only** in the context $c \_\_ d$
$a:b \Leftrightarrow c \_\_ d$	a must be realized as b in context $c \_\_ d$ and nowhere else
$a:b \;/\!\!\Leftarrow c \_\_ d$	a is **never** realized as b in the context $c \_\_ d$

The most important intuition of the two-level rules, and the mechanism that lets them avoiding feeding and bleeding, is their ability to represent constraints on *two levels*. This is based on the use of the colon (":"), which was touched in very briefly in Chapter 3. The symbol *a:b* means a lexical *a* that maps to a surface *b*. Thus *a:b* ⇔ *:c* ___ means *a* is realized as *b* after a **surface** c. By contrast *a:b* ⇔ *c:* ___ means that *a* is realized as *b* after a **lexical** c. As discussed in Chapter 3, the symbol *c* with no colon is equivalent to *c:c* that means a lexical *c* which maps to a surface *c*.

Figure 4.11 shows an intuition for how the two-level approach avoids ordering for the i-insertion and z-devoicing rules. The idea is that the z-devoicing rule maps a *lexical* z-insertion to a *surface* s and the i rule refers to the *lexical* z:

The two-level rules that model this constraint are shown in (4.6) and (4.7):

$$\varepsilon : \textit{i} \;\Leftrightarrow\; [\text{+sibilant}] : \; \hat{} \; \_\_ \; \text{z} : \# \tag{4.6}$$

$$\text{z} : \text{s} \;\Leftrightarrow\; [\text{-voice}] : \; \hat{} \; \_\_ \; \# \tag{4.7}$$

As Chapter 3 discussed, there are compilation algorithms for creating automata from rules. Kaplan and Kay (1994) give the general derivation of these algorithms, and Antworth (1990) gives one that is specific to two-level rules. The automata corresponding to the two rules are shown in Figure 4.12

---

[5] Feeding is a situation in which one rules creates the environment for another rule and so must be run beforehand.

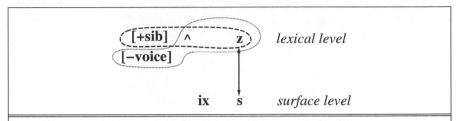

Figure 4.11   The constraints for the i-insertion and z-devoicing rules both refer to a *lexical* z, not a *surface* s.

and Figure 4.13. Figure 4.12 is based on Figure 3.14 of Chapter 3; see page 78 for a reminder of how this automaton works. Note in Figure 4.12 that the plural morpheme is represented by z:, indicating that the constraint is expressed about an lexical rather than surface z.

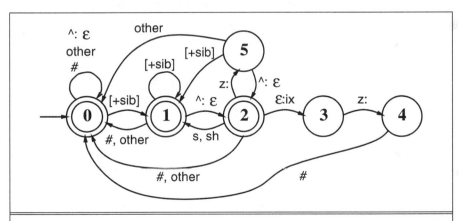

Figure 4.12   The transducer for the i-insertion rule 4.4. The rule can be read *whenever a morpheme ends in a sibilant, and the following morpheme is z, insert* [i].

Figure 4.14 shows the two automata run in parallel on the input [faksˆz] (the figure uses the ARPAbet notation [f aa k s ^ z]). Note that both the automata assuming the default mapping ^:ε to remove the morpheme boundary, and that both automata end in an accepting state.

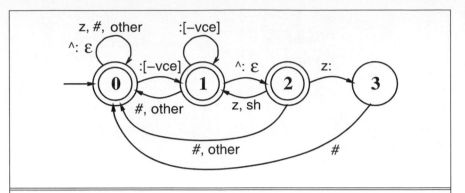

Figure 4.13   The transducer for the z-devoicing rule 4.5. This rule might be summarized *Devoice the morpheme* z *if it follows a morpheme-final voiceless consonant.*

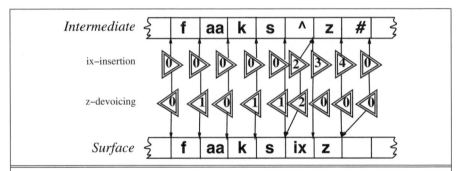

Figure 4.14   The transducer for the i-insertion rule 4.4 and the z-devoicing rule 4.5 run in parallel.

4.4   ADVANCED ISSUES IN COMPUTATIONAL PHONOLOGY

Harmony

Rules like flapping, i-insertion, and z-devoicing are relatively simple as phonological rules go. In this section we turn to the use of the two-level or finite-state model of phonology to model more sophisticated phenomena; this section will be easier to follow if the reader has some knowledge of phonology. The Yawelmani dialect of Yokuts is a Native American language spoken in California with a complex phonological system. In particular, there are three phonological rules related to the realization of vowels that had to be ordered in traditional phonology and whose interaction thus demonstrates a complicated use of finite-state phonology. These rules were first drawn up in the traditional Chomsky and Halle (1968) format by Kisseberth (1969) following the field work of Newman (1944).

First, Yokuts (like many other languages including for example Turkish and Hungarian) has a phonological phenomenon called **vowel harmony**. Vowel harmony is a process in which a vowel changes its form to look like a neighboring vowel. In Yokuts, a suffix vowel changes its form to agree in backness and roundness with the preceding stem vowel. That is, a front vowel like /i/ will appear as a backvowel [u] if the stem vowel is /u/ (examples are taken from Cole and Kisseberth (1995):[6]

Lexical		Surface	Gloss
dub+hin	→	dubhun	"tangles, non-future"
xil+hin	→	xilhin	"leads by the hand, non-future"
bok'+al	→	bok'ol	"might eat"
xat'+al	→	xat'al	"might find"

This Harmony rule has another constraint: it only applies if the suffix vowel and the stem vowel are of the same height. Thus /u/ and /i/ are both high, while /o/ and /a/ are both low.

The second relevant rule, Lowering, causes long high vowels to become low; thus /uː/ becomes [oː] in the first example below:

Lexical		Surface	Gloss
ʔuːt'+it	→	ʔoːt'ut	"steal, passive aorist"
miːk'+it	→	meːk'+it	"swallow, passive aorist"

The third rule, Shortening, shortens long vowels if they occur in closed syllables:

Lexical		Surface
sːap+hin	→	saphin
suduːk+hin	→	sudokhun

The Yokuts rules must be ordered, just as the i-insertion and z-devoicing rules had to be ordered. Harmony must be ordered before Lowering because the /uː/ in the lexical form /ʔuːt'+it/ causes the /i/ to become [u] before it lowers in the surface form [ʔoːt'ut]. Lowering must be ordered before Shortening because the /uː/ in /suduːk+hin/ lowers to [o]; if it was ordered after shortening it would appear on the surface as [u].

Goldsmith (1993) and Lakoff (1993) independently observed that the Yokuts data could be modeled by something like a transducer; Karttunen

---

[6] For purposes of simplifying the explanation, this account ignores some parts of the system such as vowel underspecification (Archangeli, 1984).

(1998) extended the argument, showing that the Goldsmith and Lakoff constraints could be represented either as a cascade of three rules in series, or in the two-level formalism as three rules in parallel; Figure 4.15 shows the two architectures. Just as in the two-level examples presented earlier, the rules work by referring sometimes to the lexical context, sometimes to the surface context; writing the rules is left as Exercise 4.10 for the reader.

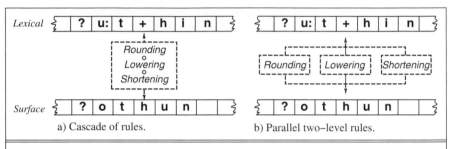

Figure 4.15   Combining the rounding, lowering, and shortening rules for Yawelmani Yokuts.

Templatic Morphology

Finite-state models of phonology/morphology have also been proposed for the templatic (non-concatenative) morphology (discussed on page 60) common in Semitic languages like Arabic, Hebrew, and Syriac. McCarthy (1981) proposed that this kind of morphology could be modeled by using different

TIERS   levels of representation that Goldsmith (1976) had called **tiers**. Kay (1987) proposed a computational model of these tiers via a special transducer which reads four tapes instead of two, as in Figure 4.16.

The tricky part here is designing a machine which aligns the various strings on the tapes in the correct way; Kay proposed that the binyan tape could act as a sort of guide for alignment. Kay's intuition has led to a number of more fully worked out finite-state models of Semitic morphology such as Beesley's (1996) model for Arabic and Kiraz's (1997) model for Syriac.

The more recent work of Kornai (1991) and Bird and Ellison (1994) showed how one-tape automata (i.e. finite-state automata rather than four-tape or even two-tape transducers) could be used to model templatic morphology and other kinds of phenomena that are handleed with the tier-based

AUTOSEGMENTAL   **autosegmental** representations of Goldsmith (1976).

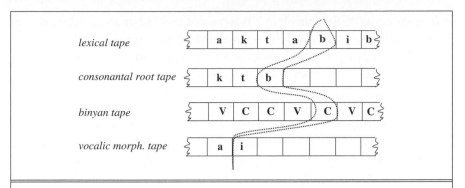

Figure 4.16   A finite-state model of templatic ("non-concatenative") morphology. Modified from Kay (1987) and Sproat (1993).

Optimality Theory

In a traditional phonological derivation, we are given an underlying lexical form and a surface form. The phonological system then consists of one component: a sequence of rules which map the underlying form to the surface form. **Optimality Theory (OT)** (Prince and Smolensky, 1993) offers an alternative way of viewing phonological derivation, based on two functions (GEN and EVAL) and a set of ranked violable constraints (CON). Given an underlying form, the GEN function produces all imaginable surface forms, even those which couldn't possibly be a legal surface form for the input. The EVAL function then applies each constraint in CON to these surface forms in order of constraint rank. The surface form which best meets the constraints is chosen.

OPTIMALITY THEORY

OT

A constraint in OT represents a wellformedness constraint on the surface form, such as a phonotactic constraint on what segments can follow each other, or a constraint on what syllable structures are allowed. A constraint can also check how **faithful** the surface form is to the underlying form.

FAITHFUL

Let's turn to our favorite complicated language, Yawelmani, for an example.[7] In addition to the interesting vowel harmony phenomena discussed above, Yawelmani has a phonotactic constraints that rules out sequences of consonants. In particular three consonants in a row (CCC) are not allowed to occur in a surface word. Sometimes, however, a word contains two consecutive morphemes such that the first one ends in two consonants and the second one starts with one consonant (or vice versa). What does the lan-

---

[7] The following explication of OT via the Yawelmani example draws heavily from Archangeli (1997) and a lecture by Jennifer Cole at the 1999 LSA Linguistic Institute.

guage do to solve this problem? It turns out that Yawelmani either deletes one of the consonants or inserts a vowel in between.

For example, if a stem ends in a C, and its suffix starts with CC, the first C of the suffix is deleted ("+" here means a morpheme boundary):

C-deletion $C \rightarrow \varepsilon / C + \underline{\quad} C$ (4.8)

Here is an example where the CCVC "passive consequent adjunctive" morpheme hneːl (actually the underlying form is /hnil/) drops the initial C if the previous morpheme ends in two consonants (and an example where it doesn't, for comparison):

underlying morphemes	gloss
diyel-neːl-aw	"guard - passive consequent adjunctive - locative"
cawa-hneːl-aw	"shout - passive consequent adjunctive - locative"

If a stem ends in CC and the suffix starts with C, the language instead inserts a vowel to break up the first two consonants:

V-insertion $\varepsilon \rightarrow V / C \underline{\quad} C + C$ (4.9)

Here are some examples in which an i is inserted into the roots ʔilk- "sing" and the roots logw- "pulverize" only when they are followed by a C-initial suffix like -hin, "past", not a V-initial suffix like -en, "future":

surface form	gloss
ʔilik-hin	"sang"
ʔilken	"will sing"
logiwhin	"pulverized"
logwen	"will pulverize"

Kisseberth (1970) suggested that it was not a coincidence that Yawelmani had these particular two rules (and for that matter other related deletion rules that we haven't presented). He noticed that these rules were functionally related; in particular, they all are ways of avoiding three consonants in a row. Another way of stating this generalization is to talk about syllable structure. Yawelmani syllables are only allowed to be of the form CVC or CV (where C means a consonant and V means a vowel). We say that languages like Yawelmani don't allow **complex onsets** or **complex codas**. From the point of view of syllabification, then, these insertions and deletions all happen so as to allow Yawelmani words to be properly syllabified. Since CVCC syllables aren't allowed on the surface, CVCC roots must be **resyllabified** when they appear on the surface. For example, here are the syllabifications

COMPLEX ONSET
COMPLEX CODA

RESYLLABIFIED

of the Yawelmani words we have discussed and some others; note, for example, that the surface syllabification of the CVCC syllables moves the final consonant to the beginning of the next syllable:

underlying morphemes	surface syllabification	gloss
ʔilk-en	ʔil.ken	"will sing"
logw-en	log.wen	"will pulverize"
logw-hin	lo.giw.hin	"will pulverize"
xat-en	xa.ten	"will eat"
diyel-hnil-aw	di.yel.neː.law	"ask - pass. cons. adjunct. - locative"

Here's where Optimality Theory comes in. The basic idea in Optimality Theory is that the language has various constraints on things like syllable structure. These constraints generally apply to the surface form. One such constraint, *COMPLEX, says "No complex onsets or codas". Another class of constraints requires the surface form to be identical to (faithful to) the underlying form. Thus FAITHV says "Don't delete or insert vowels" and FAITHC says "Don't delete or insert consonants". Given an underlying form, the GEN function produces all possible surface forms (i.e., every possible insertion and deletion of segments with every possible syllabification) and they are ranked by the EVAL function using these constraints. Figure 4.17 shows the architecture.

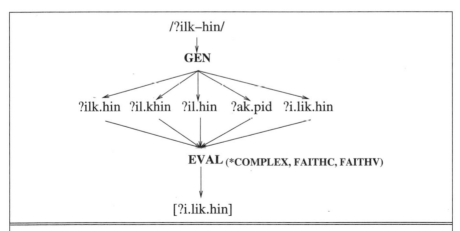

Figure 4.17   The architecture of a derivation in Optimality Theory (after Archangeli (1997)).

The EVAL function works by applying each constraint in ranked order; the optimal candidate is one which either violates no constraints, or violates less of them than all the other candidates. This evaluation is usually shown on a **tableau** (plural **tableaux**). The top left-hand cell shows the input, the constraints are listed in order of rank across the top row, and the possible outputs along the left-most column. Although there are an infinite number of candidates, it is traditional to show only the ones which are 'close'; in the tableau below we have shown the output ʔak.pid just to make it clear that even very different surface forms are to be included. If a form violates a constraint, the relevant cell contains *; a !* indicates the fatal violation which causes a candidate to be eliminated. Cells for constraints which are irrelevant (since a higher-level constraint is already violated) are shaded.

/ʔilk-hin/	*COMPLEX	FAITHC	FAITHV
ʔilk.hin	*!		
ʔil.khin	*!		
ʔil.hin		*!	
☞ ʔi.lik.hin			*
ʔak.pid		*!	

One appeal of Optimality Theoretic derivations is that the constraints are presumed to be cross-linguistic generalizations. That is all languages are presumed to have some version of faithfulness, some preference for simple syllables, and so on. Languages differ in how they rank the constraints; thus English, presumably, ranks FAITHC higher than *COMPLEX. (How do we know this?)

Can a derivation in Optimality Theory be implemented by finite-state transducers? Frank and Satta (1999), following the foundational work of Ellison (1994), showed that (1) if GEN is a regular relation (for example assuming the input doesn't contain context-free trees of some sort), and (2) if the number of allowed violations of any constraint has some finite bound, then an OT derivation can be computed by finite-state means. This second constraint is relevant because of a property of OT that we haven't mentioned: if two candidates violate exactly the same number of constraints, the winning candidate is the one which has the smallest number of violations of the relevant constraint.

One way to implement OT as a finite-state system was worked out by Karttunen (1998), following the above-mentioned work and that of Hammond (1997). In Karttunen's model, GEN is implemented as a finite-state transducer which is given an underlying form and produces a set of candidate forms. For example for the syllabification example above, GEN would generate all strings that are variants of the input with consonant deletions or vowel insertions, and their syllabifications.

Each constraint is implemented as a filter transducer that lets pass only strings which meet the constraint. For legal strings, the transducer thus acts as the identity mapping. For example, *COMPLEX would be implemented via a transducer that mapped any input string to itself, unless the input string had two consonants in the onset or coda, in which case it would be mapped to null.

The constraints can then be placed in a cascade, in which higher-ranked constraints are simply run first, as suggested in Figure 4.18.

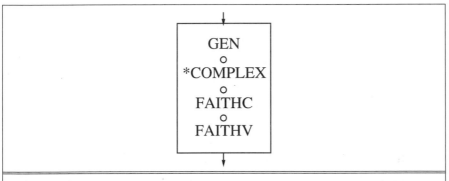

Figure 4.18   Version #1 ("merciless cascade") of Karttunen's finite-state cascade implementation of OT.

There is one crucial flaw with the cascade model in Figure 4.18. Recall that the constraints-transducers filter out any candidate which violates a constraint. But in many derivations, include the proper derivation of ʔi.lik.hin, even the optimal form still violates a constraint. The cascade in Figure 4.17 would incorrectly filter it out, leaving no surface form at all! Frank and Satta (1999) and Hammond (1997) both point out that it is essential to only enforce a constraint if it does not reduce the candidate set to zero. Karttunen (1998) formalizes this intuition with the **lenient composition** operator. Lenient composition is a combination of regular composition and an operation called **priority union**. The basic idea is that if any candidates meet the constraint these candidates will be passed through the filter as usual. If no output meets the constraint, lenient composition retains *all* of the candidates. Figure 4.19 shows the general idea; the interested reader should see Karttunen (1998) for the details. Also see Tesar (1995, 1996), Fosler (1996), and Eisner (1997) for discussions of other computational issues in OT.

LENIENT COMPOSITION

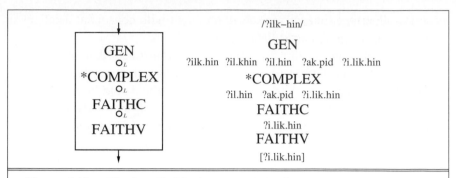

Figure 4.19   Version #2 ("lenient cascade") of Karttunen's finite-state cascade implementation of OT, showing a visualization of the candidate populations that would be passed through each FST constraint.

4.5   MACHINE LEARNING OF PHONOLOGICAL RULES

MACHINE
LEARNING

SUPERVISED

UNSUPERVISED

LEARNING
BIAS

The task of a **machine learning** system is to automatically induce a model for some domain, given some data from the domain and, sometimes, other information as well. Thus a system to learn phonological rules would be given at least a set of (surface forms of) words to induce from. A **supervised** algorithm is one which is given the correct answers for some of this data, using these answers to induce a model which can generalize to new data it hasn't seen before. An **unsupervised** algorithm does this purely from the data. While unsupervised algorithms don't get to see the correct labels for the classifications, they can be given hints about the nature of the rules or models they should be forming. For example, the knowledge that the models will be in the form of automata is itself a kind of hint. Such hints are called a **learning bias**.

This section gives a very brief overview of some models of unsupervised machine learning of phonological rules; more details about machine learning algorithms will be presented throughout the book.

Ellison (1992) showed that concepts like the consonant and vowel distinction, the syllable structure of a language, and harmony relationships could be learned by a system based on choosing the model from the set of potential models which is the simplest. Simplicity can be measured by choosing the model with the minimum coding length, or the highest probability (we will define these terms in detail in Chapter 6). Daelemans et al. (1994) used the Instance-Based Generalization algorithm (Aha et al., 1991) to learn stress rule for Dutch; the algorithm is a supervised one which is given a number of words together with their stress patterns, and which induces generalizations about the mapping from the sequences of light and heavy syllable type in the word (light syllables have no coda consonant; heavy syllables have one) to the stress pattern. Tesar and Smolensky (1993) show that a system which is given Optimality Theory constraints but not their ranking can learn the ranking from data via a simple greedy algorithm.

Johnson (1984) gives one of the first computational algorithms for phonological rule induction. His algorithm works for rules of the form

(4.10) $a \rightarrow b/C$

where C is the feature matrix of the segments around a. Johnson's algorithm sets up a system of constraint equations which C must satisfy, by considering both the positive contexts, i.e., all the contexts C_i in which a b occurs on the surface, as well as all the negative contexts C_j in which an a occurs on the surface. Touretzky et al. (1990) extended Johnson's insight by using the *version spaces* algorithm of Mitchell (1981) to induce phonological rules in their *Many Maps* architecture, which is similar to two-level phonology. Like Johnson's, their system looks at the underlying and surface realizations of single segments. For each segment, the system uses the version space algorithm to search for the proper statement of the context. The model also has a separate algorithm which handles harmonic effects by looking for multiple segmental changes in the same word, and is more general than Johnson's in dealing with epenthesis and deletion rules.

The algorithm of Gildea and Jurafsky (1996) was designed to induce transducers representing two-level rules of the type we have discussed earlier. Like the algorithm of Touretzky et al. (1990), Gildea and Jurafsky's algorithm was given sets of pairings of underlying and surface forms. The algorithm was based on the OSTIA (Oncina et al., 1993) algorithm, which is a general learning algorithm for a subtype of finite-state transducers called **subsequential transducers**. By itself, the OSTIA algorithm was too general to learn phonological transducers, even given a large corpus of underlying-form/surface-form pairs. Gildea and Jurafsky then augmented the domain-independent OSTIA system with three kinds of learning biases which are specific to natural language phonology; the main two are **Faithfulness** (underlying segments tend to be realized similarly on the surface), and **Community** (similar segments behave similarly). The resulting system was able to learn transducers for flapping in American English, or German consonant devoicing.

Finally, many learning algorithms for phonology are probabilistic. For example Riley (1991) and Withgott and Chen (1993) proposed a decision-tree approach to segmental mapping. A decision tree is induced for each segment, classifying possible realizations of the segment in terms of contextual factors such as stress and the surrounding segments. Decision trees and probabilistic algorithms in general will be defined in Chapters 5 and 6.

4.6   MAPPING TEXT TO PHONES FOR TTS

> *Dearest creature in Creation*
> *Studying English pronunciation*
> *I will teach you in my verse*
> *Sounds like corpse, corps, horse and worse.*
> *It will keep you, Susy, busy,*
> *Make your head with heat grow dizzy*
> ...
> *River, rival; tomb, bomb, comb;*
> *Doll and roll, and some and home.*
> *Stranger does not rime with anger*
> *Neither does devour with clangour.*
> ...
>
> G.N. Trenite (1870-1946) *The Chaos*, reprinted in Witten (1982).

Now that we have learned the basic inventory of phones in English and seen how to model phonological rules, we are ready to study the problem of mapping from an orthographic or text word to its pronunciation.

Pronunciation Dictionaries

An important component of this mapping is a **pronunciation dictionary**. These dictionaries are actually used in both ASR and TTS systems, although because of the different needs of these two areas the contents of the dictionaries are somewhat different.

The simplest pronunciation dictionaries just have a list of words and their pronunciations:

Word	Pronunciation	Word	Pronunciation
cat	[kæt]	goose	[gus]
cats	[kæts]	geese	[gis]
pig	[pɪg]	hedgehog	[ˈhɛdʒ.hɔg]
pigs	[pɪgz]	hedgehogs	[ˈhɛdʒ.hɔgz]
fox	[fɑx]		
foxes	[ˈfɑk.sɪz]		

Three large, commonly-used, on-line pronunciation dictionaries in this format are PRONLEX, CMUdict, and CELEX. These are used for speech recognition and can also be adapted for use in speech synthesis. The PRON-LEX dictionary (LDC, 1995) was designed for speech recognition applications and contains pronunciations for 90,694 wordforms. It covers all the words used in many years of the Wall Street Journal, as well as the Switchboard Corpus. The CMU Pronouncing Dictionary was also developed for ASR purposes and has pronunciations for about 100,000 wordforms. The CELEX dictionary (Celex, 1993) includes all the words in the Oxford Advanced Learner's Dictionary (1974) (41,000 lemmata) and the Longman Dictionary of Contemporary English (1978) (53,000 lemmata), in total it has pronunciations for 160,595 wordforms. Its pronunciations are British while the other two are American. Each dictionary uses a different phone set; the CMU and PRONLEX phonesets are derived from the ARPAbet, while the CELEX dictionary is derived from the IPA. All three represent three levels of stress: primary stress, secondary stress, and no stress. Figure 4.20 shows the pronunciation of the word *armadillo* in all three dictionaries.

Dictionary	Pronunciation	IPA Version
Pronlex	+arm.xd'Il.o	[ˌɑrməˈdɪloʊ]
CMU	AA2 R M AH0 D IH1 L OW0	[ˌɑrmʌˈdɪloʊ]
CELEX	"#-m@-'dI-l5	[ˌɑː.mə.ˈdɪ.ləʊ]

Figure 4.20   The pronunciation of the word *armadillo* in three dictionaries. Rather than explain special symbols, we have given an IPA equivalent for each pronunciation. The CMU dictionary represents unstressed vowels ([ə], [ɨ], etc.) by giving a 0 stress level to the vowel. We represented this by underlining in the IPA form. Note the r-dropping and use of the [əʊ] rather than [oʊ] vowel in the British CELEX pronunciation.

Often two distinct words are spelled the same (they are **homographs**) but pronounced differently. For example the verb *wind* ("You need to wind this up more neatly") is pronounced [waɪnd] while the noun *wind* ("blow,

blow, thou winter wind") is pronounced [wɪnd]. This is essential for TTS applications (since in a given context the system needs to say one or the other) but for some reason is usually ignored in current speech recognition systems. Printed pronunciation dictionaries give distinct pronunciations for each part-of-speech; CELEX does as well. Since they were designed for ASR, Pronlex and CMU, although they give two pronunciations for the form *wind*, don't specify which one is used for which part-of-speech.

Dictionaries often don't include many proper names. This is a serious problem for many applications; Liberman and Church (1992) report that 21% of the word tokens in their 33-million-word 1988 AP newswire corpus were names. Furthermore, they report that a list obtained in 1987 from the Donnelly marketing organization contains 1.5 million names (covering 72 million households in the United States). But only about 1000 of the 52477 lemmas in CELEX (which is based on traditional dictionaries) are proper names. By contrast Pronlex includes 20,000 names; this is still only a small fraction of the 1.5 million. Very few dictionaries give pronunciations for entries like *Dr.*, which as Liberman and Church (1992) point out can be "doctor" or "drive", or *2/3*, which can be "two thirds" or "February third" or "two slash three".

No dictionaries currently have good models for the pronunciation of function words (*and*, *I*, *a*, *the*, *of*, etc.). This is because the variation in these words due to phonetic context is so great. Usually the dictionaries include some simple baseform (such as [ði] for *the*) and use other algorithms to derive the variation due to context; Chapter 5 will treat the issue of modeling contextual pronunciation variation for words of this sort.

One significant difference between TTS and ASR dictionaries is that TTS dictionaries do not have to represent dialectal variation; thus where a very accurate ASR dictionary needs to represent both pronunciations of *either* and *tomato*, a TTS dictionary can choose one.

Beyond Dictionary Lookup: Text Analysis

Mapping from text to phones relies on the kind of pronunciation dictionaries we talked about in the last section. As we suggested before, one way to map text-to-phones would be to look up each word in a pronunciation dictionary and read the string of phones out of the dictionary. This method would work fine for any word that we can put in the dictionary in advance. But as we saw in Chapter 3, it's not possible to represent every word in English (or any other language) in advance. Both speech synthesis and speech recognition systems need to be able to guess at the pronunciation of words that are not in their dictionary. This section will first examine the kinds of words that are likely to be missing in a pronunciation dictionary, and then show how the finite-state transducers of Chapter 3 can be used to model the basic task of text-to-phones. Chapter 5 will introduce variation in pronunciation and introduce probabilistic techniques for modeling it.

Three of the most important cases where we cannot rely on a word dictionary involve **names**, **morphological productivity**, and **numbers**. As a brief example, we arbitrarily selected a brief (561 word) movie review that appeared in the July 17, 1998 issue of the New York Times. The review, of Vincent Gallo's "Buffalo '66", was written by Janet Maslin. Here's the beginning of the article:

> In Vincent Gallo's "Buffalo '66," Billy Brown (Gallo) steals a blond kewpie doll named Layla (Christina Ricci) out of her tap dancing class and browbeats her into masquerading as his wife at a dinner with his parents. Billy hectors, cajoles and tries to bribe Layla. ("You can eat all the food you want. Just make me look good.") He threatens both that he will kill her and that he won't be her best friend. He bullies her outrageously but with such crazy brio and jittery persistence that Layla falls for him. Gallo's film, a deadpan original mixing pathos with bravado, works on its audience in much the same way.

We then took two large commonly-used on-line pronunciation dictionaries; the PRONLEX dictionary, that contains pronunciations for 90,694 word-forms and includes coverage of many years of the Wall Street Journal, as well as the Switchboard Corpus, and the larger CELEX dictionary, which has pronunciations for 160,595 wordforms. The combined dictionaries have approximately 194,000 pronunciations. Of the 561 words in the movie review, 16 (3%) did not have pronunciations in these two dictionaries (not counting two hyphenated words, *baby-blue* and *hollow-eyed*). Here they are:

Names		Inflected Names	Numbers	Other
Aki	Gazzara	Gallo's	'66	c'mere
Anjelica	Kaurismaki			indie
Arquette	Kusturica			kewpie
Buscemi	Layla			sexpot
Gallo	Rosanna			

Some of these missing words can be found by increasing the dictionary size (for example Wells's (1990) definitive (but not on-line) pronunciation dictionary of English does have *sexpot* and *kewpie*). But the rest need to generated on-line.

Names are a large problem for pronunciation dictionaries. It is difficult or impossible to list in advance all proper names in English; furthermore they may come from any language, and may have variable spellings. Most potential applications for TTS or ASR involve names; for example names are essentially in telephony applications (directory assistance, call routing). Corporate names are important in many applications and are created constantly (*CoComp, Intel, Cisco*). Medical speech applications (such as transcriptions of doctor-patient interviews) require pronunciations of names of pharmaceuticals; there are some off-line medical pronunciation dictionaries but they are known to be extremely inaccurate (Markey and Ward, 1997). Recall the figure of 1.5 million names mentioned above, and Liberman and Church's (1992) finding that 21% of the word tokens in their 33 million word 1988 AP newswire corpus were names.

Morphology is a particular problem for many languages other than English. For languages with very productive morphology it is computationally infeasible to represent every possible word; recall this Turkish example:

(4.11) uygarlaştıramadıklarımızdanmışsınızcasına

uygar	*+laş*	*+tır*	*+ama*	*+dık*	*+lar*	*+ımız*
civilized	+BEC	+CAUS	+NEGABLE	+PPART	+PL	+P1PL

+dan	*+mış*	*+sınız*	*+casına*
+ABL	+PAST	+2PL	+AsIf

"(behaving) as if you are among those whom we could not civilize/cause to become civilized"

Even a language as similar to English as German has greater ability to create words; Sproat et al. (1998) note the spontaneously created German example *Unerfindlichkeitsunterstellung* ("allegation of incomprehensibility").

But even in English, morphologically simple though it is, morphological knowledge is necessary for pronunciation modeling. For example names and acronyms are often inflected (*Gallo's, IBM's, DATs, Syntex's*) as are new words (*faxes, indies*). Furthermore, we can't just add s to the pronunciation of the uninflected forms, because as the last section showed, the possessive -'s and plural -s suffix in English are pronounced differently in different contexts; *Syntex's* is pronounced [sɪntɛksɨz], *faxes* is pronounced [fæksɨz], *IBM's* is pronounced [aɪbijɛmz], and *DATs* is pronounced [dæts].

Finally, pronouncing numbers is a particularly difficult problem. The '66 in *Buffalo '66* is pronounced [sɪkstisɪks] not [sɪkssɪks]. The most natural way to pronounce the phone number "947-2020" is probably "nine"-"four"-"seven"-"twenty"-"twenty" rather than "nine"-"four"-"seven"-"two"-"zero"-"two"-"zero". Liberman and Church (1992) note that there are five main ways to pronounce a string of digits (although others are possible):

- **Serial:** Each digit is pronounced separately—*8765* is "eight seven six five".
- **Combined:** The digit string is pronounced as a single integer, with all position labels read out—"eight thousand seven hundred sixty five".
- **Paired:** Each pair of digits is pronounced as an integer; if there is an odd number of digits the first one is pronounced by itself—"eighty-seven sixty-five".
- **Hundreds:** Strings of four digits can be pronounced as counts of hundreds—"eighty-seven hundred (and) sixty-five".
- **Trailing Unit:** Strings that end in zeros are pronounced serially until the last nonzero digit, which is pronounced followed by the appropriate unit—*8765000* is "eight seven six five thousand".

Pronunciation of numbers and these five methods are discussed further in Exercises 4.5 and 4.6.

An FST-based Pronunciation Lexicon

Early work in pronunciation modeling for text-to-speech systems (such as the seminal MITalk system Allen et al. (1987)) relied heavily on **letter-to-sound** rules. Each rule specified how a letter or combination of letters was mapped to phones; here is a fragment of such a rule-base from Witten (1982):

LETTER-TO-SOUND

Fragment	Pronunciation
-p-	[p]
-ph-	[f]
-phe-	[fi]
-phes-	[fiz]
-place-	[pleɪs]
-placi-	[pleɪsi]
-plement-	[plɪmɛnt]

Such systems consisted of a long list of such rules and a very small dictionary of exceptions (often function words such as *a, are, as, both, do, does,* etc.). More recent systems have completely inverted the algorithm, relying on very large dictionaries, with letter-to-sound rules only used for the small number of words that are neither in the dictionary nor are morphological variants of words in the dictionary. How can these large dictionaries be represented in a way that allows for morphological productivity? Luckily, these morphological issues in pronunciation (adding inflectional suffixes, slight pronunciation changes at the juncture of two morphemes, etc.) are identical to the morphological issues in spelling that we saw in Chapter 3. Indeed, (Sproat, 1998b) and colleagues have worked out the use of transducers for text-to-speech. We might break down their transducer approach into five components:

1. an FST to represent the pronunciation of individual words and morphemes in the lexicon
2. FSAs to represent the possible sequencing of morphemes
3. individual FSTs for each pronunciation rule (for example expressing the pronunciation of -*s* in different contexts)
4. heuristics and letter-to-sound (LTS) rules/transducers used to model the pronunciations of names and acronyms
5. default letter-to-sound rules/transducers for any other unknown words

We will limit our discussion here to the first four components; those interested in letter-to-sound rules should see (Allen et al., 1987). These first components will turn out to be simple extensions of the FST components we saw in Chapter 3 and on page 110. The first is the representation of the lexical base form of each word; recall that base form means the uninflected form of the word. The previous base forms were stored in orthographic representation; we will need to augment each of them with the correct lexical phonological representation. Figure 4.21 shows the original and the updated lexical entries:

The second part of our FST system is the finite-state machinery to model morphology. We will give only one example: the nominal plural suffix -*s*. Figure 4.22 in Chapter 3 shows the automaton for English plurals, updated to handle pronunciation as well. The only change was the addition of the [s] pronunciation for the suffix, and ε pronunciations for all the morphological features.

We can compose the inflection FSA in Figure 4.22 with a transducer implementing the baseform lexicon in Figure 4.21 to produce an inflectionally-enriched lexicon that has singular and plural nouns. The resulting minilexicon is shown in Figure 4.23.

The lexicon shown in Figure 4.23 has two levels, an underlying or "lexical" level and an intermediate level. The only thing that remains is to add

Orthographic Lexicon	Lexicon
Regular Nouns	
cat	c|k a|æ t|t
fox	f|f o|ɑ x|ks
dog	d|d o|ɑ g|g
Irregular Singular Nouns	
goose	g|g oo|u s|s e|ɛ
Irregular Plural Nouns	
g o:e o:e s e	g|g oo|u:ee|i s|s e|ɛ

Figure 4.21   FST-based lexicon, extending the lexicon in the table on page 74 in Chapter 3. Each symbol in the lexicon is now a pair of symbols separated by "\|", one representing the "orthographic" lexical entry and one the "phonological" lexical entry. The irregular plural *geese* also pre-specifies the contents of the intermediate tape ":ee\|i".

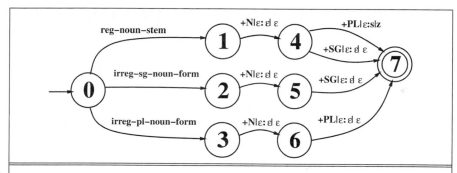

Figure 4.22   FST for the nominal singular and plural inflection. The automaton adds the morphological features [+N], [+PL], and [+SG] at the lexical level where relevant and also adds the plural suffix s\|z (at the intermediate level). We will discuss below why we represent the pronunciation of -*s* as z rather than s.

transducers which apply spelling rules and pronunciation rules to map the intermediate level into the surface level. These include the various spelling rules discussed on page 77 and the pronunciation rules starting on page 105.

The lexicon and these phonological rules and the orthographic rules from Chapter 3 can now be used to map between a lexical representation (containing both orthographic and phonological strings) and a surface representation (containing both orthographic and phonological strings). As we saw in Chapter 3, this mapping can be run from surface to lexical form, or from lexical to surface form; Figure 4.24 shows the architecture. Recall that

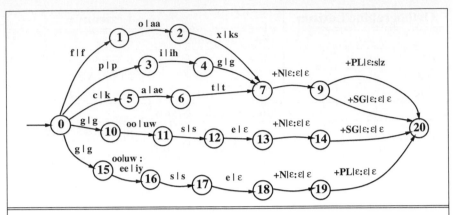

Figure 4.23   Mini-lexicon composing a transducer from the baseform lexicon of Figure 4.21 with the inflectional transducer of Figure 4.22.

the lexicon FST maps between the "lexical" level, with its stems and morphological features, and an "intermediate" level which represents a simple concatenation of morphemes. Then a host of FSTs, each representing either a single spelling rule constraint or a single phonological constraint, all run in parallel so as to map between this intermediate level and the surface level. Each level has both orthographic and phonological representations. For text-to-speech applications in which the input is a lexical form (e.g., for text generation, where the system knows the lexical identity of the word, its part-of-speech, its inflection, etc.), the cascade of FSTs can map from lexical form to surface pronunciation. For text-to-speech applications in which the input is a surface spelling (e.g., for "reading text out loud" applications), the cascade of FSTs can map from surface orthographic form to surface pronunciation via the underlying lexical form.

Finally let us say a few words about names and acronyms. Acronyms can be spelled with or without periods (*I.R.S.* or *IRS*). Acronyms with periods are usually pronounced by spelling them out ([aɪɑɾɛs]). Acronyms that usually appear without periods (AIDS, ANSI, ASCAP) may either be spelled out or pronounced as a word; so AIDS is usually pronounced the same as the third-person form of the verb *aid*. Liberman and Church (1992) suggest keeping a small dictionary of the acronyms that are pronounced as words, and spelling out the rest. Their method for dealing with names begins with a dictionary of the pronunciations of 50,000 names, and then applies a small number of affix-stripping rules (akin to the Porter Stemmer of Chapter 3), rhyming heuristics, and letter-to-sound rules to increase the coverage.

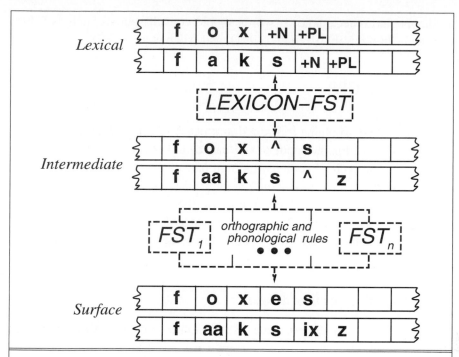

Figure 4.24   Mapping between the lexicon and surface form for orthography and phonology simultaneously. The system can be used to map from a lexical entry to its surface pronunciation or from surface orthography to surface pronunciation via the lexical entry.

Liberman and Church (1992) took the most frequent quarter million words in the Donnelly list. They found that the 50,000 word dictionary covered 59% of these 250,000 name tokens. Adding stress-neutral suffixes like *-s,* *-ville,* and *-son* (*Walters* = *Walter* + *s, Abelson* = *Abel* + *son, Lucasville* = *Lucas* + *ville*) increased the coverage to 84%. Adding name-name compounds (*Abdulhussein, Baumgaertner*) and rhyming heuristics increased the coverage to 89%. The rhyming heuristics used letter-to-sound rules for the beginning of the word and then found a rhyming word to help pronounce the end; so Plotsky was pronounced by using the LTS rule for *Pl-* and guessing *-otsky* from *Trotsky.* They then added a number of more complicated morphological rules (prefixes like *O'Brien*), stress-changing suffixes (*Adamovich*), suffix-exchanges (*Bierstadt* = *Bierbaum - baum + stadt*) and used a system of letter-to-sound rules for the remainder. This system was not implemented as an FST; Exercise 4.11 will address some of the issues in turning such a set of rules into an FST. Readers interested in further details about names, acronyms and other unknown words should consult sources such as Liberman and Church (1992), Vitale (1991), and Allen et al. (1987).

4.7   PROSODY IN TTS

The orthography to phone transduction process just described produces the main component for the input to the part of a TTS system which actually generates the speech. Another important part of the input is a specification of the **prosody**. The term **prosody** is generally used to refer to aspects of a sentence's pronunciation which aren't described by the sequence of phones derived from the lexicon. Prosody operates on longer linguistic units than phones, and hence is sometimes called the study of **suprasegmental** phenomena.

Phonological Aspects of Prosody

There are three main phonological aspects to prosody: **prominence**, **structure** and **tune**.

As page 102 discussed, prominence is a broad term used to cover **stress** and **accent**. Prominence is a property of syllables, and is often described in a relative manner, by saying one syllable is more prominent than another. Pronunciation lexicons mark lexical stress; for example *table* has its stress on the first syllable, while *machine* has its stress on the second. Function words like *there*, *the* or *a* are usually unaccented altogether. When words are joined together, their accentual patterns combine and form a larger accent pattern for the whole utterance. There are some regularities in how accents combine. For example adjective-noun combinations like *new truck* are likely to have accent on the right word (*new *truck*), while noun-noun compounds like **tree surgeon* are likely to have accent on the left. In generally, however, there are many exceptions to these rules, and so accent prediction is quite complex. For example the noun-noun compound **apple cake* has the accent on the first word while the noun-noun compound *apple *pie* or *city *hall* both have the accent on the second word (Liberman and Sproat, 1992; Sproat, 1994, 1998a). Furthermore, rhythm plays a role in keeping the accented syllables spread apart a bit; thus *city *hall* and **parking lot* combine as **city hall *parking lot* (Liberman and Prince, 1977). Finally, the location of accent is very strongly affected by the discourse factors we will describe in Chapters 18 and 19; in particular new or focused words or phrases often receive accent.

Sentences have prosodic structure in the sense that some words seem to group naturally together and some words seem to have a noticeable break or disjuncture between them. Often prosodic structure is described in terms of **prosodic phrasing**, meaning that an utterance has a prosodic phrase structure in a similar way to it having a syntactic phrase structure. For example, in the sentence *I wanted to go to London, but could only get tickets for France* there seems to be two main prosodic phrases, their boundary occurring at the comma. Commonly used terms for these larger prosodic units include **intonational phrase** or **IP** (Beckman and Pierrehumbert, 1986), **intonation unit** (Du Bois et al., 1983), and **tone unit** (Crystal, 1969). Furthermore, in the first phrase, there seems to be another set of lesser prosodic phrase boundaries (often called **intermediate phrase**s) that split up the words as follows *I wanted | to go | to London.* The exact definitions of prosodic phrases and subphrases and their relation to syntactic phrases like clauses and noun phrases and semantic units have been and still are the topic of much debate (Chomsky and Halle, 1968; Langendoen, 1975; Streeter, 1978; Hirschberg and Pierrehumbert, 1986; Selkirk, 1986; Nespor and Vogel, 1986; Croft, 1995; Ladd, 1996; Ford and Thompson, 1996; Ford et al., 1996). Despite these complications, algorithms have been proposed which attempt to automatically break an input text sentence into intonational phrases. For example Wang and Hirschberg (1992), Ostendorf and Veilleux (1994), Taylor and Black (1998), and others have built statistical models (incorporating probabilistic predictors such as the CART-style decision trees to be defined in Chapter 5) for predicting intonational phrase boundaries based on such features as the parts of speech of the surrounding words, the length of the utterance in words and seconds, the distance of the potential boundary from the beginning or ending of the utterance, and whether the surrounding words are accented.

Two utterances with the same prominence and phrasing patterns can still differ prosodically by having different **tunes**. Tune refers to the intonational melody of an utterance. Consider the utterance *oh, really*. Without varying the phrasing or stress, it is still possible to have many variants of this by varying the intonational tune. For example, we might have an excited version *oh, really!* (in the context of a reply to a statement that you've just won the lottery); a sceptical version *oh, really?*—in the context of not being sure that the speaker is being honest; to an angry *oh, really!* indicating displeasure. Intonational tunes can be broken into component parts, the most important of which is the **pitch accent**. Pitch accents occur on stressed syllables and form a characteristic pattern in the F0 contour (as explained below).

PROSODIC PHRASING

INTONATIONAL PHRASE

IP

INTERMEDIATE PHRASE

PITCH ACCENT

Depending on the type of pattern, different effects (such as those just outlined above) can be produced. A popular model of pitch accent classification is the Pierrehumbert or ToBI model (Pierrehumbert, 1980; Silverman et al., 1992), which says there are five pitch accents in English, which are made from combining two simple tones (high **H**, and low **L**) in various ways. A **H+L** pattern forms a fall, while a **L+H** pattern forms a rise. An asterisk (*) is also used to indicate which tone falls on the stressed syllable. This gives an inventory of **H***, **L***, **L+H***, **L*+H**, **H+L*** (a sixth pitch accent **H*+L** which was present in early versions of the model was later abandoned). Our three examples of *oh, really* might be marked with the accents **L+H***, **L*+H** and **L*** respectively. In addition to pitch accents, this model also has two phrase accents **L-** and **H-** and two boundary tones **L%** and **H%**, which are used at the ends of phrases to control whether the intonational tune rises or falls.

Other intonational modals differ from ToBI by not using discrete phonemic classes for intonation accents. For example the Tilt (Taylor, 2000) and Fujisaki models (Fujisaki and Ohno, 1997) use continuous parameters rather than discrete categories to model pitch accents. These researchers argue that while the discrete models are often easier to visualize and work with, continuous models may be more robust and more accurate for computational purposes.

Phonetic or Acoustic Aspects of Prosody

The three phonological factors interact and are realized by a number of different phonetic or acoustic phenomena. Prominent syllables are generally louder and longer that non-prominent syllables. Prosodic phrase boundaries are often accompanied by pauses, by lengthening of the syllable just before the boundary, and sometimes lowering of pitch at the boundary. Intonational tune is manifested in the fundamental frequency (F0) contour.

Prosody in Speech Synthesis

A major task for a TTS system is to generate appropriate linguistic representations of prosody, and from them generate appropriate acoustic patterns which will be manifested in the output speech waveform. The output of a TTS system with such a prosodic component is a sequence of phones, each of which has a duration and an F0 (pitch) value. The duration of each phone is dependent on the phonetic context (see Chapter 7). The F0 value is influenced by the factors discussed above, including the lexical stress, the accented or focused element in the sentence, and the intonational tune of the utterance (for example a final rise for questions). Figure 4.25 shows some sample TTS output from the FESTIVAL (Black et al., 1999) speech synthesis system for the sentence *Do you really want to see all of it?*. This output, together with the F0 values shown in Figure 4.26 would be the input to the **waveform synthesis** component described in Chapter 7. The durations here are computed by a CART-style decision tree (Riley, 1992).

		H*									L*	L- H%	
do		you		really				want				to	see
d	uw	y	uw	r	ih	l	iy	w	aa	n	t	t ax	s iy
110	110	50	50	75	64	57	82	57	50	72	41	43 47	54 130

	all	of	it
	ao l	ah v	ih t
	76 90	44 62	46 220

Figure 4.25   Output of the FESTIVAL (Black et al., 1999) generator for the sentence *Do you really want to see all of it?* The exact intonation contour is shown in Figure 4.26. Thanks to Paul Taylor for this figure.

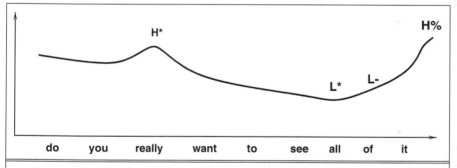

Figure 4.26   The F0 contour for the sample sentence generated by the FESTIVAL synthesis system in Figure 4.25, thanks to Paul Taylor.

As was suggested above, determining the proper prosodic pattern for a sentence is difficult, as real-world knowledge and semantic information is needed to know which syllables to accent, and which tune to apply. This sort of information is difficult to extract from the text and hence prosody modules often aim to produce a "neutral declarative" version of the input text, which assume the sentence should be spoken in a default way with no reference to discourse history or real-world events. This is one of the main reasons why intonation in TTS often sounds "wooden".

4.8   HUMAN PROCESSING OF PHONOLOGY AND MORPHOLOGY

Chapter 3 suggested that productive morphology plays a psychologically real role in the human lexicon. But we stopped short of a detailed model of how the morphology might be represented. Now that we have studied phonological structure and phonological learning, we return to the psychological question of the representation of morphological/phonological knowledge.

One view of human morphological or phonological processing might be that it distinguishes productive, regular morphology from irregular or exceptional morphology. Under this view, the regular past tense morpheme -ed, for example, could be mentally represented as a rule which would be applied to verbs like *walk* to produce *walked*. Irregular past tense verbs like *broke*, *sang*, and *brought*, on the other hand, would simply be stored as part of a lexical representation, and the rule wouldn't apply to these. Thus this proposal strongly distinguishes representation via *rules* from representation via lexical *listing*.

This proposal seems sensible, and is indeed identical to the transducer-based models we have presented in these last two chapters. Unfortunately, this simple model seems to be wrong, One problem is that the irregular verbs themselves show a good deal of phonological **subregularity**. For example, the ɪ/æ alternation relating *ring* and *rang* also relates *sing* and *sang* and *swim* and *swam* (Bybee and Slobin, 1982). Children learning the language often extend this pattern to incorrectly produce *bring-brang*, and adults often make speech errors showing effects of this subregular pattern. A second problem is that there is psychological evidence that high-frequency regular inflected forms (*needed*, *covered*) are stored in the lexicon just like the stems *cover* and *need* (Losiewicz, 1992). Finally, word and morpheme frequency in general seems to play an important role in human processing.

Arguments like these led to "data-driven" models of morphological learning and representation, which essentially store all the inflected forms they have seen. These models generalize to new forms by a kind of analogy; regular morphology is just like subregular morphology but acquires rule-like trappings simply because it occurs more often. Such models include the computational **connectionist** or **Parallel Distributed Processing** model of Rumelhart and McClelland (1986) and subsequent improvements (Plunkett and Marchman, 1991; MacWhinney and Leinbach, 1991) and the similar **network** model of Bybee (1985, 1995). In these models, the behavior of regular morphemes like -ed **emerges** from its frequent interaction with other

SUBREGU-
LARITY

CONNEC-
TIONIST
PARALLEL
DISTRIBUTED
PROCESSING

forms. Proponents of the rule-based view of morphology such as Pinker and Prince (1988), Marcus et al. (1995), and others, have criticized the connectionist models and proposed a compromise **dual processing** model, in which regular forms like *-ed* are represent as symbolic rules, but subregular examples (*broke, brought*) are represented by connectionist-style pattern associators. This debate between the connectionist and dual processing models has deep implications for mental representation of all kinds of regular rule-based behavior and is one of the most interesting open questions in human language processing. Chapter 7 will briefly discuss connectionist models of human speech processing; readers who are further interested in connectionist models should consult the references above and textbooks like Anderson (1995).

4.9 SUMMARY

This chapter has introduced many of the important notions we need to understand spoken language processing. The main points are as follows:

- We can represent the pronunciation of words in terms of units called **phones**. The standard system for representing phones is the **International Phonetic Alphabet** or **IPA**. An alternative English-only transcription system that uses ASCII letters is the **ARPAbet**.

- Phones can be described by how they are produced **articulatorily** by the vocal organs; consonants are defined in terms of their **place** and **manner** of articulation and **voicing**, vowels by their **height** and **backness**.

- A **phoneme** is a generalization or abstraction over different phonetic realizations. **Allophonic rules** express how a phoneme is realized in a given context.

- **Transducers** can be used to model phonological rules just as they were used in Chapter 3 to model spelling rules. **Two-level morphology** is a theory of morphology/phonology which models phonological rules as finite-state **well-formedness constraints** on the mapping between lexical and surface form.

- **Pronunciation dictionaries** are used for both text-to-speech and automatic speech recognition. They give the pronunciation of words as strings of phones, sometimes including syllabification and stress. Most on-line pronunciation dictionaries have on the order of 100,000 words but still lack many names, acronyms, and inflected forms.

- The **text-analysis** component of a text-to-speech system maps from orthography to strings of phones. This is usually done with a large dictionary augmented with a system (such as a transducer) for handling productive morphology, pronunciation changes, names, numbers, and acronyms.

BIBLIOGRAPHICAL AND HISTORICAL NOTES

The major insights of articulatory phonetics date to the linguists of 800–150 B.C. India. They invented the concepts of place and manner of articulation, worked out the glottal mechanism of voicing, and understood the concept of assimilation. European science did not catch up with the Indian phoneticians until over 2000 years later, in the late 19th century. The Greeks did have some rudimentary phonetic knowledge; by the time of Plato's *Theaetetus* and *Cratylus*, for example, they distinguished vowels from consonants, and stop consonants from continuants. The Stoics developed the idea of the syllable and were aware of phonotactic constraints on possible words. An unknown Icelandic scholar of the twelfth century exploited the concept of the phoneme, proposed a phonemic writing system for Icelandic, including diacritics for length and nasality. But his text remained unpublished until 1818 and even then was largely unknown outside Scandinavia (Robins, 1967). The modern era of phonetics is usually said to have begun with Sweet, who proposed what is essentially the phoneme in his *Handbook of Phonetics* (1877). He also devised an alphabet for transcription and distinguished between *broad* and *narrow* transcription, proposing many ideas that were eventually incorporated into the IPA. Sweet was considered the best practicing phonetician of his time; he made the first scientific recordings of languages for phonetic purposes, and advanced the start of the art of articulatory description. He was also infamously difficult to get along with, a trait that is well captured in the stage character that George Bernard Shaw modeled after him: Henry Higgins. The phoneme was first named by the Polish scholar Baudouin de Courtenay, who published his theories in 1894.

The idea that phonological rules could be modeled as regular relations dates to Johnson (1972), who showed that any phonological system that didn't allow rules to apply to their own output (i.e., systems that did not have recursive rules) could be modeled with regular relations (or finite-state transducers). Virtually all phonological rules that had been formulated at the time had this property (except some rules with integral-valued features, like early stress and tone rules). Johnson's insight unfortunately did not attract the attention of the community, and was independently discovered by Roland Kaplan and Martin Kay; see Chapter 3 for the rest of the history of two-level morphology. Karttunen (1993) gives a tutorial introduction to two-level morphology that includes more of the advanced details than we were able to present here.

Readers interested in phonology should consult (Goldsmith, 1995) as a reference on phonological theory in general and Archangeli and Langendoen (1997) on Optimality Theory.

Two classic text-to-speech synthesis systems are described in Allen et al. (1987) (the *MITalk* system) and Sproat (1998b) (the Bell Labs system). The pronunciation problem in text-to-speech synthesis is an ongoing research area; much of the current research focuses on prosody. Interested readers should consult the proceedings of the main speech engineering conferences: *ICSLP* (the International Conference on Spoken Language Processing), *IEEE ICASSP* (the International Conference on Acoustics, Speech, and Signal Processing), and *EUROSPEECH*.

Students with further interest in transcription and articulatory phonetics should consult an introductory phonetics textbook such as Ladefoged (1993). Pullum and Ladusaw (1996) is a comprehensive guide to each of the symbols and diacritics of the IPA. Many phonetics papers of computational interest are to be found in the *Journal of the Acoustical Society of America (JASA)*, *Computer Speech and Language*, and *Speech Communication*.

EXERCISES

4.1 Find the mistakes in the IPA transcriptions of the following words:

  a. "three" [ðri]

  b. "sing" [sɪng]

  c. "eyes" [aɪs]

  d. "study" [stʊdi]

  e. "though" [θou]

f. "planning" [plɑnɪŋ]

g. "slight" [slit]

4.2 Translate the pronunciations of the following color words from the IPA into the ARPAbet (and make a note if you think you pronounce them differently than this!):

a. [rɛd]

b. [blu]

c. [grin]

d. [ˈjɛloʊ]

e. [blæk]

f. [waɪt]

g. [ˈɔrɪndʒ]

h. [ˈpɚpl̩]

i. [pjus]

j. [toʊp]

4.3 Ira Gershwin's lyric for *Let's Call the Whole Thing Off* talks about two pronunciations of the word "either" (in addition to the tomato and potato example given at the beginning of the chapter. Transcribe Ira Gershwin's two pronunciations of "either" in IPA and in the ARPAbet.

4.4 Transcribe the following words in both the ARPAbet and the IPA:

a. dark

b. suit

c. greasy

d. wash

e. water

4.5 Write an FST which correctly pronounces strings of dollar amounts like *$45*, *$320*, and *$4100*. If there are multiple ways to pronounce a number you may pick your favorite way.

4.6 Write an FST which correctly pronounces seven-digit phone numbers like *555-1212*, *555-1300*, and so on. You should use a combination of the **paired** and **trailing unit** methods of pronunciation for the last four digits.

4.7 Build an automaton for rule (4.5).

4.8   One difference between one dialect of Canadian English and most dialects of American English is called **Canadian raising**. Bromberger and Halle (1989) note that some Canadian dialects of English raise /aɪ/ to [ʌɪ] and /aʊ/ to [ʌʊ] in stressed position before a voiceless consonant. A simplified version of the rule dealing only with /aɪ/ can be stated as:

$$/aɪ/ \rightarrow [ʌɪ] \ / \ \underline{\quad} \ \begin{bmatrix} C \\ -voice \end{bmatrix} \qquad (4.12)$$

This rule has an interesting interaction with the flapping rule. In some Canadian dialects the word *rider* and *writer* are pronounced differently: *rider* is pronounced [raɪɾɚ] while *writer* is pronounced [rʌɪɾɚ]. Write a two-level rule and an automaton for both the raising rule and the flapping rule which correctly models this distinction. You may make simplifying assumptions as needed.

4.9   Write the lexical entry for the pronunciation of the English past tense (preterite) suffix -*d*, and the two level-rules that express the difference in its pronunciation depending on the previous context. Don't worry about the spelling rules. (Hint: make sure you correctly handle the pronunciation of the past tenses of the words *add*, *pat*, *bake*, and *bag*.)

4.10   Write two-level rules for the Yawelmani Yokuts phenomena of Harmony, Shortening, and Lowering introduced on page 111. Make sure your rules are capable of running in parallel.

4.11   Find 10 stress-neutral name suffixes (look in a phone book) and sketch an FST which would model the pronunciation of names with or without suffixes.

5 PROBABILISTIC MODELS OF PRONUNCIATION AND SPELLING

> ALGERNON: *But my own sweet Cecily, I have never written you any letters.*
>
> CECILY: *You need hardly remind me of that, Ernest. I remember only too well that I was forced to write your letters for you. I wrote always three times a week, and sometimes oftener.*
>
> ALGERNON: *Oh, do let me read them, Cecily?*
>
> CECILY: *Oh, I couldn't possibly. They would make you far too conceited. The three you wrote me after I had broken off the engagement are so beautiful, and so badly spelled, that even now I can hardly read them without crying a little.*
>
> Oscar Wilde, *The Importance of being Ernest*

Like Oscar Wilde's fabulous Cecily, a lot of people were thinking about spelling during the last turn of the century. Gilbert and Sullivan provide many examples. *The Gondoliers'* Giuseppe, for example, worries that his private secretary is "shaky in his spelling" while *Iolanthe*'s Phyllis can "spell every word that she uses". Thorstein Veblen's explanation (in his 1899 classic *The Theory of the Leisure Class*) was that a main purpose of the "archaic, cumbrous, and ineffective" English spelling system was to be difficult enough to provide a test of membership in the leisure class. Whatever the social role of spelling, we can certainly agree that many more of us are like Cecily than like Phyllis. Estimates for the frequency of spelling errors in human typed text vary from 0.05% of the words in carefully edited newswire text to 38% in difficult applications like telephone directory lookup (Kukich, 1992).

In this chapter we discuss the problem of detecting and correcting spelling errors and the very related problem of modeling pronunciation variation for automatic speech recognition and text-to-speech systems. On the surface, the problems of finding spelling errors in text and modeling the variable pronunciation of words in spoken language don't seem to have much in common. But the problems turn out to be isomorphic in an important way: they can both be viewed as problems of *probabilistic transduction*. For speech recognition, given a string of symbols representing the pronunciation of a word in context, we need to figure out the string of symbols representing the lexical or dictionary pronunciation, so we can look the word up in the dictionary. But any given surface pronunciation is ambiguous; it might correspond to different possible words. For example the ARPAbet pronunciation [er] could correspond to reduced forms of the words *her*, *were*, *are*, *their*, or *your*. This ambiguity problem is heightened by **pronunciation variation**; for example the word *the* is sometimes pronounced THEE and sometimes THUH; the word *because* sometimes appears as *because*, sometimes as *'cause*. Some aspects of this variation are systematic; Section 5.7 will survey the important kinds of variation in pronunciation that are important for speech recognition and text-to-speech, and present some preliminary rules describing this variation. High-quality speech synthesis algorithms need to know when to use particular pronunciation variants. Solving both speech tasks requires extending the transduction between surface phones and lexical phones discussed in Chapter 4 with probabilistic variation.

Similarly, given the sequence of letters corresponding to a mis-spelled word, we need to produce an ordered list of possible correct words. For example the sequence *acress* might be a mis-spelling of *actress*, or of *cress*, or of *acres*. We transduce from the "surface" form *acress* to the various possible "lexical" forms, assigning each with a probability; we then select the most probable correct word.

In this chapter we first introduce the problems of detecting and correcting spelling errors, and also summarize typical human spelling error patterns. We then introduce the essential probabilistic architecture that we will use to solve both spelling and pronunciation problems: the **Bayes Rule** and the **noisy channel model**. The Bayes rule and its application to the noisy channel model will play a role in many problems throughout the book, particularly in speech recognition (Chapter 7), part-of-speech tagging (Chapter 8), and probabilistic parsing (Chapter 12).

The Bayes Rule and the noisy channel model provide the probabilistic framework for these problems. But actually solving them requires an algorithm. This chapter introduces an essential algorithm called the **dynamic**

programming algorithm, and various instantiations including the **Viterbi** algorithm, the **minimum edit distance** algorithm, and the **forward** algorithm. We will also see the use of a probabilistic version of the finite-state automaton called the **weighted automaton**.

5.1   DEALING WITH SPELLING ERRORS

The detection and correction of spelling errors is an integral part of modern word-processors. The very same algorithms are also important in applications in which even the individual letters aren't guaranteed to be accurately identified: **optical character recognition** (**OCR**) and **on-line handwriting recognition**. **Optical character recognition** is the term used for automatic recognition of machine or hand-printed characters. An optical scanner converts a machine or hand-printed page into a bitmap which is then passed to an OCR algorithm.

OCR

On-line handwriting recognition is the recognition of human printed or cursive handwriting as the user is writing. Unlike OCR analysis of handwriting, algorithms for on-line handwriting recognition can take advantage of dynamic information about the input such as the number and order of the strokes, and the speed and direction of each stroke. On-line handwriting recognition is important where keyboards are inappropriate, such as in small computing environments (palm-pilot applications, etc.) or in scripts like Chinese that have large numbers of written symbols, making keyboards cumbersome.

In this chapter we will focus on detection and correction of spelling errors, mainly in typed text, but the algorithms will apply also to OCR and handwriting applications. OCR systems have even higher error rates than human typists, although they tend to make different errors than typists. For example OCR systems often misread "D" as "O" or "ri" as "n", producing 'mis-spelled' words like *dension* for *derision*, or *POQ Bach* for *PDQ Bach*. The reader with further interest in handwriting recognition should consult sources such as Tappert et al. (1990), Hu et al. (1996), and Casey and Lecolinet (1996).

Kukich (1992), in her survey article on spelling correction, breaks the field down into three increasingly broader problems:

1. **non-word error detection:** detecting spelling errors that result in nonwords (like *graffe* for *giraffe*)

2. **isolated-word error correction:** correcting spelling errors that result in non-words, for example correcting *graffe* to *giraffe*, but looking only at the word in isolation

REAL-WORD
ERRORS

3. **context-dependent error detection and correction:** using the context to help detect and correct spelling errors even if they accidentally result in an actual word of English (**real-word errors**). This can happen from typographical errors (insertion, deletion, transposition) which accidently produce a real word (e.g., *there* for *three*), or because the writer substituted the wrong spelling of a homophone or near-homophone (e.g., *dessert* for *desert*, or *piece* for *peace*).

The next section will discuss the kinds of spelling-error patterns that occur in typed text and OCR and handwriting-recognition input.

5.2   SPELLING ERROR PATTERNS

The number and nature of spelling errors in human typed text differs from those caused by pattern-recognition devices like OCR and handwriting recognizers. Grudin (1983) found spelling error rates of between 1 and 3% in human typewritten text (this includes both non-word errors and real-word errors). This error rate goes down significantly for copy-edited text. The rate of spelling errors in handwritten text itself is similar; word error rates of between 1.5 and 2.5% have been reported (Kukich, 1992).

The errors of OCR and on-line hand-writing systems vary. Yaeger et al. (1998) propose, based on studies that they warn are inconclusive, that the on-line printed character recognition on Apple Computer's NEWTON MESSAGEPAD had a word accuracy rate of 97–98%, that is, an error rate of 2–3%, but with a high variance (depending on the training of the writer, etc.). It is not clear whether the failure of the NEWTON was because this error rate was optimistic or because a 2–3% error rate is unacceptable. More recent devices, like 3Com's Palm Pilot, often use a special input script (like the Palm Pilot's "Graffiti") instead of allowing arbitrary handwriting. OCR error rates also vary widely depending on the quality of the input; (Lopresti and Zhou, 1997) suggest that OCR letter-error rates typically range from 0.2% for clean, first-generation copy to 20% or worse for multigeneration photocopies and faxes.

In an early study, Damerau (1964) found that 80% of all misspelled words (non-word errors) in a sample of human keypunched text were caused by **single-error misspellings**: a single one of the following errors:[1]

- **insertion**: mistyping *the* as *ther*   INSERTION
- **deletion**: mistyping *the* as *th*   DELETION
- **substitution**: mistyping *the* as *thw*   SUBSTITUTION
- **transposition**: mistyping *the* as *hte*   TRANSPOSITION

Because of this study, much following research has focused on the correction of single-error misspellings. Indeed, the first algorithm we will present later in this chapter relies on the large proportion of single-error misspellings.

Kukich (1992) breaks down human typing errors into two classes. **Typographic errors** (for example misspelling *spell* as *speel*), are generally related to the keyboard. **Cognitive errors** (for example misspelling *separate* as *seperate*) are caused by writers who don't know how to spell the word. Grudin (1983) found that the keyboard was the strongest influence on the errors produced; typographic errors constituted the majority of all error types. For example consider substitution errors, which were the most common error type for novice typists, and the second most common error type for expert typists. Grudin found that immediately adjacent keys in the same row accounted for 59% of the novice substitutions and 31% of the error substitutions (e.g., *smsll* for *small*). Adding in errors in the same column and **homologous** errors (hitting the corresponding key on the opposite side of the keyboard with the other hand), a total of 83% of the novice substitutions and 51% of the expert substitutions could be considered keyboard-based errors. Cognitive errors included phonetic errors (substituting a phonetically equivalent sequence of letters (*seperate* for *separate*) and homonym errors (substituting *piece* for *peace*). Homonym errors will be discussed in Chapter 7 when we discuss real-word error correction.

While typing errors are usually characterized as substitutions, insertions, deletions, or transpositions, OCR errors are usually grouped into five classes: substitutions, multisubstitutions, space deletions or insertions, and

---

[1] In another corpus, Peterson (1986) found that single-error misspellings accounted for an even higher percentage of all misspelled words (93–95%). The difference between the 80% and the higher figure may be due to the fact that Damerau's text included errors caused in transcription to punched card forms, errors in keypunching, and errors caused by paper tape equipment (!) in addition to purely human misspellings.

failures. Lopresti and Zhou (1997) give the following example of common OCR errors:

Correct:
The quick brown fox jumps over the lazy dog.
Recognized:
'lhe q~ick brown foxjurnps ovcr tb l azy dog.

Substitutions ($e \rightarrow c$) are generally caused by visual similarity (rather than keyboard distance), as are multisubstitutions ($T \rightarrow$ 'l, $m \rightarrow rn$, $he \rightarrow b$). Multisubstitutions are also often called **framing errors**. Failures (represented by the tilde character '~': $u \rightarrow$ ~) are cases where the OCR algorithm does not select any letter with sufficient accuracy.

5.3   DETECTING NON-WORD ERRORS

Detecting non-word errors in text, whether typed by humans or scanned, is most commonly done by the use of a dictionary. For example, the word *foxjurnps* in the OCR example above would not occur in a dictionary. Some early research (Peterson, 1986) had suggested that such spelling dictionaries would need to be kept small, because large dictionaries contain very rare words that resemble misspellings of other words. For example *wont* is a legitimate but rare word but is a common misspelling of *won't*. Similarly, *veery* (a kind of thrush) might also be a misspelling of *very*. Based on a simple model of single-error misspellings, Peterson showed that it was possible that 10% of such misspellings might be "hidden" by real words in a 50,000 word dictionary, but that 15% of single-error misspellings might be "hidden" in a 350,000-word dictionary. In practice, Damerau and Mays (1989) found that this was not the case; while some misspellings were hidden by real words in a larger dictionary, in practice the larger dictionary proved more help than harm.

Because of the need to represent productive inflection (the *-s* and *ed* suffixes) and derivation, dictionaries for spelling error detection usually include models of morphology, just as the dictionaries for text-to-speech we saw in Chapters 3 and 4. Early spelling error detectors simply allowed any word to have any suffix – thus Unix SPELL accepts bizarre prefixed words like *misclam* and *antiundoggingly* and suffixed words based on *the* like *thehood* and *theness*. Modern spelling error detectors use more linguistically-motivated morphological representations (see Chapter 3).

5.4   PROBABILISTIC MODELS

This section introduces probabilistic models of pronunciation and spelling variation. These models, particularly the **Bayesian inference** or **noisy channel** model, will be applied throughout this book to many different problems.

We claimed earlier that the problem of ASR pronunciation modeling, and the problem of spelling correction for typing or for OCR, can be modeled as problems of mapping from one string of symbols to another. For speech recognition, given a string of symbols representing the pronunciation of a word in context, we need to figure out the string of symbols representing the lexical or dictionary pronunciation, so we can look the word up in the dictionary. Similarly, given the incorrect sequence of letters in a mis-spelled word, we need to figure out the correct sequence of letters in the correctly spelled word.

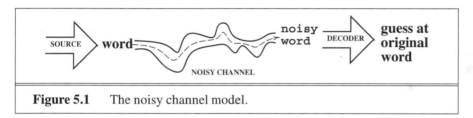

Figure 5.1   The noisy channel model.

The intuition of the **noisy channel** model (see Figure 5.1) is to treat the surface form (the "reduced"" pronunciation or misspelled word) as an instance of the lexical form (the "lexical" pronunciation or correctly-spelled word) which has been passed through a noisy communication channel. This channel introduces "noise" which makes it hard to recognize the "true" word. Our goal is then to build a model of the channel so that we can figure out how it modified this "true" word and hence recover it. For the complete speech recognition tasks, there are many sources of "noise"; variation in pronunciation, variation in the realization of phones, acoustic variation due to the channel (microphones, telephone networks, etc.). Since this chapter focuses on pronunciation, what we mean by "noise" here is the variation in pronunciation that masks the lexical or "canonical" pronunciation; the other sources of noise in a speech recognition system will be discussed in Chapter 7. For spelling error detection, what we mean by noise is the spelling errors which mask the correct spelling of the word. The metaphor of the noisy channel comes from the application of the model to speech recognition in the IBM labs in the 1970s (Jelinek, 1976). But the algorithm itself is a special case

NOISY
CHANNEL

BAYESIAN of **Bayesian inference** and as such has been known since the work of Bayes (1763). Bayesian inference or Bayesian classification was applied successfully to language problems as early as the late 1950s, including the OCR work of Bledsoe in 1959, and the seminal work of Mosteller and Wallace (1964) on applying Bayesian inference to determine the authorship of the Federalist papers.

In Bayesian classification, as in any classification task, we are given some observation and our job is to determine which of a set of classes it belongs to. For speech recognition, imagine for the moment that the observation is the string of phones which make up a word as we hear it. For spelling error detection, the observation might be the string of letters that constitute a possibly-misspelled word. In both cases, we want to classify the observations into words; thus in the speech case, no matter which of the many possible ways the word *about* is pronounced (see Chapter 4) we want to classify it as *about*. In the spelling case, no matter how the word *separate* is misspelled, we'd like to recognize it as *separate*.

Let's begin with the pronunciation example. We are given a string of phones (say [ni]). We want to know which word corresponds to this string of phones. The Bayesian interpretation of this task starts by considering all possible classes—in this case, all possible words. Out of this universe of words, we want to chose the word which is most probable given the observation we have ([ni]). In other words, we want, out of all words in the vocabulary V the single word such that $P(\text{word}|\text{observation})$ is highest. We use $\hat{w}$ to mean "our estimate of the correct w", and we'll use $\mathbf{O}$ to mean "the observation sequence [ni]" (we call it a sequence because we think of each letter as an individual observation). Then the equation for picking the best word given is:

V
$\hat{w}$
o

$$\hat{w} = \operatorname*{argmax}_{w \in V} P(w|O) \tag{5.1}$$

The function $\operatorname{argmax}_x f(x)$ means "the x such that $f(x)$ is maximized". While (5.1) is guaranteed to give us the optimal word w, it is not clear how to make the equation operational; that is, for a given word w and observation sequence O we don't know how to directly compute $P(w|O)$. The intuition of Bayesian classification is to use Bayes' rule to transform (5.1) into a product of two probabilities, each of which turns out to be easier to compute than $P(w|O)$. Bayes' rule is presented in (5.2); it gives us a way to break down $P(x|O)$ into three other probabilities:

$$P(x|y) = \frac{P(y|x)P(x)}{P(y)} \tag{5.2}$$

We can see this by substituting (5.2) into (5.1) to get (5.3):

$$\hat{w} = \underset{w \in V}{\operatorname{argmax}} \frac{P(O|w)P(w)}{P(O)} \tag{5.3}$$

The probabilities on the right-hand side of (5.3) are for the most part easier to compute than the probability $P(w|O)$ that we were originally trying to maximize in (5.1). For example, $P(w)$, the probability of the word itself, we can estimate by the frequency of the word. And we will see below that $P(O|w)$ turns out to be easy to estimate as well. But $P(O)$, the probability of the observation sequence, turns out to be harder to estimate. Luckily, we can ignore $P(O)$. Why? Since we are maximizing over all words, we will be computing $\frac{P(O|w)P(w)}{P(O)}$ for each word. But $P(O)$ doesn't change for each word; we are always asking about the most likely word string for the same observation O, which must have the same probability $P(O)$. Thus:

$$\hat{w} = \underset{w \in V}{\operatorname{argmax}} \frac{P(O|w)P(w)}{P(O)} = \underset{w \in V}{\operatorname{argmax}} P(O|w)\, P(w) \tag{5.4}$$

To summarize, the most probable word w given some observation O can be computing by taking the product of two probabilities for each word, and choosing the word for which this product is greatest. These two terms have names; $P(w)$ is called the **Prior probability**, and $P(O|w)$ is called the **likelihood**.

PRIOR

LIKELIHOOD

$$\text{\textbf{Key Concept \#3.}} \quad \hat{w} = \underset{w \in V}{\operatorname{argmax}} \quad \overbrace{P(O|w)}^{\text{likelihood}} \ \overbrace{P(w)}^{\text{prior}} \tag{5.5}$$

In the next sections we will show how to compute these two probabilities for the probabilities of pronunciation and spelling.

5.5   APPLYING THE BAYESIAN METHOD TO SPELLING

There are many algorithms for spelling correction; we will focus on the Bayesian (or noisy channel) algorithm because of its generality. Chapter 6 will show how this algorithm can be extended to model real-word spelling errors; this section will focus on non-word spelling errors. The noisy channel approach to spelling correction was first suggested by Kernighan et al. (1990); their program, `correct`, takes words rejected by the Unix `spell` program, generates a list of potential correct words, rank them according to Equation (5.5), and picks the highest-ranked one.

Let's walk through the algorithm as it applies to Kernighan et al.'s (1990) example misspelling *acress*. The algorithm has two stages: *proposing candidate corrections* and *scoring the candidates*.

In order to propose candidate corrections Kernighan et al. make the simplifying assumption that the correct word will differ from the misspelling by a single insertion, deletion, substitution, or transposition. As Damerau's (1964) results show, even though this assumption causes the algorithm to miss some corrections, it should handle most spelling errors in human typed text. The list of candidate words is generated from the typo by applying any single transformation which results in a word in a large on-line dictionary. Applying all possible transformations to *acress* yields the list of candidate words in Figure 5.2.

		Transformation			
Error	Correction	Correct Letter	Error Letter	Position (Letter #)	Type
acress	actress	t	–	2	deletion
acress	cress	–	a	0	insertion
acress	caress	ca	ac	0	transposition
acress	access	c	r	2	substitution
acress	across	o	e	3	substitution
acress	acres	–	2	5	insertion
acress	acres	–	2	4	insertion

Figure 5.2   Candidate corrections for the misspelling *acress*, together with the transformations that would have produced the error (after Kernighan et al. (1990)). "–" represents a null letter.

The second stage of the algorithm scores each correction by Equation 5.4. Let t represent the typo (the misspelled word), and let c range over the set C of candidate corrections. The most likely correction is then:

$$\hat{c} = \underset{c \in C}{\mathrm{argmax}} \quad \overbrace{P(t|c)}^{\text{likelihood}} \quad \overbrace{P(c)}^{\text{prior}} \tag{5.6}$$

As in Equation (5.4) we have omitted the denominator in Equation (5.6) since the typo t, and hence its probability $P(t)$, is constant for all c. The prior probability of each correction $P(c)$ can be estimated by counting how often NORMALIZING   the word c occurs in some corpus, and then **normalizing** these counts by the

total count of all words.[2] So the probability of a particular correction word
c is computed by dividing the count of c by the number N of words in the
corpus. Zero counts can cause problems, and so we will add .5 to all the
counts. This is called "smoothing", and will be discussed in Chapter 6; note
that in Equation (5.7) we can't just divide by the total number of words N
since we added .5 to the counts of all the words, so we add .5 for each of the
V words in the vocabulary).

$$P(c) = \frac{C(c) + 0.5}{N + 0.5V} \tag{5.7}$$

Chapter 6 will talk more about the role of corpora in computing prior
probabilities; for now let's use the corpus of Kernighan et al. (1990), which
is the 1988 AP newswire corpus of 44 million words. Thus N is 44 million.
Since in this corpus the word *actress* occurs 1343 times, the word *acres* 2879
times, and so on, the resulting prior probabilities are as follows:

c	freq(c)	p(c)
actress	1343	.0000315
cress	0	.000000014
caress	4	.0000001
access	2280	.000058
across	8436	.00019
acres	2879	.000065

Computing the likelihood term $p(t|c)$ exactly is an unsolved (unsolve-
able?) research problem; the exact probability that a word will be mistyped
depends on who the typist was, how familiar they were with the keyboard
they were using, whether one hand happened to be more tired than the other,
etc. Luckily, while $p(t|c)$ cannot be computed exactly, it can be *estimated*
pretty well, because the most important factors predicting an insertion, deletion, transposition are simple local factors like the identity of the correct
letter itself, how the letter was misspelled, and the surrounding context. For
example, the letters m and n are often substituted for each other; this is partly
a fact about their identity (these two letters are pronounced similarly and
they are next to each other on the keyboard), and partly a fact about context
(because they are pronounced similarly, they occur in similar contexts).

One simple way to estimate these probabilities is the one that Kernighan et al. (1990) used. They ignored most of the possible influences on
the probability of an error and just estimated e.g. $p(acress|across)$ using

---

[2] Normalizing means dividing by some total count so that the resulting probabilities fall
legally between 0 and 1.

CONFUSION
MATRIX
the number of times that *e* was substituted for *o* in some large corpus of errors. This is represented by a **confusion matrix**, a square 26×26 table which represents the number of times one letter was incorrectly used instead of another. For example, the cell labeled $[o,e]$ in a substitution confusion matrix would give the count of times that *e* was substituted for *o*. The cell labeled $[t,s]$ in an insertion confusion matrix would give the count of times that *t* was inserted after *s*. A confusion matrix can be computed by hand-coding a collection of spelling errors with the correct spelling and then counting the number of times different errors occurred (this has been done by Grudin (1983)). Kernighan et al. (1990) used four confusion matrices, one for each type of single-error:

- $\text{del}[x,y]$ contains the number of times in the training set that the characters *xy* in the correct word were typed as *x*.
- $\text{ins}[x,y]$ contains the number of times in the training set that the character *x* in the correct word was typed as *xy*.
- $\text{sub}[x,y]$ the number of times that *x* was typed as *y*.
- $\text{trans}[x,y]$ the number of times that *xy* was typed as *yx*.

Note that they chose to condition their insertion and deletion probabilities on the previous character; they could also have chosen to condition on the following character. Using these matrices, they estimated $p(t|c)$ as follows (where c_p is the *p*th character of the word *c*):

$$
P(t|c) = \begin{cases}
\dfrac{\text{del}_{[c_{p-1},c_p]}}{\text{count}_{[c_{p-1}c_p]}}, & \text{if deletion} \\[2ex]
\dfrac{\text{ins}_{[c_{p-1},t_p]}}{\text{count}_{[c_{p-1}]}}, & \text{if insertion} \\[2ex]
\dfrac{\text{sub}_{[t_p,c_p]}}{\text{count}_{[c_p]}}, & \text{if substitution} \\[2ex]
\dfrac{\text{trans}_{[c_p,c_{p+1}]}}{\text{count}_{[c_p c_{p+1}]}}, & \text{if transposition}
\end{cases}
\tag{5.8}
$$

Figure 5.3 shows the final probabilities for each of the potential corrections; the prior (from Equation (5.7)) is multiplied by the likelihood (computed using Equation (5.8) and the confusion matrices). The final column shows the "normalized percentage".

This implementation of the Bayesian algorithm predicts *acres* as the correct word (at a total normalized percentage of 45%), and *actress* as the second most likely word. Unfortunately, the algorithm was wrong here: The writer's intention becomes clear from the context: ... *was called a "stellar and versatile* **acress** *whose combination of sass and glamour has defined her...".* The surrounding words make it clear that *actress* and not *acres* was

c	freq(c)	p(c)	p(t|c)	p(t|c)p(c)	%
actress	1343	.0000315	.000117	3.69×10^{-9}	**37%**
cress	0	.000000014	.00000144	2.02×10^{-14}	**0%**
caress	4	.0000001	.00000164	1.64×10^{-13}	**0%**
access	2280	.000058	.000000209	1.21×10^{-11}	**0%**
across	8436	.00019	.0000093	1.77×10^{-9}	**18%**
acres	2879	.000065	.0000321	2.09×10^{-9}	**21%**
acres	2879	.000065	.0000342	2.22×10^{-9}	**23%**

Figure 5.3   Computation of the ranking for each candidate correction. Note that the highest ranked word is not *actress* but *acres* (the two lines at the bottom of the table), since *acres* can be generated in two ways. The *del*[], *ins*[], *sub*[], and *trans*[] confusion matrices are given in full in Kernighan et al. (1990).

the intended word; Chapter 6 will show how to augment the computation of the prior probability to use the surrounding words.

The algorithm as we have described it requires hand-annotated data to train the confusion matrices. An alternative approach used by Kernighan et al. (1990) is to compute the matrices by iteratively using this very spelling error correction algorithm itself. The iterative algorithm first initializes the matrices with equal values; thus any character is equally likely to be deleted, equally likely to be substituted for any other character, etc. Next the spelling error correction algorithm is run on a set of spelling errors. Given the set of typos paired with their corrections, the confusion matrices can now be recomputed, the spelling algorithm run again, and so on. This clever method turns out to be an instance of the important **EM** algorithm (Dempster et al., 1977) that we will discuss in Chapter 7 and Appendix D. Kernighan et al. (1990)'s algorithm was evaluated by taking some spelling errors that had two potential corrections, and asking three human judges to pick the best correction. Their program agreed with the majority vote of the human judges 87% of the time.

5.6   MINIMUM EDIT DISTANCE

The previous section showed that the Bayesian algorithm, as implemented with confusion matrices, was able to rank candidate corrections. But Kernighan et al. (1990) relied on the simplifying assumption that each word had only a single spelling error. Suppose we wanted a more powerful algorithm

DISTANCE

which could handle the case of multiple errors? We could think of such an algorithm as a general solution to the problem of **string distance**. The "string distance" is some metric of how alike two strings are to each other. The Bayesian method can be viewed as a way of applying such an algorithm to the spelling error correction problem; we pick the candidate word which is "closest" to the error in the sense of having the highest probability given the error.

MINIMUM EDIT
DISTANCE

One of the most popular classes of algorithms for finding string distance are those that use some version of the **minimum edit distance** algorithm, named by Wagner and Fischer (1974) but independently discovered by many people; see the History section. The minimum edit distance between two strings is the minimum number of editing operations (insertion, deletion, substitution) needed to transform one string into another. For example the gap between intention and execution is five operations, which can

ALIGNMENT

be represented in three ways; as a **trace**, an **alignment**, or a **operation list** as show in Figure 5.4.

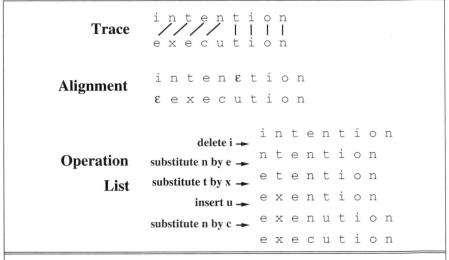

Figure 5.4   Three methods for representing differences between sequences (after Kruskal (1983))

We can also assign a particular cost or weight to each of these operations. The **Levenshtein** distance between two sequences is the simplest weighting factor in which each of the three operations has a cost of 1 (Levenshtein, 1966). Thus the Levenshtein distance between *intention* and *execution* is 5. Levenshtein also proposed an alternate version of his metric in which each insertion or deletion has a cost of one, and substitutions are not allowed (equivalent to allowing substitution, but giving each substitution a cost of 2, since any substitution can be represented by one insertion and one deletion). Using this version, the Levenshtein distance between *intention* and *execution* is 8. We can also weight operations by more complex functions, for example by using the confusion matrices discussed above to assign a probability to each operation. In this case instead of talking about the "minimum edit distance" between two strings, we are talking about the "maximum probability **alignment**" of one string with another. If we do this, an augmented minimum edit distance algorithm which multiplies the probabilities of each transformation can be used to estimate the Bayesian likelihood of a multiple-error typo given a candidate correction.

The minimum edit distance is computed by **dynamic programming**. **DYNAMIC PROGRAMMING** Dynamic programming is the name for a class of algorithms, first introduced by Bellman (1957), that apply a table-driven method to solve problems by combining solutions to subproblems. This class of algorithms includes the most commonly-used algorithms in speech and language processing, among them the **minimum edit distance** algorithm for spelling error correction the **Viterbi** algorithm and the **forward** algorithm which are used both in speech recognition and in machine translation, and the **CYK** and **Earley** algorithm used in parsing. We will introduce the minimum-edit-distance, Viterbi, and forward algorithms in this chapter and Chapter 7, the Earley algorithm in Chapter 10, and the CYK algorithm in Chapter 12.

The intuition of a dynamic programming problem is that a large problem can be solved by properly combining the solutions to various subproblems. For example, consider the sequence or "path" of transformed words that comprise the minimum edit distance between the strings *intention* and *execution*. Imagine some string (perhaps it is *exention*) that is in this optimal path (whatever it is). The intuition of dynamic programming is that if *exention* is in the optimal operation-list, then the optimal sequence must also include the optimal path from *intention* to *exention*. Why? If there were a shorter path from *intention* to *exention* then we could use it instead, resulting in a shorter overall path, and the optimal sequence wouldn't be optimal, thus leading to a contradiction.

Dynamic programming algorithms for sequence comparison work by creating a distance matrix with one column for each symbol in the target sequence and one row for each symbol in the source sequence (i.e., target along the bottom, source along the side). For minimum edit distance, this matrix is the *edit-distance* matrix. Each cell *edit-distance*[i,j] contains the distance between the first *i* characters of the target and the first *j* characters of the source. Each cell can be computed as a simple function of the surrounding cells; thus starting from the beginning of the matrix it is possible to fill in every entry. The value in each cell is computing by taking the minimum of the three possible paths through the matrix which arrive there:

$$P(t|c) = \min \begin{cases} distance[i-1,j] + \textit{ins-cost}(target_i) \\ distance[i-1,j-1] + \textit{subst-cost}(source_j, target_i) \\ distance[i,j-1] + \textit{del-cost}(source_j)) \end{cases} \quad (5.9)$$

The algorithm itself is summarized in Figure 5.5, while Figure 5.6 shows the results of applying the algorithm to the distance between *intention* and *execution* assuming the version of Levenshtein distance in which insertions and deletions each have a cost of 1 and substitutions have a cost of 2.

---

function MIN-EDIT-DISTANCE(*target*, *source*) **returns** *min-distance*

    $n \leftarrow$ LENGTH(*target*)
    $m \leftarrow$ LENGTH(*source*)
    Create a distance matrix *distance[n+1,m+1]*
    distance[0,0] $\leftarrow 0$
    for each column *i* **from** 0 **to** *n* **do**
      for each row *j* **from** 0 **to** *m* **do**
        distance[i,j] $\leftarrow$ MIN(*distance[i−1,j]* + *ins-cost*(*target_i*),
                          distance[i−1,j−1] + *subst-cost*(*source_j*, target_i),
                          distance[i,j−1] + *del-cost*(*source_j*))

Figure 5.5   The minimum edit distance algorithm, an example of the class of dynamic programming algorithms.

5.7   ENGLISH PRONUNCIATION VARIATION

> When any of the fugitives of Ephraim said: 'Let me go over,' the men of Gilead said unto him: 'Art thou an Ephraimite?' If he said: 'Nay'; then said they unto him: 'Say now Shibboleth'; and he said 'Sibboleth'; for he could not frame to pronounce it right; then they laid hold on him, and slew him at the fords of the Jordan.
>
> Judges 12:5-6

n	9	10	11	10	11	12	11	10	9	**8**
o	8	9	10	9	10	11	10	9	**8**	9
i	7	8	9	8	9	10	9	**8**	9	10
t	6	7	8	7	8	9	**8**	9	10	11
n	5	6	7	6	7	**8**	9	10	11	12
e	4	5	6	**5**	**6**	7	8	9	10	11
t	3	4	**5**	6	7	8	9	10	11	12
n	2	3	**4**	5	6	7	8	8	10	11
i	1	**2**	3	4	5	6	7	8	9	10
#	**0**	1	2	3	4	5	6	7	8	9
	#	e	x	e	c	u	t	i	o	n

Figure 5.6   Computation of minimum edit distance between *intention* and *execution* via algorithm of Figure 5.5, using Levenshtein distance with cost of 1 for insertions or deletions, 2 for substitutions. Substitution of a character for itself has a cost of 0.

This passage from Judges is a rather gory reminder of the political importance of pronunciation variation. Even in our (hopefully less political) computational applications of pronunciation, it is important to correctly model how pronunciations can vary. We have already seen that a phoneme can be realized as different allophones in different phonetic environments. We have also shown how to write rules and transducers to model these changes for speech synthesis. Unfortunately, these models significantly simplified the nature of pronunciation variation. In particular, pronunciation variation is caused by many factors in addition to the phonetic environment. This section summarizes some of these kinds of variation; the following section will introduce the probabilistic tools for modeling it.

Pronunciation variation is extremely widespread. Figure 5.7 shows the most common pronunciations of the words *because* and *about* from the hand-transcribed Switchboard corpus of American English telephone conversations. Note the wide variation in pronunciation for these two words when spoken as part of a continuous stream of speech.

What causes this variation? There are two broad classes of pronunciation variation: **lexical variation** and **allophonic variation**. We can think of lexical variation as a difference in what segments are used to represent the word in the lexicon, while allophonic variation is a difference in how the individual segments change their value in different contexts. In Figure 5.7, most of the variation in pronunciation is allophonic; that is, due to the influ-

LEXICAL VARIATION
ALLOPHONIC VARIATION

because			about		
IPA	ARPAbet	%	IPA	ARPAbet	%
[bikʌz]	[b iy k ah z]	27%	[əbaʊ]	[ax b aw]	32%
[bɪkʌz]	[b ix k ah z]	14%	[əbaʊt]	[ax b aw t]	16%
[kʌz]	[k ah z]	7%	[baʊ]	[b aw]	9%
[kəz]	[k ax z]	5%	[ʌbaʊ]	[ix b aw]	8%
[bɪkəz]	[b ix k ax z]	4%	[ɨbaʊt]	[ix b aw t]	5%
[bɪkʌz]	[b ih k ah z]	3%	[ɨbæ]	[ix b ae]	4%
[bəkʌz]	[b ax k ah z]	3%	[əbæɾ]	[ax b ae dx]	3%
[kʊz]	[k uh z]	2%	[baʊɾ]	[b aw dx]	3%
[ks]	[k s]	2%	[bæ]	[b ae]	3%
[kɨz]	[k ix z]	2%	[baʊt]	[b aw t]	3%
[kɪz]	[k ih z]	2%	[əbaʊɾ]	[ax b aw dx]	3%
[bikʌʒ]	[b iy k ah zh]	2%	[əbæ]	[ax b ae]	3%
[bikʌs]	[b iy k ah s]	2%	[bɑ]	[b aa]	3%
[bikʌ]	[b iy k ah]	2%	[bæɾ]	[b ae dx]	3%
[bikɑz]	[b iy k aa z]	2%	[ɨbaʊɾ]	[ix b aw dx]	2%
[əz]	[ax z]	2%	[ɨbɑt]	[ix b aa t]	2%

Figure 5.7   The 16 most common pronunciations of *because* and *about* from the hand-transcribed Switchboard corpus of American English conversational telephone speech (Godfrey et al., 1992; Greenberg et al., 1996).

ence of the surrounding sounds, syllable structure, and so forth. But the fact that the word *because* can be pronounced either as monosyllabic *'cause* or bisyllabic *because* is probably a lexical fact, having to do perhaps with the level of informality of speech.

SOCIOLINGUISTIC

DIALECT
VARIATION

     An important source of lexical variation (although it can also affect allophonic variation) is **sociolinguistic** variation. Sociolinguistic variation is due to extralinguistic factors such as the social identity or background of the speaker. One kind of sociolinguistic variation is **dialect variation**. Speakers of some deep-southern dialects of American English use a monophthong or near-monophthong [a] or [aɛ] instead of a diphthong in some words with the vowel [aɪ]. In these dialects *rice* is pronounced [raːs]. African-American Vernacular English (AAVE) has many of the same vowel differences from General American as does Southern American English, and also has individual words with specific pronunciations such as [bɪdnɪs] for *business* and [æks] for *ask*. For older speakers or those not from the American West or Midwest, the words *caught* and *cot* have different vowels ([kɔt] and [kɑt] respectively). Young American speakers or those from the West pronounce the two words *cot* and *caught* the same; the vowels [ɔ] and [ɑ] are usually not distinguished in these dialects. For some speakers from New York City like the first author's parents, the words *Mary* ([meɪri]), *marry* ([mæri]), and *merry* ([mɛri]) are all pronounced differently, while other New York City speakers like the second author pronounce *Mary*, and *merry* identically, but differently than *marry*. Most American speakers pronounce all three of these words identically as ([mɛri]). Students who are interested in dialects of English should consult Wells (1982), the most comprehensive study of dialects of English around the world.

Other sociolinguistic differences are due to **register** or **style** rather than dialect. In a pronunciation difference that is due to style, the same speaker might pronounce the same word differently depending on who they were talking to or what the social situation is; this is probably the case when choosing between *because* and *'cause* above. One of the most well-studied examples of style-variation is the suffix *-ing* (as in *something*), which can be pronounced [ɪŋ] or /ɪn/ (this is often written *somethin'*). Most speakers use both forms; as Labov (1966) shows, they use [ɪŋ] when they are being more formal, and [ɪn] when more casual. In fact whether a speaker will use [ɪŋ] or [ɪn] in a given situation varies markedly according to the social context, the gender of the speaker, the gender of the other speaker, and so on. Wald and Shopen (1981) found that men are more likely to use the non-standard form [ɪn] than women, that both men and women are more likely to use more of the standard form [ɪŋ] when the addressee is a women, and that men (but not women) tend to switch to [ɪn] when they are talking with friends.

REGISTER

STYLE

Where lexical variation happens at the lexical level, allophonic variation happens at the surface form and reflects phonetic and articulatory factors.[3] For example, most of the variation in the word *about* in Figure 5.7 was caused by changes in one of the two vowels or by changes to the final [t]. Some of this variation is due to the allophonic rules we have already discussed for the realization of the phoneme /t/. For example the pronunciation of *about* as [əbaʊɾ]/[ax b aw dx]) has a flap at the end because the next word was the word *it*, which begins with a vowel; the sequence *about it* was pronounced [əbaʊɾɨ]/[ax b aw dx ix]). Similarly, note that final [t] is often deleted; (*about* as [baʊ]/[b aw]). Considering these cases as "deleted" is actually a simplification; many of these "deleted" cases of [t] are actually

---

[3] For some purposes we distinguish between allophonic variation and what are called "optional phonological rules"; for the purposes of this textbook we will lump these both together as "allophonic variation".

realized as a slight change to the vowel quality called **glottalization** which are not represented in these transcriptions.

When we discussed these rules earlier, we implied that they were deterministic; given an environment, a rule always applies. This is by no means the case. Each of these allophonic rules is dependent on a complicated set of factors that must be interpreted probabilistically. In the rest of this section we summarize more of these rules and talk about the influencing factors.

COARTICULATION

Many of these rules model **coarticulation**, which is a change in a segment due to the movement of the articulators in neighboring segments. Most allophonic rules relating English phoneme to their allophones can be grouped into a small number of types: assimilation, dissimilation, deletion, flapping, vowel reduction, and epenthesis.

ASSIMILATION

Assimilation is the change in a segment to make it more like a neighboring segment. The dentalization of [t] to ([t̪]) before the dental consonant [θ] is an example of assimilation. Another common type of assimilation in English and cross-linguistically is **palatalization**. Palatalization occurs

PALATALIZATION

when the constriction for a segment occurs closer to the palate than it normally would, because the following segment is palatal or alveolo-palatal. In the most common cases, /s/ becomes [ʃ], /z/ becomes [ʒ], /t/ becomes [tʃ] and /d/ becomes dʒ]. We saw one case of palatalization in Figure 5.7 in the pronunciation of *because* as [bikʌʒ] (ARPAbet [b iy k ah zh]). Here the final segment of *because*, a lexical /z/, is realized as [ʒ], because the following word was *you've*. So the sequence *because you've* was pronounced [bikʌʒuv]. A simple version of a palatalization rule might be expressed as follows; Figure 5.8 shows examples from the Switchboard corpus.

$$
\left\{ \begin{array}{c} [s] \\ [z] \\ [t] \\ [d] \end{array} \right\} \Rightarrow \left\{ \begin{array}{c} [ʃ] \\ [ʒ] \\ [tʃ] \\ [dʒ] \end{array} \right\} \; / \; \text{---} \; \{ \, y \, \} \tag{5.10}
$$

Note in Figure 5.8 that whether a [t] is palatalized depends on lexical factors like word frequency ([t] is more likely to be palatalized in frequent words and phrases).

DELETION

Deletion is quite common in English speech. We saw examples of deletion of final /t/ above, in the words *about* and *it*. /t/ and /d/ are often deleted before consonants, or when they are part of a sequence of two or three consonants; Figure 5.9 shows some examples.

$$
\left\{ \begin{array}{c} t \\ d \end{array} \right\} \Rightarrow \emptyset \, / \, V \, \text{---} \, C \tag{5.11}
$$

The many factors that influence the deletion of /t/ and /d/ have been extensively studied. For example /d/ is more likely to be deleted than /t/.

Phrase	IPA Lexical	IPA Reduced	ARPAbet Reduced
set your	[sɛtjɔr]	[sɛtʃɚ]	[s eh ch er]
not yet	[nɑtjɛt]	[nɑtʃɛt]	[n aa ch eh t]
last year	[læstjir]	[læstʃir]	[l ae s ch iy r]
what you	[wʌtju]	[wətʃu]	[w ax ch uw]
this year	[ðɪsjir]	[ðɪʃir]	[dh ih sh iy r]
because you've	[bikʌzjuv]	[bikʌʒuv]	[b iy k ah zh uw v]
did you	[dɪdju]	[dɪdʒyʌ]	[d ih jh y ah]

Figure 5.8   Examples of palatalization from the Switchboard corpus; the lemma *you* (including *your*, *you've*, and *you'd*) was by far the most common cause of palatalization, followed by *year(s)* (especially in the phrases *this year* and *last year*).

Phrase	IPA Lexical	IPA Reduced	ARPAbet Reduced
find him	[faɪndhɪm]	[faɪnɨm]	[f ay n ix m]
around this	[əraʊndðɪs]	[ɨraʊnɪs]	[ix r aw n ih s]
mind boggling	[maɪnbɔglɪŋ]	[maɪnbɔglɪŋ]	[m ay n b ao g el ih ng]
most places	[moʊstpleɪsɨz]	[moʊspleɪsɨz]	[m ow s p l ey s ix z]
draft the	[dræftði]	[dræfði]	[d r ae f dh iy]
left me	[lɛftmi]	[lɛfmi]	[l eh f m iy]

Figure 5.9   Examples of /t/ and /d/ deletion from Switchboard. Some of these examples may have glottalization instead of being completely deleted.

Both are more likely to be deleted before a consonant (Labov, 1972). The final /t/ and /d/ in the words *and* and *just* are particularly likely to be deleted (Labov, 1975; Neu, 1980). Wolfram (1969) found that deletion is more likely in faster or more casual speech, and that younger people and males are more likely to delete. Deletion is more likely when the two words surrounding the segment act as a sort of phrasal unit, either occurring together frequently (Bybee, 1996), having a high **mutual information** or **trigram predictability** (Gregory et al., 1999), or being tightly connected for other reasons (Zwicky, 1972). Fasold (1972), Labov (1972), and many others have shown that deletion is less likely if the word-final $/t/$ or $/d/$ is the past tense ending. For example in Switchboard, deletion is more likely in the word *around* (73% $/d/$-deletion) than in the word *turned* (30% $/d/$-deletion) even though the two words have similar frequencies.

The **flapping** rule is significantly more complicated than we suggested in Chapter 4, as a number of scholars have pointed out (see especially Rhodes (1992)). The preceding vowel is highly likely to be stressed, although this is not necessary (for example there is commonly a flap in the word *thermometer* [θɚˈmɑmɪɾɚ]). The following vowel is highly likely to be unstressed, although again this is not necessary. /t/ is much more likely to flap than /d/. There are complicated interactions with syllable, foot, and word boundaries. Flapping is more likely to happen when the speaker is speaking more quickly, and is more likely to happen at the end of a word when it forms a collocation (high mutual information) with the following word (Gregory et al., 1999). Flapping is less likely to happen when a speaker **hyperar-**

HYPERARTICULATES   **ticulates**, i.e. uses a particularly clear form of speech, which often happens when users are talking to computer speech recognition systems (Oviatt et al., 1998). There is a nasal flap [r̃] whose tongue movements resemble the oral flap but in which the velum is lowered. Finally, flapping doesn't always happen, even when the environment is appropriate; thus the flapping rule, or transducer, needs to be probabilistic, as we will see below.

We have saved for last one of the most important phonological processes: **vowel reduction**, in which many vowels in unstressed syllables are

REDUCED
VOWELS   realized as **reduced vowels**, the most common of which is **schwa** ([ə]).
SCHWA   Stressed syllables are those in which more air is pushed out of the lungs; stressed syllables are longer, louder, and usually higher in pitch than unstressed syllables. Vowels in unstressed syllables in English often don't have their full form; the articulatory gesture isn't as complete as for a full vowel. As a result the shape of the mouth is somewhat neutral; the tongue is neither particularly high nor particularly low. For example the second vowels in *parakeet* is schwa: [pærəkit].

While schwa is the most common reduced vowel, it is not the only one, at least not in some dialects. Bolinger (1981) proposed three reduced vowels: a reduced mid vowel [ə], a reduced front vowel [ɨ], and a reduced rounded vowel [ɵ]. But the majority of computational pronunciation lexicons or computational models of phonology systems limit themselves to one reduced vowel ([ə]) (for example PRONLEX and CELEX) or at most two ([ə] =ARPABET [ax] and [ɨ] = ARPAbet [ix]). Miller (1998) was able to train a neural net to automatically categorize a vowel as [ə] or [ɨ] based only on the phonetic context, which suggests that for speech recognition and text-to-speech purposes, one reduced vowel is probably adequate. Indeed, Wells (1982, p. 167–168) notes that [ə] and [ɨ] are falling together in many dialects of English including General American and Irish, among others, a phenomenon he calls **weak vowel merger**.

A final note: not all unstressed vowels are reduced; any vowel, and diphthongs in particular can retain their full quality even in unstressed position. For example the vowel [eɪ] (ARPAbet [ey]) can appear in stressed position as in the word *eight*) [ˈeɪt] or unstressed position as in the word *always* [ˈɔ.weɪz]. Whether a vowel is reduced depends on many factors. For example the word *the* can be pronounced with a full vowel ði or reduced vowel ðə. It is more likely to be pronounced with the reduced vowel ðə in fast speech, in more casual situations, and when the following word begins with a consonant. It is more likely to be pronounced with the full vowel ði when the following word begins with a vowel or when the speaker is having "planning problems"; speakers are more likely to use a full vowel than a reduced one if they don't know what they are going to say next (Fox Tree and Clark, 1997). See Keating et al. (1994) and Jurafsky et al. (1998) for more details on factors effecting vowel reduction in the TIMIT and Switchboard corpora. Other factors influencing reduction include the frequency of the word, whether this is the final vowel in a phrase, and even the idiosyncracies of individual speakers.

5.8   THE BAYESIAN METHOD FOR PRONUNCIATION

HEAD KNIGHT OF NI:	Ni!
KNIGHTS OF NI:	Ni! Ni! Ni! Ni! Ni!
ARTHUR:	Who are you?
HEAD KNIGHT:	We are the Knights Who Say... 'Ni'!
RANDOM:	Ni!
ARTHUR:	No! Not the Knights Who Say 'Ni'!
HEAD KNIGHT:	The same!
BEDEVERE:	Who are they?
HEAD KNIGHT:	We are the keepers of the sacred words: 'Ni', 'Peng', and 'Neee–wom'!

Graham Chapman, John Cleese, Eric Idle, Terry Gilliam, Terry Jones, and Michael Palin, *Monty Python and the Holy Grail* 1975.

The Bayesian algorithm that we used to pick the optimal correction for a spelling error can be used to solve what is often called the **pronunciation** subproblem in speech recognition. In this task, we are given a series of phones and our job is to compute the most probable word which generated them. For this chapter, we will simplify the problem in an important way by assuming the correct string of phones. A real speech recognizer relies on probabilistic estimators for each phone, so it is never sure about the identity of any phone. We will relax this assumption in Chapter 7; for now, let's look at the simpler problem.

We'll also begin with another simplification by assuming that we already know where the word boundaries are. Later in the chapter, we'll show that we can simultaneously find word boundaries ("segment") and model pronunciation variation.

Consider the particular problem of interpreting the sequence of phones [ni], when it occurs after the word *I* at the beginning of a sentence. Stop and see if you can think of any words which are likely to have been pronounced [ni] before you read on. The word "Ni" is not allowed.

You probably thought of the word *knee*. This word is in fact pronounced [ni]. But an investigation of the Switchboard corpus produces a total of 7 words which can be pronounced [ni]! The seven words are *the*, *neat*, *need*, *new*, *knee*, *to*, and *you*.

How can the word *the* be pronounced [ni]? The explanation for this pronunciation (and all the others except the one for *knee*) lies in the contextually-induced pronunciation variation we discussed in Chapter 4. For example, we saw that [t] and [d] were often deleted word finally, especially before coronals; thus the pronunciation of *neat* as [ni] happened before the word *little* (*neat little* → [niləl]). The pronunciation of *the* as [ni] is caused by the regressive assimilation process also discussed in Chapter 4. Recall that in nasal assimilation, phones before or after nasals take on nasal manner of articulation. Thus [θ] can be realized as [n]. The many cases of *the* pronounced as [ni] in Switchboard occurred after words like *in*, *on*, and *been* (so *in the* → [mni]). The pronunciation of *new* as [ni] occurred most frequently in the word *New York*; the vowel [u] has fronted to [i] before a [y].

The pronunciation of *to* as [ni] occurred after the work *talking* (*talking to you* → [tɔkmiyu]); here the [u] is palatalized by the following [y] and the [n] is functioning jointly as the final sound of *talking* and the initial sound of *to*. Because this phone is part of two separate words we will not try to model this particular mapping; for the rest of this section let's consider only the following five words as candidate lexical forms for [ni]: *knee*, *the*, *neat*, *need*, *new*.

We saw in the previous section that the Bayesian spelling error correction algorithm had two components: candidate generation, and candidate scoring. Speech recognizers often use an alternative architecture, trading off speech for storage. In this architecture, each pronunciation is expanded in advance with all possible variants, which are then pre-stored with their scores. Thus there is no need for candidate generation; the word [ni] is simply stored with the list of words that can generate it. Let's assume this method and see how the prior and likelihood are computed for each word.

We will be choosing the word whose product of prior and likelihood is the highest, according to Equation (5.12), where y represents the sequence of phones (in this case [ni] and w represents the candidate word [*the*, *new*, etc.]). The most likely word is then:

$$\hat{w} = \operatorname*{argmax}_{w \in W} \overbrace{P(y|w)}^{\text{likelihood}} \overbrace{P(w)}^{\text{prior}} \tag{5.12}$$

We could choose to generate the likelihoods $p(y|w)$ by using a set of confusion matrices as we did for spelling error correction. But it turns out that confusion matrices don't do as well for pronunciation as for spelling. While misspelling tends to change the form of a word only slightly, the changes in pronunciation between a lexical and surface form are much greater. Confusion matrices only work well for single-errors, which, as we saw above, are common in misspelling. Furthermore, recall from Chapter 4 that pronunciation variation is strongly affected by the surrounding phones, lexical frequency, and stress and other prosodic factors. Thus probabilistic models of pronunciation variation include a lot more factors than a simple confusion matrix can include.

One simple way to generate pronunciation likelihoods is via **probabilistic rules**. Probabilistic rules were first proposed for pronunciation by PROBABILISTIC RULES (Labov, 1969) (who called them **variable rules**). The idea is to take the rules of pronunciation variation we saw in Chapter 4 and associate them with probabilities. We can then run these probabilistic rules over the lexicon and generate different possible surface forms each with its own probability. For example, consider a simple version of a nasal assimilation rule which explains why *the* can be pronounced [ni]; a word-initial [ð] becomes [n] if the preceding word ended in [n] or sometimes [m]:

$$[.15] \; ð \Rightarrow n \; / \; [+nasal] \; \#\!\_\!\_ \tag{5.13}$$

The [.15] to the left of the rule is the probability; this can be computed from a large-enough labeled corpus such as the transcribed portion of Switchboard. Let *ncount* be the number of times lexical [ð] is realized word-initially by surface [n] when the previous word ends in a nasal (91 in the Switchboard corpus). Let *envcount* be the total number of times lexical [ð] occurs (whatever its surface realization) when the previous word ends in a nasal (617 in the Switchboard corpus). The resulting probability is:

$$P(\eth \rightarrow n \; / \; [+nasal] \; \# \underline{\quad}) \; = \; \frac{ncount}{envcount}$$

$$= \; \frac{91}{617}$$

$$= \; .15$$

We can build similar probabilistic versions of the assimilation and deletion rules which account for the [ni] pronunciation of the other words. Figure 5.10 shows sample rules and the probabilities trained on the Switchboard pronunciation database.

Word	Rule Name	Rule	P
the	nasal assimilation	$\eth \Rightarrow n \; / \; [+nasal] \; \# \underline{\quad}$	[.15]
neat	final t deletion	$t \Rightarrow \emptyset \; / \; V \underline{\quad} \#$	[.52]
need	final d deletion	$d \Rightarrow \emptyset \; / \; V \underline{\quad} \#$	[.11]
new	u fronting	$u \Rightarrow i \; / \underline{\quad} \# \; [y]$	[.36]

Figure 5.10   Simple rules of pronunciation variation due to context in continuous speech accounting for the pronunciation of each of these words as [ni].

We now need to compute the prior probability $P(w)$ for each word. For spelling correction we did this by using the relative frequency of the word in a large corpus; a word which occurred 44,000 times in 44 million words receives the probability estimate $\frac{44,000}{44,000,000}$ or .001. For the pronunciation problem, let's take our prior probabilities from a collection of a written and a spoken corpus. The Brown Corpus is a 1 million word collection of samples from 500 written texts from different genres (newspaper, novels, non-fiction, academic, etc.) which was assembled at Brown University in 1963–1964 (Kučera and Francis, 1967; Francis, 1979; Francis and Kučera, 1982). The Switchboard Treebank corpus is a 1.4 million word collection of telephone conversations. Together they let us sample from both the written and spoken genres. The table below shows the probabilities for our five words; each probability is computed from the raw frequencies by normalizing by the number of words in the combined corpus (plus .5 * the number of word types; so the total denominator is 2,486,075 + 30,836):

w	freq(w)	p(w)
knee	61	.000024
the	114,834	.046
neat	338	.00013
need	1417	.00056
new	2625	.001

Now we are almost ready to answer our original question: what is the most likely word given the pronunciation [ni] and given that the previous word was *I* at the beginning of a sentence. Let's start by multiplying together our estimates for $p(w)$ and $p(y|w)$ to get an estimate; we show them sorted from most probable to least probable (*the* has a probability of 0 since the previous phone was not [n], and hence there is no other rule allowing [ð] to be realized as [n]):

Word	p(y|w)	p(w)	p(y|w)p(w)
new	.36	.001	.00036
neat	.52	.00013	.000068
need	.11	.00056	.000062
knee	1.00	.000024	.000024
the	0	.046	0

Our algorithm suggests that *new* is the most likely underlying word. But this is the wrong answer; the string [ni] following the word *I* came in fact from the word *need* in the Switchboard corpus. One way that people are able to correctly solve this task is word-level knowledge; people know that the word string *I need* ... is much more likely than the word string *I new* .... We don't need to abandon our Bayesian model to handle this fact; we just need to modify it so that our model also knows that *I need* is more likely than *I new*. In Chapter 6 we will see that we can do this by using a slightly more intelligent estimate of $p(w)$ called a **bigram** estimate; essentially we consider the probability of *need* following *I* instead of just the individual probability of *need*.

This Bayesian algorithm is in fact part of all modern speech recognizers. Where the algorithms differ strongly is how they detect individual phones in the acoustic signal, and on which search algorithm they use to efficiently compute the Bayesian probabilities to find the proper string of words in connected speech (as we will see in Chapter 7).

Decision Tree Models of Pronunciation Variation

DECISION TREE

CART

In the previous section we saw how hand-written rules could be augmented with probabilities to model pronunciation variation. Riley (1991) and Withgott and Chen (1993) suggested an alternative to writing rules by hand, which has proved quite useful: automatically inducing lexical-to-surface pronunciations mappings from a labeled corpus with a **decision tree**, particularly with the kind of decision tree called a **Classification and Regression Tree (CART)** (Breiman et al., 1984). A decision tree takes a situation described by a set of features and classifies it into a category and an associated probability. For pronunciation, a decision tree can be trained to take a lexical phone and various contextual features (surrounding phones, stress and syllable structure information, perhaps lexical identity) and select an appropriate surface phone to realize it. We can think of the confusion matrices we used in spelling error correction above as degenerate decision trees; thus the substitution matrix takes a lexical phone and outputs a probability distribution over potential surface phones to be substituted. The advantage of decision trees is that they can be automatically induced from a labeled corpus, and that they are concise: Decision trees pick out only the relevant features and thus suffer less from sparseness than a matrix, which has to condition on every neighboring phone.

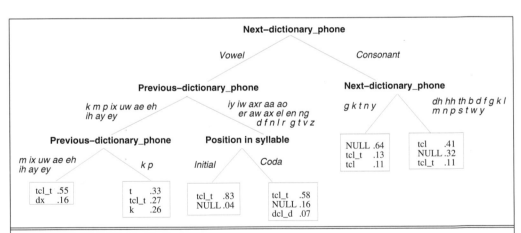

Figure 5.11   Hand-pruned decision tree for the phoneme /t/ induced from the Switchboard corpus (courtesy of Eric Fosler-Lussier). This particular decision tree doesn't model flapping since flaps were already listed in the dictionary. The tree automatically induced the categories *Vowel* and *Consonant*. We have only shown the most likely realizations at each leaf node.

For example, Figure 5.11 shows a decision tree for the pronunciation of the phoneme /t/ induced from the Switchboard corpus. While this tree doesn't including flapping (there is a separate tree for flapping) it does model the fact that /t/ is more likely to be deleted before a consonant than before a vowel. Note, in fact, that the tree automatically induced the classes *Vowel* and *Consonant*. Furthermore note that if /t/ is not deleted before a consonant, it is likely to be unreleased. Finally, notice that /t/ is very unlikely to be deleted in syllable onset position.

Readers with interest in decision tree modeling of pronunciation should consult Riley (1991), Withgott and Chen (1993), and a textbook with an introduction to decision trees such as Russell and Norvig (1995).

5.9   WEIGHTED AUTOMATA

We said earlier that for purposes of efficiency a lexicon is often stored with the most likely kinds of pronunciation variation pre-compiled. The two most common representation for such a lexicon are the **trie** and the **weighted** **finite-state automaton/transducer** (or **probabilistic FSA/FST**) (Pereira et al., 1994). We will leave the discussion of the trie to Chapter 7, and concentrate here on the weighted automaton.

WEIGHTED

The weighted automaton is a simple augmentation of the finite automaton in which each arc is associated with a probability, indicating how likely that path is to be taken. The probability on all the arcs leaving a node must sum to 1. Figure 5.12 shows two weighted automata for the word *tomato*, adapted from Russell and Norvig (1995). The top automaton shows two possible pronunciations, representing the dialect difference in the second vowel. The bottom one shows more pronunciations (how many?) representing optional reduction or deletion of the first vowel and optional flapping of the final [t].

A **Markov chain** is a special case of a weighted automaton in which the input sequence uniquely determines which states the automaton will go through. Because they can't represent inherently ambiguous problems, a Markov chain is only useful for assigning probabilities to unambiguous sequences; thus the *N*-gram models to be discussed in Chapter 6 are Markov chains since each word is treated as if it was unambiguous. In fact the weighted automata used in speech and language processing can be shown to be equivalent to **Hidden Markov Models** (HMMs). Why do we introduce weighted automata in this chapter and HMMs in Chapter 7? The

MARKOV CHAIN

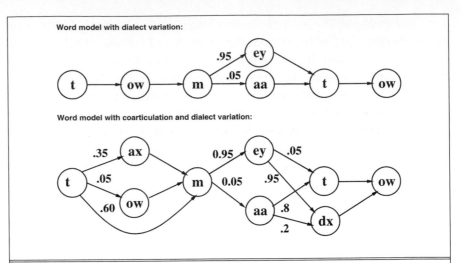

Word model with dialect variation:

Word model with coarticulation and dialect variation:

Figure 5.12   You say [t ow m ey t ow] and I say [t ow m aa t ow]. Two pronunciation networks for the word *tomato*, adapted from Russell and Norvig (1995). The top one models sociolinguistic variation (some British or eastern American dialects); the bottom one adds in coarticulatory effects. Note the correlation between allophonic and sociolinguistic variation; the dialect with the vowel [ey] is more likely to flap than the other dialect.

two models offer a different metaphor; it is sometimes easier to think about certain problems as weighted-automata than as HMMs. The weighted automaton metaphor is often applied when the input alphabet maps relatively neatly to the underlying alphabet. For example, in the problem of correcting spelling errors in typewritten input, the input sequence consists of letters and the states of the automaton can correspond to letters. Thus it is natural to think of the problem as transducing from a set of symbols to the same set of symbols with some modifications, and hence weighted automata are naturally used for spelling error correction. In the problem of correcting errors in hand-written input, the input sequence is visual, and the input alphabet is an alphabet of lines and angles and curves. Here instead of transducing from an alphabet to itself, we need to do classification on some input sequence before considering it as a sequence of states. Hidden Markov Models provide a more appropriate metaphor, since they naturally handle separate alphabets for input sequences and state sequences. But since any probabilistic automaton in which the input sequence does not uniquely specify the state sequence can be modeled as an HMM, the difference is one of metaphor rather than explanatory power.

Weighted automata can be created in many ways. One way, first proposed by Cohen (1989) is to start with on-line pronunciation dictionaries and use hand-written rules of the kind we saw above to create different potential surface forms. The probabilities can then be assigned either by counting the number of times each pronunciation occurs in a corpus, or if the corpus is too sparse, by learning probabilities for each rule and multiplying out the rule probabilities for each surface form (Tajchman et al., 1995). Finally these weighted rules, or alternatively the decision trees we discussed in the last section, can be automatically compiled into a weighted finite-state transducer (Sproat and Riley, 1996). Alternatively, for very common words, we can simply find enough examples of the pronunciation in a transcribed corpus to build the model by just combining all the pronunciations into a network (Wooters and Stolcke, 1994).

The networks for *tomato* above were shown merely as illustration and are not from any real system; Figure 5.13 shows an automaton for the word *about* which is trained on actual pronunciations from the Switchboard corpus (we discussed these pronunciations in Chapter 4).

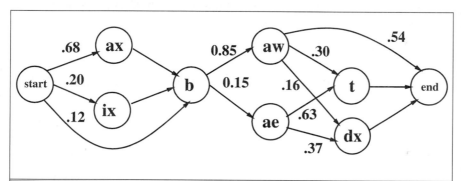

Figure 5.13   A pronunciation network for the word *about*, from the actual pronunciations in the Switchboard corpus.

Computing Likelihoods from Weighted Automata: The Forward Algorithm

One advantage of an automaton-based lexicon is that there are efficient algorithms for generating the probabilities that are needed to implement the Bayesian method of correct-word-identification of Section 5.8. These algorithms apply to weighted automata and also to the **Hidden Markov Models** that we will discuss in Chapter 7. Recall that in our example the Bayesian method is given as input a series of phones [n iy], and must choose between the words *the*, *neat*, *need*, *new*, and *knee*. This was done by computing two probabilities: the prior probability of each word, and the likelihood of the phone string [n iy] given each word. When we discussed this example earlier, we said that for example the likelihood of [n iy] given the word *need* was .11, since we computed a probability of .11 for the *final-d-deletion* rule from our Switchboard corpus. This probability is transparent for *need* since there were only two possible pronunciations ([n iy] and [n iy d]). But for words like *about*, visualizing the different probabilities is more complex. Using a precompiled weighted automata can make it simpler to see all the different probabilities of different paths through the automaton.

There is a very simple algorithm for computing the likelihood of a string of phones given the weighted automaton for a word. This algorithm, the **forward** algorithm, is an essential part of ASR systems, although in this chapter we will only be working with a simple usage of the algorithm. This is because the forward algorithm is particularly useful when there are multiple paths through an automaton which can account for the input; this is not the case in the weighted automata in this chapter, but will be true for the HMMS of Chapter 7. The forward algorithm is also an important step in defining the **Viterbi** algorithm that we will see later in this chapter.

Let's begin by giving a formal definition of a weighted automaton and of the input and output to the likelihood computation problem. A weighted automaton consists of

1. a sequence of states $q = (q_0 q_1 q_2 \ldots q_n)$, each corresponding to a phone, and

2. a set of transition probabilities between states, a_{01}, a_{12}, a_{13}, encoding the probability of one phone following another.

We represent the states as nodes, and the transition probabilities as edges between nodes; an edge exists between two nodes if there is a non-zero transition probability between the two nodes.[4] The sequences of symbols

---

4   We have used two "special" states (often called **non-emitting states**) as the start and end state; it is also possible to avoid the use of these states. In that case, an automaton must specify two more things:

1. π, an initial probability distribution over states, such that π_i is the probability that the automaton will start in state i. Of course, some states j may have $\pi_j = 0$, meaning that they cannot be initial states.

2. a set of legal accepting states.

that are input to the model (if we are thinking of it as recognizer) or which are produced by the model (if we are thinking of it as a generator) are generally called the **observation sequence**, referred to as $O = (o_1 o_2 o_3 \ldots o_t)$. (Upper-case letters are used for a sequence and lower-case letters for an individual element of a sequence). We will use this terminology when talking about weighted automata and later when talking about HMMs.

OBSERVATION SEQUENCE

Figure 5.14 shows an automaton for the word *need* with a sample observation sequence.

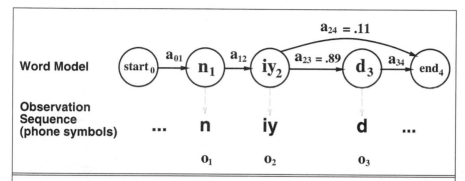

Figure 5.14   A simple weighted automaton or Markov chain pronunciation network for the word *need*, showing the transition probabilities, and a sample observation sequence. The transition probabilities a_{xy} between two states x and y are 1.0 unless otherwise specified.

This task of determining which underlying word might have produced an observation sequence is called the **decoding** problem. Recall that in order to find which of the candidate words was most probable given the observation sequence [n iy], we need to compute the product $P(O|w)P(w)$ for each candidate word (*the, need, neat, knee, new*), i.e. the likelihood of the observation sequence O given the word w times the prior probability of the word.

DECODING

The forward algorithm can be run to perform this computation for each word; we give it an observation sequence and the pronunciation automaton for a word and it will return $P(O|w)P(w)$. Thus one way to solve the decoding problem is to run the forward algorithm separately on each word and choose the word with the highest value. As we saw earlier, the Bayesian method produces the wrong result for pronunciation [n iy] as part of the word sequence *I need* (its first choice is the word *new*, and the second choice is *neat*; *need* is only the third choice). Since the forward algorithm is just a way of implementing the Bayesian approach, it will return the exact same rankings. (We will see in Chapter 6 how to augment the algorithm with **bi-gram** probabilities which will enable it to make use of the knowledge that the previous word was *I*).

The forward algorithm takes as input a pronunciation network for each candidate word. Because the word *the* only has the pronunciation [n iy] after nasals, and since we are assuming the actual context of this word was after the word *I* (no nasal), we will skip that word and look only at *new, neat, need,* and *knee.* Note in Figure 5.15 that we have augmented each network with the probability of each word, computed from the frequency that we saw on page 167.

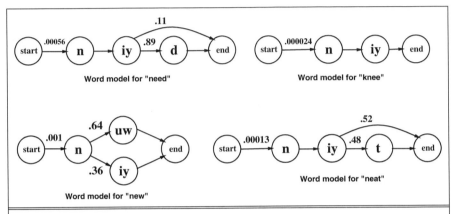

Figure 5.15   Pronunciation networks for the words *need, neat, new,* and *knee.* All networks are simplified from the actual pronunciations in the Switchboard corpus. Each network has been augmented by the unigram probability of the word (i.e., its normalized frequency from the Switchboard+Brown corpus). Word probabilities are not usually included as part of the pronunciation network for a word; they are added here to simplify the exposition of the forward algorithm.

The forward algorithm is another **dynamic programming** algorithm, and can be thought of as a slight generalization of the minimum edit distance algorithm. Like the minimum edit distance algorithm, it uses a table to store intermediate values as it builds up the probability of the observation sequence. Unlike the minimum edit distance algorithm, the rows are labeled not just by states which always occur in linear order, but implicitly by a *state-graph* which has many ways of getting from one state to another. In the minimum edit distance algorithm, we filled in the matrix by just computing the value of each cell from the three cells around it. With the forward algorithm, on the other hand, a state might be entered by any other state, and so the recurrence relation is somewhat more complicated. Furthermore, the forward algorithm computes the *sum* of the probabilities of all possible paths that could generate the observation sequence, where the minimum edit distance computed the *minimum* such probability.[5] Each cell of the forward algorithm matrix, *forward*$[t, j]$ represents the probability of being in state j after seeing the first t observations, given the automaton λ. Since we have augmented our graphs with the word probability $p(w)$, our example of the forward algorithm here is actually computing this likelihood times $p(w)$. The value of each cell *forward*$[t, j]$ is computed by summing over the probabilities of every path that could lead us to this cell. Formally, each cell expresses the following probability:

$$forward[t, j] = P(o_1, o_2 \ldots o_t, q_t = j | \lambda) \, P(w) \qquad (5.14)$$

Here $q_t = j$ means "the probability that the tth state in the sequence of states is state j". We compute this probability by summing over the extensions of all the paths that lead to the current cell. An extension of a path from a state i at time $t - 1$ is computed by multiplying the following three factors:

1. the **previous path probability** from the previous cell forward$[t - 1, i]$,

2. the **transition probability** a_{ij} from previous state i to current state j, and

3. the **observation likelihood** b_{jt} that current state j matches observation symbol t. For the weighted automata that we consider here, b_{jt} is 1 if the observation symbol matches the state, and 0 otherwise. Chapter 7 will consider more complex observation likelihoods.

The algorithm is described in Figure 5.16.

Figure 5.17 shows the forward algorithm applied to the word *need*. The algorithm applies similarly to the other words which can produce the string [n iy], resulting in the probabilities on page 167. In order to compute the most probable underlying word, we run the forward algorithm separately on each of the candidate words, and choose the one with the highest probability. Chapter 7 will give further details of the mathematics of the forward algorithm and introduce the related forward-backward algorithm.

---

[5] The forward algorithm computes the *sum* because there may be multiple paths through the network which explain a given observation sequence. Chapter 7 will take up this point in more detail.

---

function FORWARD(*observations,state-graph*) **returns** *forward-probability*

   num-states ← NUM-OF-STATES(*state-graph*)
   num-obs ← *length*(*observations*)
   Create probability matrix *forward*[*num-states* + 2, *num-obs* + 2]
   forward[0,0] ← 1.0
   for each time step *t* **from** 0 **to** *num-obs* **do**
      for each state *s* **from** 0 **to** *num-states* **do**
         for each transition *s'* from *s* specified by *state-graph*
            forward[*s',t*+1] ← *forward*[*s,t*] * *a*[*s, s'*] * *b*[*s', o_t*]
   return the sum of the probabilities in the final column of *forward*

Figure 5.16   The forward algorithm for computing likelihood of observation sequence given a word model. $a[s,s']$ is the transition probability from current state s to next state s', and $b[s',o_t]$ is the observation likelihood of s' given o_t. For the weighted automata that we consider here, $b[s',o_t]$ is 1 if the observation symbol matches the state, and 0 otherwise.

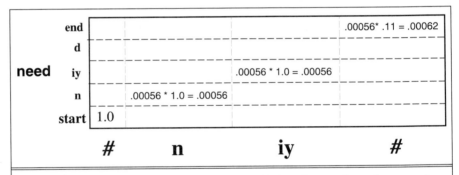

Figure 5.17   The forward algorithm applied to the word *need*, computing the probability $P(O|w)P(w)$. While this example doesn't require the full power of the forward algorithm, we will see its use on more complex examples in Chapter 7.

Decoding: The Viterbi Algorithm

The forward algorithm as we presented it seems a bit of an overkill. Since only one path through the pronunciation networks will match the input string, why use such a big matrix and consider so many possible paths? Furthermore, as a decoding method, it seems rather inefficient to run the forward algorithm once for each word (imagine how inefficient this would be if we were computing likelihoods for all possible sentences rather than all possible words!) Part of the reason that the forward algorithm seems like overkill is that we have immensely simplified the pronunciation problem by assuming that our input consists of sequences of unambiguous symbols. We will see in Chapter 7 that when the observation sequence is a set of noisy acoustic values, there are many possibly paths through the automaton, and the forward algorithm will play an important role in summing these paths.

But it is true that having to run it separately on each word makes the forward algorithm a very inefficient decoding method. Luckily, there is a simple variation on the forward algorithm called the **Viterbi** algorithm which allows us to consider all the words simultaneously and still compute the most likely path. The term **Viterbi** is common in speech and language processing, but like the forward algorithm this is really a standard application of the classic **dynamic programming** algorithm, and again looks a lot like the **minimum edit distance** algorithm. The Viterbi algorithm was first applied to speech recognition by Vintsyuk (1968), but has what Kruskal (1983) calls a 'remarkable history of multiple independent discovery and publication'; see the History section at the end of the chapter for more details. The name Viterbi is the one which is most commonly used in speech recognition, although the terms **DP alignment** (for **Dynamic Programming alignment**), **dynamic time warping** and **one-pass decoding** are also commonly used. The term is applied to the decoding algorithm for weighted automata and Hidden Markov Models on a single word and also to its more complex application to continuous speech, as we will see in Chapter 7. In this chapter we will show how the algorithm is used to find the best path through a network composed of single words, as a result choosing the word which is most probable given the observation sequence string of words.

The version of the Viterbi algorithm that we will present takes as input a single weighted automaton and a set of observed phones $o = (o_1 o_2 o_3 \ldots o_t)$ and returns the most probable state sequence $q = (q_1 q_2 q_3 \ldots q_t)$, together with its probability. We can create a single weighted automaton by combining the pronunciation networks for the four words in parallel with a single start and a single end state. Figure 5.18 shows the combined network.

Figure 5.19 shows pseudocode for the Viterbi algorithm. Like the minimum edit distance and forward algorithm, the Viterbi algorithm sets up a probability matrix, with one column for each time index t and one row for each state in the state graph. Also like the forward algorithm, each column has a cell for each state q_i in the single combined automaton for the four words. In fact, the code for the Viterbi algorithm should look exactly like the code for the forward algorithm with two modifications. First, where

VITERBI

DYNAMIC
TIME
WARPING

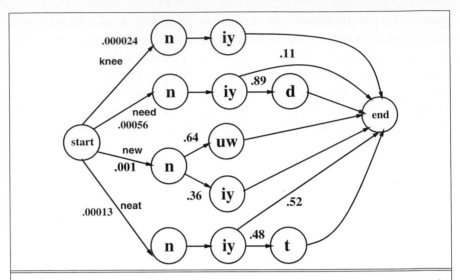

Figure 5.18   The pronunciation networks for the words *need*, *neat*, *new*, and *knee* combined into a single weighted automaton. Again, word probabilities are not usually considered part of the pronunciation network for a word; they are added here to simplify the exposition of the Viterbi algorithm.

the forward algorithm places the *sum* of all previous paths into the current cell, the Viterbi algorithm puts the *max* of the previous paths into the current cell.

The algorithm first creates $N + 2$ or four state columns. The first column is an initial pseudo-observation, the second corresponds to the first observation phone [n], the third to [iy] and the fourth to a final pseudo-observation. We begin in the first column by setting the probability of the *start* state to 1.0, and the other probabilities to 0; the reader should find this in Figure 5.20. Cells with probability 0 are simply left blank for readability.

Then we move to the next state; as with the forward algorithm, for every state in column 0, we compute the probability of moving into each state in column 1. The value *viterbi*$[t, j]$ is computed by taking the maximum over the extensions of all the paths that lead to the current cell. An extension of a path from a state i at time $t - 1$ is computed by multiplying the same three factors we used for the forward algorithm:

1. the **previous path probability** from the previous cell *forward*$[t - 1, i]$,
2. the **transition probability** a_{ij} from previous state i to current state j, and
3. the **observation likelihood** b_{jt} that current state j matches observation symbol t. For the weighted automata that we consider here, b_{jt} is 1 if

function VITERBI(*observations* of len *T*,*state-graph*) **returns** *best-path*

  num-states ← NUM-OF-STATES(*state-graph*)
  Create a path probability matrix *viterbi[num-states+2,T+2]*
  viterbi[0,0] ← 1.0
  for each time step *t* **from** 0 **to** *T* **do**
    for each state *s* **from** 0 **to** *num-states* **do**
      for each transition *s'* from *s* specified by *state-graph*
        new-score ← *viterbi[s, t]* * *a[s,s']* * $b_{s'}(o_t)$
        if ((*viterbi[s',t+1]* = 0) || (*new-score* > *viterbi[s', t+1]*))
          then
                viterbi[s', t+1] ← *new-score*
                back-pointer[s', t+1] ← *s*
  Backtrace from highest probability state in the final column of *viterbi[ ]* and
return path

Figure 5.19   Viterbi algorithm for finding optimal sequence of states in continuous speech recognition, simplified by using phones as inputs. Given an observation sequence of phones and a weighted automaton (state graph), the algorithm returns the path through the automaton which has maximum probability and accepts the observation sequence. $a[s, s']$ is the transition probability from current state s' to next state s', and $b[s', o_t]$ is the observation likelihood of s' given o_t. For the weighted automata that we consider here, $b[s', o_t]$ is 1 if the observation symbol matches the state, and 0 otherwise.

the observation symbol matches the state, and 0 otherwise. Chapter 7 will consider more complex observation likelihoods.

In Figure 5.20, in the column for the input *n*, each word starts with [n], and so each has a non-zero probability in the cell for the state *n*. Other cells in that column have zero entries, since their states don't match n. When we proceed to the next column, each cell that matches iy gets updated with the contents of the previous cell times the transition probability to that cell. Thus the value of *viterbi[2,iy_new]* for the iy state of the word *new* is the product of the "word" probability of *new* times the probability of *new* being pronounced with the vowel *iy*. Notice that if we look only at this iy column, that the word *need* is currently the "most-probable" word. But when we move to the final column, the word *new* will win out, since *need* has a smaller transition probability to *end* (.11) than *new* does (1.0). We can now follow the backpointers and backtrace to find the path that gave us this final probability of .00036.

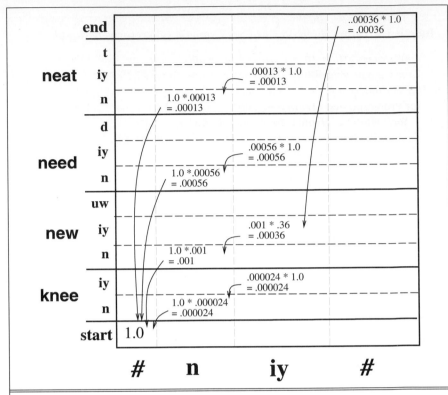

Figure 5.20   The entries in the individual state columns for the Viterbi algorithm. Each cell keeps the probability of the best path so far and a pointer to the previous cell along that path. Backtracing from the *end* state, we can reconstruct the state sequence n_{new} iy_{new}, arriving at the best word *new*.

Weighted Automata and Segmentation

SEGMENTA-
TION

Weighted automata and the Viterbi algorithm play an important in various algorithm for **segmentation**. Segmentation is the process of taking an undifferentiated sequence of symbols and "segmenting" it into chunks. For example **sentence segmentation** is the problem of automatically finding the sentence boundaries in a corpus. Similarly **word segmentation** is the problem of finding word-boundaries in a corpus. In written English there is no difficulty in segmenting words from each other because there are orthographic spaces between words. This is not the case in languages like Chinese and Japanese that use a Chinese-derived writing system. Written Chinese does not mark word boundaries. Instead, each Chinese character is written one after the other without spaces. Since each character approximately represents a single morpheme, and since words can be composed of one or more characters, it is often difficult to know where words should be segmented. Proper word-segmentation is necessary for many applications, particularly including parsing and text-to-speech. (How a sentence is broken up into words influences its pronunciation in a number of ways.)

Consider the following example sentence from Sproat et al. (1996):

(5.15) 日文章鱼怎麼说？

"How do you say 'octopus' in Japanese?"

This sentence has two potential segmentations, only one of which is correct. In the plausible segmentation, the first two characters are combined to make the word for 'Japanese language' (日文 rì-wén) (the accents indicate the **tone** of each syllable), and the next two are combined to make the word for 'octopus' (章鱼 zhāng-yú).

(5.16) 日文   章鱼   怎麼   说   ?
        rì-wén   zhāng-yú zěn-me   shuō
        Japanese octopus   how   say

"How do you say octopus in Japanese?"

(5.17) 日   文章   鱼   怎麼   说   ?
        rì   wén-zhāng yú   zěn-me   shuō
        Japan   essay   fish   how   say

"How do you say Japan essay fish?"

Sproat et al. (1996) give a very simple algorithm which selects the correct segmentation by choosing the one which contains the most-frequent words. In other words, the algorithm multiplies together the probabilities of each word in a potential segmentation and chooses whichever segmentation results in a higher product probability.

The implementation of their algorithm combines a weighted-finite-state transducer representation of a Chinese lexicon with the Viterbi algorithm. This lexicon is a slight augmentation of the FST lexicons we saw in Chapter 4; each word is represented as a series of arcs representing each character in the word, followed by a weighted arc representing the probability of the word. As is commonly true with probabilistic algorithms, they actually use the negative log probability of the word ($-\log(P(w))$). The log probability is mainly useful because the product of many probabilities gets very small, and so using the log probability can help avoid underflow. Using log probabilities also means that we are *adding costs* rather than *multiplying probabilities*, and that we are looking for the *minimum cost* solution rather than the *maximum probability* solution.

Consider the example in Figure 5.21. This sample lexicon Figure 5.21(a) consists of only five potential words:

Word	Pronunciation	Meaning	Cost $(-logp(w))$
日文	rì-wén	'Japanese'	10.63
日	rì	'Japan'	6.51
章鱼	zhāng- yú	'octopus'	13.18
文章	wén-zhāng	'essay'	9.51
鱼	yú	'fish'	10.28

The system represents the input sentence as the unweighted FSA in Figure 5.21(b). In order to compose this input with the lexicon, it needs to be converted into an FST. The algorithm uses a function *Id* which takes an FSA *A* and returns the FST which maps all and only the strings accepted by *A* to themselves. Let $D*$ represent the transitive closure of D, that is, the automaton created by adding a loop from the end of the lexicon back to the beginning. The set of all possible segmentations is $Id(I) \circ D^*$, that is, the input transducer $Id(I)$ composed with the transitive closure of the dictionary *D*, shown in Figure 5.21(c). Then the best segmentation is the lowest-cost segmentation in $Id(I) \circ D^*$, shown in Figure 5.21(d).

Finding the best path shown in Figure 5.21(d) can be done easily with the Viterbi algorithm and is left as an exercise for the reader. Furthermore, this segmentation algorithm, like the spelling error correction algorithm we saw earlier, can also be extended to incorporate the cross-word probabilities (*N*-gram probabilities) that will be introduced in Chapter 6.

Segmentation for Lexicon-Induction

The weighted automata segmentation algorithm that was presented above relies on the weights stored in the lexicon. But how is this lexicon to be learned in the first place? A number of segmentation algorithms address this "prior" problem of segmentation in the absence of a lexicon. For example de Marcken (1996) and Brent and Cartwright (1996) both propose algorithms that take an unsegmented sequence of input phones and use information-theoretic principles to iteratively induce the lexicon by trying different possible segmentations. Both rely on stochastic versions of the **Minimum Description tion Length** (**MDL**) principle and on phonotactic transition probabilities to choose between alternative models. The description length of a lexicon

MDL

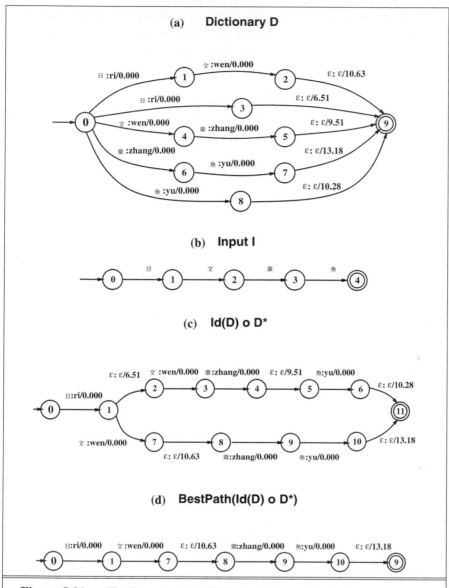

Figure 5.21   The Sproat et al. (1996) algorithm applied to four input words (after Sproat et al. (1996))

or grammar (measured, for example, in the number of symbols in it) is a heuristic measure of the information complexity in the lexicon. By preferring a lexicon with less symbols, MDL is implicitly choosing a simpler and more general lexicon. Brent and Cartwright (1996) hypothesize that children use MDL algorithms to learn a lexicon by segmenting words from speech. In fact, Saffran et al. (1996) shows that eight-month-old infants can use phone sequence probabilities as evidence for word segmentation.

5.10 PRONUNCIATION IN HUMANS

Section 5.7 discussed many factors which influence pronunciation variation in humans. In this section we very briefly summarize a computational model of the retrieval of words from the mental lexicon as part of human lexical production. The model is due to Gary Dell and his colleagues; for brevity we combine and simplify features of multiple models (Dell, 1986, 1988; Dell et al., 1997) in this single overview. First consider some data. As we suggested in Chapter 3, production errors such as slips of the tongue (*darn bore* instead *barn door*) often provide important insights into lexical production. Dell (1986) summarizes a number of previous results about such slips. The **lexical bias** effect is that slips are more likely to create words than non-words; thus slips like *dean bad*→ *bean dad* are three times more likely than slips like *deal back*→ *beal dack*. The **repeated-phoneme bias** is that two phones in two words are likely to participate in an error if there is an identical phone in both words. Thus *deal beack* is more likely to slip to *beal* than *deal back* is.

The model that Dell (1986, 1988) proposes is a network with three levels: semantics, word (lemma), and phonemes.[6] The semantics level has nodes for concepts, the lemma level has one node for each words, and the phoneme level has separate nodes for each phone, separated into onsets, vowels, and codas. Each lemma node is connected to the phoneme units which comprise the word, and the semantic units which represent the concept. Connections are used to pass activation from node to node, and are bidirectional and excitatory. Lexical production happens in two stages. In the first stage, activation passes from the semantic concepts to words. Activation will cascade down into the phonological units and then back up into other word units. At some point the most highly activated word is selected. In the second stage, this selected is given a large jolt of activation. Again this activation passes to the phonological level. Now the most highly active phoneme nodes are selected and accessed in order.

---

[6]   Dell (1988) also has a fourth level for syllable structure that we will ignore here.

Figure 5.22 shows Dell's model. Errors occur because too much activation reaches the wrong phonological node. Lexical bias, for example, is modeled by activation spreading up from the phones of the intended word to neighboring words, which then activated their own phones. Thus incorrect phones get "extra" activation if they are present in actual words.

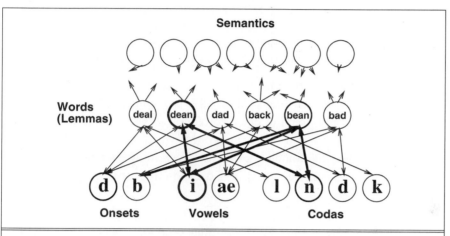

Figure 5.22   The network model of Dell (1986, 1988), showing the mechanism for lexical bias (modified from Dell (1988, p. 134)). The boldfaced nodes indicate nodes with lots of activation. The intended word *dean* has a greater chance of slipping to *bean* because of the existence of the *bean* node. The boldfaced lines show the connections which account for the possible slip.

The two-step network model also explains other facts about lexical production. **Aphasic** speakers have various troubles in language production and comprehension, often caused by strokes or accidents. Dell et al. (1997) show that weakening various connections in a network model like the one above can also account for the speech errors in aphasics. This supports the *continuity hypothesis*, which suggests that some part of aphasia is merely an extension of normal difficulties in word retrieval, and also provides further evidence for the network model. Readers interested in details of the model should see the above references and related computational models such as Roelofs (1997), which extends the network model to deal with syllabification, phonetic encoding, and more complex sequential structure, and Levelt et al. (1999).

APHASIC

5.11   SUMMARY

This chapter has introduced some essential metaphors and algorithms that will be useful throughout speech and language processing. The main points are as follows:

- We can represent many language problems as if a clean string of symbols had been corrupted by passing through a **noisy channel** and it is our job to recover the original symbol string. One powerful way to recover the original symbol string is to consider all possible original strings, and rank them by their **conditional probability**.

- The conditional probability is usually easiest to compute using the **Bayes Rule**, which breaks down the probability into a **prior** and a **likelihood**. For spelling error correction or pronunciation-modeling, the prior is computed by taking word frequencies or word bigram frequencies. The likelihood is computed by training a simple probabilistic model (like a confusion matrix, a decision tree, or a hand-written rule) on a database.

- The task of computing the distance between two strings comes up in spelling error correction and other problems. The **minimum edit distance** algorithm is an application of the **dynamic programming** paradigm to solving this problem, and can be used to produce the distance between two strings or an **alignment** of the two strings.

- The pronunciation of words is very variable. Pronunciation variation is caused by two classes of factors: **lexical variation** and **allophonic variation**. Lexical variation includes **sociolinguistic** factors like **dialect** and **register** or **style**.

- The single most important factor affecting allophonic variation is the identity of the surrounding phones. Other important factors include syllable structure, stress patterns, and the identity and frequency of the word.

- The **decoding** task is the problem of finding determining the correct "underlying" sequence of symbols that generated the "noisy" sequence of observation symbols.

- The **forward** algorithm is an efficient way of computing the likelihood of an observation sequence given a weighted automata. Like the **minimum edit distance** algorithm, it is a variant of dynamic programming. It will prove particularly in Chapter 7 when we consider Hidden

Markov Models, since it will allow us to sum multiple paths that each account for the same observation sequence.

- The **Viterbi** algorithm, another variant of dynamic programming, is an efficient way of solving the decoding problem by considering all possible strings and using the Bayes Rule to compute their probabilities of generating the observed "noisy" sequence.

- **Word segmentation** in languages without word-boundary markers, like Chinese and Japanese, is another kind of optimization task which can be solved by the Viterbi algorithm.

BIBLIOGRAPHICAL AND HISTORICAL NOTES

Algorithms for spelling error detection and correction have existing since at least Blair (1960). Most early algorithm were based on similarity keys like the Soundex algorithm discussed in the exercises on page 89 (Odell and Russell, 1922; Knuth, 1973). Damerau (1964) gave a dictionary-based algorithm for error detection; most error-detection algorithms since then have been based on dictionaries. Damerau also gave a correction algorithm that worked for single errors. Most algorithms since then have relied on dynamic programming, beginning with Wagner and Fischer (1974) (see below). Kukich (1992) is the definitive survey article on spelling error detection and correction. Only much later did probabilistic algorithms come into vogue for non-OCR spelling-error correction (for example Kashyap and Oommen (1983) and Kernighan et al. (1990)).

By contrast, the field of optical character recognition developed probabilistic algorithms quite early; Bledsoe and Browning (1959) developed a probabilistic approach to OCR spelling error correction that used a large dictionary and computed the likelihood of each observed letter sequence given each word in the dictionary by multiplying the likelihoods for each letter. In this sense Bledsoe and Browning also prefigured the modern Bayesian approaches to speech recognition. Shinghal and Toussaint (1979) and Hull and Srihari (1982) applied bigram letter-transition probabilities and the Viterbi algorithm to choose the most likely correct form for a misspelled OCR input.

The application of dynamic programming to the problem of sequence comparison has what Kruskal (1983) calls a "remarkable history of multiple independent discovery and publication".[7] Kruskal and others give at least the following independently-discovered variants of the algorithm published in four separate fields:

Citation	Field
Viterbi (1967)	information theory
Vintsyuk (1968)	speech processing
Needleman and Wunsch (1970)	molecular biology
Sakoe and Chiba (1971)	speech processing
Sankoff (1972)	molecular biology
Reichert et al. (1973)	molecular biology
Wagner and Fischer (1974)	computer science

To the extent that there is any standard to terminology in speech and language processing, it is the use of the term **Viterbi** for the application of dynamic programming to any kind of probabilistic maximization problem. For non-probabilistic problems, the plain term **dynamic programming** is often used. The history of the forward algorithm, which derives from Hidden Markov Models, will be summarized in Chapter 7. Sankoff and Kruskal (1983) is a collection exploring the theory and use of sequence comparison in different fields. Forney (1973) is an early survey paper which explores the origin of the Viterbi algorithm in the context of information and communications theory.

The weighted finite-state automata was first described by Pereira et al. (1994), drawing from a combination of work in finite-state transducers and work in probabilistic languages (Booth and Thompson, 1973).

EXERCISES

5.1 Computing minimum edit distances by hand, figure out whether *drive* is closer to *brief* or to *divers*, and what the edit distance is. You may use any version of *distance* that you like.

5.2 Now implement a minimum edit distance algorithm and use your hand-computed results to check your code.

---

[7] Seven is pretty remarkable, but see page 15 for a discussion of the prevalence of multiple discovery.

5.3   The Viterbi algorithm can be used to extend a simplified version of the Kernighan et al. (1990) spelling error correction algorithm. Recall that the Kernighan et al. (1990) algorithm only allowed a single spelling error for each potential correction. Let's simplify by assuming that we only have three confusion matrices instead of four (*del*, *ins* and *sub*; no *trans*). Now show how the Viterbi algorithm can be used to extend the Kernighan et al. (1990) algorithm to handle multiple spelling errors per word.

5.4   To attune your ears to pronunciation reduction, listen for the pronunciation of the word *the*, *a*, or *to* in the spoken language around you. Try to notice when it is reduced, and mark down whatever facts about the speaker or speech situation that you can. What are your observations?

5.5   Find a speaker of a different dialect of English than your own (even someone from a slightly different region of your native dialect) and transcribe (using the ARPAbet or IPA) 10 words that they pronounce differently than you. Can you spot any generalizations?

5.6   Implement the Forward algorithm.

5.7   Write a modified version of the Viterbi algorithm which solves the segmentation problem from Sproat et al. (1996).

5.8   Now imagine a version of English that was written without spaces. Apply your segmentation program to this "compressed English". You will need other programs to compute word bigrams or trigrams.

5.9   Two words are **confusable** if they have phonetically similar pronunciations. Use one of your dynamic programming implementations to take two words and output a simple measure of how confusable they are. You will need to use an on-line pronunciation dictionary. You will also need a metric for how close together two phones are. Use your favorite set of phonetic feature vectors for this. You may assume some small constant probability of phone insertion and deletion.

CONFUSABLE

6   N-GRAMS

But it must be recognized that the notion "probability of a sentence" is an entirely useless one, under any known interpretation of this term.

Noam Chomsky (1969, p. 57)

Anytime a linguist leaves the group the recognition rate goes up.
Fred Jelinek (then of the IBM speech group) (1988)[1]

Radar O'Reilly, the mild-mannered clerk of the 4077th M*A*S*H unit in the book, movie, and television show M*A*S*H, had an uncanny ability to guess what his interlocutor was about to say. Most of us don't have this skill, except perhaps when it comes to guessing the next words of songs written by very unimaginative lyricists. Or perhaps we do. For example what word is likely to follow this sentence fragment?

I'd like to make a collect...

Probably most of you concluded that a very likely word is *call*, although it's possible the next word could be *telephone*, or *person-to-person* or *international*. (Think of some others). The moral here is that guessing words is not as amazing as it seems, at least if we don't require perfect accuracy. Why is this important? Guessing the next word (or **word prediction**) is an essential subtask of speech recognition, hand-writing recognition, augmentative communication for the disabled, and spelling error detection. In

WORD PREDICTION

---

[1] In an address to the first Workshop on the Evaluation of Natural Language Processing Systems, December 7, 1988. While this workshop is described in Palmer and Finin (1990), the quote was not written down; some participants remember a more snappy version: *Every time I fire a linguist the performance of the recognizer improves.*

such tasks, word-identification is difficult because the input is very noisy and ambiguous. Thus looking at previous words can give us an important cue about what the next ones are going to be. Russell and Norvig (1995) give an example from *Take the Money and Run*, in which a bank teller interprets Woody Allen's sloppily written hold-up note as saying "I have a gub". A speech recognition system (and a person) can avoid this problem by their knowledge of word sequences ("a gub" isn't an English word sequence) and of their probabilities (especially in the context of a hold-up, "I have a gun" will have a much higher probability than "I have a gub" or even "I have a gull").

AUGMENTATIVE
COMMUNICATION
This ability to predict the next word is important for **augmentative communication** systems (Newell et al., 1998). These are computer systems that help the disabled in communication. For example, people who are unable to use speech or sign-language to communicate, like the physicist Steven Hawking, use systems that speak for them, letting them choose words with simple hand movements, either by spelling them out, or by selecting from a menu of possible words. But spelling is very slow, and a menu of words obviously can't have all possible English words on one screen. Thus it is important to be able to know which words the speaker is likely to want to use next, so as to put those on the menu.

Finally, consider the problem of detecting real-word spelling errors. These are spelling errors that result in real English words (although not the ones the writer intended) and so detecting them is difficult (we can't find them by just looking for words that aren't in the dictionary). Figure 6.1 gives some examples.

They are leaving in about fifteen *minuets* to go to her house.
The study was conducted mainly *be* John Black.
The design *an* construction of the system will take more than a year.
Hopefully, all *with* continue smoothly in my absence.
Can they *lave* him my messages?
I need to *notified* the bank of [this problem.]
He is trying to *fine* out.

Figure 6.1   Some attested real-word spelling errors from Kukich (1992).

These errors can be detected by algorithms which examine, among other features, the words surrounding the errors. For example, while the phrase *in about fifteen minuets* is perfectly grammatical English, it is a very unlikely combination of words. Spellcheckers can look for low probability combinations like this. In the examples above the probability of three word combinations (*they lave him*, *to fine out*, *to notified the*) is very low. Of course sentences with no spelling errors may also have low probability word sequences, which makes the task challenging. We will see in Section 6.6 that there are a number of different machine learning algorithms which make use of the surrounding words and other features to do **context-sensitive spelling error correction**.

Guessing the next word turns out to be closely related to another problem: computing the probability of a sequence of words. For example the following sequence of words has a non-zero probability of being encountered in a text written in English:

> ... all of a sudden I notice three guys standing on the sidewalk
> taking a very good long gander at me.

while this same set of words in a different order probably has a very low probability:

> good all I of notice a taking sidewalk the me long three at sudden
> guys gander on standing a a the very

Algorithms that assign a probability to a sentence can also be used to assign a probability to the next word in an incomplete sentence, and vice versa. We will see in later chapters that knowing the probability of whole sentences or strings of words is useful in part-of-speech-tagging (Chapter 8), word-sense disambiguation, and probabilistic parsing Chapter 12.

This model of word prediction that we will introduce in this chapter is the **N-gram**. An *N*-gram model uses the previous $N-1$ words to predict the next one. In speech recognition, it is traditional to use the term **language model** or **LM** for such statistical models of word sequences. In the rest of this chapter we will be using both **language model** and **grammar**, depending on the context.

N-GRAM

LANGUAGE MODEL

LM

6.1   COUNTING WORDS IN CORPORA

> [upon being asked if there weren't enough words in the English language for him]:
> *"Yes, there are enough, but they aren't the right ones."*
> James Joyce, reported in Bates (1997)

Probabilities are based on counting things. Before we talk about probabilities, we need to decide what we are going to count and where we are going to find the things to count.

As we saw in Chapter 5, statistical processing of natural language is
CORPORA
based on **corpora** (singular **corpus**), on-line collections of text and speech.
CORPUS
For computing word probabilities, we will be counting words in a training corpus. Let's look at part of the Brown Corpus, a 1 million word collection of samples from 500 written texts from different genres (newspaper, novels, non-fiction, academic, etc.), which was assembled at Brown University in 1963-64 (Kučera and Francis, 1967; Francis, 1979; Francis and Kučera, 1982). It contains sentence (6.1); how many words are in this sentence?

(6.1) He stepped out into the hall, was delighted to encounter a water
       brother.

Example (6.1) has 13 words if we don't count punctuation-marks as words, 15 if we count punctuation. Whether we treat period ("."), comma (","), and so on as words depends on the task. There are tasks such as grammar-checking, spelling error detection, or author-identification, for which the location of the punctuation is important (for checking for proper capitalization at the beginning of sentences, or looking for interesting patterns of punctuation usage that uniquely identify an author). In natural language processing applications, question-marks are an important cue that someone has asked a question. Punctuation is a useful cue for part-of-speech tagging. These applications, then, often count punctuation as words.

Unlike text corpora, corpora of spoken language usually don't have punctuation, but speech corpora do have other phenomena that we might or might not want to treat as words. One speech corpus, the Switchboard corpus of telephone conversations between strangers, was collected in the early 1990s and contains 2430 conversations averaging 6 minutes each, for a total of 240 hours of speech and 3 million words (Godfrey et al., 1992). Here's a sample utterance of Switchboard (since the units of spoken language are different than written language, we will use the word **utterance** rather than "sentence" when we are referring to spoken language):
UTTERANCE

(6.2) I do uh main- mainly business data processing

This utterance, like many or most utterances in spoken language, has
FRAGMENTS
fragments, words that are broken off in the middle, like the first instance
FILLED
PAUSES
of the word *mainly*, represented here as *main-*. It also has **filled pauses** like *uh*, which don't occur in written English. Should we consider these to be words? Again, it depends on the application. If we are building an automatic

dictation system based on automatic speech recognition, we might want to strip out the fragments. But the *uh*s and *um*s are in fact much more like words. For example, Smith and Clark (1993) and Clark (1994) have shown that *um* has a slightly different meaning than *uh* (generally speaking *um* is used when speakers are having major planning problems in producing an utterance, while *uh* is used when they know what they want to say, but are searching for the exact words to express it). Stolcke and Shriberg (1996b) also found that *uh* can be a useful cue in predicting the next word (why might this be?), and so most speech recognition systems treat *uh* as a word.

Are capitalized tokens like *They* and uncapitalized tokens like *they* the same word? For most statistical applications these are lumped together, although sometimes (for example for spelling error correction or part-of-speech-tagging) the capitalization is retained as a separate feature. For the rest of this chapter we will assume our models are not case-sensitive.

How should we deal with inflected forms like *cats* versus *cat*? Again, this depends on the application. Most current *N*-gram based systems are based on the **wordform**, which is the inflected form as it appears in the **WORDFORM** corpus. Thus these are treated as two separate words. This is not a good simplification for many domains, which might want to treat *cats* and *cat* as instances of a single abstract word, or **lemma**. A lemma is a set of lexical **LEMMA** forms having the same stem, the same major part-of-speech, and the same word-sense. We will return to the distinction between wordforms (which distinguish *cat* and *cats*) and lemmas (which lump *cat* and *cats* together) in Chapter 16.

How many words are there in English? One way to answer this question is to count in a corpus. We use **types** to mean the number of distinct **TYPES** words in a corpus, that is, the size of the vocabulary, and **tokens** to mean the **TOKENS** total number of running words. Thus the following sentence from the Brown corpus has 16 word tokens and 14 word types (not counting punctuation):

(6.3) They picnicked by the pool, then lay back on the grass and looked at the stars.

The Switchboard corpus has 2.4 million wordform tokens and approximately 20,000 wordform types. This includes proper nouns. Spoken language is less rich in its vocabulary than written language: Kučera (1992) gives a count for Shakespeare's complete works at 884,647 wordform tokens from 29,066 wordform types. Thus each of the 884,647 wordform tokens is a repetition of one of the 29,066 wordform types. The 1 million wordform tokens of the Brown corpus contain 61,805 wordform types that belong to

37,851 lemma types. All these corpora are quite small. Brown et al. (1992) amassed a corpus of 583 million wordform tokens of English that included 293,181 different wordform types.

Dictionaries are another way to get an estimate of the number of words, although since dictionaries generally do not include inflected forms they are better at measuring lemmas than wordforms. The American Heritage third edition dictionary has 200,000 "boldface forms"; this is somewhat higher than the true number of lemmas, since there can be one or more boldface form per lemma (and since the boldface forms includes multiword phrases).

The rest of this chapter will continue to distinguish between types and tokens. "Types" will mean wordform types and not lemma types, and punctuation marks will generally be counted as words.

6.2   SIMPLE (UNSMOOTHED) N-GRAMS

The models of word sequences we will consider in this chapter are probabilistic models; ways to assign probabilities to strings of words, whether for computing the probability of an entire sentence or for giving a probabilistic prediction of what the next word will be in a sequence. As we did in Chapter 5, we will assume that the reader has a basic knowledge of probability theory.

The simplest possible model of word sequences would simply let any word of the language follow any other word. In the probabilistic version of this theory, then, every word would have an equal probability of following every other word. If English had 100,000 words, the probability of any word following any other word would be $\frac{1}{100,000}$ or .00001.

In a slightly more complex model of word sequences, any word could follow any other word, but the following word would appear with its normal frequency of occurrence. For example, the word *the* has a high relative frequency, it occurs 69,971 times in the Brown corpus of 1,000,000 words (i.e., 7% of the words in this particular corpus are *the*). By contrast the word *rabbit* occurs only 11 times in the Brown corpus.

We can use these relative frequencies to assign a probability distribution across following words. So if we've just seen the string *Anyhow,* we can use the probability .07 for *the* and .00001 for *rabbit* to guess the next word. But suppose we've just seen the following string:

Just then, the white

In this context *rabbit* seems like a more reasonable word to follow *white* than *the* does. This suggests that instead of just looking at the individual relative frequencies of words, we should look at the conditional probability of a word given the previous words. That is, the probability of seeing *rabbit* given that we just saw *white* (which we will represent as $P(rabbit|white)$) is higher than the probability of *rabbit* otherwise.

Given this intuition, let's look at how to compute the probability of a complete string of words (which we can represent either as $w_1 \ldots w_n$ or w_1^n). If we consider each word occurring in its correct location as an independent event, we might represent this probability as follows:

$$P(w_1, w_2 \ldots, w_{n-1}, w_n) \tag{6.4}$$

We can use the chain rule of probability to decompose this probability:

$$
\begin{aligned}
P(w_1^n) &= P(w_1)P(w_2|w_1)P(w_3|w_1^2)\ldots P(w_n|w_1^{n-1}) \\
&= \prod_{k=1}^{n} P(w_k|w_1^{k-1})
\end{aligned}
\tag{6.5}
$$

But how can we compute probabilities like $P(w_n|w_1^{n-1})$? We don't know any easy way to compute the probability of a word given a long sequence of preceding words. (For example, we can't just count the number of times every word occurs following every long string; we would need far too large a corpus).

We solve this problem by making a useful simplification: we *approximate* the probability of a word given all the previous words. The approximation we will use is very simple: the probability of the word given the single previous word! The **bigram** model approximates the probability of a word   BIGRAM given all the previous words $P(w_n|w_1^{n-1})$ by the conditional probability of the preceding word $P(w_n|w_{n-1})$. In other words, instead of computing the probability

$$P(\text{rabbit}|\text{Just the other I day I saw a}) \tag{6.6}$$

we approximate it with the probability

$$P(\text{rabbit}|\text{a}) \tag{6.7}$$

This assumption that the probability of a word depends only on the previous word is called a **Markov** assumption. Markov models are the class   MARKOV of probabilistic models that assume that we can predict the probability of some future unit without looking too far into the past. We saw this use of the word **Markov** in introducing the **Markov chain** in Chapter 5. Recall that a

Markov chain is a kind of weighted finite-state automaton; the intuition of the term Markov in Markov chain is that the next state of a weighted FSA is always dependent on a finite history (since the number of states in a finite-state automaton is finite). The basic bigram model can be viewed as a simple kind of Markov chain which has one state for each word.

N-GRAM

FIRST-ORDER

SECOND-ORDER

We can generalize the bigram (which looks one word into the past) to the trigram (which looks two words into the past) and thus to the **N-gram** (which looks $N - 1$ words into the past). A bigram is called a **first-order** Markov model (because it looks one token into the past), a trigram is a **second-order** Markov model, and in general an N-gram is a $N - 1$th order Markov model. Markov models of words were common in engineering, psychology, and linguistics until Chomsky's influential review of Skinner's *Verbal Behavior* in 1958 (see the History section at the back of the chapter), but went out of vogue until the success of N-gram models in the IBM speech recognition laboratory at the Thomas J. Watson Research Center. brought them back to the attention of the community.

The general equation for this N-gram approximation to the conditional probability of the next word in a sequence is:

$$P(w_n|w_1^{n-1}) \approx P(w_n|w_{n-N+1}^{n-1}) \tag{6.8}$$

Equation 6.8 shows that the probability of a word w_n given all the previous words can be approximated by the probability given only the previous N words.

For a bigram grammar, then, we compute the probability of a complete string by substituting Equation (6.8) into Equation (6.5). The result:

$$P(w_1^n) \approx \prod_{k=1}^{n} P(w_k|w_{k-1}) \tag{6.9}$$

Let's look at an example from a speech-understanding system. The Berkeley Restaurant Project is a speech-based restaurant consultant; users ask questions about restaurants in Berkeley, California, and the system displays appropriate information from a database of local restaurants (Jurafsky et al., 1994). Here are some sample user queries:

I'm looking for Cantonese food.
I'd like to eat dinner someplace nearby.
Tell me about Chez Panisse.
Can you give me a listing of the kinds of food that are available?
I'm looking for a good place to eat breakfast.
I definitely do not want to have cheap Chinese food.

When is Caffe Venezia open during the day?

I don't wanna walk more than ten minutes.

Table 6.2 shows a sample of the bigram probabilities for some of the words that can follow the word *eat*, taken from actual sentences spoken by users (putting off just for now the algorithm for training bigram probabilities). Note that these probabilities encode some facts that we think of as strictly syntactic in nature (like the fact that what comes after *eat* is usually something that begins a noun phrase, that is, an adjective, quantifier or noun), as well as facts that we think of as more culturally based (like the low probability of anyone asking for advice on finding British food).

eat on	.16	eat Thai	.03
eat some	.06	eat breakfast	.03
eat lunch	.06	eat in	.02
eat dinner	.05	eat Chinese	.02
eat at	.04	eat Mexican	.02
eat a	.04	eat tomorrow	.01
eat Indian	.04	eat dessert	.007
eat today	.03	eat British	.001

Figure 6.2   A fragment of a bigram grammar from the Berkeley Restaurant Project showing the most likely words to follow *eat*.

Assume that in addition to the probabilities in Table 6.2, our grammar also includes the bigram probabilities in Table 6.3 (<s> is a special word meaning "Start of sentence").

<s> I	.25	I want	.32	want to	.65	to eat	.26	British food	.60
<s> I'd	.06	I would	.29	want a	.05	to have	.14	British restaurant	.15
<s> Tell	.04	I don't	.08	want some	.04	to spend	.09	British cuisine	.01
<s> I'm	.02	I have	.04	want thai	.01	to be	.02	British lunch	.01

Figure 6.3   More fragments from the bigram grammar from the Berkeley Restaurant Project.

Now we can compute the probability of sentences like *I want to eat British food* or *I want to eat Chinese food* by simply multiplying the appropriate bigram probabilities together, as follows:

$$P(\text{I want to eat British food}) = P(\text{I}|\text{<s>})P(\text{want}|\text{I})P(\text{to}|\text{want})$$
$$P(\text{eat}|\text{to})P(\text{British}|\text{eat})$$
$$P(\text{food}|\text{British})$$

$$= .25 * .32 * .65 * .26 * .002 * .60$$
$$= .000016$$

As we can see, since probabilities are all less than 1 (by definition), the product of many probabilities gets smaller the more probabilities we multiply. This causes a practical problem: the risk of numerical underflow. If we are computing the probability of a very long string (like a paragraph or an entire document) it is more customary to do the computation in log space; we LOGPROB take the log of each probability (the **logprob**), add all the logs (since adding in log space is equivalent to multiplying in linear space) and then take the anti-log of the result. For this reason many standard programs for computing N-grams actually store and calculate all probabilities as logprobs. In this text we will always report logs in base 2 (i.e., we will use log to mean $\log_2$).

TRIGRAM   A **trigram** model looks just the same as a bigram model, except that we condition on the two previous words (e.g., we use $P(food|eat\ British)$ instead of $P(food|British))$. To compute trigram probabilities at the very beginning of sentence, we can use two pseudo-words for the first trigram (i.e., $P(I| < start1 >< start2 >))$.

NORMALIZING N-gram models can be trained by counting and **normalizing** (for probabilistic models, normalizing means dividing by some total count so that the resulting probabilities fall legally between 0 and 1). We take some training corpus, and from this corpus take the count of a particular bigram, and divide this count by the sum of all the bigrams that share the same first word:

$$P(w_n|w_{n-1}) = \frac{C(w_{n-1}w_n)}{\sum_w C(w_{n-1}w)} \tag{6.10}$$

We can simplify this equation, since the sum of all bigram counts that start with a given word w_{n-1} must be equal to the unigram count for that word w_{n-1}. (The reader should take a moment to be convinced of this):

$$P(w_n|w_{n-1}) = \frac{C(w_{n-1}w_n)}{C(w_{n-1})} \tag{6.11}$$

For the general case of N-gram parameter estimation:

$$P(w_n|w_{n-N+1}^{n-1}) = \frac{C(w_{n-N+1}^{n-1}w_n)}{C(w_{n-N+1}^{n-1})} \tag{6.12}$$

Equation 6.12 estimates the N-gram probability by dividing the observed frequency of a particular sequence by the observed frequency of a RELATIVE FREQUENCY prefix. This ratio is called a **relative frequency**; the use of relative frequencies as a way to estimate probabilities is one example of the technique MAXIMUM LIKELIHOOD ESTIMATION known as **Maximum Likelihood Estimation** or **MLE**, because the resulting MLE parameter set is one in which the likelihood of the training set T given the model M (i.e., $P(T|M)$) is maximized. For example, suppose the word *Chinese* occurs 400 times in a corpus of a million words like the Brown corpus. What is the probability that it will occur in some other text of way a million words? The MLE estimate of its probability is $\frac{400}{1000000}$ or .0004. Now .0004 is not the best possible estimate of the probability of *Chinese* occurring in all situations; but it is the probability that makes it *most likely* that Chinese will occur 400 times in a million-word corpus.

There are better methods of estimating N-gram probabilities than using relative frequencies (we will consider a class of important algorithms in Section 6.3), but even the more sophisticated algorithms make use in some way of this idea of relative frequency. Figure 6.4 shows the bigram counts from a piece of a bigram grammar from the Berkeley Restaurant Project. Note that the majority of the values are zero. In fact, we have chosen the sample words to cohere with each other; a matrix selected from a random set of seven words would be even more sparse.

	I	want	to	eat	Chinese	food	lunch
I	8	1087	0	13	0	0	0
want	3	0	786	0	6	8	6
to	3	0	10	860	3	0	12
eat	0	0	2	0	19	2	52
Chinese	2	0	0	0	0	120	1
food	19	0	17	0	0	0	0
lunch	4	0	0	0	0	1	0

Figure 6.4   Bigram counts for seven of the words (out of 1616 total word types) in the Berkeley Restaurant Project corpus of ≈10,000 sentences.

Figure 6.5 shows the bigram probabilities after normalization (dividing each row by the following appropriate unigram counts):

I	3437
want	1215
to	3256
eat	938
Chinese	213
food	1506
lunch	459

	I	want	to	eat	Chinese	food	lunch
I	.0023	.32	0	.0038	0	0	0
want	.0025	0	.65	0	.0049	.0066	.0049
to	.00092	0	.0031	.26	.00092	0	.0037
eat	0	0	.0021	0	.020	.0021	.055
Chinese	.0094	0	0	0	0	.56	.0047
food	.013	0	.011	0	0	0	0
lunch	.0087	0	0	0	0	.0022	0

Figure 6.5   Bigram probabilities for seven of the words (out of 1616 total word types) in the Berkeley Restaurant Project corpus of $\approx$10,000 sentences.

More on N-grams and Their Sensitivity to the Training Corpus

In this section we look at a few examples of different N-gram models to get an intuition for two important facts about their behavior. The first is the increasing accuracy of N-gram models as we increase the value of N. The second is their very strong dependency on their training corpus (in particular its genre and its size in words).

We do this by borrowing a visualization technique proposed by Shannon (1951) and also used by Miller and Selfridge (1950). The idea is to train various N-grams and then use each to generate random sentences. It's simplest to visualize how this works for the unigram case. Imagine all the words of English covering the probability space between 0 and 1. We choose a random number between 0 and 1, and print out the word that covers the real value we have chosen. The same technique can be used to generate higher order N-grams by first generating a random bigram that starts with <s> (according to its bigram probability), then choosing a random bigram to follow it (again, where the likelihood of following a particular bigram is proportional to its conditional probability), and so on.

To give an intuition for the increasing power of higher order N-grams, we trained a unigram, bigram, trigram, and a quadrigram model on the complete corpus of Shakespeare's works. We then used these four grammars to generate random sentences. In the following examples we treated each punctuation mark as if it were a word in its own right, and we trained the grammars on a version of the corpus with all capital letters changed to lowercase. After generated the sentences we corrected the output for capitalization just to improve readability. Some of the resulting sentences:

1. Unigram approximation to Shakespeare

(a) To him swallowed confess hear both. Which. Of save on trail for are ay device and rote life have

(b) Every enter now severally so, let

(c) Hill he late speaks; or! a more to leg less first you enter

(d) Will rash been and by I the me loves gentle me not slavish page, the and hour; ill let

(e) Are where exeunt and sighs have rise excellency took of.. Sleep knave we. near; vile like

2. Bigram approximation to Shakespeare

(a) What means, sir. I confess she? then all sorts, he is trim, captain.

(b) Why dost stand forth thy canopy, forsooth; he is this palpable hit the King Henry. Live king. Follow.

(c) What we, hath got so she that I rest and sent to scold and nature bankrupt, nor the first gentleman?

(d) Enter Menenius, if it so many good direction found'st thou art a strong upon command of fear not a liberal largess given away, Falstaff! Exeunt

(e) Thou whoreson chops. Consumption catch your dearest friend, well, and I know where many mouths upon my undoing all but be, how soon, then; we'll execute upon my love's bonds and we do you will?

(f) The world shall- my lord!

3. Trigram approximation to Shakespeare

(a) Sweet prince, Falstaff shall die. Harry of Monmouth's grave.

(b) This shall forbid it should be branded, if renown made it empty.

(c) What is't that cried?

(d) Indeed the duke; and had a very good friend.

(e) Fly, and will rid me these news of price. Therefore the sadness of parting, as they say, 'tis done.

(f) The sweet! How many then shall posthumus end his miseries.

4. Quadrigram approximation to Shakespeare

(a) King Henry. What! I will go seek the traitor Gloucester. Exeunt some of the watch. A great banquet serv'd in;

(b) Will you not tell me who I am?

(c) It cannot be but so.

(d) Indeed the short and the long. Marry, 'tis a noble Lepidus.

(e) They say all lovers swear more performance than they are wont to keep obliged faith unforfeited!

(f) Enter Leonato's brother Antonio, and the rest, but seek the weary beds of people sick.

METHODOLOGY BOX: TRAINING SETS AND TEST SETS

The probabilities in a statistical model like an N-gram come from the corpus it is trained on. This **training corpus** needs to be carefully designed. If the training corpus is too specific to the task or domain, the probabilities may be too narrow and not generalize well to new sentences. If the training corpus is too general, the probabilities may not do a sufficient job of reflecting the task or domain.

Furthermore, suppose we are trying to compute the probability of a particular "test" sentence. If our "'test' sentence is part of the training corpus, it will have an artificially high probability. The training corpus must not be biased by including this sentence. Thus when using a statistical model of language given some corpus of relevant data, we start by dividing the data into a **training set** and a **test set**. We train the statistical parameters of the model on the training set, and then use them to compute probabilities on the test set.

This training-and-testing paradigm can also be used to **evaluate** different N-gram architectures. For example to compare the different **smoothing** algorithms we will introduce in Section 6.3, we can take a large corpus and divide it into a training set and a test set. Then we train the two different N-gram models on the training set and see which one better models the test set. But what does it mean to "model the test set"? There is a useful metric for how well a given statistical model matches a test corpus, called **perplexity**. Perplexity is a variant of **entropy**, and will be introduced on page 223.

In some cases we need more than one test set. For example, suppose we have a few different possible language models and we want first to pick the best one and then to see how it does on a fair test set, that is, one we've never looked at before. We first use a **development test set** (also called a **devtest** set) to pick the best language model, and perhaps tune some parameters. Then once we come up with what we think is the best model, we run it on the true test set.

When comparing models it is important to use statistical tests (introduced in any statistics class or textbook for the social sciences) to determine if the difference between two models is significant. Cohen (1995) is a useful reference which focuses on statistical research methods for artificial intelligence. Dietterich (1998) focuses on statistical tests for comparing classifiers.

The longer the context on which we train the model, the more coherent the sentences. In the unigram sentences, there is no coherent relation between words, and in fact none of the sentences end in a period or other sentence-final punctuation. The bigram sentences can be seen to have very local word-to-word coherence (especially if we consider that punctuation counts as a word). The trigram and quadrigram sentences are beginning to look a lot like Shakespeare. Indeed a careful investigation of the quadrigram sentences shows that they look a little too much like Shakespeare. The words *It cannot be but so* are directly from *King John*. This is because the Shakespeare oeuvre, while large by many standards, is somewhat less than a million words. Recall that Kučera (1992) gives a count for Shakespeare's complete works at 884,647 words (tokens) from 29,066 wordform types (including proper nouns). That means that even the bigram model is very sparse; with $29,066$ types, there are $29,066^2$, or more than 844 million possible bigrams, so a 1 million word training set is clearly vastly insufficient to estimate the frequency of the rarer ones; indeed somewhat under 300,000 different bigram types actually occur in Shakespeare. This is far too small to train quadrigrams; thus once the generator has chosen the first quadrigram (*It cannot be but*), there are only five possible continuations (*that, I, he, thou,* and *so*); indeed for many quadrigrams there is only one continuation.

To get an idea of the dependence of a grammar on its training set, let's look at an *N*-gram grammar trained on a completely different corpus: the Wall Street Journal (WSJ). A native speaker of English is capable of reading both Shakespeare and the Wall Street Journal; both are subsets of English. Thus it seems intuitive that our *N*-grams for Shakespeare should have some overlap with *N*-grams from the Wall Street Journal. In order to check whether this is true, here are three sentences generated by unigram, bigram, and trigram grammars trained on 40 million words of articles from the daily Wall Street Journal (these grammars are Katz backoff grammars with Good-Turing smoothing; we will learn in the next section how these are constructed). Again, we have corrected the output by hand with the proper English capitalization for readability.

1. (*unigram*) Months the my and issue of year foreign new exchange's september were recession exchange new endorsed a acquire to six executives

2. (*bigram*) Last December through the way to preserve the Hudson corporation N. B. E. C. Taylor would seem to complete the major central planners one point five percent of U. S. E. has already old M. X. corporation of living on information such as more frequently fishing to keep

her

3. (*trigram*) They also point to ninety nine point six billion dollars from two hundred four oh six three percent of the rates of interest stores as Mexico and Brazil on market conditions

Compare these examples to the pseudo-Shakespeare on the previous page; while superficially they both seem to model "English-like sentences" there is obviously no overlap whatsoever in possible sentences, and very little if any overlap even in small phrases. The difference between the Shakespeare and WSJ corpora tell us that a good statistical approximation to English will have to involve a very large corpus with a very large cross-section of different genres. Even then a simple statistical model like an *N*-gram would be incapable of modeling the consistency of style across genres. (We would only want to expect Shakespearean sentences when we are reading Shakespeare, not in the middle of a Wall Street Journal article.)

6.3   SMOOTHING

Never do I ever want
to hear another word!
There isn't one,
I haven't heard!
    Eliza   Doolittle   in
    Alan Jay Lerner's *My*
    Fair Lady lyrics

words people
never use —
could be
only I
know them
Ishikawa Takuboku 1885–1912

One major problem with standard *N*-gram models is that they must be trained from some corpus, and because any particular training corpus is finite, some perfectly acceptable English *N*-grams are bound to be missing SPARSE from it. That is, the bigram matrix for any given training corpus is **sparse**; it is bound to have a very large number of cases of putative "zero probability bigrams" that should really have some non-zero probability. Furthermore, the MLE method also produces poor estimates when the counts are non-zero but still small.

Some part of this problem is endemic to N-grams; since they can't use long-distance context, they always tend to underestimate the probability of strings that happen not to have occurred nearby in their training corpus. But there are some techniques we can use to assign a non-zero probability to these "zero probability bigrams". This task of reevaluating some of the zero-probability and low-probability N-grams, and assigning them non-zero values, is called **smoothing**. In the next few sections we will introduce some smoothing algorithms and show how they modify the Berkeley Restaurant bigram probabilities in Figure 6.5.

SMOOTHING

Add-One Smoothing

One simple way to do smoothing might be just to take our matrix of bigram counts, before we normalize them into probabilities, and add one to all the counts. This algorithm is called **add-one** smoothing. Although this algorithm does not perform well and is not commonly used, it introduces many of the concepts that we will see in other smoothing algorithms, and also gives us a useful baseline.

ADD-ONE

Let's first consider the application of add-one smoothing to unigram probabilities, since that will be simpler. The unsmoothed maximum likelihood estimate of the unigram probability can be computed by dividing the count of the word by the total number of word tokens N:

$$
\begin{aligned}
P(w_x) &= \frac{c(w_x)}{\sum_i c(w_i)} \\
&= \frac{c(w_x)}{N}
\end{aligned}
$$

The various smoothing estimates will rely on an adjusted count c^*. The count adjustment for add-one smoothing can then be defined by adding one to the count and then multiplying by a normalization factor, $\frac{N}{N+V}$, where V is the total number of word types in the language, that is, the **vocabulary size**. Since we are adding 1 to the count for each word type, the total number of tokens must be increased by the number of types. The adjusted count for add-one smoothing is then defined as:

VOCABULARY SIZE

$$
c_i^* = (c_i + 1)\frac{N}{N+V} \tag{6.13}
$$

and the counts can be turned into probabilities p_i^* by normalizing by N.

An alternative way to view a smoothing algorithm is as **discounting** (lowering) some non-zero counts in order to get the probability mass that will be assigned to the zero counts. Thus instead of referring to the discounted counts c^*, many papers also define smoothing algorithms in terms of a **discount** d_c, the ratio of the discounted counts to the original counts:

$$d_c = \frac{c^*}{c}$$

Alternatively, we can compute the probability p_i^* directly from the counts as follows:

$$p_i^* = \frac{c_i + 1}{N + V}$$

Now that we have the intuition for the unigram case, let's smooth our Berkeley Restaurant Project bigram. Figure 6.6 shows the add-one-smoothed counts for the bigram in Figure 6.4.

	I	want	to	eat	Chinese	food	lunch
I	9	1088	1	14	1	1	1
want	4	1	787	1	7	9	7
to	4	1	11	861	4	1	13
eat	1	1	3	1	20	3	53
Chinese	3	1	1	1	1	121	2
food	20	1	18	1	1	1	1
lunch	5	1	1	1	1	2	1

Figure 6.6   Add-one Smoothed Bigram counts for seven of the words (out of 1616 total word types) in the Berkeley Restaurant Project corpus of ≈10,000 sentences.

Figure 6.7 shows the add-one-smoothed probabilities for the bigram in Figure 6.5. Recall that normal bigram probabilities are computed by normalizing each row of counts by the unigram count:

$$P(w_n|w_{n-1}) = \frac{C(w_{n-1}w_n)}{C(w_{n-1})} \tag{6.14}$$

For add-one-smoothed bigram counts we need to first augment the unigram count by the number of total word types in the vocabulary V:

$$p^*(w_n|w_{n-1}) = \frac{C(w_{n-1}w_n) + 1}{C(w_{n-1}) + V} \tag{6.15}$$

We need to add V (= 1616) to each of the unigram counts:

I	3437+1616	= 5053
want	1215+1616	= 2931
to	3256+1616	= 4872
eat	938+1616	= 2554
Chinese	213+1616	= 1829
food	1506+1616	= 3122
lunch	459+1616	= 2075

The result is the smoothed bigram probabilities in Figure 6.7.

	I	want	to	eat	Chinese	food	lunch
I	.0018	.22	.00020	.0028	.00020	.00020	.00020
want	.0014	.00035	.28	.00035	.0025	.0032	.0025
to	.00082	.00021	.0023	.18	.00082	.00021	.0027
eat	.00039	.00039	.0012	.00039	.0078	.0012	.021
Chinese	.0016	.00055	.00055	.00055	.00055	.066	.0011
food	.0064	.00032	.0058	.00032	.00032	.00032	.00032
lunch	.0024	.00048	.00048	.00048	.00048	.00096	.00048

Figure 6.7   Add-one smoothed bigram probabilities for seven of the words (out of 1616 total word types) in the Berkeley Restaurant Project corpus of $\approx$10,000 sentences.

It is often convenient to reconstruct the count matrix so we can see how much a smoothing algorithm has changed the original counts. These adjusted counts can be computed by Equation (6.13). Figure 6.8 shows the reconstructed counts.

Note that add-one smoothing has made a very big change to the counts. $C(want\ to)$ changed from 786 to 331! We can see this in probability space as well: $P(to|want)$ decreases from .65 in the unsmoothed case to .28 in the smoothed case.

Looking at the discount d (the ratio between new and old counts) shows us how strikingly the counts for each prefix-word have been reduced; the bigrams starting with *Chinese* were discounted by a factor of 8!

	I	want	to	eat	Chinese	food	lunch
I	6	740	.68	10	.68	.68	.68
want	2	.42	331	.42	3	4	3
to	3	.69	8	594	3	.69	9
eat	.37	.37	1	.37	7.4	1	20
Chinese	.36	.12	.12	.12	.12	15	.24
food	10	.48	9	.48	.48	.48	.48
lunch	1.1	.22	.22	.22	.22	.44	.22

Figure 6.8   Add-one smoothed bigram counts for seven of the words (out of 1616 total word types) in the Berkeley Restaurant Project Corpus of $\approx$10,000 sentences.

I	.68
want	.42
to	.69
eat	.37
Chinese	.12
food	.48
lunch	.22

The sharp change in counts and probabilities occurs because too much probability mass is moved to all the zeros. The problem is that we arbitrarily picked the value "1" to add to each count. We could avoid this problem by adding smaller values to the counts ("add-one-half" "add-one-thousandth"), but we would need to retrain this parameter for each situation.

In general add-one smoothing is a poor method of smoothing. Gale and Church (1994) summarize a number of additional problems with the add-one method; the main problem is that add-one is much worse at predicting the actual probability for bigrams with zero counts than other methods like the Good-Turing method we will describe below. Furthermore, they show that variances of the counts produced by the add-one method are actually worse than those from the unsmoothed MLE method.

Witten-Bell Discounting

WITTEN-BELL
DISCOUNTING
A much better smoothing algorithm that is only slightly more complex than Add-One smoothing we will refer to as **Witten-Bell discounting** (it is introduced as Method C in Witten and Bell (1991)). Witten-Bell discounting is based on a simple but clever intuition about zero-frequency events. Let's think of a zero-frequency word or N-gram as one that just hasn't happened

yet. When it does happen, it will be the first time we see this new N-gram. So the probability of seeing a zero-frequency N-gram can be modeled by the probability of seeing an N-gram for the first time. This is a recurring concept in statistical language processing:

> **Key Concept #4. Things Seen Once:** Use the count of things you've seen once to help estimate the count of things you've never seen.

The idea that we can estimate the probability of "things we never saw" with help from the count of "things we saw once" will return when we discuss Good-Turing smoothing later in this chapter, and then once again when we discuss methods for tagging an unknown word with a part-of-speech in Chapter 8.

How can we compute the probability of seeing an N-gram for the first time? By counting the number of times we saw N-grams for the first time in our training corpus. This is very simple to produce since the count of "first-time" N-grams is just the number of N-gram *types* we saw in the data (since we had to see each type for the first time exactly once).

So we estimate the *total* probability mass of all the zero N-grams with the number of types divided by the number of tokens plus observed types:

$$\sum_{i:c_i=0} p_i^* = \frac{T}{N+T} \tag{6.16}$$

Why do we normalize by the number of tokens plus types? We can think of our training corpus as a series of events; one event for each token and one event for each new type. So Equation 6.16 gives the Maximum Likelihood Estimate of the probability of a new type event occurring. Note that the number of observed types T is different than the "total types" or "vocabulary size V" that we used in add-one smoothing: T is the types we have already seen, while V is the total number of possible types we might ever see.

Equation 6.16 gives the total "probability of unseen N-grams". We need to divide this up among all the zero N-grams. We could just choose to divide it equally. Let Z be the total number of N-grams with count zero (types; there aren't any tokens). Each formerly-zero unigram now gets its equal share of the redistributed probability mass:

$$Z = \sum_{i:c_i=0} 1 \tag{6.17}$$

$$p_i^* = \frac{T}{Z(N+T)} \tag{6.18}$$

If the total probability of zero N-grams is computed from Equation (6.16), the extra probability mass must come from somewhere; we get it by discounting the probability of all the seen N-grams as follows:

$$p_i^* = \frac{c_i}{N+T}\text{if } (c_i > 0) \tag{6.19}$$

Alternatively, we can represent the smoothed counts directly as:

$$c_i^* = \begin{cases} \frac{T}{Z}\frac{N}{N+T}, & \text{if } c_i = 0 \\ c_i\frac{N}{N+T}, & \text{if } c_i > 0 \end{cases} \tag{6.20}$$

Witten-Bell discounting looks a lot like add-one smoothing for unigrams. But if we extend the equation to bigrams we will see a big difference. This is because now our type-counts are conditioned on some history. In order to compute the probability of a bigram $w_{n-1}w_{n-2}$ we haven't seen, we use "the probability of seeing a new bigram starting with w_{n-1}". This lets our estimate of "first-time bigrams" be specific to a word history. Words that tend to occur in a smaller number of bigrams will supply a lower "unseen-bigram" estimate than words that are more promiscuous.

We represent this fact by conditioning T, the number of bigram types, and N, the number of bigram tokens, on the previous word w_x, as follows:

$$\sum_{i:c(w_xw_i)=0} p^*(w_i|w_x) = \frac{T(w_x)}{N(w_x) + T(w_x)} \tag{6.21}$$

Again, we will need to distribute this probability mass among all the unseen bigrams. Let Z again be the total number of bigrams with a given first word that have count zero (types; there aren't any tokens). Each formerly zero bigram now gets its equal share of the redistributed probability mass:

$$Z(w_x) = \sum_{i:c(w_xw_i)=0} 1 \tag{6.22}$$

$$p^*(w_i|w_{i-1}) = \frac{T(w_{i-1})}{Z(w_{i-1})(N+T(w_{i-1}))} \text{ if } (c_{w_{i-1}w_i} = 0) \tag{6.23}$$

As for the non-zero bigrams, we discount them in the same manner, by parameterizing T on the history:

$$\sum_{i:c(w_xw_i)>0} p^*(w_i|w_x) = \frac{c(w_xw_i)}{c(w_x) + T(w_x)} \tag{6.24}$$

To use Equation 6.24 to smooth the restaurant bigram from Figure 6.5, we will need the number of bigram types $T(w)$ for each of the first words. Here are those values:

I	95
want	76
to	130
eat	124
Chinese	20
food	82
lunch	45

In addition we will need the Z values for each of these words. Since we know how many words we have in the vocabulary ($V = 1,616$), there are exactly V possible bigrams that begin with a given word w, so the number of unseen bigram types with a given prefix is V minus the number of observed types:

$$Z(w) = V - T(w) \qquad (6.25)$$

Here are those Z values:

I	1,521
want	1,540
to	1,486
eat	1,492
Chinese	1,596
food	1,534
lunch	1,571

Figure 6.9 shows the discounted restaurant bigram counts.

	I	want	to	eat	Chinese	food	lunch
I	8	1060	.062	13	.062	.062	.062
want	3	.046	740	.046	6	8	6
to	3	.085	10	827	3	.085	12
eat	.075	.075	2	.075	17	2	46
Chinese	2	.012	.012	.012	.012	109	1
food	18	.059	16	.059	.059	.059	.059
lunch	4	.026	.026	.026	.026	1	.026

Figure 6.9   Witten-Bell smoothed bigram counts for seven of the words (out of 1616 total word types) in the Berkeley Restaurant Project corpus of $\approx$10,000 sentences.

The discount values for the Witten-Bell algorithm are much more reasonable than for add-one smoothing:

I   .97
want   .94
to   .96
eat   .88
Chinese .91
food   .94
lunch   .91

It is also possible to use Witten-Bell (or other) discounting in a different way. In Equation (6.21), we conditioned the smoothed bigram probabilities on the previous word. That is, we conditioned the number of types $T(w_x)$ and tokens $N(w_x)$ on the previous word w_x. But we could choose instead to treat a bigram as if it were a single event, ignoring the fact that it is composed of two words. Then T would be the number of types of *all* bigrams, and N would be the number of tokens of *all* bigrams that occurred. Treating the bigrams as a unit in this way, we are essentially discounting, not the conditional probability $P(w_i|w_x)$, but the **joint probability** $P(w_x w_i)$. In this way the probability $P(w_x w_i)$ is treated just like a unigram probability. This kind of discounting is less commonly used than the "conditional" discounting we walked through above starting with Equation 6.21. (Although it is often used for the Good-Turing discounting algorithm described below).

JOINT
PROBABILITY

In Section 6.4 we show that discounting also plays a role in more sophisticated language models. Witten-Bell discounting is commonly used in speech recognition systems such as Placeway et al. (1993).

Good-Turing Discounting

GOOD-
TURING

This section introduces a slightly more complex form of discounting than the Witten-Bell algorithm called **Good-Turing** smoothing. This section may be skipped by readers who are not focusing on discounting algorithms.

The Good-Turing algorithm was first described by Good (1953), who credits Turing with the original idea; a complete proof is presented in Church et al. (1991). The basic insight of Good-Turing smoothing is to re-estimate the amount of probability mass to assign to N-grams with zero or low counts by looking at the number of N-grams with higher counts. In other words, we examine N_c, the number of N-grams that occur c times. We refer to the number of N-grams that occur c times as the frequency of frequency c. So applying the idea to smoothing the joint probability of bigrams, N_0 is the number of bigrams b of count 0, N_1 the number of bigrams with count 1, and so on:

$$N_c = \sum_{b:c(b)=c} 1 \tag{6.26}$$

The Good-Turing estimate gives a smoothed count c^* based on the set of N_c for all c, as follows:

$$c^* = (c+1)\frac{N_{c+1}}{N_c} \tag{6.27}$$

For example, the revised count for the bigrams that never occurred (c_0) is estimating by dividing the number of bigrams that occurred once (the **singleton** or **hapax legomenon** bigrams N_1) by the number of bigrams that never occurred (N_0). Using the count of things we've seen once to estimate the count of things we've never seen should remind you of the Witten-Bell discounting algorithm we saw earlier in this chapter. The Good-Turing algorithm was first applied to the smoothing of N-gram grammars by Katz, as cited in Nádas (1984). Figure 6.10 gives an example of the application of Good-Turing discounting to a bigram grammar computed by Church and Gale (1991) from 22 million words from the Associated Press (AP) newswire. The first column shows the count c, i.e., the number of observed instances of a bigram. The second column shows the number of bigrams that had this count. Thus 449,721 bigrams has a count of 2. The third column shows c^*, the Good-Turing re-estimation of the count.

SINGLETON

c (MLE)	N_c	c^* (GT)
0	74,671,100,000	0.0000270
1	2,018,046	0.446
2	449,721	1.26
3	188,933	2.24
4	105,668	3.24
5	68,379	4.22
6	48,190	5.19
7	35,709	6.21
8	27,710	7.24
9	22,280	8.25

Figure 6.10   Bigram "frequencies of frequencies" from 22 million AP bigrams, and Good-Turing re-estimations after Church and Gale (1991).

Church et al. (1991) show that the Good-Turing estimate relies on the assumption that the distribution of each bigram is binomial. The estimate also assumes we know N_0, the number of bigrams we haven't seen. We know this because given a vocabulary size of V, the total number of bigrams is V^2. (N_0 is V^2 minus all the bigrams we have seen).

In practice, this discounted estimate c^* is not used for all counts c. Large counts (where $c > k$ for some threshold k) are assumed to be reliable. Katz (1987) suggests setting k at 5. Thus we define

$$c^* = c \ \text{ for } c > k \tag{6.28}$$

The correct equation for c^* when some k is introduced (from Katz (1987)) is:

$$c^* = \frac{(c+1)\frac{N_{c+1}}{N_c} - c\frac{(k+1)N_{k+1}}{N_1}}{1 - \frac{(k+1)N_{k+1}}{N_1}}, \ \text{ for } 1 \le c \le k. \tag{6.29}$$

With Good-Turing discounting as with any other, it is usual to treat N-grams with low counts (especially counts of 1) as if the count was 0.

6.4   BACKOFF

The discounting we have been discussing so far can help solve the problem of zero frequency n-grams. But there is an additional source of knowledge we can draw on. If we have no examples of a particular trigram $w_{n-2}w_{n-1}w_n$ to help us compute $P(w_n|w_{n-1}w_{n-2})$, we can estimate its probability by using the bigram probability $P(w_n|w_{n-1})$. Similarly, if we don't have counts to compute $P(w_n|w_{n-1})$, we can look to the unigram $P(w_n)$.

DELETED
INTERPOLATION

BACKOFF

There are two ways to rely on this N-gram "hierarchy", **deleted interpolation** and **backoff**. We will focus on backoff, although we give a quick overview of deleted interpolation after this section. Backoff N-gram modeling is a nonlinear method introduced by Katz (1987). In the backoff model, like the deleted interpolation model, we build an N-gram model based on an $(N-1)$-gram model. The difference is that in backoff, if we have non-zero trigram counts, we rely solely on the trigram counts and don't interpolate the bigram and unigram counts at all. We only "back off" to a lower order N-gram if we have zero evidence for a higher-order N-gram. The trigram version of backoff might be represented as follows:

$$\hat{P}(w_i|w_{i-2}w_{i-1}) = \begin{cases} P(w_i|w_{i-2}w_{i-1}), & \text{if } C(w_{i-2}w_{i-1}w_i) > 0 \\ \alpha_1 P(w_i|w_{i-1}), & \text{if } C(w_{i-2}w_{i-1}w_i) = 0 \\ & \text{and } C(w_{i-1}w_i) > 0 \\ \alpha_2 P(w_i), & \text{otherwise.} \end{cases} \tag{6.30}$$

Let's ignore the α values for a moment; we'll discuss the need for these weighting factors below. Here's a first pass at the (recursive) equation for representing the general case of this form of backoff.

$$\hat{P}(w_n|w_{n-N+1}^{n-1}) = \tilde{P}(w_n|w_{n-N+1}^{n-1})$$
$$+ \theta(P(w_n|w_{n-N+1}^{n-1}))\alpha\hat{P}(w_n|w_{n-N+2}^{n-1}) \qquad (6.31)$$

Again, ignore the α and the $\tilde{P}$ for the moment. Following Katz, we've used θ to indicate the binary function that selects a lower ordered model only if the higher-order model gives a zero probability:

$$\theta(x) = \begin{cases} 1, & \text{if } x = 0 \\ 0, & \text{otherwise.} \end{cases} \qquad (6.32)$$

and each $P(\cdot)$ is a MLE (i.e., computed directly by dividing counts). The next section will work through these equations in more detail. In order to do that, we'll need to understand the role of the α values and how to compute them.

Combining Backoff with Discounting

Our previous discussions of discounting showed how to use a discounting algorithm to assign probability mass to unseen events. For simplicity, we assumed that these unseen events were all equally probable, and so the probability mass got distributed evenly among all unseen events. Now we can combine discounting with the backoff algorithm we have just seen to be a little more clever in assigning probability to unseen events. We will use the discounting algorithm to tells us how much total probability mass to set aside for all the events we haven't seen, and the backoff algorithm to tell us how to distribute this probability in a clever way.

First, the reader should stop and answer the following question (don't look ahead): Why did we need the α values in Equation (6.30) (or Equation (6.31))? Why couldn't we just have three sets of probabilities without weights?

The answer: without α values, the result of the equation would not be a true probability! This is because the original $P(w_n|w_{n-N+1}^{n-1})$ we got from relative frequencies were true probabilities, that is, if we sum the probability of a given w_n over all N-gram contexts, we should get 1:

$$\sum_{i,j} P(w_n|w_i w_j) = 1 \qquad (6.33)$$

$\tilde{P}$ But if that is the case, if we back off to a lower order model when the probability is zero, we are adding extra probability mass into the equation, and the total probability of a word will be greater than 1!

Thus any backoff language model must also be discounted. This explains the αs and $\tilde{P}$ in Equation 6.31. The $\tilde{P}$ comes from our need to discount the MLE probabilities to save some probability mass for the lower order N-grams. We will use $\tilde{P}$ to mean discounted probabilities, and save P for plain old relative frequencies computed directly from counts. The α is used to ensure that the probability mass from all the lower order N-grams sums up to exactly the amount that we saved by discounting the higher-order N-grams. Here's the correct final equation:

$$
\begin{aligned}
\hat{P}(w_n|w_{n-N+1}^{n-1}) \;=\; & \tilde{P}(w_n|w_{n-N+1}^{n-1}) \\
& + \theta(P(w_n|w_{n-N+1}^{n-1})) \\
& \cdot \alpha(w_{n-N+1}^{n-1})\hat{P}(w_n|w_{n-N+2}^{n-1})
\end{aligned}
\tag{6.34}
$$

Now let's see the formal definition of each of these components of the equation. We define $\tilde{P}$ as the discounted (c^*) MLE estimate of the conditional probability of an N-gram, as follows:

$$
\tilde{P}(w_n|w_{n-N+1}^{n-1}) = \frac{c^*(w_{n-N+1}^n)}{c(w_1^{n-N+1})}
\tag{6.35}
$$

This probability $\tilde{P}$ will be slightly less than the MLE estimate

$$
\frac{c(w_{n-N+1}^n)}{c(w_{n-N+1}^{n-1})}
$$

(i.e., on average the c^* will be less than c). This will leave some probability mass for the lower order N-grams. Now we need to build the α weighting we'll need for passing this mass to the lower order N-grams. Let's represent the total amount of left-over probability mass by the function β, a function of the $N-1$-gram context. For a given $N-1$-gram context, the total left-over probability mass can be computed by subtracting from 1 the total discounted probability mass for all N-grams starting with that context:

$$
\beta(w_{n-N+1}^{n-1}) = 1 - \sum_{w_n:c(w_{n-N+1}^n)>0} \tilde{P}(w_n|w_{n-N+1}^{n-1})
\tag{6.36}
$$

This gives us the total probability mass that we are ready to distribute to all $N-1$-gram (e.g., bigrams if our original model was a trigram). Each individual $N-1$-gram (bigram) will only get a fraction of this mass, so we need to normalize β by the total probability of all the $N-1$-grams (bigrams) that begin some N-gram (trigram). The final equation for computing how much probability mass to distribute from an N-gram to an $N-1$-gram is represented by the function α:

$$\alpha(w_{n-N+1}^{n-1}) = \frac{1 - \sum_{w_n:c(w_{n-N+1}^{n})>0} \tilde{P}(w_n|w_{n-N+1}^{n-1})}{1 - \sum_{w_n:c(w_{n-N+1}^{n})>0} \tilde{P}(w_n|w_{n-N+2}^{n-1})} \qquad (6.37)$$

Note that α is a function of the preceding word string, that is, of w_{n-N+1}^{n-1}; thus the amount by which we discount each trigram (d), and the mass that gets reassigned to lower order N-grams (α) are recomputed for every N-gram (more accurately for every $N-1$-gram that occurs in any N-gram).

We only need to specify what to do when the counts of an $N-1$-gram context are 0, (i.e., when $c(w_{n-N+1}^{m-1}) = 0$) and our definition is complete:

$$P(w_n|w_{n-N+1}^{n-N+1}) = P(w_n|w_{n-N+1}^{n-N+2}) \qquad (6.38)$$

and

$$\tilde{P}(w_n|w_{n-N+1}^{n-1}) = 0 \qquad (6.39)$$

and

$$\tilde{\beta}(w_{n-N+1}^{n-1}) = 1 \qquad (6.40)$$

In Equation (6.35), the discounted probability $\tilde{P}$ can be computed with the discounted counts c^* from the Witten-Bell discounting (Equation (6.20)) or with the Good-Turing discounting discussed below.

Here is the backoff model expressed in a slightly clearer format in its trigram version:

$$\hat{P}(w_i|w_{i-2}w_{i-1}) = \begin{cases} \tilde{P}(w_i|w_{i-2}w_{i-1}), & \text{if } C(w_{i-2}w_{i-1}w_i) > 0 \\ \alpha(w_{n-2}^{n-1})\tilde{P}(w_i|w_{i-1}), & \text{if } C(w_{i-2}w_{i-1}w_i) = 0 \\ & \text{and } C(w_{i-1}w_i) > 0 \\ \alpha(w_{n-1})\tilde{P}(w_i), & \text{otherwise.} \end{cases}$$

In practice, when discounting, we usually ignore counts of 1, that is, we treat N-grams with a count of 1 as if they never occurred.

Gupta et al. (1992) present a variant backoff method of assigning probabilities to zero trigrams.

6.5   DELETED INTERPOLATION

The deleted interpolation algorithm, due to Jelinek and Mercer (1980), combines different N-gram orders by linearly interpolating all three models whenever we are computing any trigram. That is, we estimate the probability $P(w_n|w_{n-1}w_{n-2})$ by mixing together the unigram, bigram, and trigram probabilities. Each of these is weighted by a linear weight λ:

$$
\begin{aligned}
\hat{P}(w_n|w_{n-1}w_{n-2}) \;=\; & \lambda_1 P(w_n|w_{n-1}w_{n-2}) \\
& +\lambda_2 P(w_n|w_{n-1}) \\
& +\lambda_3 P(w_n) \qquad\qquad\qquad (6.41)
\end{aligned}
$$

such that the λs sum to 1:

$$
\sum_i \lambda_i = 1 \qquad\qquad\qquad (6.42)
$$

DELETED
INTERPOLATION

In practice, in this deleted interpolation **deleted interpolation** algorithm we don't train just three λs for a trigram grammar. Instead, we make each λ a function of the context. This way if we have particularly accurate counts for a particular bigram, we assume that the counts of the trigrams based on this bigram will be more trustworthy, and so we can make the lambdas for those trigrams higher and thus give that trigram more weight in the interpolation. So a more detailed version of the interpolation formula would be:

$$
\begin{aligned}
\hat{P}(w_n|w_{n-2}w_{n-1}) \;=\; & \lambda_1(w_{n-2}^{n-1})P(w_n|w_{n-2}w_{n-1}) \\
& +\lambda_2(w_{n-2}^{n-1})P(w_n|w_{n-1}) \\
& + \lambda_3(w_{n-2}^{n-1})P(w_n) \qquad\qquad (6.43)
\end{aligned}
$$

Given the $P(w_{...})$ values, the λ values are trained so as to maximize the likelihood of a *held-out* corpus separate from the main training corpus, using a version of the **EM** algorithm defined in Chapter 7 (Baum, 1972; Dempster et al., 1977; Jelinek and Mercer, 1980). Further details of the algorithm are described in Bahl et al. (1983).

6.6   *N*-GRAMS FOR SPELLING AND PRONUNCIATION

In Chapter 5 we saw the use of the Bayesian/noisy-channel algorithm for correcting spelling errors and for picking a word given a surface pronunciation. We saw that both these algorithms failed, returning the wrong word, because they had no way to model the probability of multiple-word strings. Now that our *n*-grams give us such a model, we return to these two problems.

Context-Sensitive Spelling Error Correction

Chapter 5 introduced the idea of detecting spelling errors by looking for words that are not in a dictionary, are not generated by some finite-state model of English word-formation, or have low probability orthotactics. But none of these techniques is sufficient to detect and correct **real-word** spelling errors. **real-word error detection**. This is the class of errors that result in an actual word of English. This can happen from typographical errors (insertion, deletion, transposition) that accidently produce a real word (e.g., *there* for *three*), or because the writer substituted the wrong spelling of a homophone or near-homophone (e.g., *dessert* for *desert*, or *piece* for *peace*). The task of correcting these errors is called **context-sensitive spelling error correction**.

REAL-WORD ERROR DETECTION

How important are these errors? By an a priori analysis of single typographical errors (single insertions, deletions, substitutions, or transpositions) Peterson (1986) estimates that 15% of such spelling errors produce valid English words (given a very large list of 350,000 words). Kukich (1992) summarizes a number of other analyses based on empirical studies of corpora, which give figures between of 25% and 40% for the percentage of errors that are valid English words. Figure 6.11 gives some examples from Kukich (1992), broken down into **local** and **global** errors. Local errors are those that are probably detectable from the immediate surrounding words, while global errors are ones in which error detection requires examination of a large context.

One method for context-sensitive spelling error correction is based on *N*-grams.

The word *N*-gram approach to spelling error detection and correction was proposed by Mays et al. (1991). The idea is to generate every possible misspelling of each word in a sentence either just by typographical modifications (letter insertion, deletion, substitution), or by including homophones as well, (and presumably including the correct spelling), and then choosing the spelling that gives the sentence the highest prior probability. That is, given a sentence $W = \{w_1, w_2, \ldots, w_k, \ldots, w_n\}$, where w_k has alternative spelling w'_k, w''_k, etc., we choose the spelling among these possible spellings that maximizes $P(W)$, using the *N*-gram grammar to compute $P(W)$. A

Local Errors
The study was conducted mainly *be* John Black.
They are leaving in about fifteen *minuets* to go to her house.
The design *an* construction of the system will take more than a year.
Hopefully, all *with* continue smoothly in my absence.
Can they *lave* him my messages?
I need to *notified* the bank of [this problem.]
He *need* to go there right *no w*.
He is trying to *fine* out.

Global Errors
Won't they *heave if* next Monday at that time?
This thesis is supported by the fact that since 1989 the system has been operating *system* with all four units on-line, but ...

Figure 6.11   Some attested real-word spelling errors from Kukich (1992), broken down into **local** and **global** errors.

class-based N-gram can be used instead, which can find unlikely part-of-speech combinations, although it may not do as well at to finding unlikely word combinations.

There are many other statistical approaches to context-sensitive spelling error correction, some proposed directly for spelling, other for more general types of lexical disambiguation (such as word-sense disambiguation or accent restoration). Beside the trigram approach we have just described, these include Bayesian classifiers, alone or combined with trigrams (Gale et al., 1993; Golding, 1997; Golding and Schabes, 1996), decision lists (Yarowsky, 1994), transformation based learning (Mangu and Brill, 1997), latent semantic analysis (Jones and Martin, 1997), and Winnow (Golding and Roth, 1999). In a comparison of these, Golding and Roth (1999) found the Winnow algorithm gave the best performance. In general, however, these algorithms are very similar in many ways; they are all based on features like word and part-of-speech N-grams, and Roth (1998, 1999) shows that many of them make their predictions using a family of linear predictors called **Linear Statistical Queries (LSQ) hypotheses**. Chapter 17 will define all these algorithms and discuss these issues further in the context of word-sense disambiguation.

N-grams for Pronunciation Modeling

The *N*-gram model can also be used to get better performance on the words-from-pronunciation task that we studied in Chapter 5. Recall that the input was the pronunciation [n iy] following the word *I*. We said that the five words that could be pronounced [n iy] were *need, new, neat, the,* and *knee*. The algorithm in Chapter 5 was based on the product of the unigram probability of each word and the pronunciation likelihood, and incorrectly chose the word *new*, based mainly on its high unigram probability.

Adding a simple bigram probability, even without proper smoothing, is enough to solve this problem correctly. In the following table we fix the table on page 167 by using a bigram rather than unigram word probability $p(w)$ for each of the five candidate words (given that the word *I* occurs 64,736 times in the combined Brown and Switchboard corpora):

Word	C('I' w)	C('I' w)+0.5	p(w|'I')
need	153	153.5	.0016
new	0	0.5	.000005
knee	0	0.5	.000005
the	17	17.5	.00018
neat	0	0.5	.000005

Incorporating this new word probability into combined model, it now predicts the correct word *need*, as the table below shows:

Word	p(y|w)	p(w)	p(y|w)p(w)
need	.11	.0016	.00018
knee	1.00	.000005	.000005
neat	.52	.000005	.0000026
new	.36	.000005	.0000018
the	0	.00018	0

6.7   ENTROPY

> *I got the horse right here*
> Frank Loesser, Guys and Dolls

Entropy and **perplexity** are the most common metrics used to evaluate *N*-gram systems. The next sections summarize a few necessary fundamental facts about **information theory** and then introduce the entropy and perplexity metrics. We strongly suggest that the interested reader consult a good information theory textbook; Cover and Thomas (1991) is one excellent example.

Entropy is a measure of information, and is invaluable in natural language processing, speech recognition, and computational linguistics. It can be used as a metric for how much information there is in a particular grammar, for how well a given grammar matches a given language, for how predictive a given N-gram grammar is about what the next word could be. Given two grammars and a corpus, we can use entropy to tell us which grammar better matches the corpus. We can also use entropy to compare how difficult two speech recognition tasks are, and also to measure how well a given probabilistic grammar matches human grammars.

Computing entropy requires that we establish a random variable X that ranges over whatever we are predicting (words, letters, parts of speech, the set of which we'll call χ), and that has a particular probability function, call it $p(x)$. The entropy of this random variable X is then

$$H(X) = - \sum_{x \in \chi} p(x) \log_2 p(x) \tag{6.44}$$

The log can in principle be computed in any base; recall that we use log base 2 in all calculations in this book. The result of this is that the entropy is measured in **bits**.

The most intuitive way to define entropy for computer scientists is to think of the entropy as a lower bound on the number of bits it would take to encode a certain decision or piece of information in the optimal coding scheme.

Cover and Thomas (1991) suggest the following example. Imagine that we want to place a bet on a horse race but it is too far to go all the way to Yonkers Racetrack, and we'd like to send a short message to the bookie to tell him which horse to bet on. Suppose there are eight horses in this particular race.

One way to encode this message is just to use the binary representation of the horse's number as the code; thus horse 1 would be `001`, horse 2 `010`, horse 3 `011`, and so on, with horse 8 coded as `000`. If we spend the whole day betting, and each horse is coded with 3 bits, on the average we would be sending 3 bits per race.

Can we do better? Suppose that the spread is the actual distribution of the bets placed, and that we represent it as the prior probability of each horse as follows:

Horse 1	$\frac{1}{2}$	Horse 5	$\frac{1}{64}$
Horse 2	$\frac{1}{4}$	Horse 6	$\frac{1}{64}$
Horse 3	$\frac{1}{8}$	Horse 7	$\frac{1}{64}$
Horse 4	$\frac{1}{16}$	Horse 8	$\frac{1}{64}$

The entropy of the random variable X that ranges over horses gives us a lower bound on the number of bits, and is:

$$
\begin{aligned}
H(X) &= -\sum_{i=1}^{i=8} p(i) \log p(i) \\
&= -\tfrac{1}{2}\log\tfrac{1}{2} - \tfrac{1}{4}\log\tfrac{1}{4} - \tfrac{1}{8}\log\tfrac{1}{8} - \tfrac{1}{16}\log\tfrac{1}{16} - 4(\tfrac{1}{64}\log\tfrac{1}{64}) \\
&= 2 \text{ bits}
\end{aligned}
\tag{6.45}
$$

A code that averages 2 bits per race can be built by using short encodings for more probable horses, and longer encodings for less probable horses. For example, we could encode the most likely horse with the code `0`, and the remaining horses as `10`, then `110`, `1110`, `111100`, `111101`, `111110`, and `111111`.

What if the horses are equally likely? We saw above that if we use an equal-length binary code for the horse numbers, each horse took 3 bits to code, and so the average was 3. Is the entropy the same? In this case each horse would have a probability of $\frac{1}{8}$. The entropy of the choice of horses is then:

$$
H(X) = -\sum_{i=1}^{i=8} \frac{1}{8}\log\frac{1}{8} = -\log\frac{1}{8} = 3 \text{ bits}
\tag{6.46}
$$

The value 2^H is called the **perplexity** (Jelinek et al., 1977; Bahl et al., 1983). Perplexity can be intuitively thought of as the weighted average number of choices a random variable has to make. Thus choosing between 8 equally likely horses (where $H = 3$ bits), the perplexity is 2^3 or 8. Choosing between the biased horses in the table above (where $H = 2$ bits), the perplexity is 2^2 or 4.

PERPLEXITY

Until now we have been computing the entropy of a single variable. But most of what we will use entropy for involves *sequences*; for a grammar, for example, we will be computing the entropy of some sequence of words $W = \{\ldots w_0, w_1, w_2, \ldots, w_n\}$. One way to do this is to have a variable that ranges over sequences of words. For example we can compute the entropy of a random variable that ranges over all finite sequences of words of length

b in some language L as follows:

$$H(w_1, w_2, \ldots, w_n) = - \sum_{W_1^n \in L} p(W_1^n) \log p(W_1^n) \qquad (6.47)$$

We could define the **entropy rate** (we could also think of this as the **per-word entropy**) as the entropy of this sequence divided by the number of words:

$$\frac{1}{n} H(W_1^n) = -\frac{1}{n} \sum_{W_1^n \in L} p(W_1^n) \log p(W_1^n) \qquad (6.48)$$

But to measure the true entropy of a language, we need to consider sequences of infinite length. If we think of a language as a stochastic process L that produces a sequence of words, its entropy rate $H(L)$ is defined as:

$$
\begin{aligned}
H(L) &= \lim_{n \to \infty} \frac{1}{n} H(w_1, w_2, \ldots, w_n) \\
&= \lim_{n \to \infty} \frac{1}{n} \sum_{W \in L} p(w_1, \ldots, w_n) \log p(w_1, \ldots, w_n) \qquad (6.49)
\end{aligned}
$$

The Shannon-McMillan-Breiman theorem (Algoet and Cover, 1988; Cover and Thomas, 1991) states that if the language is regular in certain ways (to be exact, if it is both stationary and ergodic),

$$H(L) = \lim_{n \to \infty} -\frac{1}{n} \log p(w_1 w_2 \ldots w_n) \qquad (6.50)$$

That is, we can take a single sequence that is long enough instead of summing over all possible sequences. The intuition of the Shannon-McMillan-Breiman theorem is that a long enough sequence of words will contain in it many other shorter sequences, and that each of these shorter sequences will reoccur in the longer sequence according to their probabilities.

A stochastic process is said to be **stationary** if the probabilities it assigns to a sequence are invariant with respect to shifts in the time index. In other words, the probability distribution for words at time t is the same as the probability distribution at time $t+1$. Markov models, and hence N-grams, are stationary. For example, in a bigram, P_i is dependent only on P_{i-1}. So if we shift our time index by x, P_{i+x} is still dependent on P_{i+x-1}. But natural language is not stationary, since as we will see in Chapter 9, the probability of upcoming words can be dependent on events that were arbitrarily distant and time dependent. Thus our statistical models only give an approximation to the correct distributions and entropies of natural language.

To summarize, by making some incorrect but convenient simplifying assumptions, we can compute the entropy of some stochastic process by taking a very long sample of the output, and computing its average log probability. In the next section we talk about the why and how; *why* we would want to do this (i.e., for what kinds of problems would the entropy tell us something useful), and *how* to compute the probability of a very long sequence.

Cross Entropy for Comparing Models

In this section we introduce the **cross entropy**, and discuss its usefulness in comparing different probabilistic models. The cross entropy is useful when we don't know the actual probability distribution p that generated some data. It allows us to use some m, which is a model of p (i.e., an approximation to p. The cross-entropy of m on p is defined by:

$$H(p,m) = \lim_{n \to \infty} \frac{1}{n} \sum_{W \in L} p(w_1, \ldots, w_n) \log m(w_1, \ldots, w_n) \qquad (6.51)$$

That is we draw sequences according to the probability distribution p, but sum the log of their probability according to m.

Again, following the Shannon-McMillan-Breiman theorem, for a stationary ergodic process:

$$H(p,m) = \lim_{n \to \infty} -\frac{1}{n} \log m(w_1 w_2 \ldots w_n) \qquad (6.52)$$

What makes the cross entropy useful is that the cross entropy $H(p,m)$ is an upper bound on the entropy $H(p)$. For any model m:

$$H(p) \leq H(p,m) \qquad (6.53)$$

This means that we can use some simplified model m to help estimate the true entropy of a sequence of symbols drawn according to probability p. The more accurate m is, the closer the cross entropy $H(p,m)$ will be to the true entropy $H(p)$. Thus the difference between $H(p,m)$ and $H(p)$ is a measure of how accurate a model is. Between two models m_1 and m_2, the more accurate model will be the one with the lower cross-entropy. (The cross-entropy can never be lower than the true entropy, so a model cannot err by underestimating the true entropy).

The Entropy of English

As we suggested in the previous section, the cross-entropy of some model m can be used as an upper bound on the true entropy of some process. We can use this method to get an estimate of the true entropy of English. Why should we care about the entropy of English?

METHODOLOGY BOX: PERPLEXITY

The methodology box on page 204 mentioned the idea of computing the **perplexity of a test set** as a way of comparing two probabilistic models. (Despite the risk of ambiguity, we will follow the speech and language processing literature in using the term "perplexity" rather than the more technically correct term "cross-perplexity".) Here's an example of perplexity computation as part of a "business news dictation system". We trained unigram, bigram, and trigram Katz-style backoff grammars with Good-Turing discounting on 38 million words (including start-of-sentence tokens) from the Wall Street Journal (from the WSJ0 corpus (LDC, 1993)). We used a vocabulary of 19,979 words (i.e., the rest of the words types were mapped to the unknown word token <UNK> in both training and testing). We then computed the perplexity of each of these models on a test set of 1.5 million words (where the perplexity is defined as $2^{H(p,m)}$). The table below shows the perplexity of a 1.5 million word WSJ test set according to each of these grammars.

N-gram Order	Perplexity
Unigram	962
Bigram	170
Trigram	109

In computing perplexities the model m must be constructed without any knowledge of the test set t. Any kind of knowledge of the test set can cause the perplexity to be artificially low. For example, sometimes instead of mapping all unknown words to the <UNK> token, we use a **closed-vocabulary** test set in which we know in advance what the set of words is. This can greatly reduce the perplexity. As long as this knowledge is provided equally to each of the models we are comparing, the closed-vocabulary perplexity is still a useful metric for comparing models. But this cross-perplexity is no longer guaranteed to be greater than the true perplexity of the test set, and so great care must be taken in interpreting the results. In general, the perplexity of two language models is only comparable if they use the same vocabulary.

One reason is that the true entropy of English would give us a solid lower bound for all of our future experiments on probabilistic grammars. Another is that we can use the entropy values for English to help understand what parts of a language provide the most information (for example, is the predictability of English mainly based on word order, on semantics, on morphology, on constituency, or on pragmatic cues?) This can help us immensely in knowing where to focus our language-modeling efforts.

There are two common methods for computing the entropy of English. The first was employed by Shannon (1951), as part of his groundbreaking work in defining the field of information theory. His idea was to use human subjects, and to construct a psychological experiment that requires them to guess strings of letters; by looking at how many guesses it takes them to guess letters correctly we can estimate the probability of the letters, and hence the entropy of the sequence.

The actual experiment is designed as follows: we present a subject with some English text and ask the subject to guess the next letter. The subjects will use their knowledge of the language to guess the most probable letter first, the next most probable next, and so on. We record the number of guesses it takes for the subject to guess correctly. Shannon's insight was that the entropy of the number-of-guesses sequence is the same as the entropy of English. (The intuition is that given the number-of-guesses sequence, we could reconstruct the original text by choosing the "nth most probable" letter whenever the subject took n guesses). This methodology requires the use of letter guesses rather than word guesses (since the subject sometimes has to do an exhaustive search of all the possible letters!), and so Shannon computed the **per-letter entropy** of English rather than the per-word entropy. He reported an entropy of 1.3 bits (for 27 characters (26 letters plus space)). Shannon's estimate is likely to be too low, since it is based on a single text (*Jefferson the Virginian* by Dumas Malone). Shannon notes that his subjects had worse guesses (hence higher entropies) on other texts (newspaper writing, scientific work, and poetry). More recently variations on the Shannon experiments include the use of a gambling paradigm where the subjects get to bet on the next letter (Cover and King, 1978; Cover and Thomas, 1991).

The second method for computing the entropy of English helps avoid the single-text problem that confounds Shannon's results. This method is to take a very good stochastic model, train it on a very large corpus, and use it to assign a log-probability to a very long sequence of English, using the Shannon-McMillan-Breiman theorem:

$$H(\text{English}) \leq \lim_{n \to \infty} -\frac{1}{n} \log m(w_1 w_2 \ldots w_n) \qquad (6.54)$$

For example, Brown et al. (1992) trained a trigram language model on 583 million words of English, (293,181 different types) and used it to compute the probability of the entire Brown corpus (1,014,312 tokens). The training data include newspapers, encyclopedias, novels, office correspondence, proceedings of the Canadian parliament, and other miscellaneous sources.

They then computed the character-entropy of the Brown corpus, by using their word-trigram grammar to assign probabilities to the Brown corpus, considered as a sequence of individual letters. They obtained an entropy of 1.75 bits per character (where the set of characters included all the 95 printable ASCII characters).

The average length of English written words (including space) has been reported at 5.5 letters (Nádas, 1984). If this is correct, it means that the Shannon estimate of 1.3 bits per letter corresponds to a per-word perplexity of 142 for general English. The numbers we report above for the WSJ experiments are significantly lower since the training and test set came from same subsample of English. That is, those experiments underestimate the complexity of English since the Wall Street Journal looks very little like Shakespeare.

BIBLIOGRAPHICAL AND HISTORICAL NOTES

The underlying mathematics of the N-gram was first proposed by Markov (1913), who used what are now called **Markov chains** (bigrams and trigrams) to predict whether an upcoming letter in Pushkin's *Eugene Onegin* would be a vowel or a consonant. Markov classified 20,000 letters as V or C and computed the bigram and trigram probability that a given letter would be a vowel given the previous one or two letters. Shannon (1948) applied N-grams to compute approximations to English word sequences. Based on Shannon's work, Markov models were commonly used in modeling word sequences by the 1950s. In a series of extremely influential papers starting with Chomsky (1956) and including Chomsky (1957) and Miller and Chomsky (1963), Noam Chomsky argued that "finite-state Markov processes", while a possibly useful engineering heuristic, were incapable of being a complete cognitive model of human grammatical knowledge. These arguments led many linguists and computational linguists away from statistical models altogether.

The resurgence of N-gram models came from Jelinek, Mercer, Bahl, and colleagues at the IBM Thomas J. Watson Research Center, influenced by Shannon, and Baker at CMU, influenced by the work of Baum and colleagues. These two labs independently successfully used N-grams in their speech recognition systems (Jelinek, 1976; Baker, 1975; Bahl et al., 1983). The Good-Turing algorithm was first applied to the smoothing of N-gram grammars at IBM by Katz, as cited in Nádas (1984). Jelinek (1990) summarizes this and many other early language model innovations used in the IBM language models.

While smoothing had been applied as an engineering solution to the zero-frequency problem at least as early as Jeffreys (1948) (add-one smoothing), it is only relatively recently that smoothing received serious attention. Church and Gale (1991) gives a good description of the Good-Turing method, as well as the proof, and also gives a good description of the Deleted Interpolation method and a new smoothing method. Sampson (1996) also has a useful discussion of Good-Turing. Problems with the Add-one algorithm are summarized in Gale and Church (1994). Method C in Witten and Bell (1991) describes what we called Witten-Bell discounting. Chen and Goodman (1996) give an empirical comparison of different smoothing algorithms, including two new methods, *average-count* and *one-count*, as well as Church and Gale's. Iyer and Ostendorf (1997) discuss a way of smoothing by adding in data from additional corpora.

Much recent work on language modeling has focused on ways to build more sophisticated N-grams. These approaches include giving extra weight to N-grams which have already occurred recently (the **cache LM** of Kuhn and de Mori (1990)), choosing long-distance **triggers** instead of just local N-grams (Rosenfeld, 1996; Niesler and Woodland, 1999; Zhou and Lua, 1998), and using **variable-length N-grams** (Ney et al., 1994; Kneser, 1996; Niesler and Woodland, 1996). Another class of approaches use semantic information to enrich the N-gram, including semantic word associations based on the **latent semantic indexing** described in Chapter 15 (Coccaro and Jurafsky, 1998; Bellegarda, 1999)), and from on-line dictionaries or thesauri (Demetriou et al., 1997). **Class-based** N-grams, based on word classes such as parts-of-speech, are described in Chapter 8. Language models based on more structured linguistic knowledge (such as probabilistic parsers) are described in Chapter 12. Finally, a number of augmentations to N-grams are based on discourse knowledge, such as using knowledge of the current topic (Chen et al., 1998; Seymore and Rosenfeld, 1997; Seymore et al., 1998; Florian and Yarowsky, 1999; Khudanpur and Wu, 1999) or the current speech act in dialogue (see Chapter 19).

CACHE LM

TRIGGERS

VARIABLE-LENGTH
N-GRAMS

LATENT
SEMANTIC
INDEXING

CLASS-BASED

6.8   SUMMARY

This chapter introduced the *N*-gram, one of the oldest and most broadly useful practical tools in language processing.

- An *N*-gram probability is the conditional probability of a word given
  the previous $N - 1$ words. *N*-gram probabilities can be computed by
  simply counting in a corpus and normalizing (the **Maximum Likelihood Estimate**) or they can be computed by more sophisticated algorithms. The advantage of *N*-grams is that they take advantage of lots
  of rich lexical knowledge. A disadvantage for some purposes is that
  they are very dependent on the corpus they were trained on.

- **Smoothing** algorithms provide a better way of estimating the probability of *N*-grams which never occur. Commonly-used smoothing algorithms include **backoff** or **deleted interpolation**, with **Witten-Bell**
  or **Good-Turing** discounting.

- Corpus-based **language models** like *N*-grams are evaluated by separating the corpus into a **training set** and a **test set**, training the model
  on the training set, and evaluating on the test set. The **entropy** H, or
  more commonly the **perplexity** 2^H (more properly **cross-entropy** and
  cross-perplexity) of a test set are used to compare language models.

EXERCISES

6.1   Write out the equation for trigram probability estimation (modifying
Equation 6.11).

6.2   Write out the equation for the discount $d = \frac{c*}{c}$ for add-one smoothing.
Do the same for Witten-Bell smoothing. How do they differ?

6.3   Write a program (Perl is sufficient) to compute unsmoothed unigrams
and bigrams.

6.4   Run your *N*-gram program on two different small corpora of your
choice (you might use email text or newsgroups). Now compare the statistics

of the two corpora. What are the differences in the most common unigrams between the two? How about interesting differences in bigrams?

6.5   Add an option to your program to generate random sentences.

6.6   Add an option to your program to do Witten-Bell discounting.

6.7   Add an option to your program to compute the entropy (or perplexity) of a test set.

6.8   Suppose someone took all the words in a sentence and reordered them randomly. Write a program which take as input such a **bag of words** and produces as output a guess at the original order. Use the Viterbi algorithm and an *N*-gram grammar produced by your *N*-gram program (on some corpus).

BAG OF WORDS

6.9   The field of **authorship attribution** is concerned with discovering the author of a particular text. Authorship attribution is important in many fields, including history, literature, and forensic linguistics. For example Mosteller and Wallace (1964) applied authorship identification techniques to discover who wrote *The Federalist* papers. The Federalist papers were written in 1787-1788 by Alexander Hamilton, John Jay and James Madison to persuade New York to ratify the United States Constitution. They were published anonymously, and as a result, although some of the 85 essays were clearly attributable to one author or another, the authorship of 12 were in dispute between Hamilton and Madison. Foster (1989) applied authorship identification techniques to suggest that W.S.'s *Funeral Elegy* for William Peter was probably written by William Shakespeare, and that the anonymous author of *Primary Colors* the roman à clef about the Clinton campaign for the American presidency, was journalist Joe Klein (Foster, 1996).

AUTHORSHIP ATTRIBUTION

A standard technique for authorship attribution, first used by Mosteller and Wallace, is a Bayesian approach. For example, they trained a probabilistic model of the writing of Hamilton, and another model of the writings of Madison, and computed the maximum-likelihood author for each of the disputed essays. There are many complex factors that go into these models, including vocabulary use, word-length, syllable structure, rhyme, grammar; see (Holmes, 1994) for a summary. This approach can also be used for identifying which genre a text comes from.

One factor in many models is the use of rare words. As a simple approximation to this one factor, apply the Bayesian method to the attribution of any particular text. You will need three things: a text to test, and two potential authors or genres, with a large on-line text sample of each. One of them should be the correct author. Train a unigram language model on each of the candidate authors. You are only going to use the **singleton** unigrams in each language model. You will compute $P(T|A_1)$, the probability of the text given author or genre A_1, by (1) taking the language model from A_1, (2) by multiplying together the probabilities of all the unigrams that only occur once in the "unknown" text and (3) taking the geometric mean of these (i.e., the nth root, where n is the number of probabilities you multiplied). Do the same for A_2. Choose whichever is higher. Did it produce the correct candidate?

7 HMMS AND SPEECH RECOGNITION

When Frederic was a little lad he proved so brave and daring,
His father thought he'd 'prentice him to some career seafaring.
I was, alas! his nurs'rymaid, and so it fell to my lot
To take and bind the promising boy apprentice to a **pilot** —
A life not bad for a hardy lad, though surely not a high lot,
Though I'm a nurse, you might do worse than make your boy a pilot.
I was a stupid nurs'rymaid, on breakers always steering,
And I did not catch the word aright, through being hard of hearing;
Mistaking my instructions, which within my brain did gyrate,
I took and bound this promising boy apprentice to a **pirate.**
The Pirates of Penzance, Gilbert and Sullivan, 1877

Alas, this mistake by nurserymaid Ruth led to Frederic's long indenture as a pirate and, due to a slight complication involving 21st birthdays and leap years, nearly led to 63 extra years of apprenticeship. The mistake was quite natural, in a Gilbert-and-Sullivan sort of way; as Ruth later noted, "The two words were so much alike!" True, true; spoken language understanding is a difficult task, and it is remarkable that humans do as well at it as we do. The goal of automatic speech recognition (ASR) research is to address this problem computationally by building systems that map from an acoustic signal to a string of words. Automatic speech understanding (ASU) extends this goal to producing some sort of understanding of the sentence, rather than just the words.

The general problem of automatic transcription of speech by any speaker in any environment is still far from solved. But recent years have seen ASR technology mature to the point where it is viable in certain limited domains. One major application area is in human-computer interaction. While many tasks are better solved with visual or pointing interfaces, speech has the potential to be a better interface than the keyboard for tasks where full natural language communication is useful, or for which keyboards are not appropriate. This includes hands-busy or eyes-busy applications, such as where the user has objects to manipulate or equipment to control. Another important application area is telephony, where speech recognition is already used for example for entering digits, recognizing "yes" to accept collect calls, or call-routing ("Accounting, please", "Prof. Regier, please"). In some applications, a multimodal interface combining speech and pointing can be more efficient than a graphical user interface without speech (Cohen et al., 1998). Finally, ASR is being applied to dictation, that is, transcription of extended monologue by a single specific speaker. Dictation is common in fields such as law and is also important as part of augmentative communication (interaction between computers and humans with some disability resulting in the inability to type, or the inability to speak). The blind Milton famously dictated *Paradise Lost* to his daughters, and Henry James dictated his later novels after a repetitive stress injury.

Different applications of speech technology necessarily place different constraints on the problem and lead to different algorithms. We chose to focus this chapter on the fundamentals of one crucial area: **Large-Vocabulary Continuous Speech Recognition** (**LVCSR**), with a small section on acoustic issues in speech synthesis. Large-vocabulary generally means that the systems have a vocabulary of roughly 5,000 to 60,000 words. The term **continuous** means that the words are run together naturally; it contrasts with **isolated-word** speech recognition, in which each word must be preceded and followed by a pause. Furthermore, the algorithms we will discuss are generally **speaker-independent**; that is, they are able to recognize speech from people whose speech the system has never been exposed to before.

The chapter begins with an overview of speech recognition architecture, and then proceeds to introduce the HMM, the use of the Viterbi and A* algorithms for decoding, speech acoustics and features, and the use of Gaussians and MLPs to compute acoustic probabilities. Even relying on the previous three chapters, summarizing this much of the field in this chapter requires us to omit many crucial areas; the reader is encouraged to see the suggested readings at the end of the chapter for useful textbooks and articles. This chapter also includes a short section on the acoustic component of the speech synthesis algorithms discussed in Chapter 4.

7.1   SPEECH RECOGNITION ARCHITECTURE

Previous chapters have introduced many of the core algorithms used in speech recognition. Chapter 4 introduced the notions of **phone** and **syllable**. Chap-

Margin terms: LVCSR, CONTINUOUS, ISOLATED-WORD, SPEAKER-INDEPENDENT

ter 5 introduced the **noisy channel model**, the use of the **Bayes rule**, and
the **probabilistic automaton**. Chapter 6 introduced the *N*-gram language
model and the **perplexity** metric. In this chapter we introduce the remaining
components of a modern speech recognizer: the **Hidden Markov Model
(HMM)**, the idea of **spectral features**, the **forward-backward** algorithm
for HMM training, and the **Viterbi** and **stack decoding** (also called **A* decoding** algorithms for solving the **decoding** problem: mapping from strings   A*
of phone probability vectors to strings of words.   DECODING

    Let's begin by revisiting the noisy channel model that we saw in Chap-
ter 5. Speech recognition systems treat the acoustic input as if it were a
"noisy" version of the source sentence. In order to "decode" this noisy
sentence, we consider all possible sentences, and for each one we compute
the probability of it generating the noisy sentence. We then chose the sentence with the maximum probability. Figure 7.1 shows this noisy-channel
metaphor.

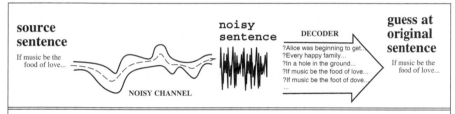

Figure 7.1   The noisy channel model applied to entire sentences (Figure 5.1
showed its application to individual words). Modern speech recognizers work
by searching through a huge space of potential "source" sentences and choosing the one which has the highest probability of generating the "noisy" sentence. To do this they must have models that express the probability of
sentences being realized as certain strings of words (*N*-grams), models that
express the probability of words being realized as certain strings of phones
(HMMs) and models that express the probability of phones being realized as
acoustic or spectral features (Gaussians/MLPs).

    Implementing the noisy-channel model as we have expressed it in Fig-
ure 7.1 requires solutions to two problems. First, in order to pick the sentence
that best matches the noisy input we will need a complete metric for a "best
match". Because speech is so variable, an acoustic input sentence will never
exactly match any model we have for this sentence. As we have suggested
in previous chapters, we will use probability as our metric, and will show
how to combine the various probabilistic estimators to get a complete estimate for the probability of a noisy observation-sequence given a candidate

sentence. Second, since the set of all English sentences is huge, we need an efficient algorithm that will not search through all possible sentences, but only ones that have a good chance of matching the input. This is the **decoding** or **search** problem, and we will summarize two approaches: the **Viterbi** or **dynamic programming** decoder, and the **stack** or **A*** decoder.

In the rest of this introduction we will introduce the probabilistic or Bayesian model for speech recognition (or more accurately re-introduce it, since we first used the model in our discussions of spelling and pronunciation in Chapter 5); we leave discussion of decoding/search for pages 244–251.

The goal of the probabilistic noisy channel architecture for speech recognition can be summarized as follows:

> *"What is the most likely sentence out of all sentences in the language L given some acoustic input O?"*

We can treat the acoustic input O as a sequence of individual "symbols" or "observations" (for example by slicing up the input every 10 milliseconds, and representing each slice by floating-point values of the energy or frequencies of that slice). Each index then represents some time interval, and successive o_i indicate temporally consecutive slices of the input (note that capital letters will stand for sequences of symbols and lower-case letters for individual symbols):

$$O = o_1, o_2, o_3, \ldots, o_t \tag{7.1}$$

Similarly, we will treat a sentence as if it were composed simply of a string of words:

$$W = w_1, w_2, w_3, \ldots, w_n \tag{7.2}$$

Both of these are simplifying assumptions; for example dividing sentences into words is sometimes too fine a division (we'd like to model facts about groups of words rather than individual words) and sometimes too gross a division (we'd like to talk about morphology). Usually in speech recognition a word is defined by orthography (after mapping every word to lowercase): *oak* is treated as a different word than *oaks*, but the auxiliary *can* ("can you tell me…") is treated as the same word as the noun *can* ("i need a can of…").   Recent ASR research has begun to focus on building more sophisticated models of ASR words incorporating the morphological insights of Chapter 3 and the part-of-speech information that we will study in Chapter 8.

The probabilistic implementation of our intuition above, then, can be expressed as follows:

$$\hat{W} = \underset{W \in \mathcal{L}}{\operatorname{argmax}} P(W|O) \qquad (7.3)$$

Recall that the function $\operatorname{argmax}_x f(x)$ means "the x such that f(x) is largest". Equation (7.3) is guaranteed to give us the optimal sentence W; we now need to make the equation operational. That is, for a given sentence W and acoustic sequence O we need to compute $P(W|O)$. Recall that given any probability $P(x|y)$, we can use Bayes' rule to break it down as follows:

$$P(x|y) = \frac{P(y|x)P(x)}{P(y)} \qquad (7.4)$$

We saw in Chapter 5 that we can substitute (7.4) into (7.3) as follows:

$$\hat{W} = \underset{W \in \mathcal{L}}{\operatorname{argmax}} \frac{P(O|W)P(W)}{P(O)} \qquad (7.5)$$

The probabilities on the right-hand side of (7.5) are for the most part easier to compute than $P(W|O)$. For example, $P(W)$, the prior probability of the word string itself is exactly what is estimated by the n-gram language models of Chapter 6. And we will see below that $P(O|W)$ turns out to be easy to estimate as well. But $P(O)$, the probability of the acoustic observation sequence, turns out to be harder to estimate. Luckily, we can ignore $P(O)$ just as we saw in Chapter 5. Why? Since we are maximizing over all possible sentences, we will be computing $\frac{P(O|W)P(W)}{P(O)}$ for each sentence in the language. But $P(O)$ doesn't change for each sentence! For each potential sentence we are still examining the same observations O, which must have the same probability $P(O)$. Thus:

$$\hat{W} = \underset{W \in \mathcal{L}}{\operatorname{argmax}} \frac{P(O|W)P(W)}{P(O)} = \underset{W \in \mathcal{L}}{\operatorname{argmax}} P(O|W)P(W) \qquad (7.6)$$

To summarize, the most probable sentence W given some observation sequence O can be computing by taking the product of two probabilities for each sentence, and choosing the sentence for which this product is greatest. These two terms have names; $P(W)$, the **prior probability**, is called the **language model**. $P(O|W)$, the **observation likelihood**, is called the **acoustic model**.

LANGUAGE
MODEL

ACOUSTIC
MODEL

$$\overset{\text{likelihood}}{} \quad \overset{\text{prior}}{}$$

Key Concept #5. $\hat{W} = \underset{W \in \mathcal{L}}{\operatorname{argmax}} \ \overbrace{P(O|W)}^{\text{likelihood}} \ \overbrace{P(W)}^{\text{prior}} \qquad (7.7)$

We have already seen in Chapter 6 how to compute the language model prior $P(W)$ by using N-gram grammars. The rest of this chapter will show

how to compute the acoustic model $P(O|W)$, in two steps. First we will make the simplifying assumption that the input sequence is a sequence of phones F rather than a sequence of acoustic observations. Recall that we introduced the **forward** algorithm in Chapter 5, which was given "observations" that were strings of phones, and produced the probability of these phone observations given a single word. We will show that these probabilistic phone automata are really a special case of the **Hidden Markov Model**, and we will show how to extend these models to give the probability of a phone sequence given an entire sentence.

One problem with the forward algorithm as we presented it was that in order to know which word was the most-likely word (the "decoding problem"), we had to run the forward algorithm again for each word. This is clearly intractable for sentences; we can't possibly run the forward algorithm separately for each possible sentence of English. We will thus introduce two different algorithms which *simultaneously* compute the likelihood of an observation sequence given each sentence, *and* give us the most-likely sentence. These are the **Viterbi** and the **A*** decoding algorithms.

Once we have solved the likelihood-computation and decoding problems for a simplified input consisting of strings of phones, we will show how the same algorithms can be applied to true acoustic input rather than pre-defined phones. This will involve a quick introduction to acoustic input and **feature extraction**, the process of deriving meaningful features from the input soundwave. Then we will introduce the two standard models for computing phone-probabilities from these features: **Gaussian** models, and **neural net (multi-layer perceptrons)** models.

Finally, we will introduce the standard algorithm for training the Hidden Markov Models and the phone-probability estimators, the **forward-backward** or **Baum-Welch** algorithm) (Baum, 1972), a special case of the the **Expectation-Maximization** or **EM** algorithm (Dempster et al., 1977).

As a preview of the chapter, Figure 7.2 shows an outline of the components of a speech recognition system. The figure shows a speech recognition system broken down into three stages. In the **signal processing** or **feature extraction** stage, the acoustic waveform is sliced up into **frames** (usually of 10, 15, or 20 milliseconds) which are transformed into **spectral features** which give information about how much energy in the signal is at different frequencies. In the **subword** or **phone recognition** stage, we use statistical techniques like neural networks or Gaussian models to tentatively recognize individual speech sounds like p or b. For a neural network, the output of this stage is a vector of probabilities over phones for each frame (i.e., "for this frame the probability of [p] is .8, the probability of [b] is .1, the probability of [f] is .02, etc."); for a Gaussian model the probabilities are slightly different. Finally, in the **decoding** stage, we take a dictionary of word pronunciations and a language model (probabilistic grammar) and use a Viterbi or A* **decoder** to find the sequence of words which has the highest probability given the acoustic events.

DECODER

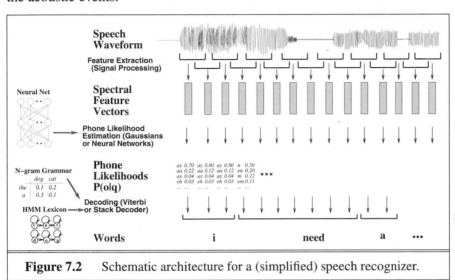

Figure 7.2   Schematic architecture for a (simplified) speech recognizer.

7.2   OVERVIEW OF HIDDEN MARKOV MODELS

In Chapter 5 we used **weighted finite-state automata** or **Markov chains** to model the pronunciation of words. The automata consisted of a sequence of states $q = (q_0 q_1 q_2 \ldots q_n)$, each corresponding to a phone, and a set of transition probabilities between states, a_{01}, a_{12}, a_{13}, encoding the probability of one phone following another. We represented the states as nodes, and the transition probabilities as edges between nodes; an edge existed between two nodes if there was a non-zero transition probability between the two nodes. We also saw that we could use the **forward** algorithm to compute the likelihood of a sequence of observed phones $o = (o_1 o_2 o_3 \ldots o_t)$. Figure 7.3 shows an automaton for the word *need* with sample observation sequence of the kind we saw in Chapter 5.

While we will see that these models figure importantly in speech recognition, they simplify the problem in two ways. First, they assume that the

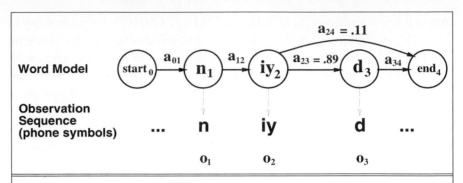

Figure 7.3   A simple weighted automaton or Markov chain pronunciation network for the word *need*, showing the transition probabilities, and a sample observation sequence. The transition probabilities a_{xy} between two states x and y are 1.0 unless otherwise specified.

input consists of a sequence of symbols! Obviously this is not true in the real world, where speech input consists essentially of small movements of air particles. In speech recognition, the input is an ambiguous, real-valued representation of the sliced-up input signal, called **features** or **spectral features**. We will study the details of some of these features beginning on page 259; acoustic features represent such information as how much energy there is at different frequencies. The second simplifying assumption of the weighted automata of Chapter 5 was that the input symbols correspond exactly to the states of the machine. Thus when seeing an input symbol [b], we knew that we could move into a state labeled [b]. In a **Hidden Markov Model** (**HMM**), by contrast, we can't look at the input symbols and know which state to move to. The input symbols don't uniquely determine the next state.[1]

HIDDEN
MARKOV
MODEL

Recall that a weighted automaton or simple Markov model is specified by the set of **states** Q , the set of **transition probabilities** A, a defined **start state** and **end state(s)**, and a set of **observation likelihoods** B. For weighted automata, we defined the probabilities $b_i(o_t)$ as 1.0 if the state i matched the observation o_t and 0 if they didn't match. An HMM formally differs from a Markov model by adding two more requirements. First, it has a separate set of *observation symbols* O, which is not drawn from the same alphabet as the

---

[1] Actually, as we mentioned in passing, by this second criterion some of the automata we saw in Chapter 5 were technically HMMs as well. This is because the first symbol in the input string [n iy] was compatible with the [n] states in the words *need* or *an*. Seeing the symbols [n], we didn't know which underlying state it was generated by, *need-n* or *an-n*.

state set Q. Second, the observation likelihood function B is not limited to the values 1.0 and 0; in an HMM the probability $b_i(o_t)$ can take on any value from 0 to 1.0.

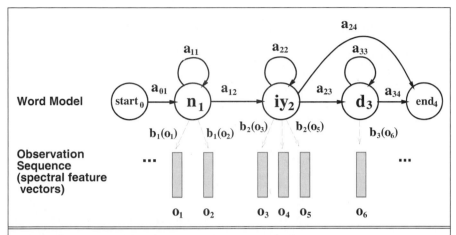

Figure 7.4   An HMM pronunciation network for the word *need*, showing the transition probabilities, and a sample observation sequence. Note the addition of the output probabilities B. HMMs used in speech recognition usually use self-loops on the states to model variable phone durations.

Figure 7.4 shows an HMM for the word *need* and a sample observation sequence. Note the differences from Figure 7.3. First, the observation sequences are now vectors of spectral features representing the speech signal. Next, note that we've also allowed one state to generate multiple copies of the same observation, by having a loop on the state. This loops allows HMMs to model the variable duration of phones; longer phones require more loops through the HMM.

In summary, here are the parameters we need to define an HMM:

- **states:** a set of states $Q = q_1 q_2 \ldots q_N$
- **transition probabilities:** a set of probabilities $A = a_{01} a_{02} \ldots a_{n1} \ldots a_{nn}$
  Each a_{ij} represents the probability of transitioning from state i to state j. The set of these is the **transition probability matrix**
- **observation likelihoods:** a set of observation likelihoods $B = b_i(o_t)$, each expressing the probability of an observation o_t being generated from a state i

In our examples so far we have used two "special" states (**non-emitting states**) as the start and end state; as we saw in Chapter 5 it is also possible to avoid the use of these states by specifying two more things:

- **initial distribution:** an initial probability distribution over states, π, such that π_i is the probability that the HMM will start in state i. Of course some states j may have $\pi_j = 0$, meaning that they cannot be initial states.
- **accepting states:** a set of legal accepting states

As was true for the weighted automata, the sequences of symbols that are input to the model (if we are thinking of it as recognizer) or which are produced by the model (if we are thinking of it as a generator) are generally called the **observation sequence**, referred to as $O = (o_1 o_2 o_3 \ldots o_T)$.

7.3   THE VITERBI ALGORITHM REVISITED

Chapter 5 showed how the forward algorithm could be used to compute the probability of an observation sequence given an automaton, and how the Viterbi algorithm can be used to find the most-likely path through the automaton, as well as the probability of the observation sequence given this most-likely path. In Chapter 5 the observation sequences consisted of a single word. But in continuous speech, the input consists of sequences of words, and we are not given the location of the word boundaries. Knowing where the word boundaries are massively simplifies the problem of pronunciation; in Chapter 5, since we were sure that the pronunciation [ni] came from one word, we only had seven candidates to compare. But in actual speech we don't know where the word boundaries are. For example, try to decode the following sentence from Switchboard (don't peek ahead!):

[ay d ih s hh er d s ah m th ih ng ax b aw m uh v ih ng r ih s en l ih]

The answer is in the footnote.[2] The task is hard partly because of coarticulation and fast speech (e.g., [d] for the first phone of *just!*). But mainly it's the lack of spaces indicating word boundaries that make the task difficult. The task of finding word boundaries in connected speech is called **segmentation** and we will solve it by using the Viterbi algorithm just as we did for Chinese word-segmentation in Chapter 5; recall that the algorithm for Chinese word-segmentation relied on choosing the segmentation that resulted in the sequence of words with the highest frequency. For speech segmentation we use the more sophisticated N-gram language models introduced in Chapter 6. In the rest of this section we show how the Viterbi algorithm can

---

2   I just heard something about moving recently.

be applied to the task of decoding and segmentation of a simple string of observations phones, using an *n*-gram language model. We will show how the algorithm is used to segment a very simple string of words. Here's the input and output we will work with:

Input	Output
[aa n iy dh ax]	*I need the*

Figure 7.5 shows word models for *I*, *need*, *the*, and also, just to make things difficult, the word *on*.

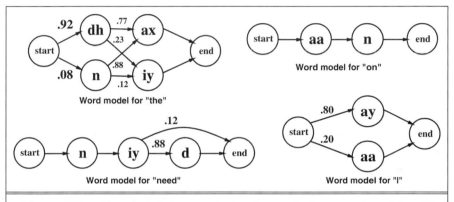

Figure 7.5   Pronunciation networks for the words *I*, *on*, *need*, and *the*. All networks (especially *the*) are significantly simplified.

Recall that the goal of the Viterbi algorithm is to find the best state sequence $q = (q_1 q_2 q_3 \ldots q_t)$ given the set of observed phones $o = (o_1 o_2 o_3 \ldots o_t)$. A graphic illustration of the output of the dynamic programming algorithm is shown in Figure 7.6. Along the *y*-axis are all the words in the lexicon; inside each word are its states. The *x*-axis is ordered by time, with one observed phone per time unit.[3] Each cell in the matrix will contain the probability of the most-likely sequence ending at that state. We can find the most-likely state sequence for the entire observation string by looking at the cell in the right-most column that has the highest probability, and tracing back the sequence that produced it.

---

[3]   This *x*-axis component of the model is simplified in two major ways that we will show how to fix in the next section. First, the observations will not be phones but extracted spectral features, and second, each phone consists of not time unit observation but many observations (since phones can last for more than one phone). The *y*-axis is also simplified in this example, since as we will see most ASR system use multiple "subphone" units for each phone.

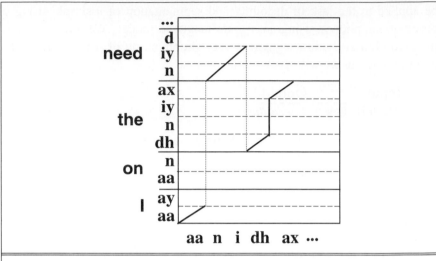

Figure 7.6   An illustration of the results of the Viterbi algorithm used to find the most-likely phone sequence (and hence estimate the most-likely word sequence).

More formally, we are searching for the best state sequence $q^* = (q_1 q_2 \ldots q_T)$, given an observation sequence $o = (o_1 o_2 \ldots o_T)$ and a model (a weighted automaton or "state graph") λ. Each cell $viterbi[i,t]$ of the matrix contains the probability of the best path which accounts for the first t observations and ends in state i of the HMM. This is the most-probable path out of all possible sequences of states of length $t-1$:

$$viterbi[t,i] = \max_{q_1, q_2, \ldots, q_{t-1}} P(q_1 q_2 \ldots q_{t-1}, q_t = i, o_1, o_2 \ldots o_t | \lambda) \qquad (7.8)$$

DYNAMIC
PROGRAMMING
INVARIANT

In order to compute $viterbi[t,i]$, the Viterbi algorithm assumes the **dynamic programming invariant**. This is the simplifying (but incorrect) assumption that if the ultimate best path for the entire observation sequence happens to go through a state q_i, that this best path must include the best path up to and including state q_i. This doesn't mean that the best path at any time t is the best path for the whole sequence. A path can look bad at the beginning but turn out to be the best path. As we will see later, the Viterbi assumption breaks down for certain kinds of grammars (including trigram grammars) and so some recognizers have moved to another kind of decoder, the **stack** or A^* decoder; more on that later. As we saw in our discussion of the minimum-edit-distance algorithm in Chapter 5, the reason for making the Viterbi assumption is that it allows us to break down the computation of the optimal path probability in a simple way; each of the best paths at time t is the best extension of each of the paths ending at time $t - 1$. In other words, the recurrence relation for the best path at time t ending in state j, $viterbi[t, j]$, is the maximum of the possible extensions of every possible previous path from time $t - 1$ to time t:

$$viterbi[t, j] = \max_i (viterbi[t - 1, i] a_{ij}) b_j(o_t) \qquad (7.9)$$

The algorithm as we describe it in Figure 7.9 takes a sequence of observations, and a single probabilistic automaton, and returns the optimal path through the automaton. Since the algorithm requires a single automaton, we will need to combine the different probabilistic phone networks for the, I, need, and a into one automaton. In order to build this new automaton we will need to add arcs with probabilities between any two words: bigram probabilities. Figure 7.7 shows simple bigram probabilities computed from the combined Brown and Switchboard corpus.

I need	0.0016	need need	0.000047	# Need	0.000018
I the	0.00018	need the	0.012	# The	0.016
I on	0.000047	need on	0.000047	# On	0.00077
I I	0.039	need I	0.000016	# I	0.079
the need	0.00051	on need	0.000055		
the the	0.0099	on the	0.094		
the on	0.00022	on on	0.0031		
the I	0.00051	on I	0.00085		

Figure 7.7   Bigram probabilities for the words the, on, need, and I following each other, and starting a sentence (i.e., following #). Computed from the combined Brown and Switchboard corpora with add-0.5 smoothing.

Figure 7.8 shows the combined pronunciation networks for the 4 words together with a few of the new arcs with the bigram probabilities. For readability of the diagram, most of the arcs aren't shown; the reader should imagine that each probability in Figure 7.7 is inserted as an arc between every two words.

The algorithm is given in Figure 5.19 in Chapter 5, and is repeated here for convenience as Figure 7.9. We see in Figure 7.9 that the Viterbi algorithm sets up a probability matrix, with one column for each time index t and one row for each state in the state graph. The algorithm first creates $T + 2$ columns; Figure 7.9 shows the first six columns. The first column is an initial pseudo-observation, the next corresponds to the first observation

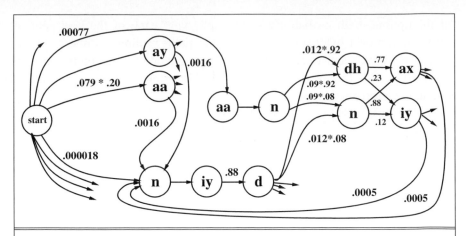

Figure 7.8   Single automaton made from the words *I*, *need*, *on*, and *the*. The arcs between words have probabilities computed from Figure 7.7. For lack of space the figure only shows a few of the between-word arcs.

phone [aa], and so on. We begin in the first column by setting the probability of the *start* state to 1.0, and the other probabilities to 0; the reader should find this in Figure 7.10. Cells with probability 0 are simply left blank for readability. For each column of the matrix, that is, for each time index t, each cell *viterbi*[t,j], will contain the probability of the most likely path to end in that cell. We will calculate this probability recursively, by maximizing over the probability of coming from all possible preceding states. Then we move to the next state; for each of the i states *viterbi*[0,i] in column 0, we compute the probability of moving into each of the j states *viterbi*[1,j] in column 1, according to the recurrence relation in (7.9). In the column for the input *aa*, only two cells have non-zero entries, since $b_1(aa)$ is zero for every other state except the two states labeled *aa*. The value of *viterbi*(1,*aa*) of the word *I* is the product of the transition probability from # to *I* and the probability of *I* being pronounced with the vowel *aa*.

Notice that if we look at the column for the observation n, that the word *on* is currently the "most-probable" word. But since there is no word or set of words in this lexicon which is pronounced *i dh ax*, the path starting with *on* is a dead end, that is, this hypothesis can never be extended to cover the whole utterance.

By the time we see the observation *iy*, there are two competing paths: *I need* and *I the*; *I need* is currently more likely. When we get to the observation *dh*, we could have arrived from either the *iy* of *need* or the *iy* of *the*.

---

function VITERBI(*observations* of len *T*,*state-graph*) **returns** *best-path*

    num-states ← NUM-OF-STATES(*state-graph*)
    Create a path probability matrix *viterbi[num-states+2,T+2]*
    viterbi[0,0] ← 1.0
    for each time step *t* **from** 0 **to** *T* **do**
        for each state *s* **from** 0 **to** *num-states* **do**
            for each transition *s'* from *s* specified by *state-graph*
                new-score ← *viterbi[s, t]* * *a[s,s']* * $b_{s'}(o_t)$
                if ((*viterbi[s',t+1]* = 0) || (*new-score* > *viterbi[s', t+1]*))
                    then
                          viterbi[s', t+1] ← *new-score*
                          back-pointer[s', t+1] ← *s*
    Backtrace from highest probability state in the final column of *viterbi[]* and
  return path.

Figure 7.9   Viterbi algorithm for finding optimal sequence of states in continuous speech recognition, simplified by using phones as inputs (duplicate of Figure 5.19). Given an observation sequence of phones and a weighted automaton (state graph), the algorithm returns the path through the automaton which has minimum probability and accepts the observation sequence. $a[s,s']$ is the transition probability from current state *s* to next state *s'* and $b_{s'}(o_t)$ is the observation likelihood of *s'* given o_t.

The probability of the *max* of these two paths, in this case the path through *I need*, will go into the cell for *dh*.

    Finally, the probability for the best path will appear in the final *ax* column. In this example, only one cell is non-zero in this column; the *ax* state of the word *the* (a real example wouldn't be this simple; many other cells would be non-zero).

    If the sentence had actually ended here, we would now need to backtrace to find the path that gave us this probability. We can't just pick the highest probability state for each state column. Why not? Because the most likely path early on is not necessarily the most likely path for the whole sentence. Recall that the most likely path after seeing *n* was the word *on*. But the most likely path for the whole sentence is *I need the*. Thus we had to rely in Figure 7.10 on the "Hansel and Gretel" method (or the "Jason and the Minotaur" method if you like your metaphors more classical): whenever we moved into a cell, we kept pointers back to the cell we came from. The reader should convince themselves that the Viterbi algorithm has simultaneously solved the segmentation and decoding problems.

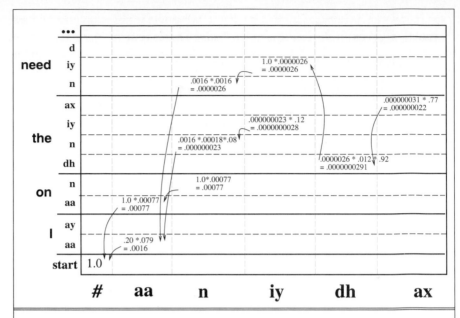

Figure 7.10   The entries in the individual state columns for the Viterbi algorithm. Each cell keeps the probability of the best path so far and a pointer to the previous cell along that path. Backtracing from the successful last word (*the*), we can reconstruct the word sequence *I need the*.

The presentation of the Viterbi algorithm in this section has been simplified; actual implementations of Viterbi decoding are more complex in three key ways that we have mentioned already. First, in an actual HMM for speech recognition, the input would not be phones. Instead, the input is a **feature vector** of spectral and acoustic features. Thus the **observation likelihood probabilities** $b_i(t)$ of an observation o_t given a state i will not simply take on the values 0 or 1, but will be more fine-grained probability estimates, computed via mixtures of Gaussian probability estimators or neural nets. The next section will show how these probabilities are computed.

Second, the HMM states in most speech recognition systems are not simple phones but rather **subphones**. In these systems each phone is divided into three states: the beginning, middle and final portions of the phone. Dividing up a phone in this way captures the intuition that the significant changes in the acoustic input happen at a finer granularity than the phone; for example the closure and release of a stop consonant. Furthermore, many

TRIPHONE   systems use a separate instance of each of these subphones for each **triphone** context (Schwartz et al., 1985; Deng et al., 1990). Thus instead of around

60 phone units, there could be as many as 60^3 context-dependent triphones. In practice, many possible sequences of phones never occur or are very rare, so systems create a much smaller number of triphones models by **clustering** the possible triphones (Young and Woodland, 1994). Figure 7.11 shows an example of the complete phone model for the triphone b(ax,aw).

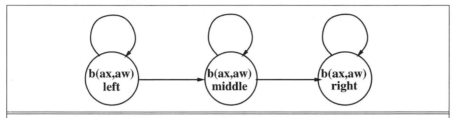

Figure 7.11   An example of the context-dependent triphone b(ax,aw) (the phone [b] preceded by a [ax] and followed by a [aw], as in the beginning of *about*, showing its left, middle, and right subphones.

Finally, in practice in large-vocabulary recognition it is too expensive to consider all possible words when the algorithm is extending paths from one state-column to the next. Instead, low-probability paths are pruned at each time step and not extended to the next state column. This is usually implemented via **beam search**: for each state column (time step), the algorithm maintains a short list of high-probability words whose path probabilities are within some percentage (**beam width**) of the most probable word path. Only transitions from these words are extended when moving to the next time step. Since the words are ranked by the probability of the path so far, which words are within the beam (active) will change from time step to time step. Making this beam search approximation allows a significant speed-up at the cost of a degradation to the decoding performance. This beam search strategy was first implemented by Lowerre (1968). Because in practice most implementations of Viterbi use beam search, some of the literature uses the term **beam search** or **time-synchronous beam search** instead of Viterbi.

BEAM SEARCH

BEAM WIDTH

7.4   ADVANCED METHODS FOR DECODING

There are two main limitations of the Viterbi decoder. First, the Viterbi decoder does not actually compute the sequence of words which is most probable given the input acoustics. Instead, it computes an approximation to this: the sequence of *states* (i.e., *phones* or *subphones*) which is most probable given the input. This difference may not always be important; the most probable sequence of phones may very well correspond exactly to the most probable sequence of words. But sometimes the most probable sequence of phones does not correspond to the most probable word sequence. For example consider a speech recognition system whose lexicon has multiple pronunciations for each word. Suppose the correct word sequence includes a word with very many pronunciations. Since the probabilities leaving the start arc of each word must sum to 1.0, each of these pronunciation-paths through this multiple-pronunciation HMM word model will have a smaller probability than the path through a word with only a single pronunciation path. Thus because the Viterbi decoder can only follow one of these pronunciation paths, it may ignore this word in favor of an incorrect word with only one pronunciation path.

A second problem with the Viterbi decoder is that it cannot be used with all possible language models. In fact, the Viterbi algorithm as we have defined it cannot take complete advantage of any language model more complex than a bigram grammar. This is because of the fact mentioned early that a trigram grammar, for example, violates the **dynamic programming invariant** that makes dynamic programming algorithms possible. Recall that this invariant is the simplifying (but incorrect) assumption that if the ultimate best path for the entire observation sequence happens to go through a state q_i, that this best path must include the best path up to and including state q_i. Since a trigram grammar allows the probability of a word to be based on the two previous words, it is possible that the best trigram-probability path for the sentence may go through a word but not include the best path to that word. Such a situation could occur if a particular word w_x has a high trigram probability given w_y, w_z, but that conversely the best path to w_y didn't include w_z (i.e., $P(w_y|w_q, w_z)$ was low for all q).

There are two classes of solutions to these problems with Viterbi decoding. One class involves modifying the Viterbi decoder to return multiple potential utterances and then using other high-level language model or pronunciation-modeling algorithms to re-rank these multiple outputs. In general this kind of **multiple-pass decoding** allows a computationally efficient, but perhaps unsophisticated, language model like a bigram to perform a rough first decoding pass, allowing more sophisticated but slower decoding algorithms to run on a reduced search space.

N-BEST

For example, Schwartz and Chow (1990) give a Viterbi-like algorithm which returns the **N-best** sentences (word sequences) for a given speech input. Suppose for example a bigram grammar is used with this N-best-Viterbi

to return the 10,000 most highly-probable sentences, each with their likelihood score. A trigram-grammar can then be used to assign a new language-model prior probability to each of these sentences. These priors can be combined with the acoustic likelihood of each sentence to generate a posterior probability for each sentence. Sentences can then be **rescored** using   RESCORED
this more sophisticated probability. Figure 7.12 shows an intuition for this algorithm.

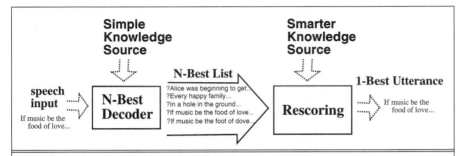

Figure 7.12   The use of *N*-best decoding as part of a two-stage decoding model. Efficient but unsophisticated knowledge sources are used to return the *N*-best utterances. This significantly reduces the search space for the second pass models, which are thus free to be very sophisticated but slow.

An augmentation of *N*-best, still part of this first class of extensions to Viterbi, is to return, not a list of sentences, but a **word lattice**. A word lattice   WORD LATTICE
is a directed graph of words and links between them which can compactly encode a large number of possible sentences. Each word in the lattice is augmented with its observation likelihood, so that any particular path through the lattice can then be combined with the prior probability derived from a more sophisticated language model. For example Murveit et al. (1993) describe an algorithm used in the SRI recognizer Decipher which uses a bigram grammar in a rough first pass, producing a word lattice which is then refined by a more sophisticated language model.

The second solution to the problems with Viterbi decoding is to employ a completely different decoding algorithm. The most common alternative algorithm is the **stack decoder**, also called the **A*** decoder (Jelinek, 1969;   STACK DECODER
Jelinek et al., 1975). We will describe the algorithm in terms of the **A***   A*
search used in the artificial intelligence literature, although the development   A* SEARCH
of stack decoding actually came from the communications theory literature and the link with AI best-first search was noticed only later (Jelinek, 1976).

A* Decoding

To see how the A* decoding method works, we need to revisit the Viterbi algorithm. Recall that the Viterbi algorithm computed an approximation of the forward algorithm. Viterbi computes the observation likelihood of the single best (MAX) path through the HMM, while the forward algorithm computes the observation likelihood of the total (SUM) of all the paths through the HMM. But we accepted this approximation because Viterbi computed this likelihood *and* searched for the optimal path simultaneously. The A* decoding algorithm, on the other hand, will rely on the complete forward algorithm rather than an approximation. This will ensure that we compute the correct observation likelihood. Furthermore, the A* decoding algorithm allows us to use any arbitrary language model.

The A* decoding algorithm is a kind of best-first search of the lattice or tree which implicitly defines the sequence of allowable words in a language. Consider the tree in Figure 7.13, rooted in the START node on the left. Each leaf of this tree defines one sentence of the language; the one formed by concatenating all the words along the path from START to the leaf. We don't represent this tree explicitly, but the stack decoding algorithm uses the tree implicitly as a way to structure the decoding search.

The algorithm performs a search from the root of the tree toward the leaves, looking for the highest probability path, and hence the highest probability sentence. As we proceed from root toward the leaves, each branch leaving a given word node represent a word which may follow the current word. Each of these branches has a probability, which expresses the conditional probability of this next word given the part of the sentence we've seen so far. In addition, we will use the forward algorithm to assign each word a likelihood of producing some part of the observed acoustic data. The A* decoder must thus find the path (word sequence) from the root to a leaf which has the highest probability, where a path probability is defined as the product of its language model probability (prior) and its acoustic match to the data (likelihood). It does this by keeping a **priority queue** of partial paths (i.e., prefixes of sentences, each annotated with a score). In a priority queue each element has a score, and the *pop* operation returns the element with the highest score. The A* decoding algorithm iteratively chooses the best prefix-so-far, computes all the possible next words for that prefix, and adds these extended sentences to the queue. The Figure 7.14 shows the complete algorithm.

PRIORITY
QUEUE

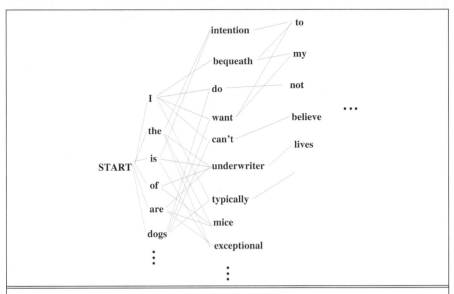

Figure 7.13   A visual representation of the implicit lattice of allowable word sequences that defines a language. The set of sentences of a language is far too large to represent explicitly, but the lattice gives a metaphor for exploring substrings of these sentences.

Let's consider a stylized example of a A* decoder working on a waveform for which the correct transcription is *If music be the food of love*. Figure 7.15 shows the search space after the decoder has examined paths of length one from the root. A **fast match** is used to select the likely next words. A fast match is one of a class of heuristics designed to efficiently winnow down the number of possible following words, often by computing some approximation to the forward probability (see below for further discussion of fast matching).

FAST MATCH

At this point in our example, we've done the fast match, selected a subset of the possible next words, and assigned each of them a score. The word *Alice* has the highest score. We haven't yet said exactly how the scoring works, although it will involve as a component the probability of the hypothesized sentence given the acoustic input $P(W|A)$, which itself is composed of the language model probability $P(W)$ and the acoustic likelihood $P(A|W)$.

Figure 7.16 show the next stage in the search. We have expanded the *Alice* node. This means that the *Alice* node is no longer on the queue, but its children are. Note that now the node labeled *if* actually has a higher score than any of the children of *Alice*.

function STACK-DECODING() **returns** *min-distance*

    Initialize the priority queue with a null sentence.
    Pop the best (highest score) sentence s off the queue.
    If (s is marked end-of-sentence (EOS)) output s and terminate.
    Get list of candidate next words by doing fast matches.
    For each candidate next word w:
        Create a new candidate sentence $s + w$.
        Use forward algorithm to compute acoustic likelihood L of $s + w$
        Compute language model probability P of extended sentence $s + w$
        Compute "score" for $s + w$ (a function of L, P, and ???)
        if (end-of-sentence) set EOS flag for $s + w$.
        Insert $s + w$ into the queue together with its score and EOS flag

Figure 7.14   The A* decoding algorithm (modified from Paul (1991) and Jelinek (1997)). The evaluation function that is used to compute the score for a sentence is not completely defined here; possibly evaluation functions are discussed below.

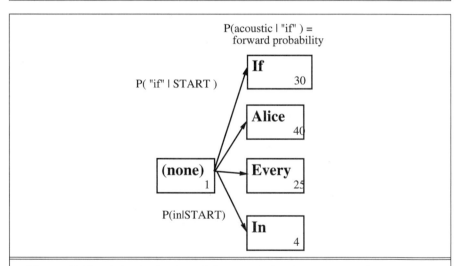

Figure 7.15   The beginning of the search for the sentence *If music be the food of love*. At this early stage *Alice* is the most likely hypothesis. (It has a higher score than the other hypotheses.)

Figure 7.17 shows the state of the search after expanding the *if* node, removing it, and adding *if music*, *if muscle*, and *if messy* on to the queue.

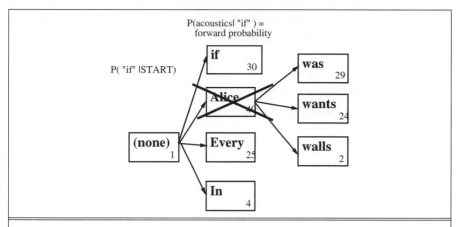

Figure 7.16   The next step of the search for the sentence *If music be the food of love*. We've now expanded the *Alice* node and added three extensions which have a relatively high score (*was*, *wants*, and *walls*). Note that now the node with the highest score is *START if*, which is not along the *START Alice* path at all!

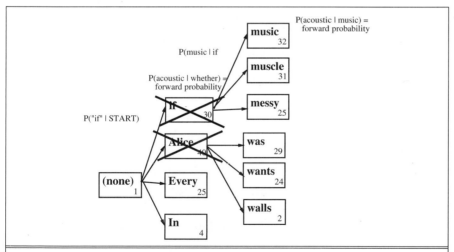

Figure 7.17   We've now expanded the *if* node. The hypothesis *START if music* currently has the highest score.

We've implied that the scoring criterion for a hypothesis is related to its probability. Indeed it might seem that the score for a string of words w_1^i given an acoustic string y_1^j should be the product of the prior and the likelihood:

$$P(y_1^j|w_1^i)P(w_1^i)$$

Alas, the score cannot be this probability because the probability will be much smaller for a longer path than a shorter one. This is due to a simple fact about probabilities and substrings; any prefix of a string must have a higher probability than the string itself (e.g., P(START the ...) will be greater than P(START the book)). Thus if we used probability as the score, the A* decoding algorithm would get stuck on the single-word hypotheses.

Instead, we use what is called the A* evaluation function (Nilsson, 1980; Pearl, 1984) called $f^*(p)$, given a partial path p:

$$f^*(p) = g(p) + h^*(p)$$

$f^*(p)$ is the *estimated* score of the best complete path (complete sentence) which starts with the partial path p. In other words, it is an estimate of how well this path would do if we let it continue through the sentence. The A* algorithm builds this estimate from two components:

- $g(p)$ is the score from the beginning of utterance to the end of the partial path p. This g function can be nicely estimated by the probability of p given the acoustics so far (i.e., as $P(A|W)P(W)$ for the word string W constituting p).

- $h^*(p)$ is an estimate of the best scoring extension of the partial path to the end of the utterance.

Coming up with a good estimate of h^* is an unsolved and interesting problem. One approach is to choose as h^* an estimate which correlates with the number of words remaining in the sentence (Paul, 1991); see Jelinek (1997) for further discussion.

We mentioned above that both the A* and various other two-stage decoding algorithms require the use of a **fast match** for quickly finding which words in the lexicon are likely candidates for matching some portion of the acoustic input. Many fast match algorithms are based on the use of a **tree-structured lexicon**, which stores the pronunciations of all the words in such a way that the computation of the forward probability can be shared for words which start with the same sequence of phones. The tree-structured lexicon was first suggested by Klovstad and Mondshein (1975); fast match algorithms which make use of it include Gupta et al. (1988), Bahl et al. (1992) in the context of A* decoding, and Ney et al. (1992) and Nguyen and Schwartz (1999) in the context of Viterbi decoding. Figure 7.18 shows an example of a tree-structured lexicon from the Sphinx-II recognizer (Ravishankar, 1996). Each tree root represents the first phone of all words begin-

TREE-STRUCTURED LEXICON

ning with that context dependent phone (phone context may or may not be preserved across word boundaries), and each leaf is associated with a word.

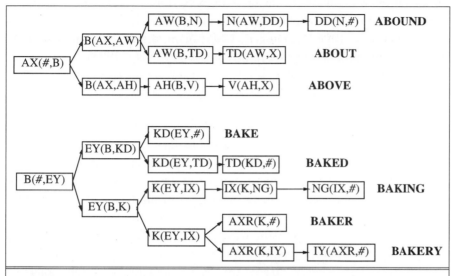

Figure 7.18   A tree-structured lexicon from the Sphinx-II recognizer (after Ravishankar (1996)). Each node corresponds to a particular triphone in a slightly modified version of the ARPAbet; thus EY(B,KD) means the phone EY preceded by a B and followed by the closure of a K.

There are many other kinds of multiple-stage search, such as the **forward-backward** search algorithm (not to be confused with the **forward-backward** algorithm for HMM parameter setting) (Austin et al., 1991) which performs a simple forward search followed by a detailed backward (i.e., time-reversed) search.

FORWARD-
BACKWARD

7.5   ACOUSTIC PROCESSING OF SPEECH

This section presents a very brief overview of the kind of acoustic processing commonly called **feature extraction** or **signal analysis** in the speech recognition literature. The term **features** refers to the vector of numbers which represent one time-slice of a speech signal. A number of kinds of features are commonly used, such as **LPC** features and **PLP** features. All of these are **spectral features**, which means that they represent the waveform in terms of the distribution of different **frequencies** which make up the waveform; such a distribution of frequencies is called a **spectrum**. We will begin with a brief

FEATURE
EXTRACTION

SIGNAL ANALYSIS

LPC

PLP

SPECTRAL FEATURES

introduction to the acoustic waveform and how it is digitized, summarize the idea of frequency analysis and spectra, and then sketch out different kinds of extracted features. This will be an extremely brief overview; the interested reader should refer to other books on the linguistics aspects of acoustic phonetics (Johnson, 1997; Ladefoged, 1996) or on the engineering aspects of digital signal processing of speech (Rabiner and Juang, 1993).

Sound Waves

The input to a speech recognizer, like the input to the human ear, is a complex series of changes in air pressure. These changes in air pressure obviously originate with the speaker, and are caused by the specific way that air passes through the glottis and out the oral or nasal cavities. We represent sound waves by plotting the change in air pressure over time. One metaphor which sometimes helps in understanding these graphs is to imagine a vertical plate which is blocking the air pressure waves (perhaps in a microphone in front of a speaker's mouth, or the eardrum in a hearer's ear). The graph measures the amount of **compression** or **rarefaction** (uncompression) of the air molecules at this plate. Figure 7.19 shows the waveform taken from the Switchboard corpus of telephone speech of someone saying "she just had a baby".

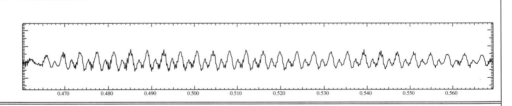

Figure 7.19   A waveform of the vowel [iy] from the utterance shown in Figure 7.20. The y-axis shows the changes in air pressure above and below normal atmospheric pressure. The x-axis shows time. Notice that the wave repeats regularly.

FREQUENCY   Two important characteristics of a wave are its **frequency** and **ampli-**
AMPLITUDE   **tude**. The frequency is the number of times a second that a wave repeats itself, or **cycles**. Note in Figure 7.19 that there are 28 repetitions of the wave in the .11 seconds we have captured. Thus the frequency of this segment of
CYCLES PER   the wave is 28/.11 or 255 **cycles per second**. Cycles per second are usually
SECOND
HERTZ   called **Hertz** (shortened to **Hz**), so the frequency in Figure 7.19 would be described as 255 Hz.

The vertical axis in Figure 7.19 measures the amount of air pressure

variation. A high value on the vertical axis (a high **amplitude**) indicates   AMPLITUDE
that there is more air pressure at that point in time, a zero value means there
is normal (atmospheric) air pressure, while a negative value means there is
lower than normal air pressure (rarefaction).

Two important perceptual properties are related to frequency and amplitude. The **pitch** of a sound is the perceptual correlate of frequency; in   PITCH
general if a sound has a higher frequency we perceive it as having a higher
pitch, although the relationship is not linear, since human hearing has different acuities for different frequencies. Similarly, the **loudness** of a sound is
the perceptual correlate of the **power**, which is related to the square of the
amplitude. So sounds with higher amplitudes are perceived as louder, but
again the relationship is not linear.

How to Interpret a Waveform

Since humans (and to some extent machines) can transcribe and understand
speech just given the sound wave, the waveform must contain enough information to make the task possible. In most cases this information is hard to
unlock just by looking at the waveform, but such visual inspection is still
sufficient to learn some things. For example, the difference between vowels
and most consonants is relatively clear on a waveform. Recall that vowels
are voiced, tend to be long, and are relatively loud. Length in time manifests
itself directly as length in space on a waveform plot. Loudness manifests
itself as high amplitude. How do we recognize voicing? Recall that voicing
is caused by regular openings and closing of the vocal folds. When the vocal
folds are vibrating, we can see regular peaks in amplitude of the kind we saw
in Figure 7.19. During a stop consonant, for example the closure of a [p], [t],
or [k], we should expect no peaks at all; in fact we expect silence.

Notice in Figure 7.20 the places where there are regular amplitude
peaks indicating voicing; from second .46 to .58 (the vowel [iy]), from second .65 to .74 (the vowel [ax]) and so on. The places where there is no
amplitude indicate the silence of a stop closure; for example from second
1.06 to second 1.08 (the closure for the first [b], or from second 1.26 to 1.28
(the closure for the second [b]).

Fricatives like [sh] can also be recognized in a waveform; they produce
an intense irregular pattern; the [sh] from second .33 to .46 is a good example
of a fricative.

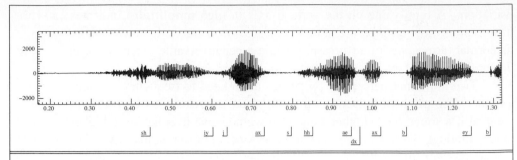

Figure 7.20   A waveform of the sentence "She just had a baby" from the Switchboard corpus (conversation 4325). The speaker is female, was 20 years old in 1991, which is approximately when the recording was made, and speaks the South Midlands dialect of American English. The phone labels show where each phone ends. The last bit of the final [iy] vowel is cut off in this figure.

Spectra

SPECTRAL

While some broad phonetic features (presence of voicing, stop closures, fricatives) can be interpreted from a waveform, more detailed classification (which vowel? which fricative?) requires a different representation of the input in terms of **spectral** features. Spectral features are based on the insight of Fourier that every complex wave can be represented as a sum of many simple waves of different frequencies. A musical analogy for this is the chord; just as a chord is composed of multiple notes, any waveform is composed of the waves corresponding to its individual "notes".

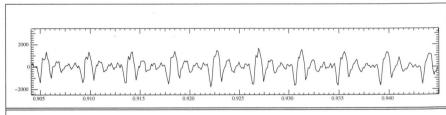

Figure 7.21   The waveform of part of the vowel [æ] from the word *had* cut out from the waveform shown in Figure 7.20.

Consider Figure 7.21, which shows part of the waveform for the vowel [æ] of the word *had* at second 0.9 of the sentence. Note that there is a complex wave which repeats about nine times in the figure; but there is also a smaller repeated wave which repeats four times for every larger pattern (notice the four small peaks inside each repeated wave). The complex wave has a frequency of about 250 Hz (we can figure this out since it repeats roughly 9 times in .036 seconds, and 9 cycles/.036 seconds = 250 Hz). The smaller wave then should have a frequency of roughly four times the frequency of the larger wave, or roughly 1000 Hz. Then if you look carefully you can see two little waves on the peak of many of the 1000 Hz waves. The frequency of this tiniest wave must be roughly twice that of the 1000 Hz wave, hence 2000 Hz.

A **spectrum** is a representation of these different frequency compo- SPECTRUM
nents of a wave. It can be computed by a **Fourier transform**, a mathematical FOURIER TRANSFORM
procedure which separates out each of the frequency components of a wave.
Rather than using the Fourier transform spectrum directly, most speech applications use a smoothed version of the spectrum called the **LPC** spectrum LPC
(Atal and Hanauer, 1971; Itakura, 1975).

Figure 7.22 shows an LPC spectrum for the waveform in Figure 7.21.
LPC (**Linear Predictive Coding**) is a way of coding the spectrum that makes
it easier to see where the **spectral peaks** are. SPECTRAL PEAKS

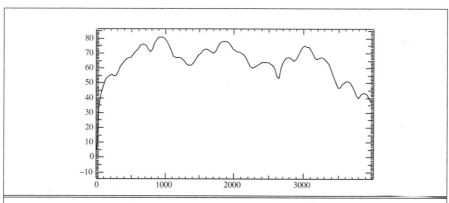

Figure 7.22   An LPC spectrum for the vowel [æ] waveform of *She just had a baby* at the point in time shown in Figure 7.21. LPC makes it easy to see **formants**.

The *x*-axis of a spectrum shows frequency while the *y*-axis shows some measure of the magnitude of each frequency component (in decibels (dB), a logarithmic measure of amplitude). Thus Figure 7.22 shows that there are important frequency components at 930 Hz, 1860 Hz, and 3020 Hz, along with many other lower-magnitude frequency components. These important components at roughly 1000 Hz and 2000 Hz are just what we predicted by looking at the wave in Figure 7.21!

Why is a spectrum useful? It turns out that these spectral peaks that are easily visible in a spectrum are very characteristic of different sounds; phones have characteristic spectral "signatures". For example different chemical elements give off different wavelengths of light when they burn, allowing us to detect elements in stars light-years away by looking at the spectrum of the light. Similarly, by looking at the spectrum of a waveform, we can detect the characteristic signature of the different phones that are present. This use of spectral information is essential to both human and machine speech recognition. In human audition, the function of the **cochlea** or **inner ear** is to compute a spectrum of the incoming waveform. Similarly, the features used as input to the HMMs in speech recognition are all representations of spectra, usually variants of LPC spectra, as we will see.

COCHLEA

INNER EAR

While a spectrum shows the frequency components of a wave at one point in time, a **spectrogram** is a way of envisioning how the different frequencies which make up a waveform change over time. The *x*-axis shows time, as it did for the waveform, but the *y*-axis now shows frequencies in Hertz. The darkness of a point on a spectrogram corresponding to the amplitude of the frequency component. For example, look in Figure 7.23 around second 0.9 and notice the dark bar at around 1000 Hz. This means that the [iy] of the word *she* has an important component around 1000 Hz (1000 Hz is just between the notes B and C). The dark horizontal bars on a spectrogram, representing spectral peaks, usually of vowels, are called **formants**.

SPECTROGRAM

FORMANTS

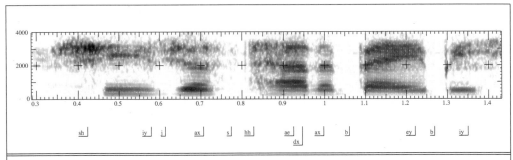

Figure 7.23   A spectrogram of the sentence "She just had a baby" whose waveform was shown in Figure 7.20. One way to think of a spectrogram is as a collection of spectra (timeslices) like Figure 7.22 placed end to end.

What specific clues can spectral representations give for phone identification? First, different vowels have their formants at characteristic places. We've seen that [æ] in the sample waveform had formants at 930 Hz, 1860 Hz, and 3020 Hz. Consider the vowel [iy], at the beginning of the utterance

in Figure 7.20. The spectrum for this vowel is shown in Figure 7.24. The first
formant of [iy] is 540 Hz; much lower than the first formant for [æ], while the
second formant (2581 Hz) is much higher than the second formant for [æ].
If you look carefully you can see these formants as dark bars in Figure 7.23
just around 0.5 seconds.

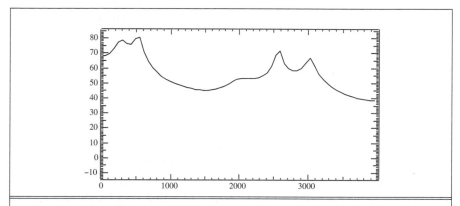

Figure 7.24   A smoothed (LPC) spectrum for the vowel [iy] at the start of
She just had a baby. Note that the first formant (540 Hz) is much lower than
the first formant for [æ] shown in Figure 7.22, while the second formant (2581
Hz) is much higher than the second formant for [æ].

The location of the first two formants (called F1 and F2) plays a large
role in determining vowel identity, although the formants still differ from
speaker to speaker. Formants also can be used to identify the nasal phones
[n], [m], and [ŋ], the lateral phone [l], and [r]. Why do different vowels have
different spectral signatures? The formants are caused by the resonant cavities of the mouth. The oral cavity can be thought of as a filter which selectively passes through some of the harmonics of the vocal cord vibrations.
Moving the tongue creates spaces of different size inside the mouth which
selectively amplify waves of the appropriate wavelength, hence amplifying
different frequency bands.

Feature Extraction

Our survey of the features of waveforms and spectra was necessarily brief,
but the reader should have the basic idea of the importance of spectral features and their relation to the original waveform. Let's now summarize the
process of extraction of spectral features, beginning with the sound wave

itself and ending with a **feature vector**.[4] An input soundwave is first **digitized**. This process of **analog-to-digital conversion** has two steps: **sampling** and **quantization**. A signal is sampled by measuring its amplitude at a particular time; the **sampling rate** is the number of samples taken per second. Common sampling rates are 8,000 Hz and 16,000 Hz. In order to accurately measure a wave, it is necessary to have at least two samples in each cycle: one measuring the positive part of the wave and one measuring the negative part. More than two samples per cycle increases the amplitude accuracy, but less than two samples will cause the frequency of the wave to be completely missed. Thus the maximum frequency wave that can be measured is one whose frequency is half the sample rate (since every cycle needs two samples). This maximum frequency for a given sampling rate is called the **Nyquist frequency**. Most information in human speech is in frequencies below 10,000 Hz; thus a 20,000 Hz sampling rate would be necessary for complete accuracy. But telephone speech is filtered by the switching network, and only frequencies less than 4,000 Hz are transmitted by telephones. Thus an 8,000 Hz sampling rate is sufficient for telephone-bandwidth speech like the Switchboard corpus.

Even an 8,000 Hz sampling rate requires 8000 amplitude measurements for each second of speech, and so it is important to store the amplitude measurement efficiently. They are usually stored as integers, either 8-bit (values from -128–127) or 16 bit (values from -32768–32767). This process of representing a real-valued number as a integer is called **quantization** because there is a minimum granularity (the quantum size) and all values which are closer together than this quantum size are represented identically.

Once a waveform has been digitized, it is converted to some set of spectral features. An LPC spectrum is represented by a vector of features; each formant is represented by two features, plus two additional features to represent spectral tilt. Thus five formants can be represented by $12\,(5 \times 2 + 2)$ features. It is possible to use LPC features directly as the observation symbols of an HMM. However, further processing is often done to the features. One popular feature set is **cepstral**, which are computed from the LPC coefficients by taking the Fourier transform of the spectrum. Another feature set, **PLP (Perceptual Linear Predictive** analysis (Hermansky, 1990)), takes the LPC features and modifies them in ways consistent with human hearing. For

SAMPLING
SAMPLING RATE

NYQUIST
FREQUENCY

QUANTIZATION

CEPSTRAL
COEFFICIENTS

PLP

---

[4] The reader might want to bear in mind Picone's (1993) reminder that the use of the word **extraction** should not be thought of as encouraging the metaphor of features as something "in the signal" waiting to be extracted.

example, the spectral resolution of human hearing is worse at high frequencies, and the perceived loudness of a sound is related to the cube rate of its intensity. So PLP applies various filters to the LPC spectrum and takes the cube root of the features.

7.6 COMPUTING ACOUSTIC PROBABILITIES

The last section showed how the speech input can be passed through signal processing transformations and turned into a series of vectors of features, each vector representing one time-slice of the input signal. How are these feature vectors turned into probabilities?

One way to compute probabilities on feature vectors is to first **cluster**
them into discrete symbols that we can count; we can then compute the probability of a given cluster just by counting the number of times it occurs in some training set. This method is usually called **vector quantization**. Vector quantization was quite common in early speech recognition algorithms but has mainly been replaced by a more direct but compute-intensive approach: computing observation probabilities on a real-valued ('continuous') input vector. This method thus computes a **probability density function** or **pdf** over a continuous space.

There are two popular versions of the continuous approach. The most widespread of the two is the use of **Gaussian** pdfs, in the simplest version of which each state has a single Gaussian function which maps the observation vector o_t to a probability. An alternative approach is the use of **neural networks** or **multi-layer perceptrons** which can also be trained to assign a probability to a real-valued feature vector. HMMs with Gaussian observation-probability-estimators are trained by a simple extension to the forward-backward algorithm (discussed in Appendix D). HMMs with neural-net observation-probability-estimators are trained by a completely different algorithm known as **error back-propagation**.

In the simplest use of Gaussians, we assume that the possible values of the observation feature vector o_t are normally distributed, and so we represent the observation probability function $b_j(o_t)$ as a Gaussian curve with mean vector μ_j and covariance matrix Σ_j; (prime denotes vector transpose). We present the equation here for completeness, although we will not cover the details of the mathematics:

$$b_j(o_t) = \frac{1}{\sqrt{(2\pi)|\Sigma j|}} e^{[(o_t - \mu_j)'\Sigma_j^{-1}(o_t - \mu_j)]} \qquad (7.10)$$

CLUSTER

VECTOR QUANTIZATION

PROBABILITY DENSITY FUNCTION

GAUSSIAN

NEURAL NETWORKS

MULTI-LAYER PERCEPTRONS

ERROR BACK-PROPAGATION

Usually we make the simplifying assumption that the covariance matrix Σ_j is diagonal, i.e., that it contains the simple variance of cepstral feature 1, the simple variance of cepstral feature 2, and so on, without worrying about the effect of cepstral feature 1 on the variance of cepstral feature 2. This means that in practice we are keeping only a single separate mean and variance for each feature in the feature vector.

Most recognizers do something even more complicated; they keep multiple Gaussians for each state, so that the probability of each feature of the observation vector is computed by adding together a variety of Gaussian curves. This technique is called **Gaussian mixtures**. In addition, many ASR systems share Gaussians between states in a technique known as **parameter tying** (or **tied mixtures**) (Huang and Jack, 1989). For example acoustically similar phone states might share (i.e., use the same) Gaussians for some features.

GAUSSIAN
MIXTURES

TIED
MIXTURES

How are the mean and covariance of the Gaussians estimated? It is helpful again to consider the simpler case of a non-hidden Markov Model, with only one state i. The vector of feature means μ and the vector of covariances Σ could then be estimated by averaging:

$$\hat{\mu}_i \;=\; \frac{1}{T} \sum_{t=1}^{T} o_t \tag{7.11}$$

$$\hat{\Sigma}_i \;=\; \frac{1}{T} \sum_{t=1}^{T} [(o_t - \mu_j)'(o_t - \mu_j)] \tag{7.12}$$

But since there are multiple hidden states, we don't know which observation vector o_t was produced by which state. Appendix D will show how the forward-backward algorithm can be modified to assign each observation vector o_t to every possible state i, prorated by the probability that the HMM was in state i at time t.

An alternative way to model continuous-valued features is the use of a **neural network, multilayer perceptron (MLP)** or **Artificial Neural Networks (ANNs)**. Neural networks are far too complex for us to introduce in a page or two here; thus we will just give the intuition of how they are used in probability estimation as an alternative to Gaussian estimators. The interested reader should consult basic neural network textbooks (Anderson, 1995; Hertz et al., 1991) as well as references specifically focusing on neural-network speech recognition (Bourlard and Morgan, 1994).

NEURAL
NETWORK

MULTILAYER
PERCEPTRON

MLP

A neural network is a set of small computation units connected by weighted links. The network is given a vector of input values and computes a vector of output values. The computation proceeds by each computational unit computing some non-linear function of its input units and passing the resulting value on to its output units.

The use of neural networks we will describe here is often called a **hybrid** HMM-MLP approach, since it uses some elements of the HMM (such as the state-graph representation of the pronunciation of a word) but the observation-probability computation is done by an MLP instead of a mixture of Gaussians. The input to these MLPs is a representation of the signal at a time t and some surrounding window; for example this might mean a vector of spectral features for a time t and eight additional vectors for times $t + 10ms$, $t + 20ms$, $t + 30ms$, $t + 40ms$, $t - 10ms$, and so on. Thus the input to the network is a set of nine vectors, each vector having the complete set of real-valued spectral features for one time slice. The network has one output unit for each phone; by constraining the values of all the output units to sum to 1, the net can be used to compute the probability of a state j given an observation vector o_t, or $P(j|o_t)$. Figure 7.25 shows a sample of such a net.

HYBRID

This MLP computes the probability of the HMM state j given an observation o_t, or $P(q_j|o_t)$. But the observation likelihood we need for the HMM, $b_j(o_t)$, is $P(o_t|q_j)$. The Bayes rule can help us see how to compute one from the other. The net is computing:

$$p(q_j|o_t) = \frac{P(o_t|q_j)p(q_j)}{p(o_t)} \tag{7.13}$$

We can rearrange the terms as follows:

$$\frac{p(o_t|q_j)}{p(o_t)} = \frac{P(q_j|o_t)}{p(q_j)} \tag{7.14}$$

The two terms on the right-hand side of (7.14) can be directly computed from the MLP; the numerator is the output of the MLP, and the denominator is the total probability of a given state, summing over all observations (i.e., the sum over all t of $\sigma_j(t)$). Thus although we cannot directly compute $P(o_t|q_j)$, we *can* use (7.14) to compute $\frac{p(o_t|q_j)}{p(o_t)}$, which is known as a **scaled likelihood** (the likelihood divided by the probability of the observation). In fact, the scaled likelihood is just as good as the regular likelihood, since the probability of the observation $p(o_t)$ is a constant during recognition and doesn't hurt us to have in the equation.

SCALED
LIKELIHOOD

The error-back-propagation algorithm for training an MLP requires that we know the correct phone label q_j for each observation o_t. Given a large training set of observations and correct labels, the algorithm iteratively adjusts the weights in the MLP to minimize the error with this training set.

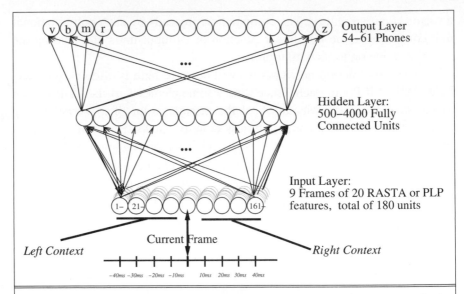

Figure 7.25   A neural net used to estimate phone state probabilities. Such a net can be used in an HMM model as an alternative to the Gaussian models. This particular net is from the MLP systems described in Bourlard and Morgan (1994); it is given a vector of features for a frame and for the four frames on either side, and estimates $p(q_j|o_t)$. This probability is then converted to an estimate of the observation likelihood $b = p(o_t|q_j)$ using the Bayes rule. These nets are trained using the error-back-propagation algorithm as part of the same **embedded training** algorithm that is used for Gaussians.

In the next section we will see where this labeled training set comes from, and how this training fits in with the **embedded training** algorithm used for HMMs. Neural nets seem to achieve roughly the same performance as a Gaussian model but have the advantage of using less parameters and the disadvantage of taking somewhat longer to train.

7.7   TRAINING A SPEECH RECOGNIZER

We have now introduced all the algorithms which make up the standard speech recognition system that was sketched in Figure 7.2 on page 241. We've seen how to build a Viterbi decoder, and how it takes 3 inputs (the observation likelihoods (via Gaussian or MLP estimation from the spectral features), the HMM lexicon, and the N-gram language model) and produces the most probable string of words. But we have not seen how all the proba-

METHODOLOGY BOX: WORD ERROR RATE

The standard evaluation metric for speech recognition systems is the **word error** rate. The word error rate is based on how much the word string returned by the recognizer (often called the **hypothesized** word string) differs from a correct or **reference** transcription. Given such a correct transcription, the first step in computing word error is to compute the **minimum edit distance** in words between the hypothesized and correct strings. The result of this computation will be the minimum number of word **substitutions**, word **insertions**, and word **deletions** necessary to map between the correct and hypothesized strings. The word error rate is then defined as follows (note that because the equation includes insertions, the error rate can be great than 100%):

$$\text{Word Error Rate} = 100 \frac{\text{Insertions} + \text{Substitutions} + \text{Deletions}}{\text{Total Words in Correct Transcript}}$$

Here is an example of **alignments** between a reference and a hypothesized utterance from the CALLHOME corpus, showing the counts used to compute the word error rate:

```
REF:  i  ***    **  UM   the  PHONE  IS            i  LEFT  THE  portable
HYP:  i  GOT    IT  TO   the  *****  FULLEST       i  LOVE  TO   portable
Eval: I   I      S        D     S                     S     S

REF:  ****   PHONE  UPSTAIRS  last  night  so  the  battery  ran  out
HYP:  FORM   OF     STORES    last  night  so  the  battery  ran  out
Eval: I       S      S
```

This utterance has six substitutions, three insertions, and one deletion:

$$\text{Word Error Rate} = 100 \frac{6 + 3 + 1}{18} = 56\%$$

As of the time of this writing, state-of-the-art speech recognition systems were achieving around 20% word error rate on natural-speech tasks like the National Institute of Standards and Technology (NIST)'s Hub4 test set from the Broadcast News corpus (Chen et al., 1999), and around 40% word error rate on NIST's Hub5 test set from the combined Switchboard, Switchboard-II, and CALLHOME corpora (Hain et al., 1999).

bilistic models that make up a recognizer get trained.

EMBEDDED
TRAINING
In this section we give a brief sketch of the **embedded training** procedure that is used by most ASR systems, whether based on Gaussians, MLPs,
or even vector quantization. Some of the details of the algorithm (like the
forward-backward algorithm for training HMM probabilities) have been removed to Appendix D.

Let's begin by summarizing the four probabilistic models we need to
train in a basic speech recognition system:

- **language model probabilities:** $P(w_i|w_{i-1}w_{i-2})$
- **observation likelihoods:** $b_j(o_t)$
- **transition probabilities:** a_{ij}
- **pronunciation lexicon:** HMM state graph structure

In order to train these components we usually have

- a training corpus of speech wavefiles, together with a word-transcription
- a much larger corpus of text for training the language model, including the word-transcriptions from the speech corpus together with many
  other similar texts
- often a smaller training corpus of speech which is phonetically labeled
  (i.e., frames of the acoustic signal are hand-annotated with phonemes)

Let's begin with the N-gram language model. This is trained in the
way we described in Chapter 6; by counting N-gram occurrences in a large
corpus, then smoothing and normalizing the counts. The corpus used for
training the language model is usually much larger than the corpus used to
train the HMM a and b parameters. This is because the larger the training
corpus the more accurate the models. Since N-gram models are much faster
to train than HMM observation probabilities, and since text just takes less
space than speech, it turns out to be feasible to train language models on
huge corpora of as much as half a billion words of text. Generally the corpus
used for training the HMM parameters is included as part of the language
model training data; it is important that the acoustic and language model
training be consistent.

The HMM lexicon structure is built by hand, by taking an off-the-shelf
pronunciation dictionary such as the PRONLEX dictionary (LDC, 1995) or
the CMUdict dictionary, both described in Chapter 4. In some systems, each
phone in the dictionary maps into a state in the HMM. So the word *cat* would
have three states corresponding to [k], [ae], and [t]. Many systems, however,
use the more complex **subphone** structure described on page 251, in which

each phone is divided into 3 states: the beginning, middle and final portions of the phone, and in which furthermore there are separate instances of each of these subphones for each **triphone** context.

The details of the embedded training of the HMM parameters varies; we'll present a simplified version. First, we need some initial estimate of the transition and observation probabilities a_{ij} and $b_j(o_t)$. For the transition probabilities, we start by assuming that for any state all the possible following states are all equiprobable. The observation probabilities can be bootstrapped from a small hand-labeled training corpus. For example, the TIMIT or Switchboard corpora contain approximately 4 hours each of phonetically labeled speech. They supply a "correct" phone state label q for each frame of speech. These can be fed to an MLP or averaged to give initial Gaussian means and variances. For MLPs this initial estimate is important, and so a hand-labeled bootstrap is the norm. For Gaussian models the initial value of the parameters seems to be less important and so the initial mean and variances for Gaussians often are just set identically for all states by using the mean and variances of the entire training set.

Now we have initial estimates for the a and b probabilities. The next stage of the algorithm differs for Gaussian and MLP systems. For MLP systems we apply what is called a **forced Viterbi** alignment. A forced Viterbi alignment takes as input the correct words in an utterance, along with the spectral feature vectors. It produces the best sequence of HMM states, with each state aligned with the feature vectors. A forced Viterbi is thus a simplification of the regular Viterbi decoding algorithm, since it only has to figure out the correct phone sequence, but doesn't have to discover the word sequence. It is called **forced** because we constrain the algorithm by requiring the best path to go through a particular sequence of words. It still requires the Viterbi algorithm since words have multiple pronunciations, and since the duration of each phone is not fixed. The result of the forced Viterbi is a set of features vectors with "correct" phone labels, which can then be used to retrain the neural network. The counts of the transitions which are taken in the forced alignments can be used to estimate the HMM transition probabilities.

FORCED VITERBI

For the Gaussian HMMs, instead of using forced Viterbi, we use the forward-backward algorithm described in Appendix D. We compute the forward and backward probabilities for each sentence given the initial a and b probabilities, and use them to re-estimate the a and b probabilities. Just as for the MLP situation, the forward-backward algorithm needs to be constrained by our knowledge of the correct words. The forward-backward algorithm computes its probabilities given a model λ. We use the "known" words sequence in a transcribed sentence to tell us which word models to string together to get the model λ that we use to compute the forward and backward probabilities for each sentence.

7.8   WAVEFORM GENERATION FOR SPEECH SYNTHESIS

Now that we have covered acoustic processing we can return to the acoustic component of a text-to-speech (TTS) system. Recall from Chapter 4 that the output of the linguistic processing component of a TTS system is a sequence of phones, each with a duration, and a F0 contour that specifies the pitch.

TARGET   This specification is often called the **target**, as it is this that we want the synthesizer to produce.

The most commonly used type of algorithm works by **waveform con-**

WAVEFORM CONCATENATION   **catenation**. Such **concatenative synthesis** is based on a database of speech that has been recorded by a single speaker. This database is then segmented into a number of short units, which can be phones, diphones, syllables, words or other units. The simplest sort of synthesizer would have phone units and the database would have a single unit for each phone in the phone inventory. By selecting units appropriately, we can generate a series of units which match the phone sequence in the input. By using signal processing to smooth joins at the unit edges, we can simply concatenate the waveforms for each of these units to form a single synthetic speech waveform.

Experience has shown that single phone concatenative systems don't produce good quality speech. Just as in speech recognition, the context of the phone plays an important role in its acoustic pattern and hence a /t/ before a /a/ sounds very different from a /t/ before an /s/.

The triphone models described in Figure 7.11 on page 251 are a popular choice of unit in speech recognition, because they cover both the left and right contexts of a phone. Unfortunately, a language typically has a very large number of triphones (tens of thousands) and it is currently pro-

DIPHONES   hibitive to collect so many units for speech synthesis. Hence **diphones** are often used in speech synthesis as they provide a reasonable balance between context-dependency and size (typically 1000–2000 in a language). In speech synthesis, diphone units normally start half-way through the first phone and end half-way through the second. This is because it is known that phones are more stable in the middle than at the edges, so that the middles of most /a/ phones in a diphone are reasonably similar, even if the acoustic patterns start to differ substantially after that. If diphones are concatenated in the middles of phones, the discontinuities between adjacent units are often negligible.

Pitch and Duration Modification

The diphone synthesizer as just described will produce a reasonable quality speech waveform corresponding to the requested phone sequence. But the pitch and duration (i.e., the prosody) of each phone in the concatenated waveform will be the same as when the diphones were recorded and will not correspond to the pitch and durations requested in the input. The next stage of the synthesis process therefore is to use signal processing techniques to change the prosody of the concatenated waveform.

The linear prediction (LPC) model described earlier can be used for prosody modification as it explicitly separates the pitch of a signal from its spectral envelope If the concatenated waveform is represented by a sequence of linear prediction coefficients, a set of pulses can be generated corresponding to the desired pitch and used to re-excite the coefficients to produce a speech waveform again. By contracting and expanding frames of coefficients, the duration can be changed. While linear prediction produces the correct F0 and durations it produces a somewhat "buzzy" speech signal.

Another technique for achieving the same goal is the time-domain pitch-synchronous overlap and add (**TD-PSOLA**) technique. TD-PSOLA works **pitch-synchronously** in that each frame is centered around a **pitchmark** in the speech, rather than at regular intervals as in normal speech signal processing. The concatenated waveform is split into a number of frames, each centered around a pitchmark and extending a pitch period either side. Prosody is changed by recombining these frames at a new set of pitchmarks determined by the requested pitch and duration of the input. The synthetic waveform is created by simply overlapping and adding the frames. Pitch is increased by making the new pitchmarks closer together (shorter pitch periods implies higher frequency pitch), and decreased by making them further apart. Speech is made longer by duplication frames and shorter by leaving frames out. The operation of TD-PSOLA can be compared to that of a tape recorder with variable speed — if you play back a tape faster than it was recorded, the pitch periods will come closer together and hence the pitch will increase. But speeding up a tape recording effectively increases the frequency of *all* the components of the speech (including the formants which characterize the vowels) and will give the impression of a "squeaky", unnatural voice. TD-PSOLA differs because it separates each frame first and then

TD-PSOLA

decreases the distance between the frames. Because the internals of each frame aren't changed, the frequency of the non-pitch components is hardly altered, and the resultant speech sounds the same as the original except with a different pitch.

Unit Selection

While signal processing and diphone concatenation can produce reasonable quality speech, the result is not ideal. There are a number of reasons for this, but they all boil down to the fact that having a single example of each diphone is not enough. First of all, signal processing inevitably incurs distortion, and the quality of the speech gets worse when the signal processing has to stretch the pitch and duration by large amounts. Furthermore, there are many other subtle effects which are outside the scope of most signal processing algorithms. For instance, the amount of vocal effort decreases over time as the utterance is spoken, producing weaker speech at the end of the utterance. If diphones are taken from near the start of an utterance, they will sound unnatural in phrase-final positions.

Unit-selection synthesis is an attempt to address this problem by collecting several examples of each unit at different pitches and durations and linguistic situations, so that the unit is close to the target in the first place and hence the signal processing needs to do less work. One technique for unit-selection (Hunt and Black, 1996) works as follows:

The input to the algorithm is the same as other concatenative synthesizers, with the addition that the F0 contour is now specified as three F0 values per phone, rather than as a contour. The technique uses phones as its units, indexing phones in a large database of naturally occurring speech Each phone in the database is also marked with a duration and three pitch values. The algorithm works in two stages. First, for each phone in the target word, a set of candidate units which match closely in terms of phone identity, duration and F0 is selected from the database. These candidates are ranked using a **target cost** function, which specifies just how close each unit actually is to the target. The second part of the algorithm works by measuring how well each candidate for each unit joins with its neighbor's candidates. Various locations for the joins are assessed, which allows the potential for units to be joined in the middle, as with diphones. These potential joins are ranked using a **concatenation cost** function. The final step is to pick the best set of units which minimize the overall target and concatenation cost for the whole sentence. This step is performed using the Viterbi algorithm in a similar way to HMM speech recognition: here the target cost is the observation probability and the concatenation cost is the transition probability.

By using a much larger database which contains many examples of each unit, unit-selection synthesis often produces more natural speech than straight diphone synthesis. Some systems then use signal processing to make sure the prosody matches the target, while others simply concatenate the units following the idea that a utterance which only roughly matches the target is better than one that exactly matches it but also has some signal processing distortion.

7.9   HUMAN SPEECH RECOGNITION

Speech recognition in humans shares some features with the automatic speech recognition models we have presented. We mentioned above that signal processing algorithms like PLP analysis (Hermansky, 1990) were in fact inspired by properties of the human auditory system. In addition, four properties of human **lexical access** (the process of retrieving a word from the mental lexicon) are also true of ASR models: **frequency**, **parallelism**, **neighborhood effects**, and **cue-based processing**. For example, as in ASR with its N-gram language models, human lexical access is sensitive to word **frequency**. High-frequency spoken words are accessed faster or with less information than low-frequency words. They are successfully recognized in noisier environments than low frequency words, or when only parts of the words are presented (Howes, 1957; Grosjean, 1980; Tyler, 1984, inter alia). Like ASR models, human lexical access is **parallel**: multiple words are active at the same time (Marslen-Wilson and Welsh, 1978; Salasoo and Pisoni, 1985, inter alia). Human lexical access exhibits **neighborhood effects** (the neighborhood of a word is the set of words which closely resemble it). Words with large frequency-weighted neighborhoods are accessed slower than words with less neighbors (Luce et al., 1990). Jurafsky (1996) shows that the effect of neighborhood on access can be explained by the Bayesian models used in ASR.

Finally, human speech perception is **cue based**: speech input is interpreted by integrating cues at many different levels. For example, there is evidence that human perception of individual phones is based on the integration of multiple cues, including acoustic cues, such as formant structure or the exact timing of voicing, (Oden and Massaro, 1978; Miller, 1994), visual cues, such as lip movement (Massaro and Cohen, 1983; Massaro, 1998),

LEXICAL
ACCESS

and lexical cues such as the identity of the word in which the phone is placed (Warren, 1970; Samuel, 1981; Connine and Clifton, 1987; Connine, 1990). For example, in what is often called the **phoneme restoration effect**, Warren (1970) took a speech sample and replaced one phone (e.g. the [s] in *legisla-ture*) with a cough. Warren found that subjects listening to the resulting tape typically heard the entire word *legislature* including the [s], and perceived the cough as background. Other cues in human speech perception include

WORD
ASSOCIATION
REPETITION
PRIMING

semantic **word association** (words are accessed more quickly if a semanti-cally related word has been heard recently) and **repetition priming** (words are accessed more quickly if they themselves have just been heard). The intuitions of both these results are incorporated into recent language models discussed in Chapter 6, such as the cache model of Kuhn and de Mori (1990), which models repetition priming, or the trigger model of Rosenfeld (1996) and the LSA models of Coccaro and Jurafsky (1998) and Bellegarda (1999), which model word association. In a fascinating reminder that good ideas are never discovered only once, Cole and Rudnicky (1983) point out that many of these insights about context effects on word and phone processing were actually discovered by William Bagley (1901). Bagley achieved his results, including an early version of the phoneme restoration effect, by recording speech on Edison phonograph cylinders, modifying it, and presenting it to subjects. Bagley's results were forgotten and only rediscovered much later.[5]

One difference between current ASR models and human speech recog-nition is the time-course of the model. It is important for the performance of the ASR algorithm that the the decoding search optimizes over the entire ut-terance. This means that the best sentence hypothesis returned by a decoder at the end of the sentence may be very different than the current-best hy-pothesis, halfway into the sentence. By contrast, there is extensive evidence

ON-LINE

that human processing is **on-line**: people incrementally segment and utter-ance into words and assign it an interpretation as they hear it. For example, Marslen-Wilson (1973) studied **close shadowers**: people who are able to shadow (repeat back) a passage as they hear it with lags as short as 250 ms. Marslen-Wilson found that when these shadowers made errors, they were syntactically and semantically appropriate with the context, indicating that word segmentation, parsing, and interpretation took place within these 250 ms. Cole (1973) and Cole and Jakimik (1980) found similar effects in their work on the detection of mispronunciations. These results have led psy-chological models of human speech perception (such as the Cohort model

---

[5] Recall the discussion on page 15 of multiple independent discovery in science.

(Marslen-Wilson and Welsh, 1978) and the computational TRACE model (McClelland and Elman, 1986)) to focus on the time-course of word selection and segmentation. The TRACE model, for example, is a **connectionist** or **neural network** interactive-activation model, based on independent computational units organized into three levels: feature, phoneme, and word. Each unit represents a hypothesis about its presence in the input. Units are activated in parallel by the input, and activation flows between units; connections between units on different levels are excitatory, while connections between units on single level are inhibitory. Thus the activation of a word slightly inhibits all other words.

CONNECTIONIST

NEURAL
NETWORK

We have focused on the similarities between human and machine speech recognition; there are also many differences. In particular, many other cues have been shown to play a role in human speech recognition but have yet to be successfully integrated into ASR. The most important class of these missing cues is prosody. To give only one example, Cutler and Norris (1988), Cutler and Carter (1987) note that most multisyllabic English word tokens have stress on the initial syllable, suggesting in their metrical segmentation strategy (MSS) that stress should be used as a cue for word segmentation.

7.10   SUMMARY

Together with Chapters 4–6, this chapter introduced the fundamental algorithms for addressing the problem of **Large Vocabulary Continuous Speech Recognition** and **Text-To-Speech synthesis**.

- The input to a speech recognizer is a series of acoustic waves. The **waveform**, **spectrogram** and **spectrum** are among the visualization tools used to understand the information in the signal.

- In the first step in speech recognition, wound waves are **sampled**, **quantized**, and converted to some sort of **spectral representation**; A commonly used spectral representation is the **LPC cepstrum**, which provides a vector of features for each time-slice of the input.

- These **feature vectors** are used to estimate the **phonetic likelihoods** (also called **observation likelihoods**) either by a mixture of **Gaussian** estimators or by a **neural net**.

- **Decoding** or **search** is the process of finding the optimal sequence of model states which matches a sequence of input observations. (The fact that are two terms for this process is a hint that speech recognition is inherently inter-disciplinary, and draws its metaphors from more than one field; **decoding** comes from information theory, and **search** from artificial intelligence).

- We introduced two decoding algorithms: time-synchronous **Viterbi** decoding (which is usually implemented with pruning and can then be called **beam search**) and **stack** or A^* decoding. Both algorithms take as input a series of feature vectors, and two ancillary algorithms: one for assigning likelihoods (e.g., Gaussians or MLP) and one for assigning priors (e.g., an N-gram language model). Both give as output a string of words.

- The **embedded training** paradigm is the normal method for training speech recognizers. Given an initial lexicon with hand-built pronunciation structures, it will train the HMM transition probabilities and the HMM observation probabilities. This HMM observation probability estimation can be done via a Gaussian or an MLP.

- One way to implement the acoustic component of a TTS system is with **concatenative synthesis**, in which an utterance is built by concatenating and then smoothing diphones taken from a large database of speech recorded by a single speaker.

BIBLIOGRAPHICAL AND HISTORICAL NOTES

The first machine which recognized speech was probably a commercial toy named "Radio Rex" which was sold in the 1920s. Rex was a celluloid dog that moved (via a spring) when the spring was released by 500 Hz acoustic energy. Since 500 Hz is roughly the first formant of the vowel in "Rex", the dog seemed to come when he was called (David and Selfridge, 1962).

By the late 1940s and early 1950s, a number of machine speech recognition systems had been built. An early Bell Labs system could recognize any of the 10 digits from a single speaker (Davis et al., 1952). This system had 10 speaker-dependent stored patterns, one for each digit, each of which roughly represented the first two vowel formants in the digit. They achieved 97–99% accuracy by choosing the pattern which had the highest relative correlation coefficient with the input. Fry (1959) and Denes (1959) built a phoneme recognizer at University College, London, which recognized four vowels and nine consonants based on a similar pattern-recognition principle.

Fry and Denes's system was the first to use phoneme transition probabilities to constrain the recognizer.

The late 1960s and early 1970s produced a number of important paradigm shifts. First were a number of feature-extraction algorithms, include the efficient Fast Fourier Transform (FFT) (Cooley and Tukey, 1965), the application of cepstral processing to speech (Oppenheim et al., 1968), and the development of LPC for speech coding (Atal and Hanauer, 1971). Second were a number of ways of handling **warping**; stretching or shrinking   WARPING
the input signal to handle differences in speaking rate and segment length when matching against stored patterns. The natural algorithm for solving this problem was dynamic programming, and, as we saw in Chapter 5, the algorithm was reinvented multiple times to address this problem. The first application to speech processing was by Vintsyuk (1968), although his result was not picked up by other researchers, and was reinvented by Velichko and Zagoruyko (1970) and Sakoe and Chiba (1971) (and (1984)). Soon afterwards, Itakura (1975) combined this dynamic programming idea with the LPC coefficients that had previously been used only for speech coding. The resulting system extracted LPC features for incoming words and used dynamic programming to match them against stored LPC templates.

The third innovation of this period was the rise of the HMM. Hidden Markov Models seem to have been applied to speech independently at two laboratories around 1972. One application arose from the work of statisticians, in particular Baum and colleagues at the Institute for Defense Analyses in Princeton on HMMs and their application to various prediction problems (Baum and Petrie, 1966; Baum and Eagon, 1967). James Baker learned of this work and applied the algorithm to speech processing (Baker, 1975) during his graduate work at CMU. Independently, Frederick Jelinek, Robert Mercer, and Lalit Bahl (drawing from their research in information-theoretical models influenced by the work of Shannon (1948)) applied HMMs to speech at the IBM Thomas J. Watson Research Center (Jelinek et al., 1975). IBM's and Baker's systems were very similar, particularly in their use of the Bayesian framework described in this chapter. One early difference was the decoding algorithm; Baker's DRAGON system used Viterbi (dynamic programming) decoding, while the IBM system applied Jelinek's stack decoding algorithm (Jelinek, 1969). Baker then joined the IBM group for a brief time before founding the speech-recognition company Dragon Systems. The HMM approach to speech recognition would turn out to completely dominate the field by the end of the century; indeed the IBM lab was the driving force in extending statistical models to natural language processing as well, including the development of class-based N-grams, HMM-based part-of-speech tagging, statistical machine translation, and the use of entropy/perplexity as an evaluation metric.

The use of the HMM slowly spread through the speech community. One cause was a number of research and development programs sponsored by the Advanced Research Projects Agency of the U.S. Department of Defense (ARPA). The first five-year program starting in 1971, and is reviewed in Klatt (1977). The goal of this first program was to build speech understanding systems based on a few speakers, a constrained grammar and lexicon (1000 words), and less than 10% semantic error rate. Four systems were funded and compared against each other: the System Development Corporation (SDC) system, Bolt, Beranek & Newman (BBN)'s HWIM system, Carnegie-Mellon University's Hearsay-II system, and Carnegie-Mellon's Harpy system (Lowerre, 1968). The Harpy system used a simplified version of Baker's HMM-based DRAGON system and was the best of the tested systems, and according to Klatt the only one to meet the original goals of the ARPA project (with a semantic error rate of 94% on a simple task).

Beginning in the mid-1980s, ARPA funded a number of new speech research programs. The first was the "Resource Management" (RM) task (Price et al., 1988), which like the earlier ARPA task involved transcription (recognition) of read-speech (speakers reading sentences constructed from a 1000-word vocabulary) but which now included a component that involved speaker-independent recognition. Later tasks included recognition of sentences read from the Wall Street Journal (WSJ) beginning with limited systems of 5,000 words, and finally with systems of unlimited vocabulary (in practice most systems use approximately 60,000 words). Later speech-recognition tasks moved away from read-speech to more natural domains; the Broadcast News (also called Hub-4) domain (LDC, 1998; Graff, 1997) (transcription of actual news broadcasts, including quite difficult passages such as on-the-street interviews) and the CALLHOME and CALLFRIEND domain (LDC, 1999) (natural telephone conversations between friends), part of what was also called Hub-5. The Air Traffic Information System (ATIS) task (Hemphill et al., 1990) was a speech understanding task whose goal was to simulate helping a user book a flight, by answering questions about potential airlines, times, dates, and so forth.

BAKE-OFF   Each of the ARPA tasks involved an approximately annual **bake-off** at which all ARPA-funded systems, and many other 'volunteer' systems from North American and Europe, were evaluated against each other in terms of word error rate or semantic error rate. In the early evaluations, for-profit corporations did not generally compete, but eventually many (especially IBM and ATT) competed regularly. The ARPA competitions resulted in widescale borrowing of techniques among labs, since it was easy to see which ideas had provided an error-reduction the previous year, and were probably an important factor in the eventual spread of the HMM paradigm to virtual every major speech recognition lab. The ARPA program also resulted in a number of useful databases, originally designed for training and testing systems for each evaluation (TIMIT, RM, WSJ, ATIS, BN, CALLHOME, Switchboard) but then made available for general research use.

There are a number of textbooks on speech recognition that are good choices for readers who seek a more in-depth understanding of the material in this chapter: Jelinek (1997), Gold and Morgan (1999), and Rabiner and Juang (1993) are the most comprehensive. The last two textbooks also have comprehensive discussions of the history of the field, and together with the survey paper of Levinson (1995) have influenced our short history discussion in this chapter. Our description of the forward-backward algorithm was modeled after Rabiner (1989). Another useful tutorial paper is Knill and Young (1997). Research in the speech recognition field often appears in the proceedings of the biennial EUROSPEECH Conference and the International Conference on Spoken Language Processing (ICSLP), held in alternating years, as well as the annual IEEE International Conference on Acoustics, Speech, and Signal Processing (ICASSP). Journals include Speech Communication, Computer Speech and Language, IEEE Transactions on Pattern Analysis and Machine Intelligence, and IEEE Transactions on Acoustics, Speech, and Signal Processing.

EXERCISES

7.1   Analyze each of the errors in the incorrectly recognized transcription of "um the phone is I left the..." on page 271. For each one, give your best guess as to whether you think it is caused by a problem in signal processing, pronunciation modeling, lexicon size, language model, or pruning in the decoding search.

7.2   In practice, speech recognizers do all their probability computation using the **log probability** (or **logprob**) rather than actual probabilities. This   LOGPROB helps avoid underflow for very small probabilities, but also makes the Viterbi algorithm very efficient, since all probability multiplications can be implemented by adding log probabilities. Rewrite the pseudocode for the Viterbi algorithm in Figure 7.9 on page 249 to make use of logprobs instead of probabilities.

7.3   Now modify the Viterbi algorithm in Figure 7.9 on page 249 to implement the beam search described on page 251. Hint: You will probably need to add in code to check whether a given state is at the end of a word or not.

7.4   Finally, modify the Viterbi algorithm in Figure 7.9 on page 249 with more detailed pseudocode implementing the array of backtrace pointers.

7.5   Implement the Stack decoding algorithm of Figure 7.14 on 256. Pick a very simple h^* function like an estimate of the number of words remaining in the sentence.

7.6   Modify the forward algorithm of Figure 5.16 to use the tree-structured lexicon of Figure 7.18 on page 259.

Part II

SYNTAX

If words are the foundation of speech and language processing, syntax is the skeleton. Syntax is the study of formal relationships between words. These six chapters study how words are clustered into classes called parts-of-speech, how they group with their neighbors into phrases, and the way words depends on other words in a sentence. This part of the book explores computational models of all of these kinds of knowledge, including context-free grammars, lexicalized grammars, feature structures, and metatheoretical issues like the Chomsky hierarchy. It introduces fundamental algorithms for dealing with this knowledge, like the Earley and CYK algorithms for parsing and the unification algorithm for feature combination. It also includes probabilistic models of this syntactic knowledge, including HMM part-of-speech taggers, and probabilistic context-free grammars. Finally, it explores psychological models of human syntactic processing.

Part II

8 WORD CLASSES AND PART-OF-SPEECH TAGGING

Conjunction Junction, what's your function?
Bob Dorough, *Schoolhouse Rock, 1973*

There are ten parts of speech, and they are all troublesome.
Mark Twain, *The Awful German Language*

The definitions [of the parts of speech] are very far from having attained the degree of exactitude found in Euclidean geometry.
Otto Jespersen, *The Philosophy of Grammar*, 1924

Dionysius Thrax of Alexandria (*c.* 100 B.C.), or perhaps someone else (exact authorship being understandably difficult to be sure of with texts of this vintage), wrote a grammatical sketch of Greek (a "*technē*") which summarized the linguistic knowledge of his day. This work is the direct source of an astonishing proportion of our modern linguistic vocabulary, including among many other words, *syntax, diphthong, clitic,* and *analogy.* Also included are a description of eight **parts-of-speech**: noun, verb, pronoun, preposition, adverb, conjunction, participle, and article. Although earlier scholars (including Aristotle as well as the Stoics) had their own lists of parts-of-speech, it was Thrax's set of eight which became the basis for practically all subsequent part-of-speech descriptions of Greek, Latin, and most European languages for the next 2000 years.

 Schoolhouse Rock was a brilliant series of 3-minute musical animated clips first aired on television in 1973. The series was designed to inspire kids to learn multiplication tables, grammar, and basic science and history. The Grammar Rock sequence, for example, included songs about parts-of-speech. Perhaps you are beginning to see why we bring this up. In

PARTS-OF-SPEECH

fact, Grammar Rock was remarkably traditional in its grammatical notation, including exactly eight songs about parts-of-speech (although the list was slightly modified from Thrax's original, substituting adjective and interjection for the original participle and article).

POS

More recent lists of parts-of-speech (also known as **POS**, **word classes**, **morphological classes**, or **lexical tags**) have much larger numbers of word classes (45 for the Penn Treebank (Marcus et al., 1993), 87 for the Brown corpus (Francis, 1979; Francis and Kučera, 1982), and 146 for the C7 tagset (Garside et al., 1997)).

The significance of the part-of-speech for language processing is that it gives a significant amount of information about the word and its neighbors. This is clearly true for major categories, (**verb** versus **noun**), but is also true for the many finer distinctions. For example these tagsets distinguish between possessive pronouns (*my, your, his, her, its*) and personal pronouns (*I, you, he, me*). Knowing whether a word is a possessive pronoun or a personal pronoun can tell us what words are likely to occur in its vicinity (possessive pronouns are likely to be followed by a noun, personal pronouns by a verb). This can be useful in a language model for speech recognition.

A word's part-of-speech can tell us something about how the word is pronounced. As Chapter 4 discussed, the word *content*, for example, can be a noun or an adjective. They are pronounced differently (the noun is pronounced *CONtent* and the adjective *conTENT*). Thus knowing the part-of-speech can produce more natural pronunciations in a speech synthesis system and more accuracy in a speech recognition system. (Other pairs like this include *OBject* (noun) and *obJECT* (verb), *DIScount* (noun) and *disCOUNT* (verb); see Cutler (1986)).

Parts-of-speech can also be used in stemming for informational retrieval (IR), since knowing a word's part-of-speech can help tell us which morphological affixes it can take, as we saw in Chapter 3. They can also help an IR application by helping select out nouns or other important words from a document. Automatic part-of-speech taggers can help in building automatic word-sense disambiguating algorithms, and POS taggers are also used in advanced ASR language models such as **class-based N-grams**, discussed in Section 8.7. Parts-of-speech are very often used for "partial parsing" texts, for example for quickly finding names or other phrases for the information extraction applications discussed in Chapter 15. Finally, corpora that have been marked for part-of-speech are very useful for linguistic research, for example to help find instances or frequencies of particular constructions in large corpora.

The remainder of this chapter begins with a summary of English word classes, followed by a description of different tagsets for formally coding these classes. The next three sections then introduce three tagging algorithms: **rule-based tagging**, **stochastic tagging**, and **transformation-based tagging**.

8.1   (MOSTLY) ENGLISH WORD CLASSES

> *Well, every person you can know,*
> *And every place that you can go,*
> *And anything that you can show,*
> *You know they're nouns.*
> Lynn Ahrens, *Schoolhouse Rock*, 1973

Until now we have been using part-of-speech terms like **noun** and **verb** rather freely. In this section we give a more complete definition of these and other classes. Traditionally the definition of parts-of-speech has been based on morphological and syntactic function; words that function similarly with respect to the affixes they take (their morphological properties) or with respect to what can occur nearby (their "distributional properties") are grouped into classes. While word classes do have tendencies toward semantic coherence (nouns do in fact often describe "people, places or things", and adjectives often describe properties), this is not necessarily the case, and in general we don't use semantic coherence as a definitional criterion for parts-of-speech.

Parts-of-speech can be divided into two broad supercategories: **closed class** types and **open class** types. Closed classes are those that have relatively fixed membership. For example, prepositions are a closed class because there is a fixed set of them in English; new prepositions are rarely coined. By contrast nouns and verbs are open classes because new nouns and verbs are continually coined or borrowed from other languages (e.g., the new verb *to fax* or the borrowed noun *futon*). It is likely that any given speaker or corpus will have different open class words, but all speakers of a language, and corpora that are large enough, will likely share the set of closed class words. Closed class words are generally also **function words**; function words are grammatical words like *of*, *it*, *and*, or *you*, which tend to be very short, occur frequently, and play an important role in grammar.

CLOSED CLASS
OPEN CLASS

FUNCTION WORDS

NOUNS There are four major open classes that occur in the languages of the
VERBS world: **nouns**, **verbs**, **adjectives**, and **adverbs**. It turns out that English has
ADJECTIVES all four of these, although not every language does. Many languages have no
ADVERBS adjectives. In the native American language Lakhota, for example, and also
possibly in Chinese, the words corresponding to English adjectives act as a
subclass of verbs.

Every known human language has at least the two categories **noun** and
verb (although in some languages, for example Nootka, the distinction is
subtle). Noun is the name given to the lexical class in which the words for
most people, places, or things occur. But since lexical classes like **noun** are
defined functionally (morphological and syntactically) rather than semantically, some words for people, places, and things may not be nouns, and
conversely some nouns may not be words for people, places, or things. Thus
nouns include concrete terms like *ship* and *chair*, abstractions like *bandwidth* and *relationship*, and verb-like terms like *pacing* in *His pacing to and
fro became quite annoying*). What defines a noun in English, then, are things
like its ability to occur with determiners (*a goat, its bandwidth, Plato's Re-
public*), to take possessives (*IBM's annual revenue*), and for most but not all
nouns, to occur in the plural form (*goats, abaci*).

PROPER NOUNS Nouns are traditionally grouped into **proper nouns** and **common nouns**.
COMMON NOUNS Proper nouns, like *Regina, Colorado*, and *IBM*, are names of specific persons
or entities. In English, they generally aren't preceded by articles (e.g., *the
book is upstairs*, but *Regina is upstairs*). In written English, proper nouns
are usually capitalized.

In many languages, including English, common nouns are divided into
COUNT NOUNS **count nouns** and **mass nouns**. Count nouns are those that allow gram-
MASS NOUNS matical enumeration; that is, they can occur in both the singular and plural
(*goat/goats, relationship/relationships*) and they can be counted (*one goat,
two goats*). Mass nouns are used when something is conceptualized as a ho-
mogeneous group. So words like *snow, salt*, and *communism* are not counted
(i.e., **two snows* or **two communisms*). Mass nouns can also appear without
articles where singular count nouns cannot (*Snow is white* but not **Goat is
white*).

The verb class includes most of the words referring to actions and processes, including main verbs like *draw, provide, differ*, and *go*. As we saw
in Chapter 3, English verbs have a number of morphological forms (non-
3rd-person-sg (*eat*), 3rd-person-sg (*eats*), progressive (*eating*), past partici-
AUXILIARIES ple *eaten*). A subclass of English verbs called **auxiliaries** will be discussed
when we turn to closed class forms.

The third open class English form is adjectives; semantically this class includes many terms that describe properties or qualities. Most languages have adjectives for the concepts of color (*white*, *black*), age (*old*, *young*), and value (*good*, *bad*), but there are languages without adjectives. As we discussed above, many linguists argue that the Chinese family of languages uses verbs to describe such English-adjectival notions as color and age.

The final open class form, adverbs, is rather a hodge-podge, both semantically and formally. For example Schachter (1985) points out that in a sentence like the following, all the italicized words are adverbs:

Unfortunately, John walked *home extremely slowly yesterday*

What coherence the class has semantically may be solely that each of these words can be viewed as modifying something (often verbs, hence the name "adverb", but also other adverbs and entire verb phrases). **Directional adverbs** or **locative adverbs** (*home*, *here*, *downhill*) specify the direction or location of some action; **degree adverbs** (*extremely*, *very*, *somewhat*) specify the extent of some action, process, or property; **manner adverbs** (*slowly*, *slinkily*, *delicately*) describe the manner of some action or process; and **temporal adverbs** describe the time that some action or event took place (*yesterday*, *Monday*). Because of the heterogeneous nature of this class, some adverbs (for example temporal adverbs like *Monday*) are tagged in some tagging schemes as nouns.

LOCATIVE

DEGREE

MANNER

TEMPORAL

The closed classes differ more from language to language than do the open classes. Here's a quick overview of some of the more important closed classes in English, with a few examples of each:

- **prepositions:** on, under, over, near, by, at, from, to, with
- **determiners:** a, an, the
- **pronouns:** she, who, I, others
- **conjunctions:** and, but, or, as, if, when
- **auxiliary verbs:** can, may, should, are
- **particles:** up, down, on, off, in, out, at, by,
- **numerals:** one, two, three, first, second, third

Prepositions occur before noun phrases; semantically they are relational, often indicating spatial or temporal relations, whether literal (*on it*, *before then*, *by the house*) or metaphorical (*on time*, *with gusto*, *beside herself*). But they often indicate other relations as well (*Hamlet was written by Shakespeare*, and [from Shakespeare] "*And I did laugh sans intermission an hour by his dial*"). Figure 8.1 shows the prepositions of English according to

PREPOSITIONS

the CELEX on-line dictionary (Celex, 1993), sorted by their frequency in the COBUILD 16 million word corpus of English. Note that this should not be considered a definitive list. Different dictionaries and different tag sets may label word classes differently. This list combines prepositions and particles; see below for more on particles.

of	540,085	through	14,964	worth	1,563	pace	12
in	331,235	after	13,670	toward	1,390	nigh	9
for	142,421	between	13,275	plus	750	re	4
to	125,691	under	9,525	till	686	mid	3
with	124,965	per	6,515	amongst	525	o'er	2
on	109,129	among	5,090	via	351	but	0
at	100,169	within	5,030	amid	222	ere	0
by	77,794	towards	4,700	underneath	164	less	0
from	74,843	above	3,056	versus	113	midst	0
about	38,428	near	2,026	amidst	67	o'	0
than	20,210	off	1,695	sans	20	thru	0
over	18,071	past	1,575	circa	14	vice	0

Figure 8.1   Prepositions (and particles) of English from the CELEX on-line dictionary. Frequency counts are from the COBUILD 16 million word corpus.

PARTICLE   A **particle** is a word that resembles a preposition or an adverb, and that
PHRASAL VERB often combines with a verb to form a larger unit called a **phrasal verb**, as in the following examples from Thoreau:

> So I *went on* for some days cutting and hewing timber. . .
> Moral reform is the effort to *throw off* sleep. . .

We can see that these are particles rather than prepositions, for in the first example, *on* is followed, not by a noun phrase, but by a true preposition phrase. With transitive phrasal verbs, as in the second example, we can tell that *off* is a particle and not a preposition because particles may appear after their objects (*throw sleep off* as well as *throw off sleep*). This is not possible for prepositions (*The horse went off its track*, but **The horse went its track off*).

Quirk et al. (1985) gives the following list of single-word particles. Since it is extremely hard to automatically distinguish particles from prepositions, some tag sets (like the one used for CELEX) do not distinguish them, and even in corpora that do (like the Penn Treebank) the distinction is very difficult to make reliably in an automatic process, so we do not give counts.

aboard	aside	besides	forward(s)	opposite	through
about	astray	between	home	out	throughout
above	away	beyond	in	outside	together
across	back	by	inside	over	under
ahead	before	close	instead	overhead	underneath
alongside	behind	down	near	past	up
apart	below	east, etc.	off	round	within
around	beneath	eastward(s),etc.	on	since	without

Figure 8.2   English single-word particles from Quirk et al. (1985).

A particularly small closed class is the **articles**: English has three: *a*, *an*, and *the* (although *this* (as in *this chapter*) and *that* (as in *that page*) are often included as well). Articles often begin a noun phrase. *A* and *an* mark a noun phrase as indefinite, while *the* can mark it as definite. We will discuss definiteness in Chapter 18. Articles are quite frequent in English; indeed *the* is the most frequent word in most English corpora. Here are COBUILD statistics, again out of 16 million words: ARTICLES

   the 1,071,676
   a   413,887
   an   59,359

Conjunctions are used to join two phrases, clauses, or sentences. Co-ordinating conjunctions like *and*, *or*, or *but*, join two elements of equal status. Subordinating conjunctions are used when one of the elements is of some sort of embedded status. For example *that* in *"I thought that you might like some milk"* is a subordinating conjunction that links the main clause *I thought* with the subordinate clause *you might like some milk*. This clause is called subordinate because this entire clause is the "content" of the main verb *thought*. Subordinating conjunctions like *that* which link a verb to its argument in this way are also called **complementizers**. Chapter 9 and Chapter 11 will discuss complementation in more detail. Table 8.3 lists English conjunctions. CONJUNCTIONS

COMPLEMENTIZERS

Pronouns are forms that often act as a kind of shorthand for referring to some noun phrase or entity or event. **Personal pronouns** refer to persons or entities (*you*, *she*, *I*, *it*, *me*, etc.). **Possessive pronouns** are forms of personal pronouns that indicate either actual possession or more often just PRONOUNS

POSSESSIVE

and	514,946	yet	5,040	considering	174	forasmuch as	0
that	134,773	since	4,843	lest	131	however	0
but	96,889	where	3,952	albeit	104	immediately	0
or	76,563	nor	3,078	providing	96	in as far as	0
as	54,608	once	2,826	whereupon	85	in so far as	0
if	53,917	unless	2,205	seeing	63	inasmuch as	0
when	37,975	why	1,333	directly	26	insomuch as	0
because	23,626	now	1,290	ere	12	insomuch that	0
so	12,933	neither	1,120	notwithstanding	3	like	0
before	10,720	whenever	913	according as	0	neither nor	0
though	10,329	whereas	867	as if	0	now that	0
than	9,511	except	864	as long as	0	only	0
while	8,144	till	686	as though	0	provided that	0
after	7,042	provided	594	both and	0	providing that	0
whether	5,978	whilst	351	but that	0	seeing as	0
for	5,935	suppose	281	but then	0	seeing as how	0
although	5,424	cos	188	but then again	0	seeing that	0
until	5,072	supposing	185	either or	0	without	0

Figure 8.3   Coordinating and subordinating conjunctions of English from the CELEX on-line dictionary. Frequency counts are from the COBUILD 16 million word corpus.

an abstract relation between the person and some object (*my, your, his, her, its, one's, our, their*). **Wh-pronouns** (*what, who, whom, whoever*) are used in certain question forms, or may also act as complementizers (*Frieda, who I met five years ago* ...). Table 8.4 shows English pronouns, again from CELEX.

WH

A closed class subtype of English verbs are the **auxiliary** verbs. Cross-linguistically, auxiliaries are words (usually verbs) that mark certain semantic features of a main verb, including whether an action takes place in the present, past or future (tense), whether it is completed (aspect), whether it is negated (polarity), and whether an action is necessary, possible, suggested, desired, etc. (mood).

AUXILIARY

English auxiliaries include the **copula** verb *be*, the two verbs *do* and *have*, along with their inflected forms, as well as a class of **modal verbs**. *Be* is called a copula because it connects subjects with certain kinds of predicate nominals and adjectives (*He is a duck*). The verb *have* is used for example to mark the perfect tenses (*I have gone, I had gone*), while *be* is used as part of the passive (*We were robbed*), or progressive (*We are leaving*) constructions. The modals are used to mark the mood associated with the event or

COPULA

MODAL

it	199,920	how	13,137	yourself	2,437	no one	106
I	198,139	another	12,551	why	2,220	wherein	58
he	158,366	where	11,857	little	2,089	double	39
you	128,688	same	11,841	none	1,992	thine	30
his	99,820	something	11,754	nobody	1,684	summat	22
they	88,416	each	11,320	further	1,666	suchlike	18
this	84,927	both	10,930	everybody	1,474	fewest	15
that	82,603	last	10,816	ourselves	1,428	thyself	14
she	73,966	every	9,788	mine	1,426	whomever	11
her	69,004	himself	9,113	somebody	1,322	whosoever	10
we	64,846	nothing	9,026	former	1,177	whomsoever	8
all	61,767	when	8,336	past	984	wherefore	6
which	61,399	one	7,423	plenty	940	whereat	5
their	51,922	much	7,237	either	848	whatsoever	4
what	50,116	anything	6,937	yours	826	whereon	2
my	46,791	next	6,047	neither	618	whoso	2
him	45,024	themselves	5,990	fewer	536	aught	1
me	43,071	most	5,115	hers	482	howsoever	1
who	42,881	itself	5,032	ours	458	thrice	1
them	42,099	myself	4,819	whoever	391	wheresoever	1
no	33,458	everything	4,662	least	386	you-all	1
some	32,863	several	4,306	twice	382	additional	0
other	29,391	less	4,278	theirs	303	anybody	0
your	28,923	herself	4,016	wherever	289	each other	0
its	27,783	whose	4,005	oneself	239	once	0
our	23,029	someone	3,755	thou	229	one another	0
these	22,697	certain	3,345	'un	227	overmuch	0
any	22,666	anyone	3,318	ye	192	such and such	0
more	21,873	whom	3,229	thy	191	whate'er	0
many	17,343	enough	3,197	whereby	176	whenever	0
such	16,880	half	3,065	thee	166	whereof	0
those	15,819	few	2,933	yourselves	148	whereto	0
own	15,741	everyone	2,812	latter	142	whereunto	0
us	15,724	whatever	2,571	whichever	121	whichsoever	0

Figure 8.4   Pronouns of English from the CELEX on-line dictionary. Frequency counts are from the COBUILD 16 million word corpus.

action depicted by the main verb. So *can* indicates ability or possibility, *may* indicates permission or possibility, *must* indicates necessity, and so on. Figure 8.5 gives counts for the frequencies of the modals in English. In addition to the copula *have* mentioned above, there is a modal verb *have* (e.g., I *have to go*), which is very common in spoken English. Neither it nor the modal verb *dare*, which is very rare, have frequency counts because the CELEX dictionary does not distinguish the main verb sense (*I have three oranges, He dared me to eat them*), from the modal sense (*There has to be some mistake, Dare I confront him?*) from the non-modal auxiliary verb sense (*I have never seen that*).

can	70,930	might	5,580	shouldn't	858
will	69,206	couldn't	4,265	mustn't	332
may	25,802	shall	4,118	'll	175
would	18,448	wouldn't	3,548	needn't	148
should	17,760	won't	3,100	mightn't	68
must	16,520	'd	2,299	oughtn't	44
need	9,955	ought	1,845	mayn't	3
can't	6,375	will	862	dare	??
have	???				

Figure 8.5   English modal verbs from the CELEX on-line dictionary. Frequency counts are from the COBUILD 16 million word corpus.

English also has many words of more or less unique function, including **interjections** (*oh, ah, hey, man, alas*), **negatives** (*no, not*), **politeness markers** (*please, thank you*), **greetings** (*hello, goodbye*), and the existential **there** (*there are two on the table*) among others. Whether these classes are assigned particular names or lumped together (as interjections or even adverbs) depends on the purpose of the labeling.

INTERJECTIONS

NEGATIVES

POLITENESS
MARKERS

GREETINGS

THERE

8.2   TAGSETS FOR ENGLISH

The previous section gave broad descriptions of the kinds of lexical classes that English words fall into. This section fleshes out that sketch by describing the actual tagsets used in part-of-speech tagging, in preparation for the various tagging algorithms to be described in the following sections.

There are a small number of popular tagsets for English, many of which evolved from the 87-tag tagset used for the Brown corpus (Francis, 1979; Francis and Kučera, 1982). Three of the most commonly used are the small 45-tag Penn Treebank tagset (Marcus et al., 1993), the medium-sized 61 tag C5 tagset used by the Lancaster UCREL project's CLAWS (the Constituent Likelihood Automatic Word-tagging System) tagger to tag the British National Corpus (BNC) (Garside et al., 1997), and the larger 146-tag C7 tagset

Tag	Description	Example	Tag	Description	Example
CC	Coordin. Conjunction	*and, but, or*	SYM	Symbol	*+,%, &*
CD	Cardinal number	*one, two, three*	TO	"to"	*to*
DT	Determiner	*a, the*	UH	Interjection	*ah, oops*
EX	Existential 'there'	*there*	VB	Verb, base form	*eat*
FW	Foreign word	*mea culpa*	VBD	Verb, past tense	*ate*
IN	Preposition/sub-conj	*of, in, by*	VBG	Verb, gerund	*eating*
JJ	Adjective	*yellow*	VBN	Verb, past participle	*eaten*
JJR	Adj., comparative	*bigger*	VBP	Verb, non-3sg pres	*eat*
JJS	Adj., superlative	*wildest*	VBZ	Verb, 3sg pres	*eats*
LS	List item marker	*1, 2, One*	WDT	Wh-determiner	*which, that*
MD	Modal	*can, should*	WP	Wh-pronoun	*what, who*
NN	Noun, sing. or mass	*llama*	WP$	Possessive wh-	*whose*
NNS	Noun, plural	*llamas*	WRB	Wh-adverb	*how, where*
NNP	Proper noun, singular	*IBM*	$	Dollar sign	*$*
NNPS	Proper noun, plural	*Carolinas*	#	Pound sign	*#*
PDT	Predeterminer	*all, both*	"	Left quote	*(' or ")*
POS	Possessive ending	*'s*	"	Right quote	*(' or ")*
PP	Personal pronoun	*I, you, he*	(	Left parenthesis	*([, (, {, <)*
PP$	Possessive pronoun	*your, one's*	)	Right parenthesis	*(],), }, >)*
RB	Adverb	*quickly, never*	,	Comma	*,*
RBR	Adverb, comparative	*faster*	.	Sentence-final punc	*(. ! ?)*
RBS	Adverb, superlative	*fastest*	:	Mid-sentence punc	*(: ; ... – -)*
RP	Particle	*up, off*			

Figure 8.6   Penn Treebank part-of-speech tags (including punctuation).

(Leech et al., 1994); the C5 and C7 tagsets are listed in Appendix C. (Also see Sampson (1987) and Garside et al. (1997) for a detailed summary of the provenance and makeup of these and other tagsets.) This section will present the smallest of them, the Penn Treebank set, and then discuss specific additional tags from some of the other tagsets that might be useful to incorporate for specific projects.

The Penn Treebank tagset, shown in Figure 8.6, has been applied to the Brown corpus and a number of other corpora. Here is an example of a tagged sentence from the Penn Treebank version of the Brown corpus (in a flat ASCII file, tags are often represented after each word, following a slash, but tags can also be represented in various other ways):

> The/DT grand/JJ jury/NN commented/VBD on/IN a/DT number/NN of/IN other/JJ topics/NNS ./.

The Penn Treebank tagset was culled from the original 87-tag tagset for the Brown corpus. This reduced set leaves out information that can be recovered from the identity of the lexical item. For example the original Brown tagset and other large tagsets like C5 include a separate tag for each of the different forms of the verbs *do* (e.g. C5 tag "VDD" for *did* and "VDG" for *doing*), *be*, and *have*. These were omitted from the Penn set.

Certain syntactic distinctions were not marked in the Penn Treebank tagset because Treebank sentences were parsed, not merely tagged, and so some syntactic information is represented in the phrase structure. For example, prepositions and subordinating conjunctions were combined into the single tag *IN*, since the tree-structure of the sentence disambiguated them (subordinating conjunctions always precede clauses, prepositions precede noun phrases or prepositional phrases).

Most tagging situations, however, do not involve parsed corpora; for this reason the Penn Treebank set is not specific enough for many uses. The C7 tagset, for example, also distinguishes prepositions (*II*) from subordinating conjunctions (*CS*) , and distinguishes the preposition *to* (*II*) from the infinite marker *to* (*TO*).

Which tagset to use for a particular application depends, of course, on how much information the application needs. The reader should see Appendix C for a listing of the C5 and C7 tagsets.

8.3   PART-OF-SPEECH TAGGING

TAGGING   Part-of-speech tagging (or just **tagging** for short) is the process of assigning a part-of-speech or other lexical class marker to each word in a corpus. Tags are also usually applied to punctuation markers; thus tagging for natural language is the same process as **tokenization** for computer languages, although tags for natural languages are much more ambiguous. As we suggested at the beginning of the chapter, taggers play an increasingly important role in speech recognition, natural language parsing and information retrieval.

TAGSET   The input to a tagging algorithm is a string of words and a specified **tagset** of the kind described in the previous section. The output is a single best tag for each word. For example, here are some sample sentences from the ATIS corpus of dialogues about air-travel reservations that we will discuss in Chapter 9. For each we have shown a potential tagged output using the Penn Treebank tagset defined in Figure 8.6 on page 297:

VB   DT NN   .
Book that flight .

VBZ DT NN   VB   NN   ?
Does that flight serve dinner ?

Even in these simple examples, automatically assigning a tag to each
word is not trivial. For example, *book* is **ambiguous**. That is, it has more   AMBIGUOUS
than one possible usage and part-of-speech. It can be a verb (as in *book that
flight* or to *book* the suspect) or a noun (as in *hand me that book*, or *a book
of matches*). Similarly *that* can be a determiner (as in *Does that flight serve
dinner*), or a complementizer (as in *I thought that your flight was earlier*).
The problem of POS-tagging is to **resolve** these ambiguities, choosing the   RESOLVE
proper tag for the context. Part-of-speech tagging is thus one of the many
disambiguation tasks we will see in this book.

How hard is the tagging problem? Most words in English are unambiguous; i.e., they have only a single tag. But many of the most common
words of English are ambiguous (for example *can* can be an auxiliary ('to
be able'), a noun ('a metal container'), or a verb ('to put something in such
a metal container')). In fact DeRose (1988) reports that while only 11.5%
of English word types in the Brown Corpus are ambiguous, over 40% of
Brown tokens are ambiguous. Based on Francis and Kučera (1982), he gives
the table of tag ambiguity in Figure 8.7.

Unambiguous (1 tag)	**35,340**	
Ambiguous (2–7 tags)	**4,100**	
2 tags	3,760	
3 tags	264	
4 tags	61	
5 tags	12	
6 tags	2	
7 tags	1	("still")

Figure 8.7   The number of word types in Brown corpus by degree of ambiguity (after DeRose (1988)).

Luckily, it turns out that many of the 40% ambiguous tokens are easy
to disambiguate. This is because the various tags associated with a word
are not equally likely. For example, *a* can be a determiner, or the letter *a*

(perhaps as part of an acronym or an initial). But the determiner sense of *a* is much more likely.

Most tagging algorithms fall into one of two classes: **rule-based** taggers and **stochastic** taggers. Rule-based taggers generally involve a large database of hand-written disambiguation rule which specify, for example, that an ambiguous word is a noun rather than a verb if it follows a determiner. The next section will describe a sample rule-based tagger, **ENGTWOL**, based on the Constraint Grammar architecture of Karlsson et al. (1995).

Stochastic taggers generally resolve tagging ambiguities by using a training corpus to compute the probability of a given word having a given tag in a given context. Section 8.5 describes a stochastic tagger called **HMM tagger**, also called a **Maximum Likelihood Tagger**, or a **Markov model tagger**, based on the Hidden Markov Model presented in Chapter 7.

HMM TAGGER

Finally, Section 8.6 will describe an approach to tagging called the **transformation-based tagger** or the **Brill tagger**, after Brill (1995). The Brill tagger shares features of both tagging architectures. Like the rule-based tagger, it is based on rules which determine when an ambiguous word should have a given tag. Like the stochastic taggers, it has a machine-learning component: The rules are automatically induced from a previously tagged training corpus.

BRILL TAGGER

8.4   RULE-BASED PART-OF-SPEECH TAGGING

The earliest algorithms for automatically assigning part-of-speech were based on a two-stage architecture (Harris, 1962; Klein and Simmons, 1963; Greene and Rubin, 1971). The first stage used a dictionary to assign each word a list of potential parts-of-speech. The second stage used large lists of hand-written disambiguation rules to winnow down this list to a single part-of-speech for each word.

ENGTWOL

The **ENGTWOL** tagger (Voutilainen, 1995) is based on the same two-stage architecture, although both the lexicon and the disambiguation rules are much more sophisticated than the early algorithms. The ENGTWOL lexicon is based on the two-level morphology described in Chapter 3, and has about 56,000 entries for English word stems (Heikkilä, 1995), counting a word with multiple parts-of-speech (e.g., nominal and verbal senses of *hit*) as separate entries, and of course not counting inflected and many derived forms. Each entry is annotated with a set of morphological and syntactic features. Figure 8.8 shows some selected words, together with a slightly simplified listing of their features.

Word	POS	Additional POS features
smaller	ADJ	COMPARATIVE
entire	ADJ	ABSOLUTE ATTRIBUTIVE
fast	ADV	SUPERLATIVE
that	DET	CENTRAL DEMONSTRATIVE SG
all	DET	PREDETERMINER SG/PL QUANTIFIER
dog's	N	GENITIVE SG
furniture	N	NOMINATIVE SG NOINDEFDETERMINER
one-third	NUM	SG
she	PRON	PERSONAL FEMININE NOMINATIVE SG3
show	V	IMPERATIVE VFIN
show	V	PRESENT -SG3 VFIN
show	N	NOMINATIVE SG
shown	PCP2	SVOO SVO SV
occurred	PCP2	SV
occurred	V	PAST VFIN SV

Figure 8.8   Sample lexical entries from the ENGTWOL lexicon described in Voutilainen (1995) and Heikkilä (1995).

Most of the features in Figure 8.8 are relatively self-explanatory; SG for singular, -SG3 for other than third-person-singular. ABSOLUTE means non-comparative and non-superlative for an adjective, NOMINATIVE just means non-genitive, and PCP2 means past participle. PRE, CENTRAL, and POST are ordering slots for determiners (predeterminers (*all*) come before determiners (*the*): *all the president's men*). NOINDEFDETERMINER means that words like *furniture* do not appear with the indefinite determiner *a*. SV, SVO, and SVOO specify the **subcategorization** or **complementation** pattern for the verb. Subcategorization will be discussed in Chapter 9 and Chapter 11, but briefly SV means the verb appears solely with a subject (*nothing occurred*); SVO with a subject and an object (*I showed the film*); SVOO with a subject and two complements: *She showed her the ball.*

SUBCATEGORIZATION

COMPLEMENTATION

In the first stage of the tagger, each word is run through the two-level lexicon transducer and the entries for all possible parts-of-speech are returned. For example the phrase *Pavlov had shown that salivation . . .* would return the following list (one line per possible tag, with the correct tag shown in boldface):

Pavlov	**PAVLOV N NOM SG PROPER**
had	**HAVE V PAST VFIN SVO**
	HAVE PCP2 SVO
shown	**SHOW PCP2 SVOO SVO SV**
that	ADV
	PRON DEM SG
	DET CENTRAL DEM SG
	CS
salivation	**N NOM SG**

...

A set of about 1,100 constraints are then applied to the input sentence to rule out incorrect parts-of-speech; the boldfaced entries in the table above show the desired result, in which the preterite (not participle) tag is applied to *had*, and the complementizer (CS) tag is applied the *that*. The constraints are used in a negative way, to eliminate tags that are inconsistent with the context. For example one constraint eliminates all readings of *that* except the ADV (adverbial intensifier) sense (this is the sense in the sentence *it isn't that odd*). Here's a simplified version of the constraint:

ADVERBIAL-THAT RULE
Given input: "that"
if
   (+1 A/ADV/QUANT); / * *if next word is adj, adverb, or quantifier* * /
   (+2 SENT-LIM);   / * *and following which is a sentence boundary,* * /
   (NOT -1 SVOC/A); / * *and the previous word is not a verb like* * /
              / * *'consider' which allows adjs as object complements* * /
then eliminate non-ADV tags
else eliminate ADV tag

The first two clauses of this rule check to see that the *that* directly precedes a sentence-final adjective, adverb, or quantifier. In all other cases the adverb reading is eliminated. The last clause eliminates cases preceded by verbs like *consider* or *believe* which can take a noun and an adjective; this is to avoid tagging the following instance of *that* as an adverb:

I consider that odd.

Another rule is used to express the constraint that the complementizer sense of *that* is most likely to be used if the previous word is a verb which expects a complement (like *believe*, *think*, or *show*), and if the *that* is followed by the beginning of a noun phrase, and a finite verb.

This description oversimplifies the ENGTWOL architecture; the system also includes probabilistic constraints, and also makes use of other syntactic information we haven't discussed. The interested reader should consult Karlsson et al. (1995).

8.5   STOCHASTIC PART-OF-SPEECH TAGGING

The use of probabilities in tags is quite old; probabilities in tagging were first used by (Stolz et al., 1965), a complete probabilistic tagger with Viterbi decoding was sketched by Bahl and Mercer (1976), and various stochastic taggers were built in the 1980s (Marshall, 1983; Garside, 1987; Church, 1988; DeRose, 1988). This section describes a particular stochastic tagging algorithm generally known as the Hidden Markov Model or HMM tagger. The intuition behind all stochastic taggers is a simple generalization of the "pick the most-likely tag for this word" approach that we discussed above, based on the Bayesian framework we saw in Chapter 5.

For a given sentence or word sequence, HMM taggers choose the tag sequence that maximizes the following formula:

$$P(\text{word}|\text{tag}) * P(\text{tag}|\text{previous } n \text{ tags}) \tag{8.1}$$

The rest of this section will explain and motivate this particular equation. HMM taggers generally choose a tag sequence for a whole sentence rather than for a single word, but for pedagogical purposes, let's first see how an HMM tagger assigns a tag to an individual word. We first give the basic equation, then work through an example, and, finally, give the motivation for the equation.

A bigram-HMM tagger of this kind chooses the tag t_i for word w_i that is most probable given the previous tag t_{i-1} and the current word w_i:

$$t_i = \underset{j}{\text{argmax}}\, P(t_j|t_{i-1}, w_i) \tag{8.2}$$

Through some simplifying Markov assumptions that we will give below, we restate Equation (8.2) to give the basic HMM equation for a single tag as follows:

$$t_i = \underset{j}{\text{argmax}}\, P(t_j|t_{i-1})P(w_i|t_j) \tag{8.3}$$

A Motivating Example

Let's work through an example, using an HMM tagger to assign the proper tag to the single word *race* in the following examples (both shortened slightly from the Brown corpus):

(8.4) Secretariat/NNP is/VBZ expected/VBN to/TO **race**/VB
       tomorrow/NN[1]

(8.5) People/NNS continue/VBP to/TO inquire/VB the/DT reason/NN
       for/IN the/DT **race**/NN for/IN outer/JJ space/NN

In the first example *race* is a verb (VB); in the second it is a noun (NN).

For the purposes of this example, let's pretend that some other mechanism has already done the best tagging job possible on the surrounding words, leaving only the word *race* untagged. A bigram version of the HMM tagger makes the simplifying assumption that the tagging problem can be solved by looking at nearby words and tags. Consider the problem of assigning a tag to *race* given just these subsequences:

       to/TO   race/???
       the/DT   race/???

Let's see how this equation applies to our example with *race*; Equation (8.3) says that if we are trying to choose between NN and VB for the sequence *to race*, we choose the tag that has the greater of these two probabilities:

$$P(\text{VB}|\text{TO})P(\text{race}|\text{VB}) \tag{8.6}$$

and

$$P(\text{NN}|\text{TO})P(\text{race}|\text{NN}) \tag{8.7}$$

Equation (8.3) and its instantiations Equations (8.6) and (8.7) each have two probabilities: a tag sequence probability $P(t_i|t_{i-1})$ and a word-likelihood $P(w_i|t_j)$. For *race*, the tag sequence probabilities $P(\text{NN}|\text{TO})$ and $P(\text{VB}|\text{TO})$ give us the answer to the question "How likely are we to expect a verb (noun) given the previous tag?" They can just be computed from a corpus by counting and normalizing. We would expect that a verb is more likely to follow TO than a noun is, since infinitives (*to race, to run, to eat*) are common in English. While it is possible for a noun to follow TO (*walk to school, related to hunting*), it is less common.

Sure enough, a look at the combined Brown and Switchboard corpora gives us the following probabilities, showing that verbs are 15 times as likely as nouns after TO:

---

[1] Some time adverbs like "tomorrow" and "Monday" are tagged as NN in some corpora, including as the Penn Treebank.

$$P(\text{NN}|\text{TO}) = .021$$
$$P(\text{VB}|\text{TO}) = .34$$

The second part of Equation (8.3) and its instantiations Equations (8.6) and (8.7) is the lexical likelihood: the likelihood of the noun *race* given each tag, $P(\text{race}|\text{VB})$ and $P(\text{race}|\text{NN})$. Note that this likelihood term is not asking "which is the most likely tag for this word". That is, the likelihood term is not $P(\text{VB}|\text{race})$. Instead we are computing $P(\text{race}|\text{VB})$. The probability, slightly counterintuitively, answers the question "If we were expecting a verb, how likely is it that this verb would be *race*?".

Here are the lexical likelihoods from the combined Brown and Switchboard corpora:

$$P(\text{race}|\text{NN}) = .00041$$
$$P(\text{race}|\text{VB}) = .00003$$

If we multiply the lexical likelihoods with the tag sequence probabilities, we see that even the simple bigram version of the HMM tagger correctly tags *race* as a VB despite the fact that it is the less likely sense of *race*:

$$P(\text{VB}|\text{TO})P(\text{race}|\text{VB}) = .00001$$
$$P(\text{NN}|\text{TO})P(\text{race}|\text{NN}) = .000007$$

The Actual Algorithm for HMM Tagging

Recall that a real HMM tagger isn't just choosing the best tag for a simple word but the best sequence of tags for an entire sentence. Now that we've seen the single-word intuition for the HMM tagger, let's give the complete equations. Generally, we make the Viterbi approximation and choose the most probable tag sequence for each sentence. This approach thus assumes that we are trying to compute for each sentence the most probable sequence of tags $T = t_1, t_2, \ldots, t_n$ given the sequence of words in the sentence (W):

$$\hat{T} = \operatorname*{argmax}_{T \in \tau} P(T|W)$$

By Bayes Law, $P(T|W)$ can be expressed as:

$$P(T|W) = \frac{P(T)P(W|T)}{P(W)}$$

Thus we are attempting to choose the sequence of tags that maximizes $\frac{P(T)P(W|T)}{P(W)}$:

$$\hat{T} = \underset{T \in \tau}{\mathrm{argmax}} \, \frac{P(T)P(W|T)}{P(W)}$$

Since we are looking for the most likely tag sequence for a sentence given a particular word sequence, the probability of the word sequence $P(W)$ will be the same for each tag sequence and we can ignore it.

$$\hat{T} = \underset{T \in \tau}{\mathrm{argmax}} \, P(T)P(W|T)$$

From the chain rule of probability:

$$P(T)P(W|T) = \prod_{i=1}^{n} P(w_i|w_1t_1 \dots w_{i-1}t_{i-1}t_i)P(t_i|w_1t_1 \dots w_{i-1}t_{i-1})$$

We make the N-gram assumption again, just as we did in Equation (6.9) for modeling the probability of word sequences. The trigram model is most often used, so let's define that one. First, we make the simplifying assumption that the probability of a word is dependent only its tag:

$$P(w_i|w_1t_1 \dots w_{i-1}t_{i-1}t_i) = p(w_i|t_i)$$

Next, we make the assumption that the tag history can be approximated by the most recent two tags:

$$P(t_i|w_1t_1 \dots w_{i-1}t_{i-1}) = P(t_i|t_{i-2}t_{i-1})$$

Thus we are choosing the tag sequence that maximizes:

$$P(t_1)P(t_2|t_1)\prod_{i=3}^{n} P(t_i|t_{i-2}t_{i-1})[\prod_{i=1}^{n} P(w_i|t_i)]$$

As usual, we can use maximum likelihood estimation from relative frequencies to estimate these probabilities.

$$P(t_i|t_{i-2}t_{i-1}) = \frac{c(t_{i-2}t_{i-1}t_i)}{c(t_{i-2}t_{i-1})}$$

$$P(w_i|t_i) = \frac{c(w_i,t_i)}{c(t_i)}$$

This model can also be smoothed (for example by the backoff or deleted interpolation algorithms of Chapter 6) to avoid zero probabilities.

Finding the most probable tag sequence can be done with the Viterbi algorithm described in Chapter 7.

Weischedel et al. (1993) and DeRose (1988) have reported accuracies of above 96% for this algorithm.

The HMM tagger we have seen so far is trained on hand-tagged data. Kupiec (1992), Cutting et al. (1992a), and others show that it is also possible to train an HMM tagger on unlabeled data, using the EM algorithm of Chapter 7 and Appendix D. These taggers still start with a dictionary which lists which tags can be assigned to which words; the EM algorithm then learns the word likelihood function for each tag, and the tag transition probabilities. An experiment by Merialdo (1994), however, indicates that with even a small amount of training data, a tagger trained on hand-tagged data worked better than one trained via EM. Thus the EM-trained "pure HMM" tagger is probably best suited in cases where no training data is available, for example when tagging languages for which there is no previously hand-tagged data.

8.6   TRANSFORMATION-BASED TAGGING

Transformation-Based Tagging, sometimes called Brill tagging, is an instance of the **Transformation-Based Learning** (TBL) approach to machine learning (Brill, 1995), and draws inspiration from both the rule-based and stochastic taggers. Like the rule-based taggers, TBL is based on rules that specify what tags should be assigned to what words. But like the stochastic taggers, TBL is a machine learning technique, in which rules are automatically induced from the data. Like some but not all of the HMM taggers, TBL is a supervised learning technique; it assumes a pre-tagged training corpus.

TRANSFORMATION-
BASED
LEARNING

Samuel et al. (1998a) offer a useful analogy for understanding the TBL paradigm, which they credit to Terry Harvey. Imagine an artist painting a picture of a white house with green trim against a blue sky. Suppose most of the picture was sky, and hence most of the picture was blue. The artist might begin by using a very broad brush and painting the entire canvas blue. Next she might switch to a somewhat smaller white brush, and paint the entire house white. She would just color in the whole house, not worrying about the brown roof, or the blue windows or the green gables. Next she takes a smaller brown brush and colors over the roof. Now she takes up the blue paint on a small brush and paints in the blue windows on the barn. Finally she takes a very fine green brush and does the trim on the gables.

The painter starts with a broad brush that covers a lot of the canvas but colors a lot of areas that will have to be repainted. The next layer colors less of the canvas, but also makes less "mistakes". Each new layer uses a

METHODOLOGY BOX: EVALUATING TAGGERS

Taggers are often evaluating by comparing them with a human-labeled **Gold Standard** test set, based on **percent correct**: the percentage of all tags in the test set where the tagger and the Gold standard agree. Most current tagging algorithms have an accuracy (percent-correct) of around 96–97% for simple tagsets like the Penn Treebank set; human annotators can then be used to manually post-process the tagged corpus.

How good is 96%? Since tag sets and tasks differ, the performance of tags can be compared against a lower-bound **baseline** and an upper-bound **ceiling**. One way to set a ceiling is to see how well humans do on the task. Marcus et al. (1993), for example, found that human annotators agreed on about 96–97% of the tags in the Penn Treebank version of the Brown Corpus. This suggests that the Gold Standard may have a 3-4% margin of error, and that it is not possible to get 100% accuracy. Two experiments by Voutilainen (1995, p. 174), however, found that if humans were allowed to discuss the tags, they reached consensus on 100% of the tags.

> **Key Concept #6. Human Ceiling:** When using a human Gold Standard to evaluate a classification algorithm, check the agreement rate of humans on the standard.

The standard **baseline**, suggested by Gale et al. (1992) (in the slightly different context of word-sense disambiguation), is to choose the **unigram most-likely tag** for each ambiguous word. The most-likely tag for each word can be computed from a hand-tagged corpus (which may be the same as the training corpus for the tagger being evaluated).

> **Key Concept #7. Unigram Baseline:** When designing a new classification algorithm, always compare it against the unigram baseline (assigning each token to the class it occurred in most often in the training set).

Charniak et al. (1993) showed that a (slightly smoothed) version of this baseline algorithm achieves an accuracy of 90–91%! Tagging algorithms since Harris (1962) have incorporated this intuition about tag-frequency.

finer brush that corrects less of the picture, but makes fewer mistakes. TBL uses somewhat the same method as this painter. The TBL algorithm has a set of tagging rules. A corpus is first tagged using the broadest rule, that is, the one that applies to the most cases. Then a slightly more specific rule is chosen, which changes some of the original tags. Next an even narrower rule, which changes a smaller number of tags (some of which might be previously changed tags).

How TBL Rules Are Applied

Let's look at one of the rules used by Brill's (1995) tagger. Before the rules apply, the tagger labels every word with its most-likely tag. We get these most-likely tags from a tagged corpus. For example, in the Brown corpus, *race* is most likely to be a noun:

$$P(\text{NN}|\text{race}) = .98$$
$$P(\text{VB}|\text{race}) = .02$$

This means that the two examples of *race* that we saw above will both be coded as NN. In the first case, this is a mistake, as NN is the incorrect tag:

(8.8) is/VBZ expected/VBN to/TO race/**NN** tomorrow/NN

In the second case this *race* is correctly tagged as an NN:

(8.9) the/DT race/**NN** for/IN outer/JJ space/NN

After selecting the most-likely tag, Brill's tagger applies its transformation rules. As it happens, Brill's tagger learned a rule that applies exactly to this mistagging of *race*:

Change NN *to* VB *when the previous tag is* TO

This rule would change *race/NN* to *race/VB* in exactly the following situation, since it is preceded by *to/TO*:

(8.10) expected/VBN to/TO race/NN → expected/VBN to/TO race/VB

How TBL Rules Are Learned

Brill's TBL algorithm has three major stages. It first labels every word with its most-likely tag. It then examines every possible transformation, and selects the one that results in the most improved tagging. Finally, it then re-tags the data according to this rule. These three stages are repeated until some stopping criterion is reached, such as insufficient improvement over the previous pass. Note that stage two requires that TBL knows the correct tag of each word; that is, TBL is a supervised learning algorithm.

The output of the TBL process is an ordered list of transformations; these then constitute a "tagging procedure" that can be applied to a new corpus. In principle the set of possible transformations is infinite, since we could imagine transformations such as "transform NN to VB if the previous word was "IBM" and the word "the" occurs between 17 and 158 words before that". But TBL needs to consider every possible transformation, in order to pick the best one on each pass through the algorithm. Thus the algorithm needs a way to limit the set of transformations. This is done by designing

TEMPLATES
a small set of **templates**, abstracted transformations. Every allowable transformation is an instantiation of one the templates. Brill's set of templates is listed in Figure 8.9. Figure 8.10 gives the details of this algorithm for learning transformations.

The preceding (following) word is tagged **z**.
The word two before (after) is tagged **z**.
One of the two preceding (following) words is tagged **z**.
One of the three preceding (following) words is tagged **z**.
The preceding word is tagged **z** and the following word is tagged **w**.
The preceding (following) word is tagged **z** and the word
         two before (after) is tagged **w**.

Figure 8.9   Brill's (1995) templates. Each begins with *"Change tag **a** to tag **b** when: ... "*. The variables **a**, **b**, **z**, and **w** range over parts-of-speech.

At the heart of Figure 8.10 are the two functions GET_BEST_TRANS-FORMATION and GET_BEST_INSTANCE. GET_BEST_TRANSFORMATION is called with a list of potential templates; for each template, it calls GET_BEST_INSTANCE. GET_BEST_INSTANCE iteratively tests every possible instantiation of each template by filling in specific values for the tag variables **a**, **b**, **z**, and **w**.

In practice, there are a number of ways to make the algorithm more efficient. For example, templates and instantiated transformations can be suggested in a data-driven manner; a transformation-instance might only be suggested if it would improve the tagging of some specific word. The search can also be made more efficient by pre-indexing the words in the training corpus by potential transformation. Roche and Schabes (1997a) show how the tagger can also be speeded up by converting each rule into a finite-state

---

function TBL(*corpus*) **returns** *transforms-queue*
INTIALIZE-WITH-MOST-LIKELY-TAGS(*corpus*)
until end condition is met **do**
  templates ← GENERATE-POTENTIAL-RELEVANT-TEMPLATES
  best-transform ← GET-BEST-TRANSFORM(*corpus, templates*)
  APPLY-TRANSFORM(*best-transform, corpus*)
  ENQUEUE(*best-transform-rule, transforms-queue*)
end
return(*transforms-queue*)

---

function GET-BEST-TRANSFORM(*corpus, templates*) **returns** *transform*
  for each *template* in *templates*
    (*instance, score*) ← GET-BEST-INSTANCE(*corpus, template*)
    if (*score > best-transform.score*) **then** *best-transform* ← (*instance, score*)
  return(*best-transform*)

---

function GET-BEST-INSTANCE(*corpus*, template) **returns** *transform*
  for *from-tag* ← **from** *tag*−1 **to** *tag*−*n* **do**
   for *to-tag* ← **from** *tag*−1 **to** *tag*−*n* **do**
    for *pos* ← **from** 1 **to** *corpus-size* **do**
     if (*correct-tag(pos)* == *to-tag* && *current-tag(pos)* == *from-tag*)
      num-good-transforms(current-tag(pos−1))++
     elseif (*correct-tag(pos)*==*from-tag* && *current-tag(pos)*==*from-tag*)
      num-bad-transforms(current-tag(pos−1))++
    end
    best-Z ← ARGMAX$_t$(*num-good-transforms*(t) - *num-bad-transforms*(t))
    if(*num-good-transforms(best-Z)* - *num-bad-transforms(best-Z)*
        > *best-instance.Z*) **then**
     best-instance ← "Change tag from *from-tag* to *to-tag*
             if previous tag is *best-Z*"
  return(*best-instance*)

---

procedure APPLY-TRANSFORM(*transform, corpus*)
for *pos* ← **from** 1 **to** *corpus-size* **do**
  if (*current-tag(pos)*==*best-rule-from*)
    && (*current-tag(pos−1)*==*best-rule-prev*))
    current-tag(pos) = *best-rule-to*

Figure 8.10   The TBL algorithm for learning to tag. GET_BEST_INSTANCE
would have to change for transformations templates other than *"Change tag
from X to Y if previous tag is Z"*. After Brill (1995).

transducer and composing all the transducers.

Figure 8.11 shows a few of the rules learned by Brill's original tagger.

	Change tags			
#	From	To	Condition	Example
1	NN	VB	Previous tag is TO	to/TO race/NN → VB
2	VBP	VB	One of the previous 3 tags is MD	might/MD vanish/VBP → VB
3	NN	VB	One of the previous 2 tags is MD	might/MD not reply/NN → VB
4	VB	NN	One of the previous 2 tags is DT	
5	VBD	VBN	One of the previous 3 tags is VBZ	

Figure 8.11   The first 20 nonlexicalized transformations from the Brill tagger (Brill, 1995).

8.7   OTHER ISSUES

Multiple Tags and Multiple Words

Two issues that arise in tagging are tag indeterminacy and multi-part words. Tag indeterminacy arises when a word is ambiguous between multiple tags and it is impossible or very difficult to disambiguate. In this case, some taggers allow the use of multiple tags. This is the case in the Penn Treebank and in the British National Corpus. Common tag indeterminacies include adjective versus preterite versus past participle (JJ/VBD/VBN), and adjective versus noun as prenominal modifier (JJ/NN).

The second issue concerns multi-part words. The C5 and C7 tagsets, for example, allow prepositions like *"in terms of"* to be treated as a single word by adding numbers to each tag:

in/II31 terms/II32 of/II33

Finally, some tagged corpora split certain words; for example the Penn Treebank and the British National Corpus splits contractions and the *'s*-genitive from their stems:

would/MD n't/RB
children/NNS 's/POS

METHODOLOGY BOX: ERROR ANALYSIS

In order to improve a computational model we need to analyze and understand where it went wrong. Analyzing the error in a pattern classifier like a part-of-speech tagger is usually done via a **confusion matrix**, also called a **contingency table**. A confusion matrix for an N-way classification task is an N-by-N matrix where the cell (x, y) contains the number of times an item with correction classification x was classified by the model as y. For example, the following table shows a portion of the confusion matrix from the HMM tagging experiments of Franz (1996). The row labels indicate correct tags, column labels indicate the tagger's hypothesized tags, and each cell indicates percentage of the overall tagging error. Thus 4.4% of the total errors were caused by mistagging a VBD as a VBN. Common errors are boldfaced in the table.

	IN	JJ	NN	NNP	RB	VBD	VBN
IN	-	.2			.7		
JJ	.2	-	**3.3**	2.1	1.7	.2	**2.7**
NN		**8.7**	-				.2
NNP	.2	**3.3**	**4.1**	-	.2		
RB	**2.2**	**2.0**	.5		-		
VBD		.3	.5			-	**4.4**
VBN		**2.8**				**2.6**	-

The confusion matrix above, and related error analyses in Franz (1996), Kupiec (1992), and Ratnaparkhi (1996), suggest that some major problems facing current taggers are:

1. **NN versus NNP versus JJ:** These are hard to distinguish prenominally. Distinguishing proper nouns is especially important for information extraction and machine translation.

2. **RP versus RB versus IN:** All of these can appear in sequences of satellites immediately following the verb.

3. **VBD versus VBN versus JJ:** Distinguishing these is important for partial parsing (participles are used to find passives), and for correctly labeling the edges of noun-phrases.

Unknown Words

All the tagging algorithms we have discussed require a dictionary that lists the possible parts-of-speech of every word. But the largest dictionary will still not contain every possible word, as we saw in Chapter 4. Proper names and acronyms are created very often, and even new common nouns and verbs enter the language at a surprising rate. Therefore in order to build a complete tagger we need some method for guessing the tag of an unknown word.

The simplest possible unknown-word algorithm is to pretend that each unknown word is ambiguous among all possible tags, with equal probability. Then the tagger must rely solely on the contextual POS-trigrams to suggest the proper tag. A slightly more complex algorithm is based on the idea that the probability distribution of tags over unknown words is very similar to the distribution of tags over words that occurred only once in a training set. an idea that was suggested by both Baayen and Sproat (1996) and Dermatas and Kokkinakis (1995). These words that only occur once are known as **hapax**

HAPAX
LEGOMENA

legomena (singular **hapax legomenon**). For example, unknown words and *hapax legomena* are similar in that they are both most likely to be nouns, followed by verbs, but are very unlikely to be determiners or interjections. Thus the likelihood $P(w_i|t_i)$ for an unknown word is determined by the average of the distribution over all singleton words in the training set. (Recall that this idea of using "things we've seen once" as an estimator for "things we've never seen" proved useful as key concept **Things Seen Once** in the Witten-Bell and Good-Turing algorithms of Chapter 6.)

The most-powerful unknown-word algorithms make use of information about how the word is spelled. For example, words that end in the letter *-s* are likely to be plural nouns (NNS), while words ending with *-ed* tend to be past participles (VBN). Words starting with capital letters are likely to be nouns. Weischedel et al. (1993) used four specific kinds of orthographic features: 3 inflectional endings (*-ed, -s, -ing*), 32 derivational endings (such as *-ion, -al, -ive*, and *-ly*), 4 values of capitalization (capitalized initial, capitalized non-initial, etc.), and hyphenation. They used the following equation to compute the likelihood of an unknown word:

$$P(w_i|t_i) = p(\text{unknown-word}|t_i) * p(\text{capital}|t_i) * p(\text{endings/hyph}|t_i)$$

Other researchers, rather than relying on these hand-designed features, have used machine learning to induce useful features. Brill (1995) used the TBL algorithm, where the allowable templates were defined orthographically (the first N letters of the words, the last N letters of the word, etc.). His algorithm induced all the English inflectional features, hyphenation, and

METHODOLOGY BOX: COMPUTING AGREEMENT VIA κ

One problem with the **percent correct** metric for evaluating taggers is that it doesn't control for how easy the tagging task is. If 99% of the tags are, say, NN, then getting 99% correct isn't very good; we could have gotten 99% correct just by guessing NN. This means that it's really impossible to compare taggers which are being run on different test sets or different tasks. As the previous methodology box noted, one factor that can help normalize different values of percent correct is to measure the difficulty of a given task via the unigram baseline for that task.

In fact, there is an evaluation statistic called **kappa** (κ) that takes this baseline into account, inherently controlling for the complexity of the task (Siegel and Castellan, 1988; Carletta, 1996). Kappa can be used instead of percent correct when comparing a tagger to a Gold Standard, or especially when comparing human labelers to each other, when there is no one correct answer. Kappa is the ratio of the proportion of times that two classifiers agree (corrected for chance agreement) to the maximum proportion of times that the classifiers could agree (corrected for chance agreement):

$$\kappa = \frac{P(A) - P(E)}{1 - P(E)}$$

P(A) is the proportion of times that the hypothesis **agrees** with the standard; i.e., percent correct. P(E) is the proportion of times that the hypothesis and the standard would be **expected** to agree by chance. P(E) can be computed from some other knowledge, or it can be computed from the actual confusion matrix for the labels being compared. The bounds for κ are just like those for percent correct; when there is no agreement (other than what would be expected by chance) κ = 0. When there is complete agreement, κ = 1.

The κ statistic is most often used when there is no "Gold Standard" at all. This occurs, for example, when comparing human labelers to each other on a difficult subjective task. In this case, κ is a very useful evaluation metric, the "average pairwise agreement corrected for chance agreement". Krippendorf (1980) suggests that a value of κ > .8 can be considered good reliability.

many derivational features such as *-ly*, *al*. Franz (1996) uses a loglinear model which includes more features, such as the length of the word and various prefixes, and furthermore includes interaction terms among various features.

Class-based N-grams

Now that we have a way of automatically assigning a class to each word in a corpus, we can use this information to augment our *N*-gram models. The **class-based N-gram** is a variant of the *N*-gram that uses the frequency of sequences of POS (or other) classes to help produce a more knowledgeable estimate of the probability of word strings. The basic class-based *N*-gram defines the conditional probability of a word w_n based on its history as the product of the two factors: the probability of the class given the preceding classes (based on an *N*-gram-of-classes), and the probability of a particular word given the class:

CLASS-BASED
N-GRAM

$$P(w_n|w_{n-N+1}^{n-1}) = P(w_n|c_n)P(c_n|c_{n-N+1}^{n-1})$$

The maximum likelihood estimate (MLE) of the probability of the word given the class and the probability of the class given the previous class can be computed as follows:

$$P(w|c) = \frac{C(w)}{C(c)}$$

$$P(c_i|c_{i-1}) = \frac{C(c_{i-1}c_i)}{\sum_c C(c_{i-1}c)}$$

A class-based *N*-gram can rely on standard tagsets like the Penn tagset to define the classes, or on application-specific sets (for example using tags like CITY and AIRLINE for an airline information system). The classes can also be automatically induced by clustering words in a corpus (Brown et al., 1992). A number of researchers have shown that class-based *N*-grams can be useful in decreasing the perplexity and word-error rate of language models, especially if they are mixed in some way with regular word-based *N*-grams (Jelinek, 1990; Kneser and Ney, 1993; Heeman, 1999; Samuelsson and Reichl, 1999).

8.8 SUMMARY

This chapter introduced the idea of **parts-of-speech** and **part-of-speech tagging**. The main ideas:

- Languages generally have a relatively small set of **closed class** words, which are often highly frequent, generally act as **function words**, and can be very ambiguous in their part-of-speech tags. Open class words generally include various kinds of **nouns**, **verbs**, **adjectives**. There are a number of part-of-speech coding schemes, based on **tagsets** of between 40 and 200 tags.

- **Part-of-speech tagging** is the process of assigning a part-of-speech label to each of a sequence of words. Taggers can be characterized as **rule-based** or **stochastic**. Rule-based taggers use hand-written rules to distinguish tag ambiguity. Stochastic taggers are either **HMM-based**, choosing the tag sequence which maximizes the product of word likelihood and tag sequence probability, or **cue-based**, using decision trees or maximum entropy models to combine probabilistic features.

- Taggers are often evaluated by comparing their output from a test-set to human labels for that test set. Error analysis can help pinpoint areas where a tagger doesn't perform well.

BIBLIOGRAPHICAL AND HISTORICAL NOTES

The earliest implemented part-of-speech assignment algorithm may have been part of the parser in Zellig Harris's Transformations and Discourse Analysis Project (TDAP), which was implemented between June 1958 and July 1959 at the University of Pennsylvania (Harris, 1962). Previous natural language processing systems had used dictionaries with part-of-speech information for words, but have not been described as performing part-of-speech disambiguation. As part of its parsing, TDAP did part-of-speech disambiguation via 14 hand-written rules, whose use of part-of-speech tag sequences prefigures all the modern algorithms, and which were run in an order based on the relative frequency of tags for a word. The parser/tagger was reimplemented recently and is described by Joshi and Hopely (1999) and Karttunen (1999), who note that the parser was essentially implemented (ironically in a very modern way) as a cascade of finite-state transducers.

Soon after the TDAP parser was the Computational Grammar Coder (CGC) of Klein and Simmons (1963). The CGC had three components: a lexicon, a morphological analyzer, and a context disambiguator. The small 1500-word lexicon included exceptional words that could not be accounted for in the simple morphological analyzer, including function words as well as irregular nouns, verbs, and adjectives. The morphological analyzer used inflectional and derivational suffixes to assign part-of-speech classes. A word was run through the lexicon and morphological analyzer to produce a candidate set of parts-of-speech. A set of 500 context rules were then used to disambiguate this candidate set, by relying on surrounding islands of unambiguous words. For example, one rule said that between an ARTICLE and a VERB, the only allowable sequences were ADJ-NOUN, NOUN-ADVERB, or NOUN-NOUN. The CGC algorithm reported 90% accuracy on applying a 30-tag tagset to articles from the Scientific American and a children's encyclopedia.

The TAGGIT tagger (Greene and Rubin, 1971) was based on the Klein and Simmons (1963) system, using the same architecture but increasing the size of the dictionary and the size of the tagset (to 87 tags). For example the following sample rule, which states that a word x is unlikely to be a plural noun (NNS) before a third person singular verb (VBZ):

x VBZ $\rightarrow$ *not* NNS

TAGGIT was applied to the Brown Corpus and, according to Francis and Kučera (1982, p. 9), "resulted in the accurate tagging of 77% of the corpus" (the remainder of the Brown Corpus was tagged by hand).

In the 1970s the Lancaster-Oslo/Bergen (LOB) Corpus was compiled as a British English equivalent of the Brown Corpus. It was tagged with the CLAWS tagger (Marshall, 1983, 1987; Garside, 1987), a probabilistic algorithm which can be viewed as an approximation to the HMM tagging approach. The algorithm used tag bigram probabilities, but instead of storing the word-likelihood of each tag, tags were marked either as *rare* ($P(\text{tag}|\text{word}) < .01$) *infrequent* ($P(\text{tag}|\text{word}) < .10$), or *normally frequent* ($P(\text{tag}|\text{word}) > .10$),

The probabilistic PARTS tagger of Church (1988) was very close to a full HMM tagger. It extended the CLAWS idea to assign full lexical probabilities to each word/tag combination, and used Viterbi decoding to find a tag sequence. Like the CLAWS tagger, however, it stored the probability of the tag given the word:

$$P(\text{tag}|\text{word}) * P(\text{tag}|\text{previous } n \text{ tags}) \tag{8.11}$$

rather than using the probability of the word given the tag, as an HMM tagger does:

$$P(\text{word}|\text{tag}) * P(\text{tag}|\text{previous } n \text{ tags}) \qquad (8.12)$$

Later taggers explicitly introduced the use of the Hidden Markov Model, often with the EM training algorithm (Kupiec, 1992; Merialdo, 1994; Weischedel et al., 1993), including the use of variable-length Markov models (Schütze and Singer, 1994).

A number of recent stochastic algorithms use various statistical and machine-learning tools to estimate the probability of a tag or tag-sequence given a large number of relevant features such as the neighboring words and neighboring parts-of-speech, as well as assorted orthographic and morphological features. These features are then combined to estimate the probability of tag either via a decision tree (Jelinek et al., 1994; Magerman, 1995), the Maximum Entropy algorithm (Ratnaparkhi, 1996), log-linear models (Franz, 1996), or networks of linear separators (SNOW) (Roth and Zelenko, 1998). Brill (1997) presents a unsupervised version of the TBL algorithm.

Readers interested in the history of parts-of-speech should consult a history of linguistics such as Robins (1967) or Koerner and Asher (1995), particularly the article by Householder (1995) in the latter.

EXERCISES

8.1 Find one tagging error in each of the following sentences that are tagged with the Penn Treebank tagset:

  a. I/PRP need/VBP a/DT flight/NN from/IN Atlanta/NN

  b. Does/VBZ this/DT flight/NN serve/VB dinner/NNS

  c. I/PRP have/VB a/DT friend/NN living/VBG in/IN Denver/NNP

  d. What/WDT flights/NNS do/VBP you/PRP have/VB from/IN Milwaukee/NNP to/IN Tampa/NNP

  e. Can/VBP you/PRP list/VB the/DT nonstop/JJ afternoon/NN flights/NNS

8.2   Use the Penn Treebank tagset to tag each word in the following sentences from Damon Runyon's short stories. You may ignore punctuation. Some of these are quite difficult; do your best.

   a. It is a nice night.

   b. This crap game is over a garage in Fifty-second Street...

   c. ...Nobody ever takes the newspapers she sells ...

   d. He is a tall, skinny guy with a long, sad, mean-looking kisser, and a mournful voice.

   e. ...I am sitting in Mindy's restaurant putting on the gefillte fish, which is a dish I am very fond of, ...

   f. When a guy and a doll get to taking peeks back and forth at each other, why there you are indeed.

8.3   Now compare your tags from the previous exercise with one or two friend's answers. On which words did you disagree the most? Why?

8.4   Implement the Kappa algorithm of page 315, and compute the agreement between you and your friends. To compute $P(A)$ and $P(E)$, you may used the following equations modified from Walker et al. (1997). These assume that you have the confusion matrix M, where the correct answers label the rows and the hypotheses label the columns (as seen in the Methodology Box on page 313):

$$P(E) = \sum_{i-1}^{n} (\frac{t_i}{T})^2$$

$$P(A) = \frac{\sum_{i-1}^{n} M(i,i)}{T}$$

where t_i is the sum of the counts in row i of M, and T is the sum of all the counts in M.

8.5   Now tag the sentences in Exercise 8.2 using the more detailed C7 tagset in Appendix C.

8.6   Implement the TBL algorithm in Figure 8.10. Create a small number of templates and train the tagger on any POS-tagged training set you can find.

8.7   Recall that the Church (1988) tagger is not an HMM tagger since it incorporates the probability of the tag given the word:

$$P(\text{tag}|\text{word}) * P(\text{tag}|\text{previous } n \text{ tags}) \tag{8.13}$$

rather than using the likelihood of the word given the tag, as an HMM tagger does:

$$P(\text{word}|\text{tag}) * P(\text{tag}|\text{previous } n \text{ tags}) \qquad (8.14)$$

As a gedanken-experiment, construct a sentence, a set of tag transition probabilities, and a set of lexical tag probabilities that demonstrate a way in which the HMM tagger can produce a better answer than the Church tagger.

8.8 Build an HMM tagger. This requires (1) that you have implemented the Viterbi algorithm from Chapter 5 or Chapter 7, (2) that you have a dictionary with part-of-speech information and (3) that you have either (a) a part-of-speech-tagged corpus or (b) an implementation of the Forward Backward algorithm. If you have a labeled corpus, train the transition and observation probabilities of an HMM tagger directly on the hand-tagged data. If you have an unlabeled corpus, train using Forward Backward.

8.9 Now run your algorithm on a small test set that you have hand-labeled. Find five errors and analyze them.

9   CONTEXT-FREE GRAMMARS FOR ENGLISH

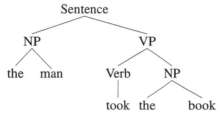

The first context-free grammar parse tree (Chomsky, 1956)

If on a winter's night a traveler by Italo Calvino
Nuclear and Radiochemistry by Gerhart Friedlander et al.
The Fire Next Time by James Baldwin
A Tad Overweight, but Violet Eyes to Die For by G. B. Trudeau
Sometimes a Great Notion by Ken Kesey
Dancer from the Dance by Andrew Holleran

           Six books in English whose titles are not constituents, from Pullum (1991, p. 195)

In her essay *The Anatomy of a Recipe*, M. F. K. Fisher (1968) wryly comments that it is "modish" to refer to the *anatomy* of a thing or problem. The similar use of *grammar* to describe the structures of an area of knowledge had a vogue in the 19th century (e.g., Busby's (1818) *A Grammar of Music* and Field's (1888) *A Grammar of Colouring*). In recent years the word *grammar* has made a reappearance, although usually now it is *the* grammar rather than *a* grammar that is being described (e.g., *The Grammar of Graphics*, *The Grammar of Conducting*). Perhaps scholars are simply less modest than they used to be? Or perhaps the word *grammar* itself has changed a

bit, from "a listing of principles or structures", to "those principles or structures as an field of inquiry". Following this second reading, in this chapter
we turn to what might be called *The Grammar of Grammar*, or perhaps *The
Grammar of Syntax*.

SYNTAX

The word **syntax** comes from the Greek *sýntaxis*, meaning "setting
out together or arrangement", and refers to the way words are arranged together. We have seen various syntactic notions in previous chapters. Chapter 8 talked about part-of-speech categories as a kind of equivalence class for
words. Chapter 6 talked about the importance of modeling word order. This
chapter and the following ones introduce a number of more complex notions of syntax and grammar. There are three main new ideas: **constituency**,
grammatical relations, and **subcategorization and dependencies**.

CONSTITUENT

The fundamental idea of constituency is that groups of words may behave as a single unit or phrase, called a **constituent**. For example we will
see that a group of words called a **noun phrase** often acts as a unit; noun
phrases include single words like *she* or *Michael* and phrases like *the house*,
Russian Hill, and *a well-weathered three-story structure*. This chapter will
introduce the use of **context-free grammars**, a formalism that will allow us
to model these constituency facts.

Grammatical relations are a formalization of ideas from traditional
grammar about SUBJECTS and OBJECTS. In the sentence:

(9.1) She ate a mammoth breakfast.

the noun phrase *She* is the SUBJECT and *a mammoth breakfast* is the OBJECT.
Grammatical relations will be introduced in this chapter when we talk about
syntactic **agreement**, and will be expanded upon in Chapter 11.

Subcategorization and **dependency relations** refer to certain kinds
of relations between words and phrases. For example the verb *want* can be
followed by an infinitive, as in *I want to fly to Detroit*, or a noun phrase, as in
I want a flight to Detroit. But the verb *find* cannot be followed by an infinitive
(**I found to fly to Dallas*). These are called facts about the *subcategory* of the
verb, which will be discussed starting on page 342, and again in Chapter 11.

All of these kinds of syntactic knowledge can be modeled by various
kinds of grammars that are based on context-free grammars. Context-free
grammars are thus the backbone of many models of the syntax of natural language (and, for that matter, of computer languages). As such they
are integral to most models of natural language understanding, of grammar
checking, and more recently of speech understanding. They are powerful
enough to express sophisticated relations among the words in a sentence, yet

computationally tractable enough that efficient algorithms exist for parsing sentences with them (as we will see in Chapter 10). Later in Chapter 12 we will introduce probabilistic versions of context-free grammars, which model many aspects of human sentence processing and which provide sophisticated language models for speech recognition.

In addition to an introduction to the grammar formalism, this chapter also provides an overview of the grammar of English. We will be modeling example sentences from the Air Traffic Information System (ATIS) domain (Hemphill et al., 1990). ATIS systems are spoken language systems that can help book airline reservations. Users try to book flights by conversing with the system, specifying constraints like *I'd like to fly from Atlanta to Denver*. The U.S. government funded a number of different research sites to build ATIS systems in the early 1990s, and so a lot of data was collected and a significant amount of research has been done on the resulting data. The sentences we will be modeling in this chapter are the user queries to the system.

9.1   CONSTITUENCY

How do words group together in English? How do we know they are really grouping together? Let's consider the standard grouping that is usually called the **noun phrase** or sometimes the **noun group**. This is a sequence   NOUN PHRASE
of words surrounding at least one noun. Here are some examples of noun   NOUN GROUP
phrases (thanks to Damon Runyon):

> three parties from Brooklyn
> a high-class spot such as Mindy's
> the Broadway coppers
> they
> Harry the Horse
> the reason he comes into the Hot Box

How do we know that these words group together (or "form a constituent")? One piece of evidence is that they can all appear in similar syntactic environments, for example before a verb.

> three parties from Brooklyn *arrive...*
> a high-class spot such as Mindy's *attracts...*
> the Broadway coppers *love...*
> they *sit*

But while the whole noun phrase can occur before a verb, this is not true of each of the individual words that make up a noun phrase. The following are not grammatical sentences of English (recall that we use an asterisk (*) to mark fragments that are not grammatical English sentences):

> *from *arrive...*
> *as *attracts...*
> *the *is...*
> *spot *is...*

Thus in order to correctly describe facts about the ordering of these words in English, we must be able to say things like *"Noun Phrases can occur before verbs"*.

PREPOSED

POSTPOSED

Other kinds of evidence for constituency come from what are called **preposed** or **postposed** constructions. For example, the prepositional phrase *on September seventeenth* can be placed in a number of different locations in the following examples, including preposed at the beginning, and postposed at the end:

> On September seventeenth, I'd like to fly from Atlanta to Denver
> I'd like to fly on September seventeenth from Atlanta to Denver
> I'd like to fly from Atlanta to Denver on September seventeenth

But again, while the entire phrase can be placed differently, the individual words making up the phrase cannot be:

> *On September, I'd like to fly seventeenth from Atlanta to Denver
> *On I'd like to fly September seventeenth from Atlanta to Denver
> *I'd like to fly on September from Atlanta to Denver seventeenth

Section 9.11 will give other motivations for context-free grammars based on their ability to model recursive structures.

There are many other kinds of evidence that groups of words often behave as a single constituent (see Radford (1988) for a good survey).

9.2   CONTEXT-FREE RULES AND TREES

The most commonly used mathematical system for modeling constituent structure in English and other natural languages is the **Context-Free Grammar**, or **CFG**. Context-free grammars are also called **Phrase-Structure**

CFG

Grammars, and the formalism is equivalent to what is also called **Backus-Naur Form** or **BNF**. The idea of basing a grammar on constituent structure dates back to the psychologist Wilhelm Wundt (1900), but was not formalized until Chomsky (1956), and, independently, Backus (1959).

A context-free grammar consists of a set of **rules** or **productions**, each of which expresses the ways that symbols of the language can be grouped and ordered together, and a **lexicon** of words and symbols. For example, the following productions express that a **NP** (or **noun phrase**), can be composed of either a *ProperNoun* or a determiner (*Det*) followed by a *Nominal*; a *Nominal* can be one or more *Noun*s.

RULES

LEXICON

NP

$$NP \rightarrow Det\ Nominal \qquad\qquad (9.2)$$

$$NP \rightarrow ProperNoun \qquad\qquad (9.3)$$

$$Nominal \rightarrow Noun \mid Noun\ Nominal \qquad\qquad (9.4)$$

Context free rules can be hierarchically embedded, so we could combine the previous rule with others like these which express facts about the lexicon:

$$Det \rightarrow a \qquad\qquad (9.5)$$

$$Det \rightarrow the \qquad\qquad (9.6)$$

$$Noun \rightarrow flight \qquad\qquad (9.7)$$

The symbols that are used in a CFG are divided into two classes. The symbols that correspond to words in the language ("the", "nightclub") are called **terminal** symbols; the lexicon is the set of rules that introduce these terminal symbols. The symbols that express clusters or generalizations of these are called **non-terminals**. In each context-free rule, the item to the right of the arrow ($\rightarrow$) is an ordered list of one or more terminals and non-terminals, while to the left of the arrow is a single non-terminal symbol expressing some cluster or generalization. Notice that in the lexicon, the non-terminal associated with each word is its lexical category, or part-of-speech, which we defined in Chapter 8.

TERMINAL

NON-TERMINAL

A CFG is usually thought of in two ways: as a device for generating sentences, or as a device for assigning a structure to a given sentence. As a generator, we could read the → arrow as "rewrite the symbol on the left with the string of symbols on the right". So starting from the symbol

NP,

we can use rule 9.2 to rewrite *NP* as

Det Nominal,

and then rule 9.4:

Det Noun,

and finally via rules 9.5 and 9.7 as

a flight,

DERIVED   We say the string *a flight* can be **derived** from the non-terminal *NP*. Thus a CFG can be used to randomly generate a series of strings. This DERIVATION   sequence of rule expansions is called a **derivation** of the string of words. PARSE TREE   It is common to represent a derivation by a **parse tree** (commonly shown inverted with the root at the top). Here is the tree representation of this derivation:

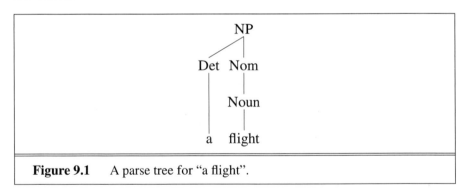

Figure 9.1   A parse tree for "a flight".

START SYMBOL   The formal language defined by a CFG is the set of strings that are derivable from the designated **start symbol**. Each grammar must have one designated start symbol, which is often called *S*. Since context-free grammars are often used to define sentences, *S* is usually interpreted as the "sentence" node, and the set of strings that are derivable from *S* is the set of sentences in some simplified version of English.

Let's add to our sample grammar a couple of higher-level rules that expand S, and a couple others. One will express the fact that a sentence can consist of a noun phrase and a **verb phrase**:   VERB PHRASE

$S \rightarrow NP\ VP$ I prefer a morning flight

A verb phrase in English consists of a verb followed by assorted other things; for example, one kind of verb phrase consists of a verb followed by a noun phrase:

$VP \rightarrow Verb\ NP$ prefer a morning flight

Or the verb phrase may have a noun phrase and a prepositional phrase:

$VP \rightarrow Verb\ NP\ PP$ leave Boston in the morning

Or the verb may be followed just by a prepositional phrase:

$VP \rightarrow Verb\ PP$ leaving on Thursday

A prepositional phrase generally has a preposition followed by a noun phrase. For example, a very common type of prepositional phrase in the ATIS corpus is used to indicate location or direction:

$PP \rightarrow Preposition\ NP$ from Los Angeles

The NP inside a PP need not be a location; PPs are often used with times and dates, and with other nouns as well; they can be arbitrarily complex. Here are ten examples from the ATIS corpus:

to Seattle	on these flights
in Minneapolis	about the ground transportation in Chicago
on Wednesday	of the round trip flight on United Airlines
in the evening	of the AP fifty seven flight
on the ninth of July	with a stopover in Nashville

Figure 9.2 gives a sample lexicon and Figure 9.3 summarizes the grammar rules we've seen so far, which we'll call $\mathcal{L}_0$. Note that we can use the or-symbol | to indicate that a non-terminal has alternate possible expansions.

We can use this grammar to generate sentences of this "ATIS-language". We start with S, expand it to $NP\ VP$, then choose a random expansion of NP (let's say to I), and a random expansion of VP (let's say to $Verb\ NP$), and so on until we generate the string *I prefer a morning flight*. Figure 9.4 shows a parse tree that represents a complete derivation of *I prefer a morning flight*.

$$Noun \rightarrow flights \mid breeze \mid trip \mid morning \mid \ldots$$
$$Verb \rightarrow is \mid prefer \mid like \mid need \mid want \mid fly$$
$$Adjective \rightarrow cheapest \mid non-stop \mid first \mid latest$$
$$\mid other \mid direct \mid \ldots$$
$$Pronoun \rightarrow me \mid I \mid you \mid it \mid \ldots$$
$$Proper\text{-}Noun \rightarrow Alaska \mid Baltimore \mid Los\ Angeles$$
$$\mid Chicago \mid United \mid American \mid \ldots$$
$$Determiner \rightarrow the \mid a \mid an \mid this \mid these \mid that \mid \ldots$$
$$Preposition \rightarrow from \mid to \mid on \mid near \mid \ldots$$
$$Conjunction \rightarrow and \mid or \mid but \mid \ldots$$

Figure 9.2   The lexicon for $\mathcal{L}_0$.

$S \rightarrow$	$NP\ VP$	I + want a morning flight
$NP \rightarrow$	$Pronoun$	I
$\mid$	$Proper\text{-}Noun$	Los Angeles
$\mid$	$Det\ Nominal$	a + flight
$Nominal \rightarrow$	$Noun\ Nominal$	morning + flight
$\mid$	$Noun$	flights
$VP \rightarrow$	$Verb$	do
$\mid$	$Verb\ NP$	want + a flight
$\mid$	$Verb\ NP\ PP$	leave + Boston + in the morning
$\mid$	$Verb\ PP$	leaving + on Thursday
$PP \rightarrow$	$Preposition\ NP$	from + Los Angeles

Figure 9.3   The grammar for $\mathcal{L}_0$, with example phrases for each rule.

BRACKETED
NOTATION

It is sometimes convenient to represent a parse tree in a more compact format called **bracketed notation**, essentially the same as LISP tree representations; here is the bracketed representation of the parse tree of Figure 9.4:

$$[_S\ [_{NP}\ [_{Pro}\ I]]\ [_{VP}\ [_V\ prefer]\ [_{NP}\ [_{Det}\ a]\ [_{Nom}\ [_N\ morning]\ [_N\ flight]]]]]$$

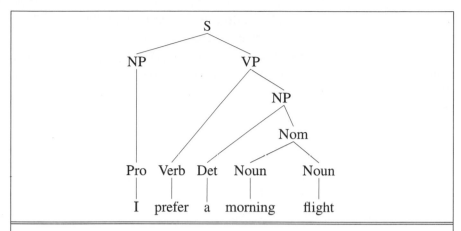

Figure 9.4   The parse tree for "I prefer a morning flight" according to grammar $\mathcal{L}_0$.

A CFG like that of $\mathcal{L}_0$ defines a formal language. We saw in Chapter 2 that a formal language is a set of strings. Sentences (strings of words) that can be derived by a grammar are in the formal language defined by that grammar, and are called **grammatical** sentences. Sentences that cannot be derived by a given formal grammar are not in the language defined by that grammar, and are referred to as **ungrammatical**. This hard line between "in" and "out" characterizes all formal languages but is only a very simplified model of how natural languages really work. This is because determining whether a given sentence is part of a given natural language (say English) often depends on the context. In linguistics, the use of formal languages to model natural languages is called **generative grammar**, since the language is defined by the set of possible sentences "generated" by the grammar.

We conclude this section by way of summary with a quick formal description of a context free grammar and the language it generates. A context-free grammar has four parameters (technically "is a 4-tuple"):

GRAMMATICAL

UNGRAMMATICAL

GENERATIVE
GRAMMAR

1. a set of non-terminal symbols (or "variables") N
2. a set of terminal symbols Σ (disjoint from N)
3. a set of productions P, each of the form $A \to \alpha$, where A is a non-terminal and α is a string of symbols from the infinite set of strings $(\Sigma \cup N)*$
4. a designated start symbol S

A language is defined via the concept of **derivation**. One string **derives** another one if it can be rewritten as the second one via some series of rule applications. More formally, following Hopcroft and Ullman (1979), if $A \rightarrow \beta$ is a production of P and α and γ are any strings in the set $(\Sigma \cup N)*$, then we say that $\alpha A\gamma$ **directly derives** $\alpha\beta\gamma$, or $\alpha A\gamma \Rightarrow \alpha\beta\gamma$. Derivation is then a generalization of direct derivation. Let $\alpha_1, \alpha_2, \ldots, \alpha_m$ be strings in $(\Sigma \cup N)*, m \geq 1$, such that

DIRECTLY DERIVES

$$\alpha_1 \Rightarrow \alpha_2, \alpha_2 \Rightarrow \alpha_3, \ldots, \alpha_{m-1} \Rightarrow \alpha_m \tag{9.8}$$

DERIVES   We say that α_1 **derives** α_m, or $\alpha_1 \overset{*}{\Rightarrow} \alpha_m$.

We can then formally define the language $\mathcal{L}_G$ generated by a grammar G as the set of strings composed of terminal symbols which can be derived from the designed start symbol S.

$$\mathcal{L}_G = W|w \text{ is in } \Sigma* \text{ and } S \overset{*}{\Rightarrow} w \tag{9.9}$$

PARSING   The problem of mapping from a string of words to its parse tree is called **parsing**; we will define algorithms for parsing in Chapter 10 and in Chapter 12.

9.3   SENTENCE-LEVEL CONSTRUCTIONS

The remainder of this chapter will introduce a few of the more complex aspects of the phrase structure of English; for consistency we will continue to focus on sentences from the ATIS domain. Because of space limitations, our discussion will necessarily be limited to highlights. Readers are strongly advised to consult Quirk et al. (1985), which is by far the best current reference grammar of English.

In the small grammar $\mathcal{L}_0$, we only gave a single sentence-level construction for declarative sentences like *I prefer a morning flight*. There are a great number of possible overall sentence structures, but four are particularly common and important: declarative structure, imperative structure, yes-no-question structure, and wh-question structure,

DECLARATIVE   Sentences with **declarative** structure have a subject noun phrase followed by a verb phrase, like "I prefer a morning flight". Sentences with this structure have a great number of different uses that we will follow up on in Chapter 19. Here are a number of examples from the ATIS domain:

> The flight should be eleven a.m. tomorrow
> I need a flight to Seattle leaving from Baltimore making a stop in Minneapolis
> The return flight should leave at around seven p.m.
> I would like to find out the flight number for the United flight that arrives in San Jose around ten p.m.

I'd like to fly the coach discount class
I want a flight from Ontario to Chicago
I plan to leave on July first around six thirty in the evening

Sentences with **imperative** structure often begin with a verb phrase, IMPERATIVE
and have no subject. They are called imperative because they are almost
always used for commands and suggestions; in the ATIS domain they are
commands to the system.

Show the lowest fare
Show me the cheapest fare that has lunch
Give me Sunday's flights arriving in Las Vegas from Memphis and
New York City
List all flights between five and seven p.m.
List all flights from Burbank to Denver
Show me all flights that depart before ten a.m. and have first class fares
Show me all the flights leaving Baltimore
Show me flights arriving within thirty minutes of each other
Please list the flights from Charlotte to Long Beach arriving after lunch
time
Show me the last flight to leave

To model this kind of sentence structure, we can add another rule for the
expansion of *S*:

$S \rightarrow VP$ Show the lowest fare

Sentences with **yes-no-question** structure are often (though not always) used to ask questions (hence the name), and begin with a auxiliary
verb, followed by a subject *NP*, followed by a *VP*. Here are some examples (note that the third example is not really a question but a command or
suggestion; Chapter 19 will discuss the **pragmatic** uses of these question
forms):

Do any of these flights have stops?
Does American's flight eighteen twenty five serve dinner?
Can you give me the same information for United?

Here's the rule:

$S \rightarrow Aux\ NP\ VP$

WH-PHRASE

WH-WORD
The most complex of the sentence-level structures we will examine are the various **wh-** structures. These are so named because one of their constituents is a **wh-phrase**, that is, one that includes a **wh-word** (who, where, what, which, how, why). These may be broadly grouped into two classes of sentence-level structures. The **wh-subject-question** structure is identical to the declarative structure, except that the first noun phrase contains some wh-word.

> What airlines fly from Burbank to Denver?
> Which flights depart Burbank after noon and arrive in Denver by six p.m?
> Which flights serve breakfast?
> Which of these flights have the longest layover in Nashville?

Here is a rule. Exercise 9.10 discusses rules for the constituents that make up the *Wh-NP*.

$$S \rightarrow Wh\text{-}NP\ VP$$

WH-NON-SUBJECT-QUESTION
In the **wh-non-subject-question** structure, the wh-phrase is not the subject of the sentence, and so the sentence includes another subject. In these types of sentences the auxiliary appears before the subject *NP*, just as in the yes-no-question structures. Here is an example:

> What flights do you have from Burbank to Tacoma Washington?

Here is a sample rule:

$$S \rightarrow Wh\text{-}NP\ Aux\ NP\ VP$$

There are other sentence-level structures we won't try to model here, like **fronting**, in which a phrase is placed at the beginning of the sentence for various discourse purposes (for example often involving topicalization and focus):

> On Tuesday, I'd like to fly from Detroit to Saint Petersburg

9.4   THE NOUN PHRASE

HEAD
We can view the noun phrase as revolving around a **head**, the central noun in the noun phrase. The syntax of English allows for both prenominal (pre-head) modifiers and post-nominal (post-head) modifiers.

Before the Head Noun

We have already discussed some of the parts of the noun phrase; the determiner, and the use of the *Nominal* constituent for representing double noun phrases. We have seen that noun phrases can begin with a determiner, as follows:

    a stop
    the flights
    that fare
    this flight
    those flights
    any flights
    some flights

There are certain circumstances under which determiners are optional in English. For example, determiners may be omitted if the noun they modify is plural:

    Show me *flights* from San Francisco to Denver on weekdays

As we saw in Chapter 8, **mass nouns** don't require determination. Recall that mass nouns often (not always) involve something that is treated like a substance (including e.g., *water* and *snow*), don't take the indefinite article "*a*", and don't tend to pluralize. Many abstract nouns are mass nouns (*music*, *homework*). Mass nouns in the ATIS domain include *breakfast*, *lunch*, and *dinner*:

    Does this flight serve dinner?

Exercise 9.4 asks the reader to represent this fact in the CFG formalism.

Word classes that appear in the NP before the determiner are called **predeterminers**. Many of these have to do with number or amount; a common predeterminer is *all*:   PREDETERMINERS

    all the flights
    all flights

A number of different kinds of word classes can appear in the NP between the determiner and the head noun (the "postdeterminers"). These include **cardinal numbers**, **ordinal numbers**, and **quantifiers**. Examples of cardinal numbers:

> two friends
> one stop

CARDINAL NUMBERS
ORDINAL NUMBERS
QUANTIFIERS

Ordinal numbers include *first*, *second*, *third*, and so on, but also words like *next*, *last*, *past*, *other*, and *another*:

> the first one
> the next day
> the second leg
> the last flight
> the other American flight
> any other fares

Some quantifiers (*many*, *(a) few*, *several*) occur only with plural count nouns:

> many fares

The quantifiers *much* and *a little* occur only with noncount nouns. Adjectives occur after quantifiers but before nouns.

> a *first-class* fare
> a *nonstop* flight
> the *longest* layover
> the *earliest* lunch flight

ADJECTIVE PHRASE
AP

Adjectives can also be grouped into a phrase called an **adjective phrase** or **AP**. APs can have an adverb before the adjective (see Chapter 8 for definitions of adjectives and adverbs):

> the *least expensive* fare

We can combine all the options for prenominal modifiers with one rule as follows:

$$NP \rightarrow (Det)\ (Card)\ (Ord)\ (Quant)\ (AP)\ Nominal \tag{9.10}$$

This simplified noun phrase rule has a flatter structure and hence is simpler than most modern theories of grammar. We present this simplified rule because there is no universally agreed-upon internal constituency for the noun phrase.

Note the use of parentheses "( )" to mark **optional constituents**. A rule with one set of parentheses is really a shorthand for two rules, one with the parentheses, one without.

After the Noun

A head noun can be followed by **postmodifiers**. Three kinds of nominal postmodifiers are very common in English:

prepositional phrases	all flights *from Cleveland*
non-finite clauses	any flights *arriving after eleven a.m.*
relative clauses	a flight *that serves breakfast*

Prepositional phrase postmodifiers are particularly common in the ATIS corpus, since they are used to mark the origin and destination of flights. Here are some examples, with brackets inserted to show the boundaries of each PP; note that more than one PP can be strung together:

any stopovers *[for Delta seven fifty one]*
all flights *[from Cleveland] [to Newark]*
arrival *[in San Jose] [before seven p.m.]*
a reservation *[on flight six oh six] [from Tampa] [to Montreal]*

Here's a new *NP* rule to account for one to three *PP* postmodifiers:

Nominal → Nominal PP (PP) (PP)

The three most common kinds of **non-finite** postmodifiers are the gerundive (*-ing*), *-ed*, and infinitive forms.

NON-FINITE

Gerundive postmodifiers are so-called because they consist of a verb phrase that begins with the gerundive (*-ing*) form of the verb. In the following examples, the verb phrases happen to all have only prepositional phrases after the verb, but in general this verb phrase can have anything in it (anything, that is, which is semantically and syntactically compatible with the gerund verb).

GERUNDIVE

any of those *[leaving on Thursday]*
any flights *[arriving after eleven a.m.]*
flights *[arriving within thirty minutes of each other]*

We can define the NP as follows, making use of a new non-terminal *GerundVP*:

Nominal → *Nominal GerundVP*

We can make rules for *GerundVP* constituents by duplicating all of our VP productions, substituting *GerundV* for *V*.

$$
\begin{aligned}
GerundVP \;\rightarrow\;& GerundV\;NP \\
\mid\;& GerundV\;PP \\
\mid\;& GerundV \\
\mid\;& GerundV\;NP\;PP
\end{aligned}
$$

GerundV can then be defined as:

GerundV → *being* | preferring | *arriving* | *leaving* | ...

The phrases in italics below are examples of the two other common kinds of non-finite clauses, infinitives and *-ed* forms:

> the last flight *to arrive in Boston*
> I need to have dinner *served*
> Which is the aircraft *used by this flight*?

RELATIVE
PRONOUN
A postnominal relative clause (more correctly a **restrictive relative clause**), is a clause that often begins with a **relative pronoun** (*that* and *who* are the most common). The relative pronoun functions as the subject of the embedded verb in the following examples:

> a flight *that serves breakfast*
> flights *that leave in the morning*
> the United flight *that arrives in San Jose around ten p.m.*
> the one *that leaves at ten thirty five*

We might add rules like the following to deal with these:

$$Nominal \;\rightarrow\; Nominal\;RelClause \tag{9.11}$$

$$RelClause \;\rightarrow\; (who \mid that)\;VP \tag{9.12}$$

The relative pronoun may also function as the object of the embedded verb, as in the following example; we leave as an exercise for the reader writing grammar rules for more complex relative clauses of this kind.

the earliest American Airlines flight that I can get

Various postnominal modifiers can be combined, as the following examples show:

a flight *[from Phoenix to Detroit] [leaving Monday evening]*
I need a flight *[to Seattle] [leaving from Baltimore] [making a stop in Minneapolis]*
evening flights *[from Nashville to Houston] [that serve dinner]*
a friend *[living in Denver] [that would like to visit me here in Washington DC]*

9.5   COORDINATION

Noun phrases and other units can be **conjoined** with **conjunctions** like *and,* CONJUNCTIONS
or, and *but*. For example a **coordinate** noun phrase can consist of two other COORDINATE
noun phrases separated by a conjunction:

Please repeat $[_{NP} [_{NP}$ the flights$]$ *and* $[_{NP}$ the costs$]]$
I need to know $[_{NP} [_{NP}$ the aircraft$]$ *and* $[_{NP}$ flight number$]]$
I would like to fly from Denver stopping in $[_{NP} [_{NP}$ Pittsburgh$]$ *and* $[_{NP}$ Atlanta$]]$

Here's a new rule for this:

$$NP \rightarrow NP \ and \ NP \qquad\qquad\qquad\qquad (9.13)$$

In addition to NPs, most other kinds of phrases can be conjoined (e.g., including sentences, VPs, and PPs):

What flights do you have $[_{VP} [_{VP}$ leaving Denver$]$ *and* $[_{VP}$ arriving in San Francisco$]]$
$[_S [_S$ I'm interested in a flight from Dallas to Washington$]$ *and* $[_S$ I'm also interested in going to Baltimore$]]$

Similar conjunction rules can be built for *VP* and *S* conjunction:

$$VP \rightarrow VP \ and \ VP \qquad\qquad\qquad\qquad (9.14)$$

$$S \rightarrow S \ and \ S \qquad\qquad\qquad\qquad (9.15)$$

9.6 AGREEMENT

In Chapter 3 we discussed English inflectional morphology. Recall that most verbs in English can appear in two forms in the present tense: the form used for third-person, singular subjects (*the flight does*), and the form used for all other kinds of subjects (*all the flights do, I do*). The third-person-singular (*3sg* form usually has a final *-s* where the non-3sg form does not. Here are some examples, again using the verb *do*, with various subjects:

Do [NP any flights] stop in Chicago?
Do [NP all of these flights] offer first class service?
Do [NP I] get dinner on this flight?
Do [NP you] have a flight from Boston to Forth Worth?
Does [NP this flight] stop in Dallas?
Does [NP that flight] serve dinner?
Does [NP Delta] fly from Atlanta to San Francisco?

Here are more examples with the verb *leave*:

What flights *leave* in the morning?
What flight *leaves* from Pittsburgh?

This agreement phenomenon occurs whenever there is a verb that has some noun acting as its subject. Note that sentences in which the subject does not agree with the verb are ungrammatical:

*[What flight] *leave* in the morning?
*Does [NP you] have a flight from Boston to Forth Worth?
*Do [NP this flight] stop in Dallas?

How can we modify our grammar to handle these agreement phenomena? One way is to expand our grammar with multiple sets of rules, one rule set for *3sg* subjects, and one for non-*3sg* subjects. For example, the rule that handled these yes-no-questions used to look like this:

$S \rightarrow Aux\ NP\ VP$

We could replace this with two rules of the following form:

$S \rightarrow 3sgAux\ 3sgNP\ VP$
$S \rightarrow Non3sgAux\ Non3sgNP\ VP$

We could then add rules for the lexicon like these:

$$3sgAux \rightarrow does \mid has \mid can \mid \dots$$
$$Non3sgAux \rightarrow do \mid have \mid can \mid \dots$$

But we would also need to add rules for *3sgNP* and *Non3sgNP*, again by making two copies of each rule for *NP*. While pronouns can be first, second, or third person, full lexical noun phrases can only be third person, so for them we just need to distinguish between singular and plural:

$$3SgNP \rightarrow (Det) (Card) (Ord) (Quant) (AP) SgNominal$$
$$Non3SgNP \rightarrow (Det) (Card) (Ord) (Quant) (AP) PlNominal$$
$$SgNominal \rightarrow SgNoun \mid SgNoun SgNoun$$
$$PlNominal \rightarrow PlNoun \mid SgNoun PlNoun$$
$$SgNoun \rightarrow flight \mid fare \mid dollar \mid reservation \mid \dots$$
$$PlNoun \rightarrow flights \mid fares \mid dollars \mid reservations \mid \dots$$

Dealing with the first and second person pronouns is left as an exercise for the reader.

A problem with this method of dealing with number agreement is that it doubles the size of the grammar. Every rule that refers to a noun or a verb needs to have a "singular" version and a "plural" version. This rule proliferation will also have to happen for the noun's **case**; for example English pronouns have **nominative** (*I, she, he, they*) and **accusative** (*me, her, him, them*) versions. We will need new versions of every *NP* and *N* rule for each of these.

CASE

NOMINATIVE

ACCUSATIVE

A more significant problem occurs in languages like German or French, which not only have noun-verb agreement like English, but also have **gender agreement**; the gender of a noun must agree with the gender of its modifying adjective and determiner. This adds another multiplier to the rule sets of the language.

GENDER
AGREEMENT

Chapter 11 will introduce a way to deal with these agreement problems without exploding the size of the grammar, by effectively **parameterizing** each non-terminal of the grammar with **feature structures**.

9.7   THE VERB PHRASE AND SUBCATEGORIZATION

The verb phrase consists of the verb and a number of other constituents. In the simple rules we have built so far, these other constituents include *NP*s and *PP*s and combinations of the two:

$$VP \rightarrow Verb \quad \text{disappear}$$
$$VP \rightarrow Verb\,NP \quad \text{prefer a morning flight}$$
$$VP \rightarrow Verb\,NP\,PP \quad \text{leave Boston in the morning}$$
$$VP \rightarrow Verb\,PP \quad \text{leaving on Thursday}$$

Verb phrases can be significantly more complicated than this. Many other kinds of constituents can follow the verb, such as an entire embedded sentence. These are called **sentential complements**:

SENTENTIAL
COMPLEMENT

You [$_{VP}$ [$_V$ said [$_S$ there were two flights that were the cheapest]]]
You [$_{VP}$ [$_V$ said [$_S$ you had a two hundred sixty six dollar fare]]
[$_{VP}$ [$_V$ Tell] [$_{NP}$ me] [$_S$ how to get from the airport in Philadelphia to downtown]]
I [$_{VP}$ [$_V$ think [$_S$ I would like to take the nine thirty flight]]

Here's a rule for these:

$$VP \rightarrow Verb\,S$$

Another potential constituent of the VP is another VP. This is often the case for verbs like *want, would like, try, intend, need*:

I want [$_{VP}$ to fly from Milwaukee to Orlando]
Hi, I want [$_{VP}$ to arrange three flights]
Hello, I'm trying [$_{VP}$ to find a flight that goes from Pittsburgh to Denver after two p.m.]

Recall from Chapter 8 that verbs can also be followed by *particles*, words that resemble a preposition but that combine with the verb to form a *phrasal verb* like *take off*). These particles are generally considered to be an integral part of the verb in a way that other post-verbal elements are not; phrasal verbs are treated as individual verbs composed of two words.

While a verb phrase can have many possible kinds of constituents, not every verb is compatible with every verb phrase. For example, the verb *want* can either be used with an NP complement (*I want a flight* ...), or with an infinitive VP complement (*I want to fly to* ...). By contrast, a verb like *find* cannot take this sort of VP complement. (* *I found to fly to Dallas*).

This idea that verbs are compatible with different kinds of complements is a very old one; traditional grammar distinguishes between **transitive** verbs like *find*, which take a direct object NP (*I found a flight*), and **intransitive** verbs like *disappear*, which do not (**I disappeared a flight*).

TRANSITIVE

INTRANSITIVE

Where traditional grammars **subcategorize** verbs into these two categories (transitive and intransitive), modern grammars distinguish as many as 100 subcategories. (In fact, tagsets for many such subcategorization frames exist; see Macleod et al. (1998) for the COMLEX tagset, Sanfilippo (1993) for the ACQUILEX tagset, and further discussion in Chapter 11). We say that a verb like *find* **subcategorizes for** an *NP*, while a verb like *want* subcategorizes for either an *NP* or a non-finite *VP*. We also call these constituents the **complements** of the verb (hence our use of the term **sentential complement** above). So we say that *want* can take a *VP* complement. These possible sets of complements are called the **subcategorization frame** for the verb. Another way of talking about the relation between the verb and these other constituents is to think of the verb as a predicate and the constituents as arguments of the predicate. So we can think of such predicate-argument relations as FIND (I, A FLIGHT), or WANT (I, TO FLY). We will talk more about this view of verbs and arguments in Chapter 14 when we talk about predicate calculus representations of verb semantics.

SUBCATEGORIZE

SUBCATEGORIZES
FOR

COMPLEMENTS

SUBCATEGORIZATION
FRAME

Here are some subcategorization frames and example verbs:

Frame	Verb	Example
∅	eat, sleep	I want to eat
NP	prefer, find, leave,	Find [$_{NP}$ the flight from Pittsburgh to Boston]
NP NP	show, give	Show [$_{NP}$ me] [$_{NP}$ airlines with flights from Pittsburgh]
PP$_{from}$ PP$_{to}$	fly, travel	I would like to fly [$_{PP}$ from Boston] [$_{PP}$ to Philadelphia]
NP PP$_{with}$	help, load,	Can you help [$_{NP}$ me] [$_{PP}$ with a flight]
VPto	prefer, want, need	I would prefer [$_{VPto}$ to go by United airlines]
VPbrst	can, would, might	I can [$_{VPbrst}$ go from Boston]
S	mean	Does this mean [$_S$ AA has a hub in Boston]?

Note that a verb can subcategorize for a particular type of verb phrase, such as a verb phrase whose verb is an infinitive (*VPto*), or a verb phrase whose verb is a bare stem (uninflected: *VPbrst*). Note also that a single verb can take different subcategorization frames. The verb *find*, for example, can take an *NP NP* frame (*find me a flight*) as well as an *NP* frame.

How can we represent the relation between verbs and their complements in a context-free grammar? One thing we could do is to do what we did with agreement features: make separate subtypes of the class Verb (*Verb-with-NP-complement*, *Verb-with-Inf-VP-complement*, *Verb-with-S-complement*, *Verb-with-NP-plus-PP-complement*, and so on):

$$Verb\text{-}with\text{-}NP\text{-}complement \ \rightarrow \ find \mid leave \mid repeat \mid \ \dots$$
$$Verb\text{-}with\text{-}S\text{-}complement \ \rightarrow \ think \mid believe \mid say \mid \ \dots$$
$$Verb\text{-}with\text{-}Inf\text{-}VP\text{-}complement \ \rightarrow \ want \mid try \mid need \mid \ \dots$$

Then each of our *VP* rules could be modified to require the appropriate verb subtype:

$$VP \ \rightarrow \ Verb\text{-}with\text{-}no\text{-}complement \quad \text{disappear}$$
$$VP \ \rightarrow \ Verb\text{-}with\text{-}NP\text{-}comp \ NP \quad \text{prefer a morning flight}$$
$$VP \ \rightarrow \ Verb\text{-}with\text{-}S\text{-}comp \ S \ \text{said there were two flights}$$

The problem with this approach, as with the same solution to the agreement feature problem, is a vast explosion in the number of rules. The standard solution to both of these problems is the **feature structure**, which will be introduced in Chapter 11. Chapter 11 will also discuss the fact that nouns, adjectives, and prepositions can subcategorize for complements just as verbs can.

9.8   AUXILIARIES

AUXILIARIES

MODAL

PERFECT

PROGRESSIVE

PASSIVE

The subclass of verbs called **auxiliaries** or **helping verbs** have particular syntactic constraints which can be viewed as a kind of subcategorization. Auxiliaries include the **modal** verbs *can, could, may, might, must, will, would, shall*, and *should*, the **perfect** auxiliary *have*, the **progressive** auxiliary *be*, and the **passive** auxiliary *be*. Each of these verbs places a constraint on the form of the following verb, and each of these must also combine in a particular order.

Modal verbs subcategorize for a *VP* whose head verb is a bare stem; for example, *can go in the morning, will try to find a flight*. The perfect verb *have* subcategorizes for a *VP* whose head verb is the past participle form: *have booked 3 flights*. The progressive verb *be* subcategorizes for a *VP* whose head verb is the gerundive participle: *am going from Atlanta*. The passive verb *be* subcategorizes for a *VP* whose head verb is the past participle: *was delayed by inclement weather*.

A sentence can have multiple auxiliary verbs, but they must occur in a particular order:

modal < perfect < progressive < passive

Here are some examples of multiple auxiliaries:

modal perfect	could have been a contender
modal passive	will be married
perfect progressive	have been feasting
modal perfect passive	might have been prevented

Auxiliaries are often treated just like verbs such as *want*, *seem*, or *intend*, which subcategorize for particular kinds of *VP* complements. Thus *can* would be listed in the lexicon as a *verb-with-bare-stem-VP-complement*. One way of capturing the ordering constraints among auxiliaries, commonly used in the **systemic grammar** of Halliday (1985), is to introduce a spe- SYSTEMIC GRAMMAR cial constituent called the **verb group**, whose subconstituents include all the VERB GROUP auxiliaries as well as the main verb. Some of the ordering constraints can also be captured in a different way. Since modals, for example, do not have a progressive or participle form, they simply will never be allowed to follow progressive or passive *be* or perfect *have*. Exercise 9.8 asks the reader to write grammar rules for auxiliaries.

The passive construction has a number of properties that make it different than other auxiliaries. One important difference is a semantic one; while the subject of non-passive (**active**) sentence is often the semantic agent of ACTIVE the event described by the verb (*I prevented a catastrophe*) the subject of the passive is often the undergoer or patient of the event (*a catastrophe was prevented*). This will be discussed further in Chapter 15.

9.9   SPOKEN LANGUAGE SYNTAX

The grammar of written English and the grammar of conversational spoken English share many features, but also differ in a number of respects. This section gives a quick sketch of a number of the characteristics of the syntax of spoken English.

the . [exhale] . . . [inhale] . . [uh] does American airlines . offer any . one way flights . [uh] one way fares, for one hundred and sixty one dollars
[mm] i'd like to leave i guess between [um] . [smack] . five o'clock no, five o'clock and [uh], seven o'clock . P M
around, four, P M
all right, [throat_clear] . . i'd like to know the . give me the flight . times . in the morning . for September twentieth . nineteen ninety one
[uh] one way
[uh] seven fifteen, please
on United airlines . . give me, the . . time . . from New York . [smack] . to Boise-, to . I'm sorry . on United airlines . [uh] give me the flight, numbers, the flight times from . [uh] Boston . to Dallas

Figure 9.5   Some sample spoken utterances from users interacting with the ATIS system.

UTTERANCE

We usually use the term **utterance** rather than **sentence** for the units of spoken language. Figure 9.5 shows some sample spoken ATIS utterances that exhibit many aspects of spoken language grammar.

This is a standard style of transcription used in transcribing speech corpora for speech recognition. The comma "," marks a short pause, each period "." marks a long pause, and the square brackets "[uh]" mark non-verbal events (breaths, lipsmacks, *uh*s and *um*s).

There are a number of ways these utterances differ from written English sentences. One is in the lexical statistics; for example spoken English is much higher in pronouns than written English; the subject of a spoken sentence is almost invariably a pronoun. Another is in the presence of various kinds of disfluencies (hesitations, repairs, restarts, etc) to be discussed below. Spoken sentences often consist of short fragments or phrases (*one way* or *around four p.m.*, which are less common in written English.

PROSODY

PITCH CONTOUR

STRESS PATTERN

Finally, these sentences were spoken with a particular **prosody**. The prosody of an utterance includes its particular **pitch contour** (the rise and fall of the fundamental frequency of the soundwave), its **stress pattern** or rhythm (the series of stressed and unstressed syllables that make up a sentence) and other similar factors like the rate (speed) of speech.

Disfluencies

Perhaps the most salient syntactic feature that distinguishes spoken and written language is the class of phenomena known as **disfluencies**. Disfluencies include the use of *uh* and *um*, word repetitions, and false starts. The ATIS sentence in Figure 9.6 shows examples of a false start and the use of *uh*. The false start here occurs when the speaker starts by asking for *one-way flights*. and then stops and corrects herself, beginning again and asking about *one-way fares*.

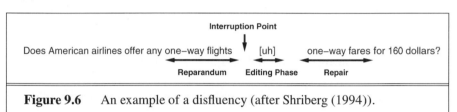

Figure 9.6   An example of a disfluency (after Shriberg (1994)).

The segment *one-way flights* is referred to as the **reparandum**, and the replacing sequence *one-way fares* is referred to as the **repair** (these terms are from Levelt (1983)). The **interruption point**, where the speaker breaks off the original word sequence, here occurs right after the word *flights*.

The words *uh* and *um* (sometimes called **filled pauses**) can be treated in the lexicon like regular words, and indeed this is often how they are modeled in speech recognition. The HMM pronunciation lexicons in speech recognizers often include pronunciation models of these words, and the *N*-gram grammars used by recognizers include the probabilities of these occurring with other words.

For speech understanding, where our goal is to build a meaning for the input sentence, it may be useful to detect these restarts in order to edit out what the speaker probably considered the "corrected" words. For example in the sentence above, if we could detect that there was a restart, we could just delete the reparandum, and parse the remaining parts of the sentence:

Does American airlines offer any one-way flights uh one-way fares
for 160 dollars?

How do disfluencies interact with the constituent structure of the sentence? Hindle (1983) showed that the repair often has the same structure as the constituent just before the interruption point. Thus in the example above, the repair is an NP, as is the reparandum. This means that if it is possible to automatically find the interruption point, it is also often possible to automatically detect the boundaries of the reparandum.

9.10   GRAMMAR EQUIVALENCE AND NORMAL FORM

A formal language is defined as a (possibly infinite) set of strings of words. This suggests that we could ask if two grammars are equivalent by asking if they generate the same set of strings. In fact it is possible to have two distinct context-free grammars generate the same language.

We usually distinguish two kinds of grammar equivalence: **weak equivalence** and **strong equivalence**. Two grammars are strongly equivalent if they generate the same set of strings *and* if they assign the same phrase structure to each sentence (allowing merely for renaming of the nonterminal symbols). Two grammars are weakly equivalent if they generate the same set of strings but do not assign the same phrase structure to each sentence.

NORMAL FORM

It is sometimes useful to have a **normal form** for grammars, in which each of the productions takes a particular form. For example a context-free grammar is in **Chomsky normal form** (CNF) (Chomsky, 1963) if it is ε-free and if in addition each production is either of the form $A \rightarrow B\ C$ or $A \rightarrow a$. That is, the righthand side of each rule either has two non-terminal symbols or one terminal symbol. Chomsky normal form grammars have binary trees (down to the prelexical nodes), which can be useful for certain algorithms.

CHOMSKY
NORMAL FORM

Any grammar can be converted into a weakly-equivalent Chomsky normal form grammar. For example a rule of the form

$$A \rightarrow B\ C\ D$$

can be converted into the following two CNF rules:

$$A \rightarrow B\ X$$
$$X \rightarrow C\ D$$

Exercise 9.11 asks the reader to formulate the complete algorithm.

9.11   FINITE-STATE AND CONTEXT-FREE GRAMMARS

We argued in Section 9.1 that a complex model of grammar would have to represent constituency. This is one reason that finite-state models of grammar are often inadequate. Now that we have explored some of the details of the syntax of noun phrases, we are prepared to discuss another problem with finite-state grammars. This problem is **recursion**. Recursion in a grammar

RECURSION

occurs when an expansion of a non-terminal includes the non-terminal itself, as we saw in rules like *Nominal → Nominal PP*.

To see why this is a problem for finite-state grammars, let's first attempt to build a finite-state model for some of the grammar rules we have seen so far. For example, we could model the noun phrase up to the head with a regular expression (= FSA) as follows:

(Det) (Card) (Ord) (Quant) (AP) Nominal

What about the postmodifiers? Let's just try adding the *PP*. We could then augment the regular expression as follows:

(Det) (Card) (Ord) (Quant) (AP) Nominal (PP)*

So to complete this regular expression we just need to expand inline the definition of *PP*, as follows:

(Det) (Card) (Ord) (Quant) (AP) Nominal (P NP)*

But wait; our definition of *NP* now presupposes an *NP*! We would need to expand the rule as follows:

(Det) (Card) (Ord) (Quant) (AP) Nominal (P (Det) (Card) (Ord) (Quant) (AP) Nominal (P NP))*

But of course the *NP* is back again! The problem is that *NP* is a **re-cursive rule**. There is actually a sneaky way to "unwind" this particular **right-recursive** rule in a finite-state automaton. In general, however, recursion cannot be handled in finite automata, and recursion is quite common in a complete model of the *NP* (for example for *RelClause* and *GerundVP*, which also have *NP* in their expansion):

RECURSIVE RULE

(Det) (Card) (Ord) (Quant) (AP) Nominal (RelClause|GerundVP|PP)*

In particular, Chomsky (1959a) proved that a context-free language L can be generated by a finite automaton if and only if there is a context-free grammar that generates L that does not have any **center-embedded** recursions (recursions of the form $A \rightarrow \alpha A \beta$).

While it thus seems at least likely that we can't model all of English syntax with a finite-state grammar, it is possible to build an FSA that approximates English (for example by expanding only a certain number of *NP*s). In fact there are algorithms for automatically generating finite-state grammars that approximate context-free grammars (Pereira and Wright, 1997).

Chapter 10 will discuss an augmented version of the finite-state automata called the **recursive transition network** or **RTN** that adds the complete power of recursion to the FSA. The resulting machine is exactly isomorphic to the context-free grammar, and can be a useful metaphor for studying CFGs in certain circumstances.

9.12 GRAMMARS AND HUMAN PROCESSING

Do people use context-free grammars in their mental processing of language? It has proved very difficult to find clear-cut evidence that they do. For example, some early experiments asked subjects to judge which words in a sentence were more closely connected (Levelt, 1970), finding that their intuitive groupings corresponded to syntactic constituents. Other experimenters examined the role of constituents in auditory comprehension by having subjects listen to sentences while also listening to short "clicks" at different times. Fodor and Bever (1965) found that subjects often mis-heard the clicks as if they occurred at constituent boundaries. They argued that the constituent was thus a "perceptual unit" which resisted interruption. Unfortunately there were severe methodological problems with the click paradigm (see e.g., Clark and Clark (1977) for a discussion).

A broader problem with all these early studies is that they do not control for the fact that constituents are often semantic units as well as syntactic units. Thus, as will be discussed further in Chapter 15, *a single odd block* is a constituent (an *NP*) but also a semantic unit (an object of type BLOCK which has certain properties). Thus experiments which show that people notice the boundaries of constituents could simply be measuring a semantic rather than a syntactic fact.

Thus it is necessary to find evidence for a constituent which is *not* a semantic unit. Furthermore, since there are many non-constituent-based theories of grammar based on lexical dependencies, it is important to find evidence that cannot be interpreted as a *lexical* fact; that is, evidence for constituency that is not based on particular words.

One suggestive series of experiments arguing for constituency has come from Kathryn Bock and her colleagues. Bock and Loebell (1990), for example, avoided all these earlier pitfalls by studying whether a subject who uses a particular syntactic constituent (e.g., a verb-phrase of a particular type, like *V NP PP*), is more likely to use the constituent in following sentences. In other words, they asked whether use of a constituent *primes* its use in subsequent sentences. As we saw in previous chapters, priming is a common way to test for the existence of a mental structure. Bock and Loebell relied on the English **ditransitive alternation**. A ditransitive verb is one like *give* which can take two arguments:

(9.16) The wealthy widow gave [$_{NP}$ the church] [$_{NP}$ her Mercedes].

The verb *give* allows another possible subcategorization frame, called a **prepositional dative** in which the indirect object is expressed as a prepositional phrase:

(9.17) The wealthy widow gave [$_{NP}$ her Mercedes] [$_{PP}$ to the church].

As we discussed on page 343, many verbs other than *give* have such **alternations** (*send*, *sell*, etc.; see Levin (1993) for a summary of many different alternation patterns). Bock and Loebell relied on these alternations by giving subjects a picture, and asking them to describe it in one sentence. The picture was designed to elicit verbs like *give* or *sell* by showing an event such as a boy handing an apple to a teacher. Since these verbs alternate, subjects might, for example, say *The boy gave the apple to the teacher* or *The boy gave the teacher an apple*.

ALTERNATIONS

Before describing the picture, subjects were asked to read an unrelated "priming" sentence out loud; the priming sentences either had *V NP NP* or *V NP PP* structure. Crucially, while these priming sentences had the same *constituent structure* as the dative alternation sentences, they did not have the same *semantics*. For example, the priming sentences might be prepositional *locatives*, rather than *datives*:

(9.18) IBM moved [$_{NP}$ a bigger computer] [$_{PP}$ to the Sears store].

Bock and Loebell found that subjects who had just read a *V NP PP* sentence were more likely to use a *V NP PP* structure in describing the picture. This suggested that the use of a particular constituent *primed* the later use of that constituent, and hence that the constituent must be mentally represented in order to prime and be primed.

In more recent work, Bock and her colleagues have continued to find evidence for this kind of constituency structure.

There is a quite different disagreement about the human use of context-free grammars. Many researchers have suggested that natural language is unlike a formal language, and in particular that the set of possible sentences in a language cannot be described by purely syntactic context-free grammar productions. They argue that a complete model of syntactic structure will prove to be impossible unless it includes knowledge from other domains (for example like semantic, intonational, pragmatic, and social/interactional domains). Others argue that the syntax of natural language can be represented by formal languages. This second position is called **modularist**: re-

MODULARIST

searchers holding this position argue that human syntactic knowledge is a distinct module of the human mind. The first position, in which grammatical knowledge may incorporate semantic, pragmatic, and other constraints, is called **anti-modularist**. We will return to this debate in Chapter 12.

ANTI-
MODULARIST

9.13   SUMMARY

This chapter has introduced a number of fundamental concepts in syntax via the **context-free grammar**.

- In many languages, groups of consecutive words act as a group or a **constituent**, which can be modeled by **context-free grammars** (also known as **phrase-structure grammars**).
- A context-free grammar consists of a set of **rules** or **productions**, expressed over a set of **non-terminal** symbols and a set of **terminal** symbols. Formally, a particular **context-free language** is the set of strings which can be **derived** from a particular **context-free grammar**.
- A **generative grammar** is a traditional name in linguistics for a formal language which is used to model the grammar of a natural language.
- There are many sentence-level grammatical constructions in English; **declarative**, **imperative**, **yes-no-question**, and **wh-question** are four very common types, which can be modeled with context-free rules.
- An English **noun phrase** can have **determiners**, **numbers**, **quantifiers**, and **adjective phrases** preceding the **head noun**, which can be followed by a number of **postmodifiers**; **gerundive** VPs, **infinitives** VPs, and **past participial** VPs are common possibilities.
- **Subjects** in English **agree** with the main verb in person and number.
- Verbs can be **subcategorized** by the types of **complements** they expect. Simple subcategories are **transitive** and **intransitive**; most grammars include many more categories than these.
- The correlate of **sentences** in spoken language are generally called **utterances**. Utterances may be **disfluent**, containing **filled pauses** like *um* and *uh*, **restarts**, and **repairs**.
- Any context-free grammar can be converted to **Chomsky normal form**, in which the right-hand-side of each rule has either two non-terminals or a single terminal.
- Context-free grammars are more powerful than finite-state automata, but it is nonetheless possible to **approximate** a context-free grammar with a FSA.

- There is some evidence that constituency plays a role in the human processing of language.

BIBLIOGRAPHICAL AND HISTORICAL NOTES

"den sprachlichen Ausdruck für die willkürliche Gliederung einer Ge-sammtvorstellung in ihre in logische Beziehung zueinander gesetzten Bestandteile"

"the linguistic expression for the arbitrary division of a total idea into its constituent parts placed in logical relations to one another"

> Wundt's (1900:240) definition of the sentence; the origin of the idea of phrasal constituency, cited in Percival (1976).

The recent historical research of Percival (1976) has made it clear that this idea of breaking up a sentence into a hierarchy of constituents appeared in the *Völkerpsychologie* of the groundbreaking psychologist Wilhelm Wundt (Wundt, 1900). By contrast, traditional European grammar, dating from the Classical period, defined relations between *words* rather than constituents. Wundt's idea of constituency was taken up into linguistics by Leonard Bloomfield in his early book *An Introduction to the Study of Language* (Bloomfield, 1914). By the time of his later book *Language* (Bloomfield, 1933), what was then called "immediate-constituent analysis" was a well-established method of syntactic study in the United States. By contrast, European syntacticians retained an emphasis on word-based or **dependency** grammars; Chapter 12 discusses some of these issues in introducing dependency grammar.

American Structuralism saw a number of specific definitions of the immediate constituent, couched in terms of their search for a "discovery procedure"; a methodological algorithm for describing the syntax of a language. In general, these attempt to capture the intuition that "The primary criterion of the immediate constituent is the degree in which combinations behave as simple units" (Bazell, 1952, p. 284). The most well-known of the specific definitions is Harris' idea of distributional similarity to individual units, with the *substitutability* test. Essentially, the method proceeded by breaking up a construction into constituents by attempting to substitute simple structures for possible constituents—if a substitution of a simple form, say *man*, was substitutable in a construction for a more complex set (like *intense young man*), then the form *intense young man* was probably a constituent. Harris's test was the beginning of the intuition that a constituent is a kind of equivalence class.

The first formalization of this idea of hierarchical constituency was the **phrase-structure grammar** defined in Chomsky (1956), and further expanded upon (and argued against) in Chomsky (1957) and Chomsky (1975). From this time on, most generative linguistic theories were based at least in part on context-free grammars (such as Head-Driven Phrase Structure Grammar (Pollard and Sag, 1994), Lexical-Functional Grammar (Bresnan, 1982), Government and Binding (Chomsky, 1981), and Construction Grammar (Kay and Fillmore, 1999), inter alia); many of these theories used schematic context-free templates known as **X-bar schemata**.

X-BAR
SCHEMATA

Shortly after Chomsky's initial work, the context-free grammar was rediscovered by Backus (1959) and independently by Naur et al. (1960) in their descriptions of the ALGOL programming language; Backus (1996) noted that he was influenced by the productions of Emil Post and that Naur's work was independent of his (Backus') own. (Recall the discussion on page 15 of multiple invention in science.) After this early work, a great number of computational models of natural language processing were based on context-free grammars because of the early development of efficient algorithms to parse these grammars (see Chapter 10).

As we have already noted, grammars based on context-free rules are not ubiquitous. One extended formalism is Tree Adjoining Grammar (TAG) (Joshi, 1985). The primary data structure in Tree Adjoining Grammar is the tree, rather than the rule. Trees come in two kinds; **initial trees** and **auxiliary trees**. Initial trees might, for example, represent simple sentential structures, while auxiliary trees are used to add recursion into a tree. Trees are combined by two operations called **substitution** and **adjunction**. See Joshi (1985) for more details. An extension of Tree Adjoining Grammar called Lexicalized Tree Adjoining Grammars will be discussed in Chapter 12.

Another class of grammatical theories that are not based on context-free grammars are instead based on the relation between words rather than constituents. Various such theories have come to be known as **dependency grammars**; representative examples include the dependency grammar of Mel'čuk (1979), the Word Grammar of Hudson (1984), and the Constraint Grammar of Karlsson et al. (1995). Dependency-based grammars have returned to popularity in modern statistical parsers, as the field has come to understand the crucial role of word-to-word relations; see Chapter 12 for further discussion.

Readers interested in general references grammars of English should waste no time in getting hold of Quirk et al. (1985). Another useful reference is McCawley (1998).

There are many good introductory textbooks on syntax. Sag and Wasow (1999) is an introduction to **formal syntax**, focusing on the use of   FORMAL SYNTAX
phrase-structure, unification, and the type-hierarchy in Head-Driven Phrase Structure Grammar. van Valin (1999) is an introduction from a less formal, more functional perspective, focusing on cross-linguistic data and on the functional motivation for syntactic structures.

EXERCISES

9.1 Draw tree structures for the following ATIS phrases:

   a. Dallas

   b. from Denver

   c. after five p.m.

   d. arriving in Washington

   e. early flights

   f. all redeye flights

   g. on Thursday

   h. a one-way fare

   i. any delays in Denver

9.2 Draw tree structures for the following ATIS sentences:

   a. Does American airlines have a flight between five a.m. and six a.m.

   b. I would like to fly on American airlines.

   c. Please repeat that.

   d. Does American 487 have a first class section?

   e. I need to fly between Philadelphia and Atlanta.

   f. What is the fare from Atlanta to Denver?

   g. Is there an American airlines flight from Philadelphia to Dallas?

9.3   Augment the grammar rules on page 341 to handle pronouns. Deal properly with person and case.

9.4   Modify the noun phrase grammar of Sections 9.4–9.6 to correctly model mass nouns and their agreement properties

9.5   How many types of *NP*s would rule (9.10) on page 336 expand to if we didn't allow parentheses in our grammar formalism?

9.6   Assume a grammar that has many *VP*s rules for different subcategorization, as expressed in Section 9.7, and differently subcategorized verb rules like *Verb-with-NP-complement*. How would the rule for post-nominal relative clauses (9.12) need to be modified if we wanted to deal properly with examples like *the earliest flight that you have*? Recall that in such examples the pronoun *that* is the object of the verb *get*. Your rules should allow this noun phrase but should correctly rule out the ungrammatical S *I get*.

9.7   Does your solution to the previous problem correctly model the NP *the earliest flight that I can get*? How about *the earliest flight that I think my mother wants me to book for her*? Hint: this phenomenon is called **long-distance dependency**.

9.8   Write rules expressing the verbal subcategory of English auxiliaries; for example you might have a rule *verb-with-bare-stem-VP-complement* → *can*.

POSSESSIVE   **9.9**   *NP*s like *Fortune's office* or *my uncle's marks* are called **possessive** or
GENITIVE   **genitive** noun phrases. A possessive noun phrase can be modeled by treated the sub-NP like *Fortune's* or *my uncle's* as a determiner of the following head noun. Write grammar rules for English possessives. You may treat *'s* as if it were a separate word (i.e., as if there were always a space before *'s*).

9.10   Page 334 discussed the need for a *Wh-NP* constituent. The simplest *Wh-NP* is one of the *Wh-pronouns* (*who, whom, whose, which*). The Wh-words *what* and *which* can be determiners: *which four will you have?*, *what credit do you have with the Duke?* Write rules for the different types of *Wh-NP*s.

9.11   Write an algorithm for converting an arbitrary context-free grammar into Chomsky normal form.

10 PARSING WITH CONTEXT-FREE GRAMMARS

There are and can exist but two ways of investigating and discovering truth. The one hurries on rapidly from the senses and particulars to the most general axioms, and from them... derives and discovers the intermediate axioms. The other constructs its axioms from the senses and particulars, by ascending continually and gradually, till it finally arrives at the most general axioms.

Francis Bacon, *Novum Organum* Book I.19 (1620)

By the seventeenth century, the western philosophical tradition had begun to distinguish two important insights about human use and acquisition of knowledge. The **empiricist** tradition, championed especially in Britain, EMPIRICIST by Bacon and Locke, focused on the way that knowledge is induced and reasoning proceeds based on data and experience from the external world. The **rationalist** tradition, championed especially on the Continent by Descartes RATIONALIST but following a tradition dating back to Plato's Meno, focused on the way that learning and reasoning is guided by prior knowledge and innate ideas.

This dialectic continues today, and has played a important role in characterizing algorithms for **parsing**. We defined parsing in Chapter 3 as a combination of recognizing an input string and assigning some structure to it. Syntactic parsing, then, is the task of recognizing a sentence and assigning a syntactic structure to it. This chapter focuses on the kind of structures assigned by the context-free grammars of Chapter 9. Since context-free grammars are a declarative formalism, they don't specify how the parse tree for a given sentence should be computed. This chapter will, therefore, present some of the many possible algorithms for automatically assigning a context-free (phrase structure) tree to an input sentence.

Parse trees are directly useful in applications such as **grammar checking** in word-processing systems; a sentence which cannot be parsed may have grammatical errors (or at least be hard to read). In addition, parsing is an important intermediate stage of representation for **semantic analysis** (as we will see in Chapter 15), and thus plays an important role in applications like **machine translation**, **question answering**, and **information extraction**. For example, in order to answer the question

What books were written by British women authors before 1800?

we'll want to know that the subject of the sentence was *what books* and that the *by-adjunct* was *British women authors* to help us figure out that the user wants a list of books (and not just a list of authors). Syntactic parsers are also used in lexicography applications for building on-line versions of dictionaries. Finally, stochastic versions of parsing algorithms have recently begun to be incorporated into **speech recognizers**, both for **language models** (Ney, 1991) and for non-finite-state acoustic and phonotactic modeling (Lari and Young, 1991).

The main parsing algorithm presented in this chapter is the **Earley** algorithm (Earley, 1970), one of the context-free parsing algorithms based on **dynamic programming**. We have already seen a number of dynamic programming algorithms—Minimum-Edit-Distance, Viterbi, Forward. The Earley algorithm is one of three commonly-used dynamic programming parsers; the others are the Cocke-Younger-Kasami (CYK) algorithm which we will present in Chapter 12, and the Graham-Harrison-Ruzzo (GHR) (Graham et al., 1980) algorithm. Before presenting the Earley algorithm, we begin by motivating various basic parsing ideas which make up the algorithm. First, we revisit the "search metaphor" for parsing and recognition, which we introduced for finite-state automata in Chapter 2, and talk about the **top-down** and **bottom-up** search strategies. We then introduce a "baseline" top-down backtracking parsing algorithm, to introduce the idea of simple but efficient parsing. While this parser is perspicuous and relatively efficient, it is unable to deal efficiently with the important problem of **ambiguity**: a sentence or words which can have more than one parse. The final section of the chapter then shows how the Earley algorithm can use insights from the top-down parser with bottom-up filtering to efficiently handle ambiguous inputs.

10.1   PARSING AS SEARCH

Chapters 2 and 3 showed that finding the right path through a finite-state automaton, or finding the right transduction for an input, can be viewed as

a search problem. For FSAs, for example, the parser is searching through
the space of all possible paths through the automaton. In syntactic parsing,
the parser can be viewed as searching through the space of all possible parse
trees to find the correct parse tree for the sentence. Just as the search space of
possible paths was defined by the structure of the FSA, so the search space
of possible parse trees is defined by the grammar. For example, consider the
following ATIS sentence:

(10.1) Book that flight.

Using the miniature grammar and lexicon in Figure 10.2, which consists of some of the CFG rules for English introduced in Chapter 9, the
correct parse tree that would be assigned to this example is shown in Figure 10.1.

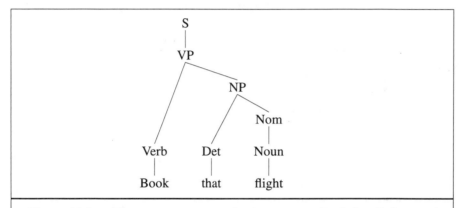

Figure 10.1   The correct parse tree for the sentence *Book that flight* according to the grammar in Figure 10.2.

How can we use the grammar in Figure 10.2 to assign the parse tree
in Figure 10.1 to Example (10.1)? (In this case there is only one parse tree,
but it is possible for there to be more than one.) The goal of a parsing search
is to find all trees whose root is the start symbol *S*, which cover exactly the
words in the input. Regardless of the search algorithm we choose, there
are clearly two kinds of constraints that should help guide the search. One
kind of constraint comes from the data, that is, the input sentence itself.
Whatever else is true of the final parse tree, we know that there must be
three leaves, and they must be the words *book*, *that*, and *flight*. The second
kind of constraint comes from the grammar. We know that whatever else is
true of the final parse tree, it must have one root, which must be the start
symbol *S*.

$S \rightarrow NP\ VP$	$Det \rightarrow that \mid this \mid a$
$S \rightarrow Aux\ NP\ VP$	$Noun \rightarrow book \mid flight \mid meal \mid money$
$S \rightarrow VP$	$Verb \rightarrow book \mid include \mid prefer$
$NP \rightarrow Det\ Nominal$	$Aux \rightarrow does$
$Nominal \rightarrow Noun$	
$Nominal \rightarrow Noun\ Nominal$	$Prep \rightarrow from \mid to \mid on$
$NP \rightarrow Proper\text{-}Noun$	$Proper\text{-}Noun \rightarrow Houston \mid TWA$
$VP \rightarrow Verb$	
$VP \rightarrow Verb\ NP$	$Nominal \rightarrow Nominal\ PP$

Figure 10.2   A miniature English grammar and lexicon.

These two constraints, recalling the empiricist/rationalist debate described at the beginning of this chapter, give rise to the two search strategies underlying most parsers: **top-down** or **goal-directed search** and **bottom-up** or **data-directed search**.

Top-Down Parsing

TOP-DOWN

A **top-down** parser searches for a parse tree by trying to build from the root node S down to the leaves. Let's consider the search space that a top-down parser explores, assuming for the moment that it builds all possible trees in parallel. The algorithm starts by assuming the input can be derived by the designated start symbol S. The next step is to find the tops of all trees which can start with S, by looking for all the grammar rules with S on the left-hand side. In the grammar in Figure 10.2, there are three rules that expand S, so the second **ply**, or level, of the search space in Figure 10.3 has three partial trees.

PLY

We next expand the constituents in these three new trees, just as we originally expanded S. The first tree tells us to expect an NP followed by a VP, the second expects an Aux followed by an NP and a VP, and the third a VP by itself. To fit the search space on the page, we have shown in the third ply of Figure 10.3 only the trees resulting from the expansion of the left-most leaves of each tree. At each ply of the search space we use the right-hand-sides of the rules to provide new sets of expectations for the parser, which are then used to recursively generate the rest of the trees. Trees are grown downward until they eventually reach the part-of-speech categories at the bottom of the tree. At this point, trees whose leaves fail to match all the words in the input can be rejected, leaving behind those trees that represent

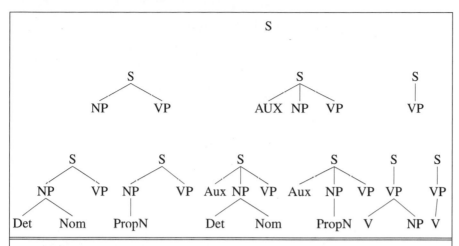

Figure 10.3   An expanding top-down search space. Each ply is created by taking each tree from the previous ply, replacing the leftmost non-terminal with each of its possible expansions, and collecting each of these trees into a new ply.

successful parses.

In Figure 10.3, only the fifth parse tree (the one which has expanded the rule *VP → Verb NP*) will eventually match the input sentence *Book that flight*. The reader should check this for themselves in Figure 10.1.

Bottom-Up Parsing

Bottom-up parsing is the earliest known parsing algorithm (it was first suggested by Yngve (1955)), and is used in the shift-reduce parsers common for computer languages (Aho and Ullman, 1972). In bottom-up parsing, the parser starts with the words of the input, and tries to build trees from the words up, again by applying rules from the grammar one at a time. The parse is successful if the parser succeeds in building a tree rooted in the start symbol *S* that covers all of the input. Figure 10.4 show the bottom-up search space, beginning with the sentence *Book that flight*. The parser begins by looking up each word (*book*, *that*, and *flight*) in the lexicon and building three partial trees with the part-of-speech for each word. But the word *book* is ambiguous; it can be a noun or a verb. Thus the parser must consider two possible sets of trees. The first two plies in Figure 10.4 show this initial bifurcation of the search space.

BOTTOM-UP

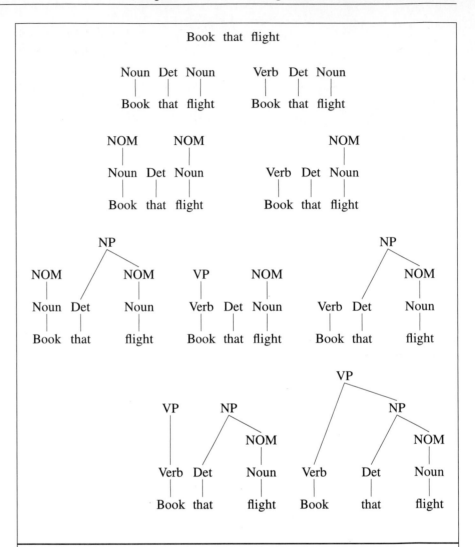

Figure 10.4   An expanding bottom-up search space for the sentence *Book that flight*. This figure does not show the final tier of the search with the correct parse tree (see Figure 10.1). Make sure you understand how that final parse tree follows from the search space in this figure.

Each of the trees in the second ply is then expanded. In the parse on the left (the one in which *book* is incorrectly considered a noun), the *Nominal → Noun* rule is applied to both of the *Noun*s (*book* and *flight*). This same rule is also applied to the sole *Noun* (*flight*) on the right, producing the trees on the third ply.

In general, the parser extends one ply to the next by looking for places in the parse-in-progress where the right-hand-side of some rule might fit. This contrasts with the earlier top-down parser, which expanded trees by applying rules when their left-hand side matched an unexpanded non-terminal. Thus in the fourth ply, in the first and third parse, the sequence *Det Nominal* is recognized as the right-hand side of the *NP → Det Nominal* rule.

In the fifth ply, the interpretation of *book* as a noun has been pruned from the search space. This is because this parse cannot be continued: there is no rule in the grammar with the right-hand side *Nominal NP*.

The final ply of the search space (not shown in Figure 10.4) is the correct parse tree (see Figure 10.1). Make sure you understand which of the two parses on the penultimate ply gave rise to this parse.

Comparing Top-Down and Bottom-Up Parsing

Each of these two architectures has its own advantages and disadvantages. The top-down strategy never wastes time exploring trees that cannot result in an *S*, since it begins by generating just those trees. This means it also never explores subtrees that cannot find a place in some *S*-rooted tree. In the bottom-up strategy, by contrast, trees that have no hope of leading to an *S*, or fitting in with any of their neighbors, are generated with wild abandon. For example the left branch of the search space in Figure 10.4 is completely wasted effort; it is based on interpreting *book* as a *Noun* at the beginning of the sentence despite the fact no such tree can lead to an *S* given this grammar.

The top-down approach has its own inefficiencies. While it does not waste time with trees that do not lead to an *S*, it does spend considerable effort on *S* trees that are not consistent with the input. Note that the first four of the six trees in the third ply in Figure 10.3 all have left branches that cannot match the word *book*. None of these trees could possibly be used in parsing this sentence. This weakness in top-down parsers arises from the fact that they can generate trees before ever examining the input. Bottom-up parsers, on the other hand, never suggest trees that are not at least locally grounded in the actual input.

Neither of these approaches adequately exploits the constraints presented by the grammar and the input words. In the next section, we present a baseline parsing algorithm that incorporates features of both the top-down and bottom-up approaches. This parser is not as efficient as the Earley or CYK parsers we will introduce later, but it is useful for showing the basic operations of parsing.

10.2   A Basic Top-Down Parser

There are any number of ways of combining the best features of top-down and bottom-up parsing into a single algorithm. One fairly straightforward approach is to adopt one technique as the primary control strategy used to generate trees and then use constraints from the other technique to filter out inappropriate parses on the fly. The parser we develop in this section uses a top-down control strategy augmented with a bottom-up filtering mechanism. Our first step will be to develop a concrete implementation of the top-down strategy described in the last section. The ability to filter bad parses based on bottom-up constraints from the input will then be grafted onto this top-down parser.

PARALLEL   In our discussions of both top-down and bottom-up parsing, we assumed that we would explore all possible parse trees in **parallel**. Thus each ply of the search in Figure 10.3 and Figure 10.4 showed all possible expansions of the parse trees on the previous plies. Although it is certainly possible to implement this method directly, it typically entails the use of an unrealistic amount of memory to store the space of trees as they are being constructed. This is especially true since realistic grammars have much more ambiguity than the miniature grammar in Figure 10.2.

DEPTH-FIRST   A more reasonable approach is to use a **depth-first strategy** such as the one used to implement the various finite-state machines in Chapter 2 and Chapter 3. The depth-first approach expands the search space incrementally by systematically exploring one state at a time. The state chosen for expansion is the most recently generated one. When this strategy arrives at a tree that is inconsistent with the input, the search continues by returning to the most recently generated, as yet unexplored, tree. The net effect of this strategy is a parser that single-mindedly pursues trees until they either succeed or fail before returning to work on trees generated earlier in the process. Figure 10.5 illustrates such a top-down, depth-first derivation using Grammar 10.2.

Note that this derivation is not fully determined by the specification of a top-down, depth-first strategy. There are two kinds of choices that have been left unspecified that can lead to different derivations: the choice of which leaf node of a tree to expand and the order in which applicable grammar rules are applied. In this derivation, the left-most unexpanded leaf node of the current tree is being expanded first, and the applicable rules of the grammar are being applied according to their textual order in the grammar. The decision to expand the left-most unexpanded node in the tree is important

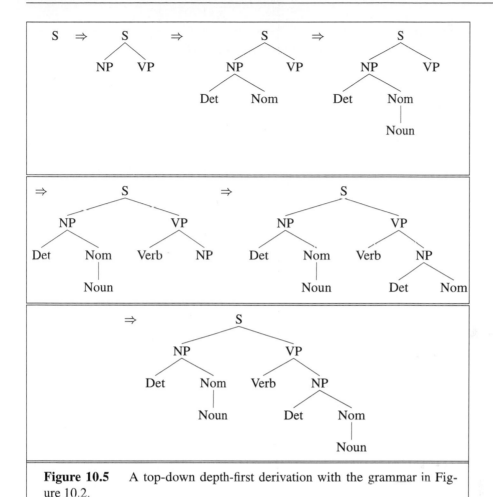

Figure 10.5   A top-down depth-first derivation with the grammar in Figure 10.2.

since it determines the order in which the input words will be consulted as the tree is constructed. Specifically, it results in a relatively natural forward incorporation of the input words into a tree. The second choice of applying rules in their textual order has consequences that will be discussed later.

Figure 10.6 presents a parsing algorithm that instantiates this top-down, depth-first, left-to-right strategy. This algorithm maintains an **agenda** of   AGENDA search-states. Each search-state consists of partial trees together with a pointer to the next input word in the sentence.

The main loop of the parser takes a state from the front of the agenda and produces a new set of states by applying all the applicable grammar rules to the left-most unexpanded node of the tree associated with that state. This

---

function TOP-DOWN-PARSE(*input, grammar*) **returns** a parse tree

  agenda ← *(Initial S tree, Beginning of input)*
  current-search-state ← POP(*agenda*)
  loop
   if SUCCESSFUL-PARSE?(*current-search-state*) **then**
    return TREE(*current-search-state*)
   else
    if CAT(NODE-TO-EXPAND(*current-search-state*)) is a POS **then**
     if CAT(*node-to-expand*)
       ⊂
       POS(CURRENT-INPUT(*current-search-state*)) **then**
      PUSH(APPLY-LEXICAL-RULE(*current-search-state*), *agenda*)
     else
      return reject
    else
     PUSH(APPLY-RULES(*current-search-state, grammar*), *agenda*)
   if *agenda* is empty **then**
    return reject
   else
    current-search-state ← NEXT(*agenda*)
  end

Figure 10.6   A top-down, depth-first left-to-right parser.

---

set of new states is then added to the front of the agenda in accordance with the textual order of the grammar rules that were used to generate them. This process continues until either a successful parse tree is found or the agenda is exhausted indicating that the input cannot be parsed.

Figure 10.7 shows the sequence of states examined by this algorithm in the course of parsing the following sentence.

(10.2) Does this flight include a meal?

In this figure, the node currently being expanded is shown in a box, while the current input word is bracketed. Words to the left of the bracketed word have already been incorporated into the tree.

The parser begins with a fruitless exploration of the *S → NP VP* rule, which ultimately fails because the word *Does* cannot be derived from any of the parts-of-speech that can begin an *NP*. The parser thus eliminates the *S → NP VP* rule. The next search-state on the agenda corresponds to the

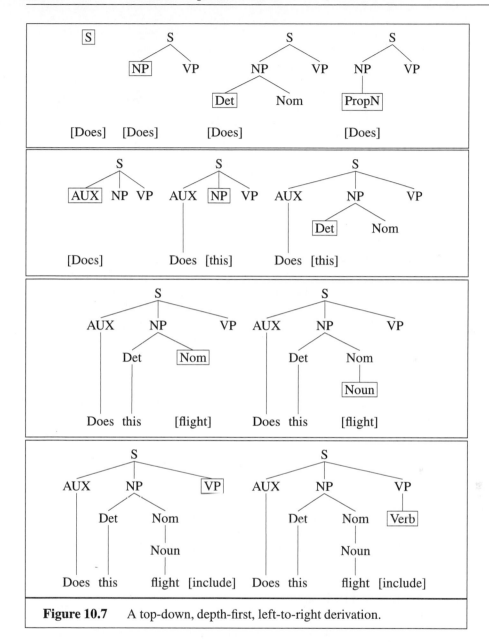

Figure 10.7   A top-down, depth-first, left-to-right derivation.

$S \rightarrow Aux\ NP\ VP$ rule. Once this state is found, the search continues in a straightforward depth-first, left-to-right fashion through the rest of the derivation.

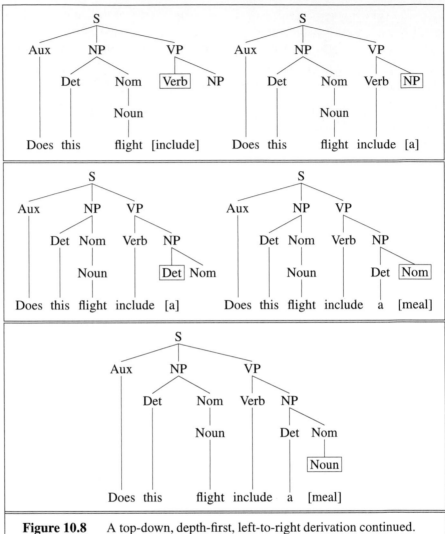

Figure 10.8   A top-down, depth-first, left-to-right derivation continued.

Adding Bottom-Up Filtering

Figure 10.7 shows an important qualitative aspect of the top-down parser. Beginning at the root of the parse tree, the parser expands non-terminal symbols along the left edge of the tree, down to the word at the bottom left edge of the tree. As soon as a word is incorporated into a tree, the input pointer moves on, and the parser will expand the new next left-most open non-terminal symbol down to the new left-corner word.

Thus in any successful parse the current input word must serve as the first word in the derivation of the unexpanded node that the parser is currently processing. This leads to an important consequence which will be useful in adding bottom-up filtering. The parser should not consider any grammar rule if the current input cannot serve as the *first word along the left edge of some derivation* from this rule. We call the first word along the left edge of a derivation the **left-corner** of the tree.   LEFT-CORNER

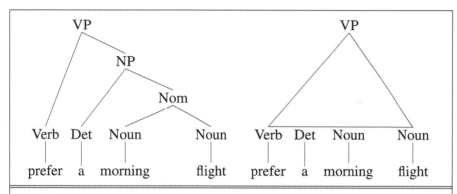

Figure 10.9   An illustration of the left-corner notion. The node *Verb* and the node *prefer* are both left-corners of *VP*.

Consider the parse tree for a *VP* shown in Figure 10.9. If we visualize the parse tree for this *VP* as a triangle with the words along the bottom, the word *prefer* lies at the lower left-corner of the tree. Formally, we can say that for non-terminals A and B, B is a left-corner of A if the following relation holds:

$$A \overset{*}{\Rightarrow} B\alpha$$

In other words, B can be a left-corner of A if there is a derivation of A that begins with a B.

We return to our example sentence *Does this flight include a meal?* The grammar in Figure 10.2 provides us with three rules that can be used to expand the category S:

$$S \rightarrow NP\ VP$$
$$S \rightarrow Aux\ NP\ VP$$
$$S \rightarrow VP$$

Using the left-corner notion, it is easy to see that only the $S \rightarrow Aux\ NP\ VP$ rule is a viable candidate since the word *Does* can not serve as the left-corner of either the *NP* or the *VP* required by the other two *S* rules. Knowing this, the parser should concentrate on the *Aux NP VP* rule, without first constructing and backtracking out of the others, as it did with the non-filtering example shown in Figure 10.7.

The information needed to efficiently implement such a filter can be compiled in the form of a table that lists all the valid left-corner categories for each non-terminal in the grammar. When a rule is considered, the table entry for the category that starts the right hand side of the rule is consulted. If it fails to contain any of the parts-of-speech associated with the current input then the rule is eliminated from consideration. The following table shows the left-corner table for Grammar 10.2.

Category	Left Corners
S	Det, Proper-Noun, Aux, Verb
NP	Det, Proper-Noun
Nominal	Noun
VP	Verb

Using this left-corner table as a filter in the parsing algorithm of Figure 10.6 is left as Exercise 10.1 for the reader.

10.3   PROBLEMS WITH THE BASIC TOP-DOWN PARSER

Even augmented with bottom-up filtering, the top-down parser in Figure 10.7 has three problems that make it an insufficient solution to the general-purpose parsing problem. These three problems are **left-recursion**, **ambiguity**, and **inefficient reparsing of subtrees**. After exploring the nature of these three problems, we will introduce the Earley algorithm, which is able to avoid all of them.

Left-Recursion

Depth-first search has a well-known flaw when exploring an infinite search space: It may dive down an infinitely deeper path and never return to visit the unexpanded states. This problem manifests itself in top-down, depth-first, left-to-right parsers when **left-recursive grammars** are used. Formally, a grammar is left-recursive if it contains at least one non-terminal A, such that $A \stackrel{*}{\Rightarrow} \alpha A \beta$, for some α and β and $\alpha \stackrel{*}{\Rightarrow} \varepsilon$. In other words, a grammar is left-recursive if it contains a non-terminal category that has a derivation

LEFT-RECURSIVE
GRAMMARS

that includes itself anywhere along its leftmost branch. The grammar of
Chapter 9 had just such a left-recursive example, in the rules for possessive
*NP*s like *Atlanta's airport*:

$$NP \rightarrow Det\ Nominal$$
$$Det \rightarrow NP\ '\ s$$

These rules introduce left-recursion into the grammar since there is a derivation for the first element of the *NP*, the *Det*, that has an *NP* as its first constituent.

A more obvious and common case of left-recursion in natural language
grammars involves immediately **left-recursive rules**. These are rules of the
form $A \rightarrow A\ \beta$, where the first constituent of the right hand side is identical to the left hand side. The following are some of the immediately left-
recursive rules that make frequent appearances in grammars of English.

LEFT-RECURSIVE
RULES

$$NP \rightarrow NP\ PP$$
$$VP \rightarrow VP\ PP$$
$$S \rightarrow S\ and\ S$$

A left-recursive non-terminal can lead a top-down, depth-first left-to-
right parser to recursively expand the same non-terminal over again in exactly the same way, leading to an infinite expansion of trees.

Figure 10.10 shows the kind of expansion that accompanies the addition of the $NP \rightarrow NP\ PP$ rule as the first *NP* rule in our small grammar.

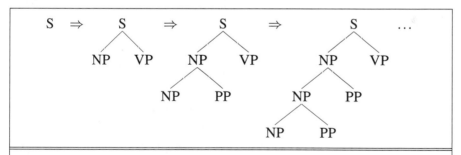

Figure 10.10   The beginning of an infinite search caused by a left-recursive
rule.

There are two reasonable methods for dealing with left-recursion in a
backtracking top-down parser: rewriting the grammar, and explicitly managing the depth of the search during parsing. Recall from Chapter 9, that
it is often possible to rewrite the rules of a grammar into a **weakly equiva-**

lent new grammar that still accepts exactly the same language as the original grammar. It is possible to eliminate left-recursion from certain common classes of grammars by rewriting a left-recursive grammar into a weakly equivalent non-left-recursive one. The intuition is to rewrite each rule of the form $A \rightarrow A\beta$ according to the following schema, using a new symbol A':

$$A \rightarrow A\beta \mid \alpha \qquad \Rightarrow \qquad \begin{array}{l} A \rightarrow \alpha A' \\ A' \rightarrow \beta A' \mid \varepsilon \end{array}$$

This transformation changes the left-recursion to a right-recursion, and changes the trees that result from these rules from left-branching structures to a right-branching ones. Unfortunately, rewriting grammars in this way has a major disadvantage: A rewritten phrase-structure rule may no longer be the most grammatically natural way to represent a particular syntactic structure. Furthermore, as we will see in Chapter 15, this rewriting may make semantic interpretation quite difficult.

Ambiguity

> *One morning I shot an elephant in my pajamas. How he got into*
> *my pajamas I don't know.*
>
> Groucho Marx, *Animal Crackers*, 1930

The second problem with the top-down parser of Figure 10.6 is that it is not efficient at handling **ambiguity**. Chapter 8 introduced the idea of **lexical category ambiguity** (words which may have more than one part-of-speech) and **disambiguation** (choosing the correct part-of-speech for a word).

AMBIGUITY

In this section we introduce a new kind of ambiguity, which arises in the syntactic structures used in parsing, called **structural ambiguity**. Structural ambiguity occurs when the grammar assigns more than one possible parse to a sentence. Groucho Marx's well-known line as Captain Spaulding is ambiguous because the phrase *in my pajamas* can be part of the *NP* headed by *elephant* or the verb-phrase headed by *shot*.

Structural ambiguity, appropriately enough, comes in many forms. Three particularly common kinds of ambiguity are **attachment ambiguity**, **coordination ambiguity**, and **noun-phrase bracketing ambiguity**.

A sentence has an attachment ambiguity if a particular constituent can be attached to the parse tree at more than one place. The Groucho Marx sentence above is an example of PP-attachment ambiguity. Various kinds of adverbial phrases are also subject to this kind of ambiguity. For example in the following example the gerundive-VP *flying to Paris* can be part of a

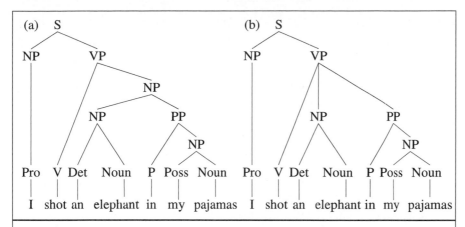

Figure 10.11   Two parse trees for an ambiguous sentence. Parse (a) corresponds to the humorous reading in which the elephant is in the pajamas, parse (b) to the reading in which Captain Spaulding did the shooting in his pajamas.

gerundive sentence whose subject is *the Eiffel Tower* or it can be an adjunct modifying the VP headed by *saw*:

(10.3) We saw the Eiffel Tower flying to Paris.

In a similar kind of ambiguity, the sentence "Can you book TWA flights" is ambiguous between a reading meaning "Can you book flights on behalf of TWA", and the other meaning "Can you book flights run by TWA". Here either one NP is attached to another to form a complex NP (*TWA flights*), or both NPs are distinct daughters of the verb phrase. Figure 10.12 shows both parses.

Another common kind of ambiguity is **coordination ambiguity**, in which there are different sets of phrases that can be conjoined by a conjunction like *and*. For example, the phrase *old men and women* can be bracketed *[old [men and women]]*, referring to *old men* and *old women*, or as *[old men] and [women]*, in which case it is only the men who are old.

These ambiguities all combine in complex ways. A program that summarized the news, for example, would need to be able to parse sentences like the following from the Brown corpus:

(10.4) President Kennedy today pushed aside other White House business to devote all his time and attention to working on the Berlin crisis address he will deliver tomorrow night to the American people over nationwide television and radio.

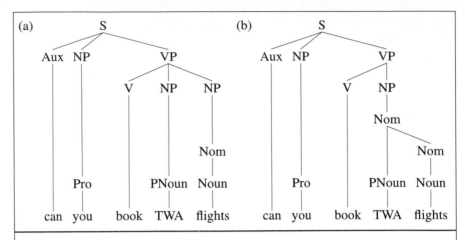

Figure 10.12   Two parse trees for an ambiguous sentence. Parse (a) corresponds to the meaning "Can you book flights on behalf of TWA?", parse (b) to "Can you book flights which are run by TWA".

This sentence has a number of ambiguities, although since they are semantically unreasonable, it requires a careful reading to see them. The last noun phrase could be parsed *[nationwide [television and radio]]* or *[[nationwide television] and radio]*. The direct object of *pushed aside* should be *other White House business* but could also be the bizarre phrase *[other White House business to devote all his time and attention to working]* (i.e., a structure like *Kennedy denied [his intention to propose a new budget to address the deficit]*). Then the phrase *on the Berlin crisis address he will deliver tomorrow night to the American people* could be an adjunct modifying the verb *pushed*. The *PP over nationwide television and radio* could be attached to any of the higher *VPs* or *NPs* (e.g., it could modify *people* or *night*).

The fact that there are many unreasonable parses for a sentence is an extremely irksome problem that affects all parsers. In practice, parsing a

DISAMBIGUATION   sentence thus requires **disambiguation**: choosing the correct parse from a multitude of possible parsers. Disambiguation algorithms generally require both statistical and semantic knowledge, so they will be introduced later, in Chapters 12 and 17.

Parsers which do not incorporate disambiguators must simply return all the possible parse trees for a given input. Since the top-down parser of Figure 10.7 only returns the first parse it finds, it would thus need to be modified to return all the possible parses. The algorithm would be changed to collect each parse as it is found and continue looking for more parses. When the search space has been exhausted, the list of all the trees found is returned. Subsequent processing or a human analyst can then decide which of the returned parses is correct.

Unfortunately, we almost certainly do not want all possible parses from the robust, highly ambiguous, wide-coverage grammars used in practical applications. The reason for this lies in the potentially exponential number of parses that are possible for certain inputs. Consider the ATIS example (10.5):

(10.5) Show me the meal on Flight UA 386 from San Francisco to Denver.

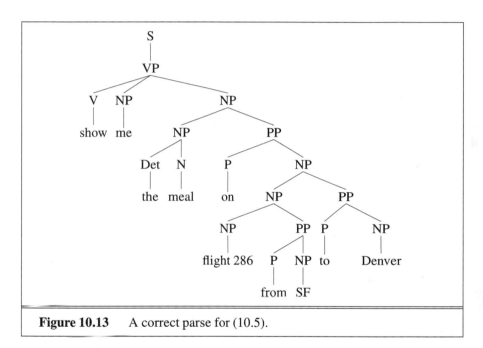

Figure 10.13   A correct parse for (10.5).

When our extremely small grammar is augmented with the recursive *VP* → *VP PP* and *NP* → *NP PP* rules introduced above, the three prepositional phrases at the end of this sentence conspire to yield a total of 14 parse trees for this sentence. For example *from San Francisco* could be part of the *VP* headed by *show* (which would have the bizarre interpretation that the showing was happening from San Francisco).

Church and Patil (1982) showed that the number of parses for sentences of this type grows at the same rate as the number of parenthesizations of arithmetic expressions. Such parenthesization problems, in turn, are known to grow exponentially in accordance with what are called the Catalan numbers:

$$C(n) = \frac{1}{n+1} \binom{2n}{n}$$

The following table shows the number of parses for a simple noun-phrase as a function of the number of trailing prepositional phrases. As can be seen, this kind of ambiguity can very quickly make it imprudent to keep every possible parse around.

Number of PPs	Number of NP Parses
2	2
3	5
4	14
5	132
6	469
7	1430
8	4867

There are two basic ways out of this dilemma: using dynamic programming to exploit regularities in the search space so that common sub-parts are derived only once, thus reducing some of the costs associated with ambiguity, and augmenting the parser's search strategy with heuristics that guide it toward likely parses first. The dynamic programming approach will be explored in the next section, while the heuristic search strategies will be covered in Chapter 12.

Even if a sentence isn't ambiguous, it can be inefficient to parse due to **local ambiguity**. Local ambiguity occurs when some part of a sentence is ambiguous, that is, has more than one parse, even if the whole sentence is not ambiguous. For example the sentence *Book that flight* is unambiguous, but when the parser sees the first word *Book*, it cannot know if it is a verb or a noun until later. Thus it must use backtracking or parallelism to consider both possible parses.

LOCAL AMBIGUITY

Repeated Parsing of Subtrees

The ambiguity problem is related to another inefficiency of the top-down parser of Section 10.2. The parser often builds valid trees for portions of the input, then discards them during backtracking, only to find that it has to rebuild them again. Consider the process involved in finding a parse for the *NP* in (10.6):

(10.6) a flight from Indianapolis to Houston on TWA

The preferred parse, which is also the one found first by the parser presented in Section 10.2, is shown as the bottom tree in Figure 10.14. While there are five distinct parses of this phrase, we will focus here on the ridiculous amount of repeated work involved in retrieving this single parse.

Because of the way the rules are consulted in our top-down, depth-first, left-to-right approach, the parser is led first to small parse trees that fail because they do not cover all of the input. These successive failures trigger backtracking events which lead to parses that incrementally cover more and more of the input. The sequence of trees attempted by our top-down parser is shown in Figure 10.14.

This figure clearly illustrates the kind of silly reduplication of work that arises in backtracking approaches. Except for its topmost component, every part of the final tree is derived more than once. The following table shows the number of times that each of the major constituents in the final tree is derived. The work done on this example would, of course, be magnified by any backtracking caused by the verb phrase or sentential level. Note that although this example is specific to top-down parsing, similar examples of wasted effort exist for bottom-up parsing as well.

a flight	4
from Indianapolis	3
to Houston	2
on TWA	1
a flight from Indianapolis	3
a flight from Indianapolis to Houston	2
a flight from Indianapolis to Houston on TWA	1

10.4 THE EARLEY ALGORITHM

The previous section presented three kinds of problems that afflict standard bottom-up or top-down parsers, even when they have been augmented with filtering and other improvements: **left-recursive rules**, **ambiguity**, and **inefficient reparsing of subtrees**. Luckily, there is a single class of algorithms which can solve all these problems. **Dynamic programming** once again

DYNAMIC PROGRAMMING

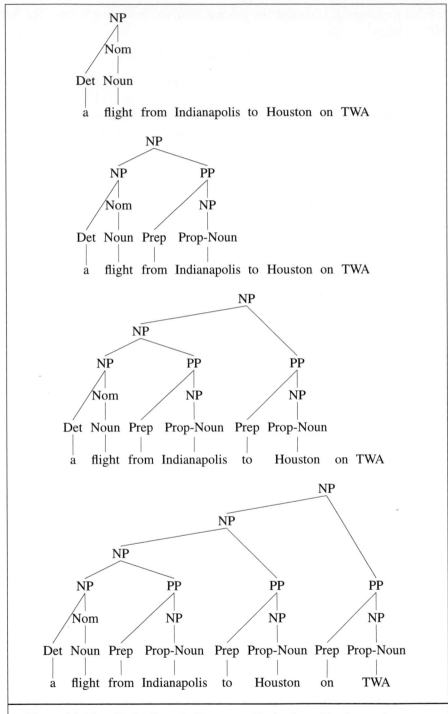

Figure 10.14   Reduplicated effort caused by backtracking in top-down parsing.

provides a framework for solving this problem, just as it helped us with the Minimum Edit Distance, Viterbi, and Forward algorithms. Recall that dynamic programming approaches systematically fill in tables of solutions to sub-problems. When complete, the tables contain the solution to all the sub-problems needed to solve the problem as a whole. In the case of parsing, such a table is used to store subtrees for each of the various constituents in the input as they are discovered. The efficiency gain arises from the fact that these subtrees are discovered once, stored, and then used in all parses calling for that constituent. This solves the reparsing problem (subtrees are looked up, not re-parsed) and the ambiguity problem (the parsing table implicitly stores all possible parses by storing all the constituents with links that enable the parses to be reconstructed). Furthermore, dynamic programming parsing algorithms also solve the problem of left-recursion. As we discussed earlier, there are three well-known dynamic programming parsers: the Cocke-Younger-Kasami (CYK) algorithm which we will present in Chapter 12, the Graham-Harrison-Ruzzo (GHR) (Graham et al., 1980) algorithm and the Earley algorithm (Earley, 1970) which we will introduce in the remainder of this chapter.

The Earley algorithm (Earley, 1970) uses a dynamic programming approach to efficiently implement a parallel top-down search of the kind discussed in Section 10.1. As with many dynamic programming solutions, this algorithm reduces an apparently exponential-time problem to a polynomial-time one by eliminating the repetitive solution of sub-problems inherent in backtracking approaches. In this case, the dynamic programming approach leads to a worst-case behavior of $O(N^3)$, where N is the number of words in the input.

The core of the Earley algorithm is a single left-to-right pass that fills an array called a **chart** that has $N + 1$ entries. For each word position in the sentence, the chart contains a list of states representing the partial parse trees that have been generated so far. By the end of the sentence, the chart compactly encodes all the possible parses of the input. Each possible subtree is represented only once and can thus be shared by all the parses that need it.

The individual states contained within each chart entry contain three kinds of information: a subtree corresponding to a single grammar rule, information about the progress made in completing this subtree, and the position of the subtree with respect to the input. Graphically, we will use a dot within the right hand side of a state's grammar rule to indicate the progress made in recognizing it. The resulting structure is called a **dotted rule**. A state's position with respect to the input will be represented by two numbers

CHART

DOTTED RULE

indicating where the state begins and where its dot lies. Consider the following three example states, which would be among those created by the Earley
algorithm in the course of parsing (10.7):

(10.7) Book that flight. (same as (10.1).)

$$S \rightarrow \bullet VP, \ [0,0]$$
$$NP \rightarrow Det \bullet Nominal, \ [1,2]$$
$$VP \rightarrow V NP \bullet, \ [0,3]$$

The first state, with its dot to the left of its constituent, represents a top-
down prediction for this particular kind of S. The first 0 indicates that the
constituent predicted by this state should begin at the start of the input; the
second 0 reflects the fact that the dot lies at the beginning as well. The second
state, created at a later stage in the processing of this sentence, indicates that
an NP begins at position 1, that a Det has been successfully parsed and that
a $Nominal$ is expected next. The third state, with its dot to the right of all its
two constituents, represents the successful discovery of a tree corresponding
to a VP that spans the entire input. These states can also be represented
graphically, in which the states of the parse are edges, or arcs, and the chart
as a whole is a directed acyclic graph, as in Figure 10.15.

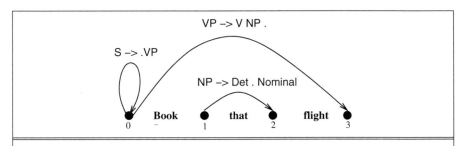

Figure 10.15   A directed acyclic graph representation of the three dotted
rules above.

The fundamental operation of an Earley parser is to march through the
$N+1$ sets of states in the chart in a left-to-right fashion, processing the states
within each set in order. At each step, one of the three operators described
below is applied to each state depending on its status. In each case, this
results in the addition of new states to the end of either the current or next set
of states in the chart. The algorithm always moves forward through the chart
making additions as it goes; states are never removed and the algorithm never

backtracks to a previous chart entry once it has moved on. The presence of a state $S \rightarrow \alpha\bullet$, $[0,N]$ in the list of states in the last chart entry indicates a successful parse. Figure 10.16 gives the complete algorithm.

---

function EARLEY-PARSE(*words, grammar*) **returns** *chart*

   ENQUEUE$((\gamma \rightarrow \bullet S, [0,0]), chart[0])$
   for $i \leftarrow$ **from** 0 **to** LENGTH(*words*) **do**
    for each *state* **in** *chart[i]* **do**
     if INCOMPLETE?(*state*) **and**
           NEXT-CAT(*state*) is not a part of speech **then**
       PREDICTOR(*state*)
     elseif INCOMPLETE?(*state*) **and**
           NEXT-CAT(*state*) is a part of speech **then**
      SCANNER(*state*)
     else
      COMPLETER(*state*)
    end
   end
   return(*chart*)

procedure PREDICTOR$((A \rightarrow \alpha \bullet B\ \beta, [i,j]))$
   for each $(B \rightarrow \gamma)$ **in** GRAMMAR-RULES-FOR($B, grammar$) **do**
    ENQUEUE$((B \rightarrow \bullet \gamma, [j,j]), chart[j])$
   end

procedure SCANNER$((A \rightarrow \alpha \bullet B\ \beta, [i,j]))$
   if B $\subset$ PARTS-OF-SPEECH($word[j]$) **then**
    ENQUEUE$((B \rightarrow word[j], [j,j+1]), chart[j+1])$

procedure COMPLETER$((B \rightarrow \gamma \bullet, [j,k]))$
   for each $(A \rightarrow \alpha \bullet B\ \beta, [i,j])$ **in** *chart[j]* **do**
    ENQUEUE$((A \rightarrow \alpha B \bullet \beta, [i,k]), chart[k])$
   end

procedure ENQUEUE(*state, chart-entry*)
   if *state* is not already in *chart-entry* **then**
    PUSH(*state, chart-entry*)
   end

Figure 10.16   The Earley algorithm.

The following three sections describe in detail the three operators used to process states in the chart. Each takes a single state as input and derives

new states from it. These new states are then added to the chart as long
as they are not already present. The PREDICTOR and the COMPLETER add
states to the chart entry being processed, while the SCANNER adds a state to
the next chart entry.

Predictor

As might be guessed from its name, the job of the PREDICTOR is to create
new states representing top-down expectations generated during the parsing
process. The PREDICTOR is applied to any state that has a non-terminal to
the right of the dot that is not a part-of-speech category. This application
results in the creation of one new state for each alternative expansion of that
non-terminal provided by the grammar. These new states are placed into the
same chart entry as the generating state. They begin and end at the point in
the input where the generating state ends.

   For example, applying the PREDICTOR to the state $S \rightarrow \bullet\, VP$, $[0,0]$
results in adding the states $VP \rightarrow \bullet\, Verb$, $[0,0]$ and $VP \rightarrow \bullet\, Verb\, NP$, $[0,0]$ to
the first chart entry.

Scanner

When a state has a part-of-speech category to the right of the dot, the SCAN-
NER is called to examine the input and incorporate a state corresponding
to the predicted part-of-speech into the chart. This is accomplished by creating a new state from the input state with the dot advanced over the predicted input category. Note that the Earley parser thus uses top-down input
to help disambiguate part-of-speech ambiguities; only those parts-of-speech
of a word that are predicted by some state will find their way into the chart.

   Returning to our example, when the state $VP \rightarrow \bullet Verb\, NP$, $[0,0]$ is processed, the SCANNER consults the current word in the input since the category following the dot is a part-of-speech. The SCANNER then notes that
book can be a verb, matching the expectation in the current state. This results
in the creation of the new state $VP \rightarrow Verb \bullet NP$, $[0,1]$. The new state is then
added to the chart entry that *follows* the one currently being processed.

Completer

The COMPLETER is applied to a state when its dot has reached the right
end of the rule. Intuitively, the presence of such a state represents the fact
that the parser has successfully discovered a particular grammatical category
over some span of the input. The purpose of the COMPLETER is to find and

advance all previously created states that were looking for this grammatical category at this position in the input. New states are then created by copying the older state, advancing the dot over the expected category and installing the new state in the current chart entry.

For example, when the state $NP \rightarrow Det\ Nominal\bullet$, $[1,3]$ is processed, the COMPLETER looks for states ending at 1 expecting an NP. In the current example, it will find the state $VP \rightarrow Verb\bullet NP$, $[0,1]$ created by the Scanner. This results in the addition of a new complete state $VP \rightarrow Verb\ NP\bullet$, $[0,3]$.

An Example

Figure 10.17 shows the sequence of states created during the complete processing of example (10.1)/(10.7). The algorithm begins by seeding the chart with a top-down expectation for an S. This is accomplished by adding a dummy state $\gamma \rightarrow \bullet S$, $[0,0]$ to Chart[0]. When this state is processed, it is passed to the PREDICTOR leading to the creation of the three states representing predictions for each possible type of S, and transitively to states for all of the left-corners of those trees. When the state $VP \rightarrow \bullet Verb$, $[0,0]$ is processed, the SCANNER is called and the first word is consulted. A state representing the verb sense of *Book* is then added to the entry for Chart[1]. Note that when the state $VP \rightarrow \bullet V\ NP$, $[0,0]$ is processed, the SCANNER is called again. However, this time a new state is not added since it would be identical to the one already in the chart. Note also that since this admittedly deficient grammar generates no predictions for the *Noun* sense of *Book*, no entries will be made for it in the chart.

When all the states of Chart[0] have been processed, the algorithm moves on to Chart[1] where it finds the state representing the verb sense of *book*. This is a complete state with its dot to the right of its constituent and is therefore passed to the COMPLETER. The COMPLETER then finds the two previously existing VP states expecting a *Verb* at this point in the input. These states are copied with their dots advanced and added to the Chart[1]. The completed state corresponding to an intransitive VP leads to the creation of the imperative S state. Alternatively, the dot in the transitive verb phrase leads to the creation of the two states predicting NPs. Finally, the state $NP \rightarrow \bullet Det\ Nominal$, $[1,1]$ causes the Scanner to consult the word *that* and add a corresponding state to Chart[2].

Moving on to Chart[2], the algorithm finds the state representing the determiner sense of *that*. This complete state leads to the advancement of the dot in the NP state predicted in Chart[1], and also to the predictions for

Chart[0]

$\gamma \rightarrow \bullet S$	[0,0]	Dummy start state
$S \rightarrow \bullet NP\ VP$	[0,0]	Predictor
$NP \rightarrow \bullet Det\ NOMINAL$	[0,0]	Predictor
$NP \rightarrow \bullet Proper\text{-}Noun$	[0,0]	Predictor
$S \rightarrow \bullet Aux\ NP\ VP$	[0,0]	Predictor
$S \rightarrow \bullet VP$	[0,0]	Predictor
$VP \rightarrow \bullet Verb$	[0,0]	Predictor
$VP \rightarrow \bullet Verb\ NP$	[0,0]	Predictor

Chart[1]

$Verb \rightarrow book \bullet$	[0,1]	Scanner
$VP \rightarrow Verb\bullet$	[0,1]	Completer
$S \rightarrow VP\bullet$	[0,1]	Completer
$VP \rightarrow Verb \bullet NP$	[0,1]	Completer
$NP \rightarrow \bullet Det\ NOMINAL$	[1,1]	Predictor
$NP \rightarrow \bullet Proper\text{-}Noun$	[1,1]	Predictor

Chart[2]

$Det \rightarrow that\bullet$	[1,2]	Scanner
$NP \rightarrow Det\bullet NOMINAL$	[1,2]	Completer
$NOMINAL \rightarrow \bullet Noun$	[2,2]	Predictor
$NOMINAL \rightarrow \bullet Noun\ NOMINAL$	[2,2]	Predictor

Chart[3]

$Noun \rightarrow flight\bullet$	[2,3]	Scanner
$NOMINAL \rightarrow Noun\bullet$	[2,3]	Completer
$NOMINAL \rightarrow Noun\bullet NOMINAL$	[2,3]	Completer
$NP \rightarrow Det\ NOMINAL \bullet$	[1,3]	Completer
$VP \rightarrow Verb\ NP \bullet$	[0,3]	Completer
$S \rightarrow VP\bullet$	[0,3]	Completer
$NOMINAL \rightarrow \bullet Noun$	[3,3]	Predictor
$NOMINAL \rightarrow \bullet Noun\ NOMINAL$	[3,3]	Predictor

Figure 10.17   Sequence of states created in chart while parsing *Book that flight*. Each entry shows the state, its start and end points, and the Earley function that placed it in the chart.

the various kinds of *Nominal*. The first of these causes the SCANNER to be called for the last time to process the word *flight*.

Moving on to Chart[3], the presence of the state representing *flight* leads in quick succession to the completion of an *NP*, transitive *VP*, and an *S*. The presence of the state $S \to VP\bullet$, $[0,3]$ in the last chart entry signals the discovery of a successful parse.

Retrieving Parse Trees from a Chart

The version of the Earley algorithm just described is actually a recognizer not a parser. After processing, valid sentences will leave the state $S \to \alpha\bullet$, $[0,N]$ in the chart. Unfortunately, as it stands we have no way of retrieving the structure of this *S*. To turn this algorithm into a parser, we must be able to extract individual parses from the chart. To do this, the representation of each state must be augmented with an additional field to store information about the completed states that generated its constituents.

This information can be gathered by making a simple change to the COMPLETER. Recall that the COMPLETER creates new states by advancing older incomplete ones when the constituent following the dot is discovered. The only change necessary is to have COMPLETER add a pointer to the older state onto the list of previous-states of the new state. Retrieving a parse tree from the chart is then merely a recursive retrieval starting with the state (or states) representing a complete *S* in the final chart entry. Figure 10.18 shows the chart produced by an appropriately updated COMPLETER.

If there are an exponential number of trees for a given sentence, the Earley algorithm can not magically *return* them all in a polynomial amount of time. The best it can do is build the chart in polynomial time. Figure 10.19 illustrates a portion of the chart from Figure 10.17 using the directed graph notation. Note that since large charts in this format can get rather confusing, this figure only includes the states that play a role in the final parse.

10.5   FINITE-STATE PARSING METHODS

Some language-processing tasks don't require complete parses. For these tasks, a **partial parse** or **shallow parse** of the input sentence may be suf- SHALLOW PARSE ficient. For example, **information extraction** algorithms generally do not extract *all* the possible information in a text; they simply extract enough to fill out some sort of template of required data. Many partial parsing sys-

Chart[0]

S0	$\gamma \to \bullet S$	[0,0]	[]	Dummy start state
S1	$S \to \bullet NP\ VP$	[0,0]	[]	Predictor
S2	$NP \to \bullet Det\ NOMINAL$	[0,0]	[]	Predictor
S3	$NP \to \bullet Proper\text{-}Noun$	[0,0]	[]	Predictor
S4	$S \to \bullet Aux\ NP\ VP$	[0,0]	[]	Predictor
S5	$S \to \bullet VP$	[0,0]	[]	Predictor
S6	$VP \to \bullet Verb$	[0,0]	[]	Predictor
S7	$VP \to \bullet Verb\ NP$	[0,0]	[]	Predictor

Chart[1]

S8	$Verb \to book \bullet$	[0,1]	[]	Scanner
S9	$VP \to Verb\bullet$	[0,1]	[S8]	Completer
S10	$S \to VP\bullet$	[0,1]	[S9]	Completer
S11	$VP \to Verb \bullet NP$	[0,1]	[S8]	Completer
S12	$NP \to \bullet Det\ NOMINAL$	[1,1]	[]	Predictor
S13	$NP \to \bullet Proper\text{-}Noun$	[1,1]	[]	Predictor

Chart[2]

S14	$Det \to that\bullet$	[1,2]	[]	Scanner
S15	$NP \to Det\bullet NOMINAL$	[1,2]	[S14]	Completer
S16	$NOMINAL \to \bullet Noun$	[2,2]	[]	Predictor
S17	$NOMINAL \to \bullet Noun\ NOMINAL$	[2,2]	[]	Predictor

Chart[3]

S18	$Noun \to flight\bullet$	[2,3]	[]	Scanner
S19	$NOMINAL \to Noun\bullet$	[2,3]	[S18]	Completer
S20	$NOMINAL \to Noun\bullet NOMINAL$	[2,3]	[S18]	Completer
S21	$NP \to Det\ NOMINAL \bullet$	[1,3]	[S14,S19]	Completer
S22	$VP \to Verb\ NP \bullet$	[0,3]	[S8,S21]	Completer
S23	$S \to VP\bullet$	[0,3]	[S22]	Completer
S24	$NOMINAL \to \bullet Noun$	[3,3]	[]	Predictor
S25	$NOMINAL \to \bullet Noun\ NOMINAL$	[3,3]	[]	Predictor

Figure 10.18   Sequence of states created in chart while parsing *Book that flight* including structural information.

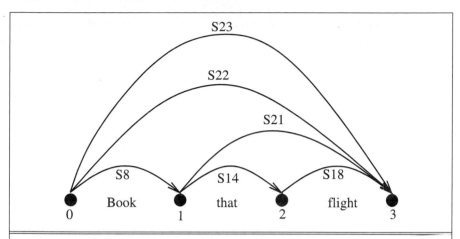

Figure 10.19   A portion of the chart shown in Figure 10.17 displayed in a directed acyclic graph notation.

tems use **cascades** of finite-state automata instead of context-free grammars. CASCADES Relying on simple finite-state automata rather than full parsing makes such systems extremely efficient. Since finite-state systems cannot model certain kinds of recursive rules, however, they trade this efficiency for a certain lack of coverage. We will discuss information extraction in Chapter 15; here we just show how finite-state automata can be used to recognize **basic phrases**, BASIC PHRASES such as noun groups, verb groups, locations, and so on. Here's the output of the FASTUS basic phrase identifier; of course the choice of which basic phrases to produce can be dependent on the application:

Company Name:	Bridgestone Sports Co.
Verb Group:	said
Noun Group:	Friday
Noun Group:	it
Verb Group:	had set up
Noun Group:	a joint venture
Preposition:	in
Location:	Taiwan
Preposition:	with
Noun Group:	a local concern
Conjunction:	and
Noun Group:	a Japanese trading house
Verb Group:	to produce
Noun Group:	golf clubs
Verb Group:	to be shipped
Preposition:	to
Location:	Japan

These basic phrases are produced by a collection finite-state rules compiled into a transducer. To give a feel for how this works, we'll give a simplified set of the FASTUS rules from Appelt and Israel (1997) used to build
NOUN GROUP   the automaton to detect **noun groups**. A noun group is like the core of a
noun phrase; it consists of the head noun and the modifiers to the left (determiner, adjectives, quantifiers, numbers, etc.). For ease of exposition we give
the rules using a notation with an arrow ($\rightarrow$) that looks like a context-free
rule formalism; but in practice these rules are compiled together into finite
automata and are not treated like context-free rules.

A noun-group can consist of just a pronoun *she, him, them* or a time-
phrase *yesterday*, or a date:

NG $\rightarrow$ Pronoun | Time-NP | Date-NP

It can also consist of certain determiners that can stand alone (*this,
that*); or a head noun (*HdNns*) preceded by optional determiner phrase
(*DETP*) and/or optional adjectives (*Adjs*) (*the quick and dirty solution, the
frustrating mathematics problem*) or a head noun modified by a gerund phrase
(*the rising index*):

NG $\rightarrow$ (DETP) (Adjs) HdNns | DETP Ving HdNns
                                      | DETP-CP (and HdNns)

The parentheses above are used to indicate optional elements, while
braces are used just for grouping. Determiner-phrases come in two varieties:

DETP $\rightarrow$ DETP-CP | DETP-INCP

Complete determiner-phrases (*DETP-CP*) are those which can stand
alone as an *NP*, such as *the only five, another three, this, many, hers, all*,
and *the most*. *Adv-pre-num* are adverbs that can appear before a number in
the determiner (*almost 5, precisely 5*), while *Pro-Poss-cp* are possessive pronouns that can stand on their own as complete *NP*s (*mine, his*). Quantifiers
(*Q*) include *many, few, much*, etc.

DETP-CP $\rightarrow$ ({ Adv-pre-num | "another" |
                          { Det | Pro-Poss } ({Adv-pre-num | "only" ("other")})}) Number
                          | Q | Q-er | ("the") Q-est | "another" | Det-cp | DetQ | Pro-Poss-cp

Incomplete determiner-phrases (*DETP-INCP*) are those which cannot
act as *NP*s alone, for example *the, his only, every, a. Pro-Poss-incomp* are
possessive pronouns which cannot stand on their own as a complete *NP* (e.g.,
my, her):

DETP-INCP → { { { Det | Pro-Poss } "only"
              | "a" | "an"
              | Det-incomp
              | Pro-Poss-incomp } ("other")
              | (DET-CP) "other"}

An adjective sequence (*Adjs*) consists of one or more adjectives or participles separated by commas and/or conjunctions (e.g., *big, bad, and ugly*, or *interesting but outdated*):

Adjs → AdjP ({ ";" | (",") Conj } { AdjP | Vparticiple}) *

Adjective phrases can be made of adjectives, participles, ordinal numbers, and noun-verb combinations, like *man-eating*, and can be modified by comparative and superlative quantifiers (Q-er: *more, fewer*; Q-est: *most, fewest*). This rule-set chooses to disallow participles as the first word in adjective-phrases or noun groups, to avoid incorrectly taking many Verb-Object combinations as noun groups.

AdjP → Ordinal
       | ({Q-er | Q-est} { Adj | Vparticiple } +
       | { N[sing,!Time-NP] ("-") { Vparticiple }
       | Number ("-") { "month" | "day" | "year"} ("-") "old"}

Nouns can be conjoined (*cats and dogs*):

HdNns → HdNn ("and" HdNn)

Finally, we need to deal with noun-noun compounds and other noun-like pre-modifiers of nouns, in order to cover head noun groups like *gasoline and oil tanks, California wines, Clinton*, and *quick-reaction strike*:

HdNn → PropN
       | { PreNs | PropN PreNs} N[!Time-NP]
       | { PropN CommonN[!Time-NP] }

Noun modifiers of nouns can be conjoined (*gasoline and oil*) or created via dash (*quick-reaction*). *Adj-noun-like* refers to adjectives that can appear in the position of a prenominal noun (e.g., *presidential retreat*):

PreNs → PreN ("and" PreN2) *
preN → (Adj "-") Common-Sing-N
preN2 → PreN | Ordinal | Adj-noun-like

Figure 10.20 shows an FSA for the *Adjs* portion of the noun-group recognizer, and an FSA for the *AdjP* portion.

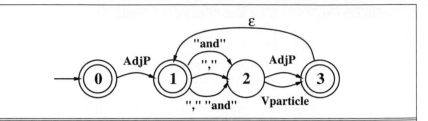

Figure 10.20   A portion of an FSA grammar, covering conjoined adjective phrases. In a real automaton, each *AdjP* node would actually be expanded with a copy of the *AdjP* automaton shown in Figure 10.21.

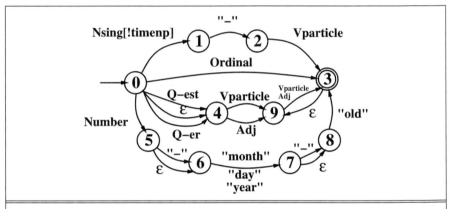

Figure 10.21   A portion of an FSA grammar, covering the internal details of adjective phrases.

The pieces of automata in Figures 10.20 and 10.21 can then be combined into a single large Noun-Group-Recognizer by starting with the *NG* automaton and iteratively expanding out each reference to another rule/automaton. This is only possible because none of these references are recursive; that is, because the expansion of *AdjP* doesn't refer to *AdjP*.

Page 349, however, showed that a more complete grammar of English requires this kind of recursion. Recall, for example, that a complete definition of *NP* needs to refer to other *NP*s in the rules for relative clauses and other post-nominal modifiers.

One way to handle recursion is by allowing only a limited amount of recursion; this is what FASTUS does, by using its automata **cascade**. The second level of FASTUS finds non-recursive noun groups; the third level combines these groups into larger *NP*-like units by adding on measure phrases:

20,000 iron and "metal wood" clubs a month,

attaching preposition phrases:

production of 20,000 iron and "metal wood" clubs a month,

and dealing with noun group conjunction:

a local concern and a Japanese trading house

In a single-level system, each of these phenomena would require recursive rules (e.g., *NP → NP and NP*). By splitting the parsing into two levels, FASTUS essentially treats the *NP* on the left-hand side as a different kind of object from the *NP*s on the right-hand side.

A second method for dealing with recursion is to use a model which looks finite-state but isn't. One such model is the **Recursive Transition Network** or **RTN**. An RTN is defined by a set of graphs like those in Figure 10.20 and Figure 10.21, in which each arc contains a terminal or non-terminal node. The difference between an RTN and an FSA lies in how the non-terminals are handled. In an RTN, every time the machine comes to an arc labeled with a non-terminal, it treats that non-terminal as a **subroutine**. It places its current location onto a stack, jumps to the non-terminal, and then jumps back when that non-terminal has been parsed. If a rule for *NP* contains a self-reference, the RTN once again puts the current location on a stack and jumps back to the beginning of the NP.

Since an RTN is exactly equivalent to a context-free grammar, traversing an RTN can thus be thought of as a graphical way to view a simple top-down parser for context-free rules. RTNs are most often used as a convenient graphical metaphor when displaying or describing grammars, or as a way to implement a system which has a small amount of recursion but is otherwise finite-state.

10.6   SUMMARY

This chapter introduced a lot of material. The most important two ideas are those of **parsing** and **partial parsing**. Here's a summary of the main points we covered about these ideas:

- Parsing can be viewed as a **search** problem.
- Two common architectural metaphors for this search are **top-down** (starting with the root *S* and growing trees down to the input words)

and **bottom-up** (staring with the words and growing trees up toward the root *S*).

- One simple parsing algorithm is the top-down depth-first left-to-right parser of Figure 10.6 on page 366.

- Top down parsers can be made more efficient by using a **left-corner** table to only suggest non-terminals which are compatible with the input.

- **Ambiguity**, **left-recursion**, and **repeated parsing of sub-trees** all pose problems for this simple parsing algorithm.

- A sentence is **structurally ambiguous** if the grammar assigns it more than one possible parse.

- Common kinds of structural ambiguity include **PP-attachment**, **coordination ambiguity** and **noun-phrase bracketing ambiguity**.

- The **dynamic programming** parsing algorithms use a table of partial-parses to efficiently parse ambiguous sentences. The **Earley** algorithm is a top-down dynamic-programming algorithm, while the **CYK** algorithm is bottom up.

- Certain **information extraction** problems can be solved without full parsing. These are often addressed via **FSA cascades**.

BIBLIOGRAPHICAL AND HISTORICAL NOTES

Writing about the history of compilers, Knuth notes:

> In this field there has been an unusual amount of parallel discovery of the same technique by people working independently.

Well, perhaps not unusual, if multiple discovery is the norm (see page 15). But there has certainly been enough parallel publication that this history will error on the side of succinctness in giving only a characteristic early mention of each algorithm; the interested reader should see Aho and Ullman (1972).

Bottom-up parsing seems to have been first described by Yngve (1955), who gave a breadth-first bottom-up parsing algorithm as part of an illustration of a machine translation procedure. Top-down approaches to parsing and translation were described (presumably independently) by at least Glennie (1960), Irons (1961), and Kuno and Oettinger (1963). Dynamic programming parsing, once again, has a history of independent discovery. According to Martin Kay (personal communication), a dynamic programming parser

containing the roots of the CYK algorithm was first implemented by John Cocke in 1960. Later work extended and formalized the algorithm, as well as proving its time complexity (Kay, 1967; Younger, 1967; Kasami, 1965). The related **well-formed substring table (WFST)** seems to have been in-   WFST
dependently proposed by Kuno (1965), as a data structure which stores the results of all previous computations in the course of the parse. Based on a generalization of Cocke's work, a similar data-structure had been independently described by Kay (1967) and Kay (1973). The top-down application of dynamic programming to parsing was described in Earley's Ph.D. dissertation (Earley, 1968) and Earley (1970). Sheil (1976) showed the equivalence of the WFST and the Earley algorithm. Norvig (1991) shows that the efficiency offered by all of these dynamic programming algorithms can be captured in any language with a *memoization* function (such as LISP) simply by wrapping the *memoization* operation around a simple top-down parser.

While parsing via cascades of finite-state automata had been common in the early history of parsing (Harris, 1962), the focus shifted to full CFG parsing quite soon afterwards. Church (1980) argued for a return to finite-state grammars as a processing model for natural language understanding; Other early finite-state parsing models include Ejerhed (1988). Abney (1991) argued for the important practical role of shallow parsing. Much recent work on shallow parsing applies machine learning to the task of learning the patterns; see for example Ramshaw and Marcus (1995), Argamon et al. (1998), Munoz et al. (1999).

The classic reference for parsing algorithms is Aho and Ullman (1972); although the focus of that book is on computer languages, most of the algorithms have been applied to natural language. A good programming languages textbook such as Aho et al. (1986) is also useful.

EXERCISES

10.1 Modify the top-down parser in Figure 10.7 to add bottom-up filtering. You can assume the use of a left-corner table like the one on page 370.

10.2 Write an algorithm for eliminating left-recursion based on the intuition on page 372.

10.3 Implement the finite-state grammar for noun-groups described on pages 388–391. Test it on some sample noun-phrases. If you have access to an on-line dictionary with part-of-speech information, start with that; if not, build a more restricted system by hand.

10.4   Augment the Earley algorithm of Figure 10.16 to enable parse trees to be retrieved from the chart by modifying the pseudocode for the COM-PLETER as described on page 385.

10.5   Implement the Earley algorithm as augmented in the previous exercise. Check it on a test sentence using a baby grammar.

10.6   Discuss the relative advantages and disadvantages of partial parsing versus full parsing.

10.7   Discuss how you would augment a parser to deal with input that may be incorrect, such as spelling errors or misrecognitions from a speech recognition system.

11 FEATURES AND UNIFICATION

FRIAR FRANCIS: *If either of you know any inward impediment why you should not be conjoined, charge you, on your souls, to utter it.*
William Shakespeare, *Much Ado About Nothing*

From a reductionist perspective, the history of the natural sciences over the last few hundred years can be seen as an attempt to explain the behavior of larger structures by the combined action of smaller primitives. In biology, the properties of inheritance have been explained by the action of genes, and then again the properties of genes have been explained by the action of DNA. In physics, matter was reduced to atoms and then again to subatomic particles. The appeal of reductionism has not escaped computational linguistics. In this chapter we introduce the idea that grammatical categories like *VPto, Sthat, Non3sgAux*, or *3sgNP*, as well as the grammatical rules like $S \rightarrow NP\ VP$ that make use of them, should be thought of as *objects* that can have complex sets of *properties* associated with them. The information in these properties is represented by **constraints**, and so these kinds of models are often called **constraint-based formalisms**.

CONSTRAINT-BASED FORMALISMS

Why do we need a more fine-grained way of representing and placing constraints on grammatical categories? One problem arose in Chapter 9, where we saw that naive models of grammatical phenomena such as agreement and subcategorization can lead to overgeneration problems. For example, in order to avoid ungrammatical noun phrases such as *this flights* and verb phrases like *disappeared a flight*, we were forced to create a huge proliferation of primitive grammatical categories such as *Non3sgVPto, NPmass, 3sgNP* and *Non3sgAux*. These new categories led, in turn, to an explosion in the number of grammar rules and a corresponding loss of generality in the grammar. A constraint-based representation scheme will allow us to represent fine-grained information about number and person, agreement, subcategorization, as well as semantic categories like mass/count.

Constraint-based formalisms have other advantages that we will not cover in this chapter, such as the ability to model more complex phenomena than context-free grammars, and the ability to efficiently and conveniently compute semantics for syntactic representations.

Consider briefly how this approach might work in the case of grammatical number. As we saw in Chapter 9, noun phrases like *this flight* and *those flights* can be distinguished based on whether they are singular or plural. This distinction can be captured if we associate a property called NUMBER that can have the value singular or plural, with appropriate members of the *NP* category. Given this ability, we can say that *this flight* is a member of the *NP* category and, in addition, has the value singular for its NUMBER property. This same property can be used in the same way to distinguish singular and plural members of the *VP* category such as *serves lunch* and *serve lunch*.

Of course, simply associating these properties with various words and phrases does not solve any of our overgeneration problems. To make these properties useful, we need the ability to perform simple operations, such as equality tests, on them. By pairing such tests with our core grammar rules, we can add various constraints to help ensure that only grammatical strings are generated by the grammar. For example, we might want to ask whether or not a given noun phrase and verb phrase have the same values for their respective number properties. Such a test is illustrated by the following kind of rule.

$S \rightarrow NP\ VP$

Only if the number of the NP is equal to the number of the VP.

The remainder of this chapter provides the details of one computational implementation of a constraint-based formalism, based on **feature structures** and **unification**. The next section describes **feature structures**, the representation used to capture the kind of grammatical properties we have in mind. Section 11.2 then introduces the **unification operator** that is used to implement basic operations over feature structures. Section 11.3 then covers the integration of these structures into a grammatical formalism. Section 11.4 then introduces the unification algorithm and its required data structures. Next, Section 11.5 describes how feature structures and the unification operator can be integrated into a parser. Finally, Section 11.6 discusses the most significant extension to this constraint-based formalism, the use of **types** and **inheritance**, as well as other extensions.

11.1 FEATURE STRUCTURES

One of the simplest ways to encode the kind of properties that we have in
mind is through the use of **feature structures**. These are simply sets of   FEATURE STRUCTURES
feature-value pairs, where features are unanalyzable atomic symbols drawn
from some finite set, and values are either atomic symbols or feature structures. Such feature structures are traditionally illustrated with the following
kind of matrix-like diagram, called a **attribute-value matrix** or **AVM**:   ATTRIBUTE-VALUE MATRIX

AVM

$$\begin{bmatrix} \text{FEATURE}_1 & \text{VALUE}_1 \\ \text{FEATURE}_2 & \text{VALUE}_2 \\ \vdots & \\ \text{FEATURE}_n & \text{VALUE}_n \end{bmatrix}$$

To be concrete, let us consider the number property discussed above.
To capture this property, we will use the symbol NUMBER to designate this
grammatical attribute, and the symbols SG and PL (introduced in Chapter 3)
to designate the possible values it can take on in English. A simple feature
structure consisting of this single feature would then be illustrated as follows:

$$\begin{bmatrix} \text{NUMBER} & \text{SG} \end{bmatrix}$$

Adding an additional feature-value pair to capture the grammatical notion of
person leads to the following feature structure:

$$\begin{bmatrix} \text{NUMBER} & \text{SG} \\ \text{PERSON} & 3 \end{bmatrix}$$

Next we can encode the grammatical category of the constituent that this
structure corresponds to through the use of the CAT feature. For example,
we can indicate that these features are associated with a noun phrase by
using the following structure:

$$\begin{bmatrix} \text{CAT} & \text{NP} \\ \text{NUMBER} & \text{SG} \\ \text{PERSON} & 3 \end{bmatrix}$$

This structure can be used to represent the *3sgNP* category introduced in
Chapter 9 to capture a restricted subcategory of noun phrases. The corresponding plural version of this structure would be captured as follows:

$$\begin{bmatrix} \text{CAT} & \text{NP} \\ \text{NUMBER} & \text{PL} \\ \text{PERSON} & 3 \end{bmatrix}$$

Note that the value of the CAT and PERSON features remains the same for these last two structures. This illustrates how the use of feature structures allows us to both preserve the core set of grammatical categories and draw distinctions among members of a single category.

As mentioned earlier in the definition of feature structures, features are not limited to atomic symbols as their values; they can also have other feature structures as their values. This is particularly useful when we wish to bundle a set of feature-value pairs together for similar treatment. As an example of this, consider that the NUMBER and PERSON features are often lumped together since grammatical subjects must agree with their predicates in both their number and person properties. This lumping together can be captured by introducing an AGREEMENT feature that takes a feature structure consisting of the NUMBER and PERSON feature-value pairs as its value. Introducing this feature into our third person singular noun phrase yields the following kind of structure.

$$\begin{bmatrix} \text{CAT} & \text{NP} \\ \text{AGREEMENT} & \begin{bmatrix} \text{NUMBER} & \text{SG} \\ \text{PERSON} & 3 \end{bmatrix} \end{bmatrix}$$

Given this kind of arrangement, we can test for the equality of the values for both the NUMBER and PERSON features of two constituents by testing for the equality of their AGREEMENT features.

FEATURE PATH This ability to use feature structures as values leads fairly directly to the notion of a **feature path**. A feature path is nothing more than a list of features through a feature structure leading to a particular value. For example, in the last feature structure, we can say that the ⟨AGREEMENT NUMBER⟩ path leads to the value SG, while the ⟨AGREEMENT PERSON⟩ path leads to the value 3. This notion of a path leads naturally to an alternative graphical way of illustrating features structures, shown in Figure 11.1, which as we will see in Section 11.4 is suggestive of how they will be implemented. In these diagrams, feature structures are depicted as directed graphs where features appear as labeled edges and values as nodes.

Although this notion of paths will prove useful in a number of settings, we introduce it here to help explain an additional important kind of feature structure: those that contain features that actually share some feature

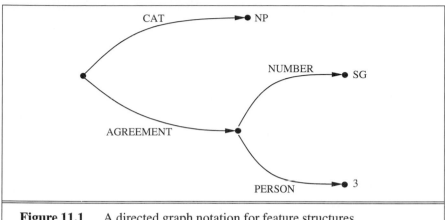

Figure 11.1   A directed graph notation for feature structures.

structure as a value. Such feature structures will be referred to as **reentrant**   REENTRANT
structures. What we have in mind here is not the simple idea that two features might have equal values, but rather that they share precisely the same
feature structure (or node in the graph). These two cases can be distinguished
clearly if we think in terms of paths through a graph. In the case of simple
equality, two paths lead to distinct nodes in the graph that anchor identical,
but distinct structures. In the case of a reentrant structure, two feature paths
actually lead to the same node in the structure.

Figure 11.2 illustrates a simple example of reentrancy. In this structure,
the ⟨HEAD SUBJECT AGREEMENT⟩ path and the ⟨HEAD AGREEMENT⟩ path
lead to the same location. Shared structures like this will be denoted in our
matrix diagrams by adding numerical indexes that signal the values to be
shared. The matrix version of the feature structure from Figure 11.2 would
be denoted as follows, using the notation of the PATR-II system (Shieber,
1986), based on Kay (1979):

$$
\begin{bmatrix}
\text{CAT} & \text{S} \\
\\
\text{HEAD} & \begin{bmatrix}
\text{AGREEMENT} & \boxed{1} \begin{bmatrix} \text{NUMBER} & \text{SG} \\ \text{PERSON} & 3 \end{bmatrix} \\
\\
\text{SUBJECT} & \begin{bmatrix} \text{AGREEMENT} & \boxed{1} \end{bmatrix}
\end{bmatrix}
\end{bmatrix}
$$

As we will see, these simple structures give us the ability to express
linguistic generalizations in surprisingly compact and elegant ways.

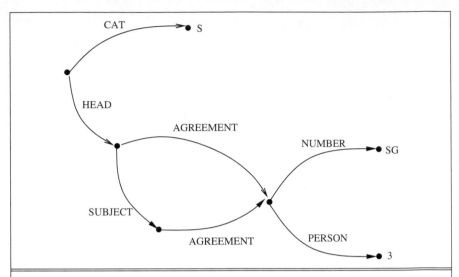

Figure 11.2   A feature structure with shared values. The location (value) found by following the ⟨HEAD SUBJECT AGREEMENT⟩ path is the same as that found via the ⟨HEAD AGREEMENT⟩ path.

11.2   UNIFICATION OF FEATURE STRUCTURES

As noted earlier, feature structures would be of little use without our being able to perform reasonably efficient and powerful operations on them. As we will show, the two principal operations we need to perform are merging the information content of two structures and rejecting the merger of structures that are incompatible. Fortunately, a single computational technique, called

UNIFICATION   **unification**, suffices for both of these purposes. The bulk of this section will illustrate through a series of examples how unification instantiates these notions of merger and compatibility. Discussion of the unification algorithm and its implementation will be deferred to Section 11.4.

We begin with the following simple application of the unification operator.

$$\begin{bmatrix} \text{NUMBER} & \text{SG} \end{bmatrix} \sqcup \begin{bmatrix} \text{NUMBER} & \text{SG} \end{bmatrix} = \begin{bmatrix} \text{NUMBER} & \text{SG} \end{bmatrix}$$

As this equation illustrates, unification is implemented as a binary operator (represented here as ⊔) that accepts two feature structures as arguments and returns a feature structure when it succeeds. In this example, unification is being used to perform a simple equality check. The unification succeeds because the corresponding NUMBER features in each structure agree as to

their values. In this case, since the original structures are identical, the output
is the same as the input. The following similar kind of check fails since the
NUMBER features in the two structures have incompatible values.

$$\begin{bmatrix} \text{NUMBER} & \text{SG} \end{bmatrix} \sqcup \begin{bmatrix} \text{NUMBER} & \text{PL} \end{bmatrix} \textit{Fails!}$$

This next unification illustrates an important aspect of the notion of
compatibility in unification.

$$\begin{bmatrix} \text{NUMBER} & \text{SG} \end{bmatrix} \sqcup \begin{bmatrix} \text{NUMBER} & [] \end{bmatrix} = \begin{bmatrix} \text{NUMBER} & \text{SG} \end{bmatrix}$$

In this situation, these features structures are taken to be compatible, and
are hence capable of being merged, despite the fact that the given values for
the respective NUMBER features are different. The [] value in the second
structure indicates that the value has been left unspecified. A feature with
such a [] value can be successfully matched to any value in a corresponding
feature in another structure. Therefore, in this case, the value SG from the
first structure can match the [] value from the second, and as is indicated by
the output shown, the result of this type of unification is a structure with the
value provided by the more specific, non-null, value.

The next example illustrates another of the merger aspects of unification.

$$\begin{bmatrix} \text{NUMBER} & \text{SG} \end{bmatrix} \sqcup \begin{bmatrix} \text{PERSON} & 3 \end{bmatrix} = \begin{bmatrix} \text{NUMBER} & \text{SG} \\ \text{PERSON} & 3 \end{bmatrix}$$

Here the result of the unification is a merger of the original two structures
into one larger structure. This larger structure contains the union of all the
information stored in each of the original structures. Although this is a simple example, it is important to understand why these structures are judged to
be compatible: they are compatible because they contain no features that are
explicitly incompatible. The fact that they each contain a feature-value pair
that the other does not is not a reason for the unification to fail.

We will now consider a series of cases involving the unification of
somewhat more complex reentrant structures. The following example illustrates an equality check complicated by the presence of a reentrant structure
in the first argument.

$$\begin{bmatrix} \text{AGREEMENT} & \boxed{1} \begin{bmatrix} \text{NUMBER} & \text{SG} \\ \text{PERSON} & 3 \end{bmatrix} \\ \text{SUBJECT} & \begin{bmatrix} \text{AGREEMENT} & \boxed{1} \end{bmatrix} \end{bmatrix}$$

$$
\sqcup \begin{bmatrix} \text{SUBJECT} & \begin{bmatrix} \text{AGREEMENT} & \begin{bmatrix} \text{PERSON} & 3 \\ \text{NUMBER} & \text{SG} \end{bmatrix} \end{bmatrix} \end{bmatrix}
$$

$$
= \begin{bmatrix} \text{AGREEMENT} & \boxed{1} \begin{bmatrix} \text{NUMBER} & \text{SG} \\ \text{PERSON} & 3 \end{bmatrix} \\ \text{SUBJECT} & \begin{bmatrix} \text{AGREEMENT} & \boxed{1} \end{bmatrix} \end{bmatrix}
$$

The important elements in this example are the SUBJECT features in the two input structures. The unification of these features succeeds because the values found in the first argument by following the $\boxed{1}$ numerical index, match those that are directly present in the second argument. Note that, by itself, the value of the AGREEMENT feature in the first argument would have no bearing on the success of unification since the second argument lacks an AGREEMENT feature at the top level. It only becomes relevant because the value of the AGREEMENT feature is shared with the SUBJECT feature.

The following example illustrates the copying capabilities of unification.

(11.1)
$$
\begin{bmatrix} \text{AGREEMENT} & \boxed{1} \\ \text{SUBJECT} & \begin{bmatrix} \text{AGREEMENT} & \boxed{1} \end{bmatrix} \end{bmatrix}
$$

$$
\sqcup \begin{bmatrix} \text{SUBJECT} & \begin{bmatrix} \text{AGREEMENT} & \begin{bmatrix} \text{PERSON} & 3 \\ \text{NUMBER} & \text{SG} \end{bmatrix} \end{bmatrix} \end{bmatrix}
$$

$$
= \begin{bmatrix} \text{AGREEMENT} & \boxed{1} \\ \text{SUBJECT} & \begin{bmatrix} \text{AGREEMENT} & \boxed{1} \begin{bmatrix} \text{PERSON} & 3 \\ \text{NUMBER} & \text{SG} \end{bmatrix} \end{bmatrix} \end{bmatrix}
$$

Here the value found via the second argument's ⟨SUBJECT AGREEMENT⟩ feature is copied over to the corresponding place in the first argument. In addition, the AGREEMENT feature of the first argument receives a value as a side-effect of the index linking it to the end of ⟨SUBJECT AGREEMENT⟩ feature.

The next example demonstrates the important difference between features that actually share values versus those that merely have similar values.

(11.2)
$$
\begin{bmatrix} \text{AGREEMENT} & \begin{bmatrix} \text{NUMBER} & \text{SG} \end{bmatrix} \\ \text{SUBJECT} & \begin{bmatrix} \text{AGREEMENT} & \begin{bmatrix} \text{NUMBER} & \text{SG} \end{bmatrix} \end{bmatrix} \end{bmatrix}
$$

$$
\sqcup \begin{bmatrix} \text{SUBJECT} & \begin{bmatrix} \text{AGREEMENT} & \begin{bmatrix} \text{PERSON} & 3 \\ \text{NUMBER} & \text{SG} \end{bmatrix} \end{bmatrix} \end{bmatrix}
$$

$$
= \begin{bmatrix} \text{AGREEMENT} & \begin{bmatrix} \text{NUMBER} & \text{SG} \end{bmatrix} \\ \text{SUBJECT} & \begin{bmatrix} \text{AGREEMENT} & \begin{bmatrix} \text{NUMBER} & \text{SG} \\ \text{PERSON} & 3 \end{bmatrix} \end{bmatrix} \end{bmatrix}
$$

The values at the end of the ⟨SUBJECT AGREEMENT⟩ path and the ⟨AGREEMENT⟩ path are the same, but not shared, in the first argument. The unification of the SUBJECT features of the two arguments adds the PERSON information from the second argument to the result. However, since there is no index linking the AGREEMENT feature to the ⟨SUBJECT AGREEMENT⟩ feature, this information is not added to the value of the AGREEMENT feature.

Finally, consider the following example of a failure to unify.

$$
\begin{bmatrix} \text{AGREEMENT} & \boxed{1} \begin{bmatrix} \text{NUMBER} & \text{SG} \\ \text{PERSON} & 3 \end{bmatrix} \\ \text{SUBJECT} & \begin{bmatrix} \text{AGREEMENT} & \boxed{1} \end{bmatrix} \end{bmatrix}
$$

$$
\sqcup \begin{bmatrix} \text{AGREEMENT} & \begin{bmatrix} \text{NUMBER} & \text{SG} \\ \text{PERSON} & 3 \end{bmatrix} \\ \text{SUBJECT} & \begin{bmatrix} \text{AGREEMENT} & \begin{bmatrix} \text{NUMBER} & \text{PL} \\ \text{PERSON} & 3 \end{bmatrix} \end{bmatrix} \end{bmatrix}
$$

Fails!

Proceeding through the features in order, we first find that the AGREEMENT features in these examples successfully match. However, when we move on to the SUBJECT features, we find that the values found at the end of the respective ⟨ SUBJECT AGREEMENT NUMBER ⟩ paths differ, causing a unification failure.

Feature structures are a way of representing partial information about some linguistic object or placing informational constraints on what the object can be. Unification can be seen as a way of merging the information in each feature structure, or describing objects which satisfy both sets of constraints. Intuitively, unifying two feature structures produces a new feature structure which is more specific (has more information) than, or is identical to, either

SUBSUMES of the input feature structures. We say that a less specific (more abstract) feature structure **subsumes** an equally or more specific one. Subsumption is represented by the operator $\sqsubseteq$. A feature structure F subsumes a feature structure G ($F \sqsubseteq G$) if and only if:

1. For every feature x in F, $F(x) \sqsubseteq G(x)$ (where $F(x)$ means "the value of the feature x of feature structure F").
2. For all paths p and q in F such that $F(p) = F(q)$, it is also the case that $G(p) = G(q)$.

For example, consider these feature structures:

(11.3) $\begin{bmatrix} \text{NUMBER} & \text{SG} \end{bmatrix}$

(11.4) $\begin{bmatrix} \text{PERSON} & 3 \end{bmatrix}$

(11.5) $\begin{bmatrix} \text{NUMBER} & \text{SG} \\ \text{PERSON} & 3 \end{bmatrix}$

(11.6) $\begin{bmatrix} \text{CAT} & \text{VP} \\ \text{AGREEMENT} & \boxed{1} \\ \text{SUBJECT} & \begin{bmatrix} \text{AGREEMENT} & \boxed{1} \end{bmatrix} \end{bmatrix}$

(11.7) $\begin{bmatrix} \text{CAT} & \text{VP} \\ \text{AGREEMENT} & \boxed{1} \\ \text{SUBJECT} & \begin{bmatrix} \text{AGREEMENT} & \begin{bmatrix} \text{PERSON} & 3 \\ \text{NUMBER} & \text{SG} \end{bmatrix} \end{bmatrix} \end{bmatrix}$

(11.8) $\begin{bmatrix} \text{CAT} & \text{VP} \\ \text{AGREEMENT} & \boxed{1} \\ \text{SUBJECT} & \begin{bmatrix} \text{AGREEMENT} & \boxed{1} \begin{bmatrix} \text{PERSON} & 3 \\ \text{NUMBER} & \text{SG} \end{bmatrix} \end{bmatrix} \end{bmatrix}$

The following subsumption relations hold among them:

$$11.3 \sqsubseteq 11.5$$
$$11.4 \sqsubseteq 11.5$$
$$11.6 \sqsubseteq 11.7 \sqsubseteq 11.8$$

Subsumption is a partial ordering; there are pairs of feature structures that neither subsume nor are subsumed by each other:

$11.3 \not\sqsubseteq 11.4$

$11.4 \not\sqsubseteq 11.3$

Since every feature structure is subsumed by the empty structure [], the relation among feature structures can be defined as a **semilattice**. The semi-   SEMILATTICE
lattice is often represented pictorially with the most general feature [] at the top and the subsumption relation represented by lines between feature structures. Unification can be defined in terms of the subsumption semilattice. Given two feature structures F and G, $F \sqcup G$ is defined as the most general feature structure H such that $F \sqsubseteq H$ and $G \sqsubseteq H$. Since the information ordering defined by unification is a semilattice, the unification operation is **monotonic** (Pereira and Shieber, 1984; Rounds and Kasper, 1986; Moshier,   MONOTONIC
1988). This means that if some description is true of a feature structure, unifying it with another feature structure results in a feature structure that still satisfies the original description. The unification operation is therefore order-independent; given a set of feature structures to unify, we can check them in any order and get the same result. Thus in the above example we could instead have chosen to check the AGREEMENT attribute first and the unification still would have failed.

To summarize, unification is a way of implementing the integration of knowledge from different constraints. Given two compatible feature structures as input, it produces the most general feature structure which nonetheless contains all the information in the inputs. Given two incompatible feature structures, it fails.

11.3 FEATURES STRUCTURES IN THE GRAMMAR

Our primary purpose in introducing feature structures and unification has been to provide a way to elegantly express syntactic constraints that would be difficult to express using the mechanisms of context-free grammars alone. Our next step, therefore, is to specify a way to integrate feature structures and unification operations into the specification of a grammar. This can be accomplished by *augmenting* the rules of ordinary context-free grammars with attachments that specify feature structures for the constituents of the rules, along with appropriate unification operations that express constraints on those constituents. From a grammatical point of view, these attachments will be used to accomplish the following goals:

- to associate complex feature structures with both lexical items and instances of grammatical categories
- to guide the composition of feature structures for larger grammatical constituents based on the feature structures of their component parts
- to enforce compatibility constraints between specified parts of grammatical constructions

We will use the following notation to denote the grammar augmentations that will allow us to accomplish all of these goals, based on the PATR-II system described in Shieber (1986):

$$\beta_0 \rightarrow \beta_1 \cdots \beta_n$$
$$\{set\ of\ constraints\}$$

The specified constraints have one of the following forms.

$$\langle \beta_i\ feature\ path \rangle = Atomic\ value$$
$$\langle \beta_i\ feature\ path \rangle = \langle \beta_j\ feature\ path \rangle$$

The notation $\langle \beta_i\ feature\ path \rangle$ denotes a feature path through the feature structure associated with the β_i component of the context-free part of the rule. The first style of constraint specifies that the value found at the end of the given path must unify with the specified atomic value. The second form specifies that the values found at the end of the two given paths must be unifiable.

To illustrate the use of these constraints, let us return to the informal solution to the number agreement problem proposed at the beginning of this chapter.

$$S \rightarrow NP\ VP$$

Only if the number of the NP is equal to the number of the VP.

Using the new notation, this rule can now be expressed as follows.

$$S \rightarrow NP\ VP$$
$$\langle NP\ \text{NUMBER} \rangle = \langle VP\ \text{NUMBER} \rangle$$

Note that in cases where there are two or more constituents of the same syntactic category in a rule, we will subscript the constituents to keep them straight, as in $VP \rightarrow V\ NP_1\ NP_2$.

Taking a step back from the notation, it is important to note that in this approach the simple generative nature of context-free rules has been fundamentally changed by this augmentation. Ordinary context-free rules are based on the simple notion of concatenation; an *NP* followed by a *VP* is an *S*, or generatively, to produce an *S* all we need to do is concatenate an *NP* to a *VP*. In the new scheme, this concatenation must be accompanied by a successful unification operation. This leads naturally to questions about the computational complexity of the unification operation and its effect on the generative power of this new grammar. These issues will be discussed in Chapter 13.

To review, there are two fundamental components to this approach.

- The elements of context-free grammar rules will have feature-based constraints associated with them. This reflects a shift from atomic grammatical categories to more complex categories with properties.

- The constraints associated with individual rules can refer to, and manipulate, the feature structures associated with the parts of the rule to which they are attached.

The following sections present applications of unification constraints to four interesting linguistic phenomena: agreement, grammatical heads, subcategorization, and long-distance dependencies.

Agreement

As discussed in Chapter 9, agreement phenomena show up in a number of different places in English. This section illustrates how unification can be used to capture the two main types of English agreement phenomena: subject-verb agreement and determiner-nominal agreement. We will use the following ATIS sentences as examples throughout this discussion to illustrate these phenomena.

(11.9) This flight serves breakfast.

(11.10) Does this flight serve breakfast?

(11.11) Do these flights serve breakfast?

Notice that the constraint used to enforce SUBJECT-VERB agreement given above is deficient in that it ignores the PERSON feature. The following constraint which makes use of the AGREEMENT feature takes care of this problem.

$$S \rightarrow NP\ VP$$

$$\langle NP\ \text{AGREEMENT} \rangle = \langle VP\ \text{AGREEMENT} \rangle$$

Examples 11.10 and 11.11 illustrate a minor variation on SUBJECT-VERB agreement. In these yes-no-questions, the subject *NP* must agree with the auxiliary verb, rather than the main verb of the sentence, which appears in a non-finite form. This agreement constraint can be handled by the following rule.

$S \rightarrow Aux\ NP\ VP$

$\langle Aux\ \text{AGREEMENT} \rangle = \langle NP\ \text{AGREEMENT} \rangle$

Agreement between determiners and nominals in noun phrases is handled in a similar fashion. The basic task is to allow the forms given above, but block the unwanted *this flights and *those flight forms where the determiners and nominals clash in their NUMBER feature. Again, the logical place to enforce this constraint is in the grammar rule that brings the parts together.

$NP \rightarrow Det\ Nominal$

$\langle Det\ \text{AGREEMENT} \rangle = \langle Nominal\ \text{AGREEMENT} \rangle$

$\langle NP\ \text{AGREEMENT} \rangle = \langle Nominal\ \text{AGREEMENT} \rangle$

This rule states that the AGREEMENT feature of the *Det* must unify with the AGREEMENT feature of the *Nominal*, and moreover, that the AGREEMENT feature of the *NP* is constrained to be the same as that of the *Nominal*.

Having expressed the constraints needed to enforce subject-verb and determiner-nominal agreement, we must now fill in the rest of the machinery needed to make these constraints work. Specifically, we must consider how the various constituents that take part in these constraints (the *Aux*, *VP*, *NP*, *Det*, and *Nominal*) acquire values for their various agreement features.

We can begin by noting that our constraints involve both lexical and non-lexical constituents. The simpler lexical constituents, *Aux* and *Det*, receive values for their respective agreement features directly from the lexicon as in the following rules.

$Aux \rightarrow do$

$\langle Aux\ \text{AGREEMENT NUMBER} \rangle = \text{PL}$

$\langle Aux\ \text{AGREEMENT PERSON} \rangle = 3$

$Aux \rightarrow does$

$\langle S\ \text{AGREEMENT NUMBER} \rangle = \text{SG}$

$\langle S\ \text{AGREEMENT PERSON} \rangle = 3$

$Determiner \rightarrow this$

$\langle Determiner\ \text{AGREEMENT NUMBER} \rangle = \text{SG}$

Determiner → *these*

⟨*Determiner* AGREEMENT NUMBER⟩ = PL

Returning to our first *S* rule, let us first consider the AGREEMENT feature for the *VP* constituent. The constituent structure for this *VP* is specified by the following rule.

VP → *Verb NP*

It seems clear that the agreement constraint for this constituent must be based on its constituent verb. This verb, as with the previous lexical entries, can acquire its agreement feature values directly from lexicon as in the following rules.

Verb → *serve*

⟨*Verb* AGREEMENT NUMBER⟩ = PL

Verb → *serves*

⟨*Verb* AGREEMENT NUMBER⟩ = SG

⟨*Verb* AGREEMENT PERSON⟩ = 3

All that remains is to stipulate that the agreement feature of the parent *VP* is constrained to be the same as its verb constituent.

VP → *Verb NP*

⟨*VP* AGREEMENT⟩ = ⟨*Verb* AGREEMENT⟩

In other words, non-lexical grammatical constituents can acquire values for at least some of their features from their component constituents.

The same technique works for the remaining *NP* and *Nominal* categories. The values for the agreement features for these categories are derived from the nouns *flight* and *flights*.

Noun → *flight*

⟨*Noun* AGREEMENT NUMBER⟩ = SG

Noun → *flights*

⟨*Noun* AGREEMENT NUMBER⟩ = PL

Similarly, the *Nominal* features are constrained to have the same values as its constituent noun, as follows.

Nominal → *Noun*

⟨*Nominal* AGREEMENT⟩ = ⟨*Noun* AGREEMENT⟩

Note that this section has only scratched the surface of the English agreement system, and that the agreement system of other languages can be considerably more complex than English.

Head Features

To account for the way compositional grammatical constituents such as noun phrases, nominals, and verb phrases come to have agreement features, the preceding section introduced the notion of copying needed feature structures from children to their parents. This use turns out to be a specific instance of a much more general phenomenon in constraint-based grammars. Specifically, the features for most grammatical categories are copied from *one* of the children to the parent. The child that provides the features is called the **head of the phrase**, and the features copied are referred to as **head features**.

HEAD OF THE PHRASE
HEAD FEATURES

To make this clear, consider the following three rules from the last section.

$VP \rightarrow Verb\ NP$

$\langle VP\ \text{AGREEMENT} \rangle = \langle Verb\ \text{AGREEMENT} \rangle$

$NP \rightarrow Det\ Nominal$

$\langle Det\ \text{AGREEMENT} \rangle = \langle Nominal\ \text{AGREEMENT} \rangle$

$\langle NP\ \text{AGREEMENT} \rangle = \langle Nominal\ \text{AGREEMENT} \rangle$

$Nominal \rightarrow Noun$

$\langle Nominal\ \text{AGREEMENT} \rangle = \langle Noun\ \text{AGREEMENT} \rangle$

In each of these rules, the constituent providing the agreement feature structure up to the parent is the head of the phrase. More specifically, the verb is the head of the verb phrase, the nominal is the head of the noun phrase, and the noun is the head of the nominal. In addition, we can say that the agreement feature structure is a head feature. We can rewrite our rules to reflect these generalizations by placing the agreement feature structure under a HEAD feature and then copying that feature upward as in the following constraints.

$VP \rightarrow Verb\ NP$ (11.12)

$\langle VP\ \text{HEAD} \rangle = \langle Verb\ \text{HEAD} \rangle$

$NP \rightarrow Det\ Nominal$ (11.13)

$\langle NP\ \text{HEAD} \rangle = \langle Nominal\ \text{HEAD} \rangle$

$\langle Det\ \text{HEAD AGREEMENT} \rangle = \langle Nominal\ \text{HEAD AGREEMENT} \rangle$

$Nominal \rightarrow Noun$ (11.14)

$\quad \langle Nominal \text{ HEAD} \rangle = \langle Noun \text{ HEAD} \rangle$

Similarly, the lexical rules that introduce these features must now reflect this HEAD notion, as in the following.

$Noun \rightarrow flights$

$\quad \langle Noun \text{ HEAD AGREEMENT NUMBER} \rangle = \text{PL}$

$Verb \rightarrow serves$

$\quad \langle Verb \text{ HEAD AGREEMENT NUMBER} \rangle = \text{SG}$

$\quad \langle Verb \text{ HEAD AGREEMENT PERSON} \rangle = 3$

The notion of a head is an extremely significant one in grammar, because it provides a way for a syntactic rule to be linked to a particular word. In this way heads will play an important role in the **dependency grammars** and **lexicalized grammars** of Chapter 12, and the **head transducers** mentioned in Chapter 21.

Subcategorization

Recall that subcategorization is the notion that verbs can be picky about the patterns of arguments they will allow themselves to appear with. In Chapter 9, to prevent the generation of ungrammatical sentences with verbs and verb phrases that do not match, we were forced to split the category of verb into multiple sub-categories. These more specific verb categories were then used in the definition of the specific verb phrases that they were allowed to occur with, as in the following rule.

$Verb\text{-}with\text{-}S\text{-}comp \rightarrow think$

$VP \rightarrow Verb\text{-}with\text{-}S\text{-}comp \ S$

Clearly, this approach introduces exactly the same undesirable proliferation of categories that we saw with the similar approach to solving the number problem. The proper way to avoid this proliferation is to introduce feature structures to distinguish among the various members of the verb category. This goal can be accomplished by associating an atomic feature called SUBCAT, with an appropriate value, with each of the verbs in the lexicon. For example, the transitive version of *serves* could be assigned the following feature structure in the lexicon.

$Verb \rightarrow serves$

$\langle Verb$ HEAD AGREEMENT NUMBER$\rangle$ = SG

$\langle Verb$ HEAD SUBCAT$\rangle$ = TRANS

The SUBCAT feature is a signal to the rest of the grammar that this verb should only appear in verb phrases with a single noun phrase argument. This constraint is enforced by adding corresponding constraints to all the verb phrase rules in the grammar, as in the following.

$VP \rightarrow Verb$

$\langle VP$ HEAD$\rangle$ = $\langle Verb$ HEAD$\rangle$

$\langle VP$ HEAD SUBCAT$\rangle$ = INTRANS

$VP \rightarrow Verb\ NP$

$\langle VP$ HEAD$\rangle$ = $\langle Verb$ HEAD$\rangle$

$\langle VP$ HEAD SUBCAT$\rangle$ = TRANS

$VP \rightarrow Verb\ NP\ NP$

$\langle VP$ HEAD$\rangle$ = $\langle Verb$ HEAD$\rangle$

$\langle VP$ HEAD SUBCAT$\rangle$ = DITRANS

The first unification constraint in these rules states that the verb phrase receives its HEAD features from its verb constituent, while the second constraint specifies what the value of that SUBCAT feature must be. Any attempt to use a verb with an inappropriate verb phrase will fail since the value of the SUBCAT feature of the *VP* will fail to unify with the atomic symbol given in second constraint. Note this approach requires unique symbols for each of the 50–100 verb phrase frames in English.

This is a somewhat opaque approach since these unanalyzable SUBCAT symbols do not directly encode either the number or type of the arguments that the verb expects to take. To see this, note that one can not simply examine a verb's entry in the lexicon and know what its subcategorization frame is. Rather, you must use the value of the SUBCAT feature indirectly as a pointer to those verb phrase rules in the grammar that can accept the verb in question.

A somewhat more elegant solution, which makes better use of the expressive power of feature structures, allows the verb entries to directly specify the order and category type of the arguments they require. The following entry for *serves* is an example of one such approach, in which the verb's subcategory feature expresses a **list** of its objects and complements.

Verb → *serves*

⟨*Verb* HEAD AGREEMENT NUMBER⟩ = SG

⟨*Verb* HEAD SUBCAT FIRST CAT⟩ = NP

⟨*Verb* HEAD SUBCAT SECOND⟩ = END

This entry uses the FIRST feature to state that the first post-verbal argument must be an *NP*; the value of the SECOND feature indicates that this verb expects only one argument. A verb like *leave Boston in the morning*, with two arguments, would have the following kind of entry.

Verb → *leaves*

⟨*Verb* HEAD AGREEMENT NUMBER⟩ = SG

⟨*Verb* HEAD SUBCAT FIRST CAT⟩ = NP

⟨*Verb* HEAD SUBCAT SECOND CAT⟩ = PP

⟨*Verb* HEAD SUBCAT THIRD⟩ = END

This scheme is, of course, a rather baroque way of encoding a list; it is also possible to use the idea of **types** defined in Section 11.6 to define a list type more cleanly.

The individual verb phrase rules must now check for the presence of exactly the elements specified by their verb, as in the following transitive rule.

VP → *Verb NP*   (11.15)

⟨*VP* HEAD⟩ = ⟨*Verb* HEAD⟩

⟨*VP* HEAD SUBCAT FIRST CAT⟩ = ⟨*NP* CAT ⟩

⟨*VP* HEAD SUBCAT SECOND⟩ = END

The second constraint in this rule's constraints states that the category of the first element of the verb's SUBCAT list must match the category of the constituent immediately following the verb. The third constraint goes on to state that this verb phrase rule expects only a single argument.

Our previous examples have shown rather simple subcategorization structures for verbs. In fact, verbs can subcategorize for quite complex **sub-categorization frames**, (e.g., *NP PP*, *NP NP*, or *NP S*) and these frames can be composed of many different phrasal types. In order to come up with a list of possible subcategorization frames for English verbs, we first need to have a list of possible phrase types that can make up these frames. Figure 11.3 shows one short list of possible phrase types for making up subcategorization

SUBCATEGORIZATION
FRAME

frames for verbs; this list is modified from one used to create verb subcategorization frames in the FrameNet project (Johnson, 1999; Baker et al., 1998),
and includes phrase types for special subjects of verbs like *there* and *it*, as
well as for objects and complements.

Noun Phrase Types		
There	nonreferential there	**There** *is still much to learn*
It	nonreferential it	**It** *was evident that my ideas*
NP	noun phrase	*As he was relating* **his story**
Preposition Phrase Types		
PP	preposition phrase	*couch their message* **in terms**
PPing	gerundive PP	*censured him* **for not having intervened**
PPpart	particle	*turn it* **off**
Verb Phrase Types		
VPbrst	bare stem VP	*she could* **discuss it**
VPto	to-marked infin. VP	*Why do you want* **to know**?
VPwh	wh-VP	*it is worth considering* **how to write**
VPing	gerundive VP	*I would consider* **using it**
Complement Clause types		
Finite Clause		
Sfin	finite clause	*maintain* **that the situation was unsatisfactory**
Swh	wh-clause	*it tells us* **where we are**
Sif	whether/if clause	*ask* **whether Aristophanes is depicting a**
Nonfinite Clause		
Sing	gerundive clause	*see* **some attention being given**
Sto	to-marked clause	*know* **themselves to be relatively unhealthy**
Sforto	for-to clause	*She was waiting* **for him to make some reply**
Sbrst	bare stem clause	*commanded* **that his sermons be published**
Other Types		
AjP	adjective phrase	*thought it* **possible**
Quo	quotes	*asked* **"What was it like?"**

Figure 11.3   A small set of potential phrase types which can be combined
to create a set of potential subcategorization frames for verbs. Modified from
the FrameNet tagset (Johnson, 1999; Baker et al., 1998). The sample sentence
fragments are from the British National Corpus.

To use the phrase types in Figure 11.3 in a unification grammar, each
phrase type would have to be described using features. For example the form
VPto, which is subcategorized for by *want* might be expressed as:

Verb → *want*

⟨*Verb* HEAD SUBCAT FIRST CAT⟩ = VP

⟨*Verb* HEAD SUBCAT FIRST FORM⟩ = INFINITIVE

Each of the 50 to 100 possible verb subcategorization frames in English would be described as a set drawn from these phrase types. For example, here's an example of the two-complement *want*. We've used this following example to demonstrate two different notational possibilities. First, lists can be represented via an angle brackets notation ⟨ and ⟩. Second, instead of using a rewrite-rule annotated with path equations, we can represent the lexical entry as a single feature structure:

$$
\begin{bmatrix}
\text{ORTH} & \text{WANT} \\
\text{CAT} & \text{VERB} \\
\text{HEAD} & \begin{bmatrix} \text{SUBCAT} & \left\langle \begin{bmatrix} \text{CAT NP} \end{bmatrix}, \begin{bmatrix} \text{CAT VP} \\ \text{HEAD} \begin{bmatrix} \text{VFORM INFINITIVE} \end{bmatrix} \end{bmatrix} \right\rangle \end{bmatrix}
\end{bmatrix}
$$

Combining even a limited set of phrase types results in a very large set of possible subcategorization frames. Furthermore, each verb allows many different subcategorization frames. For example, here are just some of the subcategorization patterns for the verb *ask*, with examples from the BNC:

Subcat	Example
Quo	asked [$_{Quo}$ "What was it like?"]
NP	asking [$_{NP}$ a question]
Swh	asked [$_{Swh}$ what trades you're interested in]
Sto	ask [$_{Sto}$ him to tell you]
PP	that means asking [$_{PP}$ at home]
Vto	asked [$_{Vto}$ to see a girl called Evelyn]
NP Sif	asked [$_{NP}$ him] [$_{Sif}$ whether he could make]
NP NP	asked [$_{NP}$ myself] [$_{NP}$ a question]
NP Swh	asked [$_{NP}$ him] [$_{Swh}$ why he took time off]

A number of comprehensive subcategorization-frame tagsets exist, such as the COMLEX set (Macleod et al., 1998), which includes subcategorization frames for verbs, adjectives, and nouns, and the ACQUILEX tagset of verb subcategorization frames (Sanfilippo, 1993). Many subcategorization-frame tagsets add other information about the complements, such as specifying the identity of the subject in a lower verb phrase that has no overt subject; this is called **control** information. For example *Temmy promised* control *Ruth to go* (at least in some dialects) implies that Temmy will do the going, while *Temmy persuaded Ruth to go* implies that Ruth will do the going. Some of the multiple possible subcategorization frames for a verb can be partially predicted by the semantics of the verb; for example many verbs of transfer (like *give*, *send*, *carry*) predictably take the two subcategorization frames *NP NP* and *NP PP*:

NP NP   sent FAA Administrator James Busey a letter
NP PP   sent a letter to the chairman of the Armed Services Committee

ALTERNATIONS

These relationships between subcategorization frames across classes of verbs are called argument-structure **alternations**, and will be discussed in Chapter 16 when we discuss the semantics of verbal argument structure. Chapter 12 will introduce probabilities for modeling the fact that verbs generally have preferences even among the different subcategorization frames they allow.

Subcategorization in Other Parts of Speech

VALENCE

Although the notion of subcategorization, or **valence** as it is often called, was originally designed for verbs, more recent work has focused on the fact that many other kinds of words exhibit forms of valence-like behavior. Consider the following contrasting uses of the prepositions *while* and *during*.

(11.16) Keep your seatbelt fastened while we are taking off.

(11.17) *Keep your seatbelt fastened *while takeoff.

(11.18) Keep your seatbelt fastened during takeoff.

(11.19) *Keep your seatbelt fastened during we are taking off.

Despite the apparent similarities between these words, they make quite different demands on their arguments. Representing these differences is left as Exercise 11.5 for the reader.

Many adjectives and nouns also have subcategorization frames. Here are some examples using the adjectives *apparent*, *aware*, and *unimportant* and the nouns *assumption* and *question*:

It was **apparent** [$_{Sfin}$ that the kitchen was the only room. . .]
It was **apparent** [$_{PP}$ from the way she rested her hand over his]
aware [$_{Sfin}$ he may have caused offense]
it is **unimportant** [$_{Swheth}$ whether only a little bit is accepted]
the **assumption** [$_{Sfin}$ that wasteful methods have been employed]
the **question** [$_{Swheth}$ whether the authorities might have decided]

See Macleod et al. (1998) and Johnson (1999) for descriptions of subcategorization frames for nouns and adjectives.

Verbs express subcategorization constraints on their subjects as well as their complements. For example, we need to represent the lexical fact that the verb *seem* can take a **Sfin** as its subject (*That she was affected seems obvious*), while the verb *paint* cannot. The SUBJECT feature can be used to express these constraints.

Long-Distance Dependencies

The model of subcategorization we have developed so far has two components. Each head word has a SUBCAT feature which contains a list of the complements it expects. Then phrasal rules like the *VP* rule in (11.16) match up each expected complement in the SUBCAT list with an actual constituent. This mechanism works fine when the complements of a verb are in fact to be found in the verb phrase.

Sometimes, however, a constituent subcategorized for by the verb is not locally instantiated, but is in a **long-distance** relationship with the predicate. Here are some examples of such **long-distance dependencies**:

LONG-DISTANCE
DEPENDENCIES

What cities does Continental service?
What flights do you have from Boston to Baltimore?
What time does that flight leave Atlanta?

In the first example, the constituent *what cities* is subcategorized for by the verb *service*, but because the sentence is an example of a **wh-non-subject-question**, the object is located at the front of the sentence. Recall from Chapter 9 that a (simple) phrase-structure rule for a **wh-non-subject-question** is something like the following:

$S \rightarrow$ *Wh-NP Aux NP VP*

Now that we have features, we'll be able to augment this phrase-structure rule to require the *Aux* and the *NP* to agree (since the *NP* is the subject). But we also need some way to augment the rule to tell it that the *Wh-NP* should fill some subcategorization slot in the *VP*. The representation of such long-distance dependencies is a quite difficult problem, because the verb whose subcategorization requirement is being filled can be quite distant from the filler. In the following (made-up) sentence, for example, the *wh*-phrase *which flight* must fill the subcategorization requirements of the verb *book*, despite the fact that there are two other verbs (*want* and *have*) in between:

Which flight do you want me to have the travel agent book?

Many solutions to representing long-distance dependencies in unification grammars involve keeping a list, often called a **gap list**, implemented

GAP LIST

as a feature GAP, which is passed up from phrase to phrase in the parse
FILLER
tree. The **filler** (for example *which flight* above) is put on the gap list, and
must eventually be unified with the subcategorization frame of some verb.
See Sag and Wasow (1999) for an explanation of such a strategy, together
with a discussion of the many other complications that must be modeled in
long-distance dependencies.

11.4   IMPLEMENTING UNIFICATION

As discussed, the unification operator takes two feature structures as input
and returns a single merged feature structure if successful, or a failure signal if the two inputs are not compatible. The input feature structures are
represented as directed acyclic graphs (DAGs), where features are depicted
as labels on directed edges, and feature values are either atomic symbols or
DAGs. As we will see, the implementation of the operator is a relatively
straightforward recursive graph matching algorithm, suitably tailored to accommodate the various requirements of unification. Roughly speaking, the
algorithm loops through the features in one input and attempts to find a corresponding feature in the other. If all of the features match, then the unification
is successful. If any single feature causes a mismatch then the unification
fails. Not surprisingly, the recursion is motivated by the need to correctly
match those features that have feature structures as their values.

One somewhat unusual aspect of the algorithm is that rather than construct a new output feature structure with the unified information from all the
information from the two arguments, it destructively alters the arguments so
that in the end they point to exactly the same information. Thus the result
of a successful call to the unification operator consists of suitably altered
versions of the arguments (failed unifications also result in alterations to the
arguments, but more on that later in Section 11.5.) As is discussed in the
next section, the destructive nature of this algorithm necessitates certain minor extensions to the simple graph version of feature structures as DAGs we
have been assuming.

Unification Data Structures

To facilitate the destructive merger aspect of the algorithm, we add a small
complication to the DAGs used to represent the input feature structures; feature structures are represented using DAGs with additional edges, or fields.

Specifically, each feature structure consists of two fields: a content field and a pointer field. The content field may be null or contain an ordinary feature structure. Similarly, the pointer field may be null or contain a pointer to another feature structure. If the pointer field of the DAG is null, then the content field of the DAG contains the actual feature structure to be processed. If, on the other hand, the pointer field is non-null, then the destination of the pointer represents the actual feature structure to be processed. The merger aspects of unification will be achieved by altering the pointer field of DAGs during processing.

To make this scheme somewhat more concrete, consider the extended DAG representation for the following familiar feature structure.

$$(11.20) \quad \begin{bmatrix} \text{NUMBER} & \text{SG} \\ \text{PERSON} & \text{3} \end{bmatrix}$$

The extended DAG representation is illustrated with our textual matrix diagrams by treating the CONTENT and POINTER fields as ordinary features, as in the following matrix.

$$(11.21) \quad \begin{bmatrix} \text{CONTENT} & \begin{bmatrix} \text{NUMBER} & \begin{bmatrix} \text{CONTENTS} & \text{SG} \\ \text{POINTER} & \text{NULL} \end{bmatrix} \\ \text{PERSON} & \begin{bmatrix} \text{CONTENTS} & \text{3} \\ \text{POINTER} & \text{NULL} \end{bmatrix} \end{bmatrix} \\ \text{POINTER} & \text{NULL} \end{bmatrix}$$

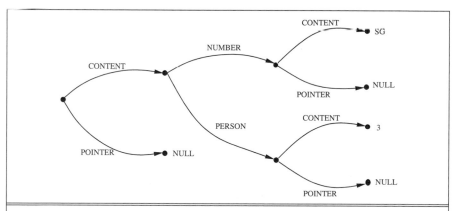

Figure 11.4   An extended DAG notation for Examples 11.20 and 11.21.

Figure 11.4 shows this extended representation in its graphical form. Note that the extended representation contains content and pointer links both for the top-level layer of features, as well as for each of the embedded feature structures all the way down to the atomic values.

Before going on to the details of the unification algorithm, we will illustrate the use of this extended DAG representation with the following simple example. The original extended representation of the arguments to this unification are shown in Figure 11.5.

(11.22) $\begin{bmatrix} \text{NUMBER} & \text{SG} \end{bmatrix} \sqcup \begin{bmatrix} \text{PERSON} & 3 \end{bmatrix} = \begin{bmatrix} \text{NUMBER} & \text{SG} \\ \text{PERSON} & 3 \end{bmatrix}$

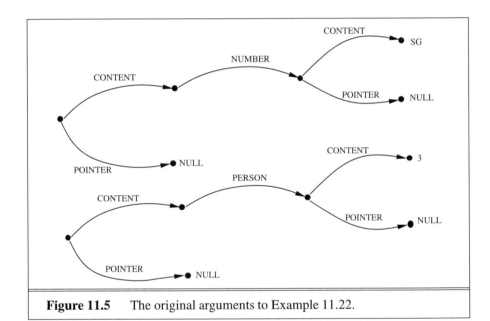

Figure 11.5   The original arguments to Example 11.22.

At a high level, we would simply say that the unification results in the creation of a new structure containing the union of the information from the two original arguments. With the extended notation, we can see how the unification is accomplished by making some additions to the original arguments and changing some of the pointers from one structure to the other so that in the end they contain the same content. In this example, this is accomplished by first adding a PERSON feature to the first argument, and assigning it a value by filling its POINTER field with a pointer to the appropriate location in the second argument, as shown in Figure 11.6.

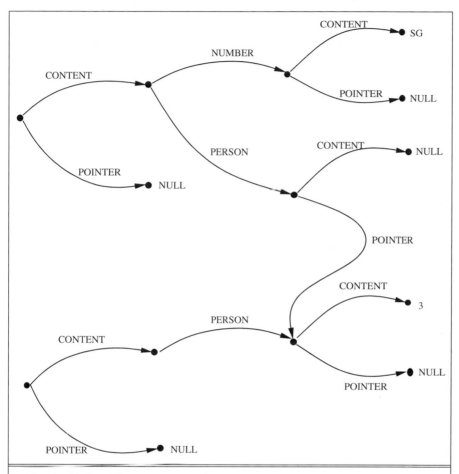

Figure 11.6   The arguments after assigning the first argument's new PER-SON feature to the appropriate value in the second argument.

The process is, however, not yet complete. While it is clear from Figure 11.6 that the first argument now contains all the correct information, the second one does not; it lacks a NUMBER feature. We could, of course, add a NUMBER feature to this argument with a pointer to the appropriate place in the first one. This change would result in the two arguments having all the correct information from this unification. Unfortunately, this solution is inadequate since it does not meet our requirement that the two arguments be truly unified. Since the two arguments are not completely unified at the top level, future unifications involving one of the arguments would not show up in the other. The solution to this problem is to simply set the POINTER field of the second argument to point at the first one. When this is done any future change to either argument will be immediately reflected in both. The result of this final change is shown in Figure 11.7.

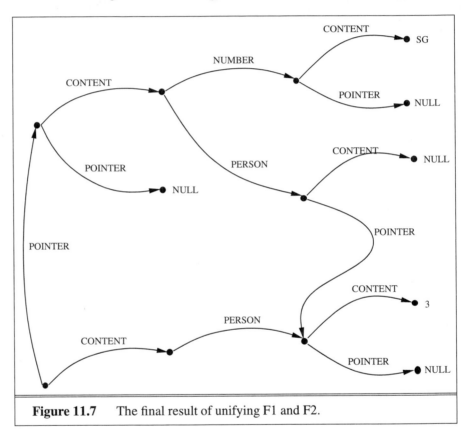

Figure 11.7   The final result of unifying F1 and F2.

The Unification Algorithm

The unification algorithm that we have been leading up to is shown in Figure 11.8. To review, this algorithm accepts two feature structures represented using the extended DAG representation. As can be seen from the code, it may return as its return either one of these arguments. This is, however, somewhat deceptive since the true effect of this algorithm is the destructive unification of the two inputs.

---

function UNIFY(*f1, f2*) **returns** *fstructure* or failure

  f1-real ← Real contents of *f1*
  f2-real ← Real contents of *f2*

  if *f1-real* is null **then**
    f1.pointer ← *f2*
    return *f2*
  else if *f2-real* is null **then**
    f2.pointer ← *f1*
    return *f1*
  else if *f1-real* and *f2-real* are identical **then**
    f1.pointer ← *f2*
    return *f2*
  else if both *f1-real* and *f2-real* are complex feature structures **then**
    f2.pointer ← *f1*
    for each *feature* **in** *f2-real* **do**
      other-feature ← Find or create
                      a feature corresponding to *feature* in *f1-real*
      if UNIFY(*feature.value, other-feature.value*) **returns** failure **then**
        return failure
    return *f1*
  else return failure

Figure 11.8   The unification algorithm.

The first step in this algorithm is to acquire the true contents of both of the arguments. Recall that if the pointer field of an extended feature structure is non-null, then the real content of that structure is found by following the pointer found in pointer field. The variables *f1-real* and *f2-real* are the result of this pointer following process, which is often referred to as **dereferencing**.

DEREFERENCING

As with all recursive algorithms, the next step is to test for the various base cases of the recursion before proceeding on to a recursive call involving some part of the original arguments. In this case, there are three possible base cases:

- One or both of the arguments has a null value.
- The arguments are identical.
- The arguments are non-complex and non-identical.

In the case where either of the arguments is null, the pointer field for the null argument is changed to point to the other argument, which is then returned. The result is that both structures now point at the same value.

If the structures are identical, then the pointer of the first is set to the second and the second is returned. It is important to understand why this pointer change is done in this case. After all, since the arguments are identical, returning either one would appear to suffice. This might be true for a single unification but recall that we want the two arguments to the unification operator to be truly unified. The pointer change is necessary since we want the arguments to be truly identical, so that any subsequent unification that adds information to one will add it to both.

If neither of the preceding tests is true then there are two possibilities: they are non-identical atomic values, or they are non-identical complex structures. The former case signals an incompatibility in the arguments that leads the algorithm to return a failure signal. In the latter case, a recursive call is needed to ensure that the component parts of these complex structures are compatible. In this implementation, the key to the recursion is a loop over all the features of the *second* argument, *f2*. This loop attempts to unify the value of each feature in *f2* with the corresponding feature in *f1*. In this loop, if a feature is encountered in *f2* that is missing from *f1*, a feature is added to *f1* and given the value NULL. Processing then continues as if the feature had been there to begin with. If *every* one of these unifications succeeds, then the pointer field of *f2* is set to *f1* completing the unification of the structures and *f1* is returned as the value of the unification.

We should note that an unfortunate aspect of this algorithm is that it is capable of producing feature structures containing cycles. This situation can arise when the algorithm is asked to unify a structure with a second structure that contains the first as a subpart. The way to avoid this situation is to employ what is called an **occur check** (Robinson, 1965). This check analyzes the input DAGs and returns *failure* when one of the arguments is contained as a subpart of the other. In practice, this check is omitted from most implementations due to its computational cost.

OCCUR CHECK

An Example

To illustrate this algorithm, let's walk through the following example.

$$(11.23) \quad \begin{bmatrix} \text{AGREEMENT} & \boxed{1}\begin{bmatrix} \text{NUMBER} & \text{SG} \end{bmatrix} \\ \text{SUBJECT} & \begin{bmatrix} \text{AGREEMENT} & \boxed{1} \end{bmatrix} \end{bmatrix}$$
$$\sqcup \begin{bmatrix} \text{SUBJECT} & \begin{bmatrix} \text{AGREEMENT} & \begin{bmatrix} \text{PERSON} & 3 \end{bmatrix} \end{bmatrix} \end{bmatrix}$$

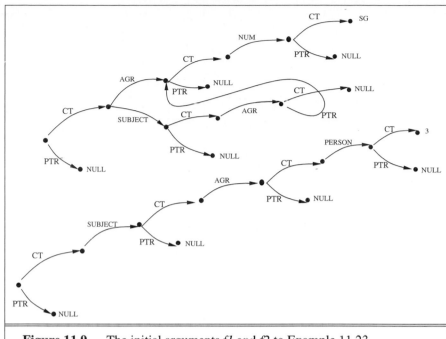

Figure 11.9   The initial arguments *f1* and *f2* to Example 11.23.

Figure 11.9 shows the extended representations for the arguments to this unification. Note how the reentrant structure in the first argument is captured through the use of the PTR field.

These original arguments are neither identical, nor null, nor atomic, so the main loop is entered. Looping over the features of *f2*, the algorithm is led to a recursive attempt to unify the values of the corresponding SUBJECT features of *f1* and *f2*.

$$\begin{bmatrix} \text{AGREEMENT} & \boxed{1} \end{bmatrix} \sqcup \begin{bmatrix} \text{AGREEMENT} & \begin{bmatrix} \text{PERSON} & 3 \end{bmatrix} \end{bmatrix}$$

These arguments are also non-identical, non-null, and non-atomic so the loop is entered again leading to a recursive check of the values of the AGREEMENT features.

$$\begin{bmatrix} \text{NUMBER} & \text{SG} \end{bmatrix} \sqcup \begin{bmatrix} \text{PERSON} & 3 \end{bmatrix}$$

In looping over the features of the second argument, the fact that the first argument lacks a PERSON feature is discovered. A PERSON feature

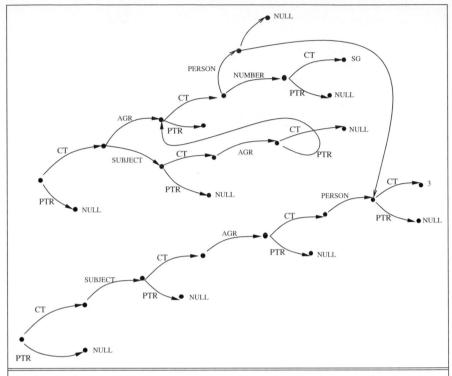

Figure 11.10   *f1* and *f2* after the recursion adds the value of the new PERSON feature.

initialized with a NULL value is, therefore, added to the first argument. This, in effect, changes the previous unification to the following.

$$\begin{bmatrix} \text{NUMBER} & \text{SG} \\ \text{PERSON} & \text{NULL} \end{bmatrix} \sqcup \begin{bmatrix} \text{PERSON} & 3 \end{bmatrix}$$

After creating this new PERSON feature, the next recursive call leads to the unification of the NULL value of the new feature in the first argument with the 3 value of the second argument. This recursive call results in the assignment of the pointer field of the first argument to the 3 value in *f2*, as shown in 11.10.

Since there are no further features to check in the *f2* argument at any level of recursion, each in turn sets the pointer for its *f2* argument to point at its *f1* argument and returns it. The result of all these assignments is shown in Figure 11.11.

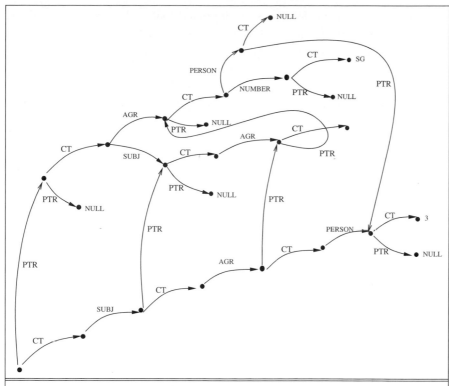

Figure 11.11   The final structures of *f1* and *f2* at the end.

11.5 PARSING WITH UNIFICATION CONSTRAINTS

We now have all the pieces necessary to integrate feature structures and unification into a parser. Fortunately, the order-independent nature of unification allows us to largely ignore the actual search strategy used in the parser.
Once we have unification constraints associated with the context-free rules
of the grammar, and feature structures with the states of the search, any of
the standard search algorithms described in Chapter 10 can be used.

Of course, this leaves a fairly large range of possible implementation
strategies. We could, for example, simply parse as we did before using the
context-free components of the rules, and then build the feature structures
for the resulting trees after the fact, filtering out those parses that contain
unification failures. Although such an approach would result in only well-
formed structures in the end, it fails to use the power of unification to reduce
the size of the parser's search space during parsing.

The next section describes an approach that makes better use of the power of unification by integrating unification constraints directly into the Earley parsing process, allowing ill-formed structures to be eliminated as soon as they are proposed. As we will see, this approach requires only minimal changes to the basic Earley algorithm. We then move on to briefly consider an approach to unification parsing that moves even further away from standard context-free methods.

Integrating Unification into an Earley Parser

We have two goals in integrating feature structures and unification into the Earley algorithm: to use feature structures to provide a richer representation for the constituents of the parse, and to block the entry into the chart of ill-formed constituents that violate unification constraints. As we will see, these goals can be accomplished via fairly minimal changes to the original Earley scheme given on page 381.

The first change involves the various representations used in the original code. Recall that the Earley algorithm operates by using a set of unadorned context-free grammar rules to fill in a data-structure called a chart with a set of states. At the end of the parse, the states that make up this chart represent all possible parses of the input. Therefore, we begin our changes by altering the representations of both the context-free grammar rules, and the states in the chart.

The rules are altered so that in addition to their current components, they also include a feature structure derived from their unification constraints. More specifically, we will use the constraints listed with a rule to build a feature structure, represented as a DAG, for use with that rule during parsing.

Consider the following context-free rule with unification constraints.

$S \rightarrow NP\ VP$

$\langle NP$ HEAD AGREEMENT$\rangle = \langle VP$ HEAD AGREEMENT$\rangle$

$\langle S$ HEAD$\rangle = \langle VP$ HEAD$\rangle$

Converting these constraints into a feature structure results in the following structure:

$$
\begin{bmatrix}
S & \begin{bmatrix} \text{HEAD} & \boxed{1} \end{bmatrix} \\
NP & \begin{bmatrix} \text{HEAD} & \begin{bmatrix} \text{AGREEMENT} & \boxed{2} \end{bmatrix} \end{bmatrix} \\
VP & \begin{bmatrix} \text{HEAD} & \boxed{1}\begin{bmatrix} \text{AGREEMENT} & \boxed{2} \end{bmatrix} \end{bmatrix}
\end{bmatrix}
$$

In this derivation, we combined the various constraints into a single structure by first creating top-level features for each of the parts of the context-free rule, S, NP, and VP in this case. We then add further components to this structure by following the path equations in the constraints. Note that this is a purely notational conversion; the DAGs and the constraint equations contain the same information. However, tying the constraints together in a single feature structure puts it in a form that can be passed directly to our unification algorithm.

The second change involves the states used to represent partial parses in the Earley chart. The original states contain fields for the context-free rule being used, the position of the dot representing how much of the rule has been completed, the positions of the beginning and end of the state, and a list of other states that represent the completed sub-parts of the state. To this set of fields, we simply add an additional field to contain the DAG representing the feature structure corresponding to the state. Note that when a rule is first used by PREDICTOR to create a state, the DAG associated with the state will simply consist of the DAG retrieved from the rule. For example, when PREDICTOR uses the above *S* rule to enter a state into the chart, the DAG given above will be its initial DAG. We'll denote states like this as follows, where *Dag* denotes the feature structure given above.

$$S \rightarrow \bullet NP\ VP,\ [0,0],[],Dag$$

Given these representational additions, we can move on to altering the algorithm itself. The most important change concerns the actions that take place when a new state is created via the extension of an existing state, which takes place in the COMPLETER routine. Recall that COMPLETER is called when a completed constituent has been added to the chart. Its task is to attempt to find, and extend, existing states in the chart that are looking for constituents that are compatible with the newly completed constituent. COMPLETER is, therefore, a function that creates new states by *combining* the information from two other states, and as such is a likely place to apply the unification operation.

To be more specific, COMPLETER adds a new state into the chart by finding an existing state whose • can be advanced by the newly completed state. A • can be advanced when the category of the constituent immediately following it matches the category of the newly completed constituent. To accommodate the use of feature structures, we can alter this scheme by unifying the feature structure associated with the newly completed state with the appropriate part of the feature structure being advanced. If this unification succeeds, then the DAG of the new state receives the unified structure and is entered into the chart. If it fails, then no new state is entered into the chart. The appropriate alterations to COMPLETER are shown in Figure 11.12.

Consider this process in the context of parsing the phrase *That flight*, where the *That* has already been seen, as is captured by the following state.

$$NP \rightarrow Det \bullet Nominal[0, 1], [S_{Det}], Dag_1$$

$$Dag_1 \begin{bmatrix} \text{NP} & \begin{bmatrix} \text{HEAD} & \boxed{1} \end{bmatrix} \\[2ex] \text{DET} & \begin{bmatrix} \text{HEAD} & \begin{bmatrix} \text{AGREEMENT} & \boxed{2} \begin{bmatrix} \text{NUMBER} & \text{SG} \end{bmatrix} \end{bmatrix} \end{bmatrix} \\[2ex] \text{NOMINAL} & \begin{bmatrix} \text{HEAD} & \boxed{1} \begin{bmatrix} \text{AGREEMENT} & \boxed{2} \end{bmatrix} \end{bmatrix} \end{bmatrix}$$

Now consider the later situation where the parser has processed *flight* and has subsequently produced the following state.

$$Nominal \rightarrow Noun \bullet, [1, 2], [S_{Noun}], Dag_2$$

$$Dag_2 \begin{bmatrix} \text{NOMINAL} & \begin{bmatrix} \text{HEAD} & \boxed{1} \end{bmatrix} \\[2ex] \text{NOUN} & \begin{bmatrix} \text{HEAD} & \boxed{1} \begin{bmatrix} \text{AGREEMENT} & \begin{bmatrix} \text{NUMBER} & \text{SG} \end{bmatrix} \end{bmatrix} \end{bmatrix} \end{bmatrix}$$

To advance the *NP* rule, the parser unifies the feature structure found under the NOMINAL feature of Dag_2, with the feature structure found under the NOMINAL feature of the *NP*'s Dag_1. As in the original algorithm, a new state is created to represent the fact that an existing state has been advanced. This new state's DAG is given the DAG that resulted from the above unification.

The final change to the original algorithm concerns the check for states already contained in the chart. In the original algorithm, the ENQUEUE function refused to enter into the chart any state that was *identical* to one already present in the chart. "Identical" meant the same rule, with the same start and finish positions, and the same position of the •. It is this check that allows the algorithm to, among other things, avoid the infinite recursion problems associated with left-recursive rules.

The problem, of course, is that our states are now more complex since they have complex feature structures associated with them. States that appeared identical under the original criteria might in fact now be different since their associated DAGs may differ. The obvious solution to this problem is to simply extend the identity check to include the DAGs associated with the states, but it turns out that we can improve on this solution.

---

function EARLEY-PARSE(*words, grammar*) **returns** *chart*

  ENQUEUE(($\gamma \rightarrow \bullet S$, [0,0], dag_γ), *chart[0]*)
  for $i \leftarrow$ **from** 0 **to** LENGTH(*words*) **do**
   for each *state* **in** *chart[i]* **do**
    if INCOMPLETE?(*state*) **and**
          NEXT-CAT(*state*) is not a part of speech **then**
      PREDICTOR(*state*)
    elseif INCOMPLETE?(*state*) **and**
          NEXT-CAT(*state*) is a part of speech **then**
      SCANNER(*state*)
    else
      COMPLETER(*state*)
   end
  end
  return(*chart*)

procedure PREDICTOR(($A \rightarrow \alpha \bullet B\ \beta$, $[i,j]$, dag_A))
  for each ($B \rightarrow \gamma$) **in** GRAMMAR-RULES-FOR(*B, grammar*) **do**
    ENQUEUE(($B \rightarrow \bullet \gamma$, $[j,j]$, dag_B), *chart[j]*)
  end

procedure SCANNER(($A \rightarrow \alpha \bullet B\ \beta$, $[i,j]$, dag_A))
  if B $\subset$ PARTS-OF-SPEECH(*word[j]*) **then**
    ENQUEUE(($B \rightarrow word[j]$, $[j,j+1]$, dag_B), *chart[j+1]*)

procedure COMPLETER(($B \rightarrow \gamma \bullet$, $[j,k]$, dag_B))
  for each ($A \rightarrow \alpha \bullet B\ \beta$, $[i,j]$, dag_A) **in** *chart[j]* **do**
    if *new-dag* $\leftarrow$ UNIFY-STATES(dag_B, dag_A, B) $\neq$ Fails!
      ENQUEUE(($A \rightarrow \alpha B \bullet \beta$, $[i,k]$, *new − dag*), *chart[k]*)
  end

procedure UNIFY-STATES(*dag1, dag2, cat*)
  dag1-cp $\leftarrow$ COPYDAG(*dag1*)
  dag2-cp $\leftarrow$ COPYDAG(*dag2*)
  UNIFY(FOLLOW-PATH(*cat, dag1-cp*), FOLLOW-PATH(*cat, dag2-cp*))

procedure ENQUEUE(*state, chart-entry*)
  if *state* is not subsumed by a state in *chart-entry* **then**
    PUSH(*state, chart-entry*)
  end

Figure 11.12   Modifications to the Earley algorithm to include unification.

The motivation for the improvement lies in the motivation for the identity check. Its purpose is to prevent the wasteful addition of a state into the chart whose effect on the parse would be accomplished by an already existing state. Put another way, we want to prevent the entry into the chart of any state that would duplicate the work that will eventually be done by other states. Of course, this will clearly be the case with identical states, but it turns out it is also the case for states in the chart that are *more general* than new states being considered.

Consider the situation where the chart contains the following state, where the *Dag* places no constraints on the *Det*.

$$NP \rightarrow \bullet Det\ NP, [i, i], [\,], Dag$$

Such a state simply says that it is expecting a *Det* at position i, and that any *Det* will do.

Now consider the situation where the parser wants to insert a new state into the chart that is identical to this one, with the exception that its DAG restricts the *Det* to be singular. In this case, although the states in question are not identical, the addition of the new state to the chart would accomplish nothing and should therefore be prevented.

To see this let's consider all the cases. If the new state is added, then a subsequent singular *Det* will match both rules and advance both. Due to the unification of features, both will have DAGs indicating that their *Det*s are singular, with the net result being duplicate states in the chart. If on the other hand, a plural *Det* is encountered, the new state will reject it and not advance, while the old rule will advance, entering a single new state into the chart. On the other hand, if the new state is not placed in the chart, a subsequent plural or singular *Det* will match the more general state and advance it, leading to the addition of one new state into the chart. Note that this leaves us in exactly the same situation as if the new state had been entered into the chart, with the exception that the duplication is avoided. In sum, nothing worthwhile is accomplished by entering into the chart a state that is more specific than a state already in the chart.

Fortunately, the notion of **subsumption** described earlier gives us a formal way to talk about the generalization and specialization relations among feature structures. This suggests that the proper way to alter ENQUEUE is to check if a newly created state is *subsumed* by any existing states in the chart. If it is, then it will not be allowed into the chart. More specifically, a new state that is identical in terms of its rule, start and finish positions, subparts, and • position, to an existing state, will be not be entered into the chart if its

DAG is subsumed by the DAG of an existing state (ie. if $Dag_{old} \sqsubseteq Dag_{new}$).
The necessary change to the original Earley ENQUEUE procedure is shown
in Figure 11.12.

The Need for Copying

The calls to COPYDAG within the UNIFY-STATE procedure require some
elaboration. Recall that one of the strengths of the Earley algorithm (and of
the dynamic programming approach in general) is that once states have been
entered into the chart they may be used again and again as part of different
derivations, including ones that in the end do not lead to successful parses.
This ability is the motivation for the fact that states already in the chart are
not updated to reflect the progress of their •, but instead are copied and then
updated, leaving the original states intact so that they can be used again in
further derivations.

   The call to COPYDAG in UNIFY-STATE is required to preserve this
behavior because of the destructive nature of our unification algorithm. If
we simply unified the DAGS associated with the existing states, those states
would be altered by the unification, and hence would not be available in the
same form for subsequent uses by the COMPLETER function. Note that this
has negative consequences regardless of whether the unification succeeds or
fails, since in either case the original states are altered.

   Let's consider what would happen if the call to COPYDAG was absent
in the following example where an early unification attempt fails.

(11.24) Show me morning flights.

Let's assume that our parser has the following entry for the ditransitive version of the verb *show*, as well as the following transitive and ditransitive verb
phrase rules.

> *Verb* → *show*
>> ⟨*Verb* HEAD SUBCAT FIRST CAT⟩ = NP
>>
>> ⟨*Verb* HEAD SUBCAT SECOND CAT⟩ = NP
>>
>> ⟨*Verb* HEAD SUBCAT THIRD⟩ = END
>
> *VP* → *Verb NP*
>> ⟨*VP* HEAD⟩ = ⟨*Verb* HEAD⟩
>>
>> ⟨*VP* HEAD SUBCAT FIRST CAT⟩ = ⟨*NP* CAT ⟩
>>
>> ⟨*VP* HEAD SUBCAT SECOND⟩ = END

$VP \rightarrow$ *Verb NP NP*

$\langle VP$ HEAD$\rangle = \langle Verb$ HEAD$\rangle$

$\langle VP$ HEAD SUBCAT FIRST CAT$\rangle = \langle NP_1$ CAT $\rangle$

$\langle VP$ HEAD SUBCAT SECOND CAT$\rangle = \langle NP_2$ CAT $\rangle$

$\langle VP$ HEAD SUBCAT THIRD$\rangle =$ END

When the word *me* is read, the state representing transitive verb phrase will be completed since its dot has moved to the end. COMPLETER will, therefore, call UNIFY-STATES before attempting to enter this complete state into the chart. This will fail since the SUBCAT structures of these two rules can not be unified. This is, of course, exactly what we want since this version of *show* is ditransitive. Unfortunately, because of the destructive nature of our unification algorithm we have already altered the DAG attached to the state representing *show*, as well as the one attached to the *VP* thereby ruining them for use with the correct verb phrase rule later on. Thus, to make sure that states can be used again and again with multiple derivations, copies are made of the dags associated with states before attempting any unifications involving them.

All of this copying can be quite expensive. As a result, a number of alternative techniques have been developed that attempt to minimize this cost (Pereira, 1985; Karttunen and Kay, 1985; Tomabechi, 1991; Kogure, 1990). Kiefer et al. (1999) describe a set of related techniques used to speed up a large unification-based parsing system.

Unification Parsing

A more radical approach to using unification in parsing can be motivated by looking at an alternative way of denoting our augmented grammar rules. Consider the following *S* rule that we have been using throughout this chapter.

$S \rightarrow NP\ VP$

$\langle NP$ HEAD AGREEMENT$\rangle = \langle VP$ HEAD AGREEMENT$\rangle$

$\langle S$ HEAD$\rangle = \langle VP$ HEAD$\rangle$

An interesting way to alter the context-free part of this rule is to change the way its grammatical categories are specified. In particular, we can place the categorical information about the parts of the rule inside the feature structure, rather than inside the context-free part of the rule. A typical instantiation of this approach would give us the following rule (Shieber, 1986).

$X_0 \rightarrow X_1 \, X_2$

$\langle X_0 \text{ CAT} \rangle = S$

$\langle X_1 \text{ CAT} \rangle = NP$

$\langle X_2 \text{ CAT} \rangle = VP$

$\langle X_1 \text{ HEAD AGREEMENT} \rangle = \langle X_2 \text{ HEAD AGREEMENT} \rangle$

$\langle X_0 \text{ HEAD} \rangle = \langle X_2 \text{ HEAD} \rangle$

Focusing solely on the context-free component of the rule, this rule now simply states that the X_0 constituent consists of two components, and that the X_1 constituent is immediately to the left of the X_2 constituent. The information about the actual categories of these components is placed inside the rule's feature structure; in this case, indicating that X_0 is an S, X_1 is an NP, and X_2 is a VP. Altering the Earley algorithm to deal with this notational change is trivial. Instead of seeking the categories of constituents in the context-free components of the rule, it simply needs to look at the CAT feature in the DAG associated with a rule.

Of course, since it is the case that these two rules contain precisely the same information, it isn't clear that there is any benefit to this change. To see the potential benefit of this change, consider the following rules.

$X_0 \rightarrow X_1 \, X_2$

$\langle X_0 \text{ CAT} \rangle = \langle X_1 \text{ CAT} \rangle$

$\langle X_2 \text{ CAT} \rangle = PP$

$X_0 \rightarrow X_1 \text{ and } X_2$

$\langle X_1 \text{ CAT} \rangle = \langle X_2 \text{ CAT} \rangle$

$\langle X_0 \text{ CAT} \rangle = \langle X_1 \text{ CAT} \rangle$

The first rule is an attempt to generalize over various rules that we have already seen, such as $NP \rightarrow NP \, PP$ and $VP \rightarrow VP \, PP$. It simply states that any category can be followed by a prepositional phrase, and that the resulting constituent has the same category as the original. Similarly, the second rule is an attempt to generalize over rules such as $S \rightarrow S \text{ and } S$, $NP \rightarrow NP \text{ and } NP$, and so on.[1] It states that any constituent can be conjoined with a constituent of the same category to yield a new category of the same type. What these

---

[1] These rules should not be mistaken for correct, or complete, accounts of the phenomena in question.

rules have in common is their use of context-free rules that contain constituents with constrained, but unspecified, categories, something that can not be accomplished with our old rule format.

Of course, since these rules rely on the use the CAT feature, their effect could be approximated in the old format by simply enumerating all the various instantiations of the rule. A more compelling case for the new approach is motivated by the existence of grammatical rules, or constructions, that contain constituents that are not easily characterized using any existing syntactic category.

Consider the following examples of the English HOW-MANY construction from the WSJ (Jurafsky, 1992).

(11.25) **How early** does it open?

(11.26) **How deep** is her Greenness?

(11.27) **How papery** are your profits?

(11.28) **How quickly** we forget.

(11.29) **How many of you** can name three famous sporting Blanchards?

As is illustrated in these examples, the HOW-MANY construction has two components: the lexical item *how*, and a lexical item or phrase that is rather hard to characterize syntactically. It is this second element that is of interest to us here. As these examples show, it can be an adjective, adverb, or some kind of quantified phrase (although not all members of these categories yield grammatical results). Clearly, a better way to describe this second element is as a *scalar* concept, a constraint can captured using feature structures, as in the following rule.

$$X_0 \rightarrow X_1 \, X_2$$
$$\langle X_1 \; \text{ORTH} \rangle = \langle how \rangle$$
$$\langle X_2 \; \text{SEM} \rangle = \langle \; \text{SCALAR} \rangle$$

A complete account of rules like this involves semantics and will therefore have to wait for Chapter 14. The key point here is that by using feature structures a grammatical rule can place constraints on its constituents in a manner that does not make any use of the notion of a syntactic category.

Of course, dealing this kind of rule requires some changes to our parsing scheme. All of the parsing approaches we have considered thus far are driven by the syntactic category of the various constituents in the input. More specifically, they are based on simple atomic matches between the categories that have been predicted, and categories that have been found. Consider, for example, the operation of the COMPLETER function shown in Figure 11.12. This function searches the chart for states that can be advanced by a newly completed state. It accomplishes this by matching the category of the newly completed state against the category of the constituent following the • in the existing state. Clearly this approach will run into trouble when there are no such categories to consult.

The remedy for this problem with COMPLETER is to search the chart for states whose DAGs *unify* with the DAG of the newly completed state. This eliminates any requirement that states or rules have a category. The PREDICTOR can be changed in a similar fashion by having it add states to the chart states whose X_0 DAG component can unify with the constituent following the • of the predicting state. Exercise 11.6 asks you to make the necessary changes to the pseudo-code in Figure 11.12 to effect this style of parsing. Exercise 11.7 asks you to consider some of the implications of these alterations, particularly with respect to prediction.

11.6   TYPES AND INHERITANCE

> *I am surprised that ancient and modern writers have not attributed greater importance to the laws of inheritance...*
>
> Alexis de Tocqueville, *Democracy in America*, 1840

The basic feature structures we have presented so far have two problems that have led to extensions to the formalism. The first problem is that there is no way to place a constraint on what can be the value of a feature. For example, we have implicitly assumed that the NUMBER attribute can take only SG and PL as values. But in our current system, there is nothing, for example, to stop NUMBER from have the value 3RD or FEMININE as values:

$$\begin{bmatrix} \text{NUMBER} & \text{FEMININE} \end{bmatrix}$$

This problem has caused many unification-based grammatical theories to add various mechanisms to try to constrain the possible values of a feature. Formalisms like Functional Unification Grammar (FUG) (Kay, 1979, 1984, 1985) and Lexical Functional Grammar (LFG) (Bresnan, 1982), for example, focused on ways to keep intransitive verb like *sneeze* from unifying with a direct object (*Marin sneezed Toby*). This was addressed in FUG by adding a special atom **none** which is not allowed to unify with anything, and in LFG   NONE by adding **coherence** conditions which specified when a feature should not be filled. Generalized Phrase Structure (GPSG) (Gazdar et al., 1985, 1988) added a class of **feature co-occurrence restrictions**, to prevent, for example, nouns from having some verbal properties.

The second problem with simple feature structures is that there is no way to capture generalizations across them. For example, the many types of English verb phrases described in the Subcategorization section on page 411 share many features, as do the many kinds of subcategorization frames for verbs. Syntactitions were looking for ways to express these generalities

TYPES

A general solution to both of these problems is the use of **types**. Type systems for unification grammars have the following characteristics:

1. Each feature structure is labeled by a type.

APPROPRIATENESS

2. Conversely, each type has **appropriateness conditions** expressing which features are appropriate for it.

TYPE HIERARCHY

3. The types are organized into a **type hierarchy**, in which more specific types inherit properties of more abstract ones.

4. The unification operation is modified to unify the types of feature structures in addition to unifying the attributes and values.

TYPED
FEATURE
STRUCTURE

SIMPLE TYPES

COMPLEX TYPES

In such **typed feature structure** systems, types are a new class of objects, just like attributes and values were for standard feature structures. Types come in two kinds: **simple types** (also called **atomic types**), and **complex types**. Let's begin with simple types. A simple type is an atomic symbol like **sg** or **pl** (we will use **boldface** for all types), and replaces the simple atomic values used in standard feature structures. All types are organized into a multiple-inheritance **type hierarchy** (a **partial order** or **lattice**). Figure 11.13 shows the type hierarchy for the new type **agr**, which will be the type of the kind of atomic object that can be the value of an AGREE feature.

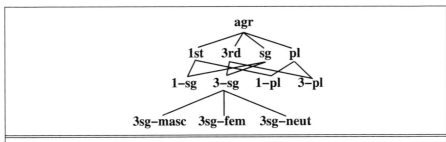

Figure 11.13   A simple type hierarchy for the subtypes of type **agr** which can be the value of the AGREE attribute. After Carpenter (1992).

SUBTYPE

In the hierarchy in Figure 11.13, **3rd** is a **subtype** of **agr**, and **3-sg** is a **subtype** of both **3rd** and **sg**. Types can be unified in the type hierarchy;

the unification of any two types is the most-general type that is more specific than the two input types. Thus:

3rd $\sqcup$ **sg = 3sg**
1st $\sqcup$ **pl = 1pl**
1st $\sqcup$ **agr = 1st**
3rd $\sqcup$ **1st** = *undefined*

The unification of two types which do not have a defined unifier is undefined, although it is also possible to explicitly represent this **fail type**   FAIL TYPE using the symbol $\perp$ (Aït-Kaci, 1984).

The second kind of types are complex types, which specify:

- a set of features that are appropriate for that type
- restrictions on the values of those features (expressed in terms of types)
- equality constraints between the values

Consider a simplified representation of the complex type **verb**, which just represents agreement and verb morphological form information. A definition of **verb** would define the two appropriate features, AGREE and VFORM, and would also define the type of the values of the two features. Let's suppose that the AGREE feature takes values of type **agr** defined in Figure 11.13 above, and the VFORM feature takes values of type **vform** (where **vform** subsumes the seven subtypes **finite**, **infinitive**, **gerund**, **base**, **present-participle**, **past-participle**, and **passive-participle**. Thus **verb** would be defined as follows (where the convention is to indicate the type either at the type of the AVM or just to the lower left of the left bracket):

$$
\begin{bmatrix}
\textbf{verb} \\
\text{AGREE} \quad \textbf{agr} \\
\text{VFORM} \quad \textbf{vform}
\end{bmatrix}
$$

By contrast, the type **noun** might be defined with the AGREE feature, but without the VFORM feature:

$$
\begin{bmatrix}
\textbf{noun} \\
\text{AGREE} \quad \textbf{agr}
\end{bmatrix}
$$

The unification operation is augmented for typed feature structures just by requiring that the type of the two structures must unify in addition to the values of the component features unifying.

$$
\begin{bmatrix}
\textbf{verb} \\
\text{AGREE} \quad \textbf{1st} \\
\text{VFORM} \quad \textbf{gerund}
\end{bmatrix}
\sqcup
\begin{bmatrix}
\textbf{verb} \\
\text{AGREE} \quad \textbf{sg} \\
\text{VFORM} \quad \textbf{gerund}
\end{bmatrix}
=
\begin{bmatrix}
\textbf{verb} \\
\text{AGREE} \quad \textbf{1-sg} \\
\text{VFORM} \quad \textbf{gerund}
\end{bmatrix}
$$

Complex types are also part of the type hierarchy. Subtypes of complex types inherit all the features of their parents, together with the constraints on their values. Sanfilippo (1993), for example, uses the type hierarchy to encode the hierarchical structure of the lexicon. Figure 11.14 shows a small part of this hierarchy, the part that models the various subcategories of verbs which take sentential complements; these are divided into the transitive ones (which take direct objects: (*ask yourself whether you have become better informed*) and the intransitive ones (*Monsieur asked whether I wanted to ride*). The type **trans-comp-cat** would introduce the required direct object, constraining it to be of type **noun-phrase**, while types like **sbase-comp-cat** would introduce the baseform (bare stem) complement and constraint its vform to be the baseform.

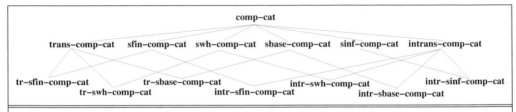

Figure 11.14   Part of the type hierarchy for the verb type **verb-cat**, showing the subtypes of the **comp-cat** type. These are all subcategories of verbs which take sentential complements. After Sanfilippo (1993).

Extensions to Typing

Typed feature structures can be extended by allowing inheritance with **defaults**. Default systems have been mainly used in lexical type hierarchies of the sort described in the previous section, in order to encode generalizations and subregular exceptions to them. In early versions of default unification the operation was order-dependent, based on the **priority union** operation (Kaplan, 1987). More recent architectures, such as Lascarides and Copestake (1997) default unification for typed feature structures, are order-independent, drawing on Young and Rounds (1993) and related to Reiter's default logic (Reiter, 1980).

DEFAULTS

PRIORITY UNION

Many unification-based theories of grammar, including HPSG (Pollard and Sag, 1987, 1994) and LFG (Bresnan, 1982) use an additional mechanism besides inheritance for capturing lexical generalizations: the **lexical rule**. Lexical rules express lexical generalizations by allowing a reduced, hence more redundancy-free lexicon to be automatically expanded by the

LEXICAL RULE

rules. Proposed originally by Jackendoff (1975), see Pollard and Sag (1994) for examples of modern lexical rules, Carpenter (1991) for a discussion of complexity issues, and Meurers and Minnen (1997) for a recent efficient implementation. Some authors have proposed using the type hierarchy to replace lexical rules, either by adding abstract types and some disjunctions (Krieger and Nerbonne, 1993) or via **type underspecification** and **dynamic typing**, in which underspecified types are combined to make new types on-line (Koenig and Jurafsky, 1995).

TYPE UNDERSPECIFICATION

DYNAMIC TYPING

Types can also be used to represent constituency. Rules like (11.13) on page 410 used a normal phrase structure rule template and added the features via path equations. Instead, it's possible to represent the whole phrase structure rule as a type. In order to do this, we need a way to represent constituents as features. One way to do this, following Sag and Wasow (1999), is to take a type **phrase** which has a feature called DTRS ("daughters"), whose value is a list of **phrases**. For example the phrase *I love New York* could have the following representation, (showing only the DTRS feature):

$$
\begin{bmatrix}
\textbf{phrase} \\
\text{DTRS} \left\langle \begin{bmatrix} \text{CAT PRO} \\ \text{ORTH I} \end{bmatrix}, \begin{bmatrix} \text{CAT VP} \\ \text{DTRS} \left\langle \begin{bmatrix} \text{CAT V} \\ \text{ORTH LOVE} \end{bmatrix}, \begin{bmatrix} \text{CAT NP} \\ \text{ORTH NEW YORK} \end{bmatrix} \right\rangle \end{bmatrix} \right\rangle
\end{bmatrix}
$$

Other Extensions to Unification

There are many other extensions to unification besides typing, including **path inequations** (Moshier, 1988; Carpenter, 1992; Carpenter and Penn, 1994) **negation** (Johnson, 1988, 1990), **set-valued features** (Pollard and Moshier, 1990), and **disjunction** Kay (1979), Kasper and Rounds (1986). In some unification systems these operations are incorporated into feature structures. Kasper and Rounds (1986) and others, by contrast, implement them in a separate metalanguage which is used to *describe* feature structures. This idea derives from the work of Pereira and Shieber (1984), and even earlier work by Kaplan and Bresnan (1982), all of whom distinguished between a metalanguage for describing feature structures and the actual feature structures themselves. The descriptions may thus use negation and disjunction to describe a set of feature structures (i.e., a certain feature must not contain a certain value, or may contain any of a set of values) but an actual instance of a feature structure that meets the description would not have negated or disjoint values.

PATH INEQUATIONS

NEGATION

SET-VALUED FEATURES

DISJUNCTION

11.7   SUMMARY

This chapter introduced feature structures and the unification operation which is used to combine them.

- A feature structure is a set of features-value pairs, where features are unanalyzable atomic symbols drawn from some finite set, and values are either atomic symbols or feature structures. They are represented either as **attribute-value matrices** (**AVMs**) or as directed acyclic graphs (**DAGs**), where features are directed labeled edges and feature values are nodes in the graph.

- **Unification** is the operation for both combining information (merging the information content of two feature structures) and comparing information (rejecting the merger of incompatible features).

- A phrase-structure rule can be augmented with feature structures, and with feature constraints expressing relations among the feature structures of the constituents of the rule. **Subcategorization** constraints can be represented as feature structures on head verbs (or other predicates). The elements which are subcategorized for by a verb may appear in the verb phrase or may be realized apart from the verb, as a **long-distance dependency**.

- Feature structures can be **typed**. The resulting **typed feature structures** place constraints on which type of values a given feature can take, and can also be organized into a **type hierarchy** to capture generalizations across types.

BIBLIOGRAPHICAL AND HISTORICAL NOTES

The use of features in linguistic theory comes originally from phonology. Anderson (1985) credits Jakobson (1939) with being the first to use features (called **distinctive features**) as an ontological type in a theory, drawing on previous uses of features by Trubetskoi (1939) and others. The semantic use of features followed soon after; see Chapter 16 for the history of componential analysis in semantics. Features in syntax were well established by the 1950s and were popularized by Chomsky (1965).

The unification operation in linguistics was developed independently by Kay (1979) (feature structure unification) and Colmerauer (1970, 1975)

(term unification) (see page 15). Both were working in machine translation and looking for a formalism for combining linguistic information which
would be reversible. Colmerauer's original Q-system was a bottom-up parser
based on a series of rewrite rules which contained logical variables, designed
for a English to French machine translation system. The rewrite rules were
reversible to allow them to work for both parsing and generation. Colmerauer, Fernand Didier, Robert Pasero, Philippe Roussel, and Jean Trudel designed the Prolog language based on extended Q-systems to full unification
based on the resolution principle of Robinson (1965), and implemented a
French analyzer based on it (Colmerauer and Roussel, 1996). The modern
use of Prolog and term unification for natural language via **Definite Clause
Grammars** was based on Colmerauer's (1975) metamorphosis grammars,
and was developed and named by Pereira and Warren (1980). Meanwhile
Martin Kay and Ron Kaplan had been working with Augmented Transition Network (**ATN**) grammars. An ATN is a Recursive Transition Network
(RTN) in which the nodes are augmented with feature registers. In an ATN
analysis of a passive, the first NP would be assigned to the subject register,
then when the passive verb was encountered, the value would be moved into
the object register. In order to make this process reversible, they restricted
assignments to registers so that certain registers could only be filled once,
that is, couldn't be overwritten once written. They thus moved toward the
concepts of logical variables without realizing it. Kay's original unification
algorithm was designed for feature structures rather than terms (Kay, 1979).
The integration of unification into an Earley-style approach given in Section
11.5 is based on Shieber (1985b).

DEFINITE
CLAUSE
GRAMMARS

ATN

See Shieber (1986) for a clear introduction to unification, and Knight
(1989) for a multidisciplinary survey of unification.

Inheritance and appropriateness conditions were first proposed for linguistic knowledge by Bobrow and Webber (1980) in the context of an extension of the KL-ONE knowledge representation system (Brachman and
Schmolze, 1985). Simple inheritance without appropriateness conditions
was taken up by number of researchers; early users include Jacobs (1985,
1987) and Flickinger et al. (1985). Aït-Kaci (1984) borrowed the notion of
inheritance in unification from the logic programming community. Typing
of feature structures, including both inheritance and appropriateness conditions, was independently proposed by Calder (1987), Pollard and Sag (1987),
and Elhadad (1990). Typed feature structures were formalized by King
(1989) and Carpenter (1992). There is an extensive literature on the use of
type hierarchies in linguistics, particularly for capturing lexical generaliza-

tions; besides the papers previously discussed, the interested reader should consult Evans and Gazdar (1996) for a description of the DATR language, designed for defining inheritance networks for linguistic knowledge representation, Fraser and Hudson (1992) for the use of inheritance in a dependency grammar, and Daelemans et al. (1992) for a general overview. Formalisms and systems for the implementation of constraint-based grammars via typed feature structures include the PAGE system using the TDL language (Krieger and Schäfer, 1994), ALE (Carpenter and Penn, 1994), and ConTroll (Götz et al., 1997).

Grammatical theories based on unification include Lexical Functional Grammar (LFG) (Bresnan, 1982), Head-Driven Phrase Structure Grammar (HPSG) (Pollard and Sag, 1987, 1994), Construction Grammar (Kay and Fillmore, 1999), and Unification Categorial Grammar (Uszkoreit, 1986).

EXERCISES

11.1   Draw the DAGs corresponding to the AVMs given in Examples 11.1–11.2.

11.2   Consider the following BERP examples, focusing on their use of pronouns.

> I want to spend lots of money.
> Tell me about Chez-Panisse.
> I'd like to take her to dinner.
> She doesn't like italian.

Assuming that these pronouns all belong to the category *Pro*, write lexical and grammatical entries with unification constraints that block the following examples.

> *Me want to spend lots of money.
> *Tell I about Chez-Panisse.
> *I would like to take she to dinner.
> *Her doesn't like italian.

11.3 Draw a picture of the subsumption semilattice corresponding to the feature structures in Examples 11.3 to 11.8. Be sure to include the most general feature structure [].

11.4 Consider the following examples.

The sheep are baaaaing.
The sheep is baaaaing.

Create appropriate lexical entries for the words *the*, *sheep*, and *baaaaing*. Show that your entries permit the correct assignment of a value to the NUM-BER feature for the subjects of these examples, as well as their various parts.

11.5 Create feature structures expressing the different subcat frames for *while* and *during* shown on page 416.

11.6 Alter the pseudocode shown in Figure 11.12 so that it performs the more radical kind of unification parsing described on page 434.

11.7 Consider the following problematic grammar suggested by Shieber (1985b).

$$S \rightarrow T$$
$$\langle T \text{ F} \rangle = \text{a}$$

$$T_1 \rightarrow T_2 \, A$$
$$\langle T_1 \text{ F} \rangle = \langle T_2 \text{ F F} \rangle$$

$$S \rightarrow A$$
$$A \rightarrow a$$

Show the first S state entered into the chart using your modified PRE-DICTOR from the previous exercise, then describe any problematic behavior displayed by PREDICTOR on subsequent iterations. Discuss the cause of the problem and how in might be remedied.

11.8 Using the list approach to representing a verb's subcategorization frame, show how a grammar could handle any number of verb subcatego-rization frames with only the following two *VP* rules. More specifically, show the constraints that would have to be added to these rules to make this work.

$$VP \rightarrow Verb$$
$$VP \rightarrow VP \, X$$

The solution to this problem involves thinking about a recursive walk down a verb's subcategorization frame. This is a hard problem; you might consult Shieber (1986) if you get stuck.

11.9   Page 441 showed how to use typed feature structure to represent constituency. Use that notation to represent rules 11.13, 11.14, and 11.15 shown on page 410.

12   LEXICALIZED AND PROBABILISTIC PARSING

> *Two roads diverged in a yellow wood,*
> *And sorry I could not travel both*
> *And be one traveler, long I stood*
> *And looked down one as far as I could*
> *To where it bent in the undergrowth...*
> Robert Frost, *The Road Not Taken*

The characters in Damon Runyon's short stories are willing to bet "on any proposition whatever", as Runyon says about Sky Masterson in *The Idyll of Miss Sarah Brown*; from the probability of getting aces back-to-back to the odds against a man being able to throw a peanut from second base to home plate. There is a moral here for language processing: with enough knowledge we can figure the probability of just about anything. The last three chapters have introduced sophisticated models of syntactic structure and its parsing. In this chapter we show that it is possible to build probabilistic models of sophisticated syntactic information and use some of this probabilistic information in efficient probabilistic parsers.

Of what use are probabilistic grammars and parsers? One key contribution of probabilistic parsing is to **disambiguation**. Recall that sentences can be very ambiguous; the Earley algorithm of Chapter 10 could represent these ambiguities in an efficient way, but was not equipped to resolve them. A probabilistic grammar offers a solution to the problem: choose the most-probable interpretation. Thus, due to the prevalence of ambiguity, probabilistic parsers can play an important role in most parsing or natural-language understanding task.

Another important use of probabilistic grammars is in **language modeling** for speech recognition or augmentative communication. We saw that

N-gram grammars were important in helping speech recognizers in predicting upcoming words, helping constrain the search for words. Probabilistic versions of more sophisticated grammars can provide additional predictive power to a speech recognizer. Indeed, since humans have to deal with the same problems of ambiguity as do speech recognizers, it is significant that we are finding psychological evidence that people use something like these probabilistic grammars in human language-processing tasks (e.g., human reading or speech understanding).

This integration of sophisticated structural and probabilistic models of syntax is at the very cutting edge of the field. Because of its newness, no single model has become standard, in the way that context-free grammar has become a standard for non-probabilistic syntax. We will explore the field by presenting a number of probabilistic augmentations to context-free grammars, showing how to parse some of them, and suggesting directions the field may take. The chapter begins with **probabilistic context-free grammars** (PCFGs), a probabilistic augmentation of context-free grammars, together with the **CYK algorithm**, a standard dynamic programming algorithm for parsing PCFGs. We then show two simple extensions to PCFGs to handle probabilistic **subcategorization** information and probabilistic **lexical dependencies**, give an evaluation metric for evaluating parsers, and then introduce some advanced issues and some discussion of human parsing.

12.1   PROBABILISTIC CONTEXT-FREE GRAMMARS

The simplest augmentation of the context-free grammar is the **Probabilistic Context-Free Grammar** (**PCFG**), also known as the **Stochastic Context-Free Grammar** (**SCFG**), first proposed by Booth (1969).

PCFG

SCFG

Recall that a context-free grammar G is defined by four parameters (N, Σ, P, S):

1. a set of non-terminal symbols (or "variables") N

2. a set of terminal symbols Σ (disjoint from N)

3. a set of productions P, each of the form $A \rightarrow \beta$, where A is a non-terminal and β is a string of symbols from the infinite set of strings $(\Sigma \cup N)*$

4. a designated start symbol S

$S \rightarrow NP\ VP$	[.80]	$Det \rightarrow that$ [.05] $\mid the$ [.80] $\mid a$ [.15]	
$S \rightarrow Aux\ NP\ VP$	[.15]	$Noun \rightarrow book$	[.10]
$S \rightarrow VP$	[.05]	$Noun \rightarrow flights$	[.50]
$NP \rightarrow Det\ Nom$	[.20]	$Noun \rightarrow meal$	[.40]
$NP \rightarrow Proper\text{-}Noun$	[.35]	$Verb \rightarrow book$	[.30]
$NP \rightarrow Nom$	[.05]	$Verb \rightarrow include$	[.30]
$NP \rightarrow Pronoun$	[.40]	$Verb \rightarrow want$	[.40]
$Nom \rightarrow Noun$	[.75]	$Aux \rightarrow can$	[.40]
$Nom \rightarrow Noun\ Nom$	[.20]	$Aux \rightarrow does$	[.30]
$Nom \rightarrow Proper\text{-}Noun\ Nom$	[.05]	$Aux \rightarrow do$	[.30]
$VP \rightarrow Verb$	[.55]	$Proper\text{-}Noun \rightarrow TWA$	[.40]
$VP \rightarrow Verb\ NP$	[.40]	$Proper\text{-}Noun \rightarrow Denver$	[.40]
$VP \rightarrow Verb\ NP\ NP$	[.05]	$Pronoun \rightarrow you$ [.40] $\mid I$ [.60]	

Figure 12.1   A PCFG; a probabilistic augmentation of the miniature English grammar and lexicon in Figure 10.2. These probabilities are not based on a corpus; they were made up merely for expository purposes.

A probabilistic context-free grammar augments each rule in P with a conditional probability:

$$A \rightarrow \beta\ [p] \tag{12.1}$$

A PCFG is thus a 5-tuple $G = (N, \Sigma, P, S, D)$, where D is a function assigning probabilities to each rule in P. This function expresses the probability p that the given non-terminal A will be expanded to the sequence β; it is often referred to as

$$P(A \rightarrow \beta)$$

or as

$$P(A \rightarrow \beta|A)$$

Formally this is conditional probability of a given expansion given the left-hand-size non-terminal A. Thus if we consider all the possible expansions of a non-terminal, the sum of their probabilities must be 1. Figure 12.1 shows a sample PCFG for a miniature grammar with only three nouns and three verbs. Note that the probabilities of all of the expansions of a non-terminal sum to 1. Obviously in any real grammar there are a great many more rules for each non-terminal and hence the probabilities of any particular rule are much smaller.

How are these probabilities used? A PCFG can be used to estimate a number of useful probabilities concerning a sentence and its parse-tree(s). For example a PCFG assigns a probability to each parse-tree T (i.e., each derivation) of a sentence S. This attribute is useful in **disambiguation**. For example, consider the two parses of the sentence "Can you book TWA flights" (one meaning "Can you book flights on behalf of TWA", and the other meaning "Can you book flights run by TWA") shown in Figure 12.2.

The probability of a particular parse T is defined as the product of the probabilities of all the rules r used to expand each node n in the parse tree:

$$P(T,S) = \prod_{n \in T} p(r(n)) \tag{12.2}$$

The resulting probability $P(T,S)$ is both the joint probability of the parse and the sentence, and also the probability of the parse $P(T)$. How can this be true? First, by the definition of joint probability:

$$P(T,S) = P(T)P(S|T) \tag{12.3}$$

But since a parse tree includes all the words of the sentence, $P(S|T)$ is 1. Thus:

$$P(T,S) = P(T)P(S|T) = P(T) \tag{12.4}$$

The probability of each of the trees in Figure 12.2 can be computed by multiplying together each of the rules used in the derivation. For example, the probability of the left tree in Figure 12.2a (call it T_l) and the right tree (Figure 12.2b or T_r) can be computed as follows:

$$
\begin{aligned}
P(T_l) &= .15 * .40 * .05 * .05 * .35 * .75 * .40 * .40 * .40 \\
&\quad * .30 * .40 * .50 \\
&= 1.5 \times 10^{-6}
\end{aligned}
\tag{12.5}
$$

$$
\begin{aligned}
P(T_r) &= .15 * .40 * .40 * .05 * .05 * .75 * .40 * .40 * .40 \\
&\quad * .30 * .40 * .50 \\
&= 1.7 \times 10^{-6}
\end{aligned}
\tag{12.6}
$$

We can see that the right tree in Figure 12.2(b) has a higher probability. Thus this parse would correctly be chosen by a disambiguation algorithm which selects the parse with the highest PCFG probability.

Let's formalize this intuition that picking the parse with the highest probability is the correct way to do disambiguation. The disambiguation

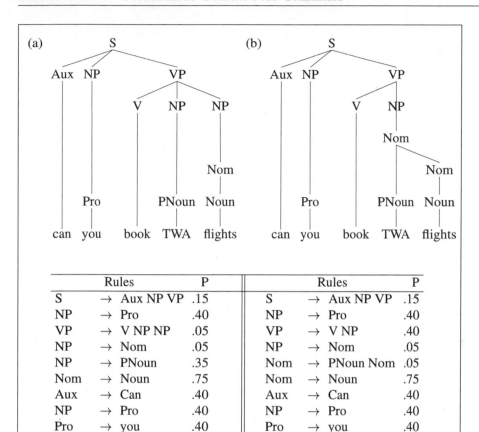

	Rules	P
S	→ Aux NP VP	.15
NP	→ Pro	.40
VP	→ V NP NP	.05
NP	→ Nom	.05
NP	→ PNoun	.35
Nom	→ Noun	.75
Aux	→ Can	.40
NP	→ Pro	.40
Pro	→ you	.40
Verb	→ book	.30
PNoun	→ TWA	.40
Noun	→ flights	.50

	Rules	P
S	→ Aux NP VP	.15
NP	→ Pro	.40
VP	→ V NP	.40
NP	→ Nom	.05
Nom	→ PNoun Nom	.05
Nom	→ Noun	.75
Aux	→ Can	.40
NP	→ Pro	.40
Pro	→ you	.40
Verb	→ book	.30
Pnoun	→ TWA	.40
Noun	→ flights	.50

Figure 12.2   Two parse trees for an ambiguous sentence. Parse (a) corresponds to the meaning "Can you book flights on behalf of TWA", parse (b) to "Can you book flights which are run by TWA".

algorithm picks the best tree for a sentence S out of the set of parse trees for S (which we'll call $\tau(S)$). We want the parse tree T which is most likely given the sentence S.

$$\hat{T}(S) = \underset{T \in \tau(S)}{\operatorname{argmax}} P(T|S) \qquad\qquad (12.7)$$

By definition the probability $P(T|S)$ can be rewritten as $P(T,S)/P(S)$, thus leading to:

$$\hat{T}(S) = \underset{T \in \tau(S)}{\operatorname{argmax}} \frac{P(T,S)}{P(S)} \qquad (12.8)$$

Since we are maximizing over all parse trees for the same sentence, $P(S)$ will be a constant for each tree, and so we can eliminate it:

$$\hat{T}(S) = \underset{T \in \tau(S)}{\operatorname{argmax}} P(T,S) \qquad (12.9)$$

Furthermore, since we showed above that $P(T,S) = P(T)$, the final equation for choosing the most likely parse neatly simplifies to choosing the parse with the highest probability:

$$\hat{T}(S) = \underset{T \in \tau(S)}{\operatorname{argmax}} P(T) \qquad (12.10)$$

A second attribute of a PCFG is that it assigns a probability to the string of words constituting a sentence. This is important in **language modeling** in speech recognition, spell-correction, or augmentative communication. The probability of an unambiguous sentence is $P(T,S) = P(T)$ or just the probability of the single parse tree for that sentence. The probability of an ambiguous sentence is the sum of the probabilities of all the parse trees for the sentence:

$$P(S) = \sum_{T \in \tau(S)} P(T,S) \qquad (12.11)$$

$$= \sum_{T \in \tau(S)} P(T) \qquad (12.12)$$

An additional useful feature of PCFGs for language modeling is that they can assign a probability to substrings of a sentence. For example, Jelinek and Lafferty (1991) give an algorithm for efficiently computing the probability of a **prefix** of a sentence. This is the probability that the grammar generates a sentence whose initial substring is $w_1 w_2 ... w_i$. Stolcke (1995) shows how the standard Earley parser can be augmented to compute these prefix probabilities, and Jurafsky et al. (1995) describes an application of a version of this algorithm as the language model for a speech recognizer.

A PCFG is said to be **consistent** if the sum of the probabilities of all sentences in the language equals 1. Certain kinds of recursive rules cause a grammar to be inconsistent by causing infinitely looping derivations for some sentences. For example a rule $S \rightarrow S$ with probability 1 would lead to

PREFIX

CONSISTENT

lost probability mass due to derivations that never terminate. See Booth and Thompson (1973) for more details on consistent and inconsistent grammars.

Probabilistic CYK Parsing of PCFGs

The parsing problem for PCFGs is to produce the most-likely parse for a given sentence, that is, to compute

$$\hat{T}(S) = \underset{T \in \tau(S)}{\operatorname{argmax}} P(T) \qquad\qquad (12.13)$$

Luckily, the algorithms for computing the most-likely parse are simple extensions of the standard algorithms for parsing. Chapter 10 introduced the use of the Earley algorithm to find all parses for a given input sentence and a given context-free grammar. It is possible to augment the Earley algorithm to compute the probability of each of its parses, and thus to find the most likely parse. Instead of presenting the probabilistic Earley algorithm here, however, we will present the **probabilistic CYK (Cocke-Younger-**   CYK
Kasami) algorithm. We do this because the probabilistic Earley algorithm is somewhat complex to present, and also because the CYK algorithm is worth understanding, and we haven't yet studied it. The reader is thus referred to Stolcke (1995) for the presentation of the probabilistic Earley algorithm.

Where the Earley algorithm is essentially a top-down parser which uses a dynamic programming table to efficiently store its intermediate results, the CYK algorithm is essentially a bottom-up parser using the same dynamic programming table. The fact that CYK is bottom-up makes it more efficient when processing lexicalized grammars, as we will see later.

Probabilistic CYK parsing was first described by Ney (1991), but the version of the probabilistic CYK algorithm that we present is adapted from Collins (1999) and Aho and Ullman (1972). Assume first that the PCFG is in Chomsky normal form; recall from page 348 that a grammar is in CNF if it is ε-free and if in addition each production is either of the form $A \rightarrow B\ C$ or $A \rightarrow a$. The CYK algorithm assumes the following input, output, and data structures:

- **Input.**

    - A Chomsky normal form PCFG $G = \{N, \Sigma, P, S, D\}$. Assume that the $|N|$ non-terminals have indices $1, 2, \ldots, |N|$, and that the start symbol S has index 1.
    - n words $w_1 \ldots w_n$.

- **Data Structure.** A dynamic programming array $\pi[i, j, a]$ holds the maximum probability for a constituent with non-terminal index a spanning words $i \ldots j$. Back-pointers in the area are used to store the links between constituents in a parse-tree.
- **Output.** The maximum probability parse will be $\pi[1, n, 1]$: the parse tree whose root is S and which spans the entire string of words $w_1 \ldots w_n$.

Like the other dynamic programming algorithms (minimum edit distance, Forward, Viterbi, and Earley), the CYK algorithm fills out the probability array by induction. In this description, we will use w_{ij}, to mean the string of words from word i to word j, following Aho and Ullman (1972):

- **base case:** Consider the input strings of length one (i.e., individual words w_i). In Chomsky normal form, the probability of a given non-terminal A expanding to a single word w_i must come only from the rule $A \to w_i$ (since $A \overset{*}{\Rightarrow} w_i$ if and only if $A \to w_i$ is a production).
- **recursive case:** For strings of words of length > 1, $A \overset{*}{\Rightarrow} w_{ij}$ if and only if there is at least one rule $A \to BC$ and some $k, 1 \le k < j$, such that B derives the first k symbols of w_{ij} and C derives the last $j - k$ symbols of w_{ij}. Since each of these strings of words is shorter than the original string w_{ij}, their probability will already be stored in the matrix π. We compute the probability of w_{ij} by multiplying together the probability of these two pieces. But there may be multiple parses of w_{ij}, and so we'll need to take the max over all the possible divisions of w_{ij} (i.e., over all values of k and over all possible rules).

Figure 12.3 gives pseudocode for this probabilistic CYK algorithm, again adapted from Collins (1999) and Aho and Ullman (1972).

Learning PCFG Probabilities

Where do PCFG probabilities come from? There are two ways to assign probabilities to a grammar. The simplest way is to use a corpus of already-parsed sentences. Such a corpus is called a **treebank**. For example the Penn Treebank (Marcus et al., 1993), distributed by the Linguistic Data Consortium, contains parse trees for the Brown Corpus, one million words from the Wall Street Journal, and parts of the Switchboard corpus. Given a treebank, the probability of each expansion of a non-terminal can be computed by counting the number of times that expansion occurs and then normalizing.

$$P(\alpha \to \beta | \alpha) = \frac{\text{Count}(\alpha \to \beta)}{\sum_\gamma \text{Count}(\alpha \to \gamma)} = \frac{\text{Count}(\alpha \to \beta)}{\text{Count}(\alpha)} \qquad (12.14)$$

TREEBANK

---

function CYK(*words,grammar*) **returns** *best_parse*

Create and clear *p*[*num_words,num_words,num_nonterminals*]

\# base case
for *i* = 1 **to** *num_words*
   for *A* = 1 **to** *num_nonterminals*
     if $A \rightarrow w_i$ is in grammar **then**
       $\pi[i, i, A] = P(A \rightarrow w_i)$

\# recursive case
for *j* = 2 **to** *num_words*
   for *i* = 1 **to** *num_words-j+1*
     for *k* = 1 **to** *j-1*
       for *A* = 1 **to** *num_nonterminals*
       for *B* = 1 **to** *num_nonterminals*
       for *C* = 1 **to** *num_nonterminals*
        $prob = \pi[i, k, B] \times p[i+k, j-k, C] \times P(A \rightarrow BC)$
        if $(prob > \pi[i, j, A])$ **then**
          $\pi[i, j, A] = prob$
          $B[i, j, A] = \{k, A, B\}$

Figure 12.3   The Probabilistic CYK algorithm for finding the maximum probability parse of a string of *num_words* words given a PCFG grammar with *num_rules* rules in Chomsky Normal Form. *B* is the array of back-pointers used to recover the best parse. After Collins (1999) and Aho and Ullman (1972).

When a treebank is unavailable, the counts needed for computing PCFG probabilities can be generated by first parsing a corpus. If sentences were unambiguous, it would be as simple as this: parse the corpus, increment a counter for every rule in the parse, and then normalize to get probabilities. However, since most sentences are ambiguous, in practice we need to keep a separate count for each parse of a sentence and weight each partial count by the probability of the parse it appears in. The standard algorithm for computing this is called the **Inside-Outside** algorithm, and was proposed [INSIDE-OUTSIDE] by Baker (1979) as a generalization of the forward-backward algorithm of Chapter 7. See Manning and Schütze (1999) for a complete description of the algorithm.

12.2   PROBLEMS WITH PCFGS

While probabilistic context-free grammars are a natural extension to context-free grammars, they have a number of problems as probability estimators. Because of these problems, most current probabilistic parsing models use some augmentation of PCFGs rather than using vanilla PCFGs. This section will summarize problems with PCFGs in modeling *structural dependencies* and in modeling *lexical dependencies*.

One problem with PCFGs comes from their fundamental independence assumption. By definition, a CFG assumes that the expansion of any one non-terminal is independent of the expansion of any other non-terminal. This independence assumption is carried over in the probabilistic version; each PCFG rule is assumed to be independent of each other rule, and thus the rule probabilities are multiplied together. But an examination of the statistics of English syntax shows that sometimes the choice of how a node expands is dependent on the location of the node in the parse tree. For example, consider the differential placement in a sentence of pronouns versus full lexical noun phrases. Beginning with Kuno (1972), many linguists have shown that there is a strong tendency in English (as well as in many other languages) for the syntactic subject of a sentence to be a pronoun. This tendency is caused by the use of subject position to realize the "topic" or old information in a sentence (Givón, 1990). Pronouns are a way to talk about old information, while non-pronominal ("lexical") noun-phrases are often used to introduce new referents. For example, Francis et al. (1999) show that of the 31,021 subjects of declarative sentences in Switchboard, 91% are pronouns (12.15a), and only 9% are lexical (12.15b). By contrast, out of the 7,489 direct objects, only 34% are pronouns (12.16a), and 66% are lexical (12.16b).

(12.15)   (a) **She's** able to take her baby to work with her.

(b) Uh, **my wife** worked until we had a family.

(12.16)   (a) Some laws absolutely prohibit **it**.

(b) All the people signed **confessions**.

These dependencies could be captured if the probability of expanding an NP as a pronoun (for example via the rule *NP → Pronoun*) versus a lexical NP (for example via the rule *NP → Det Noun*) were dependent on whether the NP was a subject or an object. But this is just the kind of probabilistic dependency that a PCFG does not allow.

An even more important problem with PCFGs is their lack of sensitivity to words. Lexical information in a PCFG can only be represented via the probability of pre-terminal nodes (*Verb*, *Noun*, *Det*) to be expanded lexically. But there are a number of other kinds of lexical and other dependencies that turn out to be important in modeling syntactic probabilities. For example a number of researchers have shown that lexical information plays an important role in selecting the correct parsing of an ambiguous prepositional-phrase attachment (Ford et al., 1982; Whittemore et al., 1990; Hindle and Rooth, 1991, inter alia). Consider the following example from Hindle and Rooth (1991):

(12.17) Moscow sent more than 100,000 soldiers into Afghanistan ...

Here the prepositional phrase *into Afghanistan* can be attached either to the NP *more than 100,000 soldiers* or to the verb-phrase headed by *sent*. In a PCFG, the attachment choice comes down to the choice between two rules: $NP \rightarrow NP\ PP$ (NP-attachment) and $VP \rightarrow NP\ PP$ (VP-attachment). The probability of these two rules depends on the training corpus; Hindle and Rooth (1991) report that NP-attachment happens about 67% compared to 33% for VP-attachment in 13 million words from the AP newswire; Collins (1999) reports 52% NP-attachment in a corpus containing a mixture of Wall Street Journal and I.B.M. computer manuals. Whether the preference is 52% or 67%, crucially in a PCFG this preference is purely structural and must be the same for all verbs.

In example (12.17), however, the correct attachment is to the verb; in this case because the verb *send* subcategorizes for a destination, which can be expressed with the preposition *into*. Indeed all of the cases of ambiguous *into*-PP-attachments with the main verb *send* in the Penn Treebank's Brown and Wall Street Journal corpora attached to the verb. Thus a model which kept separate **lexical dependency** statistics for different verbs would be able to choose the correct parse in these cases.

LEXICAL
DEPENDENCY

Coordination ambiguities are another case where lexical dependencies are the key to choosing the proper parse. Figure 12.4 shows an example from Collins (1999), with two parses for the phrase *dogs in houses and cats*. Because *dogs* is semantically a better conjunct for *cats* than *houses* (and because dogs can't fit inside cats) the parse *[dogs in [$_{NP}$ houses and cats]]* is intuitively unnatural and should be dispreferred. The two parses in Figure 12.4, however, have exactly the same PCFG rules and thus a PCFG will assign them the same probability.

In summary, probabilistic context-free grammars have a number of inadequacies as a probabilistic model of syntax. In the next section we sketch current methods for augmenting PCFGs to deal with these issues.

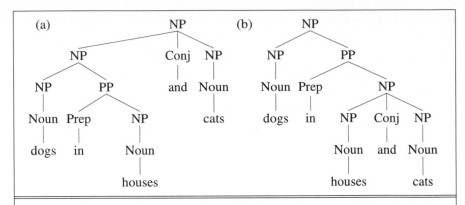

Figure 12.4   An instance of coordination ambiguity. Although the left structure is intuitively the correct one, a PCFG will assign them identically probabilities since both structure use the exact same rules. After Collins (1999).

12.3   PROBABILISTIC LEXICALIZED CFGS

We saw in Chapter 11 that syntactic constituents could be associated with a lexical **head**. This idea of a head for each constituent dates back to Bloomfield (1914), but was first used to extend PCFG modeling by Black et al. (1992). The probabilistic representation of lexical heads used in parsers such as Charniak (1997) and Collins (1999) is simpler than the complex head-feature models we saw in Chapter 11. In the simpler probabilistic representation, each non-terminal in a parse-tree is annotated with a single word which is its lexical head. Figure 12.5 shows an example of such a tree from Collins (1999), in which each non-terminal is annotated with its head. "Workers dumped sacks into a bin" is a shortened form of a WSJ sentence.

In order to generate such a tree, each PCFG rule must be augmented to identify one right-hand-side constituent to be the head daughter. The head-word for a node is then set to the headword of its head daughter. Choosing these head daughters is simple for textbook examples (*NN* is the head of *NP*) but is complicated and indeed controversial for most phrases. (Should the complementizer *to* or the verb be the head of an infinite verb-phrase?) Modern linguistic theories of syntax generally include a component that defines heads (see e.g., Pollard and Sag, 1994). Collins (1999) also gives a description of a practical set of head rules for Penn Treebank grammars modified from Magerman; for example their rule for finding the head of an NP is to return the very last word in the NP if it is tagged POS (possessive); else to

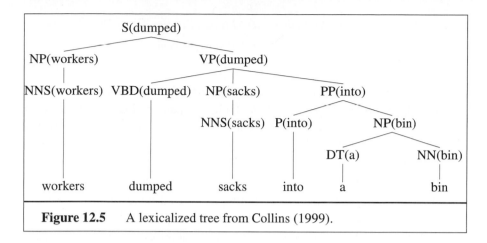

Figure 12.5   A lexicalized tree from Collins (1999).

search from right to left in the NP for the first child that is an NN, NNP, NNPS, NNS, NX, POS, or JJR; else to search from left to right for the first child that is an NP.

One way to think of these head features is as a simplified version of the head features in a unification grammar; instead of complicated re-entrant feature values, we just allow an attribute to have a single value from a finite set (in fact the set of words in the vocabulary). Technically, grammars in which each node is annotated by non-recursive features are called **attribute grammars**.

ATTRIBUTE
GRAMMARS

Another way to think of a lexicalized grammar is as a simple context-free grammar with a lot more rules; it's as if we created many copies of each rule, one copy for each possible headword for each constituent; this idea of building an expanded lexicalized grammar is due to Schabes et al. (1988) and Schabes (1990). In general there may be too many such rules to actually keep them around, but thinking about lexicalized grammars this way makes it clearer that we can parse them with standard CFG parsing algorithms.

Let's now see how these lexicalized grammars can be augmented with probabilities, and how by doing so we can represent the kind of lexical dependencies we discussed above and in Chapter 9. Suppose we were to treat a probabilistic lexicalized CFG like a normal but huge PCFG. Then we would store a probability for each rule/head combination, as in the following contrived examples:

$$VP(dumped) \rightarrow VBD(dumped)\,NP(sacks)\,PP(into)\;[3\times 10^{-10}]$$
$$VP(dumped) \rightarrow VBD(dumped)\,NP(cats)\,PP(into)\;[8\times 10^{-11}]$$

$$VP(dumped) \quad \rightarrow \quad VBD(dumped)\,NP(hats)\,PP(into)\,[4\times10^{-10}]$$

$$VP(dumped) \quad \rightarrow \quad VBD(dumped)\,NP(sacks)\,PP(above)\,[1\times10^{-12}]$$

$$\dots \hspace{6cm} (12.18)$$

The problem with this method, of course, is that there is no corpus big enough to train such probabilities. Training standard PCFG probabilities would result in zero counts for almost all the rules. To avoid this, we need to make some simplifying independence assumptions in order to cluster some of the counts.

Perhaps the main difference between various modern statistical parsers lies in exactly which independence assumptions they make. In the rest of this section we describe a simplified version of Charniak's (1997) parser, but we could also have chosen any of the other similar dependency-based statistical parsers (such as Magerman (1995), Collins (1999), and Ratnaparkhi (1997)).

Like many of these others, Charniak's parser incorporates lexical dependency information by relating the heads of phrases to the heads of their constituents. His parser also incorporates syntactic subcategorization information by conditioning the probability of a given rule expansion of a non-terminal on the head of the non-terminal. Let's look at examples of slightly simplified versions of the two kinds of statistics (simplified by being conditioned on less factors than in Charniak's complete algorithm).

First, recall that in a vanilla PCFG, the probability of a node n being expanded via rule r is conditioned on exactly one factor: the syntactic category of the node n. (For simplicity we will use the notation n to mean the syntactic category of n.) We will simply add one more conditioning factor: the headword of the node $h(n)$. Thus we will be computing the probability

$$p(r(n)|n, h(n)) \hspace{4cm} (12.19)$$

Consider for example the probability of expanding the VP in Figure Figure 12.5 via the rule r, which is:

$$VP \ \rightarrow VBD\,NP\,PP$$

This probability is $p(r|VP, dumped)$, answering the question "What is the probability that a VP headed by $dumped$ will be expanded as $VBD \ \ NP \ PP$?" This lets us capture subcategorization information about $dumped$; for example, a VP whose head is $dumped$ may be more likely to have an NP and a PP than a VP whose head is $slept$.

Now that we have added heads as a conditioning factor, we need to decide how to compute the probability of a head. The null assumption would make all heads equally likely; the probability that the head of a node would be *sacks* would be the same as the probability that the head would be *racks*. This doesn't seem very useful. The syntactic category of the node ought to matter (nouns might have different kinds of heads than verbs). And the neighboring heads might matter too. Let's condition the probability of a node *n* having a head *h* on two factors: the syntactic category of the node *n*, and the head of the node's mother $h(m(n))$. This is the probability

$$p(h(n) = word_i|n, h(m(n))) \qquad\qquad (12.20)$$

Consider for example the probability that the *NP* that is the second daughter of the *VP* in Figure 12.5 has the head *sacks*. The probability of this head is $p(head(n) = sacks|n = NP, h(m(n)) = dumped)$. This probability answers the question "What is the probability that an NP whose mother's head is *dumped* has the head *sacks*?" sketched in the following drawing:

X(dumped)
|
NP(?sacks?)

The figure shows that what this head-probability is really doing is capturing **dependency** information e.g., between the words *dumped* and *sacks*.

How are these two probabilities used to compute the probability of a complete parse? Instead of just computing the probability of a parse by multiplying each of the PCFG rule probabilities, we will modify equation (12.2) by additionally conditioning each rule on its head:

$$P(T,S) = \prod_{n \in T} p(r(n)|n, h(n)) \times p(h(n)|n, h(m(n))) \qquad (12.21)$$

Let's look at a sample parse-ambiguity to see if these lexicalized probabilities will be useful in disambiguation. Figure 12.6 shows an alternative (incorrect) parse for the sentence "Workers dumped sacks into a bin", again from Collins (1999). In this incorrect parse the *PP into a bin* modifies the *NP sacks* instead of the *VP* headed by *dumped*. This parse is incorrect because *into a bin* is extremely unlikely to be a modifier of this NP; it is much more likely to modify *dumped*, as in the original parse in Figure 12.5.

The head-head and head-rule probabilities in equation (12.21) will indeed help us correctly choose the *VP* attachment (Figure 12.5) over the NP attachment (Figure 12.6). One difference between the two trees is that *VP(dumped)* expands to *VBD NP PP* in the correct tree and *VBD NP* in the incorrect tree. Let's compute both of these by counting in the Brown corpus portion of the Penn Treebank. The first rule is quite likely:

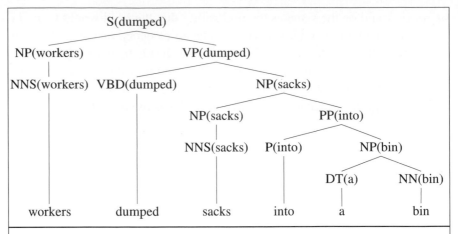

Figure 12.6   An incorrect parse of the sentence in Figure 12.5 from Collins (1999).

$$p(VP \rightarrow VBD\,NP\,PP|VP, dumped)$$
$$= \frac{C(VP(dumped) \rightarrow VBD\,NP\,PP)}{\sum_\beta C(VP(dumped) \rightarrow \beta)}$$
$$= \frac{6}{9} = .67 \qquad (12.22)$$

The second rule never happens in the Brown corpus. In practice this zero value would be smoothed somehow, but for now let's just notice that the first rule is preferred. This isn't surprising, since *dump* is a verb of caused-motion into a new location:

$$p(VP \rightarrow VBD\,NP|VP, dumped) = \frac{C(VP(dumped) \rightarrow VBD\,NP)}{\sum_\beta C(VP(dumped) \rightarrow \beta)}$$
$$= \frac{0}{9} = 0 \qquad (12.23)$$

What about the head probabilities? In the correct parse, a *PP* node whose mother's head is *dumped* has the head *into*. In the incorrect, a *PP* node whose mother's head is *sacks* has the head *into*. Once again, let's use counts from the Brown portion of the Treebank:

$$p(into|PP, dumped) = \frac{C(X(dumped) \rightarrow \ldots PP(into) \ldots)}{\sum_\beta C(X(dumped) \rightarrow \ldots PP \ldots)}$$
$$= \frac{2}{9} = .22 \qquad (12.24)$$

$$p(into|PP, sacks) = \frac{C(X(sacks) \rightarrow \ldots PP(into) \ldots)}{\sum_\beta C(X(sacks) \rightarrow \ldots PP \ldots)}$$

$$= \frac{0}{0} = ? \tag{12.25}$$

Once again, the head probabilities correctly predict that *dumped* is more likely to be modified by *into* than is *sacks*.

Of course, one example does not prove that one method is better than another. Furthermore, as we mentioned above, the probabilistic lexical grammar presented above is a simplified version of Charniak's actual algorithm. He adds additional conditioning factors (such as conditioning the rule-expansion probability on the syncat of the node's grandparent), and also proposes various backoff and smoothing algorithms, since any given corpus may still be too small to acquire these statistics. Other statistical parsers include even more factors, such as the distinction between arguments and adjuncts and giving more weight to lexical dependencies which are closer in the tree than those which are further (Collins, 1999), the three left-most parts of speech in a given constituent (Magerman and Marcus, 1991), and general structural preferences (such as the preference for right-branching structures in English) (Briscoe and Carroll, 1993).

Many of these statistical parsers have been evaluated (on the same corpus) using the methodology of the Methodology Box on page 464.

Extending the CYK algorithm to handle lexicalized probabilities is left as an exercise for the reader.

12.4   DEPENDENCY GRAMMARS

The previous section showed that constituent-based grammars could be augmented with probabilistic relations between head words, and showed that this **lexical dependency** information is important in modeling the lexical constraints that heads (such as verbs) place on their arguments or modifiers.

An important class of grammar formalisms is based purely on this **lexical dependency** information itself. In these **dependency grammars**, constituents and phrase-structure rules do not play any fundamental role. Instead, the syntactic structure of a sentence is described purely in terms of words and binary semantic or syntactic relations between these words. Dependency grammars often draw heavily from the work of Tesnière (1959), and the name **dependency** was presumably first used by David Hays. But

DEPENDENCY
GRAMMARS

DEPENDENCY

METHODOLOGY BOX: EVALUATING PARSERS

The standard techniques for evaluating parsers and grammars are called the PARSEVAL measures, and were proposed by Black et al. (1991) based on the same ideas from signal-detection theory that we saw in earlier chapters. In the simplest case, a particular parsing of the test set (for example the Penn Treebank) is defined as the correct parse. Given this "gold standard" for a test set, a given constituent in a candidate parse c of a sentence s is labeled "correctly" if there is a constituent in the treebank parse with the same starting point, ending point, and non-terminal symbol. We can then measure the precision, recall, and a new metric (crossing brackets) for each sentence s:

$$\textbf{labeled recall:} = \frac{\text{\# of correct constituents in candidate parse of } s}{\text{\# of correct constituents in treebank parse of } s}$$

$$\textbf{labeled precision:} = \frac{\text{\# of correct constituents in candidate parse of } s}{\text{\# of total constituents in candidate parse of } s}$$

cross-brackets: the number of crossed brackets (e.g., the number of constituents for which the treebank has a bracketing such as ((A B) C) but the candidate parse has a bracketing such as (A (B C))).

Using a portion of the Wall Street Journal treebank as the test set, parsers such as Charniak (1997) and Collins (1999) achieve just under 90% recall, just under 90% precision, and about 1% cross-bracketed constituents per sentence.

For comparing parsers which use different grammars, the PARSEVAL metric includes a canonicalization algorithm for removing information likely to be grammar-specific (auxiliaries, pre-infinitival "to", etc.) and computing a simplified score. The interested reader should see Black et al. (1991). There are also related evaluation metrics for dependency parses (Collins et al., 1999) and dependency-based metrics that work for any parse structure (Lin, 1995; Carroll et al., 1998).

For grammar-checking, we can compute instead the precision and recall of a simpler task: how often the parser correctly rejected an ungrammatical sentence (or recognized a grammatical sentence).

this lexical dependency notion of grammar is in fact older than the relatively recent phrase-structure or constituency grammars, and has its roots in the ancient Greek and Indian linguistic traditions. Indeed the notion in traditional grammar of "parsing a sentence into subject and predicate" is based on lexical relations rather than constituent relations.

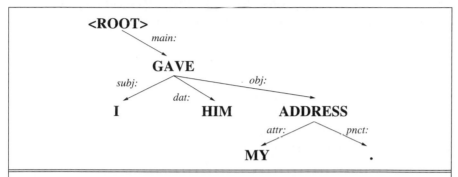

Figure 12.7   A sample dependency grammar parse, using the dependency formalism of Karlsson et al. (1995), after Järvinen and Tapanainen (1997).

Figure 12.7 shows an example parse of the sentence *I gave him my address*, using the dependency grammar formalism of Järvinen and Tapanainen (1997) and Karlsson et al. (1995). Note that there are no non-terminal or phrasal nodes; each link in the parse tree holds between two lexical nodes (augmented with the special <ROOT> node). The links are drawn from a fixed inventory of around 35 relations, most of which roughly represent grammatical functions or very general semantic relations. Other dependency-based computational grammars, such as **Link Grammar** (Sleator and Temperley, 1993), use different but roughly overlapping links. The following table shows a few of the relations used in Järvinen and Tapanainen (1997):

LINK GRAMMAR

Dependency	Description
subj	syntactic subject
obj	direct object (incl. sentential complements)
dat	indirect object
pcomp	complement of a preposition
comp	predicate nominals (complements of copulas)
tmp	temporal adverbials
loc	location adverbials
attr	premodifying (attributive) nominals (genitives, etc.)
mod	nominal postmodifiers (prepositional phrases, etc.)

We have already discussed why dependency information is important. Is there any advantage to using only dependency information and ignoring constituency? Dependency grammar researchers argue that one of the main advantages of pure dependency grammars is their ability to handle languages with relatively **free word order**. For example the word order in languages like Czech is much more flexible than in English; an *object* might occur before or after a *location adverbial* or a **comp**. A phrase-structure grammar would need a separate rule for each possible place in the parse tree that such an adverbial phrase could occur. A dependency grammar would just have one link-type representing this particular adverbial relation. Thus a dependency grammar abstracts away from word-order variation, representing only the information that is necessary for the parse.

FREE WORD ORDER

There are a number of computational implementations of dependency grammars; Link Grammar (Sleator and Temperley, 1993) and Constraint Grammar (Karlsson et al., 1995) are easily-available broad-coverage dependency grammars and parsers for English. Dependency grammars are also often used for other languages. Hajič (1998), for example, describes the 500,000 word Prague Dependency Treebank for Czech which has been used to train probabilistic dependency parsers (Collins et al., 1999).

Categorial Grammar

CATEGORIAL GRAMMAR

Categorial grammars were first proposed by Adjukiewicz (1935), and modified by Bar-Hillel (1953), Lambek (1958), Dowty (1979), Ades and Steedman (1982), and Steedman (1989) inter alia. See Bach (1988) for an introduction and the other papers in Oehrle et al. (1988) for a survey of extensions to the basic models. We will describe a simplified version of the combinatory categorial grammar of Steedman (1989). A categorial grammar has two components. The **categorial lexicon** associates each word with a syntactic and semantic category. The **combinatory rules** allow functions and arguments to be combined. There are two types of categories: functors and arguments. Arguments, like nouns, have simple categories like N. Verbs or determiners act as functors. For example, a determiner can be thought of as a function that applies to an N on its right to produce an NP. Such complex categories are built using the X/Y and X\Y operators. X/Y means a function from Y to X, that is, something which combines with a Y on its right to produce an X. Determiners thus receive the category NP/N: something that combines with an N on its right to produce an NP. Transitive verbs might have the category VP/NP; something that combines with an NP on the right to produce a VP. Ditransitive verbs like *give* might have the category (VP/NP)/NP; something which combines with an NP on its right to yield a transitive verb. The simplest **combination rules** just combine an X/Y with a Y on its right to produce an X or a X\Y with a Y on its left to produce an X.

Consider the simple sentence *Harry eats apples* from Steedman (1989). Instead of using a primitive VP category, let's assume that a finite verb phrase like *eat apples* has the category (S\NP); something which combines with an NP on the left to produce a sentence. *Harry* and *apples* are both NPs. *Eats* is a finite transitive verb which combines with an NP on the right to produce a finite VP: (S\NP)/NP. The derivation of S proceeds as follows:

(12.26)
$$
\begin{array}{ccc}
\underline{\text{Harry}} & \underline{\text{eats}} & \underline{\text{apples}} \\
\text{NP} & \text{(S\backslash NP)/NP} & \text{NP} \\
\end{array}
$$

$$
\begin{array}{c}
\text{S\backslash NP} \\
\hline
\text{S}
\end{array}
$$

Modern categorial grammars include more complex combinatory rules which are needed for coordination and other complex phenomena, and also include composition of semantic categories as well as syntactic ones. See Chapter 15 for a discussion of semantic composition, and the above-mentioned references for more details about categorial grammar.

12.5   HUMAN PARSING

How do people parse? Do we have evidence that people use any of the models of grammar and parsing developed over the last four chapters? Do people use probabilities to parse? The study of human parsing (often called human **sentence processing**) is a relatively new one, and we don't yet have complete answers to these questions. But in the last 20 years we have learned a lot about human parsing; this section will give a brief overview of some recent theories. These results are relatively recent, however, and there is still disagreement over the correct way to model human parsing, so the reader should take some of this with a grain of salt.

SENTENCE PROCESSING

An important component of human parsing is ambiguity resolution. How can we find out how people choose between two ambiguous parses of a sentence? As was pointed out in this chapter and in Chapter 9, while almost every sentence is ambiguous in some way, people rarely notice these ambiguities. Instead, they only seem to see one interpretation for a sentence. Following a suggestion by Fodor (1978), Ford et al. (1982) used this fact to show that the human sentence processor is sensitive to **lexical subcate-gorization preferences**. They presented subjects with ambiguous sentences like examples (12.27)–(12.28), in which the preposition phrase *on the beach* could attach either to a noun phrase (*the dogs*) or a verb phrase. They asked the subjects to read the sentence and check off a box indicating which of the two interpretations they got first. The results are shown after each sentence:

(12.27) The women kept the dogs on the beach

- The women kept the dogs which were on the beach. 5%
- The women kept them (the dogs) on the beach. 95%

(12.28) The women discussed the dogs on the beach

- The women discussed the dogs which were on the beach. 90%
- The women discussed them (the dogs) while on the beach. 10%

The results were that subjects preferred VP-attachment with *keep* and NP-attachment with *discuss*. This suggests that *keep* has a subcategorization preference for a VP with three constituents: ($VP \rightarrow V\ NP\ PP$) while *discuss* has a subcategorization preference for a VP with two constituents: ($VP \rightarrow V\ NP$), although both verbs still allow both subcategorizations.

GARDEN-PATH

Much of the more recent ambiguity-resolution research relies on a specific class of temporarily ambiguous sentences called **garden-path** sentences. These sentences, first described by Bever (1970), are sentences which are cleverly constructed to have three properties that combine to make them very difficult for people to parse:

1. They are **temporarily ambiguous**: The sentence is unambiguous, but its initial portion is ambiguous.
2. One of the two or more parses in the initial portion is somehow preferable to the human parsing mechanism.
3. But the dispreferred parse is the correct one for the sentence.

The result of these three properties is that people are "led down the garden path" toward the incorrect parse, and then are confused when they realize it's the wrong one. Sometimes this confusion is quite conscious, as in Bever's example (12.29); in fact this sentence is so hard to parse that readers often need to be shown the correct structure. In the correct structure *raced* is part of a reduced relative clause modifying *The horse*, and means "The horse [which was raced past the barn] fell"; this structure is also present in the sentence "Students taught by the Berlitz method do worse when they get to France".

(12.29) The horse raced past the barn fell.

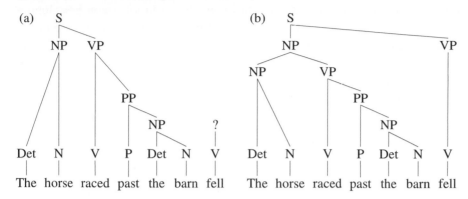

(12.30) The complex houses married and single students and their families.

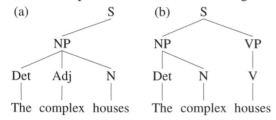

(12.31) The student forgot the solution was in the back of the book.

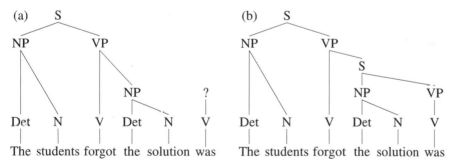

Other times the confusion caused by a garden-path sentence is so subtle that it can only be measured by a slight increase in reading time. Thus in example (12.31) from Trueswell et al. (1993) (modified from an experiment by Ferreira and Henderson (1991)), readers often mis-parse *the solution* as the direct object of *forgot* rather than as the subject of an embedded sentence. This is another subcategorization preference difference; *forgot* prefers a direct object (*VP → V NP*) to a sentential complement (*VP → V S*). But the difference is subtle, and is only noticeable because the subjects spent significantly more time reading the word *was*. How do we know how long a subject takes to read a word or a phrase? One way is by scrolling a sentence onto a computer screen one word or phrase at a time; another is by using an *eye-tracker* to track how long their eyes linger on each word. Trueswell et al. (1993) employed both methods in separate experiments. This "mini-garden-path" effect at the word *was* suggests that subjects had chosen the direct object parse and had to re-analyze or rearrange their parse now that they realize they are in a sentential complement. By contrast, a verb which prefers a sentential complement (like *hope*) didn't cause extra reading time at *was*.

These garden-path sentences are not just restricted to English. Example (12.32) shows a Spanish example from Gilboy and Sopena (1996) in which the word *que*, just like English *that*, is ambiguous between the relative clause marker and the sentential complement marker. Thus up to the phrase *dos hijas*, readers assume the sentence means "the man told the woman that he had two daughters"; after reading the second *que*, they must reparse *que tenia dos hijas* as a relative clause modifier of *mujer* rather than a complement of *dijo*.

(12.32) *El   hombre le   dijo a   la   mujer   que tenía dos hijas*
        The   man   her told to the   woman   that had   two daughters
        que la   invitaba   a   cenar.
        that her   he invited to dinner.
        "The man told the woman who had two daughters that (he) would invite her for dinner."

Example (12.33) shows a Japanese garden path from Mazuka and Itoh (1995). In this sentence, up to the verb *mikaketa* (*saw*), the reader assumes the sentence means "Yoko saw the child at the intersection." But upon reading the word *mikaketa* (*taxi-DAT*), they have to reanalyze *child* not as the object of *saw*, but as the object of *put-on*.

(12.33) *Yoko-ga   kodomo-o koosaten-de   mikaketa takusii-ni noseta.*
        Yoko-NOM child-ACC intersection-LOC saw   taxi-DAT put on
        "Yoko made the child ride the taxi she saw at the intersection."

In the Spanish and Japanese examples, and in examples (12.29) and (12.31), the garden path is caused by the **subcategorization preferences** of the verbs. The garden-path and other methodologies have been employed to study many kinds of preferences besides subcategorization preferences. Example (12.31) from Jurafsky (1996) shows that sometimes these preferences have to do with part-of-speech preferences (e.g., whether *houses* is more likely to be a verb or a noun). Many of these preferences have been shown to be probabilistic and to be related to the kinds of probabilities we have been describing in this chapter. MacDonald (1993) showed that the human processor is sensitive to whether a noun is more likely to be a head or a non-head of a constituent, and also to word-word collocation frequencies. Mitchell et al. (1995) showed that syntactic phrase-structure frequencies (such as the frequency of the relative clause construction) play a role in human processing. Juliano and Tanenhaus (1993) showed that the human processor is sensitive to a combination of lexical and phrase-structure frequency.

Besides grammatical knowledge, human parsing is affected by many other factors which we will describe later, including resource constraints (such as memory limitations, to be discussed in Chapter 13), thematic structure (such as whether a verb expects semantic *agents* or *patients*, to be discussed in Chapter 16) and semantic, discourse, and other contextual constraints (to be discussed in Chapters 15 and 17). While there is general agreement about the knowledge sources used by the human sentence processor, there is less agreement about the *time course* of knowledge use. Frazier and colleagues (most recently in Frazier and Clifton, 1996) argue that an initial interpretation is built using purely syntactic knowledge, and that semantic, thematic, and discourse knowledge only becomes available later. This view is often called a **modularist** perspective; researchers holding this MODULARIST position generally argue that human syntactic knowledge is a distinct module of the human mind. Many other researchers (including MacDonald, 1994; MacWhinney, 1987; Pearlmutter and MacDonald, 1992; Tabor et al., 1997; Trueswell and Tanenhaus, 1994; Trueswell et al., 1994) hold an **interactionist** perspective, arguing that people use multiple kinds of information INTERACTIONIST incrementally. For this latter group, human parsing is an interactive process, in which different knowledge sources interactively constrain the process of interpretation.

Some researchers, including MacDonald (1993) and Jurafsky (1996), argue that, whatever the time-course of the use of linguistic knowledge, these constraints must be fundamentally probabilistic. For example the Bayesian sentence processing model of Jurafsky (1996) and Narayanan and Jurafsky (1998) uses probabilities to explain the difficulty of examples (12.29–12.31) above, and similar garden-path sentences. In their model, the human language processor takes an ambiguous input sentence and computes multiple parallel interpretations. Each of the interpretations is assigned a probability, by combining PCFG probabilities, syntactic and thematic subcategorization

BELIEF NETWORK

probabilities, and other contextual probabilities using a Bayesian **belief network**. For example after seeing the first few words (*The horse raced*) of
example (12.29) the Bayesian model assigns probabilities to both the main
verb (MV) and reduced-relative (RR) interpretations shown in trees (12.29a)
and (12.29b), using the belief net sketched in Figure 12.8. This combines
multiple sources of probabilistic evidence, such as the probability that the
given verb *raced* is transitive (i.e., takes a direct object), the probability that
horse is the semantic *Theme* of a racing event, and the syntactic probability that a noun phrase will include a reduced relative clause. Since *race* is
more likely to be transitive (have a direct object) than not, and furthermore
since reduced relative clauses themselves are low probability, the model predicts that the probability of the main verb interpretation (12.29a) is 300 times
higher than the probability of the reduced relative interpretation.

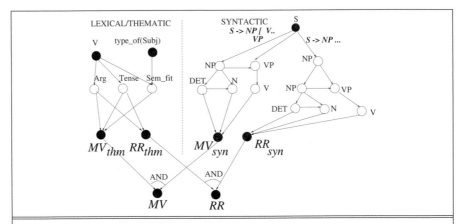

Figure 12.8   A belief net combining PCFG probabilities with subcategorization, thematic, and other lexical probabilities to represent support for the
main verb (MV) and reduced relative (RR) interpretations of a sample input.
From Narayanan and Jurafsky (1998).

The model further assumes that people are unable to maintain very
many interpretations at one time. Whether because of memory limitations,
or just because they have a strong desire to come up with a single interpretation, they prune away low-ranking interpretations (like the pruning described
in Chapter 7). Jurafsky (1996) and Narayanan and Jurafsky (1998) assume
that an interpretation is pruned if its probability is 5 times lower than the
most-probable interpretation. The result is that they sometimes prune away
the correct interpretation, leaving a highest-scoring but incorrect interpretation. This is what happens with the low-probability (but "correct") reduced-

relative interpretation of example (12.29).

The model also explains why seemingly similar sentences do not cause a garden path, such as example (12.34) (Pritchett, 1988; Gibson, 1991); since the verb *found* is transitive, the reduced-relative interpretation becomes much more likely than it was for *race*.

(12.34) The bird found in the room died.

Figure 12.9 shows the differences in the MV/RR probability ratio for *The horse raced* versus *The horse found*.

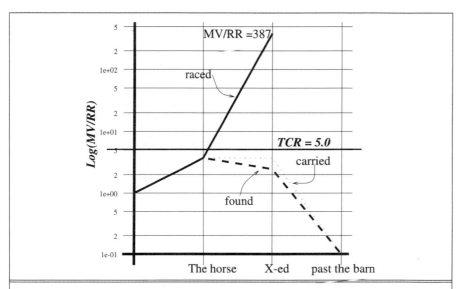

Figure 12.9   The *MV/RR* posterior probability ratio for *raced* falls above the threshold and the *RR* interpretation is pruned. For *found* and *carried*, both interpretations are active in the disambiguating region. From Narayanan and Jurafsky (1998).

The model relies on similar probability differences to explain the garden path effect in example (12.30); for example $P(N{\rightarrow}houses)$ is greater than $P(V{\rightarrow}houses)$. The Narayanan & Jurafsky model is a very preliminary one, relying on relatively simplistic independence assumptions and crude probability models; a key focus of current research is understanding exactly which probabilities are stored by the human sentence processor and how they are combined dynamically.

12.6 SUMMARY

This chapter has sketched the basics of **probabilistic** parsing, concentrating on **probabilistic context-free grammars** and **probabilistic lexicalized grammars**.

- Probabilistic grammars assign a probability to a sentence or string of words, while attempting to capture more sophisticated syntactic information than the N-gram grammars of Chapter 6.

- A **probabilistic context-free grammar** (**PCFG**) is a context-free grammar in which every rule is annotated with the probability of choosing that rule. Each PCFG rule is treated as if it were **conditionally independent**; thus the probability of a sentence is computed by **multiplying** the probabilities of each rule in the parse of the sentence.

- The **Cocke-Younger-Kasami** (**CYK**) algorithm is a bottom-up dynamic programming parsing algorithm. Both the CYK and Earley can be augmented to compute the probability of a parse while they are parsing a sentence.

- PCFG probabilities can be learning by counting in a **parsed corpus**, or by parsing a corpus. The **Inside-Outside** algorithm is a way of dealing with the fact that the sentences being parsed are ambiguous.

- **Probabilistic lexicalized CFGs** augment PCFGs with a **lexical head** for each rule. The probability of a rule can then be conditioned on the lexical head or nearby heads.

- Parsers are evaluated using three metrics: **labeled recall**, **labeled precision**, and **cross-brackets**.

- There is evidence based on **garden-path sentences** and other **on-line sentence-processing experiments** that the human parser operates probabilistically and uses probabilistic grammatical knowledge such as subcategorization information.

BIBLIOGRAPHICAL AND HISTORICAL NOTES

Many of the formal properties of probabilistic context-free grammars were first worked out by Booth (1969) and Salomaa (1969). Baker (1979) proposed the Inside-Outside algorithm for unsupervised training of PCFG probabilities, which used a CYK-style parsing algorithm to compute inside probabilities. Jelinek and Lafferty (1991) extended the CYK algorithm to compute probabilities for prefixes. Stolcke (1995) drew on both these algorithm to adopt the Earley algorithm to PCFGs.

A number of researchers starting in the early 1990s worked on adding lexical dependencies to PCFGs, and on making PCFG probabilities more sensitive to surrounding syntactic structure. Many of these papers were first presented at the DARPA Speech and Natural Language Workshop in June, 1990. A paper by Hindle and Rooth (1990) applied lexical dependencies to the problem of attaching preposition phrases; in the question session to a later paper Ken Church suggested applying this method to full parsing (Marcus, 1990). Early work on such probabilistic CFG parsing augmented with probabilistic dependency information includes Magerman and Marcus (1991), Black et al. (1992), Jones and Eisner (1992), Bod (1993), and Jelinek et al. (1994), in addition to Collins (1996), Charniak (1997), and Collins (1999) discussed above.

Probabilistic formulations of grammar other than PCFGs include probabilistic TAG grammar (Resnik, 1992; Schabes, 1992), based on the TAG grammars discussed in Chapter 9, probabilistic LR parsing (Briscoe and Carroll, 1993), and probabilistic link grammar (Lafferty et al., 1992). An approach to probabilistic parsing called **supertagging** extends the part-of-speech tagging metaphor to parsing by using very complex tags that are in fact fragments of lexicalized parse trees (Bangalore and Joshi, 1999; Joshi and Srinivas, 1994), based on the lexicalized TAG grammars of Schabes et al. (1988). For example the noun *purchase* would have a different tag as the first noun in a noun compound (where it might be on the left of a small tree dominated by Nominal) than as the second noun (where it might be on the right). See Goodman (1997) and Abney (1997) for probabilistic treatments of feature-based grammars. Another approach combines the finite-state model of parsing described in Chapter 9 with the N-gram, by doing partial parsing and then computing N-grams over basic phrases (e.g., $P(PP|NP)$) (Moore et al., 1995; Zechner and Waibel, 1998). A number of probabilistic parsers are based on dependency grammars; see for example Chelba et al. (1997), Chelba and Jelinek (1998), and Berger and Printz (1998); these parsers were also used as language models for speech recognition.

Related to probabilistic dependency grammars is the idea of learning subcategorization frames for verbs, as well as probabilities for these frames. Algorithms which learn non-probabilistic subcategorization frames for verbs include the cue-based approach of Brent (1993) and the finite-state automa-

SUPERTAGGING

ton approach of Manning (1993). Briscoe and Carroll (1997) extract more complex subcategorization frames (using 160 possible subcategorization labels) and also learn subcategorization frame frequencies, using a probabilistic LR parser and some post-processing. Roland and Jurafsky (1998) showed that it is important to compute subcategorization probabilities for the word sense ("lemma") rather than the simple orthographic word.

Many probabilistic and corpus-based approaches have been taken to the preposition-phrase attachment problem since Hindle and Rooth's study, including TBL (Brill and Resnik, 1994), Maximum Entropy (Ratnaparkhi et al., 1994), Memory-Based Learning (Zavrel and Daelemans, 1997), log-linear models (Franz, 1997), and decision trees using semantic distance between heads (computed from WordNet) (Stetina and Nagao, 1997), as well as the use of machine learning techniques like boosting (Abney et al., 1999).

Manning and Schütze (1999) is a good advanced textbook on statistical natural language processing which covers probabilistic parsing. Collins' (1999) dissertation includes a very readable survey of the field and introduction to his parser.

EXERCISES

12.1   Implement the CYK algorithm.

12.2   Sketch out how the CYK algorithm would have to be augmented to handle lexicalized probabilities.

12.3   Implement your lexicalized extension of the CYK algorithm.

12.4   Implement the PARSEVAL metrics described on page 464. Next either use a treebank or create your own hand-checked parsed testset. Now use your CFG (or other) parser and grammar and parse the testset and compute labeled recall, labeled precision, and cross-brackets.

12.5   Take any three sentences from Chapter 9 and hand-parse them into the dependency grammar formalism of Karlsson et al. (1995) shown on page 465.

13 LANGUAGE AND COMPLEXITY

This is the dog, that worried the cat, that killed the rat, that ate the malt, that lay in the house that Jack built.

Mother Goose, *The House that Jack Built*

This is the malt that the rat that the cat that the dog worried killed ate.

Victor H. Yngve (1960)

Much of the humor in musical comedy and comic operetta comes from entwining the main characters in fabulously complicated plot twists. Casilda, the daughter of the Duke of Plaza-Toro in Gilbert and Sullivan's *The Gondoliers*, is in love with her father's attendant Luiz. Unfortunately, Casilda discovers she has already been married (by proxy) as a babe of six months to "the infant son and heir of His Majesty the immeasurably wealthy King of Barataria". It is revealed that this infant son was spirited away by the Grand Inquisitor and raised by a "highly respectable gondolier" in Venice as a gondolier. The gondolier had a baby of the same age and could never remember which child was which, and so Casilda was in the unenviable position, as she puts it, of "being married to one of two gondoliers, but it is impossible to say which". By way of consolation, the Grand Inquisitor informs her that "such complications frequently occur".

Luckily, such complications don't frequently occur in natural language. Or do they? In fact there are sentences that are so complex that they are hard to understand, such as Yngve's sentence above, or the sentence:

"The Republicans who the senator who she voted for chastised were trying to cut all benefits for veterans".

Studying such sentences, and more generally understanding what level of complexity tends to occur in natural language, is an important area of language processing. Complexity plays an important role, for example, in deciding when we need to use a particular formal mechanism. Formal mechanisms like finite automata, Markov models, transducers, phonological rewrite rules, and context-free grammars, can be described in terms of their **power**, or equivalently in terms of the **complexity** of the phenomena that they can describe. This chapter introduces the Chomsky hierarchy, a theoretical tool that allows us to compare the expressive power or complexity of these different formal mechanisms. With this tool in hand, we summarize arguments about the correct formal power of the syntax of natural languages, in particular English but also including a famous Swiss dialect of German that has the interesting syntactic property called **cross-serial dependencies**. This property has been used to argue that context-free grammars are insufficiently powerful to model the morphology and syntax of natural language.

POWER

COMPLEXITY

In addition to using complexity as a metric for understanding the relation between natural language and formal models, the field of complexity is also concerned with what makes individual constructions or sentences hard to understand. For example we saw above that certain **nested** or **center-embedded** sentences are difficult for people to process. Understanding what makes some sentences difficult for people to process is an important part of understanding human parsing.

13.1   THE CHOMSKY HIERARCHY

How are automata, context-free grammars, and phonological rewrite rules related? What they have in common is that each describes a **formal language**, which we have seen is a set of strings over a finite alphabet. But the kind of grammars we can write with each of these formalism are of different **generative power**. One grammar is of greater generative power or **complexity** than another if it can define a language that the other cannot define. We will show, for example, that a context-free grammar can be used to describe formal languages that cannot be described with a finite-state automaton.

GENERATIVE
POWER

It is possible to construct a hierarchy of grammars, where the set of languages describable by grammars of greater power subsumes the set of languages describable by grammars of lesser power. There are many possible such hierarchies; the one that is most commonly used in computational linguistics is the **Chomsky hierarchy** (Chomsky, 1959a), which includes four kinds of grammars, characterized graphically in Figure 13.1.

CHOMSKY
HIERARCHY

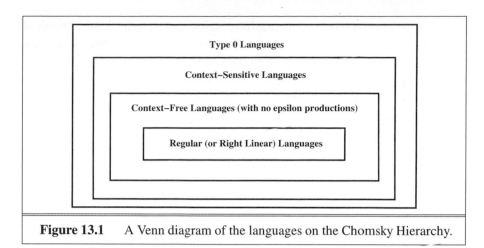

Figure 13.1   A Venn diagram of the languages on the Chomsky Hierarchy.

What is perhaps not intuitively obvious is that the decrease in the generative power of languages from the most powerful to the weakest can be accomplished merely by placing constraints on the way the grammar rules are allowed to be written. The following table shows the four types of grammars in the Chomsky hierarchy, defined by the constraints on the form that rules must take. In these examples, A is a single non-terminal, and α, β, and γ are arbitrary strings of terminal and non-terminal symbols. They may be empty unless this is specifically disallowed below. x is an arbitrary string of terminal symbols.

Type	Common Name	Rule Skeleton	Linguistic Example
0	Turing Equivalent	$\alpha \to \beta$, s.t. $\alpha \neq \varepsilon$	ATNs
1	Context Sensitive	$\alpha A \beta \to \alpha \gamma \beta$, s.t. $\gamma \neq \varepsilon$	Tree-Adjoining Grammars
2	Context Free	$A \to \gamma$	Phrase Structure Grammars
3	Regular	$A \to xB$ or $A \to x$	Finite State Automata

Figure 13.2   The Chomsky Hierarchy.

Type 0 or **unrestricted** grammars have no restrictions on the form of their rules, except that the left-hand side cannot be the empty string ε. Any (non-null) string can be written as any other string (or as ε). Type 0 grammars characterize the **recursively enumerable** languages, that is, those whose strings can be listed (enumerated) by a Turing Machine.

RECURSIVELY
ENUMERABLE

Context-sensitive grammars have rules that rewrite a non-terminal symbol A in the context $\alpha A \beta$ as any non-empty string of symbols. They can be either written in the form $\alpha A \beta \rightarrow \alpha \gamma \beta$ or in the form $A \rightarrow \gamma / \alpha \_\_\beta$. We have seen this latter version in the Chomsky-Halle representation of phonological rules (Chomsky and Halle, 1968), as the following rule of Flapping demonstrates:

$$/t/ \rightarrow [dx] / \acute{V} \_\_ V$$

While the form of these rules seems context-sensitive, Chapter 4 showed that phonological rule systems that do not have recursion are actually equivalent in power to the regular grammars. A linguistic model that is known to be context-sensitive is Tree-Adjoining Grammar (Joshi, 1985).

Another way of conceptualizing a rule in a context-sensitive grammar is as rewriting a string of symbols δ as another string of symbols ϕ in a "non-decreasing" way; such that ϕ has at least as many symbols as δ.

CONTEXT-FREE   We studied **context-free** grammars in Chapter 9. Context-free rules allow any single non-terminal to be rewritten as any string of terminals and non-terminals. A non-terminal may also be rewritten as ε, although we didn't make use of this option in Chapter 9.

Regular grammars are equivalent to regular expressions. That is, a given regular language can be characterized either by a regular expression of the type we discussed in Chapter 2, or by a regular grammar. Regular RIGHT-LINEAR   grammars can either be **right-linear** or **left-linear**. A rule in a right-linear LEFT-LINEAR   grammar has a single non-terminal on the left, and at most one non-terminal on the right-hand side. If there is a non-terminal on the right-hand side, it must be the last symbol in the string. The right-hand-side of left-linear grammars is reversed (the right-hand-side must start with (at most) a single non-terminal). All regular languages have both a left-linear and a right-linear grammar. For the rest of our discussion, we will consider only the right-linear grammars.

For example, consider the following regular (right-linear) grammar:

$$S \rightarrow aA$$
$$S \rightarrow bB$$
$$A \rightarrow aS$$
$$B \rightarrow bbS$$
$$S \rightarrow \varepsilon$$

It is regular, since the left-hand-side of each rule is a single non-terminal and each right-hand side has at most one (rightmost) non-terminal. Here is a sample derivation in the language:

$$S \Rightarrow aA \Rightarrow aaS \Rightarrow aabB \Rightarrow aabbbS \Rightarrow aabbbaA$$
$$\Rightarrow aabbbaaS \Rightarrow aabbbaa$$

We can see that each time S expands, it produces either *aaS* or *bbbS*; thus the reader should convince themself that this language corresponds to the regular expression $(aa \cup bbb)*$.

We will not present the proof that a language is regular if and only if it is generated by a regular language; it was first proved by Chomsky and Miller (1958) and can be found in textbooks like Hopcroft and Ullman (1979) and Lewis and Papadimitriou (1981). The intuition is that since the non-terminals are always at the right or left edge of a rule, they can be processed iteratively rather than recursively.

13.2   HOW TO TELL IF A LANGUAGE ISN'T REGULAR

How do we know which type of rules to use for a given problem? Could we use regular expressions to write a grammar for English? Our do we need to use context-free rules or even context-sensitive rules? It turns out that for formal languages there are methods for deciding this. That is, we can say for a given formal language whether it is representable by a regular expression, or whether it instead requires a context-free grammar, and so on.

So if we want to know if some part of natural language (the phonology of English, let's say, or perhaps the morphology of Turkish) is representable by a certain class of grammars, we need to find a formal language that models the relevant phenomena and figure out which class of grammars is appropriate for this formal language.

Why should we care whether (say) the syntax of English is representable by a regular language? One main reason is that we'd like to know which type of rule to use in writing computational grammars for English. If English is regular, we would write regular expressions, and use efficient automata to process the rules. If English is context-free, we would write context-free rules and use the Earley algorithm to parse sentences, and so on.

Another reason to care is that it tells us something about the formal properties of different aspects of natural language; it would be nice to know where a language "keeps" its complexity; whether the phonological system of a language is simpler than the syntactic system, or whether a certain kind of morphological system is inherently simpler than another kind. It would be a strong and exciting claim, for example, if we could show that the phonology of English was capturable by a finite-state machine rather than the context-sensitive rules that are traditionally used; it would mean that English phonology has quite simple formal properties. Indeed, this fact was shown by Johnson (1972), and helped lead to the modern work in finite-state methods shown in Chapters 3 and 4.

The Pumping Lemma

The most common way to prove that a language is regular is to actually build a regular expression for the language. In doing this we can rely on the fact that the regular languages are closed under union, concatenation, Kleene star, complementation, and intersection. We saw examples of union, concatenation, and Kleene star in Chapter 2. So if we can independently build a regular expression for two distinct parts of a language, we can use the union operator to build a regular expression for the whole language, proving that the language is regular.

PUMPING LEMMA
Sometimes we want to prove that a given language is *not* regular. An extremely useful tool for doing this is the **Pumping Lemma**. There are two intuitions behind this lemma. (Our description of the pumping lemma draws from Lewis and Papadimitriou (1981) and Hopcroft and Ullman (1979).) First, if a language can be modeled by a finite automaton, we must be able to decide with a bounded amount of memory whether any string was in the language or not. This amount of memory can't grow larger for different strings (since a given automaton has a fixed number of states). Thus the memory needs must not be proportional to the length of the input. This means for example that languages like $a^n b^n$ are not likely to be regular, since we would need some way to remember what n was in order to make sure that there were an equal number of a's and b's. The second intuition relies on the fact that if a regular language has any long strings (longer than the number of states in the automaton), there must be some sort of loop in the automaton for the language. We can use this fact by showing that if a language *doesn't* have such a loop, then it can't be regular.

Let's consider a language L and the corresponding deterministic FSA M, which has N states. Consider an input string also of length N. The machine starts out in state q_0; after seeing 1 symbol it will be in state q_1; after N symbols it will be in state q_n. In other words, a string of length N

will go through $N+1$ states (from q_0 to q_N). But there are only N states in the machine. This means that at least two of the states along the accepting path (call them q_i and q_j) must be the same. In other words, somewhere on an accepting path from the initial to final state, there must be a loop. Figure 13.3 shows an illustration of this point. Let x be the string of symbols that the machine reads on going from the initial state q_0 to the beginning of the loop q_i. y is the string of symbols that the machine reads in going through the loop. z is the string of symbols from the end of the loop (q_j) to the final accepting state (q_N).

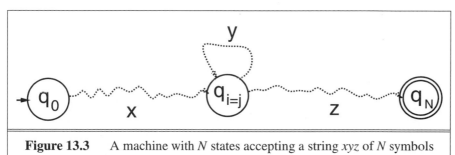

Figure 13.3   A machine with N states accepting a string xyz of N symbols

The machine accepts the concatenation of these three strings of symbols, that is, xyz. But if the machine accepts xyz it must accept xz! This is because the machine could just skip the loop in processing xz. Furthermore, the machine could also go around the loop any number of times; thus it must also accept $xyyz$, $xyyyz$, $xyyyyz$, and so on. In fact, it must accept any string of the form xy^nz for $n \geq 0$.

The version of the pumping lemma we give is a simplified one for infinite regular languages; stronger versions can be stated that also apply to finite languages, but this one gives the flavor of this class of lemmas:

Pumping Lemma. Let L be an infinite regular language. Then there are strings x, y, and z, such that $y \neq \varepsilon$ and $xy^nz \in L$ for $n \geq 0$.

The pumping lemma states that if a language is regular, then there is some string y that can be "pumped" appropriately. But this doesn't mean that if we can pump some string y, the language must be regular. Non-regular languages may also have strings that can be pumped. Thus the lemma is not used for showing that a language *is* regular. Rather it is used for showing that a language *isn't* regular, by showing that in some language there is no possible string that can be pumped in the appropriate way.

Let's use the pumping lemma to show that the language a^nb^n (i.e., the language consisting of strings of as followed by an equal number of bs) is not regular. We must show that any possible string s that we pick cannot be divided up into three parts x, y, and z such that y can be pumped. Given a random string s from $a^n b^n$, we can distinguish three ways of breaking s up, and show that no matter which way we pick, we cannot find some y that can be pumped:

1. y is composed only of as. (This implies that x is all as too, and z contains all the bs, perhaps preceded by some as.) But if y is all as, that means $xy^n z$ has more as than xyz. But this means it has more as than bs, and so cannot be a member of the language $a^n b^n$!

2. y is composed only of bs. The problem here is similar to case 1; If y is all bs, that means $xy^n z$ has more bs than xyz, and hence has more bs than as.

3. y is composed of both as and bs (this implies that x is only as, while z is only bs). This means that $xy^n z$ must have some bs before as, and again cannot be a member of the language $a^n b^n$!

Thus there is no string in $a^n b^n$ that can be divided into x, y, z in such a way that y can be pumped, and hence $a^n b^n$ is not a regular language.

But while $a^n b^n$ is not a regular language, it is a context-free language. In fact, the context-free grammar that models $a^n b^n$ only takes two rules! Here they are:

$$S \rightarrow a\ S\ b$$
$$S \rightarrow \varepsilon$$

Here's a sample parse tree using this grammar to derive the sentence *aabb*:

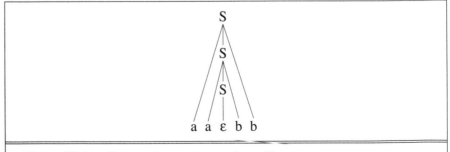

Figure 13.4   Context-free parse tree for *aabb*.

There is also a pumping lemma for context-free languages, that can be used whether or not a language is context-free; complete discussions can be found in Hopcroft and Ullman (1979) and Partee et al. (1990).

Are English and Other Natural Languages Regular Languages?

"How's business?" I asked.
"Lousy and terrible." Fritz grinned richly. "Or I pull off a new
deal in the next month or I go as a gigolo,"
"Either ... or ...," I corrected, from force of professional habit.
"I'm speaking a lousy English just now," drawled Fritz, with great
self-satisfaction. "Sally says maybe she'll give me a few lessons."

Christopher Isherwood, "Sally Bowles",
from *Goodbye to Berlin*. 1935

The pumping lemma provides us with the theoretical machinery for understanding the well-known arguments that English (or rather "the set of strings of English words considered as a formal language") is not a regular language.

The first such argument was given by Chomsky (1956, 1957). He first considers the language $\{xx^R, x \in a,b*\}$. x^R means "the reverse of x", so each sentence of this language consists of a string of as and bs followed by the reverse or "mirror image" of the string. This language is not regular; Partee et al. (1990) shows this by intersecting it with the regular language aa^*bbaa^*. The resulting language is $a^nb^2a^n$; it is left as an exercise for the reader (Exercise 13.3) to show that this is not regular by the pumping lemma.

Chomsky then showed that a particular subset of the grammar of English is isomorphic to the mirror image language. He has us consider the following English syntactic structures, where $S_1, S_2, \ldots, S_n$, are declarative sentences in English:

- If S_1, then S_2
- Either S_3, or S_4
- The man who said S_5 is arriving today

Clearly, Chomsky points out, these are English sentences. Furthermore, in each case there is a lexical dependency between one part of each structure and another. "If" must be followed by "then" (and not, e.g., "or"). "Either" must be followed by "or" (and not, e.g., "because").

Now these sentences can be embedded in English, one in another; for example, we could build sentences like the following:

If *either* the man who said S_5 is arriving today *or* the man who said S_5 is arriving tomorrow, **then** the man who said S_6 is arriving the day after...

The regular languages are closed under substitution or **homomorphism**; this just means that we can rename any of the symbols in the above sentences. Let's introduce the following substitution:

if   → a
then   → a
either   → b
or   → b
other words → ε

Now if we apply this substitution to the sentence above, we get the following sentence:

abba

This sentence has just the mirror-like property that we showed above was not capturable by finite-state methods. If we assume that *if, then, either, or,* can be nested indefinitely, then English is isomorphic to $xx^R, x \in a, b*$, and hence is not a regular language. Of course, it's not true that these structures can be nested indefinitely (sentences like this get hard to understand after a couple nestings); we will return to this issue in Section 13.4.

Partee et al. (1990) gave a second proof that English is not a regular language. This proof is based on a famous class of sentences with **center-** **embedded** structures (Yngve, 1960); here is a variant of these sentences:

The cat likes tuna fish.
The cat the dog chased likes tuna fish.
The cat the dog the rat bit chased likes tuna fish.
The cat the dog the rat the elephant admired bit chased likes tuna fish.

As was true with the either/or sentences above, these sentences get harder to understand as they get more complex. But for now, let's assume that the grammar of English allows an indefinite number of embeddings. Then in order to show that English is not regular, we need to show that sentences like these are isomorphic to some non-regular language. Since every fronted *NP* must have its associated verb, these sentences are of the form:

(the + noun)^n (transitive verb)$^{n-1}$ likes tuna fish.

The idea of the proof will be to show that sentences of these structures can be produced by intersecting English with a regular expression. We will then use the pumping lemma to prove that the resulting language isn't regular.

In order to build a simple regular expression that we can intersect with English to produce these sentences, we define regular expressions for the noun groups (A) and the verbs (B):

A = { the cat, the dog, the rat, the elephant, the kangaroo,... }
B = { chased, bit, admired, ate, befriended, ... }

Now if we take the regular expression /A* B* likes tuna fish/ and intersect it with English (considered as a set of strings), the resulting language is:

$$L = x^n y^{n-1} \text{ likes tuna fish},\ \ x \in A, y \in B$$

This language L can be shown to be non-regular via the pumping lemma (see Exercise 13.2). Since the intersection of English with a regular language is not a regular language, English cannot be a regular language either (since the regular languages are closed under intersection).

The two arguments we have seen so far are based on English syntax. There are also arguments against the finite-state nature of English based on English morphology. These morphological arguments are a different kind of argument, because they don't prove that English morphology *couldn't* be regular, only that a context-free model of English morphology is much more elegant and captures some useful descriptive generalizations. Let's summarize one from Sproat (1993) on the prefix *en-*. Like other English verbs, the verbs formed with this prefix can take the suffix *-able*. So for example the verbs *enjoy* and *enrich* can be suffixed (*enjoyable, enrichable*). But the noun or adjective stems themselves cannot take the *-able* (so **joyable, *richable*). In other words, *-able* can attach if the verb-forming prefix *en-* has already attached, but not if it hasn't.

The reason for this is very simple; *en-* creates verbs, and *-able* only attaches to verbs. But expressing this fact in a regular grammar has an annoying and inelegant redundancy; it would have to have two paths, one through *joy*, one through *enjoy*, leading to different states, as shown in Figure 13.5.

This morphological fact is easy to express in a context-free grammar; this is left as an exercise for the reader.

This kind of "elegance" argument against regular grammars also has been made for syntactic phenomena. For example a number of scholars have argued that English number agreement cannot be captured by a regular (or

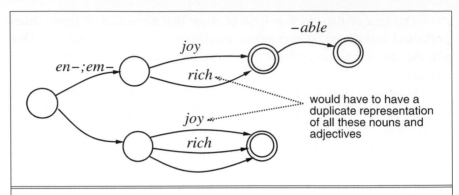

Figure 13.5   A part of an FSA for English morphology (after Sproat (1993)).

even a context-free) grammar. In fact, a simple regular grammar *can* model number agreement, as Pullum and Gazdar (1982) show. They considered the following sentences, which have a long-distance agreement dependency:

> Which *problem* did your professor say she thought *was* unsolvable?
> Which *problems* did your professor say she thought *were* unsolvable?

Here's their regular (right-linear) grammar that models these sentences:

$S \rightarrow$ Which problem did your professor say T

$S \rightarrow$ Which problems did your professor say U

$T \rightarrow$ she thought T | you thought T | was unsolvable

$U \rightarrow$ she thought U | you thought U | were unsolvable

So a regular grammar could model English agreement. The problem with such a grammar is not its computational power, but its elegance, as we saw in Chapter 9; such a regular grammar would have a huge explosion in the number of grammar rules. But for the purposes of computational complexity, agreement is not part of an argument that English is not a regular language.

13.3   IS NATURAL LANGUAGE CONTEXT-FREE?

The previous section argued that English (considered as a set of strings) doesn't seem like a regular language. The natural next question to ask is whether English is a context-free language. This question was first asked by Chomsky (1956), and has an interesting history; a number of well-known attempts to prove English and other languages non-context-free have been published, and all except two have been disproved after publication. One of these two correct (or at least not-yet disproved) arguments derives from the syntax of a dialect of Swiss German; the other from the morphology of Bambara, a Northwestern Mande language spoken in Mali and neighboring countries (Culy, 1985). The interested reader should see Pullum (1991, pp. 131–146) for an extremely witty history of both the incorrect and correct proofs; this section will merely summarize one of the correct proofs, the one based on Swiss German.

Both of the correct arguments, and most of the incorrect ones, make use of the fact that the following languages, and ones that have similar properties, are not context-free:

$$\{xx \mid x \in \{a,b\}^*\} \tag{13.1}$$

This language consists of sentences containing two identical strings concatenated. The following related language is also not context-free:

$$a^n b^m c^n d^m \tag{13.2}$$

The non-context-free nature of such languages can be shown using the pumping lemma for context-free languages.

The attempts to prove that the natural languages are not a subset of the context-free languages do this by showing that natural languages have a property of these xx languages called **cross-serial dependencies**. In a cross-serial dependency, words or larger structures are related in left-to-right order as shown in Figure 13.6. A language that has arbitrarily long cross-serial dependencies can be mapped to the xx languages.

CROSS-SERIAL
DEPENDENCIES

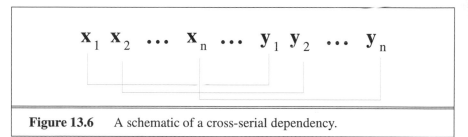

Figure 13.6   A schematic of a cross-serial dependency.

The successful proof, independently proposed by Huybregts (1984) and Shieber (1985a) (as we might expect from the prevalence of multiple discovery in science; see page 15) shows that a dialect of Swiss German spoken in Zürich has cross-serial constraints which make certain parts of that language equivalent to the non-context-free language $a^n b^m c^n d^m$. The intuition is that Swiss German allows a sentence to have a string of dative nouns followed by a string of accusative nouns, followed by a string of dative-taking verbs, followed by a string of accusative-taking verbs.

We will follow the version of the proof presented in Shieber (1985a). First, he notes that Swiss German allows verbs and their arguments to be ordered cross-serially. Assume that all the example clauses we present below are preceded by the string *"Jan säit das"* ("Jan says that"):

(13.3) ...*mer em Hans   es   huus   hälfed   aastriiche.*
       ...we   Hans/DAT the house/ACC helped   paint.

   "...we helped Hans paint the house."

Notice the cross-serial nature of the semantic dependency: both nouns precede both verbs, and *em Hans* (Hans) is the argument of *hälfed* (helped) while *es huus* (the house) is the argument of *aastriiche* (paint). Furthermore, there is a cross-serial case dependency between the nouns and verbs; *hälfed* (helped) requires the dative, and *em Hans* is dative, while *aastriiche* (paint) takes the accusative, and *es huus* (the house) is accusative.

Shieber points out that this case marking can occur even across triply embedded cross-serial clauses like the following:

(13.4) ...*mer d'chind   em Hans   es   huus   haend*
       ...we   the children/ACC Hans/DAT the house/ACC have

   wele   laa hälfe aastriiche.
   wanted to let   help   paint.

   "...we have wanted to let the children help Hans paint the house."

Shieber notes that among such sentences, those with all dative NPs preceding all accusative NPs, and all dative-subcategorizing V's preceding all accusative-subcategorizing V's are acceptable.

Jan säit das mer (d'chind)* (em Hans)* es huus haend wele laa* hälfe* aastriche.

Let's call the regular expression above R. Since it's a regular expression (you see it only has concatenation and Kleene stars) it must define a regular language, and so we can intersect R with Swiss German, and if the result is context free, so is Swiss German.

But it turns out that Swiss German requires that the number of verbs requiring dative objects (*hälfe*) must equal the number of dative NPs (*em Hans*) and similarly for accusatives. Furthermore, an arbitrary number of verbs can occur in a subordinate clause of this type (subject to performance constraints). This means that the result of intersecting this regular language with Swiss German is the following language:

L = Jan säit das mer (d'chind)^n(em Hans)^m es huus haend wele (laa)^n (hälfe)^m aastriiche.

But this language is of the form $wa^n b^m xc^n d^m y$, which is not context-free!

So we can conclude that Swiss German is not context free.

13.4   COMPLEXITY AND HUMAN PROCESSING

We noted in passing earlier that many of the sentences that were used to argue for the non-finite state nature of English (like the "center-embedded" sentences) are quite difficult to understand. If you are a speaker of Swiss German (or if you have a friend who is), you will notice that the long cross-serial sentences in Swiss German are also rather difficult to follow. Indeed, as Pullum and Gazdar (1982) point out,

> precisely those construction-types that figure in the various proofs
> that English is not context-free appear to cause massive difficulty
> in the human processing system...

This brings us to a second use of the term **complexity**. In the previous section we talked about the complexity of a language. Here we turn to a question that is as much psychological as computational: the complexity of an individual sentence. Why are certain sentences hard to comprehend? Can this tell us anything about computational processes?

Many things can make a sentence hard to understand; complicated meanings, extremely ambiguous sentences, the use of rare words, and bad handwriting are just a few. Chapter 12 introduced garden-path sentences, which are certainly complex, and showed that their complexity was due to improper choices made on temporarily ambiguous sentences by the human parser. But there is a another, particular, kind of complexity (often called "linguistic complexity" or "syntactic complexity") that bears an interesting relation to the formal-language complexity from the previous section. These are sentences whose complexity arises not from rare words or difficult meanings, but from a particular combination of syntactic structure and human memory limitations. Here are some examples of sentences (taken from a summary in Gibson (1998)) that cause difficulties when people try to read them (we will use the # to mean that a sentence causes extreme processing

difficulty). In each case the (ii) example is significantly more complex than
the (i) example:

(13.5)   (i) The cat likes tuna fish.
         (ii) #The cat the dog the rat the elephant admired bit chased
              likes tuna fish.
(13.6)   (i) If when the baby is crying, the mother gets upset, the father
              will help, so the grandmother can rest easily.
         (ii) #Because if when the baby is crying, the mother gets upset,
              the father will help, the grandmother can rest easily.
(13.7)   (i) The child damaged the pictures which were taken by the
              photographer who the professor met at the party.
         (ii) #The pictures which the photographer who the professor
              met at the party took were damaged by the child.
(13.8)   (i) The fact that the employee who the manager hired stole
              office supplies worried the executive.
         (ii) #The executive who the fact that the employee stole office
              supplies worried hired the manager.

The earliest work on sentences of this type noticed that they all exhibit
nesting or *center-embedding* (Chomsky, 1957; Yngve, 1960; Chomsky and
Miller, 1963; Miller and Chomsky, 1963). That is, they all contain examples where a syntactic category A is nested within another category B, and
surrounded by other words (X and Y):

$$[_B \text{ X } [_A] \text{ Y}]$$

In each of the examples above, part (i) has zero or one embedding,
while part (ii) has two or more embeddings. For example in (13.5ii) above,
there are three reduced relative clauses embedded inside each other:

[$_S$ The cat [$_{S'}$ the dog [$_{S'}$ the rat [$_{S'}$ the elephant admired] bit]
chased] likes tuna fish].

In (13.6ii) above, the *when* clauses are nested inside the *if* clauses inside the *because* clauses.

#[Because [if [when the baby is crying, the mother gets upset],
the father will help], [the grandmother can rest easily]].

In (13.7ii), the relative clause *who the professor met at the party* is
nested in between *the photographer* and *took*. The relative clause *which the
photographer . . . took* is then nested between *The pictures* and *were damaged
by the child.*

#The pictures [which the photographer [who the professor met at the party] took] were damaged by the child.

Could we explain the difficulty of these nested structures just by saying that they are ungrammatical in English? The answer seems to be no. The structures that are used in the complex sentences in (13.5ii)–(13.8ii) are the same ones used in the easier sentences (13.5i)–(13.8i). The difference between the easy and complex sentences seems to hinge on the *number* of embeddings. But there is no natural way to write a grammar that allows N embeddings but not $N + 1$ embeddings.

Rather, the complexity of these sentences seems to be a processing phenomenon; some fact about the human parsing mechanism is unable to deal with these kinds of multiple nestings. If complexity is a fact about "parsers" rather than grammars, we would expect sentences to be complex for similar reasons in other languages. That is, other languages have different grammars, but presumably some of the architecture of the human parser is shared from language to language.

It does seems to be the case that multiply nested structures of this kind are also difficult in other languages. For example Japanese allows a singly nested clause, but an additional nesting makes a sentence unprocessable (Cowper, 1976; Babyonyshev and Gibson, 1999).

(13.9) *Ani-ga   imooto-o   ijimeta.*
older-brother-NOM   younger-sister-ACC   bullied
"My older brother bullied my younger sister"

(13.10) *Bebiisitaa-wa   [[ani-ga   imooto-o*
babysitter-TOP   [[older-brother-NOM   younger-sister-ACC
ijimeta]   to]   itta.
bullied]   that]   said
"The babysitter said that my older brother bullied my younger sister"

(13.11) *#Obasan-wa   [[Bebiisitaa-ga   [[ani-ga*
aunt-TOP   [[babysitter-NOM   [[older-brother-NOM
imooto-o   ijimeta]   to]   itta]   to]   omotteiru.
younger-sister-ACC   bullied]   that]   said]   that]   thinks
"#My aunt thinks that the babysitter said that my older brother bullied my younger sister."

There are a number of attempts to explain these complexity effects, many of which are memory-based. That is, they rely on the intuition that each embedding requires some memory resource to store. A sentence with too much embedding either uses up too many memory resources, or creates multiple memory traces that are confusable with each other. The result is that the sentence is too hard to process at all.

For example Yngve (1960) proposed that the human parser is based on a limited-size stack. A stack-based parser places incomplete phrase-structure rules on the stack; if multiple incomplete phrases are nested, the stack will contain an entry for each of these incomplete rules. Yngve suggests that the more incomplete phrase-structure rules the parser needs to store on the stack, the more complex the sentence. Yngve's intuition was that these stack limits might mean that English is actually a regular rather than context-free language, since a context-free grammar with a finite limit on its stack-size can be modeled by a finite automaton.

SELF-EMBEDDED   An extension to this model (Miller and Chomsky, 1963) proposes that **self-embedded** structures are particularly difficult. A self-embedded structure contains a syntactic category A nested within another example of A, and surrounded by other words (X and Y):

$$[_A \ X \ [_A] \ Y]$$

Such structures might be difficult because a stack-based parser might confused two copies of the rule on the stack. This problem with self-embedding is also naturally modeled with an activation-based model, which might have only one copy of a particular rule.

Although these classic parser-based explanations have intuitive appeal, and tie in nicely to the formal language complexity issues, it seems unlikely that they are correct. One problem with them is that there are lots of syntactic complexity effects that aren't explained by these models. For example there are significant complexity differences between sentences that have the same number of embeddings, such as the well-known difference between subject-extracted relative clauses (13.12ii) and object-extracted relative clauses (13.12i):

(13.12)   (i) [$_S$ The reporter [$_{S'}$ who [$_S$ the senator attacked]] admitted
               the error].

          (ii) [$_S$ The reporter [$_{S'}$ who [$_S$ attacked the senator]] admitted
               the error].

The object-extracted relative clauses are more difficult to process (measured for example by the amount of time it takes to read them (Ford, 1983), and other factors; see for example Wanner and Maratsos (1978) and King and Just (1991), and Gibson (1998) for a survey). Different researchers have hypothesized a number of different factors that might explain this complexity difference.

For example MacWhinney and colleagues (MacWhinney, 1977, 1982; MacWhinney and Csaba Pléh, 1988) suggest that it causes difficulty for reader to *shift perspective* from one clause participant to another. Object relative require two perspective shifts (from the matrix subject to the relative clause subject and then back) while subject relatives require none (the matrix subject is the same as the relative clause subject). Another potential source of the difficulty in the object-extraction is that the first noun (*the reporter*) plays two different thematic roles—agent of one clause, patient of the other. This conflicting role-assignment may cause difficulties (Bever, 1970).

Gibson (1998) points out that there is another important difference between the object and subject extractions: the object extraction has two nouns that appear before any verb. The reader must hold on to these two nouns without knowing how they will fit into the sentences. Having multiple noun phrases lying around that aren't integrated into the meaning of the sentence presumably causes complexity for the reader.

Based on this observation, Gibson proposes the **Syntactic Prediction Locality Theory** (**SPLT**), which predicts that the syntactic memory load associated with a structure is the sum of the memory loads associated with each of the words that are obligatorily required to complete the sentence. A sentence with multiple noun phrases and no verbs will require multiple verbs before the sentence is complete, and will thus have a high load. Memory load is also based on how many other new phrases or discourse referents have to be held in memory at the same time. Thus the memory load for a word is higher if there have been many intervening *new discourse referents* since the word has been predicted. Thus while a sequence of unintegrated NPs is very complex, a sequence in which one of the two NPs is a pronoun referring to someone already in the discourse is less complex. For example the following examples of doubly nested relative clauses are processable because the innermost NP (*I*) does not introduce a new discourse entity.

(13.13)   (a) A syntax book [that some Italian [that I had never heard of]
                     wrote] was published by MIT Press (Frank, 1992)

             (b) The pictures [that the photographer [who I met at the party]
                     took] turned out very well. *(Bever, personal communication
                     to E. Gibson)*

In summary, the early suggestions that the complexity of human sentence processing is related to memory seem to be correct at some level; complexity in both natural and formal languages is caused by the need to keep many un-integrated things in memory. This is a deep and fascinating finding about language processing. But the relation between formal and natural complexity is not as simple as Yngve and others thought. Exactly which factors do play a role in complexity is an exciting research area that is just beginning to be investigated.

13.5   SUMMARY

This chapter introduced two different ideas of **complexity**: the complexity of a formal language, and the complexity of a human sentence.

- Grammars can be characterized by their **generative power**. One grammar is of greater generative power or **complexity** than another if it can define a language that the other cannot define. The **Chomsky hierarchy** is a hierarchy of grammars based on their generative power. It includes **Turing equivalent**, **context-sensitive**, **context-free**, and **regular** grammars.
- The **pumping lemma** can be used to prove that a given language is **not regular**. English is not a regular language, although the kinds of sentences that make English non-regular are exactly those that are hard for people to parse. Despite many decades of attempts to prove the contrary, English does, however, seem to be a context-free language. The syntax of Swiss-German and the morphology of Bambara, by contrast, are not context-free and seem to require context-sensitive grammars.
- **Center-embedded** sentences are hard for people to parse. Many theories agree that this difficulty is somehow caused by **memory limitations** of the human parser.

BIBLIOGRAPHICAL AND HISTORICAL NOTES

Chomsky (1956) first asked whether finite-state automata or context-free grammars were sufficient to capture the syntax of English. His suggestion in that paper that English syntax contained "examples that are not easily explained in terms of phrase structure" was a motivation for his development of syntactic transformations. Pullum (1991, pp. 131–146) is the definitive historical study of research on the non-context-free-ness of natural language. The early history of attempts to prove natural languages non-context-free is

summarized in Pullum and Gazdar (1982). The pumping lemma was originally presented by Bar-Hillel et al. (1961), who also offer a number of important proofs about the closure and decidability properties of finite-state
and context-free languages. Further details, including the pumping lemma
for context-free languages (also due to Bar-Hillel et al. (1961)) can be found
in a textbook in automata theory such as Hopcroft and Ullman (1979).

Yngve's idea that the difficulty of center-embedded sentences could
be explained if the human parser was finite-state was taken up by Church
(1980) in his master's thesis. He showed that a finite-state parser that implements this idea could also explain a number of other grammatical and
psycholinguistic phenomena. While the cognitive modeling field has turned
toward more sophisticated models of complexity, Church's work can be seen
as the beginning of the return to finite-state models in speech and language
processing that characterized the 1980s and 1990s.

There are a number of other ways of looking at complexity that we
didn't have space to go into here. One is whether language processing is
NP-complete. **NP-complete** is the name of a class of problems which are   NP-COMPLETE
suspected to be particularly difficult to process. Barton et al. (1987) prove a
number of complexity results about the NP-completeness of natural language
recognition and parsing. Among other things, they showed that

1. Maintaining lexical and agreement feature ambiguities over a potentially infinite-length sentence causes the problem of recognizing sentences in some unification-based formalisms like Lexical-Functional
   Grammar to be NP-complete.

2. Two-level morphological parsing (or even just mapping between lexical and surface form) is also NP-complete.

Recent work has also begun to link processing complexity with information-theoretic measures like Kolmogorov complexity (Juola, 1999).

EXERCISES

13.1   Is the language $a^n b^2 a^n$ context-free?

13.2   Use the pumping lemma to show this language is not regular:

$L = x^n y^{n-1} likes\ tuna\ fish, x \in A, y \in B$

13.3   Partee et al. (1990) showed that the language $xx^R, x \in a, b*$ is not regular, by intersecting it with the regular language aa^*bbaa^*. The resulting language is $a^n b^2 a^n$. Use the pumping lemma to show that this language is not regular, completing the proof that $xx^R, x \in a, b*$ is not regular.

13.4   Build a context-free grammar for the language

$$L = \{xx^R | x \in a, b*\}$$

13.5   Using a context-free grammar to represent the English morphological facts described in Figure 13.5. Assume that *en-* applies to a particular class of adjectives (call it Adj_{35}) and nouns (call it $Noun_{16}$).

Part III

SEMANTICS

Semantics is the study of the meaning of linguistic utterances. This part of the book focuses on formal representations for capturing meaning and on algorithms for mapping from utterances to these meaning representations. A key theme of the entire section is to model how the meaning of an utterance is related to the meanings of the phrases, words and morphemes that constitute it. Issues related to speakers and hearers, and the context in which utterances are found, will be deferred to Part IV, Pragmatics.

This part begins by exploring ways to represent the meaning of utterances, focusing on the use of First Order Predicate Calculus. It next explores various theoretical and practical approaches to compositional semantic analysis and their use in practical problems such as question answering and information extraction. It next turns to the topic of the meanings of individual words, the role of meaning in the organization of a lexicon, and algorithms for word-sense disambiguation. Finally, it covers the topic of information retrieval, an application area of great importance that operates almost entirely on the basis of individual word meanings.

Part III

<table>
<tr><td>

14</td><td>

REPRESENTING MEANING</td></tr>
</table>

ISHMAEL: *Surely all this is not without meaning.*
Herman Melville, *Moby Dick*

The approach to semantics that is introduced here, and is elaborated on in the next four chapters, is based on the notion that the meaning of linguistic utterances can be captured in formal structures, which we will call **meaning representations**. Correspondingly, the frameworks that are used to specify the syntax and semantics of these representations will be called **meaning representation languages**. These meaning representations play a role analogous to that of the phonological, morphological, and syntactic representations introduced in earlier chapters.

MEANING REPRESENTATIONS

MEANING REPRESENTATION LANGUAGES

The need for these representations arises when neither the raw linguistic inputs, nor any of the structures derivable from them by any of the transducers we have studied, facilitate the kind of semantic processing that is desired. More specifically, what is needed are representations that can bridge the gap from linguistic inputs to the kind of non-linguistic knowledge needed to perform a variety of tasks involving the meaning of linguistic inputs.

To illustrate this idea, consider the following everyday language tasks that require some form of semantic processing:

- answering an essay question on an exam
- deciding what to order at a restaurant by reading a menu
- learning to use a new piece of software by reading the manual
- realizing that you've been insulted
- following a recipe

It should be clear that simply having access to the kind of phonological, morphological, and syntactic representations we have discussed thus far will not get us very far on accomplishing any of these tasks. These tasks require access to representations that link the linguistic elements involved in the task to the non-linguistic *knowledge of the world* needed to successfully accomplish them. For example, some of the knowledge of the world needed to perform the above tasks includes:

- Answering and grading essay questions requires background knowledge about the topic of the question, the desired knowledge level of the students, and how such questions are *normally* answered.

- Reading a menu and deciding what to order, giving advice about where to go to dinner, following a recipe, and generating new recipes all require deep knowledge about food, its preparation, what people like to eat and what restaurants are like.

- Learning to use a piece of software by reading a manual, or giving advice about how to do the same, requires deep knowledge about current computers, the specific software in question, similar software applications, and knowledge about users in general.

In the representational approach being explored here, we take linguistic inputs and construct meaning representations that are made up of the *same kind of stuff* that is used to represent this kind of everyday commonsense knowledge of the world. The process whereby such representations SEMANTIC are created and assigned to linguistic inputs is called **semantic analysis**.
ANALYSIS

To make this notion more concrete, consider Figure 14.1, which shows sample meaning representations for the sentence *I have a car* using four frequently used meaning representation languages. The first row illustrates a sentence in **First Order Predicate Calculus**, which will be covered in detail in Section 14.3; the graph in the center illustrates a **Semantic Network**, which will be discussed further in Section 14.5; the third row contains a **Conceptual Dependency** diagram, discussed in more detail in Chapter 16, and finally a frame-based representation, also covered in Section 14.5.

While there are a number of significant differences among these four approaches to representation, at an abstract level they all share as a common foundation the notion that a meaning representation consists of structures composed from a set of symbols. When appropriately arranged, these symbol structures are taken to correspond to objects, and relations among objects, in some world being represented. In this case, all four representations make use of symbols corresponding to the speaker, a car, and a number of relations denoting the possession of one by the other.

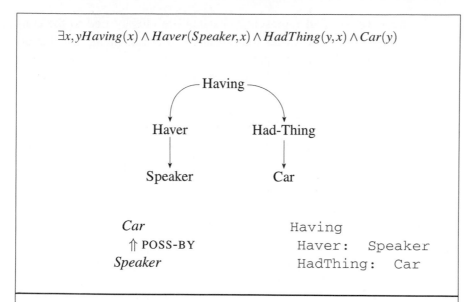

$$\exists x, y Having(x) \wedge Haver(Speaker, x) \wedge HadThing(y, x) \wedge Car(y)$$

	Having	
Haver		Had-Thing
Speaker		Car

Car
   ⇑ POSS-BY
Speaker

```
Having
  Haver:    Speaker
  HadThing: Car
```

Figure 14.1   A list of symbols, two directed graphs, and a record structure: a sampler of meaning representations for *I have a car*.

It is important to note that these representations can be viewed from at least two distinct perspectives in all four of these approaches: as representations of the meaning of the particular linguistic input *I have a car*, and as representations of the state of affairs in some world. It is this dual perspective that allows these representations to be used to link linguistic inputs to the world and to our knowledge of it.

The structure of this part of the book parallels that of the previous parts. We will alternate discussions of the nature of meaning representations with discussions of the computational processes that can produce them. More specifically, this chapter introduces the basics of what is needed in a meaning representation, while Chapter 15 introduces a number of techniques for assigning meanings to linguistic inputs. Chapter 16 explores a range of complex representational issues related to the meanings of words. Chapter 17 then explores some robust computational methods designed to exploit these lexical representations.

Note that since the emphasis of this chapter is on the basic requirements of meaning representations, we will defer a number of extremely important issues to later chapters. In particular, the focus of this chapter is on representing what is sometimes called the **literal meaning** of sentences. LITERAL MEANING

By this, we have in mind representations that are closely tied to the conventional meanings of the words that are used to create them, and that do not reflect the context in which they occur. The shortcomings of such representations with respect to phenomena such as idioms and metaphor will be discussed in the next two chapters, while the role of context in ascertaining the deeper meaning of sentences will be covered in Chapters 18 and 19.

There are three major parts to this chapter. Section 14.1 explores some of the practical computational requirements for what is needed in a meaning representation language. Section 14.2 then discusses some of the ways that language is structured to convey meaning. Section 14.3 then provides an introduction to First Order Predicate Calculus, which has historically been the principal technique used to investigate semantic issues.

14.1   COMPUTATIONAL DESIDERATA FOR REPRESENTATIONS

We begin by considering the issue of why meaning representations are needed and what they should do for us. To focus this discussion, we will consider in more detail the task of giving advice about restaurants to tourists. In this discussion, we will assume that we have a computer system that accepts spoken language queries from tourists and construct appropriate responses by using a knowledge base of relevant domain knowledge. A series of examples will serve to introduce some of the basic requirements that a meaning representation must fulfill, and some of the complications that inevitably arise in the process of designing such meaning representations. In each of these examples, we will examine the role that the representation of the meaning of the request must play in the process of satisfying it.

Verifiability

Let us begin by considering the following simple question:

(14.1) Does Maharani serve vegetarian food?

This example illustrates the most basic requirement for a meaning representation: it must be possible to use the representation to determine the relationship between the meaning of a sentence and the world as we know it. In other words, we need to be able to determine the truth of our representations. The most straightforward way to implement this notion is make it possible for a system to compare, or *match*, the representation of the meaning of an input against the representations in its **knowledge base**, its store of information

KNOWLEDGE
BASE

about its world.

In this example, let us assume that the meaning of this question contains, as a component, the meaning underlying the proposition *Maharani serves vegetarian food*. For now, we will simply gloss this representation as:

Serves(Maharani, VegetarianFood)

It is this representation of the input that will be matched against the knowledge base of facts about a set of restaurants. If the system finds a representation matching the input proposition in its knowledge base, it can return an affirmative answer. Otherwise, it must either say *No*, if its knowledge of local restaurants is complete, or say that it does not know if there is reason to believe that its knowledge is incomplete.

This notion is known as **verifiability**, and concerns a system's ability   VERIFIABILITY
to compare the state of affairs described by a representation to the state of affairs in some world as modeled in a knowledge base.[1]

Unambiguous Representations

The domain of semantics, like all the other domains we have studied, is subject to ambiguity. Specifically, single linguistic inputs can legitimately have different meaning representations assigned to them based on the circumstances in which they occur.

Consider the following example from the BERP corpus:

(14.2) I wanna eat someplace that's close to ICSI.

Given the allowable argument structures for the verb *eat*, this sentence can either mean that the speaker wants to eat *at* some nearby location, or under a Godzilla as speaker interpretation, the speaker may want to devour some nearby location. The answer generated by the system for this request will depend on which interpretation is chosen as the correct one.

Since ambiguities such as this abound in all genres of all languages, some means of determining that certain interpretations are preferable (or alternatively less preferable) than others is needed. The various linguistic phenomenon that give rise to such ambiguities, and the techniques that can be employed to deal with them, will be discussed in detail in the next four chapters.

Our concern in this chapter, however, is with the status of our meaning representations with respect to ambiguity, and not with how we arrive at

---

[1] This is a fairly practical characterization of verifiability. More theoretical views of this notion are briefly covered in Section 14.6.

correct interpretations. Since we reason about, and act upon, the semantic content of linguistic inputs, the final representation of an input's meaning should be free from any ambiguity. Therefore, regardless of any ambiguity in the raw input, it is critical that a meaning representation language support representations that have a single unambiguous interpretation.[2]

VAGUENESS   A concept closely related to ambiguity is **vagueness**. Like ambiguity, vagueness can make it difficult to determine what to do with a particular input based on its meaning representation. Vagueness, however, does not give rise to multiple representations.

Consider the following request as an example:

(14.3) I want to eat Italian food.

While the use of the phrase *Italian food* may provide enough information for a restaurant advisor to provide reasonable recommendations, it is neverthe-less quite *vague* as to what the user really wants to eat. Therefore, a vague representation of the meaning of this phrase may be appropriate for some purposes, while a more specific representation may be needed for other pur-poses. It will, therefore, be advantageous for a meaning representation lan-guage to support representations that maintain a certain level of vagueness. Note that it is not always easy to distinguish ambiguity from vagueness. Zwicky and Sadock (1975) provide a useful set of tests that can be used as diagnostics.

Canonical Form

The notion that single sentences can be assigned multiple meanings leads to the related phenomenon of distinct inputs that should be assigned the same meaning representation. Consider the following alternative ways of express-ing example (14.1):

(14.4) Does Maharani have vegetarian dishes?

(14.5) Do they have vegetarian food at Maharani?

(14.6) Are vegetarian dishes served at Maharani?

(14.7) Does Maharani serve vegetarian fare?

Given that these alternatives use different words and have widely vary-ing syntactic analyses, it would not be unreasonable to expect them to have

---

[2] This does not foreclose the use of intermediate semantic representations that maintain some level of ambiguity on the way to a single unambiguous form. Examples of such repre-sentations will be discussed in Chapter 15.

substantially different meaning representations. Such a situation would, however, have undesirable consequences for our matching approach to determining the truth of our representations. If the system's knowledge base contains only a single representation of the fact in question, then the representations underlying all but one of our alternatives will fail to produce a match. We could, of course, store all possible alternative representations of the same fact in the knowledge base, but this would lead to an enormous number of problems related to keeping such a knowledge base consistent.

The way out of this dilemma is motivated by the fact that since the answers given for each of these alternatives should be the same in all situations, we might say that they all mean the same thing, at least for the purposes of giving restaurant recommendations. In other words, at least in this domain, we can legitimately consider assigning the same meaning representation to the propositions underlying each of these requests. Taking such an approach would guarantee that our matching scheme for answering Yes-No questions will still work.

The notion that inputs that mean the same thing should have the same meaning representation is known as the doctrine of **canonical form**. This CANONICAL FORM approach greatly simplifies various reasoning tasks since systems need only deal with a single meaning representation for a potentially wide range of expressions.

Canonical form does, of course, complicate the task of semantic analysis. To see this, note that the alternatives given above use completely different words and syntax to refer to vegetarian fare and to what restaurants do with it. More specifically, to assign the same representation to all of these requests our system will have to conclude that *vegetarian fare*, *vegetarian dishes* and *vegetarian food* refer to the same thing in this context, that the use here of *having* and *serving* are similarly equivalent, and that the different syntactic parses underlying these requests are all compatible with the same meaning representation.

Being able to assign the same representation to such diverse inputs is a tall order. Fortunately there are some systematic meaning relationships among word senses and among grammatical constructions that can be exploited to make this task tractable. Consider the issue of the meanings of the words *food*, *dish* and *fare* in these examples. A little introspection, or a glance at a dictionary, reveals that these words have a fair number of distinct uses. Fortunately, it also reveals that there is at least one sense that is shared among them all. If a system has the ability to choose that shared sense, then an identical meaning representation can be assigned to the phrases contain-

WORD
SENSES

WORD SENSE
DISAMBIGUATION

ing these words.

In general, we say that these words all have various **word senses** and that some of the senses are synonymous with one another. The process of choosing the right sense in context is called **word sense disambiguation**, or word sense tagging by analogy to part-of-speech tagging. The topics of synonymy, sense tagging, and a host of other topics related to word meanings will be covered in Chapters 16 and 17. Suffice it to say here that the fact that inputs may use different words does not preclude the assignment of identical meanings to them.

Just as there are systematic relationships among the meanings of different words, there are similar relationships related to the role that syntactic analyses play in assigning meanings to sentences. Specifically, alternative syntactic analyses often have meanings that are, if not identical, at least systematically related to one another. Consider the following pair of examples:

(14.8) Maharani serves vegetarian dishes.

(14.9) Vegetarian dishes are served by Maharani.

Despite the different placement of the arguments to *serve* in these examples, we can still assign *Maharani* and *vegetarian dishes* to the same roles in both of these examples because of our knowledge of the relationship between active and passive sentence constructions. In particular, we can use knowledge of where grammatical subjects and direct objects appear in these constructions to assign *Maharani*, to the role of the server, and *vegetarian dishes* to the role of thing being served in both of these examples, despite the fact that they appear in different surface locations. The precise role of the grammar in the construction of meaning representations will be covered in Chapter 15.

Inference and Variables

Continuing with the topic of the computational purposes that meaning representations should serve, we should consider more complex requests such as the following:

(14.10) Can vegetarians eat at Maharani?

Here, it would be a mistake to invoke canonical form to force our system to assign the same representation to this request as for the previous examples. The fact that this request results in the same answer as the others arises not because they mean the same thing, but because there is a commonsense connection between what vegetarians eat and what vegetarian restaurants serve. This is a fact about the world and not a fact about any particular kind of linguistic regularity. This implies that no approach based on canonical form and simple matching will give us an appropriate answer to this request. What is needed is a systematic way to connect the meaning representation of this request with the facts about the world as they are represented in a knowledge base.

We will use the term **inference** to refer generically to a system's ability to draw valid conclusions based on the meaning representation of inputs and its store of background knowledge. It must be possible for the system to draw conclusions about the truth of propositions that are not explicitly represented in the knowledge base, but are nevertheless logically derivable from the propositions that are present.

INFERENCE

Now consider the following somewhat more complex request:

(14.11) I'd like to find a restaurant where I can get vegetarian food.

Unlike our previous examples, this request does not make reference to any particular restaurant. The user is stating that they would like information about an unknown and unnamed entity that is a restaurant that serves vegetarian food. Since this request does not mention any particular restaurant, the kind of simple matching-based approach we have been advocating is not going to work. Rather, answering this request requires a more complex kind of matching that involves the use of variables. We can gloss a representation containing such variables as follows:

$$Serves(x, VegetarianFood)$$

Matching such a proposition succeeds only if the variable x can be replaced by some known object in the knowledge base in such a way that the entire proposition will then match. The concept that is substituted for the variable can then be used to fulfill the user's request. Of course, this simple example only hints at the issues involved in the use of such variables. Suffice it to say that linguistic inputs contain many instances of all kinds of indefinite references and it is therefore critical for any meaning representation language to be able to handle this kind of expression.

Expressiveness

Finally, to be useful a meaning representation scheme must be expressive enough to handle an extremely wide range of subject matter. The ideal situation, of course, would be to have a single meaning representation language that could adequately represent the meaning of any sensible natural language utterance. Although this is probably too much to expect from any

single representational system, Section 14.3 will show that First Order Predicate Calculus is expressive enough to handle quite a lot of what needs to be
represented.

14.2   MEANING STRUCTURE OF LANGUAGE

The previous section focused on some of the purposes that meaning representations must serve, without saying much about what we will call the
meaning structure of language. By this, we have in mind the various methods by which human languages convey meaning. These include a variety of
conventional form-meaning associations, word-order regularities, tense systems, conjunctions and quantifiers, and a fundamental predicate-argument
structure. The remainder of this section focuses exclusively on this last notion of a predicate-argument structure, which is the mechanism that has had
the greatest practical influence on the nature of meaning representation languages. The remaining topics will be addressed in Chapter 15 where the
primary focus will be on how they contribute to how meaning representations are assembled, rather than on the nature of the representations.

Predicate-Argument Structure

It appears to be the case that all human languages have a form of predicate-
argument arrangement at the core of their semantic structure. To a first approximation, this predicate-argument structure asserts that specific relationships hold among the various concepts underlying the constituent words and
phrases that make up sentences. It is largely this underlying structure that
permits the creation of a single composite meaning representation from the
meanings of the various parts of an input. One of the most important jobs
of a grammar is to help organize this predicate-argument structure. Correspondingly, it is critical that our meaning representation languages support
the predicate-argument structures presented to us by language.

We have already seen the beginnings of this concept in our discussion
of verb complements in Chapters 9 and 11. There we saw that verbs dictate
specific constraints on the number, grammatical category, and location of
the phrases that are expected to accompany them in syntactic structures. To
briefly review this idea, consider the following examples:

(14.12) I want Italian food.

(14.13) I want to spend less than five dollars.

(14.14) I want it to be close by here.

These examples can be classified as having one of the following three syntactic argument frames:

NP want NP

NP want Inf-VP

NP want NP Inf-VP

These syntactic frames specify the number, position and syntactic category of the arguments that are expected to accompany a verb. For example, the frame for the variety of *want* that appears in example (14.12) specifies the following facts:

- There are two arguments to this predicate.
- Both arguments must be *NP*s.
- The first argument is pre-verbal and plays the role of the subject.
- The second argument is post-verbal and plays the role of the direct object.

As we have shown in previous chapters, this kind of information is quite valuable in capturing a variety of important facts about syntax. By analyzing easily observable semantic information associated with these frames, we can also gain considerable insight into our meaning representations. We will begin by considering two extensions of these frames into the semantic realm: semantic roles and semantic restrictions on these roles.

The notion of a semantic role can be understood by looking at the similarities among the arguments in examples (14.12) through (14.14). In each of these cases, the pre-verbal argument always plays the role of the entity doing the wanting, while the post-verbal argument plays the role of the concept that is *wanted.* By noticing these regularities and labeling them accordingly, we can associate the surface arguments of a verb with a set of discrete roles in its underlying semantics. More generally, we can say that verb subcategorization frames allow the **linking** of arguments in the surface structure with the semantic roles these arguments play in the underlying semantic representation of an input. The study of roles associated with specific verbs and across classes of verbs is usually referred to as **thematic role** or **case role** analysis and will be studied in more detail in Section 14.4 and Chapter 16.

LINKING

THEMATIC ROLE

CASE ROLE

The notion of semantic restrictions arises directly from these semantic roles. Returning to examples (14.12) through (14.14), we can see that it is not merely the case that each initial noun phrase argument will be the *wanter* but that only certain kinds, or *categories*, of concepts can play the role of

wanter in any straightforward manner. Specifically, *want* restricts the constituents appearing as the first argument to those whose underlying concepts can actually partake in a wanting. Traditionally, this notion is referred to as SELECTIONAL
RESTRICTION a **selectional restriction**. Through the use of these selectional restrictions, verbs can specify semantic restrictions on their arguments.

Before leaving this topic, we should note that verbs are by no means the only objects in a grammar that can carry a predicate-argument structure. Consider the following phrases from the BERP corpus:

(14.15) an Italian restaurant under fifteen dollars

In this example, the meaning representation associated with the preposition *under* can be seen as having something like the following structure:

$$Under(ItalianRestaurant, \$15)$$

In other words, prepositions can be characterized as two-argument predicates where the first argument is an object that is being placed in some relation to the second argument.

Another non-verb based predicate-argument structure is illustrated in the following example:

(14.16) Make a reservation for this evening for a table for two persons at 8.

Here, the predicate-argument structure is based on the concept underlying the noun *reservation*, rather than *make*, the main verb in the phrase. This example gives rise to a four argument predicate structure like the following:

$$Reservation(Hearer, Today, 8PM, 2)$$

This discussion makes it clear that any useful meaning representation language must be organized in a way that supports the specification of semantic predicate-argument structures. Specifically, it must include support for the kind of semantic information that languages present:

- variable arity predicate-argument structures
- the semantic labeling of arguments to predicates
- the statement of semantic constraints on the fillers of argument roles

14.3   FIRST ORDER PREDICATE CALCULUS

First Order Predicate Calculus (FOPC) is a flexible, well-understood, and computationally tractable approach to the representation of knowledge that satisfies many of the requirements raised in Sections 14.1 and 14.2 for a meaning representation language. Specifically, it provides a sound computational basis for the verifiability, inference, and expressiveness requirements. However, the most attractive feature of FOPC is the fact that it makes very few specific commitments as to how things ought to be represented. As we will see, the specific commitments it does make are ones that are fairly easy to live with; the represented world consists of objects, properties of objects, and relations among objects.

The remainder of this section first provides an introduction to the basic syntax and semantics of FOPC and then describes the application of FOPC to a number of linguistically relevant topics. Section 14.6 then discusses the connections between FOPC and some of the other representations shown earlier in Figure 14.1.

Elements of FOPC

We will explore FOPC in a bottom-up fashion by first examining its various atomic elements and then showing how they can be composed to create larger meaning representations. Figure 14.2, which provides a complete context-free grammar for the particular syntax of FOPC that we will be using, will be our roadmap for this section.

Let's begin by examining the notion of a **Term**, the FOPC device for representing objects. As can be seen from Figure 14.2, FOPC provides three ways to represent these basic building blocks: constants, functions, and variables. Each of these devices can be thought of as a way of naming, or pointing to, an object in the world under consideration.

TERM

Constants in FOPC refer to specific objects in the world being described. Such constants are conventionally depicted as either single capitalized letters such as *A* and *B* or single capitalized words that are often reminiscent of proper nouns such as *Maharani* and *Harry*. Like programming language constants, FOPC constants refer to exactly one object. Objects can, however, have multiple constants that refer to them.

CONSTANTS

Functions in FOPC correspond to concepts that are often expressed in English as genitives such as *the location of Maharani* or *Maharani's loca-*

FUNCTIONS

$$
\begin{aligned}
\textit{Formula} \;\rightarrow\; & \textit{AtomicFormula} \\
\mid\; & \textit{Formula Connective Formula} \\
\mid\; & \textit{Quantifier Variable,\dots Formula} \\
\mid\; & \neg\,\textit{Formula} \\
\mid\; & (\textit{Formula})
\end{aligned}
$$

$$
\textit{AtomicFormula} \;\rightarrow\; \textit{Predicate}(\textit{Term},\dots)
$$

$$
\begin{aligned}
\textit{Term} \;\rightarrow\; & \textit{Function}(\textit{Term},\dots) \\
\mid\; & \textit{Constant} \\
\mid\; & \textit{Variable}
\end{aligned}
$$

$$
\begin{aligned}
\textit{Connective} \;\rightarrow\; & \wedge \mid \vee \mid\; \Rightarrow \\
\textit{Quantifier} \;\rightarrow\; & \forall \mid \exists \\
\textit{Constant} \;\rightarrow\; & A \mid \textit{VegetarianFood} \mid \textit{Maharani}\cdots \\
\textit{Variable} \;\rightarrow\; & x \mid y \mid \cdots \\
\textit{Predicate} \;\rightarrow\; & \textit{Serves} \mid \textit{Near} \mid \cdots \\
\textit{Function} \;\rightarrow\; & \textit{LocationOf} \mid \textit{CuisineOf} \mid \cdots
\end{aligned}
$$

Figure 14.2   A context-free grammar specification of the syntax of First Order Predicate Calculus representations. Adapted from Russell and Norvig (1995).

tion. A FOPC translation of such an expression might look like the following.

$$
\textit{LocationOf}(\textit{Maharani})
$$

FOPC functions are syntactically the same as single argument predicates. It is important to remember, however, that while they have the appearance of predicates they are in fact *Terms* in that they refer to unique objects. Functions provide a convenient way to refer to specific objects without having to associate a named constant with them. This is particularly convenient in cases where many named objects, like restaurants, will have a unique concept such as a location associated with them.

VARIABLE   The notion of a **variable** is our final FOPC mechanism for referring to objects. Variables, which are normally depicted as single lower-case letters, give us the ability to make assertions and draw inferences about objects without having to make reference to any particular named object. This ability to make statements about anonymous objects comes in two flavors: making statements about a particular unknown object and making statements about all the objects in some arbitrary world of objects. We will return to the topic of variables after we have presented quantifiers, the elements of FOPC that will make them useful.

Now that we have the means to refer to objects, we can move on to the FOPC mechanisms that are used to state relations that hold among objects. As one might guess from its name, FOPC is organized around the notion of the predicate. Predicates are symbols that refer to, or name, the relations that hold among some fixed number of objects in a given domain. Returning to the example introduced informally in Section 14.1, a reasonable FOPC representation for *Maharani serves vegetarian food* might look like the following formula:

> *Serves(Maharani,VegetarianFood)*

This FOPC sentence asserts that *Serves*, a two-place predicate, holds between the objects denoted by the constants *Maharani* and *VegetarianFood*.

A somewhat different use of predicates is illustrated by the following typical representation for a sentence like *Maharani is a restaurant*:

> *Restaurant(Maharani)*

This is an example of a one-place predicate that is used, not to relate multiple objects, but rather to assert a property of a single object. In this case, it encodes the category membership of *Maharani*. We should note that while this is a commonplace way to deal with categories it is probably not the most useful. Section 14.4 will return to the topic of the representation of categories.

With the ability to refer to objects, to assert facts about objects, and to relate objects to one another, we have the ability to create rudimentary composite representations. These representations correspond to the atomic formula level in Figure 14.2. Recall that this ability to create composite meaning representations was one of the core components of the meaning structure of language described in Section 14.2.

This ability to compose complex representations is not limited to the use of single predicates. Larger composite representations can also be put together through the use of **logical connectives**. As can be seen from Figure 14.2, logical connectives give us the ability to create larger representations by conjoining logical formulas using one of three operators. Consider, for example, the following BERP sentence and one possible representation for it:

(14.17) I only have five dollars and I don't have a lot of time.

$$Have(Speaker, FiveDollars) \wedge \neg Have(Speaker, LotOfTime)$$

The semantic representation for this example is built up in a straightforward way from semantics of the individual clauses through the use of the $\wedge$ and $\neg$ operators. Note that the recursive nature of the grammar in Figure 14.2 allows an infinite number of logical formulas to be created through the use of these connectives. Thus as with syntax, we have the ability to create an infinite number of representations using a finite device.

The Semantics of FOPC

The various objects, properties, and relations represented in a FOPC knowledge base acquire their meanings by virtue of their correspondence to objects, properties, and relations out in the external world being modeled by the knowledge base. FOPC sentences can, therefore, be assigned a value of *True* or *False* based on whether the propositions they encode are in accord with the world or not.

Consider the following example:

(14.18) Ay Caramba is near ICSI.

Capturing the meaning of this example in FOPC involves identifying the *Terms* and *Predicates* that correspond to the various grammatical elements in the sentence, and creating logical formulas that capture the relations implied by the words and syntax of the sentence. For this example, such an effort might yield something like the following:

$$Near(LocationOf(AyCaramba), LocationOf(ICSI))$$

The meaning of this logical formula then arises from the relationship between the terms $LocationOf(AyCaramba)$, $LocationOf(ICSI)$, the predicate *Near*, and the objects and relation they correspond to in the world being modeled. Specifically, this sentence can be assigned a value of *True* or *False* based on whether or not the real Ay Caramba is actually close to ICSI or not. Of course, since our computers rarely have direct access to the outside world we have to rely on some other means to determine the truth of formulas like this one.

For our current purposes, we will adopt what is known as a database semantics for determining the truth of our logical formulas. Operationally, atomic formulas are taken to be true if they are literally present in the knowledge base or if they can be inferred from other formula that are in the knowledge base. The interpretations of formulas involving logical connectives is based on the meaning of the components in the formulas combined with the meanings of the connectives they contain. Figure 14.3 gives interpretations for each of the logical operators shown in Figure 14.2.

P	Q	$\neg P$	$P \wedge Q$	$P \vee Q$	$P \Rightarrow Q$
False	False	True	False	False	True
False	True	True	False	True	True
True	False	False	False	True	False
True	True	False	True	True	True

Figure 14.3   Truth table giving the semantics of the various logical connectives.

The semantics of the $\wedge$ (and), and $\neg$ (not) operators are fairly straightforward, and are correlated with at least some of the senses of their corresponding English terms. However, it is worth pointing out that the $\vee$ (or) operator is not disjunctive in the same way that the corresponding English word is, and that the $\Rightarrow$ (implies) operator is only loosely based on any commonsense notions of implication or causation. As we will see in more detail in Section 14.4, in most cases it is safest to rely directly on the entries in the truth table, rather than on intuitions arising from the names of the operators.

Variables and Quantifiers

We now have all the machinery necessary to return to our earlier discussion of variables. As noted above, variables are used in two ways in FOPC: to refer to particular anonymous objects and to refer generically to all objects in a collection. These two uses are made possible through the use of operators known as **quantifiers**. The two operators that are basic to FOPC are the existential quantifier, which is denoted $\exists$, and is pronounced as "there exists", and the universal quantifier, which is denoted $\forall$, and is pronounced as "for all".

QUANTIFIERS

The need for an existentially quantified variable is often signaled by the presence of an indefinite noun phrase in English. Consider the following example:

(14.19) a restaurant that serves Mexican food near ICSI.

Here reference is being made to an anonymous object of a specified category with particular properties. The following would be a reasonable representation of the meaning of such a phrase:

$$\exists x Restaurant(x)$$
$$\land Serves(x, MexicanFood)$$
$$\land Near((LocationOf(x), LocationOf(ICSI))$$

The existential quantifier at the head of this sentence instructs us on how to interpret the variable x in the context of this sentence. Informally, it says that for this sentence to be true there must be at least one object such that if we were to substitute it for the variable x, the resulting sentence would be true. For example, if *AyCaramba* is a Mexican restaurant near ICSI, then substituting *AyCaramba* for x results in the following logical formula:

$$Restaurant(AyCaramba)$$
$$\land Serves(AyCaramba, MexicanFood)$$
$$\land Near((LocationOf(AyCaramba), LocationOf(ICSI))$$

Based on the semantics of the $\land$ operator, this sentence will be true if all of its three component atomic formulas are true. These in turn will be true if they are either present in the system's knowledge base or can be inferred from other facts in the knowledge base.

The use of the universal quantifier also has an interpretation based on substitution of known objects for variables. The substitution semantics for the universal quantifier takes the expression *for all* quite literally; the $\forall$ operator states that for the logical formula in question to be true the substitution of *any* object in the knowledge base for the universally quantified variable should result in a true formula. This is in marked contrast to the $\exists$ operator which only insists on a single valid substitution for the sentence to be true.

Consider the following example:

(14.20) All vegetarian restaurants serve vegetarian food.

A reasonable representation for this sentence would be something like the following:

$$\forall x VegetarianRestaurant(x) \Rightarrow Serves(x, VegetarianFood)$$

For this sentence to be true, it must be the case that every substitution of a known object for x must result in a sentence that is true. We can divide up the set of all possible substitutions into the set of objects consisting of vegetarian restaurants and the set consisting of everything else. Let us first consider the case where the substituted object actually is a vegetarian restaurant; one such substitution would result in the following sentence:

$$VegetarianRestaurant(Maharani)$$
$$\Rightarrow Serves(Maharani, VegetarianFood)$$

If we assume that we know that the consequent clause,

$$Serves(Maharani, VegetarianFood)$$

is true then this sentence as a whole must be true. Both the antecedent and the consequent have the value *True* and, therefore, according to the first two rows of Figure 14.3 the sentence itself can have the value *True*. This result will, of course, be the same for all possible substitutions of *Terms* representing vegetarian restaurants for x.

Remember, however, that for this sentence to be true it must be true for all possible substitutions. What happens when we consider a substitution from the set of a objects that are not vegetarian restaurants? Consider the substitution of a non-vegetarian restaurant such as *Ay Caramba's* for the variable x:

$$VegetarianRestaurant(AyCaramba)$$
$$\Rightarrow Serves(AyCaramba, VegetarianFood)$$

Since the antecedent of the implication is *False*, we can determine from Figure 14.3 that the sentence is always *True*, again satisfying the $\forall$ constraint.

Note, that it may still be the case that *Ay Caramba* serves vegetarian food without actually being a vegetarian restaurant. Note also, that despite our choice of examples, there are no implied categorical restrictions on the objects that can be substituted for x by this kind of reasoning. In other words, there is no restriction of x to restaurants or concepts related to them. Consider the following substitution:

$$VegetarianRestaurant(Carburetor)$$
$$\Rightarrow Serves(Carburetor, VegetarianFood)$$

Here the antecedent is still false and hence the rule remains true under this kind of irrelevant substitution.

To review, variables in logical formulas must be either existentially ($\exists$) or universally ($\forall$) quantified. To satisfy an existentially quantified variable, there must be at least one substitution that results in a true sentence. Sentences with universally quantified variables must be true under all possible substitutions.

Inference

One of the most important desiderata given in Section 14.1 for a meaning representation language is that it should support inference—the ability to add valid new propositions to a knowledge base, or to determine the truth of propositions not explicitly contained within a knowledge base. This section briefly discusses **modus ponens**, the most important inference method provided by FOPC. Applications of modus ponens will be discussed in Chapter 18.

MODUS
PONENS

Modus ponens is a familiar form of inference that corresponds to what is informally known as *if-then* reasoning. We can abstractly define modus ponens as follows, where α and β should be taken as FOPC formulas:

$$\frac{\alpha}{\alpha \Rightarrow \beta}$$
$$\frac{}{\beta}$$

In general, schemas like this indicate that the formula below the line can be inferred from the formulas above the line by some form of inference. Modus ponens simply states that if the left-hand side of an implication rule is present in the knowledge base, then the right-hand side of the rule can be inferred. In the following discussions, we will refer to the left-hand side of an implication as the antecedent, and the right-hand side as the consequent.

As an example of a typical use of modus ponens, consider the following example, which uses a rule from the last section:

(14.21)

$$\frac{VegetarianRestaurant(Rudys)}{\forall x VegetarianRestaurant(x) \Rightarrow Serves(x, VegetarianFood)}$$
$$Serves(Rudys, VegetarianFood)$$

Here, the formula *VegetarianRestaurant(Rudys)* matches the antecedent of the rule, thus allowing us to use modus ponens to conclude *Serves(Rudys, VegetarianFood)*.

FORWARD
CHAINING

Modus ponens is typically put to practical use in one of two ways: forward chaining and backward chaining. In **forward chaining** systems, modus ponens is used in precisely the manner just described. As individual facts are added to the knowledge base, modus ponens is used to fire all applicable implication rules. In this kind of arrangement, as soon as a new fact is added to the knowledge base, all applicable implication rules are found and applied, each resulting in the addition new facts to the knowledge base. These new propositions in turn can be used to fire implication rules applicable to them. The process continues until no further facts can be deduced.

The forward chaining approach has the advantage that facts will be present in the knowledge base when needed, since in a sense all inference is performed in advance. This can substantially reduce the time needed to answer subsequent queries since they should all amount to simple lookups. The disadvantage of this approach is that facts may be inferred and stored that will never be needed. **Production systems**, which are heavily used in cognitive modeling work, are forward chaining inference systems augmented with additional control knowledge that governs which rules are to be fired.

PRODUCTION SYSTEMS

In **backward chaining**, modus ponens is run in reverse to prove specific propositions, called queries. The first step is to see if the query formula is true by determining if it is present in the knowledge base. If it is not, then the next step is to search for applicable implication rules present in the knowledge base. An applicable rule is one where the consequent of the rule matches the query formula. If there are such any such rules, then the query can be proved if the antecedent of any one them can be shown to be true. Not surprisingly, this can be performed recursively by backward chaining on the antecedent as a new query. The **Prolog** programming language is a backward chaining system that implements this strategy.

BACKWARD CHAINING

To see how this works, let's assume that we have been asked to verify the truth of the proposition *Serves(Rudys,VegetarianFood)*, assuming the facts given above the line in (14.21). Since it is not present in the knowledge base, a search for an applicable rule is initiated that results in the rule given above. After substituting, the constant *Rudys* for the variable x, our next task is to prove the antecedent of the rule, *VegetarianRestaurant(Rudys)*, which of course is one of the facts we are given.

Note that it is critical to distinguish between reasoning via backward chaining from queries to known facts, and reasoning backwards from known consequents to unknown antecedents. To be specific, by reasoning backwards we mean that if the consequent of a rule is known to be true, we assume that the antecedent will be as well. For example, let's assume that we know that *Serves(Rudys,VegetarianFood)* is true. Since this fact matches the consequent of our rule, we might reason backwards to the conclusion that *VegetarianRestaurant(Rudys)*.

While backward chaining is a sound method of reasoning, reasoning backwards is an invalid, though frequently useful, form of *plausible reasoning*. Plausible reasoning from consequents to antecedents is known as

ABDUCTION   **abduction**, and as we will see in Chapter 18 is often useful in accounting for
many of the inferences people make while analyzing extended discourses.

COMPLETE   While forward and backward reasoning are sound, neither is **complete**.
This means that there are valid inferences that can not be found by systems using these methods alone. Fortunately, there is an alternative infer-

RESOLUTION   ence technique called **resolution** that is sound and complete. Unfortunately,
inference systems based on resolution are far more computationally expen-
sive than forward or backward chaining systems. In practice, therefore, most
systems use some form of chaining, and place a burden on knowledge base
developers to encode the knowledge in a fashion that permits the necessary
inferences to be drawn.

14.4   SOME LINGUISTICALLY RELEVANT CONCEPTS

Entire lives have been spent studying the representation of various aspects
of human knowledge. These efforts have ranged from tightly focused efforts to represent individual domains such as time, to monumental efforts to
encode all of our commonsense knowledge of the world (Lenat and Guha,
1991). Our focus here is considerably more modest. This section provides a
brief overview of the representation of a few important topics that have clear
implications for language processing. Specifically, the following sections
provide introductions to the meaning representations of categories, events,
time, and beliefs.

Categories

As we noted in Section 14.2, words with predicate-like semantics often express preferences for the semantics of their arguments in the form of selectional restrictions. These restrictions are typically expressed in the form of
semantically-based categories where all the members of a category share a
set of relevant features.

The most common way to represent categories is to create a unary
predicate for each category of interest. Such predicates can then be asserted
for each member of that category. For example, in our restaurant discussions
we have been using the unary predicate *VegetarianRestaurant* as in:

   VegetarianRestaurant(Maharani)

Similar logical formulas would be included in our knowledge base for
each known vegetarian restaurant.

Unfortunately, in this method categories are relations, rather than full-fledged objects. It is, therefore, difficult to make assertions about categories themselves, rather than about their individual members. For example, we might want to designate the most popular member of a given category as in the following expression:

$MostPopular(Maharani, VegetarianRestaurant)$

Unfortunately, this is not a legal FOPC formula since the arguments to predicates in FOPC must be *Terms*, not other predicates.

One way to solve this problem is to represent all the concepts that we want to make statements about as full-fledged objects via a technique called **reification**. In this case, we can represent the category of *VegetarianRestaurant* as an object just as *Maharani* is. The notion of membership in such a category is then denoted via a membership relation as in the following:

REIFICATION

$ISA(Maharani, VegetarianRestaurant)$

The relation denoted by *ISA* (is a) holds between objects and the categories in which they are members. This technique can be extended to create hierarchies of categories through the use of other similar relations, as in the following:

$AKO(VegetarianRestaurant, Restaurant)$

Here, the relation *AKO* (a kind of) holds between categories and denotes a category inclusion relationship. Of course, to truly give these predicates meaning they would have to be situated in a larger set of facts defining categories as sets.

Chapter 16 discusses the practical use of such relations in databases of lexical relations, in the representation of selectional restrictions, and in word sense disambiguation.

Events

The representations for events that we have used until now have consisted of single predicates with as many arguments as are needed to incorporate all the roles associated with a given example. For example, the representation for *making a reservation* discussed in Section 14.2 consisted of a single predicate with arguments for the person making the reservation, the restaurant, the day, the time, and the number of people in the party, as in the following:

$Reservation(Hearer, Maharani, Today, 8PM, 2)$

In the case of verbs, this approach simply assumes that the predicate representing the meaning of a verb has the same number of arguments as are present in the verb's syntactic subcategorization frame.

Unfortunately, there are three problems with this approach that make it awkward to apply in practice:

- determining the correct number of roles for any given event

- representing facts about the roles associated with an event

- ensuring that all the correct inferences can be derived directly from the representation of an event

- ensuring that no incorrect inferences can be derived from the representation of an event

We will explore these, and other related issues, by considering a series of representations for events. This discussion will focus on the following examples of the verb *eat*:

(14.22) I ate.

(14.23) I ate a turkey sandwich.

(14.24) I ate a turkey sandwich at my desk.

(14.25) I ate at my desk.

(14.26) I ate lunch.

(14.27) I ate a turkey sandwich for lunch.

(14.28) I ate a turkey sandwich for lunch at my desk.

Clearly, the variable number of arguments for a predicate-bearing verb like *eat* poses a tricky problem. While we would like to think that all of these examples denote the same kind of event, predicates in FOPC have fixed

ARITY   **arity**—they take a fixed number of arguments.

One possible solution is suggested by the way that examples like these are handled syntactically. The solution given in Chapter 11 was to create one subcategorization frame for each of the configurations of arguments that a verb allows. The semantic analog to this approach is to create as many different *eating* predicates as are needed to handle all of the ways that *eat* behaves. Such an approach would yield the following kinds of representations for examples (14.22) through (14.22).

$Eating_1(Speaker)$
$Eating_2(Speaker, TurkeySandwich)$
$Eating_3(Speaker, TurkeySandwich, Desk)$
$Eating_4(Speaker, Desk)$
$Eating_5(Speaker, Lunch)$
$Eating_6(Speaker, TurkeySandwich, Lunch)$
$Eating_7(Speaker, TurkeySandwich, Lunch, Desk)$

This approach simply sidesteps the issue of how many arguments the *Eating* predicate should have by creating distinct predicates for each of the subcategorization frames. Unfortunately, this approach comes at a rather high cost. Other than the suggestive names of the predicates, there is nothing to tie these events to one another even though there are obvious logical relations among them. Specifically, if example (14.28) is true then all of the other examples are true as well. Similarly, if example (14.27) is true then examples (14.22), (14.23), and (14.26) must also be true. Such logical connections can not be made on the basis of these predicates alone. Moreover, we would expect a commonsense knowledge base to contain logical connections between concepts like *Eating* and related concepts like *Hunger* and *Food*.

One method to solve these problems involves the use of what are called **meaning postulates**. Consider the following example postulate:

MEANING
POSTULATES

$$\forall w, x, y, z \; Eating_7(w, x, y, z) \implies Eating_6(w, x, y)$$

This postulate explicitly ties together the semantics of two of our predicates. Other postulates could be created to handle the rest of the logical relations among the various *Eatings* and the connections from them to other related concepts.

Although such an approach might be made to work in small domains, it clearly has scalability problems. A somewhat more sensible approach is to say that examples (14.22) through (14.28) all reference the same predicate with some of the arguments missing from some of the surface forms. Under this approach, as many arguments are included in the definition of the predicate as ever appear with it in an input. Adopting the structure of a predicate like $Eating_7$ as an example would give us a predicate with four arguments denoting the eater, thing eaten, meal being eaten and the location of the eating. The following formulas would then capture the semantics of our examples:

$$\exists w, x, y \; Eating(Speaker, w, x, y)$$
$$\exists w, x \; Eating(Speaker, TurkeySandwich, w, x)$$
$$\exists w \; Eating(Speaker, TurkeySandwich, w, Desk)$$
$$\exists w, x \; Eating(Speaker, w, x, Desk)$$
$$\exists w, x \; Eating(Speaker, w, Lunch, x)$$
$$\exists w \; Eating(Speaker, TurkeySandwich, Lunch, w)$$
$$Eating(Speaker, TurkeySandwich, Lunch, Desk)$$

This approach directly yields the obvious logical connections among these formulas without the use of meaning postulates. Specifically, all of the sentences with ground terms as arguments logically imply the truth of the formulas with existentially bound variables as arguments.

Unfortunately, this approach still has at least two glaring deficiencies: it makes too many commitments, and it does not let us individuate events. As an example of how it makes too many commitments, consider how we accommodated the *for lunch* complement in examples (14.26) through (14.28); a third argument, the meal being eaten, was added to the *Eating* predicate. The presence of this argument implicitly makes it the case that all eating events are associated with a meal (i.e., breakfast, lunch, or dinner). More specifically, the existentially quantified variable for the meal argument in the above examples states that there is some formal meal associated with each of these eatings. This is clearly silly since one can certainly eat something independent of it being associated with a meal.

To see how this approach fails to properly individuate events, consider the following formulas.

$$\exists w, x \; Eating(Speaker, w, x, Desk)$$
$$\exists w, x \; Eating(Speaker, w, Lunch, x)$$
$$\exists w, x \; Eating(Speaker, w, Lunch, Desk)$$

If we knew that the first two formula were referring to the same event, they could be combined to create the third representation. Unfortunately, with the current representation we have no way of telling if this is possible. The independent facts that *I ate at my desk* and *I ate lunch* do not permit us to conclude that *I ate lunch at my desk*. Clearly what is lacking is some way of referring to the events in question.

As with categories, we can solve these problems if we employ reification to elevate events to objects that can be quantified and related to a other objects via sets of defined relations (Davidson, 1967; Parsons, 1990). Consider the representation of example (14.23) under this kind of approach.

$$\exists w\, ISA(w, Eating)$$
$$\wedge Eater(w, Speaker) \wedge Eaten(w, TurkeySandwich)$$

This representation states that there is an eating event where the *Speaker* is doing the eating and a *TurkeySandwich* is being eaten. The meaning representations for examples (14.22) and (14.27) can be constructed similarly.

$$\exists w\, ISA(w, Eating) \wedge Eater(w, Speaker)$$
$$\exists w\, ISA(w, Eating)$$
$$\wedge Eater(w, Speaker) \wedge Eaten(w, TurkeySandwich)$$
$$\wedge MealEaten(w, Lunch)$$

Under this reified-event approach:

- There is no need to specify a fixed number of arguments for a given surface predicate, rather as many roles and fillers can be glued on as appear in the input.

- No more roles are postulated than are mentioned in the input.

- The logical connections among closely related examples is satisfied without the need for meaning postulates.

Representing Time

In the preceding discussion of events, we did not address the issue of representing the time when the represented events are supposed to have occurred. The representation of such information in a useful form is the domain of **temporal logic**. This discussion will serve to introduce the most basic concerns of temporal logic along with a brief discussion of the means by which human languages convey temporal information, which among other things includes **tense logic**, the ways that verb tenses convey temporal information.

TEMPORAL LOGIC

TENSE LOGIC

The most straightforward theory of time hold that it flows inexorably forward, and that events are associated with either points or intervals in time, as on a timeline. Given these notions, an ordering can be imposed on distinct events by situating them on the timeline. More specifically, we can say that one event *precedes* another, if the flow of time leads from the first event to the second. Accompanying these notions in most theories is the idea of the current moment in time. Combining this notion with the idea of a temporal ordering relationship yields the familiar notions of past, present and future.

Not surprisingly, there are a large number of schemes for representing this kind of temporal information. The one presented here is a fairly simple one that stays within the FOPC framework of reified events that we have been pursuing. Consider the following examples:

(14.29) I arrived in New York.

(14.30) I am arriving in New York.

(14.31) I will arrive in New York.

These sentences all refer to the same kind of event and differ solely in the tense of the verb. In our current scheme for representing events, all three would share the following kind of representation, which lacks any temporal information:

$$\exists w \, ISA(w, Arriving)$$
$$\land Arriver(w, Speaker) \land Destination(w, NewYork)$$

The temporal information provided by the tense of the verbs can be exploited by predicating additional information about the event variable w. Specifically, we can add temporal variables representing the interval corresponding to the event, the end point of the event, and temporal predicates relating this end point to the current time as indicated by the tense of the verb. Such an approach yields the following representations for our *arriving* examples:

$$\exists i, e, w, t \, ISA(w, Arriving)$$
$$\land Arriver(w, Speaker) \land Destination(w, NewYork)$$
$$IntervalOf(w, i) \land EndPoint(i, e) \land Precedes(e, Now)$$

$$\exists i, e, w, t \, ISA(w, Arriving)$$
$$\land Arriver(w, Speaker) \land Destination(w, NewYork)$$
$$IntervalOf(w, i) \land MemberOf(i, Now)$$

$$\exists i, e, w, t \, ISA(w, Arriving)$$
$$\land Arriver(w, Speaker) \land Destination(w, NewYork)$$
$$IntervalOf(w, i) \land EndPoint(i, e) \land Precedes(Now, e)$$

This representation introduces a variable to stand for the interval of time associated with the event, and a variable that stands for the end of that interval. The two-place predicate *Precedes* represents the notion that the first time point argument precedes the second in time; the constant *Now* refers to the current time. For past events, the end point of the interval must precede the current time. Similarly, for future events the current time must precede the end of the event. For events happening in the present, the current time is contained within the event interval.

Unfortunately, the relation between simple verb tenses and points in time is by no means straightforward. Consider the following examples:

(14.32) Ok, we fly from San Francisco to Boston at 10.

(14.33) Flight 1390 will be at the gate an hour now.

In the first example, the present tense of the verb *fly* is used to refer to a future event, while in the second the future tense is used to refer to a past event.

More complications occur when we consider some of the other verb tenses. Consider the following examples:

(14.34) Flight 1902 arrived late.

(14.35) Flight 1902 had arrived late.

Although both refer to events in the past, representing them in the same way seems wrong. The second example seems to have another unnamed event lurking in the background (e.g., Flight 1902 had already arrived late *when* something else happened). To account for this phenomena, Reichenbach (1947) introduced the notion of a **reference point**. In our simple temporal scheme, the current moment in time is equated with the time of the utterance, and is used as a reference point for when the event occurred (before, at, or after). In Reichenbach's approach, the notion of the reference point is separated out from the utterance time and the event time. The following examples illustrate the basics of this approach:

REFERENCE
POINT

(14.36) When Mary's flight departed, I ate lunch.

(14.37) When Mary's flight departed, I had eaten lunch.

In both of these examples, the eating event has happened in the past, i.e. prior to the utterance. However, the verb tense in the first example indicates that the eating event began when the flight departed, while the second example indicates that the eating was accomplished prior to the flight's departure. Therefore, in Reichenbach's terms the *departure* event specifies the reference point. These facts can be accommodated by asserting additional constraints relating the *eating* and *departure* events. In the first example, the reference point precedes the *eating* event, and in the second example, the eating precedes the reference point. Figure 14.4 illustrates Reichenbach's approach with the primary English tenses. Exercise 14.9 asks you to represent these examples in FOPC.

This discussion has focused narrowly on the broad notions of past, present, and future and how they are signaled by verb tenses. Of course,

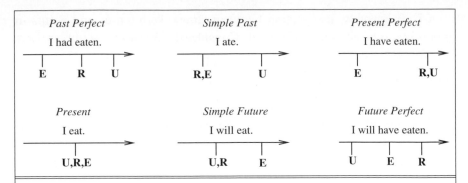

Figure 14.4   Reichenbach's approach applied to various English tenses. In these diagrams, time flows from left to right, an **E** denotes the time of the event, an **R** denotes the reference time, and an **U** denotes the time of the utterance.

languages also have many other more direct and more specific ways to convey temporal information, including the use of a wide variety of temporal expressions as in the following ATIS examples:

(14.38) I'd like to go at 6:45, in the morning.

(14.39) Somewhere around noon, please.

(14.40) Later in the afternoon, near 6PM.

As we will see in the next chapter, grammars for such temporal expressions are of considerable practical importance in information extraction and question-answering applications.

Finally, we should note that there is a systematic conceptual organization reflected in examples like these. In particular, temporal expressions in English are frequently expressed in spatial terms, as is illustrated by the various uses of *at*, *in*, *somewhere* and *near* in these examples (Lakoff and Johnson, 1980; Jackendoff, 1983) Metaphorical organizations such as these, where one domain is systematically expressed in terms of another, will be discussed in more detail in Chapter 16.

Aspect

ASPECT

In the last section, we discussed ways to represent the time of an event with respect to the time of an utterance describing it. In this section, we address the notion of **aspect**, which concerns a cluster of related topics, including whether an event has ended or is ongoing, whether it is conceptualized as happening at a point in time or over some interval, and whether or not any particular state in the world comes about because of it. Based on these and related notions, event expressions have traditionally been divided into four general classes: **statives**, **activities**, **accomplishments**, and **achievements**. The following examples provide prototypical instances of each class.

Stative: I know my departure gate.

Activity: John is flying.

Accomplishment: Sally booked her flight.

Achievement: She found her gate.

Although the earliest versions of this classification were discussed by Aristotle, the one presented here is due to Vendler (1967). In the following discussion, we'll present a brief characterization of each of the four classes, along with some diagnostic techniques suggested in Dowty (1979) for identifying examples of each kind.

    Stative expressions represent the notion of an event participant having a particular property, or being in a state, at a given point in time. As such, they can be thought of as capturing an aspect of a world at a single point in time. Consider the following ATIS examples. STATIVE EXPRESSIONS

(14.41) I like Flight 840 arriving at 10:06.

(14.42) I need the cheapest fare.

(14.43) I have a round trip ticket for $662.

(14.44) I want to go first class.

In examples like these, the event participant denoted by the subject can be seen as experiencing something at a specific point in time. Whether or not the experiencer was in the same state earlier, or will be in the future is left unspecified.

    There are a number of diagnostic tests for identifying statives. As an example, stative verbs are distinctly odd when used in the progressive form.

(14.45) *I am needing the cheapest fare on this day.

(14.46) *I am wanting to go first class.

We should note that in these and subsequent examples, we are using an * to indicate a broadened notion of ill-formedness that may include both semantic and syntactic factors.

    Statives are also odd when used as imperatives.

(14.47) *Need the cheapest fare!

    Finally, statives are not easily modified by adverbs like *deliberately* and *carefully*.

(14.48) *I deliberately like Flight 840 arriving at 10:06.

(14.49) *I carefully like Flight 840 arriving at 10:06.

ACTIVITY
EXPRESSIONS
      Activity expressions describe events undertaken by a participant that have no particular end point. Unlike statives, activities are seen as occurring over some span of time, and are therefore not associated with single points in time. Consider the following examples:

(14.50) She drove a Mazda.

(14.51) I live in Brooklyn.

These examples both specify that the subject is engaged in, or has engaged in, the activity specified by the verb for some period of time.

      Unlike statives, activity expressions are fine in both the progressive and imperative forms.

(14.52) She is living in Brooklyn.

(14.53) Drive a Mazda!

      However, like statives, activity expressions are odd when temporally modified with temporal expressions using *in*.

(14.54) *I live in Brooklyn in a month.

(14.55) *She drove a Mazda in an hour.

They can, however, successfully be used with *for* temporal adverbials, as in the following examples:

(14.56) I live in Brooklyn for a month.

(14.57) She drove a Mazda for an hour.

ACCOMPLISHMENT
EXPRESSIONS
      Unlike activities, **accomplishment expressions** describe events that have a natural end point and result in a particular state. Consider the following examples:

(14.58) He booked me a reservation.

(14.59) United flew me to New York.

In these examples, there is an event that is seen as occurring over some period of time that ends when the intended state is accomplished.

      A number of diagnostics can be used to distinguish accomplishment events from activities. Consider the following examples, which make use of the word *stop* as a test.

(14.60) I stopped living in Brooklyn.

(14.61) She stopped booking my flight.

In the first example, which is an activity, one can safely conclude that the statement *I lived in Brooklyn* even though this activity came to an end. However, from the second example, one can not conclude the statement *She booked her flight*, since the activity was stopped before the intended state was accomplished. Therefore, although stopping an activity entails that the activity took place, stopping an accomplishment event indicates that the event did not succeed.

Activities and accomplishments can also be distinguished by how they can be modified by various temporal adverbials. Consider the following examples:

(14.62) *I lived in Brooklyn in a year.

(14.63) She booked a flight in a minute.

In general, accomplishments can be modified by *in* temporal expressions, while simple activities can not.

The final aspectual class, **achievement expressions**, are similar to accomplishments in that they result in a state. Consider the following examples: ACHIEVEMENT EXPRESSIONS

(14.64) She found her gate.

(14.65) I reached New York.

Unlike accomplishments, achievement events are thought of as happening in an instant, and are not equated with any particular activity leading up to the state. To be more specific, the events in these examples may have been preceded by extended *searching* or *traveling* events, but the events corresponding directly to *found* and *reach* are conceived of as points not intervals.

The point-like nature of these events has implications for how they can be temporally modified. In particular, consider the following examples:

(14.66) I lived in New York for a year.

(14.67) *I reached New York for a few minutes.

Unlike activity and accomplishment expressions, achievements can not be modified by *for* adverbials.

Achievements can also be distinguished from accomplishments by employing the word *stop*, as we did earlier. Consider the following examples:

(14.68) I stopped booking my flight.

(14.69) *I stopped reaching New York.

As we saw earlier, using *stop* with an accomplishment expression results in a failure to reach the intended state. Note, however, that the resulting expression is perfectly well-formed. On the other hand, using *stop* with an achievement example is unacceptable.

We should note that since both accomplishments and achievements are events that result in a state, they are sometimes characterized as sub-types of a single aspectual class. Members of this combined class are known as **telic**

TELIC
EVENTUALITIES **eventualities**.

Before moving on, we should make two points about this classification scheme. The first point is that event expressions can easily be shifted from one class to another. Consider the following examples:

(14.70) I flew.

(14.71) I flew to New York.

The first example is a simple activity; it has no natural end point and can not be temporally modified by *in* temporal expressions. On the other hand, the second example is clearly an accomplishment event since it has an end point, results in a particular state, and can be temporally modified in all the ways that accomplishments can. Clearly the classification of an event is not solely governed by the verb, but by the semantics of the entire expression in context.

The second point is that while classifications such as this one are often useful, they do not *explain* why it is that events expressed in natural languages fall into these particular classes. We will revisit this issue in Chapter 16 where we will sketch a representational approach due to Dowty (1979) that accounts for these classes.

Representing Beliefs

There are a fair number of words and expressions that have what might be called a *world creating* ability. By this, we mean that their meaning representations contain logical formulas that are not intended to taken as true in the real world, but rather as part of some kind of hypothetical world. In addition, these meaning representations often denote a relation from the speaker, or some other entity, to this hypothetical world. Examples of words that have this ability are *believe*, *want*, *imagine* and *know*. World-creating words generally take various sentence-like constituents as arguments.

Consider the following example:

(14.72) I believe that Mary ate British food.

Applying our event-oriented approach we would say that there two events underlying this sentence: a believing event relating the speaker to some specific belief, and an eating event that plays the role of the believed thing. Ignoring temporal information, a straightforward application of our reified event approach would produce the following kind of representation:

$$\exists u, v \, ISA(u, Believing) \wedge ISA(v, Eating)$$
$$\wedge Believer(u, Speaker) \wedge BelievedProp(u, v)$$
$$\wedge Eater(v, Mary) \wedge Eaten(v, BritishFood)$$

This seems relatively straightforward, all the right roles are present and the two events are tied together in a reasonable way. Recall, however, that in conjunctive representations like this all of the individual conjuncts must be taken to be true. In this case, this results in a statement that there actually was an eating of British food by Mary. Specifically, by breaking this formula apart into separate formulas by conjunction elimination, the following formula can be produced:

$$\exists v \, ISA(v, Eating)$$
$$\wedge Eater(v, Mary) \wedge Eaten(v, BritishFood)$$

This is clearly more than we want to say. The fact that the speaker believes this proposition does not make it true; it is only true in the world represented by the speaker's beliefs. What is needed is a representation that has a structure similar to this, but where the *Eating* event is given a special status.

Note that reverting to the simpler predicate representations we used earlier in this chapter does not help. A common mistake using such representations would be to represent this sentence with the following kind of formula:

$$Believing(Speaker, Eating(Mary, BritishFood))$$

The problem with this representation is that it is not even valid FOPC. The second argument to the *Believing* predicate should be a FOPC term, not a formula. This syntactic error reflects a deeper semantic problem. Predicates in FOPC hold between the objects in the domain being modeled, not between the relations that hold among the objects in the domain. Therefore, FOPC lacks a meaningful way to assert relations about full propositions, which is unfortunately exactly what words like *believe*, *want*, *imagine* and *know* want to do.

The standard method for handling this situation is to augment FOPC with *operators* that allow us to make statements about full logical formulas. Let's consider how this approach might work in the case of example (14.72). We can introduce an operator called *Believes* that takes two FOPC formulas as its arguments: a formula designating a believer, and a formula designating the believed proposition. Applying this operator would result in the following meaning representation:

$$Believes(Speaker, \exists v ISA(v, Eating)$$
$$\wedge Eater(v, Mary) \wedge Eaten(v, BritishFood))$$

Under this approach, the contribution of the word *believes* to this meaning representation is not a FOPC proposition at all, but rather an operator that is applied to the believed proposition. Therefore, as we discuss in Chapter 15, these world creating verbs play quite a different role in the semantic analysis than more ordinary verbs like *eat*.

As one might expect, keeping track of who believes what about whom at any given point in time gets rather complex. As we will see in Chapter 18, this is an important task in interactive systems that must track users' beliefs as they change during the course of a dialogue.

Operators like *Believes* that apply to logical formulas are known as **modal operators**. Correspondingly, a logic augmented with such operators is known as a **modal logic**. Modal logics have found many uses in the representation of commonsense knowledge in addition to the modeling of belief, among the more prominent are representations of time and hypothetical worlds.

Not surprisingly, modal operators and modal logics raise a host of complex theoretical and practical problems that we cannot even begin to do justice to here. Among the more important issues are the following:

- How inference works in the presence of specific modal operators.
- The kinds of logical formula that particular operators can be applied to.
- How modal operators interact with quantifiers and logical connectives.
- The influence of these operators on the equality of terms across formulas.

The last issue in this list has consequences for modeling agent's knowledge and beliefs in dialogue systems and deserves some elaboration here. In standard FOPC systems, logical terms that are known to be equal to one another can be freely substituted without having any effect on the truth of sentences they occur in. Consider the following examples:

(14.73) Snow has delayed Flight 1045.

(14.74) John's sister's flight serves dinner.

Assuming that these two flights are the same, substituting *Flight 1045* for *John's sister's flight* has no effect on the truth of either sentence.

Now consider, the following variation on the first example:

(14.75) John knows that snow has delayed Flight 1045.

(14.76) John knows that his sister's flight serves dinner.

Here the substitution does not work. John may well know that Flight 1045 has been delayed without knowing that his sister's flight is delayed, simply because he may not know the number of his sister's flight. In other words, even if we assume that these sentences are true, and that John's sister is on Flight 1045, we can not say anything about the truth of the following sentence:

(14.77) John knows that snow has delayed his sister's flight.

Settings like this where a modal operator like *Know* is involved are called **referentially opaque**. In referentially opaque settings, substitution of equal terms may or may not succeed. Ordinary settings where such substitutions always work are said to be **referentially transparent**.

REFERENTIALLY OPAQUE

REFERENTIALLY TRANSPARENT

Pitfalls

As noted in Section 14.3, there are a number of common mistakes in representing the meaning of natural language utterances, that arise from confusing, or equating, elements from real languages with elements in FOPC. Consider the following example, which on the surface looks like a candidate for a standard implication rule:

(14.78) If you're interested in baseball, the Rockies are playing tonight.

A straightforward translation of this sentence into FOPC might look something like this:

$$HaveInterestIn(Hearer, Baseball)$$
$$\Rightarrow Playing(Rockies, Tonight)$$

This representation is flawed for a large number of reasons. The most obvious ones arise from the semantics of FOPC implications. In the event that the hearer is not interested in baseball, this formula becomes meaningless. Specifically, we can not draw any conclusion about the consequent clause when the antecedent is false. But of course this is a ridiculous conclusion, we know that the Rockies game will go forward regardless of whether or not the hearer happens to like baseball. Exercise 14.10 asks you to come up with a more reasonable FOPC translation of this example.

Now consider the following example:

(14.79) One more beer and I'll fall off this stool.

Again, a simple-minded translation of this sentence might consist of a conjunction of two clauses: one representing a drinking event and one representing a falling event. In this case, the surface use of the word *and* obscures the fact that this sentence instead has an implication underlying it. The lesson of both of these examples is that English words like *and*, *or* and *if* are only tenuously related to the elements of FOPC with the same names.

Along the same lines, it is important to remember the complete lack of significance of the names we make use of in representing FOPC formulas. Consider the following constant:

$$InexpensiveVegetarianIndianFoodOnTuesdays$$

Despite its impressive morphology, this term, by itself, has no more meaning than a constant like $X99$ would have. See McDermott (1976) for a discourse on the inherent dangers of such naming schemes.

14.5   RELATED REPRESENTATIONAL APPROACHES

Over the years, a fair number of representational schemes have been invented to capture the meaning of linguistic utterances for use in natural language processing systems. Other than logic, two of the most widely used schemes have been **semantic networks** and **frames**, which are also known as **slot-filler** representations. The KL-ONE (Brachman and Schmolze, 1985), and KRL (Bobrow and Winograd, 1977) systems were influential efforts to represent knowledge for use in natural language processing systems.

SEMANTIC
NETWORKS

FRAMES

In semantic networks, objects are represented as nodes in a graph, with relations between objects being represented by named links. In frame-based systems, objects are represented as feature-structures similar to those discussed in Chapter 11, which can, of course, also be naturally represented as graphs. In this approach features are called slots and the values, or fillers, of these slots can either be atomic values or other embedded frames. The following diagram illustrates how example (14.72) might be captured in a frame-based approach.

I believe Mary ate British food.

$$\begin{bmatrix} \text{BELIEVING} \\ \text{BELIEVER} \quad \text{SPEAKER} \\[4pt] \text{BELIEVED} \quad \begin{bmatrix} \text{EATING} \\ \text{EATER} \quad \text{MARY} \\ \text{EATEN} \quad \text{BRITISHFOOD} \end{bmatrix} \end{bmatrix}$$

It is now widely accepted that meanings represented in these approaches can be translated into equivalent statements in FOPC with relative ease.

14.6   ALTERNATIVE APPROACHES TO MEANING

The notion that the translation of linguistic inputs into a formal representation made up of discrete symbols adequately captures the notion of meaning is, not surprisingly, subject to a considerable amount of debate. The following sections give brief, wholly inadequate, overviews of some of the major concerns in these debates.

Meaning as Action

An approach that holds considerable appeal when we consider the semantics of imperative sentences is the notion of **meaning as action**. Under this view, utterances are viewed as actions, and the meanings of these utterances resides in **procedures** that are activated in the hearer as a result of hearing the utterance. This approach was followed in the creation of the historically important SHRDLU system, and is summed up well by its creator Terry Winograd (1972b).

MEANING AS ACTION

> One of the basic viewpoints underlying the model is that all language use can be thought of as a way of activating procedures within the hearer. We can think of an utterance as a program— one that indirectly causes a set of operations to be carried out within the hearer's cognitive system.

A recent procedural model of semantics is the **executing schema** or **x-schema** model of Bailey et al. (1997), Narayanan (1997a, 1997b), and Chang et al. (1998). The intuition of this model is that various parts of the semantics of events, including the *aspectual* factors discussed on page 530, are based on schematized descriptions of sensory-motor processes like inception, iteration, enabling, completion, force, and effort. The model represents the

X-SCHEMA

aspectual semantics of events via a kind of probabilistic automaton called a **Petri net** (Murata, 1989). The nets used in the model have states like *ready*, *process*, *finish*, *suspend*, and *result*.

The meaning representation of an example like *Jack is walking to the store* activates the *process* state of the walking event. An accomplishment event like *Jack walked to the store* activates the *result* state. An iterative activity like *Jack walked to the store every week* is simulated in the model by an iterative activation of the *process* and *result* nodes. This idea of using sensory-motor primitives as a foundation for semantic description is also based on the work of Regier (1996) on the role of visual primitives in a computational model of learning the semantics of spatial prepositions.

Meaning as Truth

The role of formal meaning representations in linguistics, natural language processing, artificial intelligence, and cognitive modeling, is quite different from its role in more philosophical circles. In the former approaches, the name of the game is getting from linguistic inputs to appropriate, unambiguous, and operationally useful representations.[3]

To philosophers, however, the mere translation of a sentence from its original natural form to another artificial form does not get us any closer to its meaning (Lewis, 1972). Formal representations may facilitate real semantic work, but are not by themselves of much interest. Under this view, the important work is in the functions, or procedures, that determine the mapping from these representations to the world being modeled. Of particular interest

TRUTH
CONDITIONS
in these approaches are the functions that determine the **truth conditions** of sentences, or their formal representations.

14.7   SUMMARY

This chapter has introduced the representational approach to meaning. The following are some of the highlights of this chapter:

- A major approach to meaning in computational linguistics involves the creation of **formal meaning representations** that capture the meaning-related content of linguistic inputs. These representations are intended to bridge the gap from language to commonsense knowledge of the

---

[3]   Of course, what counts as useful varies considerably among these areas.

world.

- The frameworks specify the syntax and semantics of these representations are called **meaning representation languages**. A wide variety of such languages are used in natural language processing and artificial intelligence.

- Such representations need to be able to support the practical computational requirements of semantic processing. Among these are the need to **determine the truth of propositions**, to support **unambiguous representations**, to represent **variables**, to support **inference**, and to be sufficiently **expressive**.

- Human languages have a wide variety of features that are used to convey meaning. Among the most important of these is the ability to convey a **predicate-argument structure**.

- **First Order Predicate Calculus** is a well-understood computationally tractable meaning representation language that offers much of what is needed in a meaning representation language.

- Important classes of meaning including bf categories, **events**, and **time** can be captured in FOPC. Propositions corresponding to such concepts as **beliefs** and **desires** require extensions to FOPC including **modal operators**.

- **Semantic networks** and **frames** can be captured within the FOPC framework.

BIBLIOGRAPHICAL AND HISTORICAL NOTES

The earliest computational use of declarative meaning representations in natural language processing was in the context of question-answering systems (Green et al., 1961; Raphael, 1968; Lindsey, 1963). These systems employed ad-hoc representations for the facts needed to answer questions. Questions were then translated into a form that could be matched against facts in the knowledge base. Simmons (1965) provides an overview of these early efforts.

Woods (1967) investigated the use of FOPC-like representations in question answering as a replacement for the ad-hoc representations in use at the time. Woods (1973) further developed and extended these ideas in the landmark Lunar system. Interestingly, the representations used in Lunar had both a truth-conditional and a procedural semantics. Winograd (1972b) employed a similar representation based on the Micro-Planner language in his SHRDLU system.

During this same period, researchers interested in the cognitive modeling of language and memory had been working with various forms of associative network representations. Masterman (1957) was probably the first to make computational use of a semantic network-like knowledge representation, although semantic networks are generally credited to Quillian (1968). A considerable amount work in the semantic network framework was carried out during this era (Norman and Rumelhart, 1975; Schank, 1972; Wilks, 1975c, 1975b; Kintsch, 1974). It was during this period that a number of researchers began to incorporate Fillmore's notion of case roles (Fillmore, 1968) into their representations. Simmons (1973) was the earliest adopter of case roles as part of representations for natural language processing.

Detailed analyses by Woods (1975) and Brachman (1979) aimed at figuring out what semantic networks actually mean led to the development of a number of more sophisticated network-like languages including KRL (Bobrow and Winograd, 1977) and KL-ONE (Brachman and Schmolze, 1985). As these frameworks became more sophisticated and well-defined it became clear that they were restricted variants of FOPC coupled with specialized inference procedures. A useful collection of papers covering much of this work can be found in (Brachman and Levesque, 1985). Russell and Norvig (1995) describe a modern perspective on these representational efforts.

Linguistic efforts to assign semantic structures to natural language sentences in the generative era began with the work of Katz and Fodor (1963). The limitations of their simple feature-based representations and the natural fit of logic to many of linguistic problems of the day quickly led to the adoption of a variety of predicate-argument structures as preferred semantic representations (Lakoff, 1972; McCawley, 1968). The subsequent introduction by Montague (1973) of truth-conditional model-theoretic framework into linguistic theory led to a much tighter integration between theories of formal syntax and a wide range of formal semantic frameworks. Good introductions to Montague semantics and its role in linguistic theory can be found in (Dowty et al., 1981; Partee, 1976).

The representation of events as reified objects is due to Davidson (1967). The approach presented here, which explicitly reifies event participants, is due to Parsons (1990). The use of modal operators and in the representation of knowledge and belief is due to Hintikka (1969). Moore (1977) was the first to make computational use of this approach. Fauconnier (1985) deals with a wide range of issues relating to beliefs and belief spaces from a cognitive science perspective. Most current computational approaches to temporal reasoning are based on Allen's notion of temporal intervals (Allen, 1984). ter Meulen (1995) provides a modern treatment of tense and aspect. Davis (1990) describes the use of FOPC to represent knowledge across a wide range of common sense domains including quantities, space, time, and beliefs.

A recent comprehensive treatment of logic and language can be found in (van Benthem and ter Meulen, 1997). The classic semantics text is (Lyons, 1977). McCawley (1993) is an indispensable textbook covering a wide range of topics concerning logic and language. Chierchia and McConnell-Ginet (1991) also provides broad coverage of semantic issues from a linguistic perspective. Heim and Kratzer (1998) is a more recent text written from the perspective of current generative theory.

EXERCISES

14.1 Choose a recipe from your favorite cookbook and try to make explicit all the common-sense knowledge that would be needed to follow it.

14.2 Proponents of information retrieval occasionally claim that natural language texts in their raw form are a perfectly suitable source of knowledge for question answering. Sketch an argument against this claim.

14.3 Peruse your daily newspaper for three examples of ambiguous sentences. Describe the various sources of the ambiguities.

14.4 Consider a domain where the word *coffee* can refer to the following concepts in a knowledge-based: a caffeinated or decaffeinated beverage, ground coffee used to make either kind of beverage, and the beans themselves. Give arguments as to which of the following uses of coffee are ambiguous and which are vague.

   a. I've had my coffee for today.

   b. Buy some coffee on your way home.

   c. Please grind some more coffee.

14.5 Encode in FOPC as much of the knowledge as you can that you came up with for Exercise 14.1

14.6   The following rule, which we gave as a translation for Example 14.20, is not a reasonable definition of what it means to be a vegetarian restaurant.

$$\forall x VegetarianRestaurant(x) \Rightarrow Serves(x, VegetarianFood)$$

Give a FOPC rule that better defines vegetarian restaurants in terms of what they serve.

14.7   Give a FOPC translations for the following sentences:

   a. Vegetarians do not eat meat.

   b. Not all vegetarians eat eggs.

14.8   Give a set of facts and inferences necessary to prove the following assertions:

   a. McDonalds is not a vegetarian restaurant.

   b. Some vegetarians can eat at McDonalds.

    Don't just place these facts in your knowledge base. Show that they can be inferred from some more general facts about vegetarians and McDonalds.

14.9   Give FOPC translations for the following sentences that capture the temporal relationships between the events.

   a. When Mary's flight departed, I ate lunch.

   b. When Mary's flight departed, I had eaten lunch.

14.10   Give a reasonable FOPC translation of the following example.

    If you're interested in baseball, the Rockies are playing tonight.

14.11   On Page 516 we gave the following FOPC translation for Example 14.17.

$$Have(Speaker, FiveDollars) \land \neg Have(Speaker, LotOfTime)$$

This literal representation would not be particularly useful to a restaurant-oriented question answering system. Give a deeper FOPC meaning representation for this example that is closer to what it really means.

14.12   On Page 516, we gave the following representation as a translation for the sentence *Ay Caramba is near ICSI*.

$$Near(LocationOf(AyCaramba), LocationOf(ICSI))$$

In our truth-conditional semantics, this formula is either true or false given the contents of some knowledge-base. Critique this truth-conditional approach with respect to the meaning of words like *near*.

15 SEMANTIC ANALYSIS

"Then you should say what you mean," the March Hare went on.
"I do," Alice hastily replied; "at least–at least I mean what I say–that's the same thing, you know."
"Not the same thing a bit!" said the Hatter. "You might just as well say that 'I see what I eat' is the same thing as 'I eat what I see'!"

Lewis Carroll, Alice in Wonderland

This chapter presents a number of computational approaches to the problem of **semantic analysis**, the process whereby meaning representations of the kind discussed in the previous chapter are composed and assigned to linguistic inputs. As we will see in this and later chapters, the creation of rich and accurate meaning representations necessarily involves a wide range of knowledge-sources and inference techniques. Among the sources of knowledge that are typically used are the meanings of words, the meanings associated with grammatical structures, knowledge about the structure of the discourse, knowledge about the context in which the discourse is occurring, and common-sense knowledge about the topic at hand.

SEMANTIC ANALYSIS

     The first approach we cover is a kind of **syntax-driven semantic analysis** that is fairly limited in its scope. It assigns meaning representations to inputs based solely on static knowledge from the lexicon and the grammar. In this approach, when we refer to an input's meaning, or meaning representation, we have in mind an impoverished representation that is both context independent and inference free. Meaning representations of this type correspond to the notion of a literal meaning introduced in the last chapter.

SYNTAX-DRIVEN SEMANTIC ANALYSIS

There are two reasons for proceeding along these lines: there are some limited application domains where such representations are sufficient to produce useful results, and these impoverished representations can serve as inputs to subsequent processes that can produce richer, more useful, meaning representations. Chapters 18 and 19 will show how these meaning representations can be used in processing extended discourses, while Chapter 21 will show how they can be used in machine translation.

Section 15.5 then presents two alternative approaches to semantic analysis that are more well-suited to practical applications. The first approach, **semantic grammars**, has been widely applied in the construction of interactive dialogue systems. In this approach, the elements of the grammars are strongly motivated by the semantic entities and relations of the domain being discussed. As we will see, the actual algorithms used in this approach are quite similar to those described in Section 15.1. The difference lies in the grammars that are used.

The final approach, presented in Section 15.5, addresses the task of extracting small amounts of pertinent information from large bodies of text. As we will see, this **information extraction** task does not require the kind of complete syntactic analysis assumed in the other approaches. Instead, a series of quite limited, mostly finite-state, automata are combined via a **cascade** to produce a robust semantic analyzer.

15.1   SYNTAX-DRIVEN SEMANTIC ANALYSIS

PRINCIPLE OF
COMPOSITIONALITY

The approach detailed in this section is based on the **principle of compositionality**.[1]   The key idea underlying this approach is that the meaning of a sentence can be composed from the meanings of its parts. Of course, when interpreted superficially, this principle is somewhat less than useful. We know that sentences are composed of words, and that words are the primary carriers of meaning in language. It would seem then that all this principle tells us is that we should compose the meaning representation for sentences from the meanings of the words that make them up.

Fortunately, the Mad Hatter has provided us with a hint as to how to make this principle useful. The meaning of a sentence is not based solely on

---

[1]   This is normally referred to as Frege's principle of compositionality. There appears to be little reason for this ascription, since the principle never explicitly appears in any of his writings. Indeed, many of his writings can be taken as supporting a decidedly non-compositional view. Janssen (1997) discusses this topic in more detail.

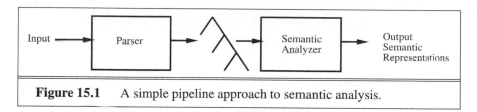

Figure 15.1   A simple pipeline approach to semantic analysis.

the words that make it up, it is based on the ordering, grouping, and relations among the words in the sentence. Of course, this is simply another way of saying that the meaning of a sentence is partially based on its syntactic structure. Therefore, in syntax-driven semantic analysis, the composition of meaning representations is guided by the syntactic *components* and *relations* provided by the kind of grammars discussed in Chapters 9, 11, and 12.

We can begin by assuming that the syntactic analysis of an input sentence will form the input to a semantic analyzer. Figure 15.1 illustrates the obvious pipeline-oriented approach that follows directly from this assumption. An input is first passed through a parser to derive its syntactic analysis. This analysis is then passed as input to a **semantic analyzer** to produce a   SEMANTIC
ANALYZER meaning representation. Note that although this diagram shows a parse tree as input, other syntactic representations such as feature structures, or lexical dependency diagrams, can be used. The remainder of this section will assume tree-like inputs.

Before moving on, we should address a major assumption about the role of ambiguity of this approach. In the syntax-driven approach presented here, ambiguities arising from the syntax and the lexicon will lead to the creation of multiple ambiguous meaning representations. It is not the job of the semantic analyzer, narrowly defined, to resolve these ambiguities. Instead, it is the job of subsequent interpretation processes with access to domain specific knowledge, and knowledge of context to *select* among competing representations. Of course, we can cut down on the number of ambiguous representations produced, through the use of robust part-of-speech taggers, prepositional phrase attachment mechanisms, and, as we will see in Chapter 17, word sense disambiguation mechanisms.

Let's consider how such an analysis might proceed with the following example:

(15.1) AyCaramba serves meat.

Figure 15.2 shows the simplified parse tree (lacking feature attachments), along with an appropriate meaning representation for this example. As suggested by the dashed arrows, a semantic analyzer given this tree as input

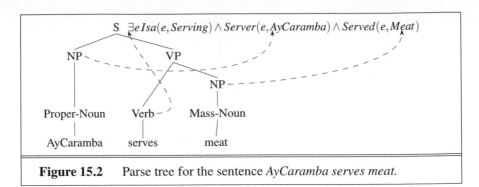

Figure 15.2   Parse tree for the sentence *AyCaramba serves meat.*

might fruitfully proceed by first retrieving a meaning representation from the subtree corresponding to the verb *serves*. The analyzer might next retrieve meaning representations corresponding to the two noun phrases in the sentence. Then using the representation acquired from the verb as a template, the noun phrase meaning representations can be used to bind the appropriate variables in the verb representation, thus producing the meaning representation for the sentence as a whole.

Unfortunately, there is a rather obvious problem with this simplified story. As described, the function used to interpret the tree in Figure 15.2 must know, among other things, that it is the verb that carries the template upon which the final representation is based, where this verb occurs in the tree, where its corresponding arguments are, and which argument fills which role in the verb's meaning representation. In other words, it requires a good deal of specific knowledge about *this particular example and its parse tree* to create the required meaning representation. Given that there are an infinite number of such trees for any reasonable grammar, any approach based on one semantic function for every possible tree is in serious trouble.

Fortunately, we have faced this problem before. Languages are not defined by enumerating the strings or trees that are permitted, but rather by specifying finite devices that are capable of generating the required set of outputs. It would seem, therefore, that the right place for semantic knowledge in a syntax-directed approach is with the finite set of devices that are used to generate trees in the first place: the grammar rules and the lexical
RULE-TO-RULE
HYPOTHESIS
entries. This is known as the **rule-to-rule hypothesis** (Bach, 1976).

Designing an analyzer based on this approach brings us back to the notion of parts and what it means for them to have meanings. The remainder of this section can be seen as an attempt to answer the following two questions:

• What does it mean for syntactic constituents to have meanings?

- What do these meanings have to be like so that they can be composed into larger meanings?

Semantic Augmentations to Context-Free Grammar Rules

In keeping with the approach used in Chapter 11, we will begin by augmenting context-free grammar rules with **semantic attachments**. These attachments can be thought of as instructions that specify how to compute the meaning representation of a construction from the meanings of its constituent parts. Abstractly, our augmented rules have the following structure:

SEMANTIC ATTACHMENTS

$$A \rightarrow \alpha_1 \ldots \alpha_n \qquad \{f(\alpha_j.sem, \ldots, \alpha_k.sem)\}$$

The semantic attachment to the basic context-free rule is shown in the $\{\ldots\}$ to the right of the rule's syntactic constituents. This notation states that the meaning representation assigned to the construction A, which we will denote as $A.sem$, can be computed by running the function f on some subset of the semantic attachments of A's constituents.

This characterization of our semantic attachments as a simple function application is rather abstract. To make this notion more concrete, we will walk through the semantic attachments necessary to compute the meaning representation for a series of examples beginning with example (15.1), shown earlier in Figure 15.2. We will begin with the more concrete entities in this example, as specified by the noun phrases, and work our way up to the more complex expressions representing the meaning of the entire sentence. The concrete entities in this example are represented by the FOPC constants *AyCaramba* and *Meat*. Our first task is to associate these constants with the constituents of the tree that introduced them. The first step toward accomplishing this is to pair them with the lexical rules representing the words that introduce them into the sentence.

$$ProperNoun \rightarrow AyCaramba \qquad \{AyCaramba\}$$

$$MassNoun \rightarrow meat \qquad \{Meat\}$$

These two rules specify that the meanings associated with the subtrees generated by these rules consist of the constants *AyCaramba* and *Meat*.

Note, however, that as the arrows in Figure 15.2 indicate, the subtrees corresponding to these rules do not directly contribute these FOPC constants to the final meaning representation. Rather, it is the *NP*s higher in the tree that contribute them to the final representation. In keeping with the principle of compositionality, we can deal with this indirect contribution by stipulating that the upper *NP*s obtain their meaning representations from the meanings of their children. In these two cases, we will assume that the meaning representations of the children are simply copied upward to the parents.

$NP \rightarrow ProperNoun \quad \{ProperNoun.sem\}$

$NP \rightarrow MassNoun \quad \{MassNoun.sem\}$

These rules state that the meaning representation of the noun phrases are the same as the meaning representations of their individual components, denoted by *ProperNoun.sem* and *MassNoun.sem*. In general, it will be the case that for non-branching grammar rules, the semantic expression associated with the child will be copied unchanged to the parent.

Before proceeding, we should point out that there is at least one potentially confusing aspect to this discussion. While the static semantic attachment to our first *NP* rule is simply *ProperNoun.sem*, the semantic value of the tree produced by that rule in this example is *AyCaramba*. It is critical to distinguish between the semantic attachment of a rule, and the semantic value associated with a tree generated by a rule. The first is a set of instructions on how to construct a meaning representation, while the second consists of the result of following those instructions.

Returning to our example, having accounted for the constants in the representation, we can move on to the event underlying this utterance as specified by *serves*. As illustrated in Figure 15.2, a generic *Serving* event involves a *Server* and something *Served*, as captured in the following logical formula:

$$\exists e, x, y \; Isa(e, Serving) \wedge Server(e, x) \wedge Served(e, y)$$

As a first attempt at this verb's semantic attachment, we can simply take this logical formula as *serve*'s semantic attachment, as in the following:

$Verb \rightarrow serves$
$\{\exists e, x, y \; Isa(e, Serving) \wedge Server(e, x) \wedge Served(e, y)\}$

Moving up the parse tree, the next constituent to be considered is the *VP* that dominates both *serves* and *meat*. Unlike the *NP*s, we can not simply copy the meaning of these children up to the parent *VP*. Rather, we need to *incorporate* the meaning of the *NP* into the meaning of the *Verb* and assign the resulting representation to the *VP.sem*. In this case, this consists of replacing the variable y with the logical term *Meat* as the second argument of the *Served* role of the *Serves* event. This yields the following meaning representation, which can be glossed as something like *someone serves meat*.

$$\exists e, x \; Isa(e, Serving) \wedge Server(e, x) \wedge Served(e, Meat)$$

To come up with this representation, the semantic attachment for the *VP* must provide a means to replace the quantified variable y within the body of *V.sem* with the logical constant *Meat*, as stipulated by *NP.sem*. Abstracting away from this specific example, the *VP* semantic attachment must have two capabilities: the means to *know* exactly which variables within the *Verb*'s semantic attachment are to be replaced by the semantics of the *Verb*'s arguments, and the ability to perform such a replacement.

Unfortunately, there is no straightforward way to do this given the mechanisms we now have at our disposal. The FOPC formula we attached to the *V.sem* does not provide any advice about when and how each of its three quantified variables should be replaced, and we have no simple way, within our current specification of FOPC, for performing such a replacement even if we did know.

Fortunately, there is a notational extension to FOPC called the **lambda notation** (Church, 1940) that provides exactly the kind of formal parameter functionality that we need. This notation extends the syntax of FOPC to include expressions of the following form:

LAMBDA
NOTATION

$$\lambda x P(x)$$

Such expressions consist of the Greek symbol λ, followed by one or more variables, followed by a FOPC expression that makes use of those variables.

The usefulness of these λ-expressions is based on the ability to **apply** them to logical terms to yield new FOPC expressions where the formal parameter variables are bound to the specified terms. This process is known as λ-reduction and is little more than a simple textual replacement of the λ variables with the specified FOPC terms, accompanied by the subsequent removal of the λ. The following expressions illustrate the application of a λ-expression to the constant A, followed by the result of performing a λ-reduction on this expression:

APPLY

$$\lambda x P(x)(A)$$

$$P(A)$$

This λ-notation provides both of the capabilities we said were needed in the *Verb* semantics: the formal parameter list makes a set of variables within the body available, and the λ-reduction process implements the desired replacement of variables with terms.

An important and useful variation of this technique is the use of one λ-expression as the body of another as in the following expression:

$$\lambda x \lambda y \; Near(x,y)$$

This fairly abstract expression can be glossed as the state of something being near something else. The following expressions illustrate a single λ-application and subsequent reduction with this kind of embedded λ-expression:

$$\lambda x \lambda y \, Near(x, y)(ICSI)$$

$$\lambda y \, Near(ICSI, y)$$

The important point here is that the resulting expression is still a λ-expression; the first reduction bound the variable x and removed the outer λ, thus revealing the inner expression. As might be expected, this resulting λ-expression can, in turn, be applied to another term to arrive at a fully specified logical formula, as in the following:

$$\lambda y \, Near(ICSI, y)(AyCaramba)$$

$$Near(ICSI, AyCaramba)$$

CURRYING

This technique, called **currying**[2] (Schönkfinkel, 1924), is a way of converting a predicate with multiple arguments into a sequence of single argument predicates. As we will see shortly, this technique is quite useful when the arguments to a predicate do not all appear together as daughters of the predicate in a parse tree.

With the λ-notation and the process of λ-reduction, we have the tools needed to return to the semantic attachments for our *VP* constituent. Recall that what was needed was a way to replace the variable representing the *Served* role with the meaning representation provided by the *NP* constituent of the *VP*. This can be accomplished in two steps: changing the semantic attachment of the *Verb* to a λ-expression, and having the semantic attachment of the *VP* apply this expression to the *NP* semantics. The first of these steps can be accomplished by designating x, the variable corresponding to the *Served* role, as the λ-variable for a λ-expression provided as the semantic attachment for *serve*.

$$Verb \rightarrow serves$$
$$\{\lambda x \exists e, y \, Isa(e, Serving) \land Server(e, y) \land Served(e, x)\}$$

This attachment makes the variable x externally available to be bound by an application of this expression to a logical term. The attachment for our

---

[2] *Currying* is the standard term, although Heim and Kratzer (1998) present an interesting argument for the term *Schönkfinkelization* over currying, since Curry *later* built on Schönfinkel's work.

transitive *VP* rule, therefore, specifies a λ-application where the λ-expression is provided by *Verb.sem* and the argument is provided by *NP.sem*.

$$VP \rightarrow Verb\,NP \qquad \{Verb.sem(NP.sem)\}$$

This λ-application results in the replacement, or binding, of x, the single formal parameter of the λ-expression, with the value contained in *NP.sem*. A λ-reduction removes the λ revealing the inner expression with the parameter x replaced by the constant *Meat*. This expression, the meaning of the verb phrase *serves meat*, is then the value of *VP.sem*.

$$\exists e,y\; Isa(e,Serving) \wedge Server(e,y) \wedge Served(e,Meat)$$

To complete this example, we must create the semantic attachment for the *S* rule. Like the *VP* rule, this rule must incorporate an *NP* argument into the appropriate role in the event representation now residing in the *VP.sem*. It should, therefore, consist of another λ-application where the value of *VP.sem* provides the λ-expression and the sentence-initial *NP.sem* provides the final argument to be incorporated.

$$S \rightarrow NP\,VP \qquad \{VP.sem(NP.sem)\}$$

Unfortunately, as it now stands the value of *VP.Sem* doesn't provide the necessary λ expression. The *lambda*-application performed at the *VP* rule resulted in a generic FOPC expression with two existentially quantified variables. The *Verb* attachment should instead have consisted of an embedded λ-expression to make the *Server* role available for binding at the *S* level of the grammar. Therefore, our revised representation of the *Verb* attachment will be the following:

$$Verb \rightarrow serves$$
$$\{\lambda x \lambda y\; \exists e\; Isa(e,Serving) \wedge Server(e,y) \wedge Served(e,x)\}$$

The body of this *Verb* attachment consists of a λ-expression inside a λ-expression. The outer expression provides the variable that is replaced by the first λ-reduction, while the inner expression can be used to bind the final variable corresponding to the *Server* role. This ordering of the variables in the multiple layers λ-expressions in semantic attachment of the verb explicitly encodes facts about the expected location of a *Verb*'s arguments in the syntax.

The parse tree for this example, with each node annotated with its corresponding semantic value, is shown in Figure 15.3.

This example has served to illustrate several of the most basic techniques used in this syntax-driven approach to semantic analysis. Section

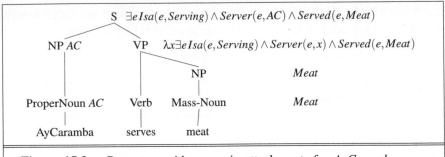

Figure 15.3   Parse tree with semantic attachments for *AyCaramba serves meat.*

15.2 will provide a more complete inventory of semantic attachments for some of the major English grammatical categories. Before proceeding to that inventory, however, we will first analyze several additional examples. These examples will serve to introduce a few more of the basic constructs needed to make this approach work, and will illustrate the general approach to developing semantic attachments for a grammar.

Let's consider the following variation on example (15.1):

(15.2) A restaurant serves meat.

Since the verb phrase of this example is unchanged from example (15.1), we can restrict our attention to the derivation of the semantics of the subject noun phrase and its subsequent integration with the verb phrase in the *S* rule. As a starting point, let's assume that the following formula is a plausible representation for the meaning of the subject in this example:

$$\exists x\, Isa(x, Restaurant)$$

Combining this new representation with the one already developed for the verb phrase, yields the following meaning representation:

$$\exists e, x\, Isa(e, Serving)$$
$$\wedge Server(e, x) \wedge Served(e, Meat) \wedge Isa(x, Restaurant)$$

In this formula, the restaurant, represented by the variable x, is specified as playing the role of the *Server* by its presence as the second argument to the *Server* predicate.

Unfortunately, the λ-application specified as the semantic attachment for the *S* rule will not produce this result. A literal interpretation of λ-reduction as a textual replacement results in the following expression, where the entire meaning representation of the noun phrase is embedded in the

Server predicate:

$$\exists\, e\, Isa(e, Serving)$$
$$\wedge Server(e, \exists x Isa(x, Restaurant)) \wedge Served(e, Meat)$$

Although this expression has a certain intuitive appeal, it is not a valid FOPC formula. Expressions like the one denoting our restaurant cannot appear as arguments to predicates; such arguments are limited to FOPC terms. In fact, since by definition λ-expressions can only be applied to FOPC terms, the application of the λ-expression attached to the *VP* to the semantics of the subject was ill-formed to begin with.

We can solve this problem in a manner similar to the way that λ-expressions were used to solve the verb phrase and *S* semantic attachment problems: by adding a new notation to the existing FOPC syntax that facilitates the compositional creation of the desired meaning representation. In this case, we will introduce the notion of a **complex-term** that allows FOPC $\quad$ COMPLEX-TERM expressions like $\exists x Isa(x, Restaurant)$ to appear in places where normally only ordinary FOPC terms would appear. Formally, a complex-term is an expression with the following three-part structure:

$$< Quantifier\ variable\ body >$$

Applying this notation to our current example, we arrive at the following representation:

$$\exists e\, Isa(e, Serving)$$
$$\wedge Server(e, < \exists x Isa(x, Restaurant) >) \wedge Served(e, Meat)$$

As was the case with λ-expressions, this notational change will only be useful if we can provide a straightforward way to convert it into ordinary FOPC syntax. This can be accomplished by rewriting any predicate using a complex-term according to the following schema:

$$P(< Quantifier\ variable\ body >)$$
$$\Rightarrow$$
$$Quantifier\ variable\ body\ Connective\ P(variable)$$

In other words, the complex-term:

1. is extracted from the predicate in which it appears,

2. is replaced by the variable that represents the object in question,

3. and has its variable, quantifier, and body prepended to the new expression through the use of an appropriate connective.

The following pair of expressions illustrates this complex-term reduction on our current example:

$$Server(e, < \exists xIsa(x, Restaurant) >)$$
$$\Rightarrow$$
$$\exists xIsa(x, Restaurant) \wedge Server(e, x)$$

The connective that is used to attach the extracted formula to the front of the new expression depends on the type of the quantifier being used: $\wedge$ is used with $\exists$, and $\Rightarrow$ is used with $\forall$.

It will also be useful to be able to access the three components of complex-terms. We will, therefore, extend the syntax used to refer to the semantics of a constituent by allowing reference to its parts. For example, if *A.sem* is a complex-term then *A.sem.quantifier*, *A.sem.variable*, and *A.sem.body* retrieve the complex-term's quantifier, variable, and body, respectively.

Returning to example (15.2), we can now address the creation of the target meaning representation for the phrase *a restaurant*. Given the simple syntactic structure of this noun phrase, the job of the *NP* semantic attachment is fairly straightforward.

$$NP \rightarrow Det\ Nominal \qquad \{< Det.sem\ x\ Nominal.sem(x) >\}$$

This attachment creates a complex-term consisting of a quantifier retrieved from the *Det*, followed by an arbitrary variable, and then an application of the λ-expression associated with the *Nominal* to that variable. This λ-application ensures that the correct variable appears within the predicate specified by the *Nominal*.

The attachment for the determiner simply specifies the quantifier to be used.

$$Det \rightarrow a \qquad \{\exists\}$$

The job of the nominal category is to create the *Isa* formula and λ-expression needed for use in the noun phrase.

$$Nominal \rightarrow Noun \qquad \{\lambda xIsa(x, Noun.sem)\}$$

Finally, the noun attachment simply provides the name of the category being discussed.

$$Noun \rightarrow restaurant \qquad \{Restaurant\}$$

In walking through this example, we have introduced five concrete mechanisms that instantiate the abstract functional characterization of semantic attachments that began this section:

1. the association of normal FOPC expressions with lexical items
2. the association of function-like λ-expressions with lexical items
3. the copying of semantic values from children to parents
4. the function-like application of λ-expressions to the semantics of one or more children of a constituent
5. the use of complex-terms to allow quantified expressions to be temporarily treated as terms

The introduction of λ-expressions and complex-terms was motivated by the gap between the syntax of FOPC and the syntax of English. These extra-logical devices serve to bring the syntax of FOPC closer to the syntax of the language being processed thus facilitating the semantic analysis process. Meaning representations that make use of these kinds of devices are usually referred to as **quasi-logical forms** or **intermediate representations**. Note, there is a subtle difference in usage between these two terms. The term quasi-logical form is usually applied to representations that can easily be converted to a logical representation via some simple syntactic transformation. The term intermediate representation is normally used to refer to meaning representations that serve as input to further analysis processes in an attempt to produce deeper meaning representations.

QUASI-LOGICAL FORMS

INTERMEDIATE REPRESENTATIONS

For the purposes of this chapter, our meaning representations are quasi-logical forms since they can easily be converted to FOPC. From a somewhat broader perspective, they are also intermediate forms since further interpretation is certainly needed to get them closer to reasonable meaning representations.

The few rules introduced in this section also serve to illustrate a principle that guides the design of semantic attachments in the compositional framework. In general, it is the lexical rules that provide content level predicates and terms for our meaning representations. The semantic attachments to grammar rules put these predicates and terms together in the right ways, but do not in general introduce predicates and terms into the representation being created.

Quantifier Scoping and the Translation of Complex-Terms

The schema given above to translate expressions containing complex-terms into FOPC expressions is, unfortunately, not unique. Consider the following example, along with its original unscoped meaning representation:

(15.3) Every restaurant has a menu.

$$\exists e Isa(e, Having)$$
$$\wedge Haver(e, < \forall x\, Isa(x, Restaurant) >)$$
$$\wedge Had(e, < \exists y\, Isa(y, Menu) >)$$

If the complex-terms filling the *Haver* and the *Had* roles are rewritten so that the quantifier for the *Haver* role has the outer scope, then the result is the following meaning representation, which corresponds to the common-sense interpretation of this sentence:

$$\forall x Restaurant(x) \Rightarrow$$
$$\exists e, y\, Having(e) \wedge Haver(e, x) \wedge Isa(y, Menu) \wedge Had(e, y)$$

On the other hand, if the terms are rewritten in the reverse order, then the following FOPC representation results, which states that there is one menu that all restaurants share:

$$\exists y\, Isa(y, Menu) \wedge \forall x\, Isa(x, Restaurant) \Rightarrow$$
$$\exists e Having(e) \wedge Haver(e, x) \wedge Had(e, y)$$

QUANTIFIER
SCOPING
This example illustrates the problem of ambiguous **quantifier scoping**—a single logical formula with two complex-terms gives rise to two distinct and incompatible FOPC representations. In the worst case, sentences with N quantifiers will have $O(N!)$ different possible quantifier scopings.

In practice, most systems employ an ad hoc set of heuristic preference rules that can be used to generate preferred forms in order of their overall likelihood. In cases where no preference rules apply, a left-to-right quantifier ordering that mirrors the surface order of the quantifiers is used. Domain specific knowledge can then be used to either accept a quantified formula, or reject it and request another formula. Alshawi (1992) presents a comprehensive approach to generating plausible quantifier scopings.

15.2   ATTACHMENTS FOR A FRAGMENT OF ENGLISH

This section describes a set of semantic attachments for a small fragment of English, the bulk of which are based on those used in the Core Language Engine (Alshawi, 1992). As in the rest of this chapter, to keep the presentation simple, we omit the feature structures associated with these rules when they are not needed. Remember that these features are needed to ensure that the correct rules are applied in the correct situations. Most importantly for this discussion, they are needed to ensure that the correct verb entries are being employed based on their subcategorization feature structures.

Sentences

For the most part, our semantic discussions have only dealt with declarative sentences. This section expands our coverage to include the other sentence types first introduced in Chapter 9: imperatives, yes-no-questions, and wh-questions. Let's start by considering the following examples:

(15.4) Flight 487 serves lunch.

(15.5) Serve lunch.

(15.6) Does Flight 207 serve lunch?

(15.7) Which flights serve lunch?

The meaning representations of these examples all contain propositions concerning the serving of lunch on flights. However, they differ with respect to the role that these propositions are intended to serve in the settings in which they are uttered. More specifically, the first example is intended to convey factual information to a listener, the second is a request for an action, and the last two are requests for information. To capture these differences, we will introduce a set of operators that can be applied to FOPC sentences in the same way that belief operators were used in Chapter 14. Specifically, the operators *DCL*, *IMP*, *YNQ*, and *WHQ* will be applied to the FOPC representations of declaratives, imperatives, yes-no-questions, and wh-questions, respectively.

Producing meaning representations that make appropriate use of these operators requires the right set of semantic attachments for each of the possible sentence types. For declarative sentences, we can simply alter the basic sentence rule we have been using as follows:

$$S \rightarrow NP\ VP \qquad \{DCL(VP.sem(NP.sem))\}$$

The normal interpretation for a representation headed by the *DCL* operator would be as a factual statement to be added to the current knowledge-base.

Imperative sentences begin with a verb phrase and lack an overt subject. Because of the missing subject, the meaning representation for the main verb phrase will consist of a λ-expression with an unbound λ-variable representing this missing subject. To deal with this, we can simply *supply* a subject to the λ-expression by applying a final λ-reduction to a dummy constant. The *IMP* operator can then be applied to this representation as in the following semantic attachment:

$$S \rightarrow VP \qquad \{IMP(VP.sem(DummyYou))\}$$

Applying this rule to example (15.5), results in the following representation:

$$IMP(\exists eServing(e) \land Server(e, DummyYou) \land Served(e, Lunch)$$

As will be discussed in Chapter 19, imperatives can be viewed as a kind of **speech act**.

As discussed in Chapter 9, **yes-no-questions** consist of a sentence-initial auxiliary verb, followed by a subject noun phrase and then a verb phrase. The following semantic attachment simply ignores the auxiliary, and with the exception of the *YNQ* operator, constructs the same representation that would be created for the corresponding declarative sentence:

$$S \rightarrow Aux\ NP\ VP \qquad \{YNQ(VP.sem(NP.sem))\}$$

The use of this rule with for example (15.6) produces the following representation:

$$YNQ(\exists eServing(e) \land Server(e, Flt207) \land Served(e, Lunch))$$

Yes-no-questions should be thought as asking whether the propositional part of its meaning is true or false given the knowledge currently contained in the knowledge-base. Adopting the kind of semantics described in Chapter 14, yes-no-questions can be answered by determining if the proposition is in the knowledge-base, or if can be inferred from the knowledge-base.

Unlike yes-no-questions, **wh-subject-questions** ask for specific information about the subject of the sentence rather than the sentence as a whole. The following attachment produces a representation that consists of the operator *WHQ*, the variable corresponding to the subject of the sentence, and the body of the proposition:

$$S \rightarrow WhWord\ NP\ VP \qquad \{WHQ(NP.sem.var, VP.sem(NP.sem))\}$$

The following representation is the result of applying this rule to example (15.7):

$$WHQ(x, \exists e, x\ Isa(e, Serving) \land Server(e, x)$$
$$\land Served(e, Lunch) \land Isa(x, Flight))$$

Such questions can be answered by returning a set of assignments for the subject variable that make the resulting proposition true with respect to the current knowledge-base.

Finally, consider the following **wh-non-subject-question**:

(15.8) How can I go from Minneapolis to Long Beach?

In examples like this, the question is not about the subject of the sentence but rather some other argument, or some aspect of the proposition as a whole.

In this case, the representation needs to provide an indication as to what the question is about. The following attachment provides this information by providing the semantics of the auxiliary as an argument to the *WHQ* operator:

$$S \rightarrow WhWord\ Aux\ NP\ VP \quad \{WHQ(\ WhWord.sem\ VP.sem(NP.sem))\}$$

The following representation would result from an application of this rule to example (15.8):

$$WHQ(How, \exists e\ Isa(e, Going) \land Goer(e, User)$$
$$\land Origin(e, Minn) \land Destination(e, LongBeach))$$

As we will discuss in Section 15.5 and Chapter 19, correctly answering this kind of question involves a fair amount of domain specific reasoning. For example, the correct way to answer example (15.8) is to search for flights with the specified departure and arrival cities. Note, however, that there is no mention of flights or flying in the actual question. The question-answerer therefore has to apply knowledge specific to this domain to the effect that questions about going places are really questions about flights to those places.

Finally, we should make it clear that this particular attachment is only useful for rather simple wh-questions without missing arguments or embedded clauses. As discussed in Chapter 11, the presence of long-distance dependencies in these questions requires additional mechanisms to determine exactly what is being asked about. Woods (1977) and Alshawi (1992) provide extensive discussions of general mechanisms for handling wh-non-subject questions. Section 15.5 presents a more ad hoc approach that is often used in practical systems.

Noun Phrases

As we have already seen, the meaning representations for noun phrases can be either normal FOPC terms or complex-terms. The following sections detail the semantic attachments needed to produce meaning representations for some of the most frequent kinds of English noun phrases. Unfortunately, as we will see, the syntax of English noun phrases provides surprisingly little insight into their meaning. It is often the case that the best we can do is provide a rather vague intermediate level of meaning representation that can serve as input to further interpretation processes.

Compound Nominals

Compound nominals, also known as noun-noun sequences, consist of simple sequences of nouns, as in the following examples:

(15.9)   Flight schedule

(15.10) Summer flight schedule

As noted in Chapter 9, the syntactic structure of this construction can be captured by the regular expression *Noun∗*, or by the following context-free grammar rules:

> *Nominal* → *Noun*
>
> *Nominal* → *Noun Nominal*

In these constructions, the final noun in the sequence is the head of the phrase and denotes an object that is semantically related in some unspecified way to the other nouns that precede it in the sequence. In general, an extremely wide range of common-sense relations can be denoted by this construction. Discerning the exact nature of these relationships is well beyond the scope of the kind of superficial semantic analysis presented in this chapter. The attachment in the following rule builds up a vague representation that simply notes the existence of a semantic relation between the head noun and the modifying nouns, by incrementally noting such a relation between the head noun and each noun to its left:

> *Nominal* → *Noun Nominal*
> $\{\lambda x\ Nominal.sem(x) \wedge NN(Noun.sem,\ x)\}$

The relation *NN* is used to specify that a relation holds between the modifying elements of a compound nominal and the head *Noun*. In the examples given above, this leads to the following meaning representations:

> $\lambda x Isa(x, Schedule) \wedge NN(x, Flight)$
>
> $\lambda x Isa(x, Schedule) \wedge NN(x, Flight) \wedge NN(x, Summer)$

Note that this representation correctly instantiates a term representing a *Schedule*, while avoiding the creation of terms representing either a *Flight* or *Summer*.

Genitive Noun Phrases

Recall from Chapter 9 that genitive noun phrases make use of complex determiners that consist of noun phrases with possessive markers, as in *Atlanta's airport* and *Maharani's menu*. It is quite tempting to represent the relation between these words as an abstract kind of possession. A little introspection, however, reveals that the relation between a city and its airport has little in common with a restaurant and its menu. Therefore, as with compound nominals, it turns out to be best to simply state an abstract semantic relation between the various constituents.

$NP \rightarrow ComplexDet\ Nominal$
$$\{< \exists xNominal.sem(x) \wedge GN(x, ComplexDet.sem) >\}$$

$ComplexDet \rightarrow NP\ 's \qquad \{NP.sem\}$

Applying these rules to *Atlanta's airport* results in the following complex-term:

$$< \exists xIsa(x, Airport) \wedge GN(x, Atlanta) >$$

Subsequent semantic interpretation would have to determine that the relation denoted by the relation *GN* is actually a location.

Adjective Phrases

English adjectives can be split into two major categories: pre-nominal and predicate. These categories are exemplified by the following BERP examples:

(15.11) I don't mind a cheap restaurant.

(15.12) This restaurant is cheap.

For the pre-nominal case, an obvious *and often incorrect* proposal for the semantic attachment is illustrated in the following rules:

$Nominal \rightarrow Adj\ Nominal$
$$\{\lambda x\ Nominal.sem(x) \wedge Isa(x, Adj.sem)\}$$

$Adj \rightarrow cheap \qquad \{Cheap\}$

This solution modifies the semantics of the nominal by applying the predicate provided by the adjective to the variable representing the nominal. For our cheap restaurant example, this yields the following fairly reasonable representation:

$$\lambda x\ Isa(x, Restaurant) \wedge Isa(x, Cheap)$$

This is an example of what is known as **intersective semantics** since the meaning of the phrase can be thought of as the intersection of the category stipulated by the nominal and the category stipulated by the adjective. In this case, this amounts to the intersection of the category of cheap things with the category of restaurants.

INTERSECTIVE SEMANTICS

Unfortunately, this solution often does the wrong thing. For example, consider the following meaning representations for the phrases *small elephant*, *former friend*, and *fake gun*:

$$\lambda x\ Isa(x, Elephant) \wedge Isa(x, Small)$$

$$\lambda x \, Isa(x, Friend) \wedge Isa(x, Former)$$

$$\lambda x \, Isa(x, Gun) \wedge Isa(x, Fake)$$

Each of these representations is peculiar in some way. The first one states that this particular elephant is a member of the general category of small things, which is probably not true. The second example is strange in two ways: it asserts that the person in question is a friend, which is false, and it makes use of a fairly unreasonable category of *former things*. Similarly, the third example asserts that the object in question is a gun despite the fact that *fake* means it is not one.

As with compound nominals, there is no clever solution to these problems within the bounds of our current compositional framework. Therefore, the best approach is to simply note the status of a specific kind of modification relation and assume that some further procedure with access to additional relevant knowledge can replace this vague relation with an appropriate representation (Alshawi, 1992).

$$Nominal \rightarrow Adj \, Nominal$$
$$\{\lambda x \, Nominal.sem(x) \wedge AM(x, Adj.sem)\}$$

Applying this rule to *a cheap restaurant* results in the following formula:

$$\exists x \, Isa(x, Restaurant) \wedge AM(x, Cheap)$$

Note that even this watered-down proposal produces representations that are logically incorrect for the *fake* and *former* examples. In both cases, it asserts that the objects in question are in fact members of their stated categories. In general, the solution to this problem has to be based on the specific semantics of the adjectives and nouns in question. For example, the semantics of *former* has to involve some form of temporal reasoning, while *fake* requires the ability to reason about the nature of concepts and categories.

Verb Phrases

The general schema for computing the semantics of verb phrases relies on the notion of function application. In most cases, the λ-expression attached to the verb is simply applied to the semantic attachments of the verb's arguments. There are, however, a number of situations that force us to depart somewhat from this general pattern.

Infinitive Verb Phrases

A fair number of English verbs take some form of verb phrase as one of their arguments. This complicates the normal verb phrase semantic schema since

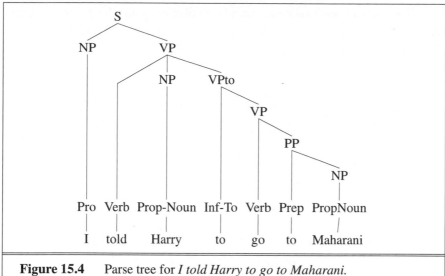

Figure 15.4   Parse tree for *I told Harry to go to Maharani.*

these argument verb phrases interact with the other arguments of the head verb in ways that are not completely obvious.

Consider the following example:

(15.13) I told Harry to go to Maharani.

The meaning representation for this example should be something like the following:

$$\exists e, f, x \, Isa(e, Telling) \wedge Isa(f, Going)$$
$$\wedge Teller(e, Speaker) \wedge Tellee(e, Harry) \wedge ToldThing(e, f)$$
$$\wedge Goer(f, Harry) \wedge Destination(f, x)$$

There are two interesting things to note about this meaning representation: the first is that it consists of two events, and the second is that one of the participants, *Harry*, plays a role in both of the two events. The difficulty in creating this complex representation falls to the verb phrase dominating the verb *tell* which will need something like the following as its semantic attachment:

$$\lambda x, y \, \lambda z \, \exists e \, Isa(e, Telling)$$
$$\wedge Teller(e, z) \wedge Tellee(e, x) \wedge ToldThing(e, y)$$

Semantically, we can interpret this subcategorization frame for *Tell* as providing three semantic roles: a person doing the telling, a recipient of the telling, and the proposition being conveyed.

The difficult part of this example involves getting the meaning representation for the main verb phrase correct. As shown in Figure 15.4, *Harry* plays the role of both the *Tellee* of the *Telling* event and the *Goer* of the *Going* event. However, *Harry* is not available when the *Going* event is created within the infinitive verb phrase.

Although there are several possible solutions to this problem, it is usually best to stick with a uniform approach to these problems. Therefore, we will start by simply applying the semantics of the verb to the semantics of the other arguments of the verb as follows:

$$VP \rightarrow Verb\ NP\ VPto \qquad \{Verb.sem(NP.sem,\ VPto.sem)\}$$

Since the *to* in the infinitive verb phrase construction does not contribute to its meaning, we simply copy the meaning of the child verb phrase up to the infinitive verb phrase. Recall, that we are relying on the unseen feature structures to ensure that only the correct verb phrases can be used with this construction.

$$VPto \rightarrow to\ VP \qquad \{VP.sem\}$$

In this solution, the verb's semantic attachment has two tasks: incorporating the *NP.sem*, the *Goer*, into the *VPto.sem*, and incorporating the *Going* event as the *ToldThing* of the *Telling*. The following attachment performs both tasks:

$$
\begin{aligned}
Verb \rightarrow\ &tell \\
&\{\lambda x, y \\
&\quad \lambda z \\
&\qquad \exists e, y.variable\ Isa(e, Telling) \\
&\qquad \wedge Teller(e, z) \wedge Tellee(e, x) \\
&\qquad \wedge ToldThing(e, y.variable) \wedge y(x)
\end{aligned}
$$

In this approach, the λ-variable x plays the role of the *Tellee* of the telling and the argument to the semantics of the infinitive, which is now contained as a λ-expression in the variable y. The expression $y(x)$ represents a λ-reduction that inserts *Harry* into the *Going* event as the *Goer*. The notation *y.variable*, is analogous to the notation used for complex-term variables, and gives us access to the event variable representing the *Going* event within the infinitive's meaning representation.

Note that this approach plays fast and loose with the definition of λ-reduction, in that it allows λ-expressions to be passed as arguments to other λ-expressions, when technically only FOPC terms can serve that role. This technique is a convenience similar to the use of complex-terms in that it allows us to temporarily treat complex expressions as terms during the creation of meaning representations.

Prepositional Phrases

At a fairly abstract level, prepositional phrases serve two distinct functions: they assert binary relations between their heads and the constituents to which they are attached, and they signal arguments to constituents that have an argument structure. These two functions argue for two distinct types of prepositional phrases that differ based on their semantic attachments. We will consider three places in the grammar where prepositional phrases serve these roles: modifiers of noun phrases, modifiers of verb phrases, and arguments to verb phrases.

Nominal Modifier Prepositional Phrases

Modifier prepositional phrases denote a binary relation between the concept being modified, which is external to the prepositional phrase, and the head of the prepositional phrase. Consider the following example and its associated meaning representation:

(15.14) A restaurant on Pearl

$$\exists x \, Isa(x, Restaurant) \land On(x, Pearl)$$

The relevant grammar rules that govern this example are the following:

$NP \rightarrow Det \, Nominal$

$Nominal \rightarrow Nominal \, PP$

$PP \rightarrow P \, NP$

Proceeding in a bottom-up fashion, the semantic attachment for this kind of relational preposition should provide a two-place predicate with its arguments distributed over two λ-expressions, as in the following:

$P \rightarrow on \quad \{\lambda y \lambda x \, On(x,y)\}$

With this kind of arrangement, the first argument to the predicate is provided by the head of prepositional phrase and the second is provided by the constituent that the prepositional phrase is ultimately attached to. The following semantic attachment provides the first part:

$PP \rightarrow P \, NP \quad \{P.sem(NP.sem)\}$

This λ-application results in a new λ-expression where the remaining argument is the inner λ-variable.

This remaining argument can be incorporated using the following nominal construction:

$$Nominal \rightarrow Nominal\ PP \qquad \{\lambda z Nominal.sem(z) \wedge PP.sem(z)\}$$

Verb Phrase Modifier Prepositional Phrases

The general approach to modifying verb phrases is similar to that of modifying nominals. The differences lie in the details of the modification in the verb phrase rule; the attachments for the preposition and prepositional phrase rules are unchanged. Let's consider the phrase *ate dinner in a hurry* which is governed by the following verb phrase rule:

$$VP \rightarrow VP\ PP$$

The meaning representation of the verb phrase constituent in this construction, *ate dinner*, is a λ-expression where the λ-variable represents the as yet unseen subject.

$$\lambda x \exists e\ Isa(e, Eating) \wedge Eater(e, x) \wedge Eaten(e, Dinner)$$

The representation of the prepositional phrase is also a λ-expression where the λ-variable is the second argument in the *PP* semantics.

$$\lambda x\ In(x, < \exists h\ Hurry(h) >)$$

The correct representation for the modified verb phrase should contain the conjunction of these two representations with the *Eating* event variable filling the first argument slot of the *In* expression. In addition, this modified representation must remain a λ-expression with the unbound *Eater* variable as the new λ-variable. The following attachment expression fulfills all of these requirements:

$$VP \rightarrow VP\ PP \qquad \{\lambda y VP.sem(y) \wedge PP.sem(VP.sem.variable)\}$$

There are two aspects of this attachment that require some elaboration. The first involves the application of the constituent verb phrases' λ-expression to the variable y. Binding the lower λ-expression's variable to a new variable allows us to *lift* the lower variable to the level of the newly created λ-expression. The result of this technique is a new λ-expression with a variable that, in effect, plays the same role as the original variable in the lower expression. In this case, this allows a λ-expression to be modified during the analysis process before the argument to the expression is actually available.

The second new aspect in this attachment involves the *VP.sem.variable* notation. This notation is used to access the event-variable representing the underlying meaning of the verb phrase, in this case, *e*. This is analogous to the notation used to provide access the various parts of complex-terms introduced earlier.

Applying this attachment to the current example yields the following representation, which is suitable for combination with a subsequent subject noun phrase:

$$\lambda y \exists e \; Isa(e, Eating) \wedge Eater(e, y) \wedge Eaten(e, Dinner)$$
$$\wedge In(e, < \exists h Hurry(h) >)$$

Verb Argument Prepositional Phrases

The prepositional phrases is this category serve to signal the role an argument plays in some larger event structure. As such, the preposition itself does not actually modify the meaning of the noun phrase. Consider the following example of role signaling prepositional phrases:

(15.15) I need to go from Boston to Dallas.

In examples like this, the arguments of *go* are expressed as prepositional phrases. However, the meaning representations of these phrases should consist solely of the unaltered representation of their head nouns. To handle this, argument prepositional phrases are treated in the same way that non-branching grammatical rules are; the semantic attachment of the noun phrase is copied unchanged to the semantics of the larger phrase.

$$PP \rightarrow P\,NP \qquad \{NP.sem\}$$

The verb phrase can then assign this meaning representation to the appropriate event role. A more complete account of how these argument bearing prepositional phrases map to underlying event roles will be presented in Chapter 16.

15.3   INTEGRATING SEMANTIC ANALYSIS INTO THE EARLEY PARSER

In Section 15.1, we suggested a simple pipeline architecture for a semantic analyzer where the results of a complete syntactic parse are passed to a semantic analyzer. The motivation for this notion stems from the fact that the compositional approach requires the syntactic parse before it can proceed. It is, however, also possible to perform semantic analysis in parallel with syntactic processing. This is possible because in our compositional framework, the meaning representation for a constituent can be created as soon as all of its constituent parts are present. This section describes just such an approach to integrating semantic analysis into the Earley parser from Chapter 10.

The integration of semantic analysis into an Earley parser is straightforward and follows precisely the same lines as the integration of unification into the algorithm given in Chapter 11. Three modifications are required to the original algorithm:

1. The rules of the grammar are given a new field to contain their semantic attachments.

2. The states in the chart are given a new field to hold the meaning representation of the constituent.

3. The ENQUEUE function is altered so that when a complete state is entered into the chart its semantics are computed and stored in the state's semantic field.

---

procedure ENQUEUE(*state, chart-entry*)
  if INCOMPLETE?(*state*) **then**
    if *state* is not already in *chart-entry* **then**
      PUSH(*state, chart-entry*)
  else if UNIFY-STATE(*state*) succeeds **then**
    if APPLY-SEMANTICS(*state*) succeeds **then**
      if *state* is not already in *chart-entry* **then**
      PUSH(*state, chart-entry*)

procedure APPLY-SEMANTICS(*state*)
  meaning-rep ← APPLY(*state.semantic-attachment, state*)
  if *meaning-rep* does not equal **failure then**
    state.meaning-rep ← *meaning-rep*

Figure 15.5   The ENQUEUE function modified to handle semantics. If the state is complete and unification succeeds then ENQUEUE calls APPLY-SEMANTICS to compute and store the meaning representation of completed states.

Figure 15.5 shows ENQUEUE modified to create meaning representations. When ENQUEUE is passed a complete state that can successfully unify its unification constraints it calls APPLY-SEMANTICS to compute and store the meaning representation for this state. Note the importance of performing feature-structure unification prior to semantic analysis. This ensures that semantic analysis will be performed only on valid trees and that features needed for semantic analysis will be present.

The primary advantage of this integrated approach over the pipeline approach lies in the fact that APPLY-SEMANTICS can fail in a manner similar to the way that unification can fail. If a semantic ill-formedness is found in the meaning representation being created, the corresponding state can be blocked from entering the chart. In this way, semantic considerations can be brought to bear during syntactic processing. Chapter 16 describes in some detail the various ways that this notion of ill-formedness can be realized.

Unfortunately, this also illustrates one of the primary disadvantages of integrating semantics directly into the parser—considerable effort may be spent on the semantic analysis of *orphan* constituents that do not in the end contribute to a successful parse. The question of whether the gains made by bringing semantics to bear early in the process outweigh the costs involved in performing extraneous semantic processing can only be answered on a case-by-case basis.

15.4 IDIOMS AND COMPOSITIONALITY

> Ce corps qui s'appelait et qui s'appelle encore le saint empire romain n'était en aucune manière ni saint, ni romain, ni empire.
>
> This body, which called itself and still calls itself the Holy Roman Empire, was neither Holy, nor Roman, nor an Empire.
>
> Voltaire[3], 1756

As innocuous as it seems, the principle of compositionality runs into trouble fairly quickly when real language is examined. There are many cases where the meaning of a constituent is not based on the meaning of its parts, at least not in the straightforward compositional sense. Consider the following WSJ examples:

(15.16) Coupons are just the tip of the iceberg.

(15.17) The SEC's allegations are only the tip of the iceberg.

---

[3] *Essai sur les moeurs et les esprit des nations.* Translation by Y. Sills, as quoted in Sills and Merton (1991).

(15.18)   Coronary bypass surgery, hip replacement and intensive-care units are but the tip of the iceberg.

The phrase *the tip of the iceberg* in each of these examples clearly doesn't have much to do with tips or icebergs. Instead, it roughly means something like *the beginning*. The most straightforward way to handle idiomatic constructions like these is to introduce new grammar rules specifically designed to handle them. These idiomatic rules mix lexical items with grammatical constituents, and introduce semantic content that is not derived from any of its parts. Consider the following rule as an example of this approach:

> *NP* → *the tip of the iceberg*
>   {*Beginning*}

The lower case items on the right-hand side of this rule are intended to represent precisely words in the input. Although, the constant *Beginning* should not be taken too seriously as a meaning representation for this idiom, it does illustrate the idea that the meaning of this idiom is not based on the meaning of any of its parts. Note that an Earley-style analyzer with this rule will now produce two parses when this phrase is encountered: one representing the idiom and one representing the compositional meaning.

As with the rest of the grammar, it may take a few tries to get these rules right. Consider the following *iceberg* examples from the WSJ corpus:

(15.19)   And that's but the tip of Mrs. Ford's iceberg.

(15.20)   These comments describe only the tip of a 1,000-page iceberg.

(15.21)   The 10 employees represent the merest tip of the iceberg.

The rule given above is clearly not general enough to handle these cases. These examples indicate that there is a vestigial syntactic structure to this idiom that permits some variation in the determiners used, and also permits some adjectival modification of both the *iceberg* and the *tip*. A more promising rule would be something like the following:

> *NP* → *TipNP of IcebergNP*
>   {*Beginning*}

Here the categories *TipNP* and *IcebergNP* can be given an internal nominal-like structure that permits some adjectival modification and some variation in the determiners, while still restricting the heads of these noun phrases to the lexical items *tip* and *iceberg*. Note that this syntactic solution ignores the thorny issue that the modifiers *mere* and *1000-page* seem to indicate that both the *tip* and *iceberg* may in fact play some compositional role in the meaning of the idiom. We will return to this topic in Chapter 16, when we take up the issue of metaphor.

To summarize, handling idioms requires at least the following changes to the general compositional framework:

- Allow the mixing of lexical items with traditional grammatical constituents.
- Allow the creation of additional idiom-specific constituents needed to handle the correct range of productivity of the idiom.
- Permit semantic attachments that introduce logical terms and predicates that are not related to any of the constituents of the rule.

This discussion is obviously only the tip of an enormous iceberg. Idioms are far more frequent and far more productive than is generally recognized and pose serious difficulties for many applications, including, as we will see in Chapter 21, machine translation.

15.5   ROBUST SEMANTIC ANALYSIS

As we noted earlier, when syntax-driven semantic analysis is applied in practice, certain compromises have to be made to facilitate system development and efficiency of operation. The following sections describe the two primary ways of instantiating a syntax-driven approach in practical systems.

Semantic Grammars

When we first introduced Frege's principle of compositionality in Section 15.1, we noted that the parts referred to in that principle are the constituents provided by a syntactic grammar. Unfortunately, the syntactic structures provided by such grammars are often not particularly well-suited for the task of compositional semantic analysis. This is not particularly surprising since capturing elegant syntactic generalizations and avoiding overgeneration carry considerably more weight in the design of grammars than semantic sensibility does. This *mismatch* between the structures provided by traditional grammars and those needed for compositional semantic analysis typically manifests itself in the following three ways:

1. Key semantic elements are often widely distributed across parse trees, thus complicating the composition of the required meaning representation.

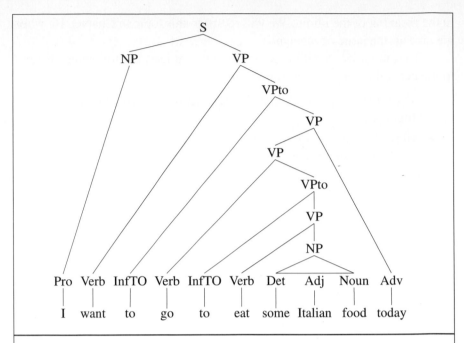

Figure 15.6　　Syntactic parse for example (15.22). This parse demonstrates the potentially wide distribution of content elements throughout a parse tree.

2. Parse trees often contain many syntactically motivated constituents that play essentially no role in semantic processing.

3. The general nature of many syntactic constituents results in semantic attachments that create nearly vacuous meaning representations.

As an example of the first two problems, consider the parse tree shown in Figure 15.6 for the following BERP example:

(15.22) I want to go to eat some Italian food today.

The branching structure of this tree distributes the key components of the meaning representation widely throughout the tree. At the same time, most of the nodes in the tree contribute almost nothing to the meaning of this sentence. This structure requires three λ-expressions and a complex-term to bring the contentful elements together at the top of the tree.

The third problem arises from the need to have uniform semantic attachments in the compositional rule-to-rule approach. This requirement often results in constituents that are at the right level of generality for the syntax, but too high a level for semantic purposes. A good example of this is the case of compound nominals and adjective phrases, where the semantic attachments are so general as to be nearly meaningless. Consider, for example, the rule governing the phrase *Italian food* in our current example:

Nominal → Adj Nominal
  {$\lambda x\ Nominal.sem(x) \wedge AM(x,\ Adj.sem)$}

Applying this attachment results in the following meaning representation:

$\exists x\ Isa(x, Food) \wedge AM(x, Italian)$

All nominals that fit this pattern receive the same vague interpretation that roughly indicates that the nominal is modified by the adjective. This is a far cry from what know that expressions like *Italian food* and *Italian restaurant* mean; they denote food prepared in a particular way, and restaurants that serve food prepared that way. Unfortunately, there is no way to get this very general rule to produce such an interpretation.

Both of these problems can be overcome through the use of **semantic grammars**, which were originally developed for text-based dialogue sys- SEMANTIC GRAMMARS tems in the domains of question answering and intelligent tutoring (Brown and Burton, 1975). Semantic grammars are more directly oriented towards serving the needs of a compositional analysis. In this approach, the rules and constituents of the grammar are designed to correspond directly to entities and relations from the domain being discussed. Such grammars are constructed so that the key semantic components occur together within single rules, and rules are made no more general than is needed to achieve sensible semantic analyses.

Let's consider how these two general strategies might be applied in the BERP domain. Consider the following candidate rule for the particular kind of information request illustrated in example (15.22):

InfoRequest → User want to go to eat FoodType TimeExpr

As with the rules introduced for idioms, rules of this type freely mix non-terminals and terminals on their right-hand side. In this case, *User*, *FoodType*, and *TimeExpr* represent semantically motivated non-terminal categories for this domain. Given this, the semantic attachment for this rule would have all the information that it needs to compose the meaning representation for requests of this type from the immediate constituents of the rule. In particular, there is no need for λ-expressions, since this flat rule elevates all the relevant arguments to the top of the tree.

Now consider the following rule that could be used to parse the phrase *Italian food* in our example:

FoodType → Nationality FoodType

The specific nature of this rule permits a far more useful semantic attachment than is possible with the generic nominal rule given above. More specifically, it can create a representation that states that the food specified by the constituent *FoodType* is to prepared in the style associated with the *Nationality* constituent.

One of the key motivations for the use of semantic grammars in these domains was the need to deal with various kinds of anaphor and ellipsis. Semantic grammars can help with these phenomena since by their nature they enable a certain amount of prediction. More specifically, they allow parsers to make highly specific predictions about upcoming input, based on the categories being actively predicted by the parser. Given this ability, anaphoric references and missing elements can be associated with specific semantic categories.

As an example of how this works consider the following ATIS examples:

(15.23) When does flight 573 arrive in Atlanta?

(15.24) When does it arrive in Dallas?

Sentences like these can be analyzed with a rule like the following, which makes use of the domain specific non-terminals *Flight* and *City*:

> *InfoRequest* → *when does Flight arrive in City*

A rule such as this gives far more information about the likely referent of the *it*, than a purely syntactic rule that would simply restrict it to anything expressible as a noun phrase. Operationally, such a system might search back in the dialogue for places where the *Flight* constituent has been recently used to find candidate references for this pronoun. Chapter 18 discusses the topic of anaphor resolution in more detail.

Not surprisingly, there are a number of drawbacks to basing a system on a semantic grammar. The primary drawback arises from an almost complete lack of **reuse** in the approach. Combining the syntax and semantics of a domain into a single representation makes the resulting grammar specific to that domain. In contrast, systems that keep their syntax and semantics separate can, in principle, reuse their grammars in new domains. A second lack of reuse arises as a consequence of eschewing syntactic generalizations in the grammar. This results in an unavoidable growth in the size of the grammar for a single domain. As an example of this, consider that whereas our original noun phrase rule was sufficient to cover both *Italian restaurant* as well as *Italian food*, we now need two separate rules for these phrases.

REUSE

In fact, inspection of the BERP corpus reveals that we would also need additional rules for *vegetarian restaurant*, *California restaurant*, and *expensive restaurant*.

Semantic grammars are susceptible to a kind of semantic overgeneration. As an example of this, consider the phrase *Canadian restaurant*. It matches the rule given above for ethnic restaurants, and would result in a meaning representation that specifies a restaurant that serves food prepared in the Canadian style. Unfortunately, this is almost certainly an incorrect interpretation of this phrase; none of the occurrences of this phrase in the WSJ corpus had this meaning, all referring instead to restaurants located within Canada. Dialogue systems that use semantic grammars rely on the rarity of such uses in restricted domains.

Finally, we should note that semantic grammars probably should have been called something else, since the grammars themselves are formally the same as in any of the other grammar formalisms we have discussed in this book. Correspondingly, there are no special algorithms for syntactic or semantic analysis specific to semantic grammars; they can use whatever algorithms are appropriate for the grammar formalism being employed, such as Earley, or any other context-free parsing algorithm.

Information Extraction

In language processing tasks such as question-answering, coming to a reasonable understanding of each input sentence is vital since giving a user a wrong answer can have serious consequences. For these tasks, the rule-to-rule approach with an eye towards semantics is a good way to build a complete interpretation of an input sentence.

However, other tasks, like extracting information about joint ventures from business news, understanding weather reports, or summarizing simple information about what happened today on the stock market from a radio report, do not necessarily require this kind of detailed understanding. Such **information extraction** tasks are characterized by two properties: the desired knowledge can be described by a relatively simple and fixed **template**, or frame, with slots that need to be filled in with material from the text, and only a small part of the information in the text is relevant for filling in this frame; the rest can be ignored.

INFORMATION EXTRACTION

TEMPLATE

For example, one of the tasks used in the fifth *Message Understanding Conference* (MUC-5) (Sundheim, 1993), a U.S. Government-organized information extraction conference, was to extract information about interna-

METHODOLOGY BOX: EVALUATING INFORMATION EX-
TRACTION SYSTEMS

The information extraction paradigm has much in common with
the field of information retrieval and has adapted several standard
evaluation metrics from information retrieval including **precision**,
recall, **fallout**, and a combined metric called an **F-measure**.

Recall is a measure of how much relevant information the system has extracted from the text; it is thus a measure of the coverage
of the system. Recall is defined as follows:

$$\textbf{Recall:} = \frac{\# \text{ of correct answers given by system}}{\text{total} \# \text{ of possible correct answers in the text}}$$

Precision is a measure of how much of the information that the system returned is actually correct, and is also known as **accuracy**. Precision is defined as follows:

$$\textbf{Precision:} = \frac{\# \text{ of correct answers given by system}}{\# \text{ of answers given by system}}$$

Fallout is a measure of the systems ability to ignore spurious information in the text. It is defined as follows:

$$\textbf{Fallout:} = \frac{\# \text{ of incorrect answers given by system}}{\# \text{ of spurious facts in the text}}$$

Note that recall and precision are antagonistic to one another
since a conservative system that strives for perfection in terms of
precision will invariably lower its recall score. Similarly, a system
that strives for coverage will get more things wrong, thus lowering
its precision score. This situation has led to the use of a combined
measure called the **F-measure** that balances recall and precision by
using a parameter β. The F-measure is defined as follows:

$$F = \frac{(\beta^2 + 1)PR}{\beta^2 P + R}$$

When β is one, precision and recall are given equal weight. When β
is greater than one, precision is favored, and when β is less than one,
recall is favored.

TIE-UP-1:
Relationship:	TIE-UP
Entities:	"Bridgestone Sports Co."
	"a local concern"
	"a Japanese trading house"
Joint Venture Company	"Bridgestone Sports Taiwan Co."
Activity	ACTIVITY-1
Amount	NT$20000000

ACTIVITY-1:
Company	"Bridgestone Sports Taiwan Co."
Product	"iron and "metal wood" clubs"
Start Date	DURING: January 1990

Figure 15.7   The templates produced by the FASTUS (Hobbs et al., 1997) information extraction engine given the input text on page 579.

---

tional joint ventures from business news. Here are the first two sentences of a sample article from Grishman and Sundheim (1995):

> Bridgestone Sports Co. said Friday it has set up a joint venture in Taiwan with a local concern and a Japanese trading house to produce golf clubs to be shipped to Japan.

> The joint venture, Bridgestone Sports Taiwan Co., capitalized at 20 million new Taiwan dollars, will start production in January 1990 with production of 20,000 iron and "metal wood" clubs a month.

The output of an information extraction system can be a single template with a certain number of slots filled in, or a more complex hierarchically related set of objects. The MUC-5 task specified this latter more complex output, requiring systems to produce hierarchically linked templates describing the participants in the joint venture, the resulting company, and its intended activity, ownership and capitalization. Figure 15.7 shows the resulting structure produced by the FASTUS system (Hobbs et al., 1997).

Many information extraction systems are built around **cascades** of finite-state automata. The FASTUS system, for example, produces the template given above, based on a cascade in which each level of linguistic processing extracts some information from the text, which is passed on to the next higher level, as shown in Figure 15.8

Many systems base all or most of these levels on finite-automata, although in practice most complete systems are not technically finite-state, either because the individual automata are augmented with feature registers

CASCADES

No.	Step	Description
1	**Tokens:**	Transfer an input stream of characters into a token sequence.
2	**Complex Words:**	Recognize multi-word phrases, numbers, and proper names.
3	**Basic phrases:**	Segment sentences into noun groups, verb groups, and particles.
4	**Complex phrases:**	Identify complex noun groups and complex verb groups.
5	**Semantic Patterns:**	Identify semantic entities and events and insert into templates.
6	**Merging:**	Merge references to the same entity or event from different parts of the text.

Figure 15.8   Levels of processing in FASTUS (Hobbs et al., 1997). Each level extracts a specific type of information which is then passed on to the next higher level.

(as in FASTUS), or because they are used only as preprocessing steps for full parsers (e.g., Gaizauskas et al., 1995; Weischedel, 1995) , or are combined with other components based on decision-trees (Fisher et al., 1995).

Let's sketch the FASTUS implementation of each of these levels, following Hobbs et al. (1997) and Appelt et al. (1995). After tokenization, the second level recognizes multiwords like *set up*, and *joint venture*, and names like *Bridgestone Sports Co.*. The name recognizer is a transducer, composed of a large set of specific mappings designed to handle locations, personal names, and names of organizations, companies, unions, performing groups, and so on. The following are typical rules for modeling names of performing organizations like *San Francisco Symphony Orchestra* and *Canadian Opera Company*. While the rules are written using a context-free syntax, there is no recursion and therefore they can be automatically compiled into finite-state transducers:

Performer-Org	$\rightarrow$	(pre-location) Performer-Noun+ Perf-Org-Suffix
pre-location	$\rightarrow$	locname | nationality
locname	$\rightarrow$	city | region
Perf-Org-Suffix	$\rightarrow$	orchestra, company
Performer-Noun	$\rightarrow$	symphony, opera
nationality	$\rightarrow$	Canadian, American, Mexican
city	$\rightarrow$	San Francisco, London

The second stage also might transduce sequences like *forty two* into the appropriate numeric value (recall the discussion of this problem on page 124 in Chapter 5).

The third FASTUS stage produces a series of **basic phrases**, such as noun groups, verb groups, and so on, using finite-state rules of the sort shown on page 390. The output of the FASTUS basic phrase identifier is shown in Figure 15.9; note the use of some domain-specific basic phrases like *Company* and *Location*. BASIC PHRASES

Company	Bridgestone Sports Co.
Verb Group	said
Noun Group	Friday
Noun Group	it
Verb Group	had set up
Noun Group	a joint venture
Preposition	in
Location	Taiwan
Preposition	with
Noun Group	a local concern
Conjunction	and
Noun Group	a Japanese trading house
Verb Group	to produce
Noun Group	golf clubs
Verb Group	to be shipped
Preposition	to
Location	Japan

Figure 15.9   The output of Stage 2 of the FASTUS basic-phrase extractor, which uses finite-state rules of the sort described by Appelt and Israel (1997) and shown on page 390.

Recall that Chapter 10 described how these basic phrases can be combined into complex noun groups and verb groups. This is accomplished in Stage 4 of FASTUS, by dealing with conjunction and with the attachment of measure phrases as in the following:

20,000 iron and "metal wood" clubs a month,

and preposition phrases:

production of 20,000 iron and "metal wood" clubs a month,

The output of Stage 4 is a list of complex noun groups and verb groups. Stage 5 takes this list, ignoring all input that has not been chunked into a complex group, recognizes entities and events in the complex groups, and

(1)	Relationship:	TIE-UP
	Entities:	"Bridgestone Sports Co."
		"a local concern"
		"a Japanese trading house"
(2)	Activity	PRODUCTION
	Product	"golf clubs"
(3)	Relationship:	TIE-UP
	Joint Venture Company	"Bridgestone Sports Taiwan Co."
	Amount	NT$20000000
(4)	Activity	PRODUCTION
	Company	"Bridgestone Sports Taiwan Co."
	Start Date	DURING: January 1990
(5)	Activity	PRODUCTION
	Product	"iron and "metal wood" clubs"

Figure 15.10   The five partial templates produced by Stage 5 of the FASTUS system. These templates will be merged by the Stage 6 merging algorithm to produce the final template shown in Figure 15.7 on page 579.

inserts the recognized objects into the proper templates. The recognition of entities and events is done by hand-coded finite-state automata whose transitions are based on particular complex-phrase types annotated by particular head words or particular features like *company*, *currency*, or *date*.

For example, the first sentence of the news story above realizes the semantic patterns based on the following two regular expressions (where NG indicates Noun-Group and VG Verb-Group):

- NG(Company/ies) VG(Set-up) NG(Joint-Venture) with NG(Company/ies)
- VG(Produce) NG(Product)

The second sentence realizes the second pattern above as well as the following two patterns:

- NG(Company) VG-Passive(Capitalized) at NG(Currency)
- NG(Company) VG(Start) NG(Activity) in/on NG(Date)

The result of processing these two sentences is the set of five draft templates shown in Figure 15.10. These five templates must then be merged into the single hierarchical structure shown in Figure 15.7. The merging algorithm decides whether two activity or relationship structures are sufficiently consistent that they might be describing the same events, and merges them if so. Since the merging algorithm must perform reference resolution (deciding when it is the case that two descriptions refer to the same entity), we defer description of this level to Chapter 18.

Domain-specific templates of the kind we have described in this section have also been used in many limited-domain semantic understanding and discourse comprehension tasks, including managing mixed dialogue in question-answering systems (Bobrow et al., 1977).

15.6 SUMMARY

This chapter explores the notion of syntax-driven semantic analysis. Among the highlights of this chapter are the following topics:

- **Semantic analysis** is the process whereby meaning representations are created and assigned to linguistic inputs.

- **Semantic analyzers** that make use of static knowledge from the lexicon and grammar can create context-independent literal, or conventional, meanings.

- The **Principle of Compositionality** states that the meaning of a sentence can be composed from the meanings of its parts.

- In **syntax-driven semantic analysis**, the parts are the syntactic constituents on an input.

- Compositional creation of FOPC formulas is possible with a few notational extensions including λ-**expressions** and **complex-terms**.

- **Natural language quantifiers** introduce a kind of ambiguity that is difficult to handle compositionally. Complex-terms can be used to compactly encode this ambiguity.

- **Idiomatic language** defies the principle of compositionality but can easily be handled by adapting the techniques used to design grammar rules and their semantic attachments.

- **Practical semantic analysis** systems adapt the strictly compositional approach in a number of ways.

  - Dialogue systems based on **semantic grammars** rely on grammars that have been written to serve the needs of semantics rather than syntactic generality.

  - **Information extraction** systems based on cascaded automata can extract pertinent information while ignoring irrelevant parts of the input.

BIBLIOGRAPHICAL AND HISTORICAL NOTES

As noted earlier, the principle of compositionality is traditionally attributed to Frege; Janssen (1997) discusses this attribution. Using the categorial grammar framework described in Chapter 12, Montague (1973) demonstrated that a compositional approach could be systematically applied to an interesting fragment of natural language. The rule-to-rule hypothesis was first articulated by Bach (1976). On the computational side of things, Woods's LUNAR system (Woods, 1977) was based on a pipelined syntax-first compositional analysis. Schubert and Pelletier (1982) developed an incremental rule-to-rule system based on Gazdar's GPSG approach (Gazdar, 1981, 1982; Gazdar et al., 1985). Main and Benson (1983) extended Montague's approach to the domain of question-answering.

In one of the all-too-frequent cases of parallel development, researchers in programming languages developed essentially identical compositional techniques to aid in the design of compilers. Specifically, Knuth (1968) introduced the notion of attribute grammars that associate semantic structures with syntactic structures in a one-to-one correspondence. As a consequence, the style of semantic attachments used in this chapter will be familiar to users of the YACC-style (Johnson and Lesk, 1978) compiler tools.

Semantic Grammars are due to Burton (Brown and Burton, 1975). Similar notions developed around the same time included Pragmatic Grammars (Woods, 1977) and Performance Grammars (Robinson, 1975). All centered around the notion of reshaping syntactic grammars to serve the needs of semantic processing. It is safe to say that most modern systems developed for use in limited domains make use of some form of semantic grammar.

Most of the techniques used in the fragment of English presented in Section 15.2 are adapted from SRI's Core Language Engine (Alshawi, 1992). Additional bits and pieces were adapted from Woods (1977), Schubert and Pelletier (1982), and Gazdar et al. (1985). Of necessity, a large number of important topics were not covered in this chapter. See Alshawi (1992) for the standard gap-threading approach to semantic interpretation in the presence of long-distance dependencies. ter Meulen (1995) presents an modern treatment of tense, aspect, and the representation of temporal information. Extensive coverage of approaches to quantifier scoping can be found in Hobbs and Shieber (1987) and Alshawi (1992).   van Lehn (1978) presents a set of human preferences for quantifier scoping. Over the years, a considerable amount of effort has been directed toward the interpretation of compound nominals. Linguistic research on this topic can be found in Lees (1970), Downing (1977), Levi (1978), and Ryder (1994), more computational approaches are described in Gershman (1977), Finin (1980), McDonald (1982), Pierre (1984), Arens et al. (1987), Wu (1992), Vanderwende (1994), and Lauer (1995).

There is a long and extensive literature on idioms. Fillmore et al. (1988) describe a general grammatical framework called Construction Grammar that places idioms at the center of its underlying theory. Makkai (1972) presents an extensive linguistic analysis of many English idioms. Hundreds of idiom dictionaries for second-language learners are also available. On the computational side, Becker (1975) was among the first to suggest the use of phrasal rules in parsers. Wilensky and Arens (1980) were among the first to successfully make use of this notion in their PHRAN system. Zernik (1987) demonstrated a system that could learn such phrasal idioms in context. A collection of papers on computational approaches to idioms appeared in (Fass et al., 1992).

The first work on information extraction was performed in the context of the Frump system (DeJong, 1982). Later work was stimulated by the U.S. government sponsored MUC conferences (Sundheim, 1991, 1992, 1993, 1995b). Chinchor et al. (1993) describes the evaluation techniques used in the MUC-3 and MUC-4 conferences. Hobbs (1997) partially credits the inspiration for FASTUS to the success of the University of Massachusetts CIRCUS system (Lehnert et al., 1991) in MUC-3. The SCISOR system is another system based loosely on cascades and semantic expectations that did well in MUC-3 (Jacobs and Rau, 1990). Due to the lack of reuse from one domain to another in information extraction, a considerable amount of work has focused on automating the process of knowledge acquisition in this area. A variety of supervised learning approaches are described in Cardie (1993), Cardie (1994), Riloff (1993), Soderland et al. (1995), Huffman (1996), and Freitag (1998).

Finally, we have skipped an entire branch of semantic analysis in which expectations driven from deep meaning representations drive the analysis process. Such systems avoid the direct representation and use of syntax, rarely making use of anything resembling a parse tree. Some of the earliest and most successful efforts along these lines were developed by Simmons (1973, 1978, 1983) and (Wilks, 1975a, 1975c). A series of similar approaches were developed by Roger Schank and his students (Riesbeck, 1975; Birnbaum and Selfridge, 1981; Riesbeck, 1986). In these approaches, the semantic analysis process is guided by detailed procedures associated with individual lexical items. The CIRCUS information extraction system (Lehnert et al., 1991) traces its roots to these systems.

EXERCISES

15.1 The attachment given on page 563 for handling noun phrases with complex determiners is not general enough to handle most possessive noun phrases. Specifically, it doesn't work for phrases like the following:

  a. My sister's flight

  b. My fiance's mother's flight

  Create a new set of semantic attachments to handle cases like these.

15.2 Develop a set of grammar rules and semantic attachments to handle predicate adjectives such as the one following:

  a. Flight 308 from New York is expensive.

  b. Murphy's restaurant is cheap.

15.3 None of the attachments given in this chapter provide temporal information. Augment a small number of the most basic rules to add temporal information along the lines sketched in Chapter 14. Use your rules to create meaning representations for the following examples:

  a. Flight 299 departed at 9 o'clock.

  b. Flight 208 will arrive at 3 o'clock.

  c. Flight 1405 will arrive late.

15.4 As noted in Chapter 14, the present tense in English can be used to refer to either the present or the future. However, it can also be used to express habitual behavior, as in the following:

  Flight 208 leaves at 3 o'clock.

  This could be a simple statement about today's Flight 208, or alternatively it might state that this flight leaves at 3 o'clock every day. Create a FOPC meaning representation along with appropriate semantic attachments for this habitual sense.

15.5   Implement an Earley-style semantic analyzer based on the discussion on page 569.

15.6   It has been claimed that it is not necessary to explicitly list the semantic attachment for most grammar rules. Instead, the semantic attachment for a rule should be inferable from the semantic types of the rule's constituents. For example, if a rule has two constituents, where one is a single argument λ-expression and the other is a constant, then the semantic attachment should obviously apply the λ-expression to the constant. Given the attachments presented in this chapter, does this *type-driven semantics* seem like a reasonable idea?

15.7   Add a simple type-driven semantics mechanism to the Earley analyzer you implemented for Exercise 15.5.

15.8   Using a phrasal search on your favorite Web search engine, collect a small corpus of *the tip of the iceberg* examples. Be certain that you search for an appropriate range of examples (i.e., don't just search for "the tip of the iceberg".) Analyze these examples and come up with a set of grammar rules that correctly accounts for them.

15.9   Collect a similar corpus of examples for the idiom *miss the boat*. Analyze these examples and come up with a set of grammar rules that correctly accounts for them.

15.10   There are now a fair number of Web-based natural language question answering services that purport to provide answers to questions on a wide range of topics (see the book's Web page for pointers to current services). Develop a corpus of questions for some general domain of interest and use it to evaluate one or more of these services. Report your results. What difficulties did you encounter in applying the standard evaluation techniques to this task?

15.11   Collect a small corpus of weather reports from your local newspaper or the Web. Based on an analysis of this corpus, create a set of frames sufficient to capture the semantic content of these reports.

15.12   Implement and evaluate a small information extraction system for the weather report corpus you collected for the last exercise.

16   LEXICAL SEMANTICS

"When I use a word", Humpty Dumpty said in rather a scornful tone, "it means just what I choose it to mean – neither more nor less."

Lewis Carroll, *Alice in Wonderland*

How many legs does a dog have if you call its tail a leg?
Four.
Calling a tail a leg doesn't make it one.

Attributed to Abraham Lincoln

The previous two chapters focused on the representation of meaning representations for entire sentences. In those discussions, we made minimal use of the notion of the meaning of a word. Words and their meanings were of interest solely to the extent that they provided the appropriate bits and pieces necessary to construct adequate meaning representations for entire sentences. This general approach is motivated by the view that while words may contribute content to the meanings of sentences, they do not themselves have meanings. By this we mean that words, by themselves, do not refer to the world, cannot be judged to be true or false, or literal or figurative, or a host of other things that are generally reserved for entire sentences and utterances. This narrow conception of the role of words in a semantic theory leads to a view of the lexicon as a simple listing of symbolic fragments devoid of any systematic structure.

The topics presented in this chapter serve to illustrate how much is missed by this narrow view. As we will see, the lexicon has a highly systematic structure that governs what words can mean, and how they can be used. This structure consists of relations among words and their meanings, as well as the internal structure of individual words. The linguistic study of this systematic, meaning related, structure is called **Lexical Semantics**.

LEXICAL
SEMANTICS

Before moving on, we will first introduce a few new terms, since the ones we have been using thus far are entirely too vague. In particular, the word *word* has by now been used in so many different ways that it will prove difficult to make unambiguous use of it in this chapter. Instead, we will focus on the notion of a **lexeme**, an individual entry in the lexicon. A lexeme should be thought of as a pairing of a particular orthographic and phonological form with some form of symbolic meaning representation. The **lexicon** is therefore a finite list of lexemes. Note that this definition allows us to include compound nouns and other non-compositional phrases as entries in the lexicon. We will use the terms **orthographic form**, and **phonological form**, to refer to the appropriate form part of a lexeme, and the term **sense** to refer to a lexeme's meaning component.

LEXEME

LEXICON

SENSE

Given this minimal nomenclature, let us turn to the topic of what facts can be discovered about lexemes that are relevant to the topic of meaning. A fruitful place to start such an exploration is a dictionary. Dictionaries are, after all, nothing if not repositories of information about the meanings of lexemes. Within dictionaries, it turns out that the most interesting place to look first is at the definitions of lexemes that no one ever actually looks up. For example, consider the following fragments from the definitions of *right*, *left*, *red*, *blood* from the *American Heritage Dictionary* (Morris, 1985).

right *adj.* located nearer the right hand esp. being on the right
           when facing the same direction as the observer.
left *adj.* located nearer to this side of the body than the right.
red *n.* the color of blood or a ruby.
blood *n.* the red liquid that circulates in the heart, arteries and
           veins of animals.

The first thing to note about these definitions is the surprising amount of circularity in them. The definition of *right* makes two direct references to itself, while the entry for *left* contains an implicit self-reference in the phrase *this side of the body*, which presumably means the *left* side. The entries for *red* and *blood* avoid this kind of direct self-reference by instead referencing each other in their definitions. Such circularity is, of course, inherent in all dictionary definitions; these examples are just extreme cases. In the end, all definitions are stated in terms of lexemes that are, in turn, defined in terms of other lexemes.

From a purely formal point of view, this inherent circularity is evidence that dictionaries entries are often not definitions at all, but rather descriptions of lexemes in terms of other lexemes. Such entries are useful when the user of the dictionary has sufficient grasp of these other terms to make the entry in question sensible. As is obvious with lexemes like *red* and *right*, this approach will fail without some ultimate grounding in the external world.

Fortunately, even with this limitation, there is still a wealth of semantic information contained in these kinds of definitions. For example, the above definitions make it clear that *right* and *left* are similar kinds of lexemes that stand in some kind of alternation, or opposition, to one another. Similarly, we can glean that *red* is a color, it can be applied to both *blood* and *rubies*, and that *blood* is a *liquid*. As we will see in this chapter, given a sufficiently large database of facts such as these, many applications are quite capable of performing sophisticated semantic tasks (even if they do not *really* know their right from their left).

To summarize, we can capture quite a bit about the semantics of individual lexemes by analyzing and labeling their relations to other lexemes in various settings. We will, in particular, be interested in accounting for the similarities and differences among different lexemes in similar settings, and the nature of the relations among lexemes in a single setting. This latter topic will lead us to examine the idea that lexemes are not unanalyzable atomic symbols, but rather have an internal structure that, in part, governs how they can be combined with other words to form sentences. Later, in Section 16.4, we will take a closer look at the notion of creativity, or generativity, and the lexicon. There we will explore the notion that the lexicon should not be thought of as a finite listing, but rather as a creative generator of infinite meanings.

Before proceeding, we should note that the view of lexical semantics presented here is not purely linguistic, nor is it oriented solely towards improving computational applications of the more restrictive "only sentences have meaning" variety. Rather, it lends itself to any application that involves the use of words, and that can be improved by some knowledge of their semantics. Therefore, a major focus of this chapter will be on those computational resources that capture lexical semantic information in a form that is useful for a wide variety of computational applications.

16.1   RELATIONS AMONG LEXEMES AND THEIR SENSES

This section explores a variety of relations that hold among lexemes and among their senses. The list of relations presented here is by no means exhaustive; the emphasis is on those relations that have had significant computational implications. As we will see, the primary analytic tool we will use involves the systematic substitution of one lexeme for another in some setting. The results of such substitutions can reveal the presence or absence of a specific relationship between the substituted lexemes.

Homonymy

HOMONYMY

We begin this section with a discussion of **homonymy**, perhaps the simplest, and semantically least interesting, relation to hold between lexemes. Traditionally, homonymy is defined as a relation that holds *between words that have the same form with unrelated meanings*. The items taking part in

HOMONYMS

such a relation are called **homonyms**. A classic example of homonymy is *bank* with its distinct financial institution and sloping mound meanings, as illustrated in the following WSJ examples:

(16.1)   Instead, a *bank* can hold the investments in a custodial account in the client's name.

(16.2)   But as agriculture burgeons on the east *bank*, the river will shrink even more.

Loosely following lexicographic tradition, we will denote this relationship by placing a superscript on the orthographic form of the word as in **bank**[1] and **bank**[2]. This notation indicates that these are two separate lexemes, with distinct and unrelated meanings, that happen to share an orthographic form.

In the following discussion, we will primarily be concerned with how well our definition of homonymy assists us in identifying and characterizing those lexemes which will lead to ambiguity problems for computational applications. Let's begin by examining our *bank* example in more detail. The first thing to note is that **bank**[1] and **bank**[2] are identical in both their orthographic *and* phonological forms. Of course, there are also pairs of lexemes with distinct meanings which do not share *both* forms. For example, pairs like *wood* and *would*, and *be* and *bee*, are pronounced the same but are spelled differently. Of course, none of these examples are traditionally considered to be good candidates for homonymy. The notion of homonymy is most closely associated with the field of lexicography, where normally

only dictionary entries with identical **citation-forms** are considered candi-   CITATION-FORMS
dates for homonymy. Citation-forms are the orthographic-forms that are
used to alphabetically index words in a dictionary, which in English correspond to what we have been calling the root form of a word. Under this
view, words with the same pronunciation but different spellings are not considered homonyms, but rather **homophones**, distinct lexemes with a shared   HOMOPHONES
pronunciation.

There are also pairs of lexemes with identical orthographic forms and
different pronunciations. Consider, for example, the distinct fish and music meanings associated with the orthographic form *bass* in the following
examples:

(16.3)   The expert angler from Dora, Mo., was fly-casting for bass rather
         than the traditional trout.

(16.4)   The curtain rises to the sound of angry dogs baying and ominous
         bass chords sounding.

While these examples more closely fit the traditional definition of homonymy,
they would only rarely appear in any traditional list of homonyms. Instead,
lexemes with the same orthographic form with unrelated meanings are called
homographs.   HOMOGRAPHS

Finally, we should note that lexemes with different parts of speech are
also typically not considered to be good candidates for homonymy. This
restriction serves to rule out examples such as *would* and *wood*, on grounds
other than their orthography. The basis for this restriction is two-fold: first
as we saw when we discussed part-of-speech tagging, lexemes with such
different parts of speech are easily distinguished based on their differing
syntactic environments, and secondly lexical items can take on many distinct
forms based on their inflectional and derivational morphology, which is in
turn largely based on part-of-speech.

To complicate matters, the issue of differing morphology can also occur with lexemes that have the same part-of-speech. Consider the lexemes
find and *found* in their locating and creating an institution meanings, as illustrated in the following WSJ examples:

(16.5)   He has looked at 14 baseball and football stadiums and found that
         only one – private Dodger Stadium – brought more money into a
         city than it took out.

(16.6)   Culturally speaking, this city has increasingly displayed its
         determination to found the sort of institutions that attract the
         esteem of Eastern urbanites.

Here we have two lexemes with distinct root forms, *find* and *found*, that nevertheless share the morphological variant *found* as the past tense of the first, and the root of the second.

As we noted earlier, homonymy is of primarily of interest to the extent that it leads an application into dealing with ambiguity. Whether or not a given pair of lexemes cause ambiguity to arise in an application is entirely dependent on the nature of the application. The critical issue is whether the nature of the form overlap is likely to cause difficulties for a given application.

In **spelling correction**, homophones can lead to real-word spelling errors, or malapropisms, as when lexemes such as *weather* and *whether* are interchanged. This is a case where a phonological overlap causes a problem for a purely text-based system. Additional problems in spelling correction are caused by such imperfect homographs as *find* and *found*, which have partially overlapping morphologies. In this case, a word-form like *founded* may represent a correct use of the past tense, or an incorrect overapplication of the regular past tense rule to an irregular verb.

In **speech recognition**, homophones such as *to*, *two* and *too* cause obvious problems. What is less clear, however, is that perfect homonyms such as *bank* are also problematic. Recall that speech recognition systems rely on language models that are often based on tables of N-gram probabilities. For perfect homonyms, the entries for all the distinct lexemes are conflated despite the fact that the different lexemes occur in different environments. This conflation results in inappropriately high probabilities to words that are cohorts of the lexeme not in use, and lower than appropriate probabilities to the correct cohorts.

Text-to-speech systems are, of course, particularly vulnerable to homographs with distinct pronunciations. This problem can be avoided through the use of part-of-speech tagging with examples such as *conduct* whose different pronunciations are associated with different parts of speech. However, for other examples like *bass*, the two lexemes must be distinguished by some other means. Note that this situation is the reverse of the one we had with spelling correction, here a fundamentally speech-oriented system is being plagued by an orthographic problem.

Finally, as we will see in detail in Chapter 17, the performance of **information retrieval** systems is degraded in the presence of homographs. Users' seeking information about saltwater *bass* are unlikely to be satisfied with documents concerning musical instruments.

Polysemy

Let's return to the topic of what it means for two meanings to be related or
unrelated. Recall that the definition of homonymy requires that the lexemes
in question have distinct and unrelated meanings. This is the crux of the
matter; if the meanings in question are related in some way then we are
dealing with a single lexeme with more than one meaning, rather than two
separate lexemes. This phenomenon of multiple related meanings within
a single lexeme is known as **polysemy**. Note that earlier we had defined a   POLYSEMY
lexeme as a pairing between a surface form and a sense. Here we will expand
that notion to be a pairing of a form with a set of related senses.

To make this notion more concrete, consider the following *bank* example from the WSJ corpus:

(16.7)   While some *banks* furnish sperm only to married women, others
         are much less restrictive.

Although this is clearly not a use of the sloping mound meaning of *bank*,
it just as clearly is not a reference to a promotional giveaway at a financial
institution. Rather, *bank* has a whole range of senses related to repositories for various biological entities, as in *blood bank*, *egg bank*, and *sperm
bank*. One way to deal with this use would be to create **bank³**, yet another
distinct lexeme associated with the form *bank*, and give it a meaning appropriate to this sperm bank usage. Unfortunately, according to our definition of
homonymy, this would require us to say that the meaning of *bank* in this example is distinct and unrelated to the financial institution sense, which seems
to be far too strong a statement. The notion of polysemy allows us to state
that this sense of *bank* is related to, and possibly derived from, the financial
institution sense, without asserting that it is a distinct lexeme.

As one might suspect, the task of distinguishing homonymy from polysemy is not quite as straightforward as we made it seem with these *bank*
examples. There are two criteria that are typically invoked to determine
whether or not the meanings of two lexemes are related or not: the history, or
etymology, of the lexemes in question, and how the lexemes are conceived of   ETYMOLOGY
by native speakers. In practice, an ill-defined combination of evidence from
these two sources is used to distinguish homonymous from polysemous lexical entries. In the case of *bank*, the etymology reveals that **bank¹** has an
Italian origin, while **bank²** is of Scandinavian origin, thus encouraging us to
list them as distinct lexemes. On the other hand, our belief that the use of
bank in example (16.7) is related to **bank¹** is based on introspection about
the similarities of their meanings, and the lack of any etymological evidence

for an independent third sense.

In the absence of detailed etymological evidence, a useful intuition to use in distinguishing homonymy from polysemy is the notion of coincidence. Cases of homonymy can usually be understood easily as accidents of history – two lexemes which have coincidentally come to share the same form. On the other hand, it is far more difficult to accept cases of polysemy as coincidences. Returning again to our *bank* example, it is difficult to accept the idea that the various uses of *bank* in all of its various repository senses are only coincidentally related to the savings institution sense.

Once we have determined that we are dealing with a polysemous lexeme, we are of course still left with the task of managing the potentially numerous polysemous senses associated with it. In particular, for any given *single* lexeme we would like to be able to answer the following questions:

- What distinct senses does it have?
- How are these senses related?
- How can they be reliably distinguished?

The answers to these questions can have serious consequences for how well semantic analyzers, search engines, generators, and machine translation systems perform their respective tasks. The first two questions will be covered here and in Section 16.4, while the final question will be covered in more detail in Chapter 17.

The issue of deciding how many senses should be associated with a given polysemous lexeme is a task that has long vexed lexicographers, who until recently have been the only people engaged in the creation of large lexical databases. Most lexicographers take the approach of creating entries with as many senses as necessary to account for all the fine distinctions in meaning observed in some very large corpus of examples. This is a reasonable approach given that the primary use for a traditional dictionary is to assist users in learning the various uses of a word. Unfortunately, it tends to err on the side of making more distinctions than are normally required for any reasonable computational application.

To make this notion of distinguishing distinct senses more concrete, consider the following uses of the verb *serve* from the WSJ corpus:

(16.8)   They rarely *serve* red meat, preferring to prepare seafood, poultry or game birds.

(16.9)   He *served* as U.S. ambassador to Norway in 1976 and 1977.

(16.10) He might have *served* his time, come out and led an upstanding life.

Reasonable arguments can be made that each of these examples represents a distinct sense of *serve*. For example, the implicit contrast between *serving red meat* and *preparing seafood* in the first example indicates a strong connection between this sense of *serve* and the related notion of food preparation. Since there is no similar component in any of the other examples, we can assume that this first use is distinct from the other two. Next, we might note that the second example has a different syntactic subcategorization from the others since its first argument, which denotes the role played by the subject, is a prepositional phrase. As will be discussed in Section 16.3, such differing syntactic behaviors are often symptomatic of differing underlying senses. Finally, the third example is specific to the domain of incarceration. This is clear since this example provides almost no specific information about prison, and yet has an obvious and clear meaning; a meaning which plays no role in the other examples.

Another practical technique, for determining if two distinct senses are present is to combine two separate uses of a lexeme into a single example using a conjunction, a device has the rather improbable name of **zeugma**.   ZEUGMA
Consider the following ATIS examples:

(16.11) Which of those flights serve breakfast?

(16.12) Does Midwest Express serve Philadelphia?

(16.13) ?Does Midwest Express serve breakfast and Philadelphia?

We'll use a (?) at the beginning of an example to mark those that are semantically ill-formed in some way. The oddness of the invented third example indicates there is no sensible way to make a single sense of *serve* work for both breakfast and Philadelphia. More precisely, the underlying concepts invoked by *serve* in the first example cannot be applied in any meaningful way to *Philadelphia*. This is an instance where we can make use of examples from a corpus along with our native intuitions in a structured way to discover the presence or distinct senses.

The issue of discovering the proper set of senses for a given lexeme is distinct from the process of determining which sense of a lexeme is being used in a given example. This latter task is called **word sense disambiguation**, and is covered in detail in Chapter 17. This task typically presumes   WORD SENSE DISAMBIGUATION
that a *fixed* set of senses can be associated with each lexical item, a dubious proposition that we will take up in Section 16.4. Note that, in practice, this task often refers to any process that identifies a word form in context with one sense chosen from a predetermined set of senses. In other words, most approaches to word sense disambiguation do not distinguish homonymy from

polysemy in any meaningful way. As we will see in Chapter 17 this has implications for how these systems are evaluated.

Finally, let us turn briefly to the topic of relatedness among the various senses of a single polysemous lexeme. Earlier, we made an appeal to the intuition that the polysemous senses of a lexeme are unlikely to have come about by coincidence. This raises the obvious question that if they are not related by coincidence, then how are they related? This question has not received much attention from those constructing large lexicons since as long as the lexicon contains the correct senses, how they came to be there is largely irrelevant. However, as soon as applications begin to deal with a wide variety of inputs, they encounter novel uses that do not correspond to any of the static senses in the system's lexicon. By examining the systematic relations among listed senses, we can gain insight into the meanings of such novel uses. These notions will be discussed in more detail in Section 16.4.

Synonymy

SYNONYMY

SUBSTITUTABILITY

The phenomenon of synonymy is sufficiently widespread to account for the popularity of both thesauri and crossword puzzles. As with homonymy, the notion of **synonymy**, has a deceptively simple definition: *different lexemes with the same meaning*. Of course, this definition leaves open the question of what it means for two lexemes to mean the same thing. Although Section 16.3 will provide some answers to this question, we can make progress without answering it directly by invoking the notion of **substitutability**: two lexemes will be considered synonyms if they can substituted for one another in a sentence without changing either the meaning or the acceptability of the sentence. The following ATIS examples illustrate this notion of substitutability:

(16.14) How big is that plane?

(16.15) Would I be flying on a large or small plane?

Exchanging *big* and *large* in these examples has no noticeable effect on either the meaning or acceptability of these sentences. We can take this as evidence for the synonymy of *big* and *large*, at least for these examples. Note that this is intended to be a very narrow statement. In particular, we are not saying anything about the relative likelihood of occurrence of *big* and *large* in contexts similar to these.

Not surprisingly, if we take the notion of substitutability to mean substitutable in all possible environments, then true synonyms in English are few and far between, as it is almost always possible to find some sentence where a purported synonym fails to substitute successfully. Given this, we will fall back on a weaker notion that allows us to call two lexemes synonyms if they are substitutable in *some* environment. This is, for all practical purposes, the notion of synonymy used in most dictionaries and thesauri.

The success or failure of the substitution of a given pair of candidate synonyms in a given setting depends primarily on four influences: polysemy, subtle shades of meaning, collocational constraints, and register. As we will see, only the first two involve the notion of meaning.

To explore the effect of polysemy on substitutability, consider the following WSJ example where a substitution of *large* for *big* clearly fails:

(16.16) Miss Nelson, for instance, became a kind of big sister to Mrs. Van Tassel's son, Benjamin.

(16.17) ?Miss Nelson, for instance, became a kind of large sister to Mrs. Van Tassel's son, Benjamin.

The source of this failure is the fact that the lexeme *big* has as one of its distinct polysemous senses the notion of being older, or grown up. Since the lexeme *large* lacks this sense among its many meanings, it is not substitutable for *big* in those environments where this sense is required. In this instance, the result is a sentence with a different meaning altogether. In other cases, such a substitution may result in a sentence that is either odd or entirely uninterpretable.

We referred to the next influence on synonymy as *shades of meaning*. By this, we have in mind cases where two lexemes share a central core meaning, but where additional ancillary facts are associated with one the lexemes. Consider the use of the lexemes *price* and *fare* in the ATIS corpus. Semantically, both have the notion of the cost for a service at the core of their meanings. They are not, however, freely interchangeable. Consider the following ATIS examples:

(16.18) What is the cheapest first class fare?

(16.19) ?What is the cheapest first class price?

Exchanging *price* for *fare* in this example leads to a certain amount of oddity. The source of this oddness is hard to pin down, but *fare* seems to be better suited to the costs for various services (ie. coach, business and first class fares), while *price* seems better applied to the tickets that represent these services. Of course, a more complete account of how these lexemes are used in this domain would require a systematic analysis of a corpus of examples. The point is that although these terms share a core meaning, there are subtle meaning-related differences that influence how they can be used.

These two influences on substitutability clearly involve the meanings of the lexical items. There are, however, other influences on the success or failure of a synonym substitution that are not based on meaning in any direct way. Collocational constraints are one such influence. By a collocational constraint, we mean the kind of associations, or attractions, between lexical items that were captured using techniques such as N-grams in Chapter 6.

Consider the following WSJ example:

(16.20) We frustrate 'em and frustrate 'em, and pretty soon they make a big mistake.

(16.21) ?We frustrate 'em and frustrate 'em, and pretty soon they make a large mistake.

As this example illustrates, there is a preference for using *big* rather than *large* when referring to mistakes of a critical or important nature. This is not due to a polysemy difference, nor does it seem to be due to any subtle shaded meaning difference between *big* and *large*. Note also, that this is clearly different than the *large sister* example in that *a large mistake* is still interpretable in the correct way; it just does not seem as natural to use *large* as *big*.

REGISTER Finally, by **register**, we mean the social factors that surround the use of possible synonyms. Here we are referring to lexemes with essentially identical meanings that are not interchangeable in all environments due to factors such as politeness, group status, and other similar social pressures. For example, multisyllabic lexemes with Latin or Greek origins are often used in place of shorter lexemes when a technical or academic style is desired.

As was the case with homonymy, these influences on synonymy have differing practical implications for computational applications. In Chapters 19 and 20, we will see that similarity of meaning, collocational constraints, and register are of great importance in natural language generation and machine translation. On the other hand, in the domains of information extraction and information retrieval, appropriateness of use is of far less consequence than the notion of identity of meaning.

Hyponymy

In our discussion of *price* and *fare*, we introduced the notion of pairs of lexemes with similar but non-identical meanings. The notion of **hyponymy** is based on a restricted class of such pairings: *pairings where one lexeme denotes a subclass of the other*. For example, the relationship between *car* and *vehicle* is one of hyponymy. Since this relation is not symmetric we will refer to the more specific lexeme as a **hyponym** of the more general one, and conversely to the more general term as a **hypernym** of the more specific one. We would therefore say that *car* is a hyponym of *vehicle*, and *vehicle* is hypernym of *car*.

HYPONYM
HYPERNYM

As with synonymy, we can explore the notion of hyponymy by making use of a restricted kind of substitution. Consider the following schema:

That is a x. ⇒ That is a y.

If *x* is a hyponym of *y*, then in any situation where the sentence on the left is true, the newly created sentence on the right must also be true, as in the following example:

That is a car. ⇒ That is a vehicle.

There a number of important differences between this kind of limited substitution and the kind of substitutions discussed with respect to synonymy. There the resulting sentence could plausibly serve as a substitute for the original sentence. Here, the new sentence is not intended to be a substitution for the original, rather it is merely serves as a diagnostic test for the presence of hyponymy.

The concept of hyponymy is closely related to a number of other notions that play central roles in biology, linguistic anthropology and computer science.

The term **ontology** usually refers to a set of distinct objects resulting from an analysis of a domain, or **microworld**. A **taxonomy** is a particular arrangement of the elements of an ontology into a tree-like class inclusion structure. Normally, there are a set of well-formedness constraints on taxonomies that go beyond their component class inclusion relations. For example, the lexemes *hound*, *mutt*, and *puppy* are all hyponyms of *dog*, but it would be odd to construct a taxonomy from those pairs since the concepts motivating the relations is different in each case. Finally, the computer science notion of an **object hierarchy** is based the notion that objects from an ontology arranged in a taxonomy, can receive, or inherit, features from their ancestors in a taxonomy. This, of course, only makes sense when the elements in the taxonomy are in fact complex structured objects with features to be inherited.

ONTOLOGY
TAXONOMY

OBJECT
HIERARCHY

Therefore, sets of hyponymy relations, by themselves, do not constitute an ontology, category structure, taxonomy, or object hierarchy. They have, however, proved to be useful as approximations to such structures.

16.2   WORDNET: A DATABASE OF LEXICAL RELATIONS

The usefulness of lexical relations in linguistic, psycholinguistic, and computational research has led to a number of efforts to create large electronic databases of such relations. Efforts to create such databases have, in general, followed one of two basic approaches: mining information from existing dictionaries and thesauri, and handcrafting a database from scratch. Despite the obvious advantages of reusing existing resources, WordNet, the most well-developed and widely used lexical database for English, was developed using the latter approach (Fellbaum, 1998).

WordNet consists of three separate databases, one each for nouns and verbs, and a third for adjectives and adverbs; closed class lexical items are not included in WordNet. Each of the three databases consists of a set of lexical entries corresponding to unique orthographic forms, accompanied by sets of senses associated with each form. Figure 16.1 gives some idea of the scope of the WordNet 1.6 release. The databases can be accessed directly with a browser (locally or over the Internet), or programmatically through the use of a set of C library functions.

In their most complete form, WordNet's sense entries consist of a set of synonyms, a dictionary-style definition, or gloss, and some example uses. Figure 16.2 shows an abbreviated version of the WordNet entry for the noun *bass*. As this entry illustrates, there are several important differences between WordNet entries and our notion of a lexeme. First, since WordNet contains no phonological information, it makes no attempt to keep separate lexemes with distinct pronunciations. For example, in this entry **bass**[4], **bass**[5], and **bass**[8] all refer to the [b ae s] fish sense, while the others refer to the [b ey s] musical sense. More generally, WordNet makes no attempt to distinguish homonymy from polysemy. For example, as far as this entry is concerned, **bass**[1] bears the same relationship to **bass**[2] as it does to

Category	Unique Forms	Number of Senses
Noun	94474	116317
Verb	10319	22066
Adjective	20170	29881
Adverb	4546	5677

Figure 16.1   Scope of the current WordNet 1.6 release in terms of unique entries and total number of senses for the four databases.

The noun "bass" has 8 senses in WordNet.
1. bass - (the lowest part of the musical range)
2. bass, bass part - (the lowest part in polyphonic music)
3. bass, basso - (an adult male singer with the lowest voice)
4. sea bass, bass - (flesh of lean-fleshed saltwater fish of the family Serranidae)
5. freshwater bass, bass - (any of various North American lean-fleshed freshwater
                              fishes especially of the genus Micropterus)
6. bass, bass voice, basso - (the lowest adult male singing voice)
7. bass - (the member with the lowest range of a family of musical instruments)
8. bass - (nontechnical name for any of numerous edible marine and
          freshwater spiny-finned fishes)

Figure 16.2   A portion of the WordNet 1.6 entry for the noun *bass*.

---

bass[4]. This is a conservative strategy that reflects the fact that although
there are fairly reliable diagnostics for discriminating among distinct word
senses, systematically organizing the resulting polysemous senses is a much
more uncertain and subjective activity. Given this, the developers of Word-
Net have opted to simply list distinct senses, without attempting to explicitly
organize them in the hierarchical manner seen in many dictionaries.

Figure 16.3 gives a rough idea of how these senses are distributed
throughout the verb database. This figures presents a sorted ranking of all
the verbs in WordNet in terms of their number of senses. The distribution is
extremely skewed, with a small number of entries having a large number of
senses, and a large number having a single sense. Distributions like this are
ubiquitous when dealing with the lexicon, and are referred to as Zipf distributions (Zipf, 1949). The degree of polysemy in the verb database is higher
than in the noun database. This is consistent with the fact that there are far
fewer verbs than nouns in English and their meanings are far more malleable
(Gentner and France, 1988).

Of course, a simple listing of lexical entries would not be much more
useful than an ordinary on-line dictionary. The power of WordNet lies in its
set of domain-independent lexical relations. These relations can hold among
WordNet entries, senses, or sets of synonyms. They are, for the most part,
restricted to items with the same part-of-speech, or more pragmatically, to
items within the same database. Figures 16.4, 16.5, and 16.6 show a subset
of the relations associated with each of the three databases, along with a brief
definition and an example. Since a full discussion of the contents of WordNet
is beyond the scope of this text, we will limit ourselves to a discussion of two

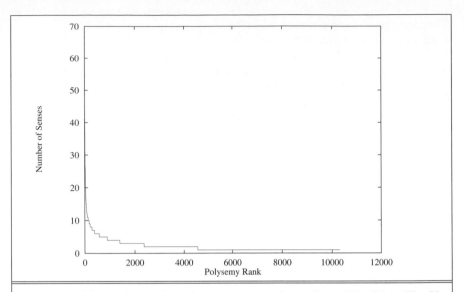

Figure 16.3   Distribution of senses among the verbs in WordNet. The Y-axis shows the number of senses per WordNet entry. The X-axis ranks the verbs according to their degree of polysemy. As can be seen, a relatively small number of verbs have a high degree of polysemy, while the majority have a single sense.

Relation	Definition	Example
Hypernym	From concepts to superordinates	*breakfast → meal*
Hyponym	From concepts to subtypes	*meal → lunch*
Has-Member	From groups to their members	*faculty → professor*
Member-Of	From members to their groups	*copilot → crew*
Has-Part	From wholes to parts	*table → leg*
Part-Of	From parts to wholes	*course → meal*
Antonym	Opposites	*leader → follower*

Figure 16.4   Noun relations in WordNet.

Relation	Definition	Example
Hypernym	From events to superordinate events	*fly → travel*
Troponym	From events to their subtypes	*walk → stroll*
Entails	From events to the events they entail	*snore → sleep*
Antonym	Opposites	*increase ⟺ decrease*

Figure 16.5   Verb relations in WordNet.

Relation	Definition	Example
Antonym	Opposite	*heavy* ⟺ *light*
Adverb	Opposite	*quickly* ⟺ *slowly*

Figure 16.6   Adjective and adverb relations in WordNet.

of its most useful and well-developed features: its sets of synonyms, and its hyponymy relations.

The fundamental basis for synonymy in WordNet is the same as that given on page 598. Two WordNet entries are considered synonyms if they can be successfully substituted in some context. The particular theory and implementation of synonymy in WordNet is organized around the notion of a **synset**, a set of synonyms. Consider the following example of a synset: SYNSET

```
{chump, fish, fool, gull, mark, patsy, fall guy,
sucker, schlemiel, shlemiel, soft touch, mug}
```

The dictionary-like definition, or gloss, of this synset describes it as *a person who is gullible and easy to take advantage of*. Each of the lexical entries included in the synset can, therefore, be used to express this notion in some setting. In practice, synsets like this one actually *constitute* the senses associated with many WordNet entries. Specifically, it is this exact synset, with its associated definition and examples, that makes up one of the senses for each of the entries listed in the synset.

Looking at this from a more theoretical perspective, each synset can be taken to represent a concept that has become lexicalized in the language. Synsets are thus somewhat analogous to the kinds of concepts we discussed in Chapter 14. Instead of representing concepts using logical terms, Word-Net represents them as lists comprised of the lexical entries that can be used to express the concept. This perspective motivates the fact that it is synsets, not lexical entries or individual senses, that participate in most of the semantic relations shown in Figures 16.4, 16.5, and 16.6.

The hyponymy relations in WordNet correspond directly to the notion of immediate hyponymy discussed on page 600. Each synset is related to its immediately more general and more specific synsets via direct hypernym and hyponym relations. To find chains of more general or more specific synsets, one can simply follow a transitive chain of hypernym and hyponym relations. To make this concrete, consider the hypernym chains for **bass**[3] and **bass**[7] shown in Figure 16.7.

In this depiction of hyponymy, successively more general synsets are shown on successive indented lines. The first chain starts from the concept of

```
Sense 3
bass, basso --
(an adult male singer with the lowest voice)
=> singer, vocalist
    => musician, instrumentalist, player
        => performer, performing artist
            => entertainer
                => person, individual, someone...
                    => life form, organism, being...
                        => entity, something
                    => causal agent, cause, causal agency
                        => entity, something

Sense 7
bass --
(the member with the lowest range of a family of
musical instruments)
=> musical instrument
    => instrument
        => device
            => instrumentality, instrumentation
                => artifact, artefact
                    => object, physical object
                        => entity, something
```

Figure 16.7   Hyponymy chains for two separate senses of the lexeme *bass*.
Note that the chains are completely distinct, only converging at *entity*.

a human bass singer. It's immediate superordinate is a synset corresponding
to the generic concept of a singer. Following this chain leads eventually to
concepts such as entertainer and person. The second chain, which starts from
musical instrument, has a completely different chain leading eventually to
such concepts as musical instrument, device and physical object. Both paths
do eventually join at the synset *entity* which basically serves as a placeholder
at the top of the hierarchy.

16.3   THE INTERNAL STRUCTURE OF WORDS

Having discussed the relations that can hold among lexemes and their meaning components, we can now turn to the topic of what these meaning com-

ponents should consist of. Recall that the approach to meaning spelled out in the last two chapters hinged on the notion that there is a fundamental predicate-argument structure underlying our meaning representations. In composing such representations, we assumed that certain classes of lexemes tend to contribute the predicate and predicate-argument structure, while others contribute the arguments. This section explores in more detail the systematic ways that the meanings of lexemes are structured to support this notion. In particular, it explores the notion that the meaning representations associated with lexemes have analyzable internal structures, and that it is these structures, combined with a grammar, that determine the relations among lexemes in well-formed sentences.

Thematic Roles

Thematic roles, first proposed by Gruber (1965) and Fillmore (1968)[1] are a set of categories which provide a shallow semantic language for characterizing certain arguments of verbs. For example consider the following two WSJ fragments:

(16.22) Houston's Billy Hatcher broke a bat.

(16.23) He opened a drawer.

In the predicate calculus event representation of Chapter 14, part of the representation of these two sentences would be the following:

$$\exists e,x,y\, Isa(e,Breaking) \land Breaker(e,BillyHatcher)$$
$$\land BrokenThing(e,y) \land Isa(y,BaseballBat)$$
$$\exists e,x,y\, Isa(e,Opening) \land Opener(e,he)$$
$$\land OpenedThing(e,y) \land Isa(y,Door)$$

In this representation, the roles of the subjects of the verbs *break* and *open* are *Breaker* and *Opener* respectively. These **deep roles** are specific to each possible kind of event; *Breaking* events have *Breakers*, *Opening* events have *Openers*, *Eating* events have *Eaters*, and so on. But *Breakers* and *Openers* have something in common. They are both volitional actors, often animate, and they have direct causal responsibility for their events. A **thematic role** is a way of expressing this commonality. We say that the subjects of both these verbs are **agents**. Thus AGENT is the thematic role which represents an abstract idea such as volitional causation. Similarly, the direct objects of both these verbs, the *BrokenThing* and *OpenedThing*, are

DEEP ROLES

THEMATIC ROLE

AGENTS

---

[1] Fillmore actually called them *deep cases*, on the metaphor of morphological case.

THEME

both prototypically inanimate objects which are affected in some way by the action. The thematic role for these participants is **theme**.

As we will discuss below, while there is no standard set of thematic roles, there are many roles that are commonly used by computational systems. For example, in any straightforward interpretation of example (16.24), Mr. Cockwell has had his collarbone broken, but there is no implication that he was the AGENT of this unfortunate event. This kind of participant

EXPERIENCER

can be labeled an **experiencer**, while the directly effected participant, the collarbone in this case, is again assigned the THEME role.

(16.24)   A company soccer game last year got so rough that Mr. Cockwell broke his collarbone and an associate broke an ankle.

In example (16.25), the earthquake is the direct cause of the glass breaking and hence might seem to be a candidate for an AGENT role. This seems odd, however, since earthquakes are not the kind of participant that can intentionally do anything. Examples such as this have been the source of considerable debate over the years among the proponents of various thematic role theories. Two approaches are common: assign the earthquake to the AGENT role and assume that the intended meaning has some kind of metaphorical connection to the core animate/volitional meaning of AGENT,

FORCE

or add a role called **force** that is similar to AGENT but lacks any notion of volitionality. We will follow this latter approach and return to the notion of metaphor in Section 16.4.

(16.25)   The quake broke glass in several downtown skyscrapers.

Finally, in the following example, the subject (*It*) refers to an event participant (in this case, someone else's elbow) whose role in the breaking event is as the instrument of some other AGENT or FORCE. Such participants

INSTRUMENTS

are called **instruments**.

(16.26)   It broke his jaw.

Figure 16.8 presents a small list of commonly-used thematic roles along with a rough description of the meaning of each. Figure 16.9 provides representative examples of each of role. Note that this list of roles is by no means definitive, and does not correspond to any single theory of thematic roles.

Applications to Linking Theory and Shallow Semantic Interpretations

One common use of thematic roles in computational systems is as a shallow semantic language. For example, as Chapter 21 will describe, thematic

Thematic Role	Definition
AGENT	The volitional causer of an event
EXPERIENCER	The experiencer of an event
FORCE	The non-volitional causer of the event
THEME	The participant most directly affected by an event
RESULT	The end product of an event
CONTENT	The proposition or content of a propositional event
INSTRUMENT	An instrument used in an event
BENEFICIARY	The beneficiary of an event
SOURCE	The origin of the object of a transfer event
GOAL	The destination of an object of a transfer event

Figure 16.8   Some commonly-used thematic roles with their definitions.

Thematic Role	Example
AGENT	*The waiter* spilled the soup.
EXPERIENCER	*John* has a headache.
FORCE	*The wind* blows debris from the mall into our yards.
THEME	Only after Benjamin Franklin broke *the ice*...
RESULT	The French government has built a *regulation-size base-ball diamond*...
CONTENT	Mona asked *"You met Mary Ann at a supermarket"?*
INSTRUMENT	He turned to poaching catfish, stunning them *with a shocking device*...
BENEFICIARY	Whenever Ann Callahan makes hotel reservations *for her boss*...
SOURCE	I flew in *from Boston*.
GOAL	I drove *to Portland*.

Figure 16.9   Prototypical examples of various thematic roles.

roles are sometimes used in machine translation systems as part of a useful intermediate language.

Another use of thematic roles, which was part of their original motivation in Fillmore (1968), was as an intermediary between semantic roles in conceptual structure or common-sense knowledge like *Breaker* and *Driven-Thing* and their more language-specific surface grammatical realization as subject and object. Fillmore noted that there are prototypical patterns governing which argument of a verb will become the subject of an active sentence, proposing the following hierarchy (often now called a **thematic hier-**

THEMATIC
HIERARCHY **archy** (Jackendoff, 1972)) for assigning the subject role:

AGENT ≻ INSTRUMENT ≻ THEME

Thus if the thematic description of a verb includes an AGENT, an IN-STRUMENT, and a THEME, it is the AGENT which will be realized as the subject. If the thematic description only includes an INSTRUMENT and a THEME, it is the INSTRUMENT which will become the subject. The thematic hierarchy is used in reverse for determining the direct object of active sentences, or the subject of passive sentences. Here are examples from Fillmore (1968) using the verb *open*:

(16.27) *John   opened   the door.*
　　　　 AGENT   THEME
(16.28) *John   opened   the door   with   the key.*
　　　　 AGENT   THEME   INSTRUMENT
(16.29) *The key   opened   the door.*
　　　　 AGENT   THEME
(16.30) *The door   was   opened   by   John.*
　　　　 THEME   AGENT

This approach led to a wide variety of work over the last thirty years on the mapping between conceptual structure and grammatical function, in an area generally referred to as **linking theory**. For example many scholars such as Talmy (1985), Jackendoff (1983), and Levin (1993) show that semantic properties of verbs help predict which surface **alternations** they can take. An alternation is a set of different mappings of conceptual (deep) roles to grammatical function. For example Fillmore (1965) and many subsequent researchers have studied the **dative alternation**, the phenomenon that certain verbs like *give*, *send*, or *read* which can take an AGENT, a THEME, and a GOAL, allow the THEME to appear as object and the GOAL in a prepositional phrase (as in example (16.31a)), or the GOAL to appear as the object, and the THEME as a sort of second object (as in example (16.31b)):

LINKING
THEORY

ALTERNATIONS

DATIVE
ALTERNATION

(16.31)   a. *Doris   gave/sent/read   the book   to   Cary.*
　　　　　　　 AGENT   THEME   GOAL
           b. *Doris   gave/sent/read   Cary   the book.*
　　　　　　　 AGENT   GOAL   THEME

Many scholars, including Green (1974), Pinker (1989), Gropen et al. (1989), Goldberg (1995) and Levin (1993) (see Levin (1993, p.45) for a full bibliography), have argued this alternation occurs with particular semantic classes of verbs, including (from Levin) "verbs of future having" (*advance, allocate, offer, owe*), "send verbs" (*forward, hand, mail*), "verbs of throwing" (*kick, pass, throw*), and many other classes.

Similarly, Talmy (1985), following Lakoff (1965, p.126), shows that "affect" verbs such as *frighten, please,* and *exasperate* can appear with the THEME as subject, as in (16.32), or with the EXPERIENCER as subject and the THEME as a prepositional object, as in (16.33):

(16.32)   a. *That   frightens   me.*
                THEME   EXPERIENCER
           b. *That   interests   me.*
                THEME   EXPERIENCER
           c. *That   surprises   me.*
                THEME   AGENT

(16.33)   a. *I   am frightened of   that.*
                EXPERIENCER   THEME
           b. *I   am interested in   that.*
                EXPERIENCER   THEME
           c. *I   am surprised at   that.*
                EXPERIENCER   THEME

Levin (1993) summarizes 80 of these alternations, including extensive lists of the verbs in each semantic class, together with the semantic constraints, exceptions, and other idiosyncrasies. This list has been used in a number of computational models (e.g., Dang et al., 1998; Jing and McKeown, 1998; Lapata and Brew, 1999).

While research of the type summarized above has shown a relationship between verbal semantic and syntactic realization, it is less clear that this relationship is mediated by a small set of thematic roles, with or without a thematic hierarchy. It turns out that semantic classes are insufficient to define the set of verbs that participate in an alternation. For example, many verbs do not allow the dative alternation despite being in the proper semantic class (e.g. *donate, return, transfer*). In addition, as shown above, many of the verbal alternations violate any standard thematic hierarchy (dative alternation sentences like *Ling sent Mary the book* have a GOAL as direct object followed by an oblique THEME, when THEME should be the best direct object).

An even greater problem, however, is that thematic roles can only play a very small role in the general mapping from semantics to syntax. This is because thematic roles are only relevant to determining the grammatical role of *NP* and *PP* arguments, and play no part in the realization of other arguments of verbs and other predicates. Many such possible arguments were described in Figure 11.3 on page 414, such as sentential complements (**Sfin**, **Swh-**, **Sforto**), verb phrases (**VPbrst**, **VPto**, etc), or quotations (**Quo**). Furthermore, thematic roles only are useful in mapping the arguments of verbs;

but nouns, for example, have arguments as well (*destruction of the city*, *father of the bride*).

There are a number of possible responses to these problems with thematic roles. Many systems continue to use them for such practical purposes as interlinguas in machine translation or as a convenient level of shallow semantic interpretation. Other researchers have argued that thematic roles should be considered an epiphenomenon, rather than a distinct representational level. For example, following Foley and van Valin (1984), Dowty (1991) argues that rather than a discrete set of thematic roles there are only two cluster-concepts, PROTO-AGENT and PROTO-PATIENT. Determining whether an argument of a verb is a PROTO-AGENT is predictable from the entailments of the deep conceptual structure meaning of the verb. The mapping from semantic role in conceptual structure to grammatical function proceeds via simple rules (the most PROTO-AGENT-like of the arguments is the subject, the most PROTO-PATIENT-like is the object (or the subject of the passive construction). Dowty's two rules make direct reference to the deep conceptual structure of the verb; thus thematic roles do not appear at any representational level at all.

One problem with Dowty's model is that the choice of thematic roles is not always predictable from the underlying conceptual structure of the event and its participants. For example Fillmore (1977) pointed out that the different verbs which can describe a **commercial event** each choose a different way to map the participants of the event. For example, a transaction between Amie and Benson involving three dollars and a sandwich can be described in any of these ways:

(16.34)   a. Amie bought the sandwich from Benson for three dollars.

           b. Benson sold Amie the sandwich for three dollars.

           c. Amie paid Benson three dollars for the sandwich.

Each of these verbs *buy*, *sell*, and *pay*, chooses a different **perspective** on the commercial event, and realizes this perspective by choosing a different mapping of underlying participants to thematic roles. The fact that these three verbs have very different mappings suggests that the thematic roles for a verb must be listed in the lexical entry for the verb, and are not predictable from the underlying conceptual structure.

This fact, together with the fact mentioned earlier that verb alternations are not completely predictable semantically (e.g. exceptions like *donate*) has led many researchers to assume that any useful computational lexicon needs to list for each verb (or adjective or other predicate) its syntactic and thematic combinatory possibilities. Another advantage of listing the combinatory possibilities for each verb is that the probability of each thematic frame can also be listed.

One recent attempt to list these elements for a number of predicates of English is the FrameNet project (Baker et al., 1998; Lowe et al., 1997). A FrameNet entry for a word lists every set of arguments it can take, including the possible sets of thematic roles, syntactic phrases, and their grammatical function. The thematic roles used in FrameNet are much more specific than the ten examples we've been describing. Each FrameNet thematic role is defined as part of a **frame**, and each **frame** as part of a domain. For example the **Cognition** domain has frames like **static cognition** (*believe, think, understand*), **cogitation** (*brood, ruminate*), **judgment**, (*accuse, admire, rebuke*), etc. All of the cognition frames define the thematic role COGNIZER. In the **judgment** frame, the COGNIZER is referred to as the JUDGE; the frame also includes an EVALUEE, a REASON, and a ROLE; here are some examples from (Johnson, 1999):

Judge	**Kim** respects Pat for being so brave
Evaluee	Kim respects **Pat** for being so brave
Reason	Kim respects Pat **for being so brave**
Role	Kim respects Pat **as a scholar**

Each entry is also labeled by one of the **phrase types** described in Figure 11.3 on page 414, and by a grammatical function (subject, object, or complement). For example, here is part of the FrameNet entry for the judgment verb *appreciate*; we have shown only the active senses of the verb; the full entry includes passives as well. Example sentences are (sometimes shortened) from the British National Corpus:

(16.35)   a.

JUDGE		REASON	EVALUEE
NP/Subj		NP/Obj	PP(in)/Comp
I	still appreciate	good manners	in men.

  b.

JUDGE		EVALUEE	REASON
NP/Subj		NP/Obj	PP(for)/Comp
I	could appreciate	it	for the music alone.

  c.

JUDGE		REASON
NP/Subj		NP/Obj
I	appreciate	your kindness.

  d.

JUDGE		EVALUEE	ROLE
NP/Subj		NP/Obj	PP(for)/Comp
He	did not appreciate	the artist	as a dissenting voice.

By contrast, another sense of the verb *appreciate* is as a verb of static cognition like *understand*; verbs of static cognition have roles like COG-NIZER and CONTENT; here are some examples:

(16.36)   a. COGNIZER   CONTENT
              NP/Subj   Sfin/Comp
              They   appreciate   that communication is a two-way process.
           b. COGNIZER   CONTENT
              NP/Subj   Swh-/Comp
              She   appreciated   how far she had fallen from grace.

It should be clear from examining the example sentences that some generalizations can be drawn about the realization of different thematic roles. JUDGES, COGNIZERS, and AGENTS in general are often realized as subjects of active sentences. ROLES are often realized as *PP*s with the preposition *as*. CONTENT is often realized as some kind of *S*. Representing thematic roles at this fine-grained level may thus make the mapping to syntax more transparent.

Gildea et al. (2000) present a stochastic algorithm trained using FrameNet for automatically assigning thematic roles to a sentence. For each constituent to be labeled, the algorithm computes the probability of each possible thematic role. These probabilities, trained on the FrameNet database of thematically labeled sentences, are conditioned on the verb, the head words of the constituents to be labeled, the mood of the verb (active, passive), and the syntactic category (*NP*, *S*, *PP*, etc.) and grammatical function (subject, object) of the constituent to be labeled.

Of course, a significant problem with a scheme like FrameNet is the extensive human effort it requires in defining thematic roles for each domain and each frame. Riloff and Schmelzenbach (1998) present an corpus-based approach to acquiring sets of thematic roles from unannotated texts.

Selectional Restrictions

The notion of a **selectional restriction** can be used to augment thematic roles by allowing lexemes to place certain semantic restrictions on the lexemes and phrases that can accompany them in a sentence. More specifically, a selectional restriction is a semantic constraint imposed by a lexeme on the concepts that can fill the various argument roles associated with it. As with many other kinds of linguistic constraints, selectional restrictions can most easily be observed in situations where they are violated. Consider the following example originally discussed in Chapter 14:

(16.37) I wanna eat someplace that's close to ICSI.

There are two possible parses for this sentence corresponding to the intransitive and transitive versions of the verb *eat*. These two parses lead, in turn, to two distinct semantic analyses. In the intransitive case, the phrase *someplace that's close to* ICSI is an adjunct that modifies the event specified by the verb phrase, while in the transitive case it provides a true argument to the eating event. This latter case is similar in structure and interpretation to examples such as the following, where the noun phrase specifies the thing to be eaten:

(16.38) I wanna eat some really cheap Chinese food right now.

Not surprisingly, attempting to analyze example (16.37) along these lines results in a kind of semantic ill-formedness. This ill-formedness signals the presence of a selectional restriction imposed by *eat* on its THEME role: it has to be something that is edible. Since the phrase being proposed as the THEME in this scenario can not easily be interpreted as edible (except in the Godzilla as speaker interpretation discussed earlier), the interpretation exhibits the semantic analog of syntactic ungrammaticality. This particular variety of ill-formedness arises from what is known as a **selectional restriction violation**: a situation where the semantics of the filler of a thematic role is not consistent with a constraint imposed on the role by the predicate.

SELECTIONAL
RESTRICTION
VIOLATION

This rather informal description of selectional restrictions needs to be refined in a number of ways before it can be put to practical use. The first refinement concerns the proper locus for stating the selectional restrictions. As discussed in Section 16.1, lexemes are often associated with a wide variety of different senses and, not surprisingly, these senses can enforce differing constraints on their arguments. Selectional restrictions therefore are associated with particular senses, not entire lexemes. Consider the following examples of the lexeme *serve*:

(16.39) Well, there was the time they served green-lipped mussels from
         New Zealand.

(16.40) Which airlines serve Denver?

(16.41) Which ones serve breakfast?

Example (16.39) illustrates the cooking sense of *serve*, which ordinarily restricts its THEME to be some kind foodstuff. Example (16.40) illustrates the *provides a commercial service to* sense of *serve*, which constrains its THEME to be some type of identifiable geographic or political entity. The sense shown in the third example is closely related to the first, and illustrates a sense of serve that is restricted to specifications of particular meals. These differing restrictions on the same thematic role of a polysemous lexeme can be accommodated by associating them with distinct senses of the same lexeme. As we will discuss in Chapter 17, this strongly suggests that selectional restrictions can be used to discriminate these senses in context.

Note that the selectional restrictions imposed by different lexemes, and different senses of the same lexeme, may occur at widely varying levels of specificity, with some lexemes expressing very general conceptual categories, and others expressing very specific ones indeed. Consider the following examples of the verbs *imagine*, *lift* and *diagonalize*:

(16.42) In rehearsal, I often ask the musicians to imagine a tennis game.

(16.43) Others tell of jumping over beds and couches they can't imagine clearing while awake.

(16.44) I cannot even imagine what this lady does all day.

(16.45) Atlantis lifted Galileo from the launch pad at 12:54 p.m. EDT and released the craft from its cargo bay about six hours later.

(16.46) When the battle was over, Mr. Kruger lifted the fish from the water, gently removed the hook from its jaw, admired it, and eased it back into the lake.

(16.47) To diagonalize a matrix is to find its eigenvalues.

Given the meaning of *imagine*, it is not surprising to find that it places few semantic restrictions on the concepts that can fill its THEME role. Its AGENT role, on the other hand, is restricted to humans and other animate entities. In contrast, the sense of *lift* shown in examples (16.45) and (16.46) limits its THEME to be something liftable, which as these examples illustrate is a notion that must cover both spacecraft and fish. For all practical purposes, this notion is best captured by the fairly general notion such as *physical object*. Finally, we have *diagonalize* which imposes a very specific constraint on the filler of its THEME role: it has to be a matrix.

These examples serve to illustrate an important fact about selectional restrictions: the concepts, categories, and features that are deployed by the lexicon as selectional restrictions are not a part of the finite language capacity. Rather, they are as open-ended as the lexicon itself. This distinguishes selectional restrictions from some of the other finite features of language that are used to define lexemes including parts-of-speech, thematic roles, and semantic primitives.

Before we move on, it is worth pointing out that verbs are not the only words that can impose selectional restrictions on their arguments. Rather, it appears to be the case that any predicate-bearing lexeme can impose arbitrary semantic constraints on the concepts that fill its argument roles. Consider the following examples, which illustrate the selectional restrictions associated with some non-verb parts-of-speech:

(16.48) Radon is a naturally occurring odorless, tasteless gas that can't be detected by human senses.

(16.49) What is the lowest fare for United Airlines flight four thirty?

(16.50) Are there any restaurants open after midnight?

The adjectives *odorless* and *tasteless* in example (16.48) are restricted to concepts that can possess an odor or a taste. Similarly, as we discussed earlier in Section 16.1, the noun *fare* is restricted to various forms of public transportation. Finally, arguments to the preposition *after* must directly or indirectly designate points in time.

Representing Selectional Restrictions

The semantics of selectional restrictions can be captured in a straightforward way by extending the event-oriented meaning representations employed in Chapter 14. Recall that the representation of an event consists of a single variable that stands for the event, a predicate that denotes the kind of event, and a series of variables and relations that designate the roles associated with the event. Ignoring the issue of the λ-structures, and using thematic roles rather than deep event roles, the semantic contribution of a verb like *eat* might look like the following:

$$\exists e, x, y \, Eating(e) \wedge Agent(e,x) \wedge Theme(e,y)$$

With this representation, all we know about y, the filler of the THEME role, is that it is associated with an *Eating* event via the *Theme* relation. To stipulate the selectional restriction that y must be something edible, we simply add a new term to that effect, as in the following:

$$\exists e, x, y \, Eating(e) \wedge Eater(e,x) \wedge Theme(e,y) \wedge Isa(y, EdibleThing)$$

When a phrase like *ate a hamburger* is encountered, a semantic analyzer can form the following kind of representation:

$$\exists e, x, y \, Eating(e) \wedge Eater(e,x) \wedge Theme(e,y) \wedge Isa(y, EdibleThing)$$
$$\wedge Isa(y, Hamburger)$$

This representation is perfectly reasonable since the membership of y in the category *Hamburger* is consistent with its membership in the category *EdibleThing*, assuming a reasonable set of facts in the knowledge base. Correspondingly, the representation for a phrase such as *ate a takeoff* would be ill-formed because membership in an event-like category such as *Takeoff* would be inconsistent with membership in the category *EdibleThing*.

While this approach adequately captures the semantics of selectional restrictions, there are two practical problems with its direct use. First, using FOPC to perform the simple task of enforcing selectional restrictions is overkill. There are far simpler formalisms that can do the job with far less computational cost. The second problem is that this approach presupposes a large logical knowledge-base of facts about the concepts that make up selectional restrictions. Unfortunately, although such common sense knowledge-bases are being developed, none are widely available and few have the kind of scope necessary to the task.

A far more practical approach, at least for English, is to exploit the hyponymy relations present in the WordNet database. In this approach, selectional restrictions on semantic roles are stated in terms of WordNet synsets, rather than logical concepts. A given meaning representation can be judged to be well-formed if the lexeme that fills a thematic role has as one of its hypernyms the synset specified by the predicate for that thematic role. Consider how this approach would work with our *ate a hamburger* example. Among its 60,000 synsets, WordNet includes the following one, which is glossed as *any substance that can be metabolized by an organism to give energy and build tissue*:

    {food, nutrient}

Given this synset, we can specify it as the selectional restriction on the THEME role of the verb *eat*, thus limiting fillers of this role to lexemes in this synset *and its hyponyms*. Luckily, the chain of hypernyms for *hamburger* shown in Figure 16.10, reveals that hamburgers are indeed food.

Note that in this approach, the filler of a role does not have to match the restriction synset exactly. Rather, a selectional restriction is satisfied if the filler has the restricting synset as one of its eventual hypernyms. Thus in the hamburger example, the selectional restriction synset is found five hypernym levels up from *hamburger*.

Of course, this approach also allows individual lexemes to satisfy restrictions at varying levels of specificity. For example, consider what happens when we apply this approach to the THEME roles of the verbs *imagine*, *lift* and *diagonalize*, discussed earlier. Let us restrict *imagine*'s THEME to the synset {entity, something}, *lift*'s THEME to {object, physical object} and *diagonalize* to {matrix}. This arrangement correctly permits *imagine a hamburger* and *lift a hamburger*, while also correctly ruling out *diagonalize*

```
Sense 1
hamburger, beefburger --
(a fried cake of minced beef served on a bun)
=> sandwich
   => snack food
      => dish
         => nutriment, nourishment, sustenance...
            => food, nutrient
               => substance, matter
                  => object, physical object
                     => entity, something
```

Figure 16.10   Evidence from WordNet that hamburgers are edible.

a hamburger.

Note that this approach relies on the presence in WordNet of exactly those lexemes that specify exactly the concepts needed for all possible selectional restrictions. Unfortunately, there is no particular reason to believe that the set of concepts used as selectional restrictions in a language is exactly subsumed by the lexemes in the language. This situation is accommodated to some extent in WordNet through the use of collocations such as *physical object* and *snack food*.

To address this problem more directly, there are a number of taxonomies that sit somewhere between common sense knowledge-bases such as CYC (Lenat and Guha, 1991) and lexical databases such WordNet. The objects contained in these hybrid models do not have to correspond to individual lexical items, but rather to those concepts that are known to be grammatically and lexically relevant. In most cases, the upper portions of these taxonomies are taken to represent domain and language-independent notions, such as physical objects, states, events and animacy. One of the most well-developed of these ontologies is the PENMAN Upper Model, discussed in more detail in Chapter 20.

Primitive Decomposition

The theories of meaning representation presented here, and in the last few chapters, have had a decidedly lexical flavor. The meaning representations for sentences have been composed of atomic symbols that appear to correspond very closely to individual lexemes. However, other than thematic roles, these lexical representations have had not much of an internal structure. The notion of **primitive decomposition**, or **componential analysis**, is an attempt to supply such a structure.

To explore these notions, consider the following examples motivated by the discussion in McCawley (1968):

(16.51) Jim killed his philodendron.

(16.52) Jim did something to cause his philodendron to become not alive.

From a truth-conditional perspective, these two sentences have the same meaning. This is not, however, a simple case of synonymy, since *kill* is not synonymous with any individual lexemes in example (16.52). Instead, this sense of *kill* is equivalent to the particular combination of *more fundamental* elements found in the second sentence. Invoking the notion of canonical form from Chapter 14 we can say that these two examples should have the *same* meaning representation — the one underlying example (16.52). Translating a simple predicate like *kill* into a more complex set of predicates can be viewed as breaking down, or decomposing, the meaning of words into combinations of simpler, more primitive, parts. In this example, the more primitive, possibly atomic, parts are the meaning representations associated with the lexemes *do*, *cause*, *become not*, and *alive*.

Interestingly, this technique has also been used to account for some of the verbal alternations discussed on page 608 (Lakoff, 1965; Dowty, 1979). Consider the following examples.

(16.53) John opened the door.

(16.54) The door opened.

(16.55) The door is open.

The decompositional approach asserts that a single state-like predicate associated with *open* underlies all of these examples. The differences among the meanings of these examples arises from the combination of this single predicate with the primitives underlying *cause* and *become*

Note that this approach to primitive decomposition is quite limited. In this approach, primitives such as DO, CAUSE, and BECOME are combined with an open-ended set of predicates corresponding to most of the verbs in a language, leaving us with a representation scheme that is still lexical in nature. A more radical approach asserts that these content predicates can themselves be broken down into sets of more primitive elements. While many such sets of primitives have been proposed, the approach known as Conceptual Dependency (CD) (Schank, 1972) has been the most widely used primitive-based representational system within natural language pro-

Primitive	Definition
ATRANS	The abstract transfer of possession or control from one entity to another.
PTRANS	The physical transfer of an object from one location to another
MTRANS	The transfer of mental concepts between entities or within an entity.
MBUILD	The creation of new information within an entity.
PROPEL	The application of physical force to move an object.
MOVE	The integral movement of a body part by an animal.
INGEST	The taking in of a substance by an animal.
EXPEL	The expulsion of something from an animal.
SPEAK	The action of producing a sound.
ATTEND	The action of focusing a sense organ.

Figure 16.11   A set of conceptual dependency primitives.

cessing. In this approach, eleven primitive predicates are used to represent all predicate-like language expressions. Figure 16.11 shows the eleven primitives with a brief explanation of their meaning.

As an example of this approach, consider the following sentence along with its CD representation:

(16.56) The waiter brought Mary the check.

$$\exists x, y \, Atrans(x) \wedge Actor(x, Waiter) \wedge Object(x, Check) \wedge To(x, Mary)$$
$$\wedge Ptrans(y) \wedge Actor(y, Waiter) \wedge Object(y, Check) \wedge To(y, Mary)$$

Here, the verb *brought* is translated into the two primitives ATRANS and PTRANS to indicate the fact that the waiter both physically conveyed the check to Mary and passed control of it to here. Note that CD also associates a fixed set of thematic roles with each primitive to represent the various participants in the action.

The compositional approach is not limited to the meanings of verbs. The same notion can be used to decompose nominals into more primitive notions. Consider the following decompositions of the lexemes *kitten*, *puppy*, and *child* into more primitive elements:

$$\exists x \, Isa(x, Feline) \wedge Isa(x, Youth)$$
$$\exists x \, Isa(x, Canine) \wedge Isa(x, Youth)$$
$$\exists x \, Isa(x, Human) \wedge Isa(x, Youth)$$

Here the primitives represent more primitive categories of objects, rather than actions. Using these primitives, the close relationship between these lexemes and the related terms *cat*, *dog* and *person* can then be captured with the following similar formulas:

$$\exists x\, Isa(x, Feline) \wedge Isa(x, Adult)$$
$$\exists x\, Isa(x, Canine) \wedge Isa(x, Adult)$$
$$\exists x\, Isa(x, Human) \wedge Isa(x, Adult)$$

The primary applications of primitives in natural language processing have been in semantic analysis and in machine translation. In semantic analysis, the principle use has been in organizing the inference process. Instead of having to encode thousands of idiosyncratic meaning postulates with particular lexical items, inference rules can be associated with a small number of primitives. We should note the use of primitive decomposition in the representation on nominals has largely been supplanted by the use of inheritance hierarchies. As we will see in Chapter 21, the emphasis in machine translation has been on the use of primitives as language independent meaning representations, or **interlinguas**.

Semantic Fields

SEMANTIC
FIELD

The lexical relations described in Section 16.1 had a decidedly local character, and made no use of the internal structure of the lexemes taking part in the relation. The notion of a **semantic field** is an attempt to capture a more integrated, or holistic, relationship among entire sets of words from a single domain. Consider the following set of words extracted from the ATIS corpus:

reservation, flight, travel, buy, price, cost, fare, rates, meal, plane

It is certainly possible to assert individual lexical relations between many of the lexemes in this list. The resulting set of relations does not, however, add up to a complete account of how these lexemes are related. They are clearly all defined with respect to a coherent chunk of common sense background information concerning air travel. Background knowledge of this kind has been studied under a variety of frameworks and is known variously as a frame (Fillmore, 1985), model (Johnson-Laird, 1983), or script (Schank and Albelson, 1977), and plays a central role in a number of computational frameworks, some of which will be discussed in Chapter 18.

The FrameNet project (Baker et al., 1998) discussed earlier, can be seen as an attempt to provide a robust resource for this kind of knowledge. In FrameNet, lexemes that refer to actions, events, thematic roles, and objects belonging to a particular domain are linked to concepts contained in frames that represent that particular domain. As in most current ontology efforts, these frames are arranged in a hierarchy so that specific frames can inherit roles from more abstract frames. The current FrameNet effort is directed at the creation of several thousand frame-semantic lexical entries. The domains to be covered include: HEALTH CARE, CHANCE, PERCEPTION, COMMU-NICATION, TRANSACTION, TIME, SPACE, BODY, MOTION, LIFE STAGES, SOCIAL CONTEXT, and COGNITION.

16.4   CREATIVITY AND THE LEXICON

The approach to lexical semantics presented thus far in this chapter accounts for word meanings by making appeal to a large static lexicon from which meaning representations are retrieved as needed. A more realistic view holds that meaning representations may need to be generated dynamically, and that the static lexicon may contribute only indirectly to its content. Under this view, much of the apparent polysemy in the lexicon is due to this generative capacity. This capacity is, of course, not unlimited or unsystematic. Rather, it is governed by a number of productive **models** that can systematically combine lexical, grammatical, contextual, and common sense knowledge to create the novel meanings we see in everyday discourse. The following discussion will briefly cover two of the more important and pervasive models: **metaphor**, and **metonymy**.

Metaphor

By **metaphor**, we have in mind situations where we refer to, and reason   METAPHOR
about, concepts using words and phrases whose meanings are appropriate to *other completely different kinds of concepts.* Metaphor is pervasive and is responsible for a large proportion of the polysemy present in any language, including many of the senses that are listed in dictionaries, as well as the more novel ones that are not. To make this notion more concrete, consider the following sentence from the WSJ corpus:

(16.57) That doesn't scare Digital, which has grown to be the world's
         second-largest computer maker by poaching customers of IBM's
         mid-range machines.

Let's consider the motivation for the use of *scare* in this example. The verb *scare* in WordNet has two closely related senses: to cause fear in, and to cause to lose courage. Although it might be interesting to consider which of these senses is the right one for this example, it is even more interesting to consider what it would mean for a corporation to lose courage, or even to have it in the first place. For this sentence to make sense with either of these senses, it has to be the case that corporations can experience emotions like fear or courage as people do. Of course they don't, but we certainly speak of them and reason about them as if they do. We can therefore say that this use of *scare* is based on a metaphor that allows us to view a corporation as a person, which we will refer to the CORPORATION AS PERSON metaphor.

This metaphor is, of course, neither novel, nor specific to this use of *scare*. Instead, it is a fairly conventional way to think about companies and motivates the use of the *resuscitate*, *hemorrhage* and *mind* in the following WSJ examples:

(16.58) Fuqua Industries Inc. said Triton Group Ltd., a company it helped **resuscitate**, has begun acquiring Fuqua shares.

(16.59) And Ford was **hemorrhaging**; its losses would hit $1.54 billion in 1980.

(16.60) But if it changed its **mind**, however, it would do so for investment reasons, the filing said.

Of course, each of these examples reflects an elaborated use of the basic CORPORATION AS PERSON metaphor. The first two examples extend it to use the notion of health to express a corporation's financial status, while the third example attributes a mind to a corporation to capture the notion of corporate strategy.

Metaphorical constructs such as CORPORATION AS PERSON are known as **conventional metaphors**. Lakoff and Johnson (1980) convincingly argue that many, if not most, of the metaphorical expressions that we encounter every day are motivated by a relatively small number of these simple conventional schemas.

CONVENTIONAL
METAPHORS

Metonymy

METONYMY

The term **metonymy** refers to those situations where we denote a concept by naming some other concept *closely related to it*. Consider the following example from the WSJ:

(16.61) GM killed the Fiero because it had dedicated a full-scale to building the plastic-bodied car...

The use of *kill* in this example roughly means to put an end to some kind of ongoing effort or activity. In this case, the ongoing activity of building, marketing, and selling a particular kind of car. The metaphor underlying this use is based on an ACTIVITY AS LIVING THING metaphor that permits the termination of the activity to be viewed as a killing. Note, however, that the example does not contain any explicit references to any activity. In particular, the THEME of *kill* is the definite reference *the Fiero*. For the metaphor to make sense, this phrase must refer not to a car, but rather to an entire sales and production effort. This is a case where the end result of an effort, *the Fiero*, is used to refer to the entire effort to produce it, which we can classify as a PRODUCT FOR THE PROCESS metonymy.

More mundane examples of metonymy include such common patterns as AUTHOR FOR AUTHOR'S WORKS, as in *He likes Shakespeare*, and PLACE FOR INSTITUTION, as in *The White House had no comment*. Note that although these schemas are superficially similar to their metaphorical counterparts, their structure and use are quite different. Unlike metaphors, which link distinct concepts, these schemas link concepts that are closely related. Similarly, whereas metaphors invite us to think of one concept it terms of another different kind of concept, metonymies are merely a way of referring to a related concept. For example, the *White House* example given above is not intended to ascribe any properties of the actual building to the administration; it is merely an indirect way of referring to the administration.

Computational Approaches to Metaphor and Metonymy

Computational approaches to metaphor and metonymy fall into two basic types: convention-based approaches, and reasoning-based approaches. Both approaches make the assumption that compositional semantic analysis using a static lexicon will fail to produce adequate meaning representations in the presence of metaphorical and metonymic inputs. It is, therefore, the job of some subsequent process to produce correct meaning representations for such inputs.

The main thrust of convention-based approaches is that the interpretation of this kind of figurative language should proceed through the direct application of specific knowledge about the conventional metaphors and metonymies in a language (Norvig, 1987; Martin, 1990; Hayes and Bayer, 1991; Veale and Keane, 1992; Jones and McCoy, 1992). The basic assumption made in these systems is that formal representations of conventional metaphors will allow a semantic analyzer to replace a meaning representation derived compositionally with another one that more closely reflects the actual meaning of the input. These approaches all make the assumption that a relatively small core set of conventional metaphors can be represented as part of a system's knowledge and that it will be sufficient to account for a wide-range of inputs.

Reasoning-based approaches eschew the notion of metaphorical and metonymic conventions. Work in this vein takes the view that figurative language processing is best approached as a problem for a general reasoning ability rather than as a specifically language related phenomenon. It follows, therefore, that the computational models following this approach are often based on pre-existing models intended for more general reasoning tasks. In the case of metaphor, the dominant approach is based on some form of analogical reasoning (Russell, 1976; Carbonell, 1982; Gentner, 1983; Fass, 1988, 1991, 1997). This approach asserts that metaphors depend on inherent structural similarities between the meaning representations derived compositionally from the input, and the correct representations that capture the intended meaning of the input.

16.5   SUMMARY

This chapter has covered a wide range of issues concerning the meanings associated with lexical items. The following are among the highlights:

- **Lexical semantics** is the study of the systematic meaning-related connections among lexemes, and the internal meaning-related structure of individual lexemes.
- **Homonymy** refers to lexemes with the same form but unrelated meanings.
- **Polysemy** refers to the notion of a single lexeme with multiple related meanings.
- **Synonymy** holds between different lexemes with the same meaning.
- **Hyponymy** relations hold between lexemes that are in class-inclusion relationship.
- **Semantic fields** are used to capture semantic connections among groups of lexemes drawn from a single domain.
- **WordNet** is a large database of lexical relations for English words.
- **Thematic roles** abstract away from the specifics of deep semantic roles by generalizing over similar roles across classes of verbs.

- Semantic **selectional restrictions** allow lexemes to post constraints on the semantic properties of the constituents that accompany them in sentences.

- **Primitive decomposition** allows the representation of the meanings of individual lexemes in terms of finite sets of sub-lexical primitives.

- Generative devices such as metaphor and metonymy are pervasive, and produce novel meanings that can not in principle be captured in a static lexicon.

BIBLIOGRAPHICAL AND HISTORICAL NOTES

Lyons (1977) and Cruse (1986) are classic linguistics texts on lexical semantics. Collections describing computational work on lexical semantics can be found in Pustejovsky and Bergler (1992), Saint-Dizier and Viegas (1995) and Klavans (1995).

Martin (1986) and Copestake and Briscoe (1995) discuss computational approaches to the representation of polysemy. The most comprehensive collection of work concerning WordNet can be found in Fellbaum (1998). There have been many efforts to use existing dictionaries as lexical resources. One of the earliest was Amsler's (1980, 1981) use of the Merriam Webster dictionary. More recently, the machine readable version of Longman's Dictionary of Contemporary English has been used in a number of systems (Boguraev and Briscoe, 1989).

Thematic roles, or case roles, can be traced back to work by Fillmore (1968) and Gruber (1965). Fillmore's work had an enormous and immediate impact on work in natural language processing. For a considerable period of time, nearly all work in natural language understanding used some version of Fillmore's case roles. Much of the early work in this vein was due to Simmons (1973, 1978, 1983).

Work on selectional restrictions as a way of characterizing semantic well-formedness began with Katz and Fodor (1963). McCawley (1968) was the first to point out that selectional restrictions could not be restricted to a finite list of semantic features, but had to be drawn from a larger base of unrestricted world knowledge.

Lehrer (1974) is a classic text on semantic fields. More recent papers addressing this topic can be found in Lehrer and Kittay (1992). Baker et al. (1998) describe ongoing work on the FrameNet project.

The use of primitives, components, and features to define lexical items is ancient. Nida (1975) presents a comprehensive overview of work on componential analysis. Wierzbicka (1996) has long been a major advocate of the use of primitives in linguistic semantics. Another prominent effort has been Jackendoff's Conceptual Semantics (1983, 1990) work which combines thematic roles and primitive decomposition. On the computational side, Schank's Conceptual Dependency (1972) remains the most widely used set of primitives in natural language processing. Wilks (1975a) was an early promoter of the use of primitives in machine translation, as well natural language understanding in general. More recently, Dorr (1993, 1992) has made considerable computational use of Jackendoff's framework in her work on machine translation.

An influential collection of papers on metaphor can be found in Ortony (1993). Lakoff and Johnson (1980) is the classic work on conceptual metaphor and metonymy. Pustejovsky (1995) introduced the notion of the *Generative Lexicon*, a conceptual framework that rejects the notion of the lexicon as a static repository in favor of a more dynamic view. Russell (1976) presents one of the earliest computational approaches to metaphor. Additional early work can be found in DeJong and Waltz (1983), Wilks (1978) and Hobbs (1979b). More recent computational efforts to analyze metaphor can be found in Fass (1988, 1991, 1997), Martin (1990), Veale and Keane (1992), Iverson and Helmreich (1992), and Chandler (1991). Martin (1996) presents a survey of computational approaches to metaphor and other types of figurative language.

EXERCISES

16.1 Collect three definitions of ordinary non-technical English words from a dictionary of your choice that you feel are flawed in some way. Explain the nature of the flaw and how it might be remedied.

16.2 Give a detailed account of similarities and differences among the following set of lexemes: *imitation*, *synthetic*, *artificial*, *fake*, and *simulated*.

16.3 Examine the entries for these lexemes in WordNet (or some dictionary of your choice). How well does it reflect your analysis?

16.4   The WordNet entry for the noun *bat* lists 6 distinct senses. Group these senses using the definitions of homonymy and polysemy given in this chapter. For any senses that are polysemous, give an argument as to how the senses are related.

16.5   Assign the various verb arguments in the following WSJ examples to their appropriate thematic roles using the set of roles shown in Figure 16.9.

  a. The intense heat buckled the highway about three feet.
  b. He melted her reserve with a husky-voiced paean to her eyes.
  c. But Mingo, a major Union Pacific shipping center in the 1890s, has melted away to little more than the grain elevator now.

16.6   Using WordNet, describe appropriate selectional restrictions on the verbs *drink*, *kiss*, and *write*.

16.7   Collect a small corpus of examples of the verbs *drink*, *kiss*, and *write*, and analyze how well your selectional restrictions worked.

16.8   Consider the following examples from (McCawley, 1968):

My neighbor is a father of three.

?My buxom neighbor is a father of three.

What does the ill-formedness of the second example imply about how constituents satisfy, or violate, selectional restrictions?

16.9   Find some articles about business, sports, or politics from your daily newspaper. Identify as many uses of conventional metaphors as you can in these articles. How many of the words used to express these metaphors have entries in either WordNet or your favorite dictionary that directly reflect the metaphor.

16.10   Consider the following example:

The stock exchange wouldn't talk publicly, but a spokesman said a news conference is set for today to introduce a new technology product.

Assuming that stock exchanges are not the kinds of things that can literally talk, give a sensible account for this phrase in terms of a metaphor or metonymy.

17 WORD SENSE DISAMBIGUATION AND INFORMATION RETRIEVAL

Oh are you from Wales?
Do you know a fella named Jonah?
He used to live in whales for a while.

Groucho Marx

This chapter introduces a number of topics related to **lexical semantic processing**. By this, we have in mind applications that make use of word meanings, but which are to varying degrees decoupled from the more complex tasks of compositional sentence analysis and discourse understanding.

LEXICAL SEMANTIC PROCESSING

The first topic we cover, **word sense disambiguation**, is of considerable theoretical and practical interest. Recall from Chapter 16 that the task of word sense disambiguation is to examine word tokens in context and specify exactly which sense of each word is being used. As we will see, this is a non-trivial undertaking given the somewhat illusive nature of a word sense. Nevertheless, there are robust algorithms that can achieve high levels of accuracy given certain reasonable assumptions.

WORD SENSE DISAMBIGUATION

The second topic we cover, **information retrieval**, is an extremely broad field, encompassing a wide-range of topics pertaining to the storage, analysis, and retrieval of all manner of media (Baeza-Yates and Ribeiro-Neto, 1999). Our concern in this chapter is solely with the storage and retrieval of text documents in response to users' requests for information. We are interested in approaches in which users' needs are expressed as words, and documents are represented in terms of the words they contain. Section 17.3 presents the **vector space model**, some variant of which is used in many current systems, including most Web search engines.

INFORMATION RETRIEVAL

17.1   SELECTIONAL RESTRICTION-BASED DISAMBIGUATION

For the most part, our discussions of compositional semantic analyzers in Chapter 15 ignored the issue of lexical ambiguity. By now it should be clear that this is not a reasonable approach. Without some means of selecting correct senses for the words in the input, the enormous amount of homonymy and polysemy in the lexicon will quickly overwhelm any approach in an avalanche of competing interpretations. As with syntactic part-of-speech tagging, there are two fundamental approaches to handling this ambiguity problem. In an integrated rule-to-rule approach to semantic analysis, the selection of correct word senses occurs during semantic analysis as a side-effect of the elimination of ill-formed semantic representations. In a stand-alone approach, sense disambiguation is performed independent of, and prior to, compositional semantic analysis. This section discusses the role of selectional restrictions in the former approach. The stand-alone approach is discussed in detail in Section 17.2.

Selectional restrictions and type hierarchies are the primary knowledge-sources used to perform disambiguation in most integrated approaches. They are used to rule out inappropriate senses and thereby reduce the amount of ambiguity present during semantic analysis. In an integrated rule-to-rule approach to semantic analysis, selectional restrictions are used to block the formation of component meaning representations that contain selectional restriction violations. By blocking such ill-formed components, the semantic analyzer will find itself dealing with fewer ambiguous meaning representations. This ability to focus on correct senses by eliminating flawed representations that result from incorrect senses can be viewed as a form of indirect word sense disambiguation. While the linguistic basis for this approach can be traced back to the work of Katz and Fodor (1963), the most sophisticated computational exploration of it is due to Hirst (1987).

As an example of this approach, consider the following pair of WSJ examples, focusing solely on their use of the lexeme *dish*:

(17.1)   "In our house, everybody has a career and none of them includes washing **dishes**," he says.

(17.2)   In her tiny kitchen at home, Ms. Chen works efficiently, stir-frying several simple **dishes**, including braised pig's ears and chicken livers with green peppers.

These examples make use of two polysemous senses of the lexeme *dish*. The first refers to the physical objects that we eat from, while the second refers to the actual meals or recipes. The fact that we perceive no ambiguity in these examples can be attributed to the selectional restrictions imposed by *wash* and *stir-fry* on their PATIENT roles, along with the semantic type information associated with the two senses of *dish*. The restrictions imposed by *wash* conflict with the food sense of dish since it does not denote something that is normally washable. Similarly, the restrictions on *stir-fry* conflict with the artifact sense of dish, since it does not denote something edible. Therefore, in both of these cases *the predicate selects the correct sense* of an ambiguous argument by eliminating the sense that fails to match one of its selectional restrictions.

Now consider the following WSJ and ATIS examples, focusing on the ambiguous predicate *serve*:

(17.3)   Well, there was the time they **served** green-lipped mussels from New Zealand.

(17.4)   Which airlines **serve** Denver?

(17.5)   Which ones **serve** breakfast?

Here the sense of *serve* in example (17.3) requires some kind of food as its PATIENT, the sense in example (17.4) requires some kind of geographical or political entity, and the sense in the last example requires a meal designator. If we assume that *mussels*, *Denver* and *breakfast* are unambiguous, then it is the arguments in these examples that select the appropriate sense of the verb.

Of course, there are also cases where both the predicate and the argument have multiple senses. Consider the following BERP example:

(17.6)   I'm looking for a restaurant that **serves** vegetarian **dishes**.

Restricting ourselves to three senses of *serve* and two senses of *dish* yields six possible sense combinations in this example. However, since only one combination of the six is free from a selectional restriction violation, determining the correct sense of both *serve* and *dish* is straightforward; the predicate and argument mutually select the correct senses.

Although there are a wide variety of ways to integrate this style of disambiguation into a semantic analyzer, the most straightforward approach follows the rule-to-rule strategy introduced in Chapter 15. In this integrated approach, fragments of meaning representations are composed and checked for selectional restriction violations as soon as their corresponding syntactic constituents are created. Those representations that contain selectional restriction violations are eliminated from further consideration.

This approach requires two additions to the knowledge structures used in semantic analyzers: access to hierarchical type information about arguments, and semantic selectional restriction information about the arguments to predicates. Recall from Chapter 16 that both of these can be encoded using knowledge from WordNet. The type information is available in the form of the hypernym information about the heads of the meaning structures being used as arguments to predicates. The selectional restriction information about argument roles can be encoded by associating the appropriate WordNet synsets with the arguments to each predicate-bearing lexical item.

Limitations of Selectional Restrictions

There are a number of practical and theoretical problems with this use of selectional restrictions. The first symptom of these problems is the fact that there are examples like the following where the available selectional restrictions are too general to uniquely select a correct sense:

(17.7)   What kind of **dishes** do you recommend?

In cases like this, we either have to rely on the stand-alone methods to be discussed in Section 17.2, or knowledge of the broader discourse context, as will be discussed in Chapter 18.

More problematic are examples that contain obvious violations of selectional restrictions but are nevertheless perfectly well-formed and interpretable. Therefore, any approach based on a strict *elimination* of such interpretations is in serious trouble. Consider the following WSJ example:

(17.8)   But it fell apart in 1931, perhaps because people realized you can't **eat** gold for lunch if you're hungry.

The phrase *eat gold* clearly violates the selectional restriction that *eat* places on its PATIENT role. Nevertheless, this example is perfectly well-formed. The key is the negative environment set up by *can't* prior to the violation of the restriction. This example makes it clear that any purely local, or rule-to-rule, analysis of selectional restrictions will fail when a wider context makes the violation of a selectional restriction acceptable.

A second problem with selectional restrictions is illustrated by the following example:

(17.9)   In his two championship trials, Mr. Kulkarni **ate** glass on an empty stomach, accompanied only by water and tea.

Although the event described in this example is somewhat unusual, the sentence itself is not semantically ill-formed, despite the violation of *eat*'s selectional restriction. Examples such as this illustrate the fact that thematic roles and selectional restrictions are merely loose approximations of the deeper concepts they represent. They cannot hope to account for uses that require deeper commonsense knowledge about what eating is all about. At best, they reflect the idea that the things that are eaten are normally edible.

Finally, as discussed in Chapter 16, metaphoric and metonymic uses challenge this approach as well. Consider the following WSJ example:

(17.10) If you want to **kill** the Soviet Union, get it to try to **eat** Afghanistan.

Here the typical selectional restrictions on the PATIENTS of both *kill* and *eat* will eliminate all possible literal senses leaving the system with no possible meanings. In many systems, such a situation serves to trigger alternative mechanisms for interpreting metaphor and metonymy (Fass, 1997).

As Hirst (1987) observes, examples like these often result in the elimination of all senses, bringing semantic analysis to a halt. One approach to alleviating this problem is to adopt the view of selectional restrictions as preferences, rather than rigid requirements. Although there have been many instantiations of this approach over the years (Wilks, 1975c, 1975b, 1978), the one that has received the most thorough empirical evaluation is Resnik's (1997) work, which uses the notion of a **selectional association**. A selectional association is a probabilistic measure of the strength of association between a predicate and a class dominating the argument to the predicate. Resnik (1997) gives a method for deriving these associations using Word-Net's hyponymy relations combined with a tagged corpus containing verb-argument relations.

Resnik (1998) shows that these selectional associations can be used to perform a limited form of word sense disambiguation. Roughly speaking the algorithm selects as the correct sense for an argument, the one that has the highest selectional association between one of its ancestor hypernyms and the predicate. Resnik (1997) reports an average of 44% correct with this technique for verb-object relationships, a result that is an improvement over the most frequent sense baseline which performs at 28%. A limitation of this approach is that it only addresses the case where the predicate is unambiguous and *selects* the correct sense of the argument. A more complex decision criteria would be needed for the situation where both the predicate and argument are ambiguous.

17.2   ROBUST WORD SENSE DISAMBIGUATION

The selectional restriction approach to disambiguation has too many requirements to be useful in large-scale practical applications. Even with the use of
WordNet, the requirements of complete selectional restriction information
for all predicate roles, and complete type information for the senses of all
possible fillers are unlikely to be met. In addition, as we saw in Chapters 10,
12, and 15, the availability of a complete and accurate parse for all inputs is
unlikely to be met in environments involving unrestricted text.

To address these concerns, a number of robust stand-alone disambiguation systems with more modest requirements have been developed over the
years. As with part-of-speech taggers, these systems are designed to operate in a stand-alone fashion and make minimal assumptions about what
information will be available from other processes. The following sections
explore the application of supervised, bootstrapping, and unsupervised machine learning approaches to this problem. We then consider the role of
machine readable dictionaries in the construction of stand-alone taggers.

Machine Learning Approaches

In machine learning approaches, systems are *trained* to perform the task
of word sense disambiguation. In these approaches, what is learned is a
classifier that can be used to assign as yet unseen examples to one of a fixed
number of senses. As we will see, these approaches vary as to the nature
of the training material, how much material is needed, the degree of human
intervention, the kind of linguistic knowledge used, and the output produced.
What they all share is an emphasis on acquiring the knowledge needed for
the task from data, rather than from human analysts. The principal question
to keep in mind as we explore these systems is whether the method scales;
that is, would it be possible to apply the method to a substantial part of the
entire vocabulary of a language?

The Inputs: Feature Vectors

In most of these approaches, the initial input consists of the word to be disambiguated, which we will refer to as the **target** word, along with a portion
of the text in which it is embedded, which we will call its **context**. This
initial input is then processed in the following ways:

- The input is normally part-of-speech tagged using one of the high accuracy methods described in Chapter 8.

- The original context may be replaced with larger or smaller segments surrounding the target word.

- Often some amount of stemming, or more sophisticated morphological processing, is performed on all the words in the context.

- Less often, some form of partial parsing, or dependency parsing, is performed to ascertain thematic or grammatical roles and relations.

After this initial processing, the input is then boiled down to a fixed set of features that capture information relevant to the learning task. This task consists of two steps: selecting the relevant linguistic features, and encoding them in a form usable in a learning algorithm. A simple **feature vector** consisting of numeric or nominal values can easily encode the most frequently used linguistic information, and is appropriate for use in most learning algorithms.

FEATURE
VECTOR

The linguistic features used in training WSD systems can be roughly divided into two classes: collocational features and co-occurrence features. In general, the term **collocation** refers to a quantifiable position-specific relationship between two lexical items. Collocational features encode information about the lexical inhabitants of *specific* positions located to the left or right of the target word. Typical features include the word, the root form of the word, and the word's part-of-speech. Such features are effective at encoding local lexical and grammatical information that can often accurately isolate a given sense.

COLLOCATION

As an example of this type of feature-encoding, consider the situation where we need to disambiguate the word *bass* in the following example:

(17.11) An electric guitar and **bass** player stand off to one side, not really part of the scene, just as a sort of nod to gringo expectations perhaps.

A feature-vector consisting of the two words to the right and left of the target word, along with their respective parts-of-speech, would yield the following vector:

```
[guitar, NN1, and, CJC, player, NN1, stand, VVB]
```

The second type of feature consists of co-occurrence data about neighboring words, ignoring their exact position. In this approach, the words themselves (or their roots) serve as features. The value of the feature is the number of times the word occurs in a region surrounding the target word.

This region is most often defined as a fixed size window with the target word at the center. To make this approach manageable, a small number of frequently used content words are selected for use as features. This kind of feature is effective at capturing the general topic of the discourse in which the target word has occurred. This, in turn, tends to identify senses of a word that are specific to certain domains.

For example, a co-occurrence vector consisting of the 12 most frequent content words from a collection of *bass* sentences drawn from the WSJ corpus would have the following words as features: *fishing, big, sound, player, fly, rod, pound, double, runs, playing, guitar, band*. Using these words as features with a window size of 10, example (17.11) would be represented by the following vector:

```
[0,0,0,1,0,0,0,0,0,0,1,0]
```

As we will see, most robust approaches to sense disambiguation make use of a combination of both collocational and co-occurrence features.

Supervised Learning Approaches

SUPERVISED
LEARNING

In supervised approaches, a sense disambiguation system is learned from a representative set of labeled instances drawn from the same distribution as the test set to be used. This is an application of the **supervised learning** approach to creating a classifier. In such approaches, a learning system is presented with a training set consisting of feature-encoded inputs *along with their appropriate label, or category*. The output of the system is a classifier system capable of assigning labels to new feature-encoded inputs.

Bayesian classifiers (Duda and Hart, 1973), decision lists (Rivest, 1987), decision trees (Quinlan, 1986), neural networks (Rumelhart et al., 1986), logic learning systems (Mooney, 1995), and nearest neighbor methods (Cover and Hart, 1967) all fit into this paradigm. We will restrict our discussion to the naive Bayes and decision list approaches, since they have been the focus of considerable work in word sense disambiguation.

NAIVE BAYES
CLASSIFIER

The **naive Bayes classifier** approach to WSD is based on the premise that choosing the best sense for an input vector amounts to choosing the most probable sense given that vector. In other words:

$$\hat{s} = \underset{s \in S}{\operatorname{argmax}} P(s|V) \qquad (17.12)$$

In this formula, S denotes the set of senses appropriate for the target associated with this vector, s denotes each of the possible senses in S, and V stands for the vector representation of the input context. As is almost always

METHODOLOGY BOX: EVALUATING WSD SYSTEMS

The basic metric used in evaluating sense disambiguation systems is simple precision: the percentage of words that are tagged correctly. The primary baseline against which this metric is compared is the **most frequent sense** metric (Gale et al., 1992): how well a system would perform if it simply chose the most frequent sense of a word.

The use of precision requires access to the correct senses for the words in a test set. Fortunately, two large sense-tagged corpora are now available: the SEMCOR corpus (Landes et al., 1998), which consists of a portion of the Brown corpus tagged with WordNet senses, and the SENSEVAL corpus (Kilgarriff and Rosenzweig, 2000), which is a tagged corpus derived from the HECTOR corpus and dictionary project.

One complication arising from the use of simple precision is that the nature of the senses used in an evaluation has a huge effect on the results. In particular, results derived from the use of coarse distinctions among homographs, such as the musical and fish senses of *bass*, can not easily be compared to results based on the use of fine-grained sense distinctions such as those found in traditional dictionaries, or lexical resources like WordNet.

A second complication has to do with metrics that go beyond simple precision and make use of **partial credit**. For example, confusing a particular musical sense of *bass* with a fish sense, is clearly worse than confusing it with another musical sense. With such a metric, an exact sense-match would receive full credit, while selecting a broader sense would receive partial credit. Of course, this kind of scheme is entirely dependent on the organization of senses in the particular dictionary being used.

Standardized evaluation frameworks for word sense disambiguation systems are now available. In particular, the SENSEVAL effort (Kilgarriff and Palmer, 2000), provides the same kind of evaluation framework for sense disambiguation, that the MUC (Sundheim, 1995b) and TREC (Voorhees and Harman, 1998) evaluations have provided for information extraction and information retrieval.

the case, it would be difficult to collect statistics for this equation directly. Instead, we rewrite it in the usual Bayesian manner as follows:

$$\hat{s} = \underset{s \in S}{\mathrm{argmax}} \frac{P(V|s)P(s)}{P(V)} \qquad (17.13)$$

Of course, the data available that associates specific vectors with senses is too sparse to be useful. However, what is available in abundance in a tagged training set is information about individual feature-value pairs in the context of specific senses. Therefore, we can make the independence assumption that gives this method its name, and that has served us well in part-of-speech tagging, speech recognition, and probabilistic parsing — naively assuming that the features are independent of one another. Making this assumption yields the following approximation for $P(V|s)$:

$$P(V|s) \approx \prod_{j=1}^{n} P(v_j|s) \qquad (17.14)$$

In other words, we can estimate the probability of an entire vector given a sense by the product of the probabilities of its individual features given that sense.

Given this equation, **training** a naive Bayes classifier amounts to collecting counts of the individual feature-value statistics with respect to each sense of the target word in a sense-tagged training corpus. To make this concrete, let's return to example (17.11). The individual statistics needed for this example might include the probability of the word *player* occurring immediately to the right of a use of each of the *bass* senses, or the probability of the word *guitar* one place to the left of a use of one of the *bass* senses.

Returning to equation (17.13), the term $P(s)$ is the prior for each sense, which just corresponds to the proportion of each sense in the sense-tagged training corpus. Finally, since $P(V)$ is the same for all possible senses, it does not effect the final ranking of senses, leaving us with the following:

$$\hat{s} = \underset{s \in S}{\mathrm{argmax}} \, P(s) \prod_{j=1}^{n} P(v_j|s) \qquad (17.15)$$

Of course, all the issues discussed in Chapter 6 with respect to zero counts and smoothing apply here as well.

In a large experiment evaluating a number of supervised learning algorithms, Mooney (1996) reports that a naive-Bayes classifier and a neural network achieved the highest performance, both achieving around 73% correct in assigning one of six senses to a corpus of examples of the word *line*.

DECISION
LIST
CLASSIFIERS   **Decision list classifiers** are equivalent to simple case statements in

Rule		Sense
fish within window	$\Rightarrow$	**bass**[1]
striped bass	$\Rightarrow$	**bass**[1]
guitar within window	$\Rightarrow$	**bass**[2]
bass player	$\Rightarrow$	**bass**[2]
piano within window	$\Rightarrow$	**bass**[2]
tenor within window	$\Rightarrow$	**bass**[2]
sea bass	$\Rightarrow$	**bass**[1]
play/V bass	$\Rightarrow$	**bass**[2]
river within window	$\Rightarrow$	**bass**[1]
violin within window	$\Rightarrow$	**bass**[2]
salmon within window	$\Rightarrow$	**bass**[1]
on bass	$\Rightarrow$	**bass**[2]
bass are	$\Rightarrow$	**bass**[1]

Figure 17.1   An abbreviated decision list for disambiguating the fish sense of bass from the music sense. Adapted from Yarowsky (1996).

most programming languages. In a decision list classifier, a sequence of tests is applied to each vector encoded input. If a test succeeds, then the sense associated with that test is returned. If the test fails, then the next test in the sequence is applied. This continues until the end of the list, where a default test simply returns the majority sense.

Figure 17.1 shows a portion of a decision list for the task of discriminating the fish sense of *bass* from the music sense. The first test says that if the word *fish* occurs anywhere within the input context then **bass**[1] is the correct answer. If it doesn't then each of the subsequent tests is consulted in turn until one returns true; as with case statements a default test that returns true is included at the end of the list.

Learning a decision list classifier consists of generating and ordering individual tests based on the characteristics of the training data. There are a wide number of methods that can be used to create such lists. In the approach used by Yarowsky (1994) every individual feature-value pair constitutes a test. These tests are then ordered according to their individual accuracy on the entire training set, where the accuracy of a test is based on its log-likelihood ratio:

$$\text{Abs}\left(\text{Log}\left(\frac{P(Sense_1|f_i = v_j)}{P(Sense_2|f_i = v_j)}\right)\right) \qquad (17.16)$$

The decision list is created from these tests by simply ordering the tests in the list according to this measure, with each test returning the appropriate sense. Yarowsky (1996) reports that this technique consistently achieves over 95% correct on a wide variety of binary decision tasks.

We should note that this training method differs quite a bit from standard decision list learning algorithms. For the details and theoretical motivation for these approaches see Rivest (1987) or Russell and Norvig (1995).

Bootstrapping Approaches

BOOTSTRAPPING
APPROACH
A major problem with supervised approaches is the need for a large sense-tagged training set. The **bootstrapping approach** (Hearst, 1991; Yarowsky, 1995) eliminates the need for a large training set by relying on a relatively small number of instances of each sense for each lexeme of interest. These labeled instances are used as **seeds** to train an initial classifier using any of the supervised learning methods mentioned in the last section. This initial classifier is then be used to extract a larger training set from the remaining untagged corpus. Repeating this process results in a series of classifiers with improving accuracy and coverage.

The key to this approach lies in its ability to create a larger training set from a small set of seeds. To succeed, it must include only those instances in which the initial classifier has a high degree of confidence. This larger training set is then used to create a new more accurate classifier with broader coverage. With each iteration of this process, the training corpus grows and the untagged corpus shrinks. As with most iterative methods, this process can be repeated until some sufficiently low error-rate on the training set is reached, or until no further examples from the untagged corpus are above threshold.

The initial seeds used in these bootstrapping methods can be generated in a number of ways. Hearst (1991) generates a seed set by simply hand-labeling a small set of examples from the initial corpus. This approach has three major advantages:

- There is a reasonable certainty that the seed instances are correct, thus ensuring that the learner does not get off on the wrong foot.
- The analyst can make some effort to choose examples that are not only correct, but in some sense prototypical of each sense.
- It is reasonably easy to carry out.

An effective alternative technique is to search for sentences containing words or phrases that are strongly associated with the target senses. Yarowsky (1995) calls this the **One Sense per Collocation** constraint and

Klucevsek **play**s Giulietti or Titano piano accordions with the more flexible, more difficult free **bass** rather than the traditional Stradella **bass** with its preset chords designed mainly for accompaniment.

We need more good teachers – right now, there are only a half a dozen who can **play** the free **bass** with ease.

An electric guitar and **bass play**er stand off to one side, not really part of the scene, just as a sort of nod to gringo expectations perhaps.

When the New Jersey Jazz Society, in a fund-raiser for the American Jazz Hall of Fame, honors this historic night next Saturday, Harry Goodman, Mr. Goodman's brother and **bass play**er at the original concert, will be in the audience with other family members.

The researchers said the worms spend part of their life cycle in such **fish** as Pacific salmon and striped **bass** and Pacific rockfish or snapper.

Associates describe Mr. Whitacre as a quiet, disciplined and assertive manager whose favorite form of escape is **bass fish**ing.

And it all started when **fish**ermen decided the striped **bass** in Lake Mead were too skinny.

Though still a far cry from the lake's record 52-pound **bass** of a decade ago, "you could fillet these **fish** again, and that made people very, very happy," Mr. Paulson says.

Saturday morning I arise at 8:30 and click on "America's best-known **fish**erman," giving advice on catching **bass** in cold weather from the seat of a bass boat in Louisiana.

Figure 17.2   Samples of *bass* sentences extracted from the WSJ using the simple correlates *play* and *fish*.

presents results that show it yields remarkably good results. As an illustration of this technique, consider the situation where we would like to generate a reasonable set of seed sentences for the fish and musical senses of *bass*. Without too much thought, we might come up with *fish* as a reasonable indicator of **bass**[1], and *play* as a reasonable indicator of **bass**[2]. Figure 17.2 shows a partial result of a such a search for the strings "fish" and "play" in a corpus of *bass* examples drawn from the WSJ.

Of course, we might also want some way to automatically suggest these associated words. Yarowsky (1995) suggests two methods to select effective correlates: deriving them from machine readable dictionary entries, and selecting seeds using collocational statistics such as those described in Chapter 6. Yarowsky (1995) reports an average performance of 96.5% on a coarse binary sense assignment involving 12 words. In these experiments, a training set derived using bootstrapping with seed sentences discovered using correlates was used to train a decision list classifier for each word.

Unsupervised Methods: Discovering Word Senses

Unsupervised approaches to sense disambiguation eschew the use of sense tagged data of any kind during training. In these approaches, feature-vector representations of unlabeled instances are taken as input and are then grouped into clusters according to a similarity metric. These clusters can then be represented as the average of their constituent feature-vectors, and labeled by hand with known word senses. Unseen feature-encoded instances can be classified by assigning them the word sense from the cluster to which they are closest according to the similarity metric.

AGGLOMERATIVE
CLUSTERING

Fortunately, clustering is a well-studied problem with a wide number of standard algorithms that can be applied to inputs structured as vectors of numerical values (Duda and Hart, 1973). A frequently used technique in language applications is known as **agglomerative clustering**. In this technique, each of the N training instances is initially assigned to its own cluster. New clusters are then formed in a bottom-up fashion by successively merging the two clusters that are most similar. This process continues until either a specified number of clusters is reached, or some global goodness measure among the clusters is achieved. In cases where the number of training instances makes this method too expensive, random sampling can be used on the original training set (Cutting et al., 1992b) to achieve similar results.

The fact that these unsupervised methods do not make use of hand-labeled data poses a number of challenges for evaluating any clustering result. The following problems are among the most important ones that have to be addressed in unsupervised approaches:

- The correct senses of the instances used in the training data may not be known.
- The clusters are almost certainly heterogeneous with respect to the senses of the training instances contained within them.
- The number of clusters is almost always different from the number of senses of the target word being disambiguated.

Schütze's experiments (Schütze, 1992, 1998) constitute an extensive application of unsupervised clustering to word sense disambiguation. Although the actual technique is quite involved, unsupervised clustering is at the core of the method. Schütze's results indicate that for coarse binary distinctions, unsupervised techniques can achieve results approaching those of supervised and bootstrap methods, in most instances approaching the 90% range. As with most of the supervised methods, this method was tested on a small sample of words.

Dictionary-Based Approaches

A major drawback with all of these approaches is the problem of scale. All require a considerable amount of work to create a classifier for each ambiguous entry in the lexicon. For this reason, most of the experiments with these methods report results ranging from 2 to 12 lexical items (The work of Ng and Lee (1996) is a notable exception reporting results disambiguating 121 nouns and 70 verbs). Scaling up any of these approaches to deal with all the ambiguous words in a language would be a large undertaking. Instead, attempts to perform large-scale disambiguation have focused on the use of **machine readable dictionaries**, of the kind discussed in Chapter 16. In this style of approach, the dictionary provides both the means for constructing a sense tagger, and the target senses to be used.

The first implementation of this approach is due to Lesk (1986). In this approach, all the sense definitions of the word to be disambiguated are retrieved from the dictionary. Each of these senses is then compared to the dictionary definitions of all the remaining words in the context. The sense with the highest overlap with these context words is chosen as the correct sense. Note that the various sense definitions of the context words are all simply lumped together in this approach.

To make this more concrete, consider Lesk's example of selecting the appropriate sense of *cone* in the phrase *pine cone* given the following definitions for *pine* and *cone*.

pine	1	kinds of evergreen tree with needle-shaped leaves
	2	waste away through sorrow or illness
cone	1	solid body which narrows to a point
	2	something of this shape whether solid or hollow
	3	fruit of certain evergreen trees

In this example, Lesk's method would select **cone**[3] as the correct sense since two of the words in its entry, *evergreen* and *tree*, overlap with words in the entry for *pine*, whereas neither of the other entries have any overlap with words in the definition of *pine*. Lesk reports accuracies of 50-70% on short samples of text selected from Austen's *Pride and Prejudice* and an AP newswire article.

The primary problem with this approach is that the dictionary entries for the target words are relatively short, and may not provide sufficient material to create adequate classifiers since the words used in the context and their definitions must have direct overlap with the words contained in the appropriate sense definition in order to be useful.[1] One way to remedy this problem is to expand the list of words used in the classifier to include words related to, but not contained in their individual sense definitions. This can be accomplished by including words whose definitions make use of the target word. For example, the word *deposit* does not occur in the definition of *bank* in the American Heritage Dictionary (Morris, 1985). However, *bank* does occur in the definition of *deposit*. Therefore, the classifier for *bank* can be expanded to include *deposit* as a relevant feature.

Of course, just knowing that *deposit* is related to *bank* does not help much since we don't know to which sense of *bank* it is related. Specifically, to make use of *deposit* as a feature, we have to know which sense of *bank* was being used in its definition. Fortunately, many dictionaries and thesauri include tags known as **subject codes** in their entries that correspond roughly to broad conceptual categories. For example, the entry for *bank* in the *Longman's Dictionary of Contemporary English* (LDOCE) (Procter, 1978) includes the subject code EC (Economics) for the financial senses of *bank*. Given such subject codes, we can guess that expanded terms with the subject code EC will be related to this sense of bank rather than any of the others. Guthrie et al. (1991) report results ranging from 47% correct for fine-grained LDOCE distinctions to 72% for more coarse distinctions.

SUBJECT
CODES

17.3   INFORMATION RETRIEVAL

Information retrieval is a growing field that encompasses a wide range of topics related to the storage and retrieval of all manner of media. The focus of this section is with the storage of text documents and their subsequent retrieval in response to users' requests for information. Of particular interest is the widespread adoption of word-based indexing and retrieval methods. Most current information retrieval systems are based on an extreme interpretation of the principle of compositional semantics. In these systems, the meaning of documents resides solely in the words that are contained within

---

[1]   Indeed, Lesk (1986) notes that the performance of his system seems to roughly correlate with the length of the dictionary entries.

them. To revisit the Mad Hatter's quote from the beginning of Chapter 16, in these systems *I see what I eat* and *I eat what I see* mean precisely the same thing. The ordering and constituency of the words that make up the sentences that make up documents play no role in determining their meaning. Because they ignore syntactic information, these approaches are often referred to as **bag of words** methods.

BAG OF
WORDS

Before moving on, we need to introduce some new terminology. In information retrieval, a **document** refers generically to the unit of text indexed in the system and available for retrieval. Depending on the application, a document can refer to anything from intuitive notions like newspaper articles, or encyclopedia entries, to smaller units such as paragraphs and sentences. In Web-based applications, it can refer to a Web page, a part of a page, or to an entire Website. A **collection** refers to a set of documents being used to satisfy user requests. A **term** refers to a lexical item that occurs in a collection, but it may also include phrases. Finally, a **query** represents a user's information need expressed as a set of terms.

DOCUMENT

COLLECTION

TERM

QUERY

The specific information retrieval task that we will consider in detail is known as **ad hoc retrieval**. In this task, it is assumed that an unaided user poses a query to a retrieval system, which then returns a possibly ordered set of potentially useful documents. Several other related, lexically oriented, information retrieval tasks will be discussed in Section 17.4.

AD HOC
RETRIEVAL

The Vector Space Model

In the **vector space model** of information retrieval, documents and queries are represented as vectors of features representing the terms that occur within them (Salton, 1971). More properly, they are represented as vectors of features consisting of the terms that occur *within the collection*, with the value of each feature indicating the presence or absence of a given term in a given document. These vectors can be represented as follows:

VECTOR
SPACE MODEL

$$\vec{d}_j = (t_{1,j}, t_{2,j}, t_{3,j}, \cdots, t_{N,j})$$
$$\vec{q}_k = (t_{1,k}, t_{2,k}, t_{3,k}, \cdots, t_{N,k})$$

In this notation, $\vec{d}_j$ and $\vec{q}_k$ denote a particular document and query, while the various t features represent the N terms that occur in the collection as a whole. Let's first consider the case where these features take on the value of one or zero, indicating the presence or absence of a term in a document or query. Given this approach, a simple way to determine the relevance of a document to a query is to determine the number of terms they have in common. This can be accomplished by the following similarity metric:

$$sim(\vec{q}_k, \vec{d}_j) = \sum_{i=1}^{N} t_{i,k} \times t_{i,j} \tag{17.17}$$

In this equation, the similarity between the query vector, $\vec{q}_k$ and the document vector, $\vec{d}_j$, is measured by simply summing the number of terms they share.

Of course, a problem with the use of binary values for features is that it fails to capture the fact that some terms are more important to the meaning of a document than others. A useful generalization is to replace the ones and zeroes with numerical **weights** that indicate the importance of the various terms in particular documents and queries. We can thus generalize our vectors as follows:

 WEIGHTS

$$\vec{d}_j = (w_{1,j}, w_{2,j}, w_{3,j}, \cdots, w_{n,j})$$
$$\vec{q}_k = (w_{1,k}, w_{2,k}, w_{3,k}, \cdots, w_{n,k})$$

This characterization of documents as vectors of term weights allows us to view the document collection as a whole as a matrix of weights, where $w_{i,j}$ represents the weight of term i in document j. This weight matrix is typically called a **term-by-document matrix** matrix. Under this view, the columns of the matrix represent the documents in the collection, and the rows represent the terms.

TERM-BY-
DOCUMENT
MATRIX

It is useful to view the features used to represent documents (and queries) in this model as dimensions in a multi-dimensional space. Correspondingly, the weights that serve as values for those features serve to locate documents in that space. When a user's query is translated into a vector it denotes a point in that space. Documents that are located close to the query can then be judged as being more relevant than documents that are farther away.

This characterization of documents and queries as vectors provides all the basic parts for an ad hoc retrieval system. A document retrieval system can simply accept a user's query, create a vector representation for it, compare it against the vectors representing all known documents, and sort the results. The result is a list of documents rank ordered by their similarity to the query.

Consider as an example of this approach, the space shown in Figure 17.3. This figure shows a simplified space consisting of the three dimensions corresponding to the terms *speech*, *language* and *processing*. The three vectors illustrated in this space represent documents derived from the chapter and section headings of Chapters 1, 7, and 13 of this text, which we will denote as **Doc1**, **Doc7**, and **Doc13**, respectively. If we use raw term frequency in document as a weight, then **Doc1** is represented by the vector $(1, 2, 1)$, **Doc7** by $(6, 0, 1)$, and **Doc13** by $(0, 5, 1)$. As is clear from the figure, this space captures certain intuitions about how these chapters are related. Chapter 1, being general, is fairly similar to both Chapters 7 and 13. Chapters 7 and 13, on the other hand, are distant from one another since they cover a different set of topics.

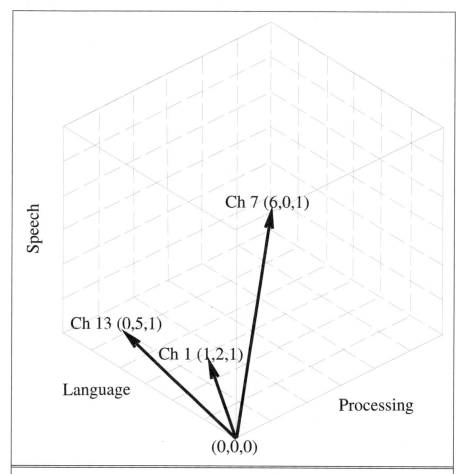

Figure 17.3   A simple vector space representation of documents derived from the text of the chapter and section headings of Chapters 1, 7, and 13 in three dimensions.

Unfortunately, this instantiation of a vector space places too much emphasis on the absolute values of the various coordinates of each document. For example, what is important about the *speech* dimension of the **Doc7**, is not the value 6 but rather that it is the dominant contributor to the meaning of that document. Similarly, the specific values of 1, 2, and 1 for **Doc1** are not important, what is important is that the three dimensions have roughly similar weights. It would be sensible, for example, to assume that a new document with weights 3, 6, and 3 would be quite similar to **Doc1** despite the magnitude differences in the term weights.

We can accomplish this effect by **normalizing** document vectors. By normalizing, we simply mean converting all the vectors to a standard length. Converting to a unit length can be accomplished by dividing each of their dimensions by the overall length of the vector, which is defined as $\sum_{i=1}^{N} w_i^2$. This, in effect, eliminates the importance of the exact length of a document's vector in the space, and emphasizes instead the direction of the document vector with respect to the origin.

Applying this technique to our three sample documents results in the following term-by-document matrix, A, where the columns represent **Doc1**, **Doc7** and **Doc13** and the rows represent the terms *speech*, *language*, and *processing*:

$$A = \begin{pmatrix} .41 & .81 & .41 \\ .98 & 0 & .16 \\ 0 & .98 & .19 \end{pmatrix}$$

You should verify that with this scheme, the normalized vectors for **Doc1** and our hypothetical $(3,6,3)$ document end up as identical vectors.

Now let's return to the topic of determining the similarity between vectors. Updating the similarity metric given earlier with numerical weights rather than binary values, gives us the following equation:

$$sim(\vec{q}_k, \vec{d}_j) = \vec{q}_k \cdot \vec{d}_j = \sum_{i=1}^{N} w_{i,k} \times w_{i,j} \tag{17.18}$$

DOT PRODUCT

This equation specifies the **dot product** between vectors. In general, the dot product between two vectors is of no use as a similarity metric, since it is too sensitive to the absolute magnitudes of the various dimensions. However, the dot product between vectors that have been normalized has a useful and

COSINE

intuitive interpretation: it computes the **cosine** of the angle between two vectors. When two documents are identical they will receive a cosine of one; when they are orthogonal (share no common terms) they will receive a cosine of zero.

Note that if for some reason the vectors are not stored in a normalized form, then the normalization can be incorporated directly into the similarity measure as follows:

$$sim(\vec{q}_k, \vec{d}_j) = \frac{\sum_{i=1}^{N} w_{i,k} \times w_{i,j}}{\sqrt{\sum_{i=1}^{N} w_{i,k}^2} \times \sqrt{\sum_{i=1}^{N} w_{i,j}^2}} \qquad (17.19)$$

Of course, in situations where the document collection is relatively static and many queries are being performed, it makes sense to normalize the document vectors once and store them, rather than include the normalization in the similarity metric.

Let's consider how this similarity metric would work in the context of some small examples. Consider the carefully selected query consisting solely of the terms *speech*, *language* and *processing*. Converting this query to a vector and normalizing it results in the vector $(.57, .57, .57)$. Computing the cosines between this vector and our three document vectors shows that **Doc1** is closest with a cosine of .92, followed by **Doc13** with a cosine of .67, and finally **Doc7** with a cosine of .65. Not surprisingly, this ranking is in close accord with our intuitions about the relationship between this query and these documents.

Now consider a shorter query consisting solely of the terms *speech* and *processing*. Processing this query yields the normalized vector $(.70, 0, .70)$. When the cosines are computed between this vector and our documents, **Doc7** is now the closest with a cosine of .80, followed by **Doc1** with a score of .58, with **Doc13** coming in a distant third with a cosine of .13.

Term Weighting

In practice, the method used to assign terms weights in the document and query vectors has an enormous impact on the effectiveness of a retrieval system. Two factors have proven to be critical in deriving effective term weights: term frequency within a single document, and the distribution of terms across a collection. We can begin with the simple notion that terms which occur frequently within a document may reflect its meaning more strongly than terms that occur less frequently and should thus have higher weights. In its simplest form, this factor is called **term frequency** and is TERM FREQUENCY simply the raw frequency of a term within a document (Luhn, 1957).

The second factor to consider is the distribution of terms across the collection as a whole. Terms that are limited to a few documents are useful for discriminating those documents from the rest of the collection. On the other hand, terms that occur frequently across the entire collection are less useful in discriminating among documents. What is needed therefore is a

METHODOLOGY BOX: EVALUATING INFORMATION RE-
TRIEVAL SYSTEMS

Information retrieval systems are evaluated with respect to the notion of **relevance** — *a judgment by a human* that a document is relevant to a query. A system's ability to retrieve relevant documents is assessed with a **recall** measure, as in Chapter 15.

$$\textbf{Recall} = \frac{\text{\# of relevant documents returned}}{\text{total \# of relevant documents in the collection}}$$

Of course, a system can achieve 100% recall by simply returning all the documents in the collection. A system's accuracy is based on how many of the documents returned for a given query are actually relevant, which can be assessed by a **precision** metric.

$$\textbf{Precision} = \frac{\text{\# of relevant documents returned}}{\text{\# of documents returned}}$$

These measures are complicated by the fact that most systems do not make explicit relevance judgments, but rather rank their collection with respect to a query. To deal with this we can specify a set of cutoffs in the output, and measure average precision for the documents ranked above the cutoff. Alternatively, we can specify a set of recall levels and measure average precision at those levels. This latter method gives rise to what are known as precision-recall curves as shown in Figure 17.4. As these curves show, comparing the performance of two systems can be difficult. In this comparison, one system is better at both high and low levels of recall, while the other is better in the middle region. An alternative to these curves are metrics that attempt to combine recall and precision into a single value. The *F* measure introduced on page 578 is one such measure.

The U.S. government-sponsored TREC (Text REtrieval Conference) evaluations have provided a rigorous testbed for the evaluation of a variety of information retrieval tasks and techniques. Like the MUC evaluations, TREC provides large document sets for both training and testing, along with a uniform scoring system. Training materials consist of sets of documents accompanied by sets of queries (called topics in TREC) and relevance judgments. Voorhees and Harman (1998) provide the details for the most recent meeting. Details of all of the meetings can be found at the TREC page on the National Institute of Standards and Technology Website.

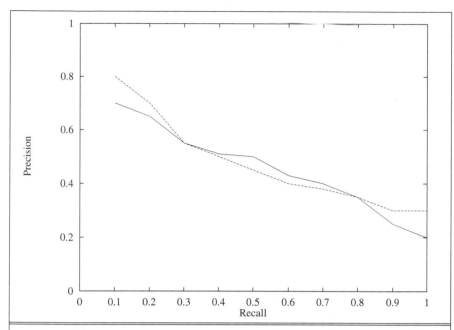

Figure 17.4   Precision-recall curves for two hypothetical systems. These curves plot the average precision of a set of returned documents at a given level of recall. For example, with both of these systems, drawing a cutoff in the return set at the document where they achieve 30% recall results in an average precision of 55%.

measure that favors terms which occur in fewer documents. The fraction N/n_i, where N is the total number of documents in the collection, and n_i is the number of documents in which term i occurs, provides exactly this measure. The fewer documents a term occurs in, the higher this weight. The lowest weight of 1 is assigned to terms that occur in all the documents. Due to the large number of documents in many collections, this measure is usually squashed with a log function leaving us with the following **inverse document frequency** term weight (Sparck Jones, 1972):

INVERSE
DOCUMENT
FREQUENCY

$$idf_i = \log\left(\frac{N}{n_i}\right) \tag{17.20}$$

Combining the term frequency factor with this factor results in a scheme known as tf · idf weighting:

$$w_{i,j} = tf_{i,j} \times idf_i \tag{17.21}$$

That is, the weight of term i in the vector for document j is the product of its overall frequency in j with the log of its inverse document frequency in the collection. With some minor variations, this weighting scheme is used to assign term weights to documents in nearly all vector space retrieval models.

Despite the fact that we use the same representations for documents and queries, it is not at all clear that the same weighting scheme should be used for both. In many ad hoc retrieval settings, such as Web search engines, user queries are not very much like documents at all. For example, an analysis of a very large set of queries (1,000,000,000 actually) from the AltaVista search engine reveals that the average query length is around 2.3 words (Silverstein et al., 1998). In such an environment, the raw term frequency in the query is not likely to be a very useful factor. Instead, Salton and Buckley (1988) recommend the following formula for weighting query terms, where $\max_j \text{tf}_{j,k}$ denotes the frequency of the most frequent term in document k.

$$w_{i,k} = \left(0.5 + \frac{0.5\text{tf}_{i,k}}{\max_j \text{tf}_{j,k}} \right) \times \text{idf}_i \tag{17.22}$$

Term Selection and Creation

Thus far, we have been assuming that it is precisely the words that occur in a collection that are used to index the documents in the collection. Two common variations on this assumption involve the use of **stemming**, and a **stop list**.

STEMMING   The notion of **stemming** takes us back to Chapter 3 and the topic of morphological analysis. The basic question addressed by stemming is whether the morphological variants of a lexical item should be listed (and counted) separately, or whether they should be collapsed into a single root form. For example, without stemming, the terms *process*, *processing* and *processed* will be treated as distinct items with separate term frequencies in a term-by-document matrix; with stemming they will be conflated to the single term *process* with a single summed frequency count. The major advantage to using stemming is that it allows a particular query term to match documents containing any of the morphological variants of the term. The Porter stemmer (Porter, 1980) described in Chapter 3 is frequently used for retrieval from collections of English documents.

A problem with this approach is that it throws away useful distinctions. For example, consider the use of the Porter stemmer on documents and queries containing the words *stocks* and *stockings*. In this case, the Porter stemmer reduces these surface forms to the single term *stock*. Of course, the result of this is that queries concerning *stock prices* will return documents about *stockings*, and queries about *stockings* will find documents about *stocks*.[2] More technically, stemming may increase recall by finding documents with terms that are morphologically related to queries, but it may also reduce precision by returning semantically unrelated documents. For this reason, few Web search engines currently make use of stemming. Hull (1996) presents results from a series of experiments that explore the efficacy of stemming.

A second common technique involves the use of stop lists, which address the issue of what words should be allowed into the index. A **stop list**   STOP LIST is simply a list of high frequency words that are eliminated from the representation of both documents and queries. Two motivations are normally given for this strategy: high frequency, closed-class terms are seen as carrying little semantic weight and are thus unlikely to help with retrieval, and eliminating them can save considerable space in the inverted index files used to map from terms to the documents that contain them. The downside of using a stop list is that it makes it difficult to search for phrases that contain words in the stop list. For example, a common stop list derived from the Brown corpus presented in Frakes and Baeza-Yates (1992), would reduce the phrase *to be or not to be* to the phrase *not*.

Homonymy, Polysemy, and Synonymy

Since the vector space model is based solely on the use of simple terms, it is useful to consider the effect that various lexical semantic phenomena may have on the model. Consider a query containing the word *canine* with its *tooth* and *dog* senses. A query containing *canine* will be judged similar to documents making use of either of these senses. However, given that users are probably only interested in one of these senses, the documents containing the other sense will be judged non-relevant. Homonymy and polysemy, therefore, can have the effect of *reducing precision* by leading a system to return documents irrelevant to the user's information need.

Now consider a query consisting of the lexeme *dog*. This query will be judged close to documents that make frequent use of the term *dog*, but may fail to match documents that use close synonyms like *canine*, as well as documents that use hyponyms such as *Malamute*. Synonymy and hyponymy, therefore, can have the effect of *reducing recall* by causing the retrieval sys-

---

[2] This example is motivated by some bad publicity received by a well-known search engine, when it returned some rather salacious sites containing extensive use of the term *stockings* in response to queries concerning *stock prices*. In response, a spokesman announced that their engineers were working hard on a solution to this strange problem with words.

tem to miss relevant documents.

Note that it is inaccurate to state flatly that polysemy reduces precision, and synonymy reduces recall since, as we discussed on page 652, both measures are relative to a fixed cutoff. As a result, every non-relevant document that rises above the cutoff due to polysemy takes up a slot in the fixed size return set, and may thus push a relevant document below threshold, thus reducing recall. Similarly, when a document is missed due to synonymy, a slot is opened in the return set for a non-relevant document, potentially reducing precision as well.

These issues lead naturally to the question of whether or not word sense disambiguation can help in information retrieval. The current evidence on this point is mixed, with some experiments reporting a gain using disambiguation-like techniques (Schütze and Pedersen, 1995), and others reporting either no gain, or a degradation in performance (Krovetz and Croft, 1992; Sanderson, 1994; Voorhees, 1998).

Improving User Queries

One of the most effective ways to improve retrieval performance is to find a way to improve user queries. The techniques presented in this section have been shown to varying degrees to be effective at this task.

RELEVANCE
FEEDBACK

The single most effective way to improve retrieval performance in the vector space model is the use of **relevance feedback** (Rocchio, 1971). In this method, a user presents a query to the system and is presented with a small set of retrieved documents. The user is then asked to specify which of these documents appears relevant to their need. The user's original query is then reformulated based on the distribution of terms in the relevant and non-relevant documents that the user examined. This reformulated query is then passed to the system as a *new* query with the new results being shown to the user. Typically an enormous improvement is seen after a single iteration of this technique.

The formal basis for the implementation of this technique falls out directly from some of the basic geometric intuitions of the vector model. In particular, we would like to *push* the vector representing the user's original query toward the documents that have been found to be relevant, and away from the documents judged not relevant. This can be accomplished by adding an averaged vector representing the relevant documents to the original query, and subtracting an averaged vector representing the non-relevant documents.

More formally, let's assume that $\vec{q}_i$ represents the user's original query, R is the number of relevant documents returned from the original query, S is the number of non-relevant documents, and documents in the relevant and non-relevant sets are denoted as $\vec{r}$ and $\vec{s}$, respectively. In addition, assume that β and γ range from 0 to 1 and that $\beta + \gamma = 1$. Given these assumptions, the following represents a standard relevance feedback update formula:

$$\vec{q}_{i+1} = \vec{q}_i + \frac{\beta}{R}\sum_{j=1}^{R}\vec{r}_j - \frac{\gamma}{S}\sum_{k=1}^{S}\vec{s}_k$$

The factors β and γ in this formula represent parameters that can be adjusted experimentally. Intuitively, β represents how far the new vector should be pushed towards the relevant documents, and γ represents how far it should be pushed away from the non-relevant ones. Salton and Buckley (1990) report good results with $\beta = .75$ and $\gamma = .25$.

We should note that evaluating systems that use relevance feedback is rather tricky. In particular, an enormous improvement is often seen in the documents retrieved by the first reformulated query. This should not be too surprising since it includes the documents that the user told the system were relevant on the first round. The preferred way to avoid this inflation is to only compute recall and precision measures for what is called the **residual collection**, the original collection without any of the documents shown to the user on any previous round. This usually has the effect of driving the system's raw performance below that achieved with the first query, since the most highly relevant documents have now been eliminated. Nevertheless, this is an effective technique to use when comparing distinct relevance feedback mechanisms.

RESIDUAL COLLECTION

An alternative approach to query improvement focuses on the terms that comprise the query vector, rather than the query vector itself. In **query expansion**, the user's original query is expanded to include terms related to the original terms. This has typically been accomplished by adding terms chosen from lists of terms that are highly correlated with the user's original terms in the collection. Such highly correlated terms are listed in what is typically called a **thesaurus**, although since it is based on correlation, rather than synonymy, it is only loosely connected to the standard references that carry the same name.

QUERY EXPANSION

THESAURUS

Unfortunately, it is usually the case that available thesaurus-like resources are not suitable for most collections. In **thesaurus generation**, a correlation-based thesaurus is generated automatically from all or a portion of the documents in the collection. Not surprisingly, one of the most popular

THESAURUS GENERATION

TERM
CLUSTERING
methods used in thesaurus generation involves the use of **term clustering**. Recall from our characterization of the term-by-document matrix that the columns in the matrix represent the documents and the rows represent the terms. Therefore, in thesaurus generation, the rows can be clustered to form sets of synonyms, which can then be added to the user's original query to improve its recall.

This technique is typically instantiated in one of two ways: a thesaurus can be generated once from the document collection as a whole (Crouch and Yang, 1992), or sets of synonym-like terms can be generated dynamically from the returned set for the original query (Attar and Fraenkel, 1977). Note that this second approach entails far more effort, since in effect a small thesaurus is generated for the documents returned for every query, rather than once for the entire collection.

17.4   OTHER INFORMATION RETRIEVAL TASKS

As noted earlier, ad-hoc retrieval is not the only word-based task in information retrieval. Some of the other more important ones include document categorization, document clustering, text segmentation, and summarization.

DOCUMENT
CATEGORIZATION
The **document categorization** task is to assign a new document to one of a pre-existing set of document classes. In this setting, the task of creating a classifier consists of discovering a useful characterization of the documents that belong in each class. Although this can be done by hand, the standard approach is to use supervised machine learning. In particular, classifiers can be trained on a set of documents that have been labeled with the correct class. Any of the supervised learning methods introduced on page 638 for word sense disambiguation can be applied to this task as well. When categorization is performed with the intent of transmitting a document to a

ROUTING
user, or set of interested users, it is usually referred to as **routing**. The term

FILTERING
filtering is used in the special case where the categorization task is to either accept or reject a document, as in e-mail filters that attempt to screen for junk mail.

DOCUMENT
CLUSTERING
The categorization task assumes an existing classification, or clustering, of documents. By contrast, the task of **document clustering** is to create, or discover, a reasonable set of clusters for a given set of documents. As was the case in word sense discovery, a reasonable cluster is defined as one that maximizes the within-cluster document similarity, and minimizes between-cluster similarity. There are two principal motivations for the use of this

technique in an ad hoc retrieval setting: efficiency, and the **cluster hypothesis**.

The efficiency motivation arises from the enormous size of many modern document collections. Recall that the retrieval method described in the last section requires every query to be compared against every document in the collection. If a collection can be divided up into a set of N conceptually coherent clusters, then queries could first be compared against representations of each of the N clusters. Ordinary retrieval could then be applied only within the top cluster or clusters, thus saving the cost of comparing the query to the documents in all of the other more distant clusters.

The **cluster hypothesis** (Jardine and van Rijsbergen, 1971) takes this argument a step further by asserting that retrieval from a clustered collection will not only be more efficient, but will in fact improve retrieval performance in terms of recall and precision. The basic notion behind this hypothesis is that by separating documents according to topic, relevant documents will be found together in the same cluster, and non-relevant documents will be avoided since they will reside in clusters that are not used for retrieval. Despite the plausibility of this hypothesis, there is only mixed empirical support for it. Results vary considerably based on the clustering algorithm and document collection in use (Willett, 1988; Shaw et al., 1996).

CLUSTER
HYPOTHESIS

A promising alternative application of clustering is to cluster the documents returned in response to a user's query, rather than the document collection as whole. Hearst and Pedersen (1996) present evidence that this technique provides many of benefits promised by the cluster hypothesis.

In **text segmentation**, larger documents are automatically broken down into smaller semantically coherent chunks. This is useful in domains where there are a significant number of large documents that cover a wide variety of topics. Text segmentation can be used to either perform retrieval below the document level, or to visually guide the user to relevant parts of retrieved documents. Again, not surprisingly, segmentation algorithms often make use of vector-like representations for the subparts of a larger document. Adjacent subparts that have similar cosines are more likely to be about the same topic than adjacent segments with more distant cosines. Roughly speaking, such discontinuities in the similarity between adjacent text segments can be used to divide larger documents into subparts (Salton et al., 1993; Hearst, 1997).

TEXT
SEGMENTATION

Finally, the task of **text summarization** (Sparck Jones, 1997) is to produce a shorter, summary version of an original document. In general, two approaches have been taken to this problem. In the **knowledge-based**

TEXT
SUMMARIZATION

approach, the original document undergoes a semantic analysis which produces a representation of the meaning of the text. This representation is then passed to a text generator which produces a summary text that conveys the important points of the original and satisfies given length restrictions. More details on text generation are presented in Chapter 20. In **selection-based summarization**, a summary document is created by first assigning a importance weight to all the sentences from the original document according to very simple word frequency and discourse structure heuristics. A summary document is then generated by determining a threshold such that the inclusion of all sentences above the threshold results in a document with the desired size.

SELECTION-BASED
SUMMARIZATION

17.5   SUMMARY

This chapter has explored two major areas of lexical semantic processing: word sense disambiguation and information retrieval.

- **Word sense disambiguation** systems assign word tokens in context to one of a pre-specified set of senses.
- **Selectional restriction-based** approaches can be used to disambiguate both predicates and arguments, but require considerable information about semantic roles restrictions and hierarchical type information about role fillers.
- **Machine learning** approaches to sense disambiguation make it possible to automatically create robust sense disambiguation systems.
  - **Supervised** approaches use collections of texts annotated with their correct senses to train classifiers.
  - **Bootstrapping** approaches permit the use of supervised methods with far fewer resources.
  - **Unsupervised** clustering-based approaches attempt to discover representations of word senses from unannotated texts.
- **Machine readable dictionaries** facilitate the creation of broad-coverage sense disambiguators.
- The dominant models of information retrieval represent the meanings of documents and queries as bags of words.
- The **vector space model** views documents and queries as vectors in a large multidimensional space. In this model, the similarity between

documents and queries, or other documents, can be measured by the cosine of the angle between the vectors.

- User queries can be improved through query reformulation using either **relevance feedback** or thesaurus-based query expansion.

BIBLIOGRAPHICAL AND HISTORICAL NOTES

Word sense disambiguation traces its roots to some of the earliest applications of digital computers. The notion of disambiguating a word by looking at a small window around it was apparently first suggested by Warren Weaver (1955), in the context of machine translation. Among the notions first proposed in this early period were the use of a thesaurus for disambiguation (Masterman, 1957), supervised training of Bayesian models for disambiguation (Madhu and Lytel, 1965), and the use of clustering in word sense analysis (Sparck Jones, 1986).

An enormous amount of work on disambiguation has been conducted within the context of AI-oriented natural language processing systems. Most natural language analysis systems of this type exhibit some form of lexical disambiguation capability, however, a number of these efforts made word sense disambiguation a larger focus of their work. Among the most influential efforts were the efforts of Quillian (1968) and Simmons (1973) with semantic networks, the work of Wilks with *Preference Semantics* Wilks (1975c, 1975b, 1975a), and the work of Small and Rieger (1982) and Riesbeck (1975) on word-based understanding systems. Hirst's ABSITY system (Hirst and Charniak, 1982; Hirst, 1987, 1988), which used a technique based on semantic networks called marker passing, represents the most advanced system of this type. As with these largely symbolic approaches, most connectionist approaches to word sense disambiguation have relied on small lexicons with hand-coded representations (Cottrell, 1985; Kawamoto, 1988).

We should note that considerable work on sense disambiguation has been conducted in the areas of Cognitive Science and psycholinguistics. Appropriately enough, it is generally described using a different name: lexical ambiguity resolution. Small et al. (1988) present a variety of papers from this perspective.

The earliest implementation of a robust empirical approach to sense disambiguation is due to Kelly and Stone (1975) who directed a team that hand-crafted a set of disambiguation rules for 1790 ambiguous English words.

Lesk (1986) was the first to use a machine readable dictionary for word sense disambiguation. The efforts at New Mexico State University using LDOCE are among the most extensive explorations of the use of machine readable dictionaries. Much of this work is described in Wilks et al. (1996). The problem of dictionary senses being too fine-grained or lacking an appropriate organization has been addressed in the work of Dolan (1994) and Chen and Chang (1998).

Modern interest in supervised machine learning approaches to disambiguation began with Black (1988), who applied decision tree learning to the task. The need for large amounts of annotated text in these methods led to investigations into the use of bootstrapping methods (Hearst, 1991; Yarowsky, 1995). The problem of how to weight and combine the disparate sources of evidence used in many robust systems is explored in Ng and Lee (1996) and McRoy (1992). There has been considerably less work in the area of unsupervised methods. The earliest attempt to use clustering in the study of word senses is due to Sparck Jones (1986). Zernik (1991) successfully applied a standard information retrieval clustering algorithm to the problem, and provided an evaluation based on improvements in retrieval performance. More extensive recent work on clustering can be found in Pedersen and Bruce (1997) and Schütze (1997, 1998).

Note that of all of these robust efforts, only three have attempted to exploit the power of mutually disambiguating all the words in a sentence. The system described in Kelly and Stone (1975) makes multiple passes over a sentence to take later advantage of easily disambiguated words; Cowie et al. (1992) use a simulated annealing model to perform a parallel search for a desirable set of senses; Veronis and Ide (1990) use inhibition and excitation in a neural network automatically constructed from a machine readable dictionary.

Ide and Veronis (1998) provide a comprehensive review of the history and current state of word sense disambiguation. Ng and Zelle (1997) provide a more focused review from a machine learning perspective. Wilks et al. (1996) describe a wide array of dictionary and corpus-based experiments, along with detailed descriptions of some very early work.

Luhn (1957) is generally credited with first advancing the notion of fully automatic indexing of documents based on their contents. Over the years Salton's SMART project (Salton, 1971) at Cornell developed or evaluated many of the most important notions in information retrieval including the vector model, term weighting schemes, relevance feedback, and the use of cosine as a similarity metric. The notion of using inverse document frequency in term weighting is due to Sparck Jones (1972). The original notion of relevance feedback is due to Rocchio (1971). An alternative to the vector model that we have not covered is the **probabilistic model**. Originally shown effective by Robinson and Sparck Jones (1976), a Bayesian network version of the probabilistic model is the basis for the widely used INQUERY system (Callan et al., 1992). Crestani et al. (1998) present a comprehensive review of probabilistic models in information retrieval.

PROBABILISTIC MODEL

The cluster hypothesis was introduced in Jardine and van Rijsbergen (1971). Willett (1988) provides a critical review of the major efforts in this area. Mather (1998) presents an algorithm-independent clustering metric that can be used to evaluate the performance of various clustering algorithms. A collection of papers on document categorization and its close siblings, filtering and routing, can be found in Lewis and Hayes (1994). A recent example of routing is AT&T's "How May I Help You?" task where the goal is to classify a user's utterance into one of fifteen possible categories, such as third number billing, or collect call. Once the system has classified the call, the system routes the caller to an appropriate human operator. The classification accuracy on this task approaches 80%, despite the fact that the speech recognizer has a word accuracy rate of only around 50% (Gorin et al., 1997).

Text segmentation has generally been investigated from one of two perspectives: approaches based on strong theories of discourse structure, and approaches based on lexical text cohesion (Morris and Hirst, 1991). Hearst (1997) describes a robust technique based on a vector model of lexical cohesion. Techniques based on strong discourse-models are discussed in Chapter 18 and Chapter 20.

Research on text summarization began with the work of Luhn (1958) on the automatic generation of abstracts. A collection of papers on text summarization can be found in Hovy and Radev (1998).

An important extension of the vector space model known as **Latent Semantic Indexing** (LSI) (Deerwester et al., 1990) uses the singular value decomposition method as means of *reducing the dimensionality* of vector models with the intent of discovering higher-order regularities in the original term-by-document matrix. Berry et al. (1999) present a useful review of numerical methods for dimensionality reduction in vector models. Although LSI began life as a retrieval method, it has been applied to a wide variety of applications including models of lexical acquisition (Landauer and Dumais, 1997), question answering (Jones, 1997), and most recently, essay grading (Landauer et al., 1997).

LATENT SEMANTIC INDEXING

Baeza-Yates and Ribeiro-Neto (1999) is a comprehensive text covering many of newest advances and trends in information retrieval. Frakes and Baeza-Yates (1992) is a more nuts and bolts text which includes a considerable amount of useful C code. Older classic texts include Salton and McGill (1983) and van Rijsbergen (1975). Many of the classic papers in the field can be found in Sparck Jones and Willett (1997). Current work is published in the annual proceedings of the ACM Special Interest Group on Information Retrieval (SIGIR). The periodic TREC conference proceedings contain results from standardized evaluations organized by the U.S. government. The primary journals in the field are the *Journal of the American Society of Information Sciences*, *ACM Transactions on Information Systems*, *Information Processing and Management*, and *Information Retrieval*.

EXERCISES

17.1 Collect a small corpus of example sentences of varying lengths from any newspaper or magazine. Using WordNet, or any standard dictionary, determine how many senses there are for each of the open-class words in each sentence. How many distinct combinations of senses are there for each sentence? How does this number seem to vary with sentence length?

17.2 Using WordNet, or a standard reference dictionary, tag each open-class word in your corpus with its correct tag. Was choosing the correct sense always a straightforward task. Report on any difficulties you encountered.

17.3 Using the same corpus, isolate the words taking part in all the verb-subject and verb-object relations. How often does it appear to be the case that the words taking part in these relations could be disambiguated using only information about the words in the relation?

17.4 Between the words *eat* and *find* which would you expect to be more effective in selectional restriction-based sense disambiguation? Why?

17.5 Implement and experiment with a decision-list sense disambiguation system. As a model, use the kinds of features shown in Figure 17.1. For more details on decision-list learning see Russell and Norvig (1995). To facilitate evaluation of your system, you should obtain one of the freely available sense-tagged corpora.

17.6   Using your favorite dictionary, simulate the word overlap disambiguation algorithm described on page 645 on the phrase *Time flies like an arrow*.
Assume that the words are to be disambiguated one at a time, from left to
right, and that the results from earlier decisions are used later in the process.

17.7   Formulate a set of detailed queries from a domain you are familiar
with, and submit them to a number of popular search engines. Using a series
of fixed cutoffs, assess the precision of each of these search engines.

17.8   For each of the returned documents that you judged **not relevant** in
Exercise 17.7, come up with an account as to why it might have been returned.

17.9   Consider the relevant documents that were returned by some, but not
all, of the search engines in Exercise 17.7. For the search engines that failed
to retrieve a relevant document:

    a. Determine if the search engine contains the relevant document.

    b. If it does, then come up with an account for why it did not return it (or
       did not rank it highly).

17.10   Investigate five of the more popular search engines and determine
which, if any, are employing some kind of morphological analysis.

17.11   Expand the queries used in Exercise 17.7 to include all of the morphological variants of each query word. Submit these expanded queries to
your original set of search engines. Does such morphological processing
seem warranted?

17.12   Using WordNet, expand your queries to include all the synonyms of
all the terms in the original query. Report on the results of submitting the
expanded queries to a set of search engines.

17.13   Using WordNet, expand your queries to include only those synonyms that are appropriate for each of the terms in the original query. In
other words, only include synonyms for the senses of terms you intended in
the original query. Submit these expanded queries to a set of search engines,
and compare the results to those you achieved in the previous exercise.

17.14   Word sense disambiguation seems to have little effect on retrieval
performance in settings where long queries are used. Suggest reasons for
why this might be the case.

17.15   Find, or create, a collection of documents that have been separated into distinct topical categories. E-mail messages that have been manually placed into distinct folders are a good source for such a collection. Using this collection, implement and evaluate a naive Bayes approach to text classification.

Part IV

PRAGMATICS

Pragmatics is the study of (some parts of) the relation between language and context-of-use. Context-of-use includes such things as the identities of people and objects, and so pragmatics includes studies of how language is used to refer (and re-refer) to people and things. Context-of-use includes the discourse context, and so pragmatics includes studies of how discourses are structured, and how the listener manages to interpret a conversational partner in a conversation. This part of the book explores algorithms for reference resolution, computational models for recovering the structure of monologue and conversational discourse, and models of how utterances in dialogue are interpreted. It also discusses the role of each of these models in building a conversational agent, as well as the design of the dialogue manager component of such an agent. Finally, it introduces natural language generation, focusing especially on the function of discourse.

Part IV

18 DISCOURSE*

Gracie: Oh yeah...and then Mr. and Mrs. Jones were having matrimonial trouble, and my brother was hired to watch Mrs. Jones.
George: Well, I imagine she was a very attractive woman.
Gracie: She was, and my brother watched her day and night for six months.
George: Well, what happened?
Gracie: She finally got a divorce.
George: Mrs. Jones?
Gracie: No, my brother's wife.

George Burns and Gracie Allen in The Salesgirl

Up to this point of the book, we have focused primarily on language phenomena that operate at the word or sentence level. Of course, language does not normally consist of isolated, unrelated sentences, but instead of collocated, related groups of sentences. We refer to such a group of sentences as a **discourse**.   DISCOURSE

The chapter you are now reading is an example of a discourse. It is in fact a discourse of a particular sort: a **monologue**. Monologues are charac-   MONOLOGUE
terized by a *speaker* (a term which will be used to include writers, as it is here), and a *hearer* (which, analogously, includes readers). The communication flows in only one direction in a monologue, that is, from the speaker to the hearer.

After reading this chapter, you may have a conversation with a friend about it, which would consist of a much freer interchange. Such a discourse is called a **dialogue**. In this case, each participant periodically takes turns   DIALOGUE

---

*This chapter was written by Andrew Kehler.

being a speaker and hearer. Unlike a typical monologue, dialogues generally consist of many different types of communicative acts: asking questions, giving answers, making corrections, and so forth.

HCI

Finally, computer systems exist and continue to be developed that allow for *human-computer interaction*, or **HCI**. HCI has properties that distinguish it from normal human-human dialogue, in part due to the present-day limitations on the ability of computer systems to participate in free, unconstrained conversation. A system capable of HCI will often employ a strategy to constrain the conversation in ways that allow it to understand the user's utterances within a limited context of interpretation.

While many discourse processing problems are common to these three forms of discourse, they differ in enough respects that different techniques have often been used to process them. This chapter focuses on techniques commonly applied to the interpretation of monologues; techniques for dialogue interpretation and HCI will be described in Chapter 19.

Language is rife with phenomena that operate at the discourse level. Consider the discourse shown in example (18.1).

(18.1) John went to Bill's car dealership to check out an Acura Integra. He looked at it for about an hour.

What do pronouns such as *he* and *it* denote? No doubt that the reader had little trouble figuring out that *he* denotes John and not Bill, and that *it* denotes the Integra and not Bill's car dealership. On the other hand, toward the end of the exchange presented at the beginning of this chapter, it appears that George had some trouble figuring out who Gracie meant when saying *she*.

What differentiates these two examples? How do hearers interpret discourse (18.1) with such ease? Can we build a computational model of this process? These are the types of questions we address in this chapter. In Section 18.1, we describe methods for interpreting *referring expressions* such as pronouns. We then address the problem of establishing the *coherence* of a discourse in Section 18.2. Finally, in Section 18.3 we explain methods for determining the *structure* of a discourse.

Because discourse-level phenomena are ubiquitous in language, algorithms for resolving them are essential for a wide range of language applications. For instance, interactions with query interfaces and dialogue interpretation systems like ATIS (see Chapter 9) frequently contain pronouns and similar types of expressions. So when a user spoke passage (18.2) to an ATIS system,

(18.2) I'd like to get from Boston to San Francisco, on either December 5th
        or December 6th. It's okay if it stops in another city along the way.

the system had to figure out that *it* denotes the flight that the user wants to
book in order to perform the appropriate action.

Similarly, information extraction systems (see Chapter 15) must frequently extract information from utterances that contain pronouns. For instance, if an information extraction system is confronted with passage (18.3),

(18.3) First Union Corp is continuing to wrestle with severe problems
        unleashed by a botched merger and a troubled business strategy.
        According to industry insiders at Paine Webber, their president, John
        R. Georgius, is planning to retire by the end of the year.

it must correctly identify *First Union Corp* as the denotation of *their* (as
opposed to *Paine Webber*, for instance) in order to extract the correct event.

Likewise, many text summarization systems employ a procedure for
selecting the important sentences from a source document and using them
to form a summary. Consider, for example, a news article that contains passage (18.3). Such a system might determine that the second sentence is
important enough to be included in the summary, but not the first. However, the second sentence contains a pronoun that is dependent on the first
sentence, so it cannot place the second sentence in the summary without first
determining the pronoun's denotation, as the pronoun would otherwise likely
receive a different interpretation within the summary. Similarly, natural language generation systems (see Chapter 20) must have adequate models for
pronominalization to produce coherent and interpretable discourse. In short,
just about any conceivable language processing application requires methods
for determining the denotations of pronouns and related expressions.

18.1   REFERENCE RESOLUTION

In this section we study the problem of **reference**, the process by which   REFERENCE
speakers use expressions like *John* and *he* in passage (18.1) to denote a person named John. Our discussion requires that we first define some terminology. A natural language expression used to perform reference is called a
referring expression, and the entity that is referred to is called the **referent**.   REFERRING
                                                                                           EXPRESSION
Thus, *John* and *he* in passage (18.1) are referring expressions, and John is   REFERENT
their referent. (To distinguish between referring expressions and their referents, we italicize the former.) As a convenient shorthand, we will sometimes

speak of a referring expression referring to a referent, e.g., we might say that *he* refers to John. However, the reader should keep in mind that what we really mean is that the speaker is performing the act of referring to John by uttering *he*. Two referring expressions that are used to refer to the same

COREFER

entity are said to **corefer**, thus *John* and *he* corefer in passage (18.1). There is also a term for a referring expression that licenses the use of another, in the way that the mention of *John* allows John to be subsequently referred to

ANTECEDENT

using *he*. We call *John* the **antecedent** of *he*. Reference to an entity that

ANAPHORA

has been previously introduced into the discourse is called **anaphora**, and

ANAPHORIC

the referring expression used is said to be **anaphoric**. In passage (18.1), the pronouns *he* and *it* are therefore anaphoric.

Natural languages provide speakers with a variety of ways to refer to entities. Say that your friend has an Acura Integra automobile and you want

DISCOURSE
CONTEXT

to refer to it. Depending on the operative **discourse context**, you might say *it, this, that, this car, that car, the car, the Acura, the Integra,* or *my friend's car*, among many other possibilities. However, you are not free to choose between any of these alternatives in any context. For instance, you cannot simply say *it* or *the Acura* if the hearer has no prior knowledge of your friend's car, it has not been mentioned before, and it is not in the immediate

SITUATIONAL
CONTEXT

surroundings of the discourse participants (i.e., the **situational context** of the discourse).

The reason for this is that each type of referring expression encodes different signals about the place that the speaker believes the referent occupies within the hearer's set of beliefs. A subset of these beliefs that has a special status form the hearer's mental model of the ongoing discourse, which

DISCOURSE
MODEL

we call a **discourse model** (Webber, 1978). The discourse model contains representations of the entities that have been referred to in the discourse and the relationships in which they participate. Thus, there are two components required by a system to successfully produce and interpret referring expressions: a method for constructing a discourse model that evolves with the dynamically-changing discourse it represents, and a method for mapping between the signals that various referring expressions encode and the hearer's set of beliefs, the latter of which includes this discourse model.

We will speak in terms of two fundamental operations to the discourse model. When a referent is first mentioned in a discourse, we say that a rep-

EVOKED

resentation for it is **evoked** into the model. Upon subsequent mention, this

ACCESSED

representation is **accessed** from the model. The operations and relationships are illustrated in Figure 18.1.

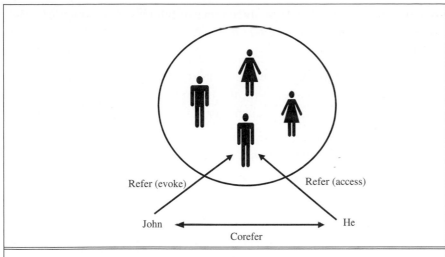

Figure 18.1   Reference operations and relationships.

We will restrict our discussion to reference to entities, although discourses include reference to many other types of referents. Consider the possibilities in example (18.4), adapted from Webber (1991).

(18.4) According to John, Bob bought Sue an Integra, and Sue bought Fred a Legend.

     a. But *that* turned out to be a lie.

     b. But *that* was false.

     c. *That* struck me as a funny way to describe the situation.

     d. *That* caused Sue to become rather poor.

     e. *That* caused them both to become rather poor.

The referent of *that* is a speech act (see Chapter 19) in (18.4a), a proposition in (18.4b), a manner of description in (18.4c), an event in (18.4d), and a combination of several events in (18.4e). The field awaits the development of robust methods for interpreting these types of reference.

Reference Phenomena

The set of referential phenomena that natural languages provide is quite rich indeed. In this section, we provide a brief description of several basic reference phenomena. We first survey five types of referring expression: *indefinite noun phrases*, *definite noun phrases*, *pronouns*, *demonstratives*, and *one-anaphora*. We then describe three types of referents that complicate the reference resolution problem: *inferrables*, *discontinuous sets*, and *generics*.

Indefinite Noun Phrases   Indefinite reference introduces entities that are new to the hearer into the discourse context. The most common form of indefinite reference is marked with the determiner *a* (or *an*), as in (18.5), but it can also be marked by a quantifier such as *some* (18.6) or even the determiner *this* (18.7).

(18.5) I saw *an Acura Integra* today.

(18.6) *Some Acura Integras* were being unloaded at the local dealership today.

(18.7) I saw *this awesome Acura Integra* today.

Such noun phrases evoke a representation for a new entity that satisfies the given description into the discourse model.

The indefinite determiner *a* does not indicate whether the entity is identifiable to the speaker, which in some cases leads to a *specific/non-specific* ambiguity. Example (18.5) only has the specific reading, since the speaker has a particular Integra in mind, particularly the one she saw. In sentence (18.8), on the other hand, both readings are possible.

(18.8) I am going to the dealership to buy an Acura Integra today.

That is, the speaker may already have the Integra picked out (specific), or may just be planning to pick one out that is to her liking (nonspecific). The readings may be disambiguated by a subsequent referring expression in some contexts; if this expression is definite then the reading is specific (*I hope they still have it*), and if it is indefinite then the reading is nonspecific (*I hope they have a car I like*). This rule has exceptions, however; for instance definite expressions in certain modal contexts (*I will park it in my garage*) are compatible with the nonspecific reading.

Definite Noun Phrases   Definite reference is used to refer to an entity that is identifiable to the hearer, either because it has already been mentioned in the discourse context (and thus is represented in the discourse model), it is contained in the hearer's set of beliefs about the world, or the uniqueness of the object is implied by the description itself.

The case in which the referent is identifiable from discourse context is shown in example (18.9).

(18.9) I saw an Acura Integra today. *The Integra* was white and needed to be washed.

Examples in which the referent is either identifiable from the hearer's set of beliefs or is inherently unique are shown in (18.10) and (18.11) respectively.

(18.10) *The Indianapolis 500* is the most popular car race in the US.

(18.11) *The fastest car in the Indianapolis 500* was an Integra.

Definite noun phrase reference requires that an entity be accessed from either the discourse model or the hearer's set of beliefs about the world. In the latter case, it also evokes a representation of the referent into the discourse model.

Pronouns   Another form of definite reference is pronominalization, illustrated in example (18.12).

(18.12) I saw an Acura Integra today. *It* was white and needed to be washed.

The constraints on using pronominal reference are stronger than for full definite noun phrases, requiring that the referent have a high degree of activation or **salience** in the discourse model. Pronouns usually (but not always) refer SALIENCE to entities that were introduced no further than one or two sentences back in the ongoing discourse, whereas definite noun phrases can often refer further back. This is illustrated by the difference between sentences (18.13d) and (18.13d').

(18.13) a. John went to Bob's party, and parked next to a beautiful Acura Integra.
         b. He went inside and talked to Bob for more than an hour.
         c. Bob told him that he recently got engaged.
         d. ?? He also said that he bought *it* yesterday.
         d.' He also said that he bought *the Acura* yesterday.

By the time the last sentence is reached, the Integra no longer has the degree of salience required to allow for pronominal reference to it.

Pronouns can also participate in **cataphora**, in which they are men- CATAPHORA tioned before their referents are, as in example (18.14).

(18.14) Before *he* bought *it*, John checked over the Integra very carefully.

Here, the pronouns *he* and *it* both occur *before* their referents are introduced.

Pronouns also appear in quantified contexts in which they are considered to be **bound**, as in example (18.15).   BOUND

(18.15) Every woman bought *her* Acura at the local dealership.

Under the relevant reading, *her* does not refer to some woman in context, but instead behaves like a variable bound to the quantified expression *every woman*. We will not be concerned with the bound interpretation of pronouns in this chapter.

Demonstratives   Demonstrative pronouns, like *this* and *that*, behave somewhat differently than simple definite pronouns like *it*. They can appear either alone or as determiners, for instance, *this Acura*, *that Acura*. The choice between two demonstratives is generally associated with some notion of spatial proximity: *this* indicating closeness and *that* signaling distance. Spatial distance might be measured with respect to the discourse participants' situational context, as in example (18.16).

(18.16) [John shows Bob an Acura Integra and a Mazda Miata]
         Bob (pointing): I like *this* better than *that*.

Alternatively, distance can be metaphorically interpreted in terms of conceptual relations in the discourse model. For instance, consider example (18.17).

(18.17) I bought an Integra yesterday. It's similar to the one I bought five
         years ago. *That one* was really nice, but I like *this one* even better.

Here, *that one* refers to the Acura bought five years ago (greater temporal distance), whereas *this one* refers to the one bought yesterday (closer temporal distance).

One Anaphora   *One*-anaphora, exemplified in (18.18), blends properties of definite and indefinite reference.

(18.18) I saw no less than 6 Acura Integras today. Now I want *one*.

This use of *one* can be roughly paraphrased by *one of them*, in which *them* refers to a plural referent (or generic one, as in the case of (18.18), see below), and *one* selects a member from this set (Webber, 1983). Thus, *one* may evoke a new entity into the discourse model, but it is necessarily dependent on an existing referent for the description of this new entity.

This use of *one* should be distinguished from the formal, non-specific pronoun usage in (18.19), and its meaning as the number one in (18.20).

(18.19) One shouldn't pay more than twenty thousand dollars for an Acura.

(18.20) John has two Acuras, but I only have one.

Inferrables   Now that we have described several types of referring expressions, we now turn our attention to a few interesting types of referents that complicate the reference resolution problem. First, we consider cases in which a referring expression does not refer to an entity that has been explicitly evoked in the text, but instead one that is inferentially related to an evoked entity. Such referents are called *inferrables* (Haviland and Clark, 1974; Prince, 1981). Consider the expressions *a door* and *the engine* in sentence (18.21).

(18.21) I almost bought an Acura Integra today, but *a door* had a dent and *the engine* seemed noisy.

The indefinite noun phrase *a door* would normally introduce a new door into the discourse context, but in this case the hearer is to infer something more: that it is not just any door, but one of the doors of the Integra. Similarly, the use of the definite noun phrase *the engine* normally presumes that an engine has been previously evoked or is otherwise uniquely identifiable. Here, no engine has been explicitly mentioned, but the hearer infers that the referent is the engine of the previously mentioned Integra.

Inferrables can also specify the results of processes described by utterances in a discourse. Consider the possible follow-ons (a-c) to sentence (18.22) in the following recipe (from Webber and Baldwin (1992)):

(18.22)   Mix the flour, butter, and water.
          a. Kneed *the dough* until smooth and shiny.
          b. Spread *the paste* over the blueberries.
          c. Stir *the batter* until all lumps are gone.

Any of the expressions *the dough* (a solid), *the batter* (a liquid), and *the paste* (somewhere in between) can be used to refer to the result of the actions described in the first sentence, but all imply different properties of this result.

Discontinuous Sets   In some cases, references using plural referring expressions like *they* and *them* (see page 678) refer to sets of entities that are evoked together, for instance, using another plural expression (*their Acuras*) or a conjoined noun phrase (*John and Mary*):

(18.23) John and Mary love their Acuras. *They* drive *them* all the time.

However, plural references may also refer to sets of entities that have been evoked by discontinuous phrases in the text:

(18.24) John has an Acura, and Mary has a Mazda. *They* drive *them* all the time.

Here, *they* refers to John and Mary, and likewise *them* refers to the Acura and the Mazda. Note also that the second sentence in this case will generally receive what is called a *pairwise* or *respectively* reading, in which John drives the Acura and Mary drives the Mazda, as opposed to the reading in which they both drive both cars.

Generics   Making the reference problem even more complicated is the existence of *generic* reference. Consider example (18.25).

(18.25) I saw no less than 6 Acura Integras today. *They* are the coolest cars.

Here, the most natural reading is not the one in which *they* refers to the particular 6 Integras mentioned in the first sentence, but instead to the class of Integras in general.

Syntactic and Semantic Constraints on Coreference

Having described a variety of reference phenomena that are found in natural language, we can now consider how one might develop algorithms for identifying the referents of referential expressions. One step that needs to be taken in any successful reference resolution algorithm is to filter the set of possible referents on the basis of certain relatively hard-and-fast constraints. We describe some of these constraints here.

Number Agreement   Referring expressions and their referents must agree in number; for English, this means distinguishing between *singular* and *plural* references. A categorization of pronouns with respect to number is shown in Figure 18.2.

Singular	Plural	Unspecified
she, her, he, him, his, it	we, us, they, them	you

Figure 18.2   Number agreement in the English pronominal system.

The following examples illustrate constraints on number agreement.

(18.26) John has a new Acura. It is red.

(18.27) John has three new Acuras. They are red.

(18.28) * John has a new Acura. They are red.

(18.29) * John has three new Acuras. It is red.

Person and Case Agreement   English distinguishes between three forms of person: first, second, and third. A categorization of pronouns with respect to person is shown in Figure 18.3.

The following examples illustrate constraints on person agreement.

(18.30) You and I have Acuras. We love them.

	First	Second	Third
Nominative	I, we	you	he, she, they
Accusative	me, us	you	him, her, them
Genitive	my, our	your	his, her, their

Figure 18.3   Person and case agreement in the English pronominal system.

(18.31) John and Mary have Acuras. They love them.

(18.32) * John and Mary have Acuras. We love them. (where *We*=John and Mary)

(18.33) * You and I have Acuras. They love them. (where *They*=You and I)

In addition, English pronouns are constrained by case agreement; different forms of the pronoun may be required when placed in subject position (nominative case, e.g., *he, she, they*), object position (accusative case, e.g., *him, her, them*), and genitive position (genitive case, e.g., *his Acura, her Acura, their Acura*). This categorization is also shown in Figure 18.3.

Gender Agreement   Referents also must agree with the gender specified by the referring expression. English third person pronouns distinguish between *male*, *female*, and *nonpersonal* genders, and unlike some languages, the first two only apply to animate entities. Some examples are shown in Figure 18.4.

masculine	feminine	nonpersonal
he, him, his	she, her	it

Figure 18.4   Gender agreement in the English pronominal system.

The following examples illustrate constraints on gender agreement.

(18.34) John has an Acura. He is attractive. (he=John, not the Acura)

(18.35) John has an Acura. It is attractive. (it=the Acura, not John)

Syntactic Constraints   Reference relations may also be constrained by the syntactic relationships between a referential expression and a possible antecedent noun phrase when both occur in the same sentence. For instance, the pronouns in all of the following sentences are subject to the constraints indicated in brackets.

(18.36) John bought himself a new Acura. [himself=John]

(18.37) John bought him a new Acura. [him≠John]

(18.38) John said that Bill bought him a new Acura. [him≠Bill]

(18.39) John said that Bill bought himself a new Acura. [himself=Bill]

(18.40) He said that he bought John a new Acura. [He≠John; he≠John]

REFLEXIVES
        English pronouns such as *himself, herself*, and *themselves* are called
reflexives. Oversimplifying the situation considerably, a reflexive corefers
with the subject of the most immediate clause that contains it (ex. 18.36),
whereas a nonreflexive cannot corefer with this subject (ex. 18.37). That
this rule applies only for the subject of the most immediate clause is shown
by examples (18.38) and (18.39), in which the opposite reference pattern is
manifest between the pronoun and the subject of the higher sentence. On the
other hand, a full noun phrase like *John* cannot corefer with the subject of
the most immediate clause nor with a higher-level subject (ex. 18.40).

        Whereas these syntactic constraints apply to a referring expression
and a particular potential antecedent noun phrase, these constraints actually
prohibit coreference between the two regardless of any other available antecedents that denote the same entity. For instance, normally a nonreflexive
pronoun like *him* can corefer with the subject of the previous sentence as
it does in example (18.41), but it cannot in example (18.42) because of its
syntactic relationship with the coreferential pronoun *he* in the second clause.

(18.41) John wanted a new car. Bill bought him a new Acura. [him=John]

(18.42) John wanted a new car. He bought him a new Acura. [he=John;
         him≠John]

These rules oversimplify the situation in a number of ways, and there
are many cases that they do not cover. Indeed, upon further inspection the
facts actually get quite complicated. In fact, it is unlikely that all of the
data can be explained using only syntactic relations (Kuno, 1987). For instance, the reflexive *himself* and the nonreflexive *him* in sentences (18.43)
and (18.44) respectively can both refer to the subject *John*, even though they
occur in identical syntactic configurations.

(18.43) John set the pamphlets about Acuras next to himself.
         [himself=John]

(18.44) John set the pamphlets about Acuras next to him. [him=John]

For the algorithms discussed later in this chapter, however, we will assume a
syntactic account of restrictions on intrasentential coreference.

Selectional Restrictions   The selectional restrictions that a verb places on
its arguments (see Chapter 16) may be responsible for eliminating referents,
as in example (18.45).

(18.45) John parked his Acura in the garage. He had driven it around for
        hours.

There are two possible referents for *it*, the Acura and the garage. The verb
drive, however, requires that its direct object denote something that can be
driven, such as a car, truck, or bus, but not a garage. Thus, the fact that the
pronoun appears as the object of *drive* restricts the set of possible referents
to the Acura. It is conceivable that a practical NLP system would include a
reasonably comprehensive set of selectional constraints for the verbs in its
lexicon.

   Selectional restrictions can be violated in the case of metaphor (see
Chapter 16); for example, consider example (18.46).

(18.46) John bought a new Acura. It drinks gasoline like you would not
        believe.

While the verb *drink* does not usually take an inanimate subject, its metaphorical use here allows *it* to refer to *a new Acura*.

   Of course, there are more general semantic constraints that may come
into play, but these are much more difficult to encode in a comprehensive
manner. Consider passage (18.47).

(18.47) John parked his Acura in the garage. It is incredibly messy, with
        old bike and car parts lying around everywhere.

Here the referent of *it* is almost certainly the garage, due in part to the fact
that a car is probably too small to have bike and car parts laying around "ev-
erywhere". Resolving this reference requires that a system have knowledge
about how large cars typically are, how large garages typically are, and the
typical types of objects one might find in each. On the other hand, one's
knowledge about Beverly Hills might lead one to assume that the Acura is
indeed the referent of *it* in passage (18.48).

(18.48) John parked his Acura in downtown Beverly Hills. It is incredibly
        messy, with old bike and car parts lying around everywhere.

In the end, just about any knowledge shared by the discourse participants
might be necessary to resolve a pronoun reference. However, due in part to
the vastness of such knowledge, practical algorithms typically do not rely on
it heavily.

Preferences in Pronoun Interpretation

In the previous section, we discussed relatively strict constraints that algorithms should apply when determining possible referents for referring ex-

pressions. We now discuss some more readily violated *preferences* that algorithms can be made to account for. These preferences have been posited to apply to pronoun interpretation in particular. Since the majority of work on reference resolution algorithms has focused on pronoun interpretation, we will similarly focus on this problem in the remainder of this section.

Recency   Most theories of reference incorporate the notion that entities introduced in recent utterances are more salient than those introduced from utterances further back. Thus, in example (18.49), the pronoun *it* is more likely to refer to the Legend than the Integra.

(18.49) John has an Integra. Bill has a Legend. Mary likes to drive it.

Grammatical Role   Many theories specify a salience hierarchy of entities that is ordered by the grammatical position of the expressions which denote them. These typically treat entities mentioned in subject position as more salient than those in object position, which are in turn more salient than those mentioned in subsequent positions.

Passages such as (18.50) and (18.51) lend support for such a hierarchy. Although the first sentence in each case expresses roughly the same propositional content, the preferred referent for the pronoun *him* varies with the subject in each case – John in (18.50) and Bill in (18.51). In example (18.52), the references to John and Bill are conjoined within the subject position. Since both seemingly have the same degree of salience, it is unclear to which the pronoun refers.

(18.50) John went to the Acura dealership with Bill. He bought an Integra.
         [he = John]

(18.51) Bill went to the Acura dealership with John. He bought an Integra.
         [he = Bill]

(18.52) John and Bill went to the Acura dealership. He bought an Integra.
         [he = ??].

Repeated Mention   Some theories incorporate the idea that entities that have been focused on in the prior discourse are more likely to continue to be focused on in subsequent discourse, and hence references to them are more likely to be pronominalized. For instance, whereas the pronoun in example (18.51) has Bill as its preferred interpretation, the pronoun in the final sentence of example (18.53) is more likely to refer to John.

(18.53) John needed a car to get to his new job. He decided that he wanted
         something sporty. Bill went to the Acura dealership with him. He
         bought an Integra. [he = John]

Parallelism   There are also strong preferences that appear to be induced by parallelism effects, as in example (18.54).

(18.54) Mary went with Sue to the Acura dealership. Sally went with her
to the Mazda dealership. [her = Sue]

The grammatical role hierarchy described above ranks Mary as more salient than Sue, and thus should be the preferred referent of *her*. Furthermore, there is no semantic reason that Mary cannot be the referent. Nonetheless, *her* is instead understood to refer to Sue.

This suggests that we might want a heuristic which says that non-subject pronouns prefer non-subject referents. However, such a heuristic may not work for cases that lack the structural parallelism of example (18.54), such as example (18.55), in which Mary is the preferred referent of the pronoun instead of Sue.

(18.55) Mary went with Sue to the Acura dealership. Sally told her not to
buy anything. [her = Mary]

Verb Semantics   Certain verbs appear to place a semantically-oriented emphasis on one of their argument positions, which can have the effect of biasing the manner in which subsequent pronouns are interpreted. Compare sentences (18.56) and (18.57).

(18.56) John telephoned Bill. He lost the pamphlet on Acuras.

(18.57) John criticized Bill. He lost the pamphlet on Acuras.

These examples differ only in the verb used in the first sentence, yet the subject pronoun in passage (18.56) is typically resolved to John, whereas the pronoun in passage (18.57) is resolved to Bill. Some researchers have claimed that this effect results from what has been called the "implicit causality" of a verb: the implicit cause of a "criticizing" event is considered to be its object, whereas the implicit cause of a "telephoning" event is considered to be its subject. This emphasis results in a higher degree of salience for the entity in this argument position, which leads to the different preferences for examples (18.56) and (18.57).

Similar preferences have been articulated in terms of the thematic roles (see Chapter 16) that the potential antecedents occupy. For example, most hearers resolve *He* to John in example (18.58) and to Bill in example (18.59). Although these referents are evoked from different grammatical role positions, they both fill the Goal thematic role of their corresponding verbs, whereas the other potential referent fills the Source role. Likewise, hearers generally resolve *He* to John and Bill in examples (18.60) and (18.61) respectively, providing evidence that fillers of the Stimulus role are preferred over fillers of the Experiencer role.

(18.58) John seized the Acura pamphlet from Bill. He loves reading about cars. (Goal=John, Source=Bill)

(18.59) John passed the Acura pamphlet to Bill. He loves reading about cars. (Goal=Bill, Source=John)

(18.60) The car dealer admired John. He knows Acuras inside and out. (Stimulus=John, Experiencer=the car dealer)

(18.61) The car dealer impressed John. He knows Acuras inside and out. (Stimulus=the car dealer, Experiencer=John)

An Algorithm for Pronoun Resolution

None of the algorithms for pronoun resolution that have been proposed to date successfully account for all of these preferences, let alone succeed in resolving the contradictions that will arise between them. However, Lappin and Leass (1994) describe a straightforward algorithm for pronoun interpretation that takes many of these into consideration. The algorithm employs a simple weighting scheme that integrates the effects of the recency and syntactically-based preferences; no semantic preferences are employed beyond those enforced by agreement. We describe a slightly simplified portion of the algorithm that applies to non-reflexive, third person pronouns.

Broadly speaking, there are two types of operations performed by the algorithm: discourse model update and pronoun resolution. First, when a noun phrase that evokes a new entity is encountered, a representation for it must be added to the discourse model and a degree of salience (which we call a **salience value**) computed for it. The salience value is calculated as the sum of the weights assigned by a set of **salience factors**. The salience factors used and their corresponding weights are shown in Figure 18.5.

SALIENCE
VALUE
SALIENCE
FACTORS

The weights that each factor assigns to an entity in the discourse model are cut in half each time a new sentence is processed. This, along with the added effect of the sentence recency weight (which initially assigns a weight of 100, to be cut in half with each succeeding sentence), captures the Recency preference described on page 682, since referents mentioned in the current sentence will tend to have higher weights than those in the previous sentence, which will in turn be higher than those in the sentence before that, and so forth.

Sentence recency	100
Subject emphasis	80
Existential emphasis	70
Accusative (direct object) emphasis	50
Indirect object and oblique complement emphasis	40
Non-adverbial emphasis	50
Head noun emphasis	80

Figure 18.5   Salience factors in Lappin and Leass's system.

Similarly, the next five factors in Figure 18.5 can be viewed as a way of encoding a grammatical role preference scheme using the following hierarchy:

> subject > existential predicate nominal > object > indirect object or oblique > demarcated adverbial PP

These five positions are exemplified by the position of the italicized phrases in examples (18.62)–(18.66) respectively.

(18.62) *An Acura Integra* is parked in the lot. (subject)

(18.63) There is *an Acura Integra* parked in the lot. (existential predicate nominal)

(18.64) John parked *an Acura Integra* in the lot. (object)

(18.65) John gave *his Acura Integra* a bath. (indirect object)

(18.66) Inside *his Acura Integra*, John showed Susan his new CD player. (demarcated adverbial PP)

The preference against referents in demarcated adverbial PPs (i.e., those separated by punctuation, as with the comma in example (18.66)) is encoded as a positive weight of 50 for every other position, listed as the non-adverbial emphasis weight in Figure 18.5. This ensures that the weight for any referent is always positive, which is necessary so that the effect of halving the weights is always to reduce them.

The head noun emphasis factor penalizes referents which are embedded in larger noun phrases, again by promoting the weights of referents that are not. Thus, the Acura Integra in each of examples (18.62)–(18.66) will receive 80 points for being denoted by a head noun, whereas the Acura Integra in example (18.67) will not, since it is embedded within the subject noun phrase.

(18.67) The owner's manual for *an Acura Integra* is on John's desk.

Each of these factors contributes to the salience of a referent based on the properties of the noun phrase that denotes it. Of course, it could be that several noun phrases in the preceding discourse refer to the same referent, each being assigned a different level of salience, and thus we need a way in which to combine the contributions of each. To address this, Lappin and Leass associate with each referent an equivalence class that contains all of the noun phrases that have been determined to refer to it. The weight that a salience factor assigns to a referent is the highest of the weights it assigns to the members of its equivalence class. The salience weight for a referent is then calculated by summing the weights for each factor. The scope of a salience factor is a sentence, so, for instance, if a potential referent is mentioned in the current sentence as well as the previous one, the sentence recency weight will be factored in for each. (On the other hand, if the same referent is mentioned more than once in the same sentence, this weight will be counted only once.) Thus, multiple mentions of a referent in the prior discourse can potentially increase its salience, which has the effect of encoding the preference for repeated mentions discussed on page 682.

Once we have updated the discourse model with new potential referents and recalculated the salience values associated with them, we are ready to consider the process of resolving any pronouns that exist within a new sentence. In doing this, we factor in two more salience weights, one for grammatical role parallelism between the pronoun and the potential referent, and one to disprefer cataphoric reference. The weights are shown in Figure 18.6. Unlike the other preferences, these two cannot be calculated independently of the pronoun, and thus cannot be calculated during the discourse model update step. We will use the term *initial salience value* for the weight of a given referent before these factors are applied, and the term *final salience value* for after they have applied.

Role Parallelism	35
Cataphora	-175

Figure 18.6   Per pronoun salience weights in Lappin and Leass's system.

We are now ready to specify the pronoun resolution algorithm. Assuming that the discourse model has been updated to reflect the initial salience values of referents as described above, the steps taken to resolve a pronoun are as follows:

1. Collect the potential referents (up to four sentences back).

2. Remove potential referents that do not agree in number or gender with the pronoun.

3. Remove potential referents that do not pass intrasentential syntactic coreference constraints (as described on page 679).

4. Compute the total salience value of the referent by adding any applicable values from Figure 18.6 to the existing salience value previously computed during the discourse model update step (i.e., the sum of the applicable values in Figure 18.5).

5. Select the referent with the highest salience value. In the case of ties, select the closest referent in terms of string position (computed without bias to direction).

We illustrate the operation of the algorithm by stepping through example (18.68).

(18.68) John saw a beautiful Acura Integra at the dealership. He showed it to Bob. He bought it.

We first process the first sentence to collect potential referents and compute their initial salience values. The following table shows the contribution to salience of each of the salience factors.

	Rec	Subj	Exist	Obj	Ind-Obj	Non-Adv	Head N	Total
John	100	80				50	80	310
Integra	100			50		50	80	280
dealership	100					50	80	230

There are no pronouns to be resolved in this sentence, so we move on to the next, degrading the above values by a factor of two as shown in the table below. The *phrases* column shows the equivalence class of referring expressions for each referent.

Referent	Phrases	Value
John	{ *John* }	155
Integra	{ *a beautiful Acura Integra* }	140
dealership	{ *the dealership* }	115

The first noun phrase in the second sentence is the pronoun *he*. Because *he* specifies male gender, Step 2 of the resolution algorithm reduces the set of possible referents to include only John, so we can stop there and take this to be the referent.

The discourse model must now be updated. First, the pronoun *he* is added in the equivalence class for John (denoted as he_1, to differentiate it from possible other mentions of *he*). Since *he* occurs in the current sentence and *John* in the previous one, the salience factors do not overlap between the two. The pronoun is in the current sentence (recency=100), subject position (=80), not in an adverbial (=50), and not embedded (=80), and so a total of 310 is added to the current weight for John:

Referent	Phrases	Value
John	{ *John*, he_1 }	465
Integra	{ *a beautiful Acura Integra* }	140
dealership	{ *the dealership* }	115

The next noun phrase in the second sentence is the pronoun *it*, which is compatible with the Integra or the dealership. We first need to compute the final salience values by adding the applicable weights from Figure 18.6 to the initial salience values above. Neither referent assignment would result in cataphora, so that factor does not apply. For the parallelism preference, both *it* and *a beautiful Acura Integra* are in object position within their respective sentences (whereas *the dealership* is not), so a weight of 35 is added to this option. With the Integra having a weight of 175 and the dealership a weight of 115, the Integra is taken to be the referent.

Again, the discourse model must now be updated. Since *it* is in a nonembedded object position, it receives a weight of 100+50+50+80=280, and is added to the current weight for the Integra.

Referent	Phrases	Value
John	{ *John*, he_1 }	465
Integra	{ *a beautiful Acura Integra*, it_1 }	420
dealership	{ *the dealership* }	115

The final noun phrase in the second sentence is *Bob*, which introduces a new discourse referent. Since it occupies an oblique argument position, it receives a weight of 100+40+50+80=270.

Referent	Phrases	Value
John	{ *John*, he_1 }	465
Integra	{ *a beautiful Acura Integra*, it_1 }	420
Bob	{ *Bob* }	270
dealership	{ *the dealership* }	115

Now we are ready to move on to the final sentence. We again degrade the current weights by one half.

Referent	Phrases	Value
John	{ *John, he*$_1$ }	232.5
Integra	{ *a beautiful Acura Integra, it*$_1$ }	210
Bob	{ *Bob* }	135
dealership	{ *the dealership* }	57.5

The reader can confirm that the referent of *he* will be resolved to John, and the referent of *it* to the Integra.

The weights used by Lappin and Leass were arrived at by experimentation on a development corpus of computer training manuals. This algorithm, when combined with several filters not described here, achieved 86% accuracy when applied to unseen test data within the same genre. It is possible that these exact weights may not be optimal for other genres (and even more so for other languages), so the reader may want to experiment with these on training data for a new application or language.

In Exercise 18.7, we consider a version of the algorithm that relies only on a noun phrase identifier (see also Kennedy and Boguraev (1996)). In the next paragraphs, we briefly summarize two other approaches to pronoun resolution.

A Tree Search Algorithm   Hobbs (1978) describes an algorithm for pronoun resolution which takes the syntactic representations of the sentences up to and including the current sentence as input, and performs a search for an antecedent noun phrase on these trees. There is no explicit representation of a discourse model or preferences as in the Lappin and Leass algorithm. However, certain of these preferences are approximated by the order in which the search on syntactic trees is performed.

An algorithm that searches parse trees must also specify a grammar, since the assumptions regarding the structure of syntactic trees will affect the results. A fragment for English that the algorithm uses is given in Figure 18.7. The steps of the algorithm are as follows:

1. Begin at the noun phrase (NP) node immediately dominating the pronoun.

2. Go up the tree to the first NP or sentence (S) node encountered. Call this node X, and call the path used to reach it *p*.

3. Traverse all branches below node X to the left of path *p* in a left-to-right, breadth-first fashion. Propose as the antecedent any NP node that is encountered which has an NP or S node between it and X.

4. If node X is the highest S node in the sentence, traverse the surface parse trees of previous sentences in the text in order of recency, the

$$S \rightarrow NP\ VP$$

$$NP \rightarrow \left\{ \begin{array}{l} (Det)\quad Nominal \\ pronoun \end{array} \right. \left(\left\{ \begin{array}{l} PP \\ Rel \end{array} \right\} \right)^{*} \Big\}$$

$$Det \rightarrow \left\{ \begin{array}{l} determiner \\ NP\ 's \end{array} \right\}$$

$$PP \rightarrow preposition\ NP$$

$$Nominal \rightarrow noun\ (PP)^{*}$$

$$Rel \rightarrow wh\text{-}word\ S$$

$$VP \rightarrow verb\ NP\ (PP)^{*}$$

Figure 18.7   A grammar fragment for the Tree Search algorithm.

most recent first; each tree is traversed in a left-to-right, breadth-first manner, and when an NP node is encountered, it is proposed as antecedent. If X is not the highest S node in the sentence, continue to step 5.

5. From node X, go up the tree to the first NP or S node encountered. Call this new node X, and call the path traversed to reach it p.

6. If X is an NP node and if the path p to X did not pass through the Nominal node that X immediately dominates, propose X as the antecedent.

7. Traverse all branches below node X to the *left* of path p in a left-to-right, breadth-first manner. Propose any NP node encountered as the antecedent.

8. If X is an S node, traverse all branches of node X to the *right* of path p in a left-to-right, breadth-first manner, but do not go below any NP or S node encountered. Propose any NP node encountered as the antecedent.

9. Go to Step 4.

Demonstrating that this algorithm yields the correct coreference assignments for example (18.68) is left as Exercise 18.3.

As stated, the algorithm depends on complete and correct syntactic structures as input. Hobbs evaluated his approach manually (with respect to both parse construction and algorithm implementation) on one hundred examples from each of three different texts, reporting an accuracy of 88.3%. (The accuracy increases to 91.7% if certain selectional restriction constraints are assumed.) Lappin and Leass encoded a version of this algorithm within their system, and reported an accuracy of 82% on their test corpus. Although this is less than the 86% accuracy achieved by their own algorithm, it should be borne in mind that the test data Lappin and Leass used was from the same genre as their development set, but different than the genres that Hobbs used in developing his algorithm.

A Centering Algorithm   As we described above, the Hobbs algorithm does not use an explicit representation of a discourse model. The Lappin and Leass algorithm does, but encodes salience as a weighted combination of preferences. Centering theory (Grosz et al., 1995, henceforth GJW), also has an explicit representation of a discourse model, and incorporates an additional claim: that there is a single entity being "centered" on at any given point in the discourse which is to be distinguished from all other entities that have been evoked.

There are two main representations tracked in the discourse model. In what follows, take U_n and U_{n+1} to be two adjacent utterances. The *backward looking center* of U_n, denoted as $C_b(U_n)$, represents the entity currently being focused on in the discourse after U_n is interpreted. The *forward looking centers* of U_n, denoted as $C_f(U_n)$, form an ordered list containing the entities mentioned in U_n, all of which could serve as the C_b of the following utterance. In fact, $C_b(U_{n+1})$ is by definition the most highly ranked element of $C_f(U_n)$ mentioned in U_{n+1}. (The C_b of the first utterance in a discourse is undefined.) As for how the entities in the $C_f(U_n)$ are ordered, for simplicity's sake we can use the grammatical role hierarchy encoded by (a subset of) the weights in the Lappin and Leass algorithm, repeated below.[1]

> subject > existential predicate nominal > object > indirect object or oblique > demarcated adverbial PP

Unlike the Lappin and Leass algorithm, however, there are no numerical weights attached to the entities on the list, they are simply ordered relative to each other. As a shorthand, we will call the highest-ranked forward-looking center C_p (for "preferred center").

We describe a centering-based algorithm for pronoun interpretation due to Brennan et al. (1987, henceforth BFP). (See also Walker et al. (1994); for other centering algorithms, see Kameyama (1986) and Strube and Hahn (1996), inter alia.) In this algorithm, preferred referents of pronouns are computed from relations that hold between the forward and backward looking centers in adjacent sentences. Four intersentential relationships between a pair of utterances U_n and U_{n+1} are defined which depend on the relationship between $C_b(U_{n+1})$, $C_b(U_n)$, and $C_p(U_{n+1})$; these are shown in Figure 18.8.

---

[1]   This is an extended form of the hierarchy used in Brennan et al. (1987), described below.

	$C_b(U_{n+1}) = C_b(U_n)$ or undefined $C_b(U_n)$	$C_b(U_{n+1}) \neq C_b(U_n)$
$C_b(U_{n+1}) = C_p(U_{n+1})$	Continue	Smooth-Shift
$C_b(U_{n+1}) \neq C_p(U_{n+1})$	Retain	Rough-Shift

Figure 18.8   Transitions in the BFP algorithm.

The following rules are used by the algorithm:

- Rule 1: If any element of $C_f(U_n)$ is realized by a pronoun in utterance U_{n+1}, then $C_b(U_{n+1})$ must be realized as a pronoun also.
- Rule 2: Transition states are ordered. Continue is preferred to Retain is preferred to Smooth-Shift is preferred to Rough-Shift.

Having defined these concepts and rules, the algorithm is defined as follows.

1. Generate possible C_b-C_f combinations for each possible set of reference assignments .
2. Filter by constraints, e.g., syntactic coreference constraints, selectional restrictions, centering rules and constraints.
3. Rank by transition orderings.

The pronominal referents that get assigned are those which yield the most preferred relation in Rule 2, assuming that Rule 1 and other coreference constraints (gender, number, syntactic, selectional restrictions) are not violated.

Let us step through passage (18.68), repeated below as (18.69), to illustrate the algorithm.

(18.69)   John saw a beautiful Acura Integra at the dealership. (U_1)
          He showed it to Bob. (U_2)
          He bought it. (U_3)

Using the grammatical role hierarchy to order the C_f, for sentence U_1 we get:

$C_f(U_1)$: {John, Integra, dealership}
$C_p(U_1)$: John
$C_b(U_1)$: undefined

Sentence U_2 contains two pronouns: *he*, which is compatible with John, and *it*, which is compatible with the Acura or the dealership. John is by definition $C_b(U_2)$, because he is the highest ranked member of $C_f(U_1)$ mentioned in U_2

(since he is the only possible referent for *he*). We compare the resulting transitions for each possible referent of *it*. If we assume *it* refers to the Integra, the assignments would be:

$C_f(U_2)$: {John, Integra, Bob}
$C_p(U_2)$: John
$C_b(U_2)$: John
Result: Continue $(C_p(U_2)=C_b(U_2); C_b(U_1)$ undefined)

If we assume *it* refers to the dealership, the assignments would be:

$C_f(U_2)$: {John, dealership, Bob}
$C_p(U_2)$: John
$C_b(U_2)$: John
Result: Continue $(C_p(U_2)=C_b(U_2); C_b(U_1)$ undefined)

Since both possibilities result in a Continue transition, the algorithm does not say which to accept. For the sake of illustration, we will assume that ties are broken in terms of the ordering on the previous C_f list. Thus, we will take *it* to refer to the Integra instead of the dealership, leaving the current discourse model as represented in the first possibility above.

In sentence U_3, *he* is compatible with either John or Bob, whereas *it* is compatible with the Integra. If we assume *he* refers to John, then John is $C_b(U_3)$ and the assignments would be:

$C_f(U_3)$: {John, Acura}
$C_p(U_3)$: John
$C_b(U_3)$: John
Result: Continue $(C_p(U_3)=C_b(U_3)=C_b(U_2))$

If we assume *he* refers to Bob, then Bob is $C_b(U_3)$ and the assignments would be:

$C_f(U_3)$: {Bob, Acura}
$C_p(U_3)$: Bob
$C_b(U_3)$: Bob
Result: Smooth-Shift $(C_p(U_3)=C_b(U_3); C_b(U_3)\neq C_b(U_2))$

Since a Continue is preferred to a Smooth-Shift per Rule 2, John is correctly taken to be the referent.

The main salience factors that the centering algorithm implicitly incorporates include the grammatical role, recency, and repeated mention preferences. Unlike the Lappin and Leass algorithm, however, the manner in which the grammatical role hierarchy affects salience is indirect, since it is the resulting transition type that determines the final reference assignments. In particular, a referent in a low-ranked grammatical role will be preferred to one in a more highly ranked role if the former leads to a more highly ranked transition. Thus, the centering algorithm may (often, but not always, incorrectly) resolve a pronoun to a referent that other algorithms would consider to be of relatively low salience (Lappin and Leass, 1994; Kehler, 1997a). For instance, in example (18.70),

(18.70) Bob opened up a new dealership last week. John took a look at the Acuras in his lot. He ended up buying one.

the centering algorithm will assign Bob as the referent of the subject pronoun *he* in the third sentence – since Bob is $C_b(U_2)$, this assignment results in a Continue relation whereas assigning John results in a Smooth-Shift relation. On the other hand, the Hobbs and Lappin/Leass algorithms will assign John as the referent.

Like the Hobbs algorithm, the centering algorithm was developed on the assumption that correct syntactic structures are available as input. In order to perform an automatic evaluation on naturally occurring data, the centering algorithm would have to be specified in greater detail, both in terms of how all noun phrases in a sentence are ordered with respect to each other on the C_f list (the current approach only includes nonembedded fillers of certain grammatical roles, generating only a partial ordering), as well as how all pronouns in a sentence can be resolved (e.g., recall the indeterminacy in resolving *it* in the second sentence of example (18.68)).

Walker (1989), however, performed a manual evaluation of the centering algorithm on a corpus of 281 examples distributed over texts from three genres, and compared its performance to the Hobbs algorithm. The evaluation assumed adequate syntactic representations, grammatical role labeling, and selectional restriction information as input. Furthermore, in cases in which the centering algorithm did not uniquely specify a referent, only those cases in which the Hobbs algorithm identified the *correct* one were counted as errors. With this proviso, Walker reports an accuracy of 77.6% for centering and 81.8% for Hobbs. See also Tetreault (1999) for a comparison between several centering-based algorithms and the Hobbs algorithm.

18.2   TEXT COHERENCE

Much of the previous section focussed on the nature of anaphoric reference and methods for resolving pronouns in discourse. Anaphoric expressions have often been called **cohesive devices** (Halliday and Hasan, 1976), since the coreference relations they establish serve to "tie" different parts of a discourse together, thus making it cohesive. While discourses often contain cohesive devices, the existence of such devices alone does not satisfy a stronger requirement that a discourse must meet, that of being *coherent*. In this section, we describe what it means for a text to be coherent, and computational mechanisms for determining coherence.

COHESIVE DEVICES

The Phenomenon

Assume that you have collected an arbitrary set of well-formed and independently interpretable utterances, for instance, by randomly selecting one sentence from each of the previous chapters of this book. Do you have a discourse? Almost certainly not. The reason is that these utterances, when juxtaposed, will not exhibit **coherence**. Consider, for example, the difference between passages (18.71) and (18.72).

COHERENCE

(18.71) John hid Bill's car keys. He was drunk.

(18.72) ?? John hid Bill's car keys. He likes spinach.

While most people find passage (18.71) to be rather unremarkable, they find passage (18.72) to be odd. Why is this so? Like passage (18.71), the sentences that make up passage (18.72) are well formed and readily interpretable. Something instead seems to be wrong with the fact that the sentences are juxtaposed. The hearer might ask, for instance, what hiding someone's car keys has to do with liking spinach. By asking this, the hearer is questioning the coherence of the passage.

Alternatively, the hearer might try to construct an explanation that makes it coherent, for instance, by conjecturing that perhaps someone offered John spinach in exchange for hiding Bill's car keys. In fact, if we consider a context in which we had known this already, the passage now sounds a lot better! Why is this? This conjecture allows the hearer to identify John's liking spinach as the cause of his hiding Bill's car keys, which would explain how the two sentences are connected. The very fact that hearers try to identify such connections is indicative of the need to establish coherence as part of discourse comprehension.

The possible connections between utterances in a discourse can be specified as a set of **coherence relations**. A few such relations, proposed by Hobbs (1979a), are given below. The terms S_0 and S_1 represent the meanings of the two sentences being related.

COHERENCE RELATIONS

Result: Infer that the state or event asserted by S_0 causes or could cause the state or event asserted by S_1.

(18.73) John bought an Acura. His father went ballistic.

Explanation: Infer that the state or event asserted by S_1 causes or could cause the state or event asserted by S_0.

(18.74) John hid Bill's car keys. He was drunk.

Parallel: Infer $p(a_1, a_2, ...)$ from the assertion of S_0 and $p(b_1, b_2, ...)$ from the assertion of S_1, where a_i and b_i are similar, for all i.

(18.75) John bought an Acura. Bill leased a BMW.

Elaboration: Infer the same proposition P from the assertions of S_0 and S_1.

(18.76) John bought an Acura this weekend. He purchased a beautiful new Integra for 20 thousand dollars at Bill's dealership on Saturday afternoon.

Occasion: A change of state can be inferred from the assertion of S_0, whose final state can be inferred from S_1, or a change of state can be inferred from the assertion of S_1, whose initial state can be inferred from S_0.

(18.77) John bought an Acura. He drove to the ballgame.

A mechanism for identifying coherence could support a number of natural language applications, including information extraction and summarization. For example, discourses that are coherent by virtue of the Elaboration relation are often characterized by a summary sentence followed by one or more sentences adding detail to it, as in passage (18.76). Although there are two sentences describing events in this passage, the fact that we infer an Elaboration relation tells us that the same event is being described in each. A mechanism for identifying this fact could tell an information extraction or summarization system to merge the information from the sentences and produce a single event description instead of two.

An Inference Based Resolution Algorithm

Each coherence relation described above is associated with one or more constraints that must be met for it to hold. How can we apply these constraints? To do this, we need a method for performing inference. Perhaps the most familiar type of inference is **deduction**; recall from Section 14.3 that the central rule of deduction is modus ponens:

DEDUCTION

$$\alpha \Rightarrow \beta$$
$$\frac{\alpha}{\beta}$$

An example of modus ponens is the following:

> All Acuras are fast.
> John's car is an Acura.
> _____
> John's car is fast.

Deduction is a form of **sound inference**: if the premises are true, then the conclusion must be true.

SOUND INFERENCE

However, much of language understanding is based on inferences that are not sound. While the ability to draw unsound inferences allows for a greater range of inferences to be made, it can also lead to false interpretations and misunderstandings. A method for such inference is logical **abduction** (Pierce, 1955). The central rule of abductive inference is:

ABDUCTION

$$\alpha \Rightarrow \beta$$
$$\frac{\beta}{\alpha}$$

Whereas deduction runs an implication relation forward, abduction runs it backward, reasoning from an effect to a potential cause. An example of abduction is the following:

> All Acuras are fast.
> John's car is fast.
> _____
> John's car is an Acura.

Obviously, this may be an incorrect inference: John's car may be made by another manufacturer yet still be fast.

In general, a given effect β may have many potential causes α_i. We generally will not want to merely reason from a fact to a *possible* explanation of it, we want to identify the *best* explanation of it. To do this, we need a method for comparing the quality of alternative abductive proofs. There are a variety of strategies one could employ for doing this. One possibility is to use a probabilistic model (Charniak and Goldman, 1988; Charniak and Shimony, 1990), although issues arise in choosing the appropriate space over which to calculate these probabilities, and in finding a way to acquire them given the lack of a corpus of events. Another method is to use a purely heuristic strategy (Charniak and McDermott, 1985, Chapter 10), such as preferring the explanation with the smallest number of assumptions, or choosing the explanation that uses the most specific characteristics of the input. While such heuristics may be easy to implement, they generally prove to be too brittle and limiting. Finally, a more general cost-based strategy can be used which combines features (both positive and negative) of the probabilistic and heuristic approaches. The approach to abductive interpretation we illustrate here, due to Hobbs et al. (1993), uses such a strategy. To simplify the discussion, however, we will largely ignore the cost component of the system, keeping in mind that one is nonetheless necessary.

Hobbs et al. (1993) apply their method to a broad range of problems in language interpretation; here we focus on its use in establishing discourse coherence, in which world and domain knowledge are used to determine the most plausible coherence relation holding between utterances. Let us step through the analysis that leads to establishing the coherence of passage (18.71). First, we need axioms about coherence relations themselves. Axiom (18.78) states that a possible coherence relation is the Explanation relation; other relations would have analogous axioms.

$$(18.78) \qquad \forall e_i, e_j \; Explanation(e_i, e_j) \Rightarrow CoherenceRel(e_i, e_j)$$

The variables e_i and e_j represent the events (or states) denoted by the two utterances being related In this axiom and those given below, quantifiers always scope over everything to their right. This axiom tells us that, given that we need to establish a coherence relation between two events, one possibility is to abductively assume that the relation is Explanation.

The Explanation relation requires that the second utterance express the cause of the effect that the first sentence expresses. We can state this as axiom (18.79).

$$(18.79) \qquad \forall e_i, e_j \; cause(e_j, e_i) \Rightarrow Explanation(e_i, e_j)$$

In addition to axioms about coherence relations, we also need axioms representing general knowledge about the world. The first axiom we use says that if someone is drunk, then others will not want that person to drive, and that the former causes the latter (for convenience, the state of not wanting is denoted by the *diswant* predicate).

$$(18.80) \qquad \begin{aligned} &\forall x, y, e_i \; drunk(e_i, x) \Rightarrow \\ &\quad \exists e_j, e_k \; diswant(e_j, y, e_k) \wedge drive(e_k, x) \wedge cause(e_i, e_j) \end{aligned}$$

Before we move on, a few notes are in order concerning this axiom and the others we will present. First, axiom (18.80) is stated using universal quantifiers to bind several of the variables, which essentially says that in all cases in which someone is drunk, all people do not want that person to drive. Although we might hope that this is generally the case, such a statement is nonetheless too strong. The way in which this is handled in the Hobbs et al. system is by including an additional relation, called an *etc* predicate, in the antecedent of such axioms. An *etc* predicate represents all the other properties that must be true for the axiom to apply, but which are too vague to state explicitly. These predicates therefore cannot be proven, they can only be assumed at a corresponding cost. Because rules with high assumption costs will be dispreferred to ones with low costs, the likelihood that the rule applies can be encoded in terms of this cost. Since we have chosen to simplify our discussion by ignoring costs, we will similarly ignore the use of *etc* predicates.

Second, each predicate has what may look like an "extra" variable in the first argument position; for instance, the *drive* predicate has two arguments instead of one. This variable is used to reify the relationship denoted by the predicate so that it can be referred to from argument places in other predicates. For instance, reifying the *drive* predicate with the variable e_k allows us to express the idea of not wanting someone to drive by referring to it in the final argument of the *diswant* predicate.

Picking up where we left off, the second world knowledge axiom we use says that if someone does not want someone else to drive, then they do not want this person to have his car keys, since car keys enable someone to drive.

$$\forall x,y,e_j,e_k\; diswant(e_j,y,e_k) \wedge drive(e_k,x) \Rightarrow$$
$$\exists z,e_l,e_m\; diswant(e_l,y,e_m) \wedge have(e_m,x,z)$$
$$\wedge carkeys(z,x) \wedge cause(e_j,e_l)$$

(18.81)

The third axiom says that if someone doesn't want someone else to have something, he might hide it from him.

(18.82)
$$\forall x,y,z,e_i,e_j\; diswant(e_l,y,e_m) \wedge have(e_m,x,z) \Rightarrow$$
$$\exists e_n\; hide(e_n,y,x,z) \wedge cause(e_l,e_n)$$

The final axiom says simply that causality is transitive, that is, if e_i causes e_j and e_j causes e_k, then e_i causes e_k.

(18.83)
$$\forall e_i,e_j,e_k\; cause(e_i,e_j) \wedge cause(e_j,e_k) \Rightarrow cause(e_i,e_k)$$

Finally, we have the content of the utterances themselves, that is, that John hid Bill's car keys (from Bill),

(18.84) $hide(e_1, John, Bill, ck) \wedge carkeys(ck, Bill)$

and that someone described using the pronoun "he" was drunk; we will represent the pronoun with the free variable *he*.

(18.85) $drunk(e_2, he)$

We can now see how reasoning with the content of the utterances along with the aforementioned axioms allows the coherence of passage (18.71) to be established under the Explanation relation. The derivation is summarized in Figure 18.9; the sentence interpretations are shown in boxes. We start by assuming there is a coherence relation, and using axiom (18.78) hypothesize that this relation is Explanation,

(18.86) $Explanation(e_1, e_2)$

which, by axiom (18.79), means we hypothesize that

(18.87) $cause(e_2, e_1)$

holds. By axiom (18.83), we can hypothesize that there is an intermediate cause e_3,

(18.88) $cause(e_2, e_3) \wedge cause(e_3, e_1)$

and we can repeat this again by expanding the first conjunct of (18.88) to have an intermediate cause e_4.

(18.89) $cause(e_2, e_4) \wedge cause(e_4, e_3)$

We can take the *hide* predicate from the interpretation of the first sentence in (18.84) and the second *cause* predicate in (18.88), and, using axiom (18.82), hypothesize that John did not want Bill to have his car keys:

(18.90) $diswant(e_3, John, e_5) \wedge have(e_5, Bill, ck)$

From this, the *carkeys* predicate from (18.84), and the second *cause* predicate from (18.89), we can use axiom (18.81) to hypothesize that John does not want Bill to drive:

(18.91) $diswant(e_4, John, e_6) \wedge drive(e_6, Bill)$

From this, axiom (18.80), and the second *cause* predicate from (18.89), we can hypothesize that Bill was drunk:

(18.92) $drunk(e_2, Bill)$

But now we find that we can "prove" this fact from the interpretation of the second sentence if we simply assume that the free variable *he* is bound to Bill. Thus, the establishment of coherence has gone through, as we have identified a chain of reasoning between the sentence interpretations – one that includes unprovable assumptions about axiom choice and pronoun assignment – that results in $cause(e_2, e_1)$, as required for establishing the Explanation relationship.

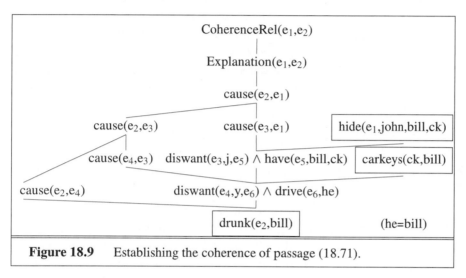

Figure 18.9   Establishing the coherence of passage (18.71).

   This derivation illustrates a powerful property of coherence establishment, namely its ability to cause the hearer to infer information about the situation described by the discourse that the speaker has left unsaid. In this case, the derivation required the assumption that John hid Bill's keys because he did not want him to drive (presumably out of fear of him having an accident, or getting stopped by the police), as opposed to some other explanation, such as playing a practical joke on him. This cause is not stated anywhere in passage (18.71); it arises only from the inference process triggered by the need to establish coherence. In this sense, the meaning of a discourse is greater than the sum of the meanings of its parts. That is, a discourse typically communicates far more information than is contained in the interpretations of the individual sentences that comprise it.

   We now return to passage (18.72), repeated below as (18.94), which was notable in that it lacks the coherence displayed by passage (18.71), repeated below as (18.93).

(18.93) John hid Bill's car keys. He was drunk.

(18.94) ?? John hid Bill's car keys. He likes spinach.

We can now see why this is: there is no analogous chain of inference capable of linking the two utterance representations, in particular, there is no causal axiom analogous to (18.80) that says that liking spinach might cause someone to not want you to drive. Without additional information that can support such a chain of inference (such as the aforementioned scenario in which someone promised John spinach in exchange for hiding Bill's car keys), the coherence of the passage cannot be established.

Because abduction is a form of unsound inference, it must be possible to subsequently retract the assumptions made during abductive reasoning, that is, abductive inferences are **defeasible**. For instance, if passage (18.93) was followed by sentence (18.95),

DEFEASIBLE

(18.95) Bill's car isn't here anyway; John was just playing a practical joke on him.

the system would have to retract the original chain of inference connecting the two clauses in (18.93), and replace it with one utilizing the fact that the hiding event was part of a practical joke.

In a more general knowledge base designed to support a broad range of inferences, one would want axioms that are more general than those we used to establish the coherence of passage (18.93). For instance, consider axiom (18.81), which says that if you do not want someone to drive, then you do not want them to have their car keys. A more general form of the axiom would say that if you do not want someone to perform an action, and an object enables them to perform that action, then you do not want them to have the object. The fact that car keys enable someone to drive would then be encoded separately, along with many other similar facts. Likewise, axiom (18.80) says that if someone is drunk, you don't want them to drive. We might replace this with an axiom that says that if someone does not want something to happen, then they don't want something that will likely cause it to happen. Again, the facts that people typically don't want other people to get into car accidents, and that drunk driving causes accidents, would be encoded separately.

While it is important to have computational models that shed light on the coherence establishment problem, large barriers remain for employing this and similar methods on a wide-coverage basis. In particular, the large number of axioms that would be required to encode all of the necessary facts about the world, and the lack of a robust mechanism for constraining inference with such a large set of axioms, makes these methods largely im-

practical in practice. Such problems have come to be informally known as **AI-complete**, a play on the term *NP-complete* in computer science. An AI-   AI-COMPLETE
complete problem is one that essentially requires all of the knowledge – and abilities to utilize it – that humans have.

Other approaches to analyzing the coherence structure of a discourse have also been proposed. One that has received broad usage is Rhetorical Structure Theory (RST) (Mann and Thompson, 1987), which proposes a set of 23 *rhetorical relations* that can hold between spans of text within a discourse. While RST is oriented more toward text description than interpretation, it has proven to be a useful tool for developing natural language generation systems. RST is described in more detail in Section 20.4.

Coherence and Coreference   The reader may have noticed another interesting property of the proof that passage (18.93) is coherent. While the pronoun *he* was initially represented as a free variable, it got bound to Bill during the derivation. In essence, a separate procedure for resolving the pronoun was not necessary; it happened as a side effect of the coherence establishment procedure. In addition to the tree-search algorithm presented on page 689, Hobbs (1978) proposes this use of the coherence establishment mechanism as a second approach to pronoun interpretation.

This approach provides an explanation for why the pronoun in passage (18.93) is most naturally interpreted as referring to Bill, but the pronoun in passage (18.96) is most naturally interpreted as referring to John.

(18.96) John lost Bill's car keys. He was drunk.

Establishing the coherence of passage (18.96) under the Explanation relation requires an axiom that says that being drunk could cause someone to lose something. Because such an axiom will dictate that the person who is drunk must be the same as the person losing something, the free variable representing the pronoun will become bound to John. The only lexico-syntactic difference between passages (18.96) and (18.93), however, is the verb of the first sentence. The grammatical positions of the pronoun and potential antecedent noun phrases are the same in both cases, so syntactically-based preferences do not distinguish between these.

Discourse Connectives   Sometimes a speaker will include a specific cue, called a **connective**, that serves to constrain the set of coherence relations   CONNECTIVE
that can hold between two or more utterances. For example, the connective *because* indicates the Explanation relationship explicitly, as in passage (18.97).

(18.97) John hid Bill's car keys because he was drunk.

The meaning of *because* can be represented as $cause(e_2, e_1)$, which would play a similar role in the proof as the *cause* predicate that was introduced abductively via axiom (18.79).

However, connectives do not always constrain the possibilities to a single coherence relation. The meaning of *and*, for instance, is compatible with the Parallel, Occasion, and Result relations introduced on page 696, as exemplified in (18.98)–(18.100) respectively.

(18.98) John bought an Acura and Bill leased a BMW.

(18.99) John bought an Acura and drove to the ballgame.

(18.100) John bought an Acura and his father went ballistic.

However, *and* is not compatible with the Explanation relation; unlike passage (18.97), passage (18.101) cannot mean the same thing as (18.93).

(18.101) John hid Bill's car keys and he was drunk.

While the coherence resolution procedure can use connectives to constrain the range of coherence relations that can be inferred between a pair of utterances, they in and of themselves do not *create* coherence. Any coherence relation indicated by a connective must still be established. Therefore, adding *because* to example (18.94), for instance, still does not make it coherent.

(18.102) ?? John hid Bill's car keys because he likes spinach.

Coherence establishment fails here for the same reason it does in example (18.72), that is, the lack of causal knowledge explaining how liking spinach would cause one to hide someone's car keys.

18.3   DISCOURSE STRUCTURE

In the previous section, we saw how the coherence of a pair of sentences can be established. We now ask how coherence can be established for longer discourses. Does one simply establish coherence relations between all adjacent pairs of sentences?

It turns out that the answer is no. Just as sentences have hierarchical structure (that is, syntax), so do discourses. Consider passage (18.103).

(18.103) John went to the bank to deposit his paycheck. (S1)

He then took a train to Bill's car dealership. (S2)

He needed to buy a car. (S3)

The company he works for now isn't near any public
transportation. (S4)

He also wanted to talk to Bill about their softball league. (S5)

Intuitively, the structure of passage (18.103) is not linear. The discourse
seems to be primarily about the sequence of events described in sentences
S1 and S2, whereas sentences S3 and S5 are related most directly to S2, and
S4 is related most directly to S3. The coherence relationships between these
sentences result in the discourse structure shown in Figure 18.10.

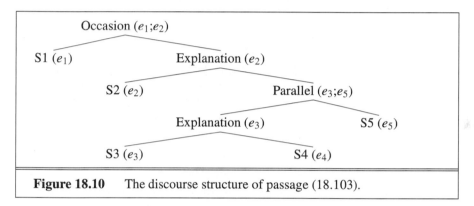

Figure 18.10   The discourse structure of passage (18.103).

Each node in the tree represents a group of locally coherent utterances,
called a **discourse segment**. Roughly speaking, one can think of discourse   DISCOURSE
segments as being analogous to constituents in sentence syntax.   SEGMENT

We can extend the set of discourse interpretation axioms used in the
last section to establish the coherence of larger, hierarchical discourses such
as (18.103). The recognition of discourse segments, and ultimately discourse
structure, results as a by-product of this process.

First, we add axiom (18.104), which states that a sentence is a discourse segment. Here, w is the string of words in the sentence, and e the
event or state described by it.

(18.104) $\forall w, e \; sentence(w,e) \Rightarrow Segment(w,e)$

Next, we add axiom (18.105), which says that two smaller segments can
be composed into a larger one if a coherence relation can be established
between the two.

(18.105) $\forall w_1, w_2, e_1, e_2, e \; Segment(w_1,e_1) \wedge Segment(w_2,e_2)$
                  $\wedge CoherenceRel(e_1,e_2,e) \Rightarrow Segment(w_1 w_2,e)$

Note that extending our axioms for longer discourses has necessitated that we add a third argument to the *CoherenceRel* predicate (*e*). The value of this variable will be a combination of the information expressed by e_1 and e_2 that represents the main assertion of the resulting segment. For our purposes

SUBORDINATING
RELATIONS

here, we will assume that **subordinating relations** such as Explanation pass along only one argument (in this case the first, that is, the effect), whereas

COORDINATING
RELATIONS

coordinating relations such as Parallel and Occasion pass a combination of both arguments. These arguments are shown in parentheses next to each relation in Figure 18.10.

Now, to interpret a coherent text W, one must simply prove that it is a segment, as expressed by statement (18.106).

(18.106) $\exists e\, Segment(W, e)$

These rules will derive any possible binary branching segmental structure for a discourse, as long as that structure can be supported by the establishment of coherence relations between the segments. Herein lies a difference between computing the syntactic structure of a sentence (see Chapter 9) and that of a discourse. Sentence-level grammars are generally complex, encoding many syntactic facts about how different constituents (noun phrases, verb phrases) can modify in each other and in what order. The "discourse grammar" above, on the contrary, is much simpler, encoding only two rules: a segment rewrites to two smaller segments, and a sentence is a segment. Which of the possible structures is actually assigned depends on how the coherence of the passage is established.

Why would we want to compute discourse structure? Several applications could benefit from it. A summarization system, for instance, might use it to select only the central sentences in the discourse, forgoing the inclusion of subordinate information. For instance, a system for creating brief summaries might only include sentences S1 and S2 when applied to passage (18.103), since the event representations for these were propagated to the top level node. A system for creating more detailed summaries might also include S3 and S5. Similarly, an information retrieval system might weight information in sentences that are propagated to higher-level parts of the discourse structure more heavily than information in ones that are not, and generation systems need knowledge of discourse structure to create coherent discourse, as described in Chapter 20.

Discourse structure may also be useful for natural language subtasks such as pronoun resolution. We already know from Section 18.1 that pronouns display a preference for recency, that is, they have a strong tendency to refer locally. But now we have two possible definitions for recency: recent in terms of the linear order of the discourse, or recent in terms of its hierarchical structure. It has been claimed that the latter definition is in fact the correct one, although admittedly the facts are not completely clear in all cases.

In this section, we have briefly described one of several possible approaches to recovering discourse structure. A different approach, one typically applied to dialogues, will be described in Section 19.4.

18.4   PSYCHOLINGUISTIC STUDIES OF REFERENCE AND COHERENCE

To what extent do the techniques described in this chapter model human discourse comprehension? A substantial body of psycholinguistic research has studied this question.

For instance, a significant amount of work has been concerned with the extent to which people use the preferences described in Section 18.1 to interpret pronouns, the results of which are often contradictory. Clark and Sengal (1979) studied the effects that sentence recency plays in pronoun interpretation using a set of **reading time experiments**. After receiving and acknowledging a three sentence context to read, human subjects were given a target sentence containing a pronoun. The subjects pressed a button when they felt that they understood the target sentence. Clark and Sengal found that the reading time was significantly faster when the referent for the pronoun was evoked from the most recent clause in the context than when it was evoked from two or three clauses back. On the other hand, there was no significant difference between referents evoked from two clauses and three clauses back, leading them to claim that "the last clause processed grants the entities it mentions a privileged place in working memory".

READING TIME EXPERIMENTS

Crawley et al. (1990) compared the grammatical role parallelism preference with a grammatical role preference, in particular, a preference for referents evoked from the subject position of the previous sentence over those evoked from object position. Unlike previous studies which conflated these preferences by considering only subject-to-subject reference effects, Crawley et al. studied pronouns in object position to see if they tended to be assigned to the subject or object of the last sentence. They found that in two task environments – a **question answering task** which revealed how the hu-

QUESTION ANSWERING

REFERENT
NAMING TASK
man subjects interpreted the pronoun, and a **referent naming task** in which the subjects identified the referent of the pronoun directly – the human subjects resolved pronouns to the subject of the previous sentence more often than the object.

However, Smyth (1994) criticized the adequacy of Crawley et al.'s data for evaluating the role of parallelism. Using data that met more stringent requirements for assessing parallelism, Smyth found that subjects overwhelmingly followed the parallelism preference in a referent naming task. The experiment supplied weaker support for the preference for subject referents over object referents, which he posited as a default strategy when the sentences in question are not sufficiently parallel.

SENTENCE
COMPLETION
TASK
Caramazza et al. (1977) studied the effect of the "implicit causality" of verbs on pronoun resolution. Verbs were categorized in terms of having subject bias or object bias using a **sentence completion task**. Subjects were given sentence fragments such as (18.107).

(18.107) John telephoned Bill because he

The subjects provided completions to the sentences, which identified to the experimenters what referent for the pronoun they favored. Verbs for which a large percentage of human subjects indicated a grammatical subject or object preference were categorized as having that bias. A sentence pair was then constructed for each biased verb: a "congruent" sentence in which the semantics supported the pronoun assignment suggested by the verb's bias, and an "incongruent" sentence in which the semantics supported the opposite prediction. For example, sentence (18.108) is congruent for the subject-bias verb "telephoned", since the semantics of the second clause supports assigning the subject *John* as the antecedent of *he*, whereas sentence (18.109) is incongruent since the semantics supports assigning the object *Bill*.

(18.108) John telephoned Bill because he wanted some information.

(18.109) John telephoned Bill because he withheld some information.

In a referent naming task, Caramazza et al. found that naming times were faster for the congruent sentences than for the incongruent ones. Perhaps surprisingly, this was even true for cases in which the two people mentioned in the first clause were of different genders, thus rendering the reference unambiguous.

FOCUS
HYPOTHESIS
Garnham et al. (1996) differentiated between two hypotheses about the manner in which implicit causality might affect pronoun resolution: the **focus hypothesis**, which says, as might be suggested by the Caramazza et al.

experiments, that such verbs have a priming effect on the filler of a particular grammatical role and thus contribute information that can be used at the point at which the pronoun is interpreted, and the **integration hypothesis**, in which this information is only used after the clause has been comprehended and is being integrated with the previous discourse. They attempted to determine which hypothesis is correct using a **probing task**. After sentences were presented to establish a context, a sentence containing a pronoun was presented one word at a time. At appropriate points during the presentation, the name of one of the possible referents was displayed, and the subject asked whether that person had been mentioned in the sentence so far. Garnham et al. found that the implicit causality information bias was generally not available right after the pronoun was given, but was utilized later in the sentence.

INTEGRATION HYPOTHESIS

PROBING TASK

Matthews and Chodorow (1988) analyzed the problem of intrasentential reference and the predictions of syntactically-based search strategies. In a question answering task, they found that subjects exhibited slower comprehension times for sentences in which a pronoun antecedent occupied an early, syntactically deep position than for sentences in which the antecedent occupied a late, syntactically shallow position. This result is consistent with the search process used in Hobbs's tree search algorithm.

There has also been psycholinguistic work concerned with testing the principles of centering theory. In a set of reading time experiments, Gordon et al. (1993) found that reading times were slower when the current backward-looking center was referred to using a full noun phrase instead of a pronoun, even though the pronouns were ambiguous and the proper names were not. This effect – which they called a **repeated name penalty** – was found only for referents in subject position, suggesting that the C_b is preferentially realized as a subject. Brennan (1995) analyzed how choice of linguistic form correlates with centering principles. She ran a set of experiments in which a human subject watched a basketball game and had to describe it to a second person. She found that the human subjects tended to refer to an entity using a full noun phrase in subject position before subsequently pronominalizing it, even if the referent had already been introduced in object position.

REPEATED NAME PENALTY

Psycholinguistic studies have also addressed the processes people use to establish discourse coherence. Some of this work has focussed on the question of **inference control**, that is, which of the potentially infinite number of possible inferences are actually made during interpretation (Singer, 1994; Garrod and Sanford, 1994). These can be categorized in terms of be-

INFERENCE CONTROL

NECESSARY
INFERENCES
ELABORATIVE
INFERENCES
ing **necessary inferences**, those which are necessary to establish coherence, and **elaborative inferences**, those which are suggested by the text but not necessary for establishing coherence. The position that only necessary inferences are made during interpretation has been called the *deferred inference theory* (Garnham, 1985) and the *minimalist position* (McKoon and Ratcliff, 1992). As with pronoun interpretation, results of studies testing these questions have yielded potentially contradictory results. Indeed, the results in each case depend to a large degree on the experimental setup and paradigm (Keenan et al., 1990).

RECOGNITION
JUDGEMENT
TASK
    Johnson et al. (1973), for instance, examined this question using a **recognition judgement task**. They presented subjects with passages such as (18.110).

(18.110)   When the man entered the kitchen he slipped on a wet spot and dropped the delicate glass pitcher on the floor. The pitcher was very expensive, and everyone watched the event with horror.

The subjects were subsequently presented either with a sentence taken directly from one of the passages, such as the first sentence of (18.110), or one that included an elaborative inference in the form of an expected consequence such as (18.111).

(18.111)   The man broke the delicate glass pitcher on the floor.

The subjects were then asked if the sentence had appeared verbatim in one of the passages. Both types of sentence received a recognition rate in the mid-60% range, whereas control sentences that substantially altered the meaning were recognized much less often (about 22%). By running a similar experiment that also measured subjects' response times, Singer (1979) addressed the question of whether these inferences were made at the time the original sentence was comprehended (and thus truly elaborative), or at the time that the expected consequence version was presented. While Singer also found that the identical and expected consequence versions yield similar rates of positive responses, the judgements about the consequence versions took 0.2-0.3 seconds longer than for the identical sentences, suggesting that the inference was not made at comprehension time.

    Singer (1980) examined the question of when different types of inferences were made using passages such as (18.112)-(18.114).

(18.112)   The dentist pulled the tooth painlessly. The patient liked the new method.

(18.113)   The tooth was pulled painlessly. The dentist used a new method.

(18.114)   The tooth was pulled painlessly. The patient liked the new method.

Each of these passages was presented to the subject, followed by the test sentence given in (18.115).

(18.115) A dentist pulled the tooth.

The information expressed in (18.115) is mentioned explicitly in (18.112), is necessary to establish coherence in (18.113), and is elaborative in (18.114). Singer found that subject verification times were approximately the same in the first two cases, but 0.25 seconds slower in the elaborative case, adding support to the deferred inference theory.

Kintsch and colleagues have proposed and analyzed a "construction-integration" model of discourse comprehension (Kintsch and van Dijk, 1978; van Dijk and Kintsch, 1983; Kintsch, 1988). They defined the concept of a **text macrostructure**, which is a hierarchical network of propositions that provides an abstract, semantic description of the global content of the text. Guindon and Kintsch (1984) evaluated whether the elaborative inferences necessary to construct the macrostructure accompany comprehension processes, using a **lexical priming** technique. Subjects read a passage and then were asked if a particular word pair was present in the text. Three types of word pairs were used: pairs that were not mentioned in the text but were related to the text macrostructure, pairs of "distractor words" that were thematically related to the text but not the macrostructure, and pairs of thematically unrelated distractor words. The number of "false alarms" – in which a subject erroneously indicated that the words appeared in the text – was significantly higher for macrostructure pairs than for thematically related pairs, which in turn was higher than for pairs of thematically unrelated words. In the remaining cases – in which the subjects correctly rejected word pairs that did not appear – response times were significantly longer for macrostructure words than thematically related pairs, which in turn were higher than for thematically unrelated words.

Myers et al. (1987) considered the question of how the degree of causal relatedness between sentences affects comprehension times and recall accuracy. Considering a target sentence such as (18.116),

(18.116) She found herself too frightened to move.

they designed four context sentences, shown in (18.117)–(18.120), which form a continuum moving from high to low causal relatedness to (18.116).

(18.117) Rose was attacked by a man in her apartment.

(18.118) Rose saw a shadow at the end of the hall.

(18.119) Rose entered her apartment to find a mess.

(18.120) Rose came back to her apartment after work.

Subjects were presented with cause-effect sentence pairs consisting of a context sentence and the target sentence. Myers et al. found that reading times were faster for more causally related pairs. After the subjects had seen a number of such pairs, Myers et al. then ran a **cued recall** experiment, in which the subjects were given one sentence from a pair and asked to recall as much as possible about the other sentence in the pair. They found that the subjects recalled more content for more causally related sentence pairs.

CUED RECALL

18.5   SUMMARY

In this chapter, we saw that many of the problems that natural language processing systems face operate between sentences, that is, at the *discourse* level. Here is a summary of some of the main points we discussed:

- Discourse interpretation requires that one build an evolving representation of discourse state, called a *discourse model*, that contains representations of the entities that have been referred to and the relationships in which they participate.
- Natural languages offer many ways to refer to entities. Each form of reference sends its own signals to the hearer about how it should be processed with respect to her discourse model and set of beliefs about the world.
- Pronominal reference can be used for referents that have an adequate degree of *salience* in the discourse model. There are a variety of lexical, syntactic, semantic, and discourse factors that appear to affect salience.
- These factors can be modeled and weighed against each other in a pronoun interpretation algorithm, due to Lappin and Leass (1994), that achieves performance in the mid-80% range on some genres.
- Discourses are not arbitrary collections of sentences; they must be *coherent*. Collections of well-formed and individually interpretable sentences often form incoherent discourses when juxtaposed.
- The process of establishing coherence, performed by applying the constraints imposed by one or more *coherence relations*, often leads to the inference of additional information left unsaid by the speaker. The unsound rule of logical *abduction* can be used for performing such inference.
- Discourses, like sentences, have hierarchical structure. Intermediate groups of locally coherent utterances are called *discourse segments*. Discourse structure recognition can be viewed as a by-product of discourse interpretation.

BIBLIOGRAPHICAL AND HISTORICAL NOTES

Building on the foundations set by early systems for natural language understanding (Woods et al., 1972; Winograd, 1972b; Woods, 1978), much of the fundamental work in computational approaches to discourse was performed in the late 70's. Webber's (1978, 1983) work provided fundamental insights into how entities are represented in the discourse model and the ways in which they can license subsequent reference. Many of the examples she provided continue to challenge theories of reference to this day. Grosz (1977a) addressed the focus of attention that conversational participants maintain as the discourse unfolds. She defined two levels of focus; entities relevant to the entire discourse were said to be in *global* focus, whereas entities that are locally in focus (i.e., most central to a particular utterance) were said to be in *immediate* focus. Sidner (1979, 1983) described a method for tracking (immediate) discourse foci and their use in resolving pronouns and demonstrative noun phrases. She made a distinction between the current discourse focus and potential foci, which are the predecessors to the backward and forward looking centers of centering theory respectively.

The roots of the centering approach originate from papers by Joshi and Kuhn (1979) and Joshi and Weinstein (1981), who addressed the relationship between immediate focus and the inferences required to integrate the current utterance into the discourse model. Grosz et al. (1983) integrated this work with the prior work of Sidner and Grosz. This led to a manuscript on centering which, while widely circulated since 1986, remained unpublished until Grosz et al. (1995). A series of papers on centering based on this manuscript/paper were subsequently published (Kameyama, 1986; Brennan et al., 1987; Di Eugenio, 1990; Walker et al., 1994; Di Eugenio, 1996; Strube and Hahn, 1996; Kehler, 1997a, inter alia) . A collection of more recent centering papers appears in Walker et al. (1998).

Researchers in the linguistics community have proposed accounts of the *information status* that referents hold in a discourse model (Chafe, 1976; Prince, 1981; Ariel, 1990; Prince, 1992; Gundel et al., 1993; Lambrecht, 1994, inter alia). Prince (1992), for instance, analyzes information status in terms of two crosscutting dichotomies: *hearer status* and *discourse status*, and shows how these statuses correlate with the grammatical position of referring expressions. Gundel et al. (1993), on the other hand, posits a unidimensional scale with six statuses (called the *givenness hierarchy*), and correlates them with the linguistic form of referring expressions.

Beginning with Hobbs's (1978) tree-search algorithm, researchers have pursued syntax-based methods for identifying reference robustly in naturally occurring text. Building on the work of Lappin and Leass (1994), Kennedy and Boguraev (1996) describe a similar system that does not rely on a full syntactic parser, but merely a mechanism for identifying noun phrases and labeling their grammatical roles. Both approaches use Alshawi's (1987) framework for integrating salience factors. An algorithm that uses this framework for resolving references in a multimodal (i.e., speech and gesture) human-computer interface is described in Huls et al. (1995). A discussion of a variety of approaches to reference in operational systems can be found in Mitkov and Boguraev (1997).

Recently, several researchers have pursued methods for reference resolution based on supervised learning (Connolly et al., 1994; Aone and Bennett, 1995; McCarthy and Lehnert, 1995; Kehler, 1997b; Ge et al., 1998, inter alia). In these studies, machine learning methods such as Bayesian model induction, decision trees, and maximum entropy modeling were used to train models from corpora annotated with coreference relations. A discussion of some issues that arise in annotating corpora for coreference can be found in Poesio and Vieira (1998).

The MUC-6 information extraction evaluation included a common evaluation on coreference (Sundheim, 1995a). The task included coreference between proper names, aliases, definite noun phrases, bare nouns, pronouns, and even coreference indicated by syntactic relations such predicate nominals (*"The Integra* is *the world's nicest looking car"*) and appositives (*"the Integra, the world's nicest looking car,"*). Performance was evaluated by calculating recall and precision statistics based on the distance between the equivalence classes of coreferent descriptions produced by a system and those in a human-annotated answer key. Five of the seven sites which participated in the evaluation achieved in the range of 51%-63% recall and 62%-72% precision. A similar evaluation was also included as part of MUC-7.

Several researchers have posited sets of coherence relations that can hold between utterances in a discourse (Halliday and Hasan, 1976; Hobbs, 1979a; Longacre, 1983; Mann and Thompson, 1987; Polanyi, 1988; Hobbs, 1990; Sanders et al., 1992, inter alia). A compendium of over 350 relations that have been proposed in the literature can be found in Hovy (1990). The Linguistic Discourse Model (Polanyi, 1988; Scha and Polanyi, 1988) is a framework in which discourse syntax is more heavily emphasized; in this approach, a discourse parse tree is built on a clause-by-clause basis in direct analogy with how a sentence parse tree is built on a constituent-by-constituent basis. A more recent line of work has applied a version of the trec-adjoining grammar formalism to discourse parsing (Webber et al., 1999, and citations therein). In addition to determining discourse structure and meaning, theories of discourse coherence have been used in algorithms for interpreting discourse-level linguistic phenomena, including pronoun resolution (Hobbs, 1979a; Kehler, 2000), verb phrase ellipsis and gapping (Prüst, 1992; Asher, 1993; Kehler, 1993, 1994a), and tense interpretation (Lascarides and Asher, 1993; Kehler, 1994b, 2000). An extensive investigation into the relationship between coherence relations and discourse connectives can be found in Knott and Dale (1994).

EXERCISES

18.1 Early work in syntactic theory attempted to characterize rules for pronominalization through purely syntactic means. A rule was proposed in which a pronoun was interpreted by deleting it from the syntactic structure of the sentence that contains it, and replacing it with the syntactic representation of the antecedent noun phrase.

Explain why the following sentences (called "Bach-Peters" sentences) are problematic for such an analysis:

(18.121) The man who deserves it gets the prize he wants.

(18.122) The pilot who shot at it hit the MIG that chased him.

What other types of reference discussed on pages 673–678 are problematic for this type of analysis?

Now, consider the following example (Karttunen, 1969):

(18.123)   The student who revised his paper did better than the student
           who handed it in as is.

What is the preferred reading for the pronoun *it*, and why is it different and interesting? Describe why the syntactic account described above can be seen to predict this reading. Is this type of reading common? Construct some superficially similar examples that nonetheless appear not to have a similar reading.

18.2 Webber (1978) offers examples in which the same referent appears to support either singular or plural agreement:

(18.124) John gave Mary five dollars. *It* was more than he gave Sue.

(18.125) John gave Mary five dollars. One of *them* was counterfeit.

What might account for this? Describe how representations of referents like *five dollars* in the discourse model could be made to allow such behavior.

Next, consider the following examples (from Webber and Baldwin (1992)):

(18.126) John made a handbag from an inner tube.

      a. He sold it for twenty dollars.
      b. He had taken it from his brother's car.
      c. Neither of them was particularly useful.
      d. * He sold them for fifty dollars.

Why is plural reference to the handbag and the inner tube possible in sentence (18.126c), but not (18.126d)? Again, discuss how representations in the discourse model could be made to support this behavior.

18.3 Draw syntactic trees for example (18.68) on page 687 and apply Hobbs's tree search algorithm to it, showing each step in the search.

18.4 Recall that Hobbs's algorithm does not have an explicit representation of a discourse model, salience, or preferences. Discuss which of the preferences we have described are approximated by the search process over syntactic representations as Hobbs has defined it, and how.

18.5 Hobbs (1977) cites the following examples from his corpus as being problematic for his tree-search algorithm:

(18.127) The positions of pillars in one hall were marked by river boulders and a shaped convex cushion of bronze that had served as <u>their</u> footings.

(18.128) They were at once assigned an important place among the scanty remains which record the physical developments of the human race from the time of <u>its</u> first appearance in Asia.

(18.129) Sites at which the coarse grey pottery of the Shang period has been discovered do not extend far beyond the southernmost reach of the Yellow river, or westward beyond <u>its</u> junction with the Wei.

(18.130) The thin, hard, black-burnished pottery, made in shapes of angular profile, which archeologists consider as the clearest hallmark of the Lung Shan culture, developed in the east. The site from which <u>it</u> takes its name is in Shantung. <u>It</u> is traced to the north-east as far as Liao-ning province.

(18.131) He had the duty of performing the national sacrifices to heaven and earth: his role as source of honours and material rewards for services rendered by feudal lords and ministers is commemorated

> in thousands of inscriptions made by the recipients on bronze
> vessels which were eventually deposited in <u>their</u> graves.

In each case, identify the correct referent of the underlined pronoun and the one that the algorithm will identify incorrectly. Discuss any factors that come into play in determining the correct referent in each case, and what types of information might be necessary to account for them.

18.6   Consider the following passage, from Brennan et al. (1987):

(18.132)   Brennan drives an Alfa Romeo.
           She drives too fast.
           Friedman races her on weekends.
           She goes to Laguna Seca.

Identify the referent that the BFP algorithm finds for the pronoun in the final sentence. Do you agree with this choice, or do you find the example ambiguous? Discuss why introducing a new noun phrase in subject position, with a pronominalized reference in object position, might lead to an ambiguity for a subject pronoun in the next sentence. What preferences are competing here?

18.7   The approaches to pronoun resolution discussed in this chapter depend on accurate parsing: Hobbs's tree search algorithm assumes a full syntactic tree, and Lappin and Leass's algorithm and centering requires that grammatical roles are assigned correctly. Given the current state of the art in syntactic processing, highly accurate syntactic structures are currently not reliably computable. Therefore, real-world algorithms must choose between one of two options: (1) use a parser to generate (often inaccurate) syntactic analyses and use them as such, or (2) to eschew full syntactic analysis altogether and base the algorithm on partial syntactic analysis, such as noun phrase recognition. The Lappin and Leass system took the first option, using a highly developed parser. However, one could take the second option, and augment their algorithm so that surface position is used to approximate a grammatical role hierarchy.

Design a set of preferences for the Lappin and Leass method that assumes that only noun phrases are bracketed in the input. Construct six examples: (1) two that are handled by both methods, (2) two examples that Lappin and Leass handle but that are not handled by your adaptation, and (3) two that are not handled correctly by either algorithm. Make sure the examples are nontrivially different.

18.8   Consider passages (18.133a-b), adapted from Winograd (1972b).

(18.133) The city council denied the demonstrators a permit because

      a. they feared violence.

      b. they advocated violence.

What are the correct interpretations for the pronouns in each case? Sketch out an analysis of each in the interpretation as abduction framework, in which these reference assignments are made as a by-product of establishing the Explanation relation.

18.9   Coherence relations may also apply *temporal* constraints to the events or states denoted by sentences in a discourse. These constraints must be compatible with the temporal information indicated by the tenses used. Consider the two follow-on sentences in example (18.134):

(18.134) John got in a car accident.

      a. He drank a six-pack of beer.

      b. He had drunk a six-pack of beer.

In what order do the events occur in each case? What coherence relation is operative in each case? Discuss what might account for this difference given the fact that causes precede effects.

18.10   The coherence relations *Result* and *Explanation* are highly related, in that Explanation is essentially the same as Result except with the opposite ordering of clauses. These two relations are exemplified in examples (18.135) and (18.136).

(18.135) Bill was drunk, so John hid his car keys.

(18.136) John hid Bill's car keys because he was drunk.

Now consider the following examples:

(18.137) Bill was drunk, but John didn't hide his car keys.

(18.138) John hid Bill's car keys, even though he wasn't drunk.

The coherence relations underlying examples (18.137) and (18.138) have been called Violated Expectation and Denial of Preventer respectively.

Define the constraints that these two relations impose, using those for Result and Explanation as a guide. Discuss how we might consider all four relations to be parameterized versions of a single relation.

18.11   Select an editorial column from your favorite newspaper, and determine the discourse structure for a 10-20 sentence portion. What problems did you encounter? Were you helped by superficial cues the speaker included (e.g., discourse connectives) in any places?

19 DIALOGUE AND CONVERSATIONAL AGENTS

C: I want you to tell me the names of the fellows on the St. Louis team.
A: I'm telling you. Who's on first, What's on second, I Don't Know is on third.
C: You know the fellows' names?
A: Yes.
C: Well, then, who's playing first?
A: Yes.
C: I mean the fellow's name on first.
A: Who.
C: The guy on first base.
A: Who is on first.
C: Well what are you askin' *me* for?
A: I'm not asking you – I'm telling you. Who is on first.

> *Who's on First* – Bud Abbott and Lou Costello's version of an old burlesque standard.

The literature of the fantastic abounds in inanimate objects magically endowed with sentience and the gift of speech. From Ovid's statue of Pygmalion to Mary Shelley's Frankenstein, Cao Xue Qin's Divine Luminescent Stone-in-Waiting in the Court of Sunset Glow to Snow White's mirror, there is something deeply touching about creating something and then having a chat with it. Legend has it that after finishing his sculpture of *Moses*, Michelangelo thought it so lifelike that he tapped it on the knee and commanded it to speak. Perhaps this shouldn't be surprising. Language itself has always been the mark of humanity and sentience, and **conversation** or **dialogue** is the most fundamental and specially privileged arena of language.

CONVERSATION

DIALOGUE

It is certainly the first kind of language we learn as children, and for most of us, it is the kind of language we most commonly indulge in, whether we are ordering curry for lunch or buying postage stamps, participating in business meetings or talking with our families, booking airline flights or complaining about the weather.

This chapter introduces the fundamental structures and algorithms in **conversational agents**, programs which communicate with users in natural language in order to book airline flights, answer questions, or act as a telephone interface to email. Many of these issues are also relevant for **business meeting summarization** systems and other spoken language understanding systems which must transcribe and summarize structured conversations like meetings. Section 19.1 begins by introducing some issues that make conversation different from other kinds of discourse, introducing the important ideas of **turn-taking**, **grounding**, and **implicature**. Section 19.2 introduces the **speech act** or **dialogue act**, and Section 19.3 gives two different algorithms for automatic speech act interpretation. Section 19.4 describes how structure and coherence in dialogue differ from the discourse structure and coherence we saw in Chapter 18. Finally, Section 19.5 shows how each of these issues must be addressed in choosing an architecture for a dialogue manager as part of a conversational agent.

19.1   WHAT MAKES DIALOGUE DIFFERENT?

Much about dialogue is similar to other kinds of discourse like the text monologues of Chapter 18. Dialogues exhibit anaphora and discourse structure and coherence, although with some slight changes from monologue. For example when resolving an anaphor in dialogue it's important to look at what the other speaker said. In the following fragment from the air travel conversation in Figure 19.1 (to be discussed below), realizing that the pronoun *they* refers to *non-stop flights* in C's utterance requires looking at A's previous utterance:

> A_4: Right. There's three non-stops today.
> C_5: What are they?

Dialogue does differ from written monologue in deeper ways, however. The next few subsections highlight some of these differences.

Turns and Utterances

One difference between monologue and dialogue is that dialogue is characterized by **turn-taking**. Speaker A says something, then speaker B, then speaker A, and so on. Figure 19.1 shows a sample dialogue broken up into labeled turns; we've chosen this human-human dialogue because it concerns travel planning, a domain that is the focus of much recent human-machine dialogue research.

TURN-TAKING

C_1:	...I need to travel in May.
A_1:	And, what day in May did you want to travel?
C_2:	OK uh I need to be there for a meeting that's from the 12th to the 15th.
A_2:	And you're flying into what city?
C_3:	Seattle.
A_3:	And what time would you like to leave Pittsburgh?
C_4:	Uh hmm I don't think there's many options for non-stop.
A_4:	Right. There's three non-stops today.
C_5:	What are they?
A_5:	The first one departs PGH at 10:00am arrives Seattle at 12:05 their time. The second flight departs PGH at 5:55pm, arrives Seattle at 8pm. And the last flight departs PGH at 8:15pm arrives Seattle at 10:28pm.
C_6:	OK I'll take the 5ish flight on the night before on the 11th.
A_6:	On the 11th? OK. Departing at 5:55pm arrives Seattle at 8pm, U.S. Air flight 115.
C_7:	OK.

Figure 19.1   A fragment from a telephone conversation between a client (C) and a travel agent (A).

How do speakers know when is the proper time to contribute their turn? Consider the timing of the utterances in conversations like Figure 19.1. First, notice that this dialogue has no noticeable overlap. That is, the beginning of each speaker's turn follows the end of the previous speaker's turn (overlap would have been indicated by surrounding it with the # symbol). The actual amount of overlapped speech in American English conversation seems to be quite small; Levinson (1983) suggests the amount is less than 5% in general, and probably less for certain kinds of dialogue like the task-oriented dialogue in Figure 19.1. If speakers aren't overlapping, perhaps they are waiting a while after the other speaker? This is also very rare. The amount of time between turns is quite small, generally less than a few hundred milliseconds even in multi-party discourse. In fact, it may take more than this few hundred milliseconds for the next speaker to plan the motor routines for producing their utterance, which means that speakers begin motor planning for their next utterance before the previous speaker has finished. For this to be possible, natural conversation must be set up in such a way that (most of the time) people can quickly figure out **who** should talk next, and exactly **when** they should talk. This kind of turn-taking behavior is generally studied in the field of **Conversation Analysis** (**CA**). In a key conversation-analytic paper, Sacks et al. (1974) argued that turn-taking behavior, at least in American English, is governed by a set of turn-taking rules. These rules apply at a **transition-relevance place**, or **TRP**; places where the structure of the language allows speaker shift to occur. Here is a simplified version of the turn-taking rules, grouped into a single three-part rule; see Sacks et al. (1974) for the complete rules:

CONVERSATION ANALYSIS

(19.1) **Turn-taking Rule.** At each TRP of each turn:

    a. If during this turn the current speaker has selected A as the next speaker then A must speak next.

    b. If the current speaker does not select the next speaker, any other speaker may take the next turn.

    c. If no one else takes the next turn, the current speaker may take the next turn.

There are a number of important implications of rule (19.1) for dialogue modeling. First, subrule (19.1a) implies that there are some utterances by which the speaker specifically selects who the next speaker will be. The most obvious of these are questions, in which the speaker selects another speaker to answer the question. Two-part structures like QUESTION-ANSWER are called **adjacency pairs** (Schegloff, 1968); other adjacency pairs include GREETING followed by GREETING, COMPLIMENT followed by DOWNPLAYER, REQUEST followed by GRANT. We will see that these pairs and the dialogue expectations they set up will play an important role in dialogue modeling.

ADJACENCY PAIRS

Subrule (19.1a) also has an implication for the interpretation of silence. While silence can occur after any turn, silence which follows the first part of an adjacency pair-part is **significant silence**. For example Levinson (1983) notes the following example from Atkinson and Drew (1979); pause lengths are marked in parentheses (in seconds):

SIGNIFICANT SILENCE

(19.2) A: Is there something bothering you or not?
        (1.0)
     A: Yes or no?
        (1.5)
     A: Eh?
     B: No.

Since A has just asked B a question, the silence is interpreted as a refusal to respond, or perhaps a **dispreferred** response (a response, like saying "no" to a request, which is stigmatized). By contrast, silence in other places, for example a lapse after a speaker finishes a turn, is not generally interpretable in this way. These facts are relevant for user interface design in spoken dialogue systems; users are disturbed by the pauses in dialogue systems caused by slow speech recognizers (Yankelovich et al., 1995).

DISPREFERRED

Another implication of (19.1) is that transitions between speakers don't occur just anywhere; the **transition-relevance places** where they tend to occur are generally at **utterance** boundaries. This brings us to the next difference between spoken dialogue and textual monologue (of course dialogue can be written and monologue spoken; but most current applications of dialogue involve speech): the spoken **utterance** versus the written **sentence**. Recall from Chapter 9 that utterances differ from written sentences in a number of ways. They tend to be shorter, are more likely to be single clauses, the subjects are usually pronouns rather than full lexical noun phrases, and they include filled pauses, repairs, and restarts.

UTTERANCE

One very important difference not discussed in Chapter 9 is that while written sentences and paragraphs are relatively easy to automatically segment from each other, utterances and turns are quite complex to segment. Utterance boundary detection is important since many computational dialogue models are based on extracting an utterance as a primitive unit. The segmentation problem is difficult because a single utterance may be spread over several turns, or a single turn may include several utterances. For example in the following fragment of a dialogue between a travel agent and a client, the agent's utterance stretches over three turns:

(19.3) A: Yeah yeah the um let me see here we've got you on American
        flight nine thirty eight
     C: Yep.
     A: leaving on the twentieth of June out of Orange County John
        Wayne Airport at seven thirty p.m.
     C: Seven thirty.
     A: and into uh San Francisco at eight fifty seven.

By contrast, the example below has three utterances in one turn:

(19.4)   A: Three two three and seven five one. OK and then does he know there is a nonstop that goes from Dulles to San Francisco? Instead of connection through St. Louis.

Algorithms for utterance segmentation are based on many boundary **cues** such as:

CUE WORDS

- **cue words:** Cue (or "clue") words like *well*, *and*, *so*, etc., tend to occur at the beginnings and ends of utterances (Reichman, 1985; Hirschberg and Litman, 1993).

- *N*-**gram word or POS sequences:** Specific word or POS sequences often indicate boundaries. *N*-gram grammars can be trained on a training set labeled with special utterance-boundary tags, and then a decoder can find the most likely utterance boundaries in a unlabeled test set (Mast et al., 1996; Meteer and Iyer, 1996; Stolcke and Shriberg, 1996a; Heeman and Allen, 1999).

- **prosody:** Prosodic features like pitch, accent, phrase-final lengthening and pause duration play a role in utterance/turn segmentation, as discussed in Chapter 4, although the relationship between utterances and prosodic units like the **intonation unit** (Du Bois et al., 1983) or **in-**

INTONATION
PHRASE

tonation phrase (Pierrehumbert, 1980; Beckman and Pierrehumbert, 1986) is complicated (Ladd, 1996; Ford and Thompson, 1996; Ford et al., 1996, inter alia) .

The relationship between turns and utterances seems to be more one-to-one in human-machine dialogue than the human-human dialogues discussed above. Probably this is because the simplicity of current systems causes people to use simpler utterances and turns. Thus while computational tasks like **meeting summarization** require solving quite difficult segmentation problems, segmentation may be easier for conversational agents.

Grounding

Another important characteristic of dialogue that distinguishes it from monologue is that it is a collective act performed by the speaker and the hearer. One implication of this collectiveness is that, unlike in monologue, the speaker

COMMON GROUND

and hearer must constantly establish **common ground** (Stalnaker, 1978), the set of things that are mutually believed by both speakers. The need to

achieve common ground means that the hearer must **ground** or **acknowl-**
edge the speaker's utterances, or else make it clear that there was a problem
in reaching common ground. For example, consider the role of the word
mm-hmm in the following fragment of a conversation between a travel agent
and a client:

> A: ... returning on U.S. flight one one one eight.
> C: Mm hmm

The word *mm-hmm* here is a **continuer**, also often called a **backchan-**
nel or an **acknowledgement token**. A continuer is a short utterance which
acknowledges the previous utterance in some way, often cueing the other
speaker to continue talking (Jefferson, 1984; Schegloff, 1982; Yngve, 1970).
By letting the speaker know that the utterance has "reached" the addressee,
a continuer/backchannel thus helps the speaker and hearer achieve common
ground. Continuers are just one of the ways that the hearer can indicate
that she believes she understands what the speaker meant. Clark and Schaefer (1989) discuss five main types of methods, ordered from weakest to
strongest:

1. **Continued attention:** B shows she is continuing to attend and therefore remains satisfied with A's presentation.
2. **Relevant next contribution:** B starts in on the next relevant contribution.
3. **Acknowledgement:** B nods or says a continuer like *uh-huh*, *yeah*, or
   the like, or an **assessment** like *that's great*.
4. **Demonstration:** B demonstrates all or part of what she has understood A to mean, for example by paraphrasing or **reformulating** A's
   utterance, or by **collaboratively completing** A's utterance.
5. **Display:** B displays verbatim all or part of A's presentation.

The following excerpt from our sample conversation shows a display
of understanding by A's repetition of *on the 11th*:

> C_6: OK I'll take the 5ish flight on the night before on the 11th.
> A_6: On the 11th?

Such repeats or reformulations are often done in the form of questions
like A_6; we return to this issue on page 739.

Not all of Clark and Shaefer's methods are available for telephone-
based conversational agents. Without eye-gaze as a visual indicator of at-

tention, for example, **continued attention** isn't an option. In fact Stifelman
et al. (1993) and Yankelovich et al. (1995) point out that users of speech-
based interfaces are often confused when the system doesn't give them an
explicit acknowledgement signal after processing the user's utterances.

REQUEST
FOR REPAIR

In addition to these acknowledgement acts, a hearer can indicate that
there were problems in understanding the previous utterance, for example by
issuing a **request for repair** like the following Switchboard example:

> A: Why is that?
> B: Huh?
> A: Why is that?

Conversational Implicature

The final important property of conversation is the way the interpretation of
an utterance relies on more than just the literal meaning of the sentences.
Consider the client's response C_2 from the sample conversation above, repeated here:

> A_1: And, what day in May did you want to travel?
> C_2: OK uh I need to be there for a meeting that's from the 12th to the 15th.

Notice that the client does not in fact answer the question. The client
merely states that he has a meeting at a certain time. The semantics for this
sentence produced by a semantic interpreter will simply mention this meeting. What is it that licenses the agent to infer that the client is mentioning
this meeting so as to inform the agent of the travel dates?

Now consider another utterance from the sample conversation, this one
by the agent:

> A_4: ... There's three non-stops today.

Now this statement would still be true if there were seven non-stops
today, since if there are seven of something, there are by definition also three.
But what the agent means here is that there are three **and not more than
three** non-stops today. How is the client to infer that the agent means **only
three** non-stops?

These two cases have something in common; in both cases the speaker
seems to expect the hearer to draw certain inferences; in other words, the
speaker is communicating more information than seems to be present in the
uttered words. These kind of examples were pointed out by Grice (1975,

IMPLICATURE

1978) as part of his theory of **conversational implicature**. **Implicature** means a particular class of licensed inferences. Grice proposed that what enables hearers to draw these inferences is that conversation is guided by a set of **maxims**, general heuristics which play a guiding role in the interpretation of conversational utterances. He proposed the following four maxims:

- **Maxim of Quantity:** Be exactly as informative as is required:
  1. Make your contribution as informative as is required (for the current purposes of the exchange).
  2. Do not make your contribution more informative than is required.

- **Maxim of Quality:** Try to make your contribution one that is true:
  1. Do not say what you believe to be false.
  2. Do not say that for which you lack adequate evidence.

- **Maxim of Relevance:** Be relevant.
- **Maxim of Manner:** Be perspicuous:
  1. Avoid obscurity of expression.
  2. Avoid ambiguity.
  3. Be brief (avoid unnecessary prolixity).
  4. Be orderly.

MAXIMS

QUANTITY

QUALITY

RELEVANCE

MANNER

It is the Maxim of Quantity (specifically Quantity 1) that allows the hearer to know that *three non-stops* did not mean *seven non-stops*. This is because the hearer assumes the speaker is following the maxims, and thus if the speaker meant seven non-stops she would have said seven non-stops ("as informative as is required"). The Maxim of Relevance is what allows the agent to know that the client wants to travel by the 12th. The agent assumes the client is following the maxims, and hence would only have mentioned the meeting if it was relevant at this point in the dialogue. The most natural inference that would make the meeting relevant is the inference that the client meant the agent to understand that his departure time was before the meeting time.

These three properties of conversation (**turn-taking**, **grounding**, and **implicature**) will play an important role in the discussion of dialogue acts, dialogue structure, and dialogue managers in the next sections.

19.2   DIALOGUE ACTS

An important insight about conversation, due to Austin (1962), is that an utterance in a dialogue is a kind of **action** being performed by the speaker.

PERFORMATIVE   This is particularly clear in **performative** sentences like the following:

(19.5) I name this ship the *Titanic*.

(19.6) I second that motion.

(19.7) I bet you five dollars it will snow tomorrow.

When uttered by the proper authority, for example, (19.5) has the effect of changing the state of the world (causing the ship to have the name *Titanic*) just as any action can change the state of the world. Verbs like *name* or *second* which perform this kind of action are called performative verbs, and

SPEECH ACTS   Austin called these kinds of actions **speech acts**. What makes Austin's work so far-reaching is that speech acts are not confined to this small class of performative verbs. Austin's claim is that the utterance of any sentence in a real speech situation constitutes three kinds of acts:

- **locutionary act:** the utterance of a sentence with a particular meaning.
- **illocutionary act:** the act of asking, answering, promising, etc., in uttering a sentence.
- **perlocutionary act:** the (often intentional) production of certain effects upon the feelings, thoughts, or actions of the addressee in uttering a sentence.

ILLOCUTIONARY
FORCE   For example, Austin explains that the utterance of example (19.8) might have the **illocutionary force** of protesting and the perlocutionary effect of stopping the addressee from doing something, or annoying the addressee.

(19.8) You can't do that.

The term **speech act** is generally used to describe illocutionary acts rather than either of the other two levels. Searle (1975b), in modifying a taxonomy of Austin's, suggests that all speech acts can be classified into one of five major classes:

- **Assertives:** committing the speaker to something's being the case (*suggesting, putting forward, swearing, boasting, concluding*).
- **Directives:** attempts by the speaker to get the addressee to do something (*asking, ordering, requesting, inviting, advising, begging*).
- **Commissives:** committing the speaker to some future course of action (*promising, planning, vowing, betting, opposing*).
- **Expressives:** expressing the psychological state of the speaker about a state of affairs *thanking, apologizing, welcoming, deploring*.
- **Declarations:** bringing about a different state of the world via the utterance (including many of the performative examples above; *I resign, You're fired.*)

While speech acts provide a useful characterization of one kind of pragmatic force, more recent work, especially in building dialogue systems, has significantly expanded this core notion, modeling more kinds of conversational functions that an utterance can play. The resulting enriched acts are called **dialogue acts** (Bunt, 1994) or **conversational moves** (Power, 1979; Carletta et al., 1997). A recent ongoing effort to develop dialogue act tagging scheme is the DAMSL (Dialogue Act Markup in Several Layers) architecture (Allen and Core, 1997; Walker et al., 1996; Carletta et al., 1997; Core et al., 1999), which codes various levels of dialogue information about utterances. Two of these levels, the **forward looking function** and the **backward looking function**, are extensions of speech acts which draw on notions of dialogue structure like the adjacency pairs mentioned earlier as well as notions of grounding and repair. For example, the forward looking function of an utterance corresponds to something like the Searle/Austin speech act, although the DAMSL tag set is hierarchical, and is focused somewhat on the kind of dialogue acts that tend to occur in task-oriented dialogue:

DIALOGUE ACT

MOVES

STATEMENT	a claim made by the speaker
INFO-REQUEST	a question by the speaker
CHECK	a question for confirming information (see below)
INFLUENCE-ON-ADDRESSEE	(=Searle's directives)
OPEN-OPTION	a weak suggestion or listing of options
ACTION-DIRECTIVE	an actual command
INFLUENCE-ON-SPEAKER	(=Austin's commissives)
OFFER	speaker offers to do something, (subject to confirmation)
COMMIT	speaker is committed to doing something
CONVENTIONAL	other
OPENING	greetings
CLOSING	farewells
THANKING	thanking and responding to thanks

The backward looking function of DAMSL focuses on the relationship of an utterance to previous utterances by the other speaker. These include accepting and rejecting proposals (since DAMSL is focused on task-oriented dialogue), as well as grounding and repair acts discussed above.

AGREEMENT	speaker's response to previous proposal
ACCEPT	accepting the proposal
ACCEPT-PART	accepting some part of the proposal
MAYBE	neither accepting nor rejecting the proposal
REJECT-PART	rejecting some part of the proposal
REJECT	rejecting the proposal
HOLD	putting off response, usually via subdialogue
ANSWER	answering a question
UNDERSTANDING	whether speaker understood previous
SIGNAL-NON-UNDER.	speaker didn't understand
SIGNAL-UNDER.	speaker did understand
ACK	demonstrated via continuer or assessment
REPEAT-REPHRASE	demonstrated via repetition or reformulation
COMPLETION	demonstrated via collaborative completion

Figure 19.2 shows a labeling of our sample conversation using versions of the DAMSL Forward and Backward tags.

19.3   AUTOMATIC INTERPRETATION OF DIALOGUE ACTS

The previous section introduced dialogue acts and other activities that utterances can perform. This section turns to the problem of identifying or interpreting these acts. That is, how do we decide whether a given input is a QUESTION, a STATEMENT, a SUGGEST (directive), or an ACKNOWLEDGEMENT?

At first glance, this problem looks simple. We saw in Chapter 9 that yes-no-questions in English have **aux-inversion**, statements have declarative syntax (no aux-inversion), and commands have imperative syntax (sentences with no syntactic subject), as in example (19.9):

(19.9)   YES-NO-QUESTION Will breakfast be served on USAir 1557?
        STATEMENT   I don't care about lunch
        COMMAND   Show me flights from Milwaukee to Orlando on Thursday night.

It seems from (19.9) that the surface syntax of the input ought to tell us what illocutionary act it is. Alas, as is clear from Abbott and Costello's famous *Who's on First* routine at the beginning of the chapter, things are not so simple. The mapping between surface form and illocutionary act is not obvious or even one-to-one.

[assert]	C$_1$:	...I need to travel in May.
[info-req,ack]	A$_1$:	And, what day in May did you want to travel?
[assert, answer]	C$_2$:	OK uh I need to be there for a meeting that's from the 12th to the 15th.
[info-req,ack]	A$_2$:	And you're flying into what city?
[assert,answer]	C$_3$:	Seattle.
[info-req,ack]	A$_3$:	And what time would you like to leave Pittsburgh?
[check,hold]	C$_4$:	Uh hmm I don't think there's many options for non-stop.
[accept,ack]	A$_4$:	Right.
[assert]		There's three non-stops today.
[info-req]	C$_5$:	What are they?
[assert, open-option]	A$_5$:	The first one departs PGH at 10:00am arrives Seattle at 12:05 their time. The second flight departs PGH at 5:55pm, arrives Seattle at 8pm. And the last flight departs PGH at 8:15pm arrives Seattle at 10:28pm.
[accept,ack]	C$_6$:	OK I'll take the 5ish flight on the night before on the 11th.
[check,ack]	A$_6$:	On the 11th?
[assert,ack]		OK. Departing at 5:55pm arrives Seattle at 8pm, U.S. Air flight 115.
[ack]	C$_7$:	OK.

Figure 19.2   A potential DAMSL labeling of the conversation fragment in Figure 19.1.

For example, the following utterance spoken to an ATIS system looks like a YES-NO-QUESTION meaning something like *Are you capable of giving me a list of... ?*:

(19.10) Can you give me a list of the flights from Atlanta to Boston?

In fact, however, this person was not interested in whether the system was *capable* of giving a list; this utterance was actually a polite form of a DIRECTIVE or a REQUEST, meaning something more like *Please give me a list of....* Thus what looks on the surface like a QUESTION can really be a REQUEST.

Similarly, what looks on the surface like a STATEMENT can really be a QUESTION. A very common kind of question, called a CHECK question (Carletta et al., 1997; Labov and Fanshel, 1977), is used to ask the other participant to confirm something that this other participant has privileged knowledge about. These CHECKs are questions, but they have declarative surface form, as the boldfaced utterance in the following snippet from another travel agent conversation:

A OPEN-OPTION	I was wanting to make some arrangements for a trip that I'm going to be taking uh to LA uh beginning of the week after next.
B HOLD	OK uh let me pull up your profile and I'll be right with you here. [pause]
B CHECK	**And you said you wanted to travel next week?**
A ACCEPT	Uh yes.

INDIRECT
SPEECH ACTS

Utterances which use a surface statement to ask a question, or a surface question to issue a request, are called **indirect speech acts**.How can a surface yes-no-question like *Can you give me a list of the flights from Atlanta to Boston?* be mapped into the correct illocutionary act REQUEST? Solutions to this problem lie along a continuum of idiomaticity. At one end of the continuum is the *idiom* approach, which assumes that a sentence structure like *Can you give me a list?* or *Can you pass the salt?* is ambiguous between a literal meaning as a YES-NO-QUESTION and an idiomatic meaning as a request. The grammar of English would simply list REQUEST as one meaning of *Can you X*. One problem with this approach is that there are many ways to make an indirect request, each of which has slightly different surface grammatical structure (see below). The grammar would have to store the REQUEST meaning in many different places. Furthermore, the idiom approach doesn't make use of the fact that there are semantic generalizations about what makes something a legitimate indirect request.

The alternative end of the continuum is the *inferential* approach, first proposed by Gordon and Lakoff (1971) and taken up by Searle (1975a). Their intuition was that a sentence like *Can you give me a list of flights from Atlanta?* is unambiguous, meaning only *Do you have the ability to give me a list of flights from Atlanta?* The directive speech act *Please give me a list*

INFERRED   *of flights from Atlanta* is **inferred** by the hearer.

The next two sections will introduce two models of dialogue act interpretation: an inferential model called the **plan inference** model, and an idiom-based model called the **cue** model.

Plan-Inferential Interpretation of Dialogue Acts

The plan-inference approach to dialogue act interpretation was first proposed by Gordon and Lakoff (1971) and Searle (1975a) when they noticed that there was a structure to what kind of things a speaker could do to make an indirect request. In particular, they noticed that a speaker could mention or question various quite specific properties of the desired activity to make an indirect request; here is a partial list with examples from the ATIS corpus:

1. The speaker can question the hearer's ability to perform the activity

   - Can you give me a list of the flights from Atlanta to Boston?
   - Could you tell me if Delta has a hub in Boston?
   - Would you be able to, uh, put me on a flight with Delta?

2. The speaker can mention speaker's wish or desire about the activity

   - I want to fly from Boston to San Francisco.
   - I would like to stop somewhere else in between.
   - I'm looking for one way flights from Tampa to Saint Louis.
   - I need that for Tuesday.
   - I wonder if there are any flights from Boston to Dallas.

3. The speaker can mention the hearer's doing the action

   - Would you please repeat that information?
   - Will you tell me the departure time and arrival time on this American flight?

4. The speaker can question the speaker's having permission to receive results of the action

   - May I get a lunch on flight U A two one instead of breakfast?
   - Could I have a listing of flights leaving Boston?

Based on this realization, Searle (1975a, p. 73) proposed that the hearer's chain of reasoning upon hearing *Can you give me a list of the flights from Atlanta to Boston?* might be something like the following (modified for our ATIS example):

1. X has asked me a question about whether I have the ability to give a list of flights.

2. I assume that X is being cooperative in the conversation (in the Gricean sense) and that his utterance therefore has some aim.

3. X knows I have the ability to give such a list, and there is no alternative reason why X should have a purely theoretical interest in my list-giving ability.

4. Therefore X's utterance probably has some ulterior illocutionary point. What can it be?

5. A preparatory condition for a directive is that the hearer have the ability to perform the directed action.

6. Therefore X has asked me a question about my preparedness for the action of giving X a list of flights.

7. Furthermore, X and I are in a conversational situation in which giving lists of flights is a common and expected activity.

8. Therefore, in the absence of any other plausible illocutionary act, X is probably requesting me to give him a list of flights.

The inferential approach has a number of advantages. First, it explains why *Can you give me a list of flights from Boston?* is a reasonable way of making an indirect request and *Boston is in New England* is not: the former mentions a precondition for the desired activity, and there is a reasonable inferential chain from the precondition to the activity itself. The inferential approach has been modeled by Allen, Cohen, and Perrault and their colleagues in a number of influential papers on what have been called **BDI** (belief, desire, and intention) models (Allen, 1995). The earliest papers, such as Cohen and Perrault (1979), offered an AI planning model for how speech acts are *generated*. One agent, seeking to find out some information, could use standard planning techniques to come up with the plan of asking the hearer to tell the speaker the information. Perrault and Allen (1980) and Allen and Perrault (1980) also applied this BDI approach to *comprehension*, specifically the comprehension of indirect speech effects, essentially cashing out Searle's (1975) promissory note in a computational formalism.

BDI

We'll begin by summarizing Perrault and Allen's formal definitions of belief and desire in the predicate calculus. We'll represent "*S* believes the proposition *P*" as the two-place predicate $B(S,P)$. Reasoning about belief is done with a number of axiom schemas inspired by Hintikka (1969) (such as $B(A,P) \wedge B(A,Q) \Rightarrow B(A,P \wedge Q)$; see Perrault and Allen (1980) for details). Knowledge is defined as "true belief"; *S knows that P* will be represented as $KNOW(S,P)$, defined as follows:

$$KNOW(S,P) \equiv P \wedge B(S,P)$$

In addition to *knowing that*, we need to define *knowing whether*. *S knows whether* (KNOWIF) a proposition *P* is true if *S* KNOWs that *P* or *S* KNOWs that $\neg P$:

$$KNOWIF(S,P) \equiv KNOW(S,P) \vee KNOW(S,\neg P)$$

The theory of desire relies on the predicate WANT. If an agent S wants P to be true, we say $WANT(S,P)$, or $W(S,P)$ for short. P can be a state or the execution of some action. Thus if ACT is the name of an action, $W(S, \text{ACT}(H))$ means that S wants H to do ACT. The logic of WANT relies on its own set of axiom schemas just like the logic of belief.

The BDI models also require an axiomatization of actions and planning; the simplest of these is based on a set of **action schema**s similar to the AI planning model STRIPS (Fikes and Nilsson, 1971). Each action schema has a set of parameters with *constraints* about the type of each variable, and three parts:

ACTION
SCHEMA

- *Preconditions:* Conditions that must already be true in order to successfully perform the action.

- *Effects:* Conditions that become true as a result of successfully performing the action.

- *Body:* A set of partially ordered goal states that must be achieved in performing the action.

In the travel domain, for example, the action of agent A booking flight $F1$ for client C might have the following simplified definition:

BOOK-FLIGHT(A,C,F):

Constraints:	Agent(A) ∧ Flight(F) ∧ Client(C)
Precondition:	Know(A,departure-date(F)) ∧ Know(A,departure-time(F)) ∧ Know(A,origin-city(F)) ∧ Know(A,destination-city(F)) ∧ Know(A,flight-type(F)) ∧ Has-Seats(F) ∧ W(C,(BOOK(A,C,F))) ∧ ...

Effect:	Flight-Booked(A,C,F)
Body:	Make-Reservation(A,F,C)

Cohen and Perrault (1979) and Perrault and Allen (1980) use this kind of action specification for speech acts. For example here is Perrault and Allen's definition for three speech acts relevant to indirect requests. IN-FORM is the speech act of informing the hearer of some proposition (the Austin/Searle *Assertive*, or DAMSL STATEMENT). The definition of IN-FORM is based on Grice's (1957) idea that a speaker informs the hearer of something merely by causing the hearer to believe that the speaker wants them to know something:

INFORM(S,H,P):
Constraints:	Speaker(S) ∧ Hearer(H) ∧ Proposition(P)
Precondition:	Know(S,P) ∧ W(S, INFORM(S, H, P))
Effect:	Know(H,P)
Body:	B(H,W(S,Know(H,P)))

INFORMIF is the act used to inform the hearer whether a proposition is true or not; like INFORM, the speaker INFORMIFs the hearer by causing the hearer to believe the speaker wants them to KNOWIF something:

INFORMIF(S,H,P):
Constraints:	Speaker(S) ∧ Hearer(H) ∧ Proposition(P)
Precondition:	KnowIf(S, P) ∧ W(S, INFORMIF(S, H, P))
Effect:	KnowIf(H, P)
Body:	B(H, W(S, KnowIf(H, P)))

REQUEST is the directive speech act for requesting the hearer to perform some action:

REQUEST(S,H,ACT):
Constraints:	Speaker(S) ∧ Hearer(H) ∧ ACT(A) ∧ H is agent of ACT
Precondition:	W(S,ACT(H))
Effect:	W(H,ACT(H))
Body:	B(H,W(S,ACT(H)))

Perrault and Allen's theory also requires what are called "surface-level acts". These correspond to the "literal meanings" of the imperative, interrogative, and declarative structures. For example the "surface-level" act S.REQUEST produces imperative utterances:

S.REQUEST (S, H, ACT):
Effect: B(H, W(S,ACT(H)))

The effects of S.REQUEST match the body of a regular REQUEST, since this is the default or standard way of doing a request (but not the only way). This "default" or "literal" meaning is the start of the hearer's inference chain. The hearer will be given an input which indicates that the speaker is requesting the hearer to inform the speaker whether the hearer is capable of giving the speaker a list:

S.REQUEST(S,H,InformIf(H,S,CanDo(H,Give(H,S,LIST))))

The hearer must figure out that the speaker is actually making a request:

REQUEST(H,S,Give(H,S,LIST))

The inference chain from the request-to-inform-if-cando to the request-to-give is based on a chain of *plausible inference*, based on heuristics called **plan inference** (PI) rules. We will use the following subset of the rules that Perrault and Allen (1980) propose:

PLAN
INFERENCE

- **(PI.AE) Action-Effect Rule:** For all agents S and H, if Y is an effect of action X and if H believes that S wants X to be done, then it is plausible that H believes that S wants Y to obtain.
- **(PI.PA) Precondition-Action Rule:** For all agents S and H, if X is a precondition of action Y and if H believes S wants X to obtain, then it is plausible that H believes that S wants Y to be done.
- **(PI.BA) Body-Action Rule:** For all agents S and H, if X is part of the body of Y and if H believes that S wants X done, then it is plausible that H believes that S wants Y done.
- **(PI.KP) Know-Desire Rule:** For all agents S and H, if H believes S wants to KNOWIF(P), then H believes S wants P to be true:

$$B(H,W(S,\text{KNOWIF}(S,P))) \overset{\text{plausible}}{\Longrightarrow} B(H,W(S,P))$$

- **(EI.1) Extended Inference Rule:** if $B(H,W(S,X)) \overset{\text{plausible}}{\Longrightarrow} B(H,W(S,Y))$ is a PI rule, then

$$B(H,W(S,B(H,(W(S,X))))) \overset{\text{plausible}}{\Longrightarrow} B(H,W(S,B(H,W(S,Y))))$$

is a PI rule. (i.e., you can prefix $B(H,W(S))$ to any plan inference rule).

Let's see how to use these rules to interpret the indirect speech act in *Can you give me a list of flights from Atlanta?* Step 0 in the table below shows the speaker's initial speech act, which the hearer initially interprets literally as a question. Step 1 then uses Plan Inference rule *Action-Effect*, which suggests that if the speaker asked for something (in this case information), they probably want it. Step 2 again uses the *Action-Effect* rule, here suggesting that if the Speaker wants an INFORMIF, and KNOWIF is an effect of INFORMIF, then the speaker probably also wants KNOWIF.

Rule	Step	Result
	0	S.REQUEST(S,H,InformIf(H,S,CanDo(H,Give(H,S,LIST))))
PI.AE	1	B(H,W(S,InformIf(H,S,CanDo(H,Give(H,S,LIST)))))
PI.AE/EI	2	B(H,W(S,KnowIf(H,S,CanDo(H,Give(H,S,LIST)))))
PI.KP/EI	3	B(H,W(S,CanDo(H,Give(H,S,LIST))))
PI.PA/EI	4	B(H,W(S,Give(H,S,LIST)))
PI.BA	5	REQUEST(H,S,Give(H,S,LIST))

Step 3 adds the crucial inference that people don't usually ask about things they aren't interested in; thus if the speaker asks whether something is true (in this case CanDo), the speaker probably wants it (CanDo) to be true. Step 4 makes use of the fact that CanDo(ACT) is a precondition for (ACT), making the inference that if the speaker wants a precondition (CanDo) for an action (Give), the speaker probably also wants the action (Give). Finally, step 5 relies on the definition of REQUEST to suggest that if the speaker wants someone to know that the speaker wants them to do something, then the speaker is probably REQUESTing them to do it.

In giving this summary of the plan-inference approach to indirect speech act comprehension, we have left out many details, including many necessary axioms, as well as mechanisms for deciding which inference rule to apply. The interested reader should consult Perrault and Allen (1980) and the other literature suggested at the end of the chapter.

Cue-based Interpretation of Dialogue Acts

The plan-inference approach to dialogue act comprehension is extremely powerful; by using rich knowledge structures and powerful planning techniques the algorithm is designed to address even subtle indirect uses of dialogue acts. The disadvantage of the plan-inference approach is that it is very time-consuming both in terms of human labor in development of the plan-inference heuristics, and in terms of system time in running these heuristics. In fact, by allowing all possible kinds of non-linguistic reasoning to play a part in discourse processing, a complete application of this approach is **AI-complete**. An AI-complete problem is one which cannot be truly solved without solving the entire problem of creating a complete artificial intelligence.

AI-COMPLETE

Thus for many applications, a less sophisticated but more efficient data-driven method may suffice. One such method is a variant of the *idiom* method discussed above. Recall that in the idiom approach, sentences like *Can you give me a list of flights from Atlanta?* have two literal meanings; one as a question and one as a request. This can be implemented in the grammar by listing sentence structures like *Can you X* with two meanings. The **cue-based** approach to dialogue act comprehension we develop in this section is based on this idiom intuition.

A number of researchers have used what might be called a cue-based approach to dialogue act interpretation, although not under that name. What characterizes a cue-based model is the use of different sources of knowledge (cues) for detecting a dialogue act, such as lexical, collocational, syntactic, prosodic, or conversational-structure cues. The models we will describe use (supervised) machine-learning algorithms, trained on a corpus of dialogues that is hand-labeled with dialogue acts for each utterance. Which cues are used depends on the individual system. Many systems rely on the fact that individual dialogue acts often have what Goodwin (1996) called a **microgrammar**; specific lexical, collocation, and prosodic features which are characteristic of them. These systems also rely on conversational structure. The dialogue-act interpretation system of Jurafsky et al. (1997), for example, relies on 3 sources of information:

MICROGRAMMAR

1. **Words and Collocations:** *Please* or *would you* is a good cue for a REQUEST, *are you* for YES-NO-QUESTIONs.

2. **Prosody:** Rising pitch is a good cue for a YES-NO-QUESTION. Loudness or stress can help distinguish the *yeah* that is an AGREEMENT from the *yeah* that is a BACKCHANNEL.

3. **Conversational Structure:** A *yeah* which follows a proposal is probably an AGREEMENT; a *yeah* which follows an INFORM is probably a BACKCHANNEL.

The previous section focused on how the plan-based approach figured out that a surface question had the illocutionary force of a REQUEST. In this section we'll look at a different kind of indirect request; the CHECK, examining the specific cues that the Jurafsky et al. (1997) system uses to solve this dialogue act identification problem. Recall that a CHECK is a subtype of question which requests the interlocutor to confirm some information; the information may have been mentioned explicitly in the preceding dialogue (as in the example below), or it may have been inferred from what the interlocutor said:

A	OPEN-OPTION	I was wanting to make some arrangements for a trip that I'm going to be taking uh to LA uh beginning of the week after next.
B	HOLD	OK uh let me pull up your profile and I'll be right with you here. [pause]
B	CHECK	**And you said you wanted to travel next week?**
A	ACCEPT	Uh yes.

Examples of possible realizations of CHECKs in English include:

1. As tag questions:

    (19.11) From the Trains corpus (Allen and Core, 1997)

    U   **and it's gonna take us also an hour to load boxcars right?**
    S   right

2. As declarative questions, usually with rising intonation (Quirk et al., 1985, p. 814)

    (19.12) From the Switchboard corpus (Godfrey et al., 1992)

    A   and we have a powerful computer down at work.
    B   Oh (laughter)
    B   **so, you don't need a personal one (laughter)?**
    A   No

3. As fragment questions (subsentential units; words, noun-phrases, clauses) (Weber, 1993)

    (19.13) From the Map Task corpus (Carletta et al., 1997)

    G   Ehm, curve round slightly to your right.
    F   **To my right?**
    G   Yes.

Studies of checks have shown that, like the examples above, they are most often realized with declarative structure (i.e., no aux-inversion), they are most likely to have rising intonation (Shriberg et al., 1998), and they often have a following **question tag**, often *right*, (Quirk et al., 1985, 810-814), as in example (19.11) above. They also are often realized as "fragments" (subsentential words or phrases) with rising intonation (Weber, 1993). In Switchboard, the REFORMULATION subtype of CHECKs have a very specific microgrammar, with declarative word order, often *you* as subject (31% of the cases), often beginning with *so* (20%) or *oh*, and sometimes ending with *then*. Some examples:

Oh so you're from the Midwest too.
So you can steady it.
You really rough it then.

Many scholars, beginning with Nagata and Morimoto (1994), realized that much of the structure of these microgrammars could be simply captured by training a separate word-N-gram grammar for each dialogue act (see e.g., Suhm and Waibel, 1994; Mast et al., 1996; Jurafsky et al., 1997; Warnke et al., 1997; Reithinger and Klesen, 1997; Taylor et al., 1998). These systems create a separate mini-corpus from all the utterances which realize the same dialogue act, and then train a separate word-N-gram language model on each of these mini-corpora. Given an input utterance u consisting of a sequence of words W, they then choose the dialogue act d whose N-gram grammar assigns the highest likelihood to W:

$$d^* = \operatorname*{argmax}_{d} P(d|W) = \operatorname*{argmax}_{d} P(d)P(W|d) \qquad (19.14)$$

This simple N-gram approach does indeed capture much of the microgrammar; for example examination of the high-frequency bigram pairs in Switchboard REFORMULATIONS shows that the most common bigrams include good cues for REFORMULATIONS like *so you*, *sounds like*, *so you're*, *oh so*, *you mean*, *so they*, and *so it's*.

Prosodic models of dialogue act microgrammar rely on phonological features like pitch or accent, or their acoustic correlates like F0, duration, and energy discussed in Chapter 4 and Chapter 7. For example many studies have shown that capturing the rise in pitch at the end of YES-NO-QUESTIONS can be a useful cue for augmenting lexical cues (Sag and Liberman, 1975; Pierrehumbert, 1980; Waibel, 1988; Daly and Zue, 1992; Kompe et al., 1993; Taylor et al., 1998). Pierrehumbert (1980) also showed that declarative utterances (like STATEMENTS) have **final lowering**: a drop in F0 at the end of the utterance. One system which relied on these results, Shriberg et al. (1998), trained CART-style decision trees on simple acoustically-based prosodic features such as the slope of F0 at the end of the utterance, the average energy at different places in the utterance, and various duration measures. They found that these features were useful, for example, in distinguishing the four dialogue acts STATEMENT (S), YES-NO QUESTION (QY), DECLARATIVE-QUESTIONS like CHECKS (QD) and WH-QUESTIONS (QW). Figure 19.3 shows the decision tree which gives the posterior probability $P(d|f)$ of a dialogue act d type given sequence of acoustic features F. Each node in the tree shows four probabilities, one for each of the four dialogue acts in the order S, QY, QW, QD; the most likely of the four is shown as the label for the node. Via the Bayes rule, this probability can be used to compute the likelihood of the acoustic features given the dialogue act: $P(f|d)$.

A final important cue for dialogue act interpretation is conversational structure. One simple way to model conversational structure, drawing on the idea of adjacency pairs (Schegloff, 1968; Sacks et al., 1974) introduced above, is as a probabilistic sequence of dialogue acts. The identity of the

FINAL LOWERING

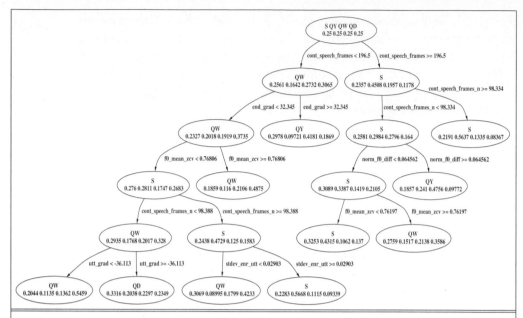

Figure 19.3   Decision tree for the classification of STATEMENT (S), YES-NO QUES-
TIONS (QY), WH-QUESTIONS (QW) and DECLARATIVE QUESTIONS (QD), after
Shriberg et al. (1998). Note that the difference between S and QY toward the right of the
tree is based on the feature `norm_f0_diff` (normalized difference between mean F0 of end
and penultimate regions), while the difference between WQ and QD at the bottom left is
based on `utt_grad`, which measures F0 slope across the whole utterance.

previous dialogue acts can then be used to help predict upcoming dialogue
acts. Many studies have modeled dialogue act sequences as dialogue-act-N-
grams (Nagata and Morimoto, 1994; Suhm and Waibel, 1994; Warnke et al.,
1997; Chu-Carroll, 1998; Stolcke et al., 1998; Taylor et al., 1998), often as
part of an HMM system for dialogue acts (Reithinger et al., 1996; Kita et al.,
1996; Woszczyna and Waibel, 1994). For example Woszczyna and Waibel
(1994) give the dialogue HMM shown in Figure 19.4 for a Verbmobil-like
appointment scheduling task.

How does the dialogue act interpreter combine these different cues to
find the most likely correct sequence of correct dialogue acts given a conversation? Stolcke et al. (1998) and Taylor et al. (1998) apply the HMM
intuition of Woszczyna and Waibel (1994) to treat the dialogue act detection
process as HMM-parsing. Given all available evidence E about a conversation, the goal is to find the dialogue act sequence $D = \{d_1, d_2 \ldots, d_N\}$ that
has the highest posterior probability $P(D|E)$ given that evidence (here we

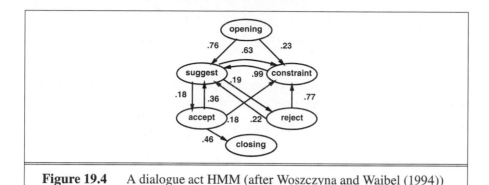

Figure 19.4   A dialogue act HMM (after Woszczyna and Waibel (1994))

are using capital letters to mean *sequences* of things). Applying Bayes' Rule
we get

$$
\begin{aligned}
D^* &= \operatorname*{argmax}_{D} P(D|E) \\
&= \operatorname*{argmax}_{D} \frac{P(D)P(E|D)}{P(E)} \\
&= \operatorname*{argmax}_{D} P(D)P(E|D)
\end{aligned}
\tag{19.15}
$$

Here $P(D)$ represents the prior probability of a sequence of dialogue acts D.
This probability can be computed by the dialogue act N-grams introduced
by Nagata and Morimoto (1994). The likelihood $P(E|D)$ can be computed
from the other two sources of evidence: the microsyntax models (for example the different word-N-gram grammars for each dialogue act) and the
microprosody models (for example the decision tree for the prosodic features of each dialogue act). The word-N-grams models for each dialogue act
can be used to estimate $P(W|D)$, the probability of the sequence of words W.
The microprosody models can be used to estimate $P(F|D)$, the probability
of the sequence of prosodic features F.

If we make the simplifying (but of course incorrect) assumption that
the prosody and the words are independent, we can estimate the evidence
likelihood for a sequence of dialogue acts D as follows:

$$
P(E|D) = P(F|D)P(W|D)
\tag{19.16}
$$

We can compute the most likely sequence of dialogue acts D^* by substituting equation (19.16) into equation (19.15), thus choosing the dialogue
act sequence which maximizes the product of the three knowledge sources
(conversational structure, prosody, and lexical/syntactic knowledge):

$$D^* = \underset{D}{\mathrm{argmax}}\, P(D)P(F|D)P(W|D)$$

Standard HMM-parsing techniques (like Viterbi) can then be used to search for this most-probable sequence of dialogue acts given the sequence of input utterances.

The HMM method is only one way of solving the problem of data-driven dialogue act identification. The link with HMM tagging suggests another approach, treating dialogue acts as *tags*, and applying other part-of-speech tagging methods. Samuel et al. (1998b), for example, applied Transformation-Based Learning to dialogue act tagging.

Summary

As we have been suggesting, the two ways of doing dialogue act interpretation (via inference and via cues) each have advantages and disadvantages. The cue-based approach may be more appropriate for systems which require relatively shallow dialogue structure which can be trained on large corpora. If a semantic interpretation is required, the cue-based approach will still need to be augmented with a semantic interpretation. The full inferential approach may be more appropriate when more complex reasoning is required.

19.4   Dialogue Structure and Coherence

Section 18.2 described an approach to determining coherence based on a set of coherence relations. In order to determine that a coherence relation holds, the system must reason about the constraints that the relation imposes on the **information** in the utterances. We will call this view the *informational* approach to coherence. Historically, the informational approach has been applied predominantly to monologues.

The BDI approach to utterance interpretation gives rise to another view of coherence, which we will call the **intentional** approach. According to this approach, utterances are understood as actions, requiring that the hearer infer the plan-based speaker intentions underlying them in establishing coherence. In contrast to the informational approach, intentional approach has been applied predominantly to dialogue.

The intentional approach we describe here is due to Grosz and Sidner (1986), who argue that a discourse can be represented as a composite of three interacting components: a **linguistic structure**, an **intentional structure**, and an **attentional state**. The linguistic structure contains the utterances in the discourse, divided into a hierarchical structure of discourse segments. (Recall the description of discourse segments in Chapter 18.) The attentional state is a dynamically-changing model of the objects, properties, and relations that are salient at each point in the discourse. This aligns closely with the notion of a discourse model introduced in the previous chapter. Centering (see Chapter 18) is considered to be a theory of attentional state in this approach.

We will concentrate here on the third component of the approach, the intentional structure, which is based on the BDI model of interpretation described in the previous section. The fundamental idea is that a discourse has associated with it an underlying purpose that is held by the person who initiates it, called the **discourse purpose** (DP). Likewise, each discourse segment within the discourse has a corresponding purpose, called a **discourse segment purpose** (DSP). Each DSP has a role in achieving the DP of the discourse in which its corresponding discourse segment appears. Listed below are some possible DPs/DSPs that Grosz and Sidner give.

1. Intend that some agent intend to perform some physical task.
2. Intend that some agent believe some fact.
3. Intend that some agent believe that one fact supports another.
4. Intend that some agent intend to identify an object (existing physical object, imaginary object, plan, event, event sequence).
5. Intend that some agent know some property of an object.

As opposed to the larger sets of coherence relations used in informational accounts of coherence, Grosz and Sidner propose only two such relations: **dominance** and **satisfaction-precedence**. DSP_1 dominates DSP_2 if satisfying DSP_2 is intended to provide part of the satisfaction of DSP_1. DSP_1 satisfaction-precedes DSP_2 if DSP_1 must be satisfied before DSP_2.

As an example, let's consider the dialogue between a client (C) and a travel agent (A) that we saw earlier, repeated here in Figure 19.5.

Collaboratively, the caller and agent successfully identify a flight that suits the caller's needs. Achieving this joint goal required that a top-level discourse intention be satisfied, listed as I1 below, in addition to several intermediate intentions that contributed to the satisfaction of I1, listed as I2-I5:

I1: (Intend C (Intend A (A find a flight for C)))
I2: (Intend A (Intend C (Tell C A departure date)))

C_1:	I need to travel in May.
A_1:	And, what day in May did you want to travel?
C_2:	OK uh I need to be there for a meeting that's from the 12th to the 15th.
A_2:	And you're flying into what city?
C_3:	Seattle.
A_3:	And what time would you like to leave Pittsburgh?
C_4:	Uh hmm I don't think there's many options for non-stop.
A_4:	Right. There's three non-stops today.
C_5:	What are they?
A_5:	The first one departs PGH at 10:00am arrives Seattle at 12:05 their time. The second flight departs PGH at 5:55pm, arrives Seattle at 8pm. And the last flight departs PGH at 8:15pm arrives Seattle at 10:28pm.
C_6:	OK I'll take the 5ish flight on the night before on the 11th.
A_6:	On the 11th? OK. Departing at 5:55pm arrives Seattle at 8pm, U.S. Air flight 115.
C_7:	OK.

Figure 19.5   A fragment from a telephone conversation between a client (C) and a travel agent (A) (repeated from Figure 19.1).

I3: (Intend A (Intend C (Tell C A destination city)))

I4: (Intend A (Intend C (Tell C A departure time)))

I5: (Intend C (Intend A (A find a nonstop flight for C)))

Intentions I2–I5 are all subordinate to intention I1, as they were all adopted to meet preconditions for achieving intention I1. This is reflected in the dominance relationships below:

I1 dominates I2

I1 dominates I3

I1 dominates I4

I1 dominates I5

Furthermore, intentions I2 and I3 needed to be satisfied before intention I5, since the agent needed to know the departure date and destination city in order to start listing nonstop flights. This is reflected in the satisfaction-precedence relationships below:

I2 satisfaction-precedes I5

I3 satisfaction-precedes I5

The dominance relations give rise to the discourse structure depicted in Figure 19.6. Each discourse segment is numbered in correspondence with the intention number that serves as its DP/DSP.

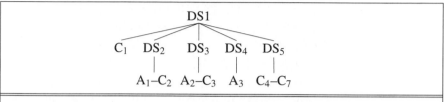

Figure 19.6   Discourse Structure of the Flight Reservation Dialogue

On what basis does this set of intentions and relationships between them give rise to a coherent discourse? It is their role in the overall *plan* that the caller is inferred to have. There are a variety of ways that plans can be represented; here we will use the simple STRIPS model described in the previous section. We make use of two simple action schemas; the first is the one for booking a flight, repeated from page 735.

BOOK-FLIGHT(A,C,F):

Constraints: Agent(A) ∧ Flight(F) ∧ Client(C)

Precondition: Know(A,departure-date(F))   ∧   Know(A,departure-time(F))   ∧   Know(A,origin-city(F))   ∧   Know(A,destination-city(F)) ∧ Know(A,flight-type(F)) ∧ Has-Seats(F) ∧ W(C,(BOOK(A,C,F))) ∧ ...

Effect: Flight-Booked(A,C,F)
Body: Make-Reservation(A,F,C)

As can be seen, booking a flight requires that the agent know a variety of parameters having to do with the flight, including the departure date and time, origin and destination cities, and so forth. The utterance with which the caller initiates the example dialogue contains the origin city and partial information about the departure date. The agent has to request the rest; the second action schema we use represents a simplified view of this action (see Cohen and Perrault (1979) for a more in-depth discussion of planning wh-questions):

REQUEST-INFO(A,C,I):

Constraints:	$Agent(A) \wedge Client(C)$
Precondition:	$Know(C,I)$
Effect:	$Know(A,I)$
Body:	$B(C,W(A,Know(A,I)))$

Because the effects of REQUEST-INFO match each precondition of BOOK-FLIGHT, the former can be used to serve the needs of the latter. Discourse segments DS2 and DS3 are cases in which performing REQUEST-INFO succeeds for identifying the values of the departure date and destination city parameters respectively. Segment DS4 is also a request for a parameter value (departure time), but is unsuccessful in that the caller takes the initiative instead, by (implicitly) asking about nonstop flights. Segment DS5 leads to the satisfaction of the top-level DP from the caller's selection of a nonstop flight from a short list that the agent produced.

SUBDIALOGUES

Subsidiary discourse segments like DS2 and DS3 are also called **subdialogues**. The type of subdialogues that DS2 and DS3 instantiate are generally called **knowledge precondition** subdialogues (Lochbaum et al., 1990; Lochbaum, 1998), since they are initiated by the agent to help satisfy preconditions of a higher-level goal (in this case addressing the client's request for travel in May). They are also called **information-sharing subdialogues** (Chu-Carroll and Carberry, 1998).

INFORMATION-SHARING SUBDIALOGUES

CORRECTION SUBDIALOGUES

Later on in a part of the conversation not given in Figure 19.5 is another kind of subdialogue, a **correction subdialogue** (Litman, 1985; Litman and Allen, 1987) (or **negotiation subdialogue**; Chu-Carroll and Carberry (1998)). Utterances C_{20} through C_{23a} constitute a correction to the previous plan of returning on May 15:

A_{17}: And you said returning on May 15th?

C_{18}: Uh, yeah, at the end of the day.

A_{19}: OK. There's #two non-stops ...#

C_{20}: #Act...actually#, what day of the week is the 15th?

A_{21}: It's a Friday.

C_{22}: Uh hmm. I would consider staying there an extra day til Sunday.

A_{23a}: OK...OK.

A_{23b}: On Sunday I have ...

SUBTASK

Finally, perhaps the earliest class of subdialogues to be addressed in the literature was the **subtask** subdialogue (Grosz, 1974), which is used to deal with subtasks of the overall task in a task-oriented dialogue.

Determining Intentional Structure   Algorithms for inferring intentional structure in dialogue (and spoken monologue) work similarly to algorithms for inferring dialogue acts.   Many algorithms apply variants of the BDI model (e.g., Litman, 1985; Grosz and Sidner, 1986; Litman and Allen, 1987; Carberry, 1990; Passonneau and Litman, 1993; Chu-Carroll and Carberry, 1998).   Others rely on similar cues to those described for utterance- and turn-segmentation on page 724, including cue words and phrases (Reichman, 1985; Grosz and Sidner, 1986; Hirschberg and Litman, 1993), prosody (Grosz and Hirschberg, 1992; Hirschberg and Pierrehumbert, 1986; Hirschberg and Nakatani, 1996), and other cues. For example Pierrehumbert and Hirschberg (1990) argue that certain **boundary tones** might be used to suggest a dominance relation between two intonational phrases.

BOUNDARY TONES

Informational vs. Intentional Coherence   As we just saw, the key to intentional coherence lies in the ability of the dialogue participants to recognize each other's intentions and how they fit into the plans they have. On the other hand, as we saw in the previous chapter, informational coherence lies in the ability to establish certain kinds of content-bearing relationships between utterances. So one might ask what the relationship between these are: does one obviate the need for the other, or do we need both?

Moore and Pollack (1992), among others, have argued that in fact both levels of analysis must co-exist. Let us assume that after our agent and caller have identified a flight, the agent makes the statement in passage (19.17).

(19.17) You'll want to book your reservations before the end of the day.
Proposition 143 goes into effect tomorrow.

This passage can be analyzed either from the intentional or informational perspective. Intentionally, the agent intends to convince the caller to book her reservation before the end of the day. One way to accomplish this is to provide motivation for this action, which is the role served by uttering the second sentence. Informationally, the two sentences satisfy the Explanation relation described in the last chapter, since the second sentence provides a cause for the effect of wanting to book the reservations before the end of the day.

Depending on the knowledge of the caller, recognition at the informational level might lead to recognition of the speaker's plan, or vice versa. Say, for instance, that the caller knows that Proposition 143 imposes a new tax on airline tickets, but did not know the intentions of the agent in uttering the second sentence. From the knowledge that a way to motivate an action is to provide a cause that has that action as an effect, the caller can surmise that the agent is trying to motivate the action described in the first sentence. Alternatively, the caller might have surmised this intention from the discourse scenario, but have no idea what Proposition 143 is about. Again, knowing the relationship between establishing a cause-effect relationship and motivating something, the caller might be led to assume an Explanation relationship, which would require that she infers that the proposition is somehow bad for airline ticket buyers (e.g., a tax). Thus, at least in some cases, both levels of analysis appear to be required.

19.5   DIALOGUE MANAGERS IN CONVERSATIONAL AGENTS

The idea of a conversational agent is a captivating one, and conversational agents like **ELIZA**, **PARRY**, or **SHRDLU** have become some of the best-known examples of natural language technology. Modern examples of conversational agents include airline travel information systems, speech-based restaurant guides, and telephone interfaces to email or calendars. The dialogue manager is the component of such conversational agents that controls the flow of the dialogue, deciding at a high level how the agent's side of the conversation should proceed, what questions to ask or statements to make, and when to ask or make them.

This section briefly summarizes some issues in dialogue manager design, discussing some simple systems based on finite-state automata and production rules, and some more complex ones based on more sophisticated BDI-style reasoning and planning techniques.

The simplest dialogue managers are based on finite-state automata. For example, imagine a trivial airline travel system whose job was to ask the user for a departure city, a destination city, a time, and any airline preference. Figure 19.7 shows a sample dialogue manager for such a system. The states of the FSA correspond to questions that the dialogue manager asks the user, and the arcs correspond to actions to take depending on what the user responds.

SINGLE INITIATIVE

SYSTEM INITIATIVE

Systems which completely control the conversation in this way are called **single initiative** or **system initiative** systems. While this simple dialogue manager architecture is sufficient for some tasks (for example for implementing a speech interface to an automatic teller machine or a simple geography quiz), it is probably too restricted for a speech based travel agent system (see the discussion in McTear (1998)). One reason is that it is convenient for users to use more complex sentences that may answer more than one question at a time, as in the following ATIS example:

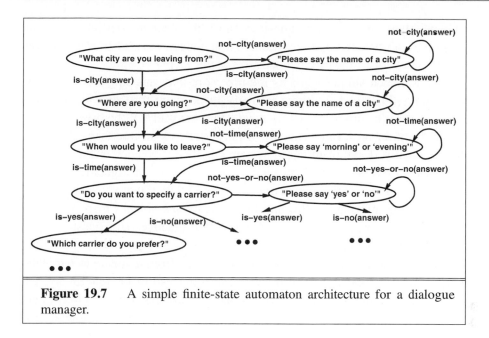

Figure 19.7   A simple finite-state automaton architecture for a dialogue manager.

> I want a flight from Milwaukee to Orlando one way leaving after five p.m. on Wednesday.

Many speech-based question answering systems, beginning with the influential GUS system for airline travel planning (Bobrow et al., 1977), and including more recent ATIS systems and other travel and restaurant guides, are **frame**- or **template**-based. For example, a simple airline system might have the goal of helping a user find an appropriate flight. It might have a frame or template with slots for various kinds of information the user might need to specify. Some of the slots come with prespecified questions to ask the user:

FRAME

TEMPLATE

Slot	Optional Question
From_Airport	"From what city are you leaving?"
To_Airport	"Where are you going?"
Dep_time	"When would you like to leave?"
Arr_time	"When do you want to arrive?"
Fare_class	
Airline	
Oneway	

Such a simple dialogue manager may just ask questions of the user, filling out the template with the answers, until it has enough information to perform a data base query, and then return the result to the user. Not every slot may have an associated question, since the dialogue designer may not want the user deluged with questions. Nonetheless, the system must be able to fill these slots if the user happens to specify them.

Even such simple domains require more than this single-template architecture. For example, there is likely to be more than one flight which meet the user's constraints. This means that the user will be given a list of choices, either on a screen or, for a purely telephone interface, by listing them verbally. A template-based system can then have another kind of template which has slots for identifying elements of lists of flights (*How much is the first one?* or *Is the second one non-stop?*). Other templates might have general route information (for questions like *Which airlines fly from Boston to San Francisco?*), information about airfare practices (for questions like *Do I have to stay a specific number of days to get a decent airfare?*) or about car or hotel reservations. Since users may switch from template to template, and since they may answer a future question instead of the one the system asked, the system must be able to disambiguate which slot of which template a given input is supposed to fill, and then switch dialogue control to that template. A template-based system is thus essentially a production rule system. Different types of inputs cause different productions to fire, each of which can flexibly fill in different templates. The production rules can then switch control based on factors such as the user's input and some simple dialogue history like the last question that the system asked.

The template or production-rule dialogue manager architecture is often used when the set of possible actions the user could want to take is relatively limited, but where the user might want to switch around a bit among these things.

The limitations of both the template-based and FSA-based dialogue managers are obvious. Consider the client's utterance C_4 in the fragment of sample dialogue of Figure 19.5 on page 746, repeated here:

A_3: And what time would you like to leave Pittsburgh?

C_4: Uh hmm I don't think there's many options for non-stop.

A_4: Right. There's three non-stops today.

C_5: What are they?

A_5: The first one departs PGH at 10:00a.m. ...

INITIATIVE   What the client is doing in C_4 is taking control or **initiative** of the dialogue. C_4 is an indirect request, asking the agent to check on non-stop flights. It would not be appropriate for the system to just set the WANTS NON-STOP field in a template and ask the user again for the departure time.

The system needs to realize that the user has indicated that a non-stop flight is a priority and that the system should focus on that next.

Conversational agents also need to use the **grounding** acts described on page 725. For example, when the user makes a choice of flights, it's important for the agent to indicate to the client that it has understood this choice. Repeated below is an example of such grounding excerpted from our sample conversation:

C_6: OK I'll take the 5ish flight on the night before on the 11th.
A_6: On the 11th? OK.

It is also important for a computational conversational agent to use requests for repairs, since given the potential for errors in the speech recognition or the understanding, there will often be times when the agent is confused or does not understand the user's request.

In order to address these and other problems, more sophisticated dialogue managers can be built on the BDI (belief, desire, intention) architecture described on page 734. Such systems are often integrated with logic-based planning models, and treat a conversation as a sequence of actions to be planned.

Let's consider the dialogue manager of the TRAINS-93 system; the system is described in Allen et al. (1995), the dialogue manager in Traum and Allen (1994). The TRAINS system is a spoken-language conversational planning agent whose task is to assist the user in managing a railway transportation system in a microworld. For example, the user and the system might collaborate in planning to move a boxcar of oranges from one city to another. The TRAINS dialogue manager maintains the flow of conversation and addresses the conversational goals (such as coming up with a operational plan for achieving the domain goal of successfully moving oranges). To do this, the manager must model the state of the dialogue, its own intentions, and the user's requests, goals, and beliefs. The manager uses a conversation act interpreter to semantically analyze the user's utterances, a domain planner and executer to solve the actual transportation domain problems, and a generator to generate sentences to the user. Figure 19.8 shows an outline of the TRAINS-93 dialogue manager algorithm.

The algorithm keeps a queue of conversation acts it needs to generate. Acts are added to the queue based on **grounding**, **dialogue obligations**, or the agent's **goals**. Let's examine each of these sources. Grounding acts were discussed on page 724; recall that a previous utterance can be grounded by an explicit backchannel (e.g., *uh-huh*, *yeah*, or under certain circumstances *ok*),

DIALOGUE_MANAGER

  while conversation is not finished
   if user has completed a turn
   then interpret user's utterance
   if system has obligations
   then address obligations
   else if system has turn
   then if system has intended conversation acts
     then call generator to produce NL utterances
     else if some material is ungrounded
     then address grounding situation
     else if high-level goals are unsatisfied
     then address goals
     else release turn or attempt to end conversation
   else if no one has turn
   then take turn
   else if long pause
   then take turn

Figure 19.8   A dialogue manager algorithm, slightly modified from Traum and Allen (1994).

or by repeating back part of the utterance. Utterances can also be grounded implicitly by "taking up" the utterance, i.e., continuing in a way which makes it clear that the utterance was understood, such as by answering a question.

Obligations are used in the TRAINS system to enable the system to correctly produce the second-pair part of an adjacency pair. That is, when a user REQUESTs something of the system (e.g., REQUEST(Give(List)), or REQUEST(InformIf(NonStop(FLIGHT-201)))), the REQUEST sets up an obligation for the system to address the REQUEST either by accepting it, and then performing it (giving the list or informing whether flight 201 is non-stop), or by rejecting it.

Finally, the TRAINS dialogue manager must reason about its own goals. For the travel agent domain, the dialogue manager's goal might be to find out the client's travel goal and then create an appropriate plan. Let's pretend that the human travel agent for the conversation in Figure 19.5 was a system and explore what the state of a TRAINS-style dialogue manager would have to be to act appropriately. Let's start with the state of the dia-

METHODOLOGY BOX: DESIGNING DIALOGUE SYSTEMS

How does a dialogue system developer choose dialogue strategies, architectures, prompts, error messages, and so on? The three design principles of Gould and Lewis (1985) can be summarized as:

Key Concept #8. User-Centered Design: Study the user and task, build simulations and prototypes, and iteratively test them on the user and fix the problems.

1. Early Focus on Users and Task: Understand the potential users and the nature of the task, via interviews with users and investigation of similar systems. Study of related human-human dialogues can also be useful, although the language in human-machine dialogues is usually simpler than in human-human dialogues. (For example pronouns are rare in human-machine dialogue and are very locally bound when they do occur (Guindon, 1988)).

2. Build Prototypes: In the children's book *The Wizard of Oz* (Baum, 1900), the Wizard turned out to be just a simulation controlled by a man behind a curtain. In Wizard-of-Oz (WOZ) or PNAMBIC (Pay No Attention to the Man BehInd the Curtain) systems, the users interact with what they think is a software system, but is in fact a human operator ("wizard") behind some disguising interface software (e.g. Gould et al., 1983; Good et al., 1984; Fraser and Gilbert, 1991) . A WOZ system can be used to test out an architecture without implementing the complete system; only the interface software and databases need to be in place. It is difficult for the wizard to exactly simulate the errors, limitations, or time constraints of a real system; results of WOZ studies are thus somewhat idealized.

3. Iterative Design: An iterative design cycle with embedded user testing is essential in system design (Nielsen, 1992; Cole et al., 1994, 1997; Yankelovich et al., 1995; Landauer, 1995). For example Stifelman et al. (1993) and Yankelovich et al. (1995) found that users of speech systems consistently tried to interrupt the system (**barge in**), suggesting a redesign of the system to recognize overlapped speech. Kamm (1994) and Cole et al. (1993) found that **directive prompts** ("Say *yes* if you accept the call, otherwise, say *no*") or the use of constrained forms (Oviatt et al., 1993) produced better results than open-ended prompts like "Will you accept the call?".

logue manager (formatted following Traum and Allen (1994)) after the first utterances in our sample conversation (repeated here):

C$_1$: I want to go to Pittsburgh in May.

The client/user has just finished a turn with an INFORM speech act. The system has the discourse goal of finding out the user's travel goal (e.g., "Wanting to go to Pittsburgh on may 15 and returning ...”), and creating a travel plan to accomplish that goal. The following table shows the five parameters of the system state: the list of obligations, the list of intended speech acts to be passed to the generator, the list of the user's speech acts that still need to be acknowledged, the list of discourse goals, and whether the system or the user holds the turn:

Discourse obligations:	NONE
Turn holder:	system
Intended speech acts:	NONE
Unacknowledged speech acts:	INFORM-1
Discourse goals:	get-travel-goal, create-travel-plan

After the utterance, the dialogue manager decides to add two conversation acts to the queue; first, to acknowledge the user's INFORM act (via "address grounding situation"), and second, to ask the next question of the user (via "address goals"). This reasoning would be worked out by the system's STRIPS-style planner as described on page 747; given the goal *get-travel-goal*, the REQUEST-INFO action schema tells the system that asking the user something is one way of finding it out. The result of adding these two conversation acts is:

Intended speech acts: REQUEST-INFORM-1, ACKNOWLEDGE-1

These would be combined by a very clever generator into the single utterance:

A$_2$: And, what day in May did you want to travel?

Note that the grounding function was achieved both by beginning with the discourse marker *and* and by repeating back the month name *May*. The request for information is achieved via the wh-question.

Let's skip ahead to the client's utterance C$_4$. Recall that C$_4$ is an indirect request, asking the agent to check on non-stop flights.

A$_3$: And what time would you like to leave Pittsburgh?

C$_4$: Uh hmm I don't think there's many options for non-stop.

Let's assume that our dialogue act interpreter correctly interprets C_4 as REQUEST-INFORM-3. The state of the agent after client utterance C_4 is then:

Discourse obligations:	address(REQUEST-INFORM-3)
Turn holder:	system
Intended speech acts:	NONE
Unacknowledged speech acts:	REQUEST-INFORM-3
Discourse goals:	get-travel-goal, create-travel-plan

The dialogue manager will first address the discourse obligation of responding to the user's request by calling the planner to find out how many non-stop flights there are. The system must now answer the question, but must also ground the user's utterance. For a direct request, the response is sufficient grounding. For an indirect request, an explicit acknowledgement is an option; since the indirect request was in the form of a *negative* check question, the form of acknowledgement will be *right* (*no* would have also been appropriate for acknowledging a negative). These two acts will then be pulled off the queue and passed to the generator:

A_4: Right. There's three non-stops today.

Dialogue managers also will need to deal with the kind of dialogue structure discussed in Section 19.4, both to recognize when the user has started a subdialogue, and to know when to initiate a subdialogue itself.

19.6   SUMMARY

Dialogue is a special kind of discourse which is particularly relevant to speech processing tasks like **conversational agents** and **automatic meeting summarization**.

- Dialogue differs from other discourse genres in exhibiting **turn-taking**, **grounding**, and **implicature**.

- An important component of dialogue modeling is the interpretation of **dialogue acts**. We introduced **plan-based** and **cue-based** algorithms for this.

- Dialogue exhibits **intentional structure** in addition to the **informational structure**, including such relations as **dominance** and **satisfaction-precedence**.

- Dialogue managers for conversational agents range from simple template- or frame-based **production systems** to complete **BDI (belief-desire-intention)** models.

METHODOLOGY BOX: EVALUATING DIALOGUE SYSTEMS

Many of the metrics that have been proposed for evaluating dialogue systems can be grouped into the following three classes:

1. User Satisfaction: Usually measured by interviewing users (Stifelman et al., 1993; Yankelovich et al., 1995) or having them fill out questionnaires asking e.g. (Shriberg et al., 1992; Polifroni et al., 1992):

- Were answers provided quickly enough?
- Did the system understand your requests the first time?
- Do you think a person unfamiliar with computers could use the system easily?

2. Task Completion Cost:

- Completion time in turns or seconds (Polifroni et al., 1992).
- Number of queries (Polifroni et al., 1992).
- Number of system non-responses (Polifroni et al., 1992) or "turn correction ratio": the number of system or user turns that were used solely to correct errors, divided by the total number of turns (Danieli and Gerbino, 1995; Hirschman and Pao, 1993).
- Inappropriateness (verbose or ambiguous) of system's questions, answers, and error messages (Zue et al., 1989).

3. Task Completion Success:

- Percent of subtasks that were completed (Polifroni et al., 1992).
- Correctness (or partial correctness) of each question, answer, error message (Zue et al., 1989; Polifroni et al., 1992).
- Correctness of the total solution (Polifroni et al., 1992).

How should these metrics be combined and weighted? The PARADISE algorithm (Walker et al., 1997) (PARAdigm for DIalogue System Evaluation) applies multiple regression to this problem. The algorithm first uses questionnaires to assign each dialogue a user satisfaction rating. A set of cost and success factors like those above is then treated as a set of independent factors; multiple regression is used to train a weight (coefficient) for each factor, measuring its importance in accounting for user satisfaction. The resulting metric can be used to compare quite different dialogue strategies.

BIBLIOGRAPHICAL AND HISTORICAL NOTES

Early work on speech and language processing had very little emphasis on the study of dialogue. One of the earliest conversational systems, ELIZA, had only a trivial production system dialogue manager; if the human user's previous sentence matched the regular-expression precondition of a possible response, ELIZA simply generated that response (Weizenbaum, 1966). The dialogue manager for the simulation of the paranoid agent PARRY (Colby et al., 1971), was a little more complex. Like ELIZA, it was based on a production system, but where ELIZA's rules were based only on the words in the user's previous sentence, PARRY's rules also rely on global variables indicating its emotional state. Furthermore, PARRY's output sometimes makes use of script-like sequences of statements when the conversation turns to its delusions. For example, if PARRY's **anger** variable is high, he will choose from a set of "hostile" outputs. If the input mentions his delusion topic, he will increase the value of his **fear** variable and then begin to express the sequence of statements related to his delusion.

The appearance of more sophisticated dialogue managers awaited the better understanding of human-human dialogue. Studies of the properties of human-human dialogue began to accumulate in the 1970's and 1980's. The Conversation Analysis community (Sacks et al., 1974; Jefferson, 1984; Schegloff, 1982) began to study the interactional properties of conversation. Grosz's (1977b) dissertation significantly influenced the computational study of dialogue with its introduction of the study of substructures in dialogues (subdialogues), and in particular with the finding that "task-oriented dialogues have a structure that closely parallels the structure of the task being performed" (p. 27). The BDI model integrating earlier AI planning work (Fikes and Nilsson, 1971) with speech act theory (Austin, 1962; Gordon and Lakoff, 1971; Searle, 1975a) was first worked out by Cohen and Perrault (1979), showing how speech acts could be generated, and Perrault and Allen (1980) and Allen and Perrault (1980), applying the approach to speech-act interpretation.

The cue-based model of dialogue act interpretation was inspired by Hinkelman and Allen (1989), who showed how lexical and phrasal cues could be integrated into the BDI model, and by the work on microgrammar in the Conversation Analysis literature (e.g. Goodwin, 1996). It was worked out at a number of mainly speech recognition labs around the world in the late 1990's (e.g. Nagata and Morimoto, 1994; Suhm and Waibel, 1994; Mast et al., 1996; Jurafsky et al., 1997; Warnke et al., 1997; Reithinger and Klesen, 1997; Taylor et al., 1998).

Models of dialogue as collaborative behavior were introduced in the late 1980's and 1990's, including the ideas of reference as a collaborative process (Clark and Wilkes-Gibbs, 1986), and models of **joint intentions** (Levesque et al., 1990), and **shared plans** (Grosz and Sidner, 1980). Related to this area is the study of **initiative** in dialogue, studying how the dialogue control shifts between participants (Walker and Whittaker, 1990; Smith and Gordon, 1997).

EXERCISES

19.1   List the dialogue act misinterpretations in the *Who's On First* routine at the beginning of the chapter.

19.2   Write a finite-state automaton for a dialogue manager for checking your bank balance and withdrawing money at an automated teller machine.

19.3   Dispreferred responses (for example turning down a request) are usually signaled by surface cues, such as significant silence. Try to notice the next time you or someone else utters a dispreferred response, and write down the utterance. What are some other cues in the response that a system might use to detect a dispreferred response? Consider non-verbal cues like eyegaze and body gestures.

19.4   When asked a question to which they aren't sure they know the answer, people use a number of cues in their response. Some of these cues overlap with other dispreferred responses. Try to notice some unsure answers to questions. What are some of the cues? If you have trouble doing this, you may instead read Smith and Clark (1993) which lists some such cues, and try instead to listen specifically for the use of these cues.

19.5   The sentence *"Do you have the ability to pass the salt?"* is only interpretable as a question, not as an indirect request. Why is this a problem for the BDI model?

19.6   Most universities require Wizard-of-Oz studies to be approved by a human subjects board, since they involve deceiving the subjects. It is a good idea (indeed it is often required) to "debrief" the subjects afterwards and tell them the actual details of the task. Discuss your opinions of the moral issues involved in the kind of deceptions of experimental subjects that take place in Wizard-of-Oz studies.

19.7   Implement a small air-travel help system. Your system should get constraints from the user about a particular flight that they want to take, expressed in natural language, and display possible flights on a screen. Make simplifying assumptions. You may build in a simple flight database or you may use an flight information system on the web as your backend.

19.8   Augment your previous system to work over the phone (or alternatively, describe the user interface changes you would have to make for it to work over the phone). What were the major differences?

19.9   Design a simple dialogue system for checking your email over the telephone. Assume that you had a synthesizer which would read out any text you gave it, and a speech recognizer which transcribed with perfect accuracy. If you have a speech recognizer or synthesizer, you may actually use them instead.

19.10   Test your email-reading system on some potential users. If you don't have an actual speech recognizer or synthesizer, simulate them by acting as the recognizer/synthesizer yourself. Choose some of the metrics described in the Methodology Box on page 758 and measure the performance of your system.

NATURAL LANGUAGE GENERATION *

"hello, world"
Kernighan & Ritchie, *The C Programming Language*

"... you, MR KEITH V LINDEN, will be a millionaire January 31!"
From a junk mailing

In one sense, language generation is the oldest subfield of language processing. When computers were able to understand only the most unnatural of command languages, they were spitting out natural texts. For example, the oldest and most famous C program, the "hello, world" program, is a generation program. It produces useful, literate English in context. Unfortunately, whatever subtle or sublime communicative force this text holds is produced not by the program itself but by the author of that program. This approach to generation, called **canned text**, is easy to implement, but is unable to adapt to new situations without the intervention of a programmer.

CANNED TEXT

Language generation is also the most pervasive subfield of language processing. Who of us has not received a form letter with our name carefully inserted in just the right places, along with eloquent appeals for one thing or another? This sort of program is easy to implement as well, but I doubt if many are fooled into thinking that such a letter is hand-written English. The inflexibility of the mechanism is readily apparent when our names are mangled, as mine is in the junk mailing shown above, or when other obvious

---

*This chapter was written by Keith Vander Linden.

mistakes are made.[1] This approach, called **template filling**, is more flexible than canned text and has been used in a variety of applications, but is still limited. For example, Weizenbaum's use of templates in ELIZA worked well in some situations, but produced nonsense in others.[2]

The success of simple generation mechanisms indicates that, to a first approximation, language generation is easier than language understanding. A language understanding system cannot generally control the complexity of the language structures it receives as input, while a generation system can limit the complexity of the structure of its output. Because of this, work in language processing initially focussed on language understanding, assuming that any generation that needed to be done could easily be handled with canned text or template filling mechanisms. Unfortunately, these simple mechanisms are not flexible enough to handle applications with any realistic variation in the information being expressed and in the context of its expression. Even the generation used in the limited domain of the "hello, world" program could use more flexibility. It might be more appropriate for the program to produce:

(20.1)   Congratulations, you've just compiled and run a simple C program
          which means that your environment is configured properly.

This text is more complex than the original and we can see a number of potential variations. If the readers are experienced systems engineers, then we might choose not to congratulate them on compiling a program. Doing so might insult them. In addition, there are a number of other ways of referring to the program in question, including "the program", "your first C program", "it" and "that lame excuse for code", each of which might or might not be appropriate in a given situation. Note also that we didn't need to conjoin "compiled and run" and we could have expressed the conclusion ("your environment is configured properly") and then the evidence ("you've compiled and run a simple C program"). These variations are not necessarily synonymous. Language has evolved a variety of ways of expressing things, all of

---

[1]   A recent example of this arose when parents of a college-bound student received an acceptance letter that read "Congratulations on 987-65-4321's admission ... as a parent you will be a partner with the university in encouraging 987-65-4321 to succeed." (from the Associated Press, March 26, 1999).

[2]   It's not difficult to "trick" ELIZA into producing nonsense, as shown in the following dialogue with ELIZA 4.3: HUMAN: "Let's talk just about you — not me. Can you think?" ELIZA: "You like to think I — not you — don't you" ... HUMAN: "I think you are an extremely stupid program." ELIZA: "Perhaps you would like to be an extremely stupid program" (Copeland, 1993, p. 40).

which are useful for expressing certain things in certain contexts. Therefore, to be useful in more complex environments, a generation system must be capable of: (1) producing an appropriate range of forms, and (2) choosing among those forms based on the intended meaning and the context. In this chapter, we will study the basic language generation techniques used to solve these problems, ignoring canned text and template-based mechanisms. This chapter will also not discuss text-to-speech synthesis, which was covered in Chapter 4.

20.1   INTRODUCTION TO LANGUAGE GENERATION

> *"Language understanding is somewhat like counting from one to infinity; language generation is like counting from infinity to one."*
>
> Yorick Wilks, quoted in Dale et al. (1998a, p. 352)

> *"Generation **from what?!**"*
> attributed to Christopher Longuet-Higgins

Natural Language Generation (NLG) is the process of constructing natural language outputs from non-linguistic inputs. The goal of this process can be viewed as the inverse of that of **natural language understanding** (NLU) in that NLG maps from meaning to text, while NLU maps from text to meaning. In doing this mapping, generation visits many of the same linguistic issues discussed in the previous chapters, but the inverse orientation distinguishes its methods from those of NLU in two important ways.

NATURAL LANGUAGE GENERATION

NATURAL LANGUAGE UNDERSTANDING

First, the nature of the input to the generation process varies widely from one application to the next. Although the linguistic input to NLU systems may vary from one text type to another, all text is governed by relatively common grammatical rules. This is not the case for the input to generation systems. Each generation system addresses a different application with a different input specification. One system may be explaining a complex set of numeric tables while another may be documenting the structure of an object-oriented software engineering model. As a result, generation systems must extract the information necessary to drive the generation process.

Second, while both NLU and NLG must be able to represent a range of lexical and grammatical forms required for the application domain, their use of these representations is different. NLU has been characterized as a process of *hypothesis management* in which the linguistic input is sequentially scanned as the system considers alternative interpretations. Its dominant concerns include ambiguity, under-specification, and ill-formed input. These concerns are not generally addressed in generation research because they don't arise. The non-linguistic representations input to an NLG system tend to be relatively unambiguous, well-specified, and well-formed. In contrast, the dominant concern of NLG is *choice*. Generation systems must make the following choices:

- **Content selection** — The system must choose the appropriate content to express from a potentially over-specified input, basing its decision on a specific communicative goal. For example, we noted that some of the content included in example (20.1) might not be appropriate for all readers. If the goal was to indicate that the environment is set up, and the reader was a systems engineer, then we'd probably express only the last clause.

- **Lexical selection** — The system must choose the lexical item most appropriate for expressing particular concepts. In example (20.1), for instance, it must choose between the word "configured" and other potential forms including "set up".

- **Sentence structure**
    - **Aggregation** — The system must apportion the selected content into phrase, clause, and sentence-sized chunks. Example (20.1) combined the actions of compiling and running into a single phrase.
    - **Referring expressions** — The system must determine how to refer to the objects being discussed. As we saw, the decision on how to refer to the program in example (20.1) was not trivial.

- **Discourse structure** — NLG systems frequently deal with multi-sentence discourse, which must have a coherent, discernible structure. Example (20.1) included two propositions in which it was clear that one was giving evidence for the other.

These issues of choice, taken together with the problem of actually putting linear sequences of words on paper, form the core of the field of NLG. Though it is a relatively young field, it has begun to develop a body of work directed at this core. This chapter will introduce this work. It will begin by presenting a simple architecture for NLG systems and will then proceed to discuss the techniques commonly used in the components of that architecture.

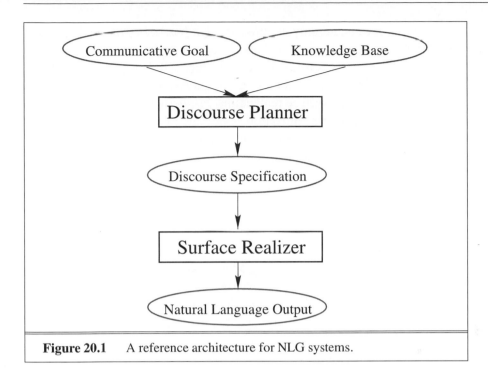

Figure 20.1   A reference architecture for NLG systems.

20.2 AN ARCHITECTURE FOR GENERATION

The nature of the architecture appropriate for accomplishing the tasks listed
in the previous section has occasioned much debate. Practical considerations, however, have frequently led to the architecture shown in Figure 20.1.
This architecture contains two pipelined components:

- **Discourse Planner** – This component starts with a communicative   DISCOURSE PLANNER
  goal and makes all the choices discussed in the previous section. It
  selects the content from the knowledge base and then structures that
  content appropriately. The resulting discourse plan will specify all the
  choices made for the entire communication, potentially spanning multiple sentences and including other annotations (including hypertext,
  figures, etc.).

- **Surface Realizer** — This component receives the fully specified dis-   SURFACE REALIZER
  course plan and generates individual sentences as constrained by its
  lexical and grammatical resources. These resources define the realizer's potential range of output. If the plan specifies multiple-sentence
  output, the surface realizer is called multiple times.

This is by no means the only architecture that has been proposed for NLG systems. Other potential mechanisms include AI-style planning and blackboard architectures. Neither is this architecture without its problems. The simple pipeline, for example, doesn't allow decisions made in the planner to be reconsidered during surface realization. Furthermore, the precise boundary between planning and realization is not altogether clear. Nevertheless, we will use it to help organize this chapter. We will start by discussing the surface realizer, the most developed of the two components, and then proceed to the discourse planner.

20.3   SURFACE REALIZATION

The surface realization component produces ordered sequences of words as constrained by the contents of a lexicon and grammar. It takes as input sentence-sized chunks of the discourse specification. This section will introduce two of the most influential approaches used for this task: Systemic Grammar and Functional Unification Grammar. Both of these approaches will be used to generate the following example:

(20.2) The system will save the document.

There is no general consensus as to the level at which the input to the surface realizer should be specified. Some approaches specify only the propositional content, so in the case of example (20.2), the discourse plan would specify a saving action done by a system entity to a document entity. Other approaches go so far as to include the specification of the grammatical form (in this case, a future tense assertion) and lexical items (in this case, "save", "system", and "document").

As we will see, systems using the two approaches discussed in this section take input at different levels. One thing they have in common, however, is that they take input that is functionally specified rather than syntactically specified. This fact, which is typical of generation systems, has tended to preclude the use of the syntactic formalisms discussed earlier in this book. Generation systems start with meaning and context, so it is most natural to

FUNCTION
FORM

specify the intended output in terms of **function** rather than of **form**. Example (20.2), for instance, could be stated in either active or passive form. Discourse planners tend not to work with these syntactic terms. They are more likely to keep track of the focus or local topic of the discourse, and thus it is more natural to specify this distinction in terms of focus. So in the example, if the document is the local topic of the discourse, it would be marked as the focus which could trigger the use of the passive. As we will see, both of the approaches discussed here categorize grammar in functional terms.

Systemic Grammar

Systemic grammar is part of **Systemic-Functional linguistics**, a branch of linguistics that views language as a resource for expressing meaning in context (Halliday, 1985). Systemic grammars represent sentences as collections of functions and maintain rules for mapping these functions onto explicit grammatical forms. This approach is well-suited to generation and has thus been widely influential in NLG. This section will start with an example of systemic sentence analysis. It will then discuss a simple systemic grammar and apply it to the running example.

SYSTEMIC-FUNCTIONAL LINGUISTICS

Systemic sentence analyses organize the functions being expressed in multiple "layers", as shown in this analysis of example (20.2):

	The system	*will*	*save*	*the document*
Mood	subject	finite	predicator	object
Transitivity	actor	process		goal
Theme	theme	rheme		

Here, the mood layer indicates a simple declarative structure with subject, finite (auxiliary), predicator (verb) and object. The transitivity layer indicates that the "system" is the actor, or doer, of the process of "saving", and that the goal, or object acted upon, is the "document".[3] The theme layer indicates that the "system" is the theme, or focus of attention, of the sentence. The concepts of theme and rheme were developed by the Prague school of linguistics (Firbas, 1966). Notice that the three layers deal with different sets of functions. These three sets, called **meta-functions**, represent three fundamental concerns in generation:

META-FUNCTIONS

- The **interpersonal meta-function** groups those functions that establish and maintain the interaction between the writer and the reader. It is represented here by the mood layer, which determines whether the writer is commanding, telling, or asking.

INTERPERSONAL META-FUNCTION

---

[3] These thematic roles are discussed in Chapter 16.

IDEATIONAL
META-FUNCTION
- The **ideational meta-function** is concerned with what is commonly called the "propositional content" of the expression. Here, the transitivity layer determines the nature of the process being expressed and the variety of case roles that must be expressed. Note that this meta-function covers much of what we previously termed "semantics".

TEXTUAL
META-FUNCTION
- The **textual meta-function** is concerned with the way in which the expression fits into the current discourse. This includes issues of thematization and reference. In our example, the theme layer represents this in that it explicitly marks "the system" as the theme of the sentence.

This explicit concern for interpersonal and textual issues as well as traditional semantics is another feature of systemic linguistics that is attractive for NLG. Many of the choices that generation systems must make depend on the context of communication, which is formalized by the interpersonal and textual metafunctions.

A systemic grammar is capable of building a sentence structure such as the one just shown. The grammar is represented using a directed, acyclic, and/or graph called a **system network**. Figure 20.2 illustrates a simple system network. Here, the large curly brace indicates "and" (i.e., parallel) systems, while the straight vertical lines represent "or" (i.e., disjoint) systems. Thus, every clause (represented as the highest level feature on the far left) will simultaneously have a set of features for mood, transitivity and theme, but will either be indicative or imperative but not both. Although the system network formalism doesn't require the use of systemic theory, we will loosely base this sample grammar on systemic categorizations. With respect to this grammar, example (20.2) is an indicative, declarative clause expressing an active material process with an unmarked theme.

SYSTEM
NETWORK

REALIZATION
STATEMENTS
A systemic grammar uses **realization statements** to map from the features specified in the grammar (e.g., Indicative, Declarative) to syntactic form. Each feature in the network can have a set of realization statements specifying constraints on the final form of the expression. These are shown in Figure 20.2 as a set of italicized statements below each feature. Realization statements allow the grammar to constrain the structure of the expression as the system network is traversed. They are specified using a simple set of operators shown here:

$+X$ Insert the function X. For example, the grammar in Figure 20.2 specifies that all clauses will have a predicator.

X/Y Conflate the functions X and Y. This allows the grammar to build a layered function structure by assigning different functions to the same

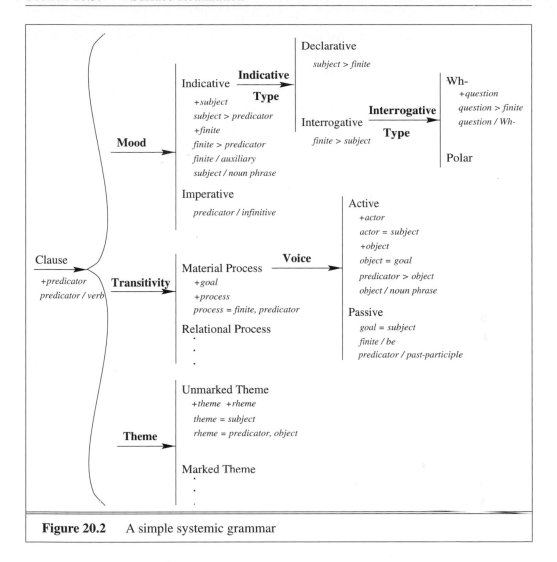

Figure 20.2   A simple systemic grammar

portion of the expression. For example, active clauses conflate the actor with the subject, while passive clauses conflate the goal with the subject.

X^Y Order function *X* somewhere before function *Y*. For example, indicative sentences place the subject before the predicator.

X : A Classify the function *X* with the lexical or grammatical feature *A*. These classifications signal a recursive pass through the grammar at a lower level. The grammar would include other networks similar to the clause network that apply to phrases, lexical items, and morphology. As an example, note that the indicative feature inserts a subject function that must be a noun phrase. This phrase will be further specified by another pass through the grammar.

$X!L$ Assign function X the lexical item L. In Figure 20.2, the finite element of the passive is assigned the lexical item "be".

Given a fully specified system network, the procedure for generation is to:

1. Traverse the network from left to right, choosing the appropriate features and collecting the associated realization statements;
2. Build an intermediate expression that reconciles the constraints set by the realization statements collected during this traversal;
3. Recurse back through the grammar at a lower level for any function that is not fully specified;

To illustrate this process, we will use the sample grammar to generate example (20.2) ("The system will save the document"). We will use the following specification as input:[4]

```
(
    :process    save-1
    :actor      system-1
    :goal       document-1
    :speechact  assertion
    :tense      future
)
```

Here, the `save-1` knowledge base instance is identified as the process of the intended expression. We will assume all knowledge base objects to be KLONE-styled instances (Brachman, 1979) for which proper lexical entries exist. The actor and goal are similarly specified as `system-1` and `document-1` respectively. The input also specifies that the expression be in the form of an assertion in the future tense.

The generation process starts with the clause feature in Figure 20.2, inserting a predicator and classifying it as a verb. It then proceeds to the mood system. The correct option for a system is chosen by a simple query or decision network associated with that system. The query or decision network bases its decision on the relevant information from the input specification and from the knowledge base. In this case, the mood system chooses the

---

[4] This input specification is loosely based on the spl-constructor interface to the PENMAN system (Mann, 1983), a systemic generation system. The Sentence Planning Language (SPL), a more flexible input language, is discussed in the bibliographical notes below.

indicative and declarative features because the input specifies an assertion. The realization statements associated with the indicative and declarative features will insert subject and finite functions, and order them as subject then finite then predicator. The resulting function structure would be as follows:

Mood	subject		finite	predicator

We will assume that the `save-1` action is marked as a material process in the knowledge base, which causes the transitivity system to choose the material process feature. This inserts the goal and process functions, and conflates the process with the finite/predicator pair. Because there is no indication in either the input or the knowledge base to use a passive, the system chooses the active feature, which: (1) inserts the actor and conflates it with the subject, and (2) inserts the object, conflating it with the goal and ordering it after the predicator. This results in:

Mood	subject		finite	predicator	object
Transitivity	actor		process		goal

Finally, because there is no thematic specification in the input, the theme network chooses unmarked theme, which inserts theme and rheme, conflating theme with subject and conflating rheme with the finite/predicator/object group. This results in the full function structure discussed above (repeated here):

Mood	subject		finite	predicator	object
Transitivity	actor		process		goal
Theme	theme		rheme		

At this point, the generation process recursively enters the grammar a number of times at lower levels to fully specify the phrases, lexical items, and morphology. The noun phrase network will use a process like the one shown here to create "the system" and "the document". Systems in the auxiliary network will insert the lexical item "will". The choice of the lexical items "system", "document", and "save" can be handled in a number of ways, most typically by retrieving the lexical item associated with the relevant knowledge base instances.

Functional Unification Grammar

Functional Unification Grammar uses unification (discussed in Chapter 11) to manipulate and reason about feature structures (Kay, 1979). With a few modifications, this technique can be applied to NLG. The basic idea is to build the generation grammar as a feature structure with lists of potential alternations, and then to unify this grammar with an input specification built using the same sort of feature structure. The unification process then takes the features specified in the input and reconciles them with those in the grammar, producing a full feature structure which can then be *linearized* to form sentence output.

In this section we will illustrate this mechanism by generating example (20.2) again. We will use the simple functional unification grammar shown in Figure 20.3. This grammar, expressed as an attribute-value matrix (cf. Chapter 11), supports simple transitive sentences in present or future tense and enforces subject-verb agreement on number. We'll now walk through the structure, explaining the features.

At its highest level, this grammar provides alternatives for sentences (cat s), noun phrases (cat np) and verb phrases (cat vp). This alternation is specified with the alt feature on the far left. We use the curly braces to indicate that any one of the three enclosed alternatives may be followed. This level also specifies a pattern that indicates the order of the features specified at this level, in this case, actor, process, then goal.

At the sentence level, this grammar supports actor, process, and goal features which are prespecified as *NP*, *VP*, and *NP* respectively. Subject-verb agreement on number is enforced using the number feature inside the process feature. Here we see that the number of the process must unify with the path {actor number}. A path is a list of features specifying a path from the root to a particular feature. In this case, the number of the process must unify with the number of the actor. While this path is given explicitly, we can also have relative paths such as the number feature of the head feature of the *NP*. The path here, {↑ ↑ number}, indicates that the number of the head of the noun phrase must unify with the number of the feature 2 levels up. We'll see how this is useful in the example below.

The *VP* level is similar in nature to the *NP* level except that it has its own alternation between present and future tense. Given the tense, which we will see specified in the input feature structure, the unification will select the alternation that matches and then proceed to unify the associated features. If the tense is present, for example, the head will be single verb. If, on the other

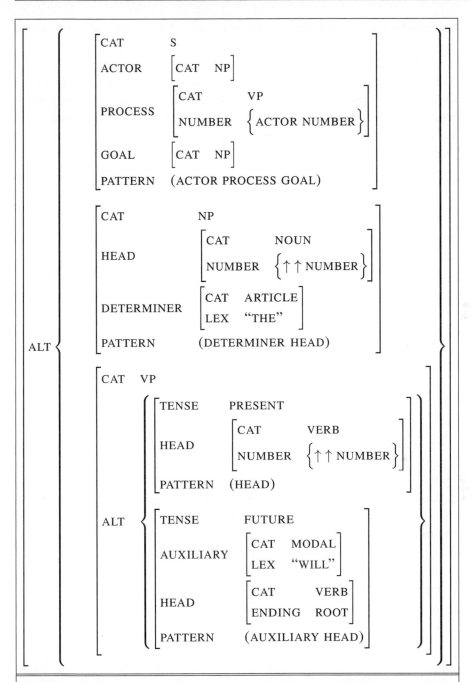

Figure 20.3   A simple FUF grammar. (FUF, or Functional Unification Formalism, is an implementation of Functional Unification Grammar developed by Elhadad (1993, 1992).)

hand, the tense is future, we will insert the modal auxiliary "will" before the head verb.

This grammar is similar to the systemic grammar from the previous section in that it supports multiple levels that are entered recursively during the generation process. We now turn to the input feature structure, which specifies the details of the particular sentence we want to generate. The input structure, called a **functional description** (FD), is a feature structure just like the grammar. An FD for example (20.2) is as follows:

FUNCTIONAL
DESCRIPTION

$$
\begin{bmatrix}
\text{CAT} & \text{S} \\
\text{ACTOR} & \begin{bmatrix} \text{HEAD} & \begin{bmatrix} \text{LEX} & \text{SYSTEM} \end{bmatrix} \end{bmatrix} \\
\text{PROCESS} & \begin{bmatrix} \text{HEAD} & \begin{bmatrix} \text{LEX} & \text{SAVE} \end{bmatrix} \\ \text{TENSE} & \text{FUTURE} \end{bmatrix} \\
\text{GOAL} & \begin{bmatrix} \text{HEAD} & \begin{bmatrix} \text{LEX} & \text{DOCUMENT} \end{bmatrix} \end{bmatrix}
\end{bmatrix}
$$

Here we see a sentence specification with a particular actor, the system, and a particular goal, the document. The process is the saving of the document by the system in the future. The input structure specifies the particular verbs and nouns to be used as well as the tense. This differs from the input to the systemic grammar. In the systemic grammar, the lexical items were retrieved from the knowledge base entities associated with the actor and goal. The tense, though not included in the example systemic grammar, would be determined by a decision network that distinguishes the relative points in time relevant to the content of the expression. This unification grammar, therefore, requires that more decisions be made by the discourse planning component.

To produce the output, this input is unified with the grammar shown in Figure 20.3. This requires multiple passes through the grammar. The preliminary unification unifies the input FD with the "S" level in the grammar (i.e., the first alternative at the top level). The result of this process is as follows:

$$
\begin{bmatrix}
\text{CAT} & \text{S} \\
\text{ACTOR} & \begin{bmatrix} \text{CAT} & \text{NP} \\ \text{HEAD} & \begin{bmatrix} \text{LEX} & \text{SYSTEM} \end{bmatrix} \end{bmatrix} \\
\text{PROCESS} & \begin{bmatrix} \text{CAT} & \text{VP} \\ \text{NUMBER} & \{ \text{ACTOR NUMBER} \} \\ \text{HEAD} & \begin{bmatrix} \text{LEX} & \text{SAVE} \end{bmatrix} \\ \text{TENSE} & \text{FUTURE} \end{bmatrix} \\
\text{GOAL} & \begin{bmatrix} \text{CAT} & \text{NP} \\ \text{HEAD} & \begin{bmatrix} \text{LEX} & \text{DOCUMENT} \end{bmatrix} \end{bmatrix} \\
\text{PATTERN} & (\text{ACTOR PROCESS GOAL})
\end{bmatrix}
$$

Here we see that the features specified in the input structure have been merged and unified with the features at the top level of the grammar. For example, the features associated with "actor" include the lexical item "system" from the input FD and the category "np" from the grammar. Similarly, the process feature combines the lexical item and tense from the input FD with the category and number features from the grammar.

The generation mechanism now recursively enters the grammar for each of the sub-constituents. It enters the *NP* level twice, once for the actor and again for the goal, and it enters the *VP* level once for the process. The FD that results from this is shown in Figure 20.4. There we see that every constituent feature that is internally complex has a pattern specification, and that every simple constituent feature has a lexical specification. The system now uses the pattern specifications to linearize the output, producing "The system will save the document."

This particular example did not specify that the actor be plural. We could do this by adding the feature-value pair "number plural" to the actor structure in the input FD. Subject-verb agreement would then be enforced by the unification process. The grammar requires that number of the heads of the *NP* and the *VP* match with the number of the actor that was specified in the input FD. The details of this process are left as an exercise.

$$
\begin{bmatrix}
\text{CAT} & \text{S} \\[2pt]
\text{ACTOR} & \begin{bmatrix}
\text{CAT} & \text{NP} \\[2pt]
\text{HEAD} & \begin{bmatrix}
\text{CAT} & \text{NOUN} \\
\text{LEX} & \text{SYSTEM} \\
\text{NUMBER} & \{\uparrow\uparrow \text{NUMBER}\}
\end{bmatrix} \\[2pt]
\text{DETERMINER} & \begin{bmatrix}
\text{CAT} & \text{ARTICLE} \\
\text{LEX} & \text{``THE''}
\end{bmatrix} \\[2pt]
\text{PATTERN} & (\text{DETERMINER HEAD})
\end{bmatrix} \\[2pt]
\text{PROCESS} & \begin{bmatrix}
\text{CAT} & \text{VP} \\[2pt]
\text{NUMBER} & \{\text{ACTOR NUMBER}\} \\[2pt]
\text{HEAD} & \begin{bmatrix}
\text{CAT} & \text{VERB} \\
\text{LEX} & \text{SAVE} \\
\text{ENDING} & \text{ROOT}
\end{bmatrix} \\[2pt]
\text{AUXILIARY} & \begin{bmatrix}
\text{CAT} & \text{MODAL} \\
\text{LEX} & \text{``WILL''}
\end{bmatrix} \\[2pt]
\text{TENSE} & \text{FUTURE} \\[2pt]
\text{PATTERN} & (\text{AUXILIARY ROOT})
\end{bmatrix} \\[2pt]
\text{GOAL} & \begin{bmatrix}
\text{CAT} & \text{NP} \\[2pt]
\text{HEAD} & \begin{bmatrix}
\text{CAT} & \text{NOUN} \\
\text{LEX} & \text{DOCUMENT} \\
\text{NUMBER} & \{\uparrow\uparrow \text{NUMBER}\}
\end{bmatrix} \\[2pt]
\text{DETERMINER} & \begin{bmatrix}
\text{CAT} & \text{ARTICLE} \\
\text{LEX} & \text{``THE''}
\end{bmatrix} \\[2pt]
\text{PATTERN} & (\text{DETERMINER HEAD})
\end{bmatrix} \\[2pt]
\text{PATTERN} & (\text{ACTOR PROCESS GOAL})
\end{bmatrix}
$$

Figure 20.4   The fully unified FD.

Summary

The two surface generation grammars we've seen in this section illustrate the nature of computational grammars for generation. Both used functional categorizations. One might wonder if it would be possible to use a single grammar for both generation and understanding. These grammars, called **bidirectional grammar**, are currently under investigation but have not found widespread use in NLG (cf. Chapter 21). This is largely due to the additional semantic and contextual information required as input to the generator.

BIDIRECTIONAL GRAMMARS

20.4   DISCOURSE PLANNING

The surface realization component discussed in the previous section takes a specified input and generates single sentences. Thus, it has little or no control over either the discourse structure in which the sentence resides or the content of the sentence itself. These things are controlled by the discourse planner. This section will introduce the two predominant mechanisms for building discourse structures: text schemata and rhetorical relations.

The focus on discourse rather than just sentences has been a key feature of much work done in NLG. Many applications require that the system produce multi-sentence or multi-utterance output. This can be done by simply producing a sentence for each component of the intended meaning, but frequently more care is required in selecting and structuring the meaning in an appropriate way. For example, consider the following alternate revision of the "hello, world" output discussed in the introduction:

(20.3)   You've just compiled a simple C program. You've just run a simple
         C program. Your environment is configured properly.

These sentences are fine in isolation, but the text is more disjointed than the one given in example (20.1) and is probably harder to understand. Although it orders the sentences in a helpful way, it doesn't give any indication of the relationship between them. These are the sorts of issues that drive discourse planning.

This section will also discuss the closely related problem of content selection, which, as we saw earlier, is the process of selecting propositional content from the input knowledge base based on a communicative goal. Because the form of this knowledge base and the nature of the communicative goal varies widely from one application to another, it is difficult to make general statements about the content selection process. To make things

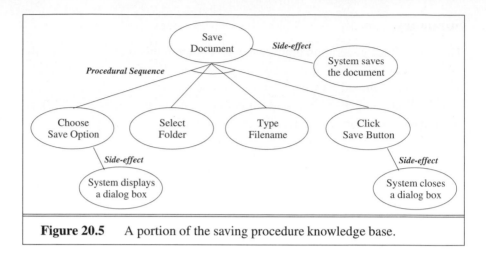

Figure 20.5   A portion of the saving procedure knowledge base.

more concrete, therefore, this section will focus on the task of generating instructions for a simple word-processing application. We'll assume that the knowledge base, whatever its underlying structure, can be viewed as a KLONE-styled knowledge base. We'll also assume that the communicative goal is to explain the represented procedure to a new user of the system. The knowledge base will represent the procedure for saving a file as a simple procedural hierarchy, as shown in Figure 20.5. The procedure specified there requires that the user choose the save option from the file menu, select the appropriate folder and file name, and then click on the save button. As a side-effect, the system automatically displays and removes the save-as dialog box in response to the appropriate user actions. This representation gives the procedural relationships between the basic actions but it doesn't show any of the domain knowledge concerning the structure of the interface (e.g., which choices are on which menus) or the particular entities that are used in the procedure (e.g., the document, the user). We'll assume that these are accessible in the knowledge base as well.

Text Schemata

Apart from the rigidly structured canned texts and slot-filler templates discussed in the opening of this chapter, the simplest way to build texts is to key the text structure to the structure of the input knowledge base. For example, we might choose to describe a game of tic-tac-toe or checkers by reviewing the moves in the sequence in which they were taken. This strategy soon breaks down, however, when we have a large amount of information that could potentially be expressed in order to achieve a variety of communicative goals. The knowledge base that contains the fragment shown in Figure 20.5, for example, could be expressed as a sequence of instructions such as one might find in a tutorial manual, or it could be expressed as an alphabetized set of program functions such as one might find in a reference manual.

One approach to this problem rests on the observation that texts tend to follow consistent structural patterns. For example, written directions explaining how to carry out an activity typically express the required actions in the order of their execution. Any preconditions of these actions are mentioned before the appropriate action. Similarly, side-effects of these actions are mentioned after the appropriate action. In some domains, patterns such as these are rarely broken. Armed with this information, we can build a **schema** representing this structure, such as the one shown in Figure 20.6. This schema is represented as an **augmented transition network** (ATN) in which each node is a state and each arc is an optional transition (see Chapter 10). Control starts in the small black node in the upper left and proceeds to follow arcs as appropriate until execution stops in the terminal node of the lower left. Node S0 allows the expression of any number of preconditions. Transitioning to S1 forces the expression of the action itself. S1 allows recursive calls to the network to express any sub-steps. The transition to S2 requires no action, and S2 allows any number of side-effects to be expressed before halting execution.

We can use this schema to plan the expression of the example procedure shown in Figure 20.5. When the system is asked to describe how to save a document, the procedure schema can be activated. We'll assume that the knowledge base specifies no preconditions for the action of saving a file, so we proceed directly to state S1, forcing the expression of the main action: "Save the document". In state S2, we recursively call the network for each of the four sub-steps specified in the input. This expresses the first sub-step, "choose the save option", along with its side-effect, "this causes the system to display the save-as dialog box". The first sub-step has no preconditions or sub-steps. Each of the other sub-steps is done in the same manner and execution finally returns to the main action execution in step S2 which expresses the result of the whole process, "this causes the system to save the document" and then terminates. Depending on the details of the planning, the final text might be as follows:

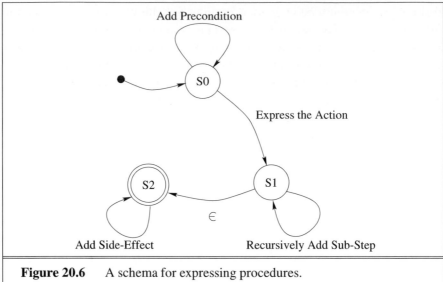

Figure 20.6   A schema for expressing procedures.

> Save the document: First, choose the save option from the
> file menu. This causes the system to display the Save-As dialog
> box. Next, choose the destination folder and type the filename.
> Finally, press the save button. This causes the system to save the
> document.

Each one of these sentences can be generated using one of the surface realizers discussed in the previous section. As we can see, the schema mechanism
is more flexible than templates or canned text. It structures the output according to known patterns of expression, but, with appropriate constraints, is able
to insert optional material collected from the knowledge base in a variety of
orders. In addition, it is not required to express everything in the knowledge
base; the side-effect of the "click save button" action, for example, was not
included.

This schema mechanism produced only a high-level discourse structure. The problem of specifying of the detailed form of each of the sentences,
commonly called microplanning, is discussed in Section 20.5.

Rhetorical Relations

Schemata are useful for discourse planning provided a discrete set of consistent patterns of expression can be found and encoded. However, they suffer
from two basic problems. First, they become impractical when the text being generated requires more structural variety and richness of expression.

For example, we may find that certain conditions dictate that we format our procedural instructions in a different manner. Some contexts may dictate that we explicitly enumerate the steps in the procedure, or that we express certain segments of the text in a different manner or in a different order. While in principle these variations could be supported either by adding constraints and operational code to the schema or by adding new schemata, the more variations that are required, the more difficult the schema-based approach becomes.

The second problem with schema-based mechanisms is that the discourse structure they produce is a simple sequence of sentence generation requests. It includes no higher-level structure relating the sentences together. In some domains, particularly in interactive ones (cf. Chapter 19), the structure of the previous discourse is relevant for future planning. For example, if we have explained a process in some detail, we might not want to do it again. It's easier to do these things when there is a record of the structure of previous discourse.

A useful approach here is to take a look under the hood of the schema in order to discover the more fundamental rhetorical dynamics at work in a text. A system informed by these dynamics could develop its own schemata based on the situations it confronts. A number of theories that attempt to formalize these rhetorical dynamics have been proposed, as discussed in some detail in Chapter 18. One such theory, **Rhetorical Structure Theory** (RST), is a descriptive theory of text organization based on the relationships that hold between parts of the text (Mann and Thompson, 1987). As an example, consider the following two texts:

(20.4)   I love to collect classic automobiles. My favorite car is my 1899 Duryea.

(20.5)   I love to collect classic automobiles. My favorite car is my 1999 Toyota.

The first text makes sense. The fact that the writer likes the 1899 Duryea follows naturally from the fact that they like classic automobiles. The second text, however, is problematic. The problem is not with the individual sentences, they work perfectly well in isolation. Rather, the problem is with their combination. The fact that the two sentences are in sequence implies that there is some coherent relationship between them. In the case of the first text, that relationship could be characterized as one of elaboration (cf. Chapter 19). The second text could be characterized as one of contrast and would thus be more appropriately expressed as:

(20.6)   I love to collect classic automobiles. However, my favorite car is my 1999 Toyota.

Here, the "however" overtly signals the contrast relation to the reader. RST claims that an inventory of 23 rhetorical relations, including ELABORATION and CONTRAST, is sufficient to describe the rhetorical structure a wide variety of texts. In practice, analysts tend to make use of a subset of the relations that are appropriate for their domain of application.

Most RST relations designate a central segment of text ("I love to collect..."), called the **nucleus**, and a more peripheral segment ("My favorite car is..."), called the **satellite**. This encodes the fact that many rhetorical relations are asymmetric. Here the second text is being interpreted in terms of the first, and not vice-versa. As we will see below, not all rhetorical relations are asymmetric. RST relations are defined in terms of the constraints they place on the nucleus, on the satellite, and on the combination of the nucleus and satellite. Here are definitions of some common RST relations:

ELABORATION   — The satellite presents some additional detail concerning the content of the nucleus. This detail may be of many forms:

- a member of a given set
- an instance of a given abstract class
- a part of a given whole
- a step of a given process
- an attribute of a given object
- a specific instance of a given generalization

CONTRAST   — The nuclei present things that, while similar in some respects, are different in some relevant way. This relation is **multi-nuclear** in that it doesn't distinguish between a nucleus and a satellite.

CONDITION   — The satellite presents something that must occur before the situation presented in the nucleus can occur.

PURPOSE   — The satellite presents the goal of performing the activity presented in the nucleus.

SEQUENCE   — This relation is multi-nuclear. The set of nuclei are realized in succession.

RESULT   — The situation presented in the nucleus results from the one presented in the satellite.

NUCLEUS

SATELLITE

MULTI-NUCLEAR

RST relations are typically graphed as follows:

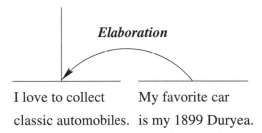

I love to collect   My favorite car

classic automobiles. is my 1899 Duryea.

Here we see a graphical representation of the rhetorical relation from example (20.4). The segments of text are ordered sequentially along the bottom of the diagram with the rhetorical relations built above them. The individual text segments are usually clauses.

Rhetorical structure analyses are built up hierarchically, so we may use one pair of related texts as a satellite or nucleus in another higher-level relation. Consider the following three-sentence structure:

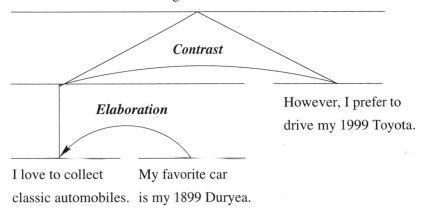

I love to collect   My favorite car

classic automobiles. is my 1899 Duryea.

Here we see that the first two clauses are related to one another via an elaboration relationship, and are related, as a pair, to the third clause via a contrast relationship. Note also how the multi-nuclear contrast relation is depicted. Recursive structuring such as this allows RST to build a single analysis tree for extended texts.

Although RST was originally proposed as a descriptive tool, it can also be used as a constructive tool for NLG. In order to do this, the rhetorical relations are typically recast as operators for an AI-style planner. As an example of this, we will look at a general-purpose, top-down, hierarchical planner that can be used for rhetorically-based text planning.[5]

---

[5] This text planner is adapted from the work of Moore and Paris (1993).

The basic approach with this sort of planner is for the generation system to post a high level communicative goal stated in terms of the effect that the text should have on the reader. For our instructional text example, we will request that the planner build a structure to achieve the goal of making the reader competent to save a file. The highest level plan operator that achieves this goal will insert a rhetorical node appropriate for the goal and insert sub-goals for the nucleus and satellite of that rhetorical relation. These sub-goals will then be recursively expanded until the planning process reaches the bottom of the rhetorical structure tree, inserting a node that can be expressed as a simple clause.

For our example, we would post the goal:

(COMPETENT hearer (DO-ACTION <some-action>))

Here, the communicative goal is to make the hearer competent to do some action. The action would be represented as an instance in the knowledge base, in this case, as the root node from the procedural hierarchy shown in Figure 20.5. A text plan operator that would fire for this goal would be as follows:

Name: Expand Purpose
Effect:
     (COMPETENT hearer (DO-ACTION ?action))
Constraints:
     (AND
          (c-get-all-substeps ?action ?sub-actions)
          (NOT (singular-list? ?sub-actions))
Nucleus:
     (COMPETENT hearer (DO-SEQUENCE ?sub-actions))
Satellites:
     (((RST-PURPOSE (INFORM s hearer (DO ?action)))
          required))

The basic idea of this plan operator is to explain how to do a particular action ("?action") by explaining how to do its substeps ("?substeps"). Note that the effect field matches the goal we posted earlier. An operator is applicable when its constraints hold. In this case, the main action ("?action") must have more than one sub-action. Because this is true in the current example (see Figure 20.5), the operator inserts a rhetorical purpose node into the discourse structure along with the goal specifications for its satellite and nucleus. The

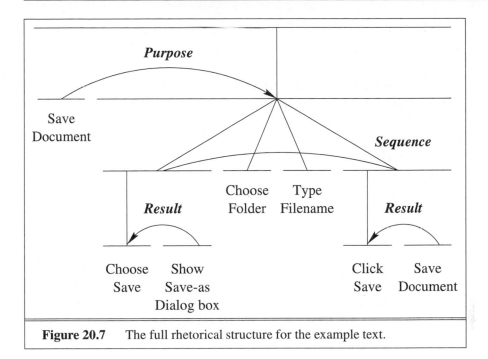

Figure 20.7   The full rhetorical structure for the example text.

satellite informs the hearer of the purpose of performing the main action, and the nucleus lists the sub-actions required to achieve this goal. Note that the effect, constraints, nucleus and satellite fields of the operator make use of variables (identifiers starting with "?") that are unified when the operator is applied. Thus, the goal action is bound to "?action" and can be accessed throughout the rest of the plan operator.

One other thing to notice about the plan operator is the way in which content selection is done. The constraint field specifies that there must be substeps and that there must be more than one of them. Determining whether the first constraint holds requires that the system retrieve the sub-steps from the knowledge base. These sub-steps are then used as the content of the nucleus node that is constructed. Thus, the plan operators themselves do the content selection as required by the discourse planning process.

The full text structure produced by the planner is shown in Figure 20.7. The root node of this tree (i.e., the horizontal line at the very top) is the node produced by the previous plan operator. The first nucleus node in Figure 20.7 is the multi-nuclear node comprising all the sub-actions. The plan operator that produces this node is as follows:

Name: Expand Sub-Actions
Effect:
    (COMPETENT hearer (DO-SEQUENCE ?actions))
Constraints:
    NIL
Nucleus:
    (foreach ?actions (RST-SEQUENCE
        (COMPETENT hearer (DO-ACTION ?actions))))
Satellites:
    NIL

This operator achieves the nucleus goal posted by the previous operator. It posts a rhetorical node with multiple nuclei, one for each sub-action required to achieve the main goal. With an appropriate set of plan operators, this planning system can produce the discourse structure shown in Figure 20.7, which could then be linearized into the following text:

To save a new file

1. Choose the save option from the file menu.
   The system will display the save-file dialog box.
2. Choose the folder.
3. Type the file name.
4. Click the save button.
   The system will save the document.

All of these sentences can be generated by a surface realizer. The last one, in particular, was identified as example 20.2 in the previous sections. As mentioned in the section on schema-based discourse planning, the problem of microplanning has been deferred to Section 20.5.

Summary

In this section, we have seen how schema-based mechanisms can take advantage of consistent patterns of discourse structure. Although this approach has proven effective in the many contexts, it is not flexible enough to handle more varied generation tasks. Discourse planning based on rhetorical relations was introduced to add the flexibility required to handle these sorts of tasks.

20.5 OTHER ISSUES

This section introduces issues that were not discussed in detail in the previous sections.

Microplanning

The previous sections did not detail the process of mapping from the discourse plans described in the examples to the inputs to the surface realizers. The discourse structures, such as the one shown in Figure 20.7, specified the high-level or macro structure of the text, but few of the details expected as input to the surface realizers. The problem of doing this more detailed planning is called **microplanning**.

MICROPLANNING

In most generation applications, microplanning is simply hard-wired. For example, in instruction generation systems, objects can be referred to in the same way in all cases, and user actions can be expressed as separate imperative sentences. This greatly simplifies the problem, but tends to produce monotonous texts such as the one shown in example (20.3). This illustrates two of the primary areas of concern in microplanning: **referring expressions** and **aggregation**.

REFERRING EXPRESSION

AGGREGATION

Planning a referring expression requires that we determine those aspects of an entity that should be used when referring to that entity in a particular context. If the object is the focus of discussion and has just been mentioned, we might be able to use a simple "it", whereas introducing a new entity may require more elaborate expressions like "a new document to hold your term paper". These issues are discussed in some detail in Chapter 18.

Aggregation is the problem of apportioning the content from the knowledge base into phrase, clause, and sentence-sized chunks. We saw an example of this in the introduction where two of the actions mentioned in example (20.1) were conjoined within the first clause as "you've just *compiled and run* a simple C program". This is more readable than the non-aggregated version given in example (20.3) ("You've just compiled a simple C program. You've just run a simple C program").

Microplanning is frequently seen as an intermediate pipelined module placed between the discourse planner and the surface realizer (see Figure 20.1) (Reiter and Dale, 2000). Indeed, more recent work has emphasized microplanning to the point that it is viewed as a task of importance equal to that of discourse planning and surface realization. It is also possible to add planning operators to the RST-based planning mechanism described in the chapter in order to perform microplanning tasks. However the microplanning is done, it serves to map from the output of the discourse planner to the input of the surface realizer.

Lexical Selection

Lexical selection refers to the general problem of choosing the appropriate words with which to express the chosen content. The surface realizers discussed in this chapter explicitly inserted closed-class lexical items as they were required, but deferred the choice of the content words to the discourse planner. Many planners simplify this issue by associating a single lexical item with each entity in the knowledge base.

Handling lexical selection in a principled way requires that the generation system deal with two issues. First, it must be able to choose the appropriate lexical item when more than one alternative exists. In the document-saving text from the previous section, for instance, the system generated "Click the save button". There are alternatives to the lexical item "click", including "hit" and "press mouse left on". The choice between these alternatives could consider: (1) style — in this case "hit" is perhaps more informal that "click", (2) collocation — in this case "click" probably co-occurs with buttons more often in this domain, and (3) user knowledge — in this case a novice computer user might need the more fully specified "press mouse left on".

Second, the generation system must be able to choose the appropriate grammatical form for the expression of the concept. For example, the system could title the section "Saving a new file" rather than "To save a new file". This choice between the participle and the infinitive form is frequently made based on the forms most commonly employed in a corpus of instructions.

Evaluating Generation Systems

In early work on NLG, the quality of the output of the system was assessed by the system builders themselves. If the output sounded good, then the system was judged a success. Because this is not a very effective test of system quality, much recent interest has been focussed on the rigorous evaluation of NLG systems. Several techniques have emerged.

One technique is to statistically compare the output of the generator with the characteristics of a corpus of target text. If the form chosen by the generator matches the form most commonly used in the corpus, it is judged as correct. The danger with this approach is that the corpus is usually produced by writers that may make errors, thus skewing the corpus statistics. The assumption is that, as Tolstoy put it in Anna Karenina, "All happy families are alike, but an unhappy family is unhappy after its own fashion." In other words, good text displays a consistent set of characteristics that arise again and again, while bad text displays idiosyncratic characteristics that will not accumulate statistically.

Another technique is to convene a panel of experts to judge the output of the generator in comparison with text produced by human authors. In this variation of the Turing test, the judges do not know which texts were generated by the system and which were written by human authors. Computer generated text typically scores lower than human written text, but its quality approaches that of human authors in some restricted domains.

A final technique is to judge how effective the generated text is at achieving its goal. For example, if the text is intended to describe some object, its quality can be measured in terms of how well readers score on a content quiz given after reading the output text. If the text is intended to explain how to perform some process, its quality can be measured in terms of the number of procedural errors made by the reader after reading the text.

Generating Speech

This chapter has focussed on generating text rather than on generating speech. There are, however, many situations in which speech output is preferable if not absolutely necessary. These include situations where there is no textual display, such as when the user is using a telephone, and situations where the users are unable to look at a textual display, such as when the user is driving or when the user is disabled.

A simplistic approach might be to pass the word string that is produced by a generation system to a text-to-speech synthesizer of the sort described in Chapter 4, Chapter 5, and Chapter 7. One problem with this approach was already discussed on page 121 and page 603: text-to-speech systems must then deal with **homographs** (i.e., words with the same spelling but different pronunciations). Consider the following example:

HOMOGRAPHS

(20.7) *Articulate* people can clearly *articulate* the issues.

Here, the two instances of the spelling "articulate" must be pronounced differently. Another problem is the treatment of **prosody**, which requires that appropriate pitch contours and stress patterns be assigned to the speech being produced.

The simplistic approach requires the text-to-speech system to solve both of these problems by analyzing the input text. Homographs can frequently be distinguished using part-of-speech tagging (the adjective and verb forms of "articulate" are pronounced differently) or by the word-sense disambiguation algorithms of Chapter 17. As Chapter 4 (page 133) suggests, automatic generation of prosody is a much harder problem. Some prosodic information can be deduced by distinguishing questions from non-questions, and by looking for commas and periods. In general, however, it is not easy to extract the required information from the input text.

An alternative to the simplistic approach is to pass a richer representation from the NLG system to the speech synthesizer. A typical NLG system knows the semantics and part-of-speech of the word it intends to generate, and can annotate the word with this information to help select the proper word pronunciation. The system could also annotate the output with discourse structure information to help synthesize the proper prosody. To date, there has been very little work on this area in NLG.

20.6   SUMMARY

Language Generation is the process of constructing natural language outputs from non-linguistic inputs. As a field of study, it usually does not include the study of simpler generation mechanisms such as **canned text** and **template filling**.

- Language generation differs from language understanding in that it focuses on linguistic **choice** rather than on resolving ambiguity. Issues of choice in generation include **content selection**, **lexical selection**, **aggregation**, **referring expression generation**, and **discourse structuring**.

- Language generation systems include a component that plans the structure of the discourse, called a **discourse planner**, and one that generates single sentences, called a **surface realizer**. Approaches for discourse planning include **text schemata** and **rhetorical relation planning**. Approaches for surface realization include **Systemic Grammar** and **Functional Unification Grammar**.

- **Microplanners** map the discourse planner output to the surface generator input, which includes the fine-grained tasks of **referring expression** generation, **aggregation**, and **lexical selection**.

BIBLIOGRAPHICAL AND HISTORICAL NOTES

Excluding canned text and template filling mechanisms, natural language generation is a young field relative to the rest of language processing. Some minor forays into the field occurred in the 1950s and 1960s, mostly in the context of machine translation, but work focusing on generation didn't arise until the 1970s. Simmons and Slocum's system (1972) used ATN's to generate discourse from semantic networks, Goldman's BABEL (1975) used decision networks to perform lexical choice, and Davey's PROTEUS (1979) produced descriptions of tic-tac-toe games. The 1980s saw the establishment of generation as a distinct field of research. Influential contributions on surface realization were made by McDonald (1980) and the PENMAN project (Mann, 1983), and on text planning by McKeown (1985) and Appelt (1985). The 1990s have seen continuing interest with the rise of generation-focussed workshops, both European and international, and organizations (cf. the Special Interest Group on language GENeration, http://www.aclweb.org/siggen). Kukich (1988) and Reiter and Dale (2000) have discussed the uses and limitations of canned text and template mechanisms.

As of this writing, no textbooks on generation exist. However, a text on applied generation is in press (Reiter and Dale, 2000), and a number of survey papers have been written (Dale et al., 1998a; Uszkoreit, 1996; McDonald, 1992; Bateman and Hovy, 1992; McKeown and Swartout, 1988). A number of these references discuss the history of NLG and its relationship to the rest of language processing. McDonald (1992) introduces the distinction between hypothesis management and choice.

Generation architectures have typically pipelined the tasks of planning and realization. The pipelining is used to constrain the search space within each of the modules and thus to make the generation task more tractable (Reiter and Dale, 2000; McDonald, 1988; Thompson, 1977). However, these architectures have the well-known problem that decisions made by the discourse planner cannot easily be undone by the realizer (Meteer, 1992). Appelt's KAMP (1985) employed a unified architecture for planning and realization based on AI planning. This approach, however, has proven computationally impractical in larger domains. Blackboard architectures have also been proposed for language generation systems (Nirenburg et al., 1989). The various concerns of microplanning itself have been the subject of considerable interest, including work on referring expressions (Dale, 1992; Appelt, 1985), aggregation (Dalianis, 1999; Mann and Moore, 1981), and other grammatical issues (Vander Linden and Martin, 1995; Meteer, 1992). The related issues of lexical selection (Stede, 1998; Reiter, 1990; Goldman, 1975) and tailoring the output text to particular audiences (Paris, 1993; Hovy, 1988a) have also received attention.

The late 1980s and early 1990s saw the construction of several reusable NLG systems, including two that have been distributed publicly: KPML

(Bateman, 1997) and FUF (Elhadad, 1993). These tools can be downloaded through the SIGGEN web site. Most of this work was done in Lisp, but recent efforts have been made to port the systems to other languages and platforms.

Systemic functional linguistics (SFL) was developed by Halliday (1985). It has remained largely independent of generative linguistics and is relatively unknown in the language processing community as a whole. Attempts to use it in parsing have had limited success (O'Donnell, 1994; Kasper, 1988). However, it has had a deep impact on NLG, being used in one form or another by a number of generation systems, including Winograd's SHRDLU (1972a), Davey's PROTEUS, Patten's SLANG (1988), PENMAN (Mann, 1983), FUF (Elhadad, 1993) and ILEX (Dale et al., 1998b). The example systemic grammar in this chapter is based in part on Winograd's discussion (1972a). SFL's most complete computational implementation is the Komet-Penman MultiLingual development environment (KPML), which is a descendent of PENMAN. KPML is packaged with NIGEL, a large English generation grammar, as well as an environment for developing multilingual grammars. It also includes a Sentence Planning Language (SPL) that forms a more usable interface to the systemic grammar itself. SPL specifications are considerably simpler to build than specifications that must include all the information required to make all the choices in the system network, but are more flexible that the spl-constructor example given in the chapter. Consider the following SPL specification:

```
(s1 / save
    :actor (a1 / system
                :determiner the)
    :actee (a2 / document
                :determiner the)
    :tense future
    )
```

The SPL interpreter will expand this into the series of feature choices required for the Nigel grammar to generate example 20.2 ("The system will save the document."). Each term in this specification gives the role of the entity (e.g., actor, actee) as well as the semantic type (e.g., save, system, document). The semantic types are KLONE-styled concepts subordinated to UPPER MODEL a general ontology (cf. Chapter 16) of concepts called the **upper model** (Bateman et al., 1990). This ontology, which represents semantic distinctions that have grammatical consequences, is used by SPL to determine the type of entity being expressed and thus to reduce the amount of information explicitly contained in the SPL specification. This example leaves out the :speechact assertion term included in the example in the chapter because SPL uses this as a default value if left unspecified.

Functional Unification Grammar was developed by Kay (1979), see Chapter 11. Its most influential implementation for generation is the Functional Unification Formalism (FUF) developed by Elhadad (Elhadad, 1993, 1992). It is distributed with the English grammar SURGE. Although the example given in the chapter used a simple phrase-structure approach to grammatical categorization (cf. (Elhadad, 1992)), the SURGE grammar uses systemic categorizations.

Another linguistic theory that has been influential in language generation is Mel'čuk's Meaning Text Theory (MTT) (1988). MTT postulates a number of levels ranging from deep syntax all the way to surface structure. Surface realizers that use it, including CoGenTex's REALPRO (Lavoie and Rambow, 1997) and ERLI's AlethGen (Coch, 1996b), start with the deep levels and map from level to level until they reach the surface level.

Discourse generation has been a concern of NLG from the beginning. Davey's PROTEUS, for example, produced paragraph-length summaries of tic-tac-toe games. His system structured its output based heavily upon the structure of the trace of the game which the application system recorded. Schema-based text structuring, pioneered by McKeown (1985), is more flexible and has been used in a number of applications (Milosavljevic, 1997; Paris, 1993; McCoy, 1985). The schema-based example presented in this chapter is based on the COMET instruction generation system (McKeown et al., 1990). Although other theories of discourse structure (cf. Chapter 18) have influenced NLG, including theories by Grosz and Sidner (1986), Hobbs (1979a), and Kamp's DRT (1981), Rhetorical Structure Theory (RST), developed by Mann and Thompson (1987), has had the most influence (Marcu, 1998; Scott and Souza, 1990; Hovy, 1988b). The classic automobile example in ths chapter is adapted from Mann and Thompson (Mann and Thompson, 1986), and the RST-based planning example is based on Moore and Paris' text planner (Moore and Paris, 1993) as it was used in the DRAFTER (Paris and Vander Linden, 1996; Paris et al., 1995), ISOLDE (Paris et al., 1998) and WIP (Wahlster et al., 1993) projects. The use of this planner in the context of an interactive dialogue system is described by Moore and Paris (1993). A more recent alternative to this approach has been developed by Marcu (1998).

Applications of NLG tend to focus on relatively restricted sublanguages (cf. Chapter 21), including weather reports (Coch, 1998; Goldberg et al.,

1994), instructions (Paris et al., 1998; Paris and Vander Linden, 1996; Wahl-ster et al., 1993), encyclopedia-like descriptions (Milosavljevic, 1997; Dale et al., 1998b), and letters (Reiter et al., 1999). The output can be delivered as simple text or hypertext (Lavoie et al., 1997; Paris and Vander Linden, 1996), dynamically generated hypertext (Dale et al., 1998b), multimedia presentation (Wahlster et al., 1993), and speech (Van Deemter and Odijk, 1997). Information on a number of these systems is available on-line at the SIGGEN web site.

The evaluation of NLG systems has received much recent attention. Evaluations have assessed the similarity of the output with a representative corpus (Yeh and Mellish, 1997; Vander Linden and Martin, 1995), convened panels of experts to review the text (Lester and Porter, 1997; Coch, 1996a), and tested how effective the text was at achieving its communicative purpose (Reiter et al., 1999). It is also becoming more common for the usability of the NLG system itself to be evaluated.

Other issues of interest in NLG include the use of connectionist and statistical techniques (Langkilde and Knight, 1998; Ward, 1994), and the viability of multilingual generation as an alternative to machine translation (Hartley and Paris, 1997; Goldberg et al., 1994).

EXERCISES

20.1   Use the systemic grammar given in the chapter to build a multiple-layer analysis of the following sentences:

   a. The document will be saved by the system.

   b. Will the document be saved by the system?

   c. Save the document.

20.2   Extend the systemic grammar given in the chapter to handle the following sentences:

   a. The document is large. (a "relational process")

   b. Give the document to Mary.

   c. Is the document saved? (a "polar interrogative")

20.3   Use the FUF grammar given in the chapter to build a fully unified FD for the following sentences:

   a. The system saves the document.

   b. The systems save the document.

   c. The system saves the documents.

20.4   Extend the FUF grammar given in the chapter to handle the following sentences:

   a. The document will be saved by the system. (i.e., the passive)

   b. Will the document be saved by the system? (i.e., wh-questions)

   c. Save the document. (i.e., imperative commands)

20.5   Select a restricted sublanguage (cf. Chapter 21) and build either a systemic or FUF generation grammar for it. The sublanguage should be subset of a restricted domain such as weather reports, instructions, or responses to simple inquires. As a test, you can download either FUF or KPML, whichever is appropriate, and implement your grammar. Both systems can be found through the SIGGEN web site. (Note that it is much easier to build test grammars with FUF than with KPML.)

20.6   Compare and contrast the SPL input to KPML (discussed in the bibliographical and historical notes) and the FD input to FUF. What decisions are required of the discourse planner for each of them? What are their relative strengths and weaknesses?

20.7   (Adapted from McKeown (1985)) Build an ATN appropriate for structuring a typical encyclopedia entry. Would it be in any way different from an ATN for a dictionary entry, and if so, could you adapt the same ATN for both purposes?

20.8   (Adapted from Bateman (1997)) Build a system network for using "dr", "mr", "ms", "mrs", "miss" in expressions like "Miss. Jones" and "Mr. Smith". What information would the knowledge base need to contain to make the appropriate choices in your network?

20.9   Do an RST analysis for the following text:

Temperature Adjustment

   Before you begin, be sure that you have administrator access to the system. If you do, you can perform the following steps:

     a. From the EMPLOYEE menu select the Adjust Temperature item. The system displays the Adjust Temperature dialog box.

b. Select the room. You may either type the room number or click on the appropriate room's icon.

c. Set the temperature. In general you shouldn't change the temperature too drastically.

d. Click the ok button. The system sets the room temperature.

By entering a desired temperature, you are pretending that you just adjusted the thermostat of the room that you are in.

The chapter lists a subset of the RST relations. Does it give you all the relations you need? How do you think your analysis would compare with the analyses produced by other analysts?

20.10   How does RST compare with Grosz and Sidner's theory of discourse presented in Chapter 18? Does one encompass the other or do they address different issues? Why do you think that RST has had a greater influence on NLG?

20.11   Would RST be useful for interactive dialog? If so, how would you use it? If not, what changes would you make to get it to work

20.12   (Adapted from ISOLDE (Paris et al., 1998)) Speculate on how you would enhance an RST-based discourse planner to plan multi-modal discourse, which would include diagrams and formatting (such as html formatting).

20.13   (Adapted from STOP (Reiter et al., 1999)). This chapter did not discuss template generators in any detail, it simply mentioned that they are easy to implement but inflexible. Try writing a simple template generator that produces persuasive letters addressed to people trying to convince them to stop smoking. The letter should include the standard elements of a letter as well as a discussion of the dangers of smoking and the advantages of quitting. For ideas, you can visit the STOP web site, available through the SIGGEN web site.

How flexible can you make the mechanism within the confines of template generation? Can you extend the system to take a case file on a particular patient that contains their medical history and produces a customized letter?

20.14   (Adapted from PEBA (Milosavljevic, 1997)). In the manner discussed in exercise 20.13, write a template generator that produces encyclopedia-like descriptions of animals. For ideas, you can visit the PEBA II web site, available through the SIGGEN web site.

21 MACHINE TRANSLATION*

"...Translation is a fine and exacting art, but there is much about it that is mechanical and routine."

Kay (1997)

This chapter introduces techniques for **machine translation** (**MT**), the use of computers to automate some or all of the process of translating from one language to another. Translation, in its full generality, is a difficult, fascinating, and intensely human endeavor, as rich as any other area of human creativity. Consider the following passage from the end of Chapter 45 of the 18th-century novel *The Story of the Stone*, also called *Dream of the Red Chamber*, by Cao Xue Qin (Cao, 1792), with the Chinese original transcribed in the Mandarin dialect, and the English translation by David Hawkes:

> As she lay there alone, Dai-yu's thoughts turned to Bao-chai... Then she listened to the insistent rustle of the rain on the bamboos and plantains outside her window. The coldness penetrated the curtains of her bed. Almost without noticing it she had begun to cry.

> *dai yu   zi   zai chuang shang   gan nian   bao chai...*
> Dai-yu alone on bed   top   think-of-with-gratitude Bao-chai

> *you   ting jian chuang wai   zhu   shao xiang   ye   zhe*
> again listen to window outside bamboo tip   plantain leaf of

> *shang, yu   sheng xi   li,   qing han   tou   mu,*
> on-top, rain sound sigh drip, clear cold penetrate curtain,

> *bu jue   you   di   xia   lei   lai.*
> not feeling again fall down tears come.

---

*This chapter mostly by Nigel Ward.

Consider some of the issues involved in this kind of literary translation. First, there is the problem of how to translate the Chinese names, complicated by Cao's frequent use of names involving wordplay. Hawkes chose to use transliterations for the names of the main characters but to translate names of servants by their meanings (Aroma, Skybright). Chinese rarely marks verbal aspect or tense; Hawkes thus had to decide to translate Chinese *tou* as *penetrated*, rather than say *was penetrating* or *had penetrated*. Hawkes also chose the possessive pronoun *her* to make *her window* more appropriate for the mood of a quiet bedroom scene than *the window*, To make the image clear for English readers unfamiliar with Chinese bed-curtains, Hawkes translated *ma* ('curtain') as *curtains of her bed*. Finally, the phrase *bamboo tip plantain leaf*, although elegant in Chinese, where such four-character phrases are a hallmark of literate prose, would be awkward if translated word-for-word into English, and so Hawkes used simply *bamboos and plantains*.

Translation of this sort clearly requires a deep and rich understanding of the source language and the input text, and a sophisticated, poetic, and creative command of the target language. The problem of automatically producing a high-quality translation of an arbitrary text from one language to another is thus far too hard to automate completely. But certain simpler translation tasks can be addressed with current computational models. In particular, machine translation systems often focus on (1) tasks for which a **rough translation** is adequate, (2) tasks where a human post-editor can be used to improve MT output, and (3) tasks limited to small **sublanguage** domains in which fully automatic high quality translation is achievable.

Information acquisition on the Web is the kind of "information pull" task where readers may be willing to settle for a very rough translation. Consider these extracts from a French web page and a machine translation:

Nous sommes une association type Loi de 1901, et notre raison d'être est de practiquer, de promouvoir, de faire découvrir le Paintball, et le cas échéant de supporter nos équipes de compétition: ...Si vous avez des questions, des envies d'organisation de parties, des envies de jouer tout courte et des envies de découvrir, n'hésitez pas à nous contacter par courrier ou par téléphone ou bien encore par eMail. ...Au sortir de la saison 97/98 et surtout au début de cette saison 98/99, les effectifs des HORS-TAXE sont modifiés.

We are a standard association Loi of 1901, and our raison d'ecirc;tre is to practice, promote, make discover Paintball, and to support our teams of competition if necessary: ...If you have questions, desires of organization of parts, desires for playing very short and desires for discovering, do not hesitate to contact us by mail or telephone or even by eMail. ...With leaving season 97/98 and especially at the beginning of this season 98/99, manpower of the HORS-TAXE are modified!

This is good enough to figure out that we have the found the home page of a paintball team, and one that seems friendly and perhaps willing to accept new members. Armed with this information, we can then try to find someone to properly translate it for us, or perhaps just go ahead and send e-mail to the organizer to ask if we can play. Incidentally, the use of MT for such document-finding purposes can sometimes be avoided or made more efficient by using **cross-language information retrieval** techniques, which focus on the retrieval of documents in a language other than that used for the query terms (Oard, 1997).

CROSS-LANGUAGE INFORMATION RETRIEVAL

Rough translation is also useful as the first stage in a complete translation process. An MT system can produce a draft translation that can be fixed up in a **post-editing** process by a human translator. Even a rough draft can sometimes speed up the overall translation process. Strictly speaking, systems used in this way are doing **computer-aided human translation** (CAHT or CAT) rather than (fully automatic) machine translation. This model of MT usage is effective especially for high volume jobs and those requiring quick turn-around. The most familiar example is perhaps the translation of software manuals for **localization** to reach new markets. Another effective application is the translation of market-moving financial news, for example from Japanese to English for use by stock traders.

POST-EDITING

COMPUTER-AIDED HUMAN TRANSLATION

LOCALIZATION

Weather forecasting is an example of a **sublanguage** domain that can be modeled completely enough to use raw MT output even without post-editing. Weather forecasts consist of phrases like *Cloudy with a chance of showers today and Thursday, Low tonight 4, high Thursday 10* and *Outlook for Friday: Sunny*. This domain has a limited vocabulary and only a few basic phrase types. Ambiguity is rare, and the senses of ambiguous words are distinct and easily disambiguated based on local context, using word classes and semantic features such as MONTH, PLACE, DIRECTION, TIME POINT, TIME DURATION, DEGREE-OF-POSSIBILITY. Other domains that are sublanguage-like include equipment maintenance manuals, air travel queries, appointment scheduling, and restaurant recommendations.

SUBLANGUAGE

This chapter breaks with the pattern of previous chapters in that the focus is less on introducing new techniques than on showing how the techniques presented earlier are used in practice. One of the themes of this chapter is that there are often trade-offs and difficult choices among alternative approaches and techniques.

Section 21.1 gives some simple illustrations of the ways in which languages differ. The following four sections are organized around four basic models for doing MT: Section 21.2 introduces the use of syntactic transformations for overcoming differences in grammar, as well as some techniques for choosing target language words. Section 21.3 introduces some ways of exploiting meaning during translation, in particular the use of thematic roles and primitive decomposition. Section 21.4 presents the minimalist "direct" approach. Section 21.5 discusses the use of statistical techniques to improve various aspects of MT. Finally, Section 21.6 discusses reasons for the gap between expectations and performance, and discusses strategies for meeting users' needs despite finite development resources.

21.1   LANGUAGE SIMILARITIES AND DIFFERENCES

When you accidentally pick up a radio program in some foreign language it seems like chaos, completely unlike the familiar languages of your everyday life. But there are patterns in this chaos, and indeed, some aspects of human language seem to be **universal**, holding true for every language. Many universals arise from the functional role of language as a communicative system by humans. Every language, for example, seems to have words for referring to people, for talking about women, men, and children, eating and drinking, for being polite or not. Other universals are more subtle; for example Chapter 8 mentioned that every language seems to have nouns and verbs.

UNIVERSAL

Even when languages differ, these differences often have systematic structure. The study of systematic cross-linguistic similarities and differences is called **typology** (Croft (1990), Comrie (1989)). This section sketches some typological facts about crosslinguistic similarity and difference. This bears on our main topic, MT, in that the difficulty of translating from one language to another depends a great deal on how similar the languages are in their vocabulary, grammar, and conceptual structure.

TYPOLOGY

Morphologically, languages are often characterized along two dimensions of variation. The first is the number of morphemes per word, ranging from **isolating** languages like Vietnamese and Cantonese, in which each word generally has one morpheme, to **polysynthetic** languages like Siberian Yupik ("Eskimo"), in which a single word may have very many morphemes,

ISOLATING

POLYSYNTHETIC

corresponding to a whole sentence in English. The second dimension is the
degree to which morphemes are segmentable, ranging from **agglutinative**
languages like Turkish (discussed in Chapter 3), in which morphemes have
relatively clean boundaries, to **fusion** languages like Russian, in which a
single affix may conflate multiple morphemes, like *-om* in the word *stolom*,
(table-SG-INSTR-DECL1) which fuses the distinct morphological categories
instrumental, singular, and first declension.

Syntactically, languages are perhaps most saliently different in the basic word order of verbs, subjects, and objects in simple declarative clauses.
German, French, English, and Mandarin, for example, are all **SVO** languages, meaning that the verb tends to come between the subject and object.
Hindi and Japanese, by contrast, are **SOV** languages, meaning that the verb
tends to come at the end of basic clauses, while Irish, Classical Arabic, and
Biblical Hebrew are **VSO** languages. Two languages that share their basic
word-order type often have other similarities. For example **SVO** languages
generally have **prepositions** while **SOV** languages generally have **postposi-
tions**; English has *to Yuriko* where Japanese has *Yuriko ni*.

Another important syntactico-morphological distinction is between
head-marking and dependent-marking languages (Nichols, 1986). Head-
marking languages tend to mark the relation between the head and its dependents on the head. Dependent-marking languages tend to mark the relation
on the non-head. Nichols (1986) for example, notes that Hungarian marks
the possessive relation with an affix (A) on the head noun (H), where English
marks it on the (non-head) possessor:

(21.1) *English*   the man-^{A}'s ^{H}house
       Hungarian   az ember ^{H}ház-^{A}a
                      the man   house-his

This syntactic distinction is related to a semantic distinction in how
languages map conceptual notions onto words. Talmy (1985) and (1991)
noted that languages can be characterized by whether direction of motion
and manner of motion are marked on the verb or on the "satellites": particles,
prepositional phrases, or adverbial phrases. For example a bottle floating out
of a cave would be described in English with the direction marked on the
particle *out* as:

(21.2) The bottle floated out.

while in Spanish the direction would be marked on the verb as:

(21.3) *La   botella   salió   flotando.*
     The bottle   exited   floating.

Languages that mark the direction of motion on the verb (leaving the satellites to mark the manner of motion) Talmy called verb-framed; Slobin (1996) gives examples like Spanish *acercarse* 'approach', *alcanzar* 'reach', *entrar* 'enter', *salir* 'exit'. Languages that mark the direction of motion on the satellite (leaving the verb to mark the manner of motion) Talmy called satellite-framed; Slobin (1996) gives examples like English *crawl out*, *float off*, *jump down*, *walk over to*, *run after*. Talmy (1991) noted that verb-framed languages include Romance, Semitic, Japanese, Tamil, Polynesian, most Bantu, most Mayan, Nez Perce, and Caddo, while satellite-framed languages include most Indo-European minus Romance, Finno-Ugric, Chinese, Ojibwa, and Warlpiri.

In addition to such properties that systematically vary across large classes of languages, there are many specific characteristics, more or less unique to single languages. English, for example, has an idiosyncratic syntactic construction involving the word *there* that is often used to introduce a new scene in a story, as in *there burst into the room three men with guns*.

To give an idea of how trivial, yet crucial, these differences can be, think of dates. Dates not only appear in various formats — typically YYM-MDD in Japanese, MM-DD-YY in American English, and DD/MM/YY in British English — but the calendars themselves may also differ. Dates in Japanese, for example, are often relative to the start of the current Emperor's reign rather than to the start of the Christian Era.

Turning now to the question of lexical organization, here too there are interesting patterns. Many words can be translated relatively directly into other languages. English *dog*, for example, translates to Mandarin *gǒu*. Where English has *chocolate*, Italian has *cioccolato* and Japanese has *choko-reeto*.[1]

Sometimes, rather than a single word, there is a fixed phrase in the target language; French *informatique* thus translates to English *computer science*. In more difficult cases, however, a word in one language does not map so simply to a word or phrase in another language.

Grammatically, for example, a word may translate best to a word of another part-of-speech in the target language. Many English sentences involving the verb *like* must be translated into German using the adverbial *gern*;

---

[1] Actually, *chokoreeto* in Japanese is perforce more formal than English *chocolate*, since Japanese also has the informal short form *choko*.

thus *she likes to sing* maps to *sie singt gerne*, where the syntactic structure is also affected.

Sometimes one language places more grammatical constraints on word choice than another. English, for example, distinguishes gender in pronouns where Mandarin does not; thus translating a third-person singular pronoun from Mandarin to English requires deciding whether the original referent was masculine or feminine. The same is true when translating from the English pronoun plural *they*, unspecified for gender, into French (masculine *ils*, feminine *elles*). In Japanese, because there is no single word for *is*, speakers must choose between *iru* or *aru*, based on whether the subject is animate[2] or not.

Such differences in specificity also occur on the semantic side: one language may divide up a particular conceptual domain in more detail than another. English, for example, has a particularly impoverished kinship vocabulary; the single word *brother* can indicate either a younger or older brother. Japanese and Chinese, by contrast, both distinguish seniority in sibling relations. Figure 21.1 gives some further examples.

English	brother	Japanese	otooto (younger)
		Japanese	oniisan (older)
		Mandarin	gege (older)
		Mandarin	didi (older)
English	wall	German	Wand (inside)
		German	Mauer (outside)
English	know	French	connaître (be acquainted with)
		French	savoir (know a proposition)
English	they	French	ils (masculine)
		French	elles (feminine)
German	berg	English	hill
		English	mountain
Mandarin	tā	English	he, she, or it

Figure 21.1   Differences in specificity.

The way that languages differ in lexically dividing up conceptual space may be more complex than this one-to-many translation problem, leading to many-to-many mappings. For example Figure 21.2 summarizes some of the complexities discussed by Hutchins and Somers (1992) in relating English *leg, foot*, and *paw*, to the French *jambe, pied, patte*, etc.

---

[2]   Taxis and buses in service sometimes count as animate for this purpose.

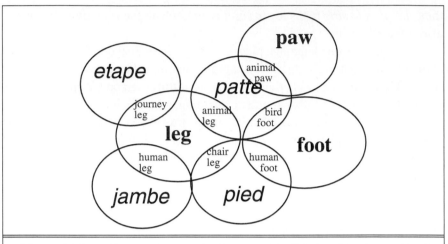

Figure 21.2   The complex overlap between English *leg*, *foot*, etc, and various French translations.

LEXICAL GAP   Further, one language may have a **lexical gap**, where no word or phrase, short of an explanatory footnote, can express the meaning of a word in the other language. For example, Japanese does not have a word for *privacy*, and English does not have a word for Japanese *oyakoko* (we make do with *filial piety*).

Moreover, dependencies on cultural context, as manifest in the background and expectations of the readers of the original and translation, further complicate matters. A number of translation theorists (Steiner, 1975; Barnstone, 1993; Hofstadter, 1997) refer to a clever story by Jorge Luis Borges showing that even two linguistic texts with the same words and grammar may have different meanings because of their different cultural contexts. Borges invents Menard, a French author in the 1930's whose aim was to recreate Cervantes' *Don Quixote* word for word:

> The text of Cervantes and that of Menard are verbally identical, but the second is almost infinitely richer. (More ambiguous, his detractors will say; but ambiguity is a richness.) It is a revelation to compare the *Don Quijote* of Menard with that of Cervantes. The latter, for instance, wrote:
>
> > ... *la verdad, cuya madre es la historia, émula del tiempo, depósito de las acciones, testigo de lo pasado, ejemplo y aviso de lo presente, advertencia de lo por venir.*
>
> Menard, on the other hand, writes:
>
> > ... *la verdad, cuya madre es la historia, émula del tiempo, depósito de*

> *las acciones, testigo de lo pasado, ejemplo y aviso de lo presente, ad-*
> *vertencia de lo por venir.*

Equally vivid is the contrast in styles. The archaic style of Menard – in the last analysis, a foreigner — suffers from a certain affectation. Not so that of his precursor, who handles easily the ordinary Spanish of his time.

These last points suggest a more general question about cultural differences and the possibility (or impossibility) of translation. A theoretical position sometimes known as the **Sapir-Whorf hypothesis** suggests that language may constrain thought — that the language you speak may affect the way you think. To the extent that this hypothesis is true, there can be no perfect translation, since speakers of the source and target languages necessarily have different conceptual systems. In any case it is clear that the differences between languages run deep, and that the process of translation is not going to be simple.

SAPIR-WHORF
HYPOTHESIS

21.2   THE TRANSFER METAPHOR

As the previous section illustrated, languages differ. One strategy for doing MT is to translate by a process of overcoming these differences, altering the structure of the input to make it conform to the rules of the target language. This can be done by applying **contrastive knowledge**, that is, knowledge about the differences between the two languages. Systems that use this strategy are sometimes said to be based on the **transfer model**.

CONTRASTIVE
KNOWLEDGE

TRANSFER MODEL

Since this requires some representation of the structure of the input, transfer presupposes a parse of some form. Moreover, since transfer only results in a structure for the target language, it must be followed by a generation phase to actually create the output sentence. Thus, on this model, MT involves three phases: **analysis**, **transfer**, and **generation**, where transfer bridges the gap between the output of the source language parser and the input to the target language generator. Figure 21.3 shows a sketch of this transfer architecture.

It is worth noting that a parse for MT may differ from parses required for other purposes. For example, suppose we need to translate *John saw the girl with the binoculars* into French. The parser does not need to bother to figure out where the prepositional phrase attaches, because both possibilities lead to the same French sentence. However this is not true for all prepositional phrase attachments, and so an MT system needs also to be able to

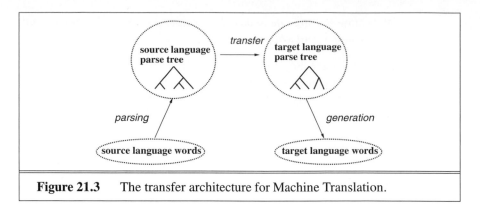

Figure 21.3   The transfer architecture for Machine Translation.

represent disambiguated parses, while still being able to work with ambiguous ones (Emele and Dorna, 1998).

Syntactic Transformations

Let us begin by considering syntactic differences. The previous section noted that in English the unmarked order in a noun-phrase had adjectives precede nouns, but in French adjectives follow nouns.[3] Temporarily postponing the question of how to translate the words, let's consider how an MT system can overcome such differences.

Figure 21.4   A simple transformation that reorders adjectives and nouns

SYNTACTIC
TRANSFORMATIONS

Figure 21.4 suggests the basic idea. Here we transform one parse tree, suitable for describing an English phrase, into another parse tree, suitable for describing a French sentence. In general, **syntactic transformations** are operations that map from one tree structure to another.

Now let's illustrate how roughly how such transformations can restructure an entire sentence, using a simplified sentence:

(21.4) There was an old man gardening.

---

[3]   There are exceptions to this generalization, such as *galore* in English and *gros* in French; furthermore in French some adjectives can appear before the noun with a different meaning; *route mauvaise* 'bad road, badly-paved road' versus *mauvaise route* 'wrong road' (Waugh, 1976).

We will assume that the parser has given us a structure like the following. We will also assume that the system starts performing transformations at the top node of the tree and works its way down:

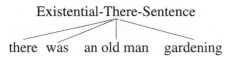

Existential-There-Sentence

there was   an old man   gardening

Since this sentence involves an "existential *there* construction", which has no analog in Japanese, we immediately have to apply a transformation that deletes the sentence-initial *there* and converts the fourth constituent to a relative clause modifying the noun, producing something like the following structure:

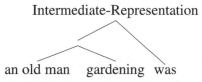

Intermediate-Representation

an old man   gardening was

The resulting structure is thus something more like the structure of a pseudo-English sentence: *an old man, who was gardening, was.*

Next, another transformation applies to reverse the order of the noun phrase and the relative clause, giving something like the following structure:

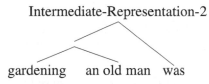

Intermediate-Representation-2

gardening   an old man   was

At this point all relevant transformations have applied, and lexical transfer takes place, substituting Japanese words for the English ones, as discussed in the next section. This gives the final structure below:

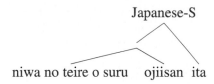

Japanese-S

niwa no teire o suru   ojiisan ita

After this, a little more syntactic work is required to produce an actual Japanese sentence, including: (1) adding the word *ga*, which is required in Japanese to mark the subject, (2) choosing the verb that agrees with the subject in terms of animacy, namely *iru*, not *aru*, and (3) inflecting the verbs. The final generation step traverses or otherwise linearizes the tree to produce a string of words. Although these generation tasks can be done by the techniques of Chapter 20, practical systems usually do them directly with simple procedures. In any case, the final output will be:

niwa   no   teire   o   shite   ita   ojiisan   ga   ita.
garden   GEN   upkeep   OBJ   do   PAST-PROG   old man   SUBJ   was

Table 21.5 shows a rough representation of the transformations we have discussed. Such transformations can be implemented as pattern-rewrite rules: if the input matches the left side of a transformation, it is rewritten according to the right side.

English to French:		
1.	NP → Adjective$_1$ Noun$_2$	
	$\Rightarrow$	
	NP → Noun$_2$ Adjective$_1$	

Japanese to English:		
2.	Existential-There-Sentence → There$_1$ Verb$_2$ NP$_3$ Postnominal$_4$	
	$\Rightarrow$	
	Sentence → (NP → NP$_3$ Relative-Clause$_4$) Verb$_2$	
3.	NP → NP$_1$ Relative Clause$_2$	
	$\Rightarrow$	
	NP → Relative-Clause$_2$ NP$_1$	

Figure 21.5   An informal description of some transformations.

Transformations in MT systems also may have more complex conditions for when they apply, and may include a "trigger", that is, a specific word that is used to index the pattern, for efficiency. One way to formalize transformations is with unification-based models; indeed as Chapter 11 discussed, the need for a reversible operation for MT was the original motivation for both feature-structure unification (Kay, 1984) and term-unification (Colmerauer and Roussel, 1996). However, unification is computationally expensive and is not commonly used.

Lexical Transfer

Some of the output words are determined in the course of syntactic transfer or generation. In the example above, the function words *ga* and *ita* are mostly grammatically controlled. Content words are another matter. The process of finding target language equivalents for the content words of the input, **lexical transfer**, is difficult for the reasons introduced in Section 21.1.   LEXICAL TRANSFER

The foundation of lexical transfer is dictionary lookup in a crosslanguage dictionary. As was discussed earlier, the translation equivalent may be a single word or it may be a phrase, as in this example where *gardening* becomes *niwa no teire o suru* ('do garden upkeep'). Furthermore, sometimes a generation process must subsequently inflect words in such phrases, as in this case.

Section 21.1 also discussed the problem of words that have several possible translations. In the example *man* is such a word. The correct choice here was *ojiisan* ('old man'), but if the input had been *man is the only linguistic animal*, the translation of *man* would have been *ningen* ('human being, man, men'); in most other cases *hito* ('person, persons, man, men') or related words would have been appropriate. Fortunately there are at least two ways to tackle this problem: in the parsing or in the generation stage. The first method is to treat words like *man* as if they were ambiguous. That is, we assume that *man* can correspond to two more concepts (perhaps HUMAN and ADULT MALE) and that choosing the correct Japanese word is like disambiguating between these concepts. This way of treating lexical transfer lets us apply all the standard techniques for lexical disambiguation (Chapter 16). A second way is to treat such words as having only one meaning, and to handle the selection among multiple possible translations (*ningen, hito, ojiisan* and so on) by using constraints imposed by the target language during generation (Whitelock, 1992). In practice, these cases are more often dealt with in the parsing stage, as the algorithms for lexical choice during generation are high-overhead (Ward, 1994), especially for content words (but see Section 21.5).

In this specific example, however, the choice of how to translate *man* is easy. Because the previous word is *old*, the correct translation is *ojiisan* ('old man'). Such inputs, where multiple source language words must be expressed with a single target language word, can be difficult to handle, requiring inference in the general case. But many such cases, including this one, can be treated simply as idioms, with their own entries in the bilingual dictionary.

21.3   THE INTERLINGUA IDEA: USING MEANING

One problem with the transfer model is that it requires a distinct set of transfer rules for each pair of languages. This is clearly suboptimal for translation systems employed in multilingual environments like the European Union, where eleven official languages need to be intertranslated.

This suggests a different perspective on the nature of translation. The transfer model treats translation as a process of altering the structure and words of an input sentence to arrive at a valid sentence of the target language. An alternative is to treat translation as a process of extracting the meaning of the input and then expressing that meaning in the target language. If this can be done, a MT system can do without contrastive knowledge, merely relying on the same syntactic and semantic rules used by a standard interpreter and generator for the language. The amount of knowledge needed is then proportional to the number of languages the system handles, rather than to the square, or so the argument goes.

INTERLINGUA

This scheme presupposes the existence of a meaning representation, or **interlingua**, in a language-independent canonical form, like the semantic representations we saw in Chapter 14. The idea is for the interlingua to represent all sentences that mean the "same" thing in the same way, regardless of the language they happen to be in. Translation in this model proceeds by performing a semantic analysis on the input from language X into the interlingual representation and generating from the interlingua to language Y.

A frequently used element in interlingual representations is the notion of a small fixed set of thematic roles, as discussed in Chapter 16. When used in an interlingua, these thematic roles are taken to be language universals. Figure 21.6 shows a possible interlingual representation for *there was an old man gardening* as a unification-style feature structure[4]. We saw in Chapter 15 how a **semantic analyzer** can produce such a structure with a AGENT relation between *man* and *gardening*. Note that since the interlingua requires such semantic interpretation in addition to syntactic parsing, it requires more analysis work than the transfer model, which only required syntactic parsing. But generation can now proceed directly from the interlingua with no need for syntactic transformations.

Note that the representation in Figure 21.6 includes the value GAR-DENING as the value for the EVENT feature, and, although such cases are familiar from Chapter 14, one might object that this looks more like an English word than it does an element in a truly interlingual representation. There is

---

[4] Of course this is seriously inadequate as an account of the meaning of the existential-there construction. In fact, the currently least incomplete account of the syntax and semantics of *there* constructions in English takes 124 pages (Lakoff, 1987).

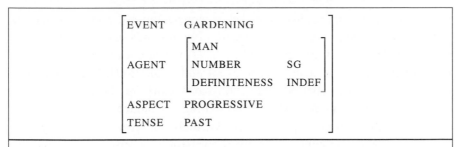

Figure 21.6   Interlingual representation of *there was an old man gardening*.

a deeper question here, that of the appropriate inventory of concepts and relations for an interlingua; that is what **ontology** to use. Certainly a meaning   ONTOLOGY
representation designer has a lot of freedom when selecting a set of tokens
and ascribing meanings to them. However, choice of an ontology for MT is
not to be undertaken lightly, since it constrains the architecture of the system as a whole. For example, recall from Chapter 16 the discussion of two
possible inventories of thematic roles, one containing AGENT and FORCE,
and one including AGENT only. The choice of which to adopt affects, for
example, the way that the system will translate *the quake broke glass* (Chapter 16) into Japanese, where *quake* needs to be marked with *de*, not the usual
subject marker *ga*, because the earthquake is not animate. If we design our
interlingua using the smaller inventory that only uses AGENT, then the representation for this sentence will place the *quake* in the AGENT role, and the
problem of *de* versus *ga* will fall to the generator. If, however, we use the
expanded inventory of Figure 16.8, then the representation will include the
FORCE role, with the work needed to make that decision being performed by
the semantic analyzer.

The interlingua idea has implications not only for syntactic transfer
but also for lexical transfer. The idea is to avoid explicit descriptions of
the relations between source language words and target language words, in
favor of mapping via concepts, that is, language-independent elements of
the ontology. Recalling our earlier problem of whether to translate *man* as
otoko, *ningen*, *ojiisan*, etc. it is clear that most of the processing involved is
not specific to the goal of translating into Japanese; there is a more general
problem of disambiguating *man* into concepts such as GENERIC-HUMAN
and MALE-HUMAN. If we commit to using such concepts in an interlingua,
then a larger part of the translation process can be done with general language processing techniques and modules, and the processing specific to the
English-to-Japanese translation task can be eliminated or at least reduced.

Some interlinguas, and some other representations, go further and use lexical decomposition, that is, the disassembly of words into their component meanings. We saw a form of this in Figure 21.6, where *was* maps to PAST and PROGRESSIVE, and *a* maps to SINGULAR and INDEFINITE. Decomposition of content words is also possible: the word *drink* can be represented by (INGEST, FLUID, BY-MOUTH)[5]. Representing a sentence by breaking down the words in such ways does seem to be actually capturing something about meaning, rather than being just a rearrangement of tokens that look like the English words of the input. Moreover, such representations are potentially useful for inference-based disambiguation. For example, it is possible to use the meanings of the words to infer what the prepositional phrase is modifying in *the policeman saw the man with a telescope*, versus *the policeman shot the man with a telescope*. It is, however, difficult to get inference of this sort to work for more than a few examples except in very small domains. In general, such high-powered interlingua-based techniques are not used in practice.

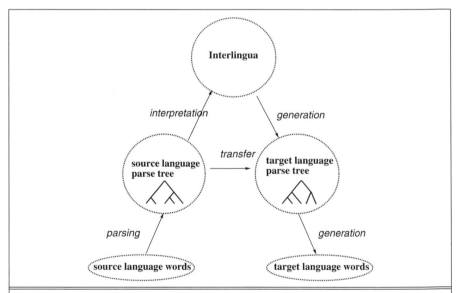

Figure 21.7   Diagram Suggesting the Relation Between the Transfer and Interlingua Models, generally credited to Vauqois.

---

[5] This use of semantic decomposition makes it clear which elements of meaning *drink* shares with *eat* and which it does not share. But as Chapter 16 discusses, lexical semantics is not so easy in general. For example, how does one express in a formal language the meaning of *heft* and the way it differs from *weight*, or the meanings of *sporadic* and *intermittent*?

Brushing over numerous important details, we can now contrast the transfer model with the interlingua model. The key implication for processing is that, by making the parser/interpreter and/or the generator do a little more work, we can eliminate the need for contrastive knowledge, as suggested in Figure 21.7.

Doing the extra work involved by the interlingua commitment, however, is not always easy. It requires the system designer to perform exhaustive analysis of the semantics of the domain and formalize that in an ontology (Levin et al., 1998). Today this is more an art than a science, although it is relatively tractable in sublanguage domains. In some cases the semantics can mostly be captured by a database model, as in the air travel, hotel reservation, or restaurant recommendation domains. In cases like these, the database definition determines the possible entities and relations; and the MT system designer's task is largely one of determining how these map to the words and structures of the two languages.

Another problem with the interlingua idea is that, in its pure form, it requires the system to fully disambiguate at all times. For a true universal interlingua, this may require some unnecessary work. For example, in order to translate from Japanese to Chinese the interlingua must include concepts such as ELDER-BROTHER and YOUNGER-BROTHER. However, to use those same concepts in the course of translating from German-to-English would require a parser to perform more disambiguation effort than is unnecessary; and will further require the system to include techniques for **preserving ambiguity**, to ensure that the output is ambiguous or vague in exactly the same way as the input. Even discounting the Sapir-Whorf idea, the idea of a universal meaning underlying all languages is clearly not without problems.

PRESERVING
AMBIGUITY

21.4 DIRECT TRANSLATION

These models are all very nice, but what happens if the analysis fails? Users do not like to receive an output of "nil" due to "no parse tree found"; in general, they would rather get something imperfect than nothing at all. This is a challenge especially for interlingua-based models, where the system should not fail to translate *it broke the glass* because it can not figure out whether *it* is a FORCE or AGENT.

Several approaches are available. One is to use the robust parsing techniques discussed in Chapter 15, which sometimes amounts to translating by fragments. Another is to give up on producing elaborate structural analyses

DIRECT

at all, and just do simple operations that can be done reliably. More radically, we could adopt the principle that an MT system should do as little work as possible. Systems built according to this philosophy are sometimes called **direct** MT systems. Typically such systems are built with only one language pair in mind, and the only processing done is that needed to get from one specific source language to one specific target language.

A direct MT system is typically composed of several stages, each focused on one type of problem. For example, we can rewrite a Japanese sentence as an English one in six stages, as seen in Figure 21.8. Figure 21.9

Stage	Action
1.	morphological analysis
2.	lexical transfer of content words
3.	various work relating to prepositions
4.	SVO rearrangements
5.	miscellany
6.	morphological generation

Figure 21.8   Six Stages for a Direct MT System for Japanese to English

illustrates how this might work for a simple example.

Stage 1 in Figure 21.9 segments the input string into words (recall that Japanese, like Chinese, does not use spaces as word boundary markers), and does morphological analysis of complex verb forms. These can be done using the finite-state techniques of Chapter 3 and segmentation algorithms like the probabilistic one described in Chapter 5.

Stage 2 chooses translation equivalents for the content words. This is done using a bilingual dictionary, or procedures that choose the correct translation based on the local context and on the target language words already chosen. Figure 21.10 illustrates such a procedure.

Input:	watashihatsukuenouenopenwojonniageta.
After stage 1:	watashi ha tsukue no ue no pen wo jon ni ageru PAST.
After stage 2:	I ha desk no ue no pen wo John ni give PAST.
After stage 3:	I ha pen on desk wo John to give PAST.
After stage 4:	I give PAST pen on desk John to.
After stage 5:	I give PAST the pen on the desk to John.
After stage 6:	I gave the pen on the desk to John.

Figure 21.9   An Example of Processing in a Direct System

In this example lexical transfer is trivial. In general, though, there may be interdependencies among target-language words, and so lexical transfer this may be done in sub-stages, for example, verbs before nouns before adjectives. For example, consider the problem of translating *nomu* from Japanese to English, where this must become either *drink* or *take* (medicine). This decision must be made before translations for modifiers are chosen, to allow translations such as *drinking heavily* and *taking a lot of medicine*, but not a scramble of the two. In general the problem of the best order in which to make decisions is a tricky one, although there are some standard solutions, as seen in Chapter 20.

Stage 3 chooses to translate *no ue no* ('at top of') to *on*, and reverses the two associated noun phrases (*desk* and *pen*), since English prepositional phrases follow, not precede, the word they modify. In accordance with the dictionary entry for *gave*, which specifies subcategorization facts, it chooses to translate *ni* as *to*.

Stage 4 invokes a procedure to move the verb from the end of the sentence to the position after the subject, and removes case marking from subjects and direct objects.

Stage 5 handles things like moving case markers before nouns and inserting articles.

Finally Stage 6 inflects the verbs.

There are several ways in which this approach differs from the approaches seen earlier. One is that it is a new way of modularizing the MT task, orthogonal to the types of modularity seen in the transfer and interlingua models in Figure 21.7. In the direct model, all the processing involving analysis of one specific problem (prepositions for example) is handled in one stage, including analysis, transfer, and generation aspects. The advantage of this is that solving specific problems one at a time may be more tractable. On the other hand, it can be advantageous to organize processing into larger modules (analysis, transfer, synthesis) if there is synergy among all the various individual analysis problems, or among all the individual generation problems, etc.

A second characteristic of direct systems is that lexical transfer may be more procedural. Lexical transfer procedures may eclectically look at the syntactic classes and semantic properties of neighboring words and dependents and heads, as seen in the decision-tree-like procedure for translating *much* and *many* into Russian in Figure 21.10.

A third characteristic of direct models is that they tend to be conservative, to only reorder words when required by obvious ungrammaticality in

---

function DIRECTLY_TRANSLATE_MUCH/MANY(Russian word) **returns**

if preceding word is *how*
   return *skol'ko*
else if preceding word is *as*
   return *stol'ko zhe*
else if word is *much*
   if preceding word is *very*
      return nil (not translated)
   else if following word is a noun
      return *mnogo*
else /* word is many */
   if preceding word is a preposition and following word is a noun
   return *mnogii*
else return *mnogo*

Figure 21.10   A procedure for translating *much* and *many* into Russian, adapted from Hutchins' (1986, pg. 133) discussion of Panov 1960.

---

the result of direct word-for-word substitution. In particular, direct systems generally do lexical transfer before syntactic processing.

   Perhaps the key characteristic of direct models is that they do without complex structures and representations. In general, they treat the input as a string of words (or morphemes), and perform various operations directly on it — replacing source language words with target language words, re-ordering words, etc. — to end up with a string of symbols in the target language.

   In practice, of course, working MT systems tend to be combinations of the direct, transfer, and interlingua methods. But of course syntactic processing is not an all-or-nothing thing. Even if the system does not do a full parse, it can adorn its input with various useful syntactic information, such as part-of-speech tags, segmentation into clauses or phrases, dependency links, and bracketings. Many systems that are often characterized as direct translation systems also adopt various techniques generally associated with the transfer and interlingua approaches (Hutchins and Somers, 1992).

21.5   USING STATISTICAL TECHNIQUES

The three architectures for MT introduced in previous sections, the transfer, interlingua, and direct models, all provide answers to the questions of what representations to use and what steps to perform to translate. But there is another way to approach the problem of translation: to focus on the result, not the process. Taking this perspective, let's consider what it means for a sentence to be a translation of some other sentence.

This is an issue to which philosophers of translation have given a lot of thought. The consensus seems to be, sadly, that it is impossible for a sentence in one language to be a translation of a sentence in other, strictly speaking. For example, one cannot really translate Hebrew *adonai roi* ('the Lord is my shepherd') into the language of a culture that has no sheep. On the one hand, we can write something that is clear in the target language, at some cost in fidelity to the original, something like *the Lord will look after me*. On the other hand, we can be faithful to the original, at the cost of producing something obscure to the target language readers, perhaps like *the Lord is for me like somebody who looks after animals with cotton-like hair*. As another example, if we translate the Japanese phrase *fukaku hansei shite orimasu*, as *we apologize*, we are not being faithful to the meaning of the original, but if we produce *we are deeply reflecting (on our past behavior, and what we did wrong, and how to avoid the problem next time)*, then our output is unclear or awkward. Problems such as these arise not only for culture-specific concepts, but whenever one language uses a metaphor, a construction, a word, or a tense without an exact parallel in the other language.

So, true translation, which is both faithful to the source language and natural as an utterance in the target language, is sometimes impossible. If you are going to go ahead and produce a translation anyway, you have to compromise. This is exactly what translators do in practice: they produce translations that do tolerably well on both criteria.

This provides us with a hint for how to do MT. We can model the goal of translation as the production of an output that maximizes some value function that represents the importance of both faithfulness and fluency. If we chose the product of fluency and faithfulness as our quality metric, we can formalize the translation problem as:

$$\text{best-translation } \hat{T} = \text{argmax}_T \; \text{fluency(T) faithfulness(T,S)}$$

where T is the target-language-sentence and S the source-language-sentence.

This model of translation was first described by researchers coming from speech recognition (Brown et al., 1990, 1993), and this model clearly resembles the Bayesian models we've used for speech recognition in Chapter 7 and for spell checking in Section 5.4. We can make the analogy perfect and apply the noisy channel model of Section 5.4 if we think of things backwards: thus we pretend that the input we must translate is a corrupted version of some target language sentence, and that our task is to discover that target language sentence:

$$\text{best-translation } \hat{T} = \text{argmax}_T \text{ P(T) } P(S|T)$$

To implement this, we need to do three things: quantify fluency, $P(T)$, quantify faithfulness, $P(S|T)$ and create an algorithm to find the sentence that maximizes the product of these two things.

There is an innovation here. In the transfer, interlingua, and direct models, each step of the process made some adjustment to the input sentence to make it closer to a fluent TL sentence, while obeying the constraint of not changing the meaning too much. In those models the process is fixed, in that there is no flexibility to trade-off a modicum of faithfulness for a smidgeon of naturalness, or conversely, based on the specific input sentence at hand. This new model, sometimes called the **statistical model of translation** allows exactly that.

Quantifying Fluency

Fortunately, we already have some useful metrics for how likely a sentence is to be a real English sentence: the language models from Chapters 6 and 8. These allow us to distinguish things that are readable but not really English (such as *that car was almost crash onto me*) from things that are more fluent (*that car almost hit me*). This is especially valuable for word order and collocations, and as such can be a useful supplement to the generation techniques of Chapter 20.

Fluency models can be arbitrarily sophisticated; any technique that can assign a better probability to a target language string is appropriate, including the more sophisticated probabilistic grammars of Chapter 12 or the statistical semantic techniques of Chapter 17.

Of course, the idea of using monolingual language knowledge to improve MT output is independent of the decision to model that knowledge statistically. Indeed, many MT systems, especially direct ones, have a final phase, in which the system uses local considerations to revise word choices in the output. For example, capitalizing every occurrence of *white house* that occurs as the subject of a verb (*the white house announced today*) is a reasonable heuristic.

Quantifying Faithfulness

Given the French sentence *ca me plaît* (*that me pleases*) and some conceivable English equivalents *that pleases me*, *I like it*, and *I'll take that one*, and *yes, good*, it is intuitively clear that the first is more faithful.

Although it is hard to quantify this intuition, one basic factor often used in metrics for fidelity is the degree to which the words in one sentence are plausible translations of the words of the other. Thus we can approximate the probability of a sentence being a good translation as the product of the probabilities that each target language word is an appropriate translation of some source language word. For this we need to know, for every source language word, the probability of it mapping to each possible target language word.

Where do we get these probabilities? Standard bilingual dictionaries do not include such information, but they can be computed from bilingual corpora, that is, parallel texts in two languages. This is not trivial, since bilingual corpora do not come with annotations specifying which word maps to which. Solving this problem requires first solving the problem of **sentence alignment** in a bilingual corpus, determining which source language sentence maps to which target language sentence, which can be done with reasonable accuracy (Kay and Röscheisen, 1993; Gale and Church, 1993; Melamed, 1999; Manning and Schütze, 1999). The second problem, **word alignment**, that is, determining which word(s) of the target correspond to each source language word or phrase, is rather more difficult (Melamed, pear), and is often addressed with EM methods (cf. Chapter 7). From bilingual corpora aligned in these ways it is possible to count how many times a word, phrase, or structure gets mapped to each of its possible translations. Such alignments are potentially useful not only for MT but also for automatic generation of bilingual dictionary entries for use by human translators (Dagan and Church, 1997; Fung and McKeown, 1997).

Let's now consider an example. Suppose we want to translate the two-word Japanese phrase *2000nen taio* into English. The most probable translation for the first word is, we will assume, *2000*, followed by *year 2000*, *Y2K*, *2000 years*, *2000 year* and some other possibilities. The most probable translation for the second word is, we will assume, *correspondence*, followed by *corresponding*, *equivalent*, *tackle*, *deal with*, *dealing with*, *countermeasures*, *respond*, *response*, *counterpart*, *antithesis* and so on. Thus, according to the translation model alone, the most highly ranked candidate will be the composition of the most highly ranked words, namely *2000 countermeasures*.

SENTENCE ALIGNMENT

WORD ALIGNMENT

But, when the contribution of the fluency model, perhaps a bigram model, is factored in, the candidate translation *dealing with Y2K* will have the highest overall score.

Of course, more complex translations models are possible: anything that generates multiple translations with a ranking associated with each. It is even possible to do "multi-engine" translation, where several translation models (for example a powerful but brittle interlingua-based one and a robust but low-quality direct one) are run in parallel to generate various translations and translation fragments, with the final output determined by assembling the pieces which have highest confidence scores (Brown and Frederking, 1995).

Search

So far we have a theory of which sentence is best, but not of how to find it. Since the number of possible translations is enormous, we must find the best output without actually generating the infinite set of all possible translations. But this is just a decoding problem, of the kind we have seen how to solve via the pruned Viterbi (beam-search) and A* algorithms of Chapter 7. For MT this decoding is done in the usual way: outputs (translations) are generated incrementally, and evaluated at each point. If at any point the probability drops below some criterion that line of attack is pruned. Generation can be left to right or outward from heads.

Good introductions to statistical MT include (Brown et al., 1990) and (Knight, 1997). One of the most influential recent systems is described in (Knight et al., 1994).

21.6   USABILITY AND SYSTEM DEVELOPMENT

Since MT systems are generally run by human operators, the human is available to help the machine. One way to use human intervention is interactively; that is, when the system runs into a problem, it can ask the user. For example, a system given the input *the chicken are ready to eat* could generate paraphrases of both possible meanings, and present the user with those alternatives, for example, asking her to decide whether the sentence means *the chicken are ready to be eaten* or *the chicken are ready to eat something*. It turns out that this is incredibly annoying — users do not like to have to answer questions from a computer, or to feel that they exist to help the computer get its work done (Cooper, 1995). On the other hand, people are comfortable with the job of fixing up poorly-written sentences, and so post-editing is the normal mode of human interaction with MT systems.

People are also able to edit sentences of the source language, and this ability can be exploited as way to improve the translatability of the input by simplifying it in various ways. Such **pre-editing** can be more cost-effective than post-editing if a single document needs to be translated into several languages, since the cost of pre-editing can then be amortized over many output languages — as is often the case for companies which sell things complete with documentation, in many countries (Mitamura and Nyberg, 1995). In order to decide what needs pre-editing, one way is to apply MT and see what comes out wrong, and then go back and rewrite those sentences in the original. Another way is to have a model of what MT ought to handle, and require input sentences to be rewritten in that sublanguage, for example, by disallowing PPs which could attach ambiguously. If such a model exists, the pre-editing phase can actually be dispensed with, by training the technical writers to only write in simple, unambiguous **controlled language**, a version of English that passes the constraints of the sublanguage grammar checker. Doing so may also make the source language text more understandable. This is interesting as a case where focusing on the larger task (getting information from tech writers to customers), rather than the problem as originally posed (to translate some existing documents), leads to improvements of the entire process.

PRE-EDITING

CONTROLLED
LANGUAGE

In general, user satisfaction is vital for MT systems. Various evaluation metrics are used to predict acceptability. Evaluation metrics for MT intended to be used raw (for information acquisition) include the percentage of sentences translated correctly, or nearly correctly, where correctness depends on both fidelity and fluency. The typical evaluation metric for MT output to be post-edited is **edit cost**, either relative to some standard translation via some automatic measure of edit-distance, similar to those seen in Chapter 7 for evaluating speech recognition, or measured directly as the amount of time (or number of keystrokes) required to correct the output to an acceptable level.

In general the content words are crucial; users can generally recover from scrambled syntax, but having the words translated properly is vital. In practice, one of the major advantages of using a MT system is that it handles most of the tedious work of looking up words in bilingual dictionaries.[6] As a result, professional MT users put great value on dictionary size and quality. Such users typically augment the basic system dictionary with the purchase of a domain-specific dictionary designed for the type of translation work they do: medical, electronic, financial, military intelligence etc. But no off-the-shelf dictionary, even one developed from a corpus of texts in the proper domain area, is more than an approximation to the dictionary needed by a specific customer, and so established translation bureaus typically invest substantial effort in augmenting the system dictionaries with entries of their own. The structure of these dictionaries is simple because the specialist **terminology** of any field is generally unambiguous — a photon is a photon is a photon, no matter what context it comes up in — and because terminology is almost invariably open-class words, with no syntactic idiosyncrasies.

TERMINOLOGY

It has also become apparent that MT systems do better if the dictionaries include not only words but also idioms, fixed phrases, and even frequent clauses and sentences. Such data can sometimes be extracted automatically from corpora. Moreover, in some situations it may be valuable to do this on-line, at translation time, rather than saving the results in a dictionary — this is they key idea behind **Example-based Machine Translation** (Sumita and Iida, 1991; Brown, 1996).

EXAMPLE-BASED
MACHINE
TRANSLATION

User satisfaction also turns out to depend on factors other than the actual quality of the translation. Many users care less about output quality than other factors, such as cost, speed, storage requirements, the ability to run transparently inside their favorite editor, the ability to preserve SGML tags, and so on. **Translation memory**, the ability to store and recall previously corrected translations, is also a big selling point.

TRANSLATION
MEMORY

Although for expository purposes the previous sections have focussed on a few basic problems that arise in translation, it is important to realize that these far from exhaust the things that MT systems have to worry about. As Section 21.1 may have suggested, language differences are a virtually inexhaustible source of complexity; and if you were reading the footnotes in the previous sections, you may have been annoyed that every "fact" we mentioned about a language was actually an oversimplification. Indeed, much of the work developing a MT system is down in the weeds, dealing with details like this, regardless of the overall system architecture chosen. Furthermore, adding more knowledge does not always help, since a working MT system,

---

[6] MT systems can also save time typing in the target language word, especially for translations into Chinese and Japanese, where it is time-consuming to enter characters.

like any huge software system, is a large, delicate piece of code. Improvement to the treatment of one phenomenon, or a correction of a bug in the translation of one sentence can cause other sentences, previously translated correctly, to go awry.

Given all this, it is surprising that MT systems so as well as they do. One development technique of proven value is iterative development: build it, evaluate it in actual use, improve it, and repeat. In the course of this process the MT system is adapted to a domain, to the working habits of its users, and to the needs of the consumers of the output.

21.7   SUMMARY

- Although MT systems exploit many standard language-processing techniques, there are also some MT-specific ones, including notably syntactic transformations.

- We have presented four models for MT, the **transfer**, **interlingua**, **direct**, and **statistical** approaches. Practical MT systems today, however, typically combine ideas from several of these models; while MT research systems are probing other niches in the design space.

- MT system design is hard work, requiring careful selection of models and algorithms and combination into a useful system. Today this is more a craft than a science, especially since this must be done while minimizing development cost.

- While MT system design today is thus fairly ad hoc, there are ongoing efforts to develop useful formal models of translation (Alshawi et al., 1998; Knight and Al-Onaizan, 1998; Wu and Wong, 1998).

- While the possibilities for improvement for MT is truly impressive, the output of today's systems is acceptable for **rough translations** for information-acquisition purposes, **draft translations** intended to be post-edited by a human translator, and translation for **sublanguage** domains.

- As for many software tasks, user interface issues in MT are crucial; the value of MT systems to users is not directly related to the sophistication of their algorithms or representations, nor even necessarily to output quality.

- Despite half a century of research, MT is far from solved. Human language is a rich and fascinating area whose treasures have only begun to be explored.

BIBLIOGRAPHICAL AND HISTORICAL NOTES

Work on models of the process and goals of translation goes back at least to Saint Jerome in the fourth century (Kelley, 1979). The development of logical languages, free of the imperfections of human languages, for reasoning correctly and for communicating truths and thereby also for translation, has been pursued at least since the 1600s (Hutchins, 1986).

By the late 1940s, scant years after the birth of the electronic computer, the idea of MT was raised seriously (Weaver, 1955). In 1954 the first public demonstration of a MT system prototype (Dostert, 1955) led to great excitement in the press (Hutchins, 1997). The next decade saw a great flowering of ideas, prefiguring most subsequent developments. But this work was ahead of its time — implementations were limited by, for example, the fact that pending the development of disks there was no good way to store dictionary information.

As high quality MT proved elusive (Bar-Hillel, 1960), a growing consensus on the need for more basic research in the new fields of formal and computational linguistics led in the mid 1960s to a dramatic cut in funding for MT research. As MT research lost academic respectability, the Association for Machine Translation and Computational Linguistics dropped MT from its name. Some MT developers, however, persevered, slowly and steadily improving their systems, and slowly garnering more customers. Systran in particular, developed initially by Peter Toma, has been continuously improved over 40 years. Its earliest uses were for information acquisition, for example by the U.S. Air Force for Russian documents; and in 1976 an English-French edition was adopted by the European Community for creating rough and post-editable translations of various administrative documents. Our translation example in the introduction was produced using the free Babelfish version of Systran on the Web. Another early successful MT system was Météo, which translated weather forecasts from English to French; incidentally, its original implementation (1976), used "Q-systems", an early unification model.

The late 1970s saw the birth of another wave of academic interest in MT. One source of excitement was the possibility of using Artificial Intelligence techniques ideas, originally developed for story understanding and knowledge engineering (Carbonell et al., 1981). This interest in meaning-based techniques was also a reaction to the dominance of syntax in computational linguistics at that time. Another motivation for the use of interlingual models was their introspective plausibility: the idea that MT systems should translate as people do (presuming that people translate by using their ability to understand). Introspection here may be misleading, since the process of human translation is enormously complex and furthermore the relevance for machine translation is unclear. Concerns about such issues were much discussed in the late 1980s and early 1990s Tsujii (1986), Nirenburg et al. (1992), Ward (1994), Carbonell et al. (1992). Meanwhile MT usage was increasing, fueled by the increase in international trade and the growth of governments with policies requiring the translation of all documents into multiple official languages, and enabled by the proliferation of word processors, and then personal computers, and then the World Wide Web.

The 1990s saw the application of statistical methods, enabled by the development of large corpora. Excitement was provided by the "grand challenge" of building speech-to-speech translation systems (Kay et al., 1992; Bub et al., 1997; Frederking et al., 1997) where MT catches up with the modern vision of computers being embedded, ubiquitous and interactive. On the practical side, with the growth of the user population, user's needs have had an increasing effect on priorities for MT research and development.

Good surveys of the early history of MT are Hutchins (1986) and (1997). The textbook by Hutchins and Somers (1992) includes a wealth of examples of language phenomena that make translation difficult, and extensive descriptions of some historically significant MT systems.

Academic papers on machine translation appear in the journal *Machine Translation* and in the proceedings of the biennial (odd years) Conferences on Theoretical and Methodological Issue in Machine Translation.

Reports on systems, markets, and user experiences can be found in *MT News International*, the newsletter of the International Association for Machine Translation, which is the umbrella organization for the three regional MT societies: the Association for MT in the Americas, the Asian-pacific Association for MT, and the European Association for MT. These societies have annual meetings which bring together developers and users. The proceedings of the biennial MT Summit (odd years) are also often published. The mainstream computational linguistics journals and conferences also occasionally report work in machine translation.

EXERCISES

21.1   Select at random a paragraph of Chapter 9 which describes a fact about English syntax. a) Describe and illustrate how your favorite foreign language differs in this respect. b) Explain how a MT system could deal with this difference.

21.2   Go to the literature section of the library, and find a foreign language novel in a language you know. Copy down the shortest sentence on the first page. Now look up the rendition of that sentence in an English translation of the novel. a) For both original and translation, draw parse trees. b) For both original and translation, draw dependency structures. c) Draw a case structure representation of the meaning which the original and translation share. d) What does this exercise suggest to you regarding intermediate representations for MT?

21.3   Pick a word from the first sentence of the top article of today's newspaper. a) List the possible equivalents found in a bilingual dictionary. b) Sketch out how a MT system could choose the appropriate translation to use based on the context of occurrence. c) Sketch out how this could be done without using contrastive knowledge.

21.4   The idea of example-based MT can be extended to "translation by analogy" (Sato and Nagao, 1990). a) Given the bilingual data in Figure 21.11, what Japanese word do you think would be appropriate as a translation of *on* in *research on gastropods*? b) Specify an algorithm for doing lexical transfer in this way. c) How is your approach similar to choice of TL words by using a TL language model (Section 21.5)? d) How is it similar to disambiguation using semantic features as in Chapter 16?

the cat **on** the mat	no ue no
more notes **on** decision making	ni tsuite
pink frosting **on** the cake	no
see boats **on** the pond	no, ni
always reading **on** the bus	de

Figure 21.11   A mini-corpus of made-up phrases involving *on* and their Japanese translations

21.5   Type a sentence into a MT system (perhaps a free demo on the Web)

and see what it outputs. a) List the problems with the translation. b) Rank these problems in order of severity. c) For the two most severe problems, suggest the probable root cause.

21.6 Since natural languages are hard to deal with, due to ambiguities, irregularities, and other complexities, it is much nicer to work with something with is more logical: something that does not have these "flaws" of natural language. As a result, various notations which are (in some ways) less ambiguous or more regular than English have been proposed. In addition to various meaning representation schemes, natural languages such as Esperanto and Sanskrit, have also been proposed for use as interlinguas for machine translation. Is this a good idea? Why or why not?

21.7 Consider the types of "understanding" needed: 1. For a natural language interface to a database, as seen in Chapter 15. 2. For an information extraction program, as seen in Chapter 15. 3. For a MT system. Which of these requires a deeper understanding? In what way?

21.8 Choose one of the generation techniques introduced in Chapter 20 and explain why it would or would not be useful for MT.

21.9 Version 1 (for native English speakers): Consider the following sentence:

> These lies are like their father that begets them; gross as a mountain, open, palpable.
>
> Henry IV, Part 1, act 2, scene 2

Translate this sentence into some dialect of modern vernacular English. For example, you might translate it into the style of a New York Times editorial or an Economist opinion piece, or into the style of your favorite television talk-show host.

Version 2 (for native speakers of other languages): Translate the following sentence into your native language.

> One night my friend Tom, who had just moved into a new apartment, saw a cockroach scurrying about in the kitchen.

For either version, now:

a) Describe how you did the translation: What steps did you perform? In what order did you do them? Which steps took the most time? b) Could you write a program that would translate using the same methods that you did? Why or why not? c) What aspects were hardest for you? Would they be hard for a MT system? d) What aspects would be hardest for a MT system? are they hard for people too? e) Which models are best for describing various aspects of your process (direct, transfer, interlingua or statistical)? f) Now compare your translation with those produced by friends or classmates. What is different? Why were the translations different?

21.10   Newspaper reports of MT systems invariably include an example of a sentence, typically a proverb, that when translated from English to language X, and then back to English, came out funny. a) Is this evidence that at least one of the two MT systems was bad? b) Why does this problem not arise with human translators? Or does it? c) On the other hand, does a successful translation to a foreign language and back indicate that the system is doing well?

21.11   Set yourself an information acquisition task: for example, to find a World-Wide Web page in your favorite foreign language reviewing a recent movie, and discover what the reviewer thought. Accomplish this task using one or two of the Web's machine translation providers. a) Give two examples each of correct and incorrect translations you encountered. b) Come up with a simple quality metric for rating the MT output, and use it to evaluate the MT systems you tried. c) Were you able to find a page of the kind you wanted? d) Were you able to figure out whether the reviewer liked the movie? e) Were the scores on your quality metric predictive of your answers to (c) and (d)?

21.12   Consider each of the following as an application for machine translation. Rank the difficulty of each from 1 (easy) to 4 (very very hard). Also, for each task, say briefly what makes it easy or hard.

   a. Letters between an American girl and her Chinese pen-pal
   b. Electronic junk mail
   c. Articles in chemistry journals
   d. Magazine advertisements
   e. Children's storybooks
   f. History books
   g. An English-speaker wanting to read articles in Japanese newsgroups
   h. An English-speaker wanting to post articles to a Japanese newsgroup

A REGULAR EXPRESSION OPERATORS

Perl	grep	MS Word	Description
Single character expressions			
\...	\...	\...	a special character
.	.	?	any single character
[...]	[...]	[...]	any single character listed
[...-...]	[...-...]	[...-...]	any single character in the range
[^...]	[^...]	[!...]	any single character not listed
[^...-...]	[^...-...]	[!...-...]	any single character not in the range
Anchors/Expressions which match positions			
^	^	^	beginning of line
$	$	$	end of line
\b	-	-	word boundary
\B	-	-	word non-boundary
-	\<	<	start of word
-	\>	>	end of word
Counters/Expressions which quantify previous expressions			
*	*	-	zero or more of previous r.e.
+	-	@	one or more of previous r.e.
?	-	-	exactly one or zero of previous r.e.
{n}	\{n\}	{n}	n of previous r.e.
{n,m}	\{n,m\}	{n,m}	from n to m of previous r.e.
{n,}	\{n,\}	{n,}	at least n of previous r.e.

Figure A.1   Basic regular expressions

Perl	grep	MS Word	Description
Other			
`.*`	`.*`	`*`	any string of characters
`...|...`	`-`	`-`	or – matches either r.e.
`(...)`	`\(...\)`	`(...)`	grouping, memory
Shortcuts			
`\d`	`[0-9]`	`[0-9]`	any digit
`\D`	`[^0-9]`	`[^0-9]`	any non-digit
`\w`	`[a-zA-Z0-9␣]`	`[a-zA-Z0-9␣]`	any alphanumeric/space
`\W`	`[^a-zA-Z0-9␣]`	`[^a-zA-Z0-9␣]`	any non-alphanumeric
`\s`	`[␣\r\t\n\f]`	`-`	whitespace (space, tab)
`\S`	`[^␣\r\t\n\f]`	`-`	non-whitespace

Figure A.2   More regular expressions

THE PORTER STEMMING ALGORITHM

For the purposes of the Porter (1980) algorithm we define a **consonant** as a letter other than A, E, I, O, and U, and other than Y preceded by a consonant. Any other letter is a **vowel**. (This is of course just an orthographic approximation.) Let c denote a consonant and v denote a vowel. C will stand for a string of one or more consonants, and V for a string of one or more vowels. Any written English word or word part can be represented by the following regular expression (where the parentheses () are used to mark optional elements):

$$(C)(VC)^m(V)$$

For example the word *troubles* maps to the following sequence:

```
troubles
C V C VC
```

with no final V. We call the Kleene operator m the **measure** of any word or word part; the measure correlates very roughly with the number of syllables in the word or word part. Some examples:

m=0	TR, EE, TREE, Y, BY
m=1	TROUBLE, OATS, TREES, IVY
m=2	TROUBLES, PRIVATE, OATEN, ORRERY

The rules that we will present below will all be in the following format:

```
(condition) S1 → S2
```

meaning "if a word ends with the suffix S1, and the stem before S1 satisfies the condition, S1 is replaced by S2". Conditions include the following and any boolean combinations of them:

m	the measure of the stem
*S	the stem ends with S (and similarly for other letters)
v	the stem contains a vowel
*d	the stem ends with a double consonant (e.g. -TT, -SS)
*o	the stem ends CVC, where the second c is not W, X, or Y (e.g. -WIL, -HOP)

The Porter algorithm consists of seven simple sets of rules, applied in order. Within each step, if more than one of the rules can apply, only the one with the longest matching suffix (S1) is followed.

Step 1: Plural Nouns and Third Person Singular Verbs

The rules in this set do not have conditions:

SSES → SS	caresses → caress
IES → I	ponies → poni
	ties → ti
SS → SS	caress → caress
S → ε	cats → cat

Step 2a: Verbal Past Tense and Progressive Forms

(m> 1) EED → EE	feed → feed
	agreed → agree
(*v*) ED → ε	plastered → plaster
	bled → bled
(*v*) ING → ε	motoring → motor
	sing → sing

Step 2b: Cleanup

If the second or third of the rules in 2a is successful, we run the following rules (that remove double letters and put the E back on -ATE/-BLE)

	AT → ATE	conflat(ed)	→	conflate
	BL → BLE	troubl(ing)	→	trouble
	IZ → IZE	siz(ed)	→	size
(*d & !(*L or *S or *Z))	→ single letter	hopp(ing)	→	hop
		tann(ed)	→	tan
		fall(ing)	→	fall
		hiss(ing)	→	hiss
		fizz(ed)	→	fizz
(m=1 & *o)	→ E	fail(ing)	→	fail
		fil(ing)	→	file

Step 3: Y → I

(*v*) Y → I	happy	→ happi
	sky	→ sky

Step 4: Derivational Morphology I: Multiple suffixes

(m > 0) ATIONAL → ATE	relational	→	relate
(m > 0) TIONAL → TION	conditional	→	condition
	rational	→	rational
(m > 0) ENCI → ENCE	valenci	→	valence
(m > 0) ANCI → ANCE	hesitanci	→	hesitance
(m > 0) IZER → IZE	digitizer	→	digitize
(m > 0) ABLI → ABLE	conformabli	→	conformable
(m > 0) ALLI → AL	radicalli	→	radical
(m > 0) ENTLI → ENT	differentli	→	different
(m > 0) ELI → E	vileli	→	vile
(m > 0) OUSLI → OUS	analogousli	→	analogous
(m > 0) IZATION → IZE	vietnamization	→	vietnamize
(m > 0) ATION → ATE	predication	→	predicate
(m > 0) ATOR → ATE	operator	→	operate
(m > 0) ALISM → AL	feudalism	→	feudal
(m > 0) IVENESS → IVE	decisiveness	→	decisive
(m > 0) FULNESS → FUL	hopefulness	→	hopeful
(m > 0) OUSNESS → OUS	callousness	→	callous
(m > 0) ALITI → AL	formaliti	→	formal
(m > 0) IVITI → IVE	sensitiviti	→	sensitive
(m > 0) BILITI → BLE	sensibiliti	→	sensible

Step 5: Derivational Morphology II: More multiple suffixes

$(m > 0)$	ICATE	$\rightarrow$	IC	triplicate	$\rightarrow$ triplic
$(m > 0)$	ATIVE	$\rightarrow$	ε	formative	$\rightarrow$ form
$(m > 0)$	ALIZE	$\rightarrow$	AL	formalize	$\rightarrow$ formal
$(m > 0)$	ICITI	$\rightarrow$	IC	electriciti	$\rightarrow$ electric
$(m > 0)$	FUL	$\rightarrow$	ε	hopeful	$\rightarrow$ hope
$(m > 0)$	NESS	$\rightarrow$	ε	goodness	$\rightarrow$ good

Step 6: Derivational Morphology III: Single suffixes

$(m > 1)$	AL	$\rightarrow$	ε	revival	$\rightarrow$ reviv
$(m > 1)$	ANCE	$\rightarrow$	ε	allowance	$\rightarrow$ allow
$(m > 1)$	ENCE	$\rightarrow$	ε	inference	$\rightarrow$ infer
$(m > 1)$	ER	$\rightarrow$	ε	airliner	$\rightarrow$ airlin
$(m > 1)$	IC	$\rightarrow$	ε	gyroscopic	$\rightarrow$ gyroscop
$(m > 1)$	ABLE	$\rightarrow$	ε	defensible	$\rightarrow$ defens
$(m > 1)$	ANT	$\rightarrow$	ε	irritant	$\rightarrow$ irrit
$(m > 1)$	EMENT	$\rightarrow$	ε	replacement	$\rightarrow$ replac
$(m > 1)$	MENT	$\rightarrow$	ε	adjustment	$\rightarrow$ adjust
$(m > 1)$	ENT	$\rightarrow$	ε	dependent	$\rightarrow$ depend
$(m > 1)$	(*S or *T) & ION	$\rightarrow$	ε	adoption	$\rightarrow$ adopt
$(m > 1)$	OU	$\rightarrow$	ε	homologou	$\rightarrow$ homolog
$(m > 1)$	ISM	$\rightarrow$	ε	communism	$\rightarrow$ commun
$(m > 1)$	ATE	$\rightarrow$	ε	activate	$\rightarrow$ activ
$(m > 1)$	ITI	$\rightarrow$	ε	angulariti	$\rightarrow$ angular
$(m > 1)$	OUS	$\rightarrow$	ε	homologous	$\rightarrow$ homolog
$(m > 1)$	IVE	$\rightarrow$	ε	effective	$\rightarrow$ effect
$(m > 1)$	IZE	$\rightarrow$	ε	bowdlerize	$\rightarrow$ bowdler

Step 7a: Cleanup

$(m > 1)$ E $\rightarrow$ ε	probate	$\rightarrow$ probat
	rate	$\rightarrow$ rate
$(m = 1$ & ! *o) E $\rightarrow$ ε	cease	$\rightarrow$ ceas

Step 7b: Cleanup

$(m > 1$ & *d *L) $\rightarrow$ [single letter]	controll	$\rightarrow$ control
	roll	$\rightarrow$ roll

C C5 AND C7 TAGSETS

Tag	Description	Example
AJ0	adjective (unmarked)	*good, old*
AJC	comparative adjective	*better, older*
AJS	superlative adjective	*best, oldest*
AT0	article	*the, a, an*
AV0	adverb (unmarked)	*often, well, longer, furthest*
AVP	adverb particle	*up, off, out*
AVQ	wh-adverb	*when, how, why*
CJC	coordinating conjunction	*and, or*
CJS	subordinating conjunction	*although, when*
CJT	the conjunction *that*	
CRD	cardinal numeral (except *one*)	*3, twenty-five, 734*
DPS	possessive determiner	*your, their*
DT0	general determiner	*these, some*
DTQ	wh-determiner	*whose, which*
EX0	existential *there*	
ITJ	interjection or other isolate	*oh, yes, mhm*
NN0	noun (neutral for number)	*aircraft, data*
NN1	singular noun	*pencil, goose*
NN2	plural noun	*pencils, geese*
NP0	proper noun	*London, Michael, Mars*
ORD	ordinal	*sixth, 77th, last*
PNI	indefinite pronoun	*none, everything*
PNP	personal pronoun	*you, them, ours*
PNQ	wh-pronoun	*who, whoever*

Figure C.1   First half of UCREL C5 Tagset for the British National Corpus (BNC) after Garside et al. (1997).

Tag	Description	Example
PNX	reflexive pronoun	*itself, ourselves*
POS	possessive *'s* or *'*	
PRF	the preposition *of*	
PRP	preposition (except *of*)	*for, above, to*
PUL	punctuation – left bracket	(or [
PUN	punctuation – general mark	. ! , : ; - ? ...
PUQ	punctuation – quotation mark	' ' "
PUR	punctuation – right bracket	) or]
TO0	infinitive marker *to*	
UNC	unclassified items (not English)	
VBB	base forms of *be* (except infinitive)	*am, are*
VBD	past form of *be*	*was, were*
VBG	-ing form of *be*	*being*
VBI	infinitive of *be*	
VBN	past participle of *be*	*been*
VBZ	-s form of *be*	*is, 's*
VDB	base form of *do*(except infinitive)	*does*
VDD	past form of *do*	*did*
VDG	-ing form of *do*	*doing*
VDI	infinitive of *do*	*to do*
VDN	past participle of *do*	*done*
VDZ	-s form of *do*	*does*
VHB	base form of *have* (except infinitive)	*have*
VHD	past tense form of *have*	*had, 'd*
VHG	-ing form of *have*	*having*
VHI	infinitive of *have*	
VHN	past participle of *have*	*had*
VHZ	-s form of *have*	*has, 's*
VM0	modal auxiliary verb	*can, could, will, 'll*
VVB	base form of lexical verb (except infin.)	*take, live*
VVD	past tense form of lexical verb	*took, lived*
VVG	-ing form of lexical verb	*taking, living*
VVI	infinitive of lexical verb	*take, live*
VVN	past participle form of lex. verb	*taken, lived*
VVZ	-s form of lexical verb	*takes, lives*
XX0	the negative *not* or *n't*	
ZZ0	alphabetical symbol	*A, B, c, d*

Figure C.2   The rest of UCREL's C5 Tagset (Garside et al., 1997).

Tag	Description	Example
!	punctuation tag - exclamation mark	
"	punctuation tag - quotation marks	
(	punctuation tag - left bracket	
)	punctuation tag - right bracket	
,	punctuation tag - comma	
-	punctuation tag - dash	
——	new sentence marker	
.	punctuation tag - full-stop	
...	punctuation tag - ellipsis	
:	punctuation tag - colon	
;	punctuation tag - semi-colon	
?	punctuation tag - question-mark	
APPGE	possessive pronoun, prenominal	*my, your, our* etc.
AT	article	*the, no*
AT1	singular article	*a, an, every*
BCL	before-clause marker	*in order [that]*
CC	coordinating conjunction	*and, or*
CCB	coordinating conjunction	*but*
CS	subordinating conjunction	*if, because, unless*
CSA	*as* as a conjunction	
CSN	*than* as a conjunction	
CST	*that* as a conjunction	
CSW	*whether* as a conjunction	
DA	post-determiner/pronoun	*such, former, same*
DA1	singular after-determiner	*little, much*
DA2	plural after-determiner	*few, several, many*
DAR	comparative after-determiner	*more, less*
DAT	superlative after-determiner	*most, least*
DB	pre-determiner/pronoun	*all, half*
DB2	plural pre-determiner/pronoun	*both*
DD	determiner/pronoun	*any, some*
DD1	singular determiner	*this, that, another*
DD2	plural determiner	*these, those*
DDQ	wh-determiner	*which, what*
DDQGE	wh-determiner, genitive	*whose*
DDQV	wh-ever determiner	*whichever, whatever*
EX	existential *there*	
FO	formula	
FU	unclassified	

Figure C.3 First part of UCREL C7 Tagset for the British National Corpus (BNC) from (Garside et al., 1997).

Tag	Description	Example
FW	foreign word	
GE	germanic genitive marker -	' or 's
IF	*for* as a preposition	
II	preposition	*in, on, to*
IO	*of* as a preposition	
IW	*with*; *without* as preposition	
JJ	general adjective	*big, old*
JJR	general comparative adjective	*older, better, bigger*
JJT	general superlative adjective	*oldest, best, biggest*
JK	adjective catenative	*able* in *be able to* *willing* in *be willing to*
MC	cardinal number (neutral for number)	*two, three...*
MC1	singular cardinal number	*one*
MC2	plural cardinal number	*tens, twenties*
MCMC	hyphenated number	*40-50, 1770-1827*
MD	ordinal number	*first, 2nd, next, last*
ND1	singular noun of direction	*north, southeast*
NN	common noun (neutral for number)	*sheep, cod*
NN1	singular common noun	*book, girl*
NN2	plural common noun	*books, girls*
NNA	following noun of title	*M.A.*
NNB	preceding noun of title	*Mr, Prof*
NNL1	singular locative noun	*street, Bay*
NNL2	plural locative noun	*islands, roads*
NNO	numeral noun (neutral for number)	*dozen, thousand*
NNO2	plural numeral noun	*hundreds, thousands*
NNT	temporal noun (neutral for number)	no known examples
NNT1	singular temporal noun	*day, week, year*
NNT2	plural temporal noun	*days, weeks, years*
NNU	unit of measurement (neutral for number)	*in., cc.*
NNU1	singular unit of measurement	*inch, centimetre*
NNU2	plural unit of measurement	*inches, centimetres*
NP	proper noun (neutral for number)	*Phillipines, Mercedes*
NP1	singular proper noun	*London, Jane, Frederick*
NP2	plural proper noun	*Browns, Reagans, Koreas*
NPD1	singular weekday noun	*Sunday*
NPD2	plural weekday noun	*Sundays*

Figure C.4   More of UCREL's C7 Tagset (Garside et al., 1997).

Tag	Description	Example
NPM1	singular month noun	*October*
NPM2	plural month noun	*Octobers*
PN	indefinite pronoun (neutral for number)	*none*
PN1	singular indefinite pronoun	*one, everything, nobody*
PNQO		*whom*
PNQS		*who*
PNQV		*whoever, whomever*
		whomsoever, whosoever
PNX1	reflexive indefinite pronoun	*oneself*
PPGE	nominal possessive personal pronoun	*mine, yours*
PPH1		*it*
PPHO1		*him, her*
PPHO2		*them*
PPHS1		*She, she*
PPHS2		*they*
PPIO1		*me*
PPIO2		*us*
PPIS1		*I*
PPIS2		*we*
PPX1	singular reflexive personal pronoun	*yourself, itself*
PPX2	plural reflexive personal pronoun	*yourselves, ourselves*
PPY		*you*
RA	adverb, after nominal head	*else, galore*
REX	adverb introducing appositional constructions	*namely, viz, eg.*
RG	degree adverb	*very, so, too*
RGQ	wh- degree adverb	*how*
RGQV	wh-ever degree adverb	*however*
RGR	comparative degree adverb	*more, less*
RGT	superlative degree adverb	*most, least*
RL	locative adverb	*alongside, forward*
RP	prepositional adverb; particle	*in, up, about*
RPK	prepositional adverb, catenative	*about* in *be about to*
RR	general adverb	*actually*
RRQ	wh- general adverb	*where, when, why, how*
RRQV	wh-ever general adverb	*wherever, whenever*
RRR	comparative general adverb	*better, longer*
RRT	superlative general adverb	*best, longest*
RT	nominal adverb of time	*now, tommorow*

Figure C.5   More of UCREL's C7 Tagset (Garside et al., 1997).

Tag	Description	Example
TO	infinitive marker	*to*
UH	interjection	*oh, yes, um*
VB0		*be*
VBDR		*were*
VBDZ		*was*
VBG		*being*
VBI	infinitive *be*	
VBM		*am*
VBN		*been*
VBR		*are*
VBZ		*is*
VD0		*do*
VDD		*did*
VDG		*doing*
VDI	infinitive *do*	
VDN		*done*
VDZ		*does*
VH0		*have*
VHD	past tense *had*	
VHG		*having*
VHI	infinitive *have*	
VHN	past participle *had*	
VHZ		*has*
VM	modal auxiliary	*can, will, would* etc.
VMK	modal catenative	*ought, used*
VV0	base form of lexical verb	*give, work* etc.
VVD	past tense form of lexical verb	*gave, worked* etc.
VVG	-ing form of lexical verb	*giving, working* etc.
VVGK	-ing form in a catenative verb	*going* in *be going to*
VVI	infinitive of lexical verb	*[to] give, [to] work* etc.
VVN	past participle form of lexical verb	*given, worked* etc.
VVNK	past part. in a catenative verb	*bound* in *be bound to*
VVZ	-s form of lexical verb	*gives, works* etc.
XX		*not, n't*
ZZ1	singular letter of the alphabet	*A, a, B,* etc.
ZZ2	plural letter of the alphabet	*As, b's,* etc.

Figure C.6   The rest of UCREL's C7 Tagset (Garside et al., 1997).

TRAINING HMMS: THE FORWARD-BACKWARD ALGORITHM

This appendix sketches the **forward-backward** or **Baum-Welch** algorithm (Baum, 1972), a special case of the **Expectation-Maximization** or **EM** algorithm (Dempster et al., 1977). The algorithm will let us train the transition probabilities a_{ij} and the emission probabilities $b_i(o_t)$ of the HMM. While it is theoretically possible to train both the network structure of an HMM and these probabilities, no good algorithm for this double-induction exists. Thus in practice the structure of most HMMs is designed by hand, and then the transition and emission probabilities are trained from a large set of observation sequences O. Furthermore, it turns out that the problem of setting the a and b parameters so as to exactly maximize the probability of the observation sequence O is unsolved. The algorithm that we give in this section is only guaranteed to find a *local* maximum. The forward-backward algorithm is used throughout speech and language processing, for example in training HMM-based part-of-speech taggers, as we saw in Chapter 8. Extensions of forward-backward are also important, like the Inside-Outside algorithm used to train stochastic context-free-grammars (Chapter 12).

Let us begin by imagining that we were training not a Hidden Markov Model but a vanilla Markov Model. We do this by running the model on the observation and seeing which transitions and observations were used. For ease of description in the rest of this section, we will pretend that we are training on a single sequence of training data (called O), but of course in a real speech recognition system we would train on hundreds of thousands of sequences (thousands of sentences). Since unlike an HMM, a vanilla Markov Model is not hidden, we can look at an observation sequence and know exactly which transitions we took through the model, and which state generated each observation symbol. Since every state can only generate one observation symbol, the observation b probabilities are all 1.0. The probability a_{ij} of a particular transition between states i and j can be computed by counting the number of times the transition was taken, which we could call $C(i \rightarrow j)$, and then normalizing by the total count of all times we took any transition from state i.

$$a_{ij} = \frac{C(i \rightarrow j)}{\sum_{q \in Q} C(i \rightarrow q)} \qquad (D.1)$$

For an HMM we cannot compute these counts directly from an observed sentence (or set of sentences), since we don't know which path of states was taken through the machine for a given input. The Baum-Welch uses two neat intuitions to solve this problem. The first idea is to *iteratively* estimate the counts. We will start with an estimate for the transition and observation probabilities, and then use these estimated probabilities to derive better and better probabilities. The second idea is that we get our estimated probabilities by computing the forward probability for an observation and then dividing that probability mass among all the different paths that contributed to this forward probability.

In order to understand the algorithm, we need to return to the forward algorithm of Chapter 5 and more formally define two related probabilities which will be used in computing the final probability: the **forward probability** and the **backward probability**. We refer to the forward probability as α and the backward probability as β. Recall that we defined the forward probability as the probability of being in state i after seeing the first t observations, given the automaton λ:

FORWARD
PROBABILITY
BACKWARD
PROBABILITY

$$\alpha_t(i) = P(o_1, o_2 \ldots o_t, q_t = i | \lambda) \qquad (D.2)$$

In Chapter 5 we used a matrix to calculate the forward probability recursively; now we will formally define the actual recursion.

1. Initialization:

$$\alpha_h(1) = a_{1j} b_j(o_1) \; 1 < j < N \qquad (D.3)$$

2. Recursion (since states 1 and N are non-emitting):

$$\alpha_j(t) = \left[\sum_{i=2}^{N-1} \alpha_i(t-1) a_{ij} \right] b_j(o_t) \; 1 < j < N, 1 < t < T \qquad (D.4)$$

3. Termination:

$$P(O|\lambda) = \alpha_N(T) = \sum_{i=2}^{N-1} \alpha_i(T) a_{iN} \qquad (D.5)$$

As we saw in Chapter 5, the forward probability is computed via a matrix or lattice, in which each column is computed by extending the paths from the previous columns. Figure D.1 illustrates the induction step for computing the value in one new cell.

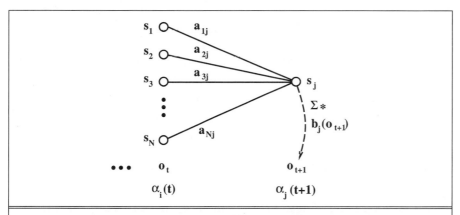

Figure D.1 The computation of $\alpha_i(t)$ by summing all the previous values α_{t-1} weighted by their transition probabilities a and multiplying by the observation probability $b_i(o_{t+1})$. Of course in any given HMM many or most of the transition probabilities will be 0, so not all previous states will contribute to the forward probability of the current state.

The second important piece of the forward-backward algorithm, the **backward** probability, is almost the mirror image of the forward probability; it computes the probability of seeing the observations from time $t+1$ to the end, given that we are in state j at time t (and of course given the automaton λ):

$$\beta_i(o_t) = P(o_{t+1}, o_{t+2} \ldots o_T | q_t = j, \lambda) \tag{D.6}$$

It is computed inductively in a similar manner to the forward algorithm.

1. Initialization:

$$\beta_i(t) = a_{iN}, \ 1 < i < N \tag{D.7}$$

2. Recursion (again since states 1 and N are non-emitting):

$$\beta_i(t) = \sum_{i=2}^{N-1} a_{ij} b_j(o_{t+1}) \beta_j(t+1) \ 1 < i < N, T > t \geq 1 \tag{D.8}$$

3. Termination:

$$P(O|\lambda) = \alpha_N(T) = \beta_1(T) = \sum_{j=2}^{N-1} a_{1j} b_j(o_1) \beta_j(1) \tag{D.9}$$

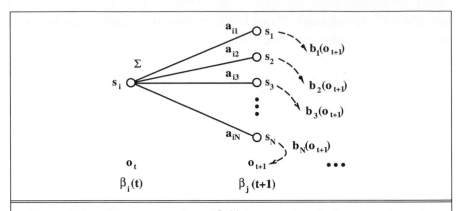

Figure D.2   The computation of $\beta_i(t)$ by summing all the successive values β_{t+1} weighted by their transition probabilities a and the observation probability $b_i(o_{t+1})$.

Figure D.2 illustrates the backward induction step.

We are now ready to understand how the forward and backward probabilities can help us compute the transition probability a_{ij} and observation probability $b_i(o_t)$ from an observation sequence, even though the actual path taken through the machine is hidden!

Let's begin by showing how to reestimate a_{ij}. We will proceed to estimate $\hat{a}_{ij}$ by a variant of (D.1):

$$\hat{a}_{ij} = \frac{\text{expected number of transitions from state } i \text{ to state } j}{\text{expected number of transitions from state } i} \quad \text{(D.10)}$$

How do we compute the numerator? Here's the intuition. Assume we had some estimate of the probability that a given transition $i \to j$ was taken at a particular point in time t in the observation sequence. If we knew this probability for each particular time t, we could sum over all times t to estimate the total count for the transition $i \to j$.

More formally, let's define the probability τ_t (τ for **t**ransition) as the probability of being in state i at time t and state j at time $t+1$, given the observation sequence and of course the model:

$$\tau_t(i,j) = P(q_t = i, q_{t+1} = j | O, \lambda) \quad \text{(D.11)}$$

In order to compute τ_t, we first compute a probability which is similar to τ_t, but differs in including the probability of the observation:

$$\text{not-quite-}\tau_t(i,j) = P(q_t = i, q_{t+1} = j, O | \lambda) \quad \text{(D.12)}$$

Figure D.3 shows the various probabilities that go into computing not-quite-τ_t: the transition probability for the arc in question, the α probability before the arc, the β probability after the arc, and the observation probability for the symbol just after the arc.

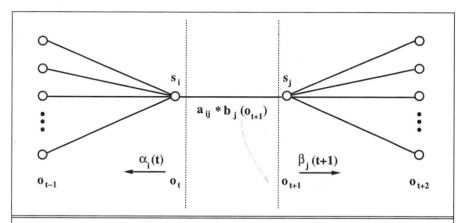

Figure D.3   Computation of the joint probability of being in state i at time t and state j at time $t+1$. The figure shows the various probabilities that need to be combined to produce $P(q_t = i, q_{t+1} = j, O|\lambda)$: the α and β probabilities, the transition probability a_{ij} and the observation probability $b_j(o_{t+1})$. After Rabiner (1989).

These are multiplied together to produce *not-quite-*τ_t as follows:

$$\text{not-quite-}\tau_t(i, j) = \alpha_i(t) a_{ij} b_j(o_{t+1}) \beta_j(t+1) \tag{D.13}$$

In order to compute τ_t from *not-quite-*τ_t, the laws of probability instruct us to divide by $P(O|\lambda)$, since:

$$P(X|O,\lambda) = \frac{P(X,O|\lambda)}{P(O|\lambda})) \tag{D.14}$$

The probability of the observation given the model is simply the forward probability of the whole utterance, (or alternatively the backward probability of the whole utterance!), which can thus be computed in a number of ways:

$$P(O|\lambda) = \alpha_N(T) = \beta_1(T) = \sum_{j=1}^{N} \alpha_j(t) \beta_j(t) \tag{D.15}$$

So, the final equation for τ_t is:

$$\tau_t(i, j) = \frac{\alpha_i(t) a_{ij} b_j(o_{t+1}) \beta_j(t+1)}{\alpha_N(T)} \tag{D.16}$$

The expected number of transitions from state i to state j is then the sum over all t of τ. For our estimate of a_{ij} in (D.10), we just need one more thing: the total expected number of transitions from state i. We can get this by summing over all transitions out of state i. Here's the final formula for $\hat{a}_{ij}$:

$$\hat{a}_{ij} = \frac{\sum_{t=1}^{T-1} \tau_t(i,j)}{\sum_{t=1}^{T-1} \sum_{j=1}^{N} \tau_t(i,j)} \qquad (D.17)$$

We also need a formula for recomputing the observation probability. This is the probability of a given symbol v_k from the observation vocabulary V, given a state j: $\hat{b}_j(v_k)$. We will do this by trying to compute:

$$\hat{b}_j(v_k) = \frac{\text{expected number of times in state } j \text{ and observing symbol } v_k}{\text{expected number of times in state } j} \qquad (D.18)$$

For this we will need to know the probability of being in state j at time t, which we will call $\sigma_j(t)$ (σ for state):

$$\sigma_j(t) = P(q_t = j|O,\lambda) \qquad (D.19)$$

Once again, we will compute this by including the observation sequence in the probability:

$$\sigma_j(t) = \frac{P(q_t = j, O|\lambda)}{P(O|\lambda)} \qquad (D.20)$$

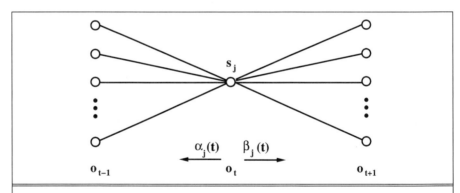

Figure D.4   The computation of $\sigma_j(t)$, the probability of being in state j at time t. Note that σ is really a degenerate case of τ and hence this figure is like a version of Figure D.3 with state i collapsed with state j.

As Figure D.4 shows, the numerator of (D.20) is just the product of the forward probability and the backward probability:

$$\sigma_j(t) = \frac{\alpha_j(t)\beta_j(t)}{P(O|\lambda)} \qquad (D.21)$$

We are ready to compute b. For the numerator, we sum $\sigma_j(t)$ for all time steps t in which the observation o_t is the symbol v_k that we are interested in. For the denominator, we sum $\sigma_j(t)$ over all time steps t. The result will be the percentage of the times that we were in state j that we saw symbol v_k (the notation $\sum_{t=1 s.t.O_t=v_k}^{T}$ means "sum over all t for which the observation at time t was v_k):

$$\hat{b}_j(v_k) = \frac{\sum_{t=1 s.t.O_t=v_k}^{T} \sigma_j(t)}{\sum_{t=1}^{T} \sigma_j(t)} \tag{D.22}$$

We now have ways to *re-estimate* the transition a and observation b probabilities from an observation sequence O assuming that we already have a previous estimate of a and b. The entire training procedure for HMMs, called **embedded training**, first chooses some estimate for a and b, and then uses equations (D.22) and (D.17) to re-estimate a and b, and then repeats until convergence. In the next sections we will see how forward-backward is extended to inputs which are non-discrete ("continuous observation densities") via Gaussian functions. Section 7.7 discussed how the embedded training algorithm gets its initial estimates for a and b.

Continuous Probability Densities

The version of the parameter reestimation that we have described so far section assumes that the input observations were discrete symbols from some reasonably-sized alphabet. This is naturally true for some uses of HMMs; for example Chapter 8 will introduce the use of HMMs for part-of-speech-tagging. Here the observations are words of English, which is a reasonably-sized finite set, say approximately 100K words. For speech recognition, the LPC cepstral features that we introduced constitute a much larger alphabet (11 features, each one say a 32-bit floating-point number), for a total vocabulary size of $2^{(11\times32)}$. In fact, since in practice, we usually use not 11 features, but delta-features and double-delta features as well, the vocabulary size would be enormous. Chapter 7 mentioned that one way to solve this problem is to **cluster** or **vector quantize** the cepstral features into a much smaller set of discrete observation symbols. A more effective approach is to use either mixtures of **Gaussian** estimators **neural networks (multi-layer perceptron)** to estimate a **probability density function** or **pdf** over a continuous space, as we suggested in Chapter 7.

HMMs with Gaussian observation-probability-estimators are trained by a simple extension to the forward-backward algorithm. Recall from Chapter 7 that in the simplest use of Gaussians, we assume that the possible values of the observation feature vector o_t are normally distributed, and so we represent the observation probability function $b_j(o_t)$ as a Gaussian curve with mean vector μ_j and covariance matrix Σ_j (prime denotes vector transpose):

$$b_j(o_t) = \frac{1}{\sqrt{(2\pi)|\Sigma j|}} e^{[(o_t - \mu_j)'\Sigma_j^{-1}(o_t - \mu_j)]} \tag{D.23}$$

Usually we make the simplifying assumption that the covariance matrix Σ_j is diagonal, which means that in practice we are keeping a single separate mean and variance for each feature in the feature vector.

How are the mean and covariance of the Gaussians estimated? It is helpful again to consider the simpler case of a non-hidden Markov Model, with only one state i. The vector of feature means μ and the vector of covariances Σ could then be estimated by averaging:

$$\hat{\mu}_i = \frac{1}{T} \sum_{t=1}^{T} o_t \tag{D.24}$$

$$\hat{\Sigma}_i = \frac{1}{T} \sum_{t=1}^{T} [(o_t - \mu_j)'(o_t - \mu_j)] \tag{D.25}$$

But since there are multiple hidden states, we don't know which observation vector o_t was produced by which state. What we would like to do is assign each observation vector o_t to every possible state i, prorated by the probability that the HMM was in state i at time t. Luckily, we already know how to do this prorating; the probability of being in state i at time t is $\sigma_i(t)$, which we saw how to compute above! Of course we'll need to do the probability computation of $\sigma_i(t)$ iteratively since getting a better observation probability b will also help us be more sure of the probability σ of being in a state at a certain time. So the actual re-estimation equations are:

$$\hat{\mu}_i = \frac{\sum_{t=1}^{T} \sigma_i(t) o_t}{\sum_{t=1}^{T} \sigma_i(t)} \tag{D.26}$$

$$\hat{\Sigma}_i = \frac{\sum_{t=1}^{T} \sigma_i(t)(o_t - \mu_i)'(o_t - \mu_i)}{\sum_{t=1}^{T} \sigma_i(t)} \tag{D.27}$$

The sums in the denominators are for the same normalization that we saw in (D.22). Equations (D.27) and (D.27) are then used in the forward-backward (Baum-Welch) training of the HMM. The values of μ_i and σ_i are first set to some initial estimate, which is then re-estimated until the numbers converge.

See Jelinek (1997) or Rabiner and Juang (1993) for a more complete description of the forward-backward algorithm. Jelinek (1997) also shows the relationship between forward-backward and EM.

Bibliography

Abbreviations and symbols:

AAAI-XX	Proceedings of the Yth National Conference on Artificial Intelligence (in year XX)
ACL-XX	Proceedings of the Yth Annual Conference of the Association for Computational Linguistics (in year XX)
CLS-XX	Papers from the Yth Annual Regional Meeting of the Chicago Linguistics Society (in year XX)
COGSCI-XX	Proceedings of the Yth Annual Conference of the Cognitive Science Society (in year XX)
COLING-XX	Proceedings of the Yth International Conference on Computational Linguistics (in year XX)
EUROSPEECH-XX	Proceedings of the Yth European Conference on Speech Communication and Technology (in year XX)
ICSLP-XX	Proceedings of the International Conference on Spoken Language Processing (in year XX)
IEEE ICASSP-XX	Proceedings of the IEEE International Conference on Acoustics, Speech, & Signal Processing (in year XX)
IJCAI-XX	Proceedings of the Yth International Joint Conference on Artificial Intelligence (in year XX)
Dagger (†)	marks references that we did not have access to; the details of these references thus may not be correct.

Abney, S. P. (1991). Parsing by chunks. In Berwick, R. C., Abney, S. P., and Tenny, C. (Eds.), *Principle-Based Parsing: Computation and Psycholinguistics*, pp. 257–278. Kluwer, Dordrecht.

Abney, S. P. (1997). Stochastic attribute-value grammars. *Computational Linguistics*, *23*(4), 597–618.

Abney, S. P., Schapire, R. E., and Singer, Y. (1999). Boosting applied to tagging and PP attachment. In *Proceedings of the 1999 Joint SIGDAT Conference on Empirical Methods in Natural Language Processing and Very Large Corpora (EMNLP/VLC-99)*, College Park, MD, pp. 38–45. ACL.

Ades, A. E. and Steedman, M. J. (1982). On the order of words. *Linguistics and Philosophy*, *4*, 517–558.

Adjukiewicz, K. (1935). Die syntaktische Konnexität. *Studia Philosophica*, *1*, 1–27. English translation "Syntactic Connexion" by H. Weber in McCall, S. (Ed.) *Polish Logic*, pp. 207–231, Oxford University Press, Oxford, 1967.

Aha, D. W., Kibler, D., and Albert, M. K. (1991). Instance-based learning algorithms. *Machine Learning*, *6*, 37–66.

Aho, A. V., Sethi, R., and Ullman, J. D. (1986). *Compilers: Principles, Techniques, and Tools*. Addison-Wesley, Reading, MA.

Aho, A. V. and Ullman, J. D. (1972). *The Theory of Parsing, Translation, and Compiling*, Vol. 1. Prentice-Hall, Englewood Cliffs, NJ.

Aït-Kaci, H. (1984). *A Lattice-Theoretic Approach to Computation Based on a Calculus of Partially Ordered Types*. Ph.D. thesis, University of Pennsylvania.

Algoet, P. H. and Cover, T. M. (1988). A sandwich proof of the Shannon-McMillan-Breiman theorem. *The Annals of Probability*, *16*(2), 899–909.

Allen, J. (1984). Towards a general theory of action and time. *Artificial Intelligence*, *23*(2), 123–154.

Allen, J. (1995). *Natural Language Understanding*. Benjamin Cummings, Menlo Park, CA.

Allen, J. and Core, M. (1997). Draft of DAMSL: Dialog act markup in several layers. Unpublished manuscript.

Allen, J., Ferguson, G., Miller, B., and Ringer, E. (1995). Spoken dialogue and interactive planning. In *Proceedings ARPA Speech and Natural Language Workshop*, Austin, TX, pp. 202–207. Morgan Kaufmann.

Allen, J. and Perrault, C. R. (1980). Analyzing intention in utterances. *Artificial Intelligence*, 15, 143–178.

Allen, J., Hunnicut, M. S., and Klatt, D. H. (1987). *From Text to Speech: The MITalk system*. Cambridge University Press, Cambridge.

Allwood, J., Nivre, J., and Ahlsén, E. (1992). On the semantics and pragmatics of linguistic feedback. *Journal of Semantics*, 9, 1–26.

Alshawi, H. (1987). *Memory and Context for Language Interpretation*. Cambridge University Press, Cambridge.

Alshawi, H. (Ed.). (1992). *The Core Language Engine*. MIT Press, Cambridge, MA.

Alshawi, H., Bangalore, S., and Douglas, S. (1998). Automatic acquisition of hierarchical transduction models for machine translation. In *COLING/ACL-98*, Montreal, pp. 41–47. ACL.

Amsler, R. A. (1980). *The Structure of the Merriam-Webster Pocket Dictionary*. Ph.D. thesis, University of Texas, Austin, Texas. Report No.

Amsler, R. A. (1981). A taxonomy of English nouns and verbs. In *ACL-81*, Stanford, CA, pp. 133–138. ACL.

Anderson, J. A. (1995). *An Introduction to Neural Networks*. MIT Press, Cambridge, MA.

Anderson, S. R. (1985). *Phonology in the Twentieth Century*. Cambridge University Press, Cambridge.

Antworth, E. L. (1990). *PC-KIMMO: A Two-level Processor for Morphological Analysis*. Summer Institute of Linguistics, Dallas, TX.

Aone, C. and Bennett, S. W. (1995). Evaluating automated and manual acquisition of anaphora resolution strategies. In *ACL-95*, Cambridge, MA, pp. 122–129. ACL.

Appelt, D. E. (1985). *Natural Language Generation*. Cambridge University Press, Cambridge.

Appelt, D. E., Hobbs, J. R., Bear, J., Israel, D., Kameyama, M., Kehler, A., Martin, D., Myers, K., and Tyson, M. (1995). SRI International FASTUS system MUC-6 test results and analysis. In *Proceedings of the Sixth Message Understanding Conference (MUC-6)*, San Francisco, pp. 237–248. Morgan Kaufmann.

Appelt, D. E. and Israel, D. (1997). ANLP-97 tutorial: Building information extraction systems. Available as www.ai.sri.com/~appelt/ie-tutorial/.

Archangeli, D. (1984). *Underspecification in Yawelmani Phonology and Morphology*. Ph.D. thesis, MIT, Cambridge, MA.

Archangeli, D. (1997). Optimality theory: An introduction to linguistics in the 1990s. In Archangeli, D. and Langendoen, D. T. (Eds.), *Optimality Theory: An Overview*. Basil Blackwell, Oxford.

Archangeli, D. and Langendoen, D. T. (Eds.). (1997). *Optimality Theory: An Overview*. Basil Blackwell, Oxford.

Arens, Y., Granacki, J., and Parker, A. (1987). Phrasal analysis of long noun sequences. In *ACL-87*, Stanford, CA, pp. 59–64. ACL.

Argamon, S., Dagan, I., and Krymolowski, Y. (1998). A memory-based approach to learning shallow natural language patterns. In *COLING/ACL-98*, Montreal, pp. 67–73. ACL.

Ariel, M. (1990). *Accessing Noun Phrase Antecedents*. Routledge.

Asher, N. (1993). *Reference to Abstract Objects in Discourse*. SLAP 50, Dordrecht, Kluwer.

Atal, B. S. and Hanauer, S. (1971). Speech analysis and synthesis by prediction of the speech wave. *Journal of the Acoustical Society of America*, 50, 637–655.

Atkinson, M. and Drew, P. (1979). *Order in Court*. Macmillan, London.

Attar, R. and Fraenkel, A. S. (1977). Local feedback in full-text retrieval systems. *Journal of the ACM*, 24(3), 398–417.

Austin, J. L. (1962). *How to Do Things with Words*. Harvard University Press, Cambridge, MA.

Austin, S., Schwartz, R., and Placeway, P. (1991). The forward-backward search algorithm. In *IEEE ICASSP-91*, Vol. 1, pp. 697–700. IEEE.

Baayen, H. and Sproat, R. (1996). Estimating lexical priors for low-frequency morphologically ambiguous forms. *Computational Linguistics*, 22(2), 155–166.

Babyonyshev, M. and Gibson, E. (1999). The complexity of nested structures in Japanese. *Language*, 75(3), 423–450.

Bach, E. (1976). An extension of classical transformational grammar. In *Problems of Linguistic Metatheory (Proceedings of the 1976 Conference)*. Michigan State University.

Bach, E. (1988). Categorial grammars as theories of language. In Oehrle, R. T., Bach, E., and Wheeler, D. (Eds.), *Categorial Grammars and Natural Language Structures*, pp. 17–34. D. Reidel, Dordrecht.

Backus, J. W. (1959). The syntax and semantics of the proposed international algebraic language of the Zurch ACM-GAMM Conference. In *Information Processing: Proceedings of the International Conference on Information Processing, Paris*, pp. 125–132. UNESCO.

Backus, J. W. (1996). Transcript of question and answer session. In Wexelblat, R. L. (Ed.), *History of Programming Languages*, p. 162. Academic Press, New York.

Bacon, F. (1620). *Novum Organum*. Annotated edition edited by Thomas Fowler published by Clarendon Press, Oxford, 1889.

Baeza-Yates, R. and Ribeiro-Neto, B. (1999). *Modern Information Retrieval*. ACM Press, New York.

Bagley, W. C. (1900–1901). The apperception of the spoken sentence: A study in the psychology of language. *The American Journal of Psychology*, 12, 80–130. †.

Bahl, L. R., de Souza, P. V., Gopalakrishnan, P. S., Nahamoo, D., and Picheny, M. A. (1992). A fast match for continuous speech recognition using allophonic models. In *IEEE ICASSP-92*, San Francisco, CA, pp. I.17–20. IEEE.

Bahl, L. R. and Mercer, R. L. (1976). Part of speech assignment by a statistical decision algorithm. In *Proceedings IEEE International Symposium on Information Theory*, pp. 88–89.

Bahl, L. R., Jelinek, F., and Mercer, R. L. (1983). A maximum likelihood approach to continuous speech recognition. *IEEE Transactions on Pattern Analysis and Machine Intelligence*, 5(2), 179–190.

Bailey, D., Feldman, J., Narayanan, S., and Lakoff, G. (1997). Modeling embodied lexical development. In *COGSCI-97*, Stanford, CA, pp. 19–24. Lawrence Erlbaum.

Baker, C. F., Fillmore, C. J., and Lowe, J. B. (1998). The Berkeley FrameNet project. In *COLING/ACL-98*, pp. 86–90.

Baker, J. K. (1979). Trainable grammars for speech recognition. In Klatt, D. H. and Wolf, J. J. (Eds.), *Speech Communication Papers for the 97th Meeting of the Acoustical Society of America*, pp. 547–550.

Baker, J. K. (1975). The DRAGON system – An overview. *IEEE Transactions on Acoustics, Speech, and Signal Processing*, ASSP-23(1), 24–29.

Bangalore, S. and Joshi, A. K. (1999). Supertagging: An approach to almost parsing. *Computational Linguistics*, 25(2), 237–265.

Bar-Hillel, Y. (1953). A quasi-arithmetical notation for syntactic description. *Language*, 29, 47–58. Reprinted in Y. Bar-Hillel. (1964). *Language and Information: Selected Essays on their Theory and Application*, Addison-Wesley 1964, 61–74.

Bar-Hillel, Y. (1960). The present status of automatic translation of languages. In Alt, F. (Ed.), *Advances in Computers 1*, pp. 91–163. Academic Press.

Bar-Hillel, Y., Perles, M., and Shamir, E. (1961). On formal properties of simple phrase structure grammars. *Zeitschrift für Phonetik, Sprachwissenschaft und Kommunikationsforschung*, 14, 143–172. Reprinted in Y. Bar-Hillel. (1964). *Language and Information: Selected Essays* on their Theory and Application, Addison-Wesley 1964, 116–150.

Barnstone, W. (1993). *The Poetics of Translation*. Yale University Press.

Barton, Jr., G. E., Berwick, R. C., and Ristad, E. S. (1987). *Computational Complexity and Natural Language*. MIT Press, Cambridge, MA.

Bateman, J. A. (1997). Enabling technology for multilingual natural language generation: the KPML development environment. *Natural Language Engineering*, *3*(1), 15–55.

Bateman, J. A. and Hovy, E. H. (1992). An overview of computational text generation. In Butler, C. S. (Ed.), *Computers and Texts: An Applied Perspective*, pp. 53–74. Basil Blackwell, Oxford.

Bateman, J. A., Kasper, R. T., Moore, J. D., and Whitney, R. (1990). A general organization of knowledge for natural language processing: The Penman Upper Model. Tech. rep., USC/ISI.

Bates, R. (1997). The corrections officer: Can John Kidd save Ulysses. *Lingua Franca*. October.

Bauer, L. (1983). *English word-formation*. Cambridge University Press, Cambridge.

Baum, L. E. (1972). An inequality and associated maximization technique in statistical estimation for probabilistic functions of Markov processes. In Shisha, O. (Ed.), *Inequalities III: Proceedings of the Third Symposium on Inequalities*, University of California, Los Angeles, pp. 1–8. Academic Press.

Baum, L. E. and Eagon, J. A. (1967). An inequality with applications to statistical estimation for probabilistic functions of Markov processes and to a model for ecology. *Bulletin of the American Mathematical Society*, *73*(3), 360–363.

Baum, L. E. and Petrie, T. (1966). Statistical inference for probabilistic functions of finite-state Markov chains. *Annals of Mathematical Statistics*, *37*(6), 1554–1563.

Bayes, T. (1763). *An Essay Toward Solving a Problem in the Doctrine of Chances*, Vol. 53. Reprinted in *Facsimiles of two papers by Bayes*, Hafner Publishing Company, New York, 1963.

Bazell, C. E. (1952). The correspondence fallacy in structural linguistics. In *Studies by Members of the English Department, Istanbul University (3)*. Reprinted in Eric P. Hamp, Fred W. Householder, and Robert Austerlitz, (Eds.), *Readings in Linguistics II* (1966), pp. 271–298. University of Chicago Press, Chicago, IL.

Becker (1975). The phrasal lexicon. In Schank, R. and Nash-Webber, B. (Eds.), *Theoretical Issues in Natural Language Processing*. Cambridge, MA.

Beckman, M. E. and Pierrehumbert, J. (1986). Intonational structure in English and Japanese. *Phonology Yearbook*, *3*, 255–310.

Beesley, K. R. (1996). Arabic finite-state morphological analysis and generation. In *COLING-96*, Copenhagen, pp. 89–94.

Bellegarda, J. R. (1999). Speech recognition experiments using multi-span statistical language models. In *IEEE ICASSP-99*, pp. 717–720. IEEE.

Bellman, R. (1957). *Dynamic Programming*. Princeton University Press, Princeton, NJ.

Berger, A. and Printz, H. (1998). Recognition performance of a large-scale dependency grammar language model. In *ICSLP-98*, Sydney, Vol. 6, pp. 2487–2490.

Berry, M. W., Drmac, Z., and Jessup, E. R. (1999). Matrices, vector spaces, and information retrieval. *SIAM Review*, *41*(2), 335–362.

Bever, T. G. (1970). The cognitive basis for linguistic structures. In Hayes, J. R. (Ed.), *Cognition and the Development of Language*, pp. 279–352. Wiley, New York.

Bird, S. and Ellison, T. M. (1994). One-level phonology: Autosegmental representations and rules as finite automata. *Computational Linguistics*, *20*(1).

Birnbaum, L. and Selfridge, M. (1981). Conceptual analysis of natural language. In Schank, R. C. and Riesbeck, C. K. (Eds.), *Inside Computer Understanding: Five Programs plus Miniatures*, pp. 318–353. Lawrence Erlbaum, Hillsdale.

Black, A. W., Taylor, P., and Caley, R. (1996-1999). The Festival Speech Synthesis System system. Manual and source code available at www.cstr.ed.ac.uk/projects/festival.html.

Black, E., Abney, S. P., Flickinger, D., Gdaniec, C., Grishman, R., Harrison, P., Hindle, D., Ingria, R., Jelinek, F., Klavans, J., Liberman, M., Marcus, M. P., Roukos, S., Santorini, B., and Strzalkowski, T. (1991). A procedure for quantitatively comparing the syntactic coverage of English grammars. In *Proceedings DARPA Speech and Natural Language Workshop*, Pacific Grove, CA, pp. 306–311. Morgan Kaufmann.

Black, E. (1988). An experiment in computational discrimination of English word senses. *IBM Journal of Research and Development*, *32*(2), 185–194.

Black, E., Jelinek, F., Lafferty, J. D., Magerman, D. M., Mercer, R. L., and Roukos, S. (1992). Towards history-based grammars: Using richer models for probabilistic parsing. In *Proceedings DARPA Speech and Natural Language Workshop*, Harriman, New York, pp. 134–139. Morgan Kaufmann.

Blair, C. R. (1960). A program for correcting spelling errors. *Information and Control, 3*, 60–67.

Bledsoe, W. W. and Browning, I. (1959). Pattern recognition and reading by machine. In *1959 Proceedings of the Eastern Joint Computer Conference*, pp. 225–232. Academic, New York.

Bloomfield, L. (1914). *An Introduction to the Study of Language*. Henry Holt and Company, New York.

Bloomfield, L. (1933). *Language*. University of Chicago Press, Chicago.

Bobrow, D. G., Kaplan, R. M., Kay, M., Norman, D. A., Thompson, H., and Winograd, T. (1977). Gus, a frame driven dialog system. *Artificial Intelligence, 8*, 155–173.

Bobrow, D. G. and Winograd, T. (1977). An overview of KRL, a knowledge representation language. *Cognitive Science, 1*(1), 3–46.

Bobrow, R. J. and Webber, B. (1980). Knowledge representation for syntactic/semantic processing. In *AAAI-80*, Stanford, CA, pp. 316–323. Morgan Kaufmann.

Bock, K. and Loebell, H. (1990). Framing sentences. *Cognition, 35*, 1–39.

Bod, R. (1993). Using an annotated corpus as a stochastic grammar. In *Proceedings of the Sixth Conference of the European Chapter of the ACL*, pp. 37–44. ACL.

Boguraev, B. and Briscoe, T. (Eds.). (1989). *Computational Lexicography for Natural Language Processing*. Longman, London.

Bolinger, D. (1981). Two kinds of vowels, two kinds of rhythm. Indiana University Linguistics Club.

Booth, T. L. (1969). Probabilistic representation of formal languages. In *IEEE Conference Record of the 1969 Tenth Annual Symposium on Switching and Automata Theory*, pp. 74–81.

Booth, T. L. and Thompson, R. A. (1973). Applying probability measures to abstract languages. *IEEE Transactions on Computers, C-22*(5), 442–450.

Bourlard, H. and Morgan, N. (1994). *Connectionist Speech Recognition: A Hybrid Approach*. Kluwer Press.

Brachman, R. J. (1979). On the epistemogical status of semantic networks. In Findler, N. V. (Ed.), *Associative Networks: Representation and Use of Knowledge by Computers*, pp. 3–50. Academic Press, New York.

Brachman, R. J. and Levesque, H. J. (Eds.). (1985). *Readings in Knowledge Representation*. Morgan Kaufmann, San Mateo, CA.

Brachman, R. J. and Schmolze, J. G. (1985). An overview of the KL-ONE knowledge representation system. *Cognitive Science, 9*(2), 171–216.

Breiman, L., Friedman, J. H., Olshen, R. A., and Stone, C. J. (1984). *Classification and Regression Trees*. Wadsworth & Brooks, Pacific Grove, California.

Brennan, S. E. (1995). Centering attention in discourse. *Language and Cognitive Processes, 10*, 137–167.

Brennan, S. E., Friedman, M. W., and Pollard, C. (1987). A centering approach to pronouns. In *ACL-87*, Stanford, CA, pp. 155–162. ACL.

Brent, M. R. (1993). From grammar to lexicon: Unsupervised learning of lexical syntax. *Computational Linguistics*, *19*(2), 243–262.

Brent, M. R. and Cartwright, T. A. (1996). Distributional regularity and phonotactic constraints are useful for segmentation. *Cognition*, *61*, 93–125.

Bresnan, J. (Ed.). (1982). *The Mental Representation of Grammatical Relations*. MIT Press, Cambridge, MA.

Bresnan, J. and Kaplan, R. M. (1982). Introduction: Grammars as mental representations of language. In Bresnan, J. (Ed.), *The Mental Representation of Grammatical Relations*. MIT Press, Cambridge, MA.

Brill, E. (1995). Transformation-based error-driven learning and natural language processing: A case study in part-of-speech tagging. *Computational Linguistics*, *21*(4), 543–566.

Brill, E. (1997). Unsupervised learning of disambiguation rules for part of speech tagging. Unpublished manuscript.

Brill, E. and Resnik, P. (1994). A rule-based approach to prepositional phrase attachment disambiguation. In *COLING-94*, Kyoto, pp. 1198–1204.

Briscoe, T. and Carroll, J. (1993). Generalized Probabilistic LR parsing of natural language (corpora) with unification-based grammars. *Computational Linguistics*, *19*(1), 25–59.

Briscoe, T. and Carroll, J. (1997). Automatic extraction of subcategorization from corpora. In *Fifth Conference on Applied Natural Language Processing*, Washington, D.C., pp. 356–363. ACL.

Bromberger, S. and Halle, M. (1989). Why phonology is different. *Linguistic Inquiry*, *20*, 51–70.

Brown, J. S. and Burton, R. R. (1975). Multiple representations of knowledge for tutorial reasoning. In Bobrow, D. G. and Collins, A. (Eds.), *Representation and Understanding*, pp. 311–350. Academic Press, New York.

Brown, P. F., Cocke, J., Della Piettra, S. A., Della Piettra, V. J., Jelinek, F., Lafferty, J. D., Mercer, R. L., and Roossin, P. S. (1990). A statistical approach to machine translation. *Computational Linguistics*, *16*(2), 79–85.

Brown, P. F., Della Pietra, S. A., Della Pietra, V. J., Lai, J. C., and Mercer, R. L. (1992). An estimate of an upper bound for the entropy of English. *Computational Linguistics*, *18*(1), 31–40.

Brown, P. F., Della Pietra, S. A., Della Pietra, V. J., and Mercer, R. L. (1993). The mathematics of statistical machine translation: Parameter estimation. *Computational Linguistics*, *19*(2), 263–311.

Brown, P. F., Della Pietra, V. J., deSouza, P. V., Lai, J. C., and Mercer, R. L. (1992). Class-based *n*-gram models of natural language. *Computational Linguistics*, *18*(4), 467–479.

Brown, R. D. (1996). Example-based machine translation in the Pangloss system. In *COLING-96*, Copenhagen, pp. 169–174.

Brown, R. D. and Frederking, R. (1995). Applying statistical English language modeling to symbolic machine translation. In *6th International Conference on Theoretical and Methodological Issues in Machine Translation*, Leuven, Belgium, pp. 221–239.

Bub, T., Wahlster, W., and Waibel, A. (1997). Verbmobil: The combination of deep and shallow processing for spontaneous speech translation. In *IEEE ICASSP-97*, pp. 71–74. IEEE.

Bunt, H. (1994). Context and dialogue control. *Think*, *3*, 19–31.

Bybee, J. L. (1985). *Morphology: A study of the relation between meaning and form*. John Benjamins, Amsterdam.

Bybee, J. L. (1995). Regular morphology and the lexicon. *Language and Cognitive Processes*, *10*(5), 425–455.

Bybee, J. L. (1996). The phonology of the lexicon: evidence from lexical diffusion. In Barlow, M. and Kemmer, S. (Eds.), *Usage-based Models of Language*.

Bybee, J. L. and Slobin, D. I. (1982). Rules and schemas in the development and use of English past tense. *Language*, *58*, 265–289.

Calder, J. (1987). Typed unification for natural language processing. In Kahn, G., MacQueen, D., and Plotkin, G. (Eds.), *Categories, Polymorphism, and Unification*. Centre for Cognitive Science, University of Edinburgh, Edinburgh, Scotland†.

Callan, J. P., Croft, W. B., and Harding, S. M. (1992). The INQUERY retrieval system. In *Proceedings of the Third International Conference on Database and Expert System Applications*, Valencia, Spain, pp. 78–83. Springer-Verlag.

Cao, X. (1792). *The Story of the Stone*. (Also known as *The Dream of the Red Chamber*). Penguin Classics, London. First published in Chinese in 1792, translated into English by David Hawkes and published by Penguin in 1973.

Caramazza, A., Grober, E., Garvey, C., and Yates, J. (1977). Comprehension of anaphoric pronouns. *Journal of Verbal Learning and Verbal Behaviour*, *16*, 601–609.

Carberry, S. (1990). *Plan Recognition in Natural Language Dialog*. MIT Press, Cambridge, MA.

Carbonell, J. (1982). Metaphor: An inescapable phenomenon in natural language comprehension. In Lehnert, W. and Ringle, M. (Eds.), *Strategies for Natural Language Processing*, pp. 415–434. Lawrence Erlbaum.

Carbonell, J., Cullingford, R. E., and Gershman, A. V. (1981). Steps toward knowledge-based machine translation. *IEEE Transactions on Pattern Analysis and Machine Intelligence*, *3*(4), 376–392.

Carbonell, J., Mitamura, T., and Nyberg, E. H. (1992). The KANT perspective: A critique of pure transfer (and pure interlingua, pure statistics, ...). In *International Conference on Theoretical and Methodological Issues in Machine Translation*.

Cardie, C. (1993). A case-based approach to knowledge acquisition for domain specific sentence analysis. In *AAAI-93*, pp. 798–803. AAAI Press.

Cardie, C. (1994). *Domain-Specific Knowledge Acquisition for Conceptual Sentence Analysis*. Ph.D. thesis, University of Massachusetts, Amherst, MA. Available as CMPSCI Technical Report 94-74.

Carletta, J., Dahlbäck, N., Reithinger, N., and Walker, M. A. (1997). Standards for dialogue coding in natural language processing. Tech. rep. Report no. 167, Dagstuhl Seminars. Report from Dagstuhl seminar number 9706.

Carletta, J. (1996). Assessing agreement on classification tasks: The Kappa statistic. *Computational Linguistics*, *22*(2), 249–254.

Carletta, J., Isard, A., Isard, S., Kowtko, J. C., Doherty-Sneddon, G., and Anderson, A. H. (1997). The reliability of a dialogue structure coding scheme. *Computational Linguistics*, *23*(1), 13–32.

Carpenter, B. (1991). The generative power of categorial grammars and head-driven phrase structure grammars with lexical rules. *Computational Linguistics*, *17*(3), 301–313.

Carpenter, B. (1992). *The Logic of Typed Feature Structures*. Cambridge University Press, Cambridge.

Carpenter, B. and Penn, G. (1994). The Attribute Logic Engine Users's Guide Version 2.0.1. Tech. rep., Carnegie Mellon University.

Carroll, J., Briscoe, T., and Sanfilippo, A. (1998). Parser evaluation: a survey and a new proposal. In *Proceedings, First International Conference on Language Resources and Evaluation*, Granada, Spain, pp. 447–454. European Language Resources Association.

Casey, R. G. and Lecolinet, E. (1996). A survey of methods and strategies in character segmentation. *IEEE Transactions on Pattern Analysis and Machine Intelligence*, *18*(7), 690–706.

Celex (1993). The CELEX lexical database. Centre for Lexical Information, Max Planck Institute for Psycholinguistics.

Chafe, W. L. (1976). Givenness, contrastiveness, definiteness, subjects, topics, and point of view. In Li, C. N. (Ed.), *Subject and Topic*, pp. 25–55. Academic Press, New York.

Chandioux, J. (1976). MÉTÉO: un système opérationnel pour la traduction automatique des bulletins météorologiques destinés au grand public. *Meta, 21,* 127–133.

Chandler, S. (1991). Metaphor comprehension: A connectionist approach to implications for the mental lexicon. *Metaphor and Symbolic Activity, 6*(4), 227–258.

Chang, N., Gildea, D., and Narayanan, S. (1998). A dynamic model of aspectual composition. In *COGSCI-98*, Madison, WI, pp. 226–231. Lawrence Erlbaum.

Charniak, E. (1993). *Statistical Language Learning*. MIT Press.

Charniak, E. and Shimony, S. E. (1990). Probabilistic semantics for cost based abduction. In Dietterich, T. S. W. (Ed.), *AAAI-90*, Boston, MA, pp. 106–111. MIT Press.

Charniak, E. (1997). Statistical parsing with a context-free grammar and word statistics. In *AAAI-97*, Menlo Park. AAAI Press.

Charniak, E. and Goldman, R. (1988). A logic for semantic interpretation. In *ACL-88*, Buffalo, NY. ACL.

Charniak, E., Hendrickson, C., Jacobson, N., and Perkowitz, M. (1993). Equations for part-of-speech tagging. In *AAAI-93*, Washington, D.C., pp. 784–789. AAAI Press.

Charniak, E. and McDermott, D. (1985). *Introduction to Artificial Intelligence*. Addison Wesley.

Chelba, C., Engle, D., Jelinek, F., Jimenez, V., Khudanpur, S., Mangu, L., Printz, H., Ristad, E. S., Rosenfeld, R., Stolcke, A., and Wu, D. (1997). Structure and performance of a dependency language model. In *EUROSPEECH-97*, Vol. 5, pp. 2775–2778.

Chelba, C. and Jelinek, F. (1998). Exploiting syntactic structure for language modeling. In *COLING/ACL-98*, Montreal, pp. 225–231. ACL.

Chen, J. N. and Chang, J. S. (1998). Topical clustering of MRD senses based on information retrieval techniques. *Computational Linguistics, 24*(1), 61–96.

Chen, S. S., Eide, E. M., Gales, M. J. F., Gopinath, R. A., Kanevsky, D., and Olsen, P. (1999). Recent improvements to IBM's speech recognition system for automatic transcription of Broadcast News. In *IEEE ICASSP-99*, pp. 37–40. IEEE.

Chen, S. F. and Goodman, J. (1996). An empirical study of smoothing techniques for language modeling. In *ACL-96*, Santa Cruz, CA, pp. 310–318. ACL.

Chen, S. F., Seymore, K., and Rosenfeld, R. (1998). Topic adaptation for language modeling using unnormalized exponential models. In *IEEE ICASSP-98*, pp. 681–684. IEEE.

Chierchia, G. and McConnell-Ginet, S. (1991). *Meaning and Grammar*. MIT Press, Cambridge, MA.

Chinchor, N., Hirschman, L., and Lewis, D. L. (1993). Evaluating Message Understanding systems: An analysis of the third Message Understanding Conference. *Computational Linguistics, 19*(3), 409–449.

Chomsky, N. (1956). Three models for the description of language. *IRI Transactions on Information Theory, 2*(3), 113–124.

Chomsky, N. (1956/1975). *The Logical Structure of Linguistic Theory*. Plenum.

Chomsky, N. (1957). *Syntactic Structures*. Mouton, The Hague.

Chomsky, N. (1959a). On certain formal properties of grammars. *Information and Control, 2,* 137–167.

Chomsky, N. (1959b). A review of B. F. Skinner's "Verbal Behavior". *Language, 35,* 26–58.

Chomsky, N. (1963). Formal properties of grammars. In Luce, R. D., Bush, R., and Galanter, E. (Eds.), *Handbook of Mathematical Psychology*, Vol. 2, pp. 323–418. Wiley, New York.

Chomsky, N. (1965). *Aspects of the Theory of Syntax*. MIT Press, Cambridge, MA.

Chomsky, N. (1969). Quine's empirical assumptions. In Davidson, D. and Hintikka,

J. (Eds.), *Words and objections. Essays on the work of W. V. Quine*, pp. 53–68. D. Reidel, Dordrecht.

Chomsky, N. (1981). *Lectures on Government and Binding*. Foris, Dordrecht.

Chomsky, N. and Halle, M. (1968). *The Sound Pattern of English*. Harper and Row, New York.

Chomsky, N. and Miller, G. A. (1958). Finite-state languages. *Information and Control*, *1*, 91–112.

Chomsky, N. and Miller, G. A. (1963). Introduction to the formal analysis of natural languages. In Luce, R. D., Bush, R., and Galanter, E. (Eds.), *Handbook of Mathematical Psychology*, Vol. 2, pp. 269–322. Wiley, New York.

Chu-Carroll, J. (1998). A statistical model for discourse act recognition in dialogue interactions. In Chu-Carroll, J. and Green, N. (Eds.), *Applying Machine Learning to Discourse Processing. Papers from the 1998 AAAI Spring Symposium*. Tech. rep. SS-98-01, pp. 12–17. AAAI Press, Menlo Park, CA.

Chu-Carroll, J. and Carberry, S. (1998). Collaborative response generation in planning dialogues. *Computational Linguistics*, *24*(3), 355–400.

Church, A. (1940). A formulation of a simple theory of types. *Journal of Symbolic Logic*, *5*, 56–68.

Church, K. W. (1988). A stochastic parts program and noun phrase parser for unrestricted text. In *Second Conference on Applied Natural Language Processing*, pp. 136–143. ACL.

Church, K. W. and Gale, W. A. (1991). A comparison of the enhanced Good-Turing and deleted estimation methods for estimating probabilities of English bigrams. *Computer Speech and Language*, *5*, 19–54.

Church, K. W., Gale, W. A., and Kruskal, J. B. (1991). Appendix A: the Good-Turing theorem. In *Computer Speech and Language* (Church and Gale, 1991), pp. 19–54.

Church, K. W. and Patil, R. (1982). Coping with syntactic ambiguity. *American Journal of Computational Linguistics*, *8*(3-4), 139–149.

Church, K. W. (1980). On memory limitations in natural language processing. Master's thesis, MIT. Distributed by the Indiana University Linguistics Club.

Clark, H. H. and Sengal, C. J. (1979). In search of referents for nouns and pronouns. *Memory and Cognition*, *7*, 35–41.

Clark, H. H. (1994). Managing problems in speaking. *Speech Communication*, *15*, 243–250.

Clark, H. H. and Clark, E. V. (1977). *Psychology and Language*. Harcourt Brace Jovanovich, San Diego.

Clark, H. H. and Schaefer, E. F. (1989). Contributing to discourse. *Cognitive Science*, *13*, 259–294.

Clark, H. H. and Wilkes-Gibbs, D. (1986). Referring as a collaborative process. *Cognition*, *22*, 1–39.

Coccaro, N. and Jurafsky, D. (1998). Towards better integration of semantic predictors in statistical language modeling. In *ICSLP-98*, Sydney, Vol. 6, pp. 2403–2406.

Coch, J. (1996a). Evaluating and comparing three text-production techniques. In *COLING-96*, Copenhagen, pp. 249–254.

Coch, J. (1996b). Overview of AlethGen. In *Demonstration overview for the Proceedings of the Eighth International Workshop on Natural Language Generation*, Herstmonceux, England, pp. 25–28.

Coch, J. (1998). Interactive generation and knowledge administration in MultiMétéo. In *Proceedings of the Ninth International Workshop on Natural Language Generation*, Ontario, Canada, pp. 300–303. System Demonstration.

Cohen, M. H. (1989). *Phonological Structures for Speech Recognition*. Ph.D. thesis, University of California, Berkeley.

Cohen, P. R., Johnston, M., McGee, D., Oviatt, S. L., Clow, J., and Smith, I. (1998). The efficiency of multimodal interaction: a case study. In *ICSLP-98*, Sydney, Vol. 2, pp. 249–252.

Cohen, P. R. (1995). *Empirical Methods for Artificial Intelligence*. MIT Press, Cambridge, MA.

Cohen, P. R. and Perrault, C. R. (1979). Elements of a plan-based theory of speech acts. *Cognitive Science*, *3*(3), 177–212.

Colby, K. M., Weber, S., and Hilf, F. D. (1971). Artificial paranoia. *Artificial Intelligence*, *2*(1), 1–25.

Cole, J. S. and Kisseberth, C. W. (1995). Restricting multi-level constraint evaluation. Rutgers Optimality Archive ROA-98.

Cole, R. A., Novick, D. G., Vermeulen, P. J. E., Sutton, S., Fanty, M., Wessels, L. F. A., de Villiers, J. H., Schalkwyk, J., Hansen, B., and Burnett, D. (1997). Experiments with a spoken dialogue system for taking the US census. *Speech Communication*, *23*, 243–260.

Cole, R. A. (1973). Listening for mispronunciations: A measure of what we hear during speech. *Perception and Psychophysics*, *13*, 153–156.

Cole, R. A. (Ed.). (1997). *Survey of the State of the Art in Human Language Technology*. Cambridge University Press, Cambridge.

Cole, R. A. and Jakimik, J. (1980). A model of speech perception. In Cole, R. A. (Ed.), *Perception and Production of Fluent Speech*, pp. 133–163. Lawrence Erlbaum, Hillsdale, NJ.

Cole, R. A., Novick, D. G., Burnett, D., Hansen, B., Sutton, S., and Fanty, M. (1994). Towards automatic collection of the U.S. census. In *IEEE ICASSP-94*, Adelaide, Australia, Vol. I, pp. 93–96. IEEE.

Cole, R. A., Novick, D. G., Fanty, M., Sutton, S., Hansen, B., and Burnett, D. (1993). Rapid prototyping of spoken language systems: The Year 2000 Census Project. In *Proceedings of the International Symposium on Spoken Dialogue*, Waseda University, Tokyo, Japan.

Cole, R. A. and Rudnicky, A. I. (1983). What's new in speech perception? The research and ideas of William Chandler Bagley. *Psychological Review*, *90*(1), 94–101.

Collins, M. J. (1996). A new statistical parser based on bigram lexical dependencies. In *ACL-96*, Santa Cruz, CA, pp. 184–191. ACL.

Collins, M. J. (1999). *Head-driven Statistical Models for Natural Language Parsing*. Ph.D. thesis, University of Pennsylvania, Philadelphia.

Collins, M. J., Hajič, J., Ramshaw, L. A., and Tillmann, C. (1999). A statistical parser for Czech. In *ACL-99*, College Park, MD, pp. 505–512. ACL.

Colmerauer, A. (1970). Les systèmes-q ou un formalisme pour analyser et synthétiser des phrase sur ordinateur. Internal publication 43, Département d'informatique de l'Université de Montréal†.

Colmerauer, A. (1975). Les grammaires de métamorphose GIA. Internal publication, Groupe Intelligence artificielle, Faculté des Sciences de Luminy, Université Aix-Marseille II, France, Nov 1975. English version, Metamorphosis grammars. In L. Bolc, (Ed.), *Natural Language Communication with Computers, Lecture Notes in Computer Science 63*, Springer Verlag, Berlin, 1978, pp. 133–189.

Colmerauer, A. and Roussel, P. (1996). The birth of Prolog. In Bergin Jr., T. J. and Gibson, Jr., R. G. (Eds.), *History of Programming Languages – II*, pp. 331–352. ACM Press/Addison-Wesley, New York.

Comrie, B. (1989). *Language Universals and Linguistic Typology*. Basil Blackwell, Oxford. Second edition.

Connine, C. M. (1990). Effects of sentence context and lexical knowledge in speech processing. In Altmann, G. T. M. (Ed.), *Cognitive Models of Speech Processing*, pp. 281–294. MIT Press, Cambridge, MA.

Connine, C. M. and Clifton, Jr., C. (1987). Interactive use of lexical information in speech perception. *Journal of Experimental Psychology: Human Perception and Performance*, *13*, 291–299.

Connolly, D., Burger, J. D., and Day, D. S. (1994). A machine learning approach to anaphoric reference. In *Proceedings of the International Conference on New Methods in Language Processing (NeMLaP)*. ACL.

Cooley, J. W. and Tukey, J. W. (1965). An algorithm for the machine calculation of complex Fourier series. *Mathematics of Computation*, *19*(90), 297–301.

Cooper, A. (1995). *About Face: The essentials of user interface design*. IDG Books.

Copeland, J. (1993). *Artificial Intelligence: A Philosophical Introduction*. Blackwell, Oxford.

Copestake, A. and Briscoe, T. (1995). Semi-productive polysemy and sense extension. *Journal of Semantics*, *12*(1), 15–68.

Core, M., Ishizaki, M., Moore, J. D., Nakatani, C., Reithinger, N., Traum, D., and Tutiya, S. (1999). The report of the third workshop of the Discourse Resource Initiative, Chiba University and Kazusa Academia Hall. Tech. rep. No.3 CC-TR-99-1, Chiba Corpus Project, Chiba, Japan.

Cottrell, G. W. (1985). *A Connectionist Approach to Word Sense Disambiguation*. Ph.D. thesis, University of Rochester, Rochester, NY. Revised version published in the same title by Pitman in 1989.

Cover, T. M. and Hart, P. E. (1967). Nearest neighbor pattern classification. *IEEE Transactions on Information Theory*, *13*(1), 21–27.

Cover, T. M. and King, R. C. (1978). A convergent gambling estimate of the entropy of English. *IEEE Transactions on Information Theory*, *24*(4), 413–421.

Cover, T. M. and Thomas, J. A. (1991). *Elements of information theory*. Wiley, New York.

Cowic, J., Guthric, J. A., and Guthrie, L. M. (1992). Lexical disambiguation using simulated annealing. In *COLING-92*, Nantes, France, pp. 359–365.

Cowper, E. A. (1976). *Constraints on Sentence Complexity: A Model for Syntactic Processing*. Ph.D. thesis, Brown University, Providence, RI†.

Crawley, R. A., Stevenson, R. J., and Kleinman, D. (1990). The use of heuristic strategies in the interpretation of pronouns. *Journal of Psycholinguistic Research*, *19*, 245–264.

Crestani, F., Lemas, M., Rijsbergen, C. J. V., and Campbell, I. (1998). "Is This Document Relevant? ...Probably": a survey of probabilistic models in information retrieval. *ACM Computing Surveys*, *30*(4), 528–552.

Croft, W. (1990). *Typology and Universals*. Cambridge University Press, Cambridge.

Croft, W. (1995). Intonation units and grammatical structure. *Linguistics*, *33*, 839–882.

Crouch, C. J. and Yang, B. (1992). Experiments in automatic statistical thesaurus construction. In *SIGIR-92*, Copenhagen, Denmark, pp. 77–88. ACM.

Cruse, D. A. (1986). *Lexical Semantics*. Cambridge University Press,, Cambridge.

Crystal, D. (1969). *Prosodic systems and intonation in English*. Cambridge University Press, Cambridge.

Cullingford, R. E. (1981). SAM. In Schank, R. C. and Riesbeck, C. K. (Eds.), *Inside Computer Understanding: Five Programs plus Miniatures*, pp. 75–119. Lawrence Erlbaum, Hillsdale, NJ.

Culy, C. (1985). The complexity of the vocabulary of Bambara. *Linguistics and Philosophy*, *8*, 345–351.

Cutler, A. (1986). Forbear is a homophone: Lexical prosody does not constrain lexical access. *Language and Speech*, *29*, 201–219.

Cutler, A. and Carter, D. M. (1987). The predominance of strong initial syllables in the English vocabulary. *Computer Speech and Language*, *2*, 133–142.

Cutler, A. and Norris, D. (1988). The role of strong syllables in segmentation for lexical access. *Journal of Experimental Psychology: Human Perception and Performance*, *14*, 113–121.

Cutting, D., Kupiec, J., Pedersen, J. O., and Sibun, P. (1992a). A practical part-of-speech tagger. In *Third Conference on Applied Natural Language Processing*, pp. 133–140. ACL.

Cutting, D., Karger, D. R., Pedersen, J. O., and Tukey, J. W. (1992b). Scatter/gather: A cluster-based approach to browsing large document collections. In *SIGIR-92*, Copenhagen, Denmark, pp. 318–329. ACM.

Daelemans, W., De Smedt, K., and Gazdar, G. (1992). Inheritance in natural language processing. *Computational Linguistics*, *18*(2), 205–218.

Daelemans, W., Gillis, S., and Durieux, G. (1994). The acquisition of stress: A data-oriented approach. *Computational Linguistics*, *20*(3), 421–451.

Dagan, I. and Church, K. W. (1997). Termight: Coordinating humans and machines in bilingual terminology acquisition. *Machine Translation*, *12*, 89–107.

Dale, R. (1992). *Generating Referring Expressions: Constructing Descriptions in a Domain of Objects and Processes*. MIT Press, Cambridge, MA.

Dale, R., Eugenio, B. D., and Scott, D. R. (1998a). Introduction to the special issue on natural language generation. *Computational Linguistics*, *24*(3), 345–353.

Dale, R., Oberlander, J., Milosavljevic, M., and Knott, A. (1998b). Integrating natural language generation and hypertext to produce dynamic documents. *Interacting with Computers*, *11*(2), 109–135.

Dalianis, H. (1999). Aggregation in natural language generation. *Computational Intelligence*, *15*(4).

Daly, N. A. and Zue, V. W. (1992). Statistical and linguistic analyses of F_0 in read and spontaneous speech. In *ICSLP-92*, Vol. 1, pp. 763–766.

Damerau, F. J. (1964). A technique for computer detection and correction of spelling errors. *Communications of the ACM*, *7*(3), 171–176.

Damerau, F. J. and Mays, E. (1989). An examination of undetected typing errors. *Information Processing and Management*, *25*(6), 659–664.

Dang, H. T., Kipper, K., Palmer, M., and Rosenzweig, J. (1998). Investigating regular sense extensions based on intersective levin classes. In *COLING/ACL-98*, Montreal, pp. 293–299. ACL.

Danieli, M. and Gerbino, E. (1995). Metrics for evaluating dialogue strategies in a spoken language system. In *Proceedings of the 1995 AAAI Spring Symposium on Empirical Methods in Discourse Interpretation and Generation*, Stanford, CA, pp. 34–39. AAAI Press, Menlo Park, CA.

Davey, A. (1979). *Discourse Production: A Computer Model of Some Aspects of a Speaker*. Edinburgh University Press.

David, Jr., E. E. and Selfridge, O. G. (1962). Eyes and ears for computers. *Proceedings of the IRE (Institute of Radio Engineers)*, *50*, 1093–1101.

Davidson, D. (1967). The logical form of action sentences. In Rescher, N. (Ed.), *The Logic of Decision and Action*. University of Pittsburgh Press.

Davis, E. (1990). *Representations of Commonsense Knowledge*. Morgan Kaufmann, San Mateo, CA.

Davis, K. H., Biddulph, R., and Balashek, S. (1952). Automatic recognition of spoken digits. *Journal of the Acoustical Society of America*, *24*(6), 637–642.

de Marcken, C. (1996). *Unsupervised Language Acquisition*. Ph.D. thesis, MIT.

de Tocqueville, A. (1840). *Democracy in America*. Doubleday, New York. The 1966 translation by George Lawrence.

Deerwester, S., Dumais, S. T., Furnas, G. W., Landauer, T. K., and Harshman, R. (1990). Indexing by latent semantic analysis. *Journal of the American Society of Information Science*, *41*, 391–407.

DeJong, G. F. (1982). An overview of the FRUMP system. In Lehnert, W. G. and Ringle, M. H. (Eds.), *Strategies for Natural Language Processing*, pp. 149–176. Lawrence Erlbaum, Hillsdale, NJ.

DeJong, G. F. and Waltz, D. L. (1983). Understanding novel language. *Computers and Mathematics with Applications*, *9*.

Dell, G. S. (1986). A spreading activation theory of retrieval in sentence production. *Psychological Review*, *93*, 283–321.

Dell, G. S. (1988). The retrieval of phonological forms in production: Tests of predictions from a connectionist model. *Journal of Memory and Language*, *27*, 124–142.

Dell, G. S., Schwarts, M. F., Martin, N., Saffran, E., and Gagnon, D. A. (1997). Lexical access in aphasic and nonaphasic speakers. *Psychological Review*, *104*(4), 801–838.

Demetriou, G., Atwell, E., and Souter, C. (1997). Large-scale lexical semantics for speech recognition support. In *EUROSPEECH-97*, pp. 2755–2758.

Dempster, A. P., Laird, N. M., and Rubin, D. B. (1977). Maximum likelihood from incomplete data via the *EM* algorithm. *Journal of the Royal Statistical Society*, *39*(1), 1–21.

Denes, P. (1959). The design and operation of the mechanical speech recognizer at University College London. *Journal of the British Institution of Radio Engineers*, *19*(4), 219–234. Appears together with companion paper (Fry 1959).

Deng, L., Lennig, M., Seitz, F., and Mermelstein, P. (1990). Large vocabulary word recognition using context-dependent allophonic hidden Markov models. *Computer Speech and Language*, *4*, 345–357.

Dermatas, E. and Kokkinakis, G. (1995). Automatic stochastic tagging of natural language texts. *Computational Linguistics*, *21*(2), 137–164.

DeRose, S. J. (1988). Grammatical category disambiguation by statistical optimization. *Computational Linguistics*, *14*, 31–39.

Di Eugenio, B. (1990). Centering theory and the Italian pronominal system. In *COLING-90*, Helsinki, pp. 270–275.

Di Eugenio, B. (1996). The discourse functions of Italian subjects: A centering approach. In *COLING-96*, Copenhagen, pp. 352–357.

Dietterich, T. G. (1998). Approximate statistical tests for comparing supervised classification learning algorithms. *Neural Computation*, *10*(7), 1895–1924.

Dolan, W. B. (1994). Word sense ambiguation: Clustering related senses. In *COLING-94*, Kyoto, Japan, pp. 712–716. ACL.

Dorr, B. (1992). The use of lexical semantics in interlingual machine translation. *Journal of Machine Translation*, *7*(3), 135–193.

Dorr, B. (1993). *Machine Translation*. MIT Press, Cambridge, MA.

Dostert, L. (1955). The Georgetown-I.B.M. experiment. In *Machine Translation of Languages: Fourteen Essays*, pp. 124–135. MIT Press.

Downing, P. (1977). On the creation and use of English compound nouns. *Language*, *53*(4), 810–842.

Dowty, D. (1991). Thematic proto-roles and argument selection. *Language*, *67*(3), 547–619.

Dowty, D. R. (1979). *Word Meaning and Montague Grammar*. D. Reidel, Dordrecht.

Dowty, D. R., Wall, R. E., and Peters, S. (1981). *Introduction to Montague Semantics*. D. Reidel, Dordrecht.

Du Bois, J. W., Schuetze-Coburn, S., Cumming, S., and Paolino, D. (1983). Outline of discourse transcription. In Edwards, J. A. and Lampert, M. D. (Eds.), *Talking Data: Transcription and Coding in Discourse Research*, pp. 45–89. Lawrence Erlbaum, Hillsdale, NJ.

Duda, R. O. and Hart, P. E. (1973). *Pattern Classification and Scene Analysis*. John Wiley and Sons, New York.

Earley, J. (1968). *An Efficient Context-Free Parsing Algorithm*. Ph.D. thesis, Carnegie Mellon University, Pittsburgh, PA.

Earley, J. (1970). An efficient context-free parsing algorithm. *Communications of the ACM*, *6*(8), 451–455. Reprinted in Grosz et al. (1986).

Eisner, J. (1997). Efficient generation in primitive optimality theory. In *ACL/EACL-97*, Madrid, Spain, pp. 313–320. ACL.

Ejerhed, E. I. (1988). Finding clauses in unrestricted text by finitary and stochastic methods. In *Second Conference on Applied Natural Language Processing*, pp. 219–227. ACL.

Elhadad, M. (1990). Types in functional unification grammars. In *ACL-90*, Pittsburgh, PA, pp. 157–164. ACL.

Elhadad, M. (1992). *Using Argumentation to Control Lexical Choice: A Functional Unification-Based Approach*. Ph.D. thesis, Columbia University.

Elhadad, M. (1993). FUF: The universal unifier — User Manual, version 5.2. Tech. rep., Ben Gurion University of the Negev.

Ellison, T. M. (1992). *The Machine Learning of Phonological Structure*. Ph.D. thesis, University of Western Australia.

Ellison, T. M. (1994). Phonological derivation in optimality theory. In *COLING-94*, Kyoto, pp. 1007–1013.

Emele, M. C. and Dorna, M. (1998). Ambiguity preserving machine translation using packed representations. In *COLING/ACL-98*, Montreal, pp. 365–371.

Evans, R. and Gazdar, G. (1996). DATR: A language for lexical knowledge representation. *Computational Linguistics*, *22*(2), 167–216.

Fasold, R. W. (1972). *Tense marking in Black English*. Center for Applied Linguistics, Washington, D.C.

Fass, D. (1988). *Collative Semantics: A Semantics for Natural Language*. Ph.D. thesis, New Mexico State University, Las Cruces, New Mexico. CRL Report No. MCCS-88-118.

Fass, D. (1991). met*: A method for discriminating metaphor and metonymy by computer. *Computational Linguistics*, *17*(1).

Fass, D. (1997). *Processing Metonymy and Metaphor*. Ablex Publishing, Greenwich, CT.

Fass, D., Martin, J. H., and Hinkelman, E. A. (Eds.). (1992). *Computational Intelligence: Special Issue on Non-Literal Language*, Vol. 8. Blackwell, Cambridge, MA.

Fauconnier, G. (1985). *Mental Spaces: Aspects of Meaning Construction in Natural Language*. MIT Press, Cambridge, MA.

Fellbaum, C. (Ed.). (1998). *WordNet: An Electronic Lexical Database*. MIT Press, Cambridge, MA.

Ferreira, F. and Henderson, J. M. (1991). How is verb information used during syntactic processing?. In Simpson, G. B. (Ed.), *Understanding Word and Sentence*, pp. 305–330. Elsevier Science.

Fikes, R. E. and Nilsson, N. J. (1971). Strips: A new approach to the application of theorem proving to problem solving. *Artificial Intelligence*, *2*, 189–208.

Fillmore, C. J. (1965). *Indirect Object Constructions in English and the Ordering of Transformations*. Mouton, The Hague.

Fillmore, C. J. (1968). The case for case. In Bach, E. W. and Harms, R. T. (Eds.), *Universals in Linguistic Theory*, pp. 1–88. Holt, Rinehart & Winston, New York.

Fillmore, C. J. (1977). Scenes-and-frames semantics. In Zampolli, A. (Ed.), *Linguistic Structures Processing*, pp. 55–79. North Holland, Amsterdam.

Fillmore, C. J. (1985). Frames and the semantics of understanding. *Quaderni di Semantica*, *VI*(2), 222–254.

Fillmore, C. J., Kay, P., and O'Connor, M. C. (1988). Regularity and idiomaticity in grammatical constructions: The case of Let Alone. *Language*, *64*(3), 510–538.

Finin, T. (1980). The semantic interpretation of nominal compounds. In *AAAI-80*, Stanford, CA, pp. 310–312.

Firbas, J. (1966). On defining the theme in functional sentence analysis. *Travaux Linguistiques de Prague*, *1*, 267–280.

Fisher, D., Soderland, S., McCarthy, J., Feng, F., and Lehnert, W. (1995). Description of the UMass system as used for MUC-6. In *Proceedings of the Sixth Message Understanding Conference (MUC-6)*, San Francisco, pp. 127–140. Morgan Kaufmann.

Fisher, M. F. K. (1968). *With Bold Knife and Fork*. Paragon Books, New York.

Flickinger, D., Pollard, C., and Wasow, T. (1985). Structure-sharing in lexical representation. In *ACL-85*, Chicago, IL, pp. 262–267. ACL.

Florian, R. and Yarowsky, D. (1999). Dynamic nonlocal language modeling via hierarchical topic-based adaptation. In *ACL-99*, College Park, MD, pp. 167–174. ACL.

Fodor, J. D. (1978). Parsing strategies and constraints on transformations. *Linguistic Inquiry*, *9*(3), 427–473.

Fodor, J. A. and Bever, T. G. (1965). The psychological reality of linguistic segments. *Journal of Verbal Learning and Verbal Behavior*, *4*, 414–420.

Foley, W. A. and van Valin, Jr., R. D. (1984). *Functional Syntax and Universal Grammar*. Cambridge University Press, Cambridge.

Ford, C., Fox, B., and Thompson, S. A. (1996). Practices in the construction of turns. *Pragmatics*, *6*, 427–454.

Ford, C. and Thompson, S. A. (1996). Interactional units in conversation: syntactic, intonational, and pragmatic resources for the management of turns. In Ochs, E., Schegloff, E. A., and Thompson, S. A. (Eds.), *Interaction and Grammar*, pp. 134–184. Cambridge University Press, Cambridge.

Ford, M. (1983). A method for obtaining measures of local parsing complexity through sentences. *Journal of Verbal Learning and Verbal Behavior*, *22*, 203–218.

Ford, M., Bresnan, J., and Kaplan, R. M. (1982). A competence-based theory of syntactic closure. In Bresnan, J. (Ed.), *The Mental Representation of Grammatical Relations*, pp. 727–796. MIT Press, Cambridge, MA.

Forney, Jr., G. D. (1973). The Viterbi algorithm. *Proceedings of the IEEE*, *61*(3), 268–278.

Fosler, E. (1996). On reversing the generation process in optimality theory. In *ACL-96*, Santa Cruz, CA, pp. 354–356. ACL.

Foster, D. W. (1989). *Elegy by W.W.: A Study in Attribution*. Associated University Presses, Cranbury, NJ.

Foster, D. W. (1996). Primary culprit. *New York*, 50–57. February 26.

Fox Tree, J. E. and Clark, H. H. (1997). Pronouncing "the" as "thee" to signal problems in speaking. *Cognition*, *62*, 151–167.

Frakes, W. B. and Baeza-Yates, R. (1992). *Information Retrieval: Data Structures and Algorithms*. Prentice Hall, Englewood Cliffs, NJ.

Francis, H. S., Gregory, M. L., and Michaelis, L. A. (1999). Are lexical subjects deviant?. In *CLS-99*. University of Chicago.

Francis, W. N. (1979). A tagged corpus – problems and prospects. In Greenbaum, S., Leech, G., and Svartvik, J. (Eds.), *Studies in English linguistics for Randolph Quirk*, pp. 192–209. Longman, London and New York.

Francis, W. N. and Kučera, H. (1982). *Frequency Analysis of English Usage*. Houghton Mifflin, Boston.

Frank, R. (1992). *Syntactic Locality and Tree Adjoining Grammar: Grammatical, Acquisition and Processing Perspectives*. Ph.D. thesis, University of Pennsylvania, Philadelphia, PA.

Frank, R. and Satta, G. (1999). Optimality theory and the generative complexity of constraint violability. *Computational Linguistics*. To appear.

Franz, A. (1996). *Automatic Ambiguity Resolution in Natural Language Processing*. Springer-Verlag, Berlin.

Franz, A. (1997). Independence assumptions considered harmful. In *ACL/EACL-97*, Madrid, Spain, pp. 182–189. ACL.

Fraser, N. M. and Gilbert, G. N. (1991). Simulating speech systems. *Computer Speech and Language*, *5*, 81–99.

Fraser, N. M. and Hudson, R. A. (1992). Inheritance in word grammar. *Computational Linguistics*, *18*(2), 133–158.

Frazier, L. and Clifton, Jr., C. (1996). *Construal*. MIT Press, Cambridge, MA.

Frederking, R., Rudnicky, A. I., and Hogan, C. (1997). Interactive speech translation in the DIPLOMAT project. In *Proceedings of the ACL-97 Spoken Language Translation Workshop*, Madrid, pp. 61–66. ACL.

Freitag, D. (1998). Multistrategy learning for information extraction. In *Proceedings of the 15th International Conference on Machine Learning*, Madison, WI, pp. 161–169.

Friedl, J. E. F. (1997). *Master Regular Expressions*. O'Reilly, Cambridge.

Fromkin, V. and Ratner, N. B. (1998). Speech production. In Gleason, J. B. and Ratner, N. B. (Eds.), *Psycholinguistics*. Harcourt Brace, Fort Worth, TX.

Fry, D. B. (1959). Theoretical aspects of mechanical speech recognition. *Journal of the British Institution of Radio Engineers*, *19*(4), 211–218. Appears together with companion paper (Denes 1959).

Fujisaki, H. and Ohno, S. (1997). Comparison and assessment of models in the study of fundamental frequency contours of speech. In *ESCA workshop on Intonation: Theory Models and Applications*.

Fung, P. and McKeown, K. R. (1997). A technical word- and term-translation aid using noisy parallel corpora. *Machine Translation*, *12*, 53–87.

Gaizauskas, R., Wakao, T., Humphreys, K., Cunningham, H., and Wilks, Y. (1995). University of Sheffield: Description of the LaSIE system as used for MUC-6. In *Proceedings of the Sixth Message Understanding Conference (MUC-6)*, San Francisco, pp. 207–220. Morgan Kaufmann.

Gale, W. A. and Church, K. W. (1993). A program for aligning sentences in bilingual corpora. *Computational Linguistics*, *19*, 75–102.

Gale, W. A. and Church, K. W. (1994). What is wrong with adding one?. In Oostdijk, N. and de Haan, P. (Eds.), *Corpus-based Research into Language*, pp. 189–198. Rodopi, Amsterdam.

Gale, W. A., Church, K. W., and Yarowsky, D. (1992). Estimating upper and lower bounds on the performance of word-sense disambiguation programs. In *ACL-92*, Newark, DE, pp. 249–256. ACL.

Gale, W. A., Church, K. W., and Yarowsky, D. (1993). A method for disambiguating word senses in a large corpus. *Computers and the Humanities*, *26*, 415–439.

Garnham, A. (1985). *Psycholinguistics*. Methuen, London.

Garnham, A., Traxler, M., Oakhill, J., and Gernsbacher, M. A. (1996). The locus of implicit causality effects in comprehension. *Journal of Memory and Language*, *35*, 517–534.

Garrett, M. F. (1975). The analysis of sentence production. In Bower, G. H. (Ed.), *The Psychology of Learning and Motivation*, Vol. 9. Academic, New York.

Garrod, S. C. and Sanford, A. J. (1994). Resolving sentences in a discourse context. In Gernsbacher, M. A. (Ed.), *Handbook of Psycholinguistics*, pp. 675–698. Academic Press, New York.

Garside, R. (1987). The CLAWS word-tagging system. In Garside, R., Leech, G., and Sampson, G. (Eds.), *The Computational Analysis of English*, pp. 30–41. Longman, London.

Garside, R., Leech, G., and McEnery, A. (1997). *Corpus Annotation*. Longman, London and New York.

Gazdar, G. (1981). Unbounded dependencies and coordinate structure. *Linguistic Inquiry*, *12*(2), 155–184.

Gazdar, G. (1982). Phrase structure grammar. In Jacobson, P. and Pullum, G. K. (Eds.), *The Nature of Syntactic Representation*, pp. 131–186. Reidel, Dordrecht.

Gazdar, G., Klein, E., Pullum, G. K., and Sag, I. A. (1985). *Generalized Phrase Structure Grammar*. Basil Blackwell, Oxford.

Gazdar, G. and Mellish, C. (1989). *Natural Language Processing in LISP*. Addison Wesley.

Gazdar, G., Pullum, G. K., Carpenter, B., Klein, E., Hukari, T. E., and Levine, R. D. (1988). Category structures. *Computational Linguistics*, *14*(1), 1–19.

Ge, N., Hale, J., and Charniak, E. (1998). A statistical approach to anaphora resolution. In *Proceedings of the Sixth Workshop on Very Large Corpora*. ACL.

Gentner, D. (1983). Structure mapping: A theoretical framework for analogy. *Cognitive Science*, *7*, 155–170.

Gentner, D. and France, I. M. (1988). The verb mutability effect: Studies of the combinatorial semantics of nouns and verbs. In *Lexical Ambiguity Resolution*, pp. 343–382. Morgan Kaufman, San Mateo, CA.

Gershman, A. V. (1977). Conceptual analysis of noun groups in English. In *IJCAI-77*, Cambridge, MA, pp. 132–138.

Gibson, E. (1991). *A Computational Theory of Human Linguistic Processing: Memory Limitations and Processing Breakdown*. Ph.D. thesis, Carnegie Mellon University, Pittsburgh, PA.

Gibson, E. (1998). Linguistic complexity: Locality of syntactic dependencies. *Cognition*, *68*, 1–76.

Gilboy, E. and Sopena, J. M. (1996). Segmentation effects in the processing of complex NPs with relative clauses. In Carreiras, M., García-Albea, J. E., and Sebastián-Gallés, N. (Eds.), *Language Processing in Spanish*, pp. 191–206. Lawrence Erlbaum, Hillsdale, NJ.

Gildea, D. and Jurafsky, D. (1996). Learning bias and phonological rule induction. *Computational Linguistics*, *22*(4), 497–530.

Gildea, D., Jurafsky, D., Roland, D., and O'Connell, M. (2000). Automatic labeling of thematic roles. Submitted manuscript.

Givón, T. (1990). *Syntax: A functional typological introduction*. John Benjamins, Amsterdam.

Glennie, A. (1960). On the syntax machine and the construction of a universal compiler. Tech. rep. No. 2, Contr. NR 049-141, Carnegie Mellon University (at the time Carnegie Institute of Technology), Pittsburgh, PA†.

Godfrey, J., Holliman, E., and McDaniel, J. (1992). SWITCHBOARD: Telephone speech corpus for research and development. In *IEEE ICASSP-92*, pp. 517–520. IEEE.

Gold, B. and Morgan, N. (1999). *Speech and Audio Signal Processing*. Wiley Press.

Goldberg, A. E. (Ed.). (1995). *Constructions: A Construction Grammar approach to Argument Structure*. University of Chicago Press, Chicago.

Goldberg, E., Driedger, N., and Kittredge, R. (1994). Using natural-language processing to produce weather forecasts. *IEEE Expert*, *9*(2), 45–53.

Golding, A. R. and Roth, D. (1999). A winnow based approach to context-sensitive spelling correction. *Machine Learning*, *34*(1-3), 107–130. Special Issue on Machine Learning and Natural Language.

Golding, A. R. (1997). A bayesian hybrid method for context-sensitive spelling correction. In *Proceedings of the Third Workshop on Very Large Corpora*, Boston, MA, pp. 39–53. ACL.

Golding, A. R. and Schabes, Y. (1996). Combining trigram-based and feature-based methods for context-sensitive spelling correction. In *ACL-96*, Santa Cruz, CA, pp. 71–78. ACL.

Goldman, N. (1975). Conceptual generation. In Schank, R. C. (Ed.), *Conceptual Information Processing*, chap. 6. North-Holland.

Goldsmith, J. (1976). *Autosegmental Phonology*. Ph.D. thesis, MIT, Cambridge, MA.

Goldsmith, J. (1993). Harmonic phonology. In Goldsmith, J. (Ed.), *The Last Phonological Rule*, pp. 21–60. University of Chicago Press, Chicago.

Goldsmith, J. (Ed.). (1995). *The Handbook of Phonological Theory*. Basil Blackwell, Oxford.

Good, I. J. (1953). The population frequencies of species and the estimation of population parameters. *Biometrika*, *40*, 16–264.

Good, M. D., Whiteside, J. A., Wixon, D. R., and Jones, S. J. (1984). Building a user-derived interface. *Communications of the ACM*, *27*(10), 1032–1043.

Goodman, J. (1997). Probabilistic feature grammars. In *Proceedings of the International Workshop on Parsing Technology*.

Goodwin, C. (1996). Transparent vision. In Ochs, E., Schegloff, E. A., and Thompson, S. A. (Eds.), *Interaction and Grammar*. Cambridge University Press, Cambridge.

Gordon, D. and Lakoff, G. (1971). Conversational postulates. In *CLS-71*, pp. 200–213. University of Chicago. Reprinted in Peter Cole and Jerry L. Morgan (Eds.), *Speech Acts: Syntax and Semantics Volume 3*, Academic, 1975.

Gordon, P. C., Grosz, B. J., and Gilliom, L. A. (1993). Pronouns, names, and the centering of attention in discourse. *Cognitive Science*, *17*(3), 311–347.

Gorin, A. L., Riccardi, G., and Wright, J. H. (1997). How may I help you?. *Speech Communication*, *23*(1), 113–127.

Götz, T., Meurers, W. D., and Gerdemann, D. (1997). The ConTroll manual. Tech. rep., Seminar für Sprachwissenschaft, Universität Tübingen.

Gould, J. D., Conti, J., and Hovanyecz, T. (1983). Composing letters with a simulated listening typewriter. *Communications of the ACM*, *26*(4), 295–308.

Gould, J. D. and Lewis, C. (1985). Designing for usability: Key principles and what designers think. *Communications of the ACM*, *28*(3), 300–311.

Graff, D. (1997). The 1996 Broadcast News speech and language-model corpus. In *Proceedings DARPA Speech Recognition Workshop*, Chantilly, VA, pp. 11–14. Morgan Kaufmann.

Graham, S. L., Harrison, M. A., and Ruzzo, W. L. (1980). An improved context-free recognizer. *ACM Transactions on Programming Languages and Systems*, 2(3), 415–462.

Grainger, J., Colé, P., and Segui, J. (1991). Masked morphological priming in visual word recognition. *Journal of Memory and Language*, 30, 370–384.

Green, B. F., Wolf, A. K., Chomsky, C., and Laughery, K. (1961). Baseball: An automatic question answerer. In *Proceedings of the Western Joint Computer Conference 19*, pp. 219–224. Reprinted in Grosz et al. (1986).

Green, G. M. (1974). *Semantics and Syntactic Regularity*. Indiana University Press, Bloomington.

Greenberg, S., Ellis, D., and Hollenback, J. (1996). Insights into spoken language gleaned from phonetic transcription of the Switchboard corpus. In *ICSLP-96*, Philadelphia, PA, pp. S24–27.

Greene, B. B. and Rubin, G. M. (1971). Automatic grammatical tagging of English. Department of Linguistics, Brown University, Providence, Rhode Island.

Gregory, M. L., Raymond, W. D., Bell, A., Fosler-Lussier, E., and Jurafsky, D. (1999). The effects of collocational strength and contextual predictability in lexical production. In *CLS-99*. University of Chicago.

Grice, H. P. (1957). Meaning. *Philosophical Review*, 67, 377–388. Reprinted in *Semantics*, edited by D. D. Steinberg & L. A. Jakobovits (1971), Cambridge University Press, pages 53–59.

Grice, H. P. (1975). Logic and conversation. In Cole, P. and Morgan, J. L. (Eds.), *Speech Acts: Syntax and Semantics Volume 3*, pp. 41–58. Academic Press, New York.

Grice, H. P. (1978). Further notes on logic and conversation. In Cole, P. (Ed.), *Pragmatics: Syntax and Semantics Volume 9*, pp. 113–127. Academic Press, New York.

Grishman, R. and Sundheim, B. (1995). Design of the MUC-6 evaluation. In *Proceedings of the Sixth Message Understanding Conference (MUC-6)*, San Francisco, pp. 1–11. Morgan Kaufmann.

Gropen, J., Pinker, S., Hollander, M., Goldberg, R., and Wilson, R. (1989). The learnability and acquisition of the dative alternation in English. *Language*, 65(2), 203–257.

Grosjean, F. (1980). Spoken word recognition processes and the gating paradigm. *Perception and Psychophysics*, 28, 267–283.

Grosz, B. and Hirschberg, J. (1992). Some intonational characteristics of discourse structure. In *ICSLP-92*, Vol. 1, pp. 429–432.

Grosz, B. J. (1974). The structure of task-oriented dialogs. In *Proceedings of the IEEE Symposium on Speech Recognition: Contributed Papers*, Pittsburgh, PA†, pp. 250–253.

Grosz, B. J. (1977a). The representation and use of focus in a system for understanding dialogs. In *IJCAI-77*, Cambridge, MA, pp. 67–76. Morgan Kaufmann. Reprinted in Grosz et al. (1986).

Grosz, B. J. (1977b). *The Representation and Use of Focus in Dialogue Understanding*. Ph.D. thesis, University of California, Berkeley.

Grosz, B. J., Jones, K. S., and Webber, B. L. (Eds.). (1986). *Readings in Natural Language Processing*. Morgan Kaufmann, Los Altos, Calif.

Grosz, B. J., Joshi, A. K., and Weinstein, S. (1983). Providing a unified account of definite noun phrases in English. In *ACL-83*, pp. 44–50. ACL.

Grosz, B. J., Joshi, A. K., and Weinstein, S. (1995). Centering: A framework for modelling the local coherence of discourse. *Computational Linguistics*, 21(2).

Grosz, B. J. and Sidner, C. L. (1980). Plans for discourse. In Cohen, P. R., Morgan, J., and Pollack, M. E. (Eds.), *Intentions in Communication*, pp. 417–444. MIT Press, Cambridge, MA.

Grosz, B. J. and Sidner, C. L. (1986). Attention, intentions, and the structure of discourse. *Computational Linguistics*, *12*(3), 175–204.

Gruber, J. S. (1965). *Studies in Lexical Relations*. Ph.D. thesis, MIT, Cambridge, MA.

Grudin, J. T. (1983). Error patterns in novice and skilled transcription typing. In Cooper, W. E. (Ed.), *Cognitive Aspects of Skilled Typewriting*, pp. 121–139. Springer-Verlag, New York.

Guindon, R. and Kintsch, W. (1984). Priming macropropositions: Evidence for the primacy of macropropositions in the memory for text. *Journal of Verbal Learning and Verbal Behavior*, *23*, 508–518.

Guindon, R. (1988). A multidisciplinary perspective on dialogue structure in user-advisor dialogues. In Guindon, R. (Ed.), *Cognitive Science And Its Applications For Human-Computer Interaction*, pp. 163–200. Lawrence Erlbaum, Hillsdale, NJ.

Gundel, J. K., Hedberg, N., and Zacharski, R. (1993). Cognitive status and the form of referring expressions in discourse. *Language*, *69*(2), 274–307.

Gupta, V., Lennig, M., and Mermelstein, P. (1988). Fast search strategy in a large vocabulary word recognizer. *Journal of the Acoustical Society of America*, *84*(6), 2007–2017.

Gupta, V., Lennig, M., and Mermelstein, P. (1992). A language model for very large-vocabulary speech recognition. *Computer Speech and Language*, *6*, 331–344.

Guthrie, J. A., Guthrie, L., Wilks, Y., and Aidinejad, H. (1991). Subject-dependent co-occurrence and word sense disambiguation. In *ACL-91*, Berkeley, CA, pp. 146–152. ACL.

Hain, T., Woodland, P. C., Niesler, T. R., and Whittaker, E. W. D. (1999). The 1998 HTK system for transcription of conversational telephone speech. In *IEEE ICASSP-99*, pp. 57–60. IEEE.

Hajič, J. (1998). *Building a Syntactically Annotated Corpus: The Prague Dependency Treebank*, pp. 106–132. Karolinum, Prague/Praha.

Halliday, M. A. K. (1985). *An Introduction to Functional Grammar*. Edward Arnold, London.

Halliday, M. A. K. and Hasan, R. (1976). *Cohesion in English*. Longman, London. English Language Series, Title No. 9.

Hammond, M. (1997). Parsing in OT. Alternative title "Parsing syllables: Modeling OT computationally". Rutgers Optimality Archive ROA-222-1097.

Hankamer, J. (1986). Finite state morphology and left to right phonology. In *Proceedings of the Fifth West Coast Conference on Formal Linguistics*, pp. 29–34.

Hankamer, J. (1989). Morphological parsing and the lexicon. In Marslen-Wilson, W. (Ed.), *Lexical Representation and Process*, pp. 392–408. MIT Press, Cambridge, MA.

Hankamer, J. and Black, H. A. (1991). Current approaches to computational morphology. Unpublished manuscript.

Harris, Z. S. (1946). From morpheme to utterance. *Language*, *22*(3), 161–183.

Harris, Z. S. (1962). *String Analysis of Sentence Structure*. Mouton, The Hague.

Hartley, A. and Paris, C. (1997). Multilingual document production: From support for translating to support for authoring. *Machine Translation*, *12*, 109–128.

Haviland, S. E. and Clark, H. H. (1974). What's new? Acquiring new information as a process in comprehension. *Journal of Verbal Learning and Verbal Behaviour*, *13*, 512–521.

Hayes, E. and Bayer, S. (1991). Metaphoric generalization through sort coercion. In *ACL-91*, Berkeley, CA, pp. 222–228. ACL.

Hearst, M. A. (1991). Noun homograph disambiguation. In *Proceedings of the 7th Annual Conference of the University of Waterloo Centre for the New OED and Text Research*, Oxford, pp. 1–19.

Hearst, M. A. (1997). TextTiling: Segmenting text into multi-paragraph subtopic passages. *Computational Linguistics*, *23*(1), 33–64.

Hearst, M. A. and Pedersen, J. O. (1996). Reexamining the cluster hypothesis: Scatter/gather on retrieval results. In *SIGIR-96*, Zurich, Switzerland, pp. 76–84. ACM.

Heeman, P. A. (1999). POS tags and decision trees for language modeling. In *Proceedings of the 1999 Joint SIGDAT Conference on Empirical Methods in Natural Language Processing and Very Large Corpora (EMNLP/VLC-99)*, College Park, MD, pp. 129–137. ACL.

Heeman, P. A. and Allen, J. (1999). Speech repairs, intonational phrases and discourse markers: Modeling speakers' utterances in spoken dialog. *Computational Linguistics*, 25(4).

Heikkilä, J. (1995). A TWOL-based lexicon and feature system for English. In Karlsson, F., Voutilainen, A., Heikkilä, J., and Anttila, A. (Eds.), *Constraint Grammar: A Language-Independent System for Parsing Unrestricted Text*, pp. 103–131. Mouton de Gruyter, Berlin.

Heim, I. and Kratzer, A. (1998). *Semantics in a Generative Grammar*. Blackwell Publishers, Malden, MA.

Hemphill, C. T., Godfrey, J., and Doddington, G. R. (1990). The ATIS spoken language systems pilot corpus. In *Proceedings DARPA Speech and Natural Language Workshop*, Hidden Valley, PA, pp. 96–101. Morgan Kaufmann.

Hermansky, H. (1990). Perceptual linear predictive (PLP) analysis of speech. *Journal of the Acoustical Society of America*, 87(4), 1738–1752.

Hertz, J., Krogh, A., and Palmer, R. G. (1991). *Introduction to the Theory of Neural Computation*. Addison-Wesley Publishing Company.

Hindle, D. (1983). Deterministic parsing of syntactic non-fluencies. In *ACL-83*, Cambridge, MA, pp. 123–128. ACL.

Hindle, D. and Rooth, M. (1990). Structural ambiguity and lexical relations. In *Proceedings DARPA Speech and Natural Language Workshop*, Hidden Valley, PA, pp. 257–262. Morgan Kaufmann.

Hindle, D. and Rooth, M. (1991). Structural ambiguity and lexical relations. In *ACL-91*, Berkeley, CA, pp. 229–236. ACL.

Hinkelman, E. A. and Allen, J. (1989). Two constraints on speech act ambiguity. In *ACL-89*, Vancouver, Canada, pp. 212–219. ACL.

Hintikka, J. (1969). Semantics for propositional attitudes. In Davis, J. W., Hockney, D. J., and Wilson, W. K. (Eds.), *Philosophical Logic*, pp. 21–45. D. Reidel, Dordrecht, Holland.

Hirschberg, J. and Litman, D. J. (1993). Empirical studies on the disambiguation of cue phrases. *Computational Linguistics*, 19(3), 501–530.

Hirschberg, J. and Nakatani, C. (1996). A prosodic analysis of discourse segments in direction-giving monologues. In *ACL-96*, Santa Cruz, CA, pp. 286–293. ACL.

Hirschberg, J. and Pierrehumbert, J. (1986). The intonational structuring of discourse. In *ACL-86*, New York, pp. 136–144. ACL.

Hirschman, L. and Pao, C. (1993). The cost of errors in a spoken language system. In *EUROSPEECH-93*, pp. 1419–1422.

Hirst, G. (1987). *Semantic Interpretation and the Resolution of Ambiguity*. Cambridge University Press, Cambridge.

Hirst, G. (1988). Resolving lexical ambiguity computationally with spreading activation and polaroid words. In Small, S. L., Cottrell, G. W., and Tanenhaus, M. K. (Eds.), *Lexical ambiguity resolution: Perspectives from psycholinguistics, neuropsychology, and artificial intelligence*, pp. 73–108. Morgan Kaufmann, San Mateo, CA.

Hirst, G. and Charniak, E. (1982). Word sense and case slot disambiguation. In *AAAI-82*, pp. 95–98.

Hobbs, J. R. (1977). 38 examples of elusive antecedents from published texts. Tech. rep. 77-2, Department of Computer Science, City University of New York.

Hobbs, J. R. (1978). Resolving pronoun references. *Lingua*, 44, 311–338. Reprinted in Grosz et al. (1986).

Hobbs, J. R. (1979a). Coherence and coreference. *Cognitive Science*, 3, 67–90.

Hobbs, J. R. (1979b). Metaphor, metaphor schemata, and selective inferencing. Tech. rep. Technical Note 204, SRI, San Mateo, CA.

Hobbs, J. R. (1990). *Literature and Cognition*. CSLI Lecture Notes 21.

Hobbs, J. R., Appelt, D., Bear, J., Israel, D., Kameyama, M., Stickel, M. E., and Tyson, M. (1997). FASTUS: A cascaded finite-state transducer for extracting information from natural-language text. In Roche, E. and Schabes, Y. (Eds.), *Finite-State Devices for Natural Language Processing*, pp. 383–406. MIT Press, Cambridge, MA.

Hobbs, J. R. and Shieber, S. M. (1987). An algorithm for generating quantifier scopings. *Computational Linguistics*, *13*(1), 47–55.

Hobbs, J. R., Stickel, M. E., Appelt, D. E., and Martin, P. (1993). Interpretation as abduction. *Artificial Intelligence*, *63*, 69–142.

Hofstadter, D. R. (1997). *Le Ton beau de Marot*. Basic Books, New York.

Holmes, D. I. (1994). Authorship attribution. *Computers and the Humanities*, *28*, 87–106.

Hopcroft, J. E. and Ullman, J. D. (1979). *Introduction to Automata Theory, Languages, and Computation*. Addison-Wesley, Reading, MA.

Householder, F. W. (1995). Dionysius Thrax, the *technai*, and Sextus Empiricus. In Koerner, E. F. K. and Asher, R. E. (Eds.), *Concise History of the Language Sciences*, pp. 99–103. Elsevier Science, Oxford.

Hovy, E. and Radev, D. (Eds.). (1998). *Intelligent Text Summarization: Papers from the 1998 AAAI Symposium*, Menlo Park, CA. AAAI, AAAI Press.

Hovy, E. H. (1988a). *Generating Natural Language Under Pragmatic Constraints*. Lawrence Erlbaum, Hillsdale, NJ.

Hovy, E. H. (1988b). Planning coherent multisentential text. In *ACL-88*, Buffalo, NY, pp. 163–169. ACL.

Hovy, E. H. (1990). Parsimonious and profligate approaches to the question of discourse structure relations. In *Proceedings of the Fifth International Workshop on Natural Language Generation*, Dawson, PA, pp. 128–136.

Howes, D. (1957). On the relation between the intelligibility and frequency of occurrence of English words. *Journal of the Acoustical Society of America*, *29*, 296–305.

Hu, J., Brown, M. K., and Turin, W. (1996). HMM based on-line handwriting recognition. *IEEE Transactions on Pattern Analysis and Machine Intelligence*, *18*(10), 1039–1045.

Huang, X. D. and Jack, M. A. (1989). Semi-continuous hidden Markov models for speech signals. *Computer Speech and Language*, *3*, 239–252.

Hudson, R. A. (1984). *Word Grammar*. Basil Blackwell, Oxford.

Huffman, D. A. (1954). The synthesis of sequential switching circuits. *Journal of the Franklin Institute*, *3*, 161–191. Continued in Volume 4.

Huffman, S. (1996). Learning information extraction patterns from examples. In Wertmer, S., Riloff, E., and Scheller, G. (Eds.), *Connectionist, Statistical, and Symbolic Approaches to Learning Natural Language Processing*, pp. 246–260. Springer, Berlin.

Hull, D. (1996). Stemming algorithms – a case study for detailed evaluation. *Journal of the American Society for Information Science*, *47*(1), 70–84.

Hull, J. J. and Srihari, S. N. (1982). Experiments in text recognition with binary *n*-gram and Viterbi algorithms. *IEEE Transactions on Pattern Analysis and Machine Intelligence*, *PAMI-4*, 520–530.

Huls, C., Bos, E., and Classen, W. (1995). Automatic referent resolution of deictic and anaphoric expressions. *Computational Linguistics*, *21*(1), 59–79.

Hunt, A. J. and Black, A. W. (1996). Unit selection in a concatenative speech synthesis system using a large speech database. In *IEEE ICASSP-96*, Atlanta, GA, Vol. 1, pp. 373–376. IEEE.

Hutchins, J. (1997). From first conception to first demonstration: the nascent years of machine translation, 1947–1954. A chronology. *Machine Translation*, *12*, 192–252.

Hutchins, W. J. and Somers, H. L. (1992). *An Introduction to Machine Translation*. Academic Press.

Hutchins, W. J. (1986). *Machine Translation: Past, Present, Future*. Ellis Horwood, Chichester, England.

Huybregts, R. (1984). The weak inadequacy of context-free phrase structure grammars. In de Haan, G., Trommele, M., and Zonneveld, W. (Eds.), *Van Periferie naar Kern*. Foris, Dordrecht†. Cited in Pullum (1991).

Ide, N. M. and Veronis, J. (Eds.). (1998). *Computational Linguistics: Special Issue on Word Sense Disambiguation*, Vol. 24. MIT Press, Cambridge, MA.

Irons, E. T. (1961). A syntax directed compiler for ALGOL 60. *Communications of the ACM*, *4*, 51–55.

Itakura, F. (1975). Minimum prediction residual principle applied to speech recognition. *IEEE Transactions on Acoustics, Speech, and Signal Processing*, *ASSP-32*, 67–72.

Iverson, E. and Helmreich, S. (1992). Metallel: An integrated approach to non-literal phrase interpretation. *Computational Intelligence*, *8*(3).

Iyer, R. and Ostendorf, M. (1997). Transforming out-of-domain estimates to improve in-domain language models. In *EUROSPEECH-97*, pp. 1975–1978.

Jackendoff, R. (1972). *Semantic Interpretation in Generative Grammar*. MIT Press, Cambridge, MA.

Jackendoff, R. (1975). Morphological and semantic regularities in the lexicon. *Language*, *51*(3), 639–671.

Jackendoff, R. (1983). *Semantics and Cognition*. MIT Press, Cambridge, MA.

Jackendoff, R. (1990). *Semantic Structures*. MIT Press, Cambridge, MA.

Jacobs, P. (1985). *A Knowledge-Based Approach to Language Generation*. Ph.D. thesis, University of California, Berkeley, CA. Available as University of California at Berkeley Computer Science Division Tech. rep. #86/254.

Jacobs, P. (1987). Knowledge-based natural language generation. *Artificial Intelligence*, *33*, 325–378.

Jacobs, P. and Rau, L. (1990). SCISOR: A system for extracting information from on-line news. *Communications of the ACM*, *33*(11), 88–97.

Jakobson, R. (1939). Observations sur le classement phonologique des consonnes.

In Blancquaert, E. and Pée, W. (Eds.), *Proceedings of the Third International Congress of Phonetic Sciences*, Ghent, pp. 34–41.

Janssen, T. M. (1997). Compositionality. In van Benthem, J. and ter Meulen, A. (Eds.), *Handbook of Logic and Language*, chap. 7, pp. 417–473. North-Holland, Amsterdam.

Jardine, N. and van Rijsbergen, C. J. (1971). The use of hierarchic clustering in information retrieval. *Information Storage and Retrieval*, *7*, 217–240.

Järvinen, T. and Tapanainen, P. (1997). A dependency parser for English. Tech. rep. TR-1, Department of General Linguistics, University of Helsinki, Helsinki.

Jefferson, G. (1984). Notes on a systematic deployment of the acknowledgement tokens 'yeah' and 'mm hm'. *Papers in Linguistics*, pp. 197–216.

Jeffreys, H. (1948). *Theory of Probability*. Clarendon Press, Oxford. 2nd edn Section 3.23.

Jelinek, F., Mercer, R. L., Bahl, L. R., and Baker, J. K. (1977). Perplexity – a measure of the difficulty of speech recognition tasks. *Journal of the Acoustical Society of America*, *62*, S63. Supplement 1.

Jelinek, F. (1969). A fast sequential decoding algorithm using a stack. *IBM Journal of Research and Development*, *13*, 675–685.

Jelinek, F. (1990). Self-organized language modeling for speech recognition. In Waibel, A. and Lee, K.-F. (Eds.), *Readings in Speech Recognition*, pp. 450–506. Morgan Kaufmann, Los Altos. Originally distributed as IBM technical report in 1985.

Jelinek, F., Lafferty, J. D., Magerman, D. M., Mercer, R. L., Ratnaparkhi, A., and Roukos, S. (1994). Decision tree parsing using a hidden derivation model. In *ARPA Human Language Technologies Workshop*, Plainsboro, N.J., pp. 272–277. Morgan Kaufmann.

Jelinek, F. and Mercer, R. L. (1980). Interpolated estimation of Markov source parameters from sparse data. In Gelsema, E. S. and Kanal, L. N. (Eds.), *Proceedings, Workshop on Pattern Recognition in Practice*, pp. 381–397. North Holland, Amsterdam.

Jelinek, F. (1976). Continuous speech recognition by statistical methods. *Proceedings of the IEEE*, *64*(4), 532–557.

Jelinek, F. (1997). *Statistical Methods for Speech Recognition*. MIT Press, Cambridge, MA.

Jelinek, F. and Lafferty, J. D. (1991). Computation of the probability of initial substring generation by stochastic context-free grammars. *Computational Linguistics*, *17*(3), 315–323.

Jelinek, F., Mercer, R. L., and Bahl, L. R. (1975). Design of a linguistic statistical decoder for the recognition of continuous speech. *IEEE Transactions on Information Theory*, *IT-21*(3), 250–256.

Jing, H. and McKeown, K. R. (1998). Combining multiple, large-scale resources in a reusable lexicon for natural language generation. In *COLING/ACL-98*, Montreal, pp. 607–613. ACL.

Johnson, C. D. (1972). *Formal Aspects of Phonological Description*. Mouton, The Hague. Monographs on Linguistic Analysis No. 3.

Johnson, C. (1999). Syntactic and semantic principles of FrameNet annotation, version 1. Tech. rep. TR-99-018, ICSI, Berkeley, CA.

Johnson, K. (1997). *Acoustic and Auditory Phonetics*. Blackwell, Cambridge, MA.

Johnson, M. K., Bransford, J. D., and Solomon, S. K. (1973). Memory for tacit implications of sentences. *Journal of Experimental Psychology*, *98*, 203–205.

Johnson, M. (1984). A discovery procedure for certain phonological rules. In *COLING-84*, Stanford, CA, pp. 344–347.

Johnson, M. (1988). *Attribute-Value Logic and the Theory of Grammar*. CSLI Lecture Notes. Chicago University Press, Chicago.

Johnson, M. (1990). Expressing disjunctive and negative feature constraints with classical first-order logic. In *ACL-90*, Pittsburgh, PA, pp. 173–179. ACL.

Johnson, S. C. and Lesk, M. E. (1978). Language development tools. *Bell System Technical Journal*, *57*(6), 2155–2175.

Johnson-Laird, P. N. (1983). *Mental Models*. Harvard University Press, Cambridge, MA.

Jones, M. A. and Eisner, J. (1992). A probabilistic parser applied to software testing documents. In *AAAI-92*, San Jose, CA, pp. 322–328.

Jones, M. A. and McCoy, K. (1992). Transparently-motivated metaphor generation. In Dale, R., Hovy, E. H., Rösner, D., and Stock, O. (Eds.), *Aspects of Automated Natural Language Generation*, Lecture Notes in Artificial Intelligence 587, pp. 183–198. Springer Verlag, Berlin.

Jones, M. P. (1997). *Spoken Language Help of High Functionality Systems*. Ph.D. thesis, University of Colorado, Boulder, CO.

Jones, M. P. and Martin, J. H. (1997). Contextual spelling correction using latent semantic analysis. In *Proceedings of the 5th Conference on Applied Natural Language Processing (ANLP'97)*, Washington, D.C., pp. 166–173. ACL.

Joshi, A. K. (1985). Tree adjoining grammars: how much context-sensitivity is required to provide reasonable structural descriptions?. In Dowty, D. R., Karttunen, L., and Zwicky, A. (Eds.), *Natural Language Parsing*, pp. 206–250. Cambridge University Press, Cambridge.

Joshi, A. K. and Hopely, P. (1999). A parser from antiquity. In Kornai, A. (Ed.), *Extended Finite State Models of Language*, pp. 6–15. Cambridge University Press, Cambridge.

Joshi, A. K. and Kuhn, S. (1979). Centered logic: The role of entity centered sentence representation in natural language inferencing. In *IJCAI-79*, pp. 435–439.

Joshi, A. K. and Srinivas, B. (1994). Disambiguation of super parts of speech (or supertags): Almost parsing. In *COLING-94*, Kyoto, pp. 154–160.

Joshi, A. K. and Weinstein, S. (1981). Control of inference: Role of some aspects of discourse structure – centering. In *IJCAI-81*, pp. 385–387.

Juliano, C. and Tanenhaus, M. K. (1993). Contingent frequency effects in syntactic ambiguity resolution. In *COGSCI-93*, Boulder, CO, pp. 593–598.

Juola, P. (1999). Measuring linguistic complexity. Presented at the 4th Conference on Conceptual Structure, Discourse, and Language (CSDL-4), Georgia.

Jurafsky, D. (1992). *An On-line Computational Model of Human Sentence Interpretation: A Theory of the Representation and Use of Linguistic Knowledge*. Ph.D. thesis, University of California, Berkeley, CA. Available as University of California at Berkeley Computer Science Division Tech. rep. #92/676.

Jurafsky, D. (1996). A probabilistic model of lexical and syntactic access and disambiguation. *Cognitive Science*, *20*, 137–194.

Jurafsky, D., Bates, R., Coccaro, N., Martin, R., Meteer, M., Ries, K., Shriberg, E., Stolcke, A., Taylor, P., and Van Ess-Dykema, C. (1997). Automatic detection of discourse structure for speech recognition and understanding. In *Proceedings of the 1997 IEEE Workshop on Speech Recognition and Understanding*, Santa Barbara, pp. 88–95.

Jurafsky, D., Bell, A., Fosler-Lussier, E., Girand, C., and Raymond, W. D. (1998). Reduction of English function words in Switchboard. In *ICSLP-98*, Sydney, Vol. 7, pp. 3111–3114.

Jurafsky, D., Wooters, C., Tajchman, G., Segal, J., Stolcke, A., Fosler, E., and Morgan, N. (1994). The Berkeley restaurant project. In *ICSLP-94*, Yokohama, Japan, pp. 2139–2142.

Jurafsky, D., Wooters, C., Tajchman, G., Segal, J., Stolcke, A., Fosler, E., and Morgan, N. (1995). Using a stochastic context-free grammar as a language model for speech recognition. In *IEEE ICASSP-95*, pp. 189–192. IEEE.

Kameyama, M. (1986). A property-sharing constraint in centering. In *ACL-86*, New York, pp. 200–206. ACL.

Kamm, C. A. (1994). User interfaces for voice applications. In Roe, D. B. and Wilpon, J. G. (Eds.), *Voice Communication Between Humans and Machines*, pp. 422–442. National Academy Press, Washington, D.C.

Kamp, H. (1981). A theory of truth and semantic representation. In Groenendijk, J.

A. G., Janssen, T. M. V., and Stokhof, M. B. J. (Eds.), *Formal Methods in the Study of Language*, Vol. 1, pp. 277–322. Mathematisch Centrum, Amsterdam.

Kaplan, R. M. (1987). Three seductions of computational psycholinguistics. In Whitelock, P., Wood, M. M., Somers, H. L., Johnson, R., and Bennett, P. (Eds.), *Linguistic Theory and Computer Applications*, pp. 149–188. Academic Press, London.

Kaplan, R. M. and Bresnan, J. (1982). Lexical-functional grammar: A formal system for grammatical representation. In Bresnan, J. (Ed.), *The Mental Representation of Grammatical Relations*, pp. 173–281. MIT Press, Cambridge, MA.

Kaplan, R. M. and Kay, M. (1981). Phonological rules and finite-state transducers. Paper presented at the Annual meeting of the Linguistics Society of America. New York.

Kaplan, R. M. and Kay, M. (1994). Regular models of phonological rule systems. *Computational Linguistics*, *20*(3), 331–378.

Karlsson, F., Voutilainen, A., Heikkilä, J., and Anttila, A. (Eds.). (1995). *Constraint Grammar: A Language-Independent System for Parsing Unrestricted Text*. Mouton de Gruyter, Berlin.

Karttunen, L. (1969). Pronouns and variables. In *CLS-69*, pp. 108–116. University of Chicago.

Karttunen, L. (1983). Kimmo: A general morphological processor. In *Texas Linguistics Forum 22*, pp. 165–186.

Karttunen, L. (1993). Finite-state constraints. In Goldsmith, J. (Ed.), *The Last Phonological Rule*, pp. 173–194. University of Chicago Press.

Karttunen, L. (1998). The proper treatment of optimality in computational phonology. In *Proceedings of FSMNLP'98: International Workshop on Finite-State Methods in Natural Language Processing*, Bilkent University. Ankara, Turkey, pp. 1–12.

Karttunen, L. (1999). Comments on Joshi. In Kornai, A. (Ed.), *Extended Finite State Models of Language*, pp. 16–18. Cambridge University Press, Cambridge.

Karttunen, L. and Kay, M. (1985). Structure sharing with binary trees. In *ACL-85*, Chicago, pp. 133–136. ACL.

Kasami, T. (1965). An efficient recognition and syntax analysis algorithm for context-free languages. Tech. rep. AFCRL-65-758, Air Force Cambridge Research Laboratory, Bedford, MA†.

Kashyap, R. L. and Oommen, B. J. (1983). Spelling correction using probabilistic methods. *Pattern Recognition Letters*, *2*, 147–154.

Kasper, R. T. (1988). An experimental parser for systemic grammars. In *COLING-88*, Budapest, pp. 309–312.

Kasper, R. T. and Rounds, W. C. (1986). A logical semantics for feature structures. In *ACL-86*, New York, pp. 257–266. ACL.

Katz, J. J. and Fodor, J. A. (1963). The structure of a semantic theory. *Language*, *39*, 170–210.

Katz, S. M. (1987). Estimation of probabilities from sparse data for the language model component of a speech recogniser. *IEEE Transactions on Acoustics, Speech, and Signal Processing*, *35*(3), 400–401.

Kawamoto, A. H. (1988). Distributed representations of ambiguous words and their resolution in connectionist networks. In Small, S. L., Cottrell, G. W., and Tanenhaus, M. (Eds.), *Lexical Ambiguity Resolution*, pp. 195–228. Morgan Kaufman, San Mateo, CA.

Kay, M. (1967). Experiments with a powerful parser. In *Proc. 2eme Conference Internationale sur le Traitement Automatique des Langues*, Grenoble.

Kay, M. (1973). The MIND system. In Rustin, R. (Ed.), *Natural Language Processing*, pp. 155–188. Algorithmics Press, New York.

Kay, M. (1979). Functional grammar. In *BLS-79*, Berkeley, CA, pp. 142–158.

Kay, M. (1980/1997). The proper place of men and machines in language translation. *Machine Translation*, *12*, 3–23. First appeared as a Xerox PARC Working paper in 1980.

Kay, M. (1984). Functional unification grammar: A formalism for machine translation. In *COLING-84*, Stanford, CA, pp. 75–78.

Kay, M. (1985). Parsing in functional unification grammar. In Dowty, D. R., Karttunen, L., and Zwicky, A. (Eds.), *Natural Language Parsing*, pp. 251–278. Cambridge University Press, Cambridge.

Kay, M. (1987). Nonconcatenative finite-state morphology. In *Proceedings of the Third Conference of the European Chapter of the ACL (EACL-87)*, Copenhagen, Denmark, pp. 2–10. ACL.

Kay, M., Gawron, J. M., and Norvig, P. (1992). *Verbmobil: A Translation System for Face-to-Face Dialog*. CSLI.

Kay, M. and Röscheisen, M. (1993). Text-translation alignment. *Computational Linguistics*, *19*, 121–142.

Kay, P. and Fillmore, C. J. (1999). Grammatical constructions and linguistic generalizations: The What's X Doing Y? construction. *Language*, *75*(1), 1–33.

Keating, P. A., Byrd, D., Flemming, E., and Todaka, Y. (1994). Phonetic analysis of word and segment variation using the TIMIT corpus of American English. *Speech Communication*, *14*, 131–142.

Keenan, J. M., Potts, G. R., Golding, J. M., and Jennings, T. M. (1990). Which elaborative inferences ar drawn during reading? A question of methodologies. In Balota, D. A., d'Arcais, G. B. F., and Rayner, K. (Eds.), *Comprehension processes in reading*, pp. 377–402. Lawrence Erlbaum, Hillsdale, NJ.

Kehler, A. (1993). The effect of establishing coherence in ellipsis and anaphora resolution. In *ACL-93*, Columbus, Ohio, pp. 62–69. ACL.

Kehler, A. (1994a). Common topics and coherent situations: Interpreting ellipsis in the context of discourse inference. In *ACL-94*, Las Cruces, New Mexico, pp. 50–57. ACL.

Kehler, A. (1994b). Temporal relations: Reference or discourse coherence?. In *ACL-94*, Las Cruces, New Mexico, pp. 319–321. ACL.

Kehler, A. (1997a). Current theories of centering for pronoun interpretation: A critical evaluation. *Computational Linguistics*, *23*(3), 467–475.

Kehler, A. (1997b). Probabilistic coreference in information extraction. In *Proceedings of the Second Conference on Empirical Methods in Natural Language Processing (EMNLP-97)*, Providence, RI, pp. 163–173.

Kehler, A. (2000). *Coherence, Reference, and the Theory of Grammar*. CSLI Publications.

Kelley, L. G. (1979). *The True Interpreter: A History of Translation Theory and Practice in the West*. St. Martin's Press, New York.

Kelly, E. F. and Stone, P. J. (1975). *Computer Recognition of English Word Senses*. North-Holland, Amsterdam.

Kennedy, C. and Boguraev, B. (1996). Anaphora for everyone: Pronominal anaphora resolution without a parser. In *COLING-96*, Copenhagen, pp. 113–118.

Kernighan, M. D., Church, K. W., and Gale, W. A. (1990). A spelling correction program base on a noisy channel model. In *COLING-90*, Helsinki, Vol. II, pp. 205–211.

Khudanpur, S. and Wu, J. (1999). A maximum entropy language model integrating n-grams and topic dependencies for conversational speech recognition. In *IEEE ICASSP-99*, pp. 553–556. IEEE.

Kiefer, B., Krieger, H.-U., Carroll, J., and Malouf, R. (1999). A bag of useful techniques for efficient and robust parsing. In *ACL-99*, College Park, MD, pp. 473–480.

Kilgarriff, A. and Palmer, M. (Eds.). (2000). *Computing and the Humanities: Special Issue on SENSEVAL*, Vol. 34. Kluwer.

Kilgarriff, A. and Rosenzweig, J. (2000). Framework and results for English SENSEVAL. *Computers and the Humanities*, *34*(1-2).

King, J. and Just, M. A. (1991). Individual differences in syntactic processing: The role of working memory. *Journal of Memory and Language*, *30*, 580–602.

King, P. (1989). *A Logical Formalism for Head-Driven Phrase Structure Grammar*. Ph.D. thesis, University of Manchester†. Cited in Carpenter (1992)).

Kintsch, W. (1974). *The Representation of Meaning in Memory*. Wiley, New York.

Kintsch, W. (1988). The role of knowledge in discourse comprehension: A construction-integration model. *Psychological Review*, *95*(2), 163–182.

Kintsch, W. and van Dijk, T. A. (1978). Toward a model of text comprehension and production. *Psychological Review*, *85*, 363–394.

Kiraz, G. A. (1997). Compiling regular formalisms with rule features into finite-state automata. In *ACL/EACL-97*, Madrid, Spain, pp. 329–336. ACL.

Kisseberth, C. W. (1969). On the abstractness of phonology: The evidence from Yawelmani. *Papers in Linguistics*, *1*, 248–282.

Kisseberth, C. W. (1970). On the functional unity of phonological rules. *Linguistic Inquiry*, *1*(3), 291–306.

Kita, K., Fukui, Y., Nagata, M., and Morimoto, T. (1996). Automatic acquisition of probabilistic dialogue models. In *ICSLP-96*, Philadelphia, PA, Vol. 1, pp. 196–199.

Klatt, D. H. (1977). Review of the ARPA speech understanding project. *Journal of the Acoustical Society of America*, *62*(6), 1345–1366.

Klavans, J. (Ed.). (1995). *Representation and Acquisition of Lexical Knowledge: Polysemy, Ambiguity and Generativity*. AAAI Press, Menlo Park, CA. AAAI Technical Report SS-95-01.

Kleene, S. C. (1951). Representation of events in nerve nets and finite automata. Tech. rep. RM-704, RAND Corporation. RAND Research Memorandum†.

Kleene, S. C. (1956). Representation of events in nerve nets and finite automata. In Shannon, C. and McCarthy, J. (Eds.), *Automata Studies*, pp. 3–41. Princeton University Press, Princeton, NJ.

Klein, S. and Simmons, R. F. (1963). A computational approach to grammatical coding of English words. *Journal of the Association for Computing Machinery*, *10*(3), 334–347.

Klovstad, J. W. and Mondshein, L. F. (1975). The CASPERS linguistic analysis system. *IEEE Transactions on Acoustics, Speech, and Signal Processing*, ASSP-23(1), 118–123.

Kneser, R. (1996). Statistical language modeling using a variable context length. In *ICSLP-96*, Philadelphia, PA, Vol. 1, pp. 494–497.

Kneser, R. and Ney, H. (1993). Improved clustering techniques for class-based statistical language modelling. In *EUROSPEECH-93*, pp. 973–976.

Knight, K. (1989). Unification: A multidisciplinary survey. *ACM Computing Surveys*, *21*(1), 93–124.

Knight, K. (1997). Automating knowledge acquisition for machine translation. *AI Magazine*, *18*(4), 81–96.

Knight, K. and Al-Onaizan, Y. (1998). Translation with finite-state devices. In Farwell, D., Gerber, L., and Hovy, E. H. (Eds.), *Machine Translation and the Information Soup*, pp. 421–437. Springer.

Knight, K., Chander, I., Haines, M., Hatzivassiloglou, V., Hovy, E. H., Iida, M., Luk, S. K., Okumura, A., Whitney, R., and Yamada, K. (1994). Integrating knowledge bases and statistics in MT. In *Proceedings of the Conference of the Association for Machine Translation in the Americas*, Columbia, MD.

Knill, K. and Young, S. J. (1997). Hidden Markov Models in speech and language processing. In Young, S. J. and Bloothooft, G. (Eds.), *Corpus-based Methods in Language and Speech Processing*, pp. 27–68. Kluwer, Dordrecht.

Knott, A. and Dale, R. (1994). Using linguistic phenomena to motivate a set of coherence relations. *Discourse Processes*, *18*(1), 35–62.

Knuth, D. E. (1968). Semantics of context-free languages. *Mathematical Systems Theory*, 2(2), 127–145.

Knuth, D. E. (1973). *Sorting and Searching: The Art of Computer Programming Volume 3*. Addison-Wesley, Reading, MA.

Koenig, J.-P. and Jurafsky, D. (1995). Type underspecification and on-line type construction in the lexicon. In Aranovich, R., Byrne, W., Preuss, S., and Senturia, M. (Eds.), *West Coast Conference on Formal Linguistics (WCCFL13)*, pp. 270–285.

Koenig, W., Dunn, H. K., , and Lacy, L. Y. (1946). The sound spectrograph. *Journal of the Acoustical Society of America*, *18*, 19–49.

Koerner, E. F. K. and Asher, R. E. (Eds.). (1995). *Concise History of the Language Sciences*. Elsevier Science, Oxford.

Kogure, K. (1990). Strategic lazy incremental copy graph unification. In *COLING-90*, Helsinki, pp. 223–228.

Kompe, R., Kießling, A., Kuhn, T., Mast, M., Niemann, H., Nöth, E., Ott, K., and Batliner, A. (1993). Prosody takes over: A prosodically guided dialog system. In *EUROSPEECH-93*, Berlin, Vol. 3, pp. 2003–2006.

Kornai, A. (1991). *Formal Phonology*. Ph.D. thesis, Stanford University, Stanford, CA†.

Koskenniemi, K. (1983). Two-level morphology: A general computational model of word-form recognition and production. Tech. rep. Publication No. 11, Department of General Linguistics, University of Helsinki.

Koskenniemi, K. and Church, K. W. (1988). Complexity, two-level morphology, and Finnish. In *COLING-88*, Budapest, pp. 335–339.

Krieger, H.-U. and Nerbonne, J. (1993). Feature-based inheritance networks for computational lexicons. In Briscoe, T., de Paiva, V., and Copestake, A. (Eds.), *Inheritance, Defaults, and the Lexicon*, pp. 90–136. Cambridge University Press, Cambridge.

Krieger, H.-U. and Schäfer, U. (1994). TDL — a type description language for HPSG. Part 1: Overview. Tech. rep. RR-94-37, DFKI, Saarbrücken.

Krippendorf, K. (1980). *Content Analysis: An Introduction to its Methodology*. Sage Publications, Beverly Hills, CA.

Krovetz, R. (1993). Viewing morphology as an inference process. In *SIGIR-93*, pp. 191–202. ACM.

Krovetz, R. and Croft, W. B. (1992). Lexical ambiguity and information retrieval. *ACM Transactions on Information Systems*, *10*(2), 115–141.

Kruskal, J. B. (1983). An overview of sequence comparison. In Sankoff, D. and Kruskal, J. B. (Eds.), *Time Warps, String Edits, and Macromolecules: The Theory and Practice of Sequence Comparison*, pp. 1–44. Addison-Wesley, Reading, MA.

Kučera, H. and Francis, W. N. (1967). *Computational analysis of present-day American English*. Brown University Press, Providence, RI.

Kuhn, R. and de Mori, R. (1990). A cache-based natural language model for speech recognition. *IEEE Transactions on Pattern Analysis and Machine Intelligence*, *12*(6), 570–583.

Kukich, K. (1988). Fluency in natural language reports. In McDonald, D. D. and Bolc, L. (Eds.), *Natural Language Generation Systems*, pp. 280–311. Springer-Verlag.

Kukich, K. (1992). Techniques for automatically correcting words in text. *ACM Computing Surveys*, *24*(4), 377–439.

Kuno, S. (1972). Functional sentence perspective: A case study from Japanese and English. *Linguistic Inquiry*, *3*(3), 269–320.

Kuno, S. (1965). The predictive analyzer and a path elimination technique. *Communications of the ACM*, *8*(7), 453–462.

Kuno, S. (1987). *Functional Syntax — Anaphora, Discourse and Empathy*. University of Chicago Press, Chicago.

Kuno, S. and Oettinger, A. G. (1963). Multiple-path syntactic analyzer. In Popplewell, C. M. (Ed.), *Information Processing 1962: Proceedings of the IFIP Congress 1962*, Munich, pp. 306–312. North-Holland. Reprinted in Grosz et al. (1986).

Kupiec, J. (1992). Robust part-of-speech tagging using a hidden Markov model. *Computer Speech and Language*, *6*, 225–242.

Kučera, H. (1992). The mathematics of language. In *The American Heritage Dictionary of the English Language*, pp. xxxi–xxxiii. Houghton Mifflin, Boston.

Labov, W. (1966). *The Social Stratification of English in New York City*. Center for Applied Linguistics, Washington, D.C.

Labov, W. (1969). Contraction, deletion, and inherent variability of the English copula. *Language*, *45*(4), 715–762.

Labov, W. (1972). The internal evolution of linguistic rules. In Stockwell, R. P. and Macaulay, R. K. S. (Eds.), *Linguistic Change and Generative Theory*, pp. 101–171. Indiana University Press, Bloomington.

Labov, W. (1975). *The quantitative study of linguistic structure*. Pennsylvania Working Papers on Linguistic Change and Variation v.1 no. 3. U.S. Regional Survey, Philadelphia, PA.

Labov, W. (1994). *Principles of linguistic change: internal factors*. Basil Blackwell, Oxford.

Labov, W. and Fanshel, D. (1977). *Therapeutic Discourse*. Academic Press, New York.

Ladd, D. R. (1996). *Intonational Phonology*. Cambridge Studies in Linguistics. Cambridge University Press.

Ladefoged, P. (1993). *A Course in Phonetics*. Harcourt Brace Jovanovich, Inc. Third Edition.

Ladefoged, P. (1996). *Elements of Acoustic Phonetics*. University of Chicago, Chicago, IL. Second Edition.

Lafferty, J. D., Sleator, D., and Temperley, D. (1992). Grammatical trigrams: A probabilistic model of link grammar. In *Proceedings of the 1992 AAAI Fall Symposium on Probabilistic Approaches to Natural Language*.

Lakoff, G. (1965). *On the Nature of Syntactic Irregularity*. Ph.D. thesis, Indiana University. Published as *Irregularity in Syntax*. Holt, Rinehart, and Winston, New York, 1970.

Lakoff, G. (1972). Linguistics and natural logic. In Davidson, D. and Harman, G. (Eds.), *Semantics for Natural Language*, pp. 545–665. D. Reidel, Dordrecht.

Lakoff, G. (1987). *Women, Fire, and Dangerous Things*. University of Chicago Press, Chicago.

Lakoff, G. (1993). Cognitive phonology. In Goldsmith, J. (Ed.), *The Last Phonological Rule*, pp. 117–145. University of Chicago Press, Chicago.

Lakoff, G. and Johnson, M. (1980). *Metaphors We Live By*. University of Chicago Press, Chicago, IL.

Lambek, J. (1958). The mathematics of sentence structure. *American Mathematical Monthly*, 65(3), 154–170.

Lambrecht, K. (1994). *Information Structure and Sentence Form*. Cambridge University Press, Cambridge.

Landauer, T. K. (Ed.). (1995). *The Trouble With Computers: Usefulness, Usability, and Productivity*. MIT Press, Cambridge, MA.

Landauer, T. K. and Dumais, S. T. (1997). A solution to Plato's problem: The Latent Semantic Analysis theory of acquisition, induction, and representation of knowledge. *Psychological Review*, 104, 211–240.

Landauer, T. K., Laham, D., Rehder, B., and Schreiner, M. E. (1997). How well can passage meaning be derived without using word order: A comparison of latent semantic analysis and humans. In *COGSCI-97*, Stanford, CA, pp. 412–417. Lawrence Erlbaum.

Landes, S., Leacock, C., and Tengi, R. I. (1998). Building semantic concordances. In Fellbaum, C. (Ed.), *WordNet: An Electronic Lexical Database*, pp. 199–216. MIT Press, Cambridge, MA.

Langendoen, D. T. (1975). Finite-state parsing of phrase-structure languages and the status of readjustment rules in the grammar. *Linguistic Inquiry*, 6(4), 533–554.

Langkilde, I. and Knight, K. (1998). The practical value of n-grams in generation. In *Proceedings of the Ninth International Workshop on Natural Language Generation*, Ontario, Canada, pp. 248–255.

Lapata, M. and Brew, C. (1999). Using subcategorization to resolve verb class ambiguity. In *Proceedings of the 1999 Joint SIGDAT Conference on Empirical Methods in Natural Language Processing and Very Large Corpora (EMNLP/VLC-99)*, College Park, MD, pp. 266–274.

Lappin, S. and Leass, H. (1994). An algorithm for pronominal anaphora resolution. *Computational Linguistics*, 20(4), 535–561.

Lari, K. and Young, S. J. (1991). Applications of stochastic context-free grammars using the Inside-Outside algorithm. *Computer Speech and Language*, 5, 237–257.

Lascarides, A. and Asher, N. (1993). Temporal interpretation, discourse relations, and common sense entailment. *Linguistics and Philosophy*, 16(5), 437–493.

Lascarides, A. and Copestake, A. (1997). Default representation in constraint-based frameworks. *Computational Linguistics*, 25(1), 55–106.

Lauer, M. (1995). Corpus statistics meet the noun compound. In *ACL-95*, Cambridge, MA, pp. 47–54.

Lavoie, B. and Rambow, O. (1997). A fast and portable realizer for text generation systems. In *Proceedings of the Fifth Conference on Applied Natural Language Processing, Washington DC*, pp. 265–268.

Lavoie, B., Rambow, O., and Reiter, E. (1997). Customizable descriptions of object-oriented models. In *Proceedings of the Fifth Conference on Applied Natural Language Processing*, Washington, DC, pp. 265–268.

LDC (1993). *LDC Catalog: CSR-I (WSJ0) Complete*. University of Pennsylvania. www.ldc.upenn.edu/Catalog/LDC93S6A.html.

LDC (1995). COMLEX English Pronunciation Dictionary Version 0.2 (COMLEX 0.2). Linguistic Data Consortium.

LDC (1998). *LDC Catalog: Hub4 project*. University of Pennsylvania. www.ldc.upenn.edu/Catalog/LDC98S71.html or www.ldc.upenn.edu/Catalog/Hub4.html.

LDC (1999). *LDC Catalog: Hub5-LVCSR project*. University of Pennsylvania. www.ldc.upenn.edu/ldc/about/chenglish.html or www.ldc.upenn.edu/Catalog/Hub5-LVCSR.html.

Leech, G., Garside, R., and Bryant, M. (1994). Claws4: The tagging of the British National Corpus. In *COLING-94*, Kyoto, pp. 622–628.

Lees, R. (1970). Problems in the grammatical analysis of English nominal compounds. In Bierwitsch, M. and Heidolph, K. E. (Eds.), *Progress in Linguistics*, pp. 174–187. Mouton, The Hague.

Lehnert, W. (1977). A conceptual theory of question answering. In *IJCAI-77*, Cambridge, MA, pp. 158–164. Morgan Kaufmann.

Lehnert, W. G., Cardie, C., Fisher, D., Riloff, E., and Williams, R. (1991). Description of the CIRCUS system as used for MUC-3. In Sundheim, B. (Ed.), *Proceedings of the Third Message Understanding Conference*, pp. 223–233. Morgan Kaufmann.

Lehrer, A. (1974). *Semantic Fields and Lexical Structure*. North-Holland, Amsterdam.

Lehrer, A. and Kittay, E. (Eds.). (1992). *Frames, Fields and Contrasts: New Essays in Semantic and Lexical Organization*. Lawrence Erlbaum, Hillsdale, NJ.

Lenat, D. B. and Guha, R. V. (1991). *Building Large Knowledge-Based Systems: Representation and Inference in CYC*. Addison-Wesley, Reading, MA.

Lerner, A. J. (1978). *The Street Where I Live*. Da Capo Press, New York.

Lesk, M. E. (1986). Automatic sense disambiguation using machine readable dictionaries: How to tell a pine cone from an ice cream cone. In *Proceedings of the Fifth International Conference on Systems Documentation*, Toronto, CA, pp. 24–26. ACM.

Lester, J. and Porter, B. (1997). Developing and empirically evaluating robust explanation generators: The KNIGHT experiments. *Computational Linguistics*, 23(2), 65–101.

Levelt, W. J. M., Roelofs, A., and Meyer, A. S. (1999). A theory of lexical access in speech production. *Behavioral and Brain Science*, 22, 1–75.

Levelt, W. J. M. (1970). A scaling approach to the study of syntactic relations. In d'Arcais, G. B. F. and Levelt, W. J. M.

(Eds.), *Advances in psycholinguistics*, pp. 109–121. North-Holland, Amsterdam.

Levelt, W. J. M. (1983). Monitoring and self-repair in speech. *Cognition*, 14, 41–104.

Levenshtein, V. I. (1966). Binary codes capable of correcting deletions, insertions, and reversals. *Cybernetics and Control Theory*, 10(8), 707–710. Original in *Doklady Akademii Nauk SSSR* 163(4): 845–848 (1965).

Levesque, H. J., Cohen, P. R., and Nunes, J. H. T. (1990). On acting together. In *AAAI-90*, Boston, MA, pp. 94–99. Morgan Kaufmann.

Levi, J. (1978). *The Syntax and Semantics of Complex Nominals*. Academic Press, New York.

Levin, B. (1993). *English Verb Classes and Alternations*. University of Chicago Press, Chicago.

Levin, L., Gates, D., Lavie, A., and Waibel, A. (1998). An interlingua based on domain actions for machine translation of task-oriented dialogues. In *ICSLP-98*, Sydney, pp. 1155–1158.

Levinson, S. C. (1983). *Pragmatics*. Cambridge University Press, Cambridge.

Levinson, S. E. (1995). Structural methods in automatic speech recognition. *Proceedings of the IEEE*, 73(11), 1625–1650.

Lewis, D. (1972). General semantics. In Davidson, D. and Harman, G. (Eds.), *Natural Language Semantics*, pp. 169–218. D. Reidel, Dordrecht.

Lewis, D. D. and Hayes, P. J. (Eds.). (1994). *ACM Transactions on Information Systems: Special Issue on Text Categorization*, Vol. 12. ACM Press.

Lewis, H. and Papadimitriou, C. (1981). *Elements of the Theory of Computation*. Prentice-Hall, Englewood Cliffs, NJ.

Liberman, M. and Church, K. W. (1992). Text analysis and word pronunciation in text-to-speech synthesis. In Furui, S. and Sondhi, M. M. (Eds.), *Advances in Speech Signal Processing*, pp. 791–832. Marcel Dekker, New York.

Liberman, M. and Prince, A. (1977). On stress and linguistic rhythm. *Linguistic Inquiry*, 8, 249–336.

Liberman, M. and Sproat, R. (1992). The stress and structure of modified noun phrases in English. In Sag, I. A. and Szabolcsi, A. (Eds.), *Lexical Matters*, pp. 131–181. CSLI, Stanford University.

Lin, D. (1995). A dependency-based method for evaluating broad-coverage parsers. In *IJCAI-95*, Montreal, pp. 1420–1425.

Lindsey, R. (1963). Inferential memory as the basis of machines which understand natural language. In Feigenbaum, E. and Feldman, J. (Eds.), *Computers and Thought*, pp. 217–233. McGraw Hill.

Litman, D. J. (1985). *Plan Recognition and Discourse Analysis: An Integrated Approach for Understanding Dialogues*. Ph.D. thesis, University of Rochester, Rochester, NY.

Litman, D. J. and Allen, J. F. (1987). A plan recognition model for subdialogues in conversation. *Cognitive Science*, *11*, 163–200.

Lochbaum, K. E. (1998). A collaborative planning model of intentional structure. *Computational Linguistics*, *24*(4), 525–572.

Lochbaum, K. E., Grosz, B. J., and Sidner, C. L. (1990). Models of plans to support communication: An initial report. In *AAAI-90*, Boston, MA, pp. 485–490. Morgan Kaufmann.

Longacre, R. E. (1983). *The Grammar of Discourse*. Plenum Press.

Lopresti, D. and Zhou, J. (1997). Using consensus sequence voting to correct OCR errors. *Computer Vision and Image Understanding*, *67*(1), 39–47.

Losiewicz, B. L. (1992). *The Effect of Frequency on Linguistic Morphology*. Ph.D. thesis, University of Texas, Austin, TX.

Lowe, J. B., Baker, C. F., and Fillmore, C. J. (1997). A frame-semantic approach to semantic annotation. In *Proceedings of ACL SIGLEX Workshop on Tagging Text with Lexical Semantics*, Washington, D.C., pp. 18–24. ACL.

Lowerre, B. T. (1968). *The Harpy Speech Recognition System*. Ph.D. thesis, Carnegie Mellon University, Pittsburgh, PA.

Luce, P. A., Pisoni, D. B., and Goldfinger, S. D. (1990). Similarity neighborhoods of spoken words. In Altmann, G. T. M. (Ed.), *Cognitive Models of Speech Processing*, pp. 122–147. MIT Press, Cambridge, MA.

Luhn, H. P. (1957). A statistical approach to the mechanized encoding and searching of literary information. *IBM Journal of Research and Development*, *1*(4), 309–317.

Luhn, H. P. (1958). The automatic creation of literature abstracts. *IBM Journal of Research and Development*, *2*(2), 159–165.

Lyons, J. (1977). *Semantics*. Cambridge University Press, New York.

MacDonald, M. C. (1993). The interaction of lexical and syntactic ambiguity. *Journal of Memory and Language*, *32*, 692–715.

MacDonald, M. C. (1994). Probabilistic constraints and syntactic ambiguity resolution. *Language and Cognitive Processes*, *9*(2), 157–201.

Macleod, C., Grishman, R., and Meyers, A. (1998). COMLEX Syntax Reference Manual Version 3.0. Linguistic Data Consortium.

MacWhinney, B. (1977). Starting points. *Language*, *53*, 152–168.

MacWhinney, B. (1982). Basic syntactic processes. In Kuczaj, S. (Ed.), *Language Acquisition: Volume 1, Syntax and Semantics*, pp. 73–136. Lawrence Erlbaum, Hillsdale, NJ.

MacWhinney, B. (1987). The competition model. In MacWhinney, B. (Ed.), *Mechanisms of Language Acquisition*, pp. 249–308. Lawrence Erlbaum, Hillsdale, NJ.

MacWhinney, B. and Csaba Pléh (1988). The processing of restrictive relative clauses in Hungarian. *Cognition*, *29*, 95–141.

MacWhinney, B. and Leinbach, J. (1991). Implementations are not conceptualizations: Revising the verb learning model. *Cognition*, *40*, 121–157.

Madhu, S. and Lytel, D. (1965). A figure of merit technique for the resolution of non-grammatical ambiguity. *Mechanical Translation*, *8*(2), 9–13.

Magerman, D. M. (1995). Statistical decision-tree models for parsing. In *ACL-95*, Cambridge, MA, pp. 276–283. ACL.

Magerman, D. M. and Marcus, M. P. (1991). Pearl: A probabilistic chart parser. In *Proceedings of the 6th Conference of the European Chapter of the ACL*, Berlin, Germany.

Main, M. G. and Benson, D. B. (1983). Denotational semantics for natural language question-answering programs. *American Journal of Computational Linguistics*, *9*(1), 11–21.

Makkai, A. (1972). *Idiom Structure in English*. Mouton, The Hague.

Mangu, L. and Brill, E. (1997). Automatic rule acquisition for spelling correction. In *Proceedings of the 14th International Conference on Machine Learning (ICML-97)*, Nashville, TN, pp. 187–194. Morgan Kaufmann.

Mann, W. C. and Moore, J. D. (1981). Computer generation of multiparagraph text. *Computational Linguistics*, *7*(1), 17–29.

Mann, W. C. (1983). An overview of the PENMAN text generation system. In *Proceedings of the National Conference on Artificial Intelligence*, pp. 261–265.

Mann, W. C. and Thompson, S. A. (1986). Relational propositions in discourse. *Discourse Processes*, *9*(1), 57–90.

Mann, W. C. and Thompson, S. A. (1987). Rhetorical structure theory: A theory of text organization. Tech. rep. RS-87-190, Information Sciences Institute.

Manning, C. D. (1993). Automatic acquisition of a large subcategorization dictionary from corpora. In *ACL-93*, Columbus, Ohio, pp. 235–242. ACL.

Manning, C. D. and Schütze, H. (1999). *Foundations of Statistical Natural Language Processing*. MIT Press, Cambridge, MA.

Marcu, D. (1998). Improving summarization through rhetorical parsing tuning. In *Proceedings of the Sixth Workshop on Very Large Corpora (WVLC-6)*, Montreal, Canada, pp. 206–215.

Marcus, G. F., Brinkman, U., Clahsen, H., Wiese, R., and Pinker, S. (1995). German inflection: The exception that proves the rule. *Cognitive Psychology*, *29*, 189–256.

Marcus, M. P. (1990). Summary of session 9: Automatic acquisition of linguistic structure. In *Proceedings DARPA Speech and Natural Language Workshop*, Hidden Valley, PA, pp. 249–250. Morgan Kaufmann.

Marcus, M. P., Santorini, B., and Marcinkiewicz, M. A. (1993). Building a large annotated corpus of English: The Penn treebank. *Computational Linguistics*, *19*(2), 313–330.

Markey, K. and Ward, W. (1997). Lexical tuning based on triphone confidence estimation. In *EUROSPEECH-97*, Vol. 5, pp. 2479–2482.

Markov, A. A. (1913). Essai d'une recherche statistique sur le texte du roman "Eugene Onegin" illustrant la liaison des epreuve en chain ('Example of a statistical investigation of the text of "Eugene Onegin" illustrating the dependence between samples in chain'). *Izvistia Imperatorskoi Akademii Nauk (Bulletin de l'Académie Impériale des Sciences de St.-Pétersbourg)*, *7*, 153–162. English translation by Morris Halle, 1956.

Marshall, I. (1983). Choice of grammatical word-class without global syntactic analysis: Tagging words in the LOB corpus. *Computers and the Humanities*, *17*, 139–150.

Marshall, I. (1987). Tag selection using probabilistic methods. In Garside, R., Leech, G., and Sampson, G. (Eds.), *The Computational Analysis of English*, pp. 42–56. Longman, London.

Marslen-Wilson, W. and Welsh, A. (1978). Processing interactions and lexical access during word recognition in continuous speech. *Cognitive Psychology*, *10*, 29–63.

Marslen-Wilson, W., Tyler, L. K., Waksler, R., and Older, L. (1994). Morphology and meaning in the English mental lexicon. *Psychological Review*, *101*(1), 3–33.

Marslen-Wilson, W. D. (1973). Linguistic structure and speech shadowing at very short latencies. *Nature*, *244*, 522–523.

Martin, J. H. (1986). The acquisition of polysemy. In *Proceedings of the Fourth International Conference on Machine Learning*, Irvine, CA, pp. 198–204.

Martin, J. H. (1990). *A Computational Model of Metaphor Interpretation*. Perspectives in Artificial Intelligence. Academic Press, San Diego, CA.

Martin, J. H. (1996). Computational approaches to figurative language. *Metaphor and Symbolic Activity*, *11*(1), 85–100.

Massaro, D. W. (1998). *Perceiving Talking Faces: From Speech Perception to a Behavioral Principle*. MIT Press.

Massaro, D. W. and Cohen, M. M. (1983). Evaluation and integration of visual and auditory information in speech perception. *Journal of Experimental Psychology: Human Perception and Performance*, *9*, 753–771.

Mast, M., Kompe, R., Harbeck, S., Kießling, A., Niemann, H., Nöth, E., Schukat-Talamazzini, E. G., and Warnke, V. (1996). Dialog act classification with the help of prosody. In *ICSLP-96*, Philadelphia, PA, Vol. 3, pp. 1732–1735.

Masterman, M. (1957). The thesaurus in syntax and semantics. *Mechanical Translation*, *4*(1), 1–2.

Mather, L. (1998). *Enhancing Cluster-Based Retrieval through Linear Algebra*. Ph.D. thesis, University of Colorado, Boulder, CO.

Matthews, A. and Chodorow, M. S. (1988). Pronoun resolution in two-clause sentences: Effects of ambiguity, antecedent location, and depth of embedding. *Journal of Memory and Language*, *27*, 245–260.

Mays, E., Damerau, F. J., and Mercer, R. L. (1991). Context based spelling correction. *Information Processing and Management*, *27*(5), 517–522.

Mazuka, R. and Itoh, K. (1995). Can Japanese speakers be led down the garden path?. In Mazuka, R. and Nagai, N. (Eds.), *Japanese Sentence Processing*, pp. 295–330. Lawrence Erlbaum, Hillsdale, NJ.

McCarthy, J. J. (1981). A prosodic theory of non-concatenative morphology. *Linguistic Inquiry*, *12*, 373–418.

McCarthy, J. F. and Lehnert, W. G. (1995). Using decision trees for coreference resolution. In *IJCAI-95*, Montreal, Canada, pp. 1050–1055.

McCawley, J. D. (1968). The role of semantics in a grammar. In Bach, E. W. and Harms, R. T. (Eds.), *Universals in Linguistic Theory*, pp. 124–169. Holt, Rinehart & Winston, New York, NY.

McCawley, J. D. (1978). Where you can shove infixes. In Bell, A. and Hooper, J. B. (Eds.), *Syllables and Segments*, pp. 213–221. North-Holland, Amsterdam.

McCawley, J. D. (1993). *Everything that Linguists have Always Wanted to Know about Logic* (2nd edition). University of Chicago Press, Chicago, IL.

McCawley, J. D. (1998). *The Syntactic Phenomena of English*. University of Chicago Press, Chicago.

McClelland, J. L. and Elman, J. L. (1986). Interactive processes in speech perception: The TRACE model. In McClelland, J. L., Rumelhart, D. E., and the PDP Research Group (Eds.), *Parallel Distributed Processing Volume 2: Psychological and Biological Models*, pp. 58–121. MIT Press, Cambridge, MA.

McCoy, K. F. (1985). *Correcting Object-Related Misconceptions*. Ph.D. thesis, University of Pennsylvania.

McCoy, K. F., Pennington, C. A., and Badman, A. L. (1998). Compansion: From research prototype to practical integration. *Natural Language Engineering*, *4*(1), 73–95.

McCulloch, W. S. and Pitts, W. (1943). A logical calculus of ideas immanent in nervous activity. *Bulletin of Mathematical Biophysics*, pp. 115–133. Reprinted in *Neurocomputing: Foundations of Research, ed. by J. A. Anderson and E Rosenfeld. MIT Press 1988*.

McDermott, D. (1976). Artificial intelligence meets natural stupidity. *SIGART Newsletter*, *57*.

McDonald, D. B. (1982). *Understanding Noun Compounds*. Ph.D. thesis, Carnegie Mellon University, Pittsburgh, PA. CMU Technical Report CS-82-102.

McDonald, D. D. (1980). *Natural Language Production as a Process of Decision Making*. Ph.D. thesis, MIT, Cambridge, MA.

McDonald, D. D. (1988). Modularity in natural language generation: Methodological issues. In *Proceedings of the AAAI Workshop on Text Planning and Realization*, pp. 91–98.

McDonald, D. D. (1992). Natural-language generation. In Shapiro, S. C. (Ed.), *Encyclopedia of Artificial Intelligence* (2nd edition)., pp. 642–655. John Wiley, New York.

McKeown, K. R. (1985). *Text Generation*. Cambridge University Press, Cambridge.

McKeown, K. R., Elhadad, M., Fukumoto, Y., Lim, J., Lombardi, C., Robin, J., and Smadja, F. (1990). Natural language generation in COMET. In Dale, R., Mellish, C., and Zock, M. (Eds.), *Current Research in Natural Language Generation*, chap. 5, pp. 103–139. Academic Press, London.

McKeown, K. R. and Swartout, W. R. (1988). Language generation and explanation. In Zock, M. and Sabah, G. (Eds.), *Advances in Natural Language Generation — An Interdisciplinary Perspective*, Vol. 1, chap. 1, pp. 1–51. Ablex, Norwood, NJ.

McKoon, G. and Ratcliff, R. (1992). Inferences during reading. *Psychological Review*, *99*, 440–466.

McRoy, S. (1992). Using multiple knowledge sources for word sense discrimination. *Computational Linguistics*, *18*(1), 1–30.

McTear, M. (1998). Modelling spoken dialogues with state transition diagrams: Experiences with the CSLU toolkit. In *ICSLP-98*, Sydney, Vol. 4, pp. 1223–1226.

Mealy, G. H. (1955). A method for synthesizing sequential circuits. *Bell System Technical Journal*, *34*(5), 1045–1079.

Melamed, I. D. (1999). Bitext maps and alignment via pattern recognition. *Computational Linguistics*, *25*(1), 107–130.

Melamed, I. D. (1999 to appear). Word-to-word models of translational equivalence. *Computational Linguistics*.

Mel'čuk, I. A. (1979). *Studies in dependency syntax*. Karoma Publishers, Ann Arbor.

Mel'čuk, I. A. (1988). *Dependency Syntax: Theory and Practice*. SUNY Series in Linguistics, Mark Aronoff, series editor. State University of New York Press, Albany.

Merialdo, B. (1994). Tagging English text with a probabilistic model. *Computational Linguistics*, *20*(2), 155–172.

Merton, R. K. (1961). Singletons and multiples in scientific discovery. *American Philosophical Society Proceedings*, *105*(5), 470–486.

Meteer, M. and Iyer, R. (1996). Modeling conversational speech for speech recognition. In *Proceedings of the Conference on Empirical Methods in Natural Language Processing*, University of Pennsylvania, pp. 33–47. ACL.

Meteer, M. W. (1992). *Expressibility and the Problem of Efficient Text Planning*. Pinter, London.

Meurers, W. D. and Minnen, G. (1997). A computational treatment of lexical rules in HPSG as covariation in lexical entries. *Computational Linguistics*, *23*(4), 543–568.

Miller, C. A. (1998). Pronunciation modeling in speech synthesis. Tech. rep. IRCS 98–09, University of Pennsylvania Institute for Research in Cognitive Science, Philadephia, PA.

Miller, G. A. and Chomsky, N. (1963). Finitary models of language users. In Luce, R. D., Bush, R. R., and Galanter, E. (Eds.), *Handbook of Mathematical Psychology*, Vol. II, pp. 419–491. John Wiley, New York.

Miller, G. A. and Selfridge, J. A. (1950). Verbal context and the recall of meaningful material. *American Journal of Psychology*, *63*, 176–185.

Miller, J. L. (1994). On the internal structure of phonetic categories: a progress report. *Cognition*, *50*, 271–275.

Milosavljevic, M. (1997). Content selection in comparison generation. In *Proceedings of the 6th European Workshop on Natural Language Generation,* Duisburg, Germany, 24–26 March, pp. 72–81.

Mitamura, T. and Nyberg, E. H. (1995). Controlled English for knowledge-based MT: Experience with the KANT system. In *6th International Conference on Theoretical and Methodological Issues in Machine Translation*, Leuven, Belgium.

Mitchell, D. C., Cuetos, F., Corley, M. M. B., and Brysbaert, M. (1995). Exposure-based models of human parsing: Evidence for the use of coarse-grained (nonlexical) statistical records. *Journal of Psycholinguistic Research*, *24*(6), 469–488.

Mitchell, T. M. (1981). Generalization as search. In Webber, B. L. and Nilsson, N. J. (Eds.), *Readings in Artificial Intelligence*, pp. 517–542. Morgan Kaufmann, Los Altos.

Mitkov, R. and Boguraev, B. (Eds.). (1997). *Proceedings of the ACL-97 Workshop on Operational Factors in Practical, Robust Anaphora Resolution for Unrestricted Texts*, Madrid, Spain. ACL.

Mohri, M. (1997). Finite-state transducers in language and speech processing. *Computational Linguistics*, *23*(2), 269–312.

Montague, R. (1973). The proper treatment of quantification in ordinary English. In Thomason, R. (Ed.), *Formal Philosophy: Selected Papers of Richard Montague*, pp. 247–270. Yale University Press, New Haven, CT.

Mooney, R. J. (1995). Encouraging experimental results on learning CNF. *Machine Learning*, *19*(1), 79–92.

Mooney, R. J. (1996). Comparative experiments on disambiguating word senses: An illustration of the role of bias in machine learning. In *Proceedings of the Conference on Empirical Methods in Natural Language Processing (EMNLP-96)*, Philadelphia, PA, pp. 82–91.

Moore, E. F. (1956). Gedanken-experiments on sequential machines. In Shannon, C. and McCarthy, J. (Eds.), *Automata Studies*, pp. 129–153. Princeton University Press, Princeton, NJ.

Moore, J. D. and Paris, C. L. (1993). Planning text for advisory dialogues: Capturing intentional and rhetorical information. *Computational Linguistics*, *19*(4), 651–694.

Moore, J. D. and Pollack, M. E. (1992). A problem for RST: The need for multi-level discourse analysis. *Computational Linguistics*, *18*(4), 537–544.

Moore, R. (1977). Reasoning about knowledge and action. In *IJCAI-77*, pp. 223–227.

Moore, R., Appelt, D., Dowding, J., Gawron, J. M., and Moran, D. (1995). Combining linguistic and statistical knowledge sources in natural-language processing for ATIS. In *Proceedings of the January 1995 ARPA Spoken Language Systems Technology Workshop*, Austin, TX, pp. 261–264. Morgan Kaufmann.

Morris, J. and Hirst, G. (1991). Lexical cohesion computed by thesaural relations as an indicator of the structure of text. *Computational Linguistics*, *17*(1), 21–48.

Morris, W. (Ed.). (1985). *American Heritage Dictionary* (2nd College Edition edition). Houghton Mifflin.

Moshier, M. A. (1988). *Extensions to Unification Grammar for the Description of Programming Languages*. Ph.D. thesis, University of Michigan, Ann Arbor, MI.

Mosteller, F. and Wallace, D. L. (1964). Inference and Disputed Authorship: The Federalist. Springer-Verlag, New York. 2nd Edition appeared in 1984 and was called *Applied Bayesian and Classical Inference*.

Mostow, J. and Aist, G. (1999). Reading and pronunciation tutor.. U.S. Patent 5,920,838.

Munoz, M., Punyakanok, V., Roth, D., and Zimak, D. (1999). A learning approach to shallow parsing. In *Proceedings of the 1999 Joint SIGDAT Conference on Empirical Methods in Natural Language Processing and Very Large Corpora (EMNLP/VLC-99)*, College Park, MD, pp. 168–178. ACL.

Murata, T. (1989). Petri nets: Properties, analysis, and applications. *Proceedings of the IEEE*, *77*(4), 541–576.

Murveit, H., Butzberger, J. W., Digalakis, V. V., and Weintraub, M. (1993). Large-vocabulary dictation using SRI's decipher speech recognition system: Progressive-search techniques. In *IEEE ICASSP-93*, Vol. 2, pp. 319–322. IEEE.

Myers, J. L., Shinjo, M., and Duffy, S. A. (1987). Degree of causal relatedness and memory. *Journal of Verbal Learning and Verbal Behavior*, *26*, 453–465.

Nádas, A. (1984). Estimation of probabilities in the language model of the ibm speech recognition system. *IEEE Transactions on Acoustics, Speech, Signal Processing, 32*(4), 859–861.

Nagata, M. and Morimoto, T. (1994). First steps toward statistical modeling of dialogue to predict the speech act type of the next utterance. *Speech Communication, 15*, 193–203.

Narayanan, S. (1997a). *Knowledge-based Action Representations for Metaphor and Aspect (KARMA)*. Ph.D. thesis, University of California, Berkeley.

Narayanan, S. (1997b). Talking the talk *is* like walking the walk: A computational model of verbal aspect. In *COGSCI-97*, Stanford, CA, pp. 548–553.

Narayanan, S. and Jurafsky, D. (1998). Bayesian models of human sentence processing. In *COGSCI-98*, Madison, WI, pp. 752–757. LEA.

Naur, P., Backus, J. W., Bauer, F. L., Green, J., Katz, C., McCarthy, J., Perlis, A. J., Rutishauser, H., Samelson, K., Vauquois, B., Wegstein, J. H., van Wijnagaarden, A., and Woodger, M. (1960). Report on the algorithmic language ALGOL 60. *Communications of the ACM, 3*(5), 299–314. Revised in CACM 6:1, 1-17, 1963.

Needleman, S. B. and Wunsch, C. D. (1970). A general method applicable to the search for similarities in the amino-acid sequence of two proteins. *Journal of Molecular Biology, 48*, 443–453.

Nespor, M. and Vogel, I. (1986). *Prosodic phonology*. Foris, Dordrecht.

Neu, H. (1980). Ranking of constraints on /t,d/ deletion in American English: A statistical analysis. In Labov, W. (Ed.), *Locating Language in Time and Space*, pp. 37–54. Academic, New York.

Newell, A., Langer, S., and Hickey, M. (1998). The rôle of natural language processing in alternative and augmentative communication. *Natural Language Engineering, 4*(1), 1–16.

Newman, S. (1944). *Yokuts Language of California*. Viking Fund Publications in Anthropology 2, New York.

Ney, H., Essen, U., and Kneser, R. (1994). On structuring probabilistic dependencies in stochastic language modelling. *Computer Speech and Language, 8*, 1–38.

Ney, H., Haeb-Umbach, R., Tran, B.-H., and Oerder, M. (1992). Improvements in beam search for 10000-word continuous speech recognition. In *IEEE ICASSP-92*, San Francisco, CA, pp. I.9–12. IEEE.

Ney, H. (1991). Dynamic programming parsing for context-free grammars in continuous speech recognition. *IEEE Transactions on Signal Processing, 39*(2), 336–340.

Ng, H. T. and Lee, H. B. (1996). Integrating multiple knowledge sources to disambiguate word senses: An exemplar-based approach. In *ACL-96*, Santa Cruz, CA, pp. 40–47. ACL.

Ng, H. T. and Zelle, J. (1997). Corpus-based approaches to semantic interpretation in NLP. *AI Magazine, 18*(4), 45–64.

Nguyen, L. and Schwartz, R. (1999). Single-tree method for grammar-directed search. In *IEEE ICASSP-99*, pp. 613–616. IEEE.

Nichols, J. (1986). Head-marking and dependent-marking grammar. *Language, 62*(1), 56–119.

Nida, E. A. (1975). *Componential Analysis of Meaning: An Introduction to Semantic Structures*. Mouton, The Hague.

Nielsen, J. (1992). The usability engineering life cycle. *IEEE Computer*, 12–22.

Niesler, T. R. and Woodland, P. C. (1996). A variable-length category-based n-gram language model. In *IEEE ICASSP-96*, Atlanta, GA, Vol. I, pp. 164–167. IEEE.

Niesler, T. R. and Woodland, P. C. (1999). Modelling word-pair relations in a category-based language model. In *IEEE ICASSP-99*, pp. 795–798. IEEE.

Nilsson, N. J. (1980). *Principles of Artificial Intelligence*. Morgan Kaufmann, Los Altos, CA.

Nirenburg, S., Lesser, V., and Nyberg, E. H. (1989). Controlling a language generation planner. In *IJCAI-89*, pp. 1524–1530.

Nirenburg, S., Carbonell, J., Tomita, M., and Goodman, K. (1992). *Machine Transla-*

tion: A Knowledge-based Approach. Morgan Kaufmann.

Norman, D. A. and Rumelhart, D. E. (1975). *Explorations in Cognition.* Freeman, San Francisco, CA.

Norvig, P. (1987). *A Unified Theory of Inference for Text Understanding.* Ph.D. thesis, University of California, Berkeley, CA. Available as University of California at Berkeley Computer Science Division Tech. rep. #87/339.

Norvig, P. (1991). Techniques for automatic memoization with applications to context-free parsing. *Computational Linguistics, 17*(1), 91–98.

Oard, D. W. (1997). Alternative approaches for cross-language text retrieval. In *AAAI Spring Symposium on Cross-Language Text and Speech Retrieval.*

Odell, M. K. and Russell, R. C. (1918/1922). U.S. Patents 1261167 (1918), 1435663 (1922)†. Cited in Knuth (1973).

Oden, G. C. and Massaro, D. W. (1978). Integration of featural information in speech perception. *Psychological Review, 85,* 172–191.

O'Donnell, M. J. (1994). *Sentence Analysis and generation: A Systemic Perspective.* Ph.D. thesis, University of Sydney.

Oehrle, R. T., Bach, E., and Wheeler, D. (Eds.). (1988). *Categorial Grammars and Natural Language Structures.* D. Reidel, Dordrecht.

Oflazer, K. (1993). Two-level description of Turkish morphology. In *Proceedings, Sixth Conference of the European Chapter of the ACL.*

Ogburn, W. F. and Thomas, D. S. (1922). Are inventions inevitable? a note on social evolution. *Political Science Quarterly, 37,* 83–98.

Oncina, J., García, P., and Vidal, E. (1993). Learning subsequential transducers for pattern recognition tasks. *IEEE Transactions on Pattern Analysis and Machine Intelligence, 15,* 448–458.

Oppenheim, A., Schafer, R., and Stockham, T. J. (1968). Nonlinear filtering of multiplied and convolved signals. *Proceedings of the IEEE, 56*(8), 1264–1291.

Orgun, O. (1995). A declarative theory of phonology-morphology interleaving. Unpublished manuscript, U. of California-Berkeley, Department of Linguistics.

Ortony, A. (Ed.). (1993). *Metaphor* (2nd edition). Cambridge University Press, Cambridge.

Ostendorf, M. and Veilleux, N. (1994). A hierarchical stochastic model for automatic prediction of prosodic boundary location. *Computational Linguistics, 20*(1).

Oviatt, S., Cohen, P. R., Wang, M. Q., and Gaston, J. (1993). A simulation-based research strategy for designing complex NL sysems. In *Proceedings DARPA Speech and Natural Language Workshop,* Princeton, NJ, pp. 370–375. Morgan Kaufmann.

Oviatt, S., MacEachern, M., and Levow, G.-A. (1998). Predicting hyperarticulate speech during human-computer error resolution. *Speech Communication, 24,* 87–110.

Packard, D. W. (1973). Computer-assisted morphological analysis of ancient Greek. In Zampolli, A. and Calzolari, N. (Eds.), *Computational and Mathematical Linguistics: Proceedings of the International Conference on Computational Linguistics,* Pisa, pp. 343–355. Leo S. Olschki.

Palmer, M. and Finin, T. (1990). Workshop on the evaluation of natural language processing systems. *Computational Linguistics, 16*(3), 175–181.

Paris, C. (1993). *User Modelling in Text Generation.* Pinter, London.

Paris, C. et al. (1995). A support tool for writing multilingual instructions. In *IJCAI-95,* pp. 1398–1404.

Paris, C. and Vander Linden, K. (1996). Drafter: An interactive support tool for writing multilingual instructions. *IEEE Computer, 29*(7), 49–56.

Paris, C., Vander Linden, K., and Lu, S. (1998). Automatic document creation from software specifications. In Kay, J. and Milosavljevic, M. (Eds.), *Proceedings of the 3rd Australian Document Computing Symposium (ADCS-98), Sydney, August,* pp. 26–31.

Parsons, T. (1990). *Events in the Semantics of English*. MIT Press, Cambridge, MA.

Partee, B. H. (Ed.). (1976). *Montague Grammar*. Academic Press, New York.

Partee, B. H., ter Meulen, A., and Wall, R. E. (1990). *Mathematical Methods in Linguistics*. Kluwer, Dordrecht.

Passonneau, R. and Litman, D. J. (1993). Intention-based segmentation: Human reliability and correlation with linguistic cues. In *ACL-93*, Columbus, Ohio, pp. 148–155. ACL.

Patten, T. (1988). *Systemic Text Generation as Problem Solving*. Cambridge University Press.

Paul, D. B. (1991). Algorithms for an optimal A* search and linearizing the search in the stack decoder. In *IEEE ICASSP-91*, Vol. 1, pp. 693–696. IEEE.

Pearl, J. (1984). *Heuristics*. Addison-Wesley, Reading, MA.

Pearlmutter, N. J. and MacDonald, M. C. (1992). Plausibility and syntactic ambiguity resolution. In *COGSCI-92*, pp. 498–503.

Pedersen, T. and Bruce, R. (1997). Distinguishing word senses in untagged text. In *Proceedings of the Conference on Empirical Methods in Natural Language Processing (EMNLP-97)*, Providence, RI.

Percival, W. K. (1976). On the historical source of immediate constituent analysis. In McCawley, J. D. (Ed.), *Syntax and Semantics Volume 7, Notes from the Linguistic Underground*, pp. 229–242. Academic Press, New York.

Pereira, F. (1985). A structure-sharing representation for unification-based grammar formalisms. In *ACL-85*, Chicago, pp. 137–144.

Pereira, F., Riley, M. D., and Sproat, R. (1994). Weighted rational transductions and their applications to human language processing. In *ARPA Human Language Technology Workshop*, Plainsboro, NJ, pp. 262–267. Morgan Kaufmann.

Pereira, F. and Shieber, S. M. (1984). The semantics of grammar formalisms seen as computer languages. In *COLING-84*, Stanford, CA, pp. 123–129.

Pereira, F. and Shieber, S. M. (1987). *Prolog and Natural-Language Analysis*, Vol. 10 of *CSLI Lecture Notes*. Chicago University Press, Chicago.

Pereira, F. and Warren, D. H. D. (1980). Definite clause grammars for language analysis— a survey of the formalism and a comparison with augmented transition networks. *Artificial Intelligence*, 13(3), 231–278.

Pereira, F. and Wright, R. N. (1997). Finite-state approximation of phrase-structure grammars. In Roche, E. and Schabes, Y. (Eds.), *Finite-State Devices for Natural Language Processing*, pp. 149–174. MIT Press, Cambridge, MA.

Perrault, C. R. and Allen, J. (1980). A plan-based analysis of indirect speech acts. *American Journal of Computational Linguistics*, 6(3-4), 167–182.

Peterson, J. L. (1986). A note on undetected typing errors. *Communications of the ACM*, 29(7), 633–637.

Picone, J. (1993). Signal modeling techniques in speech recognition. *Proceedings of the IEEE*, 81(9), 1215–1247.

Pierce, C. S. (1955). Abduction and induction. In Buchler, J. (Ed.), *Philosophical Writings of Pierce*, pp. 150–156. Dover Books, New York.

Pierre, I. (1984). Another look at nominal compounds. In *COLING-84*, Stanford, CA, pp. 509–516.

Pierrehumbert, J. and Hirschberg, J. (1990). The meaning of intonational contours in the interpretation of discourse. In Cohen, P. R., Morgan, J., and Pollack, M. (Eds.), *Intentions in Communication*, pp. 271–311. MIT Press, Cambridge, MA.

Pierrehumbert, J. (1980). *The Phonology and Phonetics of English Intonation*. Ph.D. thesis, MIT.

Pinker, S. (1989). *Learnability and Cognition: The acquisition of argument structure*. MIT Press, Cambridge.

Pinker, S. and Prince, A. (1988). On language and connectionism: Analysis of a Parallel Distributed Processing model of language acquisition. *Cognition*, 28, 73–193.

Placeway, P., Schwartz, R., Fung, P., and Nguyen, L. (1993). The estimation of powerful language models from small and large corpora. In *IEEE ICASSP-93*, Vol. 2, pp. 33–36. IEEE.

Plunkett, K. and Marchman, V. (1991). U-shaped learning and frequency effects in a multi-layered perceptron: Implications for child language acquisition. *Cognition, 38*, 43–102.

Poesio, M. and Vieira, R. (1998). A corpus-based investigation of definite description use. *Computational Linguistics, 24*(2), 183–216.

Polanyi, L. (1988). A formal model of the structure of discourse. *Journal of Pragmatics, 12*.

Polifroni, J., Hirschman, L., Seneff, S., and Zue, V. (1992). Experiments in evaluating interactive spoken language systems. In *Proceedings DARPA Speech and Natural Language Workshop*, Harriman, New York, pp. 28–33. Morgan Kaufmann.

Pollard, C. and Moshier, M. A. (1990). Unifying partial descriptions of sets. In Hanson, P. P. (Ed.), *Information, Language, and Cognition*, pp. 285–322. University of British Columbia Press, Vancouver.

Pollard, C. and Sag, I. A. (1987). *Information-Based Syntax and Semantics: Volume 1: Fundamentals*. University of Chicago Press, Chicago.

Pollard, C. and Sag, I. A. (1994). *Head-Driven Phrase Structure Grammar*. University of Chicago Press, Chicago.

Porter, M. F. (1980). An algorithm for suffix stripping. *Program, 14*(3), 130–127.

Power, R. (1979). The organization of purposeful dialogs. *Linguistics, 17*, 105–152.

Price, P., Fisher, W., Bernstein, J., and Pallet, D. (1988). The DARPA 1000-word resource management database for continuous speech recognition. In *IEEE ICASSP-88*, New York, Vol. 1, pp. 651–654. IEEE.

Prince, A. and Smolensky, P. (1993). Optimality theory: Constraint interaction in generative grammar. Tech. rep. CU-CS-696-93, Department of Computer Science, University of Colorado at Boulder, and

RuCCs Tech. rep. TR-2, Cognitive Science Center, Rutgers University. [to appear, MIT Press, Cambridge, MA].

Prince, E. (1981). Toward a taxonomy of given-new information. In Cole, P. (Ed.), *Radical Pragmatics*, pp. 223–255. Academic Press, New York, New York.

Prince, E. (1992). The ZPG letter: Subjects, definiteness, and information-status. In Thompson, S. and Mann, W. (Eds.), *Discourse Description: Diverse Analyses of a Fundraising Text*, pp. 295–325. John Benjamins, Philadelphia/Amsterdam.

Pritchett, B. (1988). Garden path phenomena and the grammatical basis of language processing. *Language, 64*(3), 539–576.

Procter, P. (Ed.). (1978). *Longman Dictionary of Contemporary English*. Longman Group, Essex, England.

Prüst, H. (1992). *On Discourse Structuring, VP Anaphora, and Gapping*. Ph.D. thesis, University of Amsterdam.

Pullum, G. K. and Gazdar, G. (1982). Natural languages and context-free languages. *Linguistics and Philosophy, 4*, 471–504.

Pullum, G. K. (1991). *The Great Eskimo Vocabulary Hoax*. University of Chicago, Chicago, IL.

Pullum, G. K. and Ladusaw, W. A. (1996). *Phonetic Symbol Guide.* University of Chicago, Chicago, IL. Second Edition.

Pustejovsky, J. (1995). *The Generative Lexicon*. MIT Press, Cambridge, MA.

Pustejovsky, J. and Bergler, S. (Eds.). (1992). *Lexical Semantics and Knowledge Representation*. Lecture Notes in Artificial Intelligence. Springer Verlag, Berlin.

Quillian, M. R. (1968). Semantic memory. In Minsky, M. (Ed.), *Semantic Information Processing*, pp. 227–270. MIT Press, Cambridge, MA.

Quinlan, J. R. (1986). Induction of decision trees. *Machine Learning, 1*, 81–106.

Quirk, R., Greenbaum, S., Leech, G., and Svartvik, J. (1985). *A Comprehensive Grammar of the English Language*. Longman, London.

Rabin, M. O. and Scott, D. (1959). Finite automata and their decision problems.

IBM Journal of Research and Development, *3*(2), 114–125.

Rabiner, L. R. (1989). A tutorial on Hidden Markov Models and selected applications in speech recognition. *Proceedings of the IEEE*, *77*(2), 257–286.

Rabiner, L. R. and Juang, B. (1993). *Fundamentals of Speech Recognition*. Prentice Hall, Englewood Cliffs, NJ.

Radford, A. (1988). *Transformational Grammar: A First Course*. Cambridge University Press, Cambridge.

Ramshaw, L. A. and Marcus, M. P. (1995). Text chunking using transformation-based learning. In *Proceedings of the Third Annual Workshop on Very Large Corpora*, pp. 82–94. ACL.

Raphael, B. (1968). SIR: A computer program for semantic information retrieval. In Minsky, M. (Ed.), *Semantic Information Processing*, pp. 33–145. MIT Press.

Ratnaparkhi, A. (1996). A maximum entropy part-of-speech tagger. In *Proceedings of the Conference on Empirical Methods in Natural Language Processing*, University of Pennsylvania, pp. 133–142. ACL.

Ratnaparkhi, A. (1997). A linear observed time statistical parser based on maximum entropy models. In *Proceedings of the Second Conference on Empirical Methods in Natural Language Processing*, Providence, Rhode Island, pp. 1–10. ACL.

Ratnaparkhi, A., Reynar, J., and Roukos, S. (1994). A Maximum Entropy model for prepositional phrase attachment. In *ARPA Human Language Technologies Workshop*, Plainsboro, N.J., pp. 250–255.

Ravishankar, M. (1996). *Efficient Algorithms for Speech Recognition*. Ph.D. thesis, School of Computer Science, Carnegie Mellon University, Pittsburgh. Available as CMU CS tech report CMU-CS-96-143.

Reeves, B. and Nass, C. (1996). *The Media Equation: How People Treat Computers, Television, and New Media Like Real People and Places*. Cambridge University Press, Cambridge.

Regier, T. (1996). *The Human Semantic Potential*. MIT Press, Cambridge, MA.

Reichenbach, H. (1947). *Elements of Symbolic Logic*. Macmillan, New York.

Reichert, T. A., Cohen, D. N., and Wong, A. K. C. (1973). An application of information theory to genetic mutations and the matching of polypeptide sequences. *Journal of Theoretical Biology*, *42*, 245–261.

Reichman, R. (1985). *Getting Computers to Talk Like You and Me*. MIT Press, Cambridge, MA.

Reiter, E. (1990). A new model for lexical choice for open-class words. In McKeown, K. R., Moore, J. D., and Nirenburg, S. (Eds.), *Proceedings of the Fifth International Workshop on Natural Language Generation*, Dawson, PA, pp. 23–30.

Reiter, E. and Dale, R. (2000). *Building Natural Language Generation Systems*. Cambridge University Press, Cambridge. To appear.

Reiter, E., Robertson, R., and Osman, L. (1999). Types of knowledge required to personalise smoking cessation letters. In *Proceedings of the Joint European Conference on Artificial Intelligence in Medicine and Medical Decision Making*. Springer-Verlag.

Reiter, R. (1980). A logic for default reasoning. *Artificial Intelligence*, *13*, 81–132.

Reithinger, N., Engel, R., Kipp, M., and Klesen, M. (1996). Predicting dialogue acts for a speech-to-speech translation system. In *ICSLP-96*, Philadelphia, PA, Vol. 2, pp. 654–657.

Reithinger, N. and Klesen, M. (1997). Dialogue act classification using language models. In *EUROSPEECH-97*, Vol. 4, pp. 2235–2238.

Resnik, P. (1992). Probabilistic tree-adjoining grammar as a framework for statistical natural language processing. In *COLING-92*, Nantes, France, pp. 418–424.

Resnik, P. (1997). Selectional preference and sense disambiguation. In *Proceedings of ACL SIGLEX Workshop on Tagging Text with Lexical Semantics*, Washington, D.C., pp. 52–57. ACL.

Resnik, P. (1998). Wordnet and class-based probabilities. In Fellbaum, C. (Ed.), *WordNet: An Electronic Lexical Database*. MIT Press, Cambridge, MA.

Rhodes, F. L. (1929). *Beginnings of telephony*. Harper and Brothers, New York.

Rhodes, R. A. (1992). Flapping in American English. In Dressler, W. U., Prinzhorn, M., and Rennison, J. (Eds.), *Proceedings of the 7th International Phonology Meeting*, pp. 217–232. Rosenberg and Sellier.

Riesbeck, C. K. (1975). Conceptual analysis. In Schank, R. C. (Ed.), *Conceptual Information Processing*, pp. 83–156. American Elsevier, New York.

Riesbeck, C. K. (1986). From conceptual analyzer to direct memory access parsing: An overview. In *Advances in Cognitive Science 1*, pp. 236–258. Ellis Horwood, Chichester.

Riley, M. D. (1991). A statistical model for generating pronunciation networks. In *IEEE ICASSP-91*, pp. 737–740. IEEE.

Riley, M. D. (1992). Tree-based modelling for speech synthesis. In Bailly, G. and Benoit, C. (Eds.), *Talking Machines: Theories, Models and Designs*. North Holland, Amsterdam.

Riloff, E. (1993). Automatically constructing a dictionary for information extraction tasks. In *AAAI-93*, Washington, D.C., pp. 811–816.

Riloff, E. and Schmelzenbach, M. (1998). An empirical approach to conceptual case frame acquisition. In *Proceedings of the Sixth Workshop on Very Large Corpora*, Montreal, Canada, pp. 49–56.

Rivest, R. L. (1987). Learning decision lists. *Machine Learning*, 2(3), 229–246.

Robins, R. H. (1967). *A Short History of Linguistics*. Indiana University Press, Bloomington.

Robinson, J. A. (1965). A machine-oriented logic based on the resolution principle. *Journal of the Association for Computing Machinery*, 12, 23–41.

Robinson, J. J. (1975). Performance grammars. In Reddy, D. R. (Ed.), *Speech Recognition: Invited Paper Presented at the 1974 IEEE Symposium*, pp. 401–427. Academic Press, New York.

Robinson, S. E. and Sparck Jones, K. (1976). Relevance weighting of search terms. *Journal of the American Society for Information Science*, 27, 129–146.

Rocchio, J. J. (1971). Relevance feedback in information retrieval. In *The SMART Retrieval System: Experiments in Automatic Indexing*, pp. 324–336. Prentice Hall, Englewood Cliffs, NJ.

Roche, E. and Schabes, Y. (1997a). Deterministic part-of-speech tagging with finite-state transducers. In Roche, E. and Schabes, Y. (Eds.), *Finite-State Devices for Natural Language Processing*, pp. 205–239. MIT Press, Cambridge, MA.

Roche, E. and Schabes, Y. (1997b). Introduction. In Roche, E. and Schabes, Y. (Eds.), *Finite-State Devices for Natural Language Processing*, pp. 1–65. MIT Press, Cambridge, MA.

Roelofs, A. (1997). The WEAVER model of word-form encoding in speech production. *Cognition*, 64, 249–284.

Roland, D. and Jurafsky, D. (1998). How verb subcategorization frequencies are affected by corpus choice. In *COLING/ACL-98*, Montreal, pp. 1122–1128. ACL.

Rosenfeld, R. (1996). A maximum entropy approach to adaptive statistical language modeling. *Computer Speech and Language*, 10, 187–228.

Roth, D. (1998). Learning to resolve natural language ambiguities: A unified approach. In *AAAI-98*, pp. 806–813.

Roth, D. (1999). Learning in natural language. In *IJCAI-99*, pp. 898–904.

Roth, D. and Zelenko, D. (1998). Part of speech tagging using a network of linear separators. In *COLING/ACL-98*, Montreal, pp. 1136–1142. ACL.

Rounds, W. C. and Kasper, R. T. (1986). A complete logical calculus for record structures representing linguistic information. In *Proceedings of the 1st Annual IEEE Symposium on Logic in Computer Science*, pp. 38–43.

Rumelhart, D. E., Hinton, G. E., and Williams, R. J. (1986). Learning internal representations by error propagation. In Rumelhart, D. E. and McClelland, J. L. (Eds.), *Parallel Distributed Processing*, Vol. 2, pp. 318–362. MIT Press.

Rumelhart, D. E. and McClelland, J. L. (1986). On learning the past tense of English verbs. In Rumelhart, D. E. and McClelland, J. L. (Eds.), *Parallel Distributed Processing*, Vol. 2, pp. 216–271. MIT Press.

Russell, S. and Norvig, P. (1995). *Artificial Intelligence: A Modern Approach*. Prentice Hall, Englewood Cliffs, NJ.

Russell, S. W. (1976). Computer understanding of metaphorically used verbs. *American Journal of Computational Linguistics*, 2. Microfiche 44.

Ryder, M. E. (1994). *Ordered Chaos: The Interpretation of English Noun-Noun Compounds*. University of California Press, Berkeley.

Sacks, H., Schegloff, E. A., and Jefferson, G. (1974). A simplest systematics for the organization of turn-taking for conversation. *Language*, 50(4), 696–735.

Saffran, J. R., Aslin, R. N., and Newport, E. L. (1996). Statistical cues in language acquisition: Word segmentation by infants. In *COGSCI-96*, pp. 376–380.

Sag, I. A. and Liberman, M. (1975). The intonational disambiguation of indirect speech acts. In *CLS-75*, pp. 487–498. University of Chicago.

Sag, I. A. and Wasow, T. (Eds.). (1999). *Syntactic Theory: A Formal Introduction*. CSLI Publications, Stanford, CA.

Saint-Dizier, P. and Viegas, E. (Eds.). (1995). *Computational Lexical Semantics*. Cambridge University Press, New York.

Sakoe, H. and Chiba, S. (1971). A dynamic programming approach to continuous speech recognition. In *Proceedings of the Seventh International Congress on Acoustics, Budapest*, Budapest, Vol. 3, pp. 65–69. Akadémiai Kiadó.

Sakoe, H. and Chiba, S. (1984). Dynamic programming algorithm optimization for spoken word recognition. *IEEE Transactions on Acoustics, Speech, and Signal Processing*, ASSP-26(1), 43–49.

Salasoo, A. and Pisoni, D. B. (1985). Interaction of knowledge sources in spoken word identification. *Journal of Memory and Language*, 24, 210–231.

Salomaa, A. (1969). Probabilistic and weighted grammars. *Information and Control*, 15, 529–544.

Salton, G. (1971). *The SMART Retrieval System: Experiments in Automatic Document Processing*. Prentice Hall, Englewood Cliffs, NJ.

Salton, G., Allan, J., and Buckley, C. (1993). Approaches to passage retrieval in full text information systems. In *SIGIR-93*, Pittsburgh, PA, pp. 49–58. ACM.

Salton, G. and Buckley, C. (1988). Term weighting approaches in automatic text retrieval. *Information Processing and Management*, 24, 513–523. Also available in Sparck Jones and Willett (1997).

Salton, G. and Buckley, C. (1990). Improving retrieval performance by relevance feedback. *Information Processing and Management*, 41, 288–297.

Salton, G. and McGill, M. J. (1983). *Introduction to Modern Information Retrieval*. McGraw-Hill, New York, NY.

Sampson, G. (1987). Alternative grammatical coding systems. In Garside, R., Leech, G., and Sampson, G. (Eds.), *The Computational Analysis of English*, pp. 165–183. Longman, London and New York.

Sampson, G. (1996). *Evolutionary Language Understanding*. Cassell, London.

Samuel, A. G. (1981). Phonemic restoration: Insights from a new methodology. *Journal of Experimental Psychology: General*, 110, 474–494.

Samuel, K., Carberry, S., and Vijay-Shanker, K. (1998a). Computing dialogue acts from features with transformation-based learning. In Chu-Carroll, J. and Green, N. (Eds.), *Applying Machine Learning to Discourse Processing. Papers from the 1998 AAAI Spring Symposium*, pp. 90–97. Technical Report SS-98-01.

Samuel, K., Carberry, S., and Vijay-Shanker, K. (1998b). Dialogue act tagging with transformation-based learning. In *COLING/ACL-98*, Montreal, Vol. 2, pp. 1150–1156. ACL.

Samuelsson, C. and Reichl, W. (1999). A class-based language model for large-vocabulary speech recognition extracted from part-of-speech statistics. In *IEEE ICASSP-99*, pp. 537–540. IEEE.

Sanders, T. J. M., Spooren, W. P. M., and Noordman, L. G. M. (1992). Toward a taxonomy of coherence relations. *Discourse Processes*, *15*, 1–35.

Sanderson, M. (1994). Word sense disambiguation and information retrieval. In *SIGIR-94*, Dublin, Ireland, pp. 142–151. ACM.

Sanfilippo, A. (1993). LKB encoding of lexical knowledge. In Briscoe, T., de Paiva, V., and Copestake, A. (Eds.), *Inheritance, Defaults, and the Lexicon*, pp. 190–222. Cambridge University Press, Cambridge.

Sankoff, D. (1972). Matching sequences under deletion-insertion constraints. *Proceedings of the Natural Academy of Sciences of the U.S.A.*, *69*, 4–6.

Sankoff, D. and Kruskal, J. B. (Eds.). (1983). *Time Warps, String Edits, and Macromolecules: The Theory and Practice of Sequence Comparison*. Addison-Wesley, Reading, MA.

Sato, S. and Nagao, M. (1990). Toward memory-based translation. In *COLING-90*, Helsinki, pp. 247–252.

Scha, R. and Polanyi, L. (1988). An augmented context free grammar for discourse. In *COLING-88*, Budapest, pp. 573–577.

Schabes, Y. (1990). *Mathematical and Computational Aspects of Lexicalized Grammars*. Ph.D. thesis, University of Pennsylvania, Philadelphia, PA†.

Schabes, Y. (1992). Stochastic lexicalized tree-adjoining grammars. In *COLING-92*, Nantes, France, pp. 426–433.

Schabes, Y., Abeillé, A., and Joshi, A. K. (1988). Parsing strategies with 'lexicalized' grammars: Applications to Tree Adjoining Grammars. In *COLING-88*, Budapest, pp. 578–583.

Schachter, P. (1985). Parts-of-speech systems. In Shopen, T. (Ed.), *Language Typology and Syntactic Description, Volume 1*, pp. 3–61. Cambridge University Press.

Schank, R. C. (1972). Conceptual dependency: A theory of natural language processing. *Cognitive Psychology*, *3*, 552–631.

Schank, R. C. and Albelson, R. P. (1977). *Scripts, Plans, Goals and Understanding*. Lawrence Erlbaum, Hillsdale, NJ.

Schank, R. C. and Riesbeck, C. K. (Eds.). (1981). *Inside Computer Understanding: Five Programs plus Miniatures*. Lawrence Erlbaum, Hillsdale, NJ.

Schegloff, E. A. (1968). Sequencing in conversational openings. *American Anthropologist*, *70*, 1075–1095.

Schegloff, E. A. (1982). Discourse as an interactional achievement: Some uses of 'uh huh' and other things that come between sentences. In Tannen, D. (Ed.), *Analyzing Discourse: Text and Talk*, pp. 71–93. Georgetown University Press, Washington, D.C.

Schönkfinkel, M. (1924). Über die Bausteine der mathematischen Logik. *Mathematische Annalen*, *92*, 305–316. English Translation appears in *From Frege to Gödel: A Source Book in Mathematical Logic*, Harvard University Press, Cambridge, MA, 1967.

Schubert, L. K. and Pelletier, F. J. (1982). From English to logic: Context-free computation of 'conventional' logical translation. *American Journal of Computational Linguistics*, *8*(1), 27–44.

Schütze, H. (1992). Dimensions of meaning. In *Proceedings of Supercomputing '92*, pp. 787–796. IEEE, IEEE Press.

Schütze, H. (1997). *Ambiguity Resolution in Language Learning: Computational and Cognitive Models*. CSLI Publications, Stanford, CA.

Schütze, H. (1998). Automatic word sense discrimination. *Computational Linguistics*, *24*(1), 97–124.

Schütze, H. and Pedersen, J. (1995). Information retrieval based on word senses. In *Proceedings of the Fourth Annual Symposium on Document Analysis and Information Retrieval*, Las Vegas, pp. 161–175.

Schütze, H. and Singer, Y. (1994). Part-of-speech tagging using a variable memory Markov model. In *ACL-94*, Las Cruces, NM, pp. 181–187. ACL.

Schwartz, R. and Chow, Y.-L. (1990). The N-best algorithm: An efficient and exact procedure for finding the N most likely sentence hypotheses. In *IEEE ICASSP-90*, Vol. 1, pp. 81–84. IEEE.

Schwartz, R., Chow, Y.-L., Kimball, O., Roukos, S., Krasnwer, M., and Makhoul, J. (1985). Context-dependent modeling for acoustic-phonetic recognition of continuous speech. In *IEEE ICASSP-85*, Vol. 3, pp. 1205–1208. IEEE.

Scott, D. R. and Souza, C. (1990). Getting the message across in RST-based text generation. In Dale, R., Mellish, C., and Zock, M. (Eds.), *Current Research in Natural Language Generation*, chap. 3. Academic Press.

Searle, J. R. (1975a). Indirect speech acts. In Cole, P. and Morgan, J. L. (Eds.), *Speech Acts: Syntax and Semantics Volume 3*, pp. 59–82. Academic Press, New York.

Searle, J. R. (1975b). A taxonomy of illocutionary acts. In Gunderson, K. (Ed.), *Language, Mind and Knowledge, Minnesota Studies in the Philosophy of Science*, Vol. VII, pp. 344–369. University of Minnesota Press, Amsterdam. Also appears in John R. Searle, *Expression and Meaning: Studies in the Theory of Speech Acts*, Cambridge University Press, 1979.

Searle, J. R. (1980). Minds, brains, and programs. *Behavioral and Brain Sciences*, *3*, 417–457.

Selkirk, E. (1986). On derived domains in sentence phonology. *Phonology Yearbook*, *3*, 371–405.

Seymore, K., Chen, S., and Rosenfeld, R. (1998). Nonlinear interpolation of topic models for language model adaptation. In *ICSLP-98*, Sydney, Vol. 6, p. 2503.

Seymore, K. and Rosenfeld, R. (1997). Using story topics for language model adaptation. In *EUROSPEECH-97*, pp. 1987–1990.

Shannon, C. E. (1938). A symbolic analysis of relay and switching circuits. *Transactions of the American Institute of Electrical Engineers*, *57*, 713–723.

Shannon, C. E. (1948). A mathematical theory of communication. *Bell System Technical Journal*, *27*(3), 379–423. Continued in following volume.

Shannon, C. E. (1951). Prediction and entropy of printed English. *Bell System Technical Journal*, *30*, 50–64.

Shaw, W. M., Burgin, R., and Howell, P. (1996). Performance standards and evaluations in ir test collections: Cluster-based retrieval models. *Information Processing and Management*, *33*(1), 1–14.

Sheil, B. A. (1976). Observations on context free parsing. *SMIL: Statistical Methods in Linguistics*, *1*, 71–109.

Shieber, S. M. (1985a). Evidence against the context-freeness of natural language. *Linguistics and Philosophy*, *8*, 333–343.

Shieber, S. M. (1985b). Using restriction to extend parsing algorithms for complex-feature-based formalisms. In *ACL-85*, Chicago, pp. 145–152.

Shieber, S. M. (1986). *An Introduction to Unification-Based Approaches to Grammar*. University of Chicago Press, Chicago.

Shieber, S. M. (1994). Lessons from a restricted Turing test. *Communications of the ACM*, *37*(6), 70–78.

Shinghal, R. and Toussaint, G. T. (1979). Experiments in text recognition with the modified Viterbi algorithm. *IEEE Transactions on Pattern Analysis and Machine Intelligence*, *PAMI-1*, 184–193.

Shoup, J. E. (1980). Phonological aspects of speech recognition. In Lea, W. A. (Ed.), *Trends in Speech Recognition*, pp. 125–138. Prentice-Hall, Englewood Cliffs, NJ.

Shriberg, E. (1994). *Preliminaries to a Theory of Speech Disfluencies*. Ph.D. thesis, University of California, Berkeley, CA.

Shriberg, E., Bates, R., Taylor, P., Stolcke, A., Jurafsky, D., Ries, K., Coccaro, N., Martin, R., Meteer, M., and Ess-Dykema, C. V. (1998). Can prosody aid the automatic classification of dialog acts in conversational speech?. *Language and Speech (Special Issue on Prosody and Conversation)*, *41*(3-4), 439–487.

Shriberg, E., Wade, E., and Price, P. (1992). Human-machine problem solving using spoken language systems (SLS): Factors affecting performance and user satisfaction. In *Proceedings DARPA Speech and Natural Language Workshop*, Harriman, New York, pp. 49–54. Morgan Kaufmann.

Sidner, C. (1979). Towards a computational theory of definite anaphora comprehension in English discourse. Tech. rep. 537, MIT Artificial Intelligence Laboratory, Cambridge, MA.

Sidner, C. (1983). Focusing in the comprehension of definite anaphora. In Brady, M. and Berwick, R. C. (Eds.), *Computational Models of Discourse*, pp. 267–330. MIT Press, Cambridge, MA.

Siegel, S. and Castellan, Jr., N. J. (1988). *Nonparametric Statistics for the Behavioral Sciences* (Second edition). McGraw-Hill, New York.

Sills, D. L. and Merton, R. K. (Eds.). (1991). *Social Science Quotations*. MacMillan, New York.

Silverman, K., Beckman, M. E., Pitrelli, J., Ostendorf, M., Wightman, C., Price, P., Pierrehumbert, J., and Hirschberg, J. (1992). ToBI: a standard for labelling English prosody. In *ICSLP-92*, Vol. 2, pp. 867–870.

Silverstein, C., Henzinger, M., Marais, H., and Moricz, M. (1998). Analysis of a very large AltaVista query log. Tech. rep. 1998-014, Digital Systems Research Center.

Simmons, R. and Slocum, J. (1972). Generating English discourse from semantic networks. *Communications of the ACM*, *15*(10), 891–905.

Simmons, R. F. (1965). Answering English questions by computer: A survey. *Communications of the ACM*, *8*(1), 53–70.

Simmons, R. F. (1973). Semantic networks: Their computation and use for understanding English sentences. In Schank, R. C. and Colby, K. M. (Eds.), *Computer Models of Thought and Language*, pp. 61–113. W.H. Freeman and Co., San Francisco.

Simmons, R. F. (1978). Rule-based computations on English. In Waterman, D. A. and Hayes-Roth, F. (Eds.), *Pattern-Directed Inference Systems*. Academic Press, New York.

Simmons, R. F. (1983). *Computations from the English*. Prentice Hall, Englewood Cliffs.

Singer, M. (1979). Processes of inference during sentence encoding. *Memory & Cognition*, *7*(3), 192–200.

Singer, M. (1980). The role of case-filling inferences in the coherence of brief passages. *Discourse Processes*, *3*, 185–201.

Singer, M. (1994). Discourse inference processes. In Gernsbacher, M. A. (Ed.), *Handbook of Psycholinguistics*, pp. 479–515. Academic Press, New York.

Sleator, D. and Temperley, D. (1993). Parsing English with a link grammar. In *Proceeedings, Third International Workshop on Parsing Technologies*, Tilburg, The Netherlands/Durbuy, Belgium.

Slobin, D. I. (1996). Two ways to travel. In Shibatani, M. and Thompson, S. A. (Eds.), *Grammatical Constructions: Their Form and Meaning*, pp. 195–220. Clarendon Press, Oxford.

Small, S. L., Cottrell, G. W., and Tanenhaus, M. (Eds.). (1988). *Lexical Ambiguity Resolution*. Morgan Kaufman, San Mateo, CA.

Small, S. L. and Rieger, C. (1982). Parsing and comprehending with Word Experts. In Lehnert, W. G. and Ringle, M. H. (Eds.), *Strategies for Natural Language Processing*, pp. 89–147. Lawrence Erlbaum, Hillsdale, NJ.

Smith, R. W. and Gordon, S. A. (1997). Effects of variable initiative on linguistic behavior in human-computer spoken natural language dialogue. *Computational Linguistics*, *23*(1), 141–168.

Smith, V. L. and Clark, H. H. (1993). On the course of answering questions. *Journal of Memory and Language*, *32*, 25–38.

Smyth, R. (1994). Grammatical determinants of ambiguous pronoun resolution. *Journal of Psycholinguistic Research*, *23*, 197–229.

Soderland, S., Fisher, D., Aseltine, J., and Lehnert, W. G. (1995). CRYSTAL: Inducing a conceptual dictionary. In *IJCAI-95*, Montreal, pp. 1134–1142.

Sparck Jones, K. (1972). A statistical interpretation of term specificity and its application in retrieval. *Journal of Documentation*, *28*(1), 11–21.

Sparck Jones, K. (1986). *Synonymy and Semantic Classification*. Edinburgh University Press, Edinburgh. Republication of 1964 PhD Thesis.

Sparck Jones, K. (1997). Summarization. In Cole, R. (Ed.), *Survey of the State of the Art in Human Language Technology*, pp. 232–235. Cambridge University Press, Cambridge.

Sparck Jones, K. and Willett, P. (Eds.). (1997). *Readings in Information Retrieval*. Morgan Kaufmann, San Francisco, CA.

Sproat, R. (1993). *Morphology and Computation*. MIT Press, Cambridge.

Sproat, R. (1994). English noun-phrase prediction for text-to-speech. *Computer Speech and Language*, *8*, 79–94.

Sproat, R. (1998a). Further issues in text analysis. In Sproat, R. (Ed.), *Multilingual Text-To-Speech Synthesis: The Bell Labs Approach*, pp. 89–114. Kluwer, Dordrecht.

Sproat, R. (Ed.). (1998b). *Multilingual Text-To-Speech Synthesis: The Bell Labs Approach*. Kluwer, Dordrecht.

Sproat, R., Möbius, B., Maeda, K., and Tzoukermann, E. (1998). Multilingual text analysis. In Sproat, R. (Ed.), *Multilingual Text-To-Speech Synthesis: The Bell Labs Approach*, pp. 31–86. Kluwer, Dordrecht.

Sproat, R. and Riley, M. D. (1996). Compilation of weighted finite-state transducers from decision trees. In *ACL-96*, Santa Cruz, CA, pp. 215–222. ACL.

Sproat, R., Shih, C., Gale, W. A., and Chang, N. (1996). A stochastic finite-state word-segmentation algorithm for Chinese. *Computational Linguistics*, *22*(3), 377–404.

Stalnaker, R. C. (1978). Assertion. In Cole, P. (Ed.), *Pragmatics: Syntax and Semantics Volume 9*, pp. 315–332. Academic Press, New York.

Stanners, R. F., Neiser, J., Hernon, W. P., and Hall, R. (1979). Memory representation for morphologically related words. *Journal of Verbal Learning and Verbal Behavior*, *18*, 399–412.

Stede, M. (1998). A generative perspective on verb alternations. *Computational Linguistics*, *24*(3), 401–430.

Steedman, M. J. (1989). Constituency and coordination in a combinatory grammar. In Baltin, M. R. and Kroch, A. S. (Eds.), *Alternative Conceptions of Phrase Structure*, pp. 201–231. University of Chicago, Chicago.

Steiner, G. (1975). *After Babel*. Oxford University Press, Oxford.

Stetina, J. and Nagao, M. (1997). Corpus based PP attachment ambiguity resolution with a semantic dictionary. In Zhou, J. and Church, K. W. (Eds.), *Proceedings of the Fifth Workshop on Very Large Corpora*, Beijing, China, pp. 66–80. ACL.

Stifelman, L. J., Arons, B., Schmandt, C., and Hulteen, E. A. (1993). VoiceNotes: A speech interface for a hand-held voice notetaker. In *Human Factors in Computing Systems: INTERCHI '93 Conference Proceedings*, Amsterdam, pp. 179–186. ACM.

Stolcke, A., Shriberg, E., Bates, R., Coccaro, N., Jurafsky, D., Martin, R., Meteer, M., Ries, K., Taylor, P., and Van Ess-Dykema, C. (1998). Dialog act modeling for conversational speech. In Chu-Carroll, J. and Green, N. (Eds.), *Applying Machine Learning to Discourse Processing. Papers from the 1998 AAAI Spring Symposium*. Tech. rep. SS-98-01, Stanford, CA, pp. 98–105. AAAI Press.

Stolcke, A. (1995). An efficient probabilistic context-free parsing algorithm that computes prefix probabilities. *Computational Linguistics*, *21*(2), 165–202.

Stolcke, A. and Shriberg, E. (1996a). Automatic linguistic segmentation of conversational speech. In *ICSLP-96*, Philadelphia, PA, pp. 1005–1008.

Stolcke, A. and Shriberg, E. (1996b). Statistical language modeling for speech disfluencies. In *IEEE ICASSP-96*, Atlanta, GA, Vol. 1, pp. 405–408. IEEE.

Stolz, W. S., Tannenbaum, P. H., and Carstensen, F. V. (1965). A stochastic approach to the grammatical coding of English. *Communications of the ACM*, *8*(6), 399–405.

Streeter, L. (1978). Acoustic determinants of phrase boundary perception. *Journal of the Acoustical Society of America*, *63*, 1582–1592.

Strube, M. and Hahn, U. (1996). Functional centering. In *ACL-96*, Santa Cruz, CA, pp. 270–277. ACL.

Suhm, B. and Waibel, A. (1994). Toward better language models for spontaneous speech. In *ICSLP-94*, Vol. 2, pp. 831–834.

Sumita, E. and Iida, H. (1991). Experiments and prospects of example-based machine translation. In *ACL-91*, Berkeley, CA, pp. 185–192. ACL.

Sundheim, B. (Ed.). (1991). *Proceedings of the Third Message Understanding Conference*, San Mateo, CA. Morgan Kaufmann.

Sundheim, B. (Ed.). (1992). *Proceedings of the Fourth Message Understanding Conference*. Morgan Kaufmann.

Sundheim, B. (Ed.). (1993). *Proceedings, Fifth Message Understanding Conference (MUC-5), Baltimore, MD*. Morgan Kaufmann, San Mateo, CA.

Sundheim, B. (1995a). Overview of results of the MUC-6 evaluation. In *Proceedings of the Sixth Message Understanding Conference (MUC-6)*, Columbia, MD, pp. 13–31.

Sundheim, B. (Ed.). (1995b). *Proceedings of the Sixth Message Understanding Conference*. Morgan Kaufmann.

Sweet, H. (1877). *A Handbook of Phonetics*. Clarendon Press, Oxford.

Tabor, W., Juliano, C., and Tanenhaus, M. K. (1997). Parsing in a dynamical system. *Language and Cognitive Processes*, *12*, 211–272.

Tajchman, G., Fosler, E., and Jurafsky, D. (1995). Building multiple pronunciation models for novel words using exploratory computational phonology. In *EUROSPEECH-95*, pp. 2247–2250.

Talmy, L. (1985). Lexicalization patterns: Semantic structure in lexical forms. In Shopen, T. (Ed.), *Language Typology and Syntactic Description, Volume 3*. Cambridge University Press. Originally appeared as UC Berkeley Cognitive Science Program Report No. 30, 1980.

Talmy, L. (1991). Path to realization: a typology of event conflation. In *BLS-91*, Berkeley, CA, pp. 480–519.

Tappert, C. C., Suen, C. Y., and Wakahara, T. (1990). The state of the art in on-line handwriting recognition. *IEEE Transactions on Pattern Analysis and Machine Intelligence*, *12*(8), 787–808.

Taylor, P. (2000). Analysis and synthesis of intonation using the Tilt model. *Journal of the Acoustical Society of America*. To appear.

Taylor, P. and Black, A. W. (1998). Assigning phrase breaks from part of speech sequences. *Computer Speech and Language*, *12*, 99–117.

Taylor, P., King, S., Isard, S., and Wright, H. (1998). Intonation and dialog context as constraints for speech recognition. *Language and Speech*, *41*(3-4), 489–508.

ter Meulen, A. (1995). *Representing Time in Natural Language*. MIT Press, Cambridge, MA.

Tesar, B. (1995). *Computational Optimality Theory*. Ph.D. thesis, University of Colorado, Boulder.

Tesar, B. (1996). Computing optimal descriptions for optimality theory grammars with context-free position structures. In *ACL-96*, Santa Cruz, CA, pp. 101–107. ACL.

Tesar, B. and Smolensky, P. (1993). The learnability of optimality theory: An algorithm and some basic complexity results. Tech. rep. CU-CS-678-93, University of Colorado at Boulder Department of Computer Science.

Tesnière, L. (1959). *Eléments de Syntaxe Structurale*. Librairie C. Klincksieck, Paris.

Tetreault, J. R. (1999). Analysis of syntax-based pronoun resolution methods. In *ACL-99*, College Park, MD, pp. 602–605.

Thompson, H. (1977). Strategy and tactics: A model for language production. In *CLS-77*, pp. 651–668.

Thompson, K. (1968). Regular expression search algorithm. *Communications of the ACM*, *11*(6), 419–422.

Tomabechi, H. (1991). Quasi-destructive graph unification. In *ACL-91*, Berkeley, CA, pp. 315–322.

Touretzky, D. S., Elvgren, III, G., and Wheeler, D. W. (1990). Phonological rule induction: An architectural solution. In *COGSCI-90*, pp. 348–355.

Traum, D. R. and Allen, J. (1994). Discourse obligations in dialogue processing. In *ACL-94*, Las Cruces, NM, pp. 1–8. ACL.

Trubetskoi, N. S. (1939). *Grundzüge der Phonologie*, Vol. 7 of *Travaux du cercle linguistique de Prague*. Available in 1969 English translation by Christiane A. M. Baltaxe as *Principles of Phonology*, University of California Press.

Trueswell, J. C. and Tanenhaus, M. K. (1994). Toward a lexicalist framework for constraint-based syntactic ambiguity resolution. In Clifton, Jr., C., Frazier, L., and Rayner, K. (Eds.), *Perspectives on Sentence Processing*, pp. 155–179. Lawrence Erlbaum, Hillsdale, NJ.

Trueswell, J. C., Tanenhaus, M. K., and Garnsey, S. M. (1994). Semantic influences on parsing: Use of of thematic role information in syntactic ambiguity resolution. *Journal of Memory and Language*, *33*, 285–318.

Trueswell, J. C., Tanenhaus, M. K., and Kello, C. (1993). Verb-specific constraints in sentence processing: Separating effects of lexical preference form garden-paths. *Journal of Experimental Psychology: Learning, Memory and Cognition*, *19*(3), 528–553.

Tsujii, J. (1986). Future directions of machine translation. In *COLING-86*, Bonn, pp. 655–668.

Turing, A. M. (1936). On computable numbers, with an application to the Entscheidungsproblem. *Proceedings of the London Mathematical Society*, *42*, 230–265. Read to the Society in 1936, but published in 1937. Correction in volume 43, 544–546.

Turing, A. M. (1950). Computing machinery and intelligence. *Mind*, *59*, 433–460.

Tyler, L. K. (1984). The structure of the initial cohort: Evidence from gating. *Perception & Psychophysics*, *36*(5), 417–427.

Usher, A. P. (1954). *A History of Mechanical Inventions*. Harvard University Press, Cambridge, MA.

Uszkoreit, H. (1986). Categorial unification grammars. In *COLING-86*, Bonn, pp. 187–194.

Uszkoreit, H. (Ed.). (1996). *Language Generation*, chap. 4. available at: http://cslu.cse.ogi.edu/HLTsurvey/.

van Benthem, J. and ter Meulen, A. (Eds.). (1997). *Handbook of Logic and Language*. MIT Press, Cambridge, MA.

Van Deemter, K. and Odijk, J. (1997). Context modeling and the generation of spoken discourse. *Speech Communication*, *21*(1/2), 101–121.

van Dijk, T. A. and Kintsch, W. (1983). *Strategies of Discourse Comprehension*. Academic Press, New York.

van Lehn, K. (1978). Determining the scope of English quantifiers. Master's thesis, MIT, Cambridge, MA. MIT Technical Report AI-TR-483.

van Rijsbergen, C. J. (1975). *Information Retrieval*. Butterworths, London.

van Santen, J. and Sproat, R. (1998). Methods and tools. In Sproat, R. (Ed.), *Multilingual Text-To-Speech Synthesis: The Bell Labs Approach*, pp. 7–30. Kluwer, Dordrecht.

van Valin, Jr., R. D. (1999). Introduction to Syntax. Unpublished textbook draft.

Vander Linden, K. and Martin, J. H. (1995). Expressing local rhetorical relations in instructional text: A case-study of the purpose relation. *Computational Linguistics*, *21*(1), 29–57.

Vanderwende, L. (1994). Algorithm for the automatic interpretation of noun sequences. In *COLING-94*, Kyoto, pp. 782–788.

Veale, T. and Keane, M. T. (1992). Conceptual scaffolding: A spatially founded meaning representation for metaphor comprehension. *Computational Intelligence*, *8*(3), 494–519.

Veblen, T. (1899). *Theory of the Leisure Class*. Macmillan Company, New York.

Velichko, V. M. and Zagoruyko, N. G. (1970). Automatic recognition of 200 words. *International Journal of Man-Machine Studies*, 2, 223–234.

Vendler, Z. (1967). *Linguistics in Philosophy*. Cornell University Press, Ithaca, NY.

Veronis, J. and Ide, N. M. (1990). Word sense disambiguation with very large neural networks extracted from machine readable dictionaries. In *COLING-90*, Helsinki, Finland, pp. 389–394.

Vintsyuk, T. K. (1968). Speech discrimination by dynamic programming. *Cybernetics*, 4(1), 52–57. Russian Kibernetika 4(1):81-88 (1968).

Vitale, T. (1991). An algorithm for high accuracy name pronunciation by parametric speech synthesizer. *Computational Linguistics*, 17(3), 257–276.

Viterbi, A. J. (1967). Error bounds for convolutional codes and an asymptotically optimum decoding algorithm. *IEEE Transactions on Information Theory*, IT-13(2), 260–269.

von Neumann, J. (1963). *Collected Works: Volume V*. Macmillan Company, New York.

Voorhees, E. M. (1998). Using WordNet for text retrieval. In Fellbaum, C. (Ed.), *WordNet: An Electronic Lexical Database*, pp. 285–303. MIT Press, Cambridge, MA.

Voorhees, E. M. and Harman, D. (Eds.). (1998). *The Seventh Text Retrieval Conference (TREC-7)*. National Institute of Standards and Technology. NIST Special Publication 500-242. Also available on the Web at NIST's TREC Web page.

Voutilainen, A. (1995). Morphological disambiguation. In Karlsson, F., Voutilainen, A., Heikkilä, J., and Anttila, A. (Eds.), *Constraint Grammar: A Language-Independent System for Parsing Unrestricted Text*, pp. 165–284. Mouton de Gruyter, Berlin.

Wagner, R. A. and Fischer, M. J. (1974). The string-to-string correction problem. *Journal of the Association for Computing Machinery*, 21, 168–173.

Wahlster, W. (1989). One word says more than a thousand pictures. On the automatic verbalization of the results of image sequence analysis systems. *Computers and Artificial Intelligence*, 8, 479–492.

Wahlster, W., André, E., Finkler, W., Profitlich, H.-J., and Rist, T. (1993). Plan-based Integration of Natural Language and Graphics Generation. *Artificial Intelligence*, 63(1–2), 387–428.

Waibel, A. (1988). *Prosody and Speech Recognition*. Morgan Kaufmann, San Mateo, CA.

Wald, B. and Shopen, T. (1981). A researcher's guide to the sociolinguistic variable (ING). In Shopen, T. and Williams, J. M. (Eds.), *Style and Variables in English*, pp. 219–249. Winthrop Publishers, Cambridge, MA.

Walker, M. A. (1989). Evaluating discourse processing algorithms. In *ACL-89*, Vancouver, Canada, pp. 251–260. ACL.

Walker, M. A., Iida, M., and Cote, S. (1994). Japanese discourse and the process of centering. *Computational Linguistics*, 20(2).

Walker, M. A., Joshi, A. K., and Prince, E. (Eds.). (1998). *Centering in Discourse*. Oxford University Press.

Walker, M. A., Litman, D. J., Kamm, C. A., and Abella, A. (1997). Paradise: A framework for evaluating spoken dialogue agents. In *ACL/EACL-97*, Madrid, Spain, pp. 271–280. ACL.

Walker, M. A., Maier, E., Allen, J., Carletta, J., Condon, S., Flammia, G., Hirschberg, J., Isard, S., Ishizaki, M., Levin, L., Luperfoy, S., Traum, D., and Whittaker, S. (1996). Penn multiparty standard coding scheme: Draft annotation manual. www.cis.upenn.edu/~ircs/discourse-tagging/newcoding.html.

Walker, M. A. and Whittaker, S. (1990). Mixed initiative in dialogue: An investigation into discourse segmentation. In *ACL-90*, Pittsburgh, PA, pp. 70–78. ACL.

Wang, M. Q. and Hirschberg, J. (1992). Automatic classification of intonational phrasing boundaries. *Computer Speech and Language*, 6(2), 175–196.

Wanner, E. and Maratsos, M. (1978). An ATN approach to comprehension. In Halle, M., Bresnan, J., and Miller, G. A. (Eds.),

Linguistic Theory and Psychological Reality, pp. 119–161. MIT Press, Cambridge, MA.

Ward, N. (1994). *A Connectionist Language Generator*. Ablex.

Warnke, V., Kompe, R., Niemann, H., and Nöth, E. (1997). Integrated dialog act segmentation and classification using prosodic features and language models. In *EUROSPEECH-97*, Vol. 1, pp. 207–210.

Warren, R. M. (1970). Perceptual restoration of missing speech sounds. *Science*, *167*, 392–393.

Waugh, L. R. (1976). The semantics and paradigmatics of word order. *Language*, *52*(1), 82–107.

Weaver, W. (1949/1955). Translation. In Locke, W. N. and Boothe, A. D. (Eds.), *Machine Translation of Languages*, pp. 15–23. MIT Press, Cambridge, MA. Reprinted from a memorandum written by Weaver in 1949.

Webber, B., Knott, A., Stone, M., and Joshi, A. (1999). Discourse relations: A structural and presuppositional account using lexicalised TAG. In *ACL-99*, College Park, MD, pp. 41–48. ACL.

Webber, B. L. (1978). *A Formal Approach to Discourse Anaphora*. Ph.D. thesis, Harvard University.

Webber, B. L. (1983). So what can we talk about now?. In Brady, M. and Berwick, R. C. (Eds.), *Computational Models of Discourse*, pp. 331–371. The MIT Press, Cambridge, MA. Reprinted in Grosz et al. (1986).

Webber, B. L. (1991). Structure and ostension in the interpretation of discourse deixis. *Language and Cognitive Processes*, *6*(2), 107–135.

Webber, B. L. and Baldwin, B. (1992). Accommodating context change. In *ACL-92*, Newark, DE, pp. 96–103. ACL.

Weber, D. J., Black, H. A., and McConnel, S. R. (1988). Ample: A tool for exploring morphology. Tech. rep. Occasional Publications in Academic Computing No. 12, Summer Institute of Linguistics, Dallas.

Weber, D. J. and Mann, W. C. (1981). Prospects for computer-assisted dialect adaptation. *American Journal of Computational Linguistics*, *7*, 165–177. Abridged from Summer Institute of Linguistics *Notes on Linguistics* Special Publication 1, 1979.

Weber, E. G. (1993). *Varieties of Questions in English Conversation*. John Benjamins, Amsterdam.

Weischedel, R. (1995). BBN: Description of the PLUM system as used for MUC-6. In *Proceedings of the Sixth Message Understanding Conference (MUC-6)*, San Francisco, pp. 55–70. Morgan Kaufmann.

Weischedel, R., Meteer, M., Schwartz, R., Ramshaw, L. A., and Palmucci, J. (1993). Coping with ambiguity and unknown words through probabilistic models. *Computational Linguistics*, *19*(2), 359–382.

Weizenbaum, J. (1966). ELIZA – A computer program for the study of natural language communication between man and machine. *Communications of the ACM*, *9*(1), 36–45.

Weizenbaum, J. (1976). *Computer Power and Human Reason: From Judgement to Calculation*. W.H. Freeman and Company, San Francisco.

Wells, J. C. (1982). *Accents of English*. Cambridge University Press.

Wells, J. C. (1990). *Pronunciation Dictionary*. Longman, London.

Whitelock, P. (1992). Shake-and-bake translation. In *COLING-92*, Nantes, France, pp. 784–791.

Whittemore, G., Ferrara, K., and Brunner, H. (1990). Empirical study of predictive powers of simple attachment schemes for post-modifier prepositional phrases. In *ACL-90*, Pittsburgh, PA, pp. 23–30. ACL.

Wierzbicka, A. (1996). *Semantics: Primes and Universals*. Oxford University Press, New York.

Wilensky, R. (1983). *Planning and Understanding*. Addison-Wesley, Reading, MA.

Wilensky, R. and Arens, Y. (1980). PHRAN: A knowledge-based natural language understander. In *ACL-80*, Philadelphia, PA, pp. 117–121. ACL.

Wilks, Y. (1975a). An intelligent analyzer and understander of English. *Communications of the ACM*, *18*(5), 264–274.

Wilks, Y. (1975b). Preference semantics. In Keenan, E. L. (Ed.), *The Formal Semantics of Natural Language*, pp. 329–350. Cambridge Univ. Press, Cambridge.

Wilks, Y. (1975c). A preferential, pattern-seeking, semantics for natural language inference. *Artificial Intelligence*, *6*(1), 53–74.

Wilks, Y. (1978). Making preferences more active. *Artificial Intelligence*, *11*(3), 197–223.

Wilks, Y., Slator, B. M., and Guthrie, L. M. (1996). *Electric Words: Dictionaries, Computers, and Meanings*. MIT Press, Cambridge, MA.

Willett, P. (1988). Recent trends in hierarchic document clustering: A critical review. *Information Processing and Management*, *24*(5), 577–597.

Winograd, T. (1972a). Understanding natural language. *Cognitive Psychology*, *3*(1). Reprinted as a book by Academic Press, 1972.

Winograd, T. (1972b). *Understanding Natural Language*. Academic Press, New York.

Withgott, M. M. and Chen, F. R. (1993). *Computational Models of American Speech*. Center for the Study of Language and Information.

Witten, I. H. and Bell, T. C. (1991). The zero-frequency problem: Estimating the probabilities of novel events in adaptive text compression. *IEEE Transactions on Information Theory*, *37*(4), 1085–1094.

Witten, I. H. (Ed.). (1982). *Principles of Computer Speech*. Academic Press, New York.

Wolfram, W. A. (1969). *A Sociolinguistic Description of Detroit Negro Speech*. Center for Applied Linguistics, Washington, D.C.

Woods, W. A. (1967). *Semantics for a Question-Answering System*. Ph.D. thesis, Harvard University.

Woods, W. A. (1973). Progress in natural language understanding. In *Proceedings of AFIPS National Conference*, pp. 441–450.

Woods, W. A. (1975). What's in a link: Foundations for semantic networks. In Bobrow, D. G. and Collins, A. M. (Eds.), *Representation and Understanding: Studies in Cognitive Science*, pp. 35–82. Academic Press, New York.

Woods, W. A. (1977). Lunar rocks in natural English: Explorations in natural language question answering. In Zampolli, A. (Ed.), *Linguistic Structures Processing*, pp. 521–569. North Holland, Amsterdam.

Woods, W. A. (1978). Semantics and quantification in natural language question answering. In Yovits, M. (Ed.), *Advances in Computers*, Vol. 17, pp. 2–87. Academic Press, New York.

Woods, W. A., Kaplan, R. M., and Nash-Webber, B. (1972). The Lunar Sciences Natural Language Information System: Final report. Tech. rep. 2378, Bolt, Beranek, and Newman, Inc., Cambridge, MA.

Wooters, C. and Stolcke, A. (1994). Multiple-pronunciation lexical modeling in a speaker-independent speech understanding system. In *ICSLP-94*, Yokohama, Japan, pp. 1363–1366.

Woszczyna, M. and Waibel, A. (1994). Inferring linguistic structure in spoken language. In *ICSLP-94*, Yokohama, Japan, pp. 847–850.

Wu, D. (1992). *Automatic Inference: A Probabilistic Basis for Natural Language Interpretation*. Ph.D. thesis, University of California, Berkeley, Berkeley, CA. UCB/CSD 92-692.

Wu, D. and Wong, H. (1998). Machine translation with a stochastic grammatical channel. In *COLING/ACL-98*, Montreal, pp. 1408–1414. ACL.

Wundt, W. (1900). *Völkerpsychologie: eine Untersuchung der Entwicklungsgesetze von Sprache, Mythus, und Sitte*. W. Engelmann, Leipzig. Band II: Die Sprache, Zweiter Teil.

Yaeger, L. S., Webb, B. J., and Lyon, R. F. (1998). Combining neural networks and context-driven search for online, printed handwriting recognition in the NEWTON. *AI Magazine*, *19*(1), 73–89.

Yankelovich, N., Levow, G.-A., and Marx, M. (1995). Designing SpeechActs: Issues in speech user interfaces. In *Human Factors in Computing Systems: CHI '95 Conference Proceedings*, Denver, CO, pp. 369–376. ACM.

Yarowsky, D. (1994). Decision lists for lexical ambiguity resolution: Application to accent restoration in Spanish and French. In *ACL-94*, Las Cruces, NM, pp. 88–95. ACL.

Yarowsky, D. (1995). Unsupervised word sense disambiguation rivaling supervised methods. In *ACL-95*, Cambridge, MA, pp. 189–196. ACL.

Yarowsky, D. (1996). Homograph disambiguation in text-to-speech synthesis. In van Santen, J., Sproat, R., Olive, J., and Hirschberg, J. (Eds.), *Progress in Speech Synthesis*, pp. 159–175. Springer-Verlag, New York.

Yeh, C.-L. and Mellish, C. (1997). An empirical study on the generation of anaphora in Chinese. *Computational Linguistics*, *23*(1), 169–190.

Yngve, V. H. (1955). Syntax and the problem of multiple meaning. In Locke, W. N. and Booth, A. D. (Eds.), *Machine Translation of Languages*, pp. 208–226. MIT Press, Cambridge, MA.

Yngve, V. H. (1960). A model and an hypothesis for language structure. *Proceedings of the American Philosophical Society*, *104*, 444–466.

Yngve, V. H. (1970). On getting a word in edgewise. In *CLS-70*, pp. 567–577. University of Chicago.

Young, M. and Rounds, W. C. (1993). A logical semantics for nonmonotonic sorts. In *ACL-93*, Columbus, OH, pp. 209–215. ACL.

Young, S. J. and Woodland, P. C. (1994). State clustering in HMM-based continuous speech recognition. *Computer Speech and Language*, *8*(4), 369–394.

Younger, D. H. (1967). Recognition and parsing of context-free languages in time n^3. *Information and Control*, *10*, 189–208.

Zappa, F. and Zappa, M. U. (1982). Valley girl. From Frank Zappa album *Ship Arriving Too Late To Save A Drowning Witch*.

Zavrel, J. and Daelemans, W. (1997). Memory-based learning: Using similarity for smoothing. In *ACL/EACL-97*, Madrid, Spain, pp. 436–443. ACL.

Zechner, K. and Waibel, A. (1998). Using chunk based partial parsing of spontaneous speech in unrestricted domains for reducing word error rate in speech recognition. In *COLING/ACL-98*, Montreal, pp. 1453–1459. ACL.

Zernik, U. (1987). *Strategies in Language Acquisition: Learning Phrases from Examples in Context*. Ph.D. thesis, University of California, Los Angeles, Computer Science Department, Los Angeles, CA.

Zernik, U. (1991). Train1 vs. train2: Tagging word senses in corpus. In *Lexical Acquisition: Exploiting On-Line Resources to Build a Lexicon*, pp. 91–112. Lawrence Erlbaum, Hillsdale, NJ.

Zhou, G. and Lua, K. (1998). Word association and MI-trigger-based language modelling. In *COLING/ACL-98*, Montreal, pp. 1465–1471. ACL.

Zipf, G. (1949). *Human Behavior and the Principle of Least Effort*. Addison–Wesley, Cambridge, MA.

Zue, V., Glass, J., Goodine, D., Leung, H., Phillips, M., Polifroni, J., and Seneff, S. (1989). Preliminary evaluation of the VOYAGER spoken language system. In *Proceedings DARPA Speech and Natural Language Workshop*, Cape Cod, MA, pp. 160–167. Morgan Kaufmann.

Zue, V., Glass, J., Goodine, D., Leung, H., Phillips, M., Polifroni, J., and Seneff, S. (1991). Integration of speech recognition and natural language processing in the MIT VOYAGER system. In *IEEE ICASSP-91*, pp. I.713–716. IEEE.

Zwicky, A. (1972). On Casual Speech. In *CLS-72*, pp. 607–615. University of Chicago.

Zwicky, A. and Sadock, J. (1975). Ambiguity tests and how to fail them. In Kimball, J. (Ed.), *Syntax and Semantics 4*, pp. 1–36. Academic Press, New York.

Index

Page numbers in **bold** are
definitions of terms and
algorithms.

⊔ unification operator, 401
ŵ, **148**
() (optional constituents),
    337
→ (derives), **327, 328**
Σ to mean finite alphabet of
    symbols, 36
δ as transition function
    between states in
    FSA, 36
ε-transitions in finite-state
    automata, **41**
#, **76**
ˆ, **76**
* (RE Kleene *), 25
+ (RE Kleene +), 26
. (RE any character), **26**
, \ (RE or symbol)27
$ (RE end-of-line), 26
((RE precedence symbol),
    27
[(RE character
    disjunction), 23
\B (RE non
    word-boundary), 26
\b (RE word-boundary), 26
] (RE character
    disjunction), 23
ˆ (RE start-of-line), 26
[ˆ] (single-char negation),
    24
∃ (there exists), 517
∀ (for all), 517
⇒ (implies), 517
λ (lambda operator), 551
λ-expressions, 551
λ-notation, 552
λ-reduction, 551, 552
∧ (and), 516
¬ (not), 516
∨ (or), 517
2001: A Space Odyssey, 1

3sg, 340
4-tuple, 331

, (short pause), 346
. (long pause), 346
[] (non-verbal events), 346

A* decoder, **237**, 238, 240,
    253
   compared to Viterbi, 254
   in MT, 822
   pseudocode, 256
A* evaluation function, **258**
abduction, **522, 697**
Abeillé, A., 459, 475
Abella, A., 320, 758
Abelson, R. P., 13
Abney, S. P., 393, 464, 475,
    476
ΛBSITY, 661
accent, 130
accented, **102**
accepting
   by finite-state automaton,
    34
accepting state, 34
accepts, 52
accomplishment
    expressions, 531,
    532
accusative, **341**
achievement expressions,
    531, **533**
acknowledge, **725**
ACL, 17
acoustic model, **239**
acoustic phonetics, 260
action schema, **735**
activity expressions, 531,
    532
add-one smoothing, **207**,
    210
Ades, A. E., 466
ad hoc retrieval, **647, 648**
adjacency pair, **722**
adjective phrase, **336**, 352
adjectives, **291**, 336

Adjukiewicz, K., 466
adjunction
   in TAG, 354
adverbs, **290, 291**, 336
   days of the week coded
    as nouns instead of,
    291
   degree, **291**
   directional, **291**
   locative, **291**
   manner, **291**
   temporal, **291**
affix, 59
affricate, **100**
agents, **607**
agglomerative clustering,
    644
agglutinative, **803**
   morphology, 61
aggregation, **789**
aggregation in generation,
    766
agreement, 340, **340**
   determiner-nominal, 407,
    408
   kappa, 315
   number, 341
   explosion of grammar
    size to deal with, 341
   subject-verb, 352, 407,
    408
Aha, D. W., 118
Ahlsén, E., 726
Aho, A. V., 361, 392, 393,
    453–455
AI-complete, **703, 738**
Aidinejad, H., 646
Aist, G., 10
Aït-Kaci, H., 439, 443
Al-Onaizan, Y., 825
Albelson, R. P., 622
Albert, M. K., 118
Algoet, P. H., 226
ALGOL, 354
alignment, **154**, 186
   word, **821**